1936 **JOHN MAYNARD KEYNES (1883–1946)**

© BETTMANN/ CORBIS

In his book *The General Theory of Employment, Interest, and Money*, Keynes developed the framework for modern macroeconomics. He also developed an explanation for the widespread unemployment of the Great Depression, and he elevated the importance of fiscal policy.

1940s **FRIEDRICH VON HAYEK (1899–1992)**

© HULTON-DEUTSCH COLLECTION/ CORBIS

In two vitally important publications, *The Road to Serfdom* (1944) and "The Use of Knowledge in Society," an article in the *American Economic Review* in 1945, Hayek explained the role of knowledge in economics, enhanced our understanding of the market process, and highlighted the fatal defects of centrally planned economies.

1960s and 1970s **MILTON FRIEDMAN (1912–)**

© BETTMANN / CORBIS

Friedman's work elevated the importance of monetary policy and convinced many that monetary instability was the major cause of both business fluctuations and inflation. His book *A Monetary History of the United States, 1867–1960* (with Anna Schwartz) was a particularly important publication.

1970s and 1980s **ROBERT LUCAS (1937–)**

© RALF-FINN HESTOFT / CORBIS

The role people's expectations play in the macroeconomy dramatically altered prior economic analysis. Although several economists made major contributions in this area, Lucas is generally recognized as the leading contributor.

11th edition

ECONOMICS
Private & Public Choice

THOMSON
™
SOUTH-WESTERN

Australia · Canada · Mexico · Singapore · Spain · United Kingdom · United States

11th edition

ECONOMICS
Private & Public Choice

JAMES D. GWARTNEY
Florida State University

•

RICHARD L. STROUP
Montana State University

•

RUSSELL S. SOBEL
West Virginia University

•

DAVID A. MACPHERSON
Florida State University

THOMSON

SOUTH-WESTERN

Australia · Canada · Mexico · Singapore · Spain · United Kingdom · United States

THOMSON
TM
SOUTH-WESTERN

Economics: Private and Public Choice, Eleventh Edition
James D. Gwartney, Richard L. Stroup, Russell S. Sobel, David A. Macpherson

VP/Editorial Director:
Jack W. Calhoun

Editor-in-Chief:
Alex von Rosenberg

Developmental Editor:
Amy Ray

Marketing Manager:
John Carey

Production Editor:
Robert Dreas

Manager of Technology, Editorial:
Vicky True

Sr. Technology Project Editor:
Peggy Buskey

Web Coordinator:
Karen Schaffer

Manufacturing Coordinator:
Sandee Milewski

Production House:
Pre-Press Company, Inc.

Printer:
Courier Kendallville, Inc.
Kendallville, Indiana

Art Director:
Michael Stratton

Internal and Cover Designer:
Nick Gliebe/Design Matters
Cincinnati, Ohio

Cover and Internal Illustrations:
© Jon Allen/Illustration Works

Photography Manager:
John Hill

Photo Researcher:
Jan Seidel

Library of Congress Control Number:
2005921020

For more information about our products, contact us at:

Thomson Learning Academic
Resource Center

1-800-423-0563

Thomson Higher Education
5191 Natorp Boulevard
Mason, OH 45040
USA

Asia (including India)
Thomson Learning
5 Shenton Way
#01-01 UIC Building
Singapore 068808

Australia/New Zealand
Thomson Learning Australia
102 Dodds Street
Southbank, Victoria 3006
Australia

Canada
Thomson Nelson
1120 Birchmount Road
Toronto, Ontario
M1K 5G4
Canada

Latin America
Thomson Learning
Seneca, 53
Colonia Polanco
11560 Mexico
D.F.Mexico

UK/Europe/Middle East/Africa
Thomson Learning
High Holborn House
50/51 Bedford Row
London WC1R 4LR

United Kingdom
Spain (including Portugal)
Thomson Paraninfo
Calle Magallanes, 25
28015 Madrid, Spain

Preface

Our main goal in this edition was to make the book both more understandable and exciting to read. Readability has been a past strength, but we worked hard to make this edition more concise and the most student-friendly edition ever. Even though we did not eliminate coverage of any topic, this edition still has about 7 percent fewer words than the previous one. In this case, we believe shorter is better.

The aim of this text is to: (a) make economics understandable, (b) illustrate the power and relevance of economics to our daily lives, and (c) explain why both individuals and nations prosper. Throughout, we seek to communicate basic and, in some cases, fairly complicated ideas in a clear and understandable manner. Clarity is a major objective, but simplicity is not substituted for in-depth analysis. We do not accept the view that economics must be either difficult or "watered down." Instead, we believe that a clear and understandable writing style reinforced with examples, illustrations, and visual aids can make the subject come alive in a way that will capture the interest of even the beginning student.

THE ORGANIZATION OF TEXT: FLEXIBLE COVERAGE OF PUBLIC CHOICE, THE KEYNESIAN MODEL, AND SPECIAL TOPICS

The organization is designed to provide instructors with maximum flexibility. Those using the full-length text for a two-semester course can cover either microeconomics or macroeconomics first. Beginning with the ninth edition, the text was divided into core chapters and a concluding special-topics section. The twenty-seven core chapters cover all of the material taught in most principles courses, and they are presented in the usual manner. Examples and data from the real world are used to reinforce the analysis. In addition, the Applying the Basics section includes fourteen relatively short discussions on high-profile topics like the growing U.S. budget deficit, reforming Social Security, and the economics of health care. Each topic is designed to be covered during a single class period. This organization has been quite popular, largely because it makes it easier for instructors to tailor their course to fit their own preferences.

Those teaching a microeconomics course who like to stress the importance of public choice will probably want to cover the first six chapters prior to beginning the core microeconomics section. Others will prefer to cover only the first four chapters and then move immediately to the core microeconomics material. The book is designed for both of these options. Instructors who like to integrate applications extensively into their micro course can pick and choose among special topics covering issues like Social Security, investing in the stock market, healthcare, school choice, income differences between men and women, and property rights and the quality of the environment.

Those teaching a macroeconomics course integrating public choice will probably want to cover Chapters 5 and 6 prior to the core macroeconomics material. Others may want to move directly from Chapter 4 (or Chapter 3) to the core macroeconomics material. The macroeconomics chapters have been written so there will be no problems with either option. Similarly, instructors who want to omit the Keynesian 45-degree aggregate expenditure model (Chapter 11) can do so without having to worry that this will cause problems for students in subsequent chapters. Special Topic 1 provides facts and figures about government spending and taxation for those who highlight this topic. Our own teaching experience indicates that the special topics on budget deficits and the national debt, European unemployment, and the "Irish miracle" can enrich a macroeconomics course.

CHANGES IN THIS EDITION

New in Macroeconomics

Chapter 8. New Application box entitled "Would Personal Savings Accounts Make Unemployment Compensation Work Better?"

Chapter 12. A new section on the politics of fiscal policy and the related box entitled "Have Supply-Side Economists Found a Way to Soak the Rich?" were added.

Chapter 15. Material on the Phillips Curve, both the early views and the current expectations view, was integrated into the chapter.

Special Topic 7, "Institutions, Policies, and the Irish Miracle," is new.

New in Microeconomics

Chapter 20. New box entitled, "Cooking the Books: How the Market Responds to Criminal Behavior."

Substantial revisions to Special Topic 4 focusing on how to best invest in the stock market.

New feature entitled, "Can Imports from Canada Reduce the Drug Prices of Americans?" in the special topic relating to health care.

Substantial updates and revisions to the special topic on the environment and natural resource use.

New in Both Microeconomics and Macroeconomics: Economics in the Movies

Economics pervades our culture—including our entertainment. Both the macroeconomics and microeconomics editions of the book contain a new boxed feature in the text called "Economics in the Movies." These boxes featured in the text include various scenes from popular movies that reflect economic concepts. A number of instructors, including the authors, now use clips from popular movies to stimulate student interest and drive home the importance of these concepts. The instructor's manual provides more ideas about how this can be done effectively.

Additional Text Features

Economics: Private and Public Choice retains several features that make the presentation of economics both more interesting and more understandable:

✗ **Keys to Economic Prosperity**—Students often fail to appreciate the organizational and institutional factors that provide the foundation for economic progress. In order to help remedy this situation, we have incorporated a "Key to Economic Prosperity" feature that highlights how important factors like the gains from trade, secure property rights, competition, and free trade are to economic prosperity. In all, twelve of the most important factors that underlie modern economic prosperity are highlighted at appropriate places throughout the text and are also listed inside the back cover.

✗ **Applications in Economics**—"Applications in Economics" boxes apply economic theory to real-world issues and controversies.

✗ **Measures of Economic Activity**—The "Measures of Economic Activity" boxes explain how important economic indicators such as the unemployment rate and the index of leading indicators are assembled and what they mean.

✗ **Outstanding Economist**—Numerous boxes in the text highlight the lives of many economists and the contributions they have made.

✘ **Myths of Economics**—These boxed articles dispel commonly held fallacies of economic reasoning. Because they are tomorrow's leaders, we believe that all students should be aware of common economic misperceptions that tend to hamper a nation's economic progress.

✘ **Chapter Focus Questions and Closing Key Point Summaries**—Each chapter begins with four or five questions that summarize the focus of the chapter. At the end of each chapter, the Key Points section provides the student with a concise statement of the material covered in the chapter (the chapter learning objectives). These two features help students better integrate the material into the broader economic picture.

✘ **Critical Analysis Questions**—Each chapter concludes with a set of discussion questions and problems designed to test the student's ability to analyze economic issues and to apply economic theory to real-world events. Appendix B at the end of the text contains suggested answers for approximately half of these questions.

SUPPLEMENTARY MATERIALS

For the Student

Coursebooks

The Coursebooks for this edition were prepared by coauthor Professor Russell Sobel and are now available in not two, but three versions, covering all three courses: Economics, Microeconomics, and Macroeconomics. The Coursebooks are more than study guides. Each includes numerous multiple-choice, true/false, and discussion questions to help students self-test their knowledge of each chapter. Answers and short explanations for most questions are provided in the back of the Coursebooks. Each chapter also contains problem and project exercises designed to improve the student's knowledge of the mechanics. Like the textbook, the Coursebooks are designed to help students develop the economic way of thinking.

Gwartney Xtra!

This Web site, which comes free with the purchase of a new book, offers a robust set of online multimedia learning tools, including Master the Learning Objectives, The Graphing Workshop, CNN Video Clips, and Xtra! Quizzing. Thirty-five questions similar to the multiple-choice questions of the Test Bank are available for each chapter. These self-testing questions provide students with ample opportunity to practice and obtain feedback prior to examinations. Students with used textbooks can purchase Xtra! by going online to **http://gwartneyxtra.swlearning.com**.

 Microeconomics Alive! **and** *Macroeconomics Alive!* **CD-ROMs.**—These CDs help students learn economics the high-tech, high-fun way. These study CDs, compatible with both Microsoft Windows and Macintosh operating systems, provide animated lessons, interactive graphing exercises, and real-life simulations. Learn economics for the first time or review the concepts in your economics course—either way, these award-winning CD-ROMs provide you with the perfect tools. Find out more at **http://econalive.swlearning.com**.

 #### InfoTrac
Students shouldn't forget to take advantage of their subscriptions to InfoTrac, which comes free with their textbooks. InfoTrac gives them anytime, anywhere online access to a database of full-text articles from hundreds of scholarly and popular periodicals using fast and easy search tools. InfoTrac is updated daily, with articles dating back as far as four years.

Support Web Site
Valuable resources can be found on the text's Internet support site found at the text's online support site at **http://gwartney.swlearning.com**. Students will find an interactive study center as well as online quizzing.

For the Instructor

We believe that many of the features incorporated into this text will help you become a better teacher. We have incorporated the Keys to Economic Prosperity series, movie clips, homework assignments, and diverse use of the online quiz questions into our own classes. We have also found that students are quite interested in the issues covered in the Special Topics section of the book. We feel sure that many of these features will help make your class more interesting to students. Of course, the full set of supplements accompanies the text. They include the following:

Test Banks

The Test Banks for the eleventh edition were prepared by the author team. The authors have worked hard to update and improve the test banks for this edition. The two Test Banks contain approximately 7,000 questions—multiple-choice and short-answer. Within each chapter, the questions correspond to the major headings of the text. The first ten questions of each chapter are suitable for use as a comprehensive quiz covering the material of the chapter. The multiple-choice questions from the Coursebook and the online practice quizzes are also included in special sections of the Test Bank. Instructors who would like to motivate their students to study the Coursebook and online quizzes can easily use these questions and incorporate them into their quizzes and exams.

Computerized Test Banks

e|v
EXAMVIEW

The computerized Test Banks for this edition have been enhanced significantly. *Exam-View*—Computerized Testing Software contains all of the questions in the printed Test Bank. *Examview* is an easy-to-use test creation software compatible with both Microsoft Windows and Macintosh. Instructors can add or edit questions, instructions, and answers and select questions by previewing them on the screen, selecting them randomly, or selecting them by number. Instructors can also create and administer quizzes online, whether over the Internet, a local-area network (LAN), or a wide-area network (WAN).

PowerPoint

We believe that our PowerPoint presentation, prepared by Chuck Skipton, is the best you will find in the principles market. It provides chapter-by-chapter lecture notes with fully animated, hyperlinked slides of the textbook's exhibits. The dynamic slides and accompanying captions make it easy for instructors to present (and students to follow) sequential changes. The dynamic graphics are also used to highlight various relationships among economic variables. In order to facilitate discussion and interaction, questions are strategically interspersed throughout each chapter to help students develop the economic way of thinking. Instructions explaining how professors can easily add, delete, and modify slides in order to tailor-make the presentation to their liking are included. If instructors want to make the PowerPoint presentation available to students, they can place it on their Web site (or the site for their course). The slides are available in two sets: Figure Slides and also Lecture Slides. These sets are available for download at the support Web site: **http://gwartney.swlearning.com**.

Instructor's Manual and Instructor's Resource CD

The *Instructor's Manual* was prepared by author David Macpherson. Instructions and information on how to use and modify the PowerPoint material is contained in the front of the manual. Also included at the front of the manual is information about *ExamView*, the computerized testing software that accompanies the book. The remainder of the manual is divided up by chapters, and each chapter is divided into three parts. The first part consists of a detailed chapter outline in lecture-note form It is designed to help instructors organize their notes to match the 11th edition of the book. Instructor's can easily prepare detailed, personalized notes by revising the computerized version of the lecture notes on the *Instructor's Resource CD*. The second part of each chapter contains teaching tips, sources of supplementary materials, and other helpful information. Part 3 of each chapter consists of in-class economic games and experiments. Contributed in part by Professor Charles Stull of Kalamazoo College, the games are an enormously popular feature with instructors. We hope you will try them.

The *Instructor's Resource CD* contains the key supplements designed to aid instructors, including the content from the instructor's manual, test banks, and PowerPoint lecture and exhibit slides for overhead use. The CD also includes an "Integrated Resource Guide," which provides a quick reference to all of South-Western's resources for teaching a principles course in economics as well as suggestions for how to incorporate the resources into all the phases of instruction.

Support Web Site for Instructors

This password-protected Web site includes some of the same essential resources that can be found on the *Instructor's Resource CD,* including instructor's manuals and test banks in Microsoft Word, and the PowerPoint lecture and exhibit slides. To get access to the site to download these supplements, register online at **http://gwartney.swlearning.com**.

WebTutor Toolbox™ and Web Tutor Advantage™ on Blackboard and WebCT

The *WebTutor Toolbox* uses the Internet to turn everyone in your class into a front-row student. It offers interactive study guide features such as quizzes, concept reviews, flashcards, discussion forums, and more. Instructor tools are also provided to facilitate communication between students and faculty. Preloaded with content, *WebTutor ToolBox* pairs all the content of the book's support Web site with all the sophisticated course management functionality of either course management platform.

More than just an interactive study guide, *WebTutor Advantage* delivers innovative learning aids that actively engage students. Benefits include automatic and immediate feedback from quizzes; interactive, multimedia-rich explanations of concepts, such as flash-animated graphing tutorials and graphing exercises that use an online graph-drawing tool; streaming video applications; online exercises; flashcards; and interaction and involvement through online discussion forums. Powerful instructor tools are also provided to facilitate communication and collaboration between students and faculty. More information on WebTutor can be found at **http://webtutor.thomsonlearning.com**. (Other platform choices are available upon request. Please visit the WebTutor Web site for details.)

Principles of Economics Videotape

Principles of Economics, a forty-minute videotape giving students an insightful overview of ten common economic principles: Trade-offs, Opportunity Cost, Marginal Thinking, Incentives, Trade, Markets, Government's Role, Productivity, Inflation, and the Phillips Curve. The video shows viewers how to apply these principles to their daily lives. It is filled with interviews from some of the leading economists, and includes profiles of real students facing economic choices.

Turner Learning/CNN Economics Video

Professors can bring the real world into the classroom by using the *Turner Learning/CNN Economics Video.* This video, which includes current news stories of economic interest, is produced in cooperation with Turner Learning, Inc. Contact your Thomson Learning sales representative for ordering information.

TEXT-SUPPLEMENT VALUE PACKAGES

Economics: Private and Public Choice can be packaged with a plethora of supplements useful to you and your students. In addition to the Coursebooks, the textbooks can be packaged with the following:

Homework Xpress! Your Homework Management Solution

http://homeworkxpress.swlearning.com

InfoTrac® with InfoMarks™

When you adopt *Economics: Private and Public Choice,* 11th edition, you and your students will gain anytime, anywhere access to reliable resources with InfoTrac College Edition, the online library. This fully searchable database offers more than twenty years' worth of full-text articles (not abstracts) from almost 5,000 diverse sources, such as top academic journals, newsletters, and up-to-the-minute periodicals, including *Time, Newsweek, Science, Forbes,* and *USA Today.*

The Wall Street Journal

Economics: Private and Public Choice, 11th edition, makes it easy for students to apply economic concepts to this authoritative publication, and for you to bring the most up-to-date, real-world events into your classroom. For a nominal additional cost, *Economics: Private and Public Choice,* 11th edition, can be packaged with a card entitling students to a fifteen-week subscription to both the print and online versions of the *Wall Street Journal.*

Favorite Ways to Learn Economics

Authors David Anderson of Centre College and Jim Chasey of Homewood Flossmoore High School use experiments to bring economic education to life. This is a growing trend, and for good reason. It works! Favorite Ways to Learn experiments and problem sets reinforce the key principles of microeconomics and macroeconomics covered in most college Advanced Placement courses. Instructors will see an improvement in their students' comprehension. This supplement comes in both student and instructor versions.

How to Think Like an Economist

Most economics instructors believe that a primary goal of this course is to teach students how economists think. There's more to thinking like an economist than knowing the concepts and technical tools of analysis. *How to Think Like an Economist* gives students unique insight into the economist's mind, allowing them to see how interesting issues are approached from an economic perspective. This soft-cover guide can be bundled free with new copies of *Economics: Private and Public Choice,* 11th edition.

Economic HITS on the Web with InfoTrac

This resource booklet supports students' research efforts on the World Wide Web. This manual includes an introduction to the Web, material on finding information and documenting Internet sources for research, and numerous economic activities along with the hottest economic URLs.

Your Thomson Learning sales representative can help you with the many text-supplement value packages available to you and your students. Completely customizable textbooks are also available via *TextChoice,* Thomson Learning's online digital content. *TextChoice* is the fastest, easiest way for instructors to create their own learning materials. You can select content from hundreds of our best-selling titles, choose material from one of our databases or add your own material.

Harvard Business Cases

Thomson is now an official distributor of Harvard Business School Publishing materials, giving you access to the richest and most respected cases and article content—at competitive prices. This comprehensive collection includes more than 9,500 Harvard Business School case studies and background notes, as well as selected case items from Babson College, Business Enterprise Trust, Design Management Institute, IESE, IMD, Richard Ivey School of Business, Stanford University, and the University of Hong Kong. For more information, contact your local Thomson South-Western Sales Representative.

Gale Business & Company Resource Center

Another expansive resource available is our Gale Business & Company Resource Center (BCRC). Our exclusive and robust online resource center allows students to conduct detailed business research and analysis from their own desks—anytime and anywhere they have an Internet connection. Through the BCRC, students gain access to a vast assortment of global business information, including competitive intelligence, career and investment opportunities, business rankings, company histories, and much more. For more information on this valuable resource, visit **http://access.gale.com/thomsonlearning/**.

A NOTE TO INSTRUCTORS

As we try to improve the book from one edition to the next, we rely heavily on our experiences as teachers. But our experience using the book is minuscule compared with that of the hundreds of instructors who use it nationwide. If you encounter problems or have suggestions for improving the book, we urge you to let us know by writing to us in care of Thomson Higher Education, 5191 Natorp Blvd., Mason, OH 45040. Such letters are invaluable, and we are glad to receive both praise and suggestions for improvement. Many such suggestions have found their way into this new book.

A NOTE TO STUDENTS

This textbook contains several features we think will help you "maximize" (a good economic term) the returns from your study efforts. Here are some of the things that will help you and a few tips for making the most of them:

Each chapter begins with a series of focus questions that communicate the central issues of the chapter. Before you read the chapter, briefly think about the focus questions, why they are important, and how they relate to the material in prior chapters.

The textbook is organized in the form of an outline. The headings within the text (highlighted with a color background) are the major points of the outline. Minor headings are subpoints under the major headings. In addition, important subpoints within sections are often set off and numbered. Bold italicized type is used to highlight material that is particularly important. Sometimes "thumbnail sketches" are included to recap material and help the reader keep the important points mentally organized. Careful use of the headings, highlighted material, and the thumbnail sketches will help you master the material.

A "Key Points" summary appears at the end of each chapter. Use the summary as a checklist to determine whether you understand the major points of the chapter.

A review of the exhibits and illustrative pictures will also provide you with a summary of the key points of each chapter. The accompanying captions briefly describe the economic phenomena illustrated by the exhibits.

The key terms introduced in each chapter are defined in the margins. As you study the chapter, go over the marginal definition of each key term as it is introduced. Later, you may also find it useful to review the marginal definitions. If you have forgotten the meaning of a term introduced earlier, consult the glossary at the end of the book.

The boxed features go into more depth on various topics without disrupting the flow of the text. In general, the topics of the boxed features have been chosen because they are a good application of the theory described in the book and because students tend to be interested in them. Reading the boxed features will supplement the text and enhance your understanding of important economic concepts.

The critical analysis questions at the end of each chapter are intended to test your understanding of the economic way of thinking. Solving these questions and problems will greatly enhance your knowledge of the material. Answers to approximately half of these questions are provided in Appendix B.

If you need more practice, be sure to obtain a Coursebook and solve the questions and problems for each chapter. The Coursebook also contains the answers to the multiple-choice questions and a brief explanation of why an answer is correct (and other choices incorrect). In most cases, if you master the concepts of the test items in the Coursebook, you will do well on the quizzes and examinations of your instructor. For extra help, in addition to the Coursebook, visit the book's student support Web site at **http:// gwartney.swlearning.com** and take advantage of the Gwartney Xtra! Web site at **http:// gwartneyxtra.swlearning.com**. Among other things, this Web site includes thirty-five multiple-choice practice questions for each chapter of the text.

ACKNOWLEDGMENTS

A project of this type is a team effort. Through the years, numerous people have assisted us in various ways. In this edition, the contributions of three people stand out. The first is developmental editor Amy Ray. She made substantial revisions to every chapter and worked as hard as we did to simplify the language and improve the readability of the text. She never gave up trying to get us to write like popular journalists rather than college professors. We really appreciate both her skillful revisions and personal commitment to the project. The contributions of Amy Gwartney and Jane Shaw Stroup were also invaluable. They edited several chapters prior to their submission to the publisher and, between the two of them, proofed every page of the text. Any future financial gain that they may derive will be well-deserved.

We are also very much indebted to the excellent team of professionals at Thomson Business and Professional Publishing, including Peter Adams, acquisitions editor, for his help and support of our efforts; Bob Dreas, production editor, who coordinated the copy-editing, proofreading, and indexing and kept the book on schedule; Jan Seidel, art and literary rights editor, who helped us locate and obtain permissions for the many photos and movie stills; Peggy Buskey, senior technology editor, who orchestrated the protection of the numerous electronic supplements, and John Carey, marketing manager, who worked hard to inform the marketplace about the advantages of the book.

We would also like to express our appreciation to Chuck Skipton of the University of Tampa for his contribution to what we believe is the very best set of PowerPoint slides accompanying an introductory economics text. We are also appreciative of the contributions of Matthew Brown, Joseph Calhoun, Kerry King, Lynn MacDonald, Dirk Mateer, Samona Bociuba, and Linda Ghent to the Test Bank, online quizzes, and other supplementary materials. Robert Lawson of Capital University assisted us with the preparation of several exhibits. The text still bears an imprint of the contributions of Woody Studenmund of Occidental College and Gary Galles of Pepperdine University, who assisted us in numerous ways with past editions. We also want to express our appreciation to Amy Gwartney, Jane Shaw Stroup, Terri Sobel, and Karen Macpherson for their patience, support, and encouragement throughout the project.

Many instructors made important contributions to the 11th edition by providing us with insightful critical reviews. The following reviewers helped us improve the textbook immensely, and we thank them for their honest feedback:

Donald Boudreaux, George Mason University; Matthew Brown, Santa Clara University; Barry Haworth, University of Louisville; Jim Hubert, Seattle Central Community College; Katherine Huger, Charleston Southern University; Derek Kellenberg, Georgia Institute of Technology; Cory Krupp, Duke University; Robert Lawson, Capital University; James Payne, Eastern Kentucky University; Jennifer Platania, Elon University; Edward Stringham, San Jose State University; and Christopher Westley, Jacksonville State University.

We have often revised material in light of suggestions made by reviewers, users, friends, and even a few competitors. In this regard, we would also like to express our appreciation to the following people for their reviews and helpful suggestions of recent editions:

Douglas Agbetsiafa, Indiana University, South Bend; James C. W. Ahiakpor, California State University, Hayward; Ali T. Akarca, University of Illinois at Chicago; Stephen A. Baker, Capital University; Alana Bhatia, University of Colorado at Boulder; Edward J. Bierhanzl, Florida A&M University; Charles A. Booth, University of Alabama at Birmingham; Ford J. Brown, University of Minnesota-Morris; Dennis Brennen, Harper College; James Bryan, Manhattanville College; Darcy R. Carr, Coastal Carolina University; Mike Cohick, Collin County Community College; David S. Collins, Virginia Highlands Community College; Jim F. Couch, University of North Alabama; Steven R. Cunningham, University of Connecticut; George W. Dollar, Clearwater Christian College; Jeff Edwards, Collin County Community College; Robert C. Eyler, Sonoma State University; James R. Fain, Oklahoma State University; Kathryn Finn, Western Washington University; Andrew W. Foshee, McNeese State University; Marsha Goldfarb, University of Maryland, Baltimore County; David Harris, Northwood University; Ronald Helgens, Golden Gate University; Robert E. Herman, Nassau Community College/SUNY; William D. Hermann, Golden Gate University, San Francisco; Brad Hobbs, Florida Gulf Coast University; Woodrow W. Hughes, Jr., Converse College; Rob H. Kamery, Christian Brothers University; Frederic R. Kolb, University of Wisconsin, Eau Claire; Barbara Kouskoulas, Lawrence Technological University; David W. Kreutzer, James Madison University; George Kuljurgis, Oakland University; Randy W. LaHote, Washtenaw Community College; Tsung-Hui Lai, Liberty University; Bob Lawson, Capital University; Don R. Leet, California State University, Fresno; George P. Lephardt, Milwaukee School of Engineering; Joe LeVesque, Northwood University; John McArthur, Wofford College; Ed Mills, Kendell College; David M. Mitchell, Oklahoma State University; Hadley T. Mitchell, Taylor University; Glen A. Moots, Northwood University; John R. Neal, Lake-Sumter Community College; Lloyd Orr, Indiana University, Bloomington; Judd W. Patton, Bellevue College; Robert Reinke, University of South Dakota; Robert C. Rencher, Jr., Liberty University; Dan Rickman, Oklahoma State University; Karin L. Russell, Keiser College; Lewis F. Schlossinger, Community College of Aurora; Thomas W. Secrest, USC Coastal Carolina; Ben S. Shippen, Jr., Mercer University; Ken Somppi, Southern Union State Community College; William A. Steiden, Jefferson Community College; Richard D. C. Trainer, Warsaw School of Economics; Scott Ward, East Texas Baptist University; Tom Lee Waterston, Northwood University; Jim Wharton, Northwood University; Edward Wolpert, University of Central Florida; Janice Yee, Wartburg College; and Anthony Zambelli, Cuyamaca College.

About the Authors

James D. Gwartney holds the Gus A. Stavros Eminent Scholar Chair at Florida State University, where he directs the Stavros Center for the Advancement of Free Enterprise and Economic Education. He served as Chief Economist of the Joint Economic Committee of the U.S. Congress during 1999-2000. He is the coauthor of *Economic Freedom of the World,* an annual report on the institutions and policies of more than 120 countries that is published by a worldwide network of institutes. His publications have appeared in both professional journals and popular media such as the *Wall Street Journal* and the *New York Times.* His Ph.D. in economics is from the University of Washington. A member of the Mont Pelerin Society, he was invited by the incoming Putin Administration in March 2000 to make presentations and have discussions with leading Russian economists concerning the future of the Russian economy. In 2004 he was the recipient of the Adam Smith Award of the Association of Private Enterprise Education for his contribution to the advancement of free market ideals.

Richard L. Stroup is Professor of Economics and Interim Department Head at Montana State University, as well as Senior Associate at the Political Economy Research Center. With a Ph.D. in economics from the University of Washington, Professor Stroup has served as director of the Office of Policy Analysis in the U.S. Department of the Interior and has been published widely in professional journals. He is a contributing editor of numerous books on the economics of resources and the environment and authored *Eco-nomics* (Cato, 2003), which won the Sir Antony Fisher International Memorial Award presented by the Atlas Economic Research Foundation. Professor Stroup has lectured throughout the United States and abroad to professional and general audiences.

Russell S. Sobel is a professor of economics and director of the Entrepreneurship Center at West Virginia University. He received his Ph.D. in economics from Florida State University in 1994. Professor Sobel regularly teaches courses in both principles of economics and public choice economics. His enthusiastic teaching style has earned him many university teaching awards. Professor Sobel regularly gives lectures at economic education outreach programs on basic economic principles. Professor Sobel has published over thirty academic articles in refereed economics journals. His research focuses on applications of economics to public policy and on how economic freedom promotes entrepreneurship in an economy.

David A. Macpherson is the Rod and Hope Brim Eminent Scholar in Economics and is the director of the Pepper Institute on Aging and Public Policy at Florida State University, where he has received two university-wide awards for teaching excellence. Professor Macpherson has written more than forty articles in leading economics journals, including the *Journal of Labor Economics, Industrial and Labor Relations Review,* and *Review of Economics and Statistics.* He is the coauthor of the annual *Union Membership and Earnings Data Book: Compilations from the Current Population Survey*, and is coauthor of *Contemporary Labor Economics.* Professor Macpherson also cowrote the book *Pensions and Productivity.* His current research interests include pensions, discrimination, labor unions, and the minimum wage. He received his undergraduate degree and Ph.D. from the Pennsylvania State University.

Brief Contents

Table of Contents

RELATIONSHIP BETWEEN MAIN EDITION AND THE MACRO/MICRO EDITIONS

1

P A R T

"Life is a series of choices"

The Economic Way of Thinking

1

Economics is about how people choose. The choices we make influence our lives and those of others. Your future will be influenced by the choices you make with regard to education, job opportunities, savings, and investment. Furthermore, changes in technology, demographics, communications, and transportation are constantly altering the attractiveness of various options and the opportunities available to us. The economic way of thinking is all about how incentives alter the choices people make. It can help you make better choices and enhance your understanding of our dynamic world.

The Economic Approach

Economist, n.—A scoundrel whose faulty vision sees things as they really are, not as they ought to be.

after Ambrose Bierce

Chapter Focus

■ What is scarcity, and why is it important even in relatively wealthy economies?

■ How does scarcity differ from poverty? Why does scarcity necessitate rationing and cause competition?

■ What is the economic way of thinking? What is different about the way economists look at choices and human decision making?

■ What is the difference between positive and normative economics?

Welcome to the world of economics. You've heard about economics in the news. Maybe you think economics has to do with the stock market or the fine print you've read in the business section of your daily newspaper. You will soon see, however, that economics is much more than that. In fact, a field trip to the fruits and vegetables section at your local grocery store could well be filled with more economics lessons than a trip to the New York Stock Exchange.

In a nutshell, economics is the study of human behavior, with a particular focus on human decision making. In economics you will learn a new and powerful way of thinking that might lead you to question some of your current views and to look at things in a different way. As the satirical definition of an economist in the chapter-opening quote suggests, economic analysis provides valuable insights about how the world really works. These insights, however, often conflict with commonly held beliefs about the way things "ought" to work.

You may have heard some of the following statements: Gas prices are so high that the government should regulate them. The government should mandate air bags in cars to increase public health and safety. The minimum wage should be increased to help the poor. Tariffs should be imposed on foreign imports to save jobs in the United States. Technology, outsourcing, and robotics lead to unemployment and hurt our standard of living.

In this course, you will gain an understanding of these issues that may well alter the way you think about them. You will also develop new insights into how and why people (including yourself) make choices. This course will better enable you to argue political and economic issues with your friends at parties. It may even help you impress your date. On a more serious note, though, the better the decisions you make in your lifetime, the better off you will be. The same goes for a society as a whole. Who knows—you may become so good at economics you discover how to improve the lives of many people around the world, in addition to your own. You could even become the next great economist of our time.

The origins of economics date back to Adam Smith, a Scottish moral philosopher, who expressed the first economic ideas in his breakthrough book, *An Inquiry into the Nature and Causes of the Wealth of Nations,* published in 1776. As the title of his book suggests, Smith sought to explain why people in some nations were wealthier than those in others. This very question is still a central issue in economics. It is so important that throughout this book we will use a special "Keys to Economic Prosperity" symbol in the margin to highlight sections that focus on this topic. ⚷ A listing of the major keys to prosperity is presented inside the front cover of the book. These keys and accompanying discussions will help you understand what factors enable economies, and their citizens, to grow wealthier and prosper. ■

WHAT IS ECONOMICS ABOUT?

While economics is about the choices *individuals* make, we often group together to form collective organizations, such as corporations, labor unions, nonprofit clubs, and governments. Individual choices, however, still underlie and direct the decisions made within these organizations. Thus, even when we study collective organizations like governments, we will still focus our analysis on the choices and decisions made by individuals within those organizations. We begin our journey into economics by discussing the constraints we face as individuals that force us to make choices.

[Economics is] the science which studies human behavior as a relationship between ends and scarce means which have alternative uses.

—*Lionel Robbins[1]*

Scarcity Means Having to Make Choices

Would you like some new clothes, a nicer car, and a larger apartment? How about better grades and more time to watch television, go skiing, and travel? Do you dream of driving

---

[1]Lionel Robbins, *An Essay on the Nature and Significance of Economic Science* (1932).

Scarcity
Fundamental concept of economics that indicates that there is less of a good freely available from nature than people would like.

your brand-new Porsche into the driveway of your oceanfront house? As individuals, our desire for goods is virtually unlimited. We may want all of these things. Unfortunately, both as individuals and as a society we face a constraint called **scarcity** that prevents us from being able to completely fulfill our desires.

Scarcity is present whenever there is less of a good or resource freely available from nature than people would like. There are some things that are not scarce—seawater comes

ECONOMICS AT THE MOVIES

Ferris Bueller's Day Off (1986)

In one scene in *Ferris Bueller's Day Off,* Ben Stein plays an economics teacher lecturing about macroeconomics. His students are bored and falling asleep. Although some parts of economics might not be as fun as others, it's a misconception that economics is boring. On the contrary, economics will enlighten you about how people make decisions and the way the world works. It will also help you make better decisions yourself, which will make you better off.

Our "Economics at the Movies" features have been inspired by G. Dirk Mateer, the author of Economics in the Movies. (Thomson South-Western Publishing, 2005).

PARAMOUNT/THE KOBAL COLLECTION

SCARCE GOODS	LIMITED RESOURCES
Food (bread, milk, meat, eggs, vegetables, coffee, etc.)	Land (various degrees of fertility)
Clothing (shirts, pants, blouses, shoes, socks, coats, sweaters, etc.)	Natural resources (rivers, trees, minerals, oceans, etc.)
Household goods (tables, chairs, rugs, beds, dressers, television sets, etc.)	Machines and other human-made physical resources
Education	Nonhuman animal resources
National defense	Technology (physical and scientific "recipes" of history)
Leisure time	Human resources (the knowledge, skill, and talent of individual human beings)
Entertainment	
Clean air	
Pleasant environment (trees, lakes, rivers, open spaces, etc.)	
Pleasant working conditions	

EXHIBIT 1
A General Listing of Scarce Goods and Limited Resources

History is a record of our struggle to transform available, but limited, resources into goods that we would like to have.

to mind; nature has provided as much of it as people want. But almost everything else you can think of—even your time—is scarce. In economics, the word *scarce* has a very specific meaning that differs slightly from the way it is commonly used. Even if large amounts of a good have been produced, it is still scarce as long as there is not as much of it *freely available from nature* as we would all like. For example, even though goods like apples and automobiles are relatively abundant in the United States, they are still scarce because we would like to have more of them than nature has freely provided. In economics, we generally wish to determine only if a good is scarce or not, and refrain from using the term to refer to the relative availability or abundance of a good or resource.

The unlimited nature of our desires, coupled with the limited nature of the goods and resources available to satisfy these desires, requires that we make choices. Should I spend the next hour studying or watching TV? Should I spend my last $20 on a new CD or on a shirt? Should this factory be used to produce clothing or furniture? **Choice,** the act of selecting among alternatives, is the logical consequence of scarcity. When we make choices, we constantly face trade-offs between meeting one desire or another. To meet one need, we must let another go unmet. The basic ideas of *scarcity* and *choice,* along with the *trade-offs* we face, provide the foundation for economic analysis.

Resources are the ingredients, or inputs, people use to produce goods and services. Our ability to produce goods and services is limited precisely because of the limited nature of our resources.

Exhibit 1 lists a number of scarce goods and the limited resources that might be used to produce them. There are three general categories of resources. First, there are *human resources*—the productive knowledge, skill, and strength of human beings. Second, there are *physical resources*—things like tools, machines, and buildings that enhance our ability to produce goods. Economists often use the term **capital** when referring to these human-made resources. Third, there are *natural resources*—things like land, mineral deposits, oceans, and rivers. The ingenuity of humans is often required to make these natural resources useful in production. For example, until recently, the yew tree was considered a "trash tree," having no value. Then, scientists discovered that the tree produces taxol, a substance that could be used to fight cancer. Human knowledge and ingenuity made yew trees a valuable resource. As you can see, natural resources are important, but knowing how to use them productively is just as important. As economist Thomas Sowell points out, cavemen had the same natural resources at their disposal that we do today. The huge difference between their standard of living and ours reflects the difference in the knowledge they could bring to bear on those resources versus what we can.[2] Over time, human

Choice
The act of selecting among alternatives.

Resource
An input used to produce economic goods. Land, labor, skills, natural resources, and capital are examples. Throughout history, people have struggled to transform available, but limited, resources into things they would like to have—economic goods.

Capital
Human-made resources (such as tools, equipment, and structures) used to produce other goods and services. They enhance our ability to produce in the future.

---

[2]Thomas Sowell, *Knowledge and Decisions* (New York: Basic Books, 1980), 47.

ingenuity, discovery, improved knowledge, and better technology have enabled us to produce more goods and services from the available resources. Nonetheless, we will never be able to produce enough goods to entirely fulfill human desires. Because scarcity can't be eliminated, people will always face choices. This is what economics is about.

Scarcity and Poverty Are Not the Same

Think for a moment what life was like in 1750. People all over the world struggled 50, 60, and 70 hours a week to obtain the basic necessities of life—food, clothing, and shelter. Manual labor was the major source of income. Animals provided the means of transportation. Tools and machines were primitive by today's standards. As the English philosopher Thomas Hobbes stated in the seventeenth century, life was "solitary, poor, nasty, brutish, and short."[3]

Throughout much of South America, Africa, and Asia, economic conditions today continue to make life difficult. In North America, Western Europe, Oceania, and some parts of Asia, however, economic progress has substantially reduced physical hardship and human drudgery. In these regions, the typical family is more likely to worry about financing their summer vacation than obtaining food and shelter. As anyone who has watched the TV reality show *Survivor* knows, we take for granted many of the items that modern technological advances have allowed us to produce at unbelievably low prices. Contestants on *Survivor* struggle with even basic things like starting a fire, finding shelter, and catching fish. They are thrilled when they win ordinary items like shampoo, rice, and toilet paper. During one episode, a contestant eagerly paid over $125 for a small chocolate bar and spoonful of peanut butter at an auction—and she considered it a great bargain!

It is important to note, however, that scarcity and poverty are not the same thing. Scarcity is an **objective** concept that describes a factual situation in which the limited nature of our resources keeps us from being able to completely fulfill our desires for goods and services. In contrast, poverty is a **subjective** concept that refers to a personal opinion of whether someone meets an arbitrarily defined level of income. This distinction is made even clearer when you realize that different people have vastly different ideas of what it

Objective
A fact based on observable phenomena that is not influenced by differences in personal opinion.

Subjective
An opinion based on personal preferences and value judgments.

The degree to which modern technology and knowledge allow us to fulfill our desires and ease the grip of scarcity is often taken for granted—as the castaways on the CBS reality series *Survivor* quickly find out when they have to struggle to meet even basic needs, such as food, shelter, and cleaning their bodies and clothes.

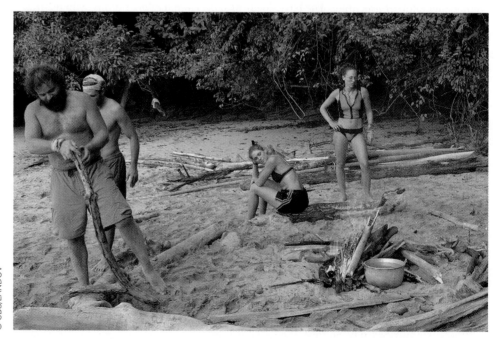

© CBS/LANDOV

---

[3]Thomas Hobbes, *Leviathan* (1651), Part I, Chapter 13.

means to be poor. The average family in the United States that meets the federal government's definition of being "in poverty" would be considered wealthy in most any country in Africa. Even in the United States as recently as the 1950s, a family was considered fairly wealthy if it had central heat and air conditioning, or more than one automobile or television set. In the United States today, the majority of families officially classified as in poverty have many, if not most, of the items that would have been viewed as symbols of wealth only 50 years ago.

The distinction between "needs" and "wants" helps us understand why it is impossible to objectively define poverty. Most people would agree that an absence of poverty means that some basic level of needs has been met. But they would disagree on what constitutes needs versus wants. In the 1920s, less than half of all households in the United States had electricity, and even fewer had a telephone or an automobile. Still, people survived and prospered. Would you consider electricity a need or a want? How about gasoline? How about other items that you generally hear people say they need, like cable television, a computer, and a $100 pair of tennis shoes—are they really needs? Although food and water are necessary for human survival, no one item (such as pizza, steak, a Big Mac, or a $1 bottle of spring water) is essential.

People always want more and better goods for themselves and others they care about—medical care, schooling, and national security are examples. Scarcity is the constraint that prevents us from having as much of *all* goods as we would like, but it is not the same as poverty. Even if every individual were rich, scarcity would still be present.

Scarcity Necessitates Rationing

Scarcity makes **rationing** a necessity. When a good or resource is scarce, some criterion must be used to determine who will receive it and who will go without. The choice of which method is used will, however, have an influence on human behavior. When rationing is done through the government sector, a person's political status and ability to manipulate the political process are the key factors. Powerful interest groups and those in good favor with influential politicians will be the ones who obtain goods and resources. When this method of rationing is used, people will devote time and resources to lobbying and favor seeking with those who have political power, rather than to productive activities.

When the criterion is first-come, first-served, goods are allocated to those who are fastest at getting in line or most willing to spend time waiting in line. Many colleges use this method to ration tickets to sporting events, and the result is students waiting in long lines (and sometimes even camping out overnight) to obtain tickets. Imagine how the behavior of students would change if tickets were instead given out to the students with the highest grade point average.

In a market economy, price is generally used to ration goods and resources only to those who are willing and able to pay the prevailing market price. Because only those goods that are scarce require rationing, in a market economy, one easy way to determine whether a good or resource is scarce is to ask if it sells for a price. If you have to pay for something, it is scarce.

Rationing
Allocating a limited supply of a good or resource among people who would like to have more of it. When price performs the rationing function, the good or resource is allocated to those willing to give up the most "other things" in order to get it.

Scarcity Leads to Competitive Behavior

Competition is a natural outgrowth of scarcity and the desire of human beings to improve their conditions. Competition exists in every economy and every society. It exists both when goods are allocated by price in markets and when they are allocated by other means—political decision making, for example.

How goods are rationed influences what competitive techniques people will use to get them. When the rationing criterion is price, individuals will engage in income-generating activities that enhance their ability to pay the price needed to buy the goods and services they want. Thus, one benefit of using price as a rationing mechanism is that it encourages individuals to engage in the production of goods and services to generate income. In contrast, rationing on the basis of first-come, first-served encourages individuals to waste a substantial amount of time unproductively waiting in line, while rationing through the political process encourages individuals to waste time attempting to influence the political process.

Within a market setting, the competition that results from scarcity is an important ingredient in economic progress. Competition among business firms for customers results in newer, better, and less expensive goods and services. Competition between employers for workers results in higher wages, benefits, and better working conditions. Further, competition encourages discovery and innovation, two important sources of growth and higher living standards.

THE ECONOMIC WAY OF THINKING

> It [economics] is a
> method rather than a
> doctrine, an apparatus of
> the mind, a technique of
> thinking which helps its
> possessor to draw correct
> conclusions.
>
> *—John Maynard Keynes[4]*

Economic theory
A set of definitions, postulates, and principles assembled in a manner that makes clear the "cause-and-effect" relationships.

One does not have to spend much time around economists to recognize that there is an "economic way of thinking." Admittedly, economists, like others, differ widely in their ideological views. A news commentator once remarked that "any half-dozen economists will normally come up with about six different policy prescriptions." Yet, in spite of their philosophical differences, the approach of economists reflects common ground.

That common ground is **economic theory,** developed from basic principles of human behavior. Economic researchers are constantly involved in testing and seeking to verify their theories. When the evidence from the testing is consistent with a theory, eventually that theory will become widely accepted among economists. Economic theory, like a road map or a guidebook, establishes reference points indicating what to look for, and how economic issues are interrelated. To a large degree, the basic economic principles are merely common sense. When applied consistently, however, these commonsense concepts can provide powerful and sometimes surprising insights.

Eight Guideposts to Economic Thinking

The economic way of thinking requires incorporating certain guidelines—some would say the building blocks of basic economic theory—into your own thought process. Once you incorporate these guidelines, economics can be a relatively easy subject to master. Students who have difficulty with economics have almost always failed to assimilate one or more of these principles. The following are eight principles that characterize the economic way of thinking. We will discuss each of these principles in more depth throughout the book so that you will be sure to understand how and when to apply them.

Opportunity cost
The highest valued alternative that must be sacrificed as a result of choosing an option.

1. The use of scarce resources is costly, so trade-offs must be made.   Economists sometimes refer to this as the "there is no such thing as a free lunch" principle. Because resources are scarce, the use of resources to produce one good diverts those resources from the production of other goods. A parcel of undeveloped land could be used for a new hospital or a parking lot, or it could simply be left undeveloped. No option is free of cost—there is always a trade-off. The choice to pursue any one of these options means the others must be sacrificed. The highest valued alternative that must be sacrificed is the **opportunity cost** of the option chosen. For example, if you use one hour of your scarce time to study economics, you will have one hour less time to watch television, read magazines, sleep, work at a job, or study other subjects. Whichever one of these options you would have chosen had you *not* spent the hour studying economics is your highest valued option forgone. If you would have been sleeping, then the opportunity cost of this hour spent studying economics is a forgone hour of sleep. In economics, the opportunity cost of an action is the highest valued option given up when a choice is made.

---

[4]John Maynard Keynes (1883–1946) was an English economist whose writings during the 1920s and 1930s exerted an enormous impact on both economic theory and policy. Keynes established the terminology and the economic framework that are still widely used when economists study problems of unemployment and inflation.

When a scarce resource is used to meet one need, other competing needs must be sacrificed. The forgone shoe store is an example of the opportunity cost of building the new drugstore.

It is important to recognize that the use of scarce resources to produce a good is always costly, regardless of who pays for the good or service produced. In many countries, various kinds of schooling are provided free of charge *to students*. However, provision of the schooling is not free *to the community as a whole*. The scarce resources used to produce the schooling—to construct the building, hire teachers, buy equipment, and so on—could have been used instead to produce more recreation, entertainment, housing, medical care, or other goods. The opportunity cost of the schooling is the highest valued option given up because the resources required for its production were instead used for schooling.

By now the central point should be obvious. As we make choices, we are continually faced with trade-offs. Using resources to do one thing leaves fewer resources to do another.

Consider one final example. Mandatory air bags in automobiles save an estimated 400 lives each year. Economic thinking, however, forces us to ask ourselves if the $50 billion spent on air bags could have been used in a better way—perhaps say, for cancer research that could have saved *more* than 400 lives per year. Most people don't like to think of air bags and cancer research as an "either/or" proposition. It's more convenient to ignore these trade-offs. But if we want to get the most out of our resources, we have to consider all of our alternatives. In this case, the appropriate analysis is not lives saved with air bags versus dollars spent on them, but the number of lives that could have been saved (or other things that could have been accomplished) if the $50 billion had been used differently. A candid consideration of hard trade-offs like this is essential to using our resources wisely.

2. Individuals choose purposefully—they try to get the most from their limited resources. People try not to deliberately waste their valuable resources. Instead, they try to choose the options that best advance their personal desires and goals at the least possible cost. This is called **economizing behavior**. Economizing behavior is the result of purposeful, or rational, decision making. When choosing among things of equal benefit, an economizer will select the cheapest option. For example, if a pizza, a lobster dinner, and a sirloin steak are expected to yield identical benefits for Mary (including the enjoyment of eating them), economizing behavior implies that Mary will select the cheapest of the three alternatives, probably the pizza. Similarly, when choosing among alternatives of equal cost, economizing decision makers will select the option that yields the greatest benefit. If the prices of several dinner specials are equal, for example, economizers will choose the one they like the best. Because of economizing behavior, the desires or preferences of individuals are revealed by the choices they make.

Purposeful choosing implies that decision makers have some basis for their evaluation of alternatives. Economists refer to this evaluation as **utility**—the benefit or satisfaction that an individual expects from the choice of a specific alternative. Utility is highly subjective, often differing widely from person to person. The steak dinner that delights one person may be repulsive to another (a vegetarian, for example).

The idea that people behave rationally to get the greatest benefit at the least possible cost is a powerful tool. It can help us understand their choices. However, we need to realize that a rational choice is not the same thing as a "right" choice. If we want to understand people's choices, we need to understand their own subjective evaluations of their options *as they see them*. As we have said, different people have different preferences. If Joan prefers $50 worth of chocolate to $50 worth of vegetables, buying the chocolate would be the rational choice for her, even though some outside observer might say that Joan is

Economizing behavior
Choosing the option that offers the greatest benefit at the least possible cost.

Utility
The subjective benefit or satisfaction a person expects from a choice or course of action.

making a "bad" decision. Similarly, some motorcycle riders choose to ride without a helmet because they believe the enjoyment they get from riding without one is greater than the cost (the risk of injury). When people weigh the benefits they receive from an activity against its cost, they are making a rational choice—even though it might not be the choice you or I would make in the same situation.

3. Incentives matter—choice is influenced in a predictable way by changes in incentives.

This is probably the most important guidepost in economic thinking. It is sometimes called the basic postulate of all economics. As the personal benefits from an option increase, a person will be more likely to choose it. On the other hand, as the personal costs associated with an option increase, a person will be less likely to choose it. This guidepost also applies to groups of people, and suggests that making an option more beneficial will predictably cause more of them to choose it. Similarly, making an option more costly will cause fewer of them to choose it.

This basic idea is a powerful tool because its usefulness is practically universal. Incentives affect behavior in virtually all aspects of our lives, ranging from market decisions about what to buy to political choices concerning for whom to vote. If beef prices rise, making beef consumption more expensive relative to other goods, consumers will be less likely to buy it. The "incentives matter" postulate also explains why a person would be unlikely to vote for a political candidate who, if elected, would raise taxes to fund a new government program he or she didn't like very much.

Most errors in economic reasoning occur because people overlook this postulate or fail to apply it consistently. With economic applications generally focusing on people trying to satisfy material desires, casual observers often argue that incentives matter only in cases of human selfishness. This view is false. People are motivated by a variety of goals, some humanitarian and some selfish, and incentives matter equally in both. Even an unselfish individual would be more likely to attempt to rescue a drowning child from a three-foot swimming pool than the rapid currents approaching Niagara Falls. Similarly, people are more likely to give a needy person their hand-me-downs rather than their favorite new clothes.

It is clear that incentives, whether monetary or nonmonetary, matter in human decision making. People will be less likely to walk down a dark alleyway than a well-lit one; they will be more likely to take a job if it has good benefits and working conditions than if

Because consumers respond to incentives, store owners know they can sell off excess inventory by reducing prices.

GETTY IMAGES

it doesn't; and they will be more likely to bend down and pick up a quarter lying on the sidewalk than they will a penny. Even a person who normally bends down to pick up pennies on the sidewalk probably would be less likely to if late for an important appointment, or on a first date.

Just how far can we push the idea that incentives matter? If asked what would happen to the number of funerals performed in your town if the price of funerals rose, how would you respond? The "incentives matter" postulate predicts that the higher cost would reduce the number of funerals. While the same number of people will still die each year, the number of funerals performed will still fall as more people choose to be cremated or buried in cemeteries in other towns. Substitutes are everywhere—even substitutes for funerals.

4. Individuals make decisions at the margin.   When making a choice between two alternatives, individuals generally focus on the *difference* in the costs and benefits between alternatives. Economists describe this process as **marginal** decision making, or "thinking at the margin." The last time you went to eat fast food, you probably faced a decision that highlights this type of thinking. Will you get the $1.50 cheeseburger and the $1.00 medium drink, or instead get the $3.00 value meal that has the cheeseburger and drink and also comes with a medium order of fries? Naturally, individual decision making focuses on the difference between the alternatives. The value meal costs 50 cents more (its marginal cost) but will give you one extra food item—the fries (its marginal benefit). Your marginal decision is whether it is worth the extra 50 cents to have the fries. If you pay attention, you'll notice yourself frequently thinking at the margin. Next time you find yourself asking a salesclerk "How much *more* is this one?" when you are choosing between two items, you are doing a marginal analysis.

Marginal
Term used to describe the effects of a change in the current situation. For example, a producer's marginal cost is the cost of producing an additional unit of a product, given the producer's current facility and production rate.

Marginal choices always involve the effects of net additions to or subtractions from current conditions. In fact, the word *additional* is often used as a substitute for *marginal*. For example, a business decision maker might ask, "What is the marginal cost of producing one more, or additional, unit?" Marginal decisions may involve large or small changes. The "one more unit" could be a new factory or a new stapler. It is marginal because it involves additional costs and additional benefits. Given the current situation, what marginal benefits (additional sales revenues, for example) can be expected from the new factory, and what will be the marginal cost of constructing it? What is the marginal benefit versus marginal cost of purchasing a new stapler? The answers to these questions will determine whether building the new factory or buying the new stapler is a good decision.

It is important to distinguish between *average* and *marginal*. A manufacturer's average cost of producing automobiles (which would be the total cost of production divided by the total number of cars the manufacturer produces) may be $25,000, but the marginal cost of producing an additional automobile (or an additional 1,000 automobiles) might be much lower, say, $10,000 per car. Costs associated with research, testing, design, molds, heavy equipment, and similar factors of production must be incurred whether the manufacturer is going to produce 1,000 units, 10,000 units, or 100,000 units. Such costs will clearly contribute to the average cost of an automobile, but they will change very little as additional units are produced. Thus, the marginal cost of additional units may be substantially less than the average cost. Should production be expanded or reduced? That choice should be based on marginal costs, which indicate the *change* in total cost due to the decision.

Confusion between marginal and total benefits or costs can also be a source of error. Almost all of the choices we make are marginal, rather than all-or-nothing decisions. For example, we don't make decisions between eating or wearing clothes—dining well in the nude versus starving in style. Instead, we choose between having a little more food at the cost of a little less clothing, or a little less of something else. So the relevant comparison is not between the total value of food and the total value of clothing but between their marginal values.

People commonly ignore the implications of marginal thinking in their comments, but seldom in their actions. Thus, the concept is far better at explaining how people act than what they say. Students are often overheard telling other students that they shouldn't skip class because they have paid to enroll in it. Of course, the tuition is not a factor relevant at the margin—it will be the same whether or not the student attends class on that particular day. The only real marginal considerations are what the student will miss that day (a quiz, information for the exam, etc.) versus what he or she could do with the extra time by skipping class. This explains why even students who tell others they paid too much for the class to skip it will ignore the tuition costs when they themselves decide to skip class.

When we confront a decision, the *marginal benefit* and *marginal cost* associated with the choice will determine our decision. Marginal analysis will be used extensively throughout this course. As we develop this concept further, you should pay special attention to understanding how to use it properly.

5. Although information can help us make better choices, its acquisition is costly.

Information that helps us make better choices is valuable. However, the time needed to gather it is scarce, making information costly to acquire. As a result, people economize on their search for information just like they do anything else. For example, when you purchase a pair of jeans, you might evaluate the quality and prices of jeans at several different stores. At some point, though, you will decide that additional comparison shopping is simply not worth the trouble. You will make a choice based on the limited information you already have.

The process is similar when individuals search for a restaurant, a new car, or a roommate. They will seek to acquire some information, but at some point, they will decide that the expected benefit derived from gathering still more information is simply not worth the cost. When differences among the alternatives are important to decision makers, they will spend more time and effort gathering information. People are much more likely to read a consumer ratings magazine before purchasing a new automobile than they are before purchasing a new can opener. Because information is costly for people to acquire, limited knowledge and uncertainty about the outcome generally characterize the decision-making process.

6. Beware of the secondary effects: Economic actions often generate indirect as well as direct effects.

In addition to direct effects that are quickly visible, people's decisions often generate indirect, or "secondary," effects that may be observable only with time. Failure to consider secondary effects is one of the most common economic errors because these effects are often quite different from initial, or direct, effects. Frederic Bastiat, a nineteenth-century French economist, stated that the difference between a good and a bad economist is that the bad economist considers only the immediate, visible effects, whereas the good economist is also aware of the **secondary effects**. The true cause of these secondary effects might not be seen, even later, except by those using the logic of good economics.

Secondary effects
The indirect impact of an event or policy that may not be easily and immediately observable. In the area of policy, these effects are often both unintended and overlooked.

Perhaps a few simple examples that involve both immediate (direct) and secondary (indirect) effects will help illustrate the point. The immediate effect of an aspirin is a bitter taste in one's mouth. The secondary effect, which is not immediately observable, is relief from a headache. The short-term direct effect of drinking twelve cans of beer might be a warm, jolly feeling. In contrast, the secondary effect is likely to be a sluggish feeling the next morning, and perhaps a pounding headache.

Sometimes, as in the case of the aspirin, the secondary effect—headache relief—is actually an intended consequence of the action. In other cases, however, the secondary effects are unintended. Changes in government policy often alter incentives, indirectly affecting how much people work, earn, invest, consume, and conserve for the future. When a change alters incentives, *unintended consequences* that are quite different from the intended consequences may occur.

Let's consider a couple of examples that illustrate the potential importance of unintended side effects. In an effort to reduce gasoline consumption, the federal government mandates that automobiles be more fuel efficient. Is this regulation a sound policy? It may be, but when evaluating the policy's overall impact, one should not overlook its secondary effects. To achieve the higher fuel efficiency, auto manufacturers will reduce the size and weight of vehicles. As a result, there will be more highway deaths—about 2,000 more per year—than would otherwise occur because these lighter cars do not offer as much protection for occupants. Furthermore, because the higher mileage standards for cars and light trucks make driving cheaper, people tend to drive more than they otherwise would. This increases congestion and results in a smaller reduction in gasoline consumption than was intended by the regulation. Once you consider the secondary effects, the fuel efficiency regulations are much less beneficial than they might first appear.

Trade restrictions between nations have important secondary effects as well. The proponents of tariffs and quotas on foreign goods almost always ignore the secondary effects of their policies. Import quotas restricting the sale of foreign-produced sugar in the U.S. market, for example, have led to sugar prices that are about three times what they are in the rest of the world. The proponents of this policy—primarily sugar producers—argue that the quotas "save jobs" and increase employment. No doubt, the employment of sugar growers in the United States is higher than it otherwise would be. But what about the secondary effects? The higher sugar prices mean it's more expensive for U.S. firms to produce candy and other products that use a lot of sugar. As a result, many candy producers, including the makers of Life Savers, Jaw Breakers, Red Hots, and Fannie May and Fanny Farmer chocolates, have moved to countries like Canada and Mexico, where sugar can be purchased at its true market price. Thus, employment among sugar-using firms in the United States is reduced. Further, because foreigners sell less sugar in the United States, they have less purchasing power with which to buy products we export to them. This, too, reduces U.S. employment.

Once the secondary effects of trade restrictions like the sugar quota program are taken into consideration, we have no reason to expect that U.S. employment will increase as a result. There may be more jobs in favored industries, but there will be less employment in others. Trade restrictions reshuffle employment rather than increase it. But those who unwittingly fail to consider the secondary effects will miss this point. Clearly, consideration of the secondary effects is an important ingredient of the economic way of thinking.

7. The value of a good or service is subjective. Preferences differ, sometimes dramatically, between individuals. How much is a ticket to see a performance of the Bolshoi Ballet worth? Some people would be willing to pay a very high price, while others might prefer to stay home, even if tickets were free! Circumstances can change from day to day, even for a given individual. Alice, a ballet fan who usually would value the ticket at more than its price of $100, is invited to a party and suddenly becomes uninterested in

Sometimes actions change the incentives people face and they respond accordingly, creating secondary effects that were not intended.

THE FAMILY CIRCUS® **By Bil Keane**

© Bill Keane, Inc. Reprinted with special permission of King Features Syndicate.

3-25
Copyright 1988
Cowles Syndicate Inc

"Everybody wants to be sick.
I'm using M&M's for pills."

attending the ballet. Now what is the ticket worth? If she knows a friend who would give her $40 for the ticket, it is worth at least that much. If she advertises the ticket on eBay and gets $60 for it, a higher value is created. But if someone who doesn't know of the ticket would have been willing to pay even more, then a potential trade creating even more value is missed. If that particular performance is sold out, perhaps someone in town would be willing to pay $120. One thing is certain: The value of the ticket depends on several things, including who uses it and under what circumstances.

Economics recognizes that people can and do value goods differently. Mike may prefer to have a grass field rather than a parking lot next to his workplace and be willing to bear the cost of walking farther from his car each day. Kim, on the other hand, may prefer the parking lot and the shorter walk. As a science, economics does not place any inherent moral judgment or value on one person's preferences over another's—in economics all individuals' preferences are counted equally. Because the subjective preferences of individuals differ, it is difficult for one person to know how much another will value an item.

Think about how hard it is to know what would make a good gift for even a close friend or family member. Thus, arranging trades, or otherwise moving items to higher valued users and uses, is not a simple task. The entrepreneurial individual, who knows how to locate the right buyers and arranges for goods to flow to their highest valued use, can sometimes create huge increases in value from existing resources. In fact, people moving goods toward those who value them most and combining resources into goods that individuals value more highly is a primary source of economic progress.

Scientific thinking
Developing a theory from basic principles and testing it against events in the real world. Good theories are consistent with and help explain real-world events. Theories that are inconsistent with the real world are invalid and must be rejected.

8. The test of a theory is its ability to predict. Economic thinking is **scientific thinking**. The proof of the pudding is in the eating. How useful an economic theory is depends on how well it predicts the future consequences of economic action. Economists develop economic theories using scientific thinking based on basic principles. The idea is to predict how incentives will affect decision makers and compare the predictions against real-world events. If the events in the real world are consistent with a theory, we say that the theory has *predictive value* and is therefore valid.

If it is impossible to test the theoretical relationships of a discipline, the discipline does not qualify as a science. Because economics deals with human beings who can think and respond in a variety of ways, can economic theories really be tested? The answer to this question is yes, if, on average, human beings respond in predictable and consistent ways to changes in economic conditions. The economist believes that this is the case, even though not all individuals will respond in the specified manner. Economists usually do not try to predict the behavior of a specific individual; instead, they focus on the general behavior of a large number of individuals.

In the 1950s, economists began to do laboratory experiments to test economic theories. Individuals were brought into laboratories to see how they would act in buying and selling situations, under differing rules. For example, cash rewards were given to individuals who, when an auction was conducted, were able to sell at high prices and buy at low prices, thus approximating real-world market incentives. These experiments have verified many of the important propositions of economic theory.

Laboratory experiments, however, cannot duplicate all real economic interactions. How can we test economic theory when controlled experiments are not feasible? This is a problem, but economics is no different from astronomy in this respect. Astronomers can use theories tested in physics laboratories, but they must also deal with the world as it is. They cannot change the course of the stars or planets to see what impact the change would have on the gravitational pull of Earth. Similarly, economists cannot arbitrarily change the prices of cars or unskilled-labor services in real markets just to observe the effects on quantities purchased or levels of employment. However, economic conditions (for example, prices, production costs, technology, and transportation costs), like the location of the planets, do change from time to time. As actual conditions change, an economic theory can be tested by comparing its predictions with real-world outcomes. Just as the universe is the main laboratory of the astronomer, the real-world economy is the primary laboratory of the economist.

POSITIVE AND NORMATIVE ECONOMICS

As a social science, economics is concerned with predicting or determining the impact of changes in economic variables on the actions of human beings. Scientific economics, commonly referred to as **positive economics,** attempts to determine "what is." Positive economic statements involve potentially verifiable or refutable propositions. For example: "If the price of gasoline rises, people will buy less gasoline." We can statistically investigate (and estimate) the relationship between gasoline prices and gallons sold. We can analyze the facts to determine the correctness of a positive economic statement. Remember, a positive economic statement need not be correct, it simply must be testable.

In contrast, **normative economics** is about "what ought to be," given the preferences and philosophical views of the advocate. Value judgments often result in disagreement about normative economic matters. Two people may differ on a policy matter because one is from one political party and the other is from another, or because one wants cheaper food while the other favors organic farming (which is more expensive), and so on. They may even agree about the expected outcome of altering an economic variable (that is, the positive economics of an issue), but disagree as to whether that outcome is desirable.

Unlike positive economic statements, normative economic statements can neither be confirmed nor proven false by scientific testing. "Business firms should not be concerned with profits." "We should have fewer parking lots and more green space on campus." "The price of gasoline is too high." These normative statements cannot be scientifically tested because their validity rests on value judgments.

Normative economic views can sometimes influence our attitude toward positive economic analysis, however. When we agree with the objectives of a policy, it's easy to overlook the warnings of positive economics. Although positive economics does not tell us which policy is best, it can provide evidence about the likely effects of a policy. Sometimes proponents unknowingly support policies that are actually in conflict with their own goals and objectives. Positive economics, based on sound economic logic, can help overcome this potential problem.

Economics can expand our knowledge of how the real world operates, in both the private and the public (government) sectors. If we do not fully understand the implications, including the secondary effects, of alternative actions, we will not be able to choose intelligently. Yet, it is not always easy to use economic thinking to isolate the impact of a change. Let's now consider some pitfalls to avoid in economic thinking.

> A positive science may be defined as a body of systematized knowledge concerning what is; a normative or regulative science is a body of systematized knowledge relating to criteria of what ought to be, and concerned therefore with the ideal as distinguished from the actual.
> —*John Neville Keynes*[5]

Positive economics
The scientific study of "what is" among economic relationships.

Normative economics
Judgments about "what ought to be" in economic matters. Normative economic views cannot be proven false because they are based on value judgments.

PITFALLS TO AVOID IN ECONOMIC THINKING

Violation of the *Ceteris Paribus* Condition Can Lead One to Draw the Wrong Conclusion

Economists often qualify their statements with the words *ceteris paribus*. *Ceteris paribus* is a Latin term meaning "other things constant." An example of a *ceteris paribus* statement would be the following: "*Ceteris paribus,* an increase in the price of housing will cause buyers to reduce their purchases of housing." Unfortunately, we live in a dynamic world, so things seldom remain constant. For example, as the price of housing rises, the income of consumers might also increase. Each of these factors—higher housing prices and increasing consumer income—will have an impact on housing purchases. In fact, we would generally expect them to have opposite effects: Higher prices are likely to reduce housing purchases, while higher consumer incomes are likely to increase them. We point out this pitfall because sometimes statistical data (or casual observations) do not support economic theories. In most of these cases, other factors have also changed. The effects observed simply reflect the combined effect of these changes.

Ceteris paribus
A Latin term meaning "other things constant," used when the effect of one change is being described, recognizing that if other things changed, they also could affect the result. Economists often describe the effects of one change, knowing that in the real world, other things might change and also exert an effect.

---

[5]John Neville Keynes, *The Scope and Method of Political Economy,* 4th ed. (1917), 34–35.

The task of sorting out the effects of two or more variables that change at the same time is difficult. However, with a strong grip on economic theory, some ingenuity, and enough data, it can usually be done. This is, in fact, precisely the day-to-day work of many professional economists.

Good Intentions Do Not Guarantee Desirable Outcomes

There is a tendency to believe that if the proponents of a policy have good intentions, their proposals must be sound. This is not necessarily the case. Proponents may be unaware of some of the adverse secondary effects of their proposals, particularly when they are indirect and observable only over time. Even if their policies would be largely ineffective, politicians may still find it advantageous to call attention to the severity of a problem and propose a program to deal with it. In other cases, proponents of a policy may actually be seeking a goal other than the one they espouse. They may tie their arguments to objectives that are widely supported by the general populace. Thus, the fact that an advocate says a program will help the poor, increase wages, improve health care, expand employment, or achieve some other highly desirable objective, does not necessarily make it so.

Let's begin with a couple of straightforward examples. Federal legislation has been introduced that would require all children, including those under age two, to be fastened in a child safety seat when traveling by air. Proponents argue the legislation will increase the survival rate of children in the case of an airline crash and thereby save lives. Certainly, saving lives is a highly desirable objective, but will this really be the case? *Some* lives will probably be saved. But what about the secondary effects? The legislation would mean that a parent traveling with a small child would have to purchase an additional ticket, which will make it more expensive to fly. As a result, many families will choose to travel by auto rather than air. Because the likelihood of a serious accident per mile traveled in an automobile is several times higher than for air travel, more automobile travel will result in more injuries and fatalities. In fact, studies indicate that the increase in injuries and fatalities from additional auto travel will exceed the number of lives saved by airline safety seats.[6] Thus, even though the intentions of the proponents may well be lofty, there is reason to believe that the net impact of their proposal will be more fatalities and injuries than would be the case in the absence of the legislation.

The stated objective of the Endangered Species Act is to protect various species that are on the verge of extinction. Certainly, this is a admirable objective, but there is nonetheless reason to question the effectiveness of the Act itself. The Endangered Species Act allows the government to regulate the use of individual private property if an endangered species is found present on *or* near his or her land. To avoid losing control of their property, many landowners have taken steps to make their land less attractive as a natural habitat for these endangered species. For example, the endangered red-cockaded woodpecker nests primarily in old trees within southern pine ecosystems. Landowners have responded by cutting down trees the woodpeckers like to nest in to avoid having one nest on their land, which would result in the owner losing control of this part of their property. The end result is that the habitat for these birds has actually been disappearing more rapidly.

As you can see, good intentions are not enough. An unsound proposal will lead to undesirable outcomes even if it is supported by proponents with good intentions. But economic thinking can help us avoid this pitfall.

Association Is Not Causation

In economics, identifying cause-and-effect relationships is very important. But statistical association alone cannot establish this causation. Perhaps an extreme example will illus-

---

[6]For a detailed analysis of this subject, see Thomas B. Newman, Brian D. Johnston, and David C. Grossman, "Effects and Costs of Requiring Child-Restraint Systems for Young Children Traveling on Commercial Airplanes," *Archives of Pediatrics and Adolescent Medicine* 157 (October 2003): 969–74.

trate the point. Suppose that each November a witch doctor performs a voodoo dance designed to summon the gods of winter, and that soon after the dance is performed, the weather in fact begins to turn cold. The witch doctor's dance is associated with the arrival of winter, meaning that the two events appear to have happened in conjunction with one another. But is this really evidence that the witch doctor's dance actually caused the arrival of winter? Most of us would answer no, even though the two events seemed to happen in conjunction with one another.

Those who argue that a causal relationship exists simply because of the presence of statistical association are committing a logical fallacy known as the *post hoc propter ergo hoc* fallacy. Sound economics warns against this potential source of error.

The Fallacy of Composition: What's True for One Might Not Be True for All

What is true for the individual (or subcomponent) may not be true for the group (or the whole). If you stand up for an exciting play during a football game, you will be better able to see. But what happens if everyone stands up at the same time? Will everyone be better able to see? The answer is, of course, no. Thus, what is true for a single individual does not necessarily apply to the group as a whole. When everyone stands up, the view for individual spectators fails to improve; in fact, it may even become worse.

People who mistakenly argue that what is true for the part is also true for the whole are said to be committing the **fallacy of composition**. What is true for the individual can be misleading and is often fallacious when applied to the entire economy. The fallacy of composition highlights the importance of considering both a micro view and a macro view in the study of economics. **Microeconomics** focuses on the decision making of consumers, producers, and resource suppliers operating in a narrowly defined market, such as that for a specific good or resource. Because individual decision makers are the moving force behind all economic action, the foundations of economics are clearly rooted in a micro view.

As we have seen, however, what is true for a small unit may not be true in the aggregate. **Macroeconomics** focuses on how the aggregation of individual micro-units affects our analysis. Like microeconomics, it is concerned with incentives, prices, and output. Macroeconomics, however, aggregates markets, lumping together all 120 million households in this country. Macroeconomics involves topics like total consumption spending, saving, and employment, in the economy as a whole. Similarly, the nation's 7 million business firms are lumped together in "the business sector." What factors determine the level of aggregate output, the rate of inflation, the amount of unemployment, and interest rates? These are macroeconomic questions. In short, macroeconomics examines the forest rather than the individual trees. As we move from the micro-components to a macro view of the whole, it is important that we beware of the fallacy of composition.

Fallacy of composition
Erroneous view that what is true for the individual (or the part) will also be true for the group (or the whole).

Microeconomics
The branch of economics that focuses on how human behavior affects the conduct of affairs within narrowly defined units, such as individual households or business firms.

Macroeconomics
The branch of economics that focuses on how human behavior affects outcomes in highly aggregated markets, such as the markets for labor or consumer products.

LOOKING AHEAD

The primary purpose of this book is to encourage you to develop the economic way of thinking so that you can separate sound reasoning from economic nonsense. Once you have developed the economic way of thinking, economics will be relatively easy. Using the economic way of thinking can also be fun. Moreover, it will help you become a better citizen. It will give you a different and fascinating perspective on what motivates people, why they act the way they do, and why their actions sometimes go against the best interest of the community or nation. It will also give you valuable insight into how people's actions can be rechanneled for the benefit of the community at large.

ECONOMICS AS A CAREER

If you find yourself doing well in this course and discover that economics interests you, you may want to think about majoring in it. Graduating with a major in economics provides a variety of career choices. Many students go on to graduate school in economics, business, public administration, or law. Graduate M.B.A. and law programs find economics majors particularly attractive because of their strong analytical skills.

A graduate degree (a master's or doctorate) in economics is typically required to pursue a career as a professional economist. About one-half of all professional economists are employed by colleges and universities as teachers and researchers. Professional economists also work for the government or private businesses. Most major corporations have a staff of economists to advise them. Governments employ economists to analyze the impact of policy alternatives. The federal government's Council of Economic Advisers provides the president with analyses of how the activities of the government influence the economy.

Students who major in economics but who do not pursue graduate school still have many job opportunities. Because economics is a way of thinking, knowledge of it is a valuable decision-making tool that can be used in almost any job. Undergraduate majors in economics typically work in business, government service, banking, or insurance. Opportunities for people with undergraduate economics degrees to teach the subject at the high school level are also increasing. Arnold Schwarzenegger, Mick Jagger, and Ronald Reagan are among the long list of famous undergraduate economics majors!

The average salary of an economics graduate is comparable to that of finance and accounting graduates and is generally higher than those with management or marketing degrees. Professional economists with graduate degrees in economics who work for private business average approximately $90,000 per year, and those who choose to work as teachers and researchers at colleges and universities earn approximately $75,000 annually. Although salaries vary substantially, the point is that a career in economics can be rewarding both personally and financially.

Even if you choose not to major in economics, you will find that your economics courses will broaden your horizons and increase your ability to understand and analyze what is going on around you in the worlds of politics, business, and human relations. Economics is a social science that often overlaps with the fields of political science, sociology, and psychology. Because the economic way of thinking is so useful in making sense of the world around us, economics has sometimes been called the "queen of the social sciences." Reflecting this, economics is the only social science for which a Nobel Prize of the Swedish Academy of Science is awarded.

! KEY POINTS

▼ Scarcity and choice are the two essential ingredients of economic analysis. A good is scarce when the human desire for it exceeds the amount freely available from nature. Scarcity requires us to choose among available alternatives. Every choice entails a trade-off.

▼ Every society will have to devise some method of rationing the scarce resources among competing uses. Markets generally use price as the rationing device. Competition is a natural outgrowth of the need to ration scarce goods.

▼ Scarcity and poverty are not the same thing. Absence of poverty implies that some basic level of need has been met. An absence of scarcity implies that our desires for goods are fully satisfied. We may someday eliminate poverty, but scarcity will always be with us.

▼ Economics is a way of thinking that emphasizes eight points:

1. The use of scarce resources to produce a good always has an opportunity cost.

2. Individuals make decisions purposefully, always seeking to choose the option they expect to be most consistent with their personal goals.

3. Incentives matter. The likelihood of people choosing an option increases as personal benefits rise and personal costs decline.

4. Economic reasoning focuses on the impact of marginal changes because it is the marginal benefits and marginal costs that influence choices.

5. Since information is scarce, uncertainty is a fact of life.

6. In addition to their direct impact, economic changes often generate secondary effects.

7. The value of a good or service is subjective and varies with individual preferences and circumstances.

8. The test of an economic theory is its ability to predict and to explain events in the real world.

▼ Economic science is positive; it attempts to explain the actual consequences of economic actions. Normative economics goes further, applying value judgments to make suggestions about what "ought to be."

▼ Microeconomics focuses on narrowly defined units, while macroeconomics is concerned with highly aggregated units. When shifting focus from micro to macro, one must beware of the fallacy of composition: What's good for the individual may not be good for the group as a whole.

▼ The origin of economics as a science dates to the publication of *The Wealth of Nations* by Adam Smith in 1776. Smith believed a market economy would bring individual self-interest and the public interest into harmony.

CRITICAL ANALYSIS QUESTIONS

1. Indicate how each of the following changes would influence the incentive of a decision maker to undertake the action described.
   a. A reduction in the temperature from 80° to 50° on one's decision to go swimming
   b. A change in the meeting time of the introductory economics course from 11:00 A.M. to 7:30 A.M. on one's decision to attend the lectures
   c. A reduction in the number of exam questions that relate directly to the text on the student's decision to read the text
   d. An increase in the price of beef on one's decision to buy steak
   e. An increase in the rental rates of apartments on one's decision to build additional rental housing units

*2. "The government should provide such goods as health care, education, and highways because it can provide them for free." Is this statement true or false? Explain your answer.

3. a. What method is used to ration goods in a market economy? How does this rationing method influence the incentive of individuals to supply goods, services, and resources to others?
   b. How are grades rationed in your economics class? How does this rationing method influence student behavior? Suppose the highest grades were rationed to those whom the teacher liked best. How would this method of rationing influence student behavior?

*4. In recent years, both the personal exemption and child tax credit have been increased in the United States. According to the basic principles of economics, how will the birthrate be affected by policies that reduce the taxes imposed on those with children?

*5. "The economic way of thinking stresses that good intentions lead to sound policy." Is this statement true or false? Explain your answer.

6. Self-interest is a powerful motivator. Does this necessarily imply that people are selfish and greedy? Do self-interest and selfishness mean the same thing?

*7. Congress and government agencies often make laws to help protect the safety of consumers. New cars, for example, are required to have many safety features before they can be sold in the United States. These rules do indeed provide added safety for buyers, although they also add to the cost of making and price of buying the new vehicles. What secondary effects can you see happening as the result of mandating that automobiles have airbags? What incentives do you see changing for drivers as the result of making cars safer? Do you think the millions of dollars spent by consumers on air bags each year could be better spent elsewhere to save even more lives?

*8. "Individuals who economize are missing the point of life. Money is not so important that it should rule the way we live." Evaluate this statement.

*9. "Positive economics cannot tell us which agricultural policy is better, so it is useless to policymakers." Evaluate this statement.

*10. "I examined the statistics for our basketball team's wins last year and found that, when the third team played more, the winning margin increased. If the coach played the third team more, we would win by a bigger margin." Evaluate this statement.

11. Which of the following are positive economic statements and which are normative?
    a. The speed limit should be lowered to 55 miles per hour on interstate highways.
    b. Higher gasoline prices cause the quantity of gasoline that consumers buy to increase.
    c. A comparison of costs and benefits should not be used to assess environmental regulations.
    d. Higher taxes on alcohol result in less drinking and driving.

12. "Economics is about trade-offs. If more scarce resources are used to produce one thing, fewer will be available to produce others." Evaluate this statement.

13. Do individuals "economize"? If so, what are they trying to do? Do you economize when you shop at the mall? Why or why not?

*14. Should the United States attempt to reduce air and water pollution to zero? Why or why not?

---

*Asterisk denotes questions for which answers are given in Appendix B.

ADDENDUM

Understanding Graphs

Economists often use graphs to illustrate economic relations. Graphs are like pictures. They are visual aids that can communicate valuable information in a small amount of space. A picture may be worth a thousand words, but only to a person who understands the picture (and the graph).

This addendum illustrates the use of simple graphs as a way to communicate. Many students, particularly those with some mathematics background, are already familiar with this material, and can safely ignore it. This addendum is for those who need to be assured that they can understand graphic illustrations of economic concepts.

The Simple Bar Graph

A simple bar graph helps us visualize comparative relationships and understand them better. It is particularly useful for illustrating how an economic indicator varies among countries, across time periods, or under alternative economic conditions.

Exhibit A-1, is a bar graph illustrating economic data. The table in part (a) presents data on the income per person in 2002 for several countries. Part (b) uses a bar graph to illustrate the same data. The horizontal scale of the graph indicates the total income per person. A bar is made for indicating the income level (see the dollar scale on the *x*-axis) of each country. The length of each bar is in pro-

COUNTRY	TOTAL INCOME PER PERSON, 2002
United States	$35,060
Switzerland	31,250
Canada	28,070
Germany	26,220
Japan	26,070
United Kingdom	25,870
Sweden	25,080
Mexico	8,540
China	4,390
India	2,570
Nigeria	780

(a)

EXHIBIT A-1
International Comparison of Income per Person

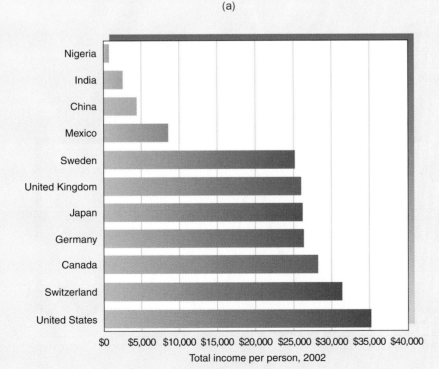

(b)

Source: The World Bank, *World Development Report 2004* (http://econ.worldbank.org/wdr/), Table 1.

portion to the per-person income of the country. Thus, the length of the bars provides a visual illustration of how per capita income varies across the countries. For example, the extremely short bar for Nigeria shows immediately that income per person there is only a small fraction of the comparable income figure for the United States, Japan, Switzerland, and several other countries

Linear Graphic Presentation

Economists often want to illustrate variations in economic variables with the passage of time. A linear graph with time on the horizontal axis and an economic variable on the vertical axis is a useful tool to indicate variations over time. **Exhibit A-2** illustrates a simple linear graph of

changes in consumer prices (the inflation rate) in the United States between 1960 and 2003. The table of the exhibit presents data on the percentage change in consumer prices for each year. Beginning with 1960, the horizontal axis indicates the time period (year). The inflation rate is plotted vertically above each year. Of course, the height of the plot (line) indicates the inflation rate during that year. For example, in 1975 the inflation rate was 9.1 percent. This point is plotted at the 9.1 percent vertical distance directly above the year 1975. In 1976 the inflation rate fell to 5.8 percent. Thus, the vertical plot of the 1976 inflation rate is lower than that for 1975. The inflation rate for each year shown in part (a) is plotted at the corresponding height directly above the year in part (b). The linear graph

EXHIBIT A-2
Changes in Level of Prices in United States, 1960–2003

The tabular data (a) of the inflation rate are presented in graphic form in (b).

YEAR	PERCENT CHANGE IN CONSUMER PRICES	YEAR	PERCENT CHANGE IN CONSUMER PRICES
1960	1.7	1982	6.2
1961	1.0	1983	3.2
1962	1.0	1984	4.3
1963	1.3	1985	3.6
1964	1.3	1986	1.9
1965	1.6	1987	3.6
1966	2.9	1988	4.1
1967	3.1	1989	4.8
1968	4.2	1990	5.4
1969	5.5	1991	4.2
1970	5.7	1992	3.0
1971	4.4	1993	3.0
1972	3.2	1994	2.6
1973	6.2	1995	2.8
1974	11.0	1996	3.0
1975	9.1	1997	2.3
1976	5.8	1998	1.6
1977	6.5	1999	2.2
1978	7.6	2000	3.4
1979	11.3	2001	2.8
1980	13.5	2002	1.6
1981	10.3	2003	2.3

(a)

(b)

Source: Bureau of Labor Statistics (http://stats.bls.gov/cpihome.htm).

is simply a line connecting the points plotted for each of the years.

The linear graph is a visual aid to understanding what happens to the inflation rate during the period. As the graph shows, the inflation rate rose sharply between 1967 and 1969, 1972 and 1974, and 1978 and 1980. It was substantially higher during the 1970s than in the early 1960s or the mid-1980s and 1990s. Most importantly, the inflation rate has been lower and more stable since 1983 than in the period before. Although the linear graph does not communicate any information not in the table, it does make it easier to see the pattern of the data. Thus, economists often use simple graphics rather than tables to communicate information.

Direct and Inverse Relationships

Economic logic often suggests that two variables are linked in a specific way. Suppose an investigation reveals that, other things being constant, farmers supply more wheat as the price of wheat increases. **Exhibit A-3** presents hypothetical data on the relationship between the price of wheat and the quantity supplied by farmers, first in tabular form in part (a) and then as a simple two-dimensional graph in part (b). Suppose we measure the quantity of wheat supplied by farmers on the x-axis (the horizontal axis) and the price of wheat on the y-axis (the vertical axis). Points indicating the value of x (quantity supplied) at alternative values of y (price of wheat) can then be plotted. The line (or curve) linking the points illustrates the relationship between the price of wheat and the amount supplied by farmers.

In the case of price and quantity supplied of wheat, the two variables are directly related. When the y-variable increases, so does the x-variable. When two variables are directly related, the graph illustrating the linkage between the two will slope upward to the right, as in the case of SS in part (b).

Sometimes the x-variable and the y-variable are inversely related. A decline in the y-variable is associated with an increase in the x-variable. Therefore, a curve picturing the inverse relationship between x and y slopes

PRICE	AMOUNT OF WHEAT SUPPLIED BY FARMERS PER YEAR (MILLIONS OF BUSHELS)
$1	45
2	75
3	100
4	120
5	140

(a)

EXHIBIT A-3
Direct Relationship Between Variables

As the table (a) indicates, farmers are willing to supply more wheat at a higher price. Thus, there is a direct relation between the price of wheat and the quantity supplied. When the x- and y-variables are directly related, a curve mapping the relationship between the two will slope upward to the right like SS.

(b)

EXHIBIT A-4
Inverse Relationship
Between Variables

As the table (a) shows, consumers will demand (purchase) more wheat as the price declines. Thus, there is an inverse relationship between the price of wheat and the quantity demanded. When the *x*- and *y*-variables are inversely related, a curve showing the relationship between the two will slope downward to the right like *DD*.

Price	Amount of Wheat Demanded by Consumers per Year (millions of bushels)
$1	170
2	130
3	100
4	75
5	60

(a)

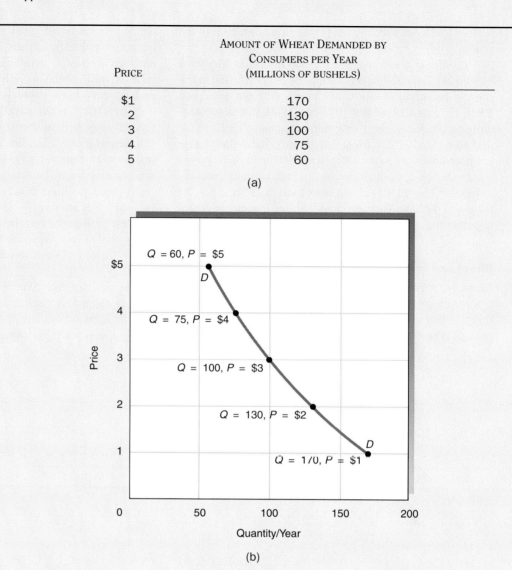

(b)

downward to the right. **Exhibit A-4** illustrates this case. As the data of the table indicate, consumers purchase more as the price of wheat declines. Measuring the price of wheat on the *y*-axis (by convention, economists always place price on the *y*-axis) and the quantity of wheat purchased on the *x*-axis, the relationship between these two variables can also be illustrated graphically. If the price of wheat were $5 per bushel, only 60 million bushels would be purchased by consumers. As the price declines to $4 per bushel, annual consumption increases to 75 million bushels. At still lower prices, the quantity purchased by consumers will expand to larger and larger amounts. As part (b) illustrates, the inverse relationship between price and quantity of wheat purchased generates a curve that slopes downward to the right.

Complex Relationships

Sometimes the initial relationship between the *x*- and *y*-variables will change. **Exhibit A-5** illustrates more complex relations of this type. Part (a) shows the typical rela-

tionship between annual earnings and age. As a young person gets work experience and develops skills, earnings usually expand. Thus, initially, age and annual earnings are directly related; annual earnings increase with age. However, beyond a certain age (approximately age 55), annual earnings generally decline as workers approach retirement. As a result, the initial direct relationship between age and earnings changes to an inverse relation. When this is the case, annual income expands to a maximum (at age 55) and then begins to decline with years of age.

Part (b) illustrates an initial inverse relation that later changes to a direct relationship. Consider the impact of travel speed on gasoline consumption per mile. At low speeds, the automobile engine will not be used efficiently. As speed increases from 5 mph to 10 mph and on to a speed of 40 mph, gasoline consumption per mile declines. In this range, there is an inverse relationship between speed of travel (*x*) and gasoline consumption per mile (*y*). However, as speed increases beyond 40 mph, air resistance increases

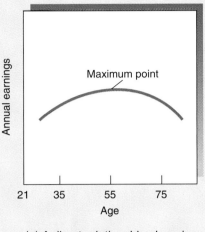

(a) A direct relationship changing to inverse

(b) An inverse relationship changing to direct

EXHIBIT A-5
Complex Relationships Between Variables

At first, an increase in age (and work experience) leads to a higher income, but later earnings decline as the worker approaches retirement (a). Thus, age and annual income are initially directly related, but at approximately age 55 an inverse relationship emerges. Part (b) illustrates the relationship between travel speed and gasoline consumption per mile. Initially, gasoline consumption per mile declines as speed increases (an inverse relationship), but as speed increases above 40 mph, gasoline consumption per mile increases with the speed of travel (direct relationship).

and more gasoline per mile is required to maintain the additional speed. At very high speeds, gasoline consumption per mile increases substantially with speed of travel. Thus, gasoline consumption per mile reaches a minimum, and a direct relationship between the x- and y-variables describes the relationship beyond that point (40 mph).

Slope of a Straight Line

In economics, we are often interested in how much the y-variable changes in response to a change in the x-variable. The slope of the line or curve reveals this information.

Mathematically, the slope of a line or curve is equal to the change in the y-variable divided by the change in the x-variable.

Exhibit A-6 illustrates the calculation of the slope for a straight line. The exhibit shows how the daily earnings (y-variable) of a worker change with hours worked (the x-variable). The wage rate of the worker is $10 per hour, so when 1 hour is worked, earnings are equal to $10. For 2 hours of work, earnings jump to $20, and so on. A 1-hour change in hours worked leads to a $10 change in earnings. Thus, the

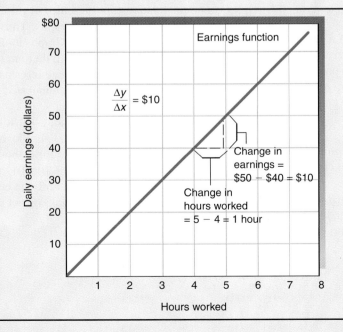

EXHIBIT A-6
Slope of a Straight Line

The slope of a line is equal to the change in y divided by the change in x. The line opposite illustrates the case in which daily earnings increase by $10 per hour worked. Thus, the slope of the earnings function is 10 ($10 ÷ 1 hr). For a straight line, the slope is constant at each point on the line.

EXHIBIT A-7
Slope of a Nonlinear Curve

The slope of a curve at any point is equal to the slope of the straight line tangent to the curve at the point. As the lines tangent to the curve at points *A* and *B* illustrate, the slope of a curve will change from point to point along the curve.

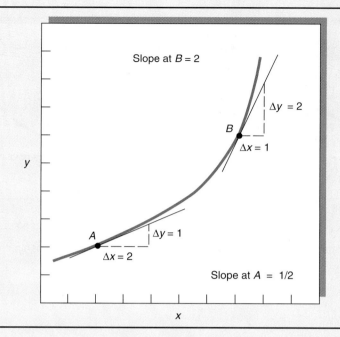

slope of the line ($\Delta y/\Delta x$) is equal to 10. (The symbol Δ means "change in.") In the case of a straight line, the change in *y,* per unit change in *x,* is equal for all points on the line. Thus, the slope of a straight line is constant for all points along the line. Exhibit A-6 illustrates a case in which a direct relation exists between the *x*- and *y*-variables. For an inverse relation, the *y*-variable decreases as the *x*-variable increases. So, when *x* and *y* are inversely related, the slope of the line will be negative.

Slope of a Curve

In contrast with a straight line, the slope of a curve is different at each point along the curve. The slope of a curve at a specific point is equal to the slope of a line tangent to the curve at the point, meaning a line that just touches the curve.

Exhibit A-7 illustrates how the slope of a curve at a specific point is determined. First, consider the slope of the curve at point *A*. A line tangent to the curve at point *A* indicates that *y* changes by one unit when *x* changes by two units at point *A*. Thus, the slope ($\Delta y/\Delta x$) of the curve at *A* is equal to 0.5.

Now consider the slope of the curve at point *B*. The line tangent to the curve at *B* indicates that *y* changes by two units for each one-unit change in *x* at point *B*. Thus, at *B* the slope ($\Delta y/\Delta x$) is equal to 2. At point *B,* a change in the *x*-variable leads to a much larger change in *y* than it does at point *A*. The greater slope of the curve at *B* re-

flects this greater change in *y* per unit change in *x* at *B* relative to *A*.

Graphs Are Not a Substitute for Economic Thinking

By now you should have a fairly good understanding of how to read a graph. If you still feel uncomfortable with graphs, try drawing (graphing) the relationship between several things with which you are familiar. If you work, try graphing the relationship between your hours worked (*x*-axis) and your weekly earnings (*y*-axis). Exhibit A-3 could guide you with this exercise. Can you graph the relationship between the price of gasoline and your expenditures on gasoline? Graphing these simple relationships will give you greater confidence in your ability to grasp more complex economic relationships presented in graphs.

This text uses only simple graphs. Thus, there is no reason for you to be intimidated. Graphs look much more complex than they really are. In fact, they are nothing more than a simple device to communicate information quickly and concisely. Nothing can be communicated with a graph that cannot be communicated verbally.

Most important, graphs are not a substitute for economic thinking. Although a graph may illustrate that two variables are related, it tells us nothing about the cause-and-effect relationship between the variables. To determine probable cause and effect, we must rely on economic theory. Thus, the economic way of thinking, not graphs, is the power station of economic analysis.

Some Tools of the Economist

Chapter Focus

■ What is opportunity cost? Why do economists place so much emphasis on it?

■ Why do people engage in exchange?

■ How does private ownership affect the use of resources? Will private owners pay any attention to the desires of others?

■ What does a production possibilities curve demonstrate?

■ What are the sources of gains from trade? How does trade influence our modern living standards?

■ What are the two major methods of economic organization? How do they differ?

The key insight of Adam Smith's Wealth of Nations *is misleadingly simple: if an exchange between two parties is voluntary, it will not take place unless both believe they will benefit from it. Most economic fallacies derive from the neglect of this simple insight, from the tendency to assume that there is a fixed pie, that one party can gain only at the expense of another.*

—Milton and Rose Friedman[1]

---

[1]Milton and Rose Friedman, *Free to Choose* (Harcourt Brace, 1990), 13.

I n the preceding chapter, you were introduced to the economic way of thinking. We will now begin to apply that approach. This chapter focuses on five topics: opportunity cost, trade, property rights, the potential output level of an economy, and the creation of wealth. These seemingly diverse topics are in fact highly interrelated. For example, the opportunity cost of goods determines which ones an individual or a nation should produce and which should be acquired through trade. In turn, the ways in which trade and property rights are structured influence the amount of output and wealth an economy can create. These tools of economics are important for answering the basic economic questions: what to produce, how to produce it, and for whom it will be produced. We will begin by first explaining in more detail what opportunity cost is. ■

WHAT SHALL WE GIVE UP?

Because of scarcity we can't have everything we want. As a result, we constantly face choices that involve trade-offs between our competing desires. Most of us would like to have more time for leisure, recreation, vacations, hobbies, education, and skill development. We would also like to have more wealth, a larger savings account, and more consumable goods. However, all these things are scarce, in the sense that they are limited. Our efforts to get more of one will conflict with our efforts to get more of others.

Opportunity Cost

An unpleasant fact of economics is that the choice to do one thing is, at the same time, a choice *not* to do something else. Your choice to spend time reading this book is a choice not to spend the time playing video games, listening to a math lecture, or going to a party. These things must be given up because you decided to read this book instead. As we indicated in Chapter 1, the highest valued alternative sacrificed in order to choose an option is called the *opportunity cost* of that choice. In economics when we refer to the "cost" of an action, we are referring to its opportunity cost.

Opportunity costs are subjective because they depend upon how the decision maker values his or her options. They are also based on the expectations of the decision maker—what he or she expects the value of the forgone alternatives will be. Because of this, opportunity cost can never be directly measured by someone other than the decision maker. Only the person choosing can know the value of what is given up.[2] This makes it difficult for someone other than the decision maker—including experts and elected officials—to make choices on that person's behalf. Moreover, not only do people differ in the trade-offs they prefer to make, but their preferences also change with time and circumstances. Thus, the decision maker is the only person who can properly evaluate the options and decide which is the best, given his or her preferences and current circumstances.

Monetary costs can be measured objectively in terms of dollars and cents (or yen, lira, and so forth). They also represent an opportunity cost. If you spend $20 on a new CD, you must now forgo the other items you could have purchased with the $20—a new shirt, for example. However, it is important to recognize that monetary costs do not represent the total opportunity cost of an option. The total cost of attending a football game, for example, is the highest valued opportunity lost as a result of both the time you spend at the game and the amount of money you pay for your ticket. In cases like the purchase of a CD, where there is minimal outlay of time, effort, and other resources to make the purchase, the monetary cost will approximate the total cost. Contrast this with a decision to sit on your sofa and listen to your new CD, which involves little or no monetary cost, but has a clear opportunity cost of your time. In this second case, the monetary cost is a poor measure of the total cost.

---

[2]See James M. Buchanan, *Cost and Choice* (Chicago: Markham, 1969), for a classic work on the relationship between cost and choice.

Opportunity Cost and the Real World

Is real-world decision making influenced by opportunity costs? Consider your own decision to attend college. Your opportunity cost of going to college is the value of the next best alternative, which could be measured as the salary you would earn if you had chosen to go directly into full-time work instead. Every year you stay in college, you give up what you could have earned by working that year. Typically, students incur opportunity costs of $80,000 or more in forgone income during their stay in college.

But what if the opportunity cost of attending college changes? How will it affect your decision? Suppose, for example, that you received a job offer today for $250,000 per year as an athlete or an entertainer, but the job would require so much travel that school would be impossible. Would this change in the opportunity cost of going to college affect your choice as to whether to continue in school? It likely would. Going to college would mean you would have to say goodbye to the huge salary you've been offered. (See the accompanying illustration on LeBron James for a good example.) You can clearly tell from this example that the monetary cost of college (tuition, books, and so forth) isn't the only factor influencing your decision. Your opportunity cost plays a part, too.

Even when their parents pay all the monetary expenses of their college education, some students are surprised to learn that they are actually incurring more of the total cost of going to college than their parents. For example, the average monetary cost (tuition, room and board, books, and so forth) for a student attending college is about $10,000 per year ($40,000 over four years). Even if the student's next best alternative were working at a job that paid only $15,000 per year, over four years, that would amount to $60,000 in forgone earnings, So, the total cost of the student's education would be $100,000 ($40,000 in monetary costs paid by the parents and $60,000 in opportunity costs incurred by the student).[3]

Now consider another decision made by college students—whether to attend a particular class meeting. The monetary cost of attending class (bus fare, parking, gasoline costs,

AP PHOTO/MARK DUNCAN

LeBron James (shown here with Cleveland Cavaliers General Manager Jim Paxson) understands opportunity cost. As a high school player, James was already one of the best basketball players in the nation. He had received numerous scholarship offers and was considering attending college at Ohio State, the University of North Carolina, Michigan State, or the University of California. However, after high school graduation, LeBron decided to go directly into the NBA because the opportunity cost of college was simply too high. He was selected as the first pick in the 2003 NBA draft, signing a three-year contract worth almost $13 million, with an option for a fourth year at $5.8 million. Had he decided to go to college instead, James would have incurred an opportunity cost of at least $19 million in forgone income to earn a four-year college degree! Would you have skipped college if your opportunity cost had been that high?

[3]From the standpoint of the family's total economic cost of sending a child to college, some of the monetary costs, such as room and board, are not costs of choosing to go to college. The cost of living does have to be covered, but it would be incurred whether or not the student went to college.

and so on) remains fairly constant from day to day. Why then do students choose to attend class on some days and not on others? Even though the monetary cost of attending class is fairly constant, a student's opportunity cost can change dramatically from day to day. Some days the next best alternative to attending class may be sleeping in or watching TV. Other days, the opportunity cost may be substantially larger, perhaps the value of attending a big football game, getting an early start on spring break, or having additional study time for a crucial exam in another class. As options like these increase the cost of attending class, more students will decide not to attend.

Failure to consider opportunity cost often leads to unwise decision making. Suppose that your community builds a beautiful new civic center. The mayor, speaking at the dedication ceremony, tells the world that the center will improve the quality of life in your community. People who understand the concept of opportunity cost may question this view. If the center had not been built, the resources might have funded construction of a new hospital, improvements to the educational system, or housing for low-income families. Will the civic center contribute more to the well-being of the people in your community than these other facilities? If so, it was a wise investment. If not, your community will be worse off than it would have been if decision makers had chosen a higher valued project.

TRADE CREATES VALUE

Why do individuals trade with each other, and what is the significance of this exchange? We have learned that value is subjective. It is wrong to assume that a particular good or service has a fixed objective value just because it exists.[4] The value of goods and services generally depends on who uses them, and on circumstances, such as when and where they are used, as well as on the physical characteristics. Some people love onions, whereas others dislike them exceedingly. Thus, when we speak of the "value of an onion," this makes sense only within the context of its value to a specific person. Similarly, to most people an umbrella is more valuable on a rainy day than on a sunny one.

Consider the case of Janet, who loves tomatoes but hates onions, and Brad, who loves onions but hates tomatoes. They go out to dinner together and the waiter brings their salads. Brad turns to Janet and says, "I'll trade you the tomatoes on my salad for the onions on yours." Janet gladly agrees to the exchange. This simple example will help us illustrate two important aspects of voluntary exchange.

OUTSTANDING ECONOMIST	Thomas Sowell (1930–)	

Thomas Sowell, a senior fellow at the Hoover Institution, recognizes the critical importance of the institutions—the "rules of the game"—that shape human interactions. His book *Knowledge and Decisions* stresses the role of knowledge in the economy and how different institutional arrangements compare at using scarce information. Sowell is the author of many books and journal articles and writes a nationally syndicated column that appears in more than 150 newspapers. His writings address subjects ranging from race preferences and cultural differences to the origins and ideology of political conflict.

[4]An illuminating discussion of this subject, termed the "physical fallacy," is found in Thomas Sowell, *Knowledge and Decisions* (New York: Basic Books, 1980), 67–72.

1. When individuals engage in a voluntary exchange, both parties are made better off.   In the above example, Janet has the option of accepting or declining Brad's offer of a trade. If she accepts his offer, she does so *voluntarily*. Janet would agree to this exchange only if she expects to be better off as a result. Because she likes tomatoes better than onions, Janet's enjoyment of her salad will be greater with this trade than without it. On the other side, Brad has voluntarily made this offer of an exchange to Janet because Brad believes he will also be better off as a result of the exchange.

People tend to think of making, building, and creating things as productive activities. Agriculture and manufacturing are like this. They create something genuinely new, something that was not there before. On the other hand, trade—the mere exchange of one thing for another—does not create new material items. You might be tempted to think that if goods are merely being traded, one party will be better off and the other worse off. A closer look at the motivation for trade helps us see through this popular fallacy. Exchange takes place because both parties expect it will make them better off. If they didn't, they wouldn't agree to do it. For example, if Janet liked onions better than tomatoes, she wouldn't have traded with Brad. The fact that she agreed to the trade means she thinks she has something to gain by doing so. Brad thinks the same thing when it comes to his tomatoes. In other words, because their exchange is voluntary, *both* Janet and Brad are made better off. As the chapter-opening quotation illustrates, most errors in economic reasoning happen when we forget that voluntary trades, like the one between Janet and Brad, make both parties better off.

2. By channeling goods and resources to those who value them most, trade creates value and increases the wealth created by a society's resources. Because preferences differ among individuals, the value of an item can vary greatly from one person to another. Therefore, trade can create value by moving goods from those who value them less to those who value them more. The simple exchange between Janet and Brad also illustrates this point. Imagine for a moment that Brad and Janet had never met and instead were both eating their salads alone. Without the ability to engage in this exchange, both would have eaten their salads but not had as much enjoyment from them. When goods are moved to individuals who value them more, the total value created by a society's limited resources is increased. The same two salads create more value when the trade occurs than when it doesn't.

It is easy to think of material things as wealth, but material things are not wealth until they are in the hands of someone who values them. A highly technical book on electronics that is of no value to an art collector may be worth several hundred dollars to an engineer. Similarly, a painting that is unappreciated by an engineer may be of great value to an art

ECONOMICS AT THE MOVIES

20TH CENTURY FOX/THE KOBAL COLLECTION

Wall Street (1987)

Michael Douglas won an Oscar for his performance in *Wall Street*, but he gets a failing grade for his understanding of economics. In response to a question Charlie Sheen poses to him about how much money is "enough," Michael Douglas replies: "It's not a question of enough, pal. It's a zero-sum game. Somebody wins; somebody loses. Money itself isn't lost or gained, it's simply transferred from one person to another." This is false. In the real world, voluntary trade is a positive-sum game, meaning that wealth is created, and both parties gain. It is not a zero-sum game, where the gains to one person result in losses to another.

collector. Therefore, a voluntary exchange that moves the electronics book to the engineer and the painting to the art collector will increase the value of both goods. By channeling goods and resources toward those who value them most, trade creates wealth for both the trading partners and for the nation.

Transaction Costs—A Barrier to Trade

Transaction costs
The time, effort, and other resources needed to search out, negotiate, and complete an exchange.

How many times have you been sitting home late at night, hungry, wishing you had a meal from your favorite fast-food restaurant? You would gladly pay the $4 price for the value meal you have in mind, but you feel it is just not worth the time and effort to get dressed and make that drive. The costs of the time, effort, and other resources necessary to search out, negotiate, and conclude an exchange are called **transaction costs**. High transaction costs can be a barrier to potentially productive exchange.

Because of transaction costs, we should not expect all potentially valuable trades to take place, any more than we expect all useful knowledge to be learned, all safety measures to be taken, or all potential "A" grades to be earned. Frequent fliers know that if they never miss a flight, they are probably spending too much time waiting in airports. Similarly, the seller of a car, a house, or a ballet ticket knows that finding the one person in the world willing to pay the most money for the good is not worth the enormous effort it would take to find him or her. Information is costly. That is one reason that perfection in exchange, as in most things we do, is seldom worth achieving.

The Internet has significantly lowered transaction costs. The auction Web site eBay enables sellers to reach millions of potential buyers with little effort and few costs. Buyers can easily search eBay for items they want to buy, even if the items are located halfway around the world. Other Web sites, such as MySimon and Pricescan, scour online shopping sites for the lowest prices so buyers don't have to. Consumers can also readily find detailed information about products on any number of sites. Amazon.com posts prices, product information provided by manufacturers, and reviews from other buyers. By reducing transaction costs, the Internet creates value and wealth. It expands the number of trades that are made, and makes it faster and easier to make them.

The Middleman as a Cost Reducer

Middleman
A person who buys and sells goods or services or arranges trades. A middleman reduces transaction costs.

Because it is costly for buyers and sellers to find each other and to negotiate the exchange, an entrepreneurial opportunity exists for people to become **middlemen**. Middlemen provide buyers and sellers information at a lower cost and arrange trades between them. Many people think middlemen just add to the buyer's expense without performing a useful function. However, because of transaction costs, without middlemen, many trades would never happen (nor would the gains from them be realized). An auto dealer, for example, is a middleman. An auto dealer helps both the manufacturer and the buyer. The dealer helps buyers by maintaining an inventory of vehicles for them to choose from. Knowledgeable salespeople hired by the dealer help car shoppers quickly learn about the vehicles they're interested in and the pros and cons of each. Car buyers also like to know that a local dealer will honor the manufacturer's warranty and provide parts and service for the car. The dealer helps manufacturers by handling tasks like these so they can concentrate on designing and making better cars.

Grocers are also middlemen. Each of us could deal with farmers directly to buy our food—probably at a lower monetary cost. But that would have a high opportunity cost. Finding and dealing with different farmers for every product we wanted to buy would take a lot of time. Alternatively, we could form consumer cooperatives, banding together to eliminate the middleman, using our own warehouses and our own volunteer labor to order, receive, display, distribute, and collect payment for the food. In fact, some cooperatives like this do exist. But most people prefer instead to pay a grocer to provide all of the goods they want rather than trying to trade with different farmers.

Stockbrokers, realtors, publishers, and merchants of all sorts are other kinds of middlemen. For a fee, they reduce transaction costs for both buyers and sellers. By making exchanges cheaper and more convenient, middlemen cause more efficient trades to happen. In so doing, they themselves create value.

THE IMPORTANCE OF PROPERTY RIGHTS

 Private ownership provides people with a strong incentive to take care of things and develop resources in ways that are highly valued by others.

Private Ownership

The buyer of an apple, a CD, a television set, or an automobile generally takes the item home. The buyer of a steamship or an office building, though, may never touch it. When exchange occurs, it's really the **property rights** of the item that change hands.

Private-property rights involve three things:

(1) the right to exclusive use of the property (that is, the owner has sole possession, control, and use of the property—including the right to exclude others);

(2) legal protection against invasion from other individuals who would seek to use or abuse the property without the owner's permission; and

(3) the right to transfer, sell, exchange, or mortgage the property.

Private owners can do anything they want with their property as long as they do not use it in a manner that invades or infringes on the rights of another. For example, I cannot throw the hammer that I own through the television set that you own. If I did, I would be violating your property right to your television. The same is true if I operate a factory spewing out pollution harming you or your land.[5] Because an owner has the right to control the use of property, the owner also must accept responsibility for the outcomes of that control.

In contrast to private ownership, common-property ownership occurs when multiple people simultaneously have or claim ownership rights to a good or resource. None of the common owners can prevent the others from using or damaging the property. Most beaches, lakes, and parks are examples of commonly owned property. The distinction between private- and common-property ownership is important because common ownership does not create the same powerful incentives as private ownership. Economists are fond of saying that when everybody owns something, nobody owns it.

Clearly defined and enforced private-property rights are a key to economic progress because of the powerful incentive effects that follow from private ownership of goods and resources. The following four incentives are particularly important:

1. Private owners can gain by employing their resources in ways that are beneficial to others, and they bear the opportunity cost of ignoring the wishes of others. Realtors often advise home owners to use neutral colors for countertops and walls in their house because they will improve the resale value of the home. As a private owner you could install bright green fixtures and paint your walls deep purple, but you will bear the cost (in terms of a lower selling price) of ignoring the wishes of others who might want to buy your house later. On the other hand, by fixing up a house and doing things to it that others find beneficial, you can reap the benefit of a higher selling price. Similarly, you could spray paint orange designs all over the outside of your brand-new car, but private ownership gives you an incentive not to do so because the resale value of the car depends on the value that *others* place on it.

Consider a parcel of undeveloped privately owned land near a university. The private owner of the land can do many things with it. For example, she could leave it undeveloped, turn it into a metered parking lot, erect a restaurant, or build rental housing. Will the wishes and desires of the nearby students be reflected in her choice, even though they are not the owners of the property? Yes. Whichever use is more highly valued by potential customers will earn her the highest investment return. If housing is relatively hard to find but there are plenty of other restaurants, the profitability of using her land for housing will be higher than

Property rights
The rights to use, control, and obtain the benefits from a good or service.

Private-property rights
Property rights that are exclusively held by an owner and protected against invasion by others. Private property can be transferred, sold, or mortgaged at the owner's discretion.

"Their house looks so nice. They must be getting ready to sell it."

A private owner has a strong incentive to do things with his or her property that increase its value to others.

---

[5]For a detailed explanation of how property rights protect the environment, with several real-world examples, see Roger E. Meiners and Bruce Yandle, *The Common Law: How It Protects the Environment* (Bozeman, Mont.: PERC, 1998), available online at http://www.perc.org.

the profitability of using it for a restaurant. Private ownership gives her a strong incentive to use her property in a way that will also fulfill the wishes of others. If she decides to leave the property undeveloped instead of erecting housing that would benefit the students, she will bear the opportunity cost of forgone rental income from the property.

As a second example, consider the owner of an apartment complex near your campus. The owner may not care much for swimming pools, workout facilities, study desks, washers and dryers, or green areas. Nonetheless, private ownership provides the owner with a strong incentive to provide these items if students and other potential customers value them more than it costs to provide them. Why? Because tenants will be willing to pay higher rents to live in a complex with amenities that they value. The owners of rental property can profit by providing an additional amenity that tenants value as long as the tenants are willing to pay enough additional rent to cover the cost of providing it. Because renters differ in their preferences and willingness to pay for amenities, some will prefer to live in less expensive apartments with fewer amenities, while others will prefer to live in more expensive apartments with a greater range of amenities. By choosing among potential apartment complexes, renters are able to buy as few or as many of these amenities as they wish.

2. Private owners have a strong incentive to care for and properly manage what they own.   Will Ed regularly change the oil in his car? Will he see to it that the seats don't get torn? Probably so, since being careless about these things would reduce the car's value, both to him and to any future owner. The car and its value—the sale price if he sells it—belong just to Ed, so he would bear the burden of a decline in the car's value if the oil ran low and ruined the engine, or if the seats were torn. Similarly, he would capture the value of an expenditure that improved the car, like a new paint job. As the owner, Ed has both the authority and the incentive to protect the car against harm or neglect and even to enhance its value. Private-property rights give owners a strong incentive for good stewardship.

Do you take equally good care not to damage an apartment you rent as you would your own house? If you share an apartment with several roommates, are the common areas of the apartment (such as the kitchen and living room) as neatly kept as the bedrooms? Based on economic theory, we guess that the answer to both of these questions is probably "No."

In 1998, the student government association at Berry College in Georgia purchased 20 bicycles to be placed around campus for everyone's use.[6] These $200 Schwinn Cruiser bicycles were painted red and were marked with a plate reading "Berry Bike." The bikes were available on a first-come, first-served basis, and students were encouraged to take them whenever they needed them and leave them anywhere on campus for others to use when they were finished. What do you think happened to these bikes? Within two months,

When apartments and other investment properties are owned privately, the owner has a strong incentive to provide amenities that others value highly relative to their cost.

[6]Daniel L. Alban and E. Frank Stephenson, "The 'Berry Bikes': A Lesson in Private Property," *Ideas on Liberty* 49, no. 10 (October 1999): 8–9.

most of these top-quality bikes were severely damaged or lost. The campus newspaper reported on the "mangled corpses of twisted red metal that lie about campus." Over the summer break the student government replaced or fixed the bikes, but despite its pleas to "treat the bikes as if they were your own property," the same thing happened the following fall precisely because the bikes weren't the students' own property. It wasn't that the students at Berry College were inherently destructive; after all, there were no problems on campus with privately owned bikes being lost or abused during this time. It was a matter of the different incentives they faced. The student government association eventually abandoned the program and began leasing the remaining bikes to individual students instead. As you can see, there is no denying the strong incentive that private ownership creates for owners to care for their property (or the lack of incentive when private ownership is not clearly defined and enforced).

The incentive for owners to care for and properly manage their property is strong. The owner of a hotel doesn't want to neglect fixing electrical or plumbing problems if it means fewer repair costs due to electrical fires or water leaks in the future. The owner knows travelers aren't going to want to stay in a charred or water-damaged hotel. Poor management will reduce the hotel's value and the owner's personal wealth. This gives the owner an incentive to manage the asset properly.

3. Private owners have an incentive to conserve for the future—particularly if the property is expected to increase in value.   People have a much stronger incentive to conserve privately owned property than they do commonly owned property. For example, when Steven was in college, the general rule among his roommates was that any food or drink in the house was common property—open game for the hungry or thirsty mouth of anyone who stumbled across it. There was never a reason for Steven to conserve food or drinks in the house because it would be quickly consumed by a roommate coming in later that night. When Steven first started living alone, he noticed a dramatic change in his behavior. When he ordered a pizza, he would save some for the next day's lunch rather than eating it all that night. Steven began counting his drinks before he had one to make sure there were enough left for the next day. When Steven was the sole owner, he began delaying his current consumption to conserve for the future because he was the one, not his roommates, who reaped the benefit from his conservation.

Similarly, when more than one individual has the right to drill oil from an underground pool of oil, each has an incentive to extract as much as possible, as quickly as possible. Any oil conserved for the future will probably be taken by someone else. In contrast, when only one owner has the right to drill, the oil will be extracted more slowly. The same applies to the common-property problems involved in overfishing of the sea compared with fisheries that use privately owned ponds.

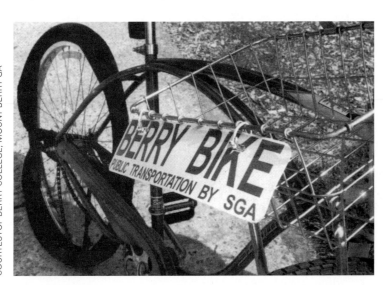

COURTESY OF BERRY COLLEGE, MOUNT BERRY GA

Without clearly defined private-property rights, there is less of an incentive to take proper care of things—as the student government administration at Berry College found out when it provided common-property bikes to be used around campus.

Someone who owns land, a house, or a factory, has a strong incentive to bear costs now, if necessary, to preserve the asset's value for the future. The owner's wealth is tied up in the value of the property, which reflects nothing more than the net benefits that will be available to a future owner. Thus, the wealth of private owners is dependent on their willingness and ability to look ahead, maintain, and conserve those things that will be more highly valued in the future. This is why private ownership is particularly important for the optimal conservation of natural resources.

4. Private owners have an incentive to lower the chance that their property will cause damage to the property of others. Private ownership links responsibility with the right of control. Private owners can be held accountable for damage done to others through the misuse of their property. A car owner has a right to drive his car, but will be held accountable if the brakes aren't maintained and the car damages someone else's property. Similarly, a chemical company has control over its products, but, exactly for that reason, it is legally liable for damages if it mishandles the chemicals. Courts of law recognize and enforce the authority granted by ownership, but they also enforce the responsibility that goes with that authority. Because private-property owners can be held accountable for damages they cause, they have an incentive to use their property responsibly and take steps to reduce the likelihood of harm to others. A property owner, for example, has an incentive to cut down a dying tree before it falls into a neighbor's house and to leash or restrain his or her dog if it's likely to bite others.

Private Ownership and Markets

Private ownership and competitive markets provide the foundation for cooperative behavior among individuals. When private-property rights are protected and enforced, the permission of the owner must be sought before anyone else can use the property. Put another way, if you want to use a good or resource, you must either buy or lease it from the owner. This means that each of us must face the cost of using scarce resources. Furthermore, market prices give private owners a strong incentive to consider the desires of others and use their resources in ways others value.

F. A. Hayek, the winner of the 1974 Nobel Prize in economics, used the expression "the extended order" to refer to the tendency for markets to lead perfect strangers from different backgrounds around the world to cooperate with one another. Let's go back to the example of the property owner who has the choice of leaving her land idle or building housing to benefit students. The landowner might not know any students in her town nor particularly care about providing them housing. However, because she is motivated by market prices, she might build an apartment complex and eventually do business with a lot of students she never intended to get to know. In the process, she will purchase materials, goods, and services produced by other strangers.

Things are different in countries that don't recognize private-ownership rights or enforce them. In these countries, whoever has the political power or authority can simply seize property from whomever might have it without compensating them. In his book *The Mystery of Capital,* economist Hernando DeSoto argues that the lack of well-defined and enforced property rights explains why some underdeveloped countries (despite being market based) have made little economic progress. DeSoto points out that in many of these nations, generations of people have squatted on the land without any legal deed giving them formal ownership. The problem is these squatters cannot borrow against the land to generate capital because they don't have a deed to it, nor can they prevent someone else from arbitrarily taking the land away from them.

Private ownership and markets can also play an important role in environmental protection and natural-resource conservation. Ocean fishing rights, tradable rights to pollute, and private ownership of endangered species are just some examples. The accompanying Applications in Economics feature, "Protecting Endangered Species and the Environment with Private-Property Rights," explores some of these issues.

APPLICATIONS IN ECONOMICS

Protecting Endangered Species and the Environment with Private-Property Rights

Column 1	Column 2
Cows	African Rhinos
Pigs	Bald Eagles
Chickens	Spotted Owls
Dogs	American Bison
Cats	African Elephants

Compare the two columns of animals above. The animals listed in column 2 are endangered species, whereas those in column 1 are not. Why the difference? The answer may surprise you—all of the animals listed in column 1 can be privately owned, whereas those in column 2 generally cannot. In this chapter you have learned about the powerful incentives for careful management and conservation created by private-property rights. This application considers how the power of these incentives is being harnessed to protect endangered species and the environment.

What do you think would happen to the total population of cows if people wanted less beef? Beef prices would fall, and the incentive for individuals to dedicate land and other resources to raising cattle would fall. It is precisely the market demand for beef that *creates* the incentive for suppliers to maintain herds of cattle and to protect them from harm.

In some ways, the rhinoceros is similar to a cow. It is large and rather unpredictable—a rhino, like a large bull in a cattle herd, may charge if disturbed. And at 3,000 pounds, a charging rhino can be very dangerous. Also like cattle, rhinos can be valuable, and they are significantly rarer. A single horn from a black rhino can sell for as much as $30,000. That makes it a favorite target of poachers—people who hunt illegally.

Rhinos are very different from cattle in one important respect: In most of Africa where they naturally range, the rhinoceros cannot be privately owned or sold by anyone who might protect them. In those areas, poachers may be assisted by local people eager to see fewer rhino present because they make life risky for humans and compete for food and water. Under these circumstances, the rhino is in danger of becoming extinct.

One reaction to this problem is to outlaw rhinoceros hunting and to forbid the sale of any rhino parts. That happened in 1977, when many nations signed an international treaty outlawing sales of black rhino products. Nearly 20 years later, however, in 1994, the black rhino was closer to

extinction than ever before. According to South African economist Michael 't Sas Rolfes, the trade ban "has not had a discernible effect on rhino numbers and does not seem to have stopped the trade in rhino horn. If anything, the . . . listings led to a sharp increase in the black market price of rhino horn, which simply fueled further poaching and encouraged speculative stockpiling of horn." Incentives for poachers and local people had not changed, and between 1970 and 1994, black rhinos suffered a 95 percent decline in Africa.[1]

Then a very different strategy for the black rhino emerged in the southern African nation of Zimbabwe. Although rhinos cannot be privately owned there, landowners can fence and manage the game animals on their property. Many of the remaining black rhinos were relocated to private land in the early 1990s. Because they could profit from protecting the big animals, some ranchers shifted their operations from cattle to wildlife protection, ecotourism, and hunting. Often, they combined several ranches into one conservancy, since some wild animals, including rhinos, range over a large area and are difficult to fence in. Revenues from the conservancies come both from hunting many big game animals—not rhinos, however—and from nonconsumptive uses of wildlife, such as photo safaris.

In 1997, a stay at the Barberton Lodge in the Bubiana Conservancy in Zimbabwe cost about $160 per night for a photo safari. Other Bubiana properties charged between $500 and $1,000 per day for a hunting safari, on top of any trophy fees (such as $3,000 or more for a leopard). No elephants were hunted in the conservancies, but elsewhere in Zimbabwe, hunters paid up to $36,000 for a three-week chance at tracking and killing an elephant. Although no black rhino could be hunted in Zimbabwe, estimates of what the fee would be, if hunting were allowed, reached $250,000. Because of the low overhead and high return, hunting is the reason that, even without the hunting of elephant and rhino, all of the ranchers in the Bubiana partnership have been able to turn a profit from their wildlife operations.

Cattle were introduced to the area in the 1950s and 1960s. When they were removed from some of the conservancies to make way for rhinos, native grasses and shrubs came back in strength, and so did other big game and other forms of wildlife. By the turn of the century, not a single animal had been poached on these private conservancies, and rhino populations climbed. A similar success story is found in South Africa for the African white rhino.[2]

In Africa, elephant numbers also show the value of property rights and market tools for conservation. Zimbabwe and Botswana have for years allowed landowners and local

---

[1]See Michael De Alessi, *Private Conservation and Black Rhinos in Zimbabwe: The Savé Valley and Bubiana Conservancies*, available online at: http://www.privateconservation.org/pubs/studies/Rhino.PDF. The rhino story is one of many case studies available from the Center for Private Conservation at www.privateconservation.org.

[2]See "The Rhinos Are Baaack!" *Smithsonian Magazine* (March 2001): 76–86..

(continued)

tribes to benefit financially from the presence of elephants. They have allowed domestic trade in ivory. Other countries, such as Kenya, have banned the ivory trade and have forbidden such gains to landowners from the elephants, instead making their government responsible for protecting them. From 1979 to 1989, property rights and market conservation helped push elephant numbers from 50,000 up to 94,000 in Zimbabwe and Botswana, while Kenya's elephant population fell from 65,000 to 19,000. The trend did not stop there. From 1989 to 1995, elephant populations in Zimbabwe and Botswana rose by about 15 percent, while the rest of Africa *lost* about 20 percent of their elephants.

The story is not entirely a happy one, however. Success is crucially dependent on protection of property rights to wildlife, and property rights are not always secure in southern Africa. Zimbabwe is currently in the midst of a virtual civil war. Terry Anderson, a resource economist and hunter, writes that the Bubiana Conservancy has experienced severe devastation: "20,000 trees have been felled, 22 buildings razed,

staff assaulted, and 50 percent of the wildlife killed." The value of the wild animals lost is estimated at $1.5 million.[3]

In South Africa, however, property rights to wildlife are much stronger. Once a landowner "game-fences" his or her property (builds a tall fence using 12 strands of high-tensile wire), wild animals become the owner's property. These owners "have an incentive to manage the wild animals as they might their cattle, paying close attention to carrying capacity, habitat, and water," writes Anderson. He observes that this is an improvement over the United States, where landowners "cannot capture the benefits of wildlife and consider it more of a nuisance than an asset." In sum, says Anderson, "My experiences in Africa show that private ownership and a focus on rewarding good stewardship are the key to protecting wildlife habitat and wildlife populations."

[3]Terry L. Anderson, "My Love Affair with Africa," *PERC Reports*, June 2004, available at http://perc.org/publications/percreports/june2004/africa.php?s=2. Much more is available on this Web site (http://www.perc.org) on ways that property rights can preserve and enhance environmental quality.

PRODUCTION POSSIBILITIES CURVE

Production possibilities curve
A curve that outlines all possible combinations of total output that could be produced, assuming (1) a fixed amount of productive resources, (2) a given amount of technical knowledge, and (3) full and efficient use of those resources. The slope of the curve indicates the amount of one product that must be given up to produce more of the other.

People try to get the most from their limited resources by making purposeful choices and engaging in economizing behavior. This can be illustrated using a conceptual tool called the **production possibilities curve**. The production possibilities curve shows the maximum amount of any two products that can be produced from a fixed set of resources, and the possible trade-offs in production between them. Admittedly, this is an oversimplified model because economies obviously produce more than just two products. Nonetheless, the production possibilities curve can help us understand a number of important economic ideas.

Exhibit 1 illustrates the production possibilities curve for Susan, an intelligent economics major. This curve indicates the combinations of English and economics grades that she thinks she can earn if she spends a total of 10 hours per week studying for the two subjects. Currently, she is choosing to study the material in each course that she expects will help her grade the most, for the time spent, and she is allocating 5 hours of study time to each course. She expects that this amount of time, carefully spent on each course, will allow her to earn a B grade in both, indicated at point *T*. But if she were to take some time away from studying one of the two subjects and spend it studying the other, she could raise her grade in the course receiving more study time. However, it would come at the cost of a lower grade in the course she spends less time studying for. If she were to move to point *S* by spending more hours on economics and fewer on English, for example, her expected economics grade would rise, while her expected English grade would fall. This illustrates the first important concept shown in the production possibilities framework—the idea of trade-offs in the use of scarce resources. Whenever more of one thing is produced, there is an opportunity cost in terms of something else that now must be forgone.

You might notice that Susan's production possibilities curve indicates that the additional study time required to raise her economics grade by one letter, from a B to an A (moving from point *T* to point *S*), would require giving up two letter grades in her English class, not just one, reducing her English grade from a B to a D. If, alternatively, Susan

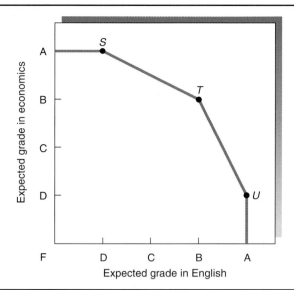

EXHIBIT 1
Production Possibilities Curve for Susan's Grades in English and Economics

The production possibilities for Susan, in terms of grades, are illustrated for 10 hours of total study time. If Susan studied 10 hours per week in these two classes, she could attain a D in English and an A in economics (point S), a B in English and a B in economics (point T), or a D in economics and an A in English (point U).

were to move from point *T* to point *U,* the opposite would be true—she would improve her English grade by one letter at the expense of two letter grades in economics. You can understand this by thinking about your own studying behavior. When you have only a limited amount of time to study a subject, you begin by studying the most important (grade-increasing) material first. As you spend additional time on that subject, you begin studying topics that are of decreasing importance for your grade. Thus, adding an hour of study time to the subject Susan studies least will have a larger impact on her grade than will taking away an hour from the subject on which she currently spends more time.

This idea of increasing opportunity cost is reflected in the slope of the production possibilities curve. The curve is flatter to the left of point *T,* and steeper to the right, showing that, as Susan takes more and more of her resources (time, in this case) from one course and puts it into the other, she must give up greater and greater amounts of productivity in the course getting fewer resources.

Of course, Susan could study more economics *without* giving up her English study time, if she gave up some leisure, or study time for other courses, or her part-time job in the campus bookstore. If she gave up leisure or her job and added those hours to the 10 hours of study time for economics and English, the entire curve in Exhibit 1 would shift outward. She could get better grades in both classes by having more time to study.

Can the production possibilities concept be applied to the entire economy? Yes. We can grow more soybeans if we grow less corn, since both can be grown on the same land. Beefing up the nation's military would mean we would have to produce fewer nonmilitary goods than we could otherwise. When scarce resources are being used efficiently, getting more of one requires that we sacrifice others.

Exhibit 2 shows a hypothetical production possibilities curve for an economy with a limited amount of resources that produces only two goods: food and clothing. The points along the curve represent all possible combinations of food and clothing that could be produced with the current level of resources and technology of the economy (assuming the resources are being used efficiently). A point outside the production possibilities curve (such as point *E*) would be considered unattainable, at the present time. A point inside the production possibilities curve (such as point *D*) is attainable, but producing that amount would mean that the economy is not making maximum use of its resources (some resources are being underutilized). Thus, point *D* is considered inefficient.

More specifically, the production possibilities curve shows all of the maximum combinations of two goods that an economy will be able to produce: (1) given a fixed quantity of resources, (2) holding the level of technology constant, and (3) assuming that all resources are used efficiently.

EXHIBIT 2
Concept of Production Possibilities Curve for an Economy

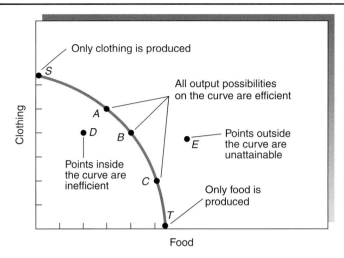

When an economy is using its limited resources efficiently, production of more clothing requires that the economy give up some other goods—such as food in this example. In time, improved technology, more resources, or improvement in its economic organization could make it possible to produce more of both goods by shifting the production possibilities curve outward.

When these three conditions are met, the economy will be at the edge of its production possibilities frontier (where points *A, B,* and *C* lie), and producing more of one good will necessitate producing less of others. If condition 3 above is not met, and resources are being used inefficiently, an economy would be operating inside its production possibilities curve. If the level of resources and technology change (conditions 1 and 2), it will result in an outward shift in the production possibilities curve. We will return to these factors that can shift the production possibilities curve in a moment.

Notice that the production possibilities curve is convex, or bowed out from the origin, just as Susan's was in Exhibit 1 because of the concept of increasing opportunity cost. Here, the convexity reflects the fact that an economy's resources are not equally well suited to produce food and clothing. If an economy were using all its resources to produce clothing (point *S*), transferring those resources least suited for producing clothing toward food production will reduce clothing output a little but increase food output a lot. Since the resources transferred would be those better-suited for producing food and less-suited for producing clothing, the opportunity cost of producing additional food (in terms of clothing forgone) is low—near point *S*. However, as more and more resources are devoted to food production, and successively larger amounts of food are produced (moving the economy from *S* to *A* to *B* and so on), the opportunity cost of food will rise. This is because, as more and more food is produced, additional food output can be achieved only by using resources that are less and less suitable for the production of food relative to clothing. Thus, as food output is expanded, successively larger amounts of clothing must be forgone per unit of additional food. This is similar to what happened to Susan when she diverted study hours from one course to another. Only this time, we are talking about an entire economy.

Shifting the Production Possibilities Curve Outward

What restricts an economy—once its resources are fully utilized—from producing more of everything? Why can't we get more of something produced without having to give up the production of something else? The same constraint that kept Susan from simultaneously making a higher grade in both English and economics—a lack of resources. As long as all current resources are being used efficiently, the only way to get more of one good is to sacrifice some of the other. Over time, however, it is possible for a country's production possibilities curve to shift outward, making it possible for more of all goods to be produced. Below we address four factors that could potentially shift the production possibilities curve outward.

1. An increase in the economy's resource base would expand our ability to produce goods and services.

If we had more or better resources, we could produce a greater amount of all goods. Resources such as machinery, buildings, tools, and education are human-made, and thus we can expand our resource base by devoting some of our efforts to producing them. This **investment** would provide us with better tools and skills and increase our ability to produce goods and services in the future. However, like with the production of other goods, devoting effort and resources toward producing these long-lasting physical assets means fewer resources are available to produce other things, in this case goods for current consumption. Thus, the choice between using resources to produce goods for current consumption and using them to produce investment goods for the future can also be illustrated within the production possibilities framework. The two economies illustrated in **Exhibit 3** begin with identical production possibilities curves (*RS*). Notice that Economy A dedicates more of its output to investment (shown by I_a) than Economy B (shown by I_b). Economy B, on the other hand, consumes more than Economy A. Because Economy A allocates more of its resources to investment and less to consumption, A's production possibilities curve shifts outward over time by a greater amount than B's. In other words, the growth rate of Economy A—the expansion of its ability to produce goods—is enhanced by this investment. But more investment in machines and human skills requires a reduction in current consumption.

2. Advancements in technology can expand the economy's production possibilities.

Technology determines the maximum amount of output an economy can produce given the resources it has. New and better technology makes it possible for us to get more output from our resources. An important form of technological change is **invention**—the use of science and engineering to create new products or processes. In recent years, for example, inventions have allowed us to develop photographs faster and more cheaply, process data more rapidly, get more oil from existing fields, and send information instantly and cheaply by satellite. Such technological advances increase our production possibilities, shifting our economy's entire production possibilities curve outward.

Investment
The purchase, construction, or development of resources, including physical assets, such as plants and machinery, and human assets, such as better education. Investment expands an economy's resources. The process of investment is sometimes called capital formation.

Technology
The technological knowledge available in an economy at any given time. The level of technology determines the amount of output we can generate with our limited resources.

Invention
The creation of a new product or process, often facilitated by the knowledge of engineering and science.

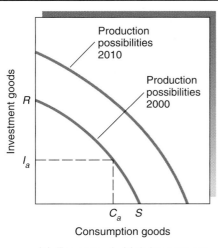

(a) Economy A, high investment

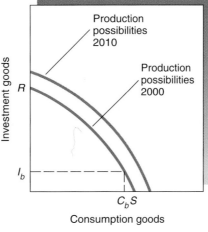

(b) Economy B, low investment

EXHIBIT 3
Investment and Production Possibilities in the Future

Here we illustrate two economies (A and B) that initially confront identical production possibilities curves (*RS*). Economy A allocates a larger share of its output to investment (I_a, compared to I_b for Economy B). As a result, the production possibilities curve of the high-investment economy (Economy A) will tend to shift outward by a larger amount over time than the low-investment economy's will.

Innovation
The successful introduction and adoption of a new product or process; the economic application of inventions and marketing techniques.

Entrepreneur
A person who introduces new products or improved technologies and decides which projects to undertake. A successful entrepreneur's actions will increase the value of resources and expand the size of the economic pie.

An economy can also benefit from technological change through **innovation**—the practical and effective adoption of new techniques. Such innovation is commonly carried out by an **entrepreneur**—a person who introduces new products or improved techniques to satisfy consumers at a lower cost. To make a profit, an entrepreneur must convert or rearrange resources in a way that increases their value. This also pushes the production possibilities curve outward.

Take, for example, Henry Ford, an entrepreneur who changed how cars were made by pioneering the assembly line. With the same amount of labor and materials, Ford made more cars, more cheaply. Another entrepreneur, the late Ray Kroc, purchased a hamburger restaurant from Richard McDonald and built it into the world's largest fast-food chain. Kroc revolutionized fast food by offering attractive food at economical prices. He also developed a franchising system that resulted in uniform quality across the many different McDonald's restaurants worldwide. More recently, entrepreneurs like Steven Jobs (Apple Computer) and Bill Gates (Microsoft) helped develop the personal computer and software programs that dramatically increased their usefulness to businesses and households. It is interesting to think about how a few famous entrepreneurs have improved our productivity and changed our lives so much.

3. An improvement in the rules under which the economy functions can also increase output. The legal system of a country influences the ability of people to cooperate with one another and produce goods. Changes in legal institutions that promote social cooperation and motivate people to produce will also push the production possibilities curve outward. On the other hand, poor institutions can reduce both the level of resources used (shifting the curve inward) and how efficiently they are used (causing the economy to operate inside its production possibilities curve).

Historically, legal innovations have been an important source of economic progress. During the eighteenth century, a system of patents was established in Europe and North America, giving inventors private-property rights to their ideas. At about the same time, laws were passed allowing businesses to establish themselves legally as corporations, reducing the cost of forming large firms that were often required for the mass production of manufactured goods. Both of these legal changes improved economic organization and accelerated the growth of output by shifting the production possibilities curve outward more rapidly.

Sometimes governments, perhaps because of ignorance or prejudice, adopt legal institutions that reduce production possibilities. Laws that restrict or prohibit trade is one example. For almost a hunderd years following the American Civil War, the laws of several southern states prohibited hiring African-Americans for certain jobs and restricted other economic exchanges between blacks and whites. The legislation not only was harmful to African-Americans, it also retarded progress and reduced the production possibilities of these states.

The collapse of communism in the 1980s also illustrates the importance of economic institutions. After the collapse, Russia was unable to develop legal institutions protecting property rights and enforcing contracts. The absence of these institutions hampered investment and the gains from trade. Investors moved their money to countries with more secure property rights, and resources within the country were used inefficiently because trade was hindered. As a result, even though Russia has a well-educated labor force and abundant natural resources, its economic performance has been poor.

4. By working harder and giving up current leisure, we could increase our production of goods and services. Hypothetically, the production possibilities curve would shift outward if everyone worked more hours and took less leisure time. Strictly speaking, however, leisure is also a good, so we would simply be giving up leisure to have more of other things. If we were to construct a production possibilities curve for leisure versus other goods, this would be shown as simply a movement along the curve. However, if we restrict our model to only material goods and services, a change in the amount we work would be shown as a shift in the curve.

How much people work depends not only on their personal preferences but also on public policy. For example, high tax rates on personal income may cause people to work less. This is because high tax rates reduce the payoff from working. When this happens, people spend more time doing other, untaxed activities—like leisure activities. This will move the production possibilities curve for material goods inward because the economy can't produce as much when people work less.

Production Possibilities and Economic Growth

Economic growth is one of the most important topics in modern economics for good reason. An economic growth rate of 3 percent per year will result in living standards doubling approximately every 24 years. On the other hand, in a country experiencing an economic growth rate of only 1 percent, it will take 75 years for living standards to double. Within the production possibilities framework, economic growth is simply an outward shift in the curve through time. The more rapidly the curve shifts outward, the more rapid is economic growth. There are other economic models that are used to analyze economic growth; however, they all share the production possibilities curve as a foundation.

TRADE, OUTPUT, AND LIVING STANDARDS

 Trade makes it possible for people to generate more output through specialization and division of labor, large-scale production processes, and the dissemination of improved products and production methods.

Gains from Trade

As we previously discussed, trade creates value by moving goods from people who value them less to people who value them more. However, this is only part of the story. Trade also makes it possible for people to expand their output through specialization and **division of labor,** large-scale production, and the dissemination of better products and production methods.

Division of labor
A method that breaks down the production of a product into a series of specific tasks, each performed by a different worker.

Gains from Specialization and Division of Labor

Businesses can achieve higher output levels and greater productivity from their workers through specialization and division of labor. More than 200 years ago, Adam Smith noted the importance of this factor. Observing the operation of a pin manufacturer, Smith noted that when each worker specialized in a separate function needed to make pins, 10 workers together were able to produce 48,000 pins per day, or 4,800 pins per worker. Smith doubted an individual worker could produce even 20 pins per day working alone from start to finish on each pin.[7]

The division of labor separates production tasks into a series of related operations. Each worker performs one or a few of perhaps hundreds of tasks necessary to produce something. This process makes it possible to assign different tasks to those individuals who are able to accomplish them most efficiently (that is, at the lowest cost). Furthermore, a worker who specializes in just one narrow area becomes more experienced and more skilled in that task over time.

Trading partners can also benefit from specialization and the division of labor. The **law of comparative advantage**, developed in the early 1800s by the great English economist David Ricardo, explains why this is true. ***The law of comparative advantage states***

Law of comparative advantage
A principle that states that individuals, firms, regions, or nations can gain by specializing in the production of goods that they produce cheaply (at a low opportunity cost) and exchanging them for goods they cannot produce cheaply (at a high opportunity cost).

---

[7]See Adam Smith, *An Inquiry into the Nature and Causes of the Wealth of Nations* (1776; Cannan's ed., Chicago: University of Chicago Press, 1976), 7–16, for additional detail on the importance of the division of labor.

that the total output of a group of individuals, an entire economy, or a group of nations will be greatest when the output of each good is produced by the person (or firm) with the lowest opportunity cost.

Comparative advantage applies to trade among individuals, business firms, regions, and even nations. When trading partners are able to use more of their time and resources to produce the things each is best at, they will be able to produce more together than would otherwise have been possible. In turn, the mutual gains they get from trading will result in higher levels of income for each. It's a win-win situation for both.

If a good or service can be obtained more economically through trade, it makes sense to get it that way rather than producing it for yourself. For example, even though most doctors might be good at record keeping and arranging appointments, it's generally better for them to hire someone to perform these services for them. That's because the time doctors spend keeping records is time they could have spent seeing patients. The revenue forgone as a result of seeing fewer patients would be greater than the cost of hiring the worker. The issue is not whether doctors are better record keepers than the assistants they could hire, but rather how they should use their time most efficiently.

If you think about it, the law of comparative advantage is common sense. If someone else is willing to supply you with a good at a lower cost than you can produce it yourself, doesn't it make sense to trade for it and use your time and resources to produce more of the things you can produce most efficiently? Consider the situation of Andrea, an attorney who earns $100 per hour providing legal services. She has several documents that need to be typed, and she is thinking about hiring a typist earning $15 per hour to do it. Andrea is an excellent typist, much faster than the prospective employee. She could do the job in 20 hours, whereas the typist would take 40 hours.

Because of her greater typing speed, some might think Andrea should handle the job herself. This is not the case. If she types the documents, the job will cost her $2,000—the opportunity cost of 20 hours of practicing law at $100 per hour. Alternatively, the cost of having the documents typed by the typist is only $600 (40 hours at $15 per hour). Andrea's comparative advantage lies in practicing law. By hiring the typist, she will increase her own productivity and make more money.

The implications of the law of comparative advantage are universal. Any group will be able to produce more output from its available resources when each good or service is produced by the person with the lowest opportunity cost. This insight is particularly important in understanding the way a market economy works. Purposeful decision making

Trade channels goods to those who value them most. Trade also helps disseminate ideas for improved products and makes production methods such as specialization, the division of labor, and mass production more feasible. Over the years, trade has enabled us to produce more with our limited resources, dramatically improving our living standards.

indicates that buyers will try to get the most for their money. They will not knowingly choose a high-cost option when a lower-cost alternative is available. This places low-cost suppliers at a competitive advantage. Thus, they will generally survive and prosper in a market economy. As a result, the production of goods and resources will naturally tend to be allocated according to comparative advantage.

Most people recognize that Americans benefit from trade among the nation's 50 states. For example, the residents of Nebraska and Florida are able to produce a larger joint output and achieve higher income levels when Nebraskans specialize in producing wheat and other grain products, and Floridians specialize in producing oranges and other citrus products. The same is true for trade among nations. Like Nebraskans and Floridians, people in different nations will be better off if they specialize in the goods and services they can produce at a low cost and trade them for goods they produce at a high cost. See the addendum to this chapter for additional evidence on this point.

Gains from Mass Production Methods

Trade also promotes economic progress by making it possible for firms to lower their per-unit costs with mass production. Say a nation isolated itself and refused to trade with other countries. In an economy like this, self-sufficiency and small-scale production would be the norm. If trade were allowed, however, the nation's firms could sell their products to customers around the world. This would make it feasible for the firms to adopt more efficient, large-scale production processes. Mass production often leads to labor and machinery efficiencies that increase enormously the output per worker. But without trade, these gains could not be achieved.

Gains from Innovation

Trade also makes it possible to realize gains from the discovery and dissemination of innovative products and production processes. Economic growth involves brain power, innovation, and the application of technology. Without trade, however, the gains derived from the discovery of better ways of doing things would be stifled. Furthermore, observing and interacting with other people using different and better technologies often encourages others to copy successful approaches. People also modify the technology they observe, adapting it for their own purposes. This sometimes results in new, and even better, technologies. Again, gains from these sources would be far more limited in a world without trade.

Can you imagine the difficulty involved in producing your own housing, clothing, and food, to say nothing of radios, television sets, dishwashers, automobiles, and telephone services? Yet, most families in North America, Western Europe, Japan, and Australia enjoy all these conveniences. They are able to do so largely because their economies are organized in such a way that individuals can cooperate, specialize, and trade, thereby reaping the benefits of the enormous increases in output—in both quantity and diversity—that can be generated. On the other hand, countries that impose obstacles that retard exchange—either domestic or international—hinder their citizens from achieving these gains and more prosperous lives.

HUMAN INGENUITY AND THE CREATION OF WEALTH

 Economic goods are the result of human ingenuity and action; thus, the size of the "economic pie" is variable, not fixed.

Human Ingenuity

The size of a country's "economic pie" is most easily thought of as the total dollar value of all goods and services produced during some period of time. This economic pie is the total amount of wealth (or value) created in the economy. It is not some fixed total waiting to be divided up among people. It is simply a statistic—a grand total, calculated by adding up the wealth created by each of the individuals in the economy. As the quotation at the chapter opening suggests, many errors in economic reasoning stem from the incorrect notion that the size of the economic pie is fixed.

On the contrary, the size of the economic pie reflects the physical effort and ingenuity of human beings. It is not an endowment from nature. Economic output expands as we discover better ways of doing things. So over time, it is human knowledge and ingenuity—perhaps more than anything else—that limits our economic progress. If Jim, a local farmer who normally produces $30,000 worth of corn each year, finds a better growing method enabling him to produce $40,000 of corn each year, he has created additional wealth. But Jim has actually created more than the $10,000 in extra wealth. The $10,000 is only his share of the gains from the additional trades made possible by the extra corn he grew. Exchange makes both buyer and seller better off, so the total wealth created by Jim includes not only his $10,000 but also the gains of all of the buyers who purchased corn from him as well.

This highlights an important point: in a market economy, a larger income for one person does not mean a smaller income for another. In fact, it is just the opposite. When a person earns income, he or she expands the economic pie by more than the amount of the slice that he or she gets, making it possible for the rest of us to have a bigger slice, too. When a wealthy entrepreneur, such as Bill Gates or Henry Ford, has an income of, say, $1 billion per year earned through voluntary exchanges in the marketplace, he has enlarged the economic pie for everyone by an even larger amount. Here's how:

Suppose that Linda, a freelance graphic artist, pays $175 for a new software program developed by Bill Gates. As a result, she can do twice as much work in the same amount of time. Because she's more productive, Linda can earn more than enough additional income with the software to justify her purchase. In addition, the businesses she serves are also likely to be better off because the software makes it possible for her to give them more and better service and a lower price for her services. Thus, while Bill Gates gained, so, too, did Linda and her customers.

Similarly, although Henry Ford certainly became rich, he also greatly increased our ability to transport goods, services, and people. In the process, he made it possible for many others to achieve higher living standards than would have been possible in his absence. Had Stephen King never written a novel, not only would he not be as rich, but we would all be poorer for never having had the opportunity to read his novels. When income is acquired through voluntary exchange, people who earn income also help others earn more income and live better, too.

ECONOMIC ORGANIZATION

Every economy faces three basic questions: (1) What will be produced? (2) How will it be produced? and (3) For whom will it be produced? These problems are highly interrelated. Throughout the book, we will consider how different types of economies solve these issues. There are two broad ways that an economy can be organized: markets and government (political) planning. Let us briefly consider each.

Market Organization

Market organization
A method of organization in which private parties make their own plans and decisions with the guidance of unregulated market prices. The basic economic questions of consumption, production, and distribution are answered through these decentralized decisions.

Capitalism
An economic system in which productive resources are owned privately and goods and resources are allocated through market prices.

Private ownership of productive assets, voluntary contracts (often verbal), and market prices are the distinguishing features of **market organization**. Market organization is also known as **capitalism**.[8] Under market organization, private parties are permitted to buy and sell ownership rights of their assets at mutually acceptable prices. The government plays the limited role of rule maker and referee. It develops the rules, or the legal structure, that recognize, define, and protect private ownership rights. It enforces contracts and protects

---

[8]*Capitalism* is a term coined by Karl Marx.

people from violence and fraud. But the government is not an active player in the economy. Ideally, it avoids modifying market outcomes in an attempt to favor some people at the expense of others. For example, it doesn't prevent sellers from slashing prices or improving the quality of their products to attract customers from other competitors. Nor does it prevent buyers from outbidding others for products and productive resources. No legal restraints limit potential buyers or sellers from producing, selling, or buying in the marketplace.

Under market organization, no single individual or group of individuals guides the economy. There is no central planning authority, only individual planning. The three basic questions are solved independently in the marketplace by individual buyers and sellers making their own decentralized decisions. Buyers and sellers decide on their own what to produce, how to produce it, and whom to trade it to, based on the prices they themselves decide to charge.

In markets, individual buyers and sellers communicate their desires and preferences both directly and indirectly. They directly voice their desires when they buy or sell by advertising, whether in print or broadcast, or informally by word of mouth, on bulletin boards, and by letters of request and complaint and other means. They communicate indirectly by exiting or entering exchange relationships, as when they stop purchasing Coke and switch to Pepsi. The indirect, or "exit," option gives special power to their voiced, or direct, statements. Indeed, sellers, when markets are competitive, often hire experts to seek out the statements and desires of potential buyers. Buyers, too, are eager to know what sellers want—special terms of payment or delivery, for example—hoping that sellers might be willing to reward cooperation with a better deal.

Political Planning

The major alternative to market organization is **collective decision making**, whereby the government, through the political process, makes decisions for buyers and sellers in an attempt to solve the basic economic questions facing the economy. The government may maintain private ownership, but uses taxes, subsidies, and regulations to resolve the basic economic questions. Alternatively, an economic system in which the government also owns the income-producing assets (machines, buildings, and land) and directly determines what goods will be produced is called **socialism**. Either way, individual planning and decisions are replaced by central planning and decisions made through the political process. These decisions can be made by a single dictator or a group of experts, or through democratic voting. Political rather than market forces direct the economy, and government officials and planning boards hand down decisions to expand or contract the output of education, medical services, automobiles, electricity, steel, consumer durables, and thousands of other commodities.

This is not to say that the preferences of individuals carry no weight. If the government officials and central planners are influenced by the democratic process, they must consider how their actions will influence their reelection prospects. That means they will listen to the voices of the voters to win over a majority of them. Otherwise, like the firm in a market economy that produces a product that consumers do not want, their tenure of service is likely to be short. However, under central planning the indirect exit method of communicating is much more difficult. Although people can use the direct or voice method to communicate their preferences by lobbying government officials or casting votes in an election, they generally cannot use the indirect exit option because they cannot refuse to pay taxes or to quit purchasing a good or service that is provided by government. For example, families who send their children to private school must continue to pay the same amount in taxes to support the public school system as they would if they kept their child in public school. Oftentimes, people "vote with their feet" and leave one political jurisdiction to move to another. This is frequently seen when people move to better school districts. It is much easier, however, to move between school districts than between states or nations.

Collective decision making
The method of organization that relies on public-sector decision making (voting, political bargaining, lobbying, and so on) to resolve basic economic questions.

Socialism
A system of economic organization in which (1) the ownership and control of the basic means of production rest with the state, and (2) resource allocation is determined by centralized planning rather than market forces.

In summary, both market organization and central planning face the same basic economic questions. A basic difference between them is that the market system, with its exit option, allows for a wider variety of products and creates constant competition among suppliers, whereas the central planning system, in a democracy, responds primarily to the votes of the majority. In varying degrees, all economies use a combination of both of these methods of economic organization. Even predominantly market economies will still use taxes, subsidies, and some government ownership to direct and control resources. Similarly, predominantly socialist economies will, to some degree, use markets to allocate certain goods and services.

LOOKING AHEAD

The next two chapters present an overview of the market sector and explain how supply and demand for goods and services work. Chapters 5 and 6 focus on potential shortcomings of the market and how the collective decision-making process works in a democracy. As we proceed, the tools of economics will be used to analyze both the market and political sectors. We think this approach is important and that you will find it both interesting and enlightening.

! KEY POINTS

▼ The highest valued activity sacrificed when a choice is made is the opportunity cost of the choice; differences (or changes) in opportunity costs help explain human behavior.

▼ Mutual gain is the foundation of trade. When two parties engage in voluntary exchange, they are both made better off. Trade creates value because it channels goods and resources to those who value them the most.

▼ Transaction costs—the time, effort, and other resources necessary to search out, negotiate, and conclude an exchange—hinder the gains from trade in an economy. Middlemen perform a productive function by reducing transaction costs.

▼ Private-property rights motivate owners to use their resources in ways that benefit others and avoid doing harm to them. These rights also motivate owners to take proper care of their resources and conserve them.

▼ The production possibilities curve shows the maximum combination of any two products that can be produced with a fixed quantity of resources.

▼ Over time, the production possibilities curve of an economy can be shifted outward by (1) investment,

(2) technological advances, (3) improved institutions, and (4) greater work effort (forgoing leisure). The size of the economic pie is variable, not fixed. It can grow (or shrink) over time.

▼ The law of comparative advantage indicates that the joint output of individuals, regions, and nations will be maximized when each productive activity is undertaken by the low-opportunity-cost supplier. When a good can be acquired through trade more economically than it can be produced directly, it makes sense to trade for it.

▼ In addition to the gains that occur when goods are moved toward those who value them most, trade also makes it possible to expand output through specialization, division of labor, mass production processes, and innovation. These improved production techniques have contributed greatly to our modern living standards.

▼ Economies can either be organized by decentralized markets (capitalism) or they can be centrally planned by government through political decision making. Under central planning, buyers and sellers are more limited in their ability to communicate their desires.

1. "If Jones trades a used car to Smith for $5,000, nothing new is created. Thus, there is no way the transaction can improve the welfare of people." Is this statement true? Why or why not?

*2. Economists often argue that wage rates reflect productivity. Yet, the wages of house painters have increased nearly as rapidly as the national average, even though these workers use approximately the same production methods as they did 50 years ago. Can you explain why the wages of painters have risen substantially even though their productivity has changed so little?

3. It takes one hour to travel from New York City to Washington, D.C., by air, but it takes five hours by bus. If the airfare is $110 and the bus fare is $70, which would be cheaper for someone whose opportunity cost of travel time is $6 per hour? For someone whose opportunity cost is $10 per hour? $14 per hour?

*4. "People in business get ahead by exploiting the needs of their consumers. The gains of business are at the expense of suffering imposed on their customers." Evaluate this statement.

5. What is the objective of the entrepreneur when it comes to the use of his or her resources? What is the major function of the middleman? Is the middleman an entrepreneur?

6. If you have a private-ownership right to something, what does this mean? Does private ownership give you the right to do anything you want with the things that you own? Explain. How does private ownership influence the incentive of individuals to (a) take care of things, (b) conserve resources for the future, and (c) develop and modify things in ways that are beneficial to others? Explain.

7. What is the law of comparative advantage? According to the law of comparative advantage, what should be the distinguishing characteristics of the goods a nation produces? What should be the distinguishing characteristics of the goods a nation imports? How will international trade influence people's production levels and living standards? Explain.

*8. Does a 60-year-old tree farmer have an incentive to plant and care for Douglas fir trees that will not reach optimal cutting size for another 50 years?

*9. What forms of competition does a private-property, market-directed economy authorize? What forms does it prohibit?

10. What are the major sources of gains from trade? Why is exchange important to a nation's prosperity? How does trade influence the quantity of output that trading partners are able to produce? In a market economy, will there be a tendency for both resources and products to be supplied by low-cost producers? Why or why not? Does this matter? Explain.

*11. Chick-fil-A's "Eat Mor Chikin" advertising campaign features three cows holding signs that say things like: "Save the cows, eat more chicken." If consumers began eating more chicken and less beef, would the cattle population increase or decrease? Explain.

*12. In many states, ticket scalping, or reselling tickets to entertainment events at prices above the original purchase price, is prohibited. Who is helped and who is hurt by such prohibitions? How can owners who want to sell their tickets get around the prohibition? Do you think it would be a good idea to prohibit the resale of other things—automobiles, books, works of art, or stock shares at prices higher than the original purchase price? Why or why not?

13. Consider the choices of two groups of women ages 30 to 50. All the women in one group have a college education. All the women in the other group have less than a high school education. Which of the two groups will participate more in the workforce? Which of the two groups will bear a larger number of children on average? Explain your answers based on the concept of opportunity cost.

14. Consider the questions below:
    a. Do you think that your work effort is influenced by whether there is a close link between personal output and personal compensation (reward)? Explain.
    b. Suppose the grades in your class were going to be determined by a random drawing at the end of the course. How would this influence your study habits?
    c. How would your study habits be influenced if everyone in the class were going to be given an A grade? How about if grades were based entirely on examinations composed of the multiple-choice questions in the course book for this textbook?
    d. Do you think the total output of a nation will be influenced by whether or not there is a close link between the productive contribution of individuals and their personal reward? Why or why not?

15. In the chapter it was stated that a private-property right also involves having the right to transfer or exchange what you own with others. However, selling your organs is a violation of federal law, a felony punishable by up to five years in prison or a $50,000 fine. In 1999 eBay intervened when a person put one of his kidneys up for sale on the auction site (the bidding

reached $5.7 million before the auction was halted). Does this lack of legal ability to exchange mean that individuals do not own their own organs? Explain.

16. During the last three decades entrepreneurs like Michael Dell, Sam Walton, and Ted Turner earned billions of dollars. Do you think the average American is better or worse off as the result of the economic activities of these individuals? Explain your response.

*__17.__ As the skill level (and therefore earnings rate) of, say, an architect, computer specialist, or chemist increases, what happens to his or her opportunity cost of doing other things? How is the time spent on leisure likely to change?

18. Two centuries ago there were more buffalo than cattle in the United States. Even though millions of

cattle are killed for beef consumption each year, the cattle population continues to grow while the buffalo are virtually extinct. Why?

19. The tables below show the production possibilities for two hypothetical countries, Italia and Nire. Which country has the comparative advantage in producing butter? Which country has the comparative advantage in producing guns? What would be a mutually agreeable rate of exchange between the countries?

Italia		Nire	
Guns	**Butter**	**Guns**	**Butter**
12	0	16	0
8	2	12	1
4	4	8	2
0	6	4	3
		0	4

*Asterisk denotes questions for which answers are given in Appendix B.

ADDENDUM

Comparative Advantage, Specialization, and Gains from Trade

This addendum is for instructors who want to assign a more detailed numerical example demonstrating comparative advantage, specialization, and mutual gains from trade. Students who are uncertain about their understanding of these topics may also find this material enlightening. The international-trade chapter later in the text provides still more information on trade and how it affects our lives.

We begin with hypothetical production possibilities curves for two countries, Slavia and Lebos, shown in **Exhibit A-1**. The numerical tables represent selected points from each country's production possibilities curve. To make calculations easier, we have assumed away increasing opportunity costs in production so that the production possibilities curves are linear.

Without trade, each country would be able to consume only what it can produce for itself. Let's arbitrarily assume

---

EXHIBIT A-1
Production Possibilities for Slavia and Lebos

For Slavia, the opportunity cost of producing 1 unit of clothing is equal to 3 units of food (1C = 3F). For Lebos, the opportunity cost of producing 3 units of clothing is equal to 3 units of food (3C = 3F or 1C = 1F). The difference in the opportunity costs of production will make possible mutually beneficial trade between the countries, with each specializing in its area of comparative advantage.

SLAVIA	
Food	Clothing
9	0
6	1
3	2
0	3

3F = 1C

LEBOS	
Food	Clothing
12	0
9	3
6	6
3	9
0	12

3F = 3C

that for survival Slavia requires 3 units of food and Lebos requires 6 units of food. As can be seen by point *A* in the exhibit, if Slavia were to produce the 3 units of food it requires, it would have enough resources remaining to produce 2 units of clothing. Similarly, if Lebos were to produce the 6 units of food it requires, it would have enough resources left to produce 6 units of clothing, again shown by point *A* in the exhibit. As we proceed we will use this outcome as our benchmark outcome that occurs in the absence of specialization and trade between the countries.

Economic analysis suggests that both countries could gain if each were to specialize in the production of the good for which they have the comparative advantage and then trade for the other. First, let's figure out which country has a comparative advantage in the production of clothing. Doing so requires calculating the opportunity cost of producing clothing for each country. Because, in this example, the opportunity costs are constant at all points along the production possibilities curve, rather than increasing, this can be found by first selecting any two points on the production possibilities curve (or equivalently by comparing any two rows of numbers in the numerical tables given in the exhibit). For Slavia, moving from the point of producing 6 food units and 1 clothing unit to the alternative point of producing 3 food units and 2 clothing units, we see that Slavia gains 1 clothing unit but must give up 3 units of food. For simplicity, the opportunity cost for Slavia can be written as 1C = 3F, where C stands for clothing and F for food. You might note that this same numerical trade-off is true for Slavia anywhere along its production possibilities curve (for example, beginning from 9 food units and 0 clothing units, it would also have to give up 3 food units to gain 1 unit of clothing).

Using a similar approach (taking any 2 points or 2 rows in the table) for Lebos shows that for every 3 units of clothing the country wishes to produce, it must give up 3 units of food (3C = 3F). This can be treated as any other mathematical equation, and can be simplified by dividing both sides by 3, resulting in an opportunity cost of 1 clothing unit equals 1 food unit (1C = 1F). Now, compare this to the opportunity cost for Slavia (1C = 3F). Slavia must give up the production of 3 units of food for every 1 unit of clothing it produces, whereas Lebos must give up only 1 unit of food for every 1 unit of clothing it produces. Thus, Lebos gives up the production of *less* food for every unit of clothing. Lebos is the low-opportunity-cost producer of clothing, and thus it has a comparative advantage in the production of clothing.

Because comparative advantage is a relative comparison, if one country has the comparative advantage in the production of one of the products, the other country must have the comparative advantage for the other good. Thus, because Lebos has the comparative advantage in clothing, it will be true that Slavia has the comparative advantage in food. However, it is worthwhile to show this here as well. To produce 1 unit of food, Lebos must give up 1 unit of clothing (recall the 1C = 1F opportunity cost). To produce

1 unit of food, Slavia must give up the production of only one-third of a unit of clothing (recall the 1C = 3F opportunity cost and rewrite the equation as 1/3 C = 1F by dividing both sides of the equation by 3). Thus, Slavia gives up the production of *less* clothing for every unit of food produced. Slavia is the low-opportunity-cost producer of food, and thus has a comparative advantage in the production of food.

Suppose that, according to their comparative advantages, Lebos specializes in producing clothing and Slavia in food. From the last row of the table for Lebos, you can see that it can produce 12 units of clothing (and 0 food) if it specializes in producing only clothing. From the top row of the table for Slavia, you can see that it can produce 9 units of food (and 0 clothing) if it specializes in producing only food. Note that this joint output (9 food and 12 clothing) is greater than the benchmark joint output (9 food and 8 clothing) produced and consumed without trade.

If they are to trade, the countries now must find a mutually agreeable rate of exchange. Any rate of exchange *between* the two opportunity costs of 1C = 3F and 3C = 3F would be mutually agreeable. Here we will use 2C = 3F.

Recall that Slavia requires 3 units of food for survival. Now, however, they are specializing and producing 9 units of food. Using the rate of exchange above, Slavia would send its extra 6 units of food to Lebos in exchange for 4 units of clothing. After trade, Slavia would then have 3 units of food and 4 units of clothing. Compare this to the situation that existed before specialization and trade, in which Slavia had only 3 units of food and 2 units of clothing to consume. Specialization and trade have created 2 additional units of clothing for Slavia that it would not have had without trade.

With specialization, Lebos is producing 12 units of clothing. In the trade with Slavia, Lebos gave up 4 units of clothing to obtain 6 units of food. After trade, Lebos has 8 units of clothing remaining and 6 units of food imported from Slavia. Compare this to the situation that existed before specialization and trade, in which Lebos had only 6 units of food and 6 units of clothing to consume. For Lebos, specialization and trade have also created 2 additional units of clothing that it would not have had without trade.

As this simple example shows, total output is greater and *both* countries are better off when they specialize in the area in which they have a comparative advantage. By doing so, each is able to consume a bundle of goods and services that exceeds what it could have achieved in the absence of trade. This concept applies equally to individuals, states, or nations. The typical worker could not begin to produce alone all of the things he or she can afford to buy with the money earned in a year by specializing and working in a single occupation. As our world has become more integrated over the past several hundred years, the gains that have occurred from specialization and trade are at the root of the significant improvements in well-being that we have experienced.

PART 2

"There are two primary methods of allocating scarce resources: markets and governments"

Markets and Government

P A R T 2

Economics has a great deal to say about how both markets and governments allocate scarce resources. It gives us insight about the conditions under which each will likely work well (and each will likely work poorly). The next four chapters will focus on this topic.

MARKET ALLOCATION OF RESOURCES

Business firms purchase resources like materials, labor services, tools, and machines from households in exchange for income, bidding the resources away from their alternate uses. The firms then transform the resources into products like shoes, automobiles, food products, and medical services and sell them to households. In a market economy, businesses will continue to supply a good or service only if the revenues from the sale of the product are sufficient to cover the cost of the resources required for its production.

GOVERNMENT ALLOCATION OF RESOURCES

Resource allocation by the government involves a more complex, three-sided exchange. In a democratic political setting, a legislative body levies taxes on voter-citizens, and these revenues are subdivided into budgets, which are allocated to government bureaus and agencies. In turn, the bureaus and agencies use the funds from their budgets to supply goods, services, and income transfers to voter-citizens. The legislative body is like a board of directors elected by the citizens. The competitive pressure to get elected gives legislators a strong incentive to cater to the wishes of voters. In turn, voters will be more likely to support a legislator if the value of the goods, services, and transfers received by them is high relative to the taxes they have to pay. In other words, goods, services, and income transfers will be supplied by the government if, and only if, a majority of legislators believe it will improve their election prospects. As you can tell, this is quite different from the way markets allocate goods and services! Now let's see just how really different it is and what impact it has on you and the rest of the economy.

CHAPTER 3

Supply, Demand, and the Market Process

I am convinced that if [the market system] were the result of deliberate human design, and if the people guided by the price changes understood that their decisions have significance far beyond their immediate aim, this mechanism would have been acclaimed as one of the greatest triumphs of the human mind.

—Friedrich Hayek, Nobel laureate[1]

From the point of view of physics, it is a miracle that [7 million New Yorkers are fed each day] without any control mechanism other than sheer capitalism.

—John H. Holland, scientist, Santa Fe Institute

Chapter Focus

- What are the laws of demand and supply?

- How do consumers decide whether to purchase a good? How do producers decide whether to supply it?

- How do buyers and sellers respond to changes in the price of a good?

- What role do profits and losses play in an economy? What must a firm do to make a profit?

- How is the market price of a good determined?

- How do markets adjust to changes in demand? How do they adjust to changes in supply?

- What is the "invisible hand" principle?

[1]Friedrich Hayek, "The Use of Knowledge in Society," *American Economic Review* 35 (September 1945): 519–30.

To those who study art, the *Mona Lisa* is much more than a famous painting of a woman. Looking beyond the overall picture, they see and appreciate the brush strokes, colors, and techniques embodied in the painting. Similarly, studying economics can help you to gain an appreciation for the details behind many things in your everyday life. During your last visit to the grocery store, you probably noticed the fruit and vegetable section. Next time, take a moment to ponder how potatoes from Idaho, oranges from Florida, apples from Washington, bananas from Honduras, kiwi fruit from New Zealand, and other items from around the world got there. Literally thousands of different individuals, *working independently,* were involved in the process. Their actions were so well coordinated, in fact, that the amount of each good was just about right to fill exactly the desires of your local community. Furthermore, even the goods shipped from halfway around the world were fresh and reasonably priced.

How does all this happen? The short answer is that it is the result of market prices and the incentives and coordination that flow from them. To the economist, the operation of markets—including your local grocery market—is like the brush strokes underlying a beautiful painting. Reflecting on this point, Professor Hayek speculates that if the market system had been deliberately designed, it would be "acclaimed as one of the greatest triumphs of the human mind." Similarly, computer scientist John H. Holland argues that, from the viewpoint of physics, the feeding of millions of New Yorkers day after day with very few shortages or surpluses is a miraculous feat (see the quotations at the chapter opening).

Amazingly, markets coordinate the actions of millions of individuals *without* central planning. There is no individual, political authority, or central planning committee in charge. Considering that there are nearly 300 million Americans with widely varying skills and desires, and roughly 25 million businesses producing a vast array of products ranging from diamond rings to toilet paper, the coordination derived from markets is indeed an awesome achievement.

This chapter focuses on supply, demand, and the determination of market prices. For now, we will analyze the operation of competitive markets—that is, markets with unrestricted numbers of buyers and sellers. We will also assume that the property rights are well defined. Later, we will consider what happens when these conditions are absent.

On eBay, sellers enter their reserve prices—the minimum prices they will accept for goods; buyers enter their maximum bids—the maximum prices they are willing to pay for goods. The process works the same way when a person runs a

The produce section of your local grocery store is a great place to see economics in action. Literally millions of individuals from around the world have been involved in the process of getting these goods to the shelves in just the right quantities. Market prices underlie this feat.

newspaper ad to sell a car. The seller has in mind a minimum price he or she will accept for the car. A potential buyer, on the other hand, has in mind a maximum price he or she will pay for the car. If the buyer's maximum price is greater than the seller's minimum price, the exchange will occur at a price somewhere in between. As these examples show, the buyers' and sellers' desires and incentives determine prices and make markets work. We will begin with the demand (buyer's) side, and then turn to the supply (seller's) side of the market. ▪

CONSUMER CHOICE AND THE LAW OF DEMAND

Law of demand
A principle that states there is an inverse relationship between the price of a good and the quantity of it buyers are willing to purchase. As the price of a good increases, consumers will wish to purchase less of it. As the price decreases, consumers will wish to purchase more of it.

Substitutes
Products that serve similar purposes. An increase in the price of one will cause an increase in demand for the other (examples are hamburgers and tacos, butter and margarine, Microsoft Xbox and Sony Play-Station, Chevrolets and Fords).

Clearly, prices influence our decisions. As the price of a good increases, we have to give up more of *other* goods if we want to buy it. Thus, as the price of a good rises, its opportunity cost increases (in terms of other goods that must be forgone to purchase it).

A basic principle of economics is that if something becomes more costly, people will be less likely to buy it. This principle is called the **law of demand**. *The law of demand states that there is an inverse (or negative) relationship between the price of a good or service and the quantity of it that consumers are willing to purchase.* This inverse relationship means that price and the quantity consumers wish to purchase move in opposite directions. As the price increases, buyers purchase less—and as the price decreases, buyers purchase more.

The availability of **substitutes**—goods that perform similar functions—helps explain this inverse relationship. No single good is absolutely essential; everything can be replaced with something else. A chicken sandwich can be substituted for a cheeseburger. Wood, aluminum, bricks, and glass can take the place of steel. Going to the movies, playing tennis, watching television, and going to a football game are substitute forms of entertainment. When the price of a good increases, people cut back on it and buy substitute products.

The Market Demand Schedule

The lower portion of **Exhibit 1** shows a hypothetical *demand schedule* for cellular telephone service.[2] A demand schedule is simply a table listing the various quantities of something consumers are willing to purchase at different prices. In Exhibit 1, notice that the price is the average monthly cost of purchasing cellular phone service. The quantity demanded is the number of people willing to subscribe to cellular service at each price. When the price of cell phone service is $143 per month, just over 2 million people subscribe. As the price falls to $85, the quantity of subscribers rises to 11 million; when the price falls to $41 per month, the quantity of subscribers increases to just over 69 million.

The upper portion of Exhibit 1 shows what the demand schedule would look like if the various prices and corresponding quantity of subscribers were plotted on a graph and connected by a line. This is called the *demand curve.* When representing the demand schedule graphically, economists measure price on the vertical or *y*-axis, and the amount demanded on the horizontal or *x*-axis. Because of the inverse relationship between price and amount purchased, the demand curve will have a negative slope—that is, it will slope downward to the right. More of a good will be purchased as its price decreases. This is the law of demand.

Read horizontally, the demand curve shows how much of a particular good consumers will buy at a given price. Read vertically, the demand curve shows how much consumers value the good. *The height of the demand curve at any quantity shows the maximum price consumers are willing to pay for an additional unit.* If consumers value highly an additional unit of a product, they will be willing to pay a large amount for it. Conversely, if they place a low value on the additional unit, they will be willing to pay only a small amount for it.

Because the amount a consumer is willing to pay for a good is directly related to the good's value to them, the demand curve indicates the marginal benefit (or value)

---

[2]These data are actual prices (adjusted to 2000 dollars) and quantities annually for 1988 to 1998 taken from *Statistical Abstract of the United States* (Washington, D.C.: U.S. Bureau of the Census, various years). *If we could assume that other demand determinants (income, prices of related goods, etc.) had remained constant,* then this hypothetical demand schedule would be accurate for that time period. Because it is possible that some of these other factors changed, we treat the numbers as hypothetical, depicting alternative prices and quantities *at a given time.*

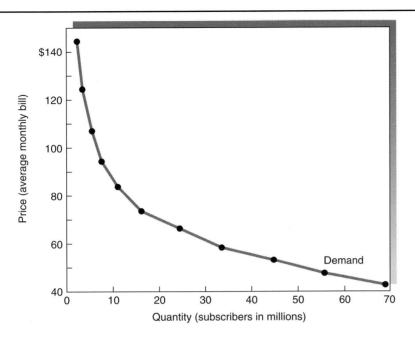

EXHIBIT 1
Law of Demand

As the demand schedule shown in the table indicates, the number of people subscribing to cellular phone service (just like the consumption of other products) is inversely related to price. The data from the table are plotted as a demand curve in the graph. The inverse relation between price and amount demanded reflects the fact that consumers will substitute away from a good as it becomes more expensive.

CELLULAR PHONE PRICE (AVERAGE MONTHLY BILL)	QUANTITY OF CELLULAR PHONE SUBSCRIBERS (IN MILLIONS)
$143	2.1
124	3.5
107	5.3
92	7.6
85	11.0
73	16.0
65	24.1
58	33.7
53	44.0
46	55.3
41	69.2

consumers receive from additional units. (Recall that we briefly discussed marginal benefit in Chapter 1.) When viewed in this manner, the demand curve reveals that as consumers have more and more of a good or service, they value additional units less and less.

Consumer Surplus

Previously, we indicated that voluntary exchanges make both buyers and sellers better off. The demand curve can be used to illustrate the gains to consumers. Suppose you value a particular good at $50, but you are able to purchase it for only $30. Your net gain from buying the good is the $20 difference. Economists call this net gain of buyers **consumer surplus**. Consumer surplus is simply the difference between the maximum amount consumers would be willing to pay and the amount they actually pay for a good.

Exhibit 2 shows the consumer surplus for an entire market. The height of the demand curve measures how much buyers in the market value each unit of the good. The price indicates the amount they actually pay. The difference between these two—the triangular area below the demand curve but above the price paid—is a measure of the total consumer surplus generated by all exchanges of the good. The size of the consumer surplus, or triangular area, is affected by the market price. If the market price for the goods falls, more of it will be purchased, resulting in a larger surplus for consumers. Conversely, if the market price rises, less of it will be purchased, resulting in a smaller surplus (net gain) for consumers.

Because the value a consumer places on a particular unit of a good is shown by the corresponding height of the demand curve, we can use the demand curve to clarify the

Consumer surplus
The difference between the maximum price consumers are willing to pay and the price they actually pay. It is the net gain derived by the buyers of the good.

EXHIBIT 2
Consumer Surplus

Consumer surplus is the area below the demand curve but above the actual price paid. This area represents the net gains to buyers from market exchange.

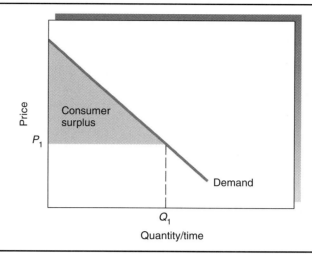

difference between the *marginal value* and *total value* of a good—a distinction we introduced briefly in Chapter 1. Returning to Exhibit 2, if consumers are currently purchasing Q_1 units, the marginal value of the good is indicated by the height of the demand curve at Q_1—the last unit consumed (or purchased). So at each quantity, the height of the demand curve shows the marginal value of that unit, which as you can see, declines along a demand curve. The *total* value of the good, however, is equal to the combined value of all units purchased. This is the sum of the value of each unit (the heights along the demand curve) on the *x*-axis, out to, and including, unit Q_1. This total value is indicated graphically as the entire area under the demand curve out to Q_1 (the triangular area representing consumer surplus *plus* the unshaded rectangular area directly below it).

You can see that the total value to consumers of a good can be far greater than the marginal value of the last unit consumed. When additional units are available at a low price, the marginal value of a good may be quite low, even though its total value to consumers is exceedingly high. This is usually the case with water, for example, because it is essential for life. The value of the first few units of water consumed per day will be exceedingly high. The consumer surplus derived from these units will also be large when water is plentiful at a low price. As more and more units are consumed, however, the *marginal value* of even something as important as water will fall to a low level. Thus, when water is cheap, people will use it not only for drinking, cleaning, and cooking, but also for washing cars, watering lawns, flushing toilets, and maintaining fish aquariums. Thus, although the total value of water is rather large, its marginal value is quite low.

Consumers will tend to expand their consumption of a good until its price and *marginal value* are equal (which occurs at Q_1 in Exhibit 2 at a price of P_1). Thus, the price of a good (which equals marginal value) reveals little about the *total value* derived from the consumption of it. This is the reason that the market price of diamonds (which reflects their high marginal value) is greater than the market price of water (which has a low marginal value), even though the total value of diamonds is far less than the total value of water. Think of it this way, beginning from your current levels of consumption, if you were offered a choice between one diamond or one gallon of water right now, which would you take? You would probably take the diamond, because at the margin it has more value to you than additional water. However, if given a choice between giving up *all* of the water you use or *all* of the diamonds you have, you would probably keep the water over diamonds, because in total water has more value to you.

Responsiveness of Quantity Demanded to Price Changes: Elastic and Inelastic Demand Curves

As we previously noted, the availability of substitutes is the main reason why the demand curve for a good slopes downward. Some goods, however, are much easier than others to substitute away from. As the price of tacos rises, most consumers find hamburgers a reasonable substitute. Because of the ease of substitutability, the quantity of tacos

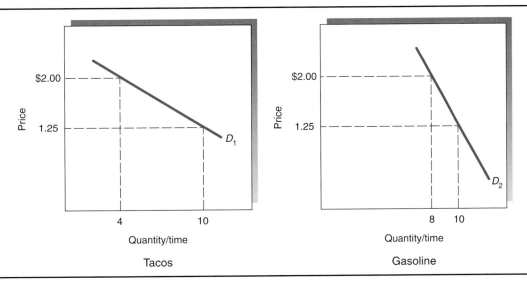

EXHIBIT 3
Elastic and Inelastic Demand Curves

The responsiveness of consumer purchases to a change in price is reflected in the steepness of the demand curve. The flatter demand curve (D_1) for tacos shows a higher degree of responsiveness and is called relatively elastic, while the steeper demand curve (D_2) for gasoline shows a lower degree of responsiveness and is called relatively inelastic.

demanded is quite sensitive to a change in their price. Economists would say that the demand for tacos is relatively *elastic* because a small price change will cause a rather large change in the amount purchased. Alternatively, goods like gasoline and electricity have fewer close substitutes. When their prices rise, it is harder for consumers to find substitutes for these products. When close substitutes are unavailable, even a large price change may not cause much of a change in the quantity demanded. In this case, an economist would say that the demand for such goods is relatively *inelastic*.

Graphically, this different degree of responsiveness is reflected in the steepness of the demand curve, as shown in **Exhibit 3**. The flatter demand curve (D_1, left frame) is for a product like tacos, for which the quantity purchased is highly responsive to a change in price. As the price increases from $1.25 to $2.00, the quantity demanded falls sharply from 10 to 4 units. The steeper demand curve (D_2, right frame) is for a product like gasoline, where the quantity purchased is much less responsive to a change in price. For gasoline, an increase in price from $1.25 to $2.00 results in only a small reduction in the quantity purchased (from 10 to 8 units). An economist would say that the flatter demand curve D_1 is "relatively elastic," whereas the steeper demand curve D_2 is "relatively inelastic." The availability of substitutes is the main determinant of a product's elasticity or inelasticity and thus how flat or steep its demand curve is.

What would a demand curve that was perfectly vertical represent? Economists refer to this as a "perfectly" inelastic demand curve. It would mean that the quantity demanded of the product never changes—regardless of its price. Although it is tempting to think that the demand curves are vertical for goods essential to human life (or goods that are addictive), this is inaccurate for two reasons. First, in varying degrees, there are substitutes for everything. As the price of a good rises, the incentive increases for suppliers to invent even more new substitutes. Thus, even for goods that currently have few substitutes, if the price were to rise high enough, alternatives would be invented and marketed, reducing the quantity demanded of the original good. Second, our limited incomes restrict our ability to afford goods when they become very expensive. As the price of a good rises to higher and higher levels, if we do not cut back on the quantity purchased, we will have less and less income to spend on other things. Eventually, this will cause us to cut back on our purchases of it. Because of these two reasons, the demand curve for every good will slope downward to the right.

CHANGES IN DEMAND VERSUS CHANGES IN QUANTITY DEMANDED

The purpose of the demand curve is to show what effect a price change will have on the quantity demanded (or purchased) of a good. Economists refer to a change in the quantity of a good purchased in response solely to a price change as a "change in *quantity demanded.*" A change in quantity demanded is simply a movement along a demand curve from one point to another.

Changes in factors other than a good's price—such as consumers' income and the prices of closely related goods—will also influence the decisions of consumers to purchase a good. If one of these other factors changes, the entire demand curve will *shift* inward or outward. Economists refer to a shift in the demand curve as a "change in *demand.*"

Failure to distinguish between a change in demand and a change in quantity demanded is one of the most common mistakes made by beginning economics students.[3] *A change in demand is a shift in the entire demand curve. A change in quantity demanded is a movement along the same demand curve.* The easiest way to distinguish between these two concepts is the following: If the change in consumer purchases is caused by a change in the price of the good, it is a change in quantity demanded—a movement along the demand curve. If the change in consumer purchases is due to a change in anything other than the price of the good (a change in consumer income, for example), it is a change in demand—a shift in the demand curve.

Let us now take a closer look at some of the factors that cause a "change in demand"—an inward or outward shift in the entire demand curve.

1. Changes in consumer income. An increase in consumer income makes it possible for consumers to purchase more goods. If you were to win the lottery, or if your boss were to give you a raise, you would respond by increasing your spending on many products. Alternatively, when the economy goes into a recession, falling incomes and rising unemployment cause consumers to reduce their purchases of many items. A change in consumer income will result in consumers buying more or less of a product at all possible *prices.* When consumer income increases, in the case of most goods, individuals will purchase more of the good even if the price is unchanged. This is shown by a shift to the right—an outward shift—in the demand curve. Such a shift is called an increase in demand. A reduction in consumer income generally causes a shift to the left—an inward shift—in the demand curve, which is called a decrease in demand. Note that the appropriate terminology here is an increase or decrease in demand, not an increase or decrease in quantity demanded.

Exhibit 4 highlights the difference between a change in demand and a change in quantity demanded. The demand curve D_1 indicates the initial demand curve for DVDs. At a price of $30, consumers will purchase Q_1 units. If the price were to decline to $10, the *quantity demanded* would increase from Q_1 to Q_3. The arrow in panel (a) indicates the change in *quantity demanded*—a movement along the original demand curve D_1 in response to the change in price. Now, alternatively suppose there were an increase in income that caused the *demand* for DVDs to shift from D_1 to D_2. As indicated by the arrows in panel (b), the entire demand curve would shift outward. At the higher income level, consumers would be willing to purchase more DVDs than before. This is true at a price of $30, $20, $10, and every other price. The increase in income leads to an increase in *demand*—a shift in the entire curve.

2. Changes in the number of consumers in the market. Businesses that sell products in college towns are greatly saddened when summer arrives. As you might expect in these towns, the demand for many items—from pizza delivery to beer—falls during the summer. **Exhibit 5** shows how the falling number of consumers in the market caused by students going home for the summer affects the demand for pizza delivery. With fewer customers, the demand curve shifts inward from D_1 to D_2. There is a decrease in demand; pizza stores sell fewer pizzas than before regardless of what price they originally charged. Had their original price been $20, then demand would fall from 200 pizzas per week to only 100. Alternatively, had their original price been $10, then demand would fall from 300 pizzas to 200. When autumn arrives and the students come back to town, there will be

---

[3]Questions designed to test the ability of students to make this distinction are favorites of many economics instructors. A word to the wise should be sufficient.

EXHIBIT 4
Change in Demand Versus Change in Quantity Demanded

Panel (a) shows a change in *quantity demanded,* a movement along the demand curve D_1, in response to a change in the price of DVD discs. Panel (b) shows a change in *demand,* a shift of the entire curve, in this case due to an increase in consumer income.

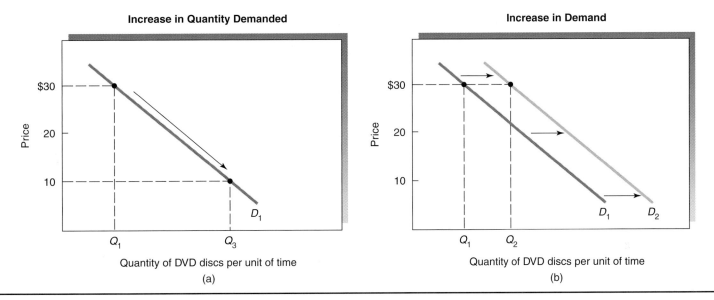

Increase in Quantity Demanded

Increase in Demand

Quantity of DVD discs per unit of time
(a)

Quantity of DVD discs per unit of time
(b)

an increase in demand that will restore the curve to about its original position. As cities grow and shrink, and as international markets open up to domestic firms, changes in the number of consumers affect the demand for many products.

3. Changes in the price of a related good.   Changes in prices of closely related products also influence the choices of consumers. Related goods may be either substitutes or complements. When two products perform similar functions or fulfill similar needs, they are substitutes. Economists define goods as substitutes when there is a direct relationship between the price of one and the demand for the other—meaning an increase in the price of one leads to an increase in demand for the other (they move in the same direction). For example, margarine is a substitute for butter. If the price of butter rises, it will increase the demand for margarine as consumers substitute margarine for the more expensive butter. Similarly, lower butter prices will reduce the demand for margarine, shifting the entire

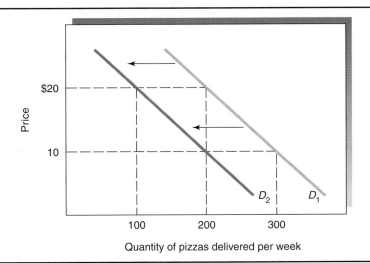

Quantity of pizzas delivered per week

EXHIBIT 5
A Decrease in Demand

In college towns the demand for pizza delivery decreases substantially when students go home for the summer. A decrease in demand is a leftward shift in the entire demand curve. Fewer pizzas are demanded at every price.

demand curve for margarine to the left. A substitute relationship exists between beef and chicken, pencils and pens, apples and oranges, coffee and tea, and so forth.

Note that although a change in the price of butter shifts the demand curve for margarine (a change in demand), it will only result in a movement along the demand curve for butter (a change in the quantity demanded). The reason is that the demand curve for butter already shows the relationship between the price of butter and the quantity of butter desired. An increase in the price of butter makes consumers willing to purchase more margarine, holding constant the price of margarine.

Complements
Products that are usually consumed jointly (for example, bread and butter, hot dogs and hot dog buns). A decrease in the price of one will cause an increase in demand for the other.

Other products are consumed jointly, so the demands for them are linked together as well. Examples of goods that "go together" include peanut butter and jelly, DVDs and DVD players, hot dogs and hot dog buns, or tents and other camping equipment. These goods are called **complements**. For complements, a decrease in the price of one will not only increase its quantity demanded, it will also increase the demand for the other good. For example, lower prices for DVD players over the past decade have substantially increased the demand for movies on DVD. The reverse is also true. As a complement becomes more expensive, the quantity demanded of it will fall, and so will the demand for its complements. For example, if the price of steak rises, grocery stores can expect to sell fewer bottles of steak sauce, even if the price of steak sauce remains unchanged.

4. Changes in expectations. Consumers' expectations about the future also can affect the current demand for a product. If consumers begin to expect that a major hurricane will strike their area, the current demand for batteries and canned food will rise. Expectations about the future direction of the economy can also affect current demand. If consumers become pessimistic about the economy, they might start spending less, causing the current demand for goods to fall. Perhaps most important is how a change in the expected future price of a good affects current demand. When consumers expect the price of a product to rise in the future, their current demand for it will increase. Gasoline is a good example. If you expect the price to increase soon, you'll want to fill up your tank now before the price goes up. On the other hand, consumers will delay a purchase if they expect the item to decrease in price. No doubt you have heard someone say, "I'll wait until it goes on sale." When consumers expect the price of a product to fall, current demand for it will decline.

5. Demographic changes. The demand for many products is strongly influenced by the demographic composition of the market. An increase in the elderly population in the United States in recent years has increased the demand for medical care, retirement housing, and vacation travel. The demand curves for these goods have shifted to the right. During the 1980s, the number of people ages 15–24 fell by more than 5 million. Because young people are a major part of the U.S. market for jeans, the demand for jeans fell by more than 100 million pairs over the course of the decade.[4]

6. Changes in consumer tastes and preferences. Why do preferences change? Preferences change because people change and because they acquire new information. Consider how consumers are responding to the popularity of the Atkins diet. The demand for high-carbohydrate foods like white bread has fallen substantially, while the demand for low-carbohydrate foods like beef has risen. This is a major change from the 1990s when the demand for beef fell because of the "heart-healthy" eating habits consumers preferred then. Trends in the markets for clothing, toys, collectibles, and entertainment are constantly causing changes in the demand for these products as well. Firms may even try to change consumer preferences for their own products through advertising and information brochures.

The accompanying **Thumbnail Sketch** summarizes the major factors that cause a change in *demand*—a shift of the entire demand curve—and points out that quantity *demanded* (but not demand) will change in response to a change in the price of a good.

---

[4]These figures are from Suzanne Tregarthen, "Market for Jeans Shrinks," *The Margin* 6, no. 3 (January–February 1991): 28.

Factors That Cause Changes in Demand and Quantity Demanded

This factor changes the quantity demanded of a good:

1. The price of the good: A higher price decreases the quantity demanded; a lower price increases the quantity demanded.

These factors change the demand for a good:

1. Consumer income: Lower consumer income decreases demand; higher consumer income increases demand.
2. Number of consumers in the market: Fewer consumers decreases demand; more consumers increases demand.
3a. Price of a substitute good: A decrease in the price of a substitute decreases the demand for the original good; an increase in the price of a substitute increases the demand for the original good.

3b. Price of a complementary good: An increase in the price of a complement decreases the demand for the original good; a decrease in the price of a complement increases the demand for the original good.
4. Expected future price of the good: If the price of a good is expected to fall in the future, the current demand for it will decrease; if the price of a good is expected to rise in the future, the current demand for it will increase.
5. Demographic changes: Population trends in age, gender, race, and other factors can increase or decrease demand for specific goods.
6. Consumer preferences: Changes in consumer tastes and preferences can increase or decrease demand for specific goods.

PRODUCER CHOICE AND THE LAW OF SUPPLY

Now let's shift our focus to producers and the supply side of the market. How does the market process determine the amount of each good that will be produced? To figure this out, we first have to understand what influences the choices of producers. Producers convert resources into goods and services by doing the following:

1. organizing productive inputs and resources, like land, labor, capital, natural resources, and intermediate goods;

2. transforming and combining these inputs into goods and services; and

3. selling the final products to consumers.

Producers have to purchase the resources at prices determined by market forces. Predictably, the owners of these resources will supply the resources only at prices at least equal to what they could earn elsewhere. Put another way, each resource the producers buy to make their product has to be bid away from all other potential uses. Its owner has to be paid its opportunity cost. *The sum of the producer's cost of each resource used to produce a good will equal the* **opportunity cost of production.**

There is an important difference between the opportunity cost of production and standard accounting measures of cost. Accountants generally do not count the cost of the firm's assets, such as its buildings, equipment, and financial resources, when they calculate a product's cost. But economists do. Economists consider the fact that these assets could be used some other way—in other words, that they have an opportunity cost. Unless these opportunity costs are covered, the resources will eventually be used in other ways.

The opportunity cost of these assets to the firm is the amount of money the firm could earn from the assets if they were used another way. Consider a manufacturer that invests $10 million in buildings and equipment to produce shirts. Instead of buying buildings and equipment, the manufacturer could simply put the $10 million in the bank and let it draw interest. If the $10 million were earning, say, 10 percent interest, the firm would make $1 million on that money in a year's time. This $1 million in forgone interest is part of the firm's opportunity cost of producing shirts. Unlike an accountant, an economist will take

Opportunity cost of production
The total economic cost of producing a good or service. The cost component includes the opportunity cost of all resources, including those owned by the firm. The opportunity cost is equal to the value of the production of other goods sacrificed as the result of producing the good.

that $1 million opportunity cost into account. If the firm plans to invest the money in shirt-making equipment, it had better earn more from making the shirts than the $1 million it could earn by simply putting the money in the bank. If the firm can't generate enough to cover all of its costs, including the opportunity cost of assets owned by the firm, it will not continue in business.

The Role of Profits and Losses

Profits and Losses

 Profits direct producers toward activities that increase the value of resources; losses impose a penalty on those who reduce the value of resources.

Profit
An excess of sales revenue relative to the opportunity cost of production. The cost component includes the opportunity cost of all resources, including those owned by the firm. Therefore, profit accrues only when the value of the good produced is greater than the value of the resources used for its production.

Firms earn a **profit** when the revenues from the goods and services that they supply exceed the opportunity cost of the resources used to make them. Consumers will not buy goods and services unless they value them at least as much as their purchase price. For example, Susan would not be willing to pay $40 for a pair of jeans unless she valued them by at least that amount. At the same time, the seller's opportunity cost of supplying a good will reflect the value consumers place on *other* goods that could have been produced with those same resources. This is true precisely because the seller has to bid those resources away from other producers wanting to use them.

Think about what it means when, for example, a firm is able to produce jeans at a cost of $30 per pair and sell them for $40, thereby reaping a profit of $10 per pair. The $30 opportunity cost of the jeans indicates that the resources used to produce the jeans could have been used to produce other items worth $30 to consumers (perhaps a denim backpack). In turn, the profit indicates that consumers value the jeans more than other goods that might have been produced with the resources used to supply the jeans.

The willingness of consumers to pay a price greater than a good's opportunity cost indicates that they value the good more than other things that could have been produced with the same resources. Viewed from this perspective, profit is a reward earned by entrepreneurs who use resources to produce goods consumers value more highly than the other goods those resources could have produced. In essence, this profit is a signal that an entrepreneur has increased the value of the resources under his or her control.

Loss
A deficit of sales revenue relative to the opportunity cost of production. Losses are a penalty imposed on those who produce goods even though they are valued less than the resources required for their production.

Business decision makers will seek to undertake production of goods and services that will generate profit. However, things do not always turn out as expected. Sometimes business firms are unable to cover their costs. **Losses** occur when the revenue derived from sales is insufficient to cover the opportunity cost of the resources used to produce a good or service. Losses indicate that the firm has reduced the value of the resources it has used. In other words, consumers would have been better off if those resources had been used to produce something else. In a market economy, losses will eventually cause firms to go out of business, and the resources they previously utilized will be directed toward other things valued more highly.

Profits and losses play a very important role in a market economy. They determine which products (and firms) will expand and survive, and which will contract and be driven from the market. Clearly, there is a positive side to business failures. As our preceding discussion highlights, losses and business failures free up resources being used unwisely so they can be put to a use producing other things that people value more highly.

Supply and the Entrepreneur

Entrepreneurs organize the production of new products. In doing so, they take on significant risk in deciding what to produce and how to produce it. Their success or failure depends upon how much consumers eventually value the products they develop relative to other products that could have been produced with the resources. Entrepreneurs figure out which projects are likely to be profitable and then try to persuade a corporation, a banker, or individual investors to invest the resources needed to give their new idea a chance. Studies indicate, however, that only about 55 to 65 percent of the new products introduced are still on the market five years later. Being an entrepreneur means you have to risk failing.

To prosper, entrepreneurs must convert and rearrange resources in a manner that will increase their value. A person who purchases 100 acres of raw land, puts in a street and a sewage-disposal system, divides the plot into 1-acre lots, and sells them for 50 percent more than the opportunity cost of all resources used is clearly an entrepreneur. This entrepreneur profits because the value of the resources has increased. Sometimes entrepreneurial activity is less complex, though. For example, a 15-year-old who purchases a power mower and sells lawn services to his neighbors is also an entrepreneur seeking to profit by increasing the value of his resources—time and equipment.

Market Supply Schedule

How will producer-entrepreneurs respond to a change in product price? Other things constant, a higher price will increase the producer's incentive to supply the good. Established producers will expand the scale of their operations, and over time new entrepreneurs, seeking personal gain, will enter the market and begin supplying the product, too. *The law of supply states that there is a direct (or positive) relationship between the price of a good or service and the amount of it that suppliers are willing to produce. This direct relationship means that price and the quantity producers wish to supply move in the same direction. As the price increases, producers will supply more—and as the price decreases, they will supply less.*

Like the law of demand, the law of supply reflects the basic economic principle that incentives matter. Higher prices increase the reward entrepreneurs get from selling their products. The more profitable producing a product becomes, the more of it they will be willing to supply. Conversely, as the price of a product falls, so does its profitability and the incentive to supply it. Just think about how many hours of tutoring services you would be willing to supply for different prices. Would you be willing to spend more time tutoring students if instead of $5 per hour, tutoring paid $50 per hour? The law of supply suggests you would, and producers of other goods and services are no different.

Exhibit 6 illustrates the law of supply. The curve shown in the exhibit is called a *supply curve*. Because there is a direct relationship between a good's price and the amount offered for sale by suppliers, the supply curve has a positive slope. It slopes upward to the right. Read horizontally, the supply curve shows how much of a particular good producers are willing to produce and sell at a given price. Read vertically, the supply curve reveals important information about the cost of production. *The height of the supply curve indicates both (1) the minimum price necessary to induce producers to supply that*

Law of supply
A principle that states there is a direct relationship between the price of a good and the quantity of it producers are willing to supply. As the price of a good increases, producers will wish to supply more of it. As the price decreases, producers will wish to supply less.

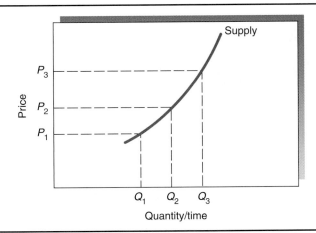

EXHIBIT 6
Supply Curve

As the price of a product increases, other things constant, producers will increase the amount of the product supplied to the market.

EXHIBIT 7
Producer Surplus

Producer surplus is the area above the supply curve but below the actual sales price. This area represents the net gains to producers and resource suppliers from production and exchange.

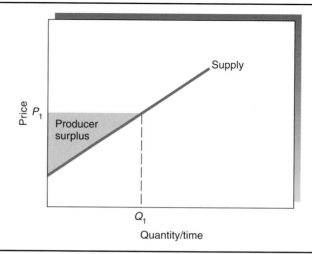

additional unit and (2) the opportunity cost of producing that additional unit. These are both measured by the height of the supply curve because the minimum price required to induce a supplier to sell a unit is precisely the marginal cost of producing it.

Producer Surplus

We previously used the demand curve to illustrate consumer surplus, the net gains of buyers from market exchanges. The supply curve can be used in a similar manner to illustrate the net gains of producers and resource suppliers. Suppose that you are an aspiring musician and are willing to perform a two-hour concert for $500. If a promoter offers to pay you $750 to perform the concert, you will accept, and receive $250 more than your minimum price. This $250 net gain represents your **producer surplus**. In effect, producer surplus is the difference between the amount a supplier actually receives (based on the market price) and the minimum price required to induce the supplier to produce the given units (their marginal cost). The measurement of producer surplus for an entire market is illustrated by the shaded area of **Exhibit 7**.

    It's important to note that producer surplus represents the gains received by all parties contributing resources to the production of a good. In this respect, producer surplus is fundamentally different from profit. Profit accrues to the owners of the business firm producing the good, whereas producer surplus encompasses the net gains derived by all people who help produce the good, including those employed by or selling resources to the firm.

Producer surplus
The difference between the minimum price suppliers are willing to accept and the price they actually receive. It measures the net gains to producers and resource suppliers from market exchange. It is not the same as profit.

OUTSTANDING ECONOMIST	**Alfred Marshall (1842–1924)**	

British economist Alfred Marshall was one of the most influential economists of his era. Many concepts and tools that form the core of modern microeconomics originated with Marshall in his famous *Principles of Economics*, first published in 1890. Marshall introduced the concepts of supply and demand, equilibrium, elasticity, consumers' and producers' surplus, and the idea of distinguishing between short-run and long-run changes.

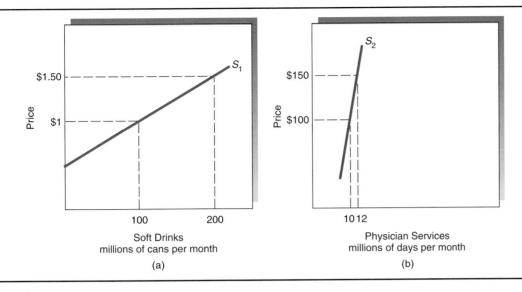

EXHIBIT 8
Elastic and Inelastic Supply Curves

Frame (a) illustrates a supply curve that is relatively elastic and therefore the quantity supplied is highly responsive to a change in price. Soft drinks provide an example. Frame (b) illustrates a relatively inelastic supply curve, one where the quantity supplied increase is by only a small amount in response to a change in price. This is the case for physician services.

Responsiveness of Quantity Supplied to Price Changes: Elastic and Inelastic Supply Curves

Like the quantity demanded, the responsiveness of the quantity supplied to a change in price is different for different goods. The supply curve is said to be elastic when a modest change in price leads to a large change in quantity supplied. This is generally true when the additional resources needed to expand output can be obtained with only a small increase in their price. Consider the supply of soft drinks. The contents of soft drinks—primarily carbonated water, sugar, and flavoring—are abundantly available. A sharp increase in the use of these ingredients by soft drink producers is unlikely to push up their price much. Therefore, as **Exhibit 8** illustrates, if the price of soft drinks were to rise from $1 to $1.50, producers would be willing to expand output sharply from 100 million to 200 million cans per month. A 50 percent increase in price leads to a 100 percent expansion in quantity supplied. The larger the increase in quantity in response to a higher price, the more elastic the supply curve. The flatness of the supply curve for soft drinks reflects the fact that it is highly elastic.

In contrast, when the quantity supplied is not very responsive to a change in price, supply is said to be inelastic. Physicians' services are an example. If the earnings of doctors increase from $100 to $150 per hour, there will be some increase in the quantity of the services they provide. Some physicians will work longer hours; others may delay retirement. Yet, these adjustments are likely to result in only a small increase in the quantity supplied because it takes a long time to train a physician and the number of qualified doctors who are working in other occupations or who are outside of the labor force is small. Therefore, as Exhibit 8 (right frame) shows, a 50 percent increase in the price of physician services leads to only a 20 percent expansion in the quantity supplied. Unlike soft drinks, higher prices for physician services do not generate much increase in quantity supplied. Economists would say that the supply of physician services is relatively inelastic.

CHANGES IN SUPPLY VERSUS CHANGES IN QUANTITY SUPPLIED

Like demand, it is important to distinguish between a change in the *quantity supplied* and a change in *supply*. When producers change the number of units they are willing to supply in response to a change in price, this movement along the supply curve is called a "change in *quantity supplied*." A change in any factor *other than the price* shifts the supply curve and is called a "change in *supply*."

As we previously discussed, profit-seeking entrepreneurs will produce a good only if its sales price is expected to exceed its opportunity cost of production. Therefore, changes that affect the opportunity cost of supplying a good will also influence the amount of it producers are willing to supply. These other factors, such as the prices of resources used to make the good and the level of technology available, are held constant when we draw the supply curve. The supply curve itself reflects quantity changes only in response to price changes. Changes in these other factors shift the supply curve. Factors that increase the opportunity cost of providing a good will discourage production and decrease supply, shifting the entire curve inward to the left. Conversely, changes that lower the opportunity cost of producers will encourage production and increase supply, shifting the entire curve outward to the right.

Let us now take a closer look at the primary factors that will cause a change in supply and shift the entire curve right or left.

1. Changes in resource prices. How will an increase in the price of a resource, such as wages of workers or the materials used to produce a product, affect the supply of a good? Higher resource prices will increase the cost of production, reducing the profitability of firms supplying the good. The higher cost will induce firms to reduce their output. With time, some may even be driven out of business. As **Exhibit 9** illustrates, higher resource prices will reduce the supply of the good, causing a shift to the left in the supply curve from S_1 to S_2. Alternatively, a reduction in the price of a resource used to produce a good will cause an increase in supply—a rightward shift in the supply curve—as firms expand output in response to the lower costs and increased profitability of supplying the good.

2. Changes in technology. Like lower resource prices, technological improvements—the discovery of new, lower-cost production techniques—reduce production costs, and thereby increase supply. Technological advances have affected the cost of almost everything. Before the invention of the printing press, books had to be handwritten. Just imagine the massive reduction in cost and increase in the supply of books caused by this single invention. Similarly, improved farm machinery has vastly expanded the supply of agricultural products through the years. Robotics have reduced the cost of producing airplanes, automobiles, and other types of machinery. Better computer chips have drastically reduced the cost of producing electronics. As recently as 35 years ago, a simple calculator cost more than $100; a microwave oven almost $500; and a VCR approximately $1,000. When introduced in the mid-1980s, a cellular telephone cost more than $4,000. You probably noticed that the prices of flat-screen computer monitors and plasma-screen televisions have fallen due to technological advances in recent years.

EXHIBIT 9
A Decrease in Supply

Crude oil is a resource used to produce gasoline. When the price of crude oil rises, it increases the cost of producing gasoline and results in a decrease in the supply of gasoline.

Factors That Cause Changes in Supply and Quantity Supplied

This factor changes the quantity supplied of a good:

1. The price of the good: A lower price decreases the quantity supplied; a higher price increases the quantity supplied.

These factors change the supply of a good:

1. Resource prices (the prices of things used to make the good): Lower resource prices increase supply; higher resource prices decrease supply.

2. Technological change: A technological improvement increases supply; a technological setback decreases supply.

3. Weather or political conditions: Favorable weather or good political conditions increase supply; adverse weather conditions or poor political conditions decrease supply.

4. Taxes imposed on the producers of a good: Lower taxes increase supply; higher taxes decrease supply.

3. Elements of nature and political disruptions.   Natural disasters and changing political conditions can also alter supply, sometimes dramatically. In some years, good weather leads to "bumper crops," increasing the supply of agricultural products. At other times, droughts lead to poor harvests, reducing supply. War and political unrest in the Middle East region have had a major impact on the supply of oil several times during the past few decades. Similarly, during the summer of 2003, massive U.S. electricity blackouts in the Midwest and along the East Coast temporarily shut down oil refineries, reducing the supply of oil. Factors such as these will reduce supply.

4. Changes in taxes.   If the government increases the taxes on the sellers of a product, the result will be the same as any other increase in the cost of doing business. The added tax that sellers have to pay will reduce their willingness to sell the product at any given price. Each unit must now be sold for a price that covers not only the opportunity cost of production, but also the tax. For example, the Superfund law, passed by Congress in 1980, placed a special tax on petroleum producers based on their output. That raised the cost of producing petroleum products, decreasing the amount producers were willing to supply.

The accompanying **Thumbnail Sketch** summarizes the major factors that change *supply*—a shift of the entire supply curve; and quantity supplied—a movement along the supply curve.

HOW MARKET PRICES ARE DETERMINED: SUPPLY AND DEMAND INTERACT

Consumer-buyers and producer-sellers make decisions independent of each other, but markets coordinate their choices and influence their actions. To the economist, a **market** is not a physical location but an abstract concept that encompasses the forces generated by the decisions of buyers and sellers. A market may be quite narrow (for example, the market for grade A jumbo eggs), or it may be quite broad like when we lump diverse goods into a single market, such as the market for all "consumer goods." There is also a wide range of sophistication among markets. The New York Stock Exchange is a highly formal, computerized market. Each weekday, buyers and sellers, who seldom meet, electronically exchange corporate shares they own worth billions of dollars. In contrast, a neighborhood market for baby-sitting services or tutoring in economics, may be highly informal, bringing together buyers and sellers primarily by word of mouth.

Equilibrium is a state in which the conflicting forces of supply and demand are in balance. When a market is in equilibrium, the decisions of consumers and producers

Market
An abstract concept encompassing the forces of supply and demand, and the interaction of buyers and sellers with the potential for exchange to occur.

Equilibrium
A state in which the conflicting forces of supply and demand are in balance. When a market is in equilibrium, the decisions of consumers and producers are brought into harmony with one another, and the quantity supplied will equal the quantity demanded.

are brought into harmony with one another, and the quantity supplied will equal the quantity demanded. In equilibrium, it is possible for both buyers and sellers to realize their choices simultaneously. What could bring these diverse interests into harmony? We will see the answer is market prices.

Market Equilibrium

As we have learned, a higher price will reduce the quantity of a good demanded by consumers. On the other hand, a higher price will increase the quantity of a good supplied by producers. The market price of a good will tend to change in a direction that will bring the quantity of a good consumers want to buy into balance with the quantity producers want to sell. If the price is too high, the quantity supplied by producers will exceed the quantity demanded. They will be unable to sell as much as they would like unless they reduce their price. Alternatively, if the price is too low, the quantity demanded by consumers will exceed the quantity supplied. Some consumers will be unable to get as much as they would like, unless they are willing to pay a higher price to bid some of the good away from other potential customers. Thus, there will be a tendency for the price in a market to move toward the price that brings the two into balance.

People have a tendency to think of consumers wanting lower prices and producers wanting higher prices. Although this is true, price changes frequently trend toward the middle of the two extremes. When a local store has an excess supply of a particular item, how does it get rid of it? By having a sale or somehow otherwise lowering its price (a "blue-light special"). Firms often lower their prices in order to get rid of excess supply.

On the other hand, excess demand is solved by consumers bidding up prices. Children's toys around Christmas provide a perfect example. When first introduced, items such as the Sony PlayStation 2, Furby, and the Tickle-Me-Elmo doll were immediate successes. The firms producing these products had not anticipated the overwhelming demand and every child wanted one for Christmas. Some stores raised their prices, but the demand was so strong that lines of parents were forming outside stores before they even opened. Often, only the first few in line were able to get the toys (a sure sign that the store had set the price below equilibrium). Out in the parking lots, in the classified ads, and on eBay, parents were offering to pay even higher prices for these items. If stores were not going to set the prices right, parents in these informal markets would! These examples show that rising prices are often the result of consumers bidding up prices when excess demand is present. A similar phenomenon can be seen in the market for Ty Beanie Babies (or concert tickets) as their immediate value on the resale market can be much higher than the original retail price if, at that price, the original quantity supplied is not adequate to meet the quantity demanded.

As these examples illustrate, whenever quantity supplied and quantity demanded are not in balance, there is a tendency for price to change in a manner that will correct the imbalance. It is possible to show this process graphically with the supply and demand curves we have developed in this chapter. **Exhibit 10** shows the supply and demand curves in the market for a basic calculator. At a high price—$12, for example—producers will plan to supply 600 calculators per day, whereas consumers will choose to purchase only 450. An excess supply of 150 calculators (shown by distance *ab* in the graph) will result. Unsold calculators will push the inventories of producers upward. To get rid of some of their calculators in inventory, some producers will cut their price to increase their sales. Other firms will have to lower their price, too, as a result, or sell even fewer calculators. This lower price will make supplying calculators less attractive to producers. Some of them will go out of business. Others will reduce their output or perhaps produce other products. How low will the price of calculators go? As the figure shows, when the price has declined to $10, the quantity supplied by producers and the quantity demanded by consumers will be in balance at 550 calculators per day. At this price ($10), the quantity demanded by consumers just equals the quantity supplied by producers, and the choices of the two groups are brought into harmony.

What will happen if the price per calculator is lower—$8, for example? In this case, the amount demanded by consumers (650 units) will exceed the amount supplied by producers (500 units). An excess demand of 150 units (shown by the distance *cd* in the graph)

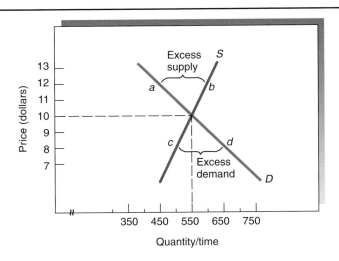

EXHIBIT 10
Supply and Demand

The table indicates the supply and demand conditions for calculators. These conditions are also illustrated by the graph. When the price exceeds $10, an excess supply is present, which places downward pressure on price. In contrast, when the price is less than $10, an excess demand results, which causes the price to rise. Thus, the market price will tend toward $10, at which point the quantity demanded will be equal to the quantity supplied.

PRICE OF CALCULATORS (DOLLARS)	QUANTITY SUPPLIED (PER DAY)	QUANTITY DEMANDED (PER DAY)	CONDITION IN THE MARKET	DIRECTION OF PRESSURE ON PRICE
$13	625	400	Excess supply	Downward
12	600	450	Excess supply	Downward
11	575	500	Excess supply	Downward
10	550	550	Balance	Equilibrium
9	525	600	Excess demand	Upward
8	500	650	Excess demand	Upward
7	475	700	Excess demand	Upward

will be the result. Some consumers who are unable to purchase the calculators at $8 per unit because of the inadequate supply would be willing to pay a higher price. Recognizing this fact, producers will raise their price. As the price increases to $10, producers will expand their output and consumers will cut down on their consumption. At the $10 price, equilibrium will be restored.

Efficiency and Market Equilibrium

When a market reaches equilibrium, all the gains from trade have been fully realized and **economic efficiency** is present. Economists often use economic efficiency as a standard to measure outcomes under alternative circumstances. The central idea of efficiency is a cost-versus-benefit comparison. Undertaking an economic action will be efficient only if it generates more benefit than cost. On the other hand, undertaking an action that generates more cost than benefit is inefficient. For a market to be efficient, all trades that generate more benefit than cost need to be undertaken. In addition, economic efficiency requires that no trades creating more cost than benefit be undertaken.

A closer look at the way in which markets work can help us understand the concept of efficiency. The supply curve reflects producers' opportunity cost. Each point along the supply curve indicates the minimum price for which the units of a good could be produced without a loss to the seller. Assuming no other third parties are affected by the production of this good, then the height of the supply curve represents the opportunity cost to society of producing and selling the good. On the other side of the market, each point along the demand curve indicates how consumers value an extra unit of the good—that is, the maximum amount the consumer is willing to pay for the extra unit. Again assuming that no other third parties are affected, the height of the demand curve represents the benefit to society of producing and selling the good. Any time the consumer's valuation of a unit (the benefit) exceeds the producer's minimum supply price (the cost), producing and selling the unit is consistent with economic efficiency. The

Economic efficiency
A situation in which all of the potential gains from trade have been realized. An action is efficient only if it creates more benefit than cost. With well-defined property rights and competition, market equilibrium is efficient.

EXHIBIT 11
Economic Efficiency

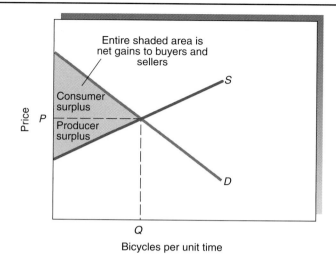

When markets are competitive and property rights are well defined, the equilibrium reached by a market satisfies economic efficiency. All units that create more benefit (the buyer's valuation shown by the height of the demand curve) than cost (opportunity cost of production shown by the height of the supply curve) are produced. This maximizes the total gains from trade, the combined area represented by consumer and producer surplus.

trade will result in mutual gain to both parties. When property rights are well defined, and only the buyers and sellers are affected by production and exchange, competitive market forces will automatically guide a market toward an equilibrium level of output that satisfies economic efficiency.

Exhibit 11 illustrates why this is true. Suppliers of bicycles will produce additional bicycles as long as the market price exceeds their opportunity cost of production (shown by the height of the supply curve). Similarly, consumers will continue to purchase additional bikes as long as their benefit (shown by the height of the demand curve) exceeds the market price. Eventually, market forces will result in an equilibrium output level of *Q* and a price of *P*. At this point all the bicycles providing benefits to consumers that exceed the costs to suppliers will be produced. Economic efficiency is met because all of the potential consumer and producer gains from exchange (shown by the shaded area) have occurred. As you can see, the point of market equilibrium is also the point where the combined area showing consumer and producer surplus is the greatest.

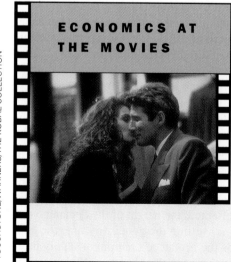

ECONOMICS AT THE MOVIES

Pretty Woman (1990)

In *Pretty Woman* Julia Roberts agrees to spend the week as Richard Gere's companion for $3,000. After Roberts and Gere agree on the price, she tells him that she would have been willing to do it for $2,000. His reply is that he would have been willing to pay $4,000. With this additional information, we know that the exchange netted Roberts $1,000 in producer surplus and Gere $1,000 in consumer surplus. This scene illustrates mutual gains from trade.

When less than Q bicycles are produced, some bicycles valued more by consumers than the opportunity cost of producing them are not being produced. This is inconsistent with economic efficiency. On the other hand, if output is expanded beyond Q, inefficiency will also result because some of the bicycles cost more to produce than consumers are willing to pay for them. Prices in competitive markets eventually guide producers and consumers to the level of output consistent with economic efficiency.

HOW MARKETS RESPOND TO CHANGES IN DEMAND AND SUPPLY

How will a market adjust to a change in demand? **Exhibit 12** shows the market adjustment to an increase in the demand for eggs around Easter time. Demand D_1 and supply S are typical throughout much of the year. During the two weeks before Easter, however, consumer demand for eggs rises because people purchase them to decorate too. This shifts egg demand from D_1 to D_2 during that time of year. As you can see, the increase in demand pushes the price upwards from P_1 to P_2 (typically by about 20 cents per dozen), and results in a larger equilibrium quantity traded (Q_2 rather than Q_1—an increase of typically around 600 million eggs). There is a new equilibrium at point b around Easter (versus point a during the rest of the year).

Although consumers may not be happy about paying a higher price for eggs around Easter, the higher price serves two essential purposes. First, it encourages consumers to conserve on their usage of eggs. Some consumers may purchase only two dozen eggs to color, rather than three; other consumers may skip having an omelet for breakfast and have cereal instead. These steps on the consumer side of the market help make the eggs that are available around Easter go further. Second, the higher price is precisely what results in the additional 600 million eggs being supplied to the market to satisfy this increased consumer demand. Without the price increase, excess demand would be present—and many consumers would simply be unable to find eggs to purchase around Easter. If the price remained at P_1 (the equilibrium price throughout most of the year) consumers at Easter time would want to purchase more eggs than producers would be willing to supply. At the higher P_2 price, however, the quantity suppliers are willing to sell is again in balance with the quantity consumers wish to purchase.

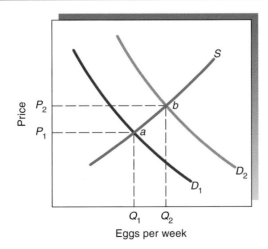

Here we illustrate how the market for eggs adjusts to an increase in demand such as generally occurs around Easter time. Initially (before the Easter season), the market for eggs reflects demand D_1 and supply S. The increase in demand (shift from D_1 to D_2) pushes price up and leads to a new equilibrium at a higher price (P_2 rather than P_1) and larger quantity traded (Q_2).

The tradition of coloring and hunting for eggs causes an increase in demand for eggs around Easter. As Exhibit 12 illustrates, this leads to higher egg prices and costly actions by producers to supply a larger quantity during this period.

© GETTY IMAGES

Why were suppliers unwilling to supply the additional 600 million eggs at the original price of P_1? Because at the original equilibrium price of P_1, suppliers were already producing and selling all the eggs that cost less to produce than that price. The additional eggs desired by consumers around Easter all cost more to produce than the old market price of P_1. The higher price of P_2 is what allows suppliers to cover their higher production costs associated with these extra eggs. Around Easter, farmers take costly steps to avoid having the hens molt because hens lay fewer eggs when they are molting. They do this by changing the quantity and types of feed and by increasing the lighting in the birds' sheds—both of which mean higher production costs. Farmers also try to build up larger than normal inventories of eggs before Easter. Eggs are typically about two days old when consumers buy them at the store, but can be up to seven days old around Easter time. Building up and maintaining this additional inventory is costly, too.

In a market economy, when the demand for a good increases, its price will rise, which will (1) motivate consumers to search for substitutes and cut back on additional purchases of the good and (2) motivate producers to supply more of the good. These two forces will eventually bring the quantity demanded and quantity supplied back into balance.

It's important to note that this response on the supply side of the egg market is not a shift in the supply curve. The supply curve remains unchanged. Rather, there is a movement along the original supply curve—a change in *quantity* supplied. The only reason suppliers are willing to alter their behavior (produce more eggs) is because the increased demand has pushed up the price of eggs. Notice that it is the change in demand (a shift of the demand curve) that leads to the change in quantity supplied (a movement along the supply curve). Producers are simply responding to the price movement caused by the change in demand. A movement along one curve (a change in quantity supplied *or* a change in quantity demanded) happens in response to a shift in the other curve (a change in demand or a change in supply).

When the demand for a product declines, the adjustment process sends buyers and sellers just the opposite signals. Take a piece of paper and see if you can diagram a decrease in demand and how it will affect price and quantity in a market. If you've done it correctly, a decline in demand (a shift to the left in the demand curve) will lead to a lower price and a lower quantity traded. What's going on in the diagram is that the lower price (caused by lower consumer demand) is reducing the incentive of producers to supply the good. When consumers no longer want as much of a good, falling market prices signal producers to cut back production. The reduced output allows these resources to be freed up to go into the production of other goods consumers want more.

How will markets respond to changes in supply? **Exhibit 13** shows the market's adjustment to a decrease in the supply of romaine lettuce. Assume that severe rains and flooding destroy a large portion of the romaine lettuce crop. This reduction in supply (shift from S_1 to S_2) will cause the price of romaine to increase sharply (P_1 to P_2). Because of the higher price, consumers will cut back on their consumption of romaine lettuce (the movement along the demand curve from *a* to *b*). Some will switch to substitutes—in this

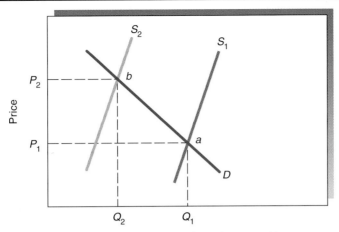

EXHIBIT 13
Market Adjustment to a Decrease in Supply

Here, using romaine lettuce as an example, we illustrate how a market adjusts to a decrease in supply. Assume adverse weather conditions substantially reduce the supply (shift from S_1 to S_2) of romaine. The reduction in supply leads to an increase in the equilibrium price (from P_1 to P_2) and a reduction in the equilibrium quantity traded (from Q_1 to Q_2).

case, probably other varieties of lettuce and leafy vegetables. The higher price also encourages the remaining romaine suppliers to take additional steps—like more careful harvesting techniques or using more fertilizer—that allow them to produce more romaine lettuce than otherwise would be the case. The higher prices will rebalance the quantity demanded and quantity supplied.

As the lettuce example illustrates, a decrease in supply will lead to higher prices and a lower equilibrium quantity. How do you think the market price and quantity would adjust to an increase in supply, as might be caused by a breakthrough in the technology used to harvest the lettuce? Again, try to draw the appropriate supply and demand curves to illustrate this case. If you do it correctly, the graph you draw will show an increase in supply (a shift to the right in the supply curve) leading to a lower market price and a larger equilibrium quantity.

The accompanying **Thumbnail Sketch** summarizes the effect of changes—both increases and decreases—in demand and supply on the equilibrium price and quantity. The cases listed in the thumbnail sketch, however, are for when only a single curve shifts. But sometimes market conditions simultaneously shift both demand and supply. For example, consumer income might increase at the same time that a technological advance in production occurs. These two changes will cause both demand and supply to increase at the same time—both curves will shift to the right. The new equilibrium will definitely be at a larger quantity, but the direction of the change in price is indeterminate. The price may either increase or decrease, depending on whether the increase in demand or increase in supply is larger—which curve shifted the most, in other words.

T H U M B N A I L   S K E T C H

How Changes in Demand and Supply Affect Market Price and Quantity

Changes in Demand

1. An increase in demand—shown by a rightward shift of the demand curve—will cause an increase in both the equilibrium price and quantity.
2. A decrease in demand—shown by a leftward shift of the demand curve—will cause a decrease in both the equilibrium price and quantity.

Changes in Supply

1. An increase in supply—shown by a rightward shift of the supply curve—will cause a decrease in the equilibrium price and an increase in the equilibrium quantity.
2. A decrease in supply—shown by leftward shift of the supply curve—will cause an increase in the equilibrium price and a decrease in the equilibrium quantity.

What will happen if supply increases but demand falls at the same time? Price will definitely fall, but the new equilibrium quantity may either increase or decrease. Draw the supply and demand curves for this case and make sure that you understand why.

INVISIBLE HAND PRINCIPLE

Invisible Hand Principle

 Market prices coordinate the actions of self-interested individuals and direct them toward activities that promote the general welfare.

More than 225 years ago, Adam Smith, the father of economics, stressed that personal self-interest *when directed by market prices* is a powerful force promoting economic progress. In a famous passage in his book *The Wealth of Nations,* Smith put it this way:

> Every individual is continually exerting himself to find out the most advantageous employment for whatever [income] he can command. It is his own advantage, indeed, and not that of the society which he has in view. But the study of his own advantage naturally, or rather necessarily, leads him to prefer that employment which is most advantageous to society. . . . He intends only his own gain, and he is in this, as in many other cases, led by an invisible hand to promote an end which was not part of his intention. By pursuing his own interest he frequently promotes that of the society more effectually than when he really intends to promote it.[5]

Smith's fundamental insight was that market forces would tend to align the actions of self-interested individuals with the best interests of society. The tendency of market forces to channel the actions of self-interested individuals into activities that promote the general betterment of society is now known as the **invisible hand principle**. Let's take a closer look at this important principle.

Invisible hand principle
The tendency of market prices to direct individuals pursuing their own interests to engage in activities promoting the economic well-being of society.

Prices and Market Order

The invisible hand principle can be difficult to grasp because there is a natural tendency to associate order with central direction and control. Surely some central authority must be in charge. But this is not the case. ***The pricing system, reflecting the choices of literally millions of consumers, producers, and resource owners, provides the direction.*** The market process works so automatically that most of us give little thought to it. We simply take it for granted.

Perhaps one example from your everyday life will help you better understand the invisible hand principle. Visualize a busy retail store with ten checkout lanes. No individual assigns shoppers to checkout lanes. Shoppers are left to choose for themselves. Nonetheless, they do not all try to get in the same lane. Why? Individuals are always alert for adjustment opportunities that offer personal gain. When one lane gets long or is held up by a price check, some shoppers will shift to other lanes and thereby smooth out the flow among the lanes. Even though central planning is absent, this process of mutual adjustment by self-interested individuals results in order and social cooperation. In fact, the degree of social cooperation is generally well beyond what could be achieved if central coordination were attempted—if, for example, stores hired someone to assign shoppers to checkout lanes in the interest of getting everyone out as quickly as possible. Shoppers *acting in their own interests* promote the most orderly and quickest flow for everyone. A similar phenomenon occurs on busy interstate highways as drivers switch between lanes for personal gain, with the end result being the quickest flow of traffic for everyone.

---

[5]Adam Smith, *An Inquiry into the Nature and Causes of the Wealth of Nations* (New York: Modern Library, 1937), 423.

Market participation is a lot like checking out at a retail store or driving on the freeway. Like the number of people in a lane, profits and losses provide market participants with information about the advantages and disadvantages of different economic activities. Losses indicate that an economic activity is congested, and, as a result, producers are unable to cover their costs. In such a case, successful market participants will shift their resources away from such activities toward other, more valuable uses. Conversely, profits are indicative of an open lane, the opportunity to experience gain if one shifts into an activity where the price is high relative to the per-unit cost. As producers and resource suppliers shift away from activities characterized by congestion and into those characterized by the opportunity for profit, they smooth out economic activity and enhance its flow. Remarkably, even though individuals are motivated by self-interest, market prices direct their actions toward activities that promote both order and economic progress. This is precisely the message of Smith's "invisible hand."

Is the concept of the invisible hand really valid? Next time you sit down to have a nice dinner, think about all the people who help make it possible. It is unlikely that any of them, from the farmer to the truck driver to the grocer, was motivated by a concern that you have an enjoyable meal. Market prices, however, bring their interest into harmony with yours. Farmers who raise the best beef or turkeys receive higher prices; truck drivers and grocers earn more money if their products are delivered fresh and in good condition; and so on. An amazing degree of cooperation and order is created by market exchanges—all without the central direction of any government official.

How do markets bring the interests of individuals into harmony with economic progress? Consider the following three vitally important functions performed by market prices.

1. Prices communicate information to decision makers. Suppose a drought in Brazil severely reduces the supply of coffee. Coffee prices will rise. Even if consumers do not know about the drought, the higher prices will provide them with all the information they need to know—it's time to cut back on coffee consumption. *Market prices register information derived from the choices of millions of consumers, producers, and resource suppliers, and provide them with everything they need to know to make wise decisions.*

Market prices provide producers with up-to-date information about which goods consumers most intensely desire, and with important information about the abundance of the resources used in the production process. The cost of production, driven by the opportunity cost of resources, tells the business decision maker the relative importance others place on the alternative uses of those resources. A boom in the housing market might cause lumber prices to rise. In turn, furniture makers seeing these higher lumber prices will utilize substitute raw materials such as metal and plastic in their production processes. Because of market prices, furniture makers will conserve on their use of lumber, just as if they had known that lumber was now more urgently needed for constructing new housing.

2. Prices coordinate the actions of market participants. Market prices also coordinate the choices of buyers and sellers, bringing their decisions into line with each other. Excess supply will lead to falling prices, which discourage production and encourage consumption until the excess supply is eliminated. Alternatively, excess demand will lead to price increases, which encourage consumers to economize on their uses of the good and suppliers to produce more of it, eliminating the excess demand. Changing market prices induce responses on both sides of the market in the proper direction to help correct these situations.

The combination of product and resource prices will determine profit (and loss) rates for alternative projects and thereby direct entrepreneurs to undertake the production projects that consumers value most intensely (relative to their cost). If consumers really want more of a good—for example, luxury apartments—the intensity of their demand will lead to a market price that exceeds the opportunity cost of constructing the apartments. The profitable opportunity thus created will soon be discovered by entrepreneurs who will undertake the construction, expanding the availability of the apartments. In contrast, if consumers want less of a good, such as large cars, the sales revenue from their production will be less than the opportunity cost of supplying them, penalizing those who undertake such unprofitable production.

3. Prices motivate economic players. Market prices establish a reward-penalty (profit-loss) structure that encourages people to work, cooperate with others, use efficient production methods, supply goods that are intensely desired by others, and invest for the future. Self-interested entrepreneurs will seek to produce only the goods consumers value enough to pay a price sufficient to cover production cost. Self-interest will also encourage producers to use efficient production methods and adopt cost-saving technologies because lower costs will mean greater profits. Firms that fail to do so will be unable to compete successfully in the marketplace.

At the beginning of this chapter, we asked you to reflect on why the grocery stores in your local community generally have on hand about the right amount of milk, bread, vegetables, and other goods. Likewise, how is it that refrigerators, automobiles, and CD players, produced at different places around the world, make their way to stores near you in approximately the same numbers that they are demanded by consumers? The invisible hand principle provides the answer, and it works without political direction. No government agency needs to tell decision makers to keep costs low or produce those goods most intensely desired by consumers. Similarly, no one has to tell individuals that they should develop skills that are highly valued by others. Once again the profit motive—in this case higher earnings—will do the job. Many of the things we take for granted in our ordinary lives reflect the invisible hand at work.

Qualifications: Competition and Property Rights

As we noted earlier in this chapter, our focus so far has been on markets where rival firms can freely enter and exit, and private-property rights are clearly defined and enforced. ***The efficiency of market organization is, in fact, dependent on these two things: (1) competitive markets and (2) well-defined and enforced private-property rights.***

Competition, the great regulator, can protect both buyer and seller. It protects consumers from sellers who would charge a price substantially above the cost of production or withhold a vital resource for an exorbitant amount of money. Similarly, it protects employees (sellers of their labor) from the power of any single employer (the buyers of labor). Competition equalizes the bargaining power between buyers and sellers.

When property rights are well defined, secure, and tradable, suppliers of goods and services have to pay resource owners for their use. They will not be permitted to seize and use scarce resources without compensating the owners. Neither will they be permitted to use violence (for example, to attack or invade the property of another) to get what they want. The efficiency of markets hinges on the presence of property rights—after all, people can't easily exchange or compete for things they don't have or can't get property rights to. Without well-defined property rights, markets simply cannot function effectively.

LOOKING AHEAD

Although we incorporated numerous examples designed to enhance your understanding of the supply-and-demand model throughout this chapter, we have only touched the surface. In various modified forms, this model is the central tool of economics. The following chapter will explore several specific applications and extensions of this important model.

KEY POINTS

▼ The law of demand states that there is an inverse (or negative) relationship between the price of a good or service and the quantity of it that consumers are willing to purchase. The height of the demand curve at any quantity shows the maximum price that consumers are willing to pay for that unit.

▼ The degree of responsiveness of consumer purchases to a change in price is shown by the steepness of the demand curve. The more responsive buyers are to a change in price, the flatter, or more elastic, the demand curve will be. Conversely, the less responsive buyers are to a change in price, the steeper, or more inelastic, the demand curve will be.

▼ A movement along a demand curve is called a change in quantity demanded. A shift of the entire curve is called a change in demand. A change in *quantity demanded* is caused by a change in the price of the good (generally in response to a shift of the supply curve). A change in *demand* can be caused by several things, including a change in consumer income or a change in the price of a closely related good.

▼ The opportunity cost of producing a good is equal to the cost of bidding away the resources needed for its production from alternative uses. Profit indicates that the producer has increased the value of the resources used, whereas a loss indicates that the producer has reduced the value of the resources used.

▼ The law of supply states that there is a direct (or positive) relationship between the price of a good or service and the quantity of it that producers are willing to supply. The height of the supply curve at any quantity shows the minimum price necessary to induce suppliers to produce that unit—that is, the opportunity cost of producing it.

▼ A movement along a supply curve is called a change in quantity supplied. A change in *quantity supplied* is caused by a change in the price of the good (generally in response to a shift of the demand curve). A shift of the entire supply curve is called a change in supply. A change in *supply* can be caused by several factors, such as a change in resource prices or an improvement in technology.

▼ The responsiveness of supply to a change in price is shown by the steepness of the supply curve. The more willing producers are to alter the quantity supplied in response to a change in price, the flatter, or more elastic, the supply curve. Conversely, the less willing producers are to alter the quantity supplied in response to a change in price, the steeper, or less elastic, the supply curve.

▼ Prices bring the conflicting forces of supply and demand into balance. There is an automatic tendency for market prices to move toward the equilibrium price, at which the quantity demanded equals the quantity supplied.

▼ Consumer surplus represents the net gain to buyers from market trades. Producer surplus represents the net gain to producers and resource suppliers from market trades. In equilibrium, competitive markets maximize these gains, a condition known as economic efficiency.

▼ Changes in the prices of goods are caused by changes in supply and demand. An increase in demand will cause the price and quantity supplied to rise. Conversely, a decrease in demand will cause the price and quantity supplied to fall. An increase in supply, on the other hand, will cause the price to fall and quantity demanded to rise. Conversely, a decrease in supply will cause the price to rise and quantity demanded to fall.

▼ Market prices communicate information, coordinate the actions of buyers and sellers, and motivate decision makers to act. As the invisible hand principle indicates, market prices are generally able to bring the self-interest of individuals into harmony with the general welfare of society. The efficiency of the system is dependent on two things, however: (1) competitive market conditions and (2) well-defined and secure property rights.

CRITICAL ANALYSIS QUESTIONS

*1. Which of the following do you think would lead to an increase in the current demand for beef?
   a. higher pork prices
   b. higher consumer income
   c. higher prices of feed grains used to feed cattle
   d. widespread outbreak of mad cow or foot-and-mouth disease
   e. an increase in the price of beef

2. What is being held constant when a demand curve for a specific product (shoes or apples, for example) is constructed? Explain why the demand curve for a product slopes downward to the right.

3. What is the law of supply? How many of the following "goods" do you think conform to the general law of supply? Explain your answer in each case.
   a. gasoline
   b. cheating on exams
   c. political favors from legislators
   d. the services of heart specialists
   e. children
   f. legal divorces

*4. Are prices an accurate reflection of a good's total value? Are prices an accurate reflection of a good's marginal value? What's the difference? Can you think of a good that has high total value but low marginal value? Use this concept to explain why professional wrestlers earn more than nurses, despite the fact that nurses probably create more total value to society.

5. What is being held constant when the supply curve is constructed for a specific good like pizza or automobiles? Explain why the supply curve for a good slopes upward to the right.

6. Define consumer and producer surplus. What is meant by economic efficiency, and how does it relate to consumer and producer surplus?

7. Recent tax reforms make college tuition partially tax deductible for certain families. This should motivate more people to attend college. How will this higher demand for a college education affect tuition prices? How will it affect the cost of college for families who don't qualify for the tax deduction?

*8. "The future of our industrial strength cannot be left to chance. Somebody has to develop notions about which industries are winners and which are losers." Is this statement by a newspaper columnist true? Who is the "somebody"?

9. What does the cost of a good or service reflect? Will producers continue to supply a good or service if consumers are unwilling to pay a price sufficient to cover the cost?

*10. "Production should be for people and not for profit." Answer the following questions concerning this statement:
    a. If production is profitable, are people helped or harmed? Explain.

    b. Are people helped more if production results in a loss than if it leads to profit? Is there a conflict between production for people and production for profit?

11. What must an entrepreneur do to earn a profit? How do the actions of firms earning profits influence the value of resources? What happens to the value of resources when losses are present? If a firm making losses goes out of business, is this bad? Why or why not?

*12. What's wrong with this way of thinking? "Economists claim that when the price of something goes up, producers increase the quantity supplied to the market. But last year, the price of oranges was really high and the supply of them was really low. Economists are wrong!"

13. What is the invisible hand principle? Does it indicate that self-interested behavior within markets will result in actions that are beneficial to others? What conditions are necessary for the invisible hand to work well? Why are these conditions important?

*14. What's wrong with this way of thinking? "Economists argue that lower prices will result in fewer units being supplied. However, there are exceptions to this rule. For example, in 1972, a very simple ten-digit electronic calculator sold for $120. By 2000, the price of the same type of calculator had declined to less than $5. Yet business firms produced and sold many more calculators in 2000 than they did in 1972. Lower prices did not result in less production or in a decline in the number of calculators supplied."

15. What is the difference between substitutes and complements? Indicate two goods that are substitutes for each other. Indicate two goods that are complements.

16. How is the market price of a good determined? When the market for a product is in equilibrium, how will consumers value an additional unit compared to the opportunity cost of producing that unit? Why is this important?

*17. Do business firms operating in competitive markets have a strong incentive to serve the interest of consumers? Are they motivated by a strong desire to help consumers? Are "good intentions" necessary if individuals are going to engage in actions that are helpful to others? Discuss.

*Asterisk denotes questions for which answers are given in Appendix B.

Supply and Demand: Applications and Extensions

Chapter Focus

■ How broadly can the supply and demand framework be used?

■ What happens when prices are set by law above or below the market equilibrium level?

■ How do rent controls affect the maintenance and quality of rental housing? How do minimum-wage rates influence the job opportunities of low-skilled workers?

■ What are "black markets"? How does the lack of a well-structured legal environment affect their operation?

■ How does a tax or subsidy affect a market? What determines the distribution of the tax burden (or subsidy benefit) between buyers and sellers?

■ What is the Laffer curve? What does it indicate about the relationship between tax rates and tax revenues?

The division of labour, from which so many advantages are derived, is not originally the effect of any human wisdom, which foresees and intends that general opulence to which it gives occasion. It is the necessary, though very slow and gradual consequence of a certain propensity in human nature . . . ; the propensity to truck, barter, and exchange one thing for another.

—Adam Smith[1]

Nations stumble upon establishments, which are indeed the result of human action, but not the execution of any human design.

—Adam Ferguson[2]

---

[1] Adam Smith, *An Inquiry into the Nature and Causes of the Wealth of Nations* (New York: Modern Library, 1937), 13.
[2] Adam Ferguson, *An Essay on the History of Civil Society* (Edinburgh: A. Millar and T. Caddel, London, 1767), 187.

Markets are everywhere. They exist in many different forms and degrees of sophistication. In elementary schools, children trade Pokémon cards; in households, individuals trade chores ("I'll clean the bathroom, if you'll clean the kitchen"); and in the stock market, individuals who have never met exchange shares of corporate stock and other financial assets worth billions of dollars each business day. Even making an activity illegal does not eliminate the market for it. Instead, the market is merely pushed underground. The exchange of illegal drugs or tickets to a big game at illegal prices illustrates this point.

Trading with other individuals is a natural part of human behavior that exists regardless of legal and societal conditions. As Adam Smith put it more than 225 years ago, human beings have a natural propensity "to truck, barter, and exchange one thing for another" (see the quotation at the chapter opening). We all want to improve our standard of living, and trade with others helps us achieve this goal—by allowing us to get the goods and services we really want and giving us the opportunity to earn the income necessary to buy them. Further, as Adam Ferguson points out, markets are a result of human action, not human design.[3] They reflect the desire of people to trade things with one another.

Market prices coordinate the actions of buyers and sellers, but sometimes the "price" of a good or service in a particular market is called something different. For example, in the labor market, the price is often called the "wage rate." In the loanable funds market, the price is generally referred to as the "interest rate." However, as Juliet observes in Shakespeare's *Romeo and Juliet,* "What's in a name? That which we call a rose by any other name would smell as sweet." The same is true for prices. When the price of something is referred to by another term, such as the wage or interest rate, it will still play the same role. Therefore, when these special terms are used, we put them along the vertical axes of supply and demand diagrams, just as we do "price"—because that's what they are.

In the previous chapter, we saw how the forces of supply and demand determine market prices and coordinate the actions of buyers and sellers in the absence of government intervention. In this chapter, we turn our attention to using the supply and demand model to understand more fully what happens when governments intervene in markets by implementing price controls, taxes, and subsidies. ■

THE LINK BETWEEN RESOURCE AND PRODUCT MARKETS

The interrelationship among markets is vitally important. A change in one market will also lead to changes in other markets. Understanding these links is important. This section addresses the important link between the labor and product markets.

The production process generally involves (a) purchasing resources—like raw materials, labor services, tools, and machines; (b) transforming these resources into products (goods and services); and (c) selling the goods and services in a product market. Production is generally undertaken by business firms. Typically, business firms will demand resources, while households will supply them. Firms demand resources *because* they contribute to the production of goods and services. In turn, households supply them in order to earn income.

Resource market
The market for inputs used to produce goods and services.

Just as in product markets, the demand curve in a **resource market** is typically downward-sloping and the supply curve upward-sloping. An inverse relationship will exist between the amount of a resource demanded and its price because businesses will substitute away from a resource as its price rises. In contrast, there will be a direct relationship between the amount of a resource supplied and its price because a higher price will make that resource more attractive to provide. As in product markets, prices will coordinate the choices of buyers and sellers in resource markets, bringing the quantity demanded into balance with the quantity supplied.

[3]This theme was a focus of much of the work of Nobel Prize–winning economist Friedrich Hayek.

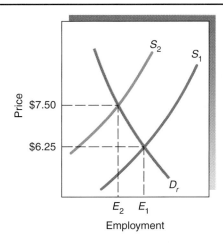

(a) Resource market
(youthful, inexperienced
labor)

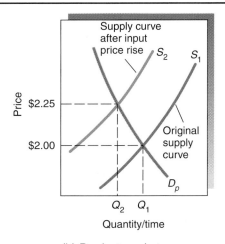

(b) Product market
(fast-food hamburgers)

EXHIBIT 1
Resource Prices,
Opportunity Cost, and
Product Markets

When the supply of young, inexperienced workers falls, it pushes the wage rates of fast-food employees upward (a). In the product market (b), the higher wage rates will increase the opportunity costs of restaurants, reducing supply (shifting from S_1 to S_2) and increasing hamburger prices.

The labor market is a large component of the broader resource market. Actually, there is not just one market for labor, but rather there are many labor markets, one for each different skill-experience-occupational category. Let's look at the labor market for low-skilled, inexperienced workers. **Exhibit 1** shows how resource and product markets are linked. The supply of young, inexperienced workers has declined in recent years in many areas of the United States. This lower supply has pushed the wages of young workers upward (for example, from $6.25 to $7.50 in Exhibit 1a). The higher price of this resource increases the opportunity cost of goods and services that young workers help produce. In turn, the higher cost reduces the supply (shifting S_1 to S_2) of products like hamburgers at McDonald's and other fast-food restaurants, pushing their price upward (Exhibit 1b). When the price of a resource increases, it will lead to higher production costs, lower supply, and higher prices for the goods and services produced with the resource.

Of course, lower resource prices have the opposite effect. Lower resource prices reduce costs and expand the supply of consumer goods made with the lower-priced resources (shifting the supply curve to the right). The increase in supply will lead to a lower price in the product market. ***Thus, when the price of a resource—such as labor—changes, the prices of goods and services produced with that resource will change in the same direction.***

Changes in product markets will also influence resource markets. ***There is a close relationship between the demand for products and the demand for the resources required for their production.*** An increase in demand for a consumer good—automobiles, for example—will lead to higher auto prices, which will increase the profitability of producing automobiles and give automakers an incentive to expand output. But the expansion in automobile output will require additional resources, causing an increase in the demand for, and prices of, the resources required for their production (steel, rubber, plastics, and the labor services of autoworkers, for example). The higher prices of these resources will cause other industries to conserve on their use, freeing them up for more automobile production.

Of course, the process will work in reverse if demand for a product falls. A decrease in demand will not only reduce the price of the product but will also reduce the demand for and prices of the resources used to produce it. ***Thus, when the demand for a product changes, the demand for (and prices of) the resources used to produce it will change in the same direction.***

THE ECONOMICS OF PRICE CONTROLS

Price controls
Government-mandated prices that are generally imposed in the form of maximum or minimum legal prices.

Buyers often complain that prices are too high, while sellers complain that they are too low. Unhappy with the prices established by market forces, various groups might try to persuade the government to intervene and impose **price controls**. Price controls force buyers or sellers to alter the prices of certain products. Price controls may be either price ceilings, which set a maximum legal price for a product, or price floors, which impose a minimum legal price. Imposing price controls might seem like a simple, easy way for the government to help buyers at the expense of sellers (or vice versa). The problem is that doing so frequently creates secondary effects that make *both* sides worse off.

Despite good intentions, price controls can, in fact, harm the very people they were intended to help because they undermine the exchange process and reduce the gains from trade. The regulation of automated teller machine (ATM) surcharge fees is one example. Many states, after being lobbied by consumer groups, enacted regulations forbidding or severely restricting the ability of ATM owners to charge fees for using their machines. The unintended consequence of these regulations is that there are now fewer ATMs available to consumers in these states because there's less incentive to own and operate them. Consumers in these states benefit by paying lower ATM fees, but they also bear the cost of reduced ATM access.

The Impact of Price Ceilings

Price ceiling
A legally established maximum price sellers can charge for a good or resource.

Shortage
A condition in which the amount of a good offered for sale by producers is less than the amount demanded by buyers at the existing price. An increase in price would eliminate the shortage.

Exhibit 2 shows the impact of imposing a **price ceiling** (P_1) for a product below its equilibrium level (P_0). At the lower price, the quantity supplied by producers decreases along the supply curve to Q_S, while the quantity demanded by consumers increases along the demand curve to Q_D. A **shortage** ($Q_D - Q_S$) of the good will result because the quantity demanded by consumers exceeds the quantity supplied by producers at the new controlled price. After the price ceiling is imposed, the quantity of the good exchanged declines from the equilibrium quantity to Q_S, and the gains from trade (consumer and producer surplus) fall as well.

Normally, a higher price would ration the good to the buyers most willing to pay for it. Because the price ceiling keeps this from happening, though, other means must be used to allocate the smaller quantity Q_S among consumers wanting to purchase Q_D. Predictably, nonprice factors will become more important in the rationing process. Sellers will be forced to discriminate on some basis other than willingness to pay as they ration their sales to eager buyers. They will be more inclined to sell their products to their friends, to buyers who do them favors, and even buyers willing to make illegal "under-the-table" payments. (The accompanying Applications in Economics box, "The Imposition of Price Ceilings During Hurricane Hugo," highlights this point.) Time might also be used as the rationing

EXHIBIT 2
The Impact of a Price Ceiling

When a price ceiling like P_1 pushes the price of a product (rental housing, for example) below the market equilibrium, a shortage will develop. Because prices are not allowed to direct the market to equilibrium, nonprice elements will become more important in rationing the good.

APPLICATIONS IN ECONOMICS

The Imposition of Price Ceilings During Hurricane Hugo

In the fall of 1989, Hurricane Hugo struck the coast of South Carolina, causing massive property damage and widespread power outages lasting for weeks. The lack of electric power meant that gasoline pumps, refrigerators, cash registers, ATMs, and many other types of electrical equipment did not work. In the hardest-hit coastal areas, such as Charleston, the demand for items such as lumber, gasoline, ice, batteries, chain saws, and electric generators increased dramatically. A bag of ice that sold for $1 before the hurricane went up in price to as much as $10; the price of plywood rose to about $200 per sheet; chain saws soared to the $600 range; and gasoline sold for as much as $10.95 per gallon. At these higher prices, individuals from other states were renting trucks, buying supplies in their home state, driving them to Charleston, and making enough money to pay for the rental truck and the purchase of the goods and to compensate them for taking time off from their regular jobs.

In response to consumer complaints of "price gouging," the mayor of Charleston signed emergency legislation making it a crime, punishable by up to 30 days in jail and a $200 fine, to sell goods at prices higher than their pre-hurricane levels in the city. The price ceilings kept prices down, but also stopped the flow of goods into the area almost immediately. Shippers of items like ice would stop and sell their goods outside the harder-hit Charleston area to avoid the price controls. Shipments that actually made it into Charleston were often greeted by long lines of consumers, many of whom would end up without goods after waiting in line for up to five hours. Many of the people at the front of the line who were able to buy the goods before supplies ran out would then drive those goods back out of the city to sell them at the higher, noncontrolled prices in areas outside of Charleston to obtain money to pay for repairs to their home. Shortages became so bad that military guards were needed to protect shipments of the goods and maintain order when a shipment did arrive.

The price controls resulted in serious misallocations of resources. Electric generators provide one of the best examples. Grocery stores couldn't open because there was no electricity. Inside stores, food was spoiling—thousands of dollars worth, in many cases. Although gas stations had gasoline in their underground storage tanks, it couldn't be pumped out without electricity. ATMs and banks couldn't operate without electricity, so people couldn't get their hands on their money—which was critical because almost all transactions in post hurricane Charleston were made with cash.

Hardware stores that sold gasoline-powered electric generators before the hurricane typically had only a few in stock, but suddenly hundreds of businesses and residents wanted to buy them. In the absence of price controls, the price of these generators would have risen to thousands of dollars to allocate the limited supply. Individual homeowners would have been outbid by businesses, which could have put the generators to use operating stores and gas stations and ATMs. It would have been these uses that could have generated enough revenue to cover the high price of the generators. People with generators at home would have found it attractive to sell them to businesses for the high sums of money involved.

However, the price ceilings prevented the generators from being allocated to those most willing to pay for them. Instead, people kept their generators at home, and it was commonplace for hardware store owners with a few generators on hand to take one home for their family and then sell the others to their close friends, neighbors, and relatives. In the absence of price rationing, nonprice factors played a larger role in the allocation process. The electric generators so critically needed for grocery stores, gasoline stations, and banks to open were instead being used by households for tasks such as running television sets, lighting, electric razors, hair dryers, and so on. As a result, hundreds of thousands of consumers couldn't get goods they urgently wanted. Moreover, the flow of new generators into the city effectively stopped, and many generators were actually taken out of the city to be sold in the less-damaged, outlying areas where price controls were not in effect. If price controls hadn't been imposed, the price of generators would quickly have been bid up to the point where they would have been (1) purchased by those with the most urgent uses for them, and (2) imported into the city fairly rapidly because of the high prices they commanded.

This dramatic example shows how important prices are. Market prices will both allocate goods to those who will put them to the highest valued uses and motivate people to supply more of the items in short supply. The secondary effects, or unintended consequences, of the price controls imposed in the Charleston area actually magnified people's suffering and retarded the recovery from the hurricane.[1] In recent years, communities hit by hurricanes and other disasters have been reluctant to impose price controls, perhaps because of what happened in Charleston.

---

[1] See David N. Laband, "In Hugo's Path, a Man-Made Disaster," *Wall Street Journal*, September 27, 1989, A22; and Tim Smith, "Economists Spurn Price Restrictions," *Greenville News*, September 28, 1989, C1.

device, with those willing to wait in line the longest being the ones able to purchase the good. In addition, the below-equilibrium price reduces the incentive of sellers to expand the future supply of the good. At the lower price, suppliers will direct resources away from production of the good and into other, more profitable areas. As a result, the product shortage will worsen through time.

What other secondary effects can be expected? *In the real world, there are two ways that sellers can raise prices. First, they can raise their money price, holding quality constant. Or, second, they can hold the money price constant while reducing the quality of the good.* (The latter might also include reducing the size of the product, say, for example, a candy bar or a loaf of bread.) Faced with a price ceiling, sellers will use quality reductions as a way to raise their prices. Because of the government-created shortage, many consumers will buy the lower quality good rather than do without it.

It is important to note that a shortage is not the same as scarcity. *Scarcity is inescapable.* Scarcity exists whenever people want more of a good than nature has provided. This means, of course, that almost everything of value is scarce. *Shortages, on the other hand, are a result of prices being set below their equilibrium values—a situation that is avoidable if prices are permitted to rise.* Removing the price ceiling will allow the price to rise back to its equilibrium level (P_0 rather than P_1 in Exhibit 2). This will stimulate additional production, discourage consumption, and increase the incentive of entrepreneurs to search for and develop substitute goods. This combination of forces will eliminate the shortage.

Rent Control: A Closer Look at a Price Ceiling

Rent controls are a price ceiling intended to protect residents from high housing prices. Rent controls are currently in place in many U.S. cities, including New York, Washington, D.C., Newark, New Jersey, and San Jose, California. Most of these measures were enacted during either World War II or the 1970s, when inflation was high. Rent controls peaked in the mid-1980s. At that time, more than 200 cities, encompassing about 20 percent of the nation's population, imposed rent controls.

Because rent controls push the price of rental housing below the equilibrium level, the amount of rental housing demanded by consumers will exceed the amount landlords will make available. Initially, if the mandated price is only slightly below equilibrium, the impact of rent controls may be barely noticeable. Over time, however, the effects will worsen. Inevitably, rent controls will lead to the following results.

1. Shortages and black markets will develop. Because the quantity of housing demanded will exceed the quantity supplied, some people who value rental housing highly will be unable to find it. Frustrated by the shortage, they will try to induce landlords to rent to them. Some will agree to prepay their rent, including a substantial damage deposit. Others might agree to rent or buy the landlord's furniture at exorbitant prices in order to get an apartment. Still others will make under-the-table (black market) payments to secure housing.

2. The future supply of rental houses will decline. The below-equilibrium price will discourage entrepreneurs from constructing new rental housing units, and private investment will flow elsewhere. In the city of Berkeley, rental units available to students at the University of California dropped by 31 percent in the first five years after the city adopted rent controls in 1978.[4] In Boston and some of its suburbs, housing and apartment construction rose dramatically following the repeal of rent controls in the late 1990s. Similar results were observed in Santa Monica, California, following removal of rent controls.

[4]William Tucker, *The Excluded Americans* (Washington, D.C.: Regnery Gateway, 1990), 162. For additional information on rent controls, see William Tucker, "Rent Control Drives Out Affordable Housing," in *USA Today Magazine* (July 1998) and Walter Block, "Rent Controls," in *Fortune Encyclopedia of Economics,* ed. David Henderson (New York: Warner Books, 1993). The latter publication can also be found online at http://www.econlib.org.

3. The quality of rental housing will deteriorate.
When apartment owners are not allowed to raise their prices, they will use quality reductions to achieve this objective. Normal maintenance and repair service will deteriorate. Tenant parking lots will be eliminated (or rented out). Eventually, the quality of the rental housing will reflect the controlled price. Cheaper housing will be of cheaper quality.

4. Nonprice methods of rationing will become more important.
Because price no longer rations rental housing, other forms of competition will develop. Landlords will rely more heavily on nonmonetary discriminating devices. They will favor friends, people of influence, and those whose lifestyles resemble their own. In contrast, applicants with many children or unconventional lifestyles, and perhaps racial

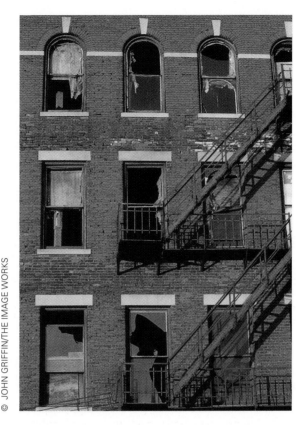

minorities, will find fewer landlords who will rent to them. Since the cost to landlords of discriminating against those they do not like is lower, discrimination will become more prevalent in the rationing process. In New York City, where rent controls are in force, a magazine article suggested that "joining a church or synagogue" could help people make the connections they need to get an apartment. Can you imagine having to devote this amount of effort to finding an apartment? If your city enacts rent controls, you just might have to.

5. Inefficient use of housing space will result.
The tenant in a rent-controlled apartment will think twice before moving. Why? Even though the tenant might want a larger or smaller space or an apartment closer to work, he or she will be less likely to move because it will be much more difficult to find a unit that's vacant. Turnover will be lower, and many people will find themselves in locations and in apartments not well suited to their needs. In a college town, students who live in the local area will have an advantage over newcomers. Local students and their parents will be more likely to have connections with apartment owners in the area. Many students from farther away, including those who value the apartments more highly, will find it extremely difficult to locate a place to rent.

6. Long-term renters will benefit at the expense of newcomers.
People who stay for lengthy periods of time in the same apartment often pay rents substantially below market value, while newcomers are faced with exorbitant prices for units sublet from other tenants. Distortions and inequities result. A book on housing and the homeless by William Tucker reports several examples: Actress Ann Turkel spends only two months each year in New York. Turkel pays $2,350 per month for a seven-room, four-and-a-half bathroom duplex she has rented for many years. Identical apartments in Turkel's building sublet for $6,500 per month.[5] Former mayor Edward Koch pays $441.49 a month for a large one-bedroom apartment that would probably rent for $1,200 in the absence of rent controls.

Rent controls lead to shortages, poor maintenance, and deterioration in the quality of rental housing.

© JOHN GRIFFIN/THE IMAGE WORKS

[5]Tucker, *The Excluded Americans,* 248.

Koch kept the apartment the entire twelve years he lived in Gracie Mansion (the official mayor's residence) because had he given up the apartment, it would have been extremely difficult to find another one.

Imposing rent control laws may sound like a simple way to deal with high housing prices. However, the secondary effects are so damaging that many cities have begun repealing them. In the words of Swedish economist Assar Lindbeck: "In many cases, rent control appears to be the most efficient technique presently known to destroy a city—except for bombing."[6] Though this may overstate the case, Lindbeck definitely has a valid point.

The Impact of Price Floors

Price floor
A legally established minimum price buyers must pay for a good or resource.

A **price floor** establishes a minimum price that can legally be charged. The government imposes price floors on some agricultural products, for example, in an effort to artificially increase the prices that farmers receive. When a price floor is imposed above the current market equilibrium price, it will alter the market's operation. **Exhibit 3** illustrates the impact of imposing a price floor (P_1) for a product above its equilibrium level (P_0). At the higher price, the quantity supplied by producers increases along the supply curve to Q_S, while the quantity demanded by consumers decreases along the demand curve to Q_D. A **surplus** ($Q_S - Q_D$) of the good will result, as the quantity supplied by producers exceeds the quantity demanded by consumers at the new controlled price. Just like a price ceiling, a price floor reduces the quantity of the good exchanged, and reduces the gains from trade.

Surplus
A condition in which the amount of a good offered for sale by producers is greater than the amount that buyers will purchase at the existing price. A decline in price would eliminate the surplus.

As in the case of the price ceiling, nonprice factors will play a larger role in the rationing process. But because there is a surplus rather than a shortage, this time buyers will be in a position to be more selective. Buyers will purchase from sellers willing to offer them nonprice favors—better service, discounts on other products, or easier credit terms, for example. When it's difficult to alter the product's quality—in this case, improve it to make it more attractive for the price that must be charged—some producers will be unable to sell it.

It is important to note that a surplus doesn't mean the good is no longer scarce. People still want more of the good than is freely available from nature, even though they want less of it *at the controlled price* than sellers want to bring to the market. A decline in price would eliminate the surplus, but the item will be scarce in either case.

EXHIBIT 3
The Impact of a Price Floor

When a price floor such as P_1 keeps the price of a good or service above the market equilibrium, a surplus will result.

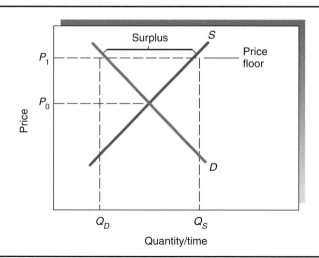

[6]Assar Lindbeck, *The Political Economy of the New Left* (New York: Harper & Row, 1972), 39.

Minimum Wage: A Closer Look at a Price Floor

In 1938 Congress passed the Fair Labor Standards Act, which mandated a national **minimum wage** of 25 cents per hour. During the past 65 years, the minimum wage has been increased many times. The current federal minimum wage is $5.15 per hour, although some states have their own higher minimum-wage rates ranging up to just over $7 per hour.

A minimum wage is a price floor. Because most employees in the United States earn wages in excess of the minimum, their employment opportunities are largely unaffected by the minimum wage law. However, low-skilled and inexperienced workers whose equilibrium wage rates are lower than the minimum wage will be affected. **Exhibit 4** shows the direct effect of a $5.15-per-hour minimum wage on the employment opportunities of a group of low-skilled workers.

Without a minimum wage, the supply of and demand for these low-skilled workers would be in balance at a wage rate of $4.00. Because the minimum wage makes low-skilled labor more expensive, employers will substitute machines and more highly skilled workers for the now more expensive low-skilled employees. Fewer low-skilled workers will be hired when the minimum wage pushes their wages up. Graphically, this is reflected in the movement up along the demand curve in Exhibit 4 from the equilibrium point to the point along the demand curve associated with the higher, $5.15 wage rate (point A). The result will be a reduction in employment of low-skilled workers from E_0 to E_1.

On the supply side of the market, as the wages of low-skilled workers are pushed above equilibrium, there will be more unskilled workers looking for jobs. Graphically, this is reflected in the movement up along the supply curve in Exhibit 4 from the equilibrium point to the point along the supply curve associated with the higher, $5.15 wage rate (point B). At the $5.15 wage rate, the quantity of workers searching for jobs will exceed the quantity of jobs available, causing excess supply. Economists generally use the term unemployment when referring to excess supply in a labor market.

In summary, economic analysis indicates that minimum-wage legislation increases the rate of unemployment among low-skilled workers. The exceedingly high unemployment rate of teenagers in the United States (one of the groups most affected by the minimum wage) is consistent with this analysis. In the United States, the unemployment rate for teenagers is more than three times the average for all workers, and the unemployment rate for black youth has generally exceeded 30 percent in recent years.

Minimum wage
Legislation requiring that workers be paid at least the stated minimum hourly rate of pay.

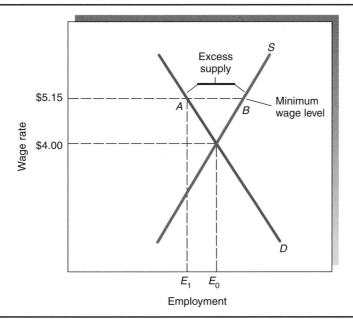

EXHIBIT 4
Employment and the Minimum Wage

If the market wage of a group of employees were $4.00 per hour, a $5.15-per-hour minimum wage will increase the earnings of workers able to retain their jobs, but reduce the employment opportunities of others as the number of jobs available shrinks from E_0 to E_1.

It is important to remember that the market price—the wage rate—is only one dimension of the transaction. When a price floor pushes the wage rate above equilibrium, employers will have less of an incentive to offer nonwage benefits to employees because they will have no trouble hiring low-skilled workers. Predictably, a higher minimum wage will lead to a deterioration of the nonwage qualities of minimum-wage jobs, and so workers in these jobs will experience less convenient working hours, fewer training opportunities, and less continuous employment.

The adverse impact of the minimum wage on the opportunity of youthful workers to acquire work experience and on-the-job training is a particularly important unintended consequence of minimum-wage laws. Low-paying, entry-level jobs can provide workers with experience that will help them move up the job ladder to higher-paying positions. Employment experience obtained at an early age, even on menial tasks, can help a person acquire self-confidence, good work habits, and skills that make them more valuable to future employers. The minimum wage makes this more difficult. Not only does the minimum wage make it harder for low-skilled workers to find jobs, it also reduces their on-the-job training opportunities. In order to pay the higher wage rate required by the law, employers will have to find other ways to cut employment costs, like reducing the amount of job training. Not surprisingly, most minimum-wage jobs are dead-end positions with little opportunity for future advancement.[7]

Workers who are able to maintain their employment at the higher minimum-wage rate—most likely the better qualified among those with low skill levels—gain from a minimum wage. But other low-skilled workers are harmed by the minimum wage, particularly those with the lowest skill levels, who will find it more difficult to get jobs.

How many fewer low-skilled workers are hired because of the minimum wage? Studies indicate that a 10 percent increase in the minimum wage reduces the employment of low-skilled workers by 1 to 3 percent. Minimum-wage supporters argue that the higher wages for low-skilled workers are worth this reduction in employment and job-training opportunities. Critics argue, however, that the reduced job opportunities for the lowest-skilled workers are reason enough to eliminate the minimum wage.

Does the minimum wage help the poor? Most minimum-wage workers belong to families with an income substantially above the poverty line. In fact, about 40 percent of minimum-wage workers are members of a family with an income in the top half of the income distribution. The typical minimum-wage worker is a spouse or a teenage member of a household with an income well above the poverty level. Therefore, even if the effects of a higher minimum wage on employment and nonwage forms of compensation were small, a higher minimum wage does little to help the poor, making it a much less attractive antipoverty program than other alternatives.[8]

BLACK MARKETS AND THE IMPORTANCE OF THE LEGAL STRUCTURE

When price controls are imposed, exchanges at prices outside of the range set by the government are illegal. Governments may also make it entirely illegal to buy and sell certain products. This is the case with drugs like marijuana and cocaine in the United States. Similarly, prostitution is illegal in all states except Nevada. However, controlling prices and making a good or service illegal doesn't eliminate market forces. When demand is strong and gains from trade can be had, markets will develop and exchanges will occur in spite of the restrictions. People will also engage in illegal exchanges in order to evade taxes. For example, the $3.39 per-pack cigarette tax in New York City has made cigarette smuggling in that city a thriving business.

---

[7]For evidence that the minimum wage limits training opportunities, see David Neumark and William Wascher, "Minimum Wages and Training Revisited," *Journal of Labor Economics* 19 (July 2001): 563–95.

[8]See William E. Even and David A. Macpherson, "Consequences of Minimum Wage Indexing," *Contemporary Economic Policy* 14 (October 1996): 67–77; David Neumark and William Wascher, "Do Minimum Wages Fight Poverty?" *Economic Inquiry* 40 (July 2002): 315–33; and David Neumark and William Wascher, "The Effects of Minimum Wages Throughout the Wage Distribution," *Journal of Human Resources* 39 (April 2004): 425–50, for evidence on this point.

Markets that operate outside the legal system are called **black markets**. How do black markets work? Can markets function without the protection of the law? As in other markets, supply and demand will determine prices in black markets, too. However, because black markets operate outside the official legal structure, enforcement of contracts and the dependability of quality will be less certain. Furthermore, participation in black markets involves greater risk, particularly for suppliers. Prices in these markets will have to be higher than they otherwise would be to compensate suppliers for the risks they are taking—the threat of arrest, possibility of a fine or prison sentence, and so on. Perhaps most important, in black markets there are no legal channels for the peaceful settlement of disputes. When a buyer or seller fails to deliver, it is the other party who must try to enforce the agreement, usually through the use or threat of physical force.

Compared to normal markets, black markets are characterized by a higher incidence of defective products, higher profit rates (for those who do not get caught), and more violence. The incidence of phony tickets purchased from street dealers selling them at illegal prices, and deaths caused by toxic, illicit drugs, are a reflection of the high presence of defective goods in these markets. Certainly the expensive clothes and automobiles of many drug dealers suggest that monetary profits are high in black-markets. Evidence of violence as a means of settling disputes arising from black market transactions is widespread. Crime statistics in urban areas show that a high percentage of the violent crimes, including murder, are associated with illegal trades gone bad and competition among dealers in the illegal drug market.

The prohibition of alcohol in the United States from 1920 to 1933 vividly illustrates how violence, deception, and fraud plague markets that operate outside the law. When the production and sale of alcohol was illegal during the Prohibition era, gangsters dominated the alcohol trade, and the murder rate soared to record highs. There were also problems with product quality (tainted or highly toxic mixtures, for example) similar to the ones present in modern-day illegal-drug markets. When Prohibition was repealed and the market for alcoholic beverages began operating once again within the legal framework, these harmful secondary effects disappeared.

The operation of black markets highlights a point often taken for granted: a legal system that provides for secure private-property rights, contract enforcement, and access to an unbiased court system for settling disputes is vitally important for the smooth operation of markets. Markets will exist in any environment, but they can be

Black market
A market that operates outside the legal system, where either illegal goods are sold or legal goods are sold at illegal prices or terms.

Black markets like those for illegal drugs are characterized by less dependable product quality and the greater use of violence to settle disputes between buyers and sellers.

GETTY IMAGES

counted on to function efficiently only when property rights are secure and contracts are enforced in an evenhanded manner.

The analysis of black markets also provides insights into the economies of Russia, Ukraine, and other parts of the former Soviet Union. Following the collapse of communism, the legal systems in these areas reflected the prior socialist nature of these economies. Both the protection of private property and the enforcement of contracts between private parties were highly uncertain. People with political connections were often able to escape their contractual responsibilities and obtain favorable rulings from legal and regulatory authorities. As a result, markets in these countries operated much like black markets. Fraud and deception were commonplace, and the incidence of violence related to business dealings was widespread. A market economy—like any other—does not work well in such an environment. Many foreign businesspeople who were initially attracted to markets in these countries soon began packing their bags and returning home. Financial capital fled, investment shrank, and these economies performed poorly. During the last few years, there has been some improvement in the legal environment, but the enforcement of contracts and conduct of business activities in the former Soviet Union still involve considerable risk. Without sound legal systems, these countries will be unable to reap the full benefits of a market economy.

THE IMPACT OF A TAX

Tax incidence
The way the burden of a tax is distributed among economic units (consumers, producers, employees, employers, and so on). The actual tax burden does not always fall on those who are statutorily assigned to pay the tax.

How do taxes affect market exchange? When governments tax goods, who bears the burden? Economists use the term **tax incidence** to indicate how the burden of a tax is *actually* shared between buyers (who pay more for what they purchase) and sellers (who receive less for what they sell). When a tax is imposed, the government can make either the buyer or the seller legally responsible for payment of the tax. The legal assignment is called the *statutory incidence* of the tax. However, the person who writes the check to the government—that is, the person statutorily responsible for the tax—is not always the one who bears the tax burden. The *actual incidence* of a tax may lie elsewhere. If, for example, a tax is placed statutorily on a seller, the seller might simply increase the price of the product. In this case, the buyers end up bearing some, or all, of the tax burden through the higher price.

To illustrate, **Exhibit 5** shows how a $1,000 tax placed on the sale of used cars would affect the market. (To simplify this example, let's assume all used cars are identical.) Here, the tax has statutorily been placed on the seller. When a tax is imposed on the seller, it shifts the supply curve upward by exactly the amount of the tax— $1,000 in this example. To understand why, remember that the height of the supply curve at a particular quantity shows the minimum price required to cause enough sellers to offer that quantity of cars for sale. Suppose you were a potential seller, willing to sell your car for any price over $6,000, but you were unwilling to sell it unless you could pocket at least $6,000 from the sale. Because you now have to pay a tax of $1,000 when you sell your car, the minimum price you will accept *from the buyer* will rise to $7,000, so that after paying the tax, you will retain $6,000. Other potential sellers will be in a similar position. The tax will push the minimum price each seller is willing to accept upward by $1,000. Thus, the after-tax supply curve will shift vertically by this amount.

Sellers would prefer to pass the entire tax on to buyers by raising prices by the full amount of the tax, rather than paying any part of it themselves. However, as sellers begin to raise prices, customers respond by purchasing fewer units. At some point, to avoid losing additional sales, sellers will find it more profitable to accept part of the tax burden themselves (in the form of a lower price net of tax), rather than to raise the price by the full amount of the tax. This process is shown in Exhibit 5.

Before the tax was imposed, used cars sold for a price of $7,000 (at the intersection of the original supply and demand curves shown by point *A*). After the $1,000 tax is imposed, the equilibrium price of used cars will rise to $7,400 (to point *B*, the intersection

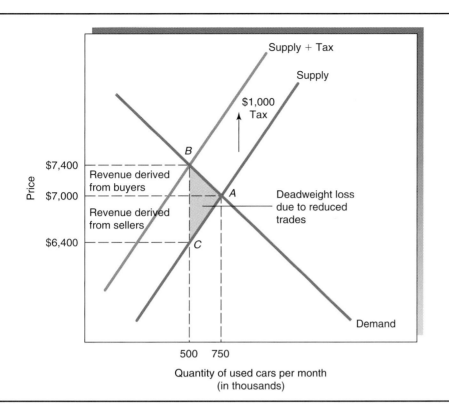

EXHIBIT 5
The Impact of a Tax
Imposed on Sellers

When a $1,000 tax is im-posed statutorily on the sellers of used cars, the supply curve shifts verti-cally upward by the amount of the tax. The price of used cars to buyers rises from $7,000 to $7,400, resulting in buyers bearing $400 of the burden of this tax. The price received by a seller falls from $7,000 to $6,400 ($7,400 minus the $1,000 tax), resulting in sellers bearing $600 of the burden.

of the new supply curve including the tax, and the demand curve). Thus, despite the tax being statutorily imposed on sellers, the higher price shifts some of the tax burden to buyers. Buyers will now pay $400 more for used cars. Sellers now receive $7,400 from the sale of their used cars. However, after sending $1,000 in taxes to the government, they retain only $6,400. This is exactly $600 less than the seller would have received had the tax not been imposed. Because the distance between the supply curves is exactly $1,000, this net price can be found in Exhibit 5 by following the vertical line down from the new equilibrium (point *B*) to the original supply curve (point *C*) and over to the price axis. In this case, each $1,000 of tax revenue transferred to the government imposes a burden of $400 on buyers (in the form of higher used-car prices) and a $600 burden on sellers (in the form of lower net receipts from a car sale)—even though sellers are responsible for actually sending the $1,000 tax payment to the government.

The tax revenue derived from a tax is equal to the **tax base** (in this case, the number of used cars exchanged) multiplied by the **tax rate**. After the tax is imposed, the quantity exchanged will fall to 500,000 cars per month because some buyers will choose not to purchase at the $7,400 price, and some sellers will decide not to sell when they are able to net only $6,400. Given the after-tax quantity sold, the monthly revenue derived from the tax will be $500 million (500,000 cars multiplied by $1,000 tax per car).

The Deadweight Loss Caused by Taxes

As Exhibit 5 shows, a $1,000 tax on used cars causes the number of units exchanged to fall from 750,000 to 500,000. It reduces the quantity of units exchanged by 250,000 units. Remember, trade results in mutual gains for both buyers and sellers. The loss of the mutual benefits that would have been derived from these additional 250,000 units also imposes a cost on buyers and sellers. But this cost—the loss of the gains from trade eliminated by the tax—does not generate any revenue for the government. Economists call this the **deadweight loss** of taxation. In Exhibit 5, the size of the triangle *ABC* measures the deadweight loss. The deadweight loss is a burden imposed on buyers and sellers over

Tax base
The level or quantity of an economic activity that is taxed. Higher tax rates reduce the level of the tax base because they make the activity less attractive.

Tax rate
The per-unit amount of the tax or the percentage rate at which the economic activity is taxed.

Deadweight loss
The loss of gains from trade to buyers and sellers that occurs when a tax is imposed. The deadweight loss imposes a burden on both buyers and sellers over and above the actual payment of the tax.

Excess burden of taxation
Another term for deadweight loss. It reflects losses that occur when beneficial activities are forgone because they are taxed.

and above the cost of the revenue transferred to the government. Sometimes it is referred to as the **excess burden of taxation**. It is composed of losses to both buyers (the lost consumer surplus consisting of the upper part of the triangle *ABC*) and sellers (the lost producer surplus consisting of the lower part of the triangle *ABC*).

The deadweight loss to sellers includes an indirect cost imposed on the people who supply resources to that industry (such as its suppliers and employees). The 1990 luxury-boat tax provides a good example. Supporters of the luxury-boat tax assumed the tax burden would fall primarily on wealthy yacht buyers. The actual effects were quite different, though. Because of the tax, luxury-boat sales fell sharply and thousands of workers lost their jobs in the yacht-manufacturing industry. The deadweight loss triangle might seem like an abstract concept, but it wasn't so abstract to the employees in the yacht industry who lost their jobs! Their losses are part of what is reflected in the triangular area. Moreover, because luxury-boat sales declined so sharply, the tax generated only a meager amount of revenue. The large deadweight loss (or excess burden) combined with meager revenue for the government eventually led to the repeal of the tax.

Actual Versus Statutory Incidence

Economic analysis indicates that the actual burden of a tax—or more precisely, the split of the burden between buyers and sellers—does not depend on whether the tax is statutorily placed on the buyer or the seller. To see this, we must first look at how the market responds to a tax statutorily placed on the buyer. Continuing with the auto tax example, let's suppose that the government places the $1,000 tax on the buyer of the car, rather than the seller. After making a used-car purchase, the buyer must send a check to the government for $1,000. Imposing a tax on buyers will shift the demand curve downward by the amount of the tax, as shown in **Exhibit 6**. This is because the height of the demand curve represents the maximum price a buyer is willing to pay for the car. If a particular buyer is willing and able to pay only $5,000 for a car, the $1,000 tax would mean that the most the

EXHIBIT 6
The Impact of a Tax Imposed on Buyers

When a $1,000 tax is imposed statutorily on the buyers of used cars, the demand curve shifts vertically downward by the amount of the tax. The price of used cars falls from $7,000 to $6,400, resulting in sellers bearing $600 of the burden. The buyer's total cost of purchasing the car rises from $7,000 to $7,400 ($6,400 plus the $1,000 tax), resulting in buyers bearing $400 of the burden of this tax. The incidence of this tax on used cars is the same regardless of whether it is statutorily imposed on buyers or sellers.

"THIS NEW TAX PLAN SOUNDS PRETTY GOOD... WE GET A 9% CUT AND BUSINESS PICKS UP THE BURDEN...."

The actual burden of a tax is independent of whether it is imposed on buyers or sellers.

buyer would be willing to pay *to the seller* would be $4,000. This is because the total cost to the buyer is now the purchase price plus the tax.

As Exhibit 6 shows, the price of used cars falls from $7,000 (point *A*) to $6,400 (point *B*) when the tax is statutorily placed on the buyer. Even though the tax is placed on buyers, the reduction in demand that results causes the price received by sellers to fall by $600. Thus, $600 of the tax is again borne by sellers, just as it was when the tax was placed statutorily on them. From the buyer's standpoint, a car now costs $7,400 ($6,400 paid to the seller plus $1,000 in tax to the government). Just as when the tax was imposed on the seller, the buyer now pays $400 more for a used car.

A comparison of Exhibits 5 and 6 makes it clear that the actual burden of the $1,000 tax is independent of its statutory incidence. In both cases, buyers pay a total price of $7,400 for the car (a $400 increase from the pretax level), and sellers receive $6,400 from the sale (a $600 decrease from the pretax level). Correspondingly, the revenue derived by the government, the number of sales eliminated by the tax, and the size of the deadweight loss are identical whether the law requires payment of the tax by the sellers or by the buyers. A similar phenomenon occurs with any tax. The 15.3 percent Social Security payroll tax, for example, is statutorily levied as 7.65 percent on the employee and 7.65 percent on the employer. The impact is to drive down the net pay received by employees and raise the employers' cost of hiring workers. Economic analysis tells us that the actual burden of this tax will probably differ from its legal assignment, and that it will be the same regardless of how the tax is statutorily assigned. Because market prices (here, workers' gross wage) will adjust, the incidence of the tax will be identical regardless of whether the 15.3 percent is levied on employees or on employers or is divided between the two parties.

Elasticity and the Incidence of a Tax

If the actual incidence of a tax is independent of its statutory assignment, what does determine the incidence? The answer: ***The incidence of a tax depends on the responsiveness of buyers and of sellers to a change in price.*** When buyers respond to even a small increase in price by leaving the market and buying other things, they will not be willing to accept a price that is much higher than it was prior to the tax. Similarly, if sellers respond to a small reduction in what they receive by shifting to the production of other goods or going out of business, they will not be willing to accept a much smaller payment, net of tax. The burden of a tax—its incidence—tends to fall more heavily on whichever side of the market has the least attractive options elsewhere—the side of the market that is less sensitive to price changes, in other words.

In the preceding chapter, we saw that the steepness of the supply and demand curves reflects how responsive producers and consumers are to a price change. Relatively inelastic

EXHIBIT 7
How the Burden of a Tax Depends on the Elasticities of Demand and Supply

In part (a), when demand is relatively more inelastic than supply, buyers bear a larger share of the burden of the tax. In part (b), when supply is relatively more inelastic than demand, sellers bear a larger share of the tax burden.

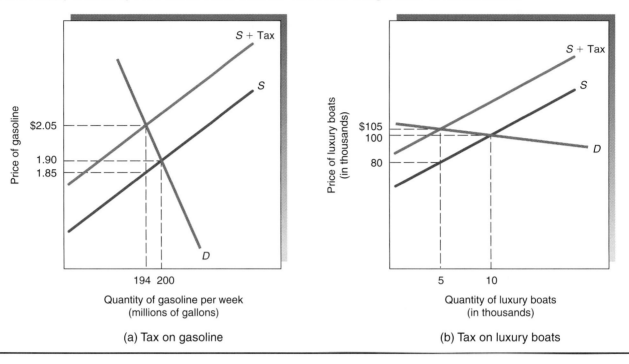

(a) Tax on gasoline

(b) Tax on luxury boats

demand or supply curves are steeper (more vertical), indicating less responsiveness to a change in price. Relatively elastic demand or supply curves are flatter (more horizontal), indicating a higher degree of responsiveness to a change in price.

Using gasoline as an example, part (a) of **Exhibit 7** illustrates the impact of a tax when demand is relatively inelastic and supply is relatively elastic. It will not be easy for gasoline consumers to shift—particularly in the short run—to other fuels in response to an increase in the price of gasoline. The inelastic demand curve shows this. When a 20-cent tax is imposed on gasoline, buyers end up paying 15 cents more per gallon ($2.05 instead of $1.90), while the net price of sellers is 5 cents less ($1.85 instead of $1.90). *When demand is relatively inelastic, or supply is relatively elastic, buyers will bear the larger share of the tax burden.*

Conversely, when demand is relatively elastic and supply is inelastic, more of the tax burden will fall on sellers and resource suppliers. The luxury-boat tax illustrates this point. As we mentioned earlier, Congress imposed a tax on the sale of luxury boats in 1990. Later, the tax was repealed because of its adverse impact on sales and employment in the industry. There are many things wealthy potential yacht owners can spend their money on other than luxury boats *sold in the United States*. For one thing, they can buy a yacht someplace else, perhaps in Mexico, England, or the Bahamas. Or they can spend more time on the golf course, travel to exotic places, or purchase a nicer car or more expensive home. Because there are attractive substitutes, the demand for domestically produced luxury boats is relatively elastic compared to supply. Therefore, as Exhibit 7b illustrates, when a $25,000 tax is imposed on luxury boats, prices rise by only $5,000 (from $100,000 to $105,000), but output falls substantially (from 10,000 to 5,000 boats). The net price received by sellers falls by $20,000 (from $100,000 to $80,000 per boat). *When demand is relatively elastic, or supply is relatively inelastic, sellers (including resource suppliers) will bear the larger share of the tax burden.*

Elasticity and the Deadweight Loss

We have seen that the elasticities of supply and demand determine how the burden of a tax is distributed between buyer and seller. They also influence the size of the deadweight loss caused by the tax because they determine the total reduction in the quantity exchanged. When either demand or supply is relatively inelastic, fewer trades will be eliminated by the tax, so the deadweight loss will be smaller. From a policy perspective, the excess burden of a tax system will therefore be lower if taxes are levied on goods and services for which either demand or supply is highly inelastic.

TAX RATES, TAX REVENUES, AND THE LAFFER CURVE

It is important to distinguish between the average and marginal rates of taxation. They can be very different, and both provide important information. The average tax rate is generally used to examine how different income groups are burdened by a tax, whereas the marginal tax rate is the key to understanding the negative economic effects created by a tax. Both can be computed with simple equations. The **average tax rate (ATR)** can be expressed as follows:

$$\text{ATR} = \text{Tax liability} / \text{Taxable income}$$

Average tax rate (ATR)
Tax liability divided by taxable income. It is the percentage of income paid in taxes.

For example, if a person's tax liability was $3,000 on an income of $20,000, her average tax rate would be 15 percent ($3,000 divided by $20,000). The average tax rate is simply the percentage of income that is paid in taxes.

In the United States, the personal income tax provides the largest single source of government revenue. This tax is particularly important at the federal level. You may have heard that the federal income tax is "progressive." A **progressive tax** is defined as a tax in which the average tax rate rises with income. In other words, people with higher income pay a larger *percentage of their income* in taxes. Alternatively, taxes can be proportional or regressive. A **proportional tax** is defined as a tax in which the average tax rate remains the same across income levels. Under a proportional tax, everyone pays the same percentage of their income in taxes. Finally, a **regressive tax** is defined as a tax in which the average tax rate falls with income. If someone making $100,000 per year paid $30,000 in taxes (an ATR of 30 percent) while someone making $30,000 per year paid $15,000 in taxes (an ATR of 50 percent), the tax code would be regressive. Note that a regressive tax merely means that the *percentage* paid in taxes declines with income; the actual dollar amount of the tax bill might still be higher for those with larger incomes.

Progressive tax
A tax in which the average tax rate rises with income. People with higher incomes will pay a higher percentage of their income in taxes.

Proportional tax
A tax in which the average tax rate is the same at all income levels. Everyone pays the same percentage of income in taxes.

Regressive tax
A tax in which the average tax rate falls with income. People with higher incomes will pay a lower percentage of their income in taxes.

Although the average tax rate is useful in determining whether a tax is progressive, proportional, or regressive, it is the marginal tax rate that concerns individuals when they are making decisions. It is the marginal tax rate that determines how much of an additional dollar of income must be paid in taxes (and thus, also, how much one gets to keep). An individual's marginal tax rate can be very different from his or her average tax rate. The **marginal tax rate (MTR)** can be expressed as follows:

$$\text{MTR} = \text{Change in tax liability} / \text{Change in taxable income}$$

Marginal tax rate (MTR)
The additional tax liability a person faces divided by his or her additional taxable income. It is the percentage of an extra dollar of income earned that must be paid in taxes. It is the marginal tax rate that is relevant in personal decision making.

The MTR reveals both how much of one's *additional* income must be turned over to the tax collector and how much is retained by the individual taxpayer. For example, when the MTR is 25 percent, $25 of every $100 of additional earnings must be paid in taxes. The individual is permitted to keep only $75 of his or her additional income, in other words. The marginal tax rate is vitally important because it affects the incentive to earn additional income. The higher the marginal tax rate, the less incentive individuals have to earn more income. At high marginal rates, for example, many spouses will choose to stay home rather than take a job, and others will choose not to take on second jobs or extra work. **Exhibit 8** shows the calculation of both the average and marginal tax rates within the framework of the 2003 income tax tables provided to taxpayers.

EXHIBIT 8

Average and Marginal Tax Rates in the Income Tax Tables

This excerpt from the 2003 federal income tax table shows that in the 25 percent federal marginal income tax bracket, each $100 of additional taxable income a single taxpayer earns ($32,100 versus $32,000, for example) causes his or her tax liability to increase by $25 (from $4,816 to $4,841). Note that the average tax rate for a single taxpayer at $32,000 is about 15 percent ($4,816 divided by $32,000)—even though the taxpayer's marginal rate is 25 percent.

2003 Tax Table—Continued

$100 of additional income . . .

. . . results in $25 of additional tax liability

If line 40 (taxable income) is—		And you are—			
At least	But less than	Single	Married filing jointly	Married filing separately	Head of a household
		Your tax is—			

32,000

At least	But less than	Single	Married filing jointly	Married filing separately	Head of a household
32,000	32,050	4,816	4,104	4,816	4,304
32,050	32,100	4,829	4,111	4,829	4,311
32,100	32,150	4,841	4,119	4,841	4,319
32,150	32,200	4,854	4,126	4,854	4,326
32,200	32,250	4,866	4,134	4,866	4,334
32,250	32,300	4,879	4,141	4,879	4,341
32,300	32,350	4,891	4,149	4,891	4,349
32,350	32,400	4,904	4,156	4,904	4,356
32,400	32,450	4,916	4,164	4,916	4,364
32,450	32,500	4,929	4,171	4,929	4,371
32,500	32,550	4,941	4,179	4,941	4,379
32,550	32,600	4,954	4,186	4,954	4,386
32,600	32,650	4,966	4,194	4,966	4,394
32,650	32,700	4,979	4,201	4,979	4,401
32,700	32,750	4,991	4,209	4,991	4,409
32,750	32,800	5,004	4,216	5,004	4,416
32,800	32,850	5,016	4,224	5,016	4,424
32,850	32,900	5,029	4,231	5,029	4,431
32,900	32,950	5,041	4,239	5,041	4,439
32,950	33,000	5,054	4,246	5,054	4,446

Generally, a person's income is subject to several different taxes, and it is the combined marginal tax rate of all of them that matters when it comes to decision making. For example, a recent college graduate with $30,000 in taxable income living in Baltimore, Maryland, would face a 25 percent marginal federal income tax rate, a 7.65 percent marginal Social Security payroll tax rate, a 4.75 percent marginal state income tax rate, and a 3.05 percent marginal local income tax rate. If we ignore the relatively small deductions that one tax can generate in calculating certain others, the result is a combined marginal tax rate of 40.45 percent, meaning that an additional $100 of gross income would result in only a $59.55 increase in net take-home income.

Governments generally levy taxes to raise revenue. The revenue derived from a tax is equal to the tax base multiplied by the tax rate. As we previously noted, taxes will lower the level of the activity taxed. When an activity is taxed more heavily, people will choose to do less of it. The higher the tax rate, the greater the shift away the activity. If taxpayers can easily escape the tax by altering their behavior (perhaps by shifting to substitutes), the tax base will shrink significantly as rates are increased. This erosion in the tax base in response to higher rates means that an increase in tax rates will generally lead to a less-than-proportional increase in tax revenue.

Economist Arthur Laffer popularized the idea that, beyond some point, higher tax rates will shrink the tax base so much that tax revenue will actually begin to decline when tax rates are increased. The curve illustrating the relationship between tax rates and tax revenues is called the **Laffer curve**. **Exhibit 9** illustrates the concept of the Laffer curve as it applies to income taxes. Obviously, tax revenue would be zero if the income tax rate were zero. What isn't so obvious is that tax revenue would also be zero (or at least very close to zero) if the tax rate were 100 percent. Confronting a 100 percent tax rate, most individuals would go fishing—or find something else to do rather than engage in taxable productive activity, since the 100 percent tax rate would eliminate all personal reward derived from earning taxable income. Why work when you have to give every penny of your earnings to the government?

As tax rates are reduced from 100 percent, the incentive to work and earn taxable income increases, income expands, and tax revenue rises. Similarly, as tax rates increase

Laffer curve
A curve illustrating the relationship between the tax rate and tax revenues. Tax revenues will be low at both very high and very low tax rates. When tax rates are quite high, lowering them can increase tax revenue.

EXHIBIT 9
Laffer Curve

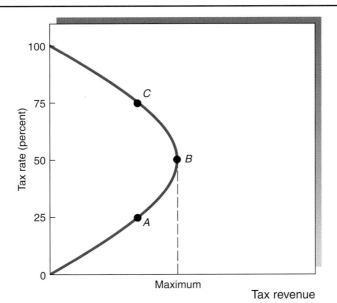

Because taxing an activity affects the amount of it people will do, a change in tax rates will not lead to a proportional change in tax revenues. As the Laffer curve indicates, beyond some point (*B*), an increase in tax rates will cause tax revenues to fall. At high tax rates, revenue can be increased by lowering tax rates. The tax rate that maximizes tax revenue is higher than the ideal tax rate for the economy as a whole because of the large deadweight loss of taxation as tax rates increase toward point *B*.

from zero, tax revenue expands. Clearly, at some rate greater than zero but less than 100 percent, tax revenue will be maximized (point *B* in Exhibit 9). This is not to imply that the tax rate that maximizes revenue is the ideal, or optimal, tax rate from the standpoint of the economy as a whole. Although it might be the tax rate that generates the most revenue for government, we must also consider the welfare reductions imposed on individuals by the deadweight loss created by the tax. As rates are increased and the maximum revenue point (*B*) is approached, relatively large tax rate increases will be necessary to expand tax revenue by even a small amount. In this range, the deadweight loss of taxation in the form of reductions in gains from trade will be exceedingly large relative to the additional tax revenue. Thus, the ideal tax rate will be well below the rate that maximizes revenue.

The Laffer curve shows that it is important to distinguish between changes in tax rates and changes in tax revenues. Higher rates will not always lead to more revenue for the government. Similarly, lower rates will not always lead to less revenue. When tax rates are already high, a rate reduction may increase tax revenues. Correspondingly, increasing high tax rates may lead to less tax revenue.

Evidence from the sharp reduction in marginal tax rates imposed on those with high incomes during the 1980s supports the Laffer curve. The top marginal rate was reduced from 70 percent at the beginning of the decade to 33 percent by the end of the decade. A person in this tax bracket who used to bring home 30 cents for each additional dollar earned now was able to bring home 67 cents for each dollar earned. Focusing on this sharp reduction in the top marginal rate, critics charged that the tax cuts of the 1980s were a bonanza for the rich. When considering the validity of this charge, however, it is important to distinguish between tax rates and tax revenues. Even though the top rates were cut sharply, tax revenues and the share of the personal income tax paid by high-income earners actually rose as a result. During the decade, revenue collected from the top 1 percent of earners rose a whopping 51.4 percent (after adjusting for inflation). In 1980, 19 percent of the personal income tax was collected from the top 1 percent of earners. By 1990 at the

The Laffer Curve and Mountain-Climbing Deaths

The Laffer curve can be used to illustrate many other relationships besides just tax rates and tax revenues. Economists J. R. Clark and Dwight Lee have used it to analyze the relationship between the safety of mountain climbing and mountain-climbing deaths on Mt. McKinley, North America's highest peak. As the risk of dying from climbing Mt. McKinley fell due to greater search-and-rescue efforts by National Park personnel, the number of people seeking to "conquer the mountain" rose significantly. The increase in the number of climbers attempting to conquer the mountain offset the lower risk, leading to a Laffer curve–type relationship. In other words, greater search-and-rescue efforts led to a *higher* number of total deaths on the mountain.

Let's look at the problem numerically. Assume that if the probability of death from an attempted climb were 90 percent, only 100 people would attempt to climb the mountain each year, leading to an annual death rate of 90. Now suppose that greater search-and-rescue efforts lower the probability of death to 50 percent. Because incentives matter, the increased safety will result in an increase in the number of people attempting to climb the mountain. Suppose

that the number of climbers increases from 100 to 200. With 200 climbers and a 50 percent probability of death, the annual number of fatalities would increase to 100, 10 more than before rescue efforts were improved. The total number of mountain-climbing deaths is actually lowest when there is both a very high and a very low probability of death—just as the Laffer curve predicts. The number of deaths is largest in the middle probability ranges. Making a very risky mountain safer can therefore result in more rather than fewer fatalities.

Clark and Lee have also explored a similar relationship between average lengths of prison sentences and total prison space occupied. Other economists have explored the Laffer curve relationship between the minimum-wage and the earnings of minimum-wage workers, as well as the regulatory costs of protecting endangered species and the habitat acres available to them.[1]

---

[1]See J. R. Clark and Dwight R. Lee, "Too Safe to Be Safe: Some Implications of Short- and Long-Run Rescue Laffer Curves," *Eastern Economic Journal* 23 no. 2 (Spring 1997): 127–37; Russell S. Sobel, "Theory and Evidence on the Political Economy of the Minimum Wage," *Journal of Political Economy* 107 no. 4 (August 1999): 761–85; and Richard L. Stroup, "The Endangered Species Act: The Laffer Curve Strikes Again," *The Journal of Private Enterprise*, vol. XIV (Special Issue 1998): 48–62.

---

lower tax rates, the top 1 percent of earners accounted for more than 25 percent of income tax revenues. The top 10 percent of earners paid just over 49 percent of total income taxes in 1980, but by 1990 the share paid by these earners had risen to 55 percent. Thus, the reduction in the exceedingly high rates increased the revenue collected from high-income taxpayers.

THE IMPACT OF A SUBSIDY

Subsidy
A payment the government makes to either the buyer or seller, usually on a per-unit basis, when a good or service is purchased or sold.

The supply and demand framework can also be used to analyze the impact of a government **subsidy**. A subsidy is a payment to either the buyer or seller of a good or service, usually on a per-unit basis. Subsidies are often granted in an effort to help buyers afford a good or service, or to increase the profitability of producers in an industry. As we have seen in other cases, however, the effect of a government program often differs substantially from its original intent. Because prices change when subsidies are imposed (just as when taxes are imposed), the benefit of a subsidy can be partially, or totally, shifted from buyer to seller, or vice versa.

Suppose that the government, in an effort to make textbooks more affordable, gives college students (buyers) a $20 subsidy for each book they buy. **Exhibit 10** shows the effect of the program. Before the subsidy was instituted, 100 million textbooks were sold each year at an average price of $80 per book. The $20-per-book subsidy paid to the buyers will increase demand by the amount of the subsidy (shift from D_1 to D_2). As the result

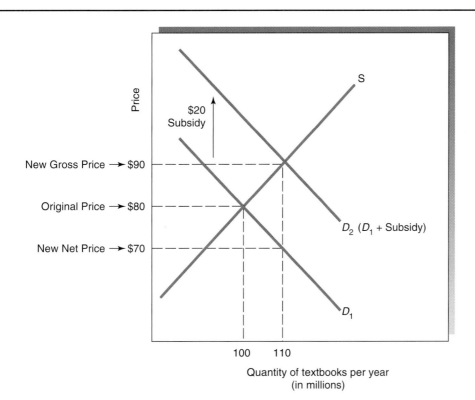

EXHIBIT 10
The Impact of a Subsidy
Granted to Buyers

When a $20-per-textbook subsidy is given to students, the demand curve for textbooks shifts vertically upward by the amount of the subsidy. The market price of textbooks rises from $80 to $90 (new gross price). With the $20 subsidy, buyers now pay a net price of $70 per textbook (the new $90 price minus the $20 subsidy), which is $10 less than before. Textbook buyers get only $10 of the benefit of the subsidy; the remaining $10 benefit accrues to the supply side of the market (sellers and resource suppliers) in the form of higher textbook prices. The distribution of the benefit from the subsidy between buyers and sellers would be the same, whether it was granted to buyers or sellers.

of the subsidy, the equilibrium price will increase from $80 to $90, and the total quantity purchased will expand to 110 million textbooks per year.

The subsidy program reduces the students' out-of-pocket cost of a textbook (from $80 to $70), but the net gain to them is less than the amount of the subsidy. Why? Even though the textbook subsidy is granted to buyers, substantial benefits also accrue to sellers. Because the subsidy program increases the demand for textbooks, pushing their price upward by $10, half of the benefits are captured by sellers (including resource suppliers like copy editors, authors, and paper suppliers).

Alternatively, if textbook suppliers had been granted a $20 payment from the government for each textbook sold, the supply curve would have shifted downward by the amount of the subsidy. This would cause the market price of textbooks to decline to $70. In this case, buyers pay $10 less than before the subsidy program, while the sellers receive $10 more (the sellers now get $90 for each book sold—the $70 market price plus the $20 government subsidy). Just like a tax, a subsidy results in the same outcome, regardless of whether the subsidy is granted to buyers or sellers.

Elasticity and the Benefit of Government Subsidy Programs

In this example, the benefit of the $20-per-textbook subsidy was split evenly between buyers and sellers. However, the actual distribution of this benefit will depend on the elasticities of supply and demand—just as it does with a tax. The benefit of the subsidy will always be shifted toward the more inelastic side of the market. Thus, the more inelastic the supply, the larger the share of the benefit that will accrue to sellers. On the other hand, the more inelastic the demand, the larger the share of the benefit that will accrue to buyers. Using our earlier examples from the section on taxation, consumers would be the main beneficiary of a subsidy on gasoline (a good for which the demand is relatively inelastic, and supply elastic), while suppliers would be the main beneficiary of a subsidy on luxury boats (a good for which demand is relatively elastic, and supply inelastic). Economic analysis indicates that the true benefit of a subsidy will: (1) be the same regardless of whether the subsidy is granted to the buyers or sellers in a market, and (2) will depend on the elasticities of supply and demand.

The Cost of Government Subsidy Programs

Policy makers and citizens alike often complain that the cost of government subsidy programs almost invariably exceeds initial projections. One reason for this is the increase in the quantity of the good purchased resulting from the subsidy. Prior to the enactment of the textbook subsidy, 100 million textbooks were sold annually. With a subsidy of $20 per textbook, one might be inclined to think that the annual cost of the program will be $2 billion ($20 × 100 million). This figure, however, will underestimate the true cost. Once the subsidy is in place, textbook sales will increase to 110 million, driving the overall cost of the program up to $2.2 billion ($20 × 110 million).

Furthermore, the expenditures on the subsidies will understate their total costs. To finance the subsidies, the government will have to raise the funds through taxation. A subsidy granted in one market will require taxation in other markets. As we have previously discussed, the taxes will generate a deadweight loss over and above the revenues transferred to the government. This excess burden is also a cost of the subsidy payments.

Real-World Subsidy Programs

The United States has a vast array of subsidy programs. Spending on these programs and the taxes that finance them are major items in the government budget. Some subsidy programs, such as Medicare and food stamps, provide payments to buyers. Others, such as the subsidies to the arts, public broadcasting, and sports stadiums, are directed toward suppliers. As we discussed, however, the party granted the subsidy may not be the one who captures the larger share of the actual benefit from the subsidy.

Still other subsidy programs are combined with price controls. Many agriculture subsidies fall into this category. The government fixes the prices of products like wheat, corn, cotton, and tobacco above the market equilibrium. To maintain the above-equilibrium price, the government purchases any amount produced that cannot be sold at the artificially high price. The government also restricts the acreage farmers are permitted to plant for these crops. If it were not for the planting restrictions, huge surpluses of these products would develop.

Sometimes government subsidies are granted only to a select group, or subset, of buyers (or sellers). Consider the structure of health-care subsidies in the United States. The Medicare program subsidizes the health-care purchases of senior citizens, and the Medicaid program provides subsidies to low-income households. These subsidies increase the demand for health care and drive up the prices of medical service for all consumers, including those ineligible for either program. In cases where only some of the buyers in a market are subsidized, groups that are ineligible for the subsidies will generally be harmed because they will have to pay higher prices for the good or service than they would otherwise have to, even though they do not receive a subsidy.

Subsidy programs are often highly complex, and it is sometimes difficult to determine whom they really benefit. As we proceed, we will analyze several of these programs in more detail. The supply and demand model presented here will facilitate our analysis.

LOOKING AHEAD

This chapter focused on how government-mandated price controls, taxes, subsidies, and prohibitions affect market outcomes. The next two chapters will apply the basic tools of economics to the political process more generally. In the chapters that follow, we will consider when intervention by the government is likely to enhance the well-being of citizens, and when it is likely to make them worse off. We will also analyze how the political process works and explain why it is sometimes a source of economic inefficiency.

! KEY POINTS

▼ Resource markets and product markets are closely linked. A change in one will generally result in changes in the other.

▼ Legally imposed price ceilings result in shortages, and legally imposed price floors will cause surpluses. Both also cause other harmful secondary effects. Rent controls, for example, will lead to shortages, less investment, poor maintenance, and deterioration in the quality of rental housing.

▼ The minimum wage is a price floor for low-skilled labor. It increases the earnings of some low-skilled workers but also reduces employment and leads to fewer training opportunities and nonwage job benefits for other low-skilled workers.

▼ Because black markets operate outside the legal system, they are often characterized by deception, fraud, and the use of violence as a means of enforcing contracts. A legal system that provides secure private-property rights and unbiased enforcement of contracts enhances the operation of markets.

▼ The division of the actual tax burden between buyers and sellers is determined by the relative elasticities of demand and supply rather than on whom the tax is legally imposed.

▼ In addition to the cost of the tax revenue transferred to the government, taxes will reduce the level of the activity taxed, eliminate some gains from trade, and thereby impose an excess burden, or deadweight loss.

▼ As tax rates increase, the size of the tax base will shrink. Initially, rates and revenues will be directly related—revenues will expand as rates increase. However, as higher and higher rates are imposed, eventually an inverse relation will develop—revenues will decline as rates are increased further. The Laffer curve illustrates this pattern.

▼ The division of the benefit from a subsidy is determined by the relative elasticities of demand and supply rather than to whom the subsidy is actually paid.

? CRITICAL ANALYSIS QUESTIONS

*1. How will a substantial increase in demand for housing affect the wages and employment of carpenters, plumbers, and electricians?

2. Suppose that college students in your town persuaded the town council to enact a law setting the maximum price for rental housing at $200 per month. Will this help or hurt college students who rent housing? In your answer, address how this price ceiling will affect (a) the quality of rental housing, (b) the amount of rental housing available, (c) the incentive of landlords to maintain their properties, (d) the amount of racial, gender, and other types of discrimination in the local rental housing market, (e) the ease with which students will be able to find housing, and finally, (f) whether a black market for housing would develop.

3. What is the difference between a price ceiling and a price floor? What will happen if a price ceiling is imposed below the market equilibrium? If a price ceiling for a good is set below the market equilibrium, what will happen to the quality and future availability of the good? Explain.

*4. To be meaningful, a price ceiling must be below the market price. Conversely, a meaningful price floor must be above the market price. What impact will a meaningful price ceiling have on the quantity exchanged? What impact will a meaningful price floor have on the quantity exchanged? Explain.

5. Congress recently passed a new program that will subsidize the purchase of prescription drugs by the elderly. What impact will this program have on the demand for and price of prescription drugs? How will people who are not elderly be affected by this program? Explain.

*6. Analyze the impact of an increase in the minimum wage from the current level to $10 per hour. How would the following be affected?
   a. Employment of people previously earning less than $10 per hour
   b. The unemployment rate of teenagers
   c. The availability of on-the-job training for low-skilled workers
   d. The demand for high-skilled workers who are good substitutes for low-skilled workers

7. What is a black market? What are some of the main differences in how black markets operate relative to legal markets?

8. How do you think the markets for organ donation and child adoption would be affected if they were made fully legal with a well-functioning price mechanism? What would be the advantages and disadvantages relative to the current system?

9. What is meant by the incidence of a tax? Explain why the statutory and actual incidence of a tax can be different.

10. What conditions must be met for buyers to bear the full burden of a tax? What conditions would cause sellers to bear the full burden? Explain.

*11. What is the nature of the deadweight loss accompanying taxes? Why is it often referred to as an "excess burden"?

12. The demand and supply curves for unskilled labor in a market are given in the accompanying table.
   a. Find the equilibrium wage and number of workers hired.
   b. Suppose that a new law is passed requiring employers to pay an unemployment insurance tax of $1.50 per hour for every employee. What happens to the equilibrium wage rate and number of workers hired? How is this tax burden distributed between employers and workers?

   c. Now suppose that, rather than being paid by employers, the tax must be paid by workers. How does this affect the equilibrium wage rate and number of workers hired? How is this tax burden distributed between employers and workers?
   d. Does it make a difference who is statutorily liable for the tax?

Demand		Supply	
Wage	Quantity Demanded	Wage	Quantity Supplied
$6.50	1,000	$6.50	1,900
$6.00	1,200	$6.00	1,800
$5.50	1,400	$5.50	1,700
$5.00	1,600	$5.00	1,600
$4.50	1,800	$4.50	1,500
$4.00	2,000	$4.00	1,400

13. Currently, the Social Security payroll tax is legally imposed equally on workers and employers: 7.65 percent for employees and 7.65 percent for employers. Show this graphically, being careful to distinguish between the total cost to the employer of hiring a worker, the employee's gross wage, and the employee's net wage. Show how the outcome would differ if all 15.3 percent were imposed on the employee or if all 15.3 percent were imposed on the employer.

*14. Suppose Congress passes legislation requiring that businesses employing workers with three or more children pay these employees at least $10 per hour. How would this legislation affect the employment level of low-skilled workers with three or more children? Do you think some workers with large families might attempt to conceal the fact? Why?

15. "We should impose a 20 percent luxury tax on expensive automobiles (those with a sales price of $50,000 or more) in order to collect more tax revenue from the wealthy." Will the burden of the proposed tax fall primarily on the wealthy? Why or why not?

*16. Should policy makers seek to set the tax on an economic activity at a rate that will maximize the revenue derived from the tax? Why or why not? Explain.

*17. During the summer of 2001, the combination of city and state taxes on cigarettes sold in New York City rose from $1.19 to more than $3.00 per pack. How will this tax increase affect (a) the quantity of cigarettes sold in New York City, (b) the revenue derived by the city and state from the tax, (c) the Internet purchases of cigarettes by New Yorkers, and (d) the incidence of smoking by New Yorkers?

*Asterisk denotes questions for which answers are given in Appendix B.

Difficult Cases for the Market, and the Role of Government

CHAPTER

5

Chapter Focus

- What is economic efficiency and how can it be used to evaluate markets?

- Why is it generally undesirable to pursue any goal to perfection?

- What is the role of government in a market economy?

- What are externalities? What are public goods?

- Why might markets fail to allocate goods and services efficiently?

- If the market has shortcomings, does this mean the government should intervene?

The principal justification for public policy intervention lies in the frequent and numerous shortcomings of market outcomes.

—Charles Wolf, Jr.[1]

[1]Charles Wolf, Jr., *Markets or Government* (Cambridge, Mass.: MIT Press, 1988), 17.

As we previously discussed, markets and government planning are the two main alternatives for the organization of economic activity. Chapters 3 and 4 introduced you to how markets work and demonstrated how the invisible hand of the market process directs the self-interest of individuals toward activities in the best interest of society. Throughout, we noted that some qualifications were in order, in terms of both the "rules of the game" that must be in place for markets to work well and the existence of special cases, in which the invisible hand might not function effectively. In this chapter, we turn our attention to discussing these potential problem areas for the market and consider their implications with regard to the role of government. In the following chapter, we will analyze how the political process works more directly. ■

A CLOSER LOOK AT ECONOMIC EFFICIENCY

Economic efficiency
A situation that occurs when (1) all activities generating more benefit than cost are undertaken, and (2) no activities are undertaken for which the cost exceeds the benefit.

Economists use the standard of **economic efficiency** to assess the desirability of economic outcomes. We briefly introduced the concept in Chapter 3. We now want to explore it in more detail. The central idea of economic efficiency is straightforward. For any given level of cost, we want to obtain the largest possible benefit. Alternatively, we want to obtain any particular benefit for the least possible cost. Economic efficiency means getting the most value from the available resources—making the largest pie from the available set of ingredients, so to speak.

Economists acknowledge that individuals generally do not regard the efficiency of the entire economy as a primary goal for themselves. Rather, each person is interested in enlarging the size of his or her own slice. But if resources are used more efficiently, the overall size of the pie will be larger, and therefore, at least potentially, *everyone* could have a larger slice. For an outcome to be consistent with ideal economic efficiency, two conditions are necessary:

Rule 1. *Undertaking an economic action is efficient if it produces more benefits than costs.* To satisfy economic efficiency, all actions generating more benefits than costs must be undertaken. Failure to undertake all such actions implies that a potential gain has been forgone.

Rule 2. *Undertaking an economic action is inefficient if it produces more costs than benefits.* To satisfy economic efficiency, no action that generates more costs than benefits should be undertaken. When such counterproductive actions are taken, society is worse off because even better alternatives were forgone.

Economic efficiency results only when both of these conditions have been met. *Either failure to undertake an efficient action (Rule 1) or the undertaking of an inefficient action (Rule 2) will result in economic inefficiency.* To illustrate, consider **Exhibit 1**, which shows the benefits and costs associated with expanding the amount of any particular activity. We have avoided using a specific example here to ensure you understand the general idea of efficiency without linking it to a specific application. As we will show, the concept has wide-ranging applications—from the evaluation of government policy to how long you choose to brush your teeth in the morning.[2]

In Exhibit 1, the marginal benefit curve shows the additional benefit associated with expanding the activity. The marginal cost curve shows the cost—including any opportu-

---

[2]Note to students who may pursue advanced study in economics: Using the concept of efficiency to compare alternative policies typically requires that the analyst estimate costs and benefits that are difficult or impossible to measure. Costs and benefits are the values of opportunities forgone or accepted by individuals, *as evaluated by those individuals.* Then these costs and benefits must be added up across all individuals and compared. But does a dollar's gain for one individual really compensate for a dollar's sacrifice by another? Some economists simply reject the validity of making such comparisons. They say that neither the estimates by the economic analyst of subjectively determined costs and benefits nor the adding up of these costs and benefits across individuals is meaningful. Their case may be valid, but most economists today nevertheless use the concept of efficiency as we present it. No other way to use economic analysis to compare policy alternatives has been found.

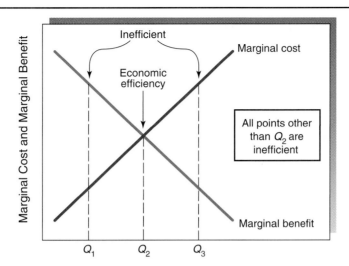

EXHIBIT 1
Economic Efficiency

As we use more time and resources to expand the level of an activity, the marginal benefits will generally decline and the marginal costs rise. From the viewpoint of efficiency, the activity should be expanded as long as the marginal benefits exceed the marginal cost. Thus, quantity Q_2 is the economically efficient level of this activity. Q_1 is inefficient because some production that could generate more benefits than costs is not undertaken. Q_3 is also inefficient because some units are produced even though their costs exceed the benefits they create. Thus, both too much and too little of an activity will result in inefficiency.

nity costs—of spending additional time, effort, and resources on the activity. At Q_1, the height of the marginal benefit curve exceeds the height of the marginal cost curve. Thus, at that point, the additional benefits of expanding the activity past Q_1 exceed the additional costs. According to Rule 1 of economic efficiency, we should continue to expand the activity until we reach Q_2. Beyond Q_2 (at Q_3, for example), the height of the marginal benefit curve is less than the height of the marginal cost curve. The additional benefits from expanding activity to that point are smaller than the additional costs. According to Rule 2, at Q_3, we have gone too far and should cut back on the activity. Q_2 is the only point consistent with both rules of economic efficiency.

IF IT'S WORTH DOING, IT'S WORTH DOING IMPERFECTLY

Eliminating pollution. Earning straight As. Being completely organized. Cleaning your apartment until it sparkles. Making automobiles completely safe. Making airplanes fully secure against terrorist attacks. All of these are worthwhile goals, right? Well, they are until you consider the costs of actually achieving them. The heading for this section is, of course, a play on the old saying, "If it's worth doing, it's worth doing to the best of your ability." Economics suggests, however, that this is not a sensible guideline. At some point, the gains from doing something even better will not be worth the cost. It will make more sense to stop short of perfection.

Exhibit 1 can also be used to illustrate this point. As more resources are dedicated to an activity, the marginal improvements (benefits) will become smaller and smaller, while the marginal costs will rise. The optimal time and effort put into the activity will be achieved at Q_2, and this will nearly always be well below one's best effort. Note that inefficiency results when either too little (for example, Q_1) or too much (for example, Q_3) time and effort are put into the activity.

Do you make decisions this way? Last time you cleaned your car or apartment, why did you decide to leave some things undone? Once the most important areas were clean, you likely began to skip over other areas (like on top of the refrigerator or under the bed), figuring that the benefits of cleaning these areas were simply not worth the cost. Very few

ECONOMICS AT THE MOVIES

Along Came Polly (2004)

Ben Stiller and Jennifer Aniston struggle to find the efficient (optimal) amount of organization in their lives. In one scene they use a knife to destroy pillows after Aniston convinces Stiller that the eight minutes a day he spends arranging decorative pillows on his bed (that nobody else sees) isn't worth the effort. In the next scene, Aniston's inefficiently low level of organization is illustrated when she spends a lot of time searching for her car keys. At the margin, Stiller's time spent arranging his pillows isn't generating enough benefit to justify the cost. Meanwhile, if Aniston were to spend just a little more time getting organized, the benefits to her would exceed the costs. The two of them would both be more efficient, and they'd probably get along better, too!

people live in a perfectly organized and clean house, wash their hands enough to prevent all colds, brush their teeth long enough to prevent all cavities, or make their home as safe as Fort Knox. They recognize that the benefit of perfection in these, and many other areas, is simply not worth the cost.

Economics is about trade-offs; it is possible to pursue even worthy activities beyond the level that is consistent with economic efficiency. People seem to be more aware of this in their personal decision making than when evaluating public policy. It is not uncommon to hear people say things like, "We ought to eliminate all pollution" or "No price is too high to save a life."

If we want to get the most out of our resources, we need to think about both marginal benefits and marginal costs and recognize that there are alternative ways of pursuing objectives. Consequently, economists do not ask whether eliminating pollution or saving lives is worth the cost *in terms of dollars* per se, but whether it is worth the cost in terms of giving up other things that could have been done with those dollars—the opportunity cost. Spending an extra $10 billion on worker safety requirements to save 100 lives isn't efficient if the funds could have been spent differently and saved 500 lives. Furthermore, it makes no more sense to have the government pursue perfection than it does for each of us personally to pursue it. Regardless of sector, achievement of perfection is virtually never worth the cost.

THINKING ABOUT THE ECONOMIC ROLE OF GOVERNMENT

For centuries, philosophers, economists, and other scholars have debated the proper role of government. While the debate continues, there is substantial agreement that at least two functions of government are legitimate: (1) protecting individuals and their property against invasions by others and (2) providing goods that cannot easily be provided through private markets. These two functions correspond to what Nobel laureate James Buchanan conceptualizes as the protective and productive functions of government.

Protective Function of Government

The most fundamental function of government is the protection of individuals and their property against acts of aggression. As John Locke wrote more than three centuries ago, individuals are constantly threatened by "the invasions of others." Therefore, each individual "is willing to join in society with others, who are already united, or have a mind to unite, for the mutual preservation of their lives, liberties, and estates."[3] ***The protective function of government involves the maintenance of a framework of security and order—an infrastructure of rules within which people can interact peacefully with one another.*** Protection of person and property is crucial. It entails providing police protection and prosecuting aggressors who take things that do not belong to them. It also involves providing for a national defense designed to protect against foreign invasions. The legal enforcement of contracts and rules against fraud are also central elements of the protective function. People and businesses that write bad checks, violate contracts, or knowingly supply others with false information, for example, are therefore subject to legal prosecution.

© BETTMANN/CORBIS

The English philosopher John Locke argued that people own themselves and, as a result of this self-ownership, they also own the fruits of their labor. Locke stressed that individuals are not subservient to governments. On the contrary, the role of governments is to protect the "natural rights" of individuals to their person and property. This view, also reflected in the "unalienable rights" section of the U.S. Declaration of Independence, is the basis for the protective function of government.

It is easy to see the economic importance of the protective function. When it is performed well, the property of citizens is secure, freedom of exchange is present, and contracts are legally enforceable. When people are assured that they will be able to enjoy the benefits of their efforts, they will be more productive. In contrast, when property rights are insecure and contracts unenforceable, productive behavior is undermined. Plunder, fraud, and economic chaos result. Governments set and enforce the "rules of the game" that enable markets to operate smoothly.

Productive Function of Government

The nature of some goods makes them difficult to provide through markets. Sometimes it is difficult to establish a one-to-one link between the payment and receipt of a good. If this link cannot be established, the incentive of market producers to supply these goods is weak. In addition, high transaction costs—particularly, the cost of monitoring use and collecting fees—can sometimes make it difficult to supply a good through the market. When either of these conditions is present, it may be more efficient for the government to supply the good and impose taxes on its citizens to cover the cost.

One of the most important productive functions of government is providing a stable monetary and financial environment. If markets are going to work well, individuals have to know the value of what they are buying or selling. For market prices to convey this information, a stable monetary system is needed. This is especially true for the many market exchanges that involve a time dimension. Houses, cars, consumer durables, land, buildings, equipment, and many other items are often paid for over a period of months or even years. When the purchasing power of money fluctuates wildly, previously determined prices do not represent their intended values. Under these circumstances, exchanges involving long-term commitments are hampered, and the smooth operation of markets is undermined.

The government's tax, spending, and monetary policies exert a powerful influence on the stability of the overall economy. If properly conducted, these policies contribute to economic stability, full and efficient utilization of resources, and stable prices. However, improper stabilization policies can cause massive unemployment, rapidly rising prices, or both. For those pursuing a course in macroeconomics, these issues will be central to that analysis.

[3]John Locke, *Treatise of Civil Government*, 1690, ed. Charles Sherman (New York: Appleton-Century-Crofts, 1937), 82.

POTENTIAL SHORTCOMINGS OF THE MARKET

As we previously discussed, the invisible hand of market forces generally gives resource owners and business firms a strong incentive to use their resources efficiently and undertake projects that create value. Will this always be true? The answer to this question is "No." There are four major factors that can undermine the invisible hand and reduce the efficiency of markets: (1) lack of competition, (2) externalities, (3) public goods, and (4) poorly informed buyers or sellers. We will now consider each of these factors and explain why they may justify government intervention.

Lack of Competition

Competition is vital to the proper operation of the pricing mechanism. The existence of competing buyers and sellers reduces the power of both to rig or alter the market in their own favor. Although competition is beneficial from a social point of view, individually each of us would prefer to be loosened from its grip. Students do not like stiff competitors in their social or romantic lives, at exam time, or when they're trying to get into graduate school. Buyers on eBay hope for few competing bidders so they can purchase the items they're bidding on at lower prices. Similarly, sellers prefer fewer competing sellers so they can sell at higher prices.

    Exhibit 2 illustrates how sellers can gain from restricting competition. In the absence of any restrictions on competition in the market, the price P_1 and output Q_1 associated with the competitive supply curve (S_1) will prevail. Here, Q_1 is the level of output consistent with economic efficiency. If a group of sellers is able to restrict competition, perhaps by forcing some firms out of the market and preventing new firms from entering, the group would be able to gain by raising the price of the product. This is illustrated by the price P_2 and output Q_2 associated with the restricted supply (S_2). Even though the output is smaller, the total revenue (price P_2 times quantity Q_2) derived by the sellers at the restricted output level is greater than at the competitive price P_1. Clearly, the sellers gain because, at the higher price, they are being paid more to produce less.

    The restricted output level, however, is clearly less efficient. At the competitive output level Q_1, all units that were valued more than their cost are produced and sold. But this is not the case at Q_2. The additional units between Q_2 and Q_1 are valued more than their cost. Nonetheless, they will not be produced if suppliers are able to limit competition and restrict output. When competition is absent, there is a potential conflict between the interests of sellers and the efficient use of resources.

EXHIBIT 2
Lack of Competition and Problems for the Market

If a group of sellers can restrict competition, it may be able to gain by reducing supply (to S_2, for example) and raising the price (to P_2, for example) rather than charging the competitive market price of P_1. Under these circumstances, output will be less than the economically efficient level.

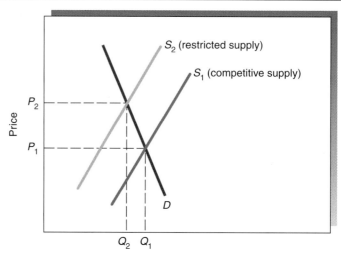

What can the government do to ensure that markets are competitive? The first guideline might be borrowed from the medical profession: Do no harm. *A productive government will refrain from using its powers to impose licenses, discriminatory taxes, price controls, tariffs, quotas, and other entry and trade restraints that lessen the intensity of competition.* In the vast majority of markets, sellers will find it difficult or impossible to limit the entry of rival firms (including rival producers from other countries). The only means by which they can limit competition is lobbying the government to impose restrictions or controls that limit competition on their behalf. In the interest of efficiency, governments should refrain from giving in to these demands.

When entering a market is very costly and there are only a few existing sellers, it may be possible for these sellers by themselves to restrict competition. In an effort to deal with cases like this, the United States has enacted a series of "antitrust laws," most notably the Sherman Antitrust Act (1890) and the Clayton Act (1914), making it illegal for firms to collude or attempt to monopolize a market.

For the most part, economists favor the general principle of government action to ensure and promote competitive markets. There is considerable debate, however, about the effectiveness of actual government policy in this area. Many economists believe that, by and large, government policy in this area has been ineffective. Others stress that government policies have often been misused to actually limit competition, rather than promote it. These laws have been used as a basis for restricting entry into markets, protecting existing producers from competitors, and limiting price competition. This is counterproductive. For those taking a microeconomics course, noncompetitive markets and related policy alternatives will be analyzed in greater detail later.

Externalities—A Failure to Account for All Costs and Benefits

When property rights are unclear or poorly enforced, the actions of an individual or group may "spill over" onto others and thereby affect their well-being without their consent. These spillover effects are called **externalities.** You are probably familiar with externalities. For example, when your neighbor's loud stereo makes it hard for you to study, you are experiencing an externality firsthand. Although your neighbors do not have a right to come in to your apartment and turn on your stereo, they do have a right to listen to their own stereo, and their listening may interfere with the quietness in your apartment. Their actions impose a cost on you, and they also raise an issue of property rights. Do your neighbors have a property right to play their stereo as loudly as they please? Or do you have a property right to quietness in your own apartment? When questions like these arise, how should the boundaries of property rights be determined, and what steps should be taken to ensure adequate enforcement? Although the volume of your neighbor's stereo may not be a major economic issue, it nonetheless illustrates the nature of the problems that arise when property rights are unclear and externalities are present.

The spillover effects may either impose a cost or create a benefit for third parties—people not directly involved in the transaction, activity, or exchange. Economists use the term **external cost** to describe a situation in which the spillover effects harm third parties. If the spillover effects enhance the welfare of the third parties, an **external benefit** is present. We will analyze both external costs and external benefits and consider why both of them can lead to problems.

External Costs   Economists worry about external costs because they may result in economic inefficiency. For example, resources may be used to produce goods that are valued less than their production costs, including the costs imposed on the nonconsenting third parties. Consider the production of paper. The firms in the market operate mills and purchase labor, trees, and other resources to produce the paper. But they also emit pollutants into the atmosphere that impose costs on residents living around the mills. The pollutants cause paint on buildings to deteriorate more rapidly. They make it difficult for some people to breathe normally, and perhaps cause other health hazards. If the residents living near a pulp mill can prove they have been harmed, they could take the mill to court and force the paper producer to cover the cost of their damages. But it might

Externalities
Spillover effects of an activity that influence the well-being of nonconsenting third parties.

External costs
Spillover effects that reduce the well-being of nonconsenting third parties.

External benefits
Spillover effects that generate benefits for nonconsenting third parties.

be difficult to prove that they were harmed and that the pulp mill is responsible for the damage. As you can see, the residents' property rights to clean air may be difficult to enforce, particularly if there are many parties emitting pollutants into the air.

If the residents are unable to enforce their property rights, the production of paper will generate an external cost that will be ignored by markets. **Exhibit 3** illustrates the implications of these external costs within the supply and demand framework. As the result of the external cost, the market supply curve S_1 will understate the true cost of producing paper. It reflects only the cost actually paid by the firms, and ignores the uncompensated costs imposed on the nearby residents. Under these circumstances, the firm will expand output to Q_1 (the intersection of the demand curve D and supply curve S_1) and the market price P_1 will emerge. Is this price and output consistent with economic efficiency? The answer is clearly "No." If all of the costs of producing the paper, including those imposed on third parties, were taken into account, the supply curve S_2 would result. From an efficiency standpoint, only the smaller quantity Q_2 should be produced. The units beyond Q_2 on out to Q_1 cost more than their value to consumers. People would be better off if the resources used to produce those units (beyond Q_2) were used to produce other things. Nonetheless, profit-maximizing firms will expand output into this range. Thus, when external costs are present, the market supply curve will understate production costs, and output will be expanded beyond the quantity consistent with economic efficiency. Moreover, resources for which property rights are poorly enforced will be overutilized and sometimes polluted. This is often the case with air and water when the property rights to these resources are poorly enforced.

What should be done about external costs? These costs arise because property rights are poorly defined or imperfectly enforced. Initially, therefore, it makes sense to think seriously about how property rights might be better defined and enforced. However, the nature of some goods will make the defining and enforcement of property rights extremely difficult. This will certainly be the case for resources like clean air and many fish species in the ocean. In cases that involve a relatively small number of people, the parties involved may be able to agree to rules and establish procedures that will minimize the external effects. For example, property owners around a small lake will generally be able to control access to the lake and prevent each other, as well as outsiders, from polluting or overfishing the lake.

However, in cases that involve large numbers of people, the transaction costs of arriving at an agreement will be prohibitively high, so it is unrealistic to expect that private contracts among the parties will handle the situation satisfactorily. For example, this will be the case when a large number of automobiles and firms emit pollutants into the atmosphere. In these "large number" cases, government regulations may be the best approach. At this

EXHIBIT 3
External Costs and Output That Is Greater Than the Efficient Level

When an activity such as paper production imposes external costs on nonconsenting third parties, these costs will not be registered by the market supply curve (S_1). As a result, output will be beyond the economically efficient level. The units between Q_2 and Q_1 will be produced, even though their cost exceeds the value they provide to consumers.

GETTY IMAGES

External costs resulting from poorly defined and enforced property rights underlie the problems of excessive air and water pollution.

point, we want you to see the nature of the problem when external costs are present. As we proceed, we will analyze a number of problems in this area in detail and consider alternative approaches that might improve economic efficiency.

External Benefits   As we mentioned, sometimes the actions of individuals and firms generate external benefits for others. The homeowner who keeps a house in good condition and maintains a neat lawn improves the beauty of the entire community. A flood-control dam built by upstream residents for their benefit might also generate gains for those who live downstream. Scientific theories benefit their authors, but the knowledge can also help others who did not contribute to the development of them.

From the standpoint of efficiency, why might external benefits be a problem? Here, inefficiency may arise because potential producers are unable to capture fully the benefits that their actions create for others. Suppose a pharmaceutical company develops a vaccine protecting users against a contagious virus or some other communal disease. Of course, the vaccine can easily be marketed to users who will benefit directly from it. However, because of the communal nature of the virus, as more and more people take the vaccine, nonusers will also be less likely to get the flu. But it will be very difficult for the pharmaceutical companies to capture any of the benefits derived by the nonusers. As a result, too little of the vaccine may be supplied.

Exhibit 4 illustrates the impact of external benefits like those generated by the vaccine within the framework of supply and demand. The market demand curve reflects the benefits derived by the users of the vaccine, while the supply curve reflects the opportunity cost of providing it. Market forces result in an equilibrium price of P_1 and output of Q_1. Is this outcome consistent with economic efficiency? Again, the answer is "No." The market demand curve D_1 will register only the benefits derived by the users. Those benefits that accrue to nonusers, who are now less likely to contract the flu, will not be taken into account by decision makers. The producer of the vaccine makes it more likely that these people will not get sick, but it doesn't derive any benefit (sales revenue) from having done so. Thus, market demand D_1 understates the total benefits derived from the production and use of the vaccine. Demand D_2 provides a measure of these total benefits, including those that accrue to the nonusers. The units between Q_1 and Q_2 are valued more highly than what it costs to produce them. Nonetheless, they will not be supplied because the suppliers of the vaccine will be unable to capture the benefits that accrue to the nonusers. Thus, when external benefits are present, market forces may supply less than the amount consistent with economic efficiency.

EXHIBIT 4
**External Benefits and
Output That Is Less
Than the Efficient Level**

A vaccine that protects users against the flu will also help nonusers by making it less likely that they will catch it. But this benefit will not be registered by the market demand curve (D_1). In cases where external benefits like this are present, output will be less than the economically efficient level. Even though the units between Q_1 and Q_2 generate more benefits than costs, they will not be supplied because sellers are unable to capture the value of these external benefits.

While external benefits are a potential source of inefficiency, entrepreneurs have a strong incentive to figure out ways to capture more fully the gains their actions generate for others. In some cases, they are able to capture what would otherwise be external benefits by extending the scope of the firm. The accompanying Application in Economics, "Capturing External Benefits: The Case of Walt Disney World," provides an interesting and informative illustration of this point.

Public Goods and Why They Pose a Problem for the Market

Public goods
Goods for which rivalry among consumers is absent and exclusion of nonpaying customers is difficult.

What are public goods? **Public goods** have two distinguishing characteristics: (1) nonrivalry in consumption and (2) nonexcludability. Let's take a closer look at both of these characteristics.

Nonrivalry in consumption means that making the good available to one consumer does not reduce its availability to others. In fact, providing it to one person simultaneously makes it available to other consumers. Thus, a consumer has no reason to compete with others for the good. A radio broadcast signal provides an example. The same signal can be shared by everyone within the listening range. Having additional listeners tune in does not detract from the availability of the signal. Clearly, most goods do not have this shared consumption characteristic, but are instead rivals-in-consumption. For example, two individuals cannot simultaneously consume the same pair of jeans. Further, if one person purchases a pair of jeans, there is one less pair available for someone else.

The second characteristic of a public good—nonexcludability—means that it is impossible (or at least very costly) to exclude nonpaying customers from receiving the good. Suppose an antimissile system were being built around the city in which you live. How could some people in the city be protected by the system and others excluded? Most people will realize there is no way the system can protect their neighbors from incoming missiles without providing similar protection to other residents. Thus, the services of the antimissile system have the nonexcludability characteristic.

It is important to note that it is the characteristic of the good, not the sector in which it is produced, that determines whether it qualifies as a public good. There is a tendency to think that if a good is provided by the government, then it is a public good. This is not the case. Many of the goods provided by governments clearly do not have the characteristics

APPLICATIONS IN ECONOMICS

Capturing External Benefits: The Case of Walt Disney World

MATT STROSHANE / BLOOMBERG NEWS / LANDOV

Sometimes projects that generate more benefits than cost are still unattractive because a substantial share of the benefits is external and therefore difficult to capture. If an entrepreneur could figure out a way to capture more of these benefits, an otherwise unprofitable project might be transformed into a profitable one. Sometimes this can be done by extending the scope of a project.

The development of golf courses is an example. Because of the beauty and openness of the courses, many people find it attractive to live nearby. Thus, constructing a golf course typically generates an external benefit—an increase in the value of the nearby property. In recent years, golf course developers have figured out how to capture this benefit. Now, they typically purchase a large tract of land around the planned course *before it is built*. This places them in a position to resell the land at a higher price after the golf course has been completed and the surrounding land has increased in value. By extending the scope of their activities to include real estate as well as golf course development, they are able to capture what would otherwise be external benefits.

Florida's Walt Disney World is an interesting case study in entrepreneurial ingenuity designed to capture external benefits more fully. When Walt Disney developed Disneyland in California, the market value of the land in the immediate area soared as a result of the increase in demand for services (food, lodging, gasoline, and so on). Because the land in the area was owned by others, the developers of Disneyland were unable to capture these external benefits. In addition, Disney felt as if some of the adult nightclubs that had opened around his existing Disneyland park were imposing external costs on him by detracting from the family image his park was trying to attain.

Because of his experience with these externalities, when Walt Disney World was developed outside of Orlando, Florida, in the mid-1960s, Walt Disney purchased far more land than was needed for the amusement park. This enabled him to capture the increased land value surrounding his development (when he resold the land for a higher price), and reduce the negative externalities imposed on him via his control of the surrounding property.

The purchases were made as secretly as possible to prevent speculators from driving up the land prices if Disney's actions were detected. Disney even created a handful of smaller companies, with names like the Latin-American Development and Managers Corporation and the Reedy Creek Ranch Corporation, to purchase the land. After his first major land purchase of 12,400 acres, Walt Disney was at a meeting at which he was offered an opportunity to purchase an additional 8,500 acres. Walt Disney's assistant was rumored to have said, "But Walt, we already own 12,000 acres, enough to build the park." Disney replied, "How would you like to own 8,000 acres around our existing Disneyland facility right now?" His assistant immediately responded, "Buy it!"

After another major acquisition of 1,250 acres, Disney began concentrating on buying smaller land parcels around his main property. By June 1965, Disney had purchased 27,400 acres, or about 43 square miles—an area 150 times larger than his existing Disneyland park, and about twice as big as Manhattan. In October 1965, when an Orlando newspaper finally broke the story that Disney was behind the land purchases, the remaining land prices around his property jumped from $183 an acre to $1,000 an acre overnight. But by then, except for several small parcels he was unable to acquire, Walt Disney had purchased all of the land he wanted.

Florida eventually gave Walt Disney permission to create an autonomous Reedy Creek Improvement District, outside the authority of any local government in Florida. In a very real sense, Walt Disney World is a jurisdiction of its own, separate from any other local government authority. Because of this, Walt Disney World can write its own zoning

(continued)

(continued)

restrictions and building codes. It can also plan its own road-ways, lakes, security, sidewalks, airports, and recreational areas. Walt Disney World is able to provide goods and ser-vices like these—that might normally be considered public goods—by charging general admission fees to its park. This helped Disney overcome the potential free-rider problems sometimes associated with producing these goods.

Just as Disney expected, the value of the land surround-ing Walt Disney World soared as the demand for hotels, restaurants, and other businesses increased along with the development of the the amusement park. Through the years, the resale of land near the park has been a major source of revenue for the company. To a large degree, the success of the Disney Corporation reflects Walt Disney's entrepreneur-ial ability to deal with externality and public-good problems.

Free rider
A person who receives the benefit of a good without paying for it. Because of their nonexcludable nature, public goods are subject to free-rider problems.

of public goods. Medical services, education, mail delivery, trash collection, and electric-ity come to mind. Although these goods are often supplied by governments, they do not have either nonrivalry or nonexcludability characteristics. Thus, they are not public goods.

Why are public goods difficult for markets to allocate efficiently? The nonexcludabil-ity characteristic provides the answer. Since those who do not pay cannot be excluded, sellers are generally unable to establish a one-to-one link between the payment and receipt of these goods. Realizing they cannot be excluded, potential consumers have little incen-tive to pay for these goods. Instead, they have an incentive to become **free riders**, people who receive the benefits of the good without helping to pay for its cost. But, when a large number of people become free riders, not very much of the good is supplied. This is pre-cisely the problem: markets will tend to undersupply public goods, even when the popula-tion in aggregate values them highly relative to their cost.

Suppose national defense were provided entirely through the market. Would you vol-untarily help to pay for it? Your contribution would have little impact on the total supply of defense available to each of us, even if you made a large personal contribution. Many citizens, even though they might value defense highly, would become free riders, and few funds would be available to finance national defense.

For most goods, it is easy to establish a link between payment and receipt. If you do not pay for a gallon of ice cream, an automobile, a television set, a DVD player, and liter-ally thousands of other items, suppliers will not provide them to you. Thus, there are very few public goods. National defense is the classic example of a public good. Radio and TV signals, software programs, flood-control projects, mosquito abatement programs, and perhaps some scientific theories also have public good characteristics. But beyond this short list, it is difficult to think of additional goods that qualify.

Just because a good is a public good does not necessarily mean that markets will fail to supply it. When the benefit of producing these goods is high, entrepreneurs will attempt to find innovative ways to gain by overcoming the free-rider problem. For example, radio and television broadcasts, which have both of the public good characteristics, are still pro-duced well by the private sector. The free-rider problem is overcome through the use of advertising (which generates indirect revenue from listeners), rather than directly charging listeners. Private entrepreneurs have developed things like scrambling devices (so nonpay-ing customers can't tune into broadcasts free of charge), copy protection on DVDs, and tie-in purchases (for example, tying the purchase of a software instruction manual to the purchase of the software itself) to overcome the free-rider problem. The marketing of computer software provides an interesting illustration. Since the same software program can be copied without reducing the amount available, and it is costly to prevent consump-tion by nonpayers, software clearly has public good characteristics. Nonetheless, Bill Gates became the richest man in the world by producing and marketing it!

In spite of the innovative efforts of entrepreneurs, however, the quantity of public goods supplied strictly through market allocation might still be smaller than the quantity consistent with economic efficiency. This creates a potential opportunity for government action to improve the efficiency of resource allocation.

Potential Information Problems

Like other goods, information is scarce. Thus, when making purchasing decisions, people are sometimes poorly informed about the price, quality, durability, and side effects of alternative products. Imperfect knowledge is not the fault of the market. In fact, the market provides consumers with a strong incentive to acquire information. If they mistakenly purchase a "lemon," they will suffer the consequences. Furthermore, sellers have a strong incentive to inform consumers about the benefits of their products, especially in comparison to competing products. However, circumstances will influence the incentive structure confronted by both buyers and sellers.

The consumer's information problem is minimal if the item is purchased regularly. Consider the purchase of soap. There is little cost associated with trying different brands. Since soap is a regularly purchased product, trial and error is an economical means of determining which brand is most suitable to one's needs. Regularly purchased items such as toothpaste, most food products, lawn service, and gasoline provide additional examples of **repeat-purchase items**. When purchasing items like these, the consumer can use past experience to acquire accurate information and make wise decisions.

Repeat-purchase item
An item purchased often by the same buyer.

Furthermore, the sellers of repeat-purchase items also have a strong incentive to supply consumers with accurate information about them because failing to do so will adversely affect future sales. Because future demand is directly related to the satisfaction level of current customers, sellers of repeat-purchase items will want to help their customers make satisfying long-run choices. This helps harmonize the interests of buyers and sellers.

But harmony will not always occur. Conflicting interests, inadequate information, and unhappy customers can arise when goods are either (1) difficult to evaluate on inspection and seldom repeatedly purchased from the same producer, or (2) potentially capable of serious and lasting harmful side effects that cannot be predicted by a typical consumer. Under these conditions, consumers might make decisions they will later regret.

When customers are unable to distinguish between high-quality and low-quality goods, business entrepreneurs have an incentive to cut costs by reducing quality. Businesses that follow this course may survive and even prosper. Consider the information problem when an automobile is purchased. Are consumers capable of properly evaluating the safety equipment? Most are not. Of course, some consumers will seek the opinion of experts, but this information will be costly and difficult to evaluate. In this case, it might be more efficient to have the government regulate automobile safety and require certain safety equipment.

Similar issues arise with regard to product effectiveness. Suppose a new wonder drug promises to reduce the probability a person will be stricken by cancer or heart disease. Even if the product is totally ineffective, many consumers will waste their money trying it. Verifying the effectiveness of the drug will be a complicated and lengthy process. Consequently, it may be better to have experts certify its effectiveness. The federal Food and Drug Administration was established to perform this function. However, letting the experts decide is also a less than ideal solution. The certification process is likely to be costly and lengthy. As a result, the introduction of products that are effective may be delayed for years, and they are likely to be more costly than they would be otherwise.

Information as a Profit Opportunity

Consumers are willing to pay for information that will help them make better decisions. This presents a profit opportunity. *Entrepreneurial publishers and other providers of information help consumers find what they seek by offering product evaluations by experts.* For example, dozens of publications provide independent expert opinions about automobiles and computers at a low cost to potential purchasers. Laboratory test results and detailed product evaluations on a wide variety of goods are provided by *Consumer Reports, Consumer Research,* and other publications.

Franchises are another way entrepreneurs have responded to the need of consumers for more and better information. A **franchise** is a right or license granted to an individual

Franchise
A right or license granted to an individual to market a company's goods or services or use its brand name. The individual firms are independently owned but must meet certain conditions to continue to use the name.

to market a company's goods or services (or use their brand name). Fast-food restaurants like McDonald's, Wendy's, and Burger King are typically organized as franchises. The individual restaurants are independently owned, but the owner pays for the right to use the company name and must offer specific products and services in a manner specified by the franchiser. Franchises help give consumers reliable information. The tourist traveling through an area for the first time with very little time to search out alternatives may find that eating at a franchised restaurant and sleeping at a franchised motel are the cheapest ways to avoid annoying and costly mistakes that might come from patronizing an unknown local establishment. The franchiser sets the standards for all firms in the chain and establishes procedures, including continuous inspections designed to maintain the standards. Franchisers have a strong incentive to maintain their reputation for quality, because if it declines, their ability to sell new franchises and to collect ongoing franchise fees is adversely affected. Even though the tourist may visit a particular establishment only once, the franchise turns that visit into a "repeat purchase," since the reputation of the entire national franchise operation is at stake.

Similarly, advertising a brand name nationally puts the brand's reputation at stake each time a purchase is made. How much would the Coca-Cola Company pay to avoid the sale of a dangerous bottle of Coke? Surely, it would be a large sum. Interbrand, a branding consulting agency that evaluates and ranks the top brand names in the world, estimates that Coke's brand name is worth $67.4 billion. The value of that brand name is a hostage to quality control. The firm would suffer enormous damage if it failed to maintain the quality of its product. For example, in 2000 and 2001, Firestone's brand name suffered an immense reduction in value after only a few Firestone tires were suspected of being defective. Firestone is still attempting to recover from its loss in brand name value.

Enterprising entrepreneurs have found ways to assure buyers that products meet high standards of quality, even when the producer is small and not so well known. Consider the case of Best Western Motels.[4] Best Western owns no motels; however, building on the franchise idea, it publishes rules and standards with which motel owners must comply if they are to use the Best Western brand name and the reservation service that the company also operates. To protect its brand name, Best Western sends out inspectors to see that each Best Western Motel meets these standards. Every disappointed customer harms the reputation and reduces the value of the Best Western name, and reduces the willingness of motel owners to pay for use of the name. The standards are designed to keep customers satisfied. Even though each motel owner has only a relatively small operation, renting the Best Western name provides the small operator with the kind of international reputation formerly available only to large firms. In effect, Best Western acts as a regulator of all motels bearing its name. It profits by requiring efficient standards—those that produce maximum visitor satisfaction for every dollar spent by the motels utilizing the franchise name. As it does so, it helps eliminate problems in the market that result from imperfect information.

Underwriters Laboratories, Inc., is another example of private-sector regulation aimed at overcoming potential information problems. UL, as it is better known, is a private-sector corporation that has been testing and certifying products for more than 100 years based on its own set of quality standards. You have probably seen the UL mark on many of your household appliances. Sellers pay a fee to have UL evaluate their products for possible certification. The value of the UL brand depends on their careful evaluation of every product they certify. If UL allows defective products to carry its mark, its brand value will diminish.

Information published by reliable sources, franchising, and brand names can help consumers make better-informed decisions. Although these options are effective, they will not always provide an ideal solution. Government regulation may sometimes be able to improve the situation, but this, too, has its shortcomings. As with other things, there is no general solution to imperfect information problems.

---

[4]This section draws from Randall G. Holcombe and Lora P. Holcombe, "The Market for Regulation," *Journal of Institutional and Theoretical Economics* 142, no. 4 (1986): 684–96.

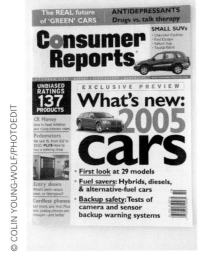

Brand names (like Coca-Cola), franchises (like McDonald's), consumer-ratings magazines (like *Consumer Reports*), and private-sector certification firms (like Underwriters Laboratories, Inc.), are ways the private sector helps buyers overcome potential information problems.

PULLING THINGS TOGETHER

Throughout this textbook, we have stressed that a sound legal system—one that protects individuals and their property and provides access to evenhanded courts for the enforcement of contracts and settlement of disputes—is vitally important for the smooth operation of markets. So, too, is a monetary regime that provides people with access to a sound currency—money that maintains its value across time periods. Beyond these functions, however, there is little justification for government action when there is reason to expect that markets will allocate resources efficiently. But a lack of competition, externalities, public goods, and information problems often pose challenges and sometimes undermine the efficient operation of markets. Market shortcomings due to these factors raise the possibility that government intervention beyond the protective function might improve things. But before jumping to that conclusion, we need better knowledge about how the political process works. We are now ready to move on to that topic.

LOOKING AHEAD

Political decision making is complex, but the tools of economics can enhance our understanding of how it works. This is the subject matter of the next chapter.

KEY POINTS

▼ Economists use the standard of economic efficiency to assess the desirability of economic outcomes. Efficiency requires both: (1) that all actions generating more benefit than cost be undertaken, and (2) that no actions generating more cost than benefit be undertaken.

▼ Although perfection is a noble goal, it is rarely worth achieving because additional time and resources devoted to an activity generally yield smaller and smaller benefits and cost more and more. Inefficiency can result when either too little or too much effort is put into an activity.

▼ Governments can enhance economic well-being by performing both protective and productive functions. The protective function involves (1) the protection of individuals and their property against aggression and (2) the provision of a legal system for the enforcement of contracts and settlement of disputes. The productive function of government can help people obtain goods that would be difficult to supply through markets.

▼ When markets fail to meet the conditions for ideal economic efficiency, the problem can generally be traced to one of four sources: absence of competition, externalities, public goods, or poor information.

▼ Externalities reflect a lack of fully defined and enforced property rights. When external costs are present, output can be too large—units are produced even though their costs exceed the benefits they generate. In contrast, external benefits can lead to an output that is too small—some units are not produced even though the benefits of doing so would exceed the cost.

▼ Public goods are goods for which (1) rivalry in consumption is absent and (2) it is difficult to exclude those who do not pay. Because of the difficulties involved in establishing a one-to-one link between payment and receipt of such goods, the market supply of public goods will often be less than the economically efficient quantity.

▼ Entrepreneurs in markets have an incentive to find solutions to each market problem, and new solutions are constantly being discovered. But problems remain that can potentially be improved through government action.

CRITICAL ANALYSIS QUESTIONS

*1. Why is it important for producers to be able to prevent nonpaying customers from receiving a good?

2. In response to the terrorist attacks of September 11, 2001, airline security screening has increased dramatically. As a result, travelers must now spend considerably more time being screened before flights. Would it make economic sense to devote enough resources to completely prevent any such future attacks? Why or why not?

3. What are the distinguishing characteristics of "public goods"? Give two examples of a public good. Why are public goods difficult for markets to allocate efficiently?

*4. Which of the following are public goods? Explain, using the definition of a public good.
   a. an antimissile system surrounding Washington, D.C.
   b. a fire department

   c. tennis courts
   d. Yellowstone National Park
   e. elementary schools

5. Explain in your own words what is meant by external costs and external benefits. Why may market outcomes be less than ideal when externalities are present?

6. English philosopher John Locke argued that the protection of each individual's person and property (acquired without the use of violence, theft, or fraud) was the primary function of government. Why is this protection important to the efficient operation of an economy?

7. "If it's worth doing, it's worth doing to the best of your ability." What is the economic explanation for why this statement is frequently said but rarely followed in practice? Explain.

8. "Unless quality and price are regulated by government, travelers would have no chance for a fair deal. Local people would be treated well, but the traveler would have no way to know, for example, who offers a good night's lodging at a fair price." Is this true or false? Explain.

*9. If sellers of toasters were able to organize themselves, reduce their output, and raise their prices, how would economic efficiency be affected? Explain.

10. What are external costs? When are they most likely to be present? When external costs are present, what is likely to be the relationship between the market output of a good and the output consistent with ideal economic efficiency?

*11. "Elementary education is obviously a public good. After all, it is provided by the government." Evaluate this statement.

12. What are the necessary conditions for economic efficiency? In what four situations might a market fail to achieve ideal economic efficiency?

13. Suppose that Abel builds a factory next to Baker's farm, and air pollution from the factory harms Baker's crops. Is Baker's property right to the land being violated? Is an externality present? What if the pollution invades Baker's home and harms her health? Are her property rights violated? Is an externality present? Explain.

*14. Apply the economic efficiency criterion to the role of government. When would a government intervention be considered economically efficient? When would a government intervention be considered economically inefficient?

*Asterisk denotes questions for which answers are given in Appendix B.

The Economics of Collective Decision Making

[Public choice] analyzes the motives and activities of politicians, civil servants and government officials as people with personal interests that may or may not coincide with the interest of the general public they are supposed to serve. It is an analysis of how people behave in the world as it is.

—*Arthur Seldon*[1]

It does not follow that whenever laissez faire falls short government interference is expedient; since the inevitable drawbacks of the latter may, in any particular case, be worse than the shortcomings of private enterprise.

—*Harry Sidgwick, 1887*[2]

Chapter Focus

■ How large is the government sector, and what are the main activities undertaken by government?

■ What are the differences and similarities between market and government actions?

■ What insights can economics provide about the behavior of voters, politicians, and bureaucrats? How will their actions affect political outcomes?

■ When is democratic representative government most likely to lead to economic efficiency?

■ Why will there sometimes be a conflict between winning politics and economic efficiency?

■ How does economic organization influence the efficiency of resource use?

[1]Preface to Gordon Tullock, *The Vote Motive* (London: Institute of Economic Affairs, 1976), x.
[2]Quoted in Charles Wolf, Jr., *Markets or Government* (Cambridge, Mass.: MIT Press, 1988), 17.

A s we have previously discussed, the protection of property rights, evenhanded enforcement of contracts, and provision of a stable monetary environment are vital for the smooth and efficient operation of markets. Governments that perform these functions well will help their citizens prosper and achieve higher levels of income. Governments may also help allocate goods difficult for markets to handle. However, it is crucially important to recognize that government is simply an alternative form of economic organization. In most industrialized nations, the activities of governments are directed by the democratic political process. In this chapter, we will use the tools of economics to analyze how this process works. ▪

THE SIZE AND GROWTH OF THE U.S. GOVERNMENT

What exactly does government do? Has its role in the economy shrunk or grown over time? Data on government spending shed light on these questions. As **Exhibit 1** illustrates, total government expenditures (federal, state, and local combined) were only 9.4 percent of the U.S. economy in 1930. (*Note:* GDP is generally how economists measure the size of the economy. The term will be explained more fully in a macroeconomics course.) In that year, federal government spending by itself was only 3 percent of the economy. At the time, this made the federal government about half the size of all state and local governments combined.

However, between 1930 and 1980, the size of government grew very rapidly. By 1980, government expenditures had risen to 32.8 percent of the economy, *more than three times* the level of 1930. Moreover, the federal government grew to about twice the size of all state and local governments combined—despite the fact that they were growing rapidly, too. Over the last two decades, total government spending as a share of the economy has been relatively constant at approximately one-third of GDP.

Exhibit 2 shows the major categories of government spending for both the federal government and state and local governments. The major categories of federal spending are health care, national defense, Social Security, and other income transfers. Education, administration, and public welfare and health constitute the largest areas of spending for state and local governments.

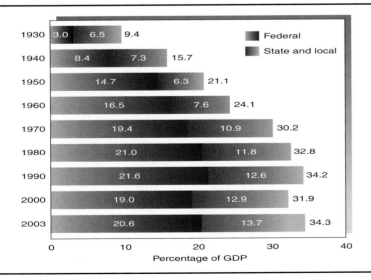

EXHIBIT 1
The Growth of Government Spending between 1930 and 2003

U.S. government expenditures as a share of the economy's gross domestic product have risen dramatically over the past seventy years.

Source: Bureau of Economic Analysis, http://www.bea.gov. Grants to state and local governments are included in federal expenditures. Individual data may not add to total due to rounding.

EXHIBIT 2
Government Spending by Category

The major categories of federal government spending are health care, Social Security, national defense, and income security (welfare programs). The major categories of state and local government spending are education, health care, and welfare programs.

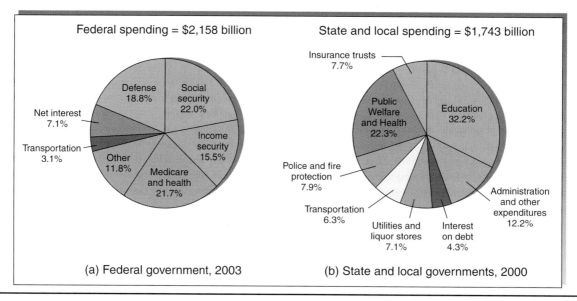

(a) Federal government, 2003   (b) State and local governments, 2000

Source: *Economic Report of the President*, 2004, and *Statistical Abstract of the United States*, 2003.

Transfer payments
Payments to individuals or institutions that are not linked to the current supply of a good or service by the recipient.

Transfer payments are transfers of income from some individuals (who pay taxes) to others (who receive government payments). Social Security, unemployment benefits, and welfare are examples of transfer payments. Direct income transfers now account for almost 40 percent of the total spending of the government. As **Exhibit 3** illustrates, government spending on income transfers has grown rapidly. In 1930, income transfers summed to only

EXHIBIT 3
The Growth of Government Transfer Payments

The government taxes approximately 13 percent of national income away from some people and transfers it to others. Means-tested income transfers—those directed toward the poor—account for only about one-sixth of all income transfers. Government income-transfer activities have grown substantially over the past seventy years.

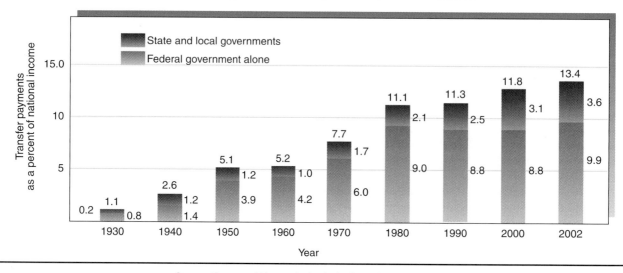

Source: Bureau of Economic Analysis, http://www.bea.gov.

1.1 percent of total income. By 1970, the figure had jumped to 7.7 percent, and by 2002 it had risen to 13.4 percent of national income. Obviously, the government has become much more involved in tax-transfer activities during the past seventy years.

Given the size and growth of government, analyzing how the political process works and what impact it is likely to have on the economy is a vitally important topic. The remainder of this chapter will address this issue.

THE DIFFERENCES AND SIMILARITIES BETWEEN GOVERNMENTS AND MARKETS

When political decisions are made democratically, the choices of individuals will influence outcomes in the government sector—just as they do in the market sector. Therefore, when we analyze the political process, we focus on individuals and how incentives influence their choices, just as we do when we analyze markets. There are both differences and similarities between political and market decision making. Let's take a look at six of them.

1. Competitive behavior is present in both the market and public sectors.   The nature of the competition and the criteria for success differ between the two sectors, but people compete in both. Politicians compete for elective office. Bureau chiefs and agency heads compete for taxpayer dollars and the authority to regulate others to meet their bureau or agency goals. Public-sector employees compete for promotions, higher incomes, and additional power, just as they do in the private sector. Lobbyists compete for program funding, for favorable bureaucratic rulings, and for legislation favorable to the interest groups they represent—including both private and government clients. The nature of the competition may differ between the two sectors, but it is present in both. (See Applications in Economics: Perspectives on the Cost of Political Competition.)

2. Public-sector organization can break the individual consumption-payment link. In the market sector, goods are allocated to those who are willing to pay the price: there is

---

Perspectives on the Cost of Political Competition: What Does It Cost to Get Elected?

Competition for elective office is fierce and campaigns are expensive. For example, in recent years, candidates for U.S. House and Senate positions raised and spent more than $1 billion. This amounts to approximately $2 million per congressional seat! Highly contested seats are often far more expensive.

During and after an election, lobbying groups compete for the attention of elected officials. In fact, the greatest portion of campaign funds raised by incumbents is not raised at election time; rather, it accrues over their entire term in office. A large campaign contribution may not be able to "buy"

a vote, but it certainly enhances the lobbyist's chance to sit down with the elected official to explain the power and "beauty" of the contributor's position. In the competitive world of politics, the politician who does not at least listen to helpful "friends of the campaign" is less likely to survive.

The U.S. Congress controls approximately $2 trillion in spending annually and imposes regulations that cost another $800 billion. That's a huge amount of money. As long as Congress wields the power to spend these sums, huge expenditures designed to influence the policies representatives make will continue.[1]

---

[1]More details on campaign finance can be found in Michael Barone and Grant Ujifusa, *The Almanac of American Politics* (Washington, D.C.: National Journal, annual), or at the Federal Election Commission's Web site.

a one-to-one relationship between a person's payment and receipt of a good. This is often not the case when decisions are made politically. Sometimes people receive very large benefits from the government even though they do not pay much of the cost to cover them. In other cases, individuals are required to pay dearly for a government program even though they derive few, if any, benefits.

3. Scarcity imposes the aggregate consumption-payment link in both sectors. Although the government can break the link between a person's payment for a good and the right to consume it, the reality of the *aggregate consumption–aggregate payment link* remains. Resources used by the government have alternative uses. Therefore, it is costly to provide goods and services through the government. This is true even if the good is provided "free of charge" to certain consumers.

4. Private-sector action is based on mutual agreement; public-sector action is based on majority rule. In the market sector, when two parties engage in trade, they do so voluntarily. Corporations like General Motors and Microsoft, no matter how large or powerful, cannot take income from you or force you to buy their products. On the other hand, when collective action occurs in a democratic setting, majority rule is the key, either through direct voting or through legislative procedures involving elected representatives. If a legislative majority decides on a particular policy, the minority must accept the policy and help pay for it, even if they strongly disagree. Similarly, if government regulators mandate that private parties must provide a wildlife habitat, wetlands, or housing at below-market prices, for example, both providers and potential buyers must comply. Although market action is based on mutual benefit, government action through the political process generates losers as well as winners.

5. When collective decisions are made legislatively, voters must choose among candidates who represent a bundle of positions on issues. On election day, the voter cannot choose the views of one politician on poverty and business welfare and simultaneously choose the views of a different politician on national defense and tariffs. This greatly limits the voter's power to make his or her preferences count on specific issues. Since the average representative is asked to vote on roughly 2,000 different issues during a two-year term, the size of the problem is obvious. The situation in markets, however, is quite different. A buyer can purchase some groceries or clothing from one store, while choosing related items from different suppliers. There is seldom a bundle-purchase problem in markets.

6. Income and power are distributed differently in the two sectors. People who supply more highly valued resources in the marketplace have larger incomes. The number of these dollar "votes" earned by a person in the marketplace will reflect his or her abilities, ambitions, skills, past savings, inheritance, good fortune, and willingness to produce for others, among other things. Bill Gates is a good example. Many people have "voted" for his products. Consequently, Gates has become quite wealthy. This process results in an unequal distribution of income and power in the market sector.

On the other hand, in a democratic government, one citizen, one vote is the rule. But there are ways other than voting to influence political outcomes. People can donate both their money and their time to help a campaign. They can also try to influence friends and neighbors, write letters to legislators, and speak in public on behalf of a candidate or cause. The greatest rewards of the political process go to those best able and most willing to use their time, persuasive skills, organizational abilities, and financial contributions to help politicians get votes. People who have more money and skills of this sort—and are willing to spend them in the political arena—can expect to benefit more handsomely for themselves and their favorite causes. Thus, while the sources of success and influence differ, there is an unequal distribution of influence and power in both sectors.

POLITICAL DECISION MAKING: AN OVERVIEW

Public-choice analysis is a branch of economics that applies the principles and methodology of economics to the operation of the political process. Public-choice analysis links the theory of *individual* behavior to political action, analyzes the implications of the theory, and tests them against events in the real world. Over the past fifty years, research in this area has greatly enhanced our understanding of political decision-making.[3] Just as economists have used the idea of self-interest to analyze markets, public-choice economists use it to analyze political choices and the operation of government. After all, the same people make decisions in both sectors. If self-interest and the structure of incentives influence market choices, there is good reason to expect that they will also influence choices in a political setting.

The collective decision-making process can be thought of as a complex interaction among voters, legislators, and bureaucrats. Voters elect a legislature, which levies taxes and allocates budgets to various government agencies and bureaus. The bureaucrats in charge of these agencies utilize the funds to supply government services and income transfers. In a representative democracy, voter support determines who is elected to the legislature. A majority vote of the legislature is generally required for the passage of taxes, budget allocations, and regulatory activities. Let's take a closer look at the incentive structure confronting the three primary political players—voters, legislators, and bureaucrats—and consider how they affect the operation of the political process.

Public-choice analysis
The study of decision making as it affects the formation and operation of collective organizations, such as governments. In general, the principles and methodology of economics are applied to political science topics.

Voters, politicians, and bureaucrats are the primary decision makers in the political arena.

---

[3]The contributions of Kenneth Arrow, James Buchanan, Duncan Black, Anthony Downs, Mancur Olson, Robert Tollison, and Gordon Tullock have been particularly important. Public choice is something of a cross between economics and political science. Thus, advanced courses are generally offered in both departments.

Incentives Confronted by the Voter

How do voters decide whom to support? Self-interest dictates that voters, like market consumers, will ask, "What can you do for me and my goals, and how much will it cost me?" The greater the voter's perceived net personal gain from a particular candidate's election, the more likely it is that the voter will favor that candidate. In contrast, the greater the perceived net economic cost imposed on the voter by the positions of a candidate, the less inclined the voter will be to support the candidate. Other things being equal, voters will tend to support those candidates whom they believe will provide them the most government services and transfer benefits, net of personal costs.

How well will voters be informed about political issues and candidates? When decisions are made collectively, the choices of a single person will not be decisive. The probability that an individual vote will decide a city, state, or national election is virtually zero. Realizing that their votes will not affect the outcome, individual voters have little incentive to spend much effort seeking the information needed to cast an informed ballot. Economists refer to this lack of incentive as the **rational ignorance effect**.

Rational ignorance effect
Because it is highly unlikely that an individual vote will decide the outcome of an election, a rational individual has little or no incentive to search for and acquire the information needed to cast an informed vote.

As the result of the rational ignorance effect, most voters simply rely on information supplied to them freely by candidates (via political advertising) and the mass media, as well as conversations with friends and coworkers. Surveys, in fact, indicate that huge numbers of voters are unable to even identify their own congressional representatives, much less know where they stand on issues like Social Security reform, tariffs, and agricultural price supports. Given that voters gain little from casting a more informed vote, their meager knowledge of political candidates and issues is not surprising.

On the other hand, when people can put information to good use, they will put forth the effort to acquire it. Consider the incentive of an automobile purchaser to make a well-informed choice. The model, the dealer, and the financial terms are a matter of personal preference. If a bad choice is made, the individual consumer will bear the consequences. As a result, auto consumers have a strong incentive to make informed decisions. Thus, they often take different models for test drives, review consumer publications, and consult with various car experts about them. On the other hand, the voter gains little or nothing in terms of a changed result from a more informed political choice. Because the person is not in a position to decide the outcome of an election, if he or she makes a mistake by casting an uninformed ballot, it won't make much difference. Thus, it is actually *reasonable* to expect people to be far better informed when choosing a car than a senatorial, congressional, or other political candidate.

OUTSTANDING ECONOMIST

James Buchanan (1919–)

James Buchanan is a key figure in the development of public-choice theory. Buchanan's most famous work, *The Calculus of Consent* (1962), coauthored with Gordon Tullock, argues that unless constitutional rules are structured in a manner that will bring the self-interests of the political players into harmony with the wise use of resources, government action will often be counterproductive.[1] This and related contributions won him the 1986 Nobel Prize in economics. Buchanan is the founder of the Center for the Study of Public Choice and a longtime professor of economics at George Mason University.

[1]J. M. Buchanan and G. Tullock, *The Calculus of Consent* (Ann Arbor: University of Michigan Press, 1962).

To get elected (or reelected), politicians have a strong incentive to provide transfers to important interest groups to secure their support.

The fact that citizens realize their individual votes will not sway the outcome of an election also explains why so many of them don't vote. Even in a presidential election, only about half of all voting-age Americans take the time to register and vote. The turnout for state and local elections is generally still lower. Given the low probability that one's vote will be decisive, low voter turn out is an expected result.

Incentives Confronted by the Politician

What motivates political candidates and officeholders? Economics indicates that the pursuit of votes will primarily shape politicians' actions and political positions. No doubt, many of them genuinely care about the "public interest" and the quality of government, but they need to get elected to achieve their objectives, whatever they might be. To be successful, a candidate's positive attributes must be brought to the attention of rationally ignorant voters focused on their families, jobs, various civic activities, and local sports teams (which are probably more entertaining). The successful candidate needs an expert staff, sophisticated polling techniques to uncover popular issues and positions, and high-quality advertising to favorably shape his or her image. This, of course, will be costly. It is not unusual for an incumbent candidate to the U.S. Senate to spend more than $15 million or more to get reelected. In other words, votes are the ultimate objective of politicians, but money helps them get those votes. Predictably, the pursuit of campaign contributions therefore shapes the actions of politicians, too.

Are we implying that politicians are selfish, caring only for their pocketbooks and reelection chances? The answer is "No." Factors other than personal political gain, narrowly defined, may well influence their actions. Sometimes an elected official may feel so strongly about an issue that he or she will knowingly take a position that is politically unpopular and damaging to his or her future electoral prospects. None of this is inconsistent with the economic view of the political process we just described. Over time, however, the politicians most likely to remain in office are the ones who focus on how their actions will influence their reelection prospects. Just as profits are the lifeblood of the market entrepreneur, votes are the lifeblood of the politician.

Politicians face competition for elected office from other candidates. Just like market suppliers, political suppliers have an incentive to find ways to gain an advantage over their competitors. Catering to the views of voters and contributors is one way of doing that. Enacting rules that put potential challengers at a disadvantage is another. When geographic political districts are redrawn, for example, politicians frequently manipulate the process to increase their chances of reelection—a process known as "gerrymandering." Incumbents can also attempt to use government resources for their reelection campaigns, an advantage challengers do not have. Campaign finance "reforms" that make it more difficult for a challenger to raise funds may also provide incumbents with an additional advantage.

Incentives Confronted by the Government Bureaucrat

Like other people, bureaucrats who staff government agencies have narrowly focused interests.[4] They usually want to see their own agency's goals furthered. Many bureaucrats believe strongly in what they are trying to do. Furthering these goals, however, usually requires larger budgets. In turn, larger budgets lead to more prestige and career opportunities for the bureaucrats. ***Economic analysis suggests there is a strong tendency for government bureaucrats and employees to want to expand their budgets to sizes well beyond what is economically efficient.***

Legislative bodies are in charge of overseeing these bureaus, but the individual legislators themselves are generally not very knowledgeable about the true costs of running these agencies. This makes it even more likely that bureaucrats will be able to get funding beyond what's economically efficient.

The political process, which begins with voter-driven elections and proceeds to legislative decisions and bureaucratic actions, brings about results that please some voters and displease others. The goals of the three major categories of participants—voters, politicians, and bureaucrats—frequently conflict with one another. Each group wants more of the government's limited supply of resources. Coalitions form and the members of each coalition hope to enhance their ability to get the government to do what they want. Sometimes this results in productive activities on the part of the government, and sometimes it does not.

WHEN THE POLITICAL PROCESS WORKS WELL

Under what conditions are voting and representative government most likely to result in productive actions? People have a tendency to believe that support by a majority makes a political action productive. However, if a government project is truly productive, it will always be possible to find a way to allocate the cost so that *all* voters gain. This would mean that, even if voting rules required unanimity or near-unanimity, all truly productive government projects would pass if the costs were allocated in the right manner. **Exhibit 4** helps illustrate this point. Column 1 presents hypothetical data on the distribution of benefits from a government road construction project. These benefits sum to $40, which exceeds the $25 cost of the road, so the project is productive. But if the project's $25 cost were allocated equally among the voters (plan A), Adams and Chan gain substantially, but Green, Lee, and Diaz lose. If the fate of the project is decided by majority vote, the project will be defeated by the "no" votes of Green, Lee, and Diaz. The reason why this productive government project fails to obtain a majority vote, however, is because of the way that the costs have been allocated.

Because the project is indeed productive, there is an alternative way to allocate its costs so that Adams, Chan, Green, Lee, and Diaz all benefit. This can be accomplished by

Just as the general does not want his Camp Swampy budget cut, most heads of agencies want expanded budgets to help them do more and do it more comfortably.

BEETLE BAILEY BY MORT WALKER. REPRINTED BY SPECIAL PERMISSION OF KING FEATURES SYNDICATE.

[4]The economic analysis of bureaucracy was pioneered by William Niskanen. Reprints of some of his classic articles along with recent updated material can be found in William A. Niskanen, Jr., *Bureaucracy and Public Economics* (Aldershot, U.K.: Edward Elgar Publishing, 1994).

EXHIBIT 4
The Benefits Derived by Voters from a Hypothetical Road Construction Project

| | | | TAX PAYMENT | |
VOTER	BENEFITS RECEIVED (1)	PLAN A (2)	PLAN B (3)
Adams	$20	$5	$12.50
Chan	12	5	7.50
Green	4	5	2.50
Lee	2	5	1.25
Diaz	2	5	1.25
Total	**$40**	**$25**	**$25.00**

When taxes are levied in proportion to benefits received (tax plan B), any efficient project can pass unanimously (and any inefficient project will fail unanimously). When taxes are not levied in accordance with benefits received (tax plan A), efficient projects can fail to win a majority vote (or inefficient projects can pass in a majority vote).

allocating the cost of the project among voters in proportion to the benefits that they receive (plan B). Under this arrangement, Adams would pay half ($12.50) of the $25 cost, since he receives half ($20) of the total benefits ($40). The other voters would all pay in proportion to the benefits they receive. Under this plan, all voters would gain from the proposal. Even though the proposal could not secure a majority when the costs were allocated equally among voters, it will be favored by all five voters when they are taxed in proportion to the benefits they receive (plan B).

This simple illustration highlights an extremely important point about voting and the efficiency of government action. ***When voters pay in proportion to benefits received, all voters will gain if the government action is productive, and all will lose if it is unproductive.***[5] ***When the benefits and costs derived by individual voters are closely related, the voting process will enact efficient projects while rejecting inefficient ones. When voters pay in proportion to the benefits they receive, there will tend to be harmony between good politics and sound economics.***

How might the cost of a government service be linked to the benefits received? **User charges**, which require people who use a service more to pay a larger share of the cost, provide one way. User charges are most likely to be levied at the local level. Local services such as electricity, water, and garbage collection are generally financed with user charges. Sometimes the intensity of the use of a service and the amount paid for it can be linked by specifying that the revenue from a specific tax be used for a designated purpose. For example, most states finance road construction and maintenance with the revenue collected from taxes on gasoline and other motor fuels. The more an individual drives, the more he or she benefits from the roads—and the more he or she pays.

Exhibit 5 provides a useful way to look at the possible linkage between the benefits and costs of government programs. The benefits from a government action may be either widespread among the general public or concentrated among a small subgroup (for example, farmers, students, business interests, senior citizens, or members of a labor union). Similarly, the costs may be either widespread or highly concentrated among voters. Thus, as the exhibit shows, there are four possible patterns of voter benefits and costs: (1) widespread benefits and widespread costs, (2) concentrated benefits and widespread costs, (3) concentrated benefits and concentrated costs, and (4) widespread benefits and concentrated costs.

When both the benefits and costs are widespread among voters (type 1 issue), essentially everyone benefits and everyone pays. Although the costs of type 1 measures may not be precisely proportional to the benefits individuals receive, there will be a rough

User charges
Payments that users (consumers) are required to make if they want to receive certain services provided by the government.

[5]The principle that productive projects generate the potential for political unanimity was initially articulated by Swedish economist Knut Wicksell in 1896. See Wicksell, "A New Principle of Just Taxation," in *Public Choice and Constitutional Economics,* James Gwartney and Richard Wagner (Greenwich, Conn.: JAI Press, Inc., 1988). Nobel laureate James Buchanan has stated that Wicksell's work provided him with the insights that led to his large role in the development of modern public-choice theory.

EXHIBIT 5
Distribution of Benefits and Costs among Voters

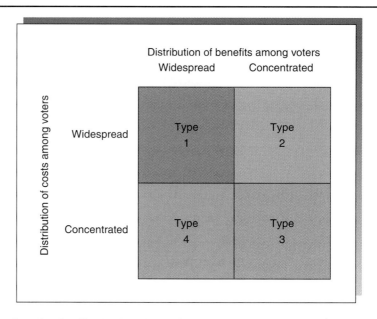

It is useful to visualize four possible combinations for the distribution of benefits and costs among voters to consider how the alternative distributions affect the operation of representative governments. When the distribution of benefits and costs is both widespread among voters (1) or both concentrated among voters (3), representative government will tend to undertake projects that are productive and reject those that are unproductive. In contrast, when the benefits are concentrated and the costs are widespread (2), representative government is biased toward the adoption of inefficient projects. Finally, when benefits are widespread but the costs concentrated (4), the political process may reject projects that are productive.

relationship. When type 1 measures are productive, almost everyone gains more than they pay. There will be little opposition, and political representatives have a strong incentive to support such proposals. In contrast, when type 1 proposals generate costs in excess of benefits, almost everyone loses, and representatives will face pressure to oppose such issues. Thus, for type 1 projects, the political process works pretty well. Productive projects will tend to be accepted and unproductive ones rejected.

Similarly, there is reason to believe that the political process will work fairly well for type 3 measures—those for which both benefits and costs are concentrated on one or more small subgroups. In some cases, the concentrated beneficiaries may be the same group of people paying for the government to provide them a service. In other cases, the subgroup of beneficiaries may differ from the subgroup footing the bill. Even in this case, however, when the benefits exceed the costs, the concentrated group of beneficiaries will have an incentive to expend more resources lobbying for the measure than those harmed by it will expend opposing it. Thus, when the benefits and costs are both concentrated, there will be a tendency for productive projects to be adopted and unproductive ones to be rejected.

WHEN THE POLITICAL PROCESS WORKS POORLY

Although the political process yields reasonable results when there is a close relationship between the receipt of benefits and the payment of costs (type 1 and type 3 projects), the harmony between good politics and sound economics breaks down when there is not (type 2 and type 4 projects). Inefficiency may also arise from other sources when governments undertake economic activities. In this section, we consider four major reasons why the political allocation of resources will often result in inefficiency.

Special-Interest Effect

Trade restrictions that limit the import of steel and lumber from abroad; subsidies for sports stadiums, the arts, and various agricultural products; federal spending on an indoor rain forest in Coralville, Iowa; a tattoo-removal program in San Luis Obispo County, California; the Rock and Roll Hall of Fame in Cleveland, Ohio; a golf awareness program in St. Augustine, Florida; and therapeutic horseback riding in Apple Valley, California. These seemingly diverse programs funded by the federal government have one thing in common: They reflect the attractiveness of special interests to vote-seeking politicians. A **special-interest issue** is one that generates substantial personal benefits for a small number of constituents while spreading the costs widely across the bulk of citizens (type 2 projects). Individually, a few people gain a great deal, but many others lose a small amount. In aggregate, the losses may exceed the benefits.

How will a vote-seeking politician respond to special-interest issues? Since their personal stake is large, members of the interest group (and lobbyists representing their interests) will feel strongly about such issues. Many of the special-interest voters will vote for or against candidates strictly on the basis of whether they are supportive of their positions. In addition, interest groups are generally an attractive source of campaign resources—including financial contributions. In contrast, most other rationally ignorant voters will

Special-interest issue
An issue that generates substantial individual benefits to a small minority while imposing a small individual cost on many other citizens. In total, the net cost to the majority might either exceed or fall short of the net benefits to the special-interest group.

APPLICATIONS IN ECONOMICS

Sweet Subsidies to Sugar Growers: A Case Study of the Special-Interest Effect

For many years, the price of sugar in the United States has been two or three times as high as the world price. For example, in February 2004, the domestic price of sugar was 20 cents per pound while the world price was less than 6 cents a pound. Why? Because the U.S. government severely restricts the quantity of sugar imported. This keeps the domestic price of sugar high. As a result, the roughly 60,000 sugar growers in the United States gain about $1.9 billion. That's more than $30,000 per grower! Most of these benefits are reaped by large growers with incomes far above the national average. On the other hand, these subsidies cost the average American household about $20 in the form of higher prices for products containing sugar. Even more important, the resources of Americans are wasted producing a good we are ill-suited to produce and one that could be obtained at a substantially lower cost through trade. As a result, Americans are worse off.

Why does Congress support this program year after year? Given the sizable impact the restrictions have on the personal wealth of sugar growers, it is perfectly sensible for them, particularly the large ones, to use their wealth and political clout to help politicians who support their interests. This is precisely what they have done. During the 2000 election cycle, the sugar lobby contributed almost

$13 million to candidates and political action committees. In contrast, it makes no sense for the average voter to investigate this issue or give it any significant weight when deciding for whom to vote. In fact, most voters are unaware that this program is costing them money. Here, as in several other areas, politicians have a strong incentive to support policies favored by special interests, solicit those parties for political contributions, and use the funds to attract the support of other voters, most of whom know nothing about the sugar program. Even though the sugar program is counterproductive, it is still a political winner.

The sugar growers are not the only ones benefiting from government programs that are economically inefficient. Taxpayers and consumers spend approximately $20 billion annually to support grain, cotton, tobacco, peanut, wool, and dairy programs, all of which have structural characteristics similar to those of the sugar program. The political power of special interests also explains the presence of tariffs and quotas on steel, textiles, lumber, and many other products. Federally funded irrigation projects, subsidized agricultural grazing rights, subsidized business loans, numerous pork-barrel spending projects (the list goes on and on) are all policies rooted in the special-interest effect rather than economic efficiency and net benefits to Americans. Although each such program individually imposes only a small drag on the economy, together they exert a sizeable negative impact on our income levels and living standards.

either not know or will care little about special-interest issues. Even if voters know about some of these programs, it will be difficult for them to punish their legislators because each politician represents a bundle of positions on many different issues. While there is little to be gained from the support of the disorganized majority, organized interest groups provide politicians with vocal supporters, campaign workers, and, most important, financial contributions.

As a result, politicians have a strong incentive to support legislation giving concentrated benefits to special-interest groups at the expense of disorganized groups (like the bulk of taxpayers and consumers). Even if supporting such legislation is counterproductive, politicians will often still be able to gain by supporting programs favored by special interests. For a real-world illustration of how the special-interest effect works, see Applications in Economics, "Sweet Subsidies to Sugar Growers: A Case Study of the Special-Interest Effect."

The power of special interests is further strengthened by logrolling and pork-barrel legislation. **Logrolling** involves the practice of trading votes by a politician to get the necessary support to pass desired legislation. **Pork-barrel legislation** is the term used to describe the bundling of unrelated projects benefiting many interests into a single bill. Both logrolling and pork-barrel legislation will often make it possible for special-interest projects to gain legislative approval, even though these projects themselves are counterproductive and individually would be unable to muster the needed votes.

Exhibit 6 provides a numeric illustration of the forces underlying logrolling and pork-barrel legislation. Here we consider the operation of a five-member legislature considering three projects: construction of a post office in district A, dredging of a harbor in district B, and spending on a military base in district C. For each district, the net benefit or cost is shown—that is, the benefit to the district minus the tax cost imposed on it. The total cost of each of the three projects exceeds the benefits (as shown by the negative number in the total row at the bottom of the table), and therefore each is counterproductive. If the projects were voted on separately, each would lose by a 4-to-1 vote because only one district would gain, and the other four would lose. However, when the projects are bundled together through either logrolling (representatives A, B, and C could agree to trade votes) or pork-barrel legislation (all three programs put on the same bill), they can all pass, despite the fact that all are inefficient.[6] This can be seen by noting that the total combined net benefit is positive for representatives A, B, and C. Given the weak incentive for voters to acquire information,

Logrolling
The exchange between politicians of political support on one issue for political support on another.

Pork-barrel legislation
A package of spending projects benefiting local areas financed through the federal government. The costs of the projects typically exceed the benefits in total, but the projects are intensely desired by the residents of a particular district, who get the benefits without having to pay much of the costs.

EXHIBIT 6
Trading Votes and Passing Counterproductive Legislation

All three projects are inefficient, and would not pass majority vote individually. However, representatives from districts A, B, and C could trade votes (logrolling) or put together pork-barrel legislation that would result in all three projects passing.

	NET BENEFITS (+) OR COSTS (−) TO VOTERS IN DISTRICT			
VOTERS OF DISTRICT[a]	CONSTRUCTION OF POST OFFICE IN A	DREDGING HARBOR IN B	CONSTRUCTION OF MILITARY BASE IN C	TOTAL
A	+$10	−$ 3	−$ 3	**+$4**
B	−$ 3	+$10	−$ 3	**+$4**
C	−$ 3	−$ 3	+$10	**+$4**
D	−$ 3	−$ 3	−$ 3	**−$9**
E	−$ 3	−$ 3	−$ 3	**−$9**
Total	**−$ 2**	**−$ 2**	**−$ 2**	**−$6**

[a]We assume the districts are of equal size.

---

[6]Logrolling and pork-barrel policies can sometimes lead to the adoption of productive measures. However, if a project is productive, there would always be a pattern of finance that would lead to its adoption even if logrolling and pork-barrel policies were absent. Thus, the tendency for logrolling and pork-barrel policies to result in the adoption of inefficient projects is the more significant point.

those harmed by pork-barrel and other special-interest policies are unlikely to even be aware of them. Thus, the incentive to support projects like these is even stronger than is implied by the simple numeric example in Exhibit 6.

Why don't representatives oppose measures that force their constituents to pay for projects that benefit others? There is some incentive to do so, but the constituents of any one elected representative can capture only a small portion of the benefits of tax savings from improved efficiency, since the savings would be spread nationwide among all tax-payers. We would not, for example, expect the president of a corporation to devote any of the firm's resources to projects not primarily benefiting its stockholders. Neither should we expect an elected representative to devote political resources to projects like defeating pork-barrel programs when the benefits of spending reductions and tax savings will be de-rived mostly by constituents in other districts. Instead, each representative has a strong incentive to work for programs that concentrate benefits among his or her own con-stituents—especially organized interest groups that can help the representative be re-elected. Heeding such incentives is a survival (reelection) tactic.

On the other hand, when the benefits of a governmental action are widespread and the costs are highly concentrated (type 4 of Exhibit 5), special-interest groups—those who stand to bear the cost—will strongly oppose and lobby against it. Most other voters will be largely uninformed and uninterested. Once again, politicians will have an incentive to respond to the views of the concentrated interests. A proposal to reduce or eliminate a tar-iff (tax) on an imported good would be an example of this type of legislation. Although many thousands of consumers would benefit from the lower prices that result, the domes-tic firms that compete with the imported good would devote substantial resources toward lobbying to keep the tariff in place. Projects of this type will tend to be rejected even when they are productive, that is, when they would generate larger benefits than costs.

The bottom line is clear: Public-choice analysis indicates that majority voting and representative democracy work poorly when concentrated interests benefit at the expense of the general public. In the case of special-interest issues, there is a conflict between good politics—getting elected—and the efficient use of resources. The special-interest effect helps explain the presence of numerous government programs that increase the size of government and reduce the overall size of the economic pie. As we discuss di-verse topics throughout this text, counterproductive political action that has its foundation in the special-interest effect will arise again and again.

Shortsightedness Effect

Because voters have a weak incentive to acquire information, current economic conditions will have a major impact on their choices at election time. Complex issues, like reforming Social Security or restructuring health care programs that involve future benefits and costs, will be difficult for voters to assess. Thus, incumbent politicians will want to make sure economic conditions look good on election day. To accomplish this, they will favor policies that provide current benefits voters can easily identify at the expense of future costs that are complicated and difficult to identify. Similarly, they will tend to oppose leg-islation that involves immediate and easily identifiable costs (and higher taxes) but yield future benefits that are complex and difficult to identify. Economists refer to this bias in-herent in the political process as the **shortsightedness effect**.

As a result of the shortsightedness effect, politicians will tend to favor programs that generate highly visible current benefits, even when the true cost of these programs outweighs the benefits. In contrast, their incentive is weak to support efficient programs that generate future benefits but involve current costs.

The shortsightedness effect sheds light on why legislators find debt financing so at-tractive. Debt financing makes it possible for officeholders to provide visible benefits to their constituents without having to levy an equivalent amount of taxes. During the last forty-five years, the federal budget has been in deficit forty times; there have been only five surpluses (1969 and 1998–2001). The bias toward budget deficits is a predictable re-sult; it reflects the shortsighted nature of the political process. Similarly, the shortsighted-

Shortsightedness effect
The misallocation of resources that results because public-sector action is biased (1) in favor of proposals yielding clearly defined current benefits in exchange for diffi-cult-to-identify future costs and (2) against proposals with clearly identifiable current costs that yield less concrete and less obvious future benefits.

ness effect indicates that vote-seeking politicians will find it attractive to promise future benefits without levying a sufficient amount of taxes to finance them. This has been the case with both the Social Security and Medicare programs. The unfunded liabilities of these two programs are nearly *three times* the size of the official outstanding federal debt. By the time the higher taxes (or benefit cuts) for these programs are confronted, the politicians who gained votes from the promised benefits will be long gone.

It is worth taking a moment to consider the differences between the public and private sectors in terms of how future benefits and costs are considered in current decisions. As we explained in Chapter 2, private-property rights provide a means by which the value of future benefits can be immediately captured (or costs borne) by a property owner. Owners who do not invest now to properly maintain their homes or cars, for example, will bear the consequences of the reduced value of those assets. Correspondingly, the value of a firm's stock will immediately rise (or fall), depending on the shareholders' perception of the expected future benefits and costs of an action taken by the company's executives today. In contrast, the public sector tends to place more weight on current benefits and costs and less weight on the future. In areas where the primary benefits are in the future, and property rights can be well defined and enforced, there is good reason to believe that the private sector will do a better job than the government sector.

When buying and selling are controlled by legislation, the first things bought and sold are legislators.

—*P. J. O'Rourke*[7]

Rent seeking
Actions by individuals and groups designed to restructure public policy in a manner that will either directly or indirectly redistribute more income to themselves or the projects they promote.

Rent Seeking

There are two ways individuals can acquire wealth: production and plunder. When individuals produce goods or services and exchange them for income, they not only enrich themselves but they also enhance the wealth of the society. Sometimes the rules—or lack of rule enforcement—also allow people to get ahead by taking, or plundering, what others have produced. This method not only fails to generate additional income—the gain of one is a loss to another—but it also consumes resources and thereby reduces the wealth of the society.

Rent seeking is the term economists use when they refer to actions taken by individuals and groups seeking to use the political process to take the wealth of others.[8] Perhaps "favor seeking" would be a more descriptive term for this type of activity, which generally involves "investing" resources in lobbying and other activities designed to gain favors from the government. The incentive for individuals to spend time and effort in rent seeking will be determined by how rewarding it is. Rent seeking will be unattractive when constitutional constraints prevent politicians from taking the property of some and transferring it to others (or forcing some to pay for things desired by others).

When a government fails to allocate the costs of public-sector projects to the primary beneficiaries (through user fees, for example), or when it becomes heavily involved in transfer activities, people will spend more time organizing and lobbying politicians and less time producing goods and services. Resources that would otherwise be used to create wealth and generate income are wasted as people fight over slices of the economic pie—a pie that is smaller than it could be if they were engaged in productive activities instead. When the government grants favors to some people at the expense of others (instead of simply acting as a neutral force protecting property rights and enforcing contracts), counterproductive activities will expand while productive activities will shrink. As a result, the overall income level will fall short of its potential.

There is ample evidence that rent-seeking consumes a substantial amount of resources. Washington, D.C., is full of organizations seeking subsidies and other favors from the federal government. More than 3,000 trade associations have offices in Washington, and they employ nearly 100,000 people seeking to alter the actions of Congress. Of course, business and labor organizations are well represented, but so, too, are agricultural interests, health care providers, trial lawyers, senior citizens, export industries, and many others.

---

[7]Quoted in P. J. O'Rourke, *Insight Magazine,* Jan. 15–25: 35.
[8]See the classic work of Charles K. Rowley, Robert D. Tollison, and Gordon Tullock, *The Political Economy of Rent-Seeking* (Boston: Kluwer Academic Publishers, 1988), for additional details on rent seeking.

As we noted earlier, income transfers have grown substantially during the last several decades. The government now taxes approximately one out of every seven dollars citizens earn, and transfers it to someone else. Rent seeking is the political "fuel" for most of these transfer activities. Interestingly, *means-tested transfers,* those directed toward the poor, constitute only about one-sixth of all transfers. No income test is applied to the other five-sixths of income transfers. These transfers are generally directed toward groups that are either well organized (like businesses and labor union interests) or easily identifiable (like the elderly and farmers). The people receiving these transfers often have incomes well above the average person.

Within the framework of public-choice analysis, the relatively small portion of income transfers directed toward the poor is not surprising. There is little reason to believe that transfers to the poor will be particularly attractive to vote-seeking politicians. After all, in the United States, the poor are less likely to vote than middle- and upper-income recipients. They are also less likely to be well informed on political issues and candidates. They are not an attractive source of political contributions. Politicians often argue that their proposed policies will help the poor, but there is little reason to believe that this will be a high priority for most of them.

There are three major reasons why government transfer activity will reduce the size of the economic pie. First, income redistribution weakens the link between productive activity and reward. When taxes take a larger share of a person's income, the reward from hard work and productive activity is reduced. Second, as public policy redistributes a larger share of income, more resources will flow into wasteful rent-seeking activities. Resources used for lobbying and other rent-seeking activities will not be available to increase the size of the economic pie. Third, higher taxes to finance income redistribution and an expansion in rent-seeking will induce taxpayers to focus less on income-producing activities, and more on actions to protect their income. More accountants, lawyers, and tax-shelter experts will be retained as people seek to limit the amount of their income redistributed to others. Like the resources allocated to rent seeking, resources allocated to protecting one's wealth from the reach of government will also be unavailable for productive activity. Predictably, the incentives created by government redistribution policies will exert a negative impact on the level of economic activity.

Inefficiency of Government Operations

Will government goods and services be produced efficiently? The pride of a job well done is likely to motivate both public- and private-sector suppliers. However, the incentive to reduce costs and operate efficiently differs substantially between the two. In the private sector, there is a strong incentive to produce efficiently because lower costs mean higher profits, and high costs mean losses and going out of business. This index of performance (profit) is unavailable in the public sector. Missing also are signals from the capital market. When a corporation announces a strategy or a plan that vigilant, personally committed investors believe to be faulty, the price of the corporation's stock will drop. There is no mechanism similar to the stock market in the public sector. Furthermore, direct competition in the form of other firms trying to woo the customers of a government agency or enterprise is largely absent in the public sector. As a result, bureaucrats have more freedom to pursue their narrow goals and interests without a strong regard for the control of costs relative to the benefits the public derives.

Bankruptcy weeds out inefficiency in the private sector, but there is no parallel mechanism to eliminate inefficiency in the public sector. In fact, failure to achieve a targeted objective (for example, a lower crime rate or improvement in student achievement scores) is often used as an argument for *increased* public-sector funding. Furthermore, public-sector managers are seldom in a position to gain personally from measures that reduce costs. The opposite is often true, in fact. If an agency fails to spend its entire budget for a given year, not only does it have to return the extra money, but its budget for the next year is likely to be cut. Because of this, government agencies typically go on a spending spree near the end of a budget period if they discover they have failed to spend all the current year's funds appropriated to them.

Just as the boy considers the quarter (his quarter) more important than the far greater cost (to the father) of the metal detector, so, too, does the leader of a bureau often consider the bureau's goals more important than the costs, even if the latter are far greater.

THE FAMILY CIRCUS   **By Bil Keane**

1-26
©1998 Bil Keane, Inc.
Dist. by Cowles Synd., Inc.

"Daddy, could you buy a new metal detector? I dropped my quarter in the snow."

It is important to note that the argument of internal inefficiency is not based on the assumption that employees of a bureaucratic government are lazy or less capable. Rather, the emphasis is on the incentives and opportunities that government managers and workers confront. Government firms do not have owners that have risked their wealth on the future success of the firm. There is no entity that will be able to reap substantial economic gain if the firm produces more efficiently or incorporates a new product or service highly valued relative to its costs. The operation of the firm and the appointment of high-level managers might be influenced by political rather than economic considerations.

Because the profitability criteria are absent, performance is difficult to evaluate. There are no tests to define economic inefficiency or measure it accurately—much less eliminate it. These perverse incentives are bound to affect efficiency.

The empirical evidence is consistent with this view. Economies dominated by government control, like those of the former Soviet bloc, India, Syria, and Nigeria (and many other African countries), have performed poorly. The level of output per unit of resource input in countries with numerous government enterprises is low. Similarly, when private firms are compared with government agencies providing the same goods or services (like garbage collection, hospitals, electric and water utilities, weather forecasting, and public transportation), studies indicate that private firms generally provide the services more economically.

ECONOMIC ORGANIZATION: WHO PRODUCES, WHO PAYS, AND WHY IT MATTERS

The structure of production and consumption will influence economic outcomes. Goods and services can be either produced by private enterprises or supplied by the government. They can be paid for either by the consumer directly or by the taxpayer or some other third party. As **Exhibit 7** shows, there are four possible combinations of production and consumption. Let's take a closer look at each and consider its impact on the allocation of resources and the incentive to economize.

In quadrant 1, goods are produced by private firms and purchased by consumers with their own money. Clearly, consumers will have a strong incentive to economize in this case. They will compare value with cost, and will make purchases only when they value items more than their purchase price. Correspondingly, the owners of private enterprises have a strong incentive to both cater to the views of consumers and supply goods efficiently. Net revenues can be increased if the output can be produced at a lower cost. Producers will continue supplying goods only if consumers are willing to pay an amount sufficient to cover their production costs. Essentially, the supply and demand analysis of Chapter 3 focused on quadrant 1 cases.

Quadrant 2 represents the case in which goods are produced privately but are paid for by the taxpayer or some other third party. Providing health care to citizens financed primarily by government (Medicare and Medicaid) or insurance is an example. If someone

	Good is paid for by:	
Good is produced by:	Consumer-Purchaser	Taxpayer or other Third Party
Private Enterprises	**(1)** Examples: apples, oranges, television sets, food, housing, most other goods	**(2)** Examples: health-care, food purchased with food stamps
Government Enterprises or Contracting	**(3)** Examples: Post Office, water and electricity in many cities, toll roads, many hospitals	**(4)** Examples: public schools, streets and roads, national defense, law enforcement

EXHIBIT 7
The Private- and Government-Sector Matrix of Production and Payment

The incentive to economize is influenced by who produces a good and who pays for it. Economizing behavior will be strongest when consumers purchase goods produced by private firms (quadrant 1). The incentive to economize is reduced when payment is made by a third party and when production is handled by the government.

else is paying the bill, consumers have little incentive to care much about the price of their health-care services. Instead of economizing, many consumers will simply purchase from suppliers they believe offer the highest quality, regardless of the price. The behavior of producers will also be affected. If consumers are largely insensitive to prices, producers have little reason to control costs and offer services at attractive prices. This can dramatically affect economic efficiency.

Quadrant 3 represents the situation in which consumers pay for a good or service, but production is handled by the government. First-class mail delivery via the U.S. Postal Service, water and electricity by municipal governments, and the operation of toll roads are examples that fall into this category. When consumers pay for a good or service directly, they will economize and seek the most value per dollar they spend. This will be true whether their purchases are from private or government enterprises. As we just discussed, however, there is reason to believe that government-operated firms will generally be less efficient than private enterprises. Cost consciousness is also likely to be reduced if the government firm is a monopolist—if it is protected from competition with potential private rivals. Competition, however, is difficult to maintain in some markets. When this is the case, government enterprises may offer a reasonable alternative. As we proceed, we will investigate this issue in more detail.

Quadrant 4 represents the case in which the government both provides the service and covers its costs through taxation. In this case, the political process determines what will be produced, how it will be produced, and how it will be allocated among the general public. Under these circumstances, consumers are in a very weak position to either discipline the suppliers or alter their production. The incentive to produce efficiently is weak, and there is likely to be a disconnect between the goods produced and the preferences of consumers. As we discussed in the previous chapter, the nature of public goods—items such as national defense—makes it difficult, if not impossible, to supply them through markets. In these cases, there may be little alternative to having the government provide them. In other instances, however, there are feasible alternatives. This is true for education.

Most goods and services in the United States are allocated under conditions approximating those of quadrant 1. Thus, most of our analysis focuses on this case. However, a sizable portion of economic activity takes place under conditions present in quadrants 2, 3, and 4, where the incentive structure often creates problems. As a result, our analysis also considers modifications that might improve the efficiency of activities currently undertaken in these quadrants.

THE ECONOMIC WAY OF THINKING ABOUT GOVERNMENT

Given its monopoly power over the legitimate use of force, people have a tendency to believe that the government, particularly a democratic representative government, can solve all types of problems. Further, if things do not go well, people tend to think that it is because the "wrong" people won the last election. Public-choice analysis suggests that the problem is more fundamental: there is sometimes a conflict between winning elections and following sound policies. For some types of activities, there is reason to believe that the political action that will help get one elected will, at the same time, reduce income levels and living standards.

Both the market and the political process have shortcomings. In Chapter 5, we focused on the shortcomings of the market and explained why markets sometimes result in the inefficient use of resources. This chapter provides a parallel analysis for the political process. The accompanying Thumbnail Sketch lists the major deficiencies of both sectors.

Understanding the strengths and weaknesses of both sectors is important if we are going to improve our current economic institutions. As we have stressed throughout this textbook, when the government protects property rights, enforces contracts, and provides a stable monetary environment, economic prosperity is more likely to ensue. The basic problem, however, is how a society can obtain the benefits of the protective functions of government and at the same time constrain it to those activities where it is a productive force. As the analysis of this chapter illustrates, this is not an easy task.

Could Constitutional Changes Help Promote Prosperity?

When we think about how to get the most out of our government, it is important to distinguish between ordinary politics and constitutional rules. Constitutions establish the procedures utilized to make political decisions. Constitutions can also limit the activities of government.

The framers of the U.S. Constitution were aware that even a democratic government might undertake counterproductive actions. Thus, they incorporated restraints on the economic role of government. They enumerated the permissible tax and spending powers of the central government (Article I, Section 8) and allocated all other powers to the states and the people (Tenth Amendment). They also prohibited states from adopting legislation "impairing the obligation of contracts" (Article I, Section 10). Furthermore, the Fifth Amendment specifies that private property shall not be "taken for public use without just compensation." Over time, however, these restraints have been significantly eroded, due in part to Supreme Court decisions that have effectively reinterpreted the Constitution. Today, it is difficult to think of an economic activity that is beyond the reach of majority rule or normal legislative procedure.

Public-choice analysis highlights the importance of constitutional rules and procedures capable of restraining government activities to those areas in which it will promote

THUMBNAIL SKETCH

What Weakens the Case for Market-Sector Allocation Versus Public-Sector Intervention, and Vice Versa?

These factors weaken the case for market-sector allocation:
1. Lack of competition
2. Externalities
3. Public goods
4. Poor information

These factors weaken the case for public-sector intervention:
1. The special-interest effect
2. The shortsightedness effect
3. Rent seeking
4. Weak incentives for operational efficiency

prosperity. If left alone, even democratic governments will tend to cater to special-interest groups and draw significant resources into rent seeking. If we can figure out how to constrain the activities of government to those areas in which it is most likely to be productive, higher income levels can be achieved. The challenge before us is to develop constitutional rules and political institutions more consistent with economic efficiency and prosperity. The theory of public choice and its applications can help us do that. Needless to say, this topic is one of the most exciting and potentially fruitful areas of research in economics.

LOOKING AHEAD

Cases involving potential government intervention will be discussed repeatedly throughout this book. The tools presented in this chapter and the previous one will help us better understand both the potential and limitations of public policy as a source for economic progress.

KEY POINTS

▼ In recent years, government spending has been about one-third the size of the U.S. economy.

▼ There are both similarities and differences between markets and governments. Competition is present in both sectors. The government can use its taxing power to break the link between payment and receipt of a good for an individual, but not for the economy as a whole. In the public sector, voters face a "bundle" purchase problem; they are unable to vote for some policies favored by one candidate and other policies favored by the candidate's opponent. Power and income are distributed differently in the public sector than in the private sector.

▼ In a representative democracy, government is controlled by voters who elect politicians to set policy and hire bureaucrats to run government agencies. The incentives faced by all three classes of participants influence political outcomes.

▼ Voters have a strong incentive to support the candidate who offers them the greatest gain relative to their personal costs. Because collective decisions break the link between the choice of the individual and the outcome of the issue, voters are likely to be poorly informed on political matters.

▼ Politicians have a strong incentive to follow a strategy that will enhance their chances of getting elected (and reelected). Political competition more or less forces them to focus on how their actions influence their support among voters and potential contributors.

▼ The distribution of the benefits and costs among voters influences how the political process works. When voters pay in proportion to the benefits they receive from a public-sector project, productive projects tend to be approved and counterproductive ones rejected. When the costs of a policy are distributed among voters differently than are the benefits, democratic decision making will tend to be less efficient.

▼ Government actions will often lead to economic inefficiency as the result of (1) the special-interest effect, (2) the shortsightedness effect, (3) rent seeking, and (4) weak incentives to keep cost low within government enterprises and agencies. Thus, just as the market sometimes fails to allocate goods efficiently, so, too, will the government.

▼ Economic organization influences efficiency. The incentive to economize is strong when consumers use their own money to purchase goods and services from private firms. Both the payment by a third party and production by the government weaken the incentive to economize.

1. Are voters likely to be well informed on issues and the positions of candidates? Why or why not?

*2. "The government can afford to take a long view when it needs to, while a private firm has a short-term outlook. Corporate officers, for example, typically care about the next 3 to 6 months, not the next 50 to 100 years. Government, not private firms, should own things like forests, which take decades to develop." Evaluate this view.

3. "If there are problems with markets, government will generally be able to intervene and correct the situation." Is this statement true or false? Explain your response.

*4. "The political process sometimes leads to economic inefficiency because we elect the wrong people to political office. If the right people were elected, a democracy governed by majority rule would allocate resources efficiently." Evaluate this statement.

5. What is rent seeking? When is it likely to be widespread? How does it influence economic efficiency? Explain.

*6. "The average person is more likely to make an informed choice when he or she purchases a personal computer than when he or she votes for a congressional candidate." Evaluate this statement.

7. "Government action is based on majority rule, whereas market action is based on mutual consent. The market allows for proportional representation of minorities, but minorities must yield to the views of the majority when activities are undertaken through government." In your own words, explain the meaning of this statement. Is the statement true? Why or why not?

*8. "Voters should simply ignore political candidates who play ball with special-interest groups and vote instead for candidates who will represent all the people when they are elected. Government will work far better when this happens." Evaluate this view.

9. If a project is efficient (if its total benefits exceed its total costs), would it be possible to allocate the cost of the project in a manner that would provide net benefits to each voter? Why or why not? Explain. Will efficient projects necessarily be favored by a majority of voters? Explain.

*10. "When an economic function is turned over to the government, social cooperation replaces personal self-interest." Is this statement true? Why or why not?

11. What is the shortsightedness effect? How does the shortsightedness effect influence the efficiency of public-sector action?

*12. What's wrong with this way of thinking? "Public policy is necessary to protect the average citizen from the power of vested interest groups. In the absence of government intervention, regulated industries such as airlines, railroads, and trucking, will charge excessive prices, products will be unsafe, and the rich would oppress the poor. Government curbs the power of special-interest groups."

13. "Since government-operated firms do not have to make a profit, they can usually produce at a lower cost and charge a lower price than privately owned enterprises." Evaluate this view.

14. What percentage of government income transfer payments go to the poor? Do you think that the political process in general works to the advantage of the poor? Why or why not?

15. Why does representative democracy often tax some people in order to provide benefits to others? When governments become heavily involved in tax-transfer activities, how will this involvement affect economic efficiency?

*16. The United States imposes highly restrictive sugar import quotas that result in a domestic price that is generally about three times as high as the world price. The quotas benefit sugar growers at the expense of consumers. Given that there are far more sugar consumers than growers, why aren't the quotas abolished? Has government action in this area improved the living standards of Americans? Why or why not?

17. "The United States is rich because it is a political democracy where the people decide what policies will be followed." Is this statement true or false? Discuss.

18. If the power of special interests were reduced, for example, through the adoption of a supra-majority voting rule, would economic efficiency improve? How would contributions to political campaigns be affected? Do you think politicians are very interested in curtailing the power of special interests? Why or why not?

*Asterisk denotes questions for which answers are given in Appendix B.

3

"Growth of output is the key to a higher living standard"

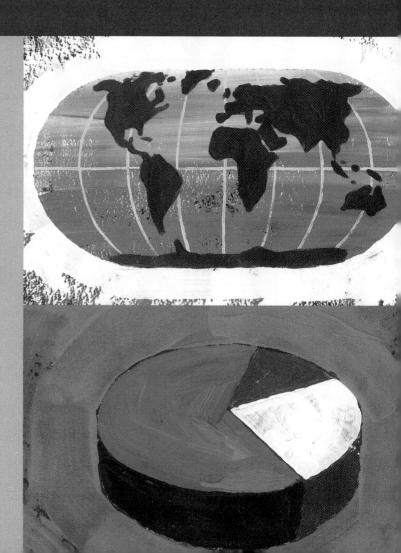

Core Macroeconomics

3

Macroeconomics is about growth of the economy and fluctuations in output, employment, and the general level of prices. Growth of output is highly important because it makes higher levels of consumption and standards of living possible. Like other countries, the United States has experienced fluctuations in output. What causes economic fluctuations? How can their frequency and intensity be reduced? What can economic policy do to promote more stability? Part 3 will focus on these questions and related issues.

CHAPTER 7

Taking the Nation's Economic Pulse

It has been said that figures rule the world; maybe. I am quite sure that it is figures which show us whether it is being ruled well or badly.

—Johann Wolfgang Goethe, 1830

Measurement is the making of distinction; precise measurement is making sharp distinctions.

—Enrico Fermi[1]

Chapter Focus

■ What is GDP? How is GDP calculated?

■ When making comparisons over time, why is it important to adjust nominal GDP for the effects of inflation?

■ What do price indexes measure? How can they be used to adjust for changes in the general level of prices?

■ Is GDP a good measure of output? What are its strengths and weaknesses?

[1]As quoted by Milton Friedman in *Economic Freedom: Toward a Theory of Measurement*, edited by Walter Block (Vancouver, B.C.: The Fraser Institute, 1991), 11.

Our society likes to keep score. The sports pages supply us with the win-loss records that reveal how well the various teams are doing. We also keep score on the performance of our economy. The scoreboard for economic performance is the *national-income accounting system.* Just as a firm's accounting statement provides information on its performance, national-income accounts supply performance information for the entire economy.

Simon Kuznets, the winner of the 1971 Nobel Prize in economics, developed the basic concepts of national-income accounting during the 1920s and 1930s (see the Outstanding Economist feature). Through the years, these procedures have been modified and improved. In this chapter, we will explain how the flow of an economy's output (and income) is measured. We will also explain how changes in the quantity of goods and services produced are separated from changes that reflect merely inflation (higher prices). Finally, we will analyze the strengths and weaknesses of the measurement tools used to assess the performance of our national economy. ▇

GDP—A MEASURE OF OUTPUT

The **gross domestic product (GDP)** *is the market value of final goods and services produced within a country during a specific time period, usually a year.* GDP is the most widely used measure of economic performance. The GDP figures are closely watched both by policy makers and by those in the business and financial communities. In the United States, the numbers are prepared quarterly and released a few weeks following the end of each quarter.

GDP is a "flow" concept. By analogy, a water gauge measures the amount of water that flows through a pipe each hour. Similarly, GDP measures the market value of production that "flows" through the economy's factories and shops each year (or quarter).

Gross domestic product (GDP)
The market value of all final goods and services produced within a country during a specific period.

What Counts toward GDP?

First and foremost, GDP is a measure of output. Thus, it cannot be arrived at merely by summing the totals on the nation's cash registers during a period. The key phrases in the definition of GDP—"market value" of "final goods and services" "produced" "within a country" "during a specific time period"—reveal a great deal about what should be included in and excluded from the calculation of GDP. Let's take a closer look at this issue.

Only final goods and services count. If output is to be measured accurately, all goods and services produced during the year must be counted once and only once. Most goods go through several stages of production before they end up in the hands of their ultimate

OUTSTANDING ECONOMIST	Simon Kuznets (1901–1985)	

Simon Kuznets provided the methodology for modern national-income accounting and developed the first reliable national-income measures for the United States. Kuznets is often referred to as the "father of national-income accounting." A native Russian, he immigrated to the United States at the age of 21 and spent his academic career teaching at the University of Pennsylvania, Johns Hopkins University, and Harvard University.

Intermediate goods
Goods purchased for resale or for use in producing another good or service.

Final market goods and services
Goods and services purchased by their ultimate user.

users. To avoid double-counting, one must take care to differentiate between **intermediate goods**—goods in intermediate stages of production—and **final market goods and services**, which are those purchased for final use rather than for resale or further processing.

Sales at intermediate stages of production are not counted by GDP because the value of the intermediate goods is embodied within the final-user good. Adding the sales price of both the intermediate good and the final-user good would exaggerate GDP. For example, when a wholesale distributor sells steak to a restaurant, the final purchase price paid by the patron of the restaurant for the steak dinner will reflect the cost of the meat. Double-counting would result if we included both the sale price of the intermediate good (the steak sold by the wholesaler to the restaurant) and the final purchase price of the steak dinner.

Exhibit 1 will help clarify the accounting method for GDP. Before the final good, bread, is in the hands of the consumer, it will go through several intermediate stages of production. The farmer produces a pound of wheat and sells it to the miller for 30 cents. The miller grinds the wheat into flour and sells it to the baker for 65 cents. The miller's actions have *added* 35 cents to the value of the wheat. The baker combines the flour with other ingredients, makes a loaf of bread, and sells it to the grocer for 90 cents. The baker has *added* 25 cents to the value of the bread. The grocer stocks the bread on the grocery shelves and provides a convenient location for consumers to shop. The grocer sells the loaf of bread for $1, *adding* 10 cents to the value of the final product. Only the final market value of the product—the $1 for the loaf of bread—is included in GDP. This price reflects the value added at each stage of production. The 30 cents *added* by the farmer, the 35 cents by the miller, the 25 cents by the baker, and the 10 cents by the grocer sum to the $1 purchase price.

Only transactions involving production count. Remember, GDP is a measure of goods and services "produced." Financial transactions and income transfers are excluded because they merely move ownership from one party to another. They do not involve current production and are therefore not included in GDP. (*Note*: If a financial transaction involves a sales commission, the commission is included in GDP because it involves a service rendered during the current period.)

EXHIBIT 1
GDP and the Stages of Production

Most goods go through several stages of production. This chart illustrates both the market value of a loaf of bread as it passes through the various stages of production (column 1) and the additional value added by each intermediate producer (column 2). GDP counts only the market value of the final product. Of course, the amount added by each intermediate producer (column 2) sums to the market value of the final product.

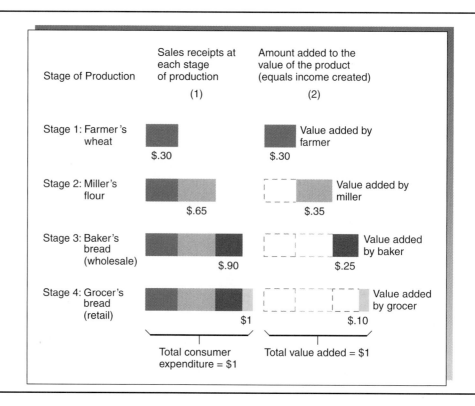

Thus, the purchases and sales of stocks, bonds, and U.S. securities are not included in GDP. Neither are private- and public-sector income transfers. If your aunt sends you $100 to help pay for your college expenses, your aunt has less wealth and you have more, but the transaction adds nothing to current production. Government income transfer payments, such as Social Security, welfare, and veterans payments, are also omitted. The recipients of these transfers are not producing goods in return for the transfers. Therefore, it would be inappropriate to add them to GDP.

Only production within the country is counted. GDP counts only goods and services produced within the geographic borders of the country. When foreigners earn income within U.S. borders, it adds to the GDP of the United States. For example, the incomes of Canadian engineers and Mexican baseball players earned in the United States are included in the U.S. GDP. On the other hand, the earnings of Americans abroad—for example, an American college professor teaching in England—do not count toward the U.S. GDP because this income is not generated within the borders of the United States.

Only goods produced during the current period are counted. As the definition indicates, GDP is a measure of output "during the current period." Transactions involving the exchange of goods or assets produced during earlier periods are omitted because they do not reflect current production. For example, the purchases of "secondhand" goods, such as a used car or a home built five years ago, are not included in this year's GDP. Production of these goods was counted at the time they were produced and initially purchased. Resale of such items produced during earlier years merely changes the ownership of the goods or assets. It does not add to current production. Thus, these transactions should not be included in current GDP. (*Note*: As in the case of financial transactions, sales commissions earned by those helping to arrange the sale of used cars, homes, or other assets are included in GDP because they reflect services provided during the current period.)

Dollars Are the Common Denominator for GDP

In elementary school, each of us was taught the difficulties of adding apples and oranges. Yet, this is precisely the nature of aggregate output. Literally millions of different commodities and services are produced each year. How can the production of apples, oranges, shoes, movies, roast beef sandwiches, automobiles, dresses, legal services, education, heart transplants, haircuts, and many other items be added together? Answer: The "market value" of each is added to GDP.

The vastly different goods and services produced in our modern world have only one thing in common: Someone pays a price for them. Therefore, when measuring output, units of each good are weighted according to their market value—the purchase price of the good or service. If a consumer pays $25,000 for a new automobile and $25 for a nice meal, production of the automobile adds 1,000 times as much to output as production of the meal. Similarly, production of a television set that is purchased for $1,000 will add 1/25 as much to output as the new automobile and 40 times the amount of the meal.

Each good produced increases output by the amount the purchaser pays for the good. The total spending on all goods and services produced during the year is then summed, in dollar terms, to obtain the annual GDP.

GDP AS A MEASURE OF BOTH OUTPUT AND INCOME

There are two ways of looking at and measuring GDP. First, the GDP of an economy can be reached by totaling the expenditures on goods and services produced during the year. National-income accountants refer to this method as the *expenditure approach*. *Alternatively, GDP can be calculated by summing the income payments to the resource suppliers of the things used to produce those goods and services.* Production of goods and services is costly because the resources required for their production must be bid away from their alternative uses. These costs generate incomes for resource suppliers. Thus, this method of calculating GDP is referred to as the *resource cost-income approach.*

The prices used to weight the goods and services included in GDP reflect both the market value of the output and the income generated by the resources. From an accounting viewpoint, when a good is produced and sold, the total payments to the factors of production (including the producer's profit or loss) must be equal to the sales price generated by the good.[2] For example, consider a beauty salon operator who leases a building and equipment, purchases various cosmetic products, and combines these items with labor to provide hairdressing services for which customers pay $500 per day. The market value of the output, $500 per day, is added to GDP. The $500 figure is also equal to the income resource owners receive from the provision of the service.

The link between the market value of a good and the income (including the profit or loss) earned by resource suppliers occurs for each good or service produced. This same link is also present in the aggregate economy. In accounting terms, the idea can be illustrated as follows:

$$\begin{array}{ccc} \text{The dollar flow of expenditures} & = & \text{The dollar flow of income (and indirect cost)} \\ \text{on final goods} & & \text{from final goods} \end{array}$$

GDP is a measure of the value of the goods and services that were purchased by households, investors, governments, and foreigners. These purchasers valued the goods and services more than the purchase price; otherwise they would not have purchased them. *GDP is also a measure of aggregate income.* Production of the goods involves human toil, wear and tear on machines, use of natural resources, risk, managerial responsibilities, and other of life's unpleasantries. Resource owners have to be compensated with income payments in order to induce them to supply these resources.

Thus, GDP is a measure of both (1) the market value of the output produced and (2) the income generated by those who produced the output. This highlights a very important point: Increases in output and growth of income are linked. An expansion in output—that is, the additional production of goods and services that people value—is the source of higher income levels.

Exhibit 2 summarizes the components of GDP for both the expenditure and resource cost-income approaches. Except for a few complicating elements that we will discuss in a moment, the revenues business firms derive from the sale of goods and services are paid

---

EXHIBIT 2
Two Ways of Measuring GDP

There are two methods of calculating GDP. It can be calculated either by summing the expenditures on the "final-user" goods and services purchased by consumers, investors, governments, and foreigners (net exports) or by summing the income payments and direct cost items that accompany the production of goods and services.

EXPENDITURE APPROACH

PERSONAL CONSUMPTION EXPENDITURES

+

GROSS PRIVATE DOMESTIC INVESTMENT

+

GOVERNMENT CONSUMPTION AND GROSS INVESTMENT

+

NET EXPORTS OF GOODS AND SERVICES

=

GDP

RESOURCE COST-INCOME APPROACH

AGGREGATE INCOME
    Compensation of employees
      (wages and salaries)
    Income of self-employed
      proprietors
    Rents
    Profits
    Interest

+

NONINCOME COST ITEMS
    Indirect business taxes
    Depreciation

+

NET INCOME OF FOREIGNERS

=

GDP

---

[2]In the national-income accounts, the terms profit and corporate profit are used in the accounting sense. Thus, they reflect both the competitive rate of return on assets (opportunity cost of capital) and the firm's economic profit and loss, which was discussed in Chapter 3.

directly to resource suppliers in the form of wages, self-employment income, rents, profits, and interest. We now turn to an examination of these components and the two alternative ways of deriving GDP.

Deriving GDP by the Expenditure Approach

When derived by the expenditure approach, GDP has four components: (1) personal consumption expenditures, (2) gross private domestic investment, (3) government consumption and gross investment, and (4) net exports to foreigners. The left side of **Exhibit 3** presents the values of these four components in 2003. Later we will discuss the right side, which deals with the resource cost-income approach.

Consumption Purchases **Personal consumption** purchases are the largest component of GDP; in 2003 they amounted to $7,761 billion. Most consumption expenditures are for nondurable goods or services. Food, clothing, recreation, medical and legal services, and fuel are included in this category. These items are used up or consumed in a relatively short time. Durable goods, such as appliances and automobiles, constitute approximately one-eighth of all consumer purchases. These products are consumed over a longer period of time, even though they are fully counted when they are purchased.

Personal consumption
Household spending on consumer goods and services during the current period. Consumption is a flow concept.

Gross Private Investment The next item in the expenditure approach, **private investment**, is the production or construction of capital goods that provide a "flow" of future service. Unlike food or medical services, they are not immediately "used." Business plants and equipment are investment goods because they will help produce goods and services in the future. Similarly, a house is an investment good because it will also provide a stream of services long into the future. Increases in business inventories are also classified as investment because they will provide future consumer benefits.

Gross investment includes expenditures for both (1) the replacement of machinery, equipment, and buildings worn out during the year and (2) net additions to the stock of capital assets. Net investment is simply gross investment minus an allowance for **depreciation** and obsolescence of machinery and other physical assets during the year.

Net investment is an important indicator of the economy's future productive capability. A substantial amount of net investment indicates that the capital stock of the economy

Private investment
The flow of private-sector expenditures on durable assets (fixed investment) plus the addition to inventories (inventory investment) during a period. These expenditures enhance our ability to provide consumer benefits in the future.

Depreciation
The estimated amount of physical capital (for example, machines and buildings) that is worn out or used up producing goods during a period.

EXHIBIT 3
Two Ways of Measuring GDP—2003 Data (Billions of Dollars)

The left side shows the flow of expenditures and the right side the flow of income payments and indirect costs. Both procedures yield GDP.

EXPENDITURE APPROACH			RESOURCE COST-INCOME APPROACH	
PERSONAL CONSUMPTION		$7,761	EMPLOYEE COMPENSATION	$6,289
Durable goods	$ 951		PROPRIETORS' INCOME	834
Nondurable goods	2,200		RENTS	154
Services	4,610		CORPORATE PROFITS	1,021
GROSS PRIVATE INVESTMENT		1,666	INTEREST INCOME	543
Fixed investment	1,667		INDIRECT BUSINESS TAXES	839
Inventories	−1		DEPRECIATION	
GOV. CONS. & GROSS INV.		2,075	(CAPITAL CONSUMPTION)[a]	1,380
Federal	752		NET INCOME OF FOREIGNERS	−55
State and local	1,323			
NET EXPORTS		−498		
GROSS DOMESTIC PRODUCT		$11,004	GROSS DOMESTIC PRODUCT	$11,004

[a]Includes $1,136 billion for the depreciation of privately owned capital, $218 billion for the depreciation of government-owned assets, and $26 billion for statistical discrepancy.
Source: U.S. Department of Commerce. These data are also online at http://www.bea.doc.gov.

is growing, thereby enhancing the economy's future productive potential (shifting the economy's production possibilities frontier outward). In contrast, a low rate of net investment, or even worse, a negative net investment, implies a stagnating or even contracting economy. Of course, the impact of investment on future income will also be affected by the productivity of investment—whether the funds invested are channeled into wealth-creating projects. Other things being the same, however, countries with a large net investment rate will tend to grow more rapidly than those with a low (or negative) rate of net investment. In 2003, gross private investment expenditures in the United States were $1,666 billion, 15.1 percent of GDP. Of course, a large portion ($1,380 billion) of this figure was for the replacement of private assets worn out during the year. Thus, net private investment was $286 billion, only 2.6 percent of GDP.

Inventory investment
Changes in the stock of unsold goods and raw materials held during a period.

Because GDP is designed to measure current production, allowance must be made for goods produced but not sold during the year—that is, for **inventory investment**, or changes during the year in the market value of unsold goods on shelves and in warehouses. If business firms have more goods on hand at the end of the year than they had at the beginning of the year, inventory investment will be positive. This inventory investment must be added to GDP. On the other hand, a decline in inventories would indicate that the purchases of goods and services exceeded current production. In this case, inventory *disinvestment* would be a subtraction from GDP. In 2003 the United States disinvested $1 billion in additional inventories.

Government Consumption and Gross Investment   In 2003, federal, state, and local government consumption and investment in the United States summed to $2,075 billion, approximately 19 percent of total GDP. The purchases of state and local governments exceeded those of the federal government by a wide margin. The government component includes both (1) expenditures on items like office supplies, law enforcement, and the operation of veterans hospitals, which are "consumed" during the current period and (2) the purchase of long-lasting capital goods, like missiles, highways, and dams for flood control. (Remember, transfer payments are excluded from GDP because they do not involve current production.) As a result, the government's total expenditures are substantially higher than its total consumption and investment expenditures. Unlike the other components of GDP, government purchases are counted at their *cost* to taxpayers rather than their *value* to those receiving them. In cases where the value of the item to citizens is low relative to the tax cost of providing it, the government expenditures will overstate the value derived from the item.

Net exports
Exports minus imports.

Exports
Goods and services produced domestically but sold to foreigners.

Imports
Goods and services produced by foreigners but purchased by domestic consumers, businesses, and governments.

Net Exports   The final item in the expenditure approach is **net exports**, or total exports minus imports. **Exports** are domestically produced goods and services sold to foreigners. **Imports** are foreign-produced goods and services purchased domestically. Remember, GDP is a measure of domestic production—output produced within the borders of a nation. Therefore, when measuring GDP by the expenditure approach, we must (1) add exports (goods produced domestically that were sold to foreigners) and (2) subtract imports (goods produced abroad that were purchased by Americans). For national-income accounting purposes, we can combine these two factors into a single entry:

$$\text{Net exports} = \text{Total exports} - \text{Total imports}$$

Net exports may be either positive or negative. When we sell more to foreigners than we buy from them, net exports are positive. In recent years, however, net exports have been negative, indicating we were buying more goods and services from foreigners than we were selling to them. In 2003 net exports were *minus* $498 billion.

Deriving GDP by the Resource Cost-Income Approach

The right side of Exhibit 3 illustrates how, rather than summing the flow of expenditures on final goods and services, we could reach GDP by summing the flow of costs incurred and income generated. Labor services play a very important role in the production process. It is therefore not surprising that employee compensation, $6,289 billion in 2003, provides the largest source of income generated by the production of goods and services.

Self-employed proprietors undertake the risks of owning their own business and simultaneously provide their own labor services to their firm. Their earnings in 2003 contributed $834 billion to GDP, 7.6 percent of the total. Together, employees and self-employed proprietors accounted for approximately two-thirds of GDP.

Machines, buildings, land, and other physical assets also contribute to the production process. Rents, corporate profits, and interest are payments to people who provide either the physical resources or the financial resources required for the purchase of physical assets. Rents are returns to resource owners who permit others to use their assets during a time period. Corporate profits are earned by stockholders, who bear the risk of the business undertaking and provide the financial capital the firm needs to purchase resources. Interest is a payment to parties who extend loans to producers.

Not all cost components of GDP result in an income payment to a resource supplier. In order to get to GDP, we also need to account for three other factors: indirect business taxes, the cost of depreciation, and the net income of foreigners.

Indirect Business Taxes   Taxes imposed on the sale of a good that increase the cost of the good to consumers are called **indirect business taxes**. The sales tax is a clear example. When you make a $1.00 purchase in a state with a 5 percent sales tax, the purchase actually costs you $1.05. The $1.00 goes to the seller to pay wages, rent, interest, and managerial costs. The 5 cents goes to the government. Indirect business taxes boost the market price of goods when GDP is calculated by the expenditure approach. Similarly, when looked at from the factor-cost viewpoint, taxes are an indirect cost of supplying the goods to the final consumers.

Depreciation   As machines are used to produce goods, they wear out and become less valuable. Even though this decline in the value of capital assets is a cost of producing goods during the current period, it does not involve a direct payment to a resource owner. Thus, it must be estimated. Depreciation is an estimate, based on the expected life of the asset, of the decline in the asset's value during the year. In 2003, depreciation (sometimes called *capital consumption allowance*) of private- and public-sector capital amounted to $1,380 billion, approximately 12.5 percent of GDP.

Net Income of Foreigners   The sum of employee compensation, proprietors' income, rents, corporate profits, and interest yields **national income**, the income of Americans, whether that income was earned domestically or abroad. If depreciation and indirect business taxes—the two indirect cost components—are added to national income, the result will be **gross national product (GNP)**, the output of Americans, whether it is generated in the United States or abroad. Put another way, GNP counts the income that Americans earn abroad, but it omits the income foreigners earn in the United States.

Because GDP is a measure of domestic output, the net income earned by foreigners must be added when GDP is derived using the resource cost-income approach. The **net income of foreigners** is equal to the income foreigners earn in the United States minus the income that Americans earn abroad. If Americans earn more abroad than foreigners earn in the United States, the net income of foreigners will be negative. In recent years, this has been the case. The net income of foreigners is generally small. In 2003, it was *minus* $55 billion, about one-half of 1 percent of GDP. As Exhibit 3 indicates, when this figure is added to the other components, the sum is equal to GDP.

The Relative Size of GDP Components

Exhibit 4 shows the relative size of each of the GDP components during 2000–2003. When the expenditure approach is used, personal consumption is by far the largest component of GDP. Consumption accounted for 70 percent of GDP during 2000–2003, compared to only 16 and 18 percent for private investment and government purchases, respectively. When GDP is measured using the resource cost-income approach, compensation to employees is the dominant component (58 percent of GDP). During 2000–2003, rents, corporate profits, and interest combined accounted for 14 percent of GDP.

Indirect business taxes
Taxes that increase a business firm's costs of production and, therefore, the prices charged to consumers. Examples are sales, excise, and property taxes.

National income
The total income earned by a country's nationals (citizens) during a period. It is the sum of employee compensation, self-employment income, rents, interest, and corporate profits.

Gross national product (GNP)
The total market value of all final goods and services produced by the citizens of a country. It is equal to GDP minus the net income of foreigners.

Net income of foreigners
The income that foreigners earn by contributing labor and capital resources to the production of goods within the borders of a country minus the income the nationals of the country earn abroad.

EXHIBIT 4
The Major Components of GDP in the United States, 2000–2003

The relative sizes of the major components of GDP usually fluctuate within a fairly narrow range. The average proportion of each component during 2000–2003 is demonstrated here for both (a) the expenditure and (b) the resource-cost approaches.

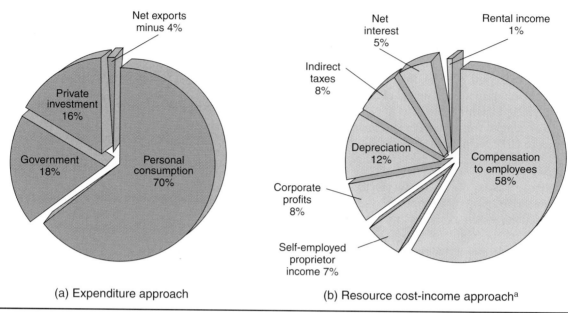

(a) Expenditure approach

(b) Resource cost-income approach[a]

[a]The net income of foreigners was negligible.
Source: http://www.economagic.com

ADJUSTING FOR PRICE CHANGES AND DERIVING REAL GDP

GDP was developed to help us better assess what is happening to output (and income) over time. This is important because expansion in the production of goods and services people value is the source of higher incomes and living standards. When comparing GDP across time periods, however we confront a problem, the nominal value of GDP may increase as the result of either (1) an expansion in the quantity of goods produced or (2) higher prices. Because only the former will improve our living standards, it is very important to distinguish between the two.

When comparing GDP and other income measures across time periods, economists use price indexes to adjust **nominal values** (or *money values,* as they are often called) for the effects of inflation—an increase in the general level of prices over time. When the term **real** accompanies GDP and income data (for example, *real GDP* or *real wages*), this means that the data have been adjusted for changes in the general level of prices through time. When comparing data at different points in time, it is nearly always the real changes that are of most interest.

What precisely is a price index, and how can it be used to adjust GDP and other figures for the effects of inflation? *A price index measures the cost of purchasing a market basket (or "bundle") of goods at a point in time relative to the cost of purchasing the identical market basket during an earlier reference period*. A base year (or period) is chosen and assigned a value of 100. As prices increase and the cost of purchasing the reference bundle of goods rises relative to the base year, the price index increases proportionally. Thus, a price index of 110 indicates that the general level of prices is 10 percent higher than during the base period. An index of 120 implies 20 percent higher prices than the base period, and so on. *Note:* See the Addendum at the end of this chapter for additional details on how price indexes are constructed.

Nominal values
Values expressed in current dollars.

Real values
Values that have been adjusted for the effects of inflation.

Two Key Price Indexes: The Consumer Price Index and the GDP Deflator

Price indexes indicate what is happening to the general level of prices. The two most widely used are the consumer price index (CPI) and the GDP deflator. Because the construction of the CPI is simpler, we will begin with it.

The **consumer price index (CPI)** *is designed to measure the impact of price changes on the cost of the typical bundle of goods purchased by households.* A bundle of 364 items that constitute the "typical bundle" purchased by urban consumers during the 1982–1984 base period provides the foundation for the CPI. The quantity of each good reflects the quantity actually purchased by the typical household during the base period. Every month, the Bureau of Labor Statistics surveys approximately 21,000 stores representative of the urban United States to derive the average price for each of the food items, consumer goods and services, housing, and property taxes included in the index. The cost of purchasing this 364-item market basket at current prices is then compared to the cost of purchasing the same market basket at base-year prices. The result is a measure of current prices compared to 1982–1984 base-period prices. In 2003, the value of the CPI was 184.0, compared to 100 during the 1982–1984 base period. This indicates that the price level in 2003 was 84.0 percent higher than the price level of 1982–1984.

The **GDP deflator** *is a broader price index than the CPI. It is designed to measure the change in the average price of the market basket of goods included in GDP.* In addition to consumer goods, the GDP deflator includes prices for capital goods and other goods and services purchased by businesses and governments. Therefore, in addition to consumer goods, the bundle used to construct the GDP deflator will include such items as large computers, airplanes, welding equipment, and office space. The overall bundle is intended to be representative of those items included in GDP.

The cost of purchasing the typical bundle of goods included in this year's GDP is always compared to the cost of purchasing that same bundle at last year's prices. Each year's inflation rate, based on the updated bundle, is then used to chain together the index. Because of this constant updating of the typical bundle, the impact of price increases is reduced when purchasers substitute away from goods that have risen in price. As a result, the GDP deflator is thought to yield a slightly more accurate measure of changes in the general level of prices than the CPI. As in the case of the CPI, a base year (currently it is the year 2000) is chosen for the GDP deflator and assigned a value of 100. As prices rise, the index increases. The year-to-year percentage change in the index provides an estimate of the rate of inflation.

Exhibit 5 presents data for both the CPI and GDP deflator during the past two decades. Even though they are based on different market baskets and procedures, the two measures of the annual rate of inflation are quite similar. An inspection of the annual rate of inflation as measured by each index indicates that the differences between these two alternative measures have been small, usually only a few tenths of a percentage point.

The CPI and GDP deflator were designed for different purposes. Choosing between the two depends on what we are trying to measure. If we want to determine how rising prices affect the money income of consumers, the CPI would be most appropriate because it includes only consumer goods. However, if we want an economy-wide measure of inflation with which to adjust GDP data, the GDP deflator is clearly the appropriate index because it includes a broader set of goods and services.

Using the GDP Deflator to Derive Real GDP

We can use the GDP deflator together with **nominal GDP** to measure **real GDP**, which is GDP in dollars of constant purchasing power. If prices are rising, we simply deflate the nominal GDP during the latter period to account for the effects of inflation.

Exhibit 6 illustrates how real GDP is measured and why it is important to adjust for price changes. Between 1998 and 2003, the nominal GDP of the United States increased from $8,747 billion to $11,004 billion, an increase of 25.8 percent. However, a large portion of this increase in nominal GDP reflected inflation rather than an increase in real output. When making GDP comparisons across time periods, we generally do so in terms of

Consumer price index (CPI)
An indicator of the general level of prices. It attempts to compare the cost of purchasing the market basket bought by a typical consumer during a specific period to the cost of purchasing the same market basket during an earlier period.

GDP deflator
A price index that reveals the cost during the current period of purchasing the items included in GDP relative to the cost during a base year (currently 2000). Unlike the consumer price index (CPI), the GDP deflator also measures the prices of capital goods and other goods and services purchased by businesses and governments. Because of this, it is thought to be a more accurate measure of changes in the general level of prices than the CPI.

Nominal GDP
GDP expressed at current prices. It is often called money GDP.

Real GDP
GDP adjusted for changes in the price level.

EXHIBIT 5
The Consumer Price
Index and GDP Deflator:
1983–2003

YEAR	CPI (1982 − 84 = 100)	INFLATION RATE (PERCENT)	GDP DEFLATOR (2000 = 100)	INFLATION RATE (PERCENT)
1983	99.6	3.2	65.2	4.0
1984	103.9	4.3	67.7	3.8
1985	107.6	3.6	69.7	3.0
1986	109.6	1.9	71.3	2.2
1987	113.6	3.6	73.2	2.7
1988	118.3	4.1	75.7	3.4
1989	124.0	4.8	78.6	3.8
1990	130.7	5.4	81.6	3.9
1991	136.2	4.2	84.4	3.5
1992	140.3	3.0	86.4	2.3
1993	144.5	3.0	88.4	2.3
1994	148.2	2.6	90.3	2.1
1995	152.4	2.8	92.1	2.0
1996	156.9	3.0	93.9	1.9
1997	160.5	2.3	95.4	1.7
1998	163.0	1.5	96.5	1.1
1999	166.6	2.2	97.9	1.4
2000	172.2	3.4	100.0	2.2
2001	177.1	2.8	102.4	2.4
2002	179.9	1.6	104.1	1.7
2003	184.0	2.3	106.0	1.8

Source: http://www.economagic.com

the purchasing power of the dollar during the base year of the GDP deflator, currently 2000. The GDP deflator, the price index that measures changes in the cost of all goods included in GDP, increased from 96.5 in 1998 to 106.0 in 2003. This indicates that prices rose by 9.8 percent between 1998 and 2003. To determine the real GDP for 2003 in terms of 1998 dollars, we deflate the 2003 nominal GDP for the rise in prices:

$$\text{Real GDP}_{2003} = \text{Nominal GDP}_{2003} \times \frac{\text{GDP deflator}_{1998}}{\text{GDP deflator}_{2003}}$$

Because prices were rising, the latter ratio is less than 1. Measured in terms of 1998 dollars, the real GDP in 2003 was $10,018 billion, only 14.5 percent more than in 1998. So although money GDP (nominal GDP) expanded by 25.8 percent, real GDP increased by only 14.5 percent.

EXHIBIT 6
Changes in Prices and Real GDP in the United States, 1998–2003

Between 1998 and 2003, nominal GDP increased by 25.8 percent. But when the 2003 GDP is deflated to account for price increases, we see that real GDP increased by only 14.5 percent.

	NOMINAL GDP (BILLIONS OF DOLLARS)	PRICE INDEX (GDP DEFLATOR, 2000 = 100)	REAL GDP (BILLIONS OF 1998 DOLLARS)
1998	$8,747	96.5	$8,747
2003	11,004	106.0	10,018
Percent Increase	25.8	9.8	14.5

Source: http://www.economagic.com

APPLICATIONS IN ECONOMICS

Converting Prior Data to Current Dollars: The Case of Gasoline

We have explained how the GDP deflator can be used to convert nominal GDP data to real GDP (measured in terms of the dollar's purchasing power during the base year of the GDP deflator). Sometimes, however, it makes more sense to convert income or other data during prior years to the purchasing power of the dollar during the current year. A price index can also be used to accomplish this task. To convert an earlier observation to current dollars, just multiply the observation by the price index during the current period and then divide it by the price index during the earlier period. If prices have risen in recent years, this will "inflate" the data for the earlier year and thereby bring it into line with the current purchasing power of the dollar.

Let's illustrate this point and at the same time analyze the changes in gasoline prices during the last several decades. As gas prices rose sharply during 2004, the media reported that they had risen to an all-time high in the United States. In nominal terms this was indeed the case, but what about the real price of gasoline?

The accompanying table presents data for the nominal price (column 1) of a gallon of unleaded regular gasoline for various years since 1973. The parallel data for the consumer price index (CPI) are presented in column 2. The nominal price of gasoline in 1973 was 39 cents. To convert this figure to the purchasing power of the dollar in May 2004, one merely multiplies the 39 cents by the ratio of the CPI in May 2004 divided by the CPI in 1973. This

real price (shown in column 3), measured in terms of the 2004 price level, is equal to $1.66 (0.39 times the ratio of 189.1/44.4).

Both crude oil prices and gasoline prices rose sharply throughout the 1970s. By 1980, the nominal price of gasoline had risen to $1.25. This would make the real price of gasoline measured in 2004 dollars equal to $2.87 ($1.25 times the ratio of 189.1/82.4), substantially higher than the figure for 2004. What was the real price of gasoline in 1976, 1985, 1990, and 1995? As an exercise, derive these figures to make sure that you understand how to convert data from an earlier time period into the purchasing power of the dollar during the current year.

Price of a Gallon of Regular Unleaded Gasoline

Year	Nominal Price (1)	CPI (1982–84 = 100) (2)	Real Price (3)
1973	$ 0.39	44.4	$1.66
1976	0.61	56.9	?
1980	1.25	82.4	2.87
1985	1.20	107.6	?
1990	1.16	130.7	?
1995	1.15	152.4	?
2000	1.51	172.2	1.66
2004 (May)	2.01	189.1	2.01

Source: U.S. Energy Information Administration, *Monthly Energy Review.* The data for regular unleaded gasoline were unavailable prior to 1976. Thus, the 1973 observation is for regular leaded gasoline, which was slightly cheaper during that period.

Data on both money GDP and price changes are essential for meaningful output comparisons between two time periods. By itself, a change in money GDP tells us nothing about what is happening to the rate of real production. For example, not even a doubling of money GDP would lead to an increase in real output if prices more than doubled during the time period. On the other hand, money income could remain constant while real GDP increased if there were a reduction in prices. Knowledge of both nominal GDP and the general level of prices is required for real income comparisons over time.

PROBLEMS WITH GDP AS A MEASURING ROD

Even real GDP is an imperfect measure of current output and income. Some productive activities are omitted because their value is difficult to determine. The introduction of new products complicates the use of GDP as a measuring rod. Also, when production involves harmful "side effects" that are not fully registered in the market prices. GDP will fail to accurately measure the level of output. Let's take a closer look at some of the limitations of GDP.

Nonmarket Production

GDP does not count household production because it does not involve a market transaction. As a result, the household services of millions of people are excluded. If you mow the yard, repair your car, paint your house, pick up relatives from school, or perform similar productive household activities, your efforts add nothing to GDP, because no market transaction is involved. Such nonmarket productive activities are sizable—10 percent to 15 percent of total GDP.

Excluding household production results in some oddities in national-income accounting. Suppose, for example, that a woman marries her gardener, and, after the marriage, the spouse-gardener works for love rather than for money. GDP will decline because the services of the spouse-gardener no longer involve a market transaction and therefore no longer contribute to GDP. On the other hand, if a family member decides to enter the labor force and hires someone to perform services previously provided by household members, there will be a double-barreled impact on GDP. It will rise as a result of (1) the market earnings of the new labor-force entrant plus (2) the amount paid to the person hired to perform the services that were previously supplied within the household.

Most important, omitting household production makes income comparisons across lengthy time periods less meaningful. Compared to the situation today, fifty years ago Americans were far more likely to produce sizable amounts of their own food and clothing. Only a small number of married women worked, and child care services were almost exclusively provided within the household. Today, people are also more likely to eat out at a restaurant than prepare their own food; hire a lawn service than mow their own lawn; and purchase an automatic dishwasher than do the dishes by hand. These and many other similar changes involve the substitution of a market transaction, which adds to GDP. Because the share of total production provided within the household has declined relative to production that involves market transactions, current GDP, even in real dollars, is overstated relative to the earlier period. Correspondingly, this factor causes an upward bias to the growth rate of real GDP.

Underground Economy

Some people attempt to conceal various economic activities in order to evade taxes or because the activities themselves are illegal. Economists call these activities, which are unreported and therefore difficult to measure, the **underground economy**.

Because cash transactions are hard for government authorities to trace, they are the lifeblood of the underground economy. This is why drug trafficking, smuggling, prostitution, and other illegal activities are generally conducted in cash. Not all underground economic activity is illegal. A large portion of the underground economy involves legal goods and services that go unreported so that people can try to evade taxes. The participants in this legal-if-reported portion of the underground economy are quite diverse. Taxicab drivers and wait staff may pocket fees and tips. Small-business owners may fail to ring up and report various cash sales. Craft and professional workers may fail to report cash income. Employees ranging from laborers to bartenders may work "off the books" and accept payment in cash in order to qualify for income-transfer benefits or evade taxes (or allow their employers to evade taxes).

Underground economy
Unreported barter and cash transactions that take place outside recorded market channels. Some are otherwise legal activities undertaken to evade taxes. Others involve illegal activities, such as trafficking drugs and prostitution.

Even though they are often productive, these unreported underground activities are not included in GDP. Estimates of the size of the underground economy in the United States range from 10 percent to 15 percent of total output. The available evidence indicates that the size of the underground economy is even larger in Western Europe (where tax rates are higher) and South America (where regulations often make it more costly to operate a business legally).

Leisure and Human Costs

GDP excludes leisure and the human cost associated with the production of goods and services. Only output matters; no allowance is made for how long or how hard people work to generate it. Simon Kuznets, the "inventor" of GDP, believed that these omissions substantially reduced the accuracy of GDP as a measure of economic well-being.

The average number of hours worked per week in the United States has declined through the years. The average nonagricultural production worker spent only 33.7 hours per week on the job in 2003, compared to more than 40 hours in 1947—a 15 percent reduction in weekly hours worked. Clearly, this reduction in the length of the workweek raised the American standard of living, even though it did not enhance GDP.

GDP also fails to take into account human costs. On average, jobs today are less physically strenuous and are generally performed in a safer, more comfortable environment than they were a generation ago.[3] To the extent that working conditions have improved through the years, GDP figures understate the growth of real income.

Quality Variation and the Introduction of New Goods

If GDP is going to measure accurately changes in real output, changes in the price level must be measured accurately. This is a difficult task in a dynamic world where new and improved products are constantly replacing old ones. Think about how much more functional today's computers are compared to yesterday's typewriters, for example. Computers also cost relatively more, even when you take inflation into account. When it comes to calculating GDP, though, a portion of the higher price of improved products like computers is probably due to quality improvements rather than pure inflation. Although statisticians attempt to make some allowance for quality improvements and new products, they are generally thought to be inadequate. Most economists believe that price indexes, including the GDP deflator, overestimate the rate of inflation by approximately 1 percent *annually* because quality improvements aren't accounted for accurately. If so, annual changes in output are underestimated by a similar amount. Although 1 percent per year might seem small, errors of this size make a huge difference over long time periods.

Harmful Side Effects and Economic "Bads"

GDP makes no adjustment for harmful side effects that sometimes arise from production, consumption, and the destructive acts of man and nature. If they do not involve market transactions, economic "bads" are ignored in the calculation of GDP. Yet, in a modern industrial economy, production and consumption sometimes generate side effects that either detract from current consumption or reduce our future production possibilities. When property rights are defined imperfectly, air and water pollution are sometimes side effects of economic activity. For example, an industrial plant may pollute the air or water while producing goods. Automobiles may put harmful chemicals into the atmosphere while providing us with transportation. GDP makes no allowance for these negative side effects. In fact, expenditures on the cleanup of air and water pollution, should they be undertaken, will add to GDP.

Similarly, GDP makes no allowance for various acts of destruction. Consider the impact of the September 11, 2001, terrorist attacks. In addition to 3,030 fatalities, property losses

---

[3]For evidence on this point, see "Have a Nice Day," *2001 Annual Report, Federal Reserve Bank of Dallas* (available online at http://www.dallasfed.org).

were estimated at approximately $20 billion, including the destruction of the World Trade Center, portions of the Pentagon, and the four commercial planes hijacked. But GDP makes no allowance for these losses. Therefore, none of this destruction influenced GDP. In fact, the cleanup cost, which continued for months, actually added to GDP. Of course, GDP was indirectly adversely affected by the attacks: some people and businesses weren't able to function for some time afterward, if ever. Air travel and tourism spending fell. Other responses to the attacks, like the increase in expenditures on security, national defense, and the reconstruction of the Pentagon, enhanced GDP. But the GDP numbers did not reflect the loss of property or life. The same is true for destruction accompanying hurricanes, earthquakes, and other acts of nature. Even if billions of dollars of assets are destroyed, there will be no adjustment made to the GDP numbers.

DIFFERENCES IN GDP OVER TIME

Per capita GDP is simply GDP divided by population. It is a measure of income per person or the average level of income. As real per capita GDP increases, so too does the average level of real income. **Exhibit 7** presents the data for per capita real GDP (measured in 2000 dollars) for the United States for various years since 1930. In 2003, per capita GDP was nearly twice the figure of 1970 and more than five times the figure for 1930. What do these figures reveal? As we previously discussed, some of the measurement deficiencies of GDP will result in an overstatement of current real GDP relative to earlier periods. For example, current per capita GDP is biased upward because, compared to earlier periods, more output now takes place in the market sector and less in the household sector. Other biases, however, are in the opposite direction. Reductions in both time and strenuousness of work as well as the introduction of improved products and new technologies provide examples of the latter. On balance, the direction of the overall bias is uncertain.

EXHIBIT 7
Per Capita GDP:
1930–2003

In 2003, per capita real GDP was 2.6 times the 1960 level, 4.6 times the 1940 level, and 5.6 times the 1930 level. What do these numbers reveal about income today relative to the earlier years?

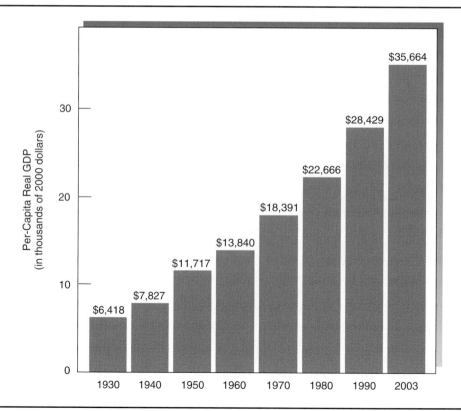

Source: Derived from U.S. Department of Commerce data.

However, one thing is clear: GDP comparisons are less meaningful when there is a dramatic difference in the bundle of goods available. This is generally the case when comparisons are made across distant time periods. Consider the 1930s, compared to today. In the 1930s, there were no jet planes, television programs, automatic dishwashers, personal computers, or MP3 players. In 1930, even a millionaire could not have purchased the typical bundle consumed by the average American in 2003.[4] When the potential goods available differ substantially between time periods (or countries), comparative GDP statistics lose some of their precision.

Shortcomings aside, however, there is evidence that GDP per person is a broad indicator of general living standards. As per capita GDP in the United States has increased over time, the quality of most goods has increased while the amount of work time required for their purchase has declined. In many cases, the changes have been dramatic. (See the boxed feature, "The Time Cost of Goods: Today and Yesterday.") Like per capita GDP, these data indicate that our income levels and living standards have improved. Various quality-of-life variables paint a similar picture. For example, as per capita GDP has risen in the United States and other countries, life expectancy and leisure time have gone up, while illiteracy and infant mortality rates have gone down. This suggests that increases in per capita GDP and improvements in living standards are closely related.

APPLICATIONS IN ECONOMICS

The Time Cost of Goods: Today and Yesterday

Many of you have heard stories from your parents or grandparents about how low prices were when they were young. A bottle of soda cost only a nickel, and a brand-new car was less than $2,000. In this chapter, you have learned that there is a difference between nominal and real values. Economists generally use the CPI or GDP deflator to adjust the nominal prices of earlier periods and figure out if a good is now cheaper or more expensive. There is, however, an alternative way of looking at this issue: you could estimate how long a person working at the average wage rate would have to work in order to earn enough to purchase various items at different points in time. For example, just after telling you that a soda used to cost a nickel, your grandfather might have noted that he used to earn only 25 cents per hour. Thus, for an hour's worth of work, he could earn enough money to purchase five bottles of soda. Today, the price of a soda is approximately $1. To earn the same real wage as your grandfather, you would need to earn only $5 per hour (exactly enough to purchase five sodas with your hour's wage).

Over time, the productivity of the average worker in America has increased substantially. This increased worker productivity is the key to higher real incomes and improved living standards. Using average wage rates, W. Michael Cox and Richard Alm of the Federal Reserve Bank of Dallas have computed the time of work required for the typical worker to purchase many common items. Their analysis shows that Americans today are able to acquire most goods with much less work time than was previously the case. Some examples are shown in the accompanying table.

In 1908, a new automobile cost $850, which took the average worker 4,696 hours to earn. In 1955, a new automobile costing $3,030 took 1,638 hours of work, and by 1997, a $17,995 new automobile cost a typical worker only 1,365 hours of work. The time cost of a new car today is less than 30 percent of the time cost in 1908. Furthermore, even today's most economical model is light-years away from the 1908 version with regard to power, performance, and dependability.

The prices of technology products, such as computers, calculators, and cellular phones, in particular, have fallen dramatically in recent years. Cellular phones and comput-

(continued)

---

[4]The following quotation from the late Mancur Olson, longtime professor of economics at the University of Maryland, illustrates this point:

> The price level has risen about eight times since 1932, so a $25,000 income then would be the "equivalent" of an income of $200,000 today—one could readily afford a Rolls-Royce, the best seats in the theater, and the care of the best physicians in the country. But the 1932 Rolls-Royce, for all its many virtues, does not embody some desirable technologies available today in the humblest Ford. Nor would the imposing dollar of 1932 buy a TV set or a home videocassette recorder. And if one got an infection, the best physicians in 1932 would not be able to prescribe an antibiotic.

APPLICATIONS IN ECONOMICS

(continued)

ers now cost only a fraction of the time required for their purchase just a few years ago. In 1984, it took the average worker more than 10 weeks of work to purchase a cellular phone; by 1997, the work time cost had fallen to 9 hours, and the figure is still lower today. In 1901, spending on food, clothing, and shelter consumed 76 percent of the typical worker's paycheck. Because of greater productivity and higher real earnings, today the average worker spends only 38 percent of earnings on these items.

As worker productivity grows, real incomes increase, and the time cost required to purchase products falls. This process generates higher living standards and brings goods that used to be luxuries, costing weeks' or months' worth of a worker's salary, within the reach of most Americans. The next time you call home, remind your parents that in 1915, a 3-minute, coast-to-coast, long-distance telephone call cost more than 2-weeks' worth of wages. Today, it costs only 1.8 minutes of work. Your parents will be happy to hear that, particularly if you are calling collect.

The Cost of Products to an Average-Wage Worker in Minutes or Hours of Work

Item	Old Cost	Cost in 1997
Eggs (1 dozen)	80 minutes in 1919	5 minutes
Sugar (5 lbs.)	72 minutes in 1919	10 minutes
Coffee (1 lb.)	55 minutes in 1919	17 minutes
Bread (1 lb.)	13 minutes in 1919	4 minutes
Mattress and box spring (twin)	161 hours in 1929	24 hours
Refrigerator	3,162 hours in 1916	68 hours
Clothes washer and dryer	256 hours in 1956	52 hours
Automobile	4,696 hours in 1908	1,365 hours
Coast-to-coast air flight	366 hours in 1930	16 hours
Big Mac	27 minutes in 1940	9 minutes
Long-distance call (3 min.)	90 hours in 1915	1.8 minutes
Calculator	31 hours in 1972	46 minutes
Microwave oven	97 hours in 1975	15 hours
Cellular phone	456 hours in 1984	9 hours
Personal computer	435 hours in 1984	76 hours

Source: W. Michael Cox and Richard Alm, "Time Well Spent: The Declining Real Cost of Living in America," *1997 Annual Report, Federal Reserve Bank of Dallas:* 2–24. Also see Michael Cox, *Myths of Rich and Poor* (New York: Basic Books, 1999).

Is an automobile really more expensive now than it was in 1955? You might be surprised to learn that in 1955 it took a typical worker 1,638 hours of work time to purchase a car. Today, a vastly improved model can be purchased after only 1,365 hours of work.

THE GREAT CONTRIBUTION OF GDP

Although GDP is a broad indicator of income levels and living standards, this is not its major purpose. ***GDP was designed to measure the value of the goods and services produced during a time period. In spite of its limitations, real GDP is a reasonably precise measure of the rate of output and the year-to-year changes in that output.***

   Adjusted for changes in prices, annual and quarterly GDP data provide the information required to track the economy's performance level. These data allow us to compare the current rate of output with that of the recent past. Without this information, policy makers would be less likely to adopt productive policies and business decision makers would be less able to determine the future direction of the demand for their products.

LOOKING AHEAD

GDP provides us with a measure of economic performance. In the next chapter, we will take a closer look at the path of real GDP in the United States and introduce other indicators of economic performance. Later, we will investigate the factors that underlie both the level of and fluctuations in real GDP.

KEY POINTS

▼ Gross domestic product (GDP) is a measure of the market value of final goods and services produced within the borders of a country during a specific time period, usually a year.

▼ Income transfers, purely financial transactions, and exchanges of goods and assets produced during earlier periods are not included in GDP because they do not involve current production.

▼ When derived by the expenditure approach, GDP has four major components: (1) personal consumption, (2) gross private investment, (3) government consumption and gross investment, and (4) net exports.

▼ When derived by the resource cost-income approach, GDP equals (1) the direct income components (wages and salaries, self-employment income, rents, interest, and corporate profits), plus (2) indirect business taxes, depreciation, and the net income of foreigners.

▼ Price indexes measure changes in the general level of prices over time. They can be used to adjust

nominal values for the effects of inflation. The two most widely used price indexes are the GDP deflator and the consumer price index (CPI).

▼ The following formula can be used to convert the nominal GDP data of the current period (2) to real GDP measured in terms of the general level of prices of an earlier period (1):

$$\text{Real GDP}_2 = \text{Nominal GDP}_2 \times \frac{\text{GDP deflator}_1}{\text{GDP deflator}_2}$$

▼ Even real GDP is an imperfect measure of current production. It excludes household production and the underground economy, fails to take leisure and human costs into account, and adjusts imperfectly for quality changes.

▼ Real GDP is vitally important because it is a reasonably accurate measure of how well the economy is doing. Per capita GDP is a broad indicator of income levels and living standards across time periods.

CRITICAL ANALYSIS QUESTIONS

*1. Indicate how each of the following activities will affect this year's GDP:
   a. The sale of a used economics textbook to the college bookstore
   b. Smith's $500 doctors bill for setting her son's broken arm
   c. Family lawn services provided by Smith's 16-year-old child
   d. Lawn services purchased by Smith from the neighbor's 16-year-old child who has a lawn-mowing business
   e. A $5,250 purchase of 100 shares of stock at $50 per share plus the sales commission of $250
   f. A multi-billion-dollar discovery of natural gas in Oklahoma
   g. A hurricane that causes $10 billion of damage in Florida
   h. $60,000 of income earned by an American college professor teaching in England

2. If nominal GDP increased by 6 percent during a year, while the GDP deflator increased by 4 percent, by how much did real GDP change during the year?

*3. A large furniture retailer sells $100,000 of household furnishings from inventories built up last year. How does this sale influence GDP? How are the components of GDP affected?

4. Suppose a group of British investors finances the construction of a plant to manufacture skateboards in St. Louis, Missouri. How will the construction of the plant affect GDP? Suppose the plant generates $100,000 in corporate profits this year. Will these profits contribute to GDP? Why or why not?

*5. Why might even real GDP be a misleading index of changes in output between 1950 and 2003 in the United States?

6. What are price indexes designed to measure? Outline how they are constructed. When GDP and other income figures are compared across time periods, explain why it is important to adjust for changes in the general level of prices.

*7. In 1982, the average hourly earnings of private nonagricultural production workers were $7.86 per hour. By 2003, the average hourly earnings had risen to $15.35. In 2003, the CPI was 184.0, compared to 96.5 in 1982. What were the real earnings of private nonagricultural production workers in 2003 measured in 1982 dollars?

8. The receipts and year of release of the four movies with the largest nominal box office revenues, along with the CPI data of each year are presented below. Assuming that the receipts for each of the movies were derived during their year of release, convert the receipts for each to real dollars for the year 2003 (2003 CPI 184.0). Which movie had the largest real box office receipts?

Movies	Box Office Receipts (Millions)	Year Released	CPI in Year Released
Titanic	$600.8	1997	160.5
Star Wars	461.0	1977	60.6
Star Wars: The Phantom Menace	431.1	1999	166.6
E. T.: The Extra-Terrestrial	399.9	1982	96.5

*9. How much do each of the following contribute to GDP?
   a. Jones pays a repair shop $1,000 to rebuild the engine of her automobile.
   b. Jones spends $200 on parts and pays a mechanic $400 to rebuild the engine of her automobile.
   c. Jones spends $200 on parts and rebuilds the engine of her automobile herself.
   d. Jones sells her four-year-old automobile for $5,000 and buys Smith's two-year-old model for $10,000.
   e. Jones sells her four-year-old automobile for $5,000 and buys a new car for $20,000.

10. What is the difference between the consumer price index (CPI) and the GDP deflator? Which would be better to use if you want to measure whether your hourly earnings this year were higher than they were last year? Why?

*11. Indicate whether the following statements are true or false:
   a. "For the economy as a whole, inventory investment can never be negative."
   b. "The net investment of an economy must always be positive."
   c. "An increase in GDP indicates that the standard of living of people has risen."

*12. How do the receipts and expenditures of a state-operated lottery affect GDP?

13. GDP does not count productive services, such as child care, food preparation, cleaning, and laundry,

provided within the household. Why are these things excluded? Is GDP a sexist measure? Does it understate the productive contributions of women relative to men? Discuss.

*14. Indicate how each of the following will affect this year's GDP:
   a. You suffer $10,000 of damage when you wreck your automobile.
   b. You win $10,000 in a state lottery.
   c. You spend $5,100 in January for 100 shares of stock ($5,000 for the stock and $100 for the sales commission) and sell the stock in August for $8,200 ($8,000 for the stock and $200 for the sales commission).
   d. You pay $500 for this month's rental of your apartment.
   e. You are paid $300 for computer services provided to a client.
   f. You receive $300 from your parents.
   g. You get a raise from $8 to $10 per hour and simultaneously decide to reduce your hours worked from 20 to 16 per week.
   h. You earn $4,000 working in Spain as an English instructor.

15. The accompanying chart presents 2003 data from the national-income accounts of the United States.

Component	Billions of Dollars
Personal consumption	$7,760.9
Employee compensation	6,289.0
Rents	153.8
Gov't consumption & investment	2,075.3
Imports	1,544.3
Depreciation	1,379.5
Corporate profits	1,021.1
Interest income	543.0
Exports	1,046.2
Gross private investment	1,665.8
Indirect business taxes	838.6
Self-employment income	834.1
Net income of foreigners	−55.2

   a. Indicate the various components of GDP when it is derived by the expenditure approach. Calculate GDP using the expenditure approach.
   b. Indicate the various components of GDP when it is derived by the resource cost-income approach. Calculate GDP using the resource cost-income approach.

*16. Fill in the blanks in the following table:

Year	Nominal GDP (In Billions)	GDP Deflator (2000 = 100)	Real GDP (Billions of 2000 Dollars)
1960	$ 526.4	21.0	a. _____
1970	$ 1,038.5	27.5	b. _____
1980	$ 2,789.5	c. _____	$5,165.7
1990	d. _____	81.6	$7,112.5
1995	$ 7,397.7	e. _____	$8,032.2
2000	$ 9,817.0	100.0	f. _____
2003	$11,004.1	106.0	g. _____

*Asterisk denotes questions for which answers are given in Appendix B.

ADDENDUM

The Construction of a Price Index

Price indexes are designed to measure the magnitude of changes in the general level of prices through time. The price index during the current year (PI_2) is

$$PI_2 = \frac{\text{Cost of purchasing the typical bundle this year}}{\text{Cost of purchasing the same bundle during the base year}} \times 100$$

The typical (representative) bundle might be the bundle actually chosen during the earlier base year. Alternatively, it could be the bundle chosen this year. *In either case, the quantities of the various goods do not change from year to year; only the prices change.*

Let's suppose that the bundle used to calculate the index was the quantity of each good actually chosen during the base year. This is how the consumer price index is calculated. In this case, the cost of purchasing the base year bundle this year would be the sum of the price of each good this year (P_2) multiplied by the quantity consumed during the base year (Q_1). The cost of purchasing the *same bundle* during the base year would be the sum of the price of each good during the base year (P_1) multiplied by the quantity of each good chosen during the base year (Q_1). Therefore, the mathematical formula for the price index during the current year (PI_2) could be written:

$$PI_2 = \frac{\Sigma P_2 Q_1}{\Sigma P_1 Q_1} \times 100$$

If prices on average are higher during the current period than they were during the base year, then this expression will be greater than 100. This indicates that it is now more costly to purchase the representative bundle than it was during the base year. Correspondingly, if the general level of prices is currently lower today than during the base period, then PI_2 would be less than 100. Thus, the current price index indicates how the current level of prices compares to the level during the base period.

Let's consider a simple example that illustrates more fully how price indexes are constructed. Suppose that your typical daily consumption bundle is 2 hamburgers, 1 order of french fries, and 3 Cokes. Initially, the price of a hamburger was $3, french fries $1, and Coke $1. The price index during this base period is assigned a value of 100. Your expenditures on the bundle during the base period (the denominator in the formula to the left) were $10 ($6 for the hamburgers, $1 for the french fries, and $3 for the 3 Cokes).

Now consider the implications if prices in the current period are $3.50 for a hamburger, $1.75 for french fries, and 75 cents for a Coke. Now the cost of purchasing this bundle (numerator to the left) is $11 ($7 for the 2 hamburgers, $1.75 for the french fries, and $2.25 for the 3 Cokes). This would yield a price index of 110 ($11 divided by $10 multiplied by 100). The price index of 110 indicates that the general level of prices for the 3-good bundle is now 10 percent higher than it was during the base period.

Of course, the number of goods and the quantities included in the consumer price index (CPI) and GDP deflator are far greater than the bundle we considered in this simple illustration. Nonetheless, the general idea is the same. The cost of purchasing the typical bundle in the current period is compared to the cost of purchasing the same bundle during a base year, which is assigned a value of 100. If the cost of purchasing the bundle is now higher than it was during the base period, then the value of this year's price index will be greater than 100. As the price index changes from year to year, it indicates the magnitude of the change in the general level of prices.

Economic Fluctuations, Unemployment, and Inflation

Chapter Focus

■ What is a business cycle? How much economic instability has the United States experienced?

■ Why do economies experience unemployment? Are some types of unemployment worse than others?

■ What do economists mean by full employment? How is full employment related to the natural rate of unemployment?

■ How are anticipated and unanticipated inflation different? What are some of the dangers that accompany inflation?

Prosperity is when the prices of things that you sell are rising; inflation is when the prices of things that you buy are rising. Recession is when other people are unemployed; depression is when you are unemployed.

—Anonymous

Threstcolumns

The performance of the economy influences our job opportunities, income levels, and quality of life. Thus, key in-dicators of economic performance, such as growth of real GDP, the rate of unemployment, and the inflation rate, are closely watched by investors, politicians, and the media. This chapter will focus on how several key eco-nomic indicators are derived and explain how changes in these measures influence our lives.

The primary objectives of macroeconomic policy are to help the economy achieve rapid growth of output, a high level of employment, and stability in the general level of prices. There is widespread agreement concerning the desirability of these goals. However, there is considerable controversy as to how they can be achieved. As we proceed, the causes of eco-nomic instability and the potential use of government policy as a stabilizing force will be analyzed in detail. ■

SWINGS IN THE ECONOMIC PENDULUM

During the last hundred years, the annual growth rate of real GDP in the United States has averaged approximately 3 percent. But there have also been considerable fluctuations in year-to-year growth. During the Great Depression of the 1930s, economic growth plunged. Real GDP declined by 7.5 percent or more each year from 1930 to 1932. In 1933, it was almost 30 percent less than it was in 1929. The 1929 level of real GDP was not reached again until 1939. The Second World War was characterized by a rapid expansion of GDP, which was followed by a decline after the war. Real GDP did not reach its 1944 level again until 1953, although the output of consumer goods did increase significantly in the years immediately following the war.

Exhibit 1 presents the growth rate figures (four-quarter moving average) for real GDP for 1960–2004. Real GDP grew rapidly throughout most of the 1960s, the periods 1972–1973, 1976–1977, and 1983–1988, and most of the 1990s. Since 1960, however, there have also been seven periods (1960, 1970, 1974–1975, 1980, 1982, 1991, and 2001) of falling real GDP. Although the economic ups and downs have continued, the fluctua-tions have been less severe in recent decades than during the first fifty years of the twenti-eth century. Figures on GDP and related data can be obtained from the Bureau of Eco-nomic Analysis on the Internet at http://www.bea.doc.gov/.

EXHIBIT 1
Instability in the Growth of Real GDP, 1960–2004

Although real GDP in the United States fluctuates substantially, periods of positive growth outweigh the periods of declining real GDP. Since 1960, the U.S. growth rate of real GDP has averaged approxi-mately 3.0 percent annu-ally. Economists refer to periods of declining real GDP as recessions. The recessionary periods are shaded.

A Hypothetical Business Cycle

The United States and other industrial economies have been characterized by instability when it comes to the growth of real GDP. Inevitably, real GDP growth has been followed by economic slowdowns. Economists refer to these swings in the rate of output as the **business cycle**. Periods of growth in real output and other aggregate measures of economic activity followed by periods of decline are the characteristics of business cycles.

Exhibit 2 shows a hypothetical business cycle. When most businesses are operating at capacity level and real GDP is growing rapidly, a *business peak,* or boom, is present. As business conditions slow, the economy begins the *contraction,* or recessionary, phase of a business cycle. During the contraction, the sales of most businesses decline, real GDP grows at a slower rate or perhaps falls, and unemployment in the labor market increases.

The bottom of the contraction phase is referred to as the *recessionary trough.* After the downturn reaches bottom and economic conditions begin to improve, the economy enters the *expansion* phase of the cycle. Here business sales rise, GDP grows rapidly, and the rate of unemployment declines. Eventually the expansion blossoms into another business peak. The peak, however, inevitably ends and turns into a contraction, beginning the cycle anew.

The term **recession** is widely used to describe conditions during the contraction and recessionary trough phases of the business cycle. This is a period during which real GDP declines. Often, a recession is defined as a decline in real GDP for two or more consecutive quarters.[1] When a recession is prolonged and has a sharp decline in economic activity, it is called a **depression**.

In one important respect, the term *business cycle* is misleading. The word *cycle* is often used to describe events of similar time length that occur regularly, like the seasons of the year, for example. As Exhibit 1 illustrates, this is not the case with the business cycle. The expansions and contractions last varying lengths of time, and the swings differ in terms of their magnitude. For example, the recessions of 1961, 1982, and 1990 were followed by eight years or more of uninterrupted growth of output. In contrast, the recession of 1980 was followed by an expansion that lasted only twelve months. The expansionary phase following the recessions of 1970 and 1974–1975 fell between these two extremes. As the accompanying feature "Expansions and Recessions" shows, the time length of real-world expansions and contractions is varied and unpredictable.

How can we know where an economy is in the business cycle? Of course, changes in real GDP will tell us. However, these numbers are available only quarterly, and it usually takes four to six weeks after the quarter is over before reliable figures are released. Various measures that are available monthly or more often can provide clues. For example,

Business cycle
Fluctuations in the general level of economic activity as measured by variables such as the rate of unemployment and changes in real GDP.

Recession
A downturn in economic activity characterized by declining real GDP and rising unemployment. In an effort to be more precise, many economists define a recession as two consecutive quarters in which there is a decline in real GDP.

Depression
A prolonged and very severe recession.

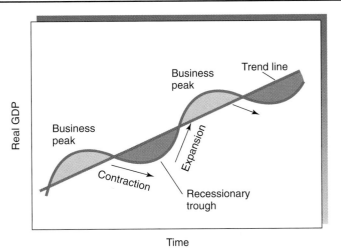

EXHIBIT 2
The Business Cycle

In the past, ups and downs have often characterized aggregate business activity. Despite these fluctuations, there has been an upward trend in real GDP in the United States and other industrial nations.

---

[1]See Geoffrey H. Moore, "Recessions," in *The Fortune Encyclopedia of Economics,* ed. David R. Henderson (New York: Time Warner Inc., 1993), for additional information on recessions in the United States. This publication is also available online at http://www.econlib.org/.

MEASURES OF ECONOMIC ACTIVITY

Expansions and Recessions

The table below indicates the periods of both expansion (rising real GDP) and recession (falling GDP) since 1950. As the table indicates, the length of both varies substantially, although the expansions have generally been longer.

Period of Expansion	Length (in Months)	Period of Recession	Length (in Months)
October 1949–July 1953	44	July 1953–May 1954	10
May 1954–August 1957	39	August 1957–April 1958	9
April 1958–April 1960	24	April 1960–February 1961	10
February 1961–December 1969	105	December 1969–November 1970	10
November 1970–November 1973	36	November 1973–March 1975	16
March 1975–January 1980	58	January 1980–July 1980	6
July 1980–July 1981	12	July 1981–November 1982	16
November 1982–July 1990	92	July 1990–March 1991	9
March 1991–March 2001	120	March 2001–November 2001	8
November 2001–?[a]	37[a]		

[a]To date, this expansion has continued through December 2004.

Source: http://www.nber.org/.

auto sales, new housing starts, new factory orders, and even the stock market will generally increase during an expansion and decline when the economy dips into a recession. As a result, these indicators are monitored carefully.

ECONOMIC FLUCTUATIONS AND THE LABOR MARKET

Fluctuations in real GDP influence the demand for labor and employment. In our modern world, people are busy with jobs, household work, school, and other activities. **Exhibit 3** illustrates how economists classify these activities in relation to the **civilian labor force**, defined as the number of people aged sixteen years and over who are either employed or seeking employment. The noninstitutional civilian adult population is divided into two broad categories: (1) people not in the labor force and (2) people in the labor force. There are various reasons why people aren't in the labor force. Some are retired. Others are working in their own households or attending school. Still others are not working because they are ill or disabled. Although many of these people are quite busy, their activities lie outside the market labor force.

As Exhibit 3 shows, **unemployed** workers who are seeking work are included in the labor force along with employed workers. The **labor force participation rate** is the number of persons in the civilian labor force (including both those who are employed and those who are unemployed) as a percentage of the civilian population 16 years of age and over. In 2003, the population (16 years of age and over) of the United States was 221.2 million, 146.5 million of whom were in the labor force. Thus, the U.S. labor force participation rate was 66.2 percent (146.5 million divided by 221.2 million).

The labor force participation rate varies substantially across countries. For example, in 2003, the labor force participation rate of fifteen- to sixty-four-year-olds was 75.8 percent in the United States, 78.1 percent in Canada, and 78.9 percent in Sweden. In contrast,

Civilian labor force
The number of people sixteen years of age and over who are either employed or unemployed. To be classified as unemployed, a person must be looking for a job.

Unemployed
The term used to describe a person not currently employed who is either (1) actively seeking employment or (2) waiting to begin or return to a job.

Labor force participation rate
The number of people in the civilian labor force sixteen years of age or over who are either employed or actively seeking employment as a percentage of the total civilian population sixteen years of age and over.

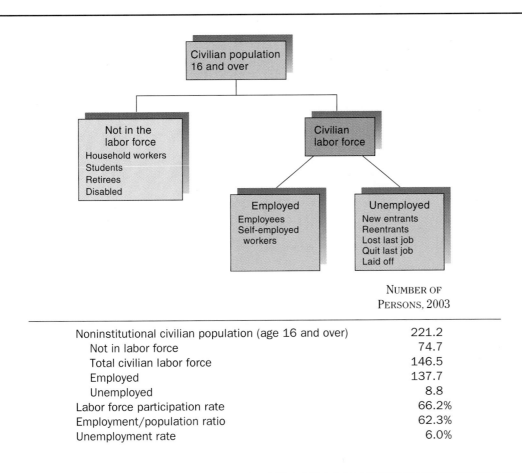

EXHIBIT 3
Population, Employment, and Unemployment, 2003

The accompanying diagram illustrates the alternative participation-status categories for the adult population. Data are measured in millions, except those expressed as percentages.

	NUMBER OF PERSONS, 2003
Noninstitutional civilian population (age 16 and over)	221.2
Not in labor force	74.7
Total civilian labor force	146.5
Employed	137.7
Unemployed	8.8
Labor force participation rate	66.2%
Employment/population ratio	62.3%
Unemployment rate	6.0%

Source: http://www.bls.gov/.

the labor force participation rate was only 61.2 percent in Mexico and 61.6 percent in Italy. The percentage of married women in the labor force is generally smaller in countries like Italy and Mexico that have low labor force participation rates.

In the United States, one of the most interesting labor force developments in recent decades is the dramatic increase in the labor force participation rate of women. **Exhibit 4** illustrates this point. In 2003, 59.5 percent of adult women worked outside the home, up from 32.7 percent in 1948. Married women accounted for most of this increase. More than half of all married women now are in the labor force, compared to only 20 percent immediately following the Second World War. While the labor force participation of women rose, the rate for men fell. In 2003, the labor force participation rate of men was 73.5 percent, down from 83.3 percent in 1960 and 86.6 percent in 1948. Clearly, the composition of workforce participation within the family has changed substantially during the past five decades.

The **unemployment rate** is a key barometer of conditions in the aggregate labor market. This notwithstanding, the term is often misunderstood. It is important to note that unemployment is different from not working. As we previously discussed, there are several reasons—including household work, school attendance, retirement, and illness or disability—that a person may be neither employed nor looking for a job. These people, though not employed, are not counted as unemployed.

Moreover, only persons employed or unemployed are counted as part of the labor force. Part-time as well as full-time workers are counted as employed members of the labor force. The rate of unemployment is the number of persons unemployed expressed as a percentage of the labor force. In 2003, the rate of unemployment in the United States was 6.0 percent (8.8 million out of a labor force of 146.5 million). (See the accompanying Applications in Economics feature for information on how the Bureau of Labor Statistics derives the unemployment rate.)

Unemployment rate
The percentage of people in the labor force who are unemployed. Mathematically, it is equal to number of people unemployed divided by the number of persons in the labor force.

EXHIBIT 4
Labor Force Participation Rate of Men and Women, 1948–2003

As the chart illustrates, the labor force participation rate for women has been steadily increasing for several decades, while the rate for men has been declining.

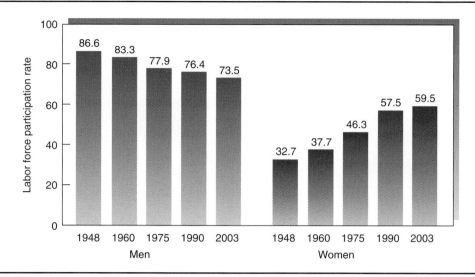

Source: http://www.bls.gov/.

Employment/population ratio
The number of people sixteen years of age and over employed as civilians divided by the total civilian population sixteen years of age and over. The ratio is expressed as a percentage.

In addition to the rate of unemployment, many economists also use the **employment/population ratio**—the number of persons employed expressed as a percentage of the population sixteen years old and over—to monitor labor market conditions. This ratio will tend to rise during an expansion and fall during a recession. Both the number of people employed and the population aged sixteen and over are well defined and readily measurable. Their measurement does not require a subjective judgment as to whether a person is actually "available for work" or "actively seeking employment." Thus, some believe that the employment/population ratio is a more objective measure of job availability than the rate of unemployment. The employment/population ratio was 62.3 percent in 2003. The accompanying Thumbnail Sketch shows the formulas that are used to calculate the major indicators of labor market conditions.

APPLICATIONS IN ECONOMICS

Deriving the Unemployment Rate

Each month, the Bureau of Labor Statistics (BLS) contacts a sample of 50,000 households that reflects the population characteristics of the United States. Specially trained interviewers pose identical questions designed to determine whether each of the approximately 90,000 adults in these households is employed, unemployed, or not in the labor force. People aged 16 years and over are considered employed if they (1) worked at all (even as little as 1 hour) for pay or profit during the survey week, (2) worked 15 hours or more without pay in a family-operated enterprise during the survey week, or (3) have a job at which they did not work during the survey week because of illness, vacation, industrial disputes, bad weather, time off, or personal reasons. People are considered unemployed if they (1) do not have a job,

(2) are available for work, and (3) have actively looked for work during the past four weeks. Looking for work may involve any of the following activities: (1) registering at a public or private employment office, (2) meeting with prospective employers, (3) checking with friends or relatives, (4) placing or answering advertisements, (5) writing letters of application, or (6) being in a union or on a professional register. In addition, those not working are classified as unemployed if they are either waiting to start a new job within 30 days or waiting to be recalled from a layoff. The BLS uses its survey data to calculate the unemployment rate and other employment-related statistics each month. States use the BLS survey and employment figures from industries covered by unemployment insurance to construct state and area employment statistics. These labor market figures are published by the U.S. Department of Labor in the *Monthly Labor Review* and on the Internet at http://www.bls.gov/.

THUMBNAIL SKETCH

Formulas for Key Labor Market Indicators

1. **Labor force** = Employed + Unemployed
2. **Labor force participation rate** = number in labor force / population (aged 16 and over)
3. **Unemployment rate** = number unemployed / number in labor force
4. **Employment / population ratio** = number employed / population (aged 16 and over)

Dynamic Change and Reasons for Unemployment

In a dynamic world, where information is scarce and people are free to choose among jobs, some unemployment is inevitable. As new products are introduced and new technologies developed, some firms are expanding while others are contracting. Similarly, some firms will be starting operations, while others will be going out of business. This process results in the creation of new jobs and the disappearance of old ones. At the same time, some potential workers will be switching from school or other nonwork activities to the labor force, while others are retiring or taking a leave from the labor force. Furthermore, workers are mobile. At any point in time, some will voluntarily quit and search for better opportunities. Although some unemployment will always be present, there is a positive side to the unemployment-job search process: it makes it possible for individuals to better match their skills and preferences with the job requirements of employers. Better-matched employees and employers increase both productivity and earnings.

Unemployment may occur for reasons other than the loss of a job, however. For example, people often experience periods of unemployment as they enter and reenter the labor force. The Department of Labor lists five reasons why workers may experience unemployment. **Exhibit 5** shows the share of unemployed workers in each of these five categories in 2003. Interestingly, 7.3 percent of the unemployed workers were first-time entrants into the labor force; 28.2 percent were reentering the labor force after exiting it to obtain additional schooling, do household work, or for other reasons. Therefore, 35.5 percent of the unemployed workers—over one-third—were unemployed because they were entering or reentering the labor force. About one out of every eleven unemployed workers (9.3 percent) quit their job. People laid off and waiting to return to their previous positions contributed 12.8 percent to the total. Workers dismissed from their job accounted for slightly more than two-fifths of unemployed workers (42.4 percent).

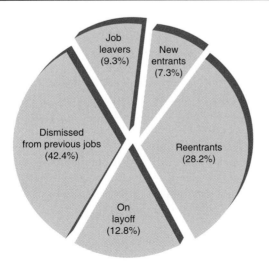

EXHIBIT 5

Composition of the Unemployed by Reason

This chart indicates the various reasons that persons were unemployed in 2003. Slightly more than two-fifths (42.4 percent) of the persons unemployed were dismissed from their last job. More than one-third (35.5 percent) of the unemployed workers were either new entrants or reentrants into the labor force.

Source: http://www.bls.gov/.

EXHIBIT 6
The Unemployment Rate by Age and Gender, 2003

GROUP	CIVILIAN RATE OF UNEMPLOYMENT 2003 (PERCENT)
Total, all workers	6.0
Men, Total	6.3
Ages 16–19	19.3
Ages 20–24	10.6
Ages 25 and over	5.0
Women, Total	5.7
Ages 16–19	15.6
Ages 20–24	9.3
Ages 25 and over	4.6

Source: http://www.bls.gov/.

Young workers often switch jobs and move between schooling and the labor force as they search for a career path that best fits their abilities and preferences. As the result of this job switching, the unemployment rate of younger workers is substantially higher than that of more established workers. As **Exhibit 6** shows, in 2003 the unemployment rate of workers twenty to twenty-four years of age was more than twice the rate for their counterparts aged twenty-five years and over. The unemployment rate for teenagers was more than three times the rate of older workers. This held true for both men and women. The unemployment rate for women, however, was less than the rate for men in each of the age categories.

THREE TYPES OF UNEMPLOYMENT

Although some unemployment is consistent with economic efficiency, this is not always the case. Abnormally high rates of unemployment generally reflect weak demand conditions for labor, counterproductive policies, and/or the inability or lack of incentive on the part of potential workers and potential employers to arrive at mutually advantageous agreements. To clarify matters, economists divide unemployment into three categories: frictional, structural, and cyclical. Let us take a closer look at each of these three classifications.

Frictional Unemployment

Frictional unemployment
Unemployment due to constant changes in the economy that prevent qualified unemployed workers from being immediately matched up with existing job openings. It results from imperfect information and search activities related to suitably matching employees with employers.

Unemployment that is caused by constant changes in the labor market is called **frictional unemployment**. It occurs because (1) employers are not fully aware of all available workers and their job qualifications and (2) available workers are not fully aware of the jobs being offered by employers. In other words, the main cause of frictional unemployment is imperfect information.

For example, an employer looking for a new worker seldom hires the first applicant who walks into its employment office. It wants to find the "best available" worker to fill the opening. It is costly to hire workers who perform poorly. It is sometimes even costly to terminate their employment. So, employers search—they expend time and resources screening applicants in an effort to find the best-qualified workers who are willing to accept their wage and employment conditions.

Similarly, job seekers search for their best option among the potential alternatives. They make telephone calls, search newspaper ads and Internet sites, submit to job interviews, use employment services, and so on. The pursuit of personal gain—landing jobs that are more attractive than the current options they face—motivates job seekers to engage in job search activities.

However, as a job seeker finds out about more and more potential job opportunities, it becomes less likely that additional searching will uncover a more attractive option. Therefore, the *marginal benefit* derived from a job search declines with the time spent searching for a job because it becomes less likely that it will lead to a better position. The *marginal*

MYTHS OF ECONOMICS

"Unemployment would not exist if the economy were operating efficiently."

Nobody likes unemployment. Certainly, being unemployed for an extended period of time can be a very painful experience for people. Looking for a job, however, performs an important labor market function: it leads to improved matches between workers' skills and employers' job requirements.

Job searchers are "shopping"—they are searching for information about the job opportunity that best fits their skills, earning capabilities, and preferences. Similarly, employers shop when they are seeking labor services. They, too, acquire information about available workers that will help them select employees whose skills and preferences match the demands of the job.

This shopping results in some unemployment, but it also provides both employees and employers with information that will help them make better choices. If the resources of an economy are going to be used effectively, the skills of workers must be matched well with the jobs of employers. Waste will result if, for example, a person with high-level computer skills ends up working as a janitor while someone else with minimal computer skills is employed as a computer programmer. Moreover, as workers try to find jobs for

which their skills are well suited, they achieve higher wage rates, and the economy is able to generate a larger output.

Perhaps thinking about the housing market will help you better understand why search time can be both beneficial and productive. Like the employment market, the housing market is characterized by imperfect information and dynamic change. New housing structures are built; older structures depreciate and are torn down. Families move from one community to another. In this dynamic world, it makes sense for renters to shop around from time to time to find the housing quality, price, and location that best fit their preferences and budgets. Similarly, landlords search among renters, seeking to rent their accommodations to those who value them most highly. As a result of this shopping, housing vacancies inevitably occur. But does this mean the housing market is inefficient? No. It is the result of imperfect information and the search for a more efficient match on the part of both landlords and renters.

Of course, some types of unemployment, particularly cyclical unemployment, are indicative of inefficiency. However, this is not the case with frictional unemployment. The job searching (as well as the frictional unemployment that accompanies it) helps both job seekers and employers make better choices, and it leads to a more efficient match of applicants with job openings than would otherwise be possible. It is perfectly consistent with economic efficiency.

cost of a job search rises as a more lengthy search leads to the discovery of more attractive job opprtunities.

As the marginal benefit of the job search declines and the marginal costs rise, eventually a rational job seeker will conclude that additional search is no longer worth the cost. He or she will then accept the best alternative available at that point. However, this process will take time, and during this time the job seeker is contributing to the frictional unemployment of the economy.

It is important to note that, even though frictional unemployment is a side effect, the job search process typically leads to improved economic efficiency and a higher real income for employees (see the accompanying Myths of Economics feature).

Changes that affect the costs and benefits of a job search influence the level of unemployment. The Internet has had an interesting effect on the job search process. Increasingly, both employers and employees are using Internet sites as a means of communicating with each other. Employers provide information about job openings in various skill and occupational categories, and employees supply information about their education, skills, and experience. This electronic job search process reduces information costs and makes it possible for both employers and employees to consider quickly a wide range of alternatives. As this method of employment search becomes more widespread, it will tend to shorten the job search process and improve the matches between employers and employees. As a result, frictional unemployment might be lower in the future.

On the other hand, a change that makes it cheaper to reject available opportunities and continue searching for jobs will increase the level of unemployment. For example, an increase in unemployment benefits would make it less costly to continue looking for a preferred job. As a result, job seekers will expand the length of their search time, and the unemployment rate will rise.

Structural Unemployment

Structural unemployment
Unemployment due to the structural characteristics of the economy that make it difficult for job seekers to find employment and for employers to hire workers. Although job openings are available, they generally require skills many unemployed workers do not have.

In the case of **structural unemployment**, changes in the basic characteristics of the economy prevent the "matching up" of available jobs with available workers. It is not always easy to distinguish between frictional and structural unemployment. In each case, job openings and potential workers searching for jobs are both present. The crucial difference between the two is that, with frictional unemployment, workers possess the necessary skills to fill the job openings; with structural unemployment, they do not. Essentially, the primary skills of a structurally unemployed worker have been rendered obsolete by changing market conditions and technology. Realistically, the structurally unemployed worker faces the prospect of either a career change or prolonged unemployment. For older workers in particular, these are bleak alternatives.

There are many causes of structural unemployment. The introduction of new products and production technologies can substantially alter the relative demand for workers with various skills. Changes of this type can affect the job opportunities of even highly skilled workers, particularly if their skills are not easily transferable to other industries and occupations. The "computer revolution" has dramatically changed the job opportunities of many workers. The alternatives available to workers with the skills required to operate and maintain high-tech equipment have improved substantially, while the prospects of those without such skills have, in some cases, deteriorated drastically.

Shifts in public-sector priorities can also cause structural unemployment. For example, environmental regulations designed to improve air quality led to a reduction in the demand for coal during the 1990s. As a result, many coal miners in West Virginia, Kentucky, and other coal-mining states lost their jobs. Unfortunately, the skills of many of the job losers were ill-suited for employment in expanding industries. Structural unemployment was the result.

Institutional factors can also make it difficult for some workers to find jobs. For example, minimum-wage legislation may push the wages of low-skilled workers above their productivity levels and thereby severely retard the job opportunities available to them. Structural unemployment would increase as a result.

Cyclical Unemployment

Cyclical unemployment
Unemployment due to recessionary business conditions and inadequate labor demand.

When there is a general downturn in business activity, **cyclical unemployment** arises. Because fewer goods are being produced, fewer workers are required to produce them. Employers lay off workers and cut back employment.

An unexpected fall in the general level of demand for goods and services will cause cyclical unemployment to rise. In a world of imperfect information, adjusting to unexpected declines in demand are often painful for people. When the demand for labor declines, workers will at first not know whether they are being laid off because their employer is experiencing lower demand or because the economy in general is experiencing lower demand. Similarly, they will not immediately know whether their poor current employment opportunities are temporary or long-term. If the downturn is limited to a single employer, the workers it lays off will generally be able to find jobs with other employers. The situation is different, however, when there is a general decline in demand. Many employers will lay off workers and few other employers will be hiring. Under these circumstances, workers' search efforts will be less fruitful, and the duration of their unemployment abnormally long. Unemployment of this type is referred to as cyclical unemployment. As we proceed, we will consider policy alternatives to deal with it.

EMPLOYMENT FLUCTUATIONS—THE HISTORICAL RECORD

Employment and output are closely linked over the business cycle. If we are going to produce more goods and services, we must either increase the number of workers or increase the output per worker. Although productivity, or output per worker, is the primary source of long-term economic growth, it changes slowly from year to year. Consequently, rapid increases in output, such as those that occur during a strong business expansion, generally require an increase in employment. As a result, output and employment tend to be positively related. Conversely, there is an inverse relationship between growth of output and the rate of unemployment.

The empirical evidence is consistent with this view. As **Exhibit 7** shows, the unemployment rate generally increases during a recession (indicated by shading), and declines during periods of expansion in output. During the recession of 1960–1961, the rate of unemployment rose to approximately 7 percent. In contrast, it declined throughout the economic boom of the 1960s, only to rise again during the recession of 1970. During the recession of 1974–1975, the unemployment rate jumped to more than 9 percent. Similarly, it soared to nearly 11 percent during the severe recession of 1982 and to 7.6 percent during the aftermath of the 1991 recession. Conversely, it declined substantially during the strong expansions of 1983–1989 and 1992–2000.

Full Employment and the Natural Rate of Unemployment

Full employment, a term widely used by economists and public officials alike, does not mean zero unemployment. As we have noted, in a world of imperfect information, both employees and employers will "shop" before they agree to accept a job or hire a new worker. Much of this shopping is efficient, since it leads to better matches between the skills of employees and the skills employers need. Some unemployment is therefore necessary for a dynamic labor market to operate efficiently. *Consequently, economists define full employment as the level of employment that results when the rate of unemployment is "normal," considering both frictional and structural factors. In the United States, full employment is currently believed to be approximately 95 percent of the labor force.*

Closely related to the concept of full employment is the **natural rate of unemployment**, the amount of unemployment reflected by job shopping and imperfect

Full employment
The level of employment that results from the efficient use of the labor force taking into account the normal (natural) rate of unemployment due to information cost, dynamic changes, and the structural conditions of the economy. For the United States, full employment is thought to exist when approximately 95 percent of the labor force is employed.

Natural rate of unemployment
The "normal" unemployment rate due to frictional and structural conditions in labor markets. It is the unemployment rate that occurs when the economy is operating at a sustainable rate of output. The current natural rate of unemployment in the United States is thought to be approximately 5 percent.

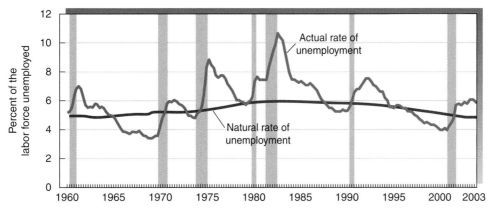

EXHIBIT 7
The Unemployment Rate, 1960–2003

Here we illustrate the rate of unemployment during the 1960–2003 period. As expected, the unemployment rate rose rapidly during each of the seven recessions. (The shaded years indicate recessions.) In contrast, soon after each recession ended, the unemployment rate began to decline as the economy moved to an expansionary phase of the business cycle. Also note that the actual rate of unemployment was substantially greater than the natural rate during and immediately following each recession.

Source: http://www.bls.gov/ and Robert J. Gordon, *Macroeconomics* (Boston: Addison-Wesley, 2003).

information. ***The natural rate of unemployment is not a temporary high or low; it is a rate that is sustainable. Economists sometimes refer to it as the unemployment rate accompanying the economy's "maximum sustainable" rate of output.*** When unemployment is at its natural rate, full employment is present, and the economy is achieving the highest rate of output that it can sustain.

The natural rate of unemployment, however, is not fixed. It is affected by the structure of the labor force and by changes in public policy. Over time, changes in the demographic composition of the labor force will influence the natural rate. The natural rate of unemployment increases when youthful workers expand as a proportion of the workforce. Because youthful workers change jobs and move in and out of the labor force often, they experience high rates of unemployment (see Exhibit 6). Therefore, the overall rate of unemployment is pushed upward as they become a larger share of the labor force. This is what happened during the 1960s and 1970s. In 1960, youthful workers (ages sixteen to twenty-four) constituted only 16 percent of the labor force. But as the postwar "baby boom" generation entered the labor market, youthful workers as a share of the labor force rose dramatically. By 1980, one out of every four workers was in the youthful-worker grouping. In contrast, prime-age workers (over age twenty-five) declined from 84 percent of the U.S. workforce in 1960 to only 75 percent in 1980. As a result of these demographic changes, studies indicate that the natural rate of unemployment rose from approximately 5 percent in the late 1950s to more than 6 percent in 1980.

During the last two decades, the situation has reversed. The natural rate of unemployment has declined as the baby boomers moved into their prime working years and youth-

---

APPLICATIONS IN ECONOMICS

Would Personal Savings Accounts Reduce the Rate of Unemployment?

Under the current unemployment insurance system, workers and their employers are required to pay taxes on wages and salaries, which are used to finance benefits for unemployed workers covered by the program. Typically, the benefits replace about 50 percent of a worker's prior pretax earnings for up to twenty-six weeks. During recent recessions, Congress has extended benefits for an additional thirteen weeks. In Europe, however, unemployment benefits are even higher, and people are permitted to draw the benefits for longer time periods—often two or three years.

Unfortunately, unemployment programs have an unintended secondary effect: they increase the unemployment rate. The benefits make it less costly for an unemployed worker to turn down available jobs and continue searching while receiving the payments. They also reduce the incentive of the unemployed to switch occupations or move to another location in order to find employment. As a result, workers stay unemployed longer and the overall unemployment rate is higher than it would be otherwise. In fact, empirical evidence indicates that there is a spike in the number of unemployed workers obtaining employment just prior to and immediately after their unemployment benefits are exhausted. The persistently higher unemployment rates in Europe (see Exhibit 8), where the benefits are more generous, also indi-

cates that the program pushes the unemployment rate upward, perhaps by as much as 2 or 3 percentage points.

To deal with this problem, Lawrence Brunner and Stephen Colarelli have proposed that a system of personal savings accounts be substituted for the current system.[1] Instead of paying a payroll tax, employees and their employers would make equivalent payments into an unemployment personal savings account owned by the employee. Workers could then access the funds in their accounts during periods of unemployment. Upon retirement, any funds remaining in the account would be available to the worker, and, in case of death, unused funds would be passed along to the worker's heirs. Because this system would mean that workers would be using their own funds rather than the government's during periods of unemployment, the approach would eliminate the perverse incentive structure caused by the current system.

Question for Thought

1. Would the proposed reform increase the incentive to search for and accept employment rather than undergo lengthy periods of unemployment? Why or why not? Can you think of problems this system would create compared to the current system?

---

[1]Lawrence Brunner and Stephen M. Colarelli, "Individual Unemployment Accounts," *Independent Review* 8 (Spring 2004): 569–85.

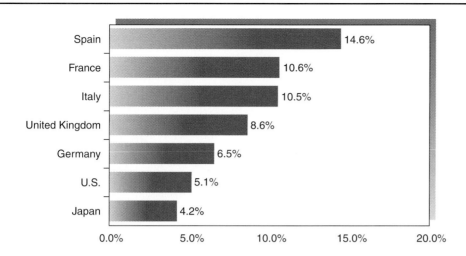

Source: Economic Outlook, OECD (June 2004).

**EXHIBIT 8
Average Unemployment
Rate for Major
Economies, 1994–2003**

ful workers shrank as a share of the labor force. Today, most researchers estimate that the natural rate is once again near 5 percent, about the same as during the late 1950s.

Public policy also affects the natural rate of unemployment. When public policy makes it more costly to employ workers and/or less costly for persons to remain unemployed, it increases the natural rate of unemployment. The large European economies are good examples. The economies of France, Germany, Italy, and Spain are characterized by high unemployment benefits and regulations that both increase the cost of dismissing workers and mandate uniform wages nationwide. Regulations of this type reduce the flexibility of labor markets and make it more costly to hire and employ workers. Thus, they lead to persistently high rates of unemployment.

As **Exhibit 8** shows, the unemployment rates of the major European economies were substantially higher during the last decade than the comparable figures for the United States and Japan, for example. High unemployment rates over such a lengthy time period are indicative of structural rather than cyclical factors. They also show the adverse effect public policy can have on the natural rate of unemployment. See the special topic "Labor Markets and Unemployment: A Cross-Country Analysis," for additional information on this topic.

The relationship between the *actual* unemployment rate and the *natural* unemployment rate for the United States over the last four decades can be observed in Exhibit 7. Note that the actual unemployment rate fluctuates around the natural rate in response to cyclical economic conditions. The actual rate generally rises above the natural rate during a recession and falls below the natural rate when the economy is in the midst of an economic boom. For example, the actual rate of unemployment was substantially above the natural rate during the recessions of 1974–1975 and 1982. The reverse was true during the latter stages of the lengthy expansions of the 1960s, 1980s, and 1990s. As we proceed, we will often compare the actual and natural rates of unemployment. In a very real sense, macroeconomics studies why the actual and natural rates differ and attempts to discern the factors that cause the natural rate to change over time.

ACTUAL AND POTENTIAL GDP

If an economy is going to realize its potential, full employment is essential. When the actual rate of unemployment exceeds the natural rate, the actual output of the economy will fall below its potential. Potential output does not represent the absolute maximum level of production that could, for example, be generated in wartime or other situations in which the level of aggregate demand is abnormally high. Rather, it is the rate that would be expected under more normal circumstances.

EXHIBIT 9
The Actual and
Potential GDP

Here we illustrate both the
actual and potential GDP.
Note the gap between the
actual and potential GDP
during recessions.

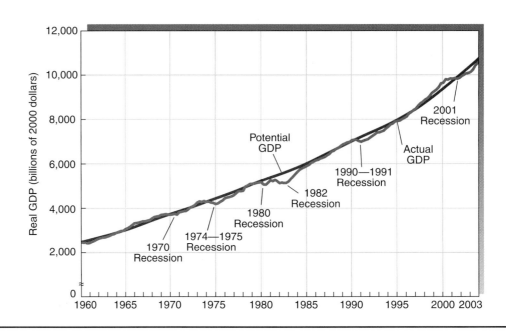

Potential output
The level of output that can be
achieved and sustained in the
future, given the size of the labor force, its expected productivity, and the natural rate of
unemployment consistent with
the efficient operation of the
labor market. Actual output
can differ from the economy's
potential output.

   Potential output can therefore be thought of as the maximum *sustainable* output
level consistent with the full employment of resources currently available in the economy.
To estimate the economy's potential output level, we need to look at three factors: the size
of the labor force, the quality (productivity) of labor, and the natural rate of unemployment. Because these factors cannot be estimated with certainty, some variation exists in
the estimated values of the potential rate of output for the U.S. economy.

   Exhibit 9 shows the relationship between the actual and potential output of the
United States since 1960. The relationship between actual and potential GDP reflects the
business cycle. Note the similarity of the actual real GDP data of Exhibit 9 and the hypothetical data of an idealized business cycle of Exhibit 2. Although the actual data of Exhibit 9 are irregular compared to the hypothetical data, periods of expansion and economic
boom followed by contraction and recession are clearly observable. During the boom
phase, actual output expands rapidly and may temporarily exceed the economy's long-run
potential. In contrast, recessions are characterized by an actual real GDP that is less than
its potential. As we proceed, we will focus on how we can achieve maximum potential
output while minimizing economic instability.

THE EFFECTS OF INFLATION

Inflation
A continuing rise in the general level of prices of goods
and services. The purchasing
power of the monetary unit,
such as the dollar, declines
when inflation is present.

Inflation is a continuing rise in the general level of prices. When inflation is on the rise, it
costs more to purchase a typical bundle of goods and services. Of course, even when the
general level of prices is stable, some prices will be rising and others will be falling. During a period of inflation, however, the impact of the rising prices will outweigh the impact
of falling prices. Because of the higher prices (on average), a dollar will purchase less than
it did previously. Inflation, therefore, can also be defined as a decline in the value (the purchasing power) of money.

   How do we determine whether prices are generally rising or falling? Essentially, we
answered that question in the preceding chapter when we indicated how a price index is
constructed. When the general level of prices is rising, the price index will also rise. The
annual inflation rate is simply the percentage change in the price index (PI) from one year
to the next. Mathematically, the inflation rate can be written as:

$$\text{Inflation rate} = \frac{\text{This year's PI} - \text{Last year's PI}}{\text{Last year's PI}} \times 100$$

If the price index this year was 220, compared to 200 last year, the inflation rate would equal 10 percent:

$$\frac{220 - 200}{200} \times 100 = 10.$$

The consumer price index (CPI) and the GDP deflator are the price indexes most widely used to measure the inflation rate in the United States. As we discussed in the preceding chapter, these two measures of the rate of inflation tend to follow a similar path.

It's important to note, however, that inflation affects the prices of things we sell as well as the prices of goods we buy. Both resource and product prices are influenced by inflation. Before we become too upset about inflation "robbing us of the purchasing power of our paychecks," we need to realize that inflation influences the size of those paychecks. For example, the weekly earnings of employees would not have risen at a sharp annual rate of 7 percent during the 1970s if the rate of inflation hadn't increased rapidly during the period, too. Wages are also a price. Inflation raises both prices and wages.

How rapidly has the general level of prices risen in the United States? Using the annual rate of change in the CPI, **Exhibit 10** shows the U.S. inflation rate since the early 1950s. During the 1950s and into the mid-1960s, the annual inflation rate was generally low. The average inflation rate during the 1953–1965 period, for example, was just 1.3 percent. Beginning in the latter half of the 1960s, however, inflation began to accelerate upward, jumping to 12 percent or more during 1974, 1979, and 1980. During the 1973–1981 period, the inflation rate averaged 9.2 percent. Price increases moderated again in the mid-1980s, and the inflation rate averaged 3.1 percent during the period 1983–2003. Additional details on inflation and related measures can be obtained on the Internet at http://www.bls.gov/.

The rate of inflation varies widely among countries. **Exhibit 11** provides data on the annual inflation rates during 1997–2003 for Canada, Germany, Singapore, the United Kingdom, and the United States—five countries with low rates of inflation. The annual inflation rates of these countries were generally less than 4 percent during this period; moreover, the year-to-year variations in inflation were relatively small—typically no more than 1 or 2 percent.

Exhibit 11 also presents parallel inflation rate data for five high-inflation countries: Romania, Russia, Turkey, Uruguay, and Venezuela. In contrast with the low-inflation

EXHIBIT 10
The Inflation Rate, 1953–2003

Here we present the annual rate of inflation for the last five decades. Between 1953 and 1965, prices increased at an annual rate of only 1.3 percent. In contrast, the inflation rate averaged 9.2 percent during the 1973–1981 era, reaching double-digit rates in several years. Since 1982, the rate of inflation has been lower (the average annual rate was 3.1 percent during the period 1983–2003) and more stable.

Source: Derived from computerized data supplied by FAME ECONOMICS. Also see *Economic Report of the President* (Washington, D.C.: Government Printing Office, published annually).

EXHIBIT 11
Variations in the Annual Inflation Rates of Selected Countries, 1997–2003

COUNTRY	1997	1998	1999	2000	2001	2002	2003
LOW INFLATION							
Canada	1.6	1.0	1.7	2.7	2.5	2.2	2.8
Germany	1.9	1.0	0.6	2.0	2.0	1.4	1.1
Singapore	2.0	−0.3	0.1	0.4	0.1	−0.5	0.5
United Kingdom	3.2	3.5	1.6	2.9	1.8	1.7	2.9
United States	2.3	1.6	2.1	3.4	2.8	1.7	2.2
HIGH INFLATION							
Romania	154.8	59.1	45.8	45.7	34.5	22.5	15.2
Russia	14.7	27.7	85.7	20.8	21.5	15.8	13.4
Turkey	85.8	−84.6	64.9	54.9	54.4	44.9	25.3
Uruguay	19.9	10.8	5.8	4.7	4.4	−13.9	19.4
Venezuela	50.0	35.8	23.6	16.2	12.5	22.5	31.1

Source: International Monetary Fund, *International Financial Statistics* (July 2004). The consumer price index was used to measure the inflation rate of each country.

countries, the inflation rate of the high-inflation countries was not only higher, it varied substantially more from one year to another. For example, consider the data for Romania. The inflation rate of Romania fell from 154.8 percent in 1997 to 59.1 percent in 1998 and receded to 45.8 percent in 1999. In 2003, it was smaller still—15.2 percent. The other countries in the high-inflation group also experienced wide fluctuations in their annual rates of inflation. The data of Exhibit 11 reflect a general pattern. ***High rates of inflation are almost always associated with substantial year-to-year swings in the inflation rate.***

Unanticipated and Anticipated Inflation

Before we examine the effects of inflation, it is important that we distinguish between unanticipated and anticipated inflation. **Unanticipated inflation** is an increase in the price level that comes as a surprise, at least to most individuals. For example, suppose that, based on the recent past, most people anticipate an inflation rate of 3 percent. If the actual inflation rate turns out to be 10 percent, it will catch people off guard. When the inflation rate is high and variable, it will be virtually impossible for people to anticipate it accurately. There are three major reasons that high and variable rates of inflation will adversely affect GDP and the overall health of the economy:

Unanticipated inflation
An increase in the general level of prices that was not expected by most decision makers.

1. High and variable inflation reduces investment. Unanticipated inflation alters the outcomes of long-term projects, such as the purchase of a machine or an investment in a business; it will increase the risks and retard the level of such productive activities. For example, when the price level rises 15 percent one year and 40 percent the next year and then increases again by 20 percent the following year, no one knows what to expect. Unanticipated changes of even 5 percent or 10 percent in the rate of inflation can often turn an otherwise profitable project into a personal economic disaster. Given the uncertainty that it creates, many decision makers will simply forgo capital investments and other transactions involving long-term commitments when the rate of inflation is highly variable and therefore unpredictable. As a result, mutually advantageous gains from trade will be lost and the efficiency of markets reduced.

2. Inflation distorts the information delivered by prices. Prices communicate important information concerning the relative scarcity of goods and resources. Some prices can be easily and regularly changed. But this will not be true for others—particularly those set by long-term contracts. For example, time delays will occur before the prices accompanying rental lease agreements, items sold in catalogs, mortgage interest rates, and collective bargaining contracts can be changed. Because some prices will respond quickly to inflation while others will change more slowly, an unanticipated change in the rate of inflation will change *relative prices* as well as the *general price level*. The distorted relative prices will be a less reliable indicator of relative scarcity. As a result of these unreliable price signals, producers and resource suppliers will often make choices that they will later regret, and the allocation of resources will be less efficient than it would have been if the general level of prices had been more stable.

3. High and variable inflation results in less productive use of resources. Failing to anticipate accurately the inflation rate can have a substantial effect on one's wealth. Because of this, when the inflation rate is high, people will spend more of their time and money gathering information about the future predicted rate of inflation and methods to cope with it—time and money that could have been used to produce goods and services demanded by the marketplace. For example, managers will spend more time coping with frequent price changes and less time improving production methods and products. Speculative market practices will occur as people try to outguess one another about the future direction of prices. As a result, funds will flow into speculative-type investments instead of more productive ones that increase output.

Anticipated inflation, on the other hand, is a change in the price level that is widely expected. Decision makers are generally able to anticipate slow, steady rates of inflation—like those in Canada, Germany, Singapore, the United Kingdom, and the United States during the period 1997–2003—with a high degree of accuracy. When the general level of prices is more stable, this will exert a positive impact on real output and the level of prosperity. The experience of the United States illustrates this point. During the 1983–2003 period, U.S. inflation was low and relatively stable. This period was characterized by strong growth and only seventeen months of recession. In contrast, when the inflation rate was high and variable during the 1970s, the United States experienced two recessions (1974–1975 and 1979–1980) and sluggish growth of real GDP.

Anticipated inflation
An increase in the general level of prices that was expected by most decision makers.

What Causes Inflation?

We need to acquire some additional tools of analysis before we can answer in detail the question of what causes inflation. However, at this point we can list two particular causes. First, economists emphasize the link between aggregate demand and supply. If aggregate demand rises more rapidly than supply, prices will rise. Second, nearly all economists believe that a rapid expansion in a nation's stock of money causes inflation. The old saying is that prices will rise because "there is too much money chasing too few goods." The hyperinflation experienced by South American countries and, more recently, by Russia and several other countries of the former Soviet Union, has mainly been the result of monetary expansion. Once we develop additional knowledge about the operation of our economy, we will consider this issue in more detail.

LOOKING AHEAD

In this chapter, we looked at business cycles and how they affect employment, and how inflation, both anticipated and unanticipated, affects output. In the next chapter, we will begin to develop a macroeconomic model that will help us better understand the factors that influence these indicators of economic performance.

KEY POINTS

▼ During the past century, real GDP in the United States has grown at an average annual rate of approximately 3 percent. Cyclical movements in real GDP have accompanied this growth of output.

▼ The four phases of the business cycle are *expansion, peak (or boom), contraction,* and *recession.* A recession is defined as two back-to-back quarters of declining real GDP. If a recession is quite severe, it is called a depression.

▼ There are three types of unemployment: (1) frictional unemployment, (2) structural unemployment, and (3) cyclical unemployment. In a world of imperfect information and dynamic change, some unemployment is inevitable.

▼ Full employment is the employment level consistent with the economy's natural rate of unemployment. Both full employment and the natural rate of unem-

ployment are associated with the economy's maximum sustainable rate of output.

▼ Potential output is the maximum *sustainable* output level consistent with the economy's resource base and current institutional arrangements.

▼ Inflation is a general rise in the level of prices in the economy. It is important to distinguish between anticipated and unanticipated inflation. Unanticipated changes in the rate of inflation often alter the intended terms of long-term agreements and cause people to regret choices they have previously made.

▼ Inflation, particularly unanticipated inflation, has harmful effects. These include: (1) adverse impact on investment and other time-dimension contracts, (2) distortion of relative prices, and (3) the shift of productive resources into activities designed to prevent inflation from eroding one's wealth.

CRITICAL ANALYSIS QUESTIONS

1. List the major phases of the business cycle and indicate how real GDP, employment, and unemployment change during these phases. Are the time periods of business cycles and the duration of the various phases relatively similar and therefore highly predictable?

*2. Explain why even an efficiently functioning economic system will have some unemployed resources.

*3. Classify each of the following as employed, unemployed, or not in the labor force:
   a. Brown is not working; she applied for a job at Wal-Mart last week and is awaiting the result of her application.
   b. Martinez is vacationing in Florida during a layoff at a General Motors plant due to a model changeover, but he expects to be recalled in a couple of weeks.
   c. Green was laid off as a carpenter when a construction project was completed. He is looking for work but has been unable to find anything except an $8-per-hour job, which he turned down.

   d. West works seventy hours per week as a homemaker for her family of nine.
   e. Carson, a seventeen-year-old, works six hours per week as a delivery person for the local newspaper.
   f. Chang works three hours in the mornings at a clinic and for the last two weeks has spent the afternoons looking for a full-time job.

4. What is full employment? When full employment is present, will the rate of unemployment be zero? Explain.

5. Is the natural rate of unemployment fixed? Why or why not? How are full employment and the natural rate of unemployment related? Is the actual rate of unemployment currently greater or less than the natural rate of unemployment? Why?

*6. How are the following related to one another?
   a. The actual rate of unemployment
   b. The natural rate of unemployment
   c. Cyclical unemployment
   d. Potential GDP

*7. Use the following data to calculate (a) the labor force participation rate, (b) unemployment rate, and (c) the employment/population ratio:

Population (aged 16 and over)	10,000
Labor force	6,000
Not currently working	4,500
Employed full-time	4,000
Employed part-time	1,500
Unemployed	500

*8. People are classified as unemployed if they are not currently working at a job and if they made an effort to find a job during the past four weeks. Does this mean that there were no jobs available? Does it mean that there were no jobs available for which the unemployed workers were qualified? What does it mean?

9. What impact will high and variable rates of inflation have on the economy? How will they influence the risk accompanying long-term contracts and related business decisions?

*10. The nominal salary paid to the president of the United States along with data for the consumer price index (CPI) are given for various years below.

Year	Presidential salary	CPI (2000 = 100)
1920	$ 75,000	11.6
1940	75,000	8.1
1960	100,000	17.2
1980	200,000	47.9
2000	400,000	100.0

a. Calculate the president's red salary measured in the purchasing power of the dollar in 2000.
b. In which year was the real presidential salary the highest?
c. The president's nominal salary was constant between 1920 and 1940. What happened to the real salary? Can you explain why?

11. "When employees are dismissed from employment for reasons other than poor performance, unemployment benefits should replace 100 percent of their prior earnings while they are searching for a new job." Evaluate this statement. Do you think the idea expressed is a good one? Would it influence how quickly laid-off workers would find new jobs? What impact would it have on the unemployment rate?

12. Suppose that the consumer price index at year-end 2003 was 150 and by year-end 2004 had risen to 160. What was the inflation rate during 2004?

*13. "My money wage rose by 6 percent last year, but inflation completely erased these gains. How can I get ahead when inflation continues to wipe out my increases in earnings?" What's wrong with this way of thinking?

14. Data for nominal GDP and the GDP deflator (2000 = 100) in 2001 and 2002 for six major industrial countries are presented in the accompanying Table A.
a. Use the data provided to calculate the 2001 and 2002 real GDP of each country measured in 2000 prices. Place the figures in the blanks provided.
b. Use the data for the GDP deflator to calculate the inflation rate of each country. Put your answers in the blanks provided.
c. Which country had the highest growth rate of real GDP? Which had the lowest?
d. Which countries had the highest and the lowest inflation rates?
e. Which one of the countries had the most inflation during this period?

*Asterisk denotes questions for which answers are given in Appendix B.

TABLE A

COUNTRY	NOMINAL GDP (BILLIONS OF LOCAL CURRENCY UNITS)		GDP DEFLATOR (2000 = 100)		REAL GDP (IN 2000 CURRENCY UNITS)		INFLATION RATE
	2001	2002	2001	2002	2001	2002	2002
United States	10,248.2	10,480.8	102.4	103.9	——	——	——
Canada	1,107.5	1,155.0	101.0	102.0	——	——	——
Japan	505,847.0	498,102.0	98.5	97.3	——	——	——
Germany	2,073.7	2,110.4	101.3	102.9	——	——	——
France	1,475.9	1,528.3	101.7	104.1	——	——	——
United Kingdom	994.0	1,043.3	102.3	105.6	——	——	——

Source: International Monetary Fund, *International Financial Statistics,* July 2004.

15. The following Table B presents the 2003 population, employment, and unemployment data for several countries.
    a. Calculate the number of people in the labor force for each country, and put the figures in the blanks provided.
    b. Calculate the labor force participation rate for each country, and put the figures in the blanks

provided. Which country had the highest labor force participation rate? Which country had the lowest?

    c. Calculate the unemployment rate for each country, and put the figures in the blanks provided. Which country had the highest unemployment rate? Which had the lowest?

TABLE B

COUNTRY	POPULATION 15 YEARS AND OVER (IN MILLIONS)	NUMBER EMPLOYED (IN MILLIONS)	NUMBER UNEMPLOYED (IN MILLIONS)	LABOR FORCE (IN MILLIONS)	LABOR FORCE PARTICIPATION RATE (PERCENT)	UNEMPLOYMENT RATE (PERCENT)
United States	230.3	139.2	8.8	_____	_____	_____
Canada	25.8	15.8	1.3	_____	_____	_____
Japan	109.7	63.2	3.5	_____	_____	_____
Germany	70.4	35.8	3.7	_____	_____	_____
France	48.6	24.6	2.6	_____	_____	_____
Australia	15.9	9.4	0.6	_____	_____	_____
Italy	49.2	22.1	2.1	_____	_____	_____

Source: http://www.oecd.org

An Introduction to Basic Macroeconomic Markets

Chapter Focus

- What is the circular flow of income? What are the major markets that coordinate macroeconomic activities?

- Why is the aggregate demand for goods and services inversely related to the price level?

- Why is an increase in the price level likely to expand output in the short run, but not in the long run?

- What determines the equilibrium level of GDP of an economy? When equilibrium is present, how will the actual rate of unemployment compare with the natural rate?

- What is the difference between the real interest rate and the money interest rate? Does inflation help borrowers relative to lenders?

- If equilibrium is present in the loanable funds and foreign exchange markets, how will this influence the leakages from and injections into the circular flow of income?

Macroeconomics is interesting . . . because it is challenging to reduce the complicated details of the economy to manageable essentials. Those essentials lie in the interactions among the goods, labor, and assets [loanable funds] markets of the economy.

—Rudiger Dornbusch and Stanley Fischer[1]

[1]Rudiger Dornbusch and Stanley Fischer, *Macroeconomics* (New York: McGraw-Hill, 1978).

As we have learned, the U.S. economy has historically grown at an annual rate of about 3 percent. This growth has improved the living standards of Americans. The growth, however, has not been steady. In some years, the economy has grown by more than the 3 percent. In others, it has grown by much less. In still other years—during recessions, for example—it has actually declined. As we noted in Chapter 8, the U.S. economy has also experienced fluctuations in employment and inflation rates. The experience of other countries is similar. All countries experience short-term fluctuations in output and employment, and varying degrees of inflation.

It is one thing to describe these fluctuations and another to understand their causes. In this chapter, we will develop a simple macroeconomic model. As we proceed, we will use this model to explain why fluctuations occur in output, employment, and prices and to analyze what might be done about them. ▧

UNDERSTANDING MACROECONOMICS: OUR GAME PLAN

A model is like a road map; it illustrates relationships between things. The simple model developed in this chapter will help us better understand macroeconomic relationships. It will also help us analyze the impact of policy changes on important economic variables, such as output, employment, and the general level of prices.

Fiscal policy
The use of government taxation and expenditure policies for the purpose of achieving macroeconomic goals.

Monetary policy
The deliberate control of the money supply, and, in some cases, credit conditions, for the purpose of achieving macroeconomic goals.

Money supply
The supply of currency, checking account funds, and traveler's checks. These items are counted as money because they are used as the means of payment for purchases.

Macroeconomic policy is usually divided into two components: fiscal policy and monetary policy. **Fiscal policy** relates to the government's taxation and spending policies to achieve macroeconomic goals. In the United States, fiscal policy is conducted by Congress and the president. It is thus a reflection of the political process. **Monetary policy** encompasses actions that alter the **money supply**—the amount of cash in our billfolds and deposits in our checking accounts. The direction of monetary policy is determined by a nation's central bank, the Federal Reserve System in the United States. Ideally, both monetary and fiscal policy are used to promote business stability, high employment, the growth of output, and a stable price level.

Initially, as we develop our basic macroeconomic model, we will assume that monetary and fiscal policies are unchanged—that Congress and the president aren't making fiscal policy changes and that the Federal Reserve is keeping the money supply stable. Of course, changes in government expenditures, taxes, and the money supply are potentially important. We will investigate their impact in detail in subsequent chapters.

FOUR KEY MARKETS: RESOURCES, GOODS AND SERVICES, LOANABLE FUNDS, AND FOREIGN EXCHANGE

Businesses generally purchase resources from households and use them to produce goods and services. In turn, households generally use a substantial portion of the income they earn from the sale of their productive services to purchase goods and services supplied by businesses. *Thus, there is a circular flow of output and income between these two key sectors, businesses and households. This circular flow of income is coordinated by four key macroeconomic markets: (1) goods and services, (2) resources, (3) loanable funds, and (4) foreign exchange.* **Exhibit 1** illustrates both the circular flow of income between the household and business sectors and the interrelationships among the key macroeconomic markets. This is a very important exhibit and really much less complicated than it might first appear. It essentially depicts the macroeconomic model explained in this chapter and used to analyze the economy. It will help you visualize more clearly the various spending flows and interrelationships among the key markets—where the money comes from and where it goes.

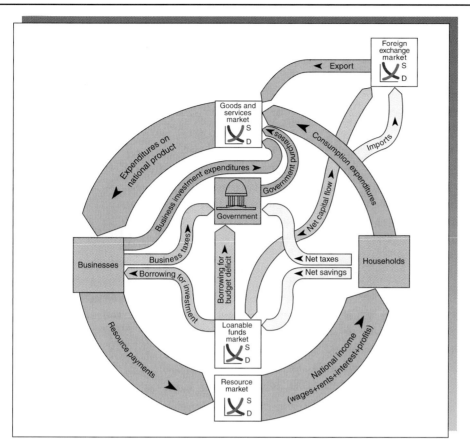

EXHIBIT 1
Four Key Markets and the Circular Flow of Income

The circular-flow diagram is a visual model of the economy. The circular flow of income is coordinated by four key markets. First, the resource market (bottom loop) coordinates businesses demanding resources and households supplying them in exchange for income. Second, the loanable funds market (lower center) brings the net saving of households plus the net inflow of foreign capital into balance with the borrowing by businesses and governments. Third, the foreign exchange market (top right) brings the purchases (imports) from foreigners into balance with sales (exports plus net inflow of capital) to them. Finally, the goods and services market (top loop) coordinates the demand (consumption, investment, government purchases, and net exports) with the supply of domestically produced goods and services (real GDP).

The bottom loop of this circular-flow diagram depicts the **resource market**, a highly aggregated market that includes the markets for labor services, natural resources, and physical capital. In the resource market, business firms demand resources because they need them to produce goods and services. Households supply labor and other resources in exchange for income. The forces of demand and supply determine prices in the resource market. The payments made to households and the suppliers of other resources sum to national income. Some of that income is taxed and used to finance the expenditures of governments. A portion is generally saved, but most of us use the bulk of our income to purchase goods and services.

The **goods and services market** constitutes the top loop of the circular-flow diagram. In this market, sometimes called the *product market*, businesses supply goods and services in exchange for sales revenue. This market counts all items in the economy's GDP. As the arrows flowing into the goods and services market (top loop) show, there are four major sources of expenditures in this market: (1) household expenditures on consumption (and new housing), (2) business investment, (3) government purchases, and (4) net exports. The expenditures of households, business investors, governments, and foreigners (net exports) compose the aggregate (total) demand for domestic output. As you can see, the goods and services market is a highly diverse market. It includes items such as cheeseburgers, pizza, hairstyling, movie tickets, clothing, television sets,

Resource market
A highly aggregated market encompassing all resources (labor, physical capital, land, and entrepreneurship) contributing to the production of current output. The labor market is the largest component of this market.

Goods and services market
A highly aggregated market encompassing the flow of all final-user goods and services. The market counts all items that enter into GDP. Thus, real output in this market is equal to real GDP.

Loanable funds market
A general term used to describe the market that coordinates the borrowing and lending decisions of business firms and households. Commercial banks, savings and loan associations, the stock and bond markets, and insurance companies are important financial institutions in this market.

Saving
The portion of after-tax income that is not spent on consumption. Saving is a "flow" concept.

Foreign exchange market
The market in which the currencies of different countries are bought and sold.

Exchange rate
The price of one unit of foreign currency in terms of the domestic currency. For example, if it takes $1.50 to purchase an English pound, the dollar-pound exchange rate is 1.50.

and DVD players—goods purchased primarily by consumers. It also includes investment goods such as tools, manufacturing equipment, and office buildings, generally purchased by business firms. Finally, things like highways, fire protection, and national defense, which are usually purchased by governments, are also part of the goods and services market.

Two other key markets help direct the flow of income between households and businesses. One is the **loanable funds market**. The loanable funds market is the market in which money is borrowed and loaned. It matches people who want to borrow money with those who want to lend it. If you borrow money to go to college or buy a car, you are participating in the loanable funds market.

The net saving *of the household sector supplies funds to the loanable funds market. The demand for funds arises from businesses, to finance investment projects, and from government, to finance budget deficits.* In an open economy like the United States, people also borrow from and lend money to foreigners. Notice the net inflow of capital from foreign economies into the loanable funds market in Exhibit 1. If the funds borrowed from foreigners exceed the loans made to them, there will be a net inflow of funds. This will increase the supply of money that can be lent out. On the other hand, if foreigners borrow more money than they supply, there will be a net outflow of funds. The price in the loanable funds market is the interest rate. Like prices in other markets, the interest rate will tend to bring the quantity demanded (funds demanded by businesses and governments) into balance with the quantity supplied (the net saving of households plus the net inflow of capital from foreigners). When the borrowed funds are spent on investment goods and government purchases, they return to the circular flow.

The other key market is the **foreign exchange market**. The foreign exchange market determines the rate—or price—at which two countries' currencies are exchanged. Firms generally want to be paid in their local currency. International transactions, therefore, generally require one of the trading partners to convert its domestic currency to that of the other partner's. Exchanges like this take place in the foreign exchange market. For example, if an American firm purchases glassware from a Mexican supplier, the firm would typically exchange dollars for pesos and then use the pesos to pay for the glassware. This generates demand for pesos. On the other hand, when foreigners buy U.S. products, it generates demand for U.S dollars. The **exchange rate**—the price of one currency relative to another—brings the purchases from foreigners into balance with the sales to them because rates of exchange are also subject to the laws of supply and demand.

Look closely at the right side of Exhibit 1 to determine what happens to the flow of income received by households. A major portion of household income is used to purchase consumer goods from domestic producers. These expenditures flow directly into the goods and services market. However, there are three types of "leakages" that can occur: households will use some of their income to purchase imports; some of the income will be taxed away by the government; and some of it will be saved. Imports, net taxes, and net saving are leakages from the circular flow of income.

However, these income leakages don't just evaporate into thin air. They tend to be channeled into the loanable funds and foreign exchange markets and back into the circular flow. The loanable funds market will tend to direct the net saving of households toward business investment and government purchases. The foreign exchange market will tend to direct import expenditures toward either spending by foreigners on exports or supplying funds to the loanable funds market. As we proceed, we will investigate in more detail how the loanable funds and foreign exchange markets influence the leakages from and injections to the circular flow of income.

As we noted in Chapter 7, there are two ways of measuring gross domestic product (GDP), the aggregate domestic output of an economy. First, GDP can be measured by adding up the spending of consumers, investors, governments, and foreigners (net exports) on goods and services produced during the year. This method is equivalent to measuring the flow of output as it moves through the top loop—the goods and services market—of the circular-flow diagram. Alternatively, GDP can be measured by summing the income payments, both direct and indirect, received by the resource suppliers who produced the goods and services. This method uses the bottom loop—the resource market—to measure the flow of output.

AGGREGATE DEMAND FOR GOODS AND SERVICES

What goes on in the aggregate goods and services market is central to the health of an economy. Indeed, if we could keep our eye on just one market in an economy, we would choose the goods and services market. It is important to note that the "quantity" and "price" in this highly aggregated, or combined, market differ from their counterparts in markets for specific goods. In the aggregate market for goods and services, the "quantity" (graphed on the *x*-axis) refers to the output of the entire economy—its GDP, in other words. The "price" (graphed on the *y*-axis) refers to the price level in the entire economy, which is measured by a general price index (such as the GDP deflator or consumer price index).

Demand and supply can help us understand highly aggregated markets just as they do markets for specific goods (say, for MP3 players or Starbucks coffee). Because demand in the goods and services market aggregates, or combines together, the purchases of all consumers, investors, governments, and foreigners, it is called "aggregate demand." The **aggregate demand curve** shows the various quantities of *domestically produced* goods and services purchasers are willing to buy at different price levels. As **Exhibit 2** illustrates, the aggregate demand curve (*AD*) slopes downward to the right, indicating an inverse relationship between the amount of goods and services demanded and the price level.

Aggregate demand curve
A downward-sloping curve showing the relationship between the price level and the quantity of domestically produced goods and services all households, business firms, governments, and foreigners (net exports) are willing to purchase.

Why Does the Aggregate Demand Curve Slope Downward?

The reason the aggregate demand curve slopes downward is different from the reason the demand curve for a single product does. The inverse relationship between price and the amount demanded of a specific commodity—television sets, for example—reflects the fact that consumers will buy the good in lieu of substitute goods when its price goes down. This is because the good becomes less expensive relative to others. In contrast, a price reduction in the aggregate goods and services market indicates that the level of prices in the entire economy has declined. When this happens, the prices of *all* goods are lower. When the prices of all goods produced domestically fall by the same proportion, there will be no incentive for *domestic* buyers to substitute one good for another.

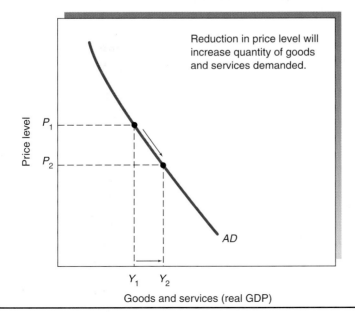

Reduction in price level will increase quantity of goods and services demanded.

EXHIBIT 2
The Aggregate Demand Curve

The quantity of goods and services purchased will increase (to Y_2) as the price level declines (to P_2). Other things being constant, the lower price level will increase the wealth of people holding money, lead to lower interest rates, and make domestically produced goods cheaper relative to foreign goods. All these factors will tend to increase the quantity of goods and services purchased at the lower price level.

There are three major reasons a lower price level will lead to an increase in the aggregate quantity of goods and services demanded by purchasers.

1. A lower price level will increase the purchasing power of money. As the level of prices declines, the purchasing power of money increases. For example, suppose that you have $2,000 in your bank account. Consider how a 20 percent reduction in the level of prices will influence your wealth and spending. At the lower price level, your $2,000 will buy more goods and services. In fact, your $2,000 will buy as much as $2,500 would have purchased at the previous higher price level. Other people will be in the same position you are. They will be wealthier and able to buy more. *(Note*: Remember we are assuming that the supply of money is fixed—that the Federal Reserve is keeping it stable.) Because of this increase in wealth, people will purchase more goods and services. Economists refer to this inverse relationship between the price level and the wealth of households and businesses (given a fixed supply of money as the **real balance effect**). It helps explain why a fall in the price level will lead to an increase in the quantity demanded of goods and services.

Real balance effect
The increase in wealth that occurs when the price level falls and the purchasing power of money increases (assuming the supply of money in the economy is stable). The wealth effect leads to an inverse relationship between price (level) and quantity demanded in the goods and services market: when the price level falls, people will demand more goods and services.

2. The interest-rate effect: A lower price level will reduce the demand for money and lower the real interest rate, which will stimulate additional purchases. When the average price of everything is lower, consumers and businesses will need less money to conduct their normal activities. Households will be able to get by just fine with a smaller money balance because, at the lower price level, they will be spending a smaller amount on food, clothing, and other items they regularly purchase. Similarly, businesses will need less money to pay employee wages, taxes, and other business expenses. At the lower price level, both consumers and businesses will attempt to reduce their money balances and shift more funds to interest-earning assets like bonds and savings deposits. This will channel more funds into the loanable funds market, placing downward pressure on interest rates.

What impact will a lower interest rate have on the demand for goods and services? A reduction in the interest rate will make it cheaper to purchase goods and services on credit. Both households and businesses will demand more goods and services as a result. Households can be expected to increase their purchases of interest-sensitive consumption goods, like automobiles and consumer durables. Similarly, firms will invest more in business expansion and new construction. This effect on the interest rate also contributes to the downward slope of the aggregate demand curve.

3. Other things being constant, a lower price level will make domestically produced goods less expensive relative to foreign goods. At a lower price level, imports will decline as Americans find that many domestically produced goods are now cheaper than products produced abroad. At the lower price level, Americans will tend to purchase fewer Japanese automobiles, Korean textiles, Italian shoes, and other imports because these items are now more expensive relative to domestically produced goods. At the same time, foreigners will increase their purchases of American-made goods that are now relatively cheaper. Therefore, net exports (exports minus imports) will tend to rise.[2] The increase in net exports at the lower U.S. price level will directly increase the quantity demanded of domestically produced goods. This international-substitution effect is a third reason the aggregate demand curve slopes downward.

The Downward-Sloping Aggregate Demand Curve: A Summary

The accompanying Thumbnail Sketch summarizes the reasons why a lower price level increases the quantity demanded of domestically produced goods and services. A lower

[2]An increase in exports and a decline in imports will place some upward pressure on the foreign exchange value of the currency. However, the lower interest rates (point 2 above) will result in an outflow of capital, which will place downward pressure on the foreign exchange value of the currency. Most economists believe that this latter effect will dominate. If it does, a depreciation in the nation's currency will stimulate net exports, which will also increase the quantity demanded of goods and services.

price level will (1) increase the purchasing power of money, (2) lower interest rates, and (3) reduce the price of domestically produced goods relative to goods produced abroad. Each of these factors will tend to increase the quantity demanded in the goods and services market.

If the price level were to rise, the effects would be just the opposite. At a higher price level, (1) the wealth of people holding money would be less, (2) the demand for money would be greater, which would lead to higher interest rates, and (3) domestic goods would be more expensive relative to those produced abroad. Each of these factors would tend to reduce the quantity demanded of domestically produced goods.

AGGREGATE SUPPLY OF GOODS AND SERVICES

In light of our discussion of aggregate demand, it shouldn't surprise you that the general shape of the **aggregate supply curve** differs from the shape of the supply curve for a single good. As we already noted, when the price level rises, the prices of all goods rise, rather than the price of one good relative to other goods. Thus, the general shape of the aggregate supply (*AS*) curve is not a reflection of changes in the relative prices of goods.

When we examine aggregate supply, it is particularly important to distinguish between the short run and the long run. In the short run, some prices, particularly those in labor markets, are set by prior contracts and agreements. Households and businesses are unable to adjust these prices when unexpected changes occur, including unexpected changes in the price level. In contrast, the long run is a time period long enough that people are able to modify their behavior in response to price changes. We now consider both the short-run and long-run aggregate supply curves.

Aggregate supply curve
The curve showing the relationship between a nation's price level and the quantity of goods supplied by its producers. In the short run, it is an upward-sloping curve, but in the long run the aggregate supply curve is vertical.

Aggregate Supply in the Short Run

*The short-run aggregate supply (***SRAS***) curve shows the various quantities of goods and services domestic firms will supply in response to changing demand conditions that alter the level of prices in the goods and services market.* As **Exhibit 3** shows, the *SRAS* curve in the goods and services market slopes upward to the right. The upward slope reflects the fact that, in the short run, an unanticipated increase in the price level will, on average, improve the profitability of firms. They will respond with an expansion in output.

The *SRAS* curve is based on a specific expected price level, P_{100} in the case of Exhibit 3, and rate of inflation that generates that price level. When the expected price level is actually achieved, the profitability rate of firms, on average, will be normal, and they will supply output Y_0.

Consider how firms would respond if strong demand led to an unexpected increase in the price level (to P_{105}, for example). *Important components of producers' costs are determined by long-term contracts.* These components include interest rates on their

THUMBNAIL SKETCH

Why is the aggregate quantity demanded inversely related to the price level?

A decrease in the price level will raise the aggregate quantity demanded because:
1. The real wealth of people holding money will increase when prices fall; this will encourage additional consumption.

2. A fall in the demand for money at the lower price level will reduce interest rates, which will encourage current investment and consumption.
3. Net exports will expand (since the prices of domestic goods will have fallen relative to foreign goods).

EXHIBIT 3
The Short-Run
Aggregate Supply
Curve

The short-run aggregate supply (*SRAS*) curve shows the relationship between the price level and the quantity supplied of goods and services by domestic producers. In the short run, firms will generally expand output as the price level increases; the higher prices will improve their profit margins because many of their cost components will be temporarily fixed as the result of prior long-term commitments.

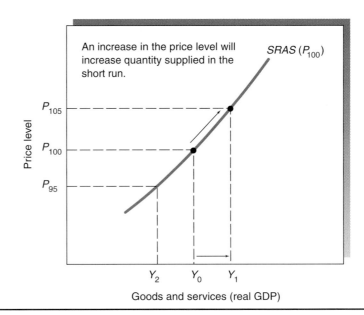

loans, collective bargaining agreements with their employees, lease agreements on buildings and machines, and other contracts with resource suppliers. The prices incorporated into these long-term contracts at the time of the agreement are based on the expectation of price level (P_{100}) for the current period and tend to be temporarily fixed. So, in the short run, the higher prices enhance producers' profitability because the prices for which they can sell their products rise but some of their costs (like labor) don't. When this happens, firms will happily respond by expanding their output (to Y_1). Their profits will be higher if they do.[3]

Conversely, an unexpected reduction in the price level to P_{95} will have the opposite effect. It will decrease product prices relative to costs and thereby reduce profitability. In response, firms would reduce output to Y_2. As you can see, there is a direct relationship between the amount producers will supply and the price level in the goods and services market—in the short run, that is.

Aggregate Supply in the Long Run

Things are different, though, when it comes to aggregate supply in the long run. In the long run, a higher price level won't change the relationship between product and resource prices. Once people have time to fully adjust their prior commitments, competitive forces will restore the usual relationship between product prices and costs. Profit rates will return to normal, and firms will not have any additional incentive to pump out extra goods and services. *The long-run aggregate supply (**LRAS**) curve shows the relationship between the price level and quantity of output after decision makers have had time to adjust their prior commitments, or take steps to counterbalance them, when the price level changes.* Therefore, as **Exhibit 4** illustrates, the *LRAS* curve is vertical.

---

[3]Other factors may also contribute to the positive relationship between the price level and output in the short run. In response to a general increase in demand, some firms may expand output without much of an increase in price because they believe that their current strong sales are only temporary and that a price increase would drive some of their regular customers to rival suppliers. Other firms may expand output because they mistakenly believe that the demand for their product has increased relative to other products. In the long run, higher costs relative to product prices will make it impossible to sustain such expansions in output.

EXHIBIT 4
The Long-Run Aggregate
Supply Curve

In the long run, a higher price level will not expand an economy's rate of output. Once people have had time to adjust their prior long-term commitments, resource markets (and costs) will adjust to the higher level of prices and firms will no longer have an incentive to supply a larger output at the higher price level. An economy's full-employment rate of output—Y_F, the maximum output rate that is sustainable—is determined by the supply of resources, level of technology, and structure of institutions, factors that are insensitive to changes in the price level. The vertical *LRAS* curve illustrates this point.

In the long run, once people have time to adjust their choices, the forces that provide for an upward-sloping **SRAS** *curve are no longer present.* Costs that are temporarily fixed as the result of contractual agreements will eventually rise. With time, the long-term contracts will expire and be renegotiated. Once the contracts are renegotiated, resource prices will increase in the same proportion as product prices. A proportional increase in costs and product prices will leave the incentive to produce unchanged. Consider how a firm with a selling price of $50 and per-unit costs of $50 will be affected when both the price it can sell its product for and the resources used to make it double. After the price increase, the firm's sales price per unit will be $100, but so, too, will its per-unit costs. Thus, neither the firm's profit rate nor its incentive to produce more of the good has changed. Therefore, in the long run, an increase in the price level will fail to exert a lasting impact on aggregate output.

As we discussed in Chapter 2, at a point in time, the production possibilities of a nation are constrained by the supply of resources, level of technology, and institutional arrangements that influence the efficiency of resource use. *The long-run aggregate supply curve is an alternative way to visualize the economy's production possibilities.* Rather than showing the output of physical units like the production possibilities curve does, the long-run aggregate supply curve shows the real dollar value of the units produced. The vertical long-run supply curve indicates that a change in the price level doesn't loosen the constraints limiting our production possibilities. For example, a doubling of prices will not improve technology. Neither will it expand the availability of productive resources, nor improve the efficiency of our economic institutions.

Thus, there is no reason a higher price level would increase our ability to produce goods and services in the long run. Firms are going to continue to produce the same amount of goods and services they're able to, given their resources, no matter what the price level is. This is precisely what the vertical *LRAS* curve implies. The temporary hike in aggregate supply—shown by the upward slope of the *SRAS* curve—is purely a short-run phenomenon. It can't last. The accompanying Thumbnail Sketch summarizes the factors that underlie both the short-run and long-run aggregate supply curves.

Why is the short-run aggregate quantity supplied directly related to the price level?

As the general level of sales prices for products increases, profit margins will improve because some costs of production are temporarily fixed by long-term contracts.

Why is the long-run aggregate supply curve vertical?

1. Once people have had time to adjust fully to a new price level, the normal relationship between product prices and resource costs will be restored.

2. The sustainable potential output of an economy is determined by its quantity of resources, level of technology, and the efficiency of its institutional structures—not by the price level.

Equilibrium
A balance of forces permitting the simultaneous fulfillment of plans by buyers and sellers.

EQUILIBRIUM IN THE GOODS AND SERVICES MARKET

We are now ready to combine our analysis of aggregate demand and aggregate supply to see how they determine the price level and rate of output in the economy. When a market is in **equilibrium**, the forces exerted by buyers and sellers balance one another. Buyers are willing to purchase all the units that sellers are willing to supply *at the current price level*. Because the equilibrium price clears the market—all units produced are sold—some refer to it as the "market-clearing price."

Equilibrium in the Short Run

As **Exhibit 5** illustrates, short-run equilibrium is present in the goods and services market at the price level *P*, at which the aggregate quantity demanded is equal to the aggregate quantity supplied. This occurs at the output rate *Y*, where the *AD* and *SRAS* curves intersect. At the price level *P*, the amount that buyers want to purchase is just equal to the quantity that sellers are willing to supply.

EXHIBIT 5
Short-Run Equilibrium in the Goods and Services Market

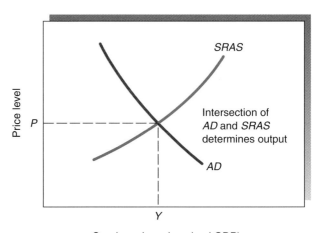

Short-run equilibrium in the goods and services market occurs at the price level *P*, where the *AD* and *SRAS* curves intersect. If the price level were lower than *P*, excess demand in goods and services markets would push prices upward. Conversely, if the price level were higher than *P*, excess supply would result in falling prices.

If a price level lower than *P* were present, the aggregate quantity demanded would exceed the aggregate quantity supplied. Purchasers would want to buy more goods and services than producers would be willing to produce. This excess demand would place upward pressure on prices, causing the price level to rise toward *P*. On the other hand, at a price level greater than *P,* the aggregate quantity supplied would exceed the aggregate quantity demanded. Producers would be unable to sell all the goods they produce. This would result in downward pressure (toward *P*) on prices. Only at the price level *P* will there be a balance of forces between the amount of goods demanded by consumers, investors, governments, and foreigners, and the amount supplied by domestic firms.

Equilibrium in the Long Run

In the short run, the goods and services market will gravitate toward a price level that brings quantity demanded and quantity supplied in the economy into balance. ***However, a second condition is required for long-run equilibrium: decision makers who agreed to long-term contracts influencing current prices and costs must have correctly anticipated the current price level at the time they arrived at the agreements.*** If this is not the case, buyers and sellers will want to modify the agreements when their long-term contracts expire. In turn, their modifications will affect costs, profit margins, and output.

Exhibit 6 illustrates a long-run equilibrium in the goods and services market. Like in Exhibit 3, the subscripts attached to the *SRAS* and *AD* curves indicate the price level (the price index) that decision makers anticipated at the time they made their decisions about their long-term contracts. In this case, when buyers and sellers made their purchasing and production choices, they anticipated that the price level during the period would be P_{100}. As the intersection of the *AD* and *SRAS* curves reveals, P_{100} was actually attained. In long-run equilibrium, aggregate demand (*AD*) intersects with *SRAS* along the economy's vertical *LRAS*.

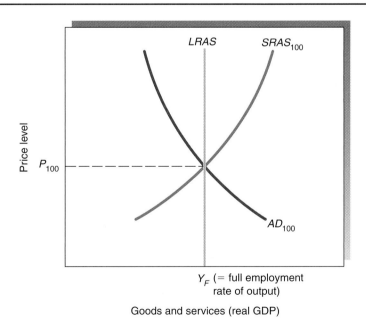

EXHIBIT 6
Long-Run Equilibrium in the Goods and Services Market

When the goods and services market is in long-run equilibrium, two conditions must be present. First, the quantity demanded must equal the quantity supplied at the current price level. Second, the price level anticipated by decision makers must equal the actual price level. The subscripts on the *SRAS* and *AD* curves indicate that buyers and sellers alike anticipated the price level P_{100}, where the 100 represents an index of prices during an earlier base year. When the anticipated price level is actually attained, current output (Y_F) will equal the economy's potential GDP, and full employment will be present.

When the price level expectations about the long-term contracts turn out to be correct, then the current resource prices and real interest rates will tend to persist into the future. Profit rates will be normal. The choices of buyers and sellers will harmonize, and neither will have reason to modify their previous contractual agreements when they come up for renegotiation. Thus, the current rate of output (Y_F) is sustainable in the future. This also corresponds to full employment in the economy. Long-run equilibrium is present, and it will persist into the future until changes in other factors alter *AD* or *SRAS*.

Long-Run Equilibrium, Potential Output, and Full Employment

As we discussed in Chapter 8, potential GDP is equal to the economy's *maximum sustainable output* consistent with its resource base, current technology, and institutional structure. Potential GDP is neither a temporary high nor an abnormal low. When long-run equilibrium is present, the actual output achieved is equal to the economy's potential GDP.

The long-run equilibrium output rate (Y_F in Exhibit 6) also corresponds with the full employment of resources. When full-employment output is present, the job search time of unemployed workers will be normal, given the characteristics of the labor force and the institutional structure of the economy. Only frictional and structural unemployment will be present; cyclical unemployment will be absent.

When an economy is in long-run equilibrium, the *actual* rate of unemployment will be equal to the natural rate. Remember, the *natural* rate of unemployment reflects the normal job search process of employees and employers, given the structure of the economy and the laws and regulations that affect the operation of markets. It is a rate that is neither abnormally high nor abnormally low; it can be sustained into the future. If long-run equilibrium is present, unemployment will be at its natural rate.

Let's summarize what we've learned: In long-run equilibrium, (1) output will be equal to its potential, (2) full employment will be achieved, and (3) the actual rate of unemployment will be equivalent to the natural rate of unemployment. It is this long-run maximum sustainable output that economists are referring to when they speak of "full employment output" or "potential GDP."

What Happens When the Economy's Output Differs from Its Long-Run Potential?

Scenario 1: Output Is Greater Than Long-Run Potential What happens when changes in the price level catch buyers and sellers by surprise? When the actual price level differs from the level forecast by buyers and sellers, some decision makers will enter into agreements that they will later regret—agreements that they will want to change as soon as they have an opportunity to do so.

Consider the situation when the price level *increases* more than was anticipated. Failing to foresee the strong demand and higher product prices, many resource suppliers will have agreed to long-term contracts that are not as attractive as they initially thought they would be. For example, many union officials and employees will have made commitments to money wages that are now unattractive, given the strong demand and higher general level of prices. Other resource suppliers will find themselves in a similar position. In the short run, the atypically low resource costs relative to product prices make profit margins abnormally high. In this case, firms will pump out more output to boost their profits. Employment expands and unemployment falls below its natural rate.

But this abnormally large output and high level of employment are not sustainable. The "mistakes," based on a failure to predict the strength of current demand, will be recognized and corrected when contracts expire. Real wages (and other resource prices) will increase and eventually reflect the higher price level and rate of inflation. Profit margins will return to normal. When these adjustments are completed, the temporarily large output rate and high employment level will decline and return to normal.

How can output, even temporarily, be pushed beyond the economy's potential GDP? Remember, potential GDP is a sustainable rate of output; it can be maintained. Motivated by strong demand and high profitability, firms can expand output through intensive supervision, more overtime work, a reduction in downtime for maintenance, and similar measures. However, this intense pace cannot be maintained over lengthy periods. The situation is much like that of students who stay up later, watch less television, and spend less time on social and leisure activities in order to increase their study time prior to a major exam. They are able to increase their "productivity" temporarily, but the hectic schedule cannot be maintained. Similarly, business firms can temporarily push output beyond long-run potential. But, given the constraints of the current resource base, the higher output rate cannot be sustained. Markets will adjust and output will recede to its long-run potential.

Scenario 2: Output Is Less Than Long-Run Potential What will happen if product prices either decline or increase less rapidly than anticipated? Given the lower than expected price level, many employers will find themselves committed to wages and other resource prices that are extremely high relative to the prices they can get for their products. Profit margins will be squeezed, causing producers to reduce output and lay off employees. Unemployment will rise above its *natural rate,* and current output will fall short of the economy's potential GDP.

Many economists think that high costs of producing products (relative to the prices they can sell them for) because of prior long-term commitments actually *cause* recessions. The 1982 recession provides a vivid illustration of why this is likely to be the case. After inflation rates of 13 percent in 1979, and 12 percent in 1980, price increases in the economy plummeted to 4 percent in 1982. This sharp reduction in the inflation rate caught many decision makers by surprise. Unable to pass along to consumers the large increases in money wages agreed to in 1980 and 1981, employers cut back production and laid off workers. The unemployment rate soared to 10.8 percent in late 1982, up from 7.6 percent in 1981. Eventually, new agreements provided for smaller money wage increases and even wage reductions in 1983 and 1984. Unemployment then fell. Nevertheless, in 1982, unemployment was well above its natural rate. The necessary adjustments could not be made instantaneously.

Again, let's summarize what we've learned: An unexpected change in the price level (rate of inflation) will alter the rate of output in the short run. An unexpected *increase* in the price level will stimulate output and employment during the next year or two, whereas an unexpected *decrease* in the price level will cause output and employment to fall.

The expected rate of inflation influences the prices incorporated into long-term contracts, like collective bargaining agreements. If the actual price level differs from what was expected, output will differ from long-run equilibrium.

© GETTY IMAGES

RESOURCE MARKET

As we have said, in addition to the aggregate goods and services market, the resource market, loanable funds market, and foreign exchange market help coordinate the circular flow of income between households and businesses. All four of these markets are interrelated—changes in one will have repercussions in the others. We will now turn to an analysis of the resource, loanable funds, and foreign exchange markets and how they work in tandem with the goods and services market.

The resource market is the place where labor, raw materials, machines, and other factors of production are bought and sold. Within the framework of our circular-flow analysis, households supply resources (like their labor) in exchange for income. Business firms demand resources to produce goods and services, as Exhibit 1 showed. By far, labor is the largest component of the resource market. In the United States, labor costs make up approximately 70 percent of production costs. Because of the labor market's size and importance, we will focus considerable attention on it.

An increase in the price of labor and other resources will increase the cost of production and make it less profitable for firms to employ resources. As a result, businesses will demand less labor and other resources as the prices of those resources increase. Thus, the demand curve in the resource market will have the usual downward slope to the right. Although working and supplying resources generates income, it also requires a person to give up other things—like leisure. Higher resource prices—like higher wages—will make it more attractive for people to give up some leisure and supply labor and other resources instead. Therefore, the quantity supplied of labor and other resources expands as resource prices increase.

As **Exhibit 7** illustrates, there will be a tendency to move toward a price level that will bring the amount of resources demanded by business firms into balance with the amount supplied by resource owners—just as goods and services are brought into balance between consumers and producers. At this price (P_r), the choices of both buyers and sellers in the aggregate resource market harmonize—they are consistent with each other. If the market price were greater than P_r, an excess supply of resources would occur. In turn, this excess supply would push resource prices downward toward equilibrium. In contrast, if resource prices were below equilibrium (less than P_r), excess demand would place upward pressure on the price of resources. Market forces thus tend to move resource prices toward the price that clears the market and brings the amount demanded into equality with the amount supplied.

The markets for resources and products are closely related. The demand for resources is directly linked to the demand for goods and services. An increase in demand in the goods and services market will generate additional demand for resources. Similarly, a reduction in aggregate demand in the goods and services market will reduce the demand for resources.

EXHIBIT 7
Equilibrium in the Resource Market

In general, as resource prices increase, the amount demanded by producers declines and the amount supplied by resource owners expands. In equilibrium, resource price brings the amount demanded into balance with the amount supplied in the aggregate-resource market. The labor market is a major component of the resource market.

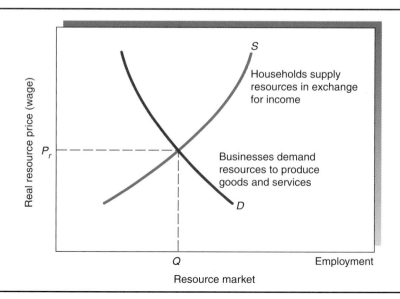

Changes in resource markets will also exert an effect on the goods and services market. The cost of producing goods and services is influenced directly by the price of resources. Other things constant, an increase in resource prices will increase costs and squeeze profit margins, causing the supply curve (*SRAS*) in the product market to shift to the left. If inputs are costing firms more, higher product prices will be required to provide firms with the same incentive to supply any given level of output. Conversely, a reduction in resource prices will lower costs and improve profit margins in the goods and services market. An increase in aggregate supply (a shift to the right in *SRAS*) will result. As we analyze the macroeconomy, the interrelations between these two markets will arise again and again.

*When an economy is in long-run equilibrium, the price of resources relative to the price of goods and services firms can receive will be such that, on average, firms will **be just able** to cover their costs of production, including a competitive return on their investment. If this were not the case, producers would seek to either contract or expand output.* For example, if the prices of resources were so high (relative to product prices) that firms were unable to cover their costs, many producers would cut back output or perhaps even discontinue production. Aggregate output would change. Conversely, if resource prices were so low that firms were able to earn an above-market return, profit-seeking firms would expand output. New firms would begin production. Again, these forces would alter conditions in the goods and services market.

LOANABLE FUNDS MARKET

As we have said, the loanable funds market is the market where borrowers demand funds and lenders supply them. The price in this market is the interest rate. To keep things simple, we will assume that there is a single interest rate. In reality, of course, borrowers and lenders make deals at many different interest rates. Those interest rates depend on what a person or firm is buying, the length of time they want to borrow the money for, and the level of risk involved. Banks, insurance companies, and brokerage firms often act as intermediaries between lenders and borrowers in the loanable funds market.

Essentially, borrowers are exchanging future income to get purchasing power now. Most of us are impatient; we want things now rather than in the future. *From the viewpoint of borrowers, interest is the price they have to pay to get money now. From the viewpoint of lenders, interest is the reward they get for waiting—for not being able to spend their money now because they've loaned it to someone else.*

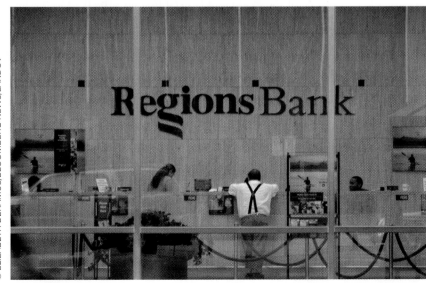

Banks, savings and loan associations, and brokerage firms help coordinate saving and borrowing in the loanable funds market.

© ELIZABETH DERAMUS/BLOOMBERG NEWS/LANDOV

EXHIBIT 8
Interest Rates and the Loanable Funds Market

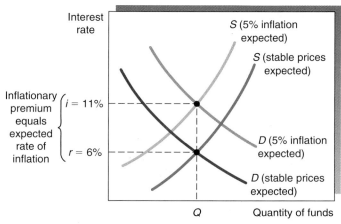

a) Interest Rate Determination

b) Inflation and Nominal Interest Rate

The interest rate in the loanable funds market will bring the quantity of funds demanded by borrowers into balance with the quantity supplied by lenders (part a). As part (b) illustrates, inflation will influence the nominal interest rate. Suppose that when people expect the general level of prices to be stable (zero inflation) in the future, a 6 percent interest rate brings quantity demand ͟   ͟ ͟ ͟ balance with quantity supplied. Under these conditions, the money interest rate and real interest rate will be equa͟ ͟rate, however, the money rate of interest (*i*) will rise to 11 percent even ͟ ͟ ͟ ͟ ͟ ͟ ͟ ͟ ͟ ͟ ͟ ͟ ͟ ͟ ͟ 5 percent.

͟ ͟ ͟ ͟rates, more funds will be borrowed at lower interest ͟ ͟ ͟ke it cheaper for households to purchase consumption ͟ ͟ ͟rtake investment projects. They will borrow more at ͟ ͟ ͟ ͟ curve for loanable funds slopes downward to the right. ͟ ͟ ͟rates make it more attractive to save (and lend funds). ͟ ͟ ͟ funds slopes upward to the right, indicating that there ͟ ͟ ͟he interest rate and the quantity of funds supplied by ͟ ͟ ͟rdinate the actions of borrowers and lenders. It will tend ͟ ͟ ͟te (in the case of Exhibit 8a, 6 percent). This is the rate ͟ ͟ ͟plied by lenders just equals the quantity demanded by ͟ ͟ ͟

Money interest ͟ ͟ ͟ ͟ ͟ ͟ ͟ ͟he interest rate in two ways. First, there is the **money** ͟ ͟ ͟the amount borrowed that must be paid to the lender in ͟ ͟ ͟principal. Money interest rates are those typically quoted in newspapers and business publications. Second, there is the **real interest rate**, which reflects the actual burden to borrowers and the payoff to lenders after inflation has had an impact.

Money interest rate
The percentage of the amount borrowed that must be paid to the lender in addition to the repayment of the principal. The money interest rate overstates the real cost of borrowing during an inflationary period. When inflation is anticipated, an inflationary premium will be incorporated into this rate. The money interest rate is often called the nominal interest rate.

Real interest rate
The interest rate adjusted for expected inflation; it indicates the real cost of borrowing and lending money after inflation has been factored in.

The rate of inflation expected by borrowers and lenders will influence the attractiveness of various interest rates. Perhaps an example will illustrate this point and highlight the distinction between the money interest rate and the real interest rate. Suppose that a borrower and lender—both anticipating that the general level of prices will be stable—agree to a 6 percent interest rate for a one-year loan of $1,000. After a year, the borrower must pay the lender $1,060—the $1,000 principal plus the 6 percent interest. Now, suppose during the year prices rise 5 percent as the result of inflation. Because of this, the $1,060 repayment after a year commands only about 1 percent more purchasing power than the original $1,000 did when it was loaned. The lender receives only a 1 percent return for making the purchasing power available to the borrower. In this case, the real interest return to the lender (and real cost to the borrower) is just 1 percent. Lenders are unlikely to continue making funds available at such bargain rates. They are going to begin charging higher rates.

When inflation is persistent, people will come to anticipate it. Once borrowers and lenders expect a rate of inflation—5 percent, for example—they will build that rate into their loanable funds agreements. Lenders will demand (and borrowers will agree to pay) a higher money interest rate to compensate for the impact of inflation. This premium for the expected decline in purchasing power of the dollar is called the **inflationary premium**. It is equal to the expected rate of inflation. The relationship between the real interest rate and money interest rate is:

$$\text{Real interest rate} = \text{Money interest rate} - \text{Inflationary premium}$$

Part (b) of Exhibit 8 illustrates how people's expectations about inflation influence money interest rates. Here we consider a situation in which a 6 percent market rate of interest would emerge when borrowers and lenders anticipate stable prices. Because the expected rate of inflation is zero, there will be no inflationary premium and, under these conditions, the money interest rates and real interest rates are equal. Now consider how a persistent inflation rate of 5 percent will influence the choices of both borrowers and lenders. Compared to the situation where the inflation rate was zero and the interest rate 6 percent, an 11 percent interest rate will now be required to provide lenders with the same incentive to loan funds. Similarly, an 11 percent interest rate will provide borrowers with the same incentive to demand funds. When people expect a 5 percent rate of inflation, both the supply and demand curves will shift vertically by this amount to compensate for the expected rate of inflation. As a result, the money rate of interest will increase to 11 percent: 5 percent of that is the inflationary premium; 6 percent is the real return that lenders earn.

Of course, the expected rate of inflation and inflationary premium cannot be directly observed. Therefore, neither can the real interest rate. Nonetheless, it is easy to see why the money interest rate can be misleading. It doesn't reflect what the real cost of borrowing money is. (Remember: *real* always means adjusted for inflation.) What people expect inflation to be and what it actually ends up being can be different. Even though this is problematic, the money interest rate will nonetheless vary directly with what people expect inflation to be. If they expect inflation will be higher, the inflationary premium will be higher, too, as will the money rate of interest. Only the *real* interest rate reflects the true cost of borrowing and the true return of lending money.

Does Inflation Help Borrowers?

In a world of uncertainty, decision makers will not always be able to forecast accurately the future rate of inflation. If the actual rate of inflation is higher than was expected, borrowers will tend to gain relative to lenders. For example, suppose borrowers and lenders expect a 3 percent future rate of inflation and therefore agree to an 8 percent interest rate on a loan—5 percent representing the real interest rate and 3 percent the inflationary premium. If the actual rate of inflation turns out to be higher than 3 percent—6 percent, for example—the real amount paid by the borrower and received by the lender will decline. *When the actual rate of inflation is greater than was anticipated, borrowers gain at the expense of lenders.*

But the converse is true when the actual rate of inflation is less than expected. Suppose that after the borrower and lender agree to the 8 percent loan, the price level remains stable. In this case, the borrower ends up paying an 8 percent real interest rate, rather than the 5 percent they thought they were going to pay. *When the actual rate of inflation is less than anticipated, lenders gain at the expense of borrowers.*

Some people argue that inflation helps borrowers relative to lenders. But this neglects the fact that loans have an inflationary premium built into them. Borrowers would only gain relative to lenders if both borrowers and lenders underestimate the rate of inflation and don't allow enough of an inflationary premium. This is highly unlikely to happen on a regular basis. Of course, forecasting errors will be made. Sometimes the inflation rate will be higher than decision makers anticipated, whereas in other instances it will be lower. *There is no reason, however, to expect that everyone will underestimate inflation and what the inflationary premium should be. Thus, there is no reason why inflation will help either borrowers or lenders in a systematic manner.*

Inflationary premium
A component of the money interest rate that reflects compensation to the lender for the expected decrease, due to inflation, in the purchasing power of the principal and interest during the course of the loan. It is determined by the expected rate of future inflation.

Interest Rates and Macroeconomic Markets

The circular-flow diagram (Exhibit 1) illustrates both the inflow and outflow to the loanable funds market. The net saving of households and net capital inflow from foreigners provide the inflow—the supply of funds—into the loanable funds market. Borrowing by businesses and governments generates the demand for loanable funds.

Businesses and governments often borrow money by issuing bonds on which they pay interest on. Issuing bonds is simply a method of demanding loanable funds. In turn, the purchasers of bonds are supplying loanable funds. There is an inverse relationship between bond prices and interest rates. *When interest rates rise, the market value of bonds previously issued will fall. Conversely, lower interest rates will push the market value of bonds previously issued upward.* (For a detailed explanation of this point, see the Applications in Economics box on bonds and interest rates).

In an open economy like that of the United States, domestic residents are also able to borrow from and lend to foreigners. When foreigners supply more loanable funds to the domestic market than Americans supply to foreigners, there will be a net inflow of foreign capital that will supplement domestic saving. On the other hand, if Americans are net lenders, there will be a net outflow of capital from the domestic market. The real interest rate in the loanable funds market will move toward the rate that will bring the quantity of funds demanded into equality with the quantity supplied, *including the net inflow or outflow of capital.*

In today's global financial markets, the flow of capital to the domestic loanable funds market will be directly related to the real interest rate. As **Exhibit 9** shows, when domestic demand is weak (D_1, for example) and the real interest rate low (r_1), capital will flow outward toward other markets where the rate of return is expected to be higher. In contrast, strong domestic demand (D_2, for example) for loanable funds and high real interest rates will lead to an inflow of capital.

Like the resource market, the loanable funds market is interrelated with the goods and services market. We saw that the interest rate generally falls when the price level falls, which helps explain why the *AD* curve slopes downward to the right. In addition, the real interest rate may change for other reasons. When it does, it will affect the aggregate demand schedule. The real interest rate influences how households allocate their income between saving and current consumption. An increase in the interest rate will discourage current consumption by making it more attractive to save and more expensive to borrow. This will reduce aggregate demand. Lower interest rates will have the opposite effect. As we proceed, we will analyze in more detail the interrelationship between the loanable funds market and the goods and services market.

When an economy is in long-run equilibrium, the relationship between interest rates in the loanable funds market and prices in product and resource markets will be such that the typical firm is just able to earn normal returns on its investments. In other words, the typical producer's return to capital must equal the interest rate, that is, the opportunity cost of capital. *Higher returns would induce producers to expand output, whereas lower returns would cause them to cut back on production.*

FOREIGN EXCHANGE MARKET

Look back at Exhibit 1 and note the various transactions with foreigners. Households import some goods and services from foreigners, reducing the flow of spending into the domestic product market. But foreigners buy some of the goods produced by the domestic firms, and these exports add to the flow of spending into the domestic product market. In addition, there is an inflow of money from foreigners into the loanable funds market and an outflow of money to foreigners. As we just discussed, the size and direction of this net flow of money depends on the real interest rate.

Exhibit 10 illustrates how the foreign exchange market tends to bring purchases and sales between countries into balance. The dollar price of foreign currency is

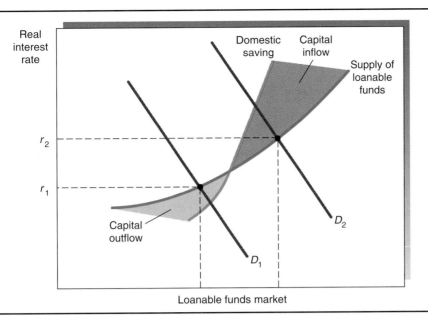

EXHIBIT 9
Interest Rates and the Inflow and Outflow of Capital

Demand and supply in the loanable funds market determine interest rates. When the demand for loanable funds is strong (such as D_2), the real interest rate will be high (such as r_2), and there will be a net inflow of capital. In contrast, weak demand (such as D_1) and low interest rates (such as r_1) will lead to net capital outflow.

APPLICATIONS IN ECONOMICS

Bonds, Interest Rates, and Bond Prices

Bonds are simply IOUs issued by firms and governments. Issuing bonds is a method of borrowing in the loanable funds market. The entity issuing the bond promises to pay interest at a fixed rate on the amount borrowed (called principal) while the loan is outstanding and to repay the principal on a specified date in the future (for example, five or ten years after the bond is issued). The date when the principal comes due is called the bond's *maturity* date. Each year until that time, the issuing entity usually makes regular interest payments (for example, quarterly or semi-annually) to bondholders.

Even though interest rates may change over time, *the bondholder will receive the fixed interest rate specified on the face of the bond.* Although bonds are issued for lengthy periods of time—the U.S. Treasury issues bonds for up to thirty years—they can be sold to another party at any time prior to their maturity. Each day, most of the bonds sold in the bond market are ones that have been issued previously.

When overall interest rates rise, the prices of these previously issued bonds will fall. Suppose you bought a newly issued $1,000 bond that pays 8 percent per year in perpetuity (forever). (*Note:* Bonds that pay interest in perpetuity

are called "consols" and are available in the United Kingdom.) As long as you own the bond, you are entitled to a fixed return of $80 per year. Let's also assume that after you have held the bond for one year and collected your $80 interest for that year, the market rate of interest for newly issued bonds like yours increases to 10 percent. How will this increase in the interest rate affect the market price of your bond? Because bond purchasers can now earn 10 percent interest if they buy newly issued bonds, they will be unwilling to pay more than $800 for your bond, which pays only $80 interest per year. After all, why would anyone pay $1,000 for a bond that yields only $80 interest per year when the same $1,000 will now purchase a bond that yields $100 (10 percent) per year? The increase in the interest rate to 10 percent will therefore cause the *market price* of your $1,000 bond (which earns only 8 percent annually) to fall to $800. At that price, the new owner of your bond would earn the 10 percent market rate of interest. This is why rising market interest rates cause bond prices to fall.

Conversely, falling interest rates will cause bond prices to rise. If the market interest rate had fallen to 6 percent, what would have happened to the market value of your bond? (*Hint:* $80 is 6 percent of $1,333.) As you can see, bond prices and interest rates are inversely linked to each other.

EXHIBIT 10
Foreign Exchange Market

Americans demand foreign currencies to pay for goods and services they import and investments they make abroad. Foreigners demand U.S. dollars in order to purchase American exports and make investments in the United States. The exchange rate will bring the quantity demanded into balance with the quantity supplied. This will also bring imports plus capital outflow into equality with exports plus capital inflow.

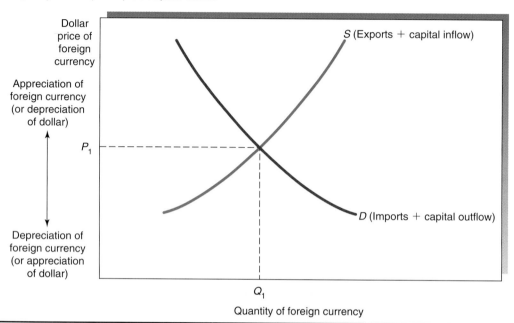

measured along the vertical axis. A fall in the dollar price of foreign currency—shown by a movement down the vertical axis—means a dollar will buy more units of various foreign currencies. This will make it cheaper for Americans to purchase things from foreigners. Thus, we say that the dollar has **appreciated**, meaning that it will now buy more foreign goods than it previously could. As the dollar price for foreign exchange falls (movement down the vertical axis), Americans buy more from foreigners and therefore demand a larger quantity of foreign currency in order to make the purchases. The demand curve for foreign currency therefore slopes downward to the right.

In contrast, an increase in the dollar price of foreign currency—shown by movement up the vertical axis—means that more dollars are needed to purchase a unit of foreign currency. This makes foreign purchases more expensive for Americans. Thus, we say the dollar has **depreciated**. As the dollar depreciates, a unit of foreign currency will purchase a larger quantity of dollars. This depreciation in the dollar makes American goods less expensive for foreigners. As the dollar depreciates (movement up the vertical axis), foreigners buy more from Americans and supply more foreign currency in exchange for dollars. The supply curve for foreign currency therefore slopes upward to the right. The forces of supply and demand in the foreign exchange market will move the exchange rate toward the equilibrium price (P_1 in Exhibit 10). In equilibrium, the quantity demanded of foreign currency will just equal the quantity supplied. Imports plus the outflow of capital for investment abroad to foreign countries will equal exports plus the inflow of capital from the investments of foreigners in the United States.[4]

Appreciation
An increase in the value of a currency relative to foreign currencies. An appreciation increases the purchasing power of the currency over foreign goods.

Depreciation
A reduction in the value of a currency relative to foreign currencies. A depreciation reduces the purchasing power of the currency over foreign goods.

---

[4]There are two other small items, gifts to and from foreigners and net income from investments abroad, that also influence the demand for and supply of foreign exchange. Because these factors are so small, however, their omission will not alter the general analysis presented here.

Mathematically, when the exchange market is in equilibrium, the following relationship exists:

$$\text{Imports} + \text{Capital outflow} = \text{Exports} - \text{Capital inflow} \qquad \textbf{(9-1)}$$

This relationship can be rewritten as:

$$\text{Imports} - \text{Exports} = \text{Capital inflow} - \text{Capital outflow} \qquad \textbf{(9-2)}$$

The right side of Equation 9-2 is also called *net capital inflow*. Because it is a net figure, it can be either positive (indicating an inflow of capital) or negative (indicating an outflow of capital).

The left side of the equation (imports minus exports) indicates the nation's balance of trade. When imports exceed exports, this is referred to as a **trade deficit**. On the other hand, when exports exceed imports, this is referred to as a **trade surplus**. There is an interesting relationship between the flow of trade and the flow of capital: when a trade deficit is present, there must be an inflow of capital. The reverse is also true: an inflow of capital implies a trade deficit. Conversely, when a trade surplus (exports are greater than imports) is present, there must also be an outflow of capital.

When the exchange rate is determined by market forces, trade deficits will be closely linked with an inflow of capital. Conversely, trade surpluses will be closely linked with an outflow of capital.

Exhibit 11 shows the relationship between the inflow of capital and trade deficits in the United States in recent decades, measured as a share of GDP. Notice how large capital inflows (shown in part a) are closely associated with correspondingly large trade deficits (shown in part b). In the late 1970s and early 1980s, the net inflow of capital was relatively small; so too was the trade deficit. Between 1983 and 1987, the net inflow of capital soared, reaching more than 3 percent of GDP during the latter part of the period. Again, the trade deficit increased by a similar amount. Between 1988 and 1992, the inflow of capital slowed to a trickle and the trade deficit shrank to about to 0.5 percent of GDP. During the last decade, however, the inflow of capital soared once again, reaching 4 percent of GDP; the trade deficit increased hugely, too. Clearly, these two factors are closely related; this is to be expected when a country's exchange rate is determined by market forces.

Are trade deficits bad? The term deficit certainly has negative connotations, and many people, particularly those in the media, often assume it means there's something wrong with the economy. However, understanding the link between capital inflows and trade deficits casts things in a different light. If investors, both domestic and foreign, weren't optimistic about an economy's future, there wouldn't be a net inflow of capital into that economy. Thus, trade deficits often reflect something positive: a net inflow of capital that results because investors have substantial confidence in the future strength of the domestic economy.

Trade deficit
The situation when a country's imports of goods and services are greater than its exports.

Trade surplus
The situation when a country's exports of goods and services are greater than its imports.

LEAKAGES AND INJECTIONS FROM THE CIRCULAR FLOW OF INCOME

As we explained earlier, there are three leakages of income in the circular-flow diagram: saving, taxes, and imports. However, there are also "injections." Refer again to Exhibit 1, and notice that, in addition to consumption expenditures, there are three other arrows showing flows, or injections, into the goods and services market. They are investment, government purchases, and exports.

For macroequilibrium to be present, the flow of expenditures on goods and services (top loop of Exhibit 1) must equal the flow of income to resource owners (bottom loop). *This will be true if the injections (investment, government purchases, and exports) into the circular flow equal the leakages (saving, taxes, and imports).* Interestingly, this will be the case when the loanable funds and foreign exchange markets are also in equilibrium. Let's analyze why this is so.

As Exhibit 1 shows, the net saving of households plus net capital inflow from foreigners provide the supply in the loanable funds market. Business investment and government

EXHIBIT 11
**Net Capital Inflow and
the Trade Deficit**

When a country's exchange rate is determined by market forces, the size of the net inflow of capital and trade deficit will be closely linked, as the figures here show. Notice that when the United States has experienced an increase in net capital inflow, its trade deficit has increased by a similar magnitude.

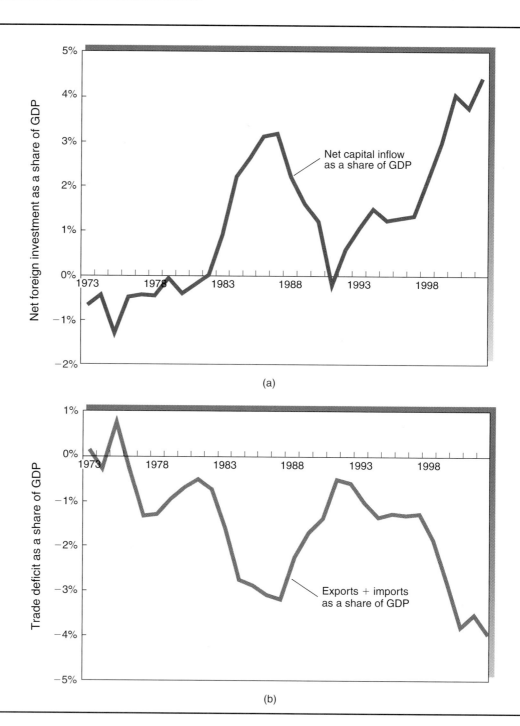

borrowing to finance budget deficits generate the demand. When the interest rate brings these two forces into balance, the following relationship is present:

(9-3)

$$\text{Net saving} + \text{Net capital inflow} = \text{Investment} + \text{Budget deficit}$$

The foreign exchange market brings imports plus capital outflow into equality with exports plus capital inflow (Equation 9-1 above). As a result, the net inflow of capital (capital inflow minus capital outflow) is equal to imports minus exports (see Equation 9-2 above). Substituting imports minus exports for the net capital inflow in Equation 9-3 yields:

(9-4)

$$\text{Net saving} + \text{Imports} - \text{Exports} = \text{Investment} + \text{Budget deficit}$$

Because the budget deficit is merely government purchases minus net taxes, Equation 9-4 can be rewritten as:

$$\text{Net saving} + \text{Imports} - \text{Exports} = \text{Investment} + \text{Government purchases} - \text{Taxes} \qquad \textbf{(9-5)}$$

Finally, moving exports and taxes to opposite sides of the equation yields:

$$\text{Net saving} + \text{Imports} + \text{Taxes} = \text{Investment} + \text{Government purchases} + \text{Exports} \qquad \textbf{(9-6)}$$

Of course, the derivation of Equation 9-6 is based on the presence of equilibrium in both the loanable funds and foreign exchange markets. When interest rates and exchange rates bring these markets into equilibrium, they will also bring into balance the leakages from (left side of Equation 9-6) and injections into (right side of Equation 9-6) the circular flow of income.

We have now discussed all four basic macroeconomic markets: goods and services, resources, loanable funds, and foreign exchange. Like the legs of a chair, these four macroeconomic markets are dependent on each other. When an economy is in long-run equilibrium, the interrelationships among these four markets will be in harmony. The relationship among resource prices, interest rates, and product prices will be such that firms will earn, on average, only a competitive rate of return. Correspondingly, the interest rates and exchange rates will bring the injections into the circular flow of income into balance with the leakages from it. When people correctly anticipate the current price level (rate of inflation), there are reasons to believe that market adjustments will move an economy toward long-run equilibrium.

LOOKING AHEAD

In this chapter, we focused on macroequilibrium. We introduced the four basic macroeconomic markets and analyzed the implications of their equilibriums. However, we live in a world of dynamic change, and unexpected events that continually war against macroequilibrium. The next chapter explains how changing conditions influence economic performance. The model developed in this chapter will help us better analyze these changes.

! KEY POINTS

▼ The circular flow of income and expenditures shows how money flows through the four basic markets that make up the macroeconomy. Those four markets are the (a) goods and services market, (b) resources market, (c) loanable funds market, and (d) foreign exchange market.

▼ The aggregate demand curve shows the various quantities of domestically produced goods and services that purchasers are willing to buy at different price levels. It slopes downward to the right because the quantity purchased by consumers, investors, governments, and foreigners (net exports) will be larger at lower price levels.

▼ The aggregate supply (*AS*) curve shows the various quantities of goods and services that domestic suppliers will produce at different price levels. The short-run aggregate supply (*SRAS*) curve will slope upward to the right because higher product prices will improve profit margins when important cost components like labor are temporarily fixed in the short run.

▼ In the long run, output is constrained by the economy's resource base, current technology, and efficiency of its existing institutions. A higher price level does not loosen these constraints. Thus, the long-run aggregate supply (*LRAS*) curve is vertical.

▼ Two conditions are necessary for long-run equilibrium in the goods and services market: (a) the quantity demanded must equal the quantity supplied, and (b) the *actual* price level must equal the price level decision makers *anticipated* when they entered into their long-term agreements. When long-run equilibrium is present, output will be at its maximum sustainable level.

▼ The aggregate demand–aggregate supply model reveals the determinants of the price level and real output. In the short run, price and output will move toward the intersection of the aggregate demand (*AD*) and short-run aggregate supply (*SRAS*) curves. In the long run, price and output will gravitate to the levels represented by the intersection of the *AD, SRAS,* and *LRAS* curves.

▼ When the economy is in long-run equilibrium, potential output will be achieved and full employment will be present (the actual rate of unemployment will equal the natural rate).

▼ It is important to distinguish between real interest rates and money interest rates. The real interest rate reflects the real burden to borrowers and the payoff to lenders after inflation. It is equal to the money rate of interest minus the inflationary premium. The inflationary premium depends on the expected rate of inflation.

▼ When equilibrium is present in the loanable funds and foreign exchange markets, the injections (investment, government purchases, and exports) into the circular flow of income will equal the leakages (saving, taxes, and imports) from it.

▼ Macroeconomic equilibrium requires that equilibrium be achieved in all four key macroeconomic markets and that they be in harmony with one another.

CRITICAL ANALYSIS QUESTIONS

1. In your own words, explain why aggregate demand is inversely related to the price level. Why does the explanation for the inverse relationship between price and quantity demanded for the aggregate demand curve differ from that of a demand curve for a specific good?

2. What major factors influence our ability to produce goods and services in the long run? Why is the long-run aggregate supply curve vertical?

3. Why does the short-run aggregate supply curve slope upward to the right? If the prices of both (a) resources and (b) goods and services increased proportionally (by the same percentage), would business firms be willing to expand output? Why or why not?

*4. Suppose prices had been rising at 3 percent annually in recent years. A major union signs a three-year contract calling for increases in money wage rates of 6 percent annually. What will happen to the real wages of the union members if the price level is constant (unchanged) during the next three years? If other unions sign similar contracts, what will probably happen to the unemployment rate? Why? Answer the same questions under conditions in which the price level increases at an annual rate of 8 percent during the next three years.

5. What is the current money interest rate on ten-year government bonds? Is this also the real interest rate? Why or why not?

*6. If the real interest rate in the loanable funds market increases, what will happen to the net inflow of foreign capital? Explain.

7. Explain why it's possible to temporarily achieve output levels beyond the economy's long-run potential. Why can't the high rates of output be sustained?

*8. If the price level in the current period is higher than buyers and sellers anticipated, what will tend to happen to real wages and the level of employment? How will the profit margins of businesses be affected? How will the actual rate of unemployment compare with the natural rate of unemployment? Will the current rate of output be sustainable in the future? Why or why not?

9. Suppose you purchase a $5,000 bond that pays 7 percent interest annually and matures in five years. If the inflation rate in recent years has been steady at 3 percent annually, what is the estimated real rate of interest? If the inflation rate during the next five years remains steady at 3 percent, what real rate of return will you earn? If the inflation rate during the next five years is 6 percent, what will happen to your real rate of return?

*10. How are the following related to each other?
   a. The long-run equilibrium rate of output
   b. The potential real GDP of the economy
   c. The output rate at which the actual and natural rates of unemployment are equal

11. How will an increase in the inflation rate affect (a) the money rate of interest and (b) the real rate of interest? Explain. Does inflation transfer wealth from lenders to borrowers? Why or why not?

*12. If a bond pays $1,000 per year in perpetuity (each year in the future), what will the market price of the bond be when the long-term interest rate is 10 percent? What would it be if the interest rate were 5 percent?

*13. How are bond prices related to interest rates? Why are they related?

14. When the price of a specific product increases, individual firms can generally expand their output by a larger amount in the long run than in the short run. For the economy as a whole, however, an unexpected increase in the price level leads to a larger expansion in output in the short run than in the long run. Can you explain this apparent paradox?

15. Show that when equilibrium is present in the loanable funds and foreign exchange markets, leakages from the circular flow of income will just equal injections.

*16. The following chart indicates the aggregate demand (*AD*) and short-run aggregate supply (*SRAS*) schedules of decision makers for the current period. Both buyers and sellers previously anticipated that the price level during the current period would be P_{105}.
   a. Indicate the quantity of GDP that will be produced during this period.
   b. Will it be a long-run equilibrium level of GDP? Why or why not?
   c. What will the relationship between the actual and natural rates of unemployment be during the period? Explain your answer.

AD_{105}	Price Level	$SRAS_{105}$
6,900	90	4,500
6,600	95	4,800
6,300	100	5,100
6,000	105	5,400
5,700	110	5,700
5,400	115	6,000

17. Consider an economy with the following aggregate demand (*AD*) and short-run aggregate supply (*SRAS*) schedules. Decision makers have previously made decisions anticipating that the price level during the current period will be P_{105}.
   a. Indicate the quantity of GDP that will be produced during the period.
   b. Is it a long-run equilibrium level of GDP? Why or why not?
   c. How will the unemployment rate during the current period compare with the natural rate of unemployment?
   d. Will the current rate of GDP be sustainable into the future? Why or why not?

AD_{105}	Price Level	$SRAS_{105}$
6,300	90	4,500
6,000	95	4,800
5,700	100	5,100
5,400	105	5,400
5,100	110	5,700
4,800	115	6,000

---

*Asterisk denotes questions for which answers are given in Appendix B.

CHAPTER 1

Working with Our Basic Aggregate Demand and Aggregate Supply Model

We might as well reasonably dispute whether it is the upper or under blade of a pair of scissors that cuts a piece of paper, as whether value is governed by [demand] or [supply].

—Alfred Marshall[1]

Chapter Focus

- What factors change aggregate demand? What factors change aggregate supply?

- How does the goods and services market adjust to changes in aggregate demand?

- How does the economy adjust to changes in aggregate supply?

- What causes recessions and booms?

- Does a market economy have a self-correcting mechanism that will lead it to full employment?

[1]Alfred Marshall, *Principles of Economics,* 8th ed. (London: Macmillan, 1920), 348.

In Chapter 9, we focused on the equilibrium conditions in the four basic macroeconomic markets. Equilibrium is important, but we live in a dynamic world that continually wars against it. Markets are always being affected by unexpected changes. Some of these changes might include the development of a vastly improved computer chip, shifts in consumer confidence, a drought in midwestern agricultural states, or changes in defense expenditures as the result of national security conditions. Consequently, equilibrium is continually disrupted. Thus, if we want to understand how the real world works, we need to know how macroeconomic markets adjust to change. In this chapter, as in Chapter 9, we will assume that the government's tax, spending, and monetary policies don't change. First, we want to help you understand how macroeconomic markets work without these complications. Then we will show you what impact government policies have. ▪

ANTICIPATED AND UNANTICIPATED CHANGES

In Chapter 8, we stated that it is important to distinguish between price level changes that are anticipated and those that are not. This distinction is important in several areas of economics. **Anticipated changes** are foreseen by economic participants. Decision-makers have time to adjust to them before they occur. For example, suppose that, under normal weather conditions, a new drought-resistant hybrid seed is expected to expand grain production in the Midwest by 10 percent next year. As a result, buyers and sellers will plan for a larger supply of grain and lower grain prices in the future. They will adjust their decision-making behavior accordingly.

In contrast, **unanticipated changes** catch people by surprise. New products are introduced, technological discoveries alter production costs, droughts reduce crop yields, and demand expands for some goods and contracts for others. It is impossible for decision makers to foresee many of these changes. As we will explain in a moment, there is good reason to expect that the path of the adjustment process will be influenced by whether or not a change is anticipated.

Anticipated change
A change that is foreseen by decision makers in time for them to make adjustments.

Unanticipated change
A change that decision makers could not reasonably foresee. The choices they made prior to the change did not take it into account.

FACTORS THAT SHIFT AGGREGATE DEMAND

The aggregate demand curve isolates the effect of the price level on the quantity demanded of goods and services. As we discussed in the previous chapter, a reduction in the price level will (1) increase the wealth of people holding a fixed quantity of money, (2) reduce the real rate of interest, and (3) make domestically produced goods cheaper than those produced abroad. All three of these factors will lead to an increase in the quantity of goods and services demanded at the lower price level.

The price level, however, is not the only factor that influences the demand for goods and services. When we constructed the aggregate demand curve, we assumed that several other factors affecting the choices of buyers in the goods and services market were constant. Changes in these "other factors" will shift the entire aggregate demand schedule, altering the amount purchased at each price level. Let us take a closer look at the major factors that alter aggregate demand and shift the *AD* curve.

1. Changes in real wealth. Between 1994 and 1999, stock prices in the United States approximately tripled. This stock market boom increased the real wealth of stockholders. In contrast, during 2000–2002, stock prices plummeted, reducing the wealth of many Americans.

EXHIBIT 1
Shifts in Aggregate Demand

An increase in real wealth that would result from a stock market boom, for example, will increase aggregate demand, shifting the entire curve to the right (from AD_0 to AD_1). In contrast, a reduction in real wealth decreases the demand for goods and services, causing AD to shift to the left (from AD_0 to AD_2).

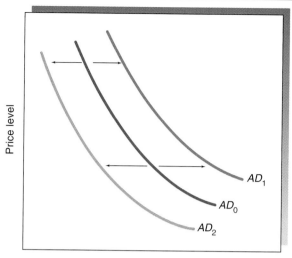

How will changes in the wealth of households affect the demand for goods and services? If the real wealth of households increases, perhaps as the result of higher prices in stock, housing, and/or real estate markets, people will demand more goods and services. As **Exhibit 1** illustrates, this increase in wealth will shift the entire aggregate demand (AD) curve to the right (from AD_0 to AD_1). More goods and services are purchased at each price level. Conversely, a reduction in wealth will reduce the demand for goods and services, shifting the AD curve to the left (to AD_2).

2. Changes in the real interest rate. As we discussed in Chapter 9, the major macroeconomic markets are closely related. A change in the real interest rate in the loanable funds market will influence the choices of consumers and investors in the goods and services market. A lower real interest rate makes it cheaper for consumers to buy major appliances, automobiles, and houses now rather than in the future. Simultaneously, a lower interest rate will also stimulate business spending on capital goods (investment). The interest rate influences the opportunity cost of all investment projects. If the firm must borrow, the real interest rate will contribute directly to the cost of a project. Even if the firm uses its own funds, it sacrifices interest that could have been earned by loaning the funds to someone else. Therefore, a lower interest rate reduces the opportunity cost of a project, regardless of whether it is financed with internal funds or by borrowing.

Because a fall in the real interest rate makes both consumer and investment goods cheaper, both households and investors will increase their current expenditures in response. In turn, their additional expenditures will increase aggregate demand, shifting the entire AD curve to the right. In contrast, a higher real interest rate makes current consumption and investment goods more expensive, which leads to a reduction in aggregate demand, shifting the AD curve to the left.

3. Change in the expectations of businesses and households about the future direction of the economy. What people think will happen in the future influences current purchasing decisions. Optimism about the future direction of the economy will stimulate current investment. Business decision makers know that an expanding economy will mean strong sales and improved profit margins. Investment today may be necessary if business firms are going to benefit fully from these opportunities. Similarly, consumers are more likely to buy big-ticket items, such as automobiles and houses, when they expect an expanding economy to provide them with both job security and rising income in the future. Increased optimism encourages additional current expenditures by both investors and consumers, increasing aggregate demand.

Source: http://www.economagic.com

EXHIBIT 2
Consumer Sentiment Index, 1978–2004

The consumer sentiment index developed by the University of Michigan is shown here. It is designed to measure whether consumers are becoming more optimistic or more pessimistic about the economy. Note how the index has turned down (shaded areas) sharply prior to and during the early stages of recent recessions.

Of course, pessimism about the future of the economy exerts just the opposite effect. When investors and consumers expect an economic downturn (a recession), they will cut back on their current spending to avoid overextending themselves. This pessimism leads to a decline in aggregate demand, shifting the *AD* schedule to the left.

The University of Michigan conducts a monthly survey of consumers and uses the information to develop a **consumer sentiment index**. **Exhibit 2** presents this index for the 1978–2004 period. An increase in the consumer sentiment index indicates that consumers are more optimistic about the future. A decline indicates increased consumer pessimism. Notice how the index fell sharply prior to and during the early stages of the recessions that occurred during this period.

Consumer sentiment index
A measure of the optimism of consumers based on their responses to a set of five questions about their current and expected future personal economic situation. Conducted by the University of Michigan, it is based on a representative sample of U.S. households.

4. Change in the expected rate of inflation.   When consumers and investors believe that the inflation is going to go up in the future, they have an incentive to spend more during the current period. "Buy now before prices go higher" becomes the order of the day. This expectation of higher inflation will stimulate current aggregate demand, shifting the *AD* curve to the right.

In contrast, if people expect inflation to decline in the future, this will discourage current spending. When prices are expected to stabilize (or at least increase less rapidly), people will have an incentive to wait until they do before they buy things. This expectation of lower inflation will cause current aggregate demand to fall, shifting the *AD* curve to the left.

5. Changes in income abroad.   Changes in the income of a nation's trading partners will influence the demand for its exports. If the income of a nation's trading partners increases rapidly, the demand for its exports will expand. This will stimulate its aggregate demand. For example, rapid growth of income in Europe, Canada, and Mexico increases the demand of consumers in these areas for U.S.-produced goods. This will cause U.S. exports to expand, increasing aggregate demand (shifting the *AD* curve to the right).

Conversely, when a nation's trading partners are experiencing recessionary conditions, citizens in these countries reduce their purchases, including their purchases of foreign-produced goods. Thus, a decline in the income of a nation's trading partners will reduce its exports and the aggregate demand for its products.

Currently, approximately 12 percent of the goods and services produced in the United States are sold to purchasers abroad. Canada, Mexico, and most Western European countries export an even larger share of what they produce. The larger the size of the trade sector, the greater the potential importance of fluctuations in income abroad as a source of instability in aggregate demand. However, if the demand of foreign buyers does not rise and fall at the same time as domestic demand, the diversity of markets will reduce the fluctuations in demand for a nation's exports, and thereby exert a stabilizing affect on aggregate demand.

T H U M B N A I L   S K E T C H

What Factors Affect Aggregate Demand?

These factors *increase* aggregate demand (*AD*).[1]
1. An increase in real wealth
2. A decrease in the real rate of interest
3. Optimism about future economic conditions
4. A rise in the expected rate of inflation
5. Higher real incomes abroad
6. A fall in the value of a nation's currency

These factors *decrease* aggregate demand (*AD*).
1. Lower real wealth
2. An increase in the real rate of interest
3. Pessimism about future economic conditions
4. A fall in the expected rate of inflation
5. Lower real incomes abroad
6. A rise in the value of a nation's currency

---

[1] The impact of macroeconomic policy will be considered later.

---

6. Changes in exchange rates.   As we previously explained, changes in exchange rates influence the relative price of both imports and exports. If the dollar appreciates, imported goods will be cheaper for Americans to buy, and goods exported from the United States will be more expensive for foreigners to purchase. As a result, U.S. imports will rise and exports will fall. This decline in net exports (exports minus imports) will reduce aggregate demand (shifting the *AD* curve to the left).

Consider what happened when the dollar increased in value relative to the Mexican peso in the mid-1990s. In late 1994 and early 1995, the number of pesos that could be purchased with a dollar nearly doubled in just a few months. The appreciation of the dollar relative to the peso made imports from Mexico cheaper for Americans and U.S. exports more expensive for Mexicans. As U.S. imports rose and exports fell, there was downward pressure on aggregate demand in the United States.

If the dollar depreciates, the effect will be just the opposite. When the value of the dollar falls, foreign-produced goods become more expensive for U.S. consumers, while U.S.-produced goods become cheaper for foreigners. This is precisely what happened during 2002–2003, when the dollar depreciated by about 30 percent relative to the euro. When the dollar depreciates, imports will tend to fall and exports rise. In turn, this increase in net exports will stimulate aggregate demand in the United States (shifting the *AD* curve to the right).[2]

The accompanying Thumbnail Sketch summarizes the major factors that change aggregate demand and shift the *AD* curve. Other factors include the government's spending, taxing, and monetary policies. In subsequent chapters, we will analyze the impact of fiscal and monetary policy on aggregate demand and economic performance. We now turn to the analysis of the factors that alter aggregate supply. Then we will be in a position to consider how macroeconomic markets adjust and whether these adjustments will help keep output and employment high.

SHIFTS IN AGGREGATE SUPPLY

What factors will cause the aggregate supply curve to shift? The answer to this question will differ depending on whether the change in supply is long run and sustainable or short run and only temporary. A long-run change in aggregate supply indicates that it will be

---

[2] Later, when discussing international demand finance, we will analyze the determinants of the exchange rate and consider in more detail how changes in exchange rates affect both trade and macroeconomic markets.

possible to achieve and sustain a larger rate of output. For example, the discovery of a lower-cost source of energy would cause a long-run change in aggregate supply. If this happened, both long-run (*LRAS*) and short-run (*SRAS*) aggregate supply would change.

In contrast, changes that temporarily alter the production capacity of an economy will shift the *SRAS* curve, but not the *LRAS* curve. A drought in California would be an example of such a short-run change. The drought will hurt in the short run, but it will eventually end, and output will return to the long-run normal rate. Changes that are temporary in nature shift only the *SRAS* curve. Now let's look at the other kinds of things that change both long-run and short-run aggregate supply.

Changes in Long-Run Aggregate Supply

Remember, the long-run aggregate supply curve shows the maximum rate of sustainable output of an economy, given its current (1) resource base, (2) level of technology, and (3) institutional arrangements that affect its **productivity** and the efficient use of its resources. Changes in any of these three determinants of output will cause the *LRAS* curve to shift.

As part (a) of **Exhibit 3** illustrates, changes that increase the economy's production capacity will shift the *LRAS* curve to the right. Over time, net investment will expand the supply of physical capital, natural resources, and labor (human resources). Physical capital investment expands the supply of buildings, machines, and other physical assets an economy has. Education and training improve the quality of its labor force and expand its human capital. Because investment in physical and human capital enhances output both now and in the future, it increases both long-run and short-run aggregate supply, causing both curves to shift to the right. But things can work the other way around, too. If less is invested in physical and human capital over time, both the current and long-term production capacity of the economy will fall, shifting the *SRAS* and *LRAS* curves to the left. Note that demographic changes affecting labor force participation can also affect short- and long-run supply one way or the other because labor is a resource.

Improvements in technology—the discovery of economical new products or less costly ways of producing goods and services—also permit us to squeeze a larger output from a given resource supply. The enormous improvement in our living standards during the last 250 years is largely the result of the discovery and adoption of technologically superior ways of transforming resources into goods and services. The development of the internal combustion engine, electricity, and nuclear power has vastly altered our energy sources (and consumption). The railroad, automobile, and airplane dramatically changed both the speed and cost of transportation. More recently, high-tech products like personal

Productivity
The average output produced per worker during a specific time period. It is usually measured in terms of output per hour worked.

(a) Increase in *LRAS*   (b) Increase in *SRAS*

EXHIBIT 3
Shifts in Aggregate Supply

Factors like an increase in the stock of capital or an improvement in technology will expand the economy's potential output and shift the *LRAS* curve to the right as shown in part (a). Factors like favorable weather or falling resource prices (say, a temporary drop in the price of a major import like oil) will shift the *SRAS* curve to the right, as shown in part (b).

computers, fax machines, e-mail, and the Internet have cut the cost of doing business and expanded our production capacity. Technological improvements of this type enhance productivity and thereby shift both *LRAS* and *SRAS* curves to the right.

Finally, institutional changes can affect productivity and efficiency and change both short- and long-run aggregate supply. Depending on how well a government's institutional, or policy, changes are designed, they can increase aggregate supply by enhancing economic efficiency and productivity or decrease it by encouraging waste and making production more costly.

The long-run growth of real GDP in the United States has been about 3 percent per year. In other words, we have been able to steadily expand our productivity over the years. Hence, the *LRAS* and *SRAS* curves have gradually drifted to the right at about a 3 percent annual rate, sometimes a little faster and sometimes a little slower.

Changes in Short-Run Aggregate Supply

Changes can sometimes influence current output without altering the economy's long-run capacity. When this is the case, the *SRAS* curve will shift even though the *LRAS* curve remains unchanged. What types of changes would do this?

1. Changes in resource prices. When we derived the *SRAS* schedule in Chapter 9, we held resource prices constant. But a change in resource prices will alter *SRAS*, although not necessarily *LRAS*. A reduction in resource prices will lower production costs and therefore shift the *SRAS* curve to the right, as illustrated in part (b) of Exhibit 3. However, unless the lower cost of resources reflects a long-term increase in their supply, *LRAS* won't change. Conversely, an increase in the price of resources used in production will increase firms' costs, shifting the *SRAS* curve to the left. But unless the higher prices are the result of a long-term reduction in the size of the economy's resource base, they will not reduce *LRAS*.[3]

2. Changes in the expected rate of inflation. As we learned, a change in the expected rate of inflation will affect aggregate demand (*AD*) in the goods and services market. It will also alter short-run aggregate supply (*SRAS*). If sellers in the goods and services market expect the future rate of inflation to increase, they will be less motivated to sell their products at lower prices in the current period. After all, goods that they do not

Net investment, technological advances, and improvements in institutional arrangements expand an economy's production capacity, shifting *LRAS* to the right.

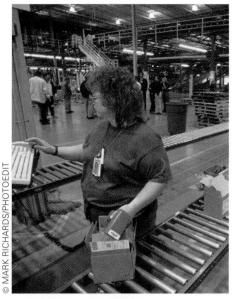

---

[3]In subsequent chapters, we will explain how stable prices can be achieved as real output increases.

What Factors Affect Long-Run and Short-Run Aggregate Supply?

These factors *increase* long-run aggregate supply (*LRAS*).[1]
1. An increase in the supply of resources
2. Technology and productivity improvements
3. Institutional changes that improve the efficiency of resource use

These factors *decrease* long-run aggregate supply (*LRAS*).[1]
1. A decrease in the supply of resources
2. Technology and productivity deteriorations
3. Institutional changes that reduce the efficiency of resource use

These factors increase short-run aggregate supply (*SRAS*).[1]
1. A fall in resource prices (production costs)
2. A fall in the expected rate of inflation
3. Favorable supply shocks, such as good weather or lower prices of important imported resources

These factors *decrease* short-run aggregate supply (*SRAS*).[1]
1. A rise in resource prices (production costs)
2. A rise in the expected rate of inflation
3. Unfavorable supply shocks, such as bad weather or higher prices of important imported resources

[1] The impact of macroeconomic policy will be considered later.

---

sell today will be available for sale in the future at what they anticipate will be even higher prices because of inflation. But they will have produced them earlier at lower costs. Therefore, an increase in the expected rate of inflation will reduce the *current* supply of goods, thereby shifting the *SRAS* curve to the left. Of course, a reduction in the expected rate of inflation will have just the opposite effect. When sellers scale back their expectations of future price increases, their incentive to sell in the current period rises. Why should they wait to sell what they've produced now, if prices aren't going to go up very much in the future? Thus, a reduction in the expected rate of inflation will increase short-run aggregate supply, shifting the *SRAS* curve to the right.

3. Supply shocks. Supply shocks can also alter current output without directly affecting the productive capacity of the economy. **Supply shocks** are surprise occurrences that temporarily increase or decrease current output. For example, adverse weather conditions, a natural disaster, or a temporary rise in the price of imported resources (for example, oil in the case of the United States) will reduce current supply, even though they do not alter the economy's long-term production capacity. They lower short-run aggregate supply (shift the *SRAS* curve to the left) without directly affecting *LRAS,* in other words. On the other hand, favorable weather conditions or a temporary fall in the world price of major resources imported by a country will expand current output, even though the economy's long-run capacity remains unchanged.

Supply shock
An unexpected event that temporarily increases or decreases aggregate supply.

The Thumbnail Sketch above summarizes the major factors that influence both long-run and short-run aggregate supply. Of course, macroeconomic policy can also influence aggregate supply. Like aggregate demand, we will study the impact macroeconomic policies have on aggregate supply in subsequent chapters.

STEADY ECONOMIC GROWTH AND ANTICIPATED CHANGES IN LONG-RUN AGGREGATE SUPPLY

As we've said, changes that people anticipate affect the economy differently than changes they don't. When a change takes place slowly and predictably, decision makers will make choices based on their anticipation of the event. These changes do not generally disrupt equilibrium in markets. With time, net investment and improvements in technology and institutional efficiency will lead to increases in the sustainable rate of output and shift the economy's *LRAS* curve to the right.

EXHIBIT 4
Growth of Aggregate Supply

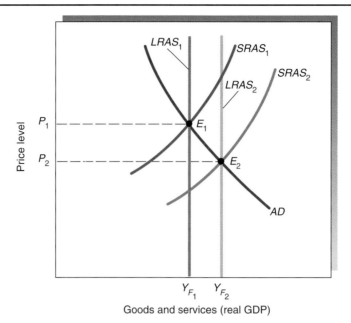

Here we illustrate the impact of economic growth due to capital formation or a technological advancement, for example. The full-employment output of the economy expands from Y_{F1} to Y_{F2}. Thus, both *LRAS* and *SRAS* increase (to *LRAS₂* and *SRAS₂*). A sustainable, higher level of real output and real income is the result. If the money supply is held constant, a new long-run equilibrium will emerge at a larger output rate (Y_{F2}) and lower price level (P_2).

Exhibit 4 illustrates the impact of economic growth on the goods and services market. Initially, the economy is in long-run equilibrium at price level P_1 and output Y_{F1}. The growth expands the economy's potential output, shifting both the *LRAS* and *SRAS* curves to the right (to *LRAS₂* and *SRAS₂*). Because these changes are gradual, decision makers have time to anticipate the changing market conditions and adjust their behavior accordingly.

When economic growth expands the economy's production possibilities, a higher rate of real output can be achieved and sustained. The larger output can be attained even while unemployment remains at its natural rate. If the money supply is held constant, the increase in aggregate supply will lead to a lower price level (P_2).

During the past fifty years, real output has expanded significantly in the United States and other countries. However, contrary to the presentation of Exhibit 4, the price level has generally not declined. This is because the Federal Reserve has expanded the supply of money. As we will see later, an increase in the money supply stimulates aggregate demand, shifting *AD* to the right and pushing the price level upward.[4]

UNANTICIPATED CHANGES AND MARKET ADJUSTMENTS

In contrast to anticipated changes, unanticipated changes in aggregate demand and aggregate supply will disrupt long-run equilibrium in the goods and services market. If

[4]Thoughtful students may wonder how output (and, by implication, the quantity of resources) can be increased, even temporarily, when real wages and resource prices have fallen. As we noted in the last chapter, firms may temporarily be able to achieve high rates of output through more intense supervision, greater use of overtime, and reduction in downtime for maintenance. In addition, two other factors may contribute to temporary output levels beyond long-run potential. First, in an inflationary environment, workers (and other resource suppliers) may be fooled, at least temporarily, by an increase in money wages (and resource prices) that is less rapid than the inflation rate. Responding to the higher money wages, workers may supply more labor even though their real wages have fallen. Although we have presented the analysis within the framework of a noninflationary environment, the basic linkage between real wages (costs) and *SRAS* still holds. A reduction in the real wage rate, even when it takes the form of a nominal wage increase that is less than the inflation rate, will reduce real costs and thereby increase *SRAS*. Second, the resource base may temporarily expand in response to strong demand conditions because the cost of entering the labor force will decline during this boom phase of the business cycle. Potential new labor force entrants will be able to find jobs quickly during an economic expansion, causing the size of the labor force to grow rapidly. Conversely, the labor force will tend to shrink (or grow less rapidly) during a business contraction, when the cost of entering the labor force will be high.

a change isn't anticipated, initially, it may be unclear to decision makers whether the change—an increase in sales, for example—reflects a random occurrence or a real change in demand conditions. It will also take businesses some time to differentiate between temporary fluctuations and more permanent changes. Even after decision makers are convinced that market conditions have changed, it will take some time for them to make new decisions and carry them out. In some cases, long-term contracts will delay the adjustment process.

Equilibrium may be disrupted by unexpected changes in either aggregate demand or aggregate supply. We will next consider the impact of an unanticipated change in aggregate demand.

Unanticipated Increases in Aggregate Demand

Part (a) of **Exhibit 5** shows how an economy that is initially in long-run equilibrium will adjust to an unanticipated increase in aggregate demand. Initially, at output Y_F and price level P_{100} (point E_1), the economy is in long-run equilibrium. Aggregate demand and aggregate supply are in balance. Decision makers have correctly anticipated the current price level, and the economy is operating at its full-employment level of output.

What would happen if this equilibrium were disrupted by an unanticipated increase in aggregate demand (a shift from AD_1 to AD_2), which might result from a stock market boom or the rapid growth of income abroad? An excess demand for goods and services would result at the initial price level (P_{100}). Responding to the strong sales and excess demand, businesses would increase their prices. Their profit margins would improve (since product prices increase relative to the cost of the resources used to make them), and they would expand output along the *SRAS* curve. As part (a) of Exhibit 5 shows, the economy would move to a short-run equilibrium (e_2), at a larger output (Y_2) and higher price level (P_{105}). (*Note:* A short-run equilibrium is indicated with a lowercase *e*, whereas a capital *E* is used to designate a long-run equilibrium. This convention will be followed throughout the text.)

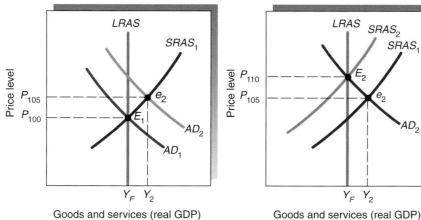

(a) Short-run effects of increase in *AD*

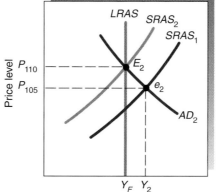

(b) Long-run effects of increase in *AD*

EXHIBIT 5
An Unanticipated Increase in Aggregate Demand

In response to an unanticipated increase in aggregate demand for goods and services that shifts AD_1 to AD_2 (shown in part a), prices will rise to P_{105} in the short run and output will increase temporarily to Y_2, exceeding full-employment capacity. However, over time, prices in resource markets, including the labor market, will rise as the result of the strong demand. The higher resource prices will mean higher production costs, which will reduce aggregate supply to $SRAS_2$ (as shown in part b). In the long run, a new equilibrium will emerge at a higher price level (P_{110}) and an output consistent with the economy's sustainable capacity. Thus, the increase in aggregate demand will expand output only temporarily.

In the short run, the economy's output will deviate from full-employment capacity when prices in the goods and services market deviate from the price level people antici-pated. This will happen when unusually strong demand pushes prices up more than was expected. For a time, resource prices like wage rates, interest payments, and rents will re-main at the initial price level (P_{100}), lagging behind the prices producers can get for their products. The higher price level will temporarily improve firms' profit margins, which will motivate them to expand both output and employment in the short run. As a result, the unemployment rate will drop below its natural rate, and the economy's output will temporarily exceed its long-run potential.[5]

This isn't the end of the story, though. *The increase in GDP above the economy's long-run potential will last only until temporarily fixed resource prices (and interest rates) can be adjusted upward by people in light of the new stronger demand conditions.* The strong demand accompanying the high level of output (rates beyond Y_F) will put up-ward pressure on prices in the resource and loanable funds markets. As part (b) of Exhibit 5 shows, eventually the rising resource prices and costs will shift the short-run aggregate supply curve to the left (to $SRAS_2$). Given sufficient time, wages, other resource prices, and interest rates will completely adjust. When this happens, a new long-run equilibrium (E_2) will be established at a higher price level (P_{110}). Correspondingly, profit margins will return to their normal levels, output will recede to the economy's long-run potential, and unemployment will return to its natural rate.

Notice that because an increase in aggregate demand doesn't change the economy's production capacity, it cannot permanently expand output (beyond Y_F). The increase in demand temporarily expands output, but in the long term, it only increases the price level.

Unanticipated Reductions in Aggregate Demand

How would the goods and services market adjust to an unanticipated reduction in aggregate demand? For example, suppose decision makers become more pessimistic about the future or that an unexpected decline in income abroad reduces demand for their products. **Exhibit 6** will help us analyze what happens in this situation. In part (a) of Exhibit 6, the economy is in long-run equilibrium (E_1) at output Y_F and the price level P_{100}. Long-run equilibrium is disturbed by a fall in aggregate demand, and the aggregate demand curve shifts from AD_1 to AD_2. As the result of the decline in demand, businesses will be unable to sell Y_F units of output at the initial price level of P_{100}. In the short run, business firms will reduce their output (to Y_2) and cut their prices (to P_{95}) in response to the weak demand conditions. Because many business costs are temporarily fixed, profit margins will fall. Predictably, firms will cut back on output and lay off workers, causing the unemployment rate to rise. The actual rate of unemployment will rise above the economy's natural rate of unemployment. Weak demand and excess supply will be widespread in resource markets. These forces will place downward pressure on resource prices.

If resource prices quickly adjust downward in response to weak demand and rising unemployment, then the decline in output to Y_2 will be brief. Lower resource prices will reduce costs and increase aggregate supply, shifting the $SRAS_1$ curve to $SRAS_2$, as part (b) shows. The result will be a new long-run equilibrium (E_2) at the economy's full-employment output rate (Y_F) and a lower price level (P_{90}). Lower interest rates may also play a role. Given the excess production capacity of many firms, weak demand for capital goods (investment) will reduce the demand for loanable funds, which will put downward pressure on interest rates. The lower rates will stimulate current spending, which will help offset the lower demand and direct the economy back to full employment.

---

[5] The definition of long-run aggregate supply helps clarify why a change in resource prices will affect short-run aggregate supply, but not long-run aggregate supply. When an economy is operating on its *LRAS* curve, the relationship between resource prices (costs) and product prices will reflect normal competitive market conditions. Because both profit and unemployment rates are at their normal levels, there is no tendency for resource prices to change relative to product prices when current output is equal to the economy's long-run potential. Therefore, when an economy is operating on its *LRAS* schedule, any change in resource prices will be matched by a proportional change in product prices, leaving the incentive to supply resources (and output) unchanged.

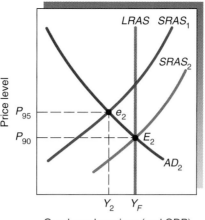

EXHIBIT 6
An Unanticipated Reduction in Aggregate Demand

(a) Short-run effects of decline in *AD*

(b) Long-run effects of decline in *AD*

The short-run impact of an unanticipated fall in aggregate demand, shifting AD_1 to AD_2, will be a decline in output to Y_2 and a lower price level of P_{95} (as shown in part a). Temporarily, profit margins will decline, output will fall, and unemployment will rise above its natural rate. In the long run, weak demand and excess supply in the resource market will lead to lower wages and resource prices. This will lower production costs, leading to an expansion in short-run aggregate supply, shifting it to $SRAS_2$ (as shown in part b). However, this method of restoring equilibrium (E_2) may be both highly painful and quite lengthy.

Resource prices and interest rates, however, might not adjust quickly. Long-term contracts and uncertainty about whether the weak demand is only temporary will slow down the adjustment process. Moreover, workers and unions might be reluctant to accept lower wages. If resource prices are downwardly inflexible, as many economists believe, the adjustment process might be lengthy and painful. Pessimism on the part of both investors and consumers might also complicate the adjustment process. This is what has happened in recent recessions. As Exhibit 2 shows, consumer confidence remained at a low level for twelve to eighteen months after the 1990–1991 and 2001 recessions were over. This pessimism acted as a drag on the growth of aggregate demand, and, as a result, the economy rebounded more slowly than it would have otherwise.

Unanticipated Increases in Short-Run Aggregate Supply

Supply shocks catch people by surprise. That is, in part, why they're called "shocks." What would happen if the nation's output expanded because of a favorable shock like good weather conditions or a temporary fall in the world price of oil? **Exhibit 7** provides the answer. Because the temporarily favorable supply conditions can't be counted on in the future, they won't change the economy's long-term production capacity. Short-run aggregate supply will increase (to $SRAS_2$), but *LRAS* will remain unchanged. Output (and income) will temporarily expand beyond the economy's full-employment constraints. This increase in current supply will put downward pressure on the price level.

Over time, however, the favorable conditions will come to an end. As this happens, the *SRAS* curve will return to its original position, and long-run equilibrium will be restored. The expansion in output will be only temporary. Knowing this, many households will save a substantial portion of the extra income they earn during the expansion for a time when things aren't so prosperous.

What would happen if the favorable conditions increasing supply reflected long-term factors? For example, suppose adoption of a new oil production technology resulted in a decline in the price of oil that was expected to be permanent rather than temporary. In this case, both the *LRAS* and the *SRAS* would increase (shift to the right).

EXHIBIT 7

An Unanticipated, Temporary Increase in Aggregate Supply

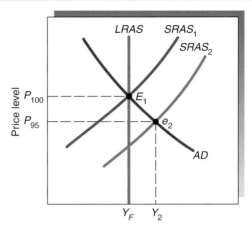

Goods and services (real GDP)

Here we show the impact of an unanticipated, but temporary, increase in aggregate supply that might result from a bumper crop caused by favorable weather, for example. The increase in aggregate supply, shifting it to $SRAS_2$, will lead to a lower price level of P_{95} and an increase in current GDP to Y_2. Since the favorable supply conditions cannot be counted on in the future, the economy's long-run aggregate supply will not increase.

This case would parallel the analysis of Exhibit 4. A new long-run equilibrium at a higher output would result.

Unanticipated Reductions in Short-Run Aggregate Supply

In recent decades, the U.S. economy has been jolted by several unfavorable supply-side factors. During the summer of 1988, the worst drought to hit the country in fifty years made for an extremely poor harvest in the U.S. agricultural belt. In 1973, 1979, and again in 1990, the United States, which imports more than half of the oil it consumes, was hit with sharply higher oil prices due to instability in the Middle East. The higher oil prices had a significant impact because they raised the transportation costs of virtually everything as well as the production costs of numerous items, such as plastics, fertilizer, and asphalt. Then, after trending downward for almost a decade, the price of crude oil jumped from $18 to almost $35 per barrel during 2000. Persistently high crude oil prices, along with regulations inadvertently lowering the supply of electricity, resulted in soaring energy prices and even blackouts in some areas during 2001. In 2004, the uncertainties accompanying the war in Iraq pushed the world price of crude oil above $50 per barrel and, for the first time in the United States, the average price of a gallon of gasoline rose above $2.

How do unfavorable supply shocks like this affect macroeconomic markets? As **Exhibit 8** (part a) illustrates, an unfavorable supply shock, such as might result from adverse weather or a higher world price of oil, will reduce supply (from S_1 to S_2) in the domestic resource market. Resource prices will rise to P'_r. In turn, the higher resource prices will reduce short-run aggregate supply (the shift from $SRAS_1$ to $SRAS_2$ in part b) in the goods and services market. Because supply shocks of this type are generally unanticipated, initially they will reduce output and put upward pressure on prices in the goods and services market.

If an unfavorable supply shock is expected to be temporary, as will generally be the case, long-run aggregate supply will be unaffected. For example, unfavorable weather conditions for a year or two do not represent a permanent change in the climate. As normal weather returns, supply and prices in the resource market will return to normal, and the economy will return to long-run equilibrium at output Y_F.

When an adverse supply-side factor is more permanent, the long-run supply curve will also shift to the left. For example, an oil price increase that is expected to continue for several years will reduce long-run as well as short-run aggregate supply. Under these

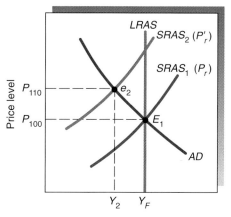

(a) Resource market (b) Goods and services (real GDP)

EXHIBIT 8
The Effects of an
Adverse Supply Shock

Suppose that there's an unanticipated fall in the economy's supply of resources, perhaps because of a crop failure or sharp increase in the price of a major imported resource like oil. Resource prices will rise from P_r to P'_r, as shown in part (a). The higher resource prices will shift the *SRAS* curve to the left, as shown in part (b). In the short run, the price level will rise to P_{110}, and output will decline to Y_2. What happens in the long run depends on whether the reduction in the supply of resources is temporary or permanent. If it is temporary, resource prices will fall in the future, permitting the economy to return to its initial equilibrium (E_1). Conversely, if it is permanent, the production capacity of the economy will shrink, shifting *LRAS* to the left, and e_2 will become the new long-run equilibrium.

circumstances, the economy will have to adjust to a lower level of output. Whether the decline in aggregate supply is temporary or permanent, other things being constant, the price level will rise. Similarly, output will decline, at least temporarily.

The Price Level, Inflation, and the *AD-AS* Model

In the basic *AD-AS* model, the price level is measured on the *y*-axis in both the goods and services and resource markets. This approach makes it easier to visualize relative price changes. If prices change in one of the markets, goods and services, for example, this indicates that prices in that market have changed *relative* to those in other markets. It is important to note, however, that this structure implicitly incorporates the assumption that the actual and expected rates of inflation are initially zero.

As we have previously discussed, when persistent inflation is present, it will be anticipated and incorporated into long-term contracts that affect important components of production costs in the short run. When the actual and anticipated rates of inflation are equal, persistent price increases will be present in both goods and services and resource markets, even though the relative prices between the two markets are unchanged.

However, once decision makers anticipate a given rate of inflation and build it into long-term contracts, an actual rate of inflation that is less than expected is essentially the equivalent of a reduction in the price level when price stability (zero inflation) is anticipated. For example, consider the situation in which 5 percent inflation has been present over a lengthy time period and therefore the 5 percent rate has been built into long-term contracts, including those in resource markets. If weak demand causes the inflation rate to fall to, say, 2 percent, the adjustments will be the same as those for a reduction in product prices when zero inflation is anticipated (see Exhibit 6). In both cases, prices in the goods and services market will fall relative to resource prices. In the short run, profit margins will be squeezed, and firms will cut back on output. Workers will be laid off and the economy may well fall into a recession.

Similarly, the impact of an inflation rate that is greater than was anticipated will be like that of an increase in the price level when price stability is anticipated. Both will increase product prices relative to resource prices, which will enhance profits and thereby induce firms to expand output and employment.

THE BUSINESS CYCLE REVISITED

It's interesting to look at the business cycle within the *AD-AS* framework. Unanticipated shifts in aggregate demand and aggregate supply are what cause economic fluctuations, according to the *AD-AS* model. These unexpected shifts lead to a misalignment between prices and costs because markets don't instantly adjust, and decision makers aren't always able to accurately anticipate changes in the price level (and inflation rate).

Recessions occur because prices in the goods and services market are low relative to costs of production (and resource prices). There are two reasons that this might occur: (1) an unanticipated fall in aggregate demand and (2) unfavorable supply shocks. An unanticipated fall in aggregate demand (illustrated by part a of Exhibit 6) leads to a lower-than-expected price level in the goods and services market. Given the weak demand and lower-than-expected prices, many firms will confront losses, which will force them to reduce output and, in some cases, terminate production. Correspondingly, an adverse supply shock (illustrated by Exhibit 8) leads to higher-than-expected resource prices and costs. This, too, will cause firms to incur losses and reduce output.

In contrast, economic booms—high rates of output that are unsustainable— occur when prices in the goods and services market are high relative to costs (and resource prices). The two causes of booms are: (1) unanticipated increases in aggregate demand and (2) favorable supply shocks. An unanticipated increase in aggregate demand (see part a of Exhibit 5) leads to a higher-than-expected price level in the goods and services market. The strong demand, high prices, and attractive profit margins induce firms to expand output to rates that are unsustainable in the long run. Similarly, a favorable supply shock (see Exhibit 7) leads to lower-than-expected costs and unsustainable rates of output.

Exhibit 9 presents a picture of the economic fluctuations in the United States during the past forty-five years. Let's look at the fluctuations in terms of the *AD-AS* model. During this lengthy period, real GDP grew substantially. This is what one would expect of an economy characterized by net investment and improvements in technology. Recessions were experienced, however, during 1970, 1974–1975, 1979, 1982, 1990–1991, and 2001. As output fell during these periods, unemployment rose above its natural rate (part b). (*Note:* Because the natural rate of unemployment is not directly observable, a range of estimates is provided in part b of Exhibit 9.)

The timing of the recessions is particularly interesting. The 1970 recession occurred as the Vietnam War was winding down. The more severe recession of 1974–1975 followed the doubling of crude oil prices (a supply shock) and sharp fall in the rate of inflation (probably due to an unanticipated fall in *AD*). Sharp changes in oil prices and the inflation rate also played a role in the recessions of 1979 and 1982. Oil prices doubled once again in 1978–1979, pushing up costs unexpectedly prior to and during the recession of 1979. The 1982 recession was associated with a sharp reduction in the inflation rate from 12.5 percent in 1980 (and 13.3 percent in 1979) to only 3.8 percent in 1982, suggesting that there was an abrupt, and therefore unexpected, decline in aggregate demand during this period. The 1990 recession was associated with substantial cuts in U.S. defense spending following the collapse of communism, and economic readjustments accompanying the military buildup and war in Kuwait. The 2001 recession followed the collapse of stock prices in 2000 and 2001. During the mid- and late 1990s, many people figured the upward spiral of the stock market would continue unabated. They were caught by surprise when this did not happen. Clearly, supply shocks and unanticipated changes in aggregate demand underpinned these recessions.

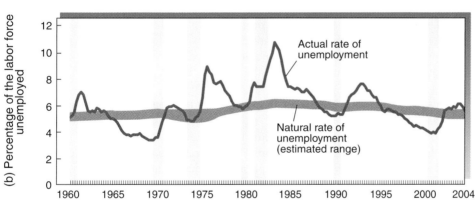

EXHIBIT 9
Expansions, Recessions, and the Rate of Unemployment

Here we show the periods of expansion and contraction (recession) since 1960. Notice how the falls in real GDP (the shaded periods) in the top graph correspond with unemployment rates well above the natural rate, shown in the bottom graph. The *AD-AS* model indicates that recessions are caused by unanticipated falls in aggregate demand that are likely to accompany abrupt falls in inflation and/or adverse supply shocks.

Plant closings, employee layoffs, and high unemployment are hallmarks of recessions. Unanticipated falls in aggregate demand and/or adverse supply shocks are the primary causes of recessions.

DOES A MARKET ECONOMY HAVE A SELF-CORRECTING MECHANISM?

Are there market forces that can help stabilize an economy and cushion the effects of economic shocks without the government having to intervene? Does a market economy have a built-in mechanism preventing an economic downturn from plunging it into a depression? There are three reasons to believe that the answer to both of these questions is "Yes."

Permanent income hypothesis
The hypothesis that people's consumption depends on their long-run expected (permanent) income rather than their current income.

1. Consumption demand is relatively stable. Consumption is by far the largest component of aggregate demand. There is good reason to believe that consumption spending is considerably more stable than aggregate income. The **permanent income hypothesis**, developed by Nobel Prize–winning economist Milton Friedman, explains why. According to the permanent income hypothesis, the consumption of households is largely determined by their long-range expected, or permanent, income. People base their spending on what they think their long-term income prospects are—not temporary increases in their income due to an economic boom that eventually will end.[6] During a boom, for example, they will allocate a substantial amount of their extra income to saving. (Remember that "saving" is income that is not spent on current consumption.) Because of this, consumption demand in the economy will increase less rapidly than income does during the expansion phase of the business cycle. Similarly, when households experience a temporary decline in income during a recession, they will reduce their current saving (and draw on their prior savings) to maintain their living standards. Thus, consumer demand will increase less than income during a boom and decline by a smaller amount than income during a recession. This relative stability of the large consumption component will help stabilize, or even out, aggregate demand over the business cycle—without any sort of intervention by the government.

2. Changes in real interest rates help stabilize aggregate demand and redirect economic fluctuations. Real interest rates tend to reflect business conditions. During an economic downturn, businesses borrow less money for new investment projects. The demand for loanable funds is weak, and real interest rates generally fall. In turn, the lower interest rates lead to higher consumption and make investment projects cheaper, motivating businesses to undertake them. This helps offset the decline in aggregate demand and redirect output toward the full-employment level.

On the other hand, during an economic boom, businesses borrow more money to invest in projects that will help them meet the stronger demand for their goods and services. The demand for loanable funds will strengthen, putting upward pressure on real interest rates. In turn, the higher interest rates will make it more expensive to purchase consumer durables and undertake investment projects. This helps restrain aggregate demand and redirect output down toward the full-employment level.

In summary, interest rate movements help stabilize the economy when it's out of equilibrium. Lower real interest rates during recessionary periods of weak demand will stimulate current spending and thereby help direct the economy back to the full-employment equilibrium. Conversely, higher real interest rates during economic booms restrain aggregate demand and help direct the economy toward the full-employment output level that can be sustained into the future.

---

[6]Perhaps a personal application will help explain why it is important to distinguish between temporary and long-term changes in income. Think for a moment how you would adjust your current spending on goods and services if an aunt left you a gift of $10,000 next month. No doubt you would spend some of the money almost immediately. Perhaps you would buy a new laptop or take a nice vacation. However, you would probably also use a significant portion of this temporary (one-time only) increase in income to pay bills or save for future education. Now, consider how you would alter your current spending if your aunt indicated that you were to receive $10,000 per year for the next thirty years. Compared to the one-time gift, the annual gift for thirty years increases your long-term expected income by a much larger amount. In this case, you are likely to spend most of this year's $10,000 almost immediately. You might even borrow money to buy an automobile or make some major expenditures, and thereby expand your spending on goods and services this year by more than $10,000.

EXHIBIT 10

Changes in Real Interest Rates and Resource Prices over the Business Cycle

When aggregate output is less than the economy's full-employment potential (Y_F), weak demand for investment leads to lower real interest rates, and slack demand in resource markets puts downward pressure on wages and other resource prices (P_r). Conversely, when output exceeds Y_F, strong demand for capital goods (investment) and tight labor market conditions will result in rising real interest rates and resource prices.

Interest rate adjustments will also help offset potential economic disturbances when people suddenly change their expectations about the future. Suppose consumers and business operators suddenly become more pessimistic and, as a result, reduce their current level of spending. This will lower consumer spending and increase saving. Demand in the loanable funds market will be weak. Thus, the supply of loanable funds will increase relative to the demand. This will lead to lower real interest rates, which will help offset the lower spending caused by the pessimism.

Just the opposite will happen if consumers and businesses suddenly became more optimistic. If they suddenly decide to spend more of their current income, this will reduce the supply of loanable funds relative to the demand, causing the real interest rates to rise. The higher rates will then make current spending less attractive and will help stabilize aggregate demand.

3. Changes in real resource prices will help redirect economic fluctuations.
Price adjustments in the resource market also help keep the economy on an even keel. When the economy's output is less than its full-employment potential, weak demand for resources used in production will place downward pressure on real resource prices (like wages). In contrast, when an economy is operating beyond its full-employment capacity—when unemployment is less than the natural unemployment rate—strong demand will rapidly push up the real price of labor (wages) and other resources.

A Graphic Presentation of the Self-Correcting Mechanism

Exhibits 10 and 11 provide a graphic summary of the economy's self-correcting mechanism. **Exhibit 10** shows how real interest rates and resource prices respond as market conditions change. When an economy is operating below its full-employment potential (Y_F), real interest rates and real resource prices tend to decline. This will help direct output toward long-run equilibrium (along the vertical *LRAS* curve). Conversely, when the economy's output exceeds its long-run sustainable level, rising real interest rates and resource prices will cause output to recede to the full-employment level.

Exhibit 11 shows how the economy's self-correcting mechanism works within the *AS-AD* framework. Part (a) illustrates the supply and demand conditions in the goods and services market for an economy initially operating beyond full-employment capacity,

EXHIBIT 11
The Economy's Self-Correcting Mechanism

In the short run, output may either exceed or fall short of the economy's full-employment capacity (Y_F). If output is temporarily greater than the economy's potential, as shown in part (a), higher real interest rates and resource prices will lead to lower output. The higher interest rates will reduce aggregate demand, shifting it from AD_1 to AD_2. At the same time, the higher resource prices will increase production costs and reduce short-run aggregate supply, shifting it to $SRAS_2$. These forces will direct output toward its full-employment potential.

When output is less than capacity, as shown in part (b), lower interest rates (reflecting the weak demand for investment funds) will stimulate aggregate demand, shifting it to AD_2. Lower resource prices (because of weak demand and abnormally high unemployment) will reduce production costs and stimulate short-run aggregate supply, shifting it to $SRAS_2$. Thus, output will move toward the economy's full-employment capacity. However, this self-correction process might require considerable time. In upcoming chapters, we will look at policy alternatives that might shorten the adjustment process.

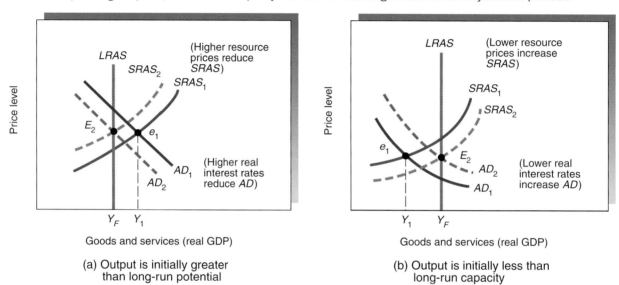

(a) Output is initially greater than long-run potential

(b) Output is initially less than long-run capacity

perhaps as the result of an unanticipated increase in aggregate demand. These are the conditions one would expect when the expansionary phase of the business cycle results in an unsustainable economic boom. When this happens, the strong demand for goods and services will lead to both high employment and strong demand for investment funds as firms try to expand their output. As a result, the actual rate of unemployment will be less than the natural rate. However, the strong demand for both loanable funds and resources will put upward pressure on real interest rates and resource prices, causing both to rise. The higher interest rates will increase the cost of both investment projects and consumer durables, which will tend to retard the strong demand (shifting AD_1 to AD_2 in part a). At the same time, the rising cost of labor and other resources will push production costs upward, reducing short-run aggregate supply (shifting $SRAS_1$ to $SRAS_2$). As resource prices and costs rise, profit margins will decline to normal competitive rates, and output will recede to its long-run potential. *Eventually, these forces—higher real interest rates and resource prices—will direct the output of an overemployed economy back to its long-run capacity.*

Part (b) of Exhibit 11 shows an economy initially in a recession. The initial short-run equilibrium (e_1 of part b) takes place at a rate of output (Y_1) well below the economy's full-employment capacity. When current output is less than an economy's long-run potential, the demand for investment funds will be extremely weak. This weak demand will result in lower real interest rates, which will lead to an increase in aggregate demand (shifting AD_1 to AD_2). At the same time, abnormally high unemployment and weak demand for resources will place downward pressure on real wages and resource prices. Eventually, the excess supply in resource markets will motivate suppliers to accept lower wages and prices for their resources. The decline in resource prices will lower costs and lead to an increase in short-run aggregate supply (shifting $SRAS_1$ to $SRAS_2$ in part b).

Eventually, lower interest rates and resource prices will restore the economy's full-employment rate of output (equilibrium E_2).

The AD-AS model shows that changes in real interest rates and real resource prices (like wages) will redirect the economy during booms and recessions. The economy won't continue to spiral upward when a boom occurs, and it won't continue to spiral downward when a recession occurs. Eventually, it will correct itself. The experience of the U.S. economy is consistent with this view. Real interest rates have tended to decline during recessions and rise during booms. Correspondingly, the real hourly compensation of employees has tended to increase rapidly during economic booms, but only slowly, if at all, during recessionary periods.

The Great Debate: How Rapidly Does the Self-Correcting Mechanism Work?

Following the Great Depression of the 1930s, many economists thought that market economies were inherently unstable.[7] They argued that, unless monetary and fiscal policy were used to stimulate and guide the macroeconomy, prolonged recessions would result. Influenced by both a reevaluation of the 1930s and the experience of the last sixty years, most modern economists reject this stagnation view. Today, there is a widespread consensus that market economies possess a self-corrective mechanism—that changes in interest rates and resource prices will direct macro markets back to equilibrium in the manner outlined above.

However, economists are divided about how rapidly this self-corrective mechanism works. This is a key issue. If the self-corrective process works slowly, then market economies will still experience lengthy periods of abnormally high unemployment and below-capacity output. Many economists believe this is the case. As a result, they have a good deal of confidence that discretionary monetary and fiscal policy can help promote stability and prosperity.

Conversely, other economists believe that the self-corrective mechanism of a market economy works reasonably well when monetary and fiscal policy follow a stable course. This latter group argues that macroeconomic policy mistakes are a major source of economic instability. Thus, they focus on the importance of stable, predictable monetary and fiscal policies, while relying mostly on the self-corrective mechanism of markets to keep the economy on track. When we analyze the impact of monetary and fiscal policy, we will return to this debate.

LOOKING AHEAD

The study of macroeconomics has evolved over the years. The Great Depression and the prolonged unemployment that accompanied it had an enormous impact on macroeconomics. During the Great Depression, John Maynard Keynes, the brilliant English economist, shed new light on why economies experience high unemployment. The next chapter explains Keynes's theory.

---

[7]A detailed analysis of the forces causing and prolonging the Great Depression is presented in Chapter 15.

KEY POINTS

▼ It is important to distinguish between anticipated and unanticipated changes.

▼ An increase in aggregate demand involves a shift of the entire *AD* curve to the right. Major factors causing an increase in aggregate demand (other than government policies) are (1) an increase in real wealth, (2) a lower real interest rate, (3) increased optimism on the part of businesses and consumers, (4) an increase in the expected rate of inflation, (5) higher real income abroad, and (6) a depreciation in the exchange rate. Conversely, if these factors change in the opposite direction, a decrease in aggregate demand will result.

▼ It is important to distinguish between long-run and short-run aggregate supply. The following factors will increase long-run aggregate supply (*LRAS*): (1) increases in the supply of labor and capital resources, (2) improvements in technology and productivity, and (3) institutional changes improving the efficiency of resource use. Changes in resource prices, the expected rate of inflation, and supply shocks will cause shifts in short-run aggregate supply (*SRAS*).

▼ An increase in output due to economic growth (an increase in the economy's production capacity) will increase both short-run and long-run aggregate supply, permitting the economy to achieve and sustain a larger output level.

▼ Unanticipated changes in either aggregate demand or aggregate supply will disrupt long-run equilibrium

and cause current output to differ from the economy's long-run potential.

▼ Unanticipated increases in aggregate demand and favorable supply shocks can cause economic booms that push output beyond the economy's long-run potential and unemployment below its natural rate. However, as decision makers adjust to the strong demand, resource prices and interest rates will rise, and output will recede to long-run capacity.

▼ Unanticipated reductions in aggregate demand and adverse supply shocks can lead to below-capacity output and abnormally high rates of unemployment. Eventually, lower resource prices (and lower real interest rates) will direct the economy back to long-run equilibrium. However, the process may be both lengthy and painful, particularly if wages and prices are downwardly inflexible.

▼ Changes in real interest rates and resource prices help the economy correct itself. During a recession, lower interest rates will stimulate aggregate demand, and lower resource prices (including wages) will increase short-run aggregate supply. Both of these forces will help direct output toward its full-employment potential. Similarly, when current output exceeds potential GDP, higher real interest rates and rising real resource prices cause output to recede to the economy's potential capacity.

▼ There is considerable debate among economists concerning how rapidly the economy's self-correcting mechanism works.

CRITICAL ANALYSIS QUESTIONS

*1. Explain how and why each of the following factors would influence current aggregate demand in the United States:
 a. Increased fear of recession
 b. Increased fear of inflation
 c. Rapid growth of real income in Canada and Western Europe
 d. A reduction in the real interest rate
 e. A higher price level (Be careful.)

*2. Indicate how each of the following would influence U.S. aggregate supply in the short run:
 a. An increase in real wage rates
 b. A severe freeze that destroys half the orange trees in Florida

 c. An increase in the expected rate of inflation in the future
 d. An increase in the world price of oil, a major import
 e. Abundant rainfall during the growing season of agricultural states

3. What is the difference between the production possibilities constraint and the long-run aggregate supply curve? How would changes in conditions that move the production possibilities curve affect the *SRAS* and *LRAS*? What impact has computer technology had on the cost of doing business during the last fifteen years? How has this affected production possibilities and the long-run aggregate supply curve?

*4. When current output is less than full-employment capacity, explain how the self-correcting mechanism will direct output toward the economy's long-run potential. Can you think of any reason that this mechanism might not work? Discuss.

5. What is the difference between an anticipated and an unanticipated increase in aggregate demand? Provide an example of each. Which is more likely to result in a temporary spurt in the growth of real output?

*6. Assume that both union and management representatives agree to wage increases because they expect prices to rise 10 percent during the next year. Explain why the unemployment rate will probably increase if the actual rate of inflation next year is only 3 percent.

7. During 2000, there was a sharp reduction in stock prices and a sharp increase in the world price of crude oil. How will aggregate demand and aggregate supply in the United States be influenced by these two factors? Using the *AD-AS* model, explain the expected impact on output.

*8. When the actual output exceeds the long-run potential of the economy, how will the self-correcting mechanism direct the economy to long-run equilibrium? Why can't the above-normal output be maintained?

*9. Are the real wages of workers likely to increase more rapidly when the unemployment rate is high or when it is low? Why?

10. When an economy dips into a recession, consumers will often be relatively pessimistic about the future for an extended period of time. How will this pessimism affect the speed and strength of the recovery? Feel free to use the data of Exhibit 2 in your response to this question.

11. How will (a) an unexpected 3 percent fall in the price level in the goods and services market differ from (b) 1 percent inflation when 4 percent inflation had been expected? What impact would (a) and (b) have on the real price of resources, profit margins, output, and employment? Explain.

*12. Suppose that unexpectedly rapid growth in real income abroad leads to a sharp increase in the demand for U.S. exports. What impact will this change have on the price level, output, and employment in the short run in the United States? In the long run?

13. If the real interest rate increases, how will this affect the incentive of consumers and investors to purchase goods and services? How will it affect the *AD* curve?

14. Construct the *AD, SRAS,* and *LRAS* curves for an economy experiencing (a) full employment, (b) an economic boom, and (c) a recession.

*15. As the result of changing international conditions, real national defense expenditures declined approximately 15 percent between 1989 and 1991. What would you expect the impact of this decline to be on aggregate demand and output in the short run? If the United States spends less on national defense in the future, how will this factor influence the standard of living of Americans? Discuss.

16. Consider an economy with the following aggregate demand (*AD*) and aggregate supply (*AS*) schedules. These schedules reflect the fact that, prior to the period we're examining, decision makers entered into contracts and made choices anticipating that the price level would be P_{105}.

AD_{105} (in trillions)	Price Level	$SRAS_{105}$ (in trillions)
$5.1	95	$3.5
4.9	100	3.8
4.7	105	4.2
4.5	110	4.5
4.3	115	4.8

a. Indicate the quantity of GDP that will be produced and the price level that will emerge during this period.
b. Is the economy in long-run equilibrium? Why or why not?
c. How will the unemployment rate during the current period compare with this economy's natural rate of unemployment?
d. What will tend to happen to resource prices in the future? How will this affect the equilibrium rate of output?
e. Will the rate of GDP produced during this period be sustainable into the future? Why or why not?

17. Suppose that the price level that emerges from aggregate demand and aggregate supply conditions during the current period is lower than decision makers had anticipated.
a. Construct *AD, SRAS,* and *LRAS* schedules that reflect these conditions.
b. During the current period, how will the actual rate of unemployment compare with the natural rate? How will actual output compare with the economy's potential?
c. As the result of the current conditions, what will tend to happen to resource prices and interest rates? Why?

*18. What effect did the events of September 11, 2001, have on aggregate demand, aggregate supply, and the long-run potential real output of the United States?

---

*Asterisk denotes questions for which answers are given in Appendix B.

CHAPTER

11

Keynes and the Evolution of Macroeconomics

I believe myself to be writing a book on economic theory which will largely revolutionize not, I suppose, at once but in the course of the next ten years the way the world thinks about economic problems.

—John Maynard Keynes[1]

Chapter Focus

- What did John Maynard Keynes and his followers think happened during the Great Depression?

- What are the major components of the Keynesian model? What is the major factor that causes the level of output and employment to change?

- What determines the equilibrium level of output in the Keynesian model?

- What is the multiplier principle? Why is it important?

- Why do Keynesians believe that market economies experience business instability?

[1]Letter from John Maynard Keynes to George Bernard Shaw, New Year's Day, 1935.

odern macroeconomics is the product of an evolutionary process. Prior to the Great Depression of the 1930s, most economists thought market adjustments would automatically guide an economy to full employment in a relatively brief time. But double-digit unemployment rates throughout the 1930s undermined this view. The experience of the Great Depression also led to the development of a new theory, one designed to explain the persistently high unemployment levels during the Great Depression. The new theory, developed by the English economist John Maynard Keynes (pronounced "canes"), provided a reasonable explanation for the problem.[2] It also had an enormous influence on the development of macroeconomics. Several basic concepts of theory and much of the terminology we use today in macroeconomics can be traced to Keynes. In fact, macroeconomics as we now know it today is built around Keynes's analysis. ■

THE GREAT DEPRESSION AND MACROECONOMICS

Mainstream economists before Keynes (often called **classical economists**) emphasized the importance of the economy's total production (aggregate supply) and paid little attention to aggregate demand. Classical economists adhered to **Say's Law**, named for nineteenth-century French economist J. B. Say. According to Say's Law, a general overproduction of goods relative to total demand is impossible because supply (production) *creates* its own demand. The reasoning here is that the purchasing power necessary for people to buy, or demand, the products they want is generated by production. A farmer's supply of wheat generates the income to meet his or her demand for shoes, clothes, automobiles, and other goods. Similarly, the supply of shoes generates the purchasing power that gives shoemakers (and their employees) the ability to demand the farmer's wheat and other goods they want.

Of course, producers might produce too much of some goods and not enough of others. But the pricing system would correct such imbalances. The prices of goods in excess supply would fall, and the prices of products in excess demand would rise. According to the classical view, deficient total demand could never be a problem because the production of the goods would always generate a demand sufficient to purchase the goods produced.

Classical economists believed that markets would always adjust and quickly direct the economy toward equilibrium and full employment. If unemployment were temporarily high, wages would fall, which would reduce costs and lower prices until the excess supply of labor was eliminated. Similarly, market-determined interest rates would bring saving and investment into balance.

Before the Great Depression, the classical view seemed reasonable. But the severity and duration of the decline during the 1930s led people to challenge the view's validity and laid the foundation for what we now call Keynesian economics. For those who are familiar only with the relative stability of recent decades, the depth of the economic decline during the 1930s is difficult to comprehend: between 1930 and 1933, real GDP in the United States fell by more than 30 percent. In 1933, nearly 25 percent—one-quarter—of the U.S. labor force was unemployed. The depressed conditions continued throughout the decade. In 1939, a decade after the plunge began, per capita income was still nearly 10 percent less than in 1929. Other industrial countries experienced similar conditions during the 1930s.

Classical economists
Economists from Adam Smith to the time of Keynes who focused their analyses on economic efficiency and production. With regard to business instability, they thought market prices and wages would decline during a recession quickly enough to bring the economy back to full employment within a short period of time.

Say's Law
The view that production creates its own demand. Demand will always be sufficient to purchase the goods produced because the income payments to the resource suppliers will equal the value of the goods produced.

Keynesian View of the Great Depression

Keynes developed a theory explaining why depressed conditions like those of the 1930s might exist for a lengthy period of time. He offered a completely new concept of output

[2]See the classic book by Keynes, *The General Theory of Employment, Interest, and Money* (London: Macmillan, 1936), for the presentation of this theory.

The Keynesian model was an outgrowth of the Great Depression. It provided an explanation for the widespread, prolonged unemployment of the 1930s.

determination: Keynes believed that spending motivated firms to supply goods and services. He argued that, if total spending fell—as it might, for example, if consumers and investors became pessimistic about the future or tried to save more of their current income for the future—then firms would respond by cutting back production. Less spending would thus lead to less output.

Keynes and his followers rejected the classical view that lower wages and interest rates would get the economy back on track and eliminate abnormally high rates of unemployment. What was the basis of their argument? First, they argued that wages and prices are highly inflexible, particularly in a downward direction. Even if demand were weak, Keynesians believed powerful trade unions and large corporations would be able to maintain their wages and prices at a high level. Further, even if wages did decline, this would reduce incomes and exert a negative impact on aggregate demand.

Second, Keynesians also rejected the potential effectiveness of interest rate cuts to get the economy back on track. They argued that when excess capacity is widespread and people are extremely pessimistic about the future, lower interest rates will fail to stimulate additional investment. Moreover, after nominal interest rates had fallen to extremely low levels—rates near zero, for example—significant additional reductions capable of stimulating the economy would be impossible. Keynes believed that all of these conditions were present during the Great Depression. Under these circumstances, he did not believe that market forces would direct the economy back to full employment.

Keynes also introduced a different concept of equilibrium and a different mechanism for its achievement. ***In the Keynesian view, equilibrium takes place when the level of total spending in the economy is equal to its current output. When this is the case, producers will have no reason to either expand or contract output.*** Keynesians believe that changes in output rather than changes in prices direct the economy to equilibrium. If total spending is less than full-employment output, output will be cut back to the level of spending, and, most significantly, it will remain there until the level of spending changes.

OUTSTANDING ECONOMIST	John Maynard Keynes (1883–1946)	

Keynes might properly be referred to as the "father of macroeconomics." The son of a prominent nineteenth-century economist (John Neville Keynes), he earned a degree in mathematics from King's College, Cambridge, where he would later return and spend most of his career as an economist. His *General Theory of Employment, Interest, and Money,* published in 1936, revolutionized the way that economists think about macroeconomics. This work, written in the midst of the Great Depression, provided both a plausible explanation for the massive unemployment and a strategy for ending it. Keynes married an idea with a moment in time.

Although Keynes's work was groundbreaking, it was also controversial. Keynes thought governments should run budget deficits during a recession to stimulate demand and direct the economy back to full employment (we'll discuss more about how this works in the next chapter). But this challenged the entrenched views of both policy makers and classical economists. Nonetheless, he correctly predicted that his ideas would be influential (see the chapter's opening quotation). This was certainly the case for three decades following his untimely death due to a heart attack in 1946. His influence eventually waned because his theory could not simultaneously explain the inflation, unemployment, and instability of the 1970s. Nonetheless, macroeconomic thought and practice continue to reflect his ideas.

Therefore, if total spending is deficient, equilibrium output will be less than full-employment output, and high rates of unemployment will continue. This is precisely what Keynes believed was happening during the 1930s.

The central message of Keynes can be summarized as follows: businesses will produce only the quantity of goods and services they believe consumers, investors, governments, and foreigners will plan to buy. If these planned aggregate expenditures are less than the economy's full-employment output, output will fall short of its potential. When aggregate expenditures are deficient, there are no automatic forces capable of returning the economy to full employment. Prolonged unemployment will persist. Against the background of the Great Depression, this was a compelling argument.

The Keynesian Model of Spending and Output

All models make simplifying assumptions. As we develop the Keynesian model, we want to be explicit about several of the key assumptions. First, as with the *AD-AS* model developed in Chapters 9 and 10, we will assume that there is a specific full-employment level of output. Only the natural rate of unemployment is present when full-employment capacity is attained. Second, following in the Keynesian tradition, we will assume that wages and prices are completely inflexible until full employment is reached. Once full employment is achieved, though, additional demand will lead only to higher prices. Strictly speaking, extreme assumptions like these will not hold in the real world. For example, some suppliers will probably lower their prices if the economy isn't operating at full capacity. In the short run, however, these wage and price inflexibility conditions may be approximated. Finally, we will continue to assume that the government's taxing, spending, and monetary policies are constant.

The key to understanding the basic Keynesian model, what we today call the *aggregate expenditure* (AE) *model*, is the concept of *planned* aggregate expenditures. Like aggregate demand, the four components of *planned* aggregate expenditures are consumption, investment, government purchases, and net exports. Let's consider each.

Planned Consumption Expenditures

The largest component of planned aggregate expenditures is *planned* consumption (*C*). Keynes believed that people's current income primarily determines their consumption spending. As he stated:

> Men are disposed, as a rule and on the average, to increase their consumption as their income increases, but not by as much as the increase in their income.[3]

According to Keynes, disposable income—one's income after taxes—is by far the most important determinant of current consumption. If disposable income increases, consumers will increase their planned expenditures.

This positive relationship between disposable income and consumption spending is called the **consumption function**. **Exhibit 1** illustrates this relationship for an economy. At low levels of aggregate income (less than $7 trillion), the consumption expenditures of households will exceed their disposable income. When income is low, households *dissave*—they either borrow money or draw from their past savings to purchase consumption goods. Because consumption does not increase as rapidly as income, the slope of the consumption function will be less than 1—less than the slope of a 45-degree line. That means that the aggregate consumption line will be flatter than the 45-degree line in Exhibit 1. As income increases, household aggregate income eventually equals and exceeds current consumption. For aggregate income above $7 trillion, saving increases as income rises.

Consumption function
The fundamental relationship between disposable income and consumption. When disposable income increases, current consumption expenditures rise, but by a smaller amount than the increase in income.

---

[3]Keynes, *The General Theory of Employment, Interest, and Money*, 96.

EXHIBIT 1
Aggregate Consumption Function

The Keynesian model assumes that there is a positive relationship between consumption and income. However, as income increases, consumption expands by a smaller amount. Thus, the slope of the consumption function (line *C*) is less than 1 (less than the slope of the 45-degree line).

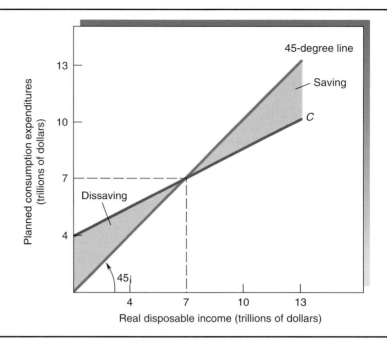

Autonomous expenditures
Expenditures that do not vary with the level of income. They are determined by factors (such as business expectations and economic policy) that are outside the basic aggregate expenditure model.

Planned Investment Expenditures

Investment (*I*) encompasses (1) expenditures on fixed assets, such as buildings and machines, and (2) changes in the inventories of raw materials and final products not yet sold. Keynes argued that, in the short run, investment was best viewed as an **autonomous expenditure**, one independent of people's income. In other words, business investment decisions, at least in the short run, don't hinge on people's current income and spending. Instead, investment is primarily a function of current sales relative to plant capacity, expected future sales, and the interest rate. To isolate the forces pushing an economy toward an equilibrium level of output, Keynes's model assumed there was a constant level of planned investment expenditures.

Planned Government Expenditures

Like investment, planned government (*G*) expenditures in the basic Keynesian model are assumed to be independent of income. These expenditures need not change with the level of income. In the Keynesian model, government expenditures are a policy variable determined by the political process—not consumers' income or spending. Governments can, and often do, spend more than they receive in taxes. Viewing the government's expenditures as independent of income allows us to focus more clearly on the stabilizing forces of a private economy. Later, we will analyze how changes in government expenditures influence output and employment within the framework of the Keynesian model.

Planned Net Exports

Exports are dependent on spending choices and income levels abroad. These decisions are, by and large, unaffected by changes in a nation's domestic income level and spending. Therefore, as **Exhibit 2** illustrates, exports remain constant (at $1.2 trillion) when income changes. In contrast, increases in domestic income will induce consumers to purchase more foreign as well as domestic goods. So the level of imports increases as income rises. Because exports remain constant but imports increase as aggregate income expands, a nation's net exports (*NX*) will decline as income rises (see Exhibit 2). Thus, Keynes theorized that there is a negative relationship between a nation's net exports and its aggregate income. When its aggregate income rises, its net exports fall; when its aggregate income falls, its net exports rise.

TOTAL OUTPUT (REAL GDP IN TRILLIONS)	PLANNED EXPORTS (TRILLIONS)	PLANNED IMPORTS (TRILLIONS)	PLANNED NET EXPORTS (TRILLIONS)
$ 9.4	$1.2	$1.00	$0.20
9.7	1.2	1.05	0.15
10.0	1.2	1.10	0.10
10.3	1.2	1.15	0.05
10.6	1.2	1.20	0.0

EXHIBIT 2
Income and Net Exports

Because exports are determined by income abroad, they are constant at $1.2 trillion. Imports increase as domestic income expands. Thus, planned net exports fall as domestic income increases.

Planned Versus Actual Expenditures

Now let's explain the difference between planned and *actual* expenditures. Planned expenditures reflect the choices of consumers, investors, governments, and foreigners, *given their expectations about the choices of other decision makers*. Planned expenditures, though, need not equal actual expenditures. If buyers spend a different amount on goods and services than firms anticipate, the firms will experience unplanned changes in inventories.

Consider what would happen if the planned expenditures of consumers, investors, governments, and foreigners on goods and services were less than what business firms thought they would be. If this were the case, business firms would be unable to sell as much of their current output as they had anticipated. Their *actual* inventories would increase as they unintentionally made larger inventory investments than they *planned*. On the other hand, consider what would happen if purchasers bought more goods and services than businesses expected. The unexpected brisk sales would draw down inventories and result in less inventory investment than business firms planned. In this case, actual inventory investment would be less than was planned for by business decision makers.

Actual and *planned* expenditures are equal only when purchasers buy the quantity of goods and services that business decision makers anticipated they would purchase. Only then will the plans of buyers and sellers in the goods and services market harmonize.

KEYNESIAN EQUILIBRIUM

Equilibrium is present in the Keynesian model when planned aggregate expenditures equal the value of actual output. When this is the case, businesses are able to sell the total amount of goods and services that they produce. There are no unexpected changes in inventories. Thus, producers have no incentive to either expand or contract their output during the next period. In equation form, Keynesian macroequilibrium is attained when:

$$\underbrace{\text{Total output}}_{\text{Real GDP}} = \underbrace{\text{Planned } C + I + G + NX}_{\text{Planned aggregate expenditures}}$$

For an example of Keynesian macroeconomic equilibrium, let's take a look at the hypothetical economy described by **Exhibit 3.** First, look at columns 1 and 2. At what level of total output is this economy in Keynesian macroeconomic equilibrium? Stop now and attempt to figure out the answer.

The answer is $10 trillion, because only there is total output exactly equal to planned aggregate expenditures. When real GDP is equal to $10 trillion, the planned expenditures of consumers, investors, governments, and foreigners (net exports) are precisely equal to the value of the output produced by business firms. To see this, note that only at $10 trillion do columns 3, 4, and 5 combined equal column 1. At $10 trillion in output, the spending plans of purchasers mesh with the production plans of businesses.

What happens at other output levels? At any output other than equilibrium, the plans of producers and purchasers will conflict. If output is $9.7 trillion, for example, planned aggregate expenditures will be $9.85 trillion—$150 billion more than the current level of

EXHIBIT 3
Example of Keynesian Macroeconomic Equilibrium

Note: All figures are in trillions of dollars. Column 2 equals the sum of columns 3, 4, and 5.

TOTAL OUTPUT (REAL GDP) (1)	PLANNED AGGREGATE EXPENDITURES (2)	PLANNED CONSUMPTION (3)	PLANNED INVESTMENT + GOVERNMENT EXPENDITURES (4)	PLANNED NET EXPORTS (5)	TENDENCY OF OUTPUT (6)
$ 9.4	$ 9.70	$ 7.1	$ 2.4	$ 0.20	Expand
9.7	9.85	7.3	2.4	0.15	Expand
10.0	10.00	7.5	2.4	0.10	Equilibrium
10.3	10.15	7.7	2.4	0.05	Contract
10.6	10.30	7.9	2.4	0.00	Contract

output. When expenditures (purchases) exceed output, inventories will decline. Firms will then expand their output to get their inventories back up to normal levels. Therefore, when aggregate expenditures exceed current output, there will be a tendency for output to expand toward the equilibrium output ($10 trillion).

On the other hand, if aggregate expenditures are less than current output, firms will cut back on production. For example, if output is $10.3 trillion, it will be greater than planned aggregate expenditures, and excess inventories will accumulate. Of course, business firms will not continue to produce goods they cannot sell, so they will reduce production, and output will recede toward the $10 trillion equilibrium.

Equilibrium at Less Than Full Employment

Because Keynesian equilibrium hinges on planned aggregate expenditures and output being equal, it need not take place at full employment. If an economy is in Keynesian equilibrium, there will be no tendency for output to change—even if output is well below full-employment capacity.

To see this using our example, assume that full employment is at an output of $10.3 trillion, in Exhibit 3. Given the current planned spending, the economy will fail to achieve full employment. The rate of unemployment will be high. In the Keynesian model, neither wages nor interest rates will decline in the face of abnormally high unemployment and excess capacity. Therefore, output will remain at less than the full-employment rate as long as insufficient spending prevents the economy from reaching its full potential.

This is precisely what Keynes thought was happening during the Great Depression. He believed that Western economies were in equilibrium at an employment rate substantially below capacity. Unless aggregate expenditures increased, therefore, the prolonged unemployment had to continue—and, in fact, it did, throughout the 1930s.

Keynesian Equilibrium—a Graphic Presentation

The Keynesian analysis is presented graphically in **Exhibit 4.** Notice that planned aggregate consumption, investment, government, and net export expenditures are measured on the *y*-axis, and total output is measured on the *x*-axis. The 45-degree line that extends from the origin maps out all the points at which aggregate expenditures (*AE*) are equal to total output (GDP).

Because aggregate expenditures equal total output for all points along the 45-degree line, the line maps out all possible equilibrium income levels. As long as the economy is operating at less than its full-employment capacity, producers will produce any output along the 45-degree line that they believe purchasers will buy. Producers, though, will supply a level of output only if they believe planned expenditures will be large enough to purchase it. Depending on the level of aggregate expenditures, each point along the 45-degree line is a potential equilibrium. Using the data of Exhibit 3, **Exhibit 5** shows the Keynesian equilibrium in our hypothetical economy. The $C + I + G + NX$ (*AE*) line indicates the total planned expenditures of consumers, investors, governments, and

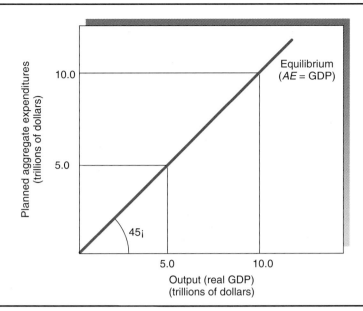

EXHIBIT 4
Aggregate Expenditures (*AE*)

Aggregate expenditures will be equal to total output for all points along a 45-degree line from the origin. The 45-degree line thus maps out potential equilibrium levels of output for the Keynesian model.

foreigners (net exports) at each income level. Remember, the aggregate expenditure (*AE*) line is flatter than the 45-degree line because, as income rises, consumption also increases, but by less than the increase in income. Therefore, as income expands, total expenditures increase by less than the expansion in income.

The equilibrium level of output will be $10.0 trillion, the point at which total expenditures (measured vertically) are just equal to total output (measured horizontally). Of course, the aggregate expenditures function $C + I + G + NX$ will cross the 45-degree line at the $10.0 trillion Keynesian equilibrium level of output. As long as the aggregate expenditures function remains unchanged, no other level of output can be

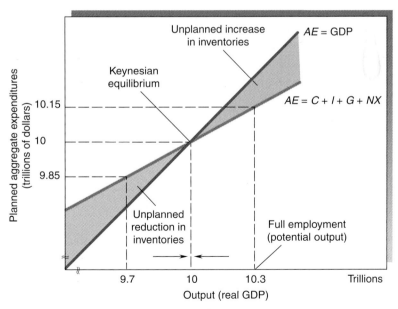

EXHIBIT 5
Aggregate Expenditures and Keynesian Equilibrium

Here the data of Exhibit 3 are presented within the Keynesian graphic framework. The equilibrium level of output is $10.0 trillion because planned expenditures ($C + I + G + NX$) are just equal to output at that level of income. At a lower level of income, $9.7 trillion, for example, unplanned inventory reduction would cause business firms to expand output (right-pointing arrow). Conversely, at a higher income level, such as $10.3 trillion, accumulation of inventories would lead to lower future output (left-pointing arrow). Given current aggregate expenditures, only the $10.0 trillion output would be sustainable in the future. Note that the $10.0 trillion equilibrium income level is less than the economy's potential of $10.3 trillion.

sustained. When total output exceeds $10.0 trillion—for example, when it's $10.3 trillion—the aggregate expenditure line ($C + I + G + NX$) lies below the 45-degree line. Remember that, when the $C + I + G + NX$ line is less than the 45-degree line, total spending is less than total output. People aren't willing to buy as much as is produced. Excess inventories will then accumulate, leading businesses to reduce their future production. Employment will subsequently decline. Output will fall back from $10.3 trillion to the equilibrium level of $10.0 trillion. Note that the change in total spending, followed by changes in output and employment, is what will restore equilibrium in the Keynesian model—not changes in prices.

In contrast, if total output is temporarily below equilibrium, there will be a tendency for aggregate income to rise. Here's how: Suppose output is temporarily at $9.7 trillion. At that output level, the $C + I + G + NX$ function lies above the 45-degree line. At this point, aggregate expenditures exceed aggregate output. Businesses are selling more than they currently produce. Their inventories are falling. Excess demand is present. They will react by hiring more workers and expanding production. This will increase the nation's aggregate income. Only at the equilibrium level—the point at which the $C + I + G + NX$ function crosses the 45-degree line ($10.0 trillion)—though, will the spending plans of consumers, investors, governments, and foreigners equal the output of firms. Only this level of output can be sustained.

Notice (from Exhibit 5) that the economy's full-employment potential level is actually $10.3 trillion—not $10.0 trillion, where equilibrium exists between the amount buyers are willing to purchase and the amount producers are willing to sell. At $10.3 trillion, though, aggregate expenditures are insufficient to purchase the output produced. Given the aggregate expenditures function, output will remain below its potential. Unemployment will persist. Within the Keynesian model, equilibrium need not coincide with full employment.

How Can Full Employment Be Achieved?

According to the Keynesian model, an output equal to the economy's full-employment capacity cannot be achieved unless aggregate demand is sufficiently high. Because the Keynesian model assumes that prices are fixed until potential capacity is reached, wage and price reductions are ruled out as a feasible mechanism for directing the economy to full employment. Neither is the interest rate capable of stimulating demand and directing the economy to full employment.

However, if consumers, investors, governments, and foreigners could be induced to expand their expenditures, output would expand to full-employment capacity. **Exhibit 6** illustrates this point. If additional spending shifted the aggregate expenditures schedule (AE) upward to AE_2, equilibrium output would expand to its potential capacity. At the higher level of expenditures, AE_2, total spending would equal output at $10.3 trillion.

What would happen if aggregate expenditures were to exceed the economy's production capacity? For example, suppose aggregate expenditures rose to AE_3. Within the basic Keynesian model, aggregate expenditures in excess of output lead to a higher price level once the economy reaches full employment. Nominal output will increase, but it merely reflects higher prices, rather than additional real output. Total spending in excess of full-employment capacity is inflationary within the Keynesian model.

Aggregate expenditures are the catalyst of the Keynesian model. Changes in expenditures make things happen. If the economy is operating below full employment, supply is always accommodative. An increase in aggregate expenditures, caused, for example, by an increase in government expenditures, will thus lead to an increase in real output and employment. Once full employment is reached, though, additional aggregate expenditures lead merely to higher prices.

Keynesians argue that regulating aggregate expenditures is the crux of sound macroeconomic policy. If we could ensure that aggregate expenditures were large enough to achieve capacity output, but not so large as to result in inflation, then maximum output, full employment, and price stability could be attained.

EXHIBIT 6
Shifts in Aggregate Expenditures and Changes in Equilibrium Output

When equilibrium output is less than the economy's capacity, only an increase in expenditures (a shift in *AE*) will lead to full employment. If consumers, investors, governments, or foreigners would spend more and thereby shift the aggregate expenditures schedule to AE_2, output would reach its full-employment potential ($10.3 trillion). Once full employment is reached, further increases in aggregate expenditures, like those shown by the shift to AE_3, will lead only to higher prices. Nominal output will expand (the dotted segment of the *AE*-GDP schedule), but real output will not.

The Keynesian model was an outgrowth of the Great Depression. It provided an explanation for the widespread and prolonged unemployment of the 1930s.

THE KEYNESIAN MODEL WITHIN THE *AD-AS* FRAMEWORK

The Keynesian model can also be presented within the now familiar aggregate demand–aggregate supply (*AD-AS*) framework of the previous two chapters. The only difference in the graphic analysis is that the short-run aggregate supply curve (*SRAS*) has a different shape than in previous chapters because of the assumptions of the Keynesian model. Take a look at **Exhibit 7.** Note that the *SRAS* is completely flat at the existing price level until full-employment capacity is reached. This is because the Keynesian model assumes that, at less than full-employment output levels, prices (and wages) are fixed because they are inflexible in a downward direction. In essence, firms have a horizontal supply curve when operating below normal capacity, so any change in aggregate demand will lead to a corresponding change in output. Economists sometimes refer to this horizontal segment as the *Keynesian range* of the aggregate supply curve.

What happens to the *SRAS* in Exhibit 7 when capacity is reached? In this situation, firms raise their prices to allocate the capacity output to those willing to pay the highest prices. Thus, the economy's *SRAS* is vertical at full-employment capacity. So both *SRAS* and *LRAS* are vertical at the full-employment rate of output (Y_F in Exhibit 7).

Part (a) of **Exhibit 8** illustrates the impact of a change in aggregate demand within the polar assumptions of the Keynesian model. When aggregate demand is less than AD_2 (for example, AD_1), the economy will languish below potential capacity. Because prices and wages are inflexible downward, below-capacity output rates (Y_1, for example) and abnormally high unemployment will persist unless there is an increase in aggregate demand. When output is below its potential, any increase in aggregate demand (for example, the shift from AD_1 to AD_2) brings previously idle resources into the productive process at an unchanged price level. In this range, the Keynesian analysis essentially turns Say's Law (supply creates an equivalent amount of demand) on its head. In the Keynesian range, an increase in demand creates its own supply. Of course, once the economy's potential output constraint (Y_F) is reached, additional demand would merely lead to higher prices rather than to more output. Because both the *SRAS* and *LRAS* curves are vertical at capacity output, an increase in aggregate demand to AD_3 fails to expand real output.

When constructing models, we often make polar assumptions to illustrate various points. The Keynesian model is no exception. In the real world, prices will not be completely inflexible. Similarly, in the short run, unanticipated increases in demand will

EXHIBIT 7
Keynesian Aggregate
Supply Curves

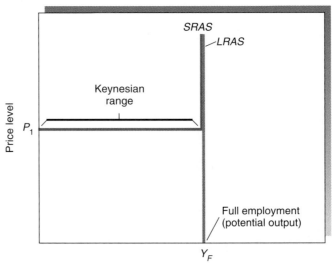

The Keynesian model theorizes that because of the downward inflexibility in wages and prices, the *SRAS* curve is flat for outputs less than potential GDP (Y_F). In this range, often referred to as the Keynesian range, output is entirely dependent on the level of aggregate demand. But once full employment is attained, real output rates beyond full employment are unattainable. Thus, both *SRAS* and *LRAS* are vertical at the economy's full-employment potential output.

EXHIBIT 8
AD-AS Presentation of Keynesian Model

Part (a) illustrates the extreme implications of the Keynesian model. When output is less than capacity (for example, Y_1), an increase in aggregate demand, shown by the shift from AD_1 to AD_2, will expand output without increasing prices. But increases in demand beyond AD_2 (like the shift to AD_3) lead only to a higher price level (P_2). Part (b) relaxes the assumption of complete price inflexibility and short-run output inflexibility beyond Y_F. Notice that in part (b) the *SRAS* curve turns from horizontal to vertical more gradually. Part (b) is more realistic.

(a) Polar assumption

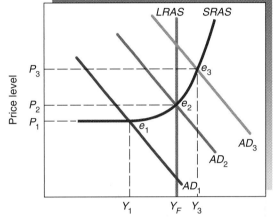

(b) Central implication

not lead solely to higher prices. Nevertheless, the Keynesian model implies an important point that is illustrated more realistically by part (b) of Exhibit 8. The horizontal segment of the *SRAS* curve is an oversimplification intended to reinforce the idea that changes in aggregate demand exert little impact on prices and substantial impact on output when an economy is operating well below capacity. *In other words, under conditions like those of the 1930s—when idle factories and widespread unemployment are rampant—an increase in aggregate demand will primarily affect output.*

Similarly, the vertical segment of the aggregate supply curve is a simplifying assumption meant to illustrate the concept that there is an attainable output rate beyond which increases in demand will lead almost exclusively to price increases (and only small increases in real output). *When aggregate demand is already quite strong (for example, AD_3), increases in aggregate demand will predictably exert their primary impact on prices rather than on output.*

THE MULTIPLIER

The multiplier occupies a central position in the Keynesian model. It focuses on the impact that changes in autonomous expenditures have on the level of income. Changes in autonomous expenditures—for example, an increase in the level of investment due to improved business expectations or an increase in net exports as the result of higher incomes abroad—will change the entire aggregate expenditure schedule and generally lead to an expansion in income even *greater* than the initial shift in expenditures. The **expenditure multiplier** is defined as the change in total income (equilibrium output) divided by the autonomous expenditure change that brought about the larger income.

The multiplier principle builds on the point that one individual's expenditure becomes the income of another. As we previously discussed, consumption expenditures are directly related to income—an increase in income (or wealth) will lead to an increase in consumption. Predictably, income recipients will spend a portion of their additional earnings on consumption. In turn, their consumption expenditures will generate additional income for others who will also spend a portion of it.

Expenditure multiplier
The ratio of the change in equilibrium output to the independent change in investment, consumption, or government spending that brings about the change. Numerically, the multiplier is equal to 1 *divided by* (1 − MPC) when the price level is constant.

Perhaps an example will illuminate the multiplier concept. Suppose an entrepreneur decided to undertake a $1 million investment project. Because investment is a component of aggregate demand, the project will increase demand directly by $1 million. This is not the entire story, however. The investment project will require plumbers, carpenters, masons, lumber, cement, and many other resources. The incomes of the suppliers of these resources will increase by $1 million. What will they do with this additional income? After setting aside (saving) a portion of this additional income, the resource suppliers will predictably spend a fraction of the additional income. They will buy more food, clothing, recreation, medical care, and thousands of other items. How will this spending influence the incomes of those who supply these products and services? Their incomes will increase, also. These people will save a portion of it and will spend some of it on current consumption. Their consumption spending will result in still more additional income for other goods and services suppliers.

The term *multiplier* is also used to indicate the number by which the initial investment would be multiplied to obtain the total increases in the economy's income. If the $1 million investment resulted in $4 million of additional income, the multiplier would be 4. The total increase in income would be four times the amount of the initial increase in spending. Similarly, if total income increased by $3 million, the multiplier would be 3.

The Size of the Multiplier

Marginal propensity to consume (MPC)
Additional current consumption divided by additional current disposable income.

The size of the multiplier depends on the proportion of the additional income that households choose to spend on consumption.[4] Keynes referred to this fraction as the **marginal propensity to consume (MPC)**. Mathematically:

$$\text{MPC} = \frac{\text{Additional consumption}}{\text{Additional income}}$$

For example, if your income increases by $100 and you increase your current consumption expenditures by $75 as a result, your marginal propensity to consume is 3/4, or 0.75. **Exhibit 9** illustrates why the size of the multiplier is dependent on the MPC. Suppose the MPC is equal to 3/4, meaning that consumers spend 75 cents of each additional dollar earned. Continuing with our previous example, we know that a $1 million investment

---

EXHIBIT 9
The Multiplier Principle

EXPENDITURE STAGE	ADDITIONAL INCOME (DOLLARS)	ADDITIONAL CONSUMPTION (DOLLARS)	MARGINAL PROPENSITY TO CONSUME
Round 1	1,000,000 ⟶	750,000	3/4
Round 2	750,000 ⟵⟶	562,500	3/4
Round 3	562,500 ⟵⟶	421,875	3/4
Round 4	421,875 ⟵⟶	316,406	3/4
Round 5	316,406 ⟵⟶	237,305	3/4
Round 6	237,305 ⟵⟶	177,979	3/4
Round 7	177,979 ⟵⟶	133,484	3/4
Round 8	133,484 ⟵⟶	100,113	3/4
Round 9	100,113 ⟵⟶	75,085	3/4
Round 10	75,085 ⟵⟶	56,314	3/4
All Others	225,253 ⟵⟶	168,939	3/4
Total	4,000,000	3,000,000	3/4

---

[4]For the purposes of simplicity when calculating the size of the multiplier, we will assume that all additions to income are either (1) spent on domestically produced goods or (2) saved. This assumption means that we are ignoring the impact of taxes and spending on imports as income expands via the multiplier process. At the conclusion of our analysis, we will indicate the significance of this assumption.

would initially result in $1 million of additional income in round 1. Because the MPC is 3/4, consumption would increase by $750,000 (the other $250,000 would flow into saving), and turn into other people's income in round 2. The recipients of the round 2 income of $750,000 would spend three-fourths of it on current consumption. Hence, their spending would increase income by $562,500 in round 3. Exhibit 9 illustrates the additions to income through other rounds. In total, income would increase by $4 million, given an MPC of 3/4. The multiplier is 4.

If the MPC had been greater, income recipients would have spent a larger share of their additional income on current consumption during each round. Thus, the additional income generated in each round would have been greater, increasing the size of the multiplier. There is a precise relationship between the MPC and the multiplier, in other words: The expenditure multiplier, *M,* is

$$M = \frac{1}{1 - \text{MPC}}$$

Exhibit 10 indicates the size of the multiplier for several different values of MPC.

Real-World Significance of the Multiplier

The multiplier is important in the Keynesian model because it explains why even small changes in investment, government, or consumption spending can trigger much larger changes in output. The multiplier magnifies the fluctuations in output and employment that emanate from autonomous changes in spending.

There are both positive and negative sides to the amplified effects. On the negative side, the multiplier means that a small fall in investment expenditures (perhaps due to a decline in business optimism) can lead to much larger changes in income. As a result, many Keynesians believe that the stability of a market economy is quite fragile and constantly susceptible to even modest disruptions. On the positive side, the multiplier shows how policy changes that provide only a small amount of demand stimulus can exert a sizeable impact and help direct an economy back to full employment.

It's important to keep in mind three points related to the multiplier's impact. *First, in addition to saving, leakages in the form of taxes and spending on imports will also reduce the size of the multiplier.* To keep things simple, we assumed throughout our analysis that all income was either saved or spent on domestically produced goods. Like saving, taxes and imports will siphon some of the additional income away from spending on domestic goods and services. These leakages from the flow of spending will dampen the effects of the multiplier. Therefore, the actual multiplier will be somewhat smaller than the simple expenditure multiplier of our analysis.

Second, it takes time for the multiplier to work. In the real world, several weeks or perhaps even months will be required for each successive round of spending. Only a

MPC	SIZE OF MULTIPLIER
9/10	10
4/5	5
3/4	4
2/3	3
1/2	2
1/3	1.5

EXHIBIT 10
A Higher MPC Means a Larger Multiplier

fraction of the multiplier effect will be observed quickly. Most researchers believe that only about one-half the total multiplier effect will be felt during the first six months following a change in expenditures.

Third, the multiplier implies that the additional spending brings idle resources into production, leading to additional real output rather than to increased prices. When unemployment is widespread, this is a realistic assumption. However, when there is an absence of abundant idle resources, the multiplier effect will be dampened by an increase in the price level.

APPLICATIONS IN ECONOMICS

Sports Stadiums, Development Subsidies, and the Multiplier

Many local governments have constructed or heavily subsidized sports stadiums, civic and arts centers, and even hotels, arguing that they will promote economic development and employment. The multiplier concept is often used to bolster these arguments. Proponents buttress their case by claiming, for example, that a $100 million project will promote additional spending of three or four times this amount, and thereby generate additional income and tax revenue for the financing of the project.

The construction of GABP (Great American Ball Park) is typical. This 42,036-seat baseball stadium is the home of the Cincinnati Reds. Opened in 2003, the facility cost $297 million, nearly all of which was financed with taxpayer funds generated by a half-cent increase in the local sales tax (the tax increase also paid for a new stadium for the Cincinnati Bengals football team).

Does the multiplier make projects like GABP more attractive? As you think about this, keep two points in mind: first, the multiplier applies only in the case of expenditures that otherwise would not have taken place. Economists refer to spending of this type as "exogenous expenditures." But was the $297 million spent on the stadium money that was just lying around? Probably not. The tax increase (and government borrowing) drained about $280 million from the pockets of local taxpayers. If the money hadn't been used to finance GABP, taxpayers would have used a substantial portion of these funds to purchase more food, housing, recreation, health care, and other items in the local economy. Clearly, this reduction in spending as the result of the higher taxes to finance the stadium is a partial offset against the spending for the construction of the new ballpark.

Second, if the multiplier is going to work its magic and expand real income, resources that would otherwise have been unemployed must be brought into the production process. Unless this is the case, the expansion in demand will merely lead to higher prices. At the time of GABP's construction, unemployment of construction workers in Cincinnati and other areas of the country was low. Given these conditions, a large portion of any increased demand derived from the stadium construction was bound to push prices upward, rather than expanding employment and real income.

What about the spending of people attending the games? Again, a substantial portion of this spending would likely have been spent on something else—on basketball and football games, movies, other forms of entertainment, and eating out, for example. The composition of spending is affected, but there is little reason to believe that there will be much impact on the overall level of expenditures in the city of Cincinnati. Of course, there will be *some* increase in local spending generated by those attending games from out of town. This spending will generate a multiplier effect for the local economy. However, Reds fans in the Cincinnati area may follow the team to other cities, and, as a result, spend less in Cincinnati. This would, at least partially, offset the additional spending in the Cincinnati area by those from out of town.

Several economists have examined the impact of sports teams and the construction of sports stadiums on economic activity. A recent survey of eight such studies concludes that there is no evidence that sports teams and facilities generate any additional economic growth.[1] This indicates that the multiplier for sports teams is zero.

The fact is, local government spending projects for sports, entertainment, and the arts are generally more about rent seeking—more about trying to exact favors from the government than economic development. All of us would like to have others help us pay for the things we want, or things that will increase the value of assets we own. But does it really help the economy? The answer is "No."

---

[1]See John Siegfried and Andrew Zimbalist, "The Economics of Sports Facilities and Their Communities," *Journal of Economic Perspectives*, Summer 2000, 95–114.

Do government expenditures on projects like the construction of the Great American Ball Park in Cincinnati, Ohio, exert a multiplier effect?

© GETTY IMAGES

KEYNESIAN VIEW OF THE BUSINESS CYCLE

Keynesian economists believe that a market economy, if left to its own devices, is unstable and likely to experience prolonged periods of recession. The Keynesian view emphasizes the destabilizing potential of autonomous changes in expenditures powered by the multiplier and changes in optimism. Suppose there is an increase in aggregate demand triggered by what appears to be a relatively minor disruption—for example, higher incomes abroad, an increase in consumer optimism, or a burst of business optimism generated by a new innovation. Keynesians believe that changes like these will often lead to an expansion in output that will feed on itself. The initial increase in demand, *magnified by the multiplier,* will lead to an expansion in employment and a rapid growth of income. In turn, the higher incomes will lead to additional consumption and strong business sales. Inventories will decline, and businesses will expand output (to rebuild inventories) and move investment projects forward as they become more optimistic about the future. Unemployment will decline to a low level as the economy experiences a boom.

Can this expansionary phase continue indefinitely? The answer is "No." Eventually, full-employment capacity will be reached. Constrained by the availability of both labor and machines, the growth rate of the economy will slow. The slower growth will dampen the optimism of business decision makers and cause them to cut back on fixed investments. In turn, the multiplier will magnify the impact of the change in investment. Thus, even a modest decline in investment spending will often lead to a substantial fall in output. As the economy slides into a recession, inventories will rise as businesses are unable to sell their goods because of the low level of demand. Employment will decline and workers will be laid off. As employment opportunities deteriorate, consumers will become more pessimistic and cut back on their purchases, particularly for those big-ticket items like automobiles and appliances. This will also reduce aggregate demand and cause the economy to plunge *deeper* into recession. When the plunge is severe, the economy might not recover for a prolonged period of time.

Keynes believed that this is what happened during the 1930s. Consumers did not spend much because their incomes had fallen, and they were extremely pessimistic about the future. Similarly, businesses did not produce much because there was little demand for their products. Investment came to a complete standstill because underutilized resources and capacity were abundantly available.

Wide fluctuation in private investment is the villain of Keynesian business cycle theory. An economic expansion accelerates into a boom because investment, amplified by the multiplier, stimulates other sectors of the economy. At the first sign of a slowdown, though, investment plans are sharply curtailed. The reduction in investment exerts a multiplier impact, leading to an even larger decline in aggregate demand. Workers are laid off, firms operate with excess capacity, and output falls below its potential. Eventually, machines will wear out and the capital stock will decline to a level consistent with the current level of income. At that point, *additional* investment will be necessary for replacement purposes. The new investment will stimulate additional output and employment, and start the cycle anew.

Keynesians believe that market economies will tend to sway back and forth between recession and boom. They have little confidence that changes in wages and interest rates will keep the economy on a path of steady growth.

EVOLUTION OF MODERN MACROECONOMICS
Major Insights of Keynesian Economics

Keynesian economics and the aggregate expenditure (*AE*) model dominated the thinking of macroeconomists for three decades following the Second World War. Three major insights of the Keynesian model stand out.

1. Market forces may fail to restore full employment quickly. In the classical model, wage and interest rate changes help restore the economy to its full-employment potential. But the Keynesian model theorizes that in the short run, wage rates may be inflexible, particularly in a downward direction. Furthermore, if substantial excess capacity is present and decision-makers are pessimistic about the future, lower interest rates may fail to stimulate additional investment. Under these circumstances, recessions may drag on for extended periods of time.

2. The responsiveness of aggregate supply to changes in demand will be directly related to the availability of unemployed resources. Keynesian analysis emphasizes that, when idle resources are present, output will be highly responsive to changes in aggregate demand. Conversely, when an economy is operating at or near its capacity, output will be much less sensitive to changes in demand. So the *SRAS* curve is relatively flat when an economy is well below capacity and relatively steep when the economy is operating near and beyond capacity (see Exhibit 8).

3. Fluctuations in aggregate demand are an important potential source of business instability. Abrupt changes in demand are a potential source of both recession and inflation. Policies that effectively stabilize aggregate demand—that minimize abrupt changes in demand—will substantially reduce economic instability.

The Diminished Popularity of the *AE* Model

As we have stressed, both Keynesian economics and the *AE* model were an outgrowth of the Great Depression. Keynesian analysis provides an explanation for what happened during the 1930s. However, other explanations are also possible. Many economists believe misguided economic policies, particularly monetary policy, contributed to the depth and duration of the Great Depression. According to this view, markets were unable to restore full employment within a reasonable length of time during the 1930s because policies that were adopted not only inadvertently hampered recovery, but actually depressed economic conditions. This monetary view of the business cycle will be presented in Chapters 14 and 15.

In recent years, the popularity of the Keynesian aggregate expenditure model has diminished. There are two major reasons for this. First, the model is unable to explain the simultaneous occurrence of inflation and high unemployment. In the *AE* model, aggregate expenditures are either too low (resulting in recession) or too high (leading to inflation). Thus, it is unable to explain the simultaneous presence of both—something that occurred in the United States during the 1970s.

The second factor contributing to the decline of the aggregate expenditure model is the stability of recent years. The *AE* model was designed to explain lengthy recessions—equilibrium at less than full employment—and the fragile nature of business stability. This was an important consideration in the aftermath of the Great Depression. But several of the expansions during the last four decades have been quite lengthy and the recessions have been relatively short, at least by the standards of the Great Depression. Just as the classical model appeared to have little relevance to the 1930s, a model that focuses on why market economies are constantly gyrating between inflationary booms and prolonged recessions seems out of place today.

The Hybrid Nature of Modern Macroeconomics

Modern macroeconomics is a hybrid, reflecting elements of both classical and Keynesian analysis as well as some unique insights from other areas of economics. With regard to the business cycle, the dominant view among economists today might be summarized in the following manner. As we discussed in the previous chapter, various shocks (unanticipated changes in *AD* or *AS*) can disrupt full-employment equilibrium and lead either to recessionary unemployment or to an inflationary boom in the short run. Furthermore, macroeconomic markets don't adjust instantaneously. In the short run, misperceptions about the current price level and "sticky" wages and prices can lead to output levels that differ from long-run equilibrium. This latter fact reflects the Keynesian view.

Most economists today believe that changes in real wages and interest rates will act as a stabilizing force, directing a market economy toward full employment. Of course, unexpected reductions in demand and adverse supply shocks will from time to time throw an economy into a recession. However, if the government doesn't aggravate the problem by implementing poorly designed policies, the economy will not spiral downward for prolonged periods of time. Falling real interest rates and wage rates will prevent that from happening. Most modern economists believe that the self-correcting mechanism of a market economy works more effectively than the early Keynesians thought. Furthermore, they believe that the impact of economic change is more complex than either the earlier classical or Keynesian economists realized. When the impact of a change is analyzed, it makes a difference whether the change is anticipated or unanticipated. It is also important whether people expect the change to be temporary or permanent. Today, both Keynesians and non-Keynesians build these factors into their analysis.

Finally, several key elements of modern macroeconomics are more easily visualized within the framework of the multimarket *AD-AS* model we developed in Chapters 9 and 10 than the *AE* model. The *AD-AS* model also makes it easier to understand and distinguish between long-run and short-run conditions. Put plainly, the classical model is a long-run equilibrium model, whereas the Keynesian aggregate expenditure model is a short-run, excess-capacity model. But the *AD-AS* model accounts for both the short and long run. It is more flexible, and it can be used to address a broader range of topics than either the classical or Keynesian models. As a result, it will be the primary tool we use as we learn about other macroeconomic issues.

LOOKING AHEAD

In the Keynesian model, full employment is dependent upon aggregate demand remaining at the proper level. Keynesian analysis helped explain what classical economics couldn't—the prolonged unemployment of the Great Depression. It also theorized that fiscal (tax and expenditure) policy could restore the economy to full employment. The following chapter will show specifically how governments use fiscal policy as a stabilization tool.

KEY POINTS

▼ Classical economists believed that production created an equivalent amount of current demand (Say's Law) and that flexible wages, prices, and interest rates would always lead to full employment. The Great Depression undermined the credibility of the classical view.

▼ The concept of planned aggregate expenditures is central to Keynesian analysis. In the Keynesian model, as income expands, consumption increases, but by a lesser amount than the expansion in income. Both planned investment and government expenditures are independent of income in the Keynesian model. Planned net exports decline as income increases.

▼ The Keynesian model theorizes that firms will produce the amount of goods and services they believe consumers, investors, governments, and foreigners (net exports) plan to buy. Equilibrium is present when planned total expenditures equal total output.

▼ When total expenditures are less than current output, firms will accumulate excess inventories that will cause them to cut back on future output and employment. On the other hand, when total expenditures are greater than output, inventories will fall, and firms will respond by expanding their output to restore their inventories to their normal levels.

▼ A key point of Keynesian economics is that equilibrium need not occur at the full-employment level of output. This is different than classical economics.

▼ Changes in aggregate expenditures are the catalyst of the Keynesian model. When an economy is operating below full-employment capacity, increases in aggregate expenditures lead to an expansion in both output and employment. Once capacity is reached, further expansions in expenditures lead only to higher prices. The Keynesian model highlights the importance of maintaining demand at a level consistent with full-employment equilibrium.

▼ The expenditure multiplier shows that increases in investment, government, and consumption spending will cause income (and output) to increase by some multiple of the initial increase in spending. (The increase in income and output will be more than the initial increase in spending, in other words.) The multiplier is the number by which the initial change in spending is multiplied to obtain the total amplified increase in income. The size of the multiplier increases with the marginal propensity to consume.

▼ There are three points to keep in mind when it comes to the power of the multiplier: (1) taxes and spending on imports will dampen the size of the multiplier; (2) it takes time for the multiplier to work; and (3) the amplified effect on real output is based on the assumption that the additional spending will bring idle resources into production without price changes.

▼ According to the Keynesian view of the business cycle, upswings and downswings tend to feed on themselves. During a downturn, business pessimism, declining investment, and the multiplier combine to plunge the economy deeper into recession. During an economic upswing, business and consumer optimism and expanding investment interact with the multiplier to propel the economy to an inflationary boom. The theory suggests that a market-directed economy, left to its own devices, will tend to fluctuate between economic recessions and inflationary booms.

▼ Modern macroeconomics incorporates elements of both Keynesian and classical economics. It also underscores the role people's expectations play in the economy, and why distinguishing between the short and long run is important.

CRITICAL ANALYSIS QUESTIONS

1. What determines the equilibrium rate of output in the Keynesian model? Explain why an equilibrium level of output will continue to persist. What did Keynes think caused the prolonged, high level of unemployment of the Great Depression?

*2. How will each of the following factors influence the consumption function?
   a. The expectation that consumer prices will rise more rapidly in the future
   b. Pessimism about future employment conditions
   c. Lower income taxes
   d. An increase in the interest rate
   e. A decline in stock prices
   f. A redistribution of income from older workers (age forty-five and over) to younger workers (under thirty-five)
   g. A redistribution of income from the wealthy to the poor

3. What do Keynesians think cause fluctuations in output? What must be done to maintain full-employment capacity?

*4. What is the multiplier principle? What determines the size of the multiplier? Does the multiplier make it more or less difficult to stabilize the economy? Explain.

5. In the Keynesian *AE* model, why does an increase in aggregate spending lead to an equal increase in real GDP as long as output is at less than full-employment capacity? What does this imply about the shape of the aggregate supply curve?

6. The Great Depression undermined the credibility of the classical view. Correspondingly, the high rates of inflation and unemployment during the 1970s undermined the Keynesian view. Can you explain why both of these phenomena occurred?

*7. How do declining real wages and resource prices restore full employment in the Keynesian model? If output is currently below the full-employment rate, what will direct the economy to full employment in the Keynesian model?

*8. Suppose that individuals suddenly decided to spend less on consumption and save more of their current income. Compare and contrast this change within the framework of the Keynesian *AE* and the *AD-AS* models.

9. Would an increase in federal spending on the space program generate a multiplier effect on the U.S. economy? What impact would the additional spending have in Houston, Huntsville, Florida's, Space Coast, and similar areas with a heavy concentration of space facilities? What impact would higher taxes to finance the additional spending have in other areas of the country?

*10. As the U.S. economy began to expand following the recessions of 1990–1991 and 2001, real GDP grew slowly during the first eighteen months of these recoveries. Why might a Keynesian economist expect real GDP to grow slowly during the initial phase of a recovery?

11. Economists often say that the *AE* model is most relevant in the short run, whereas the classical model is most relevant to the long run. In what sense is this true?

*12. In recent years, approximately 40 percent of the income of Canadians has been spent on imports. In the United States, spending on imports constitutes about 12 percent of income. Would you expect the size of the multiplier to be larger or smaller in Canada than in the United States? Explain.

13. Who is helped and who is hurt when local and regional governments raise taxes in order to finance stadiums for major-league sports teams? How do these subsidies influence the income of team owners and professional athletes? What impact do they have on income inequality? Indicate why you either support or oppose the subsidies.

14. The constructed stadium of the San Francisco Giants was financed privately. Will the multiplier effects of privately funded projects differ from those financed through taxes and government subsidies? Why or why not?

*15. The rate of output and planned expenditures for an economy are shown in the accompanying table.

Total Output (Real GDP in billions)	Planned Aggregate Expenditures (in billions)
$5,000	$5,250
5,500	5,500
6,000	5,750
6,500	6,000
7,000	6,250

a. If the current output rate is $5.0 trillion, what will tend to happen to business inventories, future output, and employment?

b. If the current output rate is $6.5 trillion, what will tend to happen to inventories, future output, and employment?

c. What is the equilibrium rate of income of this economy?

d. If the economy's full-employment rate of output is $6.0 trillion, will the rate of unemployment be high, low, or normal, assuming the current planned demand persisted into the future?

e. What would happen if there were an autonomous increase in investment of $250 billion?

*Asterisk denotes questions for which answers are given in Appendix B.

CHAPTER

12

Fiscal Policy

In the early stages of the Keynesian revolution, macroeconomists emphasized fiscal policy as the most powerful and balanced remedy for demand management. Gradually, shortcomings of fiscal policy became apparent. The shortcomings stem from timing, politics, macroeconomic theory, and the deficit itself.[1]

—Paul Samuelson,
Nobel laureate

Chapter Focus

■ How does fiscal policy affect aggregate demand? How does it affect aggregate supply?

■ What is the Keynesian view of fiscal policy? How do the crowding-out and new classical models modify the basic Keynesian analysis?

■ How difficult is it to time fiscal policy properly? Why is proper timing important?

■ Is there a synthesis view of fiscal policy? What are its major elements?

■ Are there supply-side effects of fiscal policy?

[1]Paul A. Samuelson and William D. Nordhaus, *Economics,* 15th ed. (New York: McGraw-Hill, 1995), 644.

A s we indicated in Chapter 9, fiscal policy involves the use of the government's spending and taxing authority. Until now, we have assumed that the government's fiscal policy remained unchanged. We are now ready to relax this assumption and investigate the effect of fiscal policy on output, prices, and employment. There is some disagreement among economists about both how fiscal policy works and its potential to improve the performance of a market economy. In fact, views on this topic have changed in recent decades. This chapter will cover four alternative fiscal policy models—the Keynesian, crowding-out, new classical, and supply-side models. We will consider how and why views on these models have changed in recent decades. The basic *AD-AS* macroeconomic model will be used to illustrate each of the fiscal policy perspectives.

We want to isolate the impact of changes in fiscal policy from changes in monetary policy. Thus, we will continue to assume that the monetary authorities maintain a constant supply of money. The next two chapters will focus on the conduct of monetary policy. ■

BUDGET DEFICITS AND SURPLUSES

Fiscal policy relates to the government's spending, taxing, and borrowing policies. It is one of the major tools that can be used to help promote the goals of full employment, price stability, and rapid economic growth. When the supply of money is constant, government expenditures must be financed with either (1) taxes and other revenues derived from the sale of services or assets or (2) borrowing.

When the government's revenues from taxes and sales are equal to its total expenditures, the government has a **balanced budget**. The budget need not be in balance, however. A **budget deficit** occurs when total government spending exceeds total government revenue from all sources. When this happens, the government must borrow funds to finance the excess of its spending relative to revenue. It borrows by issuing interest-bearing bonds that become part of what we call the national debt, the total amount of outstanding government bonds. Conversely, a **budget surplus** is present when the government's revenues exceed its total expenditures. The surplus allows the government to reduce its outstanding debt.

The federal budget is much more than a mere revenue and expenditure statement of a large organization. It is the primary tool of fiscal policy. Unlike private organizations, which are directed by the pursuit of income and profit, the federal government can alter its budget with an eye to influencing the future direction of the economy.

Changes in the size of the federal deficit or surplus are often used to gauge whether fiscal policy is stimulating aggregate demand or restraining it. It is important to note, however, that changes in the size of the deficit or surplus can have two different sources. *First, changes in the size of the deficit or surplus may merely reflect the state of the economy.* During a recession, tax revenues generally fall and expenditures on transfer programs increase because of the weak economic conditions. This will shift the budget toward a deficit—even with no changes in fiscal policy. Just the opposite will happen during the expansionary phase of the business cycle. Tax revenues will increase and transfer payments decline as the result of the rapid growth of income. This will shift the budget toward a surplus (or smaller deficit), even if there are no changes in fiscal policy. *Second, changes in the deficit or surplus may reflect* discretionary fiscal policy. Policy makers can institute deliberate changes in tax laws or government spending in order to alter the size of the budget deficit (or surplus). When we speak of "changes in fiscal policy," we are referring to changes of this type—deliberate changes in government expenditures or tax policy (or both) designed to affect the size of the budget deficit or surplus.

Balanced budget
A situation in which current government revenue from taxes, fees, and other sources is just equal to current government expenditures.

Budget deficit
A situation in which total government spending exceeds total government revenue during a specific time period, usually one year.

Budget surplus
A situation in which total government spending is less than total government revenue during a time period, usually a year.

Discretionary fiscal policy
A change in laws or appropriation levels that alters government revenues and/or expenditures.

THE KEYNESIAN VIEW OF FISCAL POLICY

Like economists prior to the time of Keynes, nearly all policy makers and business leaders in the 1950s thought that the government should balance its budget. Keynesian economists, though, were highly critical of this view. Keynesians argued that the federal budget should be used to promote a level of aggregate demand consistent with the full-employment rate of output. Beginning with the Kennedy administration, the Keynesian view began to exert a major impact on budgetary policy.

How might policy makers use the budget to stimulate aggregate demand? First, an increase in government purchases of goods and services will directly increase aggregate demand. As the government spends more on highways, flood-control projects, education, and national defense, for example, these expenditures will increase demand in the goods and services market. Second, changes in tax policy will also influence aggregate demand. For example, a reduction in personal taxes will increase the current disposable income of households. As their after-tax income rises, people will spend more on consumption. In turn, this increase in consumption will stimulate aggregate demand. Similarly, a reduction in business taxes increases after-tax profitability, which will stimulate both business investment and aggregate demand.

Expansionary fiscal policy
An increase in government expenditures and/or a reduction in tax rates such that the expected size of the budget deficit expands.

When an economy is operating below its potential capacity, Keynesians believe the government should institute **expansionary fiscal policy**. In other words, the government should increase its purchases of goods and services or cut taxes or both. Of course, this policy will increase the government's budget deficit. To finance the enlarged budget deficit, the government will have to borrow from either private domestic sources or foreigners.[2]

Exhibit 1 illustrates the case for expansionary fiscal policy when an economy is experiencing abnormally high unemployment caused by deficient aggregate demand. Initially, the economy is operating at e_1. Output is below potential capacity, Y_F, and un-

EXHIBIT 1
Expansionary Fiscal Policy to Promote Full Employment

Here we illustrate an economy operating in the short run at Y_1, below its potential capacity of Y_F. There are two routes to a long-run, full-employment equilibrium. First, policy makers could wait for lower wages and resource prices to reduce costs, increase supply to $SRAS_3$, and restore equilibrium at E_3. Keynesians believe this market-adjustment method will be slow and uncertain. Alternatively, expansionary fiscal policy could stimulate aggregate demand (shift it to AD_2) and guide the economy to E_2.

[2]Alternatively, the government could borrow from its central bank—the Federal Reserve Bank in the United States. However, as we will see in the following chapter, this method of financing a budget deficit would expand the money supply. Since we want to differentiate between fiscal and monetary effects, we must hold the supply of money constant. So for now, we assume that the government deficit must be financed by borrowing from private sources.

employment exceeds its natural rate. As we discussed in Chapter 10, if there is no change in policy, abnormally high unemployment and excess supply in the resource market will eventually reduce real wages and other resource prices, which will lower costs and direct the economy toward a full-employment equilibrium like E_3. In addition, interest rates would decline as the result of the weak demand for investment. In turn, the lower interest rates will stimulate spending on interest-rate-sensitive items, like automobiles, housing, and consumer durables. This will increase aggregate demand and also help direct the economy back to full employment.

However, as noted in the previous chapter, Keynesians believe that this self-corrective process will work slowly, if at all. They argue that wages and prices are inflexible, particularly in a downward direction. Neither do they believe that lower interest rates will stimulate much additional spending in a recessionary economy dominated by consumer pessimism and excess production capacity. Thus, they have little confidence that lower wages and interest rates will restore full employment, at least not very quickly.

Rather than depending on the economy's self-corrective mechanism, Keynesians recommend government action. During a recession, Keynesians favor a shift to a more expansionary fiscal policy—an increase in government spending or a reduction in taxes, or some combination of the two. Put another way, they advocate a deliberate increase in the budget deficit in order to stimulate aggregate demand. Furthermore, they argue that the multiplier process will magnify the initial increase in spending. Suppose that the government holds taxes constant and increases its spending on highways and school construction by $20 billion. The additional spending will enhance the incomes of those undertaking the construction by $20 billion. As these individuals use a portion of this income to buy consumer goods, they will provide additional demand stimulus. Thus, Keynesians expect that the total increase in aggregate demand will be substantially greater than the initial $20 billion increase in government purchases.

When an economy is operating below its potential capacity, the Keynesian prescription calls for expansionary fiscal policy—a deliberate change in expenditures and/or taxes that will increase the size of the government's budget deficit. An appropriate dose of expansionary fiscal policy, if timed properly, will stimulate aggregate demand (shift the curve to AD_2 in Exhibit 1) and guide the economy to full-employment equilibrium (E_2).

The Keynesian view also provides a fiscal policy remedy for inflation. Suppose that an economy is experiencing an inflationary economic boom as the result of excessive aggregate demand. As **Exhibit 2** illustrates, in the absence of a change in policy, the strong demand (AD_1) will push up wages and other resource prices. In time, the higher resource prices will increase costs, reduce aggregate supply (from $SRAS_1$ to $SRAS_3$), and lead to a

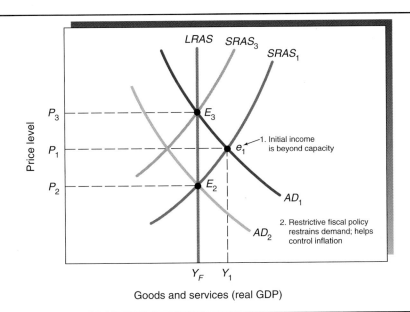

EXHIBIT 2
Restrictive Fiscal Policy to Combat Inflation

Strong demand such as AD_1 will temporarily lead to an output rate beyond the economy's long-run potential (Y_F). If the high level of demand persists, it will lead to a long-run equilibrium (E_3) at a higher price level. However, restrictive fiscal policy could restrain demand to AD_2 (or better still, prevent demand from expanding to AD_1 in the first place) and thereby guide the economy to a noninflationary equilibrium (E_2).

The first American to win the Nobel Prize in Economics, Paul Samuelson played a central role in the development and acceptance of Keynesian economics in the 1950s and 1960s. Through the years, his views regarding the effectiveness of fiscal policy have gradually changed (see the chapter-opening quotation). A professor of economics at MIT for more than four decades, Samuelson's *Collected Scientific Papers* encompasses five lengthy volumes.[1]

[1]Paul Samuelson, *Collected Papers of Paul Samuelson* (Cambridge: MIT Press, 1966).

Restrictive fiscal policy
A reduction in government expenditures and/or an increase in tax rates such that the expected size of the budget deficit declines (or the budget surplus increases).

higher price level (P_3). Keynesians argue, however, that **restrictive fiscal policy** can be used to reduce aggregate demand (shift it to AD_2) and guide the economy to a noninflationary equilibrium (E_2). A reduced level of government purchases will diminish aggregate demand directly. Alternatively, higher taxes on households and businesses could be used to dampen consumption and private investment. The restrictive fiscal policy—a spending reduction and/or an increase in taxes—will shift the government budget toward a surplus (or smaller deficit). *Keynesians believe that a shift toward a more restrictive fiscal policy is the proper prescription with which to combat inflation generated by excessive aggregate demand.*

The Keynesian revolution challenged the view that a responsible government should constrain spending within the bounds of its revenues. Rather than balancing the budget annually, Keynesians stressed the importance of countercyclical policy, *that is, policy designed to "counter" or offset fluctuations in aggregate demand.* When an economy is threatened by a recession, the government should shift to a more expansionary fiscal policy, increasing spending or reducing taxes in a manner that will increase the size of the budget deficit. On the other hand, fiscal policy should become more restrictive—the budget should be shifted toward a smaller deficit or larger surplus—in response to a threat of inflation. According to the Keynesian view, fluctuations in aggregate demand are the major source of economic disturbances. Moreover, wise use of fiscal policy can help stabilize and maintain demand at or near the full-employment rate of output.

Countercyclical policy
A policy that tends to move the economy in an opposite direction from the forces of the business cycle. Such a policy would stimulate demand during the contraction phase of the business cycle and restrain demand during the expansion phase.

FISCAL POLICY AND THE CROWDING-OUT EFFECT

By the 1960s, the Keynesian view was widely accepted by both economists and policy makers. At that time, it was generally believed that changes in the size of the budget deficit exerted a powerful impact on aggregate demand and output. More recently, however, economists have noted that there are secondary effects that tend to weaken the potency of fiscal policy.

When the size of the budget deficit increases, the government will have to borrow more funds to finance its deficit. The higher level of government borrowing will increase the demand for funds in the loanable funds market and place upward pressure on interest rates. How will the higher real interest rates influence private spending? Consumers will reduce their purchases of interest-rate-sensitive goods, such as automobiles and consumer durables. A higher interest rate will also increase the opportunity cost of investment projects. Businesses will postpone spending on plant expansions, heavy equipment, and capital improvements. Residential-housing construction and sales will also be hurt. Thus, the higher real interest rates caused by the larger deficit will retard private spending. Economists refer to this squeezing out of private spending by a deficit-induced increase in the real interest rate as the **crowding-out effect**.

Crowding-out effect
A reduction in private spending as a result of higher interest rates generated by budget deficits that are financed by borrowing in the private loanable funds market.

The crowding-out effect suggests that budget deficits will have less effect on aggregate demand than the basic Keynesian model implies. Because financing the deficit pushes up interest rates, budget deficits will tend to retard private spending, particularly spending on investment and consumer durables. This reduction in private spending as the result of higher interest rates will at least partially offset additional spending emanating from the deficit. Thus, the crowding-out effect implies that expansionary fiscal policy will have little, if any, effect on demand, output, and employment.

Furthermore, as private investment is crowded out by the higher interest rates, the output of capital goods will decline. As a result, the future stock of capital (for example, heavy equipment, other machines, and buildings) available to future workers will be smaller than it would have been otherwise. In other words, deficits will have an adverse effect on capital formation and tend to retard the growth of productivity and income.

Keynesians believe that, although crowding-out may occur when an economy is at or near full employment, it is unlikely to be very important during a recession, particularly a serious one. When widespread unemployment is present during a serious recession, Keynesians argue that an increase in government purchases financed by a deficit will exert a strong multiplier effect on output, employment, and real income. As the incomes of households increase, people will save more, and this will make it possible for the government to finance its enlarged deficits without much upward pressure on interest rates. Moreover, when applied during a recession, the demand stimulus may improve business profit expectations and thereby stimulate additional private investment.

The implications of the crowding-out analysis are symmetrical. Restrictive fiscal policy will "crowd in" private spending. If the government increases taxes and/or reduces its spending, the budget will shift toward a surplus (or smaller deficit). As a result, the government's demand for loanable funds will decrease, placing downward pressure on the real interest rate. The lower real interest rate will stimulate additional private investment and consumption. So the fiscal policy restraint will be at least partially offset by an expansion in private spending. *As the result of this crowding-in, restrictive fiscal policy may be largely ineffective as a weapon against inflation.*

Do Global Financial Markets Minimize the Crowding-Out Effect?

Today, financial capital can rapidly move in and out of countries. Suppose the budget deficit of the United States increases and additional borrowing by the U.S. Treasury pushes real interest rates upward, just as the crowding-out theory implies. Think about how investors will respond to this situation. The higher real interest yields on bonds and other financial assets will attract funds from abroad. In turn, this inflow of financial capital will increase the supply of loanable funds and thereby moderate the rise in real interest rates in the United States.[3]

At first glance, the crowding-out effect would appear to be weakened because the inflow of funds from abroad will moderate the upward pressure on domestic interest rates. Closer inspection, though, reveals that this will not be the case. Foreigners cannot buy more U.S. bonds and financial assets without "buying" more dollars. Thus, additional bond purchases will increase the demand for U.S. dollars (and the supply of foreign currencies) in the foreign exchange market—the market that coordinates exchanges of the various national currencies. As foreigners demand more dollars to buy financial investments in the United States, this will increase the demand for the dollar, causing it to appreciate. The appreciation of the dollar will make imports cheaper for Americans. Simultaneously, it will make U.S. exports more expensive for foreigners. Predictably, the United States will import more and export less. Thus, net exports will decline (or net imports increase), causing a reduction in aggregate demand. Therefore, while the inflow of capital from abroad will moderate the increase in the interest rate and the crowding-out of private domestic investment, it will also reduce net exports and thereby retard aggregate demand.

---

[3]For students who are unsure about the demand for and supply of loanable funds, this would be a good time to review the topic within the framework of our basic macro model outlined by Exhibit 1 in Chapter 9. As this exhibit indicates, household saving and the inflow of financial capital from abroad supply loanable funds. In turn, private investment and borrowing by the government to finance budget deficits generate the demand for these funds.

EXHIBIT 3
A Visual Presentation of the Crowding-Out Effect in an Open Economy

An increase in government borrowing to finance an enlarged budget deficit will put upward pressure on real interest rates. This will retard private investment and aggregate demand. In an open economy, the higher interest rates will also increase the inflow of capital from abroad, which will cause the dollar to appreciate and net exports to decline. Thus, the higher interest rates will trigger reductions in both private investment and net exports, which will weaken the expansionary impact of a budget deficit.

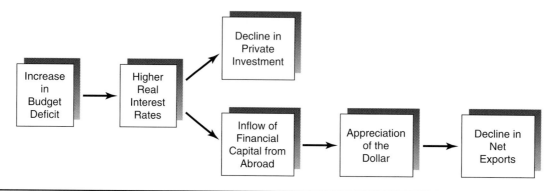

Exhibit 3 summarizes the crowding-out view of budget deficits in an open economy. The additional government borrowing triggered by the budget deficits will cause interest rates to rise, and this will lead to two secondary effects that will dampen the stimulus impact of the deficits. First, the higher interest rates will reduce private investment, which will directly restrain aggregate demand. Second, the higher interest returns will also attract an inflow of foreign capital, which will moderate the increase in interest rates, but it will also cause the dollar to appreciate. In turn, the appreciation of the dollar will reduce both net exports and aggregate demand. *According to the crowding-out theory, these two factors will largely, if not entirely, offset the stimulus effects of a larger budget deficit.*

THE NEW CLASSICAL VIEW OF FISCAL POLICY

Thus far, we have implicitly assumed that the current consumption and saving decisions of taxpayers are unaffected by budget deficits. This may not be the case. Robert Lucas (University of Chicago), the 1995 Nobel laureate, Thomas Sargent (New York University), and Robert Barro (Harvard University) have been leaders among a group of economists arguing that budget deficits imply higher future taxes and that taxpayers will reduce their current consumption just as they would have if the taxes had been collected during the current period. Because this position has its foundation in classical economics, these economists and their followers are referred to as **new classical economists**.

In the Keynesian model, a tax cut financed by borrowing will increase the current income of households, and they respond by increasing their consumption. New classical economists argue that this analysis is incorrect because it ignores the impact of the higher future tax liability implied by the budget deficit and the interest payments required to service the additional debt. Rather than increasing their consumption in response to a larger budget deficit, new classical economists believe that households will save all or most of their increase in disposable income so they will be able to pay the higher future taxes implied by the additional government debt. Thus, new classical economists do not believe that budget deficits will stimulate additional consumption and aggregate demand.

The new classical economists stress that debt financing simply substitutes higher future taxes for lower current taxes. Thus, budget deficits affect the timing of the taxes, but not their magnitude. A mere change in the timing of taxes will not alter the wealth of households. Therefore, there is no reason to believe that current consumption will change when current taxes are cut and government debt and future taxes are increased by an equivalent amount. This view that taxes and debt financing are essentially equivalent is

New classical economists
Economists who believe that there are strong forces pushing a market economy toward full-employment equilibrium and that macroeconomic policy is an ineffective tool with which to reduce economic instability.

known as **Ricardian equivalence**, after the nineteenth-century economist, David Ricardo, who initially developed the idea.[4]

Perhaps an illustration will help explain the underlying logic of the new classical view. Suppose you knew that your taxes were going to be cut by $1,000 this year, but that next year they were going to be increased by $1,000 plus the interest on that figure. Would this year's $1,000 tax cut cause you to increase your consumption spending? New classical economists argue that it would not. They believe that most people would recognize that their wealth is unchanged and would therefore save most of this year's tax cut to be better able to pay next year's higher taxes. Correspondingly, new classical economists argue that when debt is substituted for taxes, people will recognize that the additional debt means higher future taxes and that therefore they will save more in order to pay them.

Exhibit 4 illustrates the implications of the new classical view on the potency of fiscal policy. Suppose that the fiscal authorities issue $50 billion of additional debt in order to cut taxes by an equal amount. The government borrowing increases the demand for loanable funds (D_1 shifts to D_2 in part b of Exhibit 4) by $50 billion. If taxpayers didn't think that higher future taxes would result from the debt, they would expand their consumption in response to the lower taxes and the increase in their current disposable income. Under these circumstances, aggregate demand in the goods and services market would expand to AD_2 (part a). In the new classical model, though, this will not be the case. Realizing that the $50 billion in additional debt will mean higher future taxes, taxpayers will maintain their initial level of consumption spending and use the tax cut to increase their savings in order to generate the additional income required to pay the higher future taxes. Because consumption is unchanged, aggregate demand also remains constant (at AD_1). At the same time, the additional saving (to pay the implied increase in future taxes) allows the government to finance its deficit without an increase in the real interest rate.

According to the new classical view, changes in fiscal policy have little effect on the economy. Debt financing and larger budget deficits will not stimulate aggregate demand. Neither will they affect output and employment. Similarly, the real interest rate is unaffected by deficits since people will save more in order to pay the higher future taxes. In the new classical model, fiscal policy is completely impotent.

Ricardian equivalence
The view that a tax reduction financed with government debt will exert no effect on current consumption and aggregate demand because people will fully recognize the higher future taxes implied by the additional debt.

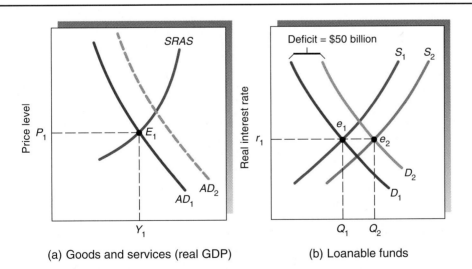

(a) Goods and services (real GDP) (b) Loanable funds

EXHIBIT 4
The New Classical View—Higher Expected Future Taxes Crowd Out Private Spending

New classical economists emphasize that budget deficits merely substitute future taxes for current taxes. If households did not anticipate the higher future taxes, aggregate demand would increase to AD_2. However, demand remains unchanged at AD_1 when households fully anticipate the future increase in taxes (part a). Simultaneously, the additional saving to meet the higher future taxes will increase the supply of loanable funds to S_2 and allow the government to borrow the funds to finance its deficit without pushing up the real interest rate (part b). In this model, fiscal policy exerts no effect. The real interest rate, real GDP, and level of employment all remain unchanged.

[4]See Robert J. Barro, "The Ricardian Approach to Budget Deficits," *Journal of Economic Perspectives* (Spring 1989): 37–44; and John J. Seater, "Ricardian Equivalence," *Journal of Economic Literature* (March 1993): 142–90.

You may be wondering which of the three theories is right. Each of them has both merits and shortcomings. Each may be valid under some conditions, but not others. Later in the chapter, we will return to this issue.

FISCAL POLICY CHANGES AND PROBLEMS OF TIMING

If fiscal policy is going to reduce economic instability, changes in policy must stimulate the economy during a recession and restrain it during an inflationary boom. But proper timing of fiscal policy is not an easy task. There are three major reasons that this is so.

First, a change in fiscal policy will require legislative action. But the political process moves slowly. This is particularly true in a country like the United States that has a number of checks and balances built into its political system.[5] Congressional committees must meet, hear testimony, and draft legislation. Key legislators may choose to delay action in an attempt to amend the legislation so that it benefits their own constituents and supporters. Furthermore, a majority of the lawmakers must be convinced that the legislation will not adversely affect their particular constituents and supporters. Predictably, this will all require a significant amount of time.

Second, a change in policy will not immediately impact the macroeconomy. Even after a policy change is adopted, another six to twelve months will generally pass before it will have much impact on the economy. If government expenditures are going to be increased, time will be required for competitive bids to be submitted and government contracts granted. Contractors might not be able to begin work right away. Although a tax cut might exert some stimulus more quickly, typically several months will pass before the primary effects of the cut are felt throughout the economy.

Third, because of these delays, if fiscal policy is going to exert a stabilizing influence, policy makers need to know what economic conditions are going to be like twelve to eighteen months in the future. But this is a big problem because our ability to forecast when

Congress and the president are in charge of fiscal policy. Given the difficulties involved in forecasting the future direction of the economy, and the inevitable delays associated with political action, it is unlikely that changes in fiscal policy will be an effective stabilization tool.

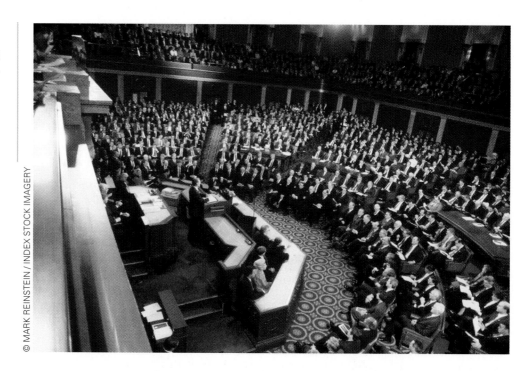

© MARK REINSTEIN / INDEX STOCK IMAGERY

---

[5]The time required for the institution of a change in fiscal policy may be shorter under a parliamentary political system, such as that of Canada or the United Kingdom. This is highly likely to be the case if a single party has a parliamentary majority.

the economy is about to dip into a recession or experience an economic boom is extremely limited. Therefore, in a world of dynamic change and unpredictable events, macroeconomic policy making is a little bit like lobbing a ball at a target that often moves in unforeseen directions. Clearly, policy-making errors will occur.

Exhibit 5 illustrates the implications of the difficulties involved in the proper timing of fiscal policy. Suppose policy makers attempt to use expansionary fiscal policy to stimulate aggregate demand during an economic downturn. If forecasting a recession and adopting a policy change take a substantial amount of time, the economy's self-correcting mechanism may already have restored full employment by the time the policy begins to stimulate aggregate demand. This will lead to excessive demand and inflation. Conversely, restrictive fiscal policy to cool an overheated economy can cause a recession if aggregate demand declines prior to the policy having an effect.

In the real world, a discretionary change in fiscal policy is like a two-edged sword— it has the potential to do harm as well as good. If timed correctly, it will reduce economic instability. If timed incorrectly, however, it will increase rather than reduce economic instability.

Automatic Stabilizers

Fortunately, there are a few fiscal programs that tend automatically to apply demand stimulus during a recession and demand restraint during an economic boom. Programs of this type are called **automatic stabilizers**. They are automatic in that, without any new legislative action, they tend to increase the budget deficit (or reduce the surplus) during a recession and increase the surplus (or reduce the deficit) during an economic boom.

Automatic stabilizers
Built-in features that tend automatically to promote a budget deficit during a recession and a budget surplus during an inflationary boom, even without a change in policy.

Goods and services (real GDP)

EXHIBIT 5
Why Proper Timing of Fiscal Policy Is Difficult

Here we consider an economy that experiences shifts in aggregate demand that are not easy to forecast. Initially, the economy is in long-run equilibrium (E_0) at price level P_0 and at output Y_0. At this output, only the natural rate of unemployment is present. However, an investment slump and business pessimism result in an unanticipated decline in aggregate demand (to AD_1). Output falls and unemployment increases. After a time, policy makers institute expansionary fiscal policy to shift aggregate demand back to AD_0. By the time fiscal policy begins to exert its primary effect, though, private investment has recovered and decision makers have become increasingly optimistic about the future. So aggregate demand is already, on its own, shifting back to AD_0. Thus, the expansionary fiscal policy "overshifts" aggregate demand to AD_2 rather than AD_0. Prices rise because the economy is now overheated. Unless the expansionary fiscal policy is reversed, wages and other resource prices will eventually increase, shifting SRAS to the left, pushing the price level still higher (to P_3). Alternatively, suppose an investment boom disrupts the equilibrium. The increase in investment shifts aggregate demand to AD_2, placing upward pressure on prices. Policy makers respond by increasing taxes and cutting government expenditures. By the time the restrictive fiscal policy exerts its primary impact, though, investment returns to its normal rate. As a result, the restrictive fiscal policy overshifts aggregate demand to AD_1 and throws the economy into a recession. Because fiscal policy does not work instantaneously and dynamic factors are constantly influencing private demand, proper timing of fiscal policy is not an easy task.

The major advantage of automatic stabilizers is that they institute countercyclical fiscal policy without the delays associated with legislative action. They minimize the problem of proper timing, in other words. When unemployment is rising and business conditions are slow, these stabilizers automatically reduce tax revenues collected and increase government spending, giving the economy a shot in the arm. On the other hand, automatic stabilizers help apply the brakes to an economic boom, increasing tax revenues and decreasing government spending. Three of these built-in stabilizers deserve specific mention: unemployment compensation, the corporate profit tax, and the progressive income tax.

Unemployment Compensation

When an economy begins to dip into a recession, the government will pay out more money in unemployment benefits as the number of laid-off and unemployed workers expands. Simultaneously, the receipts from the employment tax that finances the unemployment compensation system will decline because fewer workers are paying into the system. Therefore, this program will automatically run a deficit during a business slowdown. In contrast, during an economic boom, the tax receipts from the program will increase because more people are now working, and the amount paid out in benefits will decline because fewer people are unemployed. Thus, the program will automatically tend to run a surplus during good times. So without any change in policy, the unemployment compensation program has the desired countercyclical effect on aggregate demand.[6]

The Corporate Profit Tax

Tax studies show that the corporate profit tax is the most important countercyclical automatic stabilizer because corporate profits are highly sensitive to cyclical conditions. During a recession, corporate profits decline sharply, and so, too, do corporate tax payments. In turn, the decline in tax revenues will enlarge the size of the budget deficit. In contrast, when the economy is expanding, corporate profits typically increase much more rapidly than wages, income, or consumption. This increase in corporate profits will result in a rapid increase in the "tax take" from the business sector during the expansion phase of the business cycle. Thus, corporate tax payments will go up during an expansion and fall rapidly during a contraction, even though no new legislative action has been instituted.

The Progressive Income Tax

When incomes grow rapidly, the average personal income tax liability of individuals and families increases. With rising incomes, more people will find their income above the "no tax due" cutoff. Others will jump up into higher tax brackets. Therefore, during an economic expansion, personal income tax revenues increase more rapidly than income, because income will grow at a more incremental pace. Other things constant, the budget moves toward a surplus (or smaller deficit), even though the economy's tax rate structure is unchanged. On the other hand, when incomes decline, many individuals will be taxed at lower rates or not at all. Income tax revenues will fall more rapidly than income, automatically enlarging the size of the budget deficit during a recession.

HOW POLITICS HAMPERS THE EFFECTIVENESS OF FISCAL POLICY

In addition to the practical problems that make it difficult to time fiscal policy changes appropriately, the structure of political incentives also reduces the likelihood that fiscal

---

[6]Although unemployment compensation has the desired countercyclical effect on demand, it also reduces the incentive to accept available employment opportunities. Research in this area indicates that the existing unemployment compensation system increases the length of job search by unemployed workers and thereby increases the long-run natural (normal) unemployment rate.

policy will be instituted in a stabilizing manner. As our analysis of public choice stressed, politicians—at least those who survive for very long—will be attracted to policies that will help them win the next election. Predictably, legislators will be delighted to spend money on programs that benefit their constituents but reluctant to raise taxes since they impose a visible cost on voters. Because politicians are rewarded for providing programs that benefit their constituencies and punished for raising taxes, they are far more inclined to spend than to tax; they will find deficits substantially more attractive than surpluses. As a result, it is unrealistic to expect that fiscal policy will be instituted evenhandedly. Instead, politicians will be highly agreeable to legislation that calls for additional spending and lower taxes, but quite reluctant to cut spending and increase taxes. Because of this, deficits will be far more common than surpluses. Furthermore, politicians will be far more likely to find a reason to shift toward fiscal expansion than to institute fiscal restriction, even when a more restrictive policy is needed to deal with an inflationary boom.

FISCAL POLICY AS A STABILIZATION TOOL: A MODERN SYNTHESIS

During the 1960s, the basic Keynesian view was widely accepted. Fiscal policy was thought to be highly potent. Furthermore, it was widely believed that political decision makers, with the assistance of their economic advisers, were fully capable of instituting discretionary fiscal policy changes in a manner that would help stabilize the economy. During the 1970s and 1980s, however, fiscal policy and its efficacy as a stabilization tool were analyzed and hotly debated by economists. A synthesis view has emerged from that debate. Most macroeconomists—both Keynesian and non-Keynesian—now accept the following four elements of the modern synthesis view.

1. *Proper timing of discretionary fiscal policy is both difficult to achieve and crucially important.* Given our limited ability to forecast ups and downs in the business cycle, and the political delays that inevitably accompany a change in fiscal policy, the effectiveness of discretionary fiscal policy as a stabilization tool is limited. In addition, the incentive structure confronted by elected political officials reduces the likelihood that fiscal policy changes will be instituted in a stabilizing manner. Therefore, most macroeconomists now place less emphasis on the use of fiscal policy as a stabilization tool. (*Note:* The chapter-opening quotation from Paul Samuelson, a long-time Keynesian, highlights this point.)

2. *Automatic stabilizers reduce fluctuations in aggregate demand and help direct the economy toward full employment.* Since they are not dependent on legislative action, automatic stabilizers are able consistently to shift the budget toward a deficit during a recession and toward a surplus during an economic boom. They add needed stimulus during a recession and act as a restraining force during an inflationary boom. Although some economists question their potency, nearly all agree that they exert a stabilizing influence.

3. *Fiscal policy is much less potent than the early Keynesian view implied.* The current debate among macroeconomists concerning the impact of fiscal policy during normal times is not whether crowding-out takes place, but rather how it takes place. The crowding-out and new classical models highlight this point. Both models indicate that there are side effects of budget deficits that will substantially, if not entirely, offset their impact on aggregate demand. In the crowding-out model, higher real interest rates and a decline in net exports as the result of currency appreciation reduce private demand and offset the expansionary effects of budget deficits. In the new classical model, higher anticipated future taxes lead to the same result. Both models indicate that fiscal policy will have little, if any, effect on current aggregate demand, employment, and real output during normal economic times.

4. Each of the three demand-side models of fiscal policy is valid under some circumstances but not others. During normal times, when there is a strong demand for loanable funds, the crowding-out view is largely correct. Under these conditions, budget deficits will lead to higher interest rates and appreciation in the foreign exchange value of the domestic currency, which will tend to offset the expansionary effects of the budget deficits, just as the crowding-out model implies. However, when the demand for loanable funds is weak, as it is likely to be during a recession, deficits will not raise interest rates much, and expansionary fiscal policy can stimulate demand and increase output as the Keynesian model implies. Finally, when it is announced that a tax cut is temporary or that taxpayers will be given a "one-time-only" tax rebate, the key assumption of the new classical model is likely to be valid. For a tax cut of this type, households can be reasonably sure that although taxes are lower this year, they will be higher in the future. Predictably, households will save a large portion of this year's tax cut, so that they will be in a better position to pay the higher future taxes. In this case, the budget deficit will exert little impact on either interest rates or aggregate demand, just as the new classical model implies. Thus, depending upon the current conditions, each of the three demand-side models can add to our understanding of how fiscal policy works.

THE SUPPLY-SIDE EFFECTS OF FISCAL POLICY

So far, we have focused on the potential demand-side effects of fiscal policy. However, when fiscal changes alter tax rates, they influence people's incentives to work, invest, and use resources efficiently. Thus, tax changes also influence aggregate supply. Prior to 1980, macroeconomists generally ignored the supply-side effects of changes in tax rates, thinking they were of little importance. **Supply-side economists** challenged this view. The supply-side argument was central to the tax rate reductions of the 1980s, and it also affected tax legislation passed in both 2001 and 2002.

Supply-side economists
Modern economists who believe that changes in marginal tax rates exert important effects on aggregate supply.

From a supply-side viewpoint, the marginal tax rate is crucially important. As we discussed in Chapter 4, the marginal tax rate determines the breakdown of a person's additional income between tax payments on the one hand and personal income on the other. Lower marginal tax rates mean that individuals get to keep a larger share of their additional earnings. For example, reducing the marginal tax rate from 40 percent to 30 percent allows individuals to keep 70 cents of each additional dollar they earn, instead of only 60 cents. In turn, the lower tax rates and accompanying increase in take-home pay provide them with a greater incentive to earn. Supply-side economists believe that these incentive effects are important. Most significantly, they argue that high marginal rates—for example, rates of 50 percent or more—seriously discourage people from working harder and engaging in productive activities.

Tax policy changes affect the supply side of the economy differently than the demand side of the economy, though. On the demand side, lower taxes stimulate spending by consumers and increase aggregate demand. *On the supply side, lower taxes encourage people to work more, increasing aggregate supply.*

Exhibit 6 graphically depicts the impact of a supply-side tax cut, one that reduces marginal tax rates. The lower marginal tax rates increase aggregate supply because the new incentive structure encourages taxpayers to earn more and use resources more efficiently. If taxpayers think the cut will be permanent, both long- and short-run aggregate supply (*LRAS* and *SRAS*) will increase. Real output and income will expand. As real income expands, aggregate demand will also increase (shift to AD_2). If the lower marginal rates are financed by a budget deficit, though, aggregate demand may increase by a larger amount than aggregate supply, putting upward pressure on the price level.

Supply-side economics should not be viewed as a short-run countercyclical tool. It will take time for people to react to the tax cuts and move their resources out of investments designed to lower their taxes and into higher-yielding, production-oriented activities. The full positive effects of lower marginal tax rates will not be observed until both labor and capital markets have time to adjust fully to the new incentive structure. *Clearly, supply-side economics is a long-run, growth-oriented strategy, not a short-run stabilization tool.*

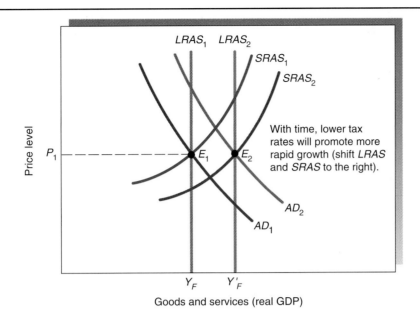

EXHIBIT 6
Tax Rate Effects and Supply-Side Economics

Here we illustrate the supply-side effects of lower marginal tax rates. The lower marginal tax rates increase the incentive to earn and use resources efficiently. Because these are long-run as well as short-run effects, both *LRAS* and *SRAS* increase (shift to the right). Real output expands. In turn, the higher income levels accompanying the expansion in real output will stimulate aggregate demand (shift it to AD_2).

Why Do High Tax Rates Retard Output?

There are three major reasons that high tax rates are likely to retard the growth of output. First, as we have explained, high marginal tax rates discourage work effort and productivity. When marginal tax rates soar to 55 percent or 60 percent, people get to keep less than half of what they earn, so they tend to work less. Some (for example, those with a working spouse) will drop out of the labor force. Others will simply work fewer hours. Still others will decide to take longer vacations, forgo overtime opportunities, retire earlier, or forget about pursuing that promising but risky business venture. In some cases, high tax rates will even drive highly productive citizens to other countries where taxes are lower. In recent years, high-tax countries such as Belgium, France, Sweden, and even Canada have experienced an outflow of highly successful professionals, business entrepreneurs, and athletes.

    Second, high tax rates will adversely affect the rate of capital formation and the efficiency of its use. When tax rates are high, foreign investors will look for other places to put their money, and domestic investors will look for investment projects abroad where taxes are lower. In addition, domestic investors will direct more of their time and effort into hobby businesses (like collecting antiques, raising horses, or giving golf lessons) that may not earn much money but are enjoyable and have tax-shelter advantages. This will divert resources away from projects with higher rates of return but fewer tax-avoidance benefits. As a result, scarce capital will be wasted and resources channeled away from their most productive uses.

    Third, high marginal tax rates encourage people to substitute less-desired tax-deductible goods for more-desired nondeductible goods. High marginal tax rates make tax-deductible expenditures cheap for people in high tax brackets. Since the personal cost (but not the cost to society) is cheap, these taxpayers will spend more money on pleasurable, tax-deductible items, like plush offices, professional conferences held in favorite vacation spots, and various other fringe benefits (say a company-paid luxury automobile and business entertainment). Because purchasing tax-deductible goods lowers their taxes, people will often buy them even though they do not value them as much as it costs to produce them. Business and professional people are often able to engage in tax-avoidance activities like these.

How Important Are the Supply-Side Effects?

There is considerable debate among economists about the strength of the supply-side incentive effects. Critics of supply-side economics argue that the tax cuts of the 1980s reduced real federal tax revenues and led to large budget deficits, without having much

APPLICATIONS IN ECONOMICS

Have Supply-Side Economists Found a Way to Soak the Rich?

Under a progressive rate structure, marginal tax rates rise with income level. The highest marginal tax rates are imposed on those with the largest incomes. The supply-side view stresses that high marginal rates have such a negative effect on the incentive to earn (and the taxable income base) that reducing these high rates can actually increase the revenues collected from high-income taxpayers. The Laffer Curve analysis presented in Chapter 4 highlights this point. The Laffer Curve indicates that as tax rates are increased from zero, rate increases will increase the revenue

derived from the tax. Eventually, however, higher and higher rates will lead to a maximum revenue point, and rate increases beyond this level will actually reduce the revenue collected. Thus, when tax rates are exceedingly high, more revenue could be collected from these high-income taxpayers if their rates were reduced.

Since 1960, the personal income tax rate imposed on high-income earners has varied considerably. What effect have the rate changes had on the revenue collected from them? **Exhibit 7** presents data on the share of the personal income tax collected from the top one-half percent of income recipients. When the top marginal tax rate was sliced from 91 percent to 70 percent by the Kennedy-Johnson tax cut of 1964, the share of the personal income

EXHIBIT 7
How Have Changes in Marginal Tax Rates Affected the Share of Taxes Paid by the Rich?

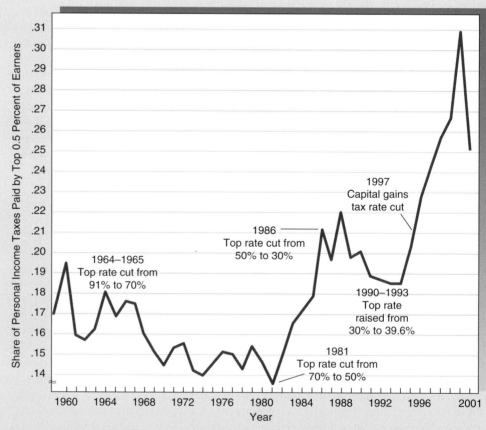

The accompanying graph shows the share of the personal income taxes paid by the top one-half percent of earners from 1960 to 2001. During this period, there were four major reductions in marginal tax rates. First, the Kennedy-Johnson tax cut reduced the top rate from 91 percent in 1963 to 70 percent in 1965. During the Reagan years, the top rate was reduced from 70 percent in 1980 to 50 percent in 1982 and to approximately 30 percent in 1986. In 1997, the capital gains tax rate was sliced from 28 to 20 percent. Interestingly, the share of the tax bill paid by these "super-rich" earners increased after each of these tax cuts. These findings suggest that, at least for this group of high-income recipients, strong supply-side effects accompanied the rate cuts. Perhaps surprising to some, these high-income taxpayers paid a larger portion of the tax bill when the top marginal rate was less than 40 percent (1986–2001) than when it was 70 percent or more.

APPLICATIONS IN ECONOMICS

tax paid by these earners rose from 16 percent to 18 percent. In contrast, as inflation pushed more and more taxpayers into higher brackets during the 1970s, the share paid by the top one-half percent declined. When the tax cuts of the 1980s once again reduced the top rates, the share paid by the top one-half percent climbed to more than 20 percent of the total. As the top marginal rate was increased in 1991 and again in 1993, there was little change in the share of taxes paid by the top group. Beginning in 1997, the tax rate on income from capital gains was cut from 28 percent to 20 percent. This rate reduction was accompanied by a substantial increase in revenues derived from the capital gains taxes and personal income taxes collected from high-income taxpayers.[1]

Supply-side economists argue that high marginal tax rates, like those of the 1960s and 1970s, are counterproductive; they reduce productive activity without raising any appreciable revenue. Since 1986, the top marginal personal income tax rate in the United States has been less than 40 percent; prior to 1981, it was 70 percent or higher. Nonetheless, those with high incomes are now paying more. In fact, the top one-half percent of earners has paid more than 25 percent of the personal income tax every year since 1997. This is well above the 14 percent to 19 percent collected from these taxpayers in the 1960s and 1970s, when much higher marginal rates were imposed on the rich. Perhaps the supply-siders have found a way to "soak the rich"—keep their marginal tax rates relatively low.[2]

[1]In 1996, capital gains income was $261 billion, which yielded tax revenues of $66 billion. By 2000, income due to capital gains had risen to $652 billion, with corresponding tax revenues of $129 billion.

[2]For additional evidence on the impact of tax rates on both output and revenue, see Lawrence Lindsey, *The Growth Experiment: How the New Tax Policy Is Transforming the U.S. Economy* (New York: Basic Books, 1990). For a critical analysis of supply-side policies, see Joel Slemro (ed.), *Does Atlas Shrug: The Economic Consequences of Taxing the Rich* (New York: Russell Sage Foundation, 2000).

impact on economic growth. This suggests that the supply-side effects are not very strong. Defenders of the supply-side position respond by noting that rate reductions in both the 1960s and the 1980s resulted in impressive growth and lengthy economic expansions. They also stress that the supply-side response in top income brackets—where lower rates have the largest incentive effects—is particularly strong.[7] See the boxed feature "Have Supply-Side Economists Found a Way to Soak the Rich?"

Supply-side critics also point out that most elasticity estimates indicate that a 10 percent change in after-tax wages increases the quantity of labor supplied by only 1 or 2 percent. This suggests that changes in tax rates exert only a small effect on the amount of labor supplied. Supply-side advocates, however, argue that these estimates reflect only the adjustments that occur over relatively short time periods. In the long run, they claim that tax cuts increase the labor supply by much more. Recent work by Nobel laureate Edward Prescott at Arizona State University supports this view. Prescott used marginal tax differences between France and the United States to estimate the labor supply response in the long run. Prescott found that the elasticity of labor supply in the long run was substantially greater than in the short run. He also found that France's higher tax rates explained why the labor supply in that country is nearly 30 percent less than it is in the United States.[8]

Although researchers continue to study and debate the impact of changes in tax rates, there is considerable evidence that the supply-side view has influenced tax policy throughout the world. During the last two decades, there has been a dramatic shift away from high

[7]The incentive effects are greater in the upper brackets because a similar percentage rate reduction will have a greater impact on take-home pay in this area. For example, if a 70 percent marginal tax rate is cut to 50 percent, take-home pay per additional dollar of earnings will increase from 30 cents to 50 cents, a 67 percent increase in the incentive to earn. On the other hand, if a 14 percent marginal rate is reduced to 10 percent, take-home pay per dollar of additional earnings will increase from 86 cents to 90 cents, only a 5 percent increase in the incentive to earn.

[8]Prescott concludes, *I find it remarkable that virtually all of the large difference in labor supply between France and the United States is due to differences in tax systems. I expected institutional constraints on the operation of labor markets and the nature of the unemployment benefit system to be more important. I was surprised that the welfare gain from reducing the intratemporal tax wedge is so large.* (Prescott, 2002, 9)

See Edward C. Prescott, "Richard T. Ely Lecture: Prosperity and Depression," *American Economic Review,* Papers and Proceedings 92, no. 2 (May 2002): 1–15.

marginal tax rates. In 1980, 62 countries had a personal income tax with a top marginal rate of 50 percent or more; by 2002, only 13 countries imposed such a high rate. Many countries with exceedingly high rates cut them substantially. For example, in 1980 the top marginal rate in the United Kingdom was 83 percent; in 2002 it was 40 percent. In Italy, the top rate was 75 percent in 1980, but only 47 percent in 2002. In Germany, the top rate was 65 percent in 1980, but it was 51 percent in 2002. By 2002, the top marginal rate of virtually every country with a personal income tax was at least 10 percentage points lower than it was in 1980. Moreover, there is virtually no support among either political leaders or economists for a return to the 50 percent, 60 percent, and higher marginal tax rates of the early 1980s.

THE FISCAL POLICY OF THE UNITED STATES

The accompanying Thumbnail Sketch summarizes the major schools of economic thought with regard to expansionary fiscal policy. In general, the effects of restrictive fiscal policy would be just the opposite. As we previously mentioned, economists use changes in the size of the deficit or surplus, rather than the absolute amount, to determine whether fiscal policy is shifting toward expansion or restriction. Movement toward a larger deficit (or a smaller surplus) relative to GDP indicates that fiscal policy is becoming more expansionary. Conversely, a reduction in the deficit as a share of GDP (or increase in the surplus) would imply that a more restrictive fiscal policy has been implemented.

Exhibit 8 shows federal expenditures, revenues, and deficits in the United States as a share of GDP since 1960. Although the federal government ran deficits throughout most of the 1960s and 1970s, the deficits were small relative to the size of the economy, except during the recessions of 1970 and 1974–1975. Budget deficits have generally increased during recessions (indicated by the shaded bars) and shrunk during expansions. However, the changes in the size of the deficit over the business cycle have been primarily the result of automatic stabilizers rather than discretionary use of fiscal policy. Major changes in discretionary spending motivated by economic conditions have generally come too late to have much countercyclical effect. For example, this was the case with the 1968 tax increase that was designed to combat inflation during the Vietnam War. It was also the case with the antirecession tax rebate of 1975.

Business-cycle conditions are not the only factor underlying fiscal policy. Sometimes external conditions like the threat of war have a strong impact on spending and revenue levels. This has been the case during the last couple of decades. Fiscal policy during the first half of the 1980s was driven by a supply-side tax cut and higher defense spending. These two factors, along with the severe recession of 1982, pushed the federal deficit to

THUMBNAIL SKETCH

The Impact of Expansionary Fiscal Policy—A Summary of Four Views

1. **The basic Keynesian view:** An increase in government spending and/or a reduction in taxes will be magnified by the multiplier process and lead to a substantial increase in aggregate demand. When an economy is operating below capacity, real output and employment will also increase substantially.

2. **Crowding-out view:** Expansionary fiscal policy will exert little or no effect on aggregate demand and employment because borrowing to finance the budget deficit will push up interest rates and crowd out private spending, particularly investment. In an open economy, the higher interest rates will lead to an inflow of capital, a currency appreciation, and a decline in net exports.

3. **New classical view:** Expansionary fiscal policy will exert little or no effect on aggregate demand and employment because households will anticipate the higher future taxes that might result from the debt and reduce their spending (and increase their saving) in order to pay them. Like current taxes, debt (future taxes) will crowd out private spending.

4. **Supply-side view:** Lower marginal tax rates will increase the incentive to earn (produce) and improve the efficiency of resource use, leading to an increase in aggregate supply (real output) in the long run.

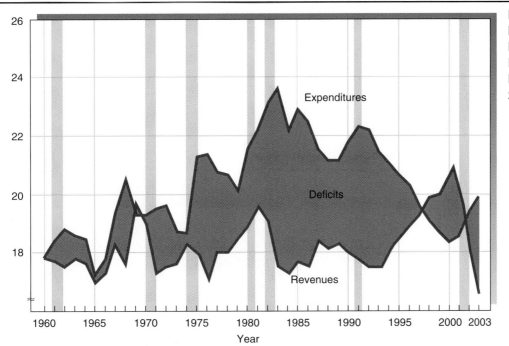

EXHIBIT 8
Federal Government Expenditures and Revenues as a Percentage of GDP, 1960–2003

Except during recessions (indicated by shaded bars), budget deficits were small as a share of the economy prior to 1980. After a period of persistently large deficits during the 1980s, the federal deficit shrank, and by the late 1990s a surplus was present. Deficits reemerged in 2002. Increased government spending on defense and homeland security, coupled with revenue reductions due to a recession and the Bush tax cuts, led to the recent deficits.

Source: Economic Report of the President, 2004, tables B-1 and B-79.

peacetime highs in the mid-1980s. The deficit declined as the economy grew rapidly during the latter half of the 1980s, but increased once again during the recession and sluggish growth of the early 1990s.

Although increases in defense spending expanded the deficit in the 1980s, the opposite was true during the 1990s. Following the collapse of communism and the end of the Cold War, defense spending was cut sharply. This helped reduce the deficit and eventually led to a budget surplus at the end of the decade. Modest tax increases in both 1990 and 1993 and the strong growth throughout most of the decade also contributed to the budget surpluses of 1998–2001. The budgetary situation again changed dramatically following the terrorist attacks of September 11, 2001. The combination of the 2001 recession and sluggish recovery, increases in defense spending, and the Bush administration's tax cut quickly moved the budget from surplus to deficit.

It is interesting to compare and contrast fiscal policy during and following the recessions of 1990–1991 and 2001. During the earlier recession, the administrations of both George H. W. Bush and Bill Clinton raised taxes. In both cases, the tax increases were based on the premise that higher taxes would shrink the budget deficit, reduce government borrowing, and lower interest rates. These tax increases were grounded in the crowding-out theory. In contrast, taxes were cut and government expenditures increased during and following the recession of 2001. As Exhibit 8 illustrates, the budget shifted from surplus to deficit. Thus, the fiscal policy response to the 2001 recession reflected the Keynesian perspective. Even though the fiscal policy responses to the two recessions were essentially polar opposites, there's little evidence that they made much difference. Both recessions were mild and relatively short (8 to 12 months). In both cases, the initial recovery phase was rather sluggish. Even though the fiscal policies differed substantially, the two recessions' similarities suggest that fiscal policy is not very potent. At least this is the case during relatively normal times.

Defense expenditures increased sharply during the 1980s, declined substantially during the 1990s after the collapse of communism, and then increased once again following the September 11, 2001, terrorism attacks. These fluctuations had a major impact on the size of the federal deficit.

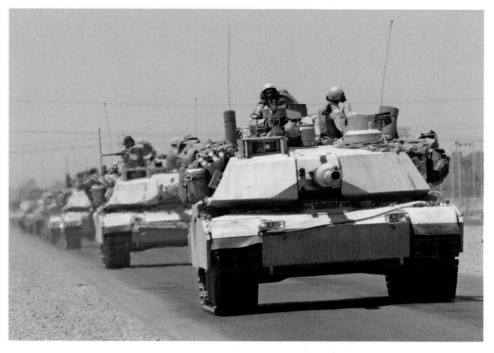

RADU SIGHETI/REUTERS/LANDOV

It is also interesting to compare fiscal policy during the 1980s with that of the 1990s. Propelled by both the Reagan tax cuts and defense buildup, fiscal policy was highly expansionary during the 1980s. As Exhibit 8 shows, the budget deficit was approximately 5 percent of GDP during 1982–1986. In spite of this expansionary fiscal policy, the inflation rate fell from the double-digit levels of 1979–1980 to 4 percent in 1983. As the economy rebounded from the 1982 recession, inflation remained in check, and the recovery was both strong and lengthy, lasting nearly eight years.

In contrast with the 1980s, fiscal policy was restrictive in the 1990s. Between 1994 and 2000, federal expenditures declined as a share of GDP, and a large budget deficit was transformed into a modest surplus. As during the 1980s, the expansion of the 1990s was both strong and lengthy. Thus, in spite of the differences in fiscal policy between the two decades, the performance of the economy was quite similar. These results do not indicate that fiscal policy—either expansionary or restrictive—exerts a strong effect on either aggregate demand or real output. In that respect, they are more consistent with the crowding-out and new classical theories than the Keynesian view.

During the last four decades, we have pretty much come full circle with regard to fiscal policy. In the 1960s, most economists thought that fiscal policy was highly potent and that it could be used successfully to smooth the business cycle. Few now adhere to that view. Confidence in the ability of Congress and the president to institute fiscal policy in a countercyclical manner has waned. There is also greater awareness of offsetting secondary effects—the factors highlighted by both the crowding-out and new classical models. Thus, most economists now believe that fiscal policy exerts only a modest effect on aggregate demand, at least during normal times.

LOOKING AHEAD

If fiscal policy is either impotent or difficult to employ effectively, then monetary policy—the other major stabilization weapon—becomes more important. We are now ready to integrate the monetary system into our analysis. Chapter 13 will focus on the operation of the banking system and the factors that determine the supply of money. In Chapter 14, we will analyze the impact of monetary policy on real output, interest rates, and the price level.

KEY POINTS

▼ The federal budget is the primary tool of fiscal policy. Discretionary fiscal policy encompasses deliberate changes in the government's spending and tax policies. It is designed to alter the size of the budget deficit and thereby influence the overall level of economic activity.

▼ According to the Keynesian view, fluctuations in aggregate demand are the major source of economic instability. Rather than balancing the budget annually, Keynesians believe that fiscal policy should reflect business cycle conditions. During a recession, fiscal policy should become more expansionary (a larger deficit should be run). During an inflationary boom, fiscal policy should become more restrictive (shift toward a budget surplus).

▼ The crowding-out model indicates that expansionary fiscal policy will lead to higher real interest rates and less private spending, particularly for investment. In an open economy, the higher interest rates will also lead to the following secondary effects: an inflow of capital, appreciation of the dollar, and a reduction in net exports. The crowding-out theory implies that these secondary effects will largely offset the demand stimulus of expansionary fiscal policy. The secondary effects of restrictive fiscal policy will also render it impotent.

▼ The new classical model stresses that financing government spending with debt rather than taxes changes the timing, but not the level, of taxes. According to this view, people will expect higher future taxes, which will lead to more saving and less private spending. This will offset the expansionary effects of the deficit.

▼ Changes in fiscal policy must be timed properly if they are going to exert a stabilizing influence on an economy. The ability of policy makers to time fiscal policy changes in a countercyclical manner is reduced by (1) the inability of the political process to act rapidly, (2) the time lag between when a policy change is instituted and when it affects the economy, and (3) inability to forecast the future direction of the economy.

▼ The problem of proper timing is less severe because of automatic stabilizers—forces that stimulate the economy during a recession and restrain it during a boom, even though no legislative action has been taken.

▼ The major points of the modern synthesis view of fiscal policy as a stabilization tool are: (1) Proper timing of discretionary fiscal policy is both difficult to achieve and crucially important; (2) automatic stabilizers reduce the fluctuation of aggregate demand and help promote economic stability; (3) fiscal policy is much less potent than the early Keynesians thought; and (4) each of the three demand-side models of fiscal policy is valid under some circumstances but not others.

▼ When fiscal policy changes marginal tax rates, it influences aggregate supply by altering the attractiveness of productive activity relative to leisure and tax avoidance. Other things being constant, lower marginal tax rates will increase aggregate supply. Supply-side economics should be viewed as a long-run strategy, not a countercyclical tool.

▼ Fiscal policy is often influenced by external factors. During the 1980s, defense expenditures increased substantially and large budget deficits resulted. Following the collapse of communism, defense spending fell sharply during the 1990s, shifting the budget toward a surplus. In the aftermath of September 11, 2001, spending on defense and homeland security increased sharply and large budget deficits again were incurred. Even though fiscal policy was expansionary during the 1980s and restrictive during the 1990s, both decades were characterized by a lengthy economic expansion and strong economic growth.

CRITICAL ANALYSIS QUESTIONS

1. Suppose that you are a member of the Council of Economic Advisers. The president has asked you to prepare a statement on the question, "What is the proper fiscal policy for the next 12 months?" Prepare such a statement, indicating (a) the current state of the economy (that is, the unemployment rate, growth in real income, and rate of inflation) and (b) your fiscal policy suggestions. Should the budget be in balance? Explain the reasoning behind your suggestions.

*2. What is the crowding-out effect? How does it modify the implications of the basic Keynesian model with regard to fiscal policy? How does the new classical theory of fiscal policy differ from the crowding-out model?

3. From a stabilization standpoint, why is proper timing of a change in fiscal policy important? Is it easy to time fiscal policy changes properly? Why or why not?

*4. What are automatic stabilizers? Explain their major advantage.

5. Outline the supply-side view of fiscal policy. How does this view differ from the various demand-side theories? Would a supply-side economist be more likely to favor a $500 tax credit or an equivalent reduction in marginal tax rates? Why?

*6. According to the Keynesian view, what fiscal policy actions should be taken if the unemployment rate is high and current GDP is well below the economy's potential output rate?

7. Are discretionary changes in fiscal policy likely to be instituted in a manner that will help smooth the ups and downs of the business cycle? Why or why not?

*8. "If we set aside our reluctance to use fiscal policy as a stabilization force, it is quite easy to achieve full employment and price stability. When output is at less than full employment, we run a budget deficit. If inflation is a problem, we run a budget surplus. Quick implementation of proper fiscal policy will stabilize the economy." Evaluate this statement.

9. Suppose that the government provides each taxpayer with a $1,000 tax rebate financed by issuing additional Treasury bonds. Outline alternative views that predict how this fiscal action will influence interest rates, aggregate demand, output, and employment.

*10. Some people argue that the growth of output and employment in the 1980s was the result of the large budget deficits. As one politician put it, "Anyone could create prosperity if he wrote $200 billion of hot checks every year." Evaluate this statement. If stimulating aggregate demand created the prosperity, what would you expect to happen to the rate of inflation? Did this happen during the 1980s?

11. During the 1990s, the federal budget moved from a deficit to a surplus. What factors accounted for this change? Were the budget surpluses of the late 1990s good for the economy? Would it have been better to have reduced taxes and balanced the budget during 1999–2000? Why or why not?

12. Marginal tax rates were cut substantially during the 1980s, and although rates were increased in the early 1990s, the marginal rates applicable in the highest income brackets were still well below the top rates of the 1960s and 1970s. How did the lower rates of the 1980s and 1990s affect the share of taxes paid by high-income taxpayers? Were the lower rates of the 1980s and 1990s good or bad for the economy? Discuss.

*13. If the impact on tax revenues is the same, does it make any difference whether the government cuts taxes by (a) reducing marginal tax rates or (b) increasing the personal exemption allowance? Explain.

14. Does fiscal policy have a strong impact on aggregate demand? Did the large budget deficits of the 1980s lead to excessive aggregate demand? Did the budget surpluses of the late 1990s restrain aggregate demand? Discuss.

*15. How do persistently large budget deficits affect capital formation and the long-run rate of economic growth? Do the proponents of the Keynesian, crowding-out, and new classical theories agree on the answer to this question? Discuss.

16. Review the chapter-opening quotation by Paul Samuelson. Professor Samuelson mentions four shortcomings of fiscal policy as a stabilization tool: (a) timing, (b) politics, (c) macroeconomic theory, and (d) the deficit itself. Explain why each of these four factors reduces the effectiveness of fiscal policy as a stabilization tool.

---

*Asterisk denotes questions for which answers are given in Appendix B.

Money and the Banking System

Chapter Focus

- What is money? How is the money supply defined?

- What is a fractional reserve banking system? How does it influence the ability of banks to create money?

- What are the major functions of the Federal Reserve System?

- What are the major tools with which the Federal Reserve controls the supply of money?

- How are financial innovations and other changes affecting the nature of money? What will money be like in the future?

Money is whatever is generally accepted in exchange for goods and services—accepted not as an object to be consumed but as an object that represents a temporary abode of purchasing power to be used for buying still other goods and services.

—Milton Friedman[1]

[1]Milton Friedman, *Money Mischief: Episodes in Monetary History* (New York: Harcourt Brace Jovanovich, 1992), 16.

The simple macroeconomic model we have developed so far has four major markets: (1) the goods and services market, (2) the resources market, (3) the loanable funds market, and (4) the foreign exchange market. When people make exchanges in any of these markets, they generally use money. Money is used to purchase all types of goods, services, physical assets like houses, and financial assets like stocks and bonds. This chapter focuses on the nature of money, how the banking system works, and how the **central bank**—the Federal Reserve System in the United States—controls the supply of money. ▪

Central bank
An institution that regulates the banking system and controls the supply of a country's money.

WHAT IS MONEY?

Money is the item commonly used to pay for goods, services, assets, and outstanding debts. (See the chapter-opening quotation by Milton Friedman.) Paradoxically, most modern money has no intrinsic worth. In other words, if we as a society didn't agree among ourselves that it's valuable, in and of itself it would be worth very little. Nonetheless, most of us would like to have more of it. Why? Because money is an asset that performs three basic functions: it serves as a medium of exchange, it provides a means of storing value for future use, and it is used as an accounting unit.

Money as a Medium of Exchange

Medium of exchange
An asset that is used to buy and sell goods or services.

Money is one of the most important inventions in human history because of its role as a **medium of exchange**. Money simplifies and reduces the costs of transactions. Think what it would be like to live in a barter economy—one without money, where goods were traded for goods. If you wanted to buy a pair of jeans, for example, you would first have to find someone willing to trade you the jeans for your labor services or something else you were willing to supply. Such an economy would be highly inefficient.

Money "oils the wheels" of trade and makes it possible for each of us to specialize in the supply of those things that we do best and easily buy the many goods and services we want. It frees us from cumbersome barter procedures.

Money is the item commonly used to buy and sell things. During the Second World War, prisoners of war used cigarettes as money in POW camps.

© BETTMAN/CORBIS

At various times in the past, societies have used gold, silver, beads, seashells, and other commodities as a medium of exchange. However, when a commodity is used as money, people will employ scarce resources (resources perhaps better used elsewhere) to produce more of that particular commodity. Because of this, the opportunity cost of commodity-based money is high. Here's why. Think about how much it costs to create a thousand dollar bill: just a cent or two, perhaps. But if gold bars were used instead of bills as money, think about how many of them a society would have to produce to facilitate even a small amount of trade. This would also prevent much of the gold in the economy from being used for other purposes.

When societies use something as money that costs little or nothing to produce, more scarce resources, like precious metals and so forth, are available to produce other goods and services. Thus, most modern nations use **fiat money**—money with no intrinsic value. Checking account deposits are nothing more than accounting numbers. Coins have some intrinsic value as metal, but in most cases this value is considerably less than their value as money. Why is fiat money valuable? Its value is based on the confidence of the people who use it. People are willing to accept fiat money because they know it can be used to purchase real goods and services. Governments that issue fiat money often designate it as "legal tender," meaning it is acceptable for the payment of debts.

Money as a Store of Value

Money is also a financial asset—a method of storing value for use in the future. Put another way, it provides readily available purchasing power for dealing with an uncertain future. Thus, most people hold some of their wealth in the form of money. Moreover, it is the most **liquid** of all assets. It can be easily and quickly transformed into other goods at a low transaction cost, usually without an appreciable loss in value.

However, there are some disadvantages of using money as a **store of value**. The value of a unit of money—a dollar, for example—is measured in terms of what it will buy. Its value, therefore, is inversely related to the price level in the economy. When inflation rises, the purchasing power of money declines—as does its usefulness as a store of value. This imposes a cost on people holding money.

Other assets, like land, houses, stocks, or bonds, also serve as a store of value, but they aren't as liquid as money. It will take time to locate an acceptable buyer for a house, a plot of land, or an office building. Stocks and bonds are quite liquid—they can usually be sold quickly for only a small commission—but they are not readily acceptable as a direct means of payment.

Money as a Unit of Account

Money also serves as a **unit of account**. Just as we use yards or meters to measure distance, we use units of money to measure the exchange value and costs of goods, services, assets, and resources. The value (and cost) of movie tickets, personal computers, labor services, automobiles, houses, and numerous other items is measured in units of money. Money serves as a common denominator for the expression of both costs and benefits. If consumers are going to spend their income wisely, they must be able to compare the costs of a vast array of goods and services. Prices measured in units of money help them make such comparisons. Similarly, sound business decisions require cost and revenue comparisons among vastly different productive services. Resource prices and accounting procedures measured in money units facilitate this task.

HOW THE SUPPLY OF MONEY AFFECTS ITS VALUE

The main thing that makes money valuable is the same thing that generates value for other commodities: demand relative to supply. People demand money because it reduces the cost of exchanges. When the supply of money is limited relative to the demand, money will become more valuable. Conversely, when the supply of money is large relative to demand, it will become less valuable.

Fiat money
Money that has neither intrinsic value nor the backing of a commodity with intrinsic value; paper currency is an example.

Liquid asset
An asset that can be easily and quickly converted to purchasing power.

Store of value
An asset that will allow people to transfer purchasing power from one period to the next.

Unit of account
A unit of measurement used by people to post prices and keep track of revenues and costs.

If the purchasing power of money is to remain stable over time, the supply of money must be limited. If the supply of money grows more rapidly than the growth in real output of goods and services in the economy, prices will rise. In layman's terms, "too much money is chasing too few goods."

When government authorities rapidly expand the supply of money, it becomes less valuable in exchange and is virtually useless as a store of value. The rapid growth in the supply of money in Germany following the First World War provides a dramatic illustration of this point. During the period 1922–1923, the supply of German marks increased by 250 percent in some months. The German government was printing money almost as fast as the printing presses would run. Since money became substantially more plentiful in relation to goods and services, it quickly lost its value. As a result, an egg cost 80 billion marks and a loaf of bread 200 billion. Workers picked up their wages in suitcases. Shops closed at the lunch hour to change price tags. The value of money had eroded. More recently (in the 1980s and 1990s), Argentina, Bolivia, Brazil, Israel, Yugoslavia, Russia, and Ukraine followed this same pattern. These countries expanded the supply of money rapidly to pay for government expenditures and, as a result, experienced hyperinflation.

HOW IS THE MONEY SUPPLY MEASURED?

How is the money supply defined and measured? There is not a single answer to this question. Economists and policy makers have developed several alternative measures. We will briefly describe the two most widely used measures.

The M1 Money Supply

M1 (money supply)
The sum of (1) currency in circulation (including coins), (2) checkable deposits maintained in depository institutions, and (3) traveler's checks.

Currency
Medium of exchange made of metal or paper.

Demand deposits
Non-interest-earning checking deposits that can be either withdrawn or made payable on demand to a third party. Like currency, these deposits are widely used as a means of payment.

Other checkable deposits
Interest-earning deposits that are also available for checking.

M2 (money supply)
Equal to M1 plus (1) savings deposits, (2) time deposits (accounts of less than $100,000) held in depository institutions, and (3) money market mutual fund shares.

Depository institutions
Businesses that accept checking and savings deposits and use a portion of them to extend loans and make investments. Banks, savings and loan associations, and credit unions are examples.

Above all else, money is a medium of exchange. The narrowest definition of the money supply, **M1**, focuses on this function. Based on its role as a medium of exchange, it is clear that **currency**—coins and paper bills—falls into this definition. But currency isn't the only form of money readily used for exchange. If you go to a store and you are out of currency, many of them will let you write a check. Therefore checkable deposits—bank deposits that can be withdrawn by writing a check—should be included in the M1 money supply measure.

There are two kinds of checkable deposits. First, there are **demand deposits**, non-interest-earning deposits with banking institutions that are available for withdrawal ("on demand") at any time without restrictions. Demand deposits are usually withdrawn by writing a check. Second, there are **other checkable deposits** that earn interest but carry some restrictions on their transferability. Interest-earning checkable deposits generally either limit the number of checks depositors can write each month or require the depositor to maintain a substantial minimum balance ($1,000, for example).

Like currency and demand deposits, interest-earning checkable deposits are available for use as a medium of exchange. Traveler's checks are also a means of payment. They can be freely converted to cash at parity (equal value). ***Thus, the M1 money supply comprises (1) currency in circulation, (2) checkable deposits (both demand deposits and interest-earning checkable deposits), and (3) traveler's checks***.

As **Exhibit 1** shows, the total M1 money supply in the United States was $1,293 billion at year-end 2003. Demand and other checkable deposits accounted for almost one-half of the M1 money supply. This large share reflects the fact that most of the nation's business is conducted by check.

The Broader M2 Money Supply

In modern economies, several financial assets can be easily converted into checking deposits or currency; therefore, the line between money and "near monies" is often blurred. Broader definitions of the money supply include various assets that can be easily converted to checking account funds and cash. The most common broad definition of the money supply is **M2**. It includes all the items included in M1 plus (1) savings deposits, (2) time deposits of less than $100,000 at all **depository institutions**, and (3) money market mutual funds.

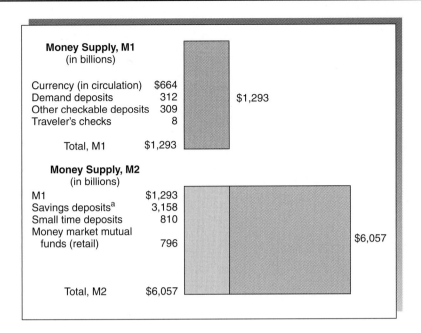

EXHIBIT 1
The Composition of Money Supply in the United States

The size and composition (as of December 2003) of the two most widely used measures of the money supply are shown. M1, the narrowest definition of the money supply, is composed of currency, checking deposits, and traveler's checks. M2, which contains M1 plus the various savings components indicated, is approximately four times the size of M1.

---

[a]Including money market deposit accounts.
Source: http://www.federalreserve.gov

Although the non-M1 components of the M2 money supply are not generally used as a means of making payment, they can be easily and quickly converted to currency or checking deposits for such use. For example, if you maintain funds in a savings account, you can easily transfer the funds to your checking account. **Money market mutual funds** are interest-earning accounts offered by brokerage firms that pool depositors' funds and invest them in highly liquid short-term securities. Because these securities can be quickly converted to cash, depositors are permitted to write checks against these accounts.

Many economists—particularly those who stress the store-of-value function of money—prefer the broader M2 definition of the money supply to the narrower M1 concept. As Exhibit 1 shows, at year-end 2003 the M2 money supply was $6,057 billion, more than four times the M1 money supply. Other definitions of the money supply have been developed for specialized purposes, but the M1 and M2 definitions are the most important and most widely used.

Credit Cards Versus Money

It is important to distinguish between money and credit. Money is a financial asset that provides the holder with future purchasing power. **Credit** is a liability acquired when one borrows funds. This distinction sheds light on a question students frequently ask: "Because credit cards are often used to make purchases, why aren't credit card expenditures part of the money supply?" In contrast with money, credit cards are not purchasing power. They are merely a convenient way of arranging a loan. When you use your Visa or MasterCard to buy a DVD player, for example, you are not really paying for the player. Instead, you are taking out a loan from the institution issuing your card, and that institution is paying for the player. You haven't payed for the DVD player until you've paid your credit card bill down far enough to cover its cost. The same goes for your other credit card purchases. Thus, credit cards are not money because they don't represent purchasing power. Instead, the outstanding balance on your credit card is a liability, money you owe to the company that issued the card.

Money market mutual funds
Interest-earning accounts offered by brokerage firms that pool depositors' funds and invest them in highly liquid short-term securities. Since these securities can be quickly converted to cash, depositors are permitted to write checks (which reduce their share holdings) against their accounts.

Credit
Funds acquired by borrowing.

Money is an asset; it is part of the wealth of the people who hold it. In contrast, credit card purchases create a liability. They are merely a convenient method of arranging a short-term loan.

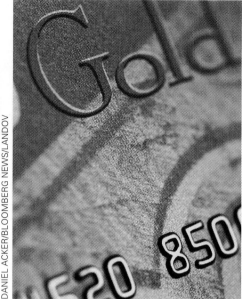

Although credit cards are not money, their use will influence the amount of money people will want to hold. Credit cards make it possible for people to buy things throughout the month and then pay for them in a single transaction at the end of the month. This makes it possible for people to conduct their regular business affairs with less money than would otherwise be needed. Thus, widespread use of credit cards will tend to reduce the average quantity of money people hold.

THE BUSINESS OF BANKING

We must understand a few things about the business of banking before we can explain the factors that influence the supply of money. The banking industry in the United States operates under the jurisdiction of the **Federal Reserve System**, the nation's central bank. We will discuss the Federal Reserve System in detail later in this chapter.

The banking system is an important component of the capital market. Like other private businesses, banks are profit-seeking operations. Banks provide services (for example, the safekeeping of funds and checking account services) and pay interest to attract both checking and savings depositors. *They help bring together people who want to save for the future and those who want to borrow in order to undertake investment projects.* The primary source of revenue for banks is the interest income derived from the loans they make.

When deciding whether or not to fund a project, bankers have a strong incentive to take into account the project's expected profitability and the borrower's creditworthiness. If the borrowed funds are channeled into unprofitable projects, the borrower might be unable to repay them. This will hurt the bank's profitability. The efficient allocation of investment funds by banks is an important source of economic growth. Profitable business projects increase the value of resources and promote economic growth; unprofitable projects have the opposite effect and tie up resources better used elsewhere. Thus, an efficiently operating capital market—of which the banking system is an integral part—is an important ingredient for economic growth.

In the United States, the banking system consists of savings and loan institutions, credit unions, and commercial banks. **Savings and loan associations** accept deposits in exchange for shares that pay dividends. **Credit unions** are cooperative financial

Federal Reserve System
The central bank of the United States; it carries out banking regulatory policies and is responsible for the conduct of monetary policy.

Savings and loan associations
Financial institutions that accept deposits in exchange for shares that pay dividends. Historically, these funds were channeled into residential mortgage loans. Under banking legislation adopted in 1980, S&Ls are permitted to offer a broad range of services similar to those of commercial banks.

Credit unions
Financial cooperative organizations of individuals with a common affiliation (such as an employer or a labor union). They accept deposits, including checkable deposits, pay interest (or dividends) on them out of earnings, and lend funds primarily to members.

organizations composed of individuals with a common affiliation (such as an employer). Credit unions accept deposits, pay interest (or dividends) on them, and generate earnings primarily by extending loans to members. **Commercial banks** offer a wide range of services—including checking and savings accounts and extension of loans—and are owned by stockholders.

Prior to 1980, both credit unions and savings and loan associations were severely restricted in the types of financial products they could offer. Legislation passed in 1980, however, enabled these depository institutions to offer both checking and savings accounts and extend a wide variety of loans to their customers. All of these institutions are now under the jurisdiction of the Federal Reserve System, which applies similar regulations and offers similar services to each. ***Therefore, when we speak of the banking industry, we are referring not only to commercial banks, but to savings and loan associations and credit unions as well.***

Exhibit 2 presents the consolidated balance sheet of commercial banking institutions. These figures illustrate the major banking functions. Note that the major liabilities of banks are transaction (checking), savings, and time deposits. *From the viewpoint of a bank,* these are liabilities because they represent an obligation of the bank to its depositors. Outstanding interest-earning loans constitute the major class of banking assets. In addition, most banks own sizable amounts of interest-earning securities—bonds issued by either governments or private corporations. As these figures show, banks use the deposits of their customers to earn income by extending loans. Banks also invest some of the deposits in low-risk assets, such as U.S. government securities.

Banking differs from most businesses in that a large portion of the liabilities are payable on demand. However, even though it would be possible for all depositors to demand the money in their checking accounts on the same day, the probability of this occurring is generally quite remote. Typically, while some individuals are making withdrawals, others are making deposits. These transactions tend to balance out, eliminating sudden changes in demand deposits.

It's important to note that banks maintain only a fraction of their assets in reserves to meet the requirements of depositors. As Exhibit 2 illustrates, **bank reserves**—vault cash plus reserve deposits with the Federal Reserve—were only $34 billion at year-end 2003, compared to checking deposits of $485 billion. Thus, on average, banks were maintaining only about 7 percent of their assets in reserve against the checking deposits of their customers. We will now explain why this is so.

Commercial banks
Financial institutions that offer a wide range of services (for example, checking accounts, savings accounts, and loans) to their customers. Commercial banks are owned by stockholders and seek to operate at a profit.

Bank reserves
Vault cash plus deposits of banks with Federal Reserve banks.

CONSOLIDATED BALANCE SHEET OF COMMERCIAL BANKING INSTITUTIONS, YEAR-END 2003 (BILLIONS OF DOLLARS)

ASSETS		LIABILITIES	
Vault cash	$ 25	Deposits	$ 485
Reserves at the Fed	9	Savings and time deposits	4,117
Loans outstanding	4,399	Borrowings	1,480
U.S. government securities	1,105	Other liabilities	679
Other securities	752	Net worth	530
Other assets	1,001		
Total	$7,291		$7,291

EXHIBIT 2
The Functions of Commercial Banking Institutions

The consolidated balance sheet of commercial banks shown here illustrates the primary banking functions. Banks provide services and pay interest to attract deposits (both checking and saving) that are liabilities from the standpoint of the bank. Most of these deposits are invested and loaned out, providing the bank with interest income. Banks hold a portion of their assets as reserves (either cash or deposits with the Fed) to meet their daily obligations toward their depositors.

Source: http://www.federalreserve.gov

Fractional Reserve Banking

Economists often draw an analogy between our current banking system and the goldsmiths of the past. In the past, gold was used as the means of making payments. It was money. People would store their money with a goldsmith for safekeeping, just as many of us open a checking account for safety reasons. Gold owners received a certificate granting them the right to withdraw their gold any time they wished. If they wanted to buy something, they would go to the goldsmith, withdraw gold, and use it as a means of making a payment. Thus, the money supply was equal to the amount of gold in circulation plus the gold deposited with goldsmiths.

It was inconvenient to make a trip to the goldsmith every time one wanted to buy something. Because the certificates were redeemable in gold, they began to circulate as a means of payment. The depositors were pleased with this arrangement because it eliminated the need for a trip to the goldsmith every time something was purchased. As long as they had confidence in the goldsmith, sellers were glad to accept the certificates as payment.

As gold certificates began to circulate, the daily withdrawals and deposits with goldsmiths declined even more. This makes sense because the only way the goldsmiths could earn money was by lending out gold. They made nothing on the gold just sitting in their vaults. Consequently, local goldsmiths would keep only about 20 percent of the total gold deposited with them so they could meet the current requests to redeem the gold certificates in circulation. The remaining 80 percent of their gold deposits would be loaned out to merchants, traders, and other citizens. One hundred percent of the gold certificates were circulating as money, along with that portion of gold that had been loaned out—80 percent of total deposits, in other words. Therefore the *total* money supply circulating in the economy—gold certificates plus actual gold—was 1.8 times the amount of gold deposited with the goldsmiths. By issuing loans and retaining only a fraction of the total gold in their vaults, goldsmiths were actually able to increase the money supply.

Fractional reserve banking
A system that permits banks to hold reserves of less than 100 percent against their deposits.

In principle, our modern banking system is very similar to goldsmithing. The United States has a **fractional reserve banking** system. Banks are required to maintain only a fraction of their deposits in the form of vault cash and other reserves. These are called **required reserves.** Just as the early goldsmiths did not have enough gold to pay all their depositors simultaneously, our banks also do not have enough reserves to pay all depositors at once. To make money, the early goldsmiths expanded the money supply by issuing loans. So do present-day bankers. They earn no income on money sitting in their vaults. Reserve requirements, however, limit the expansion today, just as they did back in the days of goldsmithing.

Required reserves
The minimum amount of reserves that a bank is required by law to keep on hand to back up its deposits. If reserve requirements were 15 percent, banks would be required to keep $150,000 in reserves against each $1 million of deposits.

There are important differences between modern banking and early goldsmithing, though. Today, the actions of individual banks are regulated by a central bank. The central bank is supposed to follow policies designed to promote a healthy economy. It also acts as a lender of last resort. If all of a bank's depositors attempted to withdraw their funds simultaneously, the central bank would intervene and supply the bank with enough funds to meet the demand.

Bank Runs, Bank Failures, and Deposit Insurance

Compared to other businesses, banks are more vulnerable to failure because their liabilities to depositors are current but most of their assets are illiquid. This means that if a significant share of depositors lose confidence and withdraw their funds from a bank, it will quickly lead to problems. In turn, when a bank fails, it affects not only the bank's owners and employees, of course, but its depositors as well. These secondary effects can undermine the operation of an economy if many banks fail.

The U.S. economy has had its share of banking problems. Between 1922 and 1933, more than 10,000 banks (one-third of the total) failed. Most of these failures were the result of "bank runs"—panic withdrawals when people lost confidence in the banking system. Remember, under a fractional reserve system, banks do not have a sufficient amount of reserves to redeem the funds of all (or even most) depositors if they should seek to withdraw their funds at the same time.

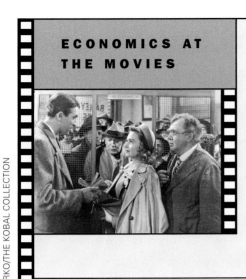

ECONOMICS AT THE MOVIES

It's a Wonderful Life (1946)

In this classic movie from 1946 (which often airs on TV during the winter holidays), there is a bank run. When everyone shows up and wants to withdraw their money, James Stewart explains, "Your money is not in the vault. It's in Bert's house and in Ernie's house." Thus, he cannot give everyone their money because the bank uses the deposits to make loans to other people. In essence, Stewart is giving everyone a lesson in fractional reserve banking.

The bank failures of the 1920s and 1930s led to the establishment of the **Federal Deposit Insurance Corporation (FDIC)** in 1934. The FDIC guarantees the deposits of banking customers up to some limit—currently $100,000 per account. Even if the bank should fail, depositors will be able to get their money (up to the $100,000 limit). Member banks pay an insurance premium to the FDIC for each dollar deposited with them, and the FDIC uses these premiums to reimburse depositors when a bank fails. The FDIC restored confidence in the banking system and brought bank runs to a halt. As a result, bank failures are now extremely rare.

Federal Deposit Insurance Corporation (FDIC)
A federally chartered corporation that insures the deposits held by commercial banks, savings and loans, and credit unions.

HOW BANKS CREATE MONEY BY EXTENDING LOANS

Let us consider a banking system without a central bank, one in which only currency acts as a reserve against deposits. Initially, we will assume that all banks are required by law to maintain 20 percent or more of their deposits as cash in their vaults. This proportion of the percentage of reserves that must be maintained against checkable transaction deposits is called the **required reserve ratio**. The required reserve ratio in our example is 20 percent.

Now suppose that you find $1,000 your long-deceased uncle had apparently hidden in the basement of his house. You take the bills to the First National Bank and open a checking account. How much will the $1,000 in your newly opened account expand the economy's money supply? First National is now required to keep $200 of the $1,000 in vault cash—20 percent of your deposit. So after placing $200 in the bank vault, First National has $800 of **excess reserves**—reserves over and above the amount the law requires it to retain. Given its current excess reserves, First National can now extend an $800 loan. Suppose it loans $800 to a local citizen to help pay for a car. At the time the loan is extended, the money supply will increase by $800 as the bank adds the funds to the checking account of the borrower. No one else has less money. You still have your $1,000 checking account, and the borrower has $800 for a new car.

When the borrower buys a new car, the seller accepts a check and deposits the $800 in a bank, Citizen's State Bank. What happens when the check clears? The temporary excess reserves of the First National Bank will be eliminated when it pays $800 to the Citizen's State Bank. But when Citizen's State Bank receives $800 in currency, it will now have excess reserves. It must keep 20 percent of it, or $160, as required reserves, but the remaining $640 can be loaned out. Because Citizen's State, like other banks, is in business to make money, it will be quite happy to "extend a helping hand" to someone who wants to borrow that money. When the second bank loans out its excess reserves, the deposits of the person borrowing the money will increase by $640. Another $640 has now been added to the money supply.

Required reserve ratio
A percentage of a specified liability category (for example, checkable deposits) that banking institutions are required to hold as reserves against that type of liability.

Excess reserves
Actual reserves that exceed the legal requirement.

EXHIBIT 3
Creating Money from New Reserves

When banks are required to maintain 20 percent reserves against demand deposits, the creation of $1,000 of new reserves will potentially increase the supply of money by $5,000.

BANK	NEW CASH DEPOSITS: ACTUAL RESERVES	NEW REQUIRED RESERVES	POTENTIAL DEMAND DEPOSITS CREATED BY EXTENDING NEW LOANS
Initial deposit (Bank A)	$1,000.00	$ 200.00	$ 800.00
Second stage (Bank B)	800.00	160.00	640.00
Third stage (Bank C)	640.00	128.00	512.00
Fourth stage (Bank D)	512.00	102.40	409.60
Fifth stage (Bank E)	409.60	81.92	327.68
Sixth stage (Bank F)	327.68	65.54	262.14
Seventh stage (Bank G)	262.14	52.43	209.71
All others (other banks)	1,048.58	209.71	838.87
Total	$5,000.00	$1,000.00	$4,000.00

Deposit expansion multiplier
The multiple by which an increase in reserves will increase the money supply. It is inversely related to the required reserve ratio.

Potential deposit expansion multiplier
The maximum potential increase in the money supply as a ratio of the new reserves injected into the banking system. It is equal to the inverse of the required reserve ratio.

You still have your $1,000, the automobile seller has an additional $800, and the new borrower has just received an additional $640. Because you found the $1,000 and deposited it in the bank, the money supply has increased by $1,440 ($800 + $640).

Of course, the process can continue. **Exhibit 3** shows what happens when the money creation process continues through several more stages. When the reserve requirement is 20 percent, the money supply can expand to a maximum of $5,000, the initial $1,000 plus an additional $4,000 in demand deposits that can be created by extending new loans.

The multiple by which new reserves increase the stock of money is called the **deposit expansion multiplier**. It is determined by the ratio of required reserves to deposits. In fact, the **potential deposit expansion multiplier** is merely the reciprocal of the required reserve ratio (r). Mathematically, the potential deposit expansion multiplier is equal to $1/r$. In our example, the required reserves are 20 percent, or one-fifth of the total deposits. So the potential deposit expansion multiplier is 5. If only 10 percent reserves were required, the potential deposit expansion multiplier would be 10, the reciprocal of one-tenth. *The lower the percentage of reserves required, the more the money supply will expand. However, the fractional reserve requirement puts a ceiling on the expansion.*

The Actual Deposit Multiplier

Will the introduction of new currency reserves fully expand the money supply by the amount of the multiplier? The answer is "No." The actual deposit multiplier will generally be less than its potential for two reasons.

First, the deposit expansion multiplier will be reduced if some people decide to hold the currency rather than deposit it in a bank. For example, suppose the person who borrowed the $800 in the preceding example spends only $700 and stashes the remaining $100 away for a possible emergency. Only $700 can then end up as a deposit in the second stage and contribute to the excess reserves that underlie the expansion of the money supply. The potential of new loans in the second stage and in all subsequent stages will be reduced proportionally. When currency remains in circulation outside of banks, it reduces the size of the deposit expansion multiplier.

Second, the actual deposit multiplier will be less than its maximum potential when banks fail to use all the new excess reserves to extend loans. Banks, though, have a strong incentive to loan out or invest most of their new excess reserves. Idle excess reserves do not earn interest. Because banks are in business to earn income, they will maintain only a very small portion of their assets—mostly currency needed for daily transactions—in the form of excess reserves. In recent years, excess reserves have accounted for less than 1 percent of the total reserves of banks.

However, because people generally keep most of their money in banks (rather than in their wallets) and because banks try to keep their excess reserves to a minimum, the injection of new reserves into the system can be counted on to expand the supply of money. As you will see, these "money injections" are an important tool of the Federal Reserve, which we discuss next.

THE FEDERAL RESERVE SYSTEM

Most countries have a central banking authority that controls the money supply and conducts monetary policy. As we previously noted, the central bank of the United States is the Federal Reserve System. In the United Kingdom, the central bank is the Bank of England; in Canada, it is the Bank of Canada; in Japan, it is the Bank of Japan. Central banks are responsible for the conduct of their nation's monetary policy.

Structure of the Fed

The major purpose of the Federal Reserve System (and other central banks) is to regulate the money supply and provide a monetary climate that is in the best interest of the entire economy. Congress has instructed the Federal Reserve, or the Fed, as it is often called, to conduct monetary policy in a manner that promotes both full employment and price stability. Unlike commercial banks, the Federal Reserve is not a profit-making institution. The earnings of the Fed, over and above its expenses, belong to the U.S. Treasury.

Exhibit 4 illustrates the structure of the Fed. There are three major centers of decision making within the Federal Reserve: (1) the Board of Governors, (2) the district and regional banks, and (3) the Federal Open Market Operations Committee.

EXHIBIT 4
Structure of Federal Reserve System

The Board of Governors of the Federal Reserve System is at the center of the banking system in the United States. The board sets the rules and regulations for all depository institutions. The seven members of the Board of Governors also serve on the Federal Open Market Committee, which establishes Fed policy with regard to the buying and selling of government securities, the primary mechanism used to control the money supply in the United States.

The Board of Governors

The Board of Governors is the decision-making center of the Fed. This powerful board consists of seven members, each appointed to a staggered fourteen-year term by the nation's president with the advice and consent of the U.S. Senate. The president designates one of the seven members as chair for a four-year term. (See the Outstanding Economist box about Alan Greenspan.) The Board of Governors establishes the rules and regulations that apply to all depository institutions. It sets the reserve requirements and regulates the composition of the asset holdings of depository institutions. The board is the rule maker, and often the umpire, of the banking industry.

The Federal Reserve District Banks

There are twelve Federal Reserve District banks with twenty-five regional branches spread throughout the nation. **Exhibit 5** shows the regions covered by each of the twelve district banks. These district and regional banks operate under the supervision of the Board of Governors. Federal Reserve banks are bankers' banks; they provide banking services for commercial banks. Despite the fact that the Fed is a bankers' bank, it does not pay interest to banks on the reserves they must keep with it. Private citizens and corporations do not bank with the Fed.

The district banks are primarily responsible for the monitoring of the commercial banks in their region. They audit the books of depository institutions regularly to ensure their compliance with reserve requirements and other regulations of the Fed. The district banks also play an important role in the clearing of checks throughout the banking system.

EXHIBIT 5
The Twelve Federal Reserve Districts

The map shows the twelve Federal Reserve districts and the city in which the district bank is located. These district banks monitor the commercial banks in their region and assist them with the clearing of checks. If you look at any dollar bill, it will identify the Federal Reserve district bank that initially issued the currency. The Board of Governors of the Fed is located in Washington, D.C.

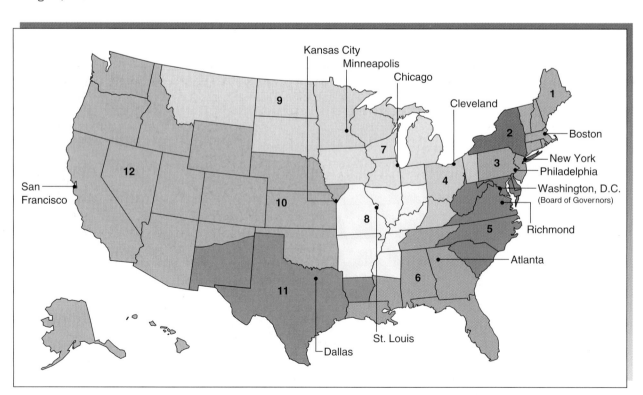

Most depository institutions, regardless of their Fed membership status, maintain deposits with Federal Reserve Banks. As a result, the clearing of checks through the Federal Reserve System becomes merely an accounting transaction. The district and regional banks handle approximately 85 percent of all check-clearing services of the banking system.

The Federal Open Market Committee

The **Federal Open Market Committee (FOMC)** is a powerful committee that determines the Fed's policy with respect to the purchase and sale of government bonds. As we shall soon see, this is the Fed's most frequently used method of controlling the money supply in the United States. The seven members of the Board of Governors, plus the twelve presidents of the Federal Reserve district banks, participate in the FOMC meetings, but at any point in time, only twelve of the nineteen members will get to vote. The twelve voting members of this important policy-making arm of the Fed are (1) the seven members of the Board of Governors, (2) the president of the New York district bank, and (3) four (of the remaining eleven) additional presidents of the Fed's district banks, who rotate as voting members. The FOMC meets every four to six weeks in the huge conference room of the Federal Reserve Building in Washington, D.C.

Federal Open Market Committee (FOMC)
A committee of the Federal Reserve system that establishes Fed policy with regard to the buying and selling of government securities—the primary mechanism used to control the money supply. It is composed of the seven members of the Board of Governors and the twelve district bank presidents of the Fed.

The Independence of the Fed

Like the Supreme Court, the Federal Reserve operates with considerable independence from both Congress and the executive branch of government. Several factors contribute to this independence. The lengthy terms—fourteen years—protect the seven members of the Fed's Board of Governors from political pressures. Because their terms are staggered—a new governor is appointed only every two years—even two-term presidents are well into their second term before they are able to appoint a majority of the Fed's governing board. The Fed's earnings on its financial assets, mostly government bonds, provide it with substantially more funding than is needed to cover its operating costs. Thus, it is not dependent on Congress for funding allocations. The Fed does not even have to undergo audits from the General Accounting Office, a government agency that audits the books of most

OUTSTANDING ECONOMIST	Alan Greenspan (1926–)	

From 1954 to 1974, Alan Greenspan ran a very successful economic consulting firm in New York City. After serving as the chair of the Council of Economic Advisers (1974–1977) during the Ford administration, Greenspan returned to his consulting firm for the following ten years. During this period, he also served as Chairman of the National Commission on Social Security Reform and as a board member of many corporations. In 1987, President Reagan appointed him to a four-year term as chairman of the Fed's Board of Governors. Later, he was reappointed to that position by Presidents George H. W. Bush, Bill Clinton, and George W. Bush. The Fed chairman directs the Federal Reserve staff, presides over Board meetings, and testifies frequently before Congress. Because of the importance of monetary policy and the power of the position, the Fed chairman is often said to be the second most influential person—next to the president—in the United States. As the result of the low rate of inflation and relatively stable growth of the economy, Greenspan is given high marks for his tenure as chairman.

government operations. This independence of the Fed is designed to reduce the likelihood that political pressures will adversely affect its ability to follow a stable, noninflationary monetary policy.

Does the independence of a central bank affect policy? There is considerable variation in the independence of central banks. Like the Fed, the central banks of Japan, England, and Canada also have considerable independence from the other branches of their governments. So, too, does the recently established European Central Bank. In other instances, however, central banks are directly beholden to political officials. The central banks of many Latin American countries fall into this category. Studies indicate that when a country's central bank is strongly influenced by political considerations, the bank is more likely to follow inflationary policies. For example, politicians in a country with high budget deficits might lobby their central bank to expand the money supply to help finance the government's spending. If the bank succumbs to this pressure, inflation will quickly set in and undermine the economy.

How the Fed Controls the Money Supply

The Fed controls the money supply in three ways: by (1) establishing reserve requirements for depository institutions, (2) buying and selling U.S. government securities in the open market, and (3) setting the interest rate at which it loans funds to commercial banks and other depository institutions. We will analyze in detail how each of these tools can be used to regulate the amount of money in circulation.

Reserve Requirements

The Federal Reserve System requires banking institutions (including credit unions and savings and loan associations) to maintain reserves against the demand deposits of their customers. The reserves of banking institutions are composed of (1) currency held by the bank (vault cash) and (2) deposits of the bank with the Federal Reserve System. A bank can always obtain additional currency by drawing on its deposits with the Federal Reserve. So, both the bank's cash-on-hand and its deposits with the Fed can be used to meet the demands of depositors. Both therefore count as reserves.

Exhibit 6 indicates the required reserve ratio—the percentage of each deposit category that banks are required to keep in reserve (either as vault cash or deposits with the Fed). As of December 2003, the reserve requirement for checking accounts was set at 3 percent for amounts above $6.6 million and up to $45.4 million and 10 percent for amounts in excess of $45.4 million. Currently, banks are not required to keep reserves against their savings and time deposits or against the first $6.6 million of their checking deposits.

Why are commercial banks required to maintain assets in the form of reserves? One reason is to prevent imprudent bankers from overextending loans and thereby placing themselves in a poor position to deal with any sudden increase in withdrawals by

EXHIBIT 6
The Required Reserve Ratio of Banking Institutions

	Checking ACCOUNTS[a]		
	$0–$6.6 MILLION	$6.6–$45.4 MILLION	OVER $45.4 MILLION
Required reserves as a percent of deposits	0%	3%	10%

Banking institutions are required to maintain 3 percent reserves against checking account deposits of over $6.6 million and up to $45.4 million and 10 percent reserves for transaction deposits over $45.4 million (in effect December 2003).

[a]The dividing points are adjusted each year to reflect changes in total checking account deposits in all banking institutions.
Source: http://www.federalreserve.gov

depositors. The quantity of reserves needed to meet such emergencies is not left totally to the judgment of individual bankers, obviously. The Fed sets the rules.

The Fed's control over reserve requirements, however, is important for another reason. By altering reserve requirements, the Fed can alter the money supply. The law does not prevent banks from holding reserves over and above those required by the Fed, but, as we previously noted, banking institutions will want to hold interest-earning assets (like loans to customers and bonds) rather than excess reserves. Because reserves draw no interest, profit-seeking banks will shave their excess reserves to a low level. As a result, an increase in reserve requirements will typically force banks to reduce their outstanding loans and investments. As the volume of loans (and other forms of credit) extended by banks declines, so, too, will the money supply. ***Thus, an increase in the reserve requirements will reduce the supply of money.***

A reduction in reserve requirements will have the opposite effect. When the Fed reduces the reserve requirements, it creates additional excess reserves for banks. Predictably, profit-seeking banks will use a large portion of these newly created excess reserves to extend additional loans and undertake other investments. As they do so, their actions will expand the supply of money. ***Thus, lower reserve requirements increase the money supply.***

In recent years, the Fed has seldom used its regulatory power over reserve requirements to alter the supply of money. Why? For one thing, changes in reserve requirements can be disruptive to banking operations. An increase in the required reserve ratio may force many banks to sell securities quickly or call in loans, even if there has been no change in the level of their deposits. Furthermore, reserve requirement changes are a blunt instrument—small changes in reserve requirements can sometimes lead to large changes in the money supply. The magnitude and timing of a change in the money supply resulting from a change in reserve requirements is difficult to predict with precision. For these reasons, the Fed has usually preferred to use other monetary tools.

Open Market Operations

The most common tool used by the Fed to alter the money supply is **open market operations**—the buying and selling of U.S. securities on the open market. As we indicated earlier, Fed policy in this area is conducted by the Federal Open Market Committee (FOMC). This committee meets every few weeks to map out the Fed's policy. Open market operations can be undertaken easily and quietly. Because they influence the money supply either directly or through their impact on bank reserves, open market operations are less disruptive than changes in reserve requirements.

If the Fed wanted to expand the money supply, for example, it would merely instruct its bond traders at the New York Federal Reserve Bank to buy bonds. (Because of its location near major financial markets, the New York bank handles the Fed's bond trading.) ***When the Fed purchases U.S. securities, it injects "new money" into the economy in the form of additional currency in circulation and deposits with commercial banks.***

Let's consider a hypothetical case. Suppose the Fed purchases $10,000 of U.S. securities from Maria Valdez. The Fed receives the securities and Valdez receives a check for $10,000. If she merely cashes the check drawn on the Federal Reserve, the amount of currency in circulation would expand by $10,000, increasing the money supply by that amount. If, as is more likely to be the case, she deposits the funds in her checking account at City Bank, her checking account will increase by $10,000, and new excess reserves will be created. City Bank is required to increase its reserve holdings by only a fraction of Valdez's $10,000 deposit. Assuming that the bank is required to keep 10 percent in reserves, it can now extend new loans of up to $9,000 while maintaining its initial reserve position. As the new loans are extended, they, too, will contribute to a further expansion in the money supply. Part of the new loans will eventually be deposited in other banks, and these banks will also be able to extend additional loans. As the process continues, the money supply expands by a multiple of the securities purchased by the Fed.

Open market operations can also be used to reduce the money supply. ***If the Fed wants to reduce the money supply, it sells some of its current holdings of government securities.*** When the Fed sells securities, a buyer like Maria Valdez will pay for them with

Open market operations
The buying and selling of U.S. government securities in the open market by the Federal Reserve.

EXHIBIT 7
The Monetary Base and Money Supply (Year-end 2003)

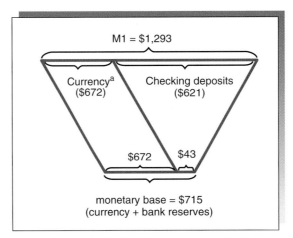

The monetary base (currency plus bank reserves) provides the foundation for the money supply. The currency in circulation contributes directly to the money supply, while the bank reserves provide the underpinnings for checking deposits. Fed actions that alter the monetary base will affect the money supply. (All figures are in billions.)

Traveler's checks are included in this category.

a check drawn on a commercial bank. As the check clears, both the buyer's checking deposits and the reserves of the bank on which the check was written will decline. Thus, the action will reduce the money supply both directly (by reducing checking deposits) and indirectly (by reducing the quantity of reserves available to the banking system).

The Fed's purchase and sale of U.S. securities influence the size of the **monetary base**. The monetary base is equal to the reserves of commercial banks (vault cash and reserve deposits with the Fed) plus the currency in circulation. As **Exhibit 7** illustrates, the monetary base provides the foundation for the money supply of the United States. Of course, the currency in circulation ($672 billion in December 2003) contributes directly to the money supply. In turn, the reserves ($43 billion in December 2003) underpin the checking deposits ($621 billion). Fed purchases of U.S. securities increase the monetary base. Some of the proceeds (received by those selling bonds to the Fed) will circulate as currency. Each new dollar of currency in circulation will increase the money supply by exactly $1. In addition, many of those receiving proceeds from bond sales to the Fed will deposit the funds in a bank. When this happens, the bank's excess reserves increase. Most of the excess reserves will be used to extend loans, which will cause the money supply to expand.

By how much will the money supply change as the Fed injects and withdraws reserves through open market operations? Given the reserve requirements present in the early 2000s (see Exhibit 6), an increase in the monetary base could potentially expand the money supply (M1) by a multiple of 10 or more. However, leakages in the form of additional currency in circulation and excess bank reserves that don't get lent out will cause the actual deposit expansion multiplier to be substantially less than its potential. Exhibit 7 shows that the M1 was approximately twice the size of the monetary base in 2003. This suggests that M1 will increase by about $2 for every $1 change in the monetary base that occurs when the Fed sells bonds.

The Discount Rate and Federal Funds Rate

When banking institutions borrow from the Federal Reserve, they must pay interest on the loans. The interest rate that banks pay on loans from the Federal Reserve is called the **discount rate**. Banks borrow from the Fed primarily to meet temporary shortages of reserves. They are most likely to borrow from the Fed for a brief period of time while they are making other adjustments in their loan and investment portfolios that enable them to meet their reserve requirement.

Monetary base
The sum of currency in circulation plus bank reserves (vault cash and reserves with the Fed). It reflects the stock of U.S. securities held by the Fed.

Discount rate
The interest rate the Federal Reserve charges banking institutions for borrowing funds.

The discount rate is closely related to the interest rate in the **federal funds market**. The federal funds market is a private loanable funds market in which banks with excess reserves extend short-term loans (sometimes for as little as a day) to other banks trying to meet their reserve requirements. The interest rate in the federal funds market fluctuates with the demand for loanable funds.

Prior to January 2003, the discount rate was often lower than the interest rate in the federal funds market. As a result, banks had an incentive to borrow from the Fed. This is no longer the case. Under new operating procedures, the Fed now charges banks a discount rate that is greater than the federal funds rate. The new procedures were adopted because the Fed wanted to discourage banks from borrowing from the Fed.

The precise rate the Fed charges is determined by the financial conditions of the bank borrowing the funds—how likely it is to be able to repay the loan. The Fed charges financially sound banks an interest rate that is 1 percentage point above the federal funds rate. The interest rate charged to financially troubled banks is 1.5 percentage points above the federal funds rate. Small banks in agricultural or vacation areas that experience substantial seasonal swings in deposits and loans can borrow from the Fed at the same interest rate as the federal funds rate. Of course, the Fed sets the size of the differential between the discount rate and the federal funds rate, and it can alter this differential any time it wants.

Announcements following the regular meetings of the Federal Open Market Committee often focus on the Fed's target for the federal funds rate. If the Fed wants to lower the federal funds interest rate, it will purchase government securities and thereby inject additional reserves into the banking system. This will expand the supply of money and reduce the federal funds rate. Conversely, if the Fed wants to increase the federal funds rate, it will sell some of its bond holdings and thereby drain reserves from the system. In turn, reducing the supply of reserves will lower the money supply and place upward pressure on the federal funds rate.

Federal funds market
A loanable funds market in which banks seeking additional reserves borrow short-term funds (generally for seven days or less) from banks with excess reserves. The interest rate in this market is called the federal funds rate.

Controlling the Money Supply—A Summary

Exhibit 8 summarizes the monetary tools of the Federal Reserve. If the Fed wants to increase the money supply, it can decrease reserve requirements, purchase additional U.S. securities, and/or lower the discount rate. If it wants to reduce the money supply, it can increase the reserve requirements, sell U.S. securities, and/or raise the discount rate. Because the Fed typically seeks only small changes in the money stock (or its rate of increase), at any point in time, it typically uses only one of these tools, usually open market operations, to accomplish a desired objective.

The Fed and the Treasury

Many students tend to confuse the Federal Reserve with the U.S. Treasury, probably because both sound like monetary agencies. The Treasury is a budgetary agency. If there is a budgetary deficit, the Treasury will issue U.S. securities as a method of financing the deficit. Newly issued U.S. securities are almost always sold to private investors (or government trust funds). Bonds issued by the Treasury to finance a budget deficit are seldom purchased directly by the Fed. In any case, the Treasury is primarily interested in obtaining funds so it can pay Uncle Sam's bills. Except for nominal amounts, mostly coins, the Treasury does not issue money. Borrowing—the public sale of new U.S. securities—is the primary method used by the Treasury to cover any excess of expenditures in relation to revenues from taxes and other sources.

Whereas the Treasury is concerned with the revenues and expenditures of the government, the Fed is concerned primarily with the availability of money and credit for the entire economy. The Fed does not issue U.S. securities. It merely purchases and sells government securities issued by the Treasury as a means of controlling the economy's money supply. Unlike the Treasury, the Fed can purchase government bonds by writing a check on itself without having deposits, gold, or anything else to back it up. In doing so,

EXHIBIT 8
Summary of Monetary Tools of the Federal Reserve

FEDERAL RESERVE POLICY	EXPANSIONARY MONETARY POLICY	RESTRICTIVE MONETARY POLICY
1. Reserve requirements	*Reduce reserve requirements,* because this will create additional excess reserves and induce banks to extend additional loans, which will expand the money supply.	*Raise reserve requirements,* because this will reduce the excess reserves of banks, causing them to make fewer loans; as the outstanding loans of banks decline, the money stock will be reduced.
2. Open market operations	*Purchase additional U.S. securities,* which will expand the money stock directly, and increase the reserves of banks, inducing bankers in turn to extend more loans; this will expand the money stock indirectly.	*Sell previously purchased U.S. securities,* which will reduce both the money stock and excess reserves; the decline in excess reserves will indirectly lead to an additional reduction in the money supply.
3. Discount rate	*Lower the discount rate,* which will encourage more borrowing from the Fed; banks will tend to reduce their reserves and extend more loans because of the lower cost of borrowing from the Fed if they temporarily run short on reserves.	*Raise the discount rate,* thereby discouraging borrowing from the Fed; banks will tend to extend fewer loans and build up their reserves so they will not have to borrow from the Fed.

the Fed creates money out of thin air. The Treasury does not have this power. The Fed does not have an obligation to meet the financial responsibilities of the U.S. government. That is the domain of the Treasury. Although the two agencies cooperate with each other, they are distinctly different institutions established for different purposes (see the accompanying Thumbnail Sketch).

It is important to recognize that the buying and selling of bonds by the Treasury and by the Fed have different effects on the supply of money. The key point here is that the Treasury and the Fed handle revenues collected from the selling of bonds in different ways. When the Treasury issues and sells bonds, it does so to pay for federal government expenditures. After all, the Treasury issues the bonds in order to generate additional revenues to cover its spending. The people who buy the bonds from the Treasury have less money, but when the Treasury spends, the recipients of its spending will have more money. Thus, Treasury borrowing and spending does not change the supply of money.

THUMBNAIL SKETCH

What are the differences between the U.S. Treasury and the Federal Reserve banking system?

The U.S. Treasury

1. Is concerned with the finances of the federal government
2. Issues bonds to the general public to finance the budget deficits of the federal government
3. Does not determine the money supply

The Federal Reserve

1. Is concerned with the monetary climate of the economy
2. Does not issue bonds
3. Determines the money supply—primarily through its buying and selling of bonds issued by the U.S. Treasury

In contrast, when the Fed sells bonds, in effect, it takes the revenues and holds them, keeping them out of circulation. Because this money is out of circulation and can no longer be used for the purchase of goods and services, the money supply shrinks. On the other hand, if the Fed later wishes to increase the money supply, it can buy bonds, which will increase the availability of bank reserves and the money supply.

AMBIGUITIES IN THE MEANING AND MEASUREMENT OF THE MONEY SUPPLY

In the past, economists have generally used the *growth rate* of the money supply (either M1 or M2) to gauge the direction of monetary policy. A rapid growth rate of the money supply was indicative of expansionary monetary policy—a policy that was adding stimulus to the economy. Conversely, slow growth, or a decline, in the money stock implied a more restrictive monetary policy. However, financial innovations have altered our methods of payment and the nature of money many times in the past. Sometimes these innovations affect the significance of the growth rate figures for the various measures of the money supply. Consider the changes during the last several decades.

Throughout most of the 1970s, M1 consisted almost entirely of currency and demand deposits. At the time, regulations virtually prohibited banks from offering their customers interest-earning checking accounts. Increased competition from mutual funds led to the repeal of the regulatory restraints in 1980, and, as **Exhibit 9** illustrates, this repeal was followed by rapid growth of interest-earning checking deposits. In turn, growth of these deposits pushed up the growth rate of the M1 money supply. The growth of M1 during the 1980s, however, was deceptive. To a degree, it reflected a change in the nature of the M1 money supply. Interest-earning checking accounts are less costly to hold than currency and demand deposits. In essence, interest-earning checking accounts are partly medium-of-exchange money and partly savings. As a result, the M1 money supply of the 1980s is not precisely comparable with the figures for earlier years.

Another innovation influenced the M1 money supply in the 1990s. Beginning in 1994, a number of banks began to encourage customers to move deposits from interest-earning checking accounts into money market deposit accounts. Each of these accounts provides customers with similar services. However, because interest-earning checking deposits are included in M1 but money market deposits are not, this shift reduced the size of the M1 money supply figures. It was largely responsible for the decline in the M1 money supply during the period 1995–1997 (see Exhibit 9). As with the introduction of interest-earning checking during the 1980s, these shifts distorted the M1 money supply statistics and reduced their comparability across time periods.

Other structural changes and financial innovations—some of which are already present and others of which are likely to develop in the near future—continue to alter the nature of money, and therefore the usefulness of money growth figures (both M1 and M2) as an indicator of monetary policy. Let's consider three of these factors.

1. Widespread use of the U.S. dollar outside of the United States.   The U.S. dollar is widely used in other countries. To a degree, this has been true for a long time. However, in recent years, a number of countries have relaxed legal restraints that limited the domestic use of foreign currencies (and the maintenance of foreign currency bank accounts).[2] As noted earlier, the currency component of the M1 money supply was approximately $664 billion at year-end 2003. According to a recent study by the Federal Reserve, more than one-half and perhaps as much as two-thirds of this currency is held overseas. The movement of these funds abroad (and our inability to measure them with any degree of precision) substantially reduces the reliability of the M1 money supply figures. (*Note:* There is also some impact on M2. However, since the currency component is a much smaller proportion of M2 than M1, the distortion of M2 is less severe.)

---

[2]The number of countries where it is legal for citizens to maintain a foreign currency bank account rose from 38 in 1985 to 69 in 2002. See James Gwartney and Robert Lawson, *Economic Freedom of the World: 2004 Annual Report* (Vancouver, B.C.: Fraser Institute, 2004).

EXHIBIT 9
The Changing Nature of the M1 Money Supply

As a result of deregulation during the 1980s, interest-earning checkable deposits grew rapidly, and they now account for approximately one-quarter of the M1 money supply. Since the opportunity cost of holding these other checkable deposits is less than it is for other forms of money, strictly speaking, the money supply today is not exactly comparable to the money supply prior to 1980.

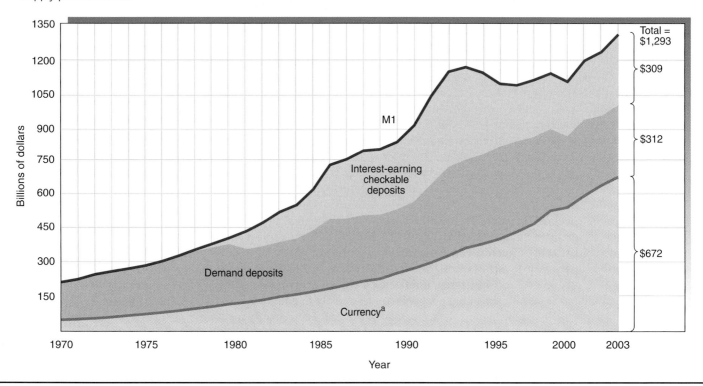

[a]Traveler's checks are included in this category.
Source: http://www.federalreserve.gov

2. The increasing availability of low-fee stock and bond mutual funds. Until recently, financial investors were generally required to pay a substantial start-up, or "load," fee when purchasing stock and bond mutual funds. This reduced their attractiveness relative to the various savings instruments included in the M2 money supply. No-load stock and bond mutual funds—that is, funds without an initial fee—are now increasingly available. Because stock and bond mutual fund investments are not counted in any of the monetary aggregates, movement of funds from various M2 components (money market mutual funds, for example) will distort the M2 money supply figures.[3]

3. Debit cards and electronic money. Financial innovators are currently developing a more convenient and versatile debit card. A card of this type would transfer funds from the cardholder's bank account to that of the seller. If more and more businesses accept payment via debit cards in the future, Americans will have less reason to hold currency. As less money is held in the form of currency—and more as bank deposits—unless the Fed takes offsetting actions, the money supply will grow rapidly. This is because of the effect the deposit expansion multiplier has. Like other changes in the nature of money, innovations in this area will reduce the future reliability of the money supply data, particularly the M1 figures, as indicators of monetary policy.

[3] For additional information on this topic, see Sean Collins and Cheryl L. Edwards, "Redefining M2 to Include Bond and Equity Mutual Funds," Federal Reserve Bank of St. Louis *Review,* November/December 1994: 7–30, and John V. Duca, "Should Bond Funds Be Included in M2?" *Journal of Banking and Finance* 19 (April 1995): 131–52.

APPLICATIONS IN ECONOMICS

Will Money Be Electronic in the Future?

The world today is becoming a place where your "paycheck" can be deposited in an electronic cash account accessible through your personal computer, but protected with a personal code. With the touch of a few computer keys, you can transfer funds to pay your monthly utility bill, mortgage and auto loan payments, and other regular expenditures. You can also shop on the Internet and use your deposits to pay for magazines, financial advice, and numerous consumer goods. Your funds can also be used to purchase stocks, bonds, mutual funds, and other financial investments. Like your paycheck, earnings from (or future sales of) these investments can be automatically deposited into your electronic cash account. Now suppose you want to withdraw some electronic cash. In the future, you might merely insert a card in your computer and load it up with transferable purchasing power, which is widely accepted by restaurants, recreation facilities, retail stores, and other business establishments. If you want to give or receive funds from family or friends, you simply merge their "cash cards" with yours, and funds can be added to one card and subtracted from another. In effect, your electronic money allows you to do anything you can currently do with currency or checking deposits—and you can do it faster, safer, and more conveniently.

Many think that this world, or something very much like it, is only a few years away. Already at more than forty colleges and universities, such as Colby College, Florida State University, and Pennsylvania State University, student identification cards have become so-called Smart Cards. Students can store money on these Smart Cards, which can be used to make purchases at retail stores as well as pay university fees such as parking tickets and tuition. Electronic money and similar innovations may well alter the nature of money and perhaps even the conduct of monetary policy in the future.

Finally, there is the expected development of electronic money. (See the Applications in Economics feature "Will Money Be Electronic in the Future?") It is difficult to forecast the nature of changes in this area. However, if individuals and businesses can economically and safely use electronic cash instead of checking deposits and currency, the nature of money and the meaning of the monetary aggregates will clearly change. If, as is anticipated, these electronic deposits can be maintained safely outside the banking system, the development might substantially change the banking system as we know it.

Because of the factors we have just discussed, M1 figures have recently shown more variability than the M2 figures. Most analysts now rely on M2 (rather than M1) when they use money supply growth rates as an indicator of what the Fed should do when it comes to monetary policy making. We will follow this convention in this textbook. However, we should keep in mind that future innovations are likely to alter the nature of money and the reliability of M2 as well.

THE CHANGING NATURE OF MONEY AROUND THE WORLD

The Euro

In the past, if you traveled from country to country in Europe, you had to exchange currencies in order to do business. Starting in January 2002, this was no longer necessary. Twelve European nations (Austria, Belgium, Finland, France, Germany, Greece, Ireland, Italy, Luxembourg, Netherlands, Portugal, and Spain) now use a single European currency called the euro.

This new currency is managed by a new central bank, the European Central Bank (ECB). The ECB, located in the Eurotower in Frankfurt, Germany, is directed by a six-member executive committee and an eighteen-member council comprised of six executive committee members plus the central bank governor from each of the twelve countries that uses the euro. The relationship between the ECB and the former central banks of the twelve countries is much like that between the Board of Governors of the Fed and the District Federal Reserve banks. The ECB sets policy, and the national central banks are expected to carry it out. The prime objective of the ECB is price stability. Its current target rate of inflation is 2 percent or less. The euro is expected not only to reduce transaction costs in these countries, but also to challenge the use of the dollar and the yen in international markets.

Movement Toward Fewer Currencies

The move toward a single currency in Europe is not unusual. In fact, the number of independent currencies in the world is shrinking. Smaller countries have been linking their currencies to those of larger countries. For example, Hong Kong ties its domestic currency—the Hong Kong dollar—to the U.S. dollar at a 7.7-to-1 rate. Other countries adopting a similar strategy include Lithuania, Bosnia, Bulgaria, and Estonia. When a country ties its currency to a strong foreign currency and backs each unit with assets denominated in the foreign currency, people are more likely to be persuaded that the currency will maintain its future value. This increased credibility is an important benefit, particularly for countries with a long history of hyperinflation and monetary instability.

Another factor reducing the number of currencies is the informal use or outright adoption of a strong foreign currency as a means of payment. The U.S. dollar has been formally adopted as the official currency in Panama, El Salvador, and Ecuador, for example. Currently, dollars are also widely held and, in some cases, used as a means of exchange in Russia (and several other countries of the former Soviet Union), Argentina, Bolivia, Mexico, and still other Latin American countries. As we previously noted, an estimated $300 billion of U.S. currency—more than half of the total—is held abroad.

How do these holdings of dollars by foreigners affect the U.S. economy? Foreigners acquired the dollars by providing goods and services to Americans. In effect, Americans got valuable goods and services by simply issuing pieces of paper—dollar bills. The dollars held abroad are very much like an interest-free loan to the U.S. government and, indirectly, the taxpayers of the United States. If foreigners were not willing to hold these dollars at a zero interest rate, the U.S. Treasury would have to issue more bonds (perhaps as much as $300 billion more) and pay interest to the bondholders. As a result, the annual interest costs of the federal government would be about $15 billion higher.

What is likely to happen to the number of currencies in the future? The U.S. dollar is likely to become the dominant currency in the Americas. As the euro gains credibility, other European countries that do not currently belong to the European Monetary Union are likely to either adopt the euro or link their currency to it. Likewise, either the Japanese yen or the Chinese yuan are likely to emerge as the primary currency in Asia. Therefore, in the relatively near future, most of the world's trade—both domestic and foreign—may well be conducted with only three or four currencies.

LOOKING AHEAD

In this chapter, we focused on the banking industry and the mechanics of monetary policy. The following chapter will analyze how monetary policy affects output, growth, and the general level of prices.

KEY POINTS

▼ Money is a financial asset that is widely accepted as a medium of exchange. It is a means of storing purchasing power for the future and is used as a unit of account. Without money, exchange would be both costly and tedious. Money derives its value from its scarcity (supply) relative to its usefulness (demand).

▼ Economists use alternative measures of the money supply to gauge how effective the Fed's monetary policies are. The narrowest definition of the money supply (M1) includes only (1) currency in the hands of the public, (2) checkable deposits (both demand and interest-earning) held in depository institutions, and (3) traveler's checks

▼ The broader M2 money supply includes M1 plus (1) savings deposits, (2) time deposits (of less than $100,000), and (3) money market mutual fund shares.

▼ Banking is a business. Banks provide their depositors with the safekeeping of money, check-clearing services on demand deposits, and interest payments on time (and some checking) deposits. Banks get most of their income by extending loans and investing in interest-earning securities.

▼ Under legislation adopted in 1980, savings and loan associations and credit unions provide the same services and confront similar regulations as commercial banks. In essence, all of these institutions are part of an integrated banking system.

▼ Under a fractional reserve banking system, banks are required to maintain only a fraction of their deposits in the form of reserves (vault cash or deposits with the Fed). Excess reserves may be invested or loaned to customers. When banks extend loans, they create additional deposits and thereby expand the money supply.

▼ The Federal Reserve System is a central banking authority designed to provide a stable monetary framework for the entire economy. The Fed is a banker's bank. The structure of the Fed is designed to insulate it from political pressures so that it will have greater freedom to follow policies more consistent with economic stability.

▼ The Fed has three major tools with which to control the money supply: (1) the establishment of reserve requirements, (2) open market operations, and (3) the setting of the discount rate. If the Fed wanted to increase the money supply, it could increase the reserves banks are required to hold, buy U.S. securities in the open market, or reduce the discount rate. Open market operations—the buying or selling of bonds—is the primary tool used by the Fed to alter the money supply.

▼ The Federal Reserve and the U.S. Treasury are distinct agencies. The Fed is concerned primarily with the money supply and the establishment of a stable monetary climate, whereas the Treasury focuses on budgetary matters—tax revenues, government expenditures, and the financing of government debt.

▼ Historically, the rate of change of the money supply has been used to judge the direction and intensity of a central bank's monetary policy. However, recent financial innovations and other structural changes (for example, the widespread use of U.S. currency in other countries) have blurred the meaning of money and reduced the reliability of the various money supply measures. In the computer age, continued change in this area is likely.

CRITICAL ANALYSIS QUESTIONS

*1. What is meant by the statement, "This asset is illiquid"? List some things you own and rank them from most liquid to most illiquid.

2. What determines whether or not a financial asset is included in the M1 money supply? Why are interest-earning checkable deposits included in M1, while interest-earning savings accounts and Treasury bills are not?

*3. What makes money valuable? Does money perform an economic service? Explain. Could money perform its function better if there were twice as much of it? Why or why not?

4. "People are poor because they don't have very much money. Yet, central bankers keep money scarce. If people had more money, poverty could be eliminated." Evaluate this view. Do you think it reflects sound economics?

5. Why can banks continue to hold reserves that are only a fraction of the demand deposits of their customers? Is your money safe in a bank? Why or why not?

*6. Suppose you withdraw $100 from your checking account. How does this transaction affect (a) the supply of money, (b) the reserves of your bank, and (c) the excess reserves of your bank?

7. Explain how the creation of excess reserves would cause the money supply to increase by some multiple of the newly created excess reserves.

*8. How will the following actions affect the money supply?
   a. A reduction in the discount rate
   b. An increase in the reserve requirements
   c. Purchase by the Fed of $100 million in U.S. securities from a commercial bank
   d. Sale by the U.S. Treasury of $100 million in newly issued bonds to a commercial bank
   e. An increase in the discount rate
   f. Sale by the Fed of $200 million in U.S. securities to a private investor

9. What's wrong with this way of thinking? "When the government runs a budget deficit, it simply pays its bills by printing more money. As the newly printed money works its way through the economy, it waters down the value of paper money already in circulation. Thus, it takes more money to buy things. Budget deficits are the major cause of inflation."

*10. If the Federal Reserve does not take any offsetting action, what would happen to the supply of money if the general public decided to increase its holdings of currency and decrease its checking deposits by an equal amount?

11. What is the federal funds interest rate? If the Fed wants to use open market operations to lower the federal funds rate, what action should it take? Explain.

*12. If the Fed wants to expand the money supply, why is it more likely to do so by purchasing bonds rather than by lowering reserve requirements?

*13. Are the following statements true or false?
   a. "You can never have too much money."
   b. "When you deposit currency in a commercial bank, cash goes out of circulation and the money supply declines."
   c. "If the Fed would create more money, Americans would achieve a higher standard of living."

14. How has the nature of the M1 money supply changed in recent years? How have these changes influenced the usefulness of M1 as an indicator of monetary policy? Why do many analysts prefer to use M2 rather than M1 when comparing the monetary policy of the 1990s with that of earlier periods?

15. Why do foreigners often hold U.S. dollars? How does the holding of dollars by foreigners affect the welfare of Americans?

*16. Suppose that the Federal Reserve purchases a bond for $100,000 from Donald Truck, who deposits the proceeds in the Manufacturer's National Bank.
   a. What will be the impact of this transaction on the supply of money?
   b. If the reserve requirement ratio is 20 percent, what is the maximum amount of additional loans that the Manufacturer's Bank will be able to extend as the result of Truck's deposit?
   c. Given the 20 percent reserve requirement, what is the maximum increase in the quantity of checkable deposits that could result throughout the entire banking system because of the Fed's action?
   d. Would you expect this to happen? Why or why not? Explain.

17. Suppose that the reserve requirement is 10 percent and the balance sheet of the People's National Bank looks like the accompanying example.
   a. What are the required reserves of People's National Bank? Does the bank have any excess reserves?
   b. What is the maximum loan that the bank could extend?
   c. Indicate how the bank's balance sheet would be altered if it extended this loan.
   d. Suppose that the required reserves were 20 percent. If this were the case, would the bank be in a position to extend any additional loans? Explain.

Assets		Liabilities	
Vault cash	$ 20,000	Checking deposits	$200,000
Deposits at Fed	30,000	Net worth	15,000
Securities	45,000		
Loans	120,000		

*18. Suppose that the reserve requirements are 10 percent and that the Federal Reserve purchases $2 billion in securities on a given day.
   a. How will this transaction affect the M1 money supply?
   b. If the brokerage firm that sold the bonds to the Fed deposits the proceeds of the sale into its account with City Bank, what is the maximum amount of additional loans that City Bank will be able to extend as the result of this deposit?
   c. If additional loans are extended throughout the banking system and the proceeds are always redeposited back into a checking account, by how

much will the M1 money supply increase if banks use all their additional reserves to extend new loans?

d. Why is the actual money deposit multiplier generally less than the potential multiplier?

19. How would the following influence the growth rates of the M1 and M2 money supply figures over time?

   a. An increase in the quantity of U.S. currency held overseas

   b. A shift of funds from interest-earning checking deposits to money market mutual funds

c. A reduction in the holdings of currency by the general public because debit cards have become more popular and widely accepted

d. The shift of funds from money market mutual funds into stock and bond mutual funds because the fees to invest in the latter have declined

*Asterisk denotes questions for which answers are given in Appendix B.

CHAPTER
14

Modern Macroeconomics and Monetary Policy

The conventional wisdom once held that money doesn't matter. Now there is wide agreement that monetary policy can significantly affect real economic activity in the short run, though only price level in the long run.

—Daniel L. Thornton and
David C. Wheelock[1]

Chapter Focus

- What are the determinants of the demand for money? How is the supply of money determined?

- How does monetary policy affect interest rates, output, and employment?

- Can monetary policy stimulate real GDP in the short run? Can it do so in the long run?

- Does it make any difference whether people quickly anticipate the effects of a change in monetary policy? Why?

- Does an increase in the supply of money cause inflation?

[1]Daniel L. Thornton and David C. Wheelock, "Editor's Introduction," *Federal Reserve Bank of St. Louis: Review* (May/June 1995): vii.

I n the preceding chapter, we noted that many consider the chairman of the Federal Reserve System to be the second most important person—next to the president—in the United States. Why is this so? Along with other members of the Fed's Board of Governors and Federal Open Market Committee, the Fed chairman is in charge of monetary policy. When monetary policy keeps prices stable—that is, when it keeps the inflation rate at a persistently low level—markets operate more smoothly. On the other hand, the consequences of monetary instability and high rates of inflation are often disastrous. This makes the conduct of monetary policy extremely important.

Until now, within the framework of the aggregate demand–aggregate supply model, we assumed that the supply of money was constant. We now relax this assumption. The previous chapter identified the tools the Fed has to alter the supply of money. This chapter focuses on how monetary policy works—how changes in the supply of money affect interest rates, output, and prices. ■

THE IMPACT OF MONETARY POLICY ON OUTPUT AND INFLATION

Like the modern view of fiscal policy, the modern view of monetary policy has evolved over the years. In the aftermath of the Great Depression and Keynesian Revolution, there was great debate about the importance of monetary policy. During the 1950s and 1960s, most Keynesians argued that monetary policy could be used to control inflation, but that it was often ineffective as a means of stimulating aggregate demand. It was popular to draw an analogy between monetary policy and the workings of a string. Like a string, monetary policy could be used to "pull" (hold back) price increases and thereby control inflation. However, just as one cannot "push" with a string, monetary policy could not be used to push (stimulate) aggregate demand.

Beginning in the late 1950s, this view was hotly contested by Milton Friedman, who later became a Nobel laureate, and a group of economists, who, along with Friedman, became known as **monetarists**. Monetarists argue that changes in the stock (supply) of money have a powerful influence on the economy's output in the short run, and prices in the long run. Monetarists believe, in fact, that erratic monetary policy is actually the primary *source* of both business instability and inflation. Milton Friedman summarized the monetarists' position in his 1967 presidential address to the American Economic Association in which he stated,

> Every major contraction in this country has been either produced by monetary disorder or greatly exacerbated by monetary disorder. Every major inflation episode has been produced by monetary expansion.[2]

A modern view of monetary policy emerged from this debate. Although minor disagreements remain, both modern Keynesians and monetarists now agree that monetary policy has a major impact on the economy.[3] The following sections present the modern consensus view of this impact.

Monetarists
Economists who believe that (1) monetary instability is the major cause of fluctuations in real GDP and (2) rapid growth of the money supply is the major cause of inflation.

The Demand and Supply of Money

Why do individuals and businesses want to hold cash and checking account money rather than bonds, stocks, automobiles, buildings, and consumer durables? As you think about this question, don't confuse (1) the desire to hold money balances with (2) the desire for

---

[2]Milton Friedman, "The Role of Monetary Policy," *American Economic Review* (March 1968): 12.

[3]The evolution of the views of Paul Samuelson, who might properly be regarded as the father of American Keynesian economics, best illustrates the change in the Keynesian view with regard to the relative importance of monetary and fiscal policy. Commenting on the twelfth edition of his classic text in 1985, Samuelson stated: "In the early editions of the book, fiscal policy was top banana. In later editions that emphasis changed to equality. In this edition we've taken a stand that monetary policy is most important."

Milton Friedman (1912–)

Milton Friedman, the 1976 recipient of the Nobel Prize, is widely regarded as the most influential spokesman for a free market economy in the twentieth century. He was also a pioneering researcher and the leading spokesman for the monetarist perspective. At a time when the role of money was largely ignored by the dominant Keynesian perspective, Friedman almost single-handedly convinced the economics profession that monetary policy exerted a powerful impact on the economy. He and other monetarists maintain that business fluctuations are primarily the result of monetary instability. Even his critics eventually concluded that, by and large, he was right.

His popular books *Capitalism and Freedom* (1962) and *Free to Choose* (1980), coauthored with his wife, Rose, are classical treatises in support of economic freedom. After spending years at the University of Chicago, he is currently on the faculty at Stanford University. Now in his nineties, he continues to be an active scholar and writer.

more wealth (or income). Of course, all of us would like to have more wealth, but we may be perfectly satisfied with our holdings of money in relation to our holdings of other goods, *given our current level of wealth*. When we say people want to hold more (or less) money, we mean that they want to restructure their wealth toward larger (smaller) money balances.

People hold money for several reasons. At the most basic level, we hold money so we can buy things. Households hold money balances so they can pay for the weekly groceries, the monthly house payment, gasoline for the car, lunch for the kids, and other items they purchase regularly. Businesses demand money so they can pay their workers, buy supplies, and conduct other transactions. People also hold money for unexpected expenses like an accident or a medical emergency. Economists call this the *precautionary motive* for holding money. In addition, money is an asset—a means of storing value. Holding money is a convenient way to set aside purchasing power for future use.

Higher interest rates make it more costly to hold money, however. Consider the cost of holding $1,000 in currency and demand deposits (which do not earn interest) rather than in interest-earning bonds, for example. If the interest rate is 10 percent, it will cost you $100 per year to hold an additional $1,000 of non-interest-earning money. In contrast, if the interest rate is 1 percent, the annual cost of holding the $1,000 money balance will be only $10. Even if you put the $1,000 in an interest-earning checking account, you could probably earn more interest if you purchased a bond or some other less liquid form of savings with it. Thus, the opportunity cost of holding money is directly related to the nominal interest rate.

A curve that outlines the relationship between the interest rate (measured on the y-axis) and the quantity of money (measured on the x-axis) is called the **demand for money.** *As part (a) of* **Exhibit 1** *shows, there is an inverse relationship between the interest rate and the quantity of money demanded.* This inverse relationship reflects the fact that higher interest rates make it more costly to hold money instead of interest-earning assets like bonds. Therefore, as interest rates rise, individuals and businesses will try to manage their affairs with smaller money balances.

The demand for money balances will generally increase with the nominal value of transactions. If wages and prices increase, people will need more money in their wallets (or checking accounts) to make their regular daily, weekly, and monthly purchases.

Demand for money
A curve that indicates the relationship between the interest rate and the quantity of money people want to hold. Because higher interest rates increase the opportunity cost of holding money, the quantity of money demanded will be inversely related to the interest rate.

(a) Demand for money

(b) Supply of money

EXHIBIT 1
The Demand and Supply of Money

The demand for money is inversely related to the money interest rate (a). The supply of money is determined by the monetary authorities (the Fed) through their open market operations, discount-rate policy, and reserve requirements (b).

Businesses will also require more money to pay their bills. Similarly, if prices remain constant but the quantity of goods bought and sold in the economy increases, larger money balances will be needed to conduct those transactions. In other words, as nominal GDP increases as the result of *either* higher prices or the growth of real output, the demand for money balances will also increase. When this happens, the entire demand curve for money will shift to the right. Conversely, a decline in nominal GDP will decrease the demand for money, shifting the curve to the left.

Changes in institutional factors can also affect the demand for money. For example, the greater availability and widespread use of credit cards in recent years has made it easier for households to manage their affairs with less money. The increased availability of short-term loans has had a similar effect. Both of these factors have gradually reduced the demand for money (shifting the entire curve to the left).

As we discussed in the previous chapter, the amount of money in the economy is determined by the monetary authorities—the Fed in the case of the United States. The Fed can use reserve requirements, the discount rate, and especially open market operations to set the supply of money at whatever level it wants. Changes in the interest rate do not alter the Fed's ability to determine the supply of money. Therefore, as Exhibit 1 (part b) shows, the money supply schedule is vertical. The vertical supply curve reflects that the quantity of money is determined by Fed policy and is not affected by changes in the interest rate.

The Equilibrium Between Money Demand and Money Supply

Exhibit 2 brings money demand and money supply together and shows how they determine the equilibrium rate of interest. The money interest rate will move toward i_e, when the quantity of money demanded by households and businesses is just equal to the quantity supplied by the Fed. At the equilibrium interest rate, people are willing to hold the stock of money the Fed has supplied to the economy.

At an interest rate above equilibrium, i_2, for example, people will not want to hold as much money as the Fed has supplied. Accordingly, they will try to reduce their money balances. A number of people (and businesses) will do so by using some of their money balances to buy bonds. This increase in demand for bonds will drive bond prices up and interest rates down. (*Remember*: Higher bond prices imply lower interest rates.) As a result, the money interest rate will move toward the i_e equilibrium. On the other hand, at a below-equilibrium money interest rate, i_3, for example, an excess demand for money will

**EXHIBIT 2
Money Supply, Money Demand, and Equilibrium**

The money interest rate will tend to gravitate toward equilibrium, i_e, where the quantity of money demanded by households and businesses will equal the quantity of money supplied by the Fed.

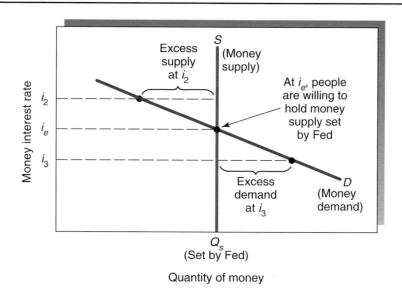

be present. People would like to hold a larger quantity of money than the Fed has supplied. In this case, people will sell some of the bonds they own to get more money. In turn, the sale of their bonds will reduce bond prices and put upward pressure on interest rates. This will cause the interest rate to move once again toward i_e.

How Does Monetary Policy Affect the Economy?

How will a change in the money supply affect the economy? As we previously discussed, the Fed typically uses open market operations to control the supply of money. If the Fed wants to shift to a more **expansionary monetary policy**, it will buy bonds. **Exhibit 3** shows the impact of an expansionary monetary policy on the economy. Let's first consider the situation in which the money interest rate (i_1 in the money balances market) is equal to the real interest rate (r_1 in the loanable funds market). This indicates that the expected rate of inflation is zero. When the Fed purchases bonds in order to increase the money supply (shifting S_1 to S_2 in part a), it bids up bond prices and injects additional reserves into the banking system. Profit-seeking banks will not let the additional reserves lie idle; they will loan them out to customers in order to earn interest on them. This combination of factors—higher bond prices and excess reserves—will increase the supply of loanable funds (shift from S_1 to S_2 in part b). In the short run, this will cause the real interest rate to fall to r_2.

How will the Fed's bond purchases, the creation of additional bank reserves, and a lower real interest rate influence the demand for goods and services? As part (c) of Exhibit 3 shows, aggregate demand will increase (shift from AD_1 to AD_2). Economists stress the importance of three factors that contribute to this increase in aggregate demand:[4]

1. The lower real interest rate will make current investment and consumption cheaper. At the lower interest rate, entrepreneurs will undertake some investment projects they otherwise wouldn't have. Spending by firms on structures and equipment will increase. Likewise, consumers will decide to expand their purchases of automobiles and consumer durables, which can now be bought with smaller monthly payments.

Expansionary monetary policy A shift in monetary policy designed to stimulate aggregate demand. Bond purchases by the Fed, the creation of additional bank reserves, and an increase in the growth rate of the money supply generally indicate a shift to a more expansionary monetary policy.

---

[4]See the *Federal Reserve Bank of St. Louis: Review* (May/June 1995) and the *Journal of Economic Perspectives* (Fall 1995) for additional details on how changes in monetary policy affect aggregate demand.

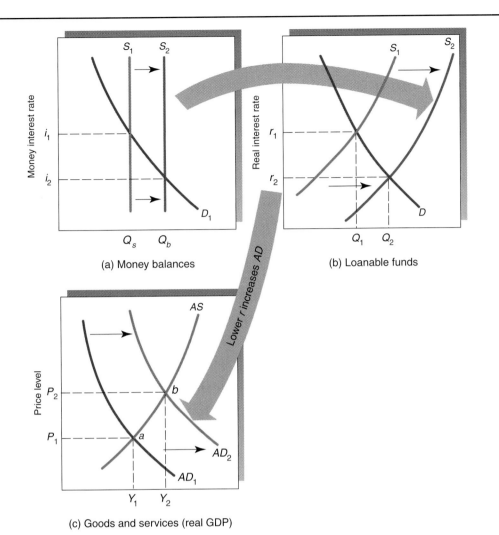

(a) Money balances

(b) Loanable funds

(c) Goods and services (real GDP)

Lower r increases AD

EXHIBIT 3
The Transmission of Monetary Policy

When the Fed shifts to a more expansionary monetary policy, it will generally buy additional bonds. This will supply the banking system with additional reserves. Both the Fed's bond purchases and the banks' use of the additional reserves to extend new loans will increase the supply of loanable funds (shift it from S_1 to S_2, part b) and put downward pressure on the real rate of interest. As the real interest rate falls (to r_2), aggregate demand increases (to AD_2 in part c). Because the effects of the monetary expansion were unanticipated, the expansion in AD leads to both an increase in current output (to Y_2) and higher prices (inflation) in the short run. The increase in output, however, will be only temporary.

2. The lower interest rate will tend to cause financial capital to move abroad, the foreign exchange rate of the dollar to depreciate, and net exports to expand. Here's how: As domestic interest rates fall, both domestic and foreign investors will shift some of their financial investments to countries where interest rates are higher and they can get better returns on their investments. As investors shift funds abroad, they will supply dollars and demand foreign currency to purchase the new foreign assets. This will cause the dollar to depreciate in the foreign exchange market. In turn, the depreciation in the exchange-rate value of the dollar will make imports more expensive for Americans and U.S. exports cheaper for foreigners. As a result, U.S. imports will decline and exports will expand. This increase in net exports will also stimulate the nation's aggregate demand as foreigners buy more U.S. goods and services.

3. The lower interest rate will tend to increase asset prices—for example, the prices of stocks, houses, and other structures people own—which will also increase aggregate demand. Here's how this works: As the prices of real and financial assets rise because they are now relatively more attractive investments, household wealth will increase. Because people are wealthier, they will, in turn, increase their consumption spending. Perhaps more important, the higher prices of houses and other physical assets will make their production more profitable and motivate entrepreneurs to expand their investment spending on them. This additional investment by entrepreneurs will also increase aggregate demand.

THUMBNAIL SKETCH

The Transmission of Monetary Policy—A Summary

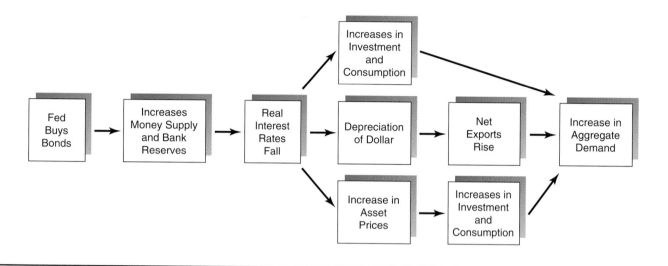

The accompanying Thumbnail Sketch outlines the complex sequence of events through which Fed bond purchases expand the money supply and increase aggregate demand. This sequence is sometimes referred to as the interest rate transmission mechanism of monetary policy.[5]

The Effects of an Unanticipated Expansionary Monetary Policy

As we have previously discussed, modern macroeconomic analysis emphasizes whether a change is anticipated or unanticipated. If people do not anticipate the increase in aggregate demand accompanying an expansionary monetary policy, the prices of products will rise more quickly than the costs of producing them in the short run. As a result, the profit margins of businesses will improve, and they will respond by expanding their output (as the increase in real output from Y_1 to Y_2 in part c of Exhibit 3 shows).

An unexpected increase in the supply of money will reduce the real rate of interest, thereby triggering an increase in the demand for goods and services. In turn, the increase in aggregate demand will expand real output and employment in the short run.

Exhibit 4 part (a) shows the potential of expansionary monetary policy to direct a recessionary economy to full employment. Consider an economy initially at output Y_1, which is below full-employment capacity (Y_F). Expansionary monetary policy will lower interest rates and increase aggregate demand (to AD_2). Real output will then expand (to Y_F). In essence, the expansionary monetary policy provides an alternative to the economy's self-corrective mechanism. If demand is unchanged, declining resource prices and real interest rates will eventually restore full employment. Because businesses will be selling more goods and services and earning higher profits, they will therefore want to hire more workers. For these reasons, many economists believe that expansionary monetary policy can speed up the return to full-employment equilibrium.

---

[5]There is also a more direct route through which expansionary monetary policy may stimulate aggregate demand. When the Fed expands the supply of money, it will create an "excess supply of money" *at the initial money interest rate*. People may respond by directly increasing their purchases of goods and services in an effort to reduce their money balances to desired levels. Obviously, this will increase aggregate demand. This direct path is most relevant when the government expands the supply of money by paying its bills with newly created currency. Because the money supply of the United States is generally expanded via open market operations, we have focused on the transmission of monetary policy through the interest rate. The implications of both the direct and indirect paths are identical—both indicate that expansionary monetary policy will stimulate aggregate demand.

EXHIBIT 4
The Effects of
Expansionary Monetary
Policy

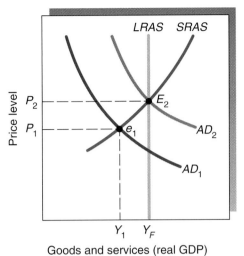

(a) Output is initially at less
than full employment

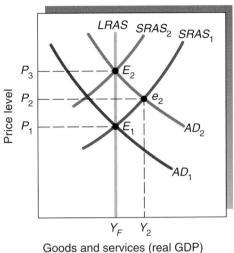

(b) Output is initially at full
employment

If the impact of an increase in aggregate demand accompanying an expansionary monetary policy is felt when the economy is operating below capacity, the policy will help direct the economy to a long-run full-employment equilibrium (E_2 in part a). In this case, the increase in output from Y_1 to Y_F will be long term. In contrast, if the stimulus on aggregate demand is imposed on an economy already at full employment (part b), it will lead to excess demand and higher product prices. Output will temporarily increase (to Y_2). However, in the long run, the strong demand will push up resource prices, shifting short-run aggregate supply to $SRAS_2$. The price level will rise to P_3 and output will recede (to Y_F) from its temporary high.

How will an expansion of the money supply by the Fed influence the price level and output if the economy is already at full employment? Although this is not a desirable strategy, it is interesting to analyze the outcome. As part (b) of Exhibit 4 shows, an unanticipated shift to a more expansionary monetary policy will increase aggregate demand, causing the prices of products to rise relative to the costs of making them. Keep in mind that important production components, such as labor, are sometimes temporarily fixed by long-term contracts. When this is the case, real output will initially increase to Y_2, which is beyond the economy's long-run capacity of Y_F. However, the high rate of output (Y_2) will not be sustainable. Eventually, the long-term contracts based on the previously weaker demand (AD_1) will end. The new agreements will reflect the new, stronger demand. As a result, resource prices (such as labor costs) will rise, shifting $SRAS$ upward and to the left. Eventually, a new long-run equilibrium (E_2) will be established at a higher price level (P_3). Output will fall to Y_F. Thus, when an economy is already at full employment, an unexpected shift to a more expansionary monetary policy will temporarily increase output, but in the long run it leads only to higher prices.

The Effects of an Unanticipated Restrictive Monetary Policy

Suppose the Fed moves toward a more **restrictive monetary policy** by selling bonds to the general public. The sale of bonds will reduce both the supply of money and the reserves of banks as people take money out of their accounts to buy the bonds. **Exhibit 5** shows the impact of the more restrictive monetary policy on the loanable funds and goods and services markets. The Fed's sale of bonds reduces bond prices because it puts more bonds in the market. It also drains reserves from the banking system as people buy the bonds (reducing the ability of banks to extend loans). As a result, the supply of loanable funds will fall, causing the real interest rate to rise (from r_1 to r_2 in part a of Exhibit 5). The higher real interest rate will reduce spending on both investment goods and consumer durables because they'll be more costly to finance. The higher rate will also cause an inflow of capital from abroad

Restrictive monetary policy
A shift in monetary policy designed to reduce aggregate demand and put downward pressure on the general level of prices (or the rate of inflation). Bond sales by the Fed, a decline in bank reserves, and a reduction in the growth rate of the money supply generally indicate a shift to a restrictive monetary policy.

and lead to the appreciation in the exchange rate of the dollar. In turn, this appreciation of the dollar will encourage U.S. citizens to buy imported products (which will become cheaper for them) and discourage foreigners from buying U.S. exports (because they will be more costly for them). This will then lead to lower net U.S. exports (and lower aggregate demand in the United States). The higher interest rates will also reduce housing and other asset prices, discouraging new construction and investment. All of these factors will tend to reduce aggregate demand (shift it from AD_1 to AD_2 in part b of Exhibit 5).

The unexpected decline in the demand for goods and services will put downward pressures on prices, squeeze profit margins, and reduce output. As part (b) of Exhibit 5 shows, the price level will decline (to P_2), and output will fall (to Y_2) as the result of the restrictive monetary policy.

The appropriateness of a restrictive policy depends on the state of the economy. **Exhibit 6** illustrates this point. When there is upward pressure on prices because of strong demand, restrictive policy is an effective weapon against inflation. Suppose that, as illustrated by part (a) of Exhibit 6, an economy is temporarily operating at e_1 and Y_1—beyond its full-employment real GDP of Y_F. Strong aggregate demand is putting upward pressure on prices. In this case, a restrictive policy will help keep the price level constant and offset the inflationary forces. If a proper "dose" of a restrictive policy is administered at the right time, it will lower aggregate demand (to AD_2) and direct the economy to a noninflationary, long-run equilibrium at P_2 and Y_F (that is, E_2).

As part (b) of Exhibit 6 shows, however, an unanticipated shift to restrictive policy will be damaging to an economy operating at full-employment equilibrium. If the output of an economy is at full employment (or worse still, at less than full employment), a restrictive policy will reduce aggregate demand (shift it to AD_2) and output will decline from Y_F to Y_2. This output will fall below the economy's full-employment capacity and throw the economy into a recession.

Why Is Timing Important?

Like fiscal policy, monetary policy must be properly timed to help stabilize an economy. Exhibits 4 and 6 highlight this point. When an economy is operating below its long-run capacity, expansionary monetary policy can increase aggregate demand and push the

---

EXHIBIT 5
The Short-Run Effects of a More Restrictive Monetary Policy

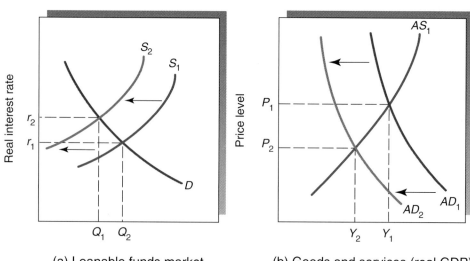

(a) Loanable funds market   (b) Goods and services (real GDP)

When the Fed shifts to a more restrictive policy, it sells bonds, which reduces the reserves available to banks, decreases the supply of loanable funds, and puts upward pressure on interest rates (a). The higher interest rates decrease aggregate demand (shift it to AD_2 in b). When the reduction in aggregate demand is unanticipated, real output will decline (to Y_2) and downward pressure on prices will result.

EXHIBIT 6
The Effects of a
Restrictive Monetary
Policy

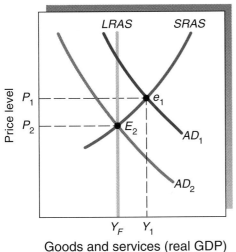

(a) Restrictive policy to
control inflation

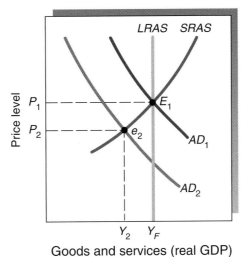

(b) Restrictive policy that
causes a recession

The stabilization effects of restrictive monetary policy depend on the state of the economy when the policy exerts its primary effect. Restrictive monetary policy will reduce aggregate demand. If the restraint takes effect when aggregate demand is strong and the economy is overheated, it will limit or even prevent the occurrence of an inflationary boom (a). In contrast, if the restraint in aggregate demand takes effect when the economy is at full employment, it will disrupt the long-run equilibrium, reduce output, and result in a recession (b).

output of the economy to its sustainable potential (part a of Exhibit 4). Similarly, if properly timed, restrictive monetary policy can help control (or prevent) inflation (part a of Exhibit 6).

If it is timed improperly, however, monetary policy can be destabilizing. Expansionary monetary policy will cause inflation if the effects of the policy are felt when the economy is already at or beyond its capacity (part b of Exhibit 4). Similarly, if the effects of a restrictive policy come when an economy is operating at its potential GDP, a recession is the likely outcome (part b of Exhibit 6). Worse still, the impact of a restrictive policy can be disastrous if it is imposed on an economy that's already in a recession.

Properly timing monetary policy is not an easy task for the Fed. Although the Fed can change a policy rapidly, there will be a time lag before it has a significant impact on aggregate demand. Economists estimate the lag will generally be at least five or six months. Some economists, particularly monetarists, believe it may be as much as twelve to eighteen months. The impact on the price level and inflation rate will likely take even longer, perhaps as long as thirty-six months. Given our limited ability to forecast the future, these lengthy time lags clearly reduce the effectiveness of discretionary monetary policy as a stabilization tool.

MONETARY POLICY IN THE LONG RUN
The Quantity Theory of Money

Since the middle of the eighteenth century, economists have argued that excessive money growth leads to inflation. Nearly a hundred years ago, Englishman Alfred Marshall and American Irving Fisher formalized the **quantity theory of money** in support of this view. ***The quantity theory of money predicts that an increase in the supply of money will cause a proportional increase in the price level.***

The quantity theory of money can be more easily understood once we recognize that there are two ways of viewing GDP. As the *AD-AS* model shows, nominal GDP is the sum

Quantity theory of money
A theory that hypothesizes that a change in the money supply will cause a proportional change in the price level because velocity and real output are unaffected by the quantity of money.

of the price, *P*, times the output, *Y*, of each final-product good purchased during the period. In aggregate, *P* represents the economy's price level, whereas *Y* indicates real income or real GDP. There is also a second way of visualizing GDP. When the existing money stock, *M*, is multiplied by the number of times, *V*, that money is used to buy final products, this, too, yields the economy's nominal GDP. Therefore,

$$PY = \text{GDP} = MV$$

Velocity of money
The average number of times a dollar is used to purchase final goods and services during a year. It is equal to GDP divided by the stock of money.

The **velocity of money** (*V*) is simply the average number of times a dollar is used to purchase a final product or service during a year. Velocity is equal to nominal GDP divided by the size of the money stock. For example, in 2003, GDP was equal to $10,988 billion, while the M1 money supply was $1,293 billion. Therefore, the velocity of the M1 money stock was 8.5 ($10,988 billion divided by $1,293 billion). The velocity of the M2 money stock can be derived in a similar manner. In 2003, the M2 money stock was $6,063 billion. Thus, the velocity of M2 was 1.8 ($10,988 billion divided by $6,063 billion).

The concept of velocity is closely related to the demand for money. When decision makers conduct a specific amount of business with a smaller amount of money, their demand for money balances is reduced. Each dollar, though, is being used more often, so the velocity of the money increases. Thus, for a given GDP level, when the demand for money declines, the velocity of money increases. Correspondingly, an increase in the demand for money is a reflection of a reduction in velocity.

When considering the behavior of prices, output, money, and velocity over time, we can write the quantity theory equation in terms of growth rates:

Rate of inflation + Growth rate of real output = Growth rate of the money supply + Growth rate of velocity

Equation of exchange
MV = *PY*, where *M* is the money supply, *V* is the velocity of money, *P* is the price level, and *Y* is the output of goods and services produced in an economy.

Economists call the *MV* = *PY* relationship the **equation of exchange**, because it reflects both the monetary and real sides of each final-product exchange. The quantity theory of money, though, assumes that *Y* and *V* are determined by factors other than the amount of money in circulation. Classical economists believed that real output, *Y*, was determined by factors such as technology, the size of the economy's resource base, and the skill of its labor force. These factors were thought to be unrelated to changes in the money supply. Likewise, the velocity of money, *V*, was thought to be determined primarily by institutional factors, such as the organization of banking and credit, the frequency of income payments, transportation speed, and the communication system. These factors change quite slowly.

Thus, classical economists thought that, for all practical purposes, both *Y* and *V* were constant (or changed by only small amounts) over periods of two, three, or four years. If both *Y* and *V* are constant, then the *MV* = *PY* relationship indicates that an increase in the money supply (*M*) will lead to a proportional increase in the price level (*P*). Correspondingly, an increase in the growth rate of the money supply can be expected to cause a similar increase in the rate of inflation.

The Long-Run Impact of Monetary Policy: The Modern View

How will expansionary monetary policy impact an economy in the long run? Let's begin with a simple case. Suppose real GDP is growing at a 3 percent annual rate and that the monetary authorities (the Fed in the U.S.) are expanding the money supply by 3 percent each year. In addition, let's assume that the velocity of money is constant. This would imply that the 3 percent annual increase in output, or GDP, would lead to a 3 percent annual increase in the demand for money. In this case, the 3 percent monetary growth would be consistent with stable prices (zero inflation). Initially, we will assume that the economy's real interest rate is 4 percent. Because the inflation rate is zero, the nominal rate of interest is also equal to 4 percent. **Exhibits 7** and **8** illustrate an economy initially (period 1) characterized by these conditions.

EXHIBIT 7
The Long-Run Effects of a More Rapid Expansion in the Money Supply on the Goods and Services Market

Here we illustrate the long-term impact of an increase in the annual growth rate of the money supply from 3 to 8 percent. Initially, prices are stable (P_{100}) when the money supply is expanding by 3 percent annually. The acceleration in the growth rate of the money supply increases aggregate demand (shifts it to AD_2). At first, real output may expand beyond the economy's potential (Y_F). However, abnormally low unemployment and strong demand conditions will create upward pressure on wages and other resource prices, shifting aggregate supply to AS_2. Output will return to its long-run potential and the price level will increase to P_{105} (E_2). If the more rapid monetary growth continues in subsequent periods, AD and AS will continue to shift upward, leading to still higher prices (E_3 and periods beyond). The net result of the process is sustained inflation.

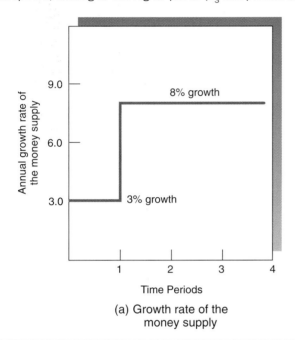

(a) Growth rate of the money supply

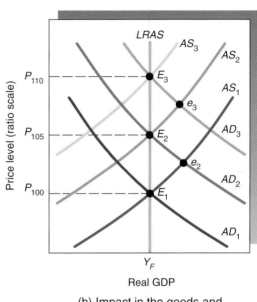

(b) Impact in the goods and services market

What will happen if the monetary authorities permanently increase the growth rate of the money supply from 3 percent to 8 percent annually (see part a of Exhibit 7, beginning in period 2)?[6] In the short run, the expansionary monetary policy will reduce the real interest rate and stimulate aggregate demand (shift it to AD_2 in part b of Exhibit 7), just as we previously explained (in Exhibits 3 and 4). For a time, real output will exceed the economy's potential. However, many resource suppliers will want to modify their long-term agreements as soon as they can in light of the strong demand conditions. Over time, more and more resource suppliers (including workers represented by union officials) will have the opportunity to alter their prior contracts. As this happens, wages and other resource prices will increase. As they do, costs will rise and profit margins will fall back to normal levels. The higher costs will reduce aggregate supply (shift it to AS_2). As the rapid monetary growth continues in subsequent periods (periods 3, 4, and so on), both AD and AS will shift upward. The price level will rise to P_{105}, P_{110}, and still higher levels as the money supply continues to grow more rapidly than the monetary growth rate consistent with stable prices. The continuation of the expansionary monetary policy leads to a higher and higher price level—that is, a sustained inflation.

Suppose an inflation rate of 5 percent eventually emerges from the more rapid growth rate of the money supply (8 percent rather than 3 percent). In the long run, more and more people will make decisions based on the persistent 5 percent inflation because it will be what they come to expect. In the resource market, both buyers and sellers will eventually

---

[6]In the preceding chapter, we noted the difficulties involved in the measurement of the money supply (both M1 and M2). Changes in the growth rate of the money supply may not always be indicative of a shift in monetary policy. More generally, the example presented here assumes that the Fed has shifted to a more expansionary monetary policy—one that will lead to an increase in the rate of inflation—whether or not the monetary aggregates as currently measured reflect this shift.

include the 5 percent expected inflation rate in long-term contracts, such as collective bargaining agreements. Once this happens, resource prices and costs will rise as rapidly as prices in the goods and services market. ***When the inflation rate is what it's expected to be in the long run, it will fail to either reduce real wages or improve profit margins. Unemployment will return to its natural rate.***

Exhibit 8 shows the long-run adjustments in the loanable funds market once borrowers and lenders expect the 5 percent inflation rate. When lenders expect a 5 percent annual increase in the price level, a 9 percent interest rate will be necessary to provide them with as much incentive to supply loanable funds as a 4 percent rate did *when stable prices were expected*. Thus, the supply of loanable funds will shift vertically by the 5 percent expected rate of inflation. Simultaneously, borrowers who were willing to pay 4 percent interest on their loans when stable prices were expected will be willing to pay 9 percent when they expect prices to increase by 5 percent annually. The demand for loanable funds will therefore also increase (shift vertically) by the expected inflation rate. Once borrowers and lenders anticipate the higher (5 percent) inflation rate, the equilibrium money interest rate will rise to 9 percent. Of course, the real interest rate is equal to the money interest rate (9 percent) minus the expected rate of inflation (5 percent). In the long run, a 4 percent real interest rate will emerge with inflation, just as it did with stable prices.[7] Inflation, then, will fail to reduce the real interest rate in the long run.

The long-run implications of modern analysis are consistent with those of the earlier quantity theory of money. ***In the long run, the main consequence of rapid money growth is inflation. An unanticipated shift to a more expansionary policy will increase output and employment in the short run, but not in the long run. In the long run, rapid monetary growth will neither reduce unemployment nor raise real output.***

EXHIBIT 8
The Long-Run Effects of More Rapid Expansion in the Money Supply on the Loanable Funds Market

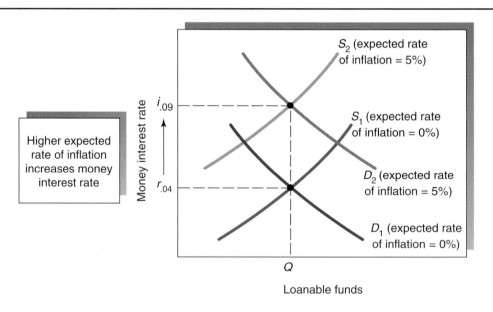

When prices are stable, supply and demand in the loanable funds market are in balance at a real and nominal interest rate of 4 percent. If a more rapid monetary expansion leads to a long-term 5 percent inflation rate, borrowers and lenders will build the higher inflation rate into their decision making. As a result, the nominal interest rate (*i*) will rise to 9 percent—the 4 percent real rate plus a 5 percent inflationary premium.

---

[7]Higher rates of inflation are generally associated with an increase in the variability of the inflation rate. Thus, greater risk (the possibility of either a substantial gain or loss associated with a sharp change in the inflation rate) accompanies exchange in the loanable funds market when inflation rates are high. This additional risk may result in higher real interest rates than would prevail at lower rates of inflation. The text discussion does not introduce this consideration.

MONETARY POLICY WHEN THE EFFECTS ARE ANTICIPATED

So far, we have assumed that decision makers come to anticipate the effects of a monetary policy only after they begin to occur. For example, we assumed that borrowers and lenders began to anticipate a higher inflation rate only after prices began to rise more rapidly. Similarly, we assumed that resource suppliers anticipated the inflation only after it had begun.

What if enough decision makers in the market catch on to the link between expansionary monetary policy and an increase in the inflation rate even before the initial effects are felt? Suppose that borrowers and lenders start paying attention to the money supply figures and other monetary policy indicators. Seeing a more expansionary monetary policy, they revise their inflation expectations upward. When this happens, lenders will become more reluctant to supply loanable funds at current rates because they know they won't be able to raise them later. Simultaneously, borrowers will be eager to demand loanable funds to lock in their loans at the current low rates before inflation sends them higher. Under these circumstances, lower supply and higher demand for loanable funds will quickly push up the money interest rate. If borrowers and lenders quickly and accurately forecast the future rate of inflation that accompanies the monetary expansion, the real interest rate will remain unchanged.

If buyers and sellers in the goods and services market also anticipate a shift to a more expansionary monetary policy, they, too, may anticipate its inflationary consequences. As buyers anticipate future price increases, many of them will buy now rather than later. Current aggregate demand will rise. Similarly, expecting an acceleration in the inflation rate, sellers will be reluctant to sell except at premium prices. Current aggregate supply will fall. This combination of factors will quickly push prices of goods and services upward.

Simultaneously, if buyers and sellers in the resource market believe that more rapid monetary growth will lead to a higher rate of inflation, they too will build this view into long-term contracts. Union officials will demand and employers will pay an inflationary premium for future money wages, based on their expectation of inflation. Alternatively, they may write an **escalator clause** (sometimes called a cost-of-living adjustment, or COLA) into their collective bargaining agreements. Such a provision will automatically raise money wages when the inflation transpires. If decision makers in the resource market correctly anticipate the inflation, real resource prices will not decline once prices accelerate upward.

Escalator clause
A contractual agreement that periodically and automatically adjusts money wage rates upward as the price level rises. It is sometimes referred to as a cost-of-living adjustment, or COLA.

As **Exhibit 9** shows, when people correctly anticipate the effects of expansionary monetary policy *prior to their occurrence,* the short-run impact of monetary policy is like its impact in the long run. The price level will increase, pushing up money income (P_2Y_1), but real income (Y_1) will be unchanged. Nominal interest rates will rise, but real interest rates will be unchanged. Thus, when the effects of expansionary monetary policy are fully anticipated, they exert little effect on real economic activity.

Are people likely to anticipate the effects of monetary policy? This is a topic of hot debate among economists, and we will consider it in more detail in the next chapter. Because the effects of monetary policy differ substantially depending on whether they are anticipated, clearly this question is an important one.

INTEREST RATES AND MONETARY POLICY

Can the Fed control interest rates? How quickly will a shift in monetary policy have a significant impact on output and prices in the goods and services market? These two questions are linked. Let us begin with the interest rate question. To simplify matters, we have proceeded as if there were only a single interest rate in the loanable funds market. In the real world, of course, there are numerous interest rates reflecting loans of differing risk and time length. For example, there are short-term interest rates, such as those for federal funds, Treasury bills, and savings deposits. In addition, there are longer-term rates, such as those for home mortgages and long-term bonds.

EXHIBIT 9
The Short-Run Effects
of an Anticipated
Monetary Expansion

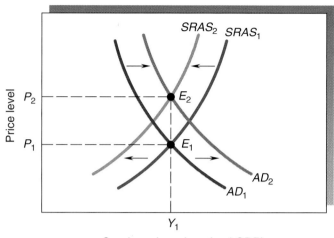

When decision makers fully anticipate the effects of monetary expansion, the expansion does not alter real output even in the short run because suppliers, including resource suppliers, build the expected price rise into their decisions from the out-set. The anticipated inflation leads to a rise in nominal costs (including wages), causing aggregate supply to decline (shift to $SRAS_2$). Nominal wages, prices, and interest rates rise, but their real values remain unchanged. The result is inflation with-out any change in real output (Y_1).

When the Fed moves toward a more expansionary policy (for example, when it pur-chases bonds and injects additional reserves into the system) there is an immediate effect on short-term interest rates, like the rate in the federal funds market—the market where banks with excess reserves extend short-term loans to banks with insufficient reserves. As the federal funds rate declines, so, too, will other short-term interest rates, such as rates on savings deposits, three-month Treasury bills, and bank certificates of deposit (CDs).

However, the impact of the expansionary monetary policy on long-term interest rates like those on home mortgages and ten-year bonds, will be more modest and less predictable. There are two reasons for this: ***First, the long-term rates are influenced more by real factors like the demand for investment funds than by monetary factors. Second, to the extent that monetary factors influence long-term interest rates, they operate primarily through their effect on the expected rate of inflation.*** The expected long-term future rate of inflation is a crucial component of long-term nominal interest rates. If people expect a higher future rate of inflation as the result of the shift to a more expansionary policy, long-term rates may rise rather than fall. Thus, although the Fed policy is able to quickly and significantly affect short-term interest rates, its impact on longer-term rates is both less certain and likely to occur with a substantially longer time lag. Because long- and medium-term rates are most relevant for the investment decisions of businesses and households, the ambiguity concern-ing the impact of monetary policy on these rates is particularly important.

Short-Term Interest Rates, the Velocity of Money, and Time Lags

How will changes in short-term interest rates influence the velocity of money and aggre-gate demand? This is an important question because it is the short-term interest rates that will be most sensitive to shifts in monetary policy.

When a shift to a more expansionary monetary policy reduces short-term interest rates, the lower rates will also reduce the opportunity cost of holding money balances. Pre-dictably, the velocity of money will decline. This will tend to dampen the initial stimulus effects of the monetary expansion. For a time, total spending (aggregate demand) may not change much because the lower velocity is at least partially offsetting the increase in the growth rate of money. Of course, if the more expansionary monetary policy persists, a combination of the lower real interest rates and more readily available credit will eventu-ally stimulate aggregate demand (see Exhibit 3). Over time, the additional demand will put upward pressure on prices, which will also increase both the expected rate of inflation and nominal interest rates, including short-term nominal rates. When this happens—and several quarters may pass before it does—the higher short-term nominal interest rates will increase the velocity of money and amplify the demand-stimulus effects of the policy. It is at this point in time that the effects of the expansionary monetary policy will be strongest.

The same forces also work in reverse. When the Fed shifts to a more restrictive policy, it typically drains reserves from the banking system, which will quickly put upward pressure on the federal funds rate and other short-term interest rates. The restrictive policy, however, will generally have less effect on longer-term interest rates. If people perceive that inflation is a smaller threat as the result of the more restrictive monetary policy, this factor will put downward pressure on long-term interest rates, which will at least partially offset the restraining effects of the increase in the short-term rates.

At the same time, the higher short-term rates will increase the opportunity cost of holding money and, as a result, its velocity. This increase in the velocity of money will promote additional spending, which will, *for a time,* tend to dampen the restrictive effects of the policy. Of course, the restrictive policy, if continued, will eventually begin to lower inflation and reduce nominal interest rates (including short-term rates), which will reduce the velocity of money. Once this happens, and many months may pass before it does, the restrictive policy will be very powerful—it will substantially reduce aggregate demand, output, and prices.

All these factors suggest that the linkage between a change in monetary policy and a change in output and prices is likely to be both lengthy and variable. When there is a shift in monetary policy, the potency of the short-run effects may differ substantially from the potency of the policy shift over a longer period of time. Obviously, these factors will complicate the job of monetary policy makers and make it more difficult for them to institute changes in a manner that will exert a stabilizing influence on the economy.

The Money Supply and the Federal Funds Rate

Throughout, we have used shifts in the money supply to indicate the direction of changes in monetary policy. In recent years, however, the Fed has mainly used the federal funds rate to implement changes in monetary policy. If the Fed wants to shift toward a more expansionary policy, it reduces its target for the federal funds interest rate. The Fed controls this rate through its open market operations. To get the lower rate, it buys more bonds and thereby puts additional reserves into the system, which places downward pressure on the federal funds rate. Of course, the Fed's buying of bonds also increases the money supply. Therefore, even though the news media and others may highlight the change in the federal funds rate, the impact on the economy will be the same as it is for an increase in the money supply.

On the other hand, when the Fed shifts to a more restrictive policy, it usually seeks to increase the federal funds rate. But the Fed achieves this goal through its sale of bonds, which will reduce the reserves available to the banking system. Again, the result will be the same as it is for a reduction in the money supply.

The Danger of Using Interest Rates as an Indicator of Monetary Policy

Can interest rates be used to determine the direction of monetary policy? For example, do low interest rates show that the Fed is following an expansionary policy? Here, it is very important to distinguish between the short run and the long run. When the Fed shifts to a more expansionary policy, it generally injects additional reserves into the banking system. As we have said, in the short run, more money puts downward pressure on interest rates—particularly short-term rates. However, think what would happen if the Fed continued on a highly expansionary course, seeking to push interest rates down over a long period of time. In the long run, rapid monetary growth will lead to inflation. As people come to expect the inflation, nominal interest rates will rise instead of fall. Conversely, a shift to a more restrictive policy will increase interest rates in the short run. But when pursued over a lengthy time period, restrictive policy will eventually lead to deflation (falling prices) and low interest rates.

Thus, interest rates are often a misleading gauge of monetary policy. In the United States, interest rates were high during the 1970s, a period of expansionary monetary policy and inflation. On the other hand, interest rates were relatively low during the 1960s and 1990s, periods of more restrictive monetary policy. Similarly, during the Great Depression, interest rates fell to less than 1 percent. But this was not indicative of expansionary monetary policy either. On the contrary, it was reflective of a highly restrictive monetary policy that caused deflation and the expectation of a falling price level.

Internationally, the picture is the same. The highest interest rates in the world are found in countries experiencing hyperinflation due to very rapid money supply growth: Argentina and Brazil in the 1980s and Russia in the 1990s, for example. If the central banks of these countries had put a damper on money growth, both the inflation rate and the interest rate would have been lower. On the other hand, the lowest interest rates are found in countries that are follow a highly restrictive monetary policy. For example, in the late 1990s, several interest rates in Japan fell below 1 percent. Like the United States's interest rate during the Great Depression, the low Japanese interest rates were reflective of a highly restrictive monetary policy, one that led to a falling price level and the expectation of deflation.

THE EFFECTS OF MONETARY POLICY—A SUMMARY

The accompanying Thumbnail Sketch shows the impact of monetary policy on the economy under three different scenarios: (1) the short run, when the effects are unanticipated, (2) the short run, when the effects are anticipated, and (3) the long run. Note that the impact of monetary policy in the latter two cases is the same. When decision makers quickly anticipate the effects of monetary policy, the adjustment process speeds up, and therefore the short-run effects are identical to the long-run effects. Under these circumstances, only nominal variables such as money interest rates and the inflation rate are affected. Real variables like real GDP, employment, and the real interest rate are unaffected.

THUMBNAIL SKETCH

What Are the Effects of Monetary Policy?

	Short-Term Effects When Policy Is Unanticipated (1)	Short-Term Effects When Policy Is Anticipated[a] (2)	Long-Term Effects (3)
The Effect of Expansionary Monetary Policy on			
Inflation rate	Only a small increase, particularly if excess capacity is present	Increase	
Real output and employment	Increase, particularly if excess capacity is present	No change	
Money interest rate	Short-term rates will probably decline	Increase	
Real interest rate	Decrease	No change	
The Effect of Restrictive Monetary Policy on			
Inflation rate	Only a small decrease	Decrease	
Real output and employment	Decrease, particularly if economy at less than capacity	No change	
Money interest rate	Short-term rates will probably increase	Decrease	
Real interest rate	Increase	No change	

[a]Beginning from long-term equilibrium

Five major predictions flow from our analysis:

1. An unanticipated shift to a more expansionary monetary policy will temporarily stimulate output and employment. As Exhibits 3 and 4 illustrate, an increase in aggregate demand due to an unanticipated increase in the money supply will lead to a short-run expansion in real output and employment. Conversely, as Exhibit 5 shows, an unanticipated move toward a more restrictive monetary policy reduces aggregate demand and retards real output.

2. The stabilizing effects of a change in monetary policy are dependent upon the state of the economy when the effects of the policy change are observed. If the effects of an expansionary policy hit when the economy is operating at less than capacity, then the demand stimulus will push the economy toward full employment. However, if the demand stimulus hits when the economy is operating at or beyond capacity, it will contribute to an acceleration in the inflation rate. Conversely, a restrictive policy will help control inflation if the demand-restraining effects are felt when output is beyond the economy's long-run capacity. On the other hand, a restrictive policy will lead to a recession if the lower aggregate demand hits when the economy is at or below long-run capacity.

3. Persistent growth of the money supply at a rapid rate will cause inflation. Although the short-run effects of an expansionary monetary policy will primarily affect output, persistent expansion in the money supply at a rate greater than the growth of real output will cause inflation. The more rapid the sustained growth rate of the money supply (relative to real output), the higher the accompanying rate of inflation.

4. Money interest rates and the inflation rate will be directly related. As the inflation rate rises, money interest rates will eventually increase because both borrowers and lenders will begin to expect the higher rate of inflation and build it into their decision making. Conversely, as the inflation rate declines, a reduction in the expected rate of inflation will eventually lead to lower money interest rates. Therefore, when monetary expansion leads to an acceleration in the inflation rate, it will also result in an increase in nominal interest rates.

5. There will be only a loose year-to-year relationship between shifts in monetary policy and changes in output and prices. It takes time for markets to adjust to changing demand conditions. Some prices in both product and resource markets are set by long-term contracts. Obviously, price responses in these markets will take time. In some cases, people will anticipate the effects of a policy change and adjust quickly; in others, the reaction to a policy change will take more time. Differences in this area will weaken the year-to-year relationship between monetary indicators and important economic variables like output and prices.

In addition, a monetary policy shift will initially have a far greater impact on short-term interest rates than on longer-term rates. Movements in the short-term nominal rates are likely to cause changes in the velocity of money, which will tend to dampen the initial effects of a monetary policy shift. This, too, will tend to weaken the year-to-year link between changes in monetary policy and changes in output and prices. Therefore, even though our analysis indicates that monetary policy does influence output and prices, the year-to-year relationships are likely to be weak.

TESTING THE MAJOR IMPLICATIONS OF MONETARY THEORY

Is the real world consistent with our analysis? The next four exhibits provide evidence on this topic. Our analysis indicates that a shift to a more expansionary monetary policy will initially stimulate output, whereas a shift to monetary restriction will retard it. **Exhibit 10** shows the relationship between changes in the growth rate of the money supply and real

EXHIBIT 10
Monetary Policy and Real GDP

Sharp declines in the growth rate of the money supply, such as those of 1968–1969, 1973–1974, 1977–1978, 1988–1991, and 1999–2000, have generally preceded periods of lower real GDP and recession(indicated by shading) (Notice that the dips occur near the shaded areas.) Conversely, periods of sharp acceleration in the growth rate of the money supply, like those of 1971–1972 and in 1976, have often been followed by a rapid growth in GDP. The Fed has generally increased the growth rate of the money supply during recessions. Note that the growth rate of the money supply has been slower and more stable in the last decade, and so has GDP.

Source: Federal Reserve Bank of St. Louis, http://www.stls.frb.org. Also see *Economic Report of the President* (published annually).

output since 1960 for the United States. In order to smooth the temporary quarterly fluctuations, we use a four-quarter moving average for the annual rates for both figures. Because the introduction of interest-earning checking accounts dramatically changed the nature of M1 (and affected its growth rate) during the 1980s, the M2 money-supply measure is used here. Of course, changes in the growth rate of M2 might not always accurately reflect the direction of monetary policy. Other factors, such as supply shocks and fiscal policy changes, will also influence the growth of output. Thus, the relationship between changes in the money supply and the growth of real GDP will probably be fairly loose. However, close inspection of the data shows that periods of sharp acceleration in the growth rate of the money supply were generally associated with an acceleration in the growth rate of real GDP. For example, an acceleration in the growth rate of the money supply during 1961–1964, 1971–1972, 1976, 1983, and 2001 was associated with an increase in the growth rate of real GDP.

The converse was also true: periods of sharp deceleration in the growth rate of the money supply were generally associated with (or followed by) economic recession. A decline in the growth rate of the money supply preceded the recessions of 1960, 1970, and 1974–1975. Similarly, a sharp decline in the growth rate of the money stock from 13 percent in 1976–1977 to less than 8 percent in 1978–1979 preceded the back-to-back recessions and sluggish growth of 1979–1982. Prior to the 1990 recession, the growth rate of the money supply fell from 8.9 percent in 1987 (first quarter) to only 3.1 percent in 1989 (second quarter). Between October 1999 and July 2000, the Fed increased its discount rate and target federal funds rate five times. The more restrictive monetary policy of 1999–2000 preceded the recession of 2001. Just as our theory predicts, there does appear to be a relationship between shifts in monetary policy and changes in real GDP.

Exhibit 11 presents a graphic picture of the relationship between monetary policy and the inflation rate of the United States. Although our theory indicates that persistent, long-term growth of the money supply will be closely associated with inflation, it also indicates that time is required for a monetary expansion (or contraction) to alter demand relationships and affect prices. Most economists believe that the time lag between shifts in monetary policy and observable changes in the level of prices is often two or three years. To illustrate this relationship, Exhibit 11 compares the current money supply (M2) data with the inflation rate three years in the future. Once again, though the linkage is far from tight, it definitely exists. Most noticeably, the rapid monetary acceleration during 1971–1972 was followed by a similar acceleration in the inflation rate during 1973–1974. Similarly, the sharp monetary contraction of 1973–1974 was accompanied by not only the recession of 1974–1975, but also a substantial reduction in the inflation rate during 1975–1976. However, as monetary policy again shifted toward expansion in 1976–1977, the double-digit inflation rates of 1979–1980 were soon to follow.

During the 1980–1986 period, the link between monetary growth and the inflation rate a few years later appeared to weaken. This may merely reflect the financial innovations and changing nature of money during this period, particularly the move by consumers to interest-earning checking accounts. There is evidence that the relationship once again became more predictable after the transition to interest-earning checking accounts

EXHIBIT 11
The Effect of Changes in Money Supply on Inflation

Here we illustrate the relationship between the money supply (M2) growth rate and the annual inflation rate three years later. Although the two are not perfectly correlated, the data do indicate that periods of monetary acceleration (for example, 1971–1972 and 1975–1976) tend to be associated with an increase in the inflation rate about three years later. Similarly, a slower growth rate of the money supply, like that of the 1990s, is generally associated with a lower rate of inflation.

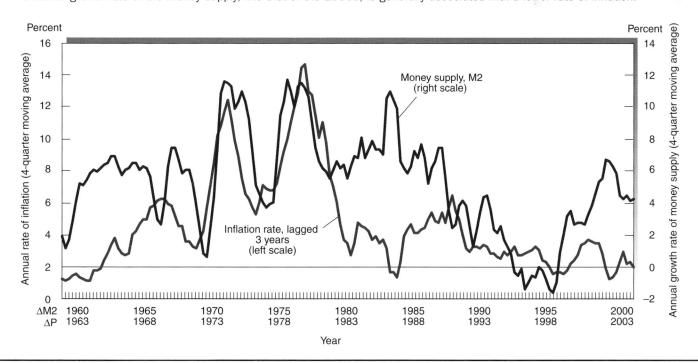

Source: Federal Reserve Bank of St. Louis, http://www.stls.frb.org. Also see *Economic Report of the President* (published annually). The consumer price index was used to measure the rate of inflation.

had been completed. During the 1987–1993 period, the annual growth rate of the money supply (M2) decelerated from more than 8 percent to less than 2 percent. With a lag, the inflation rate followed a similar path, which is more what we would expect. Furthermore, the low rate of money growth during the 1990s and early 2000s—the money growth rate averaged approximately 4 percent during this period—has been associated with low rates of inflation.

Exhibit 12 shows the relationship between the inflation rate (as measured by the consumer price index) and the nominal interest rate. Because our measure of inflation is the rate of change in the price level during the last year, we will compare it with a short-term nominal interest rate—the three-month Treasury bill rate. Our theory implies that nominal interest rates will rise with the inflation rate. The empirical evidence shows that this indeed is the case. As the inflation rate rose significantly during the late 1960s, so also did the nominal interest rate. During the 1970s, sharp increases in the inflation rate, particularly during 1977–1980, were accompanied by substantial increases in the nominal interest rate. Similarly, as the inflation rate decelerated from the double-digit levels of the late 1970s, the money interest rate also plunged during 1981–1987. Later, a modest increase in the inflation rate during 1988–1990 resulted in a similar modest increase in short-term interest rates. Finally, as the inflation rate hovered around 2 to 3 percent during 1994–2003, the short-term nominal interest rate averaged about 4 percent. These data provide strong evidence that, just as our theory predicts, the choices of borrowers and lenders are strongly influenced by the inflation rate and expectations concerning its path in the future.

A major implication of our analysis is that rapid growth rates in the money supply over long periods of time will be associated with high rates of inflation. **Exhibit 13** pre-

EXHIBIT 12
The Inflation Rate and the Money Interest Rate

The expectation of inflation (a) reduces the supply and (b) increases the demand for loanable funds, causing the money interest rates to rise (see Exhibit 8). Notice how the short-term interest rate (on three-month Treasury bills) has tended to increase when the inflation rate accelerates (and decline as the inflation rate falls).

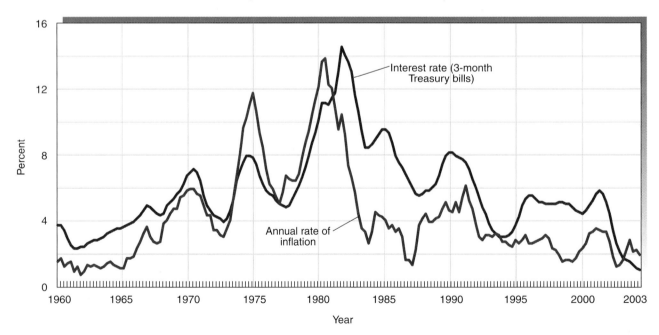

Source: Federal Reserve Bank of St. Louis, http://www.stls.frb.org. Also see *Economic Report of the President* (published annually). The consumer price index was used to measure the rate of inflation.

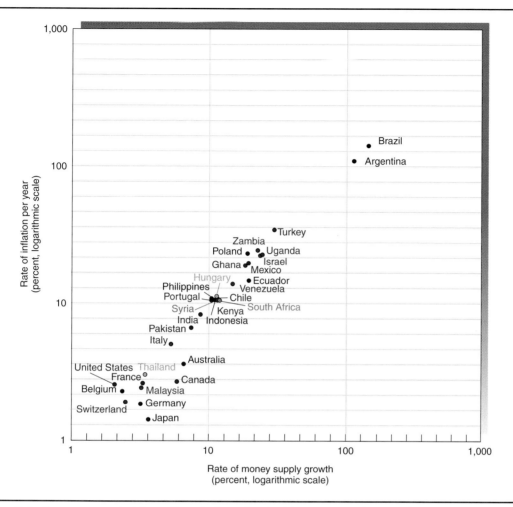

EXHIBIT 13
Money and Inflation—
An International
Comparison,
1980–2002

The relationship between the average annual growth rate of the money supply and the rate of inflation is shown here for the 1980–2002 period. Clearly, there is a close relationship between the two. Higher rates of money growth lead to higher rates of inflation.

Note: The money supply data are the actual growth rate of the money supply minus the growth rate of real GDP.
Source: World Bank, *World Development Indicators,* 2004.

sents data on the annual growth rate of the money supply (adjusted for the growth rate of the nation's output) and the rate of inflation for a diverse set of countries during the 1980–2002 period. The results clearly illustrate the link between monetary policy and inflation. Countries with single-digit rates of money growth—for example, Belgium, Germany, Japan, Malaysia, Switzerland, and the United States—experienced single-digit rates of inflation. Similarly, countries with rates of money growth in the 10 percent to 20 percent range experienced rates of inflation in this same range. The data for the Philippines, South Africa, Kenya, Hungary, and Chile illustrate this point. Countries like Mexico, Ghana, and Poland with money growth rates in the 30 percent to 50 percent range had inflation rates within this same range. Finally, look at the data for Argentina and Brazil. The average annual rate of money growth of these two countries exceeded 100 percent during this period. So, too, did their average inflation rate. Most of the money growth of Argentina and Brazil occurred during the 1980s. Predictably, the substantially lower rates of money growth during the 1990s resulted in substantially lower rates of inflation.

When viewed over a lengthy time period, the link between money growth and inflation is one of the most consistent relationships in all of economics. Inflation is a monetary phenomenon. Persistently low rates of money growth lead to low rates of inflation. Similarly, high rates of money growth lead to high rates of inflation.

LOOKING AHEAD

As we discussed in this chapter, theory indicates that the impact of monetary policy will be influenced by whether people anticipate its effects. So far, we have said little about how decision makers form expectations about the future. The next chapter will consider this important issue.

KEY POINTS

▼ The quantity of money people want to hold is inversely related to the money interest rate. Higher interest rates make it more costly to hold money instead of interest-earning assets like bonds. The supply of money is vertical because it is determined by the Fed. The money interest rate will gravitate toward the rate at which the quantity of money people want to hold is just equal to the quantity supplied by the Fed.

▼ The impact of a shift in monetary policy is transmitted through interest rates, exchange rates, and asset prices.

▼ When instituting a more expansionary monetary policy, the Fed generally buys bonds, which both increases bond prices and creates additional bank reserves, putting downward pressure on real interest rates. In the short run, an *unanticipated* shift to a more expansionary policy will stimulate aggregate demand and thereby increase output and employment.

▼ When instituting a more restrictive monetary policy, the Fed sells bonds, which depresses bond prices and drains reserves from the banking system. An unanticipated shift to a more restrictive monetary policy will increase real interest rates and reduce aggregate demand, output, and employment in the short run.

▼ The quantity theory of money postulates that the velocity of money is constant (or approximately so) and that real output is independent of monetary factors. When these assumptions hold, an increase in the stock of money will lead to a proportional increase in the price level.

▼ In the long run, the primary effect of monetary policy will be on prices rather than on real output.

▼ When expansionary monetary policy leads to rising prices, decision makers eventually anticipate the higher inflation rate and build it into their choices. As this happens, money interest rates, wages, and incomes will reflect the expectation of the inflation, but real interest rates, wages, and output will return to their long-run normal levels.

▼ When the effects of expansionary monetary policy are anticipated, the short-run impact of an increase in the money supply is similar to its impact in the long run. Nominal prices and interest rates rise, but real output remains unchanged.

▼ Although the Fed can strongly influence short-term interest rates, its impact on long-term rates is much more limited. Interest rates can be a misleading indicator of monetary policy because the rates react differently in the short run than in the long run. In the short run, expansionary monetary policy leads to lower interest rates. In the long run, however, it leads to inflation and high, rather than low, interest rates. Conversely, although restrictive monetary policy leads to higher interest rates in the short run, a persistently restrictive policy will result in deflation and lower interest rates in the long run.

▼ The empirical evidence is consistent with the theory. In the short run, changes in monetary policy tend to cause real GDP to change in the same direction, typically with a time lag of twelve to eighteen months. In the long run, however, rapid growth of the money supply leads to inflation. Inflation is a monetary phenomenon. Countries with persistently high growth rates of the money supply experience high rates of inflation.

CRITICAL ANALYSIS QUESTIONS

1. Why do people hold money? How will an increase in the interest rate influence the amount of money that people will want to hold?

*2. How would each of the following influence the quantity of money you would like to hold?
   a. An increase in the interest rate on checking deposits
   b. An increase in the expected rate of inflation
   c. An increase in income
   d. An increase in the differential interest rate between money market mutual funds and checking deposits

*3. What is the opportunity cost of the following: (a) obtaining a $100,000 house, (b) holding the house for one year, (c) obtaining $1,000, and (d) holding the $1,000 in your checking account for one year?

4. Historically, shifts toward a more expansionary monetary policy have often been associated with increases in real output.

   Why? Would a more expansionary policy increase the long-term growth rate of real GDP? Why or why not?

5. What impact will an unanticipated increase in the money supply have on the real interest rate, real output, and employment in the short run? How will expansionary monetary policy affect the economy when the effects are widely anticipated? Why does it make a difference whether or not the effects of a monetary policy are anticipated?

6. How rapidly has the money supply (M1) grown during the past twelve months? How rapidly has M2 grown? Do you think the monetary authorities should increase or decrease the growth rate of the money supply during the next year? Why? (The data necessary to answer this question for the United States are available in the *Federal Reserve Bulletin*. They may also be found at the Web site of the Federal Reserve Bank of St. Louis, http://www.stls.frb.org.)

*7. If the Fed shifts to a more restrictive monetary policy, it will generally sell bonds in the open market. How will this action influence each of the following? Briefly explain each of your answers.
   a. The reserves available to banks
   b. Real interest rates
   c. Household spending on consumer durables
   d. The exchange rate value of the dollar
   e. Net exports
   f. The prices of stocks and real assets like apartment or office buildings
   g. Real GDP

8. Will a budget deficit be more expansionary if it is financed by borrowing from the Federal Reserve or from the general public? Explain.

9. Political officials often call on the monetary authorities to expand the money supply more rapidly so that interest rates can be reduced. Will expanding the money supply lower interest rates in the short run? What about the long run? Explain. The highest interest rates in the world are found in countries that expand the supply of money rapidly. Can you explain why?

*10. Many economists believe that there is a "long and variable time lag" between the time a change in monetary policy is instituted and the time its primary impact on output, employment, and prices is felt. If true, how does this long and variable time lag affect the ability of policy makers to use monetary policy as a stabilization tool?

*11. "Historically, when interest rates are high, the inflation rate is high. High interest rates are a major cause of inflation." Evaluate this statement.

*12. If the supply of money is constant, how will an increase in the demand for money influence aggregate demand?

13. a. What is the quantity theory of money?
    b. Is the quantity theory of money valid?
    c. Does it explain the impact of shifts in monetary policy on the economy? Why or why not?

*14. The accompanying chart presents data on the money supply, price level, and real GDP for three countries during the 2000–2003 period.
   a. Fill in the missing data.
   b. Which country followed the most expansionary monetary policy (highest average rate of growth in the money supply) between 2000 and 2003?
   c. Which country experienced the highest average annual rate of inflation during the 2000-2003 period?
   d. Which country experienced the most rapid increase in real output during the 2000–2003 period?

---

*Asterisk denotes questions for which answers are given in Appendix B.

	MONEY SUPPLY (IN BILLIONS OF LOCAL CURRENCY)	GDP DEFLATOR (2000 = 100)	NOMINAL GDP (IN CURRENT CURRENCY UNITS)	REAL GDP (IN 2000 CURRENCY UNITS)	PERCENT RATE OF CHANGE	
					MONEY SUPPLY	PRICE LEVEL
United States						
2000	1,088	100.0	9,817		X	X
2001	1,179	102.4	10,100.8			
2002	1,217	103.9	10,480.8			
2003	1,293	105.7	10,987.9			
Chile						
2000	3,645	100.0	40,575		X	X
2001	4,062	103.4	43,441			
2002	4,431	105.7	46,411			
2003	4,931	109.1	49,819			
Turkey						
2000	7,407	100.0	124,583		X	X
2001	10,840	154.5	178,412			
2002	14,814	221.8	276,003			
2003	21,194	272.8	359,763			

Source: International Monetary Fund, *International Financial Yearbook*, July 2004. The figures for Turkey are measured in trillions of currency units.

15. As signs of economic weakness appeared during the first half of 2001, the Fed reduced its discount rate and the federal funds interest rate several times. What was the Fed trying to do? What was the expected impact on aggregate demand, output, employment, and the general level of prices? Will the Fed's actions cause inflation in the future? Looking back, how would you evaluate the Fed's actions? Did they help or harm the economy?

Stabilization Policy, Output, and Employment

CHAPTER 15

Chapter Focus

■ Can discretionary use of monetary and fiscal policy reduce the ups and downs of the business cycle? Why or why not?

■ How are expectations formed? Do expectations influence how macroeconomic policy works?

■ What is the Phillips curve? Why were the early views about the Phillips curve wrong?

■ What is the modern view of stabilization policy? How has this influenced macroeconomic policy in recent years?

■ Did perverse macroeconomic policy cause the Great Depression?

Unfortunately, policymakers cannot act as if the economy is an automobile that can quickly be steered back and forth. Rather, the procedure of changing aggregate demand is much closer to that of a captain navigating a giant supertanker. Even if he gives a signal for a hard turn, it takes a mile before he can see a change, and ten miles before the ship makes the turn.

—Robert J. Gordon[1]

[1]Robert J. Gordon, *Macroeconomics* (Boston: Little, Brown, 1978), 334.

In previous chapters, we analyzed the effect of both fiscal and monetary policy on output, employment, and prices. We also noted that the initial effect of a policy change is often different from the effect over a more lengthy time period. We now want to consider the potential of macro policy as a stabilization tool. Can active management of fiscal and/or monetary policy reduce economic instability? This chapter will focus on stabilization policy and examine the factors that both enhance and limit its successful application. ▦

ECONOMIC FLUCTUATIONS—THE HISTORICAL RECORD

Wide fluctuations in the general level of business activity—income, employment, and the price level—make personal economic planning extremely difficult. Such changes can cause even well-devised investment plans to go awry. The tragic stories of unemployed workers begging for food and newly impoverished investors jumping out of windows during the Great Depression vividly portray the enormous personal and social costs of economic instability and the uncertainty that it generates.

Historically, there have been substantial fluctuations in real output. **Exhibit 1** illustrates the growth record of real GDP in the United States during the past ninety-five years. Prior to the Second World War, double-digit swings in real GDP during a single

EXHIBIT 1
Decline in Economic Instability Following World War II

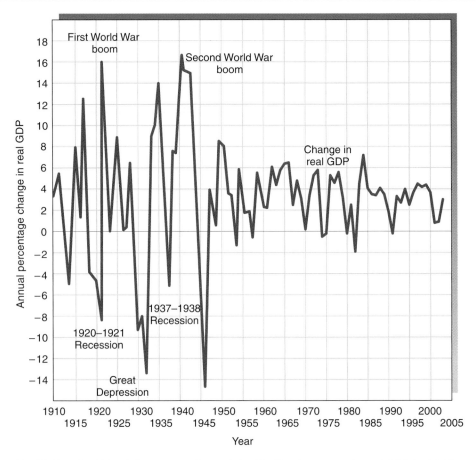

Prior to the conclusion of the Second World War, the United States experienced double-digit increases in real GDP in 1918, 1922, 1935–1936, and 1941–1943. In contrast, real output fell by 5 percent or more in 1920–1921, 1930–1932, 1938, and 1946. As illustrated here, fluctuations in real GDP have moderated during the last five decades. Most economists believe that more appropriate macroeconomic policy—particularly monetary policy—deserves much of the credit for the increased stability of recent decades.

Sources: Historical Statistics of the United States, 224; and Bureau of Economic Analysis, http://www.bea.doc.gov/.

year were not uncommon. Real GDP rose by more than 10 percent annually during the First World War, during an economic boom in 1922, during a mid-1930s recovery, and again during the Second World War. In contrast, output fell at an annual rate of 5 percent or more during the 1920–1921 recession, in the depression years of 1930–1932 and 1938, and again following the Second World War. Since 1950, economic ups and downs have been more moderate. Nevertheless, substantial fluctuations are still observable.

CAN DISCRETIONARY POLICY PROMOTE ECONOMIC STABILITY?

There is widespread agreement about the goals of macroeconomic policy. Economists of almost all persuasions favor the goals of steady growth, price stability, and full employment (unemployment at the natural rate). However, there are disagreements about how to achieve these objectives. Most of these disagreements focus on the potential and limitations of discretionary macro policy as a stabilization tool.

If monetary and fiscal policies could inject stimulus during economic slowdowns and apply restraint during inflationary booms, this would help reduce the ups and downs of the business cycle. Some macroeconomists, sometimes called **activists**, believe this is possible. The activists believe that policy makers will be able to manage demand and respond to various disruptions and changing economic conditions in a manner that will promote economic stability. Other economists, called **nonactivists**, argue that the discretionary use of monetary and fiscal policy in response to changing economic conditions is likely to do more harm than good. The nonactivists have confidence in the economy's self-corrective mechanism and note that erratic use of macro policy has been a major cause of economic instability in the past. Thus, activists argue that the economy will be more stable if policy makers merely follow a steady course rather than trying to respond to turns in the economic road.

Both activists and nonactivists recognize that conducting macro policy in a stabilizing manner is not an easy task. Let's take a closer look at some of the complicating factors and the tools available to help policy makers deal with them.

Time Lag Problem

If monetary and fiscal policy are going to exert a stabilizing impact, proper timing is crucially important. Three different types of time lags complicate the achievement of proper timing.

First, there is the **recognition lag**, the time period between a change in economic conditions and recognition of the change by policy makers. It generally takes a few months to gather and tabulate reliable information on the recent performance of the economy in order to determine whether it has dipped into a recession, whether the inflation rate has accelerated, and so forth.

Second, even after the need for a policy change is recognized, there is generally an additional time period before the policy change is instituted. Economists refer to this delay as **administrative lag**. In the case of monetary policy, the administrative lag is generally quite short. The Federal Open Market Committee meets every few weeks and is in a position to institute a change in monetary policy quickly. This is a major advantage of monetary policy. For discretionary fiscal policy, the administrative lag is likely to be much longer. Congressional committees must meet. Legislation must be proposed and debated. Congress must act, and the president must consent. Each of these steps typically takes several months.

Finally, there is the **impact lag**, the time period between the implementation of a macro policy change and the primary effect of that change on the economy. Although the impact of a change in tax rates is generally felt quickly, the expansionary effects of an increase in government spending are usually much less rapid. It will take time for contractors to submit competitive bids and new contracts to be signed. Several months may pass before work on a new project actually begins. The impact lag in the case of monetary policy is likely to be even longer. The time period between a shift in monetary policy, a change in interest rates, and, in turn, a change in the level of spending may be quite lengthy.

Activists
Economists who believe that discretionary changes in monetary and fiscal policy can reduce the degree of instability in output and employment.

Nonactivists
Economists who believe that discretionary macroeconomic policy adjustments in response to cyclical conditions are likely to increase, rather than reduce, instability. Nonactivitsts favor steady and predictable policies regardless of business conditions.

Recognition lag
The time period after a policy change is needed from a stabilization standpoint but before the need is recognized by policy makers.

Administrative lag
The time period after the need for a policy change is recognized but before the policy is actually implemented.

Impact lag
The time period after a policy change is implemented but before the change begins to exert its primary effects.

Economists who have studied this topic, including Milton Friedman and Robert Gordon, conclude that the combined duration of these time lags is generally twelve to eighteen months in the case of monetary policy, and even longer in the case of fiscal policy. This means that, if a policy is going to exert the desired effect at the proper time, policy makers cannot wait to act until a problem develops. Rather, they must correctly forecast the future direction of the economy and act before there is a contraction in real GDP or an observable increase in the rate of inflation.

Forecasting Tools and Macro Policy

Because it takes time for macroeconomic policy to work, policy makers need to know what economic conditions will be like six to fifteen months in the future. They need to know whether a business recession or an inflationary boom is around the corner. How can they predict? Forecasting tools can provide them with some information. Let's consider some of the forecasting devices available to policy makers.

Index of Leading Indicators

Index of leading indicators
An index of economic variables that historically has tended to turn down prior to the beginning of a recession and turn up prior to the beginning of a business expansion.

The **index of leading indicators** is the single most widely used and closely watched forecasting tool. The index is a composite statistic based on ten key variables that generally turn down prior to a recession and turn up before the beginning of a business expansion (see the accompanying Measures of Economic Activity, "Index of Leading Indicators"). The index is published monthly, and a decline for three consecutive months is considered a warning that the economy is about to dip into a recession.

Exhibit 2 illustrates the path of the index during the 1959–2003 period. The index has correctly forecasted each of the seven recessions since 1959. On four occasions, the

EXHIBIT 2
Index of Leading Indicators

The shaded periods represent recessions. The index of leading indicators forecasted each of the seven recessions during the 1959–2003 period. As the arrows show, however, the time lag varied between when the index turned down and when the economy fell into a recession. In addition, on five occasions (1962, 1966, 1984, 1987, and 1995), the index predicted a recession that did not occur.

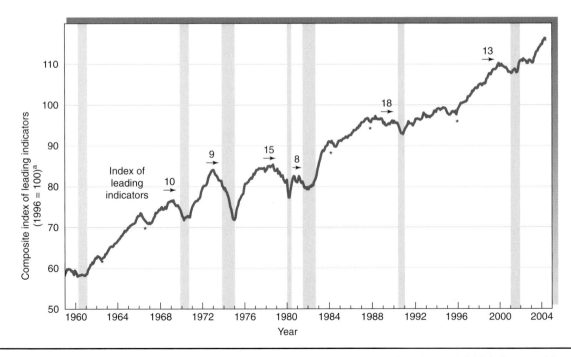

[a] The arrows indicate the number of months that the downturn in the index preceded a recession. An asterisk (*) indicates a false signal of a recession.
Source: http://www.globalindicators.org/.

MEASURES OF ECONOMIC ACTIVITY

The Index of Leading Indicators

History indicates that no single indicator is able to forecast accurately the future direction of the economy. However, several economic variables do tend to reach a high or low prior to the peak of a business expansion or the trough of an economic recession. Such variables are called leading economic indicators.

To provide more reliable information on the future direction of the economy, economists have devised an index of ten such indicators:

1. Length of the average workweek in hours

2. Initial weekly claims for unemployment compensation

3. New orders placed with manufacturers

4. Percentage of companies receiving slower deliveries from suppliers

5. Contracts and orders for new plants and equipment

6. Permits for new housing starts

7. Interest rate spread, ten-year Treasury bonds less Fed funds rate

8. Index of consumer expectations

9. Change in the index of stock prices (500 common stocks)

10. Change in the money supply (M2)

The variables included in the index were chosen both because of their tendency to lead (or predict) turns in the business cycle and because they are available frequently and promptly. In some cases, it is easy to see why a change in an economic indicator precedes a change in general economic activity. Consider the indicator of "new orders placed with manufacturers" (measured in constant dollars). An expansion in the volume of orders is generally followed by an expansion in manufacturing output. Similarly, manufacturers will tend to scale back their future production when a decline in new orders signals the probability of weak future demand for their products. The index of leading indicators can be found in *Business Cycle Indicators,* published by the Conference Board, a nonprofit business and research organization.

downturn occurred eight to eleven months prior to a recession, providing policy makers with sufficient lead time to modify policy, particularly monetary policy. In other instances, the downturn in the index preceded the recession by an even longer period. For example, it turned down eighteen months prior to the 1990–1991 recession.

A downturn in the index, however, is not always an accurate indicator of the future. On five occasions (1962, 1966, 1984, 1987, and 1995), a decline in the index of leading indicators forecasted a future recession that did not materialize. This has given rise to the quip that the index has accurately predicted twelve of the last seven recessions.

Forecasting Models

Economists have developed highly complex econometric (statistical) models to improve the accuracy of macroeconomic forecasts. In essence, these models use past data on economic interrelationships to project how currently observed changes will influence the future path of key economic variables, such as real GDP, employment, and the price level. The most elaborate models use hundreds of variables and equations to simulate the future direction of various sectors and the economy's overall output and employment. Powerful, high-speed computers are employed to analyze the effects of policy alternatives and attempt to predict the future.

To date, the record of computer forecasting models is mixed. When economic conditions are relatively stable (for example, when the growth of real GDP and the rate of inflation follow a steady trend), the models have generally provided accurate forecasts for both aggregate economic variables and important subcomponents of the economy. Unfortunately, however, they have generally missed the major turns in the economic road. For example, none of the major computer models forecasted the recessions of either 1990 or 2001.

Other Forecasting Information

Many policy makers have favorite indicators, such as the consumer confidence index or the number of first-time applicants for unemployment benefits, that they believe are particularly good forecasting tools. Information supplied by certain markets can also sound an early warning that a change in policy is needed. For example, since they fluctuate daily and are determined in auction markets, changes in commodity prices often foretell future changes in the general price level. An increase in a broad index of commodity prices implies that money is plentiful (relative to demand). This suggests that the Fed should shift toward a more restrictive policy in order to offset future inflation. In contrast, falling commodity prices indicate that deflation is a potential future danger, in which case the Fed might want to shift toward a more expansionary policy.

Changes in exchange rates are also a source of information about the relative scarcity of money and fear of inflation. Because exchange rates, to a degree, reflect the willingness of foreigners to hold U.S. dollars, a decline in the exchange rate value of the dollar (the value of the dollar relative to other currencies) suggests a fear of higher inflation and a reluctance to hold dollars. This would signal the need to shift to a more restrictive policy. Conversely, an increase in the exchange rate value of the dollar would indicate that the Fed has some leeway to shift to a more expansionary monetary policy. Most policy makers view market signals such as commodity prices and exchange rates as supplements to, rather than substitutes for, other forecasting devices.

Is Accurate Forecasting Feasible?

Many economists maintain that accurate forecasts of turns in the economy are beyond the reach of economics. Two major factors underlie this view. First, turns in the economic road often reflect economic shocks and unforeseen events—for example, an unexpected policy change, discovery of a new resource or technology, abnormal weather, or political upheaval in an important oil-exporting nation. There is no reason to believe that economists or anyone else will be able to predict these changes accurately and consistently. Thus, while economic theory helps predict the implications of unforeseen events, it cannot foretell what those events will be and when they might occur. Second, the critics of forecasting models argue that the future will differ from the past because people will often make different choices as the result of what they learned from previous events. Therefore, forecasting models based on past relationships—including elaborate computer models—will never be able to generate consistently accurate predictions.

One thing is for sure: forecasting the future direction of the economy is an imperfect science, and it is likely to remain so in the foreseeable future. But this is not the only deterrent to effective stabilization policy. Policy makers must also deal with expectations. A change may exert a very different effect, depending on whether it is widely expected or catches people by surprise. Given the importance of expectations, we need to analyze how they are formed. We now turn to that topic.

HOW ARE EXPECTATIONS FORMED?

There are two general theories about how expectations are formed. Let's consider both of them.

Adaptive-expectations hypothesis
The hypothesis that economic decision makers base their future expectations on actual outcomes observed during recent periods. For example, according to this view, the rate of inflation actually experienced during the past two or three years would be the major determinant of the rate of inflation expected for the next year.

Adaptive Expectations

The simplest theory concerning the formation of expectations is that people rely on the past to predict future trends. According to this theory, which economists call the **adaptive-expectations hypothesis**, decision makers believe that the best indicator of the future is what has happened in the recent past. For example, individuals would expect the price level to be stable next year if stable prices had been present during the past two or three years. Similarly, if prices had risen at an annual rate of 4 or 5 percent during the past several years, people would expect similar increases next year.

EXHIBIT 3
Adaptive-Expectations Hypothesis

According to the adaptive-expectations hypothesis, the actual occurrence during the most recent period (or set of periods) determines people's future expectations. Thus, the expected future rate of inflation (b) lags behind the actual rate of inflation (a) by one period as expectations are altered over time.

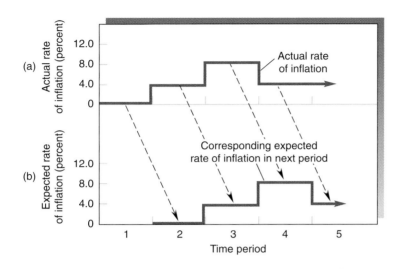

Exhibit 3 graphically illustrates the adaptive-expectations hypothesis. In period 1, prices were stable (part a). Therefore, on the basis of the experience of period 1, decision makers assume that prices will be stable in period 2 (part b). Suppose, however, that the actual rate of inflation in period 2 jumps to 4 percent. If the 4 percent inflation rate continues throughout the period (periods may range in length from six months to two or three years), decision makers will change their expectations about the next period. Relying on the experience of period 2, they anticipate 4 percent inflation in period 3. When their expectations turn out to be incorrect (the actual rate of inflation during period 3 is 8 percent), they again alter their expectations accordingly. Then, during period 4, the actual rate of inflation declines to 4 percent, less than the expected rate. Again, decision makers adjust their expectations about the rate of inflation, this time for period 5.

Of course, we would not expect the precise mechanical link between past occurrences and future expectations outlined in Exhibit 3. Rather than simply using the inflation rate of the immediate past period, people may use a weighted average of recent inflation rates when forming their expectations. It is the structure, however, that is important. With adaptive expectations, people expect that the future will be pretty much like the recent past.

Rational Expectations

The idea that people form their expectations about the future on the basis of all available information, including knowledge about policy changes and how they affect the economy, is called the **rational-expectations hypothesis**. According to this view, rather than merely assuming that the future will be like the immediate past, people also consider the expected effects of changes in policy. Based on their understanding of economic policy, people alter their expectations with regard to the future when the government, for example, runs a larger deficit or expands the supply of money more rapidly.

Perhaps an example will help clarify the rational-expectations hypothesis. Suppose that prices had increased at an annual rate of 3 percent during each of the past three years. In addition, assume that decision makers believe there is a relationship between the growth rate of the money supply and rising prices. They note that the money stock has expanded at a 12 percent annual rate during the last nine months, up from the 4 percent rate of the past several years. According to the rational-expectations hypothesis,

Rational-expectations hypothesis
The hypothesis that economic decision makers weigh all available evidence, including information concerning the probable effects of current and future economic policy, when they form their expectations about future economic events (such as the probable future inflation rate).

they will integrate the recent monetary acceleration into their forecast of the future in-flation rate. For example, they might project an increase in the inflation rate, perhaps to the 6 to 10 percent range. In other words, they will expect the future inflation rate to re-spond to the more rapid growth of the money supply. In contrast, under the adaptive-expectations hypothesis, the shift to a more expansionary monetary policy would have no effect on people's expectations.

The rational-expectations hypothesis does not assume that forecasts will always be correct. We live in a world of uncertainty. Even rational decision makers will err. But they will not continue to make the same errors. Thus, the rational-expectations hypothesis assumes that the errors of decision makers will tend to be random. For example, sometimes decision makers may overestimate the increase in the inflation rate caused by monetary expansion, and at other times they may underestimate it. But because they learn from experience, people will not continue to make the same types of mistakes year after year.

What Are the Major Differences between the Two Theories?

The adaptive- and rational-expectations theories differ in two major respects: (1) how quickly people adjust to a change and (2) the likelihood of systematic forecasting errors. If the adaptive-expectations theory is correct, people will adjust more slowly. When a more expansionary policy leads to inflation, for example, there will be a significant time lag, perhaps two or three years, before people come to expect the inflation and incorporate it into their decision making. In contrast, the rational-expectations theory implies that people will begin to anticipate more inflation as soon as they observe a move toward a more expansionary policy—perhaps even before there is an actual increase in the rate of inflation. Therefore, the time lag between a shift in policy and a change in expectations will be shorter under rational than under adaptive expectations.

Second, systematic errors will occur under adaptive, but not under rational expecta-tions. For example, when the inflation rate is rising, decision makers will systematically tend to underestimate the future rate of inflation. In contrast, when the rate of inflation is falling, individuals will tend systematically to overestimate its future rate. On the other hand, the errors will be random under rational expectations. With rational expectations, people will be as likely to overestimate as to underestimate the inflationary impact of a shift to a more expansionary policy.

MACRO POLICY IMPLICATIONS OF ADAPTIVE AND RATIONAL EXPECTATIONS

When it comes to setting macro policy, does it make any difference how quickly people alter their expectations and whether errors are random or systematic? The *AD-AS* model can be used to address this question. Suppose there is a shift to a more expansionary macro

EXHIBIT 4
Expectations and the Short-Run Effects of Demand Stimulus

Because people with adaptive expectations do not anticipate inflation until after it occurs, a shift to a more expansionary policy will increase aggregate demand and lead to a temporary increase in real GDP from Y_F to Y_2 (part a). In contrast, people who have rational expectations quickly anticipate the inflationary impact of demand-stimulus policies, and therefore resource prices and production costs rise as rapidly as prices. In this case, both *AD* and *SRAS* shift upward, leading to an increase in the general level of prices (inflation), but there is no change in real output, even in the short run (part b).

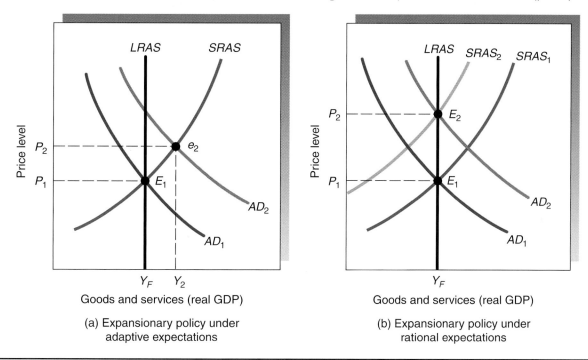

(a) Expansionary policy under
adaptive expectations

(b) Expansionary policy under
rational expectations

policy—an increase in the money growth rate, for example. As part (a) of **Exhibit 4** illustrates, the policy shift will stimulate aggregate demand and place upward pressure on the price level (or the inflation rate in the dynamic case). Under adaptive expectations, people will initially fail to anticipate the higher prices. Therefore, as we have previously discussed, output will temporarily increase to Y_2, beyond the economy's long-run potential. Correspondingly, employment will expand and unemployment will recede below the economy's natural rate. When the effects of expansionary policy are unanticipated, both output and employment increase in the short run.

However, the output rate beyond the economy's capacity will be unsustainable even when people have adaptive expectations. As the expansionary policies persist and the rate of inflation increases, people will eventually begin to anticipate the higher rate of inflation. Once this happens, resource prices will rise as rapidly as product prices, and output will return to its long-run potential (Y_F). As a result, the high level of output and employment will be only temporary.

Part (b) of Exhibit 4 illustrates the impact of expansionary macroeconomic policy when people have rational expectations. Remember that decision makers with rational expectations will quickly begin to anticipate the probable effects of the more expansionary policy—stronger demand and a rising rate of inflation, for example—and alter their choices accordingly. Agreements specifying future wage rates and resource prices will quickly make allowance for an expected increase in the price level. These agreements might even incorporate escalator clauses providing for automatic increases in nominal wages as the general price level rises. When buyers and sellers in the resource market anticipate fully and adjust quickly to the effects of the demand-stimulus policies, wage rates and resource prices will rise as rapidly as product prices. Hence, the short-run aggregate supply curve will shift upward (to $SRAS_2$) as rapidly as the aggregate demand curve. When people quickly and accurately anticipate the inflationary effects of the more expansionary policy, the result will merely be an increase in the general level of prices (move from E_1 to E_2 in part b of Exhibit 4). Even in the short run, demand-stimulus policies will fail to increase output and employment under rational expectations.

Policy Implications of the Two Hypotheses Differ in the Short Run, but Not in the Long Run

The short-run implications of the adaptive and rational expectations hypotheses differ substantially. In the short run, demand-stimulus policies will expand output and employment under adaptive expectations, but not under rational expectations. In the long run, however, the implications of the two hypotheses are identical. Like rational expectations, the adaptive-expectations hypothesis indicates that decision makers will eventually anticipate the inflationary effects of the more expansionary policy. Once this happens, output will recede to the economy's long-run potential. Therefore, both theories imply that the long-run effects of a more expansionary macro policy will be inflation, rather than sustainable increases in output.

PHILLIPS CURVE: THE VIEW OF THE 1960s VERSUS TODAY

Phillips curve
A curve that illustrates the relationship between the rate of inflation and the rate of unemployment.

In the late 1950s, British economist A. W. Phillips examined the historical data on the relationship between wage inflation and unemployment in the United Kingdom. [2] As a result, a curve indicating the relationship between the rate of inflation and the rate of unemployment is known as the **Phillips curve**. **Exhibit 5** uses a graphic from the 1969 *Economic Report of the President* to illustrate the idea of the Phillips curve. When the unemployment rate was plotted against the rate of inflation in the U.S during the period 1954–1968, the points mapped out a curve showing an inverse relationship between the rate of inflation and the rate of unemployment. When inflation was high, the unemployment rate tended to be low. Correspondingly, when the inflation rate was low, the unemployment rate tended to be high.

In the 1960s, most macroeconomists ignored the potential impact of expectations. Instead, they believed there was a direct trade-off between inflation and unemployment—that a lower rate of unemployment could be achieved if we were willing to tolerate a little more inflation. [3] This view became the foundation for the policies of the 1970s.

Beginning in the latter part of the 1960s, both monetary and fiscal policy became more expansionary. The inflation rate rose to the 3 percent to 6 percent range, but as the higher rates of inflation persisted, the unemployment rate also began to rise. As macroeconomic policy became even more expansionary, the unemployment rate dipped briefly, but it soon returned to exceedingly high levels. By the end of the 1970s, the U.S. economy was characterized by high rates of both inflation and unemployment. The inflation rate in 1979 was 11.3 percent and in 1980 it jumped to 13.5 percent, about 10 percentage points higher than the rates of the late 1960s. But even these high rates of inflation failed to reduce the unemployment rate. In 1980, the rate of unemployment stood at 7.1 percent, well above the 4.9 percent registered during the recessionary year of 1970.

What went wrong? Given what we know about expectations today, this is now an easy question to answer. As both the adaptive- and rational-expectations hypotheses indicate, the alleged trade-off between inflation and unemployment will dissipate once

---

[2] A. W. Phillips, "The Relationship between Unemployment and the Rate of Change of Money Wages in the United Kingdom, 1861–1957," *Economica* 25 (1958): 238–99.

[3] For example, Nobel Prize winners Paul Samuelson and Robert Solow told the 1959 meeting of the American Economic Association,

> In order to achieve the nonperfectionist's goal of high enough output to give us no more than 3 percent unemployment, the price index might have to rise by as much as 4 to 5 percent per year. That much price rise [inflation] would seem to be the necessary cost of high employment and production in the years immediately ahead.

See Paul A. Samuelson and Robert Solow, "Our Menu of Policy Changes," *American Economic Review* (May 1960).

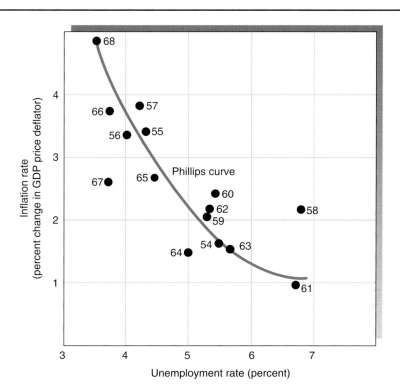

EXHIBIT 5
Early View of the
Phillips Curve

The Phillips curve shows the relationship between inflation and unemployment. The dots on this diagram from the 1969 *Economic Report of the President* represent the inflation rate and unemployment rate for each year between 1954 and 1968. Note that the chart suggests that higher rates of inflation are associated with lower rates of unemployment. Because they failed to recognize the importance of expectations, many economists and policy makers in the 1960s and 1970s thought this relationship was stable. Thus, they believed that expansionary (inflationary) policies could permanently reduce the rate of unemployment. As the record of the 1970s shows, this view is fallacious.

Source: Economic Report of the President, 1969, page 95. The Phillips curve was fitted to the points.

people anticipate a higher rate of inflation. Put another way, the Phillips curve is not fixed. When the inflation rate increases, people will come to anticipate the higher rate of inflation, and this will cause the Phillips curve to shift upward and to the right. The adaptive-expectations hypothesis implies that there will be a time lag—perhaps one to three years—before people are able to anticipate and adjust fully to a higher rate of inflation. But once the higher inflation rate is anticipated, neither output nor employment will be stimulated. The rational-expectations hypothesis indicates that the adjustment period will be shorter. Both theories of expectations, however, imply that people will eventually anticipate the higher rate of inflation and once this happens, the inflationary policies will fail to expand output and employment. With expectations, there is no trade-off between inflation and unemployment. Expectations undermine the simple Phillips curve analysis of the 1960s.[4]

Expectations and the Modern View of the Phillips Curve

If accurately anticipated by decision makers, even high rates of inflation—rates of 10 or 15 percent for example—will fail to reduce unemployment below its natural rate.[5] Of course,

[4]Even during the 1960s, there were some critics of the inflation versus unemployment trade-off view. See Edmund S. Phelps, "Phillips Curves, Expectations of Inflation and Optimal Employment over Time," *Economica* 3 (1967): 254–81; and Milton Friedman, "The Role of Monetary Policy," *American Economic Review* (May 1968): 1–17.

[5]Empirically, higher rates of inflation are generally associated with greater variability in the inflation rate. Erratic variability increases economic uncertainty. It is likely to inhibit business activity, reduce the volume of mutually advantageous exchange, and cause the level of employment to fall. Thus, higher, more variable inflation rates may well increase the rate of unemployment.

people won't always correctly anticipate the rate of inflation, particularly if there is an abrupt change in the rate. Within the expectations framework, it is the difference between the actual and expected inflation rate that will influence output and employment. When inflation is greater than anticipated, profit margins will improve, output will expand, and unemployment will fall below its natural rate. On the other hand, when the actual rate of inflation is less than the expected rate, profits will be abnormally low, output will recede, and unemployment will rise above its natural rate.

Exhibit 6 recasts the Phillips curve within the expectations framework. When people underestimate the actual rate of inflation, abnormally low unemployment will occur. Conversely, when decision makers expect a higher rate of inflation than what actually occurs—when they overestimate the inflation rate—unemployment will rise above its natural rate. When the actual and expected rates are equal, the economy's output will be at its potential and unemployment at its natural rate.

When the inflation rate is steady—when it is neither rising nor falling—people will come to anticipate the rate accurately. The steady rate will be built into long-term contracts, such as collective bargaining agreements, building leases, and bank loans. Under these conditions, profit margins will be normal, and output will move toward the economy's long-run potential. Correspondingly, the actual rate of unemployment will move toward its natural rate—its minimum sustainable rate. In fact, the natural rate of unemployment is sometimes defined as the unemployment rate present when the inflation rate is neither rising nor falling. In contrast with the early Phillips curve views, the modern view indicates that, if policy makers want to keep the unemployment rate low, they should follow policies consistent with a low and steady rate of inflation—one that people will be able to forecast accurately.

Exhibit 7 illustrates the impact of both abrupt changes and low steady rates of inflation during the last three decades. The inflation measure is the change in the inflation rate (the four-quarter moving average). When this variable spikes upward, it means there has been a sharp increase in the rate of inflation during the last twelve months. Conversely, a spike downward means that the rate of inflation has fallen sharply during the last twelve months. Predictably, these abrupt changes will be difficult for people to

EXHIBIT 6
Modern Expectational
Phillips Curve

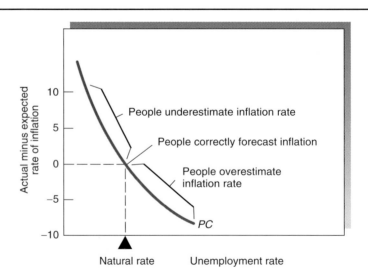

It is the difference between the actual and expected rates of inflation that influences the unemployment rate, not the size of the inflation rate, as the earlier, naive Phillips curve analysis implied. When inflation is greater than anticipated (people underestimate it), unemployment will fall below the natural rate. In contrast, when inflation is less than people anticipate (people overestimate it) unemployment will rise above the natural rate. If the inflation rate is correctly anticipated by decision makers, the natural rate of unemployment will result.

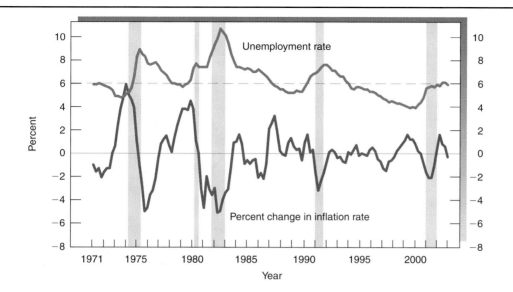

EXHIBIT 7
Unemployment and Changes in the Rate of Inflation

Here we show the relationship between changes in the inflation rate (four-quarter moving average) and the rate of unemployment. Abrupt changes in the inflation rate will be difficult for people to anticipate correctly. Notice how the sharp declines in the inflation rate during 1974, 1980–1981, and 1988–1989 preceded recessions and substantial increases in the unemployment rate. Also notice that the steadier (and lower) inflation rates since the early 1990s have been associated with lower and more stable rates of unemployment.

Source: http://www.economagic.com/.

forecast accurately. The actual rate of inflation is likely to rise above the expected rate when the inflation rate increases abruptly and fall below it when there is an abrupt downturn in the rate of inflation. If that is true, our analysis indicates that the unemployment rate will tend to fall when there is a sharp upturn in the inflation rate and rise when there is a sharp downturn.

History bears this out. Notice how the substantial increases in the rate of inflation during 1973, 1976–1978, and even the more moderate increases of the 1980s were associated with downturns in the rate of unemployment. On the other hand, the sharp reductions in the rate of inflation during 1974, 1980–1981, and 1989 preceded substantial increases in the rate of unemployment. The changes in the inflation rate since 1980, and particularly since the early 1990s, have been more moderate than those during the 1970s. Note how the lower and steadier rates of inflation during the last decade were associated with lower and steadier rates of unemployment.

Just as our analysis indicates, abrupt swings in the inflation rate tend to cause abrupt swings in the economy, including the rate of unemployment. In contrast, when the inflation rate is steadier, the unemployment rate tends to be lower and more stable.

Experience, Theory, and Stabilization Policy

Right or wrong, the views of economists have had a major impact on stabilization policy. In the 1930s, there was little understanding of how changes in the money supply influenced output and employment. At the same time, economists also believed that the federal government should balance its budget annually. These two factors led to disastrous policies during that decade. (See the accompanying Applications in Economics, "Perverse Macroeconomic Policy and the Great Depression.") More recently, the failure to integrate expectations into macro analysis laid the foundation for the policies that caused the inflation of the 1970s.

APPLICATIONS IN ECONOMICS

Perverse Macroeconomic Policy and the Great Depression

As we previously discussed, the Great Depression exerted an enormous effect on both economic thought and economic institutions. **Table 1** presents data that illustrate both the severity and length of the economic contraction. For four successive years (1930–1933), real output fell. Unemployment soared to nearly one-quarter of the workforce in 1932 and 1933. Although real output expanded and the rate of unemployment declined during the 1934–1937 period, the economy again fell into the depths of a depression in 1938. Ten years after the catastrophe started, real GDP was virtually the same as it had been in 1929.[1]

Armed with knowledge you now have about how monetary and fiscal policies work, you can clearly see that the severity of the calamity was the result of perverse macroeconomic policy. Three important factors contributed to the economic collapse of the 1930s.

1. A sharp reduction in the supply of money during the 1930–1933 period reduced aggregate demand and real output.

The supply of money expanded slowly but steadily throughout the 1920s.[2] As Table 1 shows, monetary policy suddenly shifted in 1930. The money supply fell by 6.9 percent during 1930, by 10.9 percent in 1931, and by 4.7 percent in 1932. As banks failed and the money supply collapsed, the Fed failed to inject new reserves into the system. Neither did it act as a lender of last resort. The quantity of money in 1933 was 27 percent less than in 1929! Our analysis indicates that a drastic reduction in the money supply, such as that of the early 1930s, will reduce both aggregate demand and real output. This is precisely what happened. Real output plunged. By 1933, real GDP was 29 percent lower than the 1929 level.

2. A large tax increase in the midst of a severe recession made a bad situation worse.

Prior to the Keynesian revolution, the dominant view was that the federal budget should be balanced. Reflecting the ongoing economic downturn, the federal budget ran a deficit in

© BETTMANN/CORBIS

Perhaps the most catastrophic example of inappropriate stabilization policy was that of the Great Depression. A sharp reduction in the supply of money, a huge tax increase, and protectionist trade policies turned a recession into the worst depression in U.S. history.

1931, and an even larger deficit was shaping up for 1932. Assisted by the newly elected Democratic majority in the House of Representatives, the Republican Hoover administration passed the largest peacetime tax rate increase in the history of the United States. At the bottom of the income scale, marginal tax rates were raised from 1.5 percent to 4 percent in 1932. At the top of the scale, tax rates were raised from 25 percent to 63 percent. As our prior analysis of fiscal policy suggests, a huge tax increase in the midst of a severe recession will further reduce aggregate demand and the incentive to earn. Table 1 shows the degree to which this happened. As tax rates were increased in 1932, real GDP fell by 13.3 percent. Unemployment rose from 15.9 percent in 1931 to 23.6 percent in 1932.

3. Tariff increases retarded international exchange.

Concerned about low agricultural prices, an influx of imports, rising unemployment, and declining tax revenues, Congress adopted various trade restraints. Tariffs (taxes on imported goods) on a wide range of products were increased substantially in early 1930.[3] Other countries promptly responded by increasing their tariffs, further reducing the volume of trade between nations. As the flow of trade diminished, so, too, did the mutual gains that trading partners derived from specialization and exchange.

---

[1]See Robert J. Samuelson, "Great Depression," in *The Fortune Encyclopedia of Economics,* ed. David R. Henderson (New York: Warner Books, 1993), for an interesting and informative commentary on this time period. This publication can also be found online at http://www.econlib.org/.

[2]From 1921 through 1929, the money stock expanded at an annual rate of 2.7 percent, slightly less rapidly than the growth in the output of goods and services. Thus, the 1920s were a decade of price stability, even of slight deflation.

[3] The high-tariff policy was ineffective as a revenue measure. Even though the taxes on imported goods were increased by approximately 50 percent, imports declined so sharply that tariff revenues fell from $602 million in 1929 to $328 million in 1932.

TABLE 1
Economic Record of the Great Depression

Year	Real GDP in 1989 Dollars (billions)	Implicit GDP Deflator (1929 = 100)	Unemployment Rate	Percent Change in the Money Supply (M1)
1929	821.8	100.0	3.2	+1.0
1930	748.9	96.8	8.7	−6.9
1931	691.3	88.0	15.9	−10.9
1932	599.7	77.6	23.6	−4.7
1933	587.1	76.0	24.9	−2.9
1934	632.6	82.4	21.7	+10.0
1935	681.3	84.8	20.1	+18.2
1936	777.9	84.8	16.9	+13.9
1937	811.4	89.6	14.3	+4.7
1938	778.9	87.2	19.0	−1.3
1939	840.7	86.4	17.2	+12.1

Source: Economic Report of the President: 1993 (Washington, D.C.: U.S. Government Printing Office, 1993); and Bureau of the Census, *The Statistical History of the United States from Colonial Times to the Present* (New York: Basic Books, 1976).

When discussing the Great Depression, historians often stress the role of the 1929 stock market crash. Because the stock market crash diminished the wealth of many, it was a contributing factor to the reduction in aggregate demand and output. However, the severity of the Great Depression was the result of disastrous macroeconomic policy, not an inevitable consequence of a stock market crash. A stock market crash decades later, in October 1987, illustrates this point. In just a few days, the stock market lost a third of its value in 1987, just as it did in 1929. But that is where the parallel ends. In contrast with the response to the 1929 crash, in 1987 the Fed moved quickly to supply reserves to the banking system. The money supply did not fall. Tax rates were not increased. And even though there was a lot of political rhetoric about "the need to protect American businesses," trade barriers were not raised. In short, sensible policies were followed subsequent to the crash of 1987. Continued growth and stability were the result.

ECONOMICS AT THE MOVIES

Seabiscuit (2003)

Seabiscuit is set during the Great Depression. It shows the frustration people felt when one in four persons were unemployed, despite the many new government policies put in place to "fix" the economy. Today we realize that the government's policies actually made the Great Depression much worse and longer than it otherwise would have been.

Today, however, expectations are taken into account. This has significantly influenced the way economists and policy makers think about stabilization policy. The performance of the U.S. economy during the relative price stability of the last two decades, particularly the low inflation of the 1990s, has also been influential. Substantial agreement about what constitutes sound stabilization policy has emerged from this process. We now turn to that topic.

MODERN CONSENSUS VIEW OF STABILIZATION POLICY

There are four major elements of the modern consensus view.

1. Demand-stimulus policies cannot reduce the rate of unemployment below the natural rate—at least not for long. Once people come to expect inflation, the inflation versus unemployment trade-off dissipates. While the adaptive-expectations hypothesis implies that an unanticipated shift to a more expansionary policy can temporarily reduce the unemployment rate, the rational-expectations hypothesis indicates that even the temporary reduction in the unemployment-rate might not occur. Given the uncertainty of the short-run trade-off and clear absence of a long-lasting trade-off, most economists now believe that stimulating inflation in an effort to reduce unemployment is both destabilizing and shortsighted.

2. Wide swings in both monetary and fiscal policy should be avoided. Given our limited forecasting ability and knowledge about how quickly changes in monetary and fiscal policy impact the economy, policy makers should not attempt to respond to every turn in the economic road. Major changes in tax policy, budget deficits, and the money supply *in response to business cycle conditions* are likely to increase rather than reduce instability. More stability will result if the policy makers adopt a long-range strategy and stick with it.

3. Using discretionary fiscal policy as an effective stabilization tool is impractical, particularly in countries like the United States. Proper timing is essential for the effective use of stabilization policy. Given the checks and balances built into the U.S. political structure, it is unrealistic to expect speedy changes in fiscal policy. Moreover, the crowding-out effect creates additional uncertainty about how potent a fiscal policy change will be. These shortcomings have caused even longtime Keynesians like Paul Samuelson to conclude that fiscal policy is an impractical stabilization tool.

4. Monetary policy should focus on price stability. Inflation is caused by expansionary monetary policy and therefore the control of inflation is the responsibility of monetary policy makers. When the Fed keeps the inflation rate at a low and therefore easily predictable rate, it lays the groundwork for the smooth operation of markets and long-term healthy growth. In fact, price stability is so important that it is one of our twelve keys to economic prosperity.

Price Stability

 When monetary policy makers consistently achieve price stability, they are laying the foundation for both economic stability and the efficient operation of markets.

The high standard of living that Americans enjoy is the result of gains from specialization, division of labor, and mass-production processes. Price stability and the smooth operation of the pricing system will help individuals more fully realize the potential gains from these sources. In contrast, high and variable rates of inflation create uncertainty, distort relative prices, and reduce the efficiency of a market economy.

There is no conflict between price stability and full employment. When the general level of prices is relatively stable, the uncertainties of time-related activities such as investment diminish. This helps promote both full employment and strong economic growth. When price stability is achieved and maintained, monetary policy makers have done their job well.

Who Deserves Credit for the Recent Stability?

The stability of the U.S. economy during the last two decades has been unprecedented. **Exhibit 8** illustrates this point. From 1910 to 1959, the U.S. economy was in recession 32.8 percent of the time. Between 1960 and 1982, recession was present 22.8 percent of the time. By way of comparison, during the period 1983–2004, the U.S. economy was in recession only 6.1 percent of the time—just sixteen months.

What accounts for the recent stability? The public tends to credit as well as blame the president for the state of the economy. In contrast, economists would be more inclined to examine the policies of the Federal Reserve. Most economists credit the recent stability to the Fed. In contrast with the 1970s, in recent years the Fed has focused on price stability. Under the leadership of first Paul Volcker and later Alan Greenspan, it has avoided wide swings in the rate of inflation. In turn, the low, stable rates of inflation have enhanced the overall stability of the U.S. economy.

LOOKING AHEAD

The following chapter will focus on economic growth. It will explain why income levels and growth rates differ across countries and analyze what policy makers can do to create an environment conducive to prosperity.

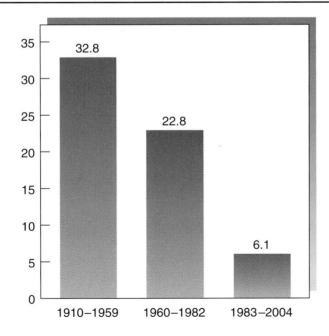

EXHIBIT 8
Reduction in the Incidence of Recession

The U.S. economy was in recession 32.8 percent of the time during the 1910–1959 period and 22.8 percent of the time between 1960 and 1982, but only 6.1 percent of the time during the 1983–2004 period.

Sources: R.E. Lipsey and D. Preston, *Source Book of Statistics Relating to Construction* (1966); and National Bureau of Economic Research, http://www.nber.org/.

KEY POINTS

▼ Historically, the United States has experienced substantial swings in real output. Prior to the Second World War, year-to-year changes in real GDP of 5 to 10 percent were experienced on several occasions. Fluctuations during the last five decades have been more moderate.

▼ If stimulus could be injected during periods of recession and restraint during inflationary booms, macro policy could moderate the ups and downs of the business cycle. Proper timing, however, is difficult to achieve because it takes time to recognize and institute a policy change, and the effects of the change are not immediate.

▼ To time a change properly, policy makers need to know where the economy will be six to eighteen months in the future. Forecasting devices such as the index of leading indicators will be helpful, but forecasting is a highly imperfect science.

▼ There are two major theories about how expectations are formed. According to the adaptive-expectations hypothesis, individuals form their expectations about the future on the basis of data from the recent past. The rational-expectations hypothesis assumes that people use all pertinent information, including data on the conduct of current policy, when forming their expectations about the future.

▼ When people have adaptive expectations, an unanticipated shift to a more expansionary policy will tem-porarily stimulate output and employment. In contrast, when people have rational expectations, expansionary policy will fail, even temporarily, to systematically increase output. However, both expectations theories indicate that sustained expansionary policies will lead to inflation without permanently increasing output and employment.

▼ The Phillips curve outlines the relationship between inflation and unemployment. In the 1960s, it was widely believed that higher rates of inflation could be used to reduce the unemployment rate. This view provided the foundation for the expansionary policies and inflation of the 1970s. Once expectations are integrated into macro analysis, it is clear that this early view of the Phillips curve is fallacious.

▼ While debate about macro policy continues, most economists now believe that monetary policy consistent with relative price stability is the key ingredient of effective stabilization policy. In contrast with the 1960s, today's economists think that using fiscal policy as an effective stabilization tool is impractical.

▼ An analysis of the Great Depression reveals that the severity and length of the economic plunge, if not its onset, were the result of perverse policies—a sharp contraction in the money supply, a huge tax increase, and a sharp rise in tariff rates.

CRITICAL ANALYSIS QUESTIONS

1. The chair of the Council of Economic Advisers has requested that you write a short paper explaining how economic policy can be used to stabilize the economy and achieve a high level of economic growth during the next five years. Be sure to make specific proposals. Indicate why your recommendations will work. You may submit your paper to your instructor.

*2. How does economic instability during the past four decades compare with instability prior to the Second World War? Is there any evidence that stabilization policy has either increased or decreased economic stability during recent decades?

3. State in your own words the adaptive-expectations hypothesis. How does the hypothesis of rational expectations differ from that of adaptive expectations?

4. What is the index of leading indicators? Why is it useful to macro policy makers?

*5. How would you expect the actual unemployment rate to compare with the natural unemployment rate in the following cases?
   a. Prices are stable and have been stable for the last four years.
   b. The current inflation rate is 3 percent, and this rate was widely anticipated more than a year ago.

c. Expansionary policies lead to an unexpected increase in the inflation rate from 3 percent to 7 percent.

d. There is an unexpected reduction in the inflation rate from 7 percent to 2 percent.

6. Compare and contrast the impact of an unexpected shift to a more expansionary monetary policy under both rational and adaptive expectations. Are the implications of the two theories different in the short run? Are the long-run implications different? Explain.

*7. What are some of the practical problems that limit the effectiveness of discretionary monetary and fiscal policy as stabilization tools?

8. Many central banks now indicate that their primary objective is to keep inflation at a persistently low rate. If the rate of inflation is persistently low, will this help reduce the instability of the business cycle? Why or why not?

*9. "The Great Depression indicates that the self-correcting mechanism of a market economy is weak and unreliable." Evaluate this statement.

10. Prior to the mid-1970s, many economists thought a higher rate of unemployment would reduce the in-

flation rate. Why? How does the modern view of the Phillips curve differ from the earlier view?

*11. a. What is the most important thing the Fed can do to promote economic stability?

b. Can expansionary monetary policy reduce interest rates and stimulate a higher growth rate of real output in the long run?

c. If monetary policy is too expansionary, how will nominal interest rates and the general level of prices be affected?

12. What were the major causes of the Great Depression? Did the stock market crash of October 1929 make the Great Depression inevitable? Have advances in macroeconomic understanding made the prospects of another Great Depression unlikely? Why or why not?

13. How did integration of expectations into the Phillips curve analysis and rejection of the view that higher inflation will reduce the unemployment rate affect macroeconomic policy in the last two decades?

---

*Asterisk denotes questions for which answers are given in Appendix B.

CHAPTER 16

Economic Growth and the Wealth of Nations

*Certain fundamental principles—
formulating sound monetary and
fiscal policies, removing domestic
price controls, opening the economy to international market
forces, ensuring property rights
and private property, creating
competition, and reforming and
limiting the role of government—
are essential for a healthy market
economy.*

—*Economic Report of the
President, 1991*

Chapter Focus

- Why is economic growth important?

- How does sustained economic growth change income levels and the lives of people?

- Why do some countries grow and prosper while others remain poor?

- Can governments enhance growth? If so, how? When governments are large, how does this influence growth?

Throughout history, most of the world's population has struggled fifty, sixty, and seventy hours per week just to obtain the basic necessities of life—food, clothing, and shelter. During the last two centuries, sustained economic growth has changed that situation for most people in North America, Europe, Oceania, and Japan. Rising incomes and improving living standards have not always been present in Western countries. According to Phelps Brown, a twentieth-century British economist and author, the real income of English building-trade workers was virtually unchanged between 1215 and 1798, a period of nearly six centuries.[1] In other parts of Europe, workers experienced a similar stagnation of real earnings throughout much of this period. Low incomes and widespread poverty are still the norm in most countries—particularly those of South and Central America, Africa, and South-Central Asia. Why do some countries grow and achieve high levels of income while others stagnate? The keys to economic prosperity series has already addressed several dimensions of this issue, but we now want to consider it more directly, and in a more comprehensive manner. ■

IMPORTANCE OF ECONOMIC GROWTH

Economic growth is important because it is a necessary ingredient for higher incomes and living standards. Remember, GDP is a measure of both output and income. The linkage between output and income highlights a very important point: growth of output is necessary for the growth of income. Without more output, it will be impossible to achieve higher levels of income.

Economic growth expands the productive capacity of an economy. As **Exhibit 1** shows, an expansion in output can be illustrated within the framework of both the

EXHIBIT 1
Economic Growth, Production Possibilities, and Long-Run Aggregate Supply

Economic growth expands the sustainable output level of an economy. This can be illustrated by either an outward shift in the production possibilities curve (part a) or an increase in the long-run aggregate supply curve (a shift from $LRAS_{95}$ to $LRAS_{2005}$ in part b).

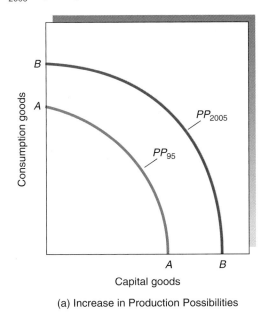

(a) Increase in Production Possibilities

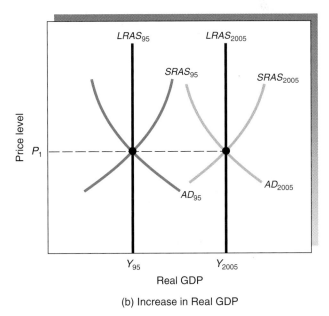

(b) Increase in Real GDP

[1]Phelps Brown, *A Century of Pay: The Course of Pay and Production in France, Germany, Sweden, the United Kingdom, and the United States* (London: Macmillan, 1968).

production possibilities and the *AD-AS* models. If a country experienced economic growth during the last decade, this means that it will now be possible to produce a larger quantity of both consumer and capital goods in 2005 than it could in 1995. As part (a) of Exhibit 1 shows, this growth will shift the economy's production possibilities curve outward (from *AA* to *BB*). Within the framework of the *AD-AS* model, the long-run aggregate supply curve indicates what the economy's maximum sustainable rate of output will be. As part (b) of Exhibit 1 shows, growth will shift the long-run aggregate supply curve to the right (move it from $LRAS_{95}$ to $LRAS_{2005}$), and the equilibrium level of output will expand from Y_{95} to Y_{2005}.

> **When a nation's GDP is increasing more rapidly than its population,** per capita **GDP—*that is, GDP per person—will also expand. Growth of per capita GDP means more goods and services per person.*** In most cases, this will mean that the typical person has a higher standard of living— a better diet, improved health and access to medical services, a longer life expectancy, and greater educational opportunity.

per capita GDP
Income per person. Increases in income per person are vital for the achievement of higher living standards.

Impact of Sustained Economic Growth

People have a tendency to think that a 1 percent or 2 percent difference in growth is of little consequence. When sustained over a lengthy period, however, seemingly small differences in growth can exert a huge effect. If the income per person in Country A grows at an annual rate of 3.5 percent, per capita income will double every twenty years. In contrast, if the growth rate of Country B is 1.75 percent, it will take forty years for per capita income to double. If the two countries start out at the same income level, after forty years the income of Country A will be twice that of Country B. The principle of compound return is at work here.

Rule of 70
If a variable grows at a rate of *x* percent per year, 70/*x* will approximate the number of years required for the variable to double.

The **rule of 70** makes it easy to figure how many years it will take for income to double at various rates of growth. If you divide 70 by a country's average growth rate, it will approximate the number of years required for an income level to double.[2] For example, at an average annual growth rate of 5 percent, it will take fourteen years (70 divided by 5) for the income level to double. As we just noted, when the growth rate is 3.5 percent, income will double in twenty years (70 divided by 3.5). At a 1 percent growth rate, it will take seventy years for income to double. (*Note:* The rule of 70 also applies to the rate of return on savings and investments. As you can see, over a long period of time, small differences in rates of return can make a big difference in the accumulated value of your savings or investment.)

> ***Differences in sustained growth rates over a few decades will substantially alter the relative incomes of countries.*** Nations that experience sustained periods of rapid economic growth will rapidly move up the income ladder and eventually achieve high-income status. On the other hand, nations that grow slowly or experience declines in real GDP per capita will slide down the economic ladder.

Using the actual per capita real income figures (measured in 1985 dollars) for Venezuela, Argentina, Mexico, Japan, Hong Kong, and Singapore, **Exhibit 2** vividly illustrates how sustained growth over a lengthy period influences relative incomes. Look at the figures for 1960. The per capita incomes of Hong Kong and Singapore were substantially less than those of the three Latin American countries. In 1960, Japan's per capita income was about the same as that of Mexico and well below the comparable figures for Argentina and Venezuela. During the next forty-two years, Venezuela's real income per capita receded, Argentina's grew slowly (0.5 percent annual rate), and Mexico's increased at a modest rate (2.2 percent). During the same period, the annual growth of per capita income averaged 4.2 percent in Japan, 5.3 percent in Hong Kong, and 5.9 percent in Singapore.

Now look at the per capita income figures of the six countries in 2002. The rapid growth rates of Hong Kong and Singapore paid off in a big way. The per capita incomes of these two countries, which were the lowest in 1960, were the highest among the six in 2002. In fact, the 2002 per capita incomes of Hong Kong and Singapore were three times those of

---

[2]Sometimes this rule is called the rule of 72, rather than 70. Although 70 yields more accurate estimates for growth rates of less than 5 percent, 72 yields slightly more accurate estimates when the annual rate of growth exceeds 5 percent.

EXHIBIT 2
Differences in Long-Term Growth Rates and Changes in Per Capita Income

The impact of long-term growth on income levels is illustrated here. During the 1960–2002 period, the per capita growth rates of Japan, Hong Kong, and Singapore were 4.2 percent, 5.3 percent, and 5.9 percent, respectively. Conversely, the growth rates of Mexico, Argentina, and Venezuela were 2.2 percent, 0.5 percent, and minus 0.3 percent, respectively, during the same period. Notice how the more rapid growth rates of the three Asian countries dramatically increased their income levels relative to the three Latin American nations.

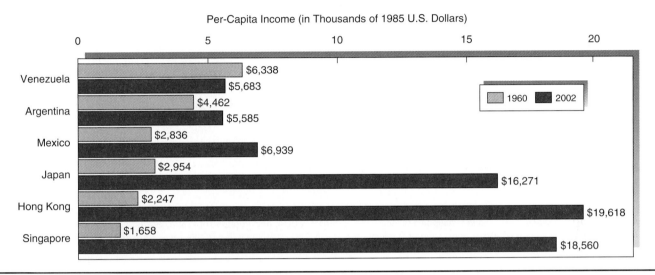

Per-Capita Income (in Thousands of 1985 U.S. Dollars)

Source: Robert Summers and Alan Heston, *Penn World Tables, Mark 5.6* (Cambridge, MA: National Bureau of Economic Research, 1994); and World Bank, *World Development Indicators,* CD-ROM, 2004.

Venezuela and Argentina and about two and a half times the figure for Mexico. Japan's income level, which was about the same as that of Mexico in 1960 ($2,954 versus $2,836), was now $16,271 compared to $6,939 for Mexico. Even though Japan's growth rate was only two percentage points higher than Mexico's, this differential made a dramatic impact over the forty-two-year period. The income levels of Venezuela and Argentina, which were the highest in 1960, were the lowest among the six countries in 2002. Clearly, the differences in growth rates among these countries dramatically altered their relative incomes.

BEST AND WORST GROWTH RECORDS

Observing the income differences between the wealthy industrial nations and **less developed countries (LDCs)**, some have argued that the rich are consistently getting richer while the poor are getting poorer. Is this true? Which countries are growing most rapidly? Which are falling behind? **Exhibit 3** presents data on the growth of per capita GDP for (1) high-growth economies, (2) high-income industrial nations, and (3) the economies with the worst growth records.

Only ten countries (shown in the left side of Exhibit 3) were able to achieve an average growth rate of 3.5 percent or more during the 1980–2002 period. China, South Korea, Taiwan, Ireland, Singapore, and Thailand head the list. Except for Ireland, all of the high-growth countries were classified as LDCs at the beginning of the period. One-third of the world's population lives in the two most populated countries, China and India. Both of these countries are included in the high-growth list. Remember, a 3.5 percent annual growth rate means that per capita GDP doubles every twenty years. As a result, per person incomes in the high-growth economies increased sharply in these countries during the last couple of decades, and living standards improved dramatically.

Among the high-income industrial economies, growth rates were tightly bunched. The nine most populated high-income countries all had growth rates between 1.6 percent and 2.2

Less-developed countries (LDCs)
Low-income countries generally characterized by rapid population growth and an agriculture-household sector that dominates the economy. Sometimes these countries are referred to as developing countries.

EXHIBIT 3

Growth of Per Capita GDP for High-Income Industrial Countries, High-Growth LDCs, and Low-Growth LDCs (1980–2002)

HIGH-GROWTH LDCs*	GROWTH OF PER CAPITA GDP 1980–2002	HIGH-INCOME INDUSTRIAL COUNTRIES	GROWTH OF PER CAPITA GDP 1980–2002	LOW-GROWTH LDCs**	GROWTH OF PER CAPITA GDP 1980–2002
China	8.1%	United Kingdom	2.2%	Congo (Zaire)	−4.9%
South Korea	6.1%	Japan	2.1%	Sierra Leone	−3.3%
Taiwan	6.0%	Australia	1.9%	Haiti	−2.8%
Ireland	4.8%	United States	1.9%	Madagascar	−2.1%
Botswana	4.6%	Netherlands	1.8%	Niger	−2.0%
Thailand	4.6%	Italy	1.8%	Côte d'Ivoire	−1.8%
Mauritius	4.4%	France	1.7%	Togo	−1.7%
Singapore	4.2%	Germany	1.7%	Nicaragua	−1.4%
Hong Kong	3.7%	Canada	1.6%	Venezuela	−1.3%
India	3.6%	Switzerland	0.7%	Nigeria	−1.1%

*Countries classified as LDC in 1980 with 1980–2002 growth rates of more than 3.5%.
**Countries classified as LDC in 1980 with 1980–2002 negative growth rates of more than –1%.

Source: Data are from World Bank, *World Development Indicators*, CD-ROM, 2004; and Republic of China, *Statistical Yearbook of the Republic of China, 2004*. Only countries with a population of 2 million or more in 2002 were included in this table.

percent over the twenty-two-year period. Switzerland's growth, 0.7 percent annually, lagged behind. Most of the other smaller high-income economies (not included in the exhibit) also had growth rates between 1 percent and 2 percent during the period. Thus, per capita incomes in the high-growth economies—most of which were LDCs at the beginning of the period—expanded at two or three times the rate of the high-income industrial countries.

Unfortunately, LDCs dominate not only the high-growth list but also the list with the worst economic record (right side of Exhibit 3). The income levels of this latter group have not only failed to grow, they have regressed.

The per capita incomes of eleven LDCs have declined at an annual rate of more than 1 percent during the last twenty-two years. In the case of Congo (formerly Zaire), Sierra Leone, Niger, Haiti, and Madagascar, the income reductions averaged 2 percent or more. This implies that the per person income level of these countries in 2002 was only about half the level of 1980.

The growth picture of LDCs is clearly one of diversity. The fastest-growing countries in the world, including two with a third of the world's population (China and India), are LDCs. These rapidly growing countries have closed the income gap relative to their wealthier counterparts.[3] At the same time, other LDCs are doing very poorly and falling further and further behind.

WHAT DETERMINES WHETHER A COUNTRY WILL GROW OR STAGNATE?

The process of economic growth, is complex. Several factors contribute to growth, and they are often interrelated. Much as the performance of an athletic team reflects the joint output of the team members, economic growth is jointly determined by several factors. And just as one or two weak players can substantially reduce overall team performance, weakness in one or two key areas can substantially harm the overall performance of an economy.

[3]In fact, the income levels of two of the high-growth countries, Hong Kong and Singapore, have risen so much that they are no longer classified as less developed.

APPLICATIONS IN ECONOMICS

China: Is It a Special Case?

You might be surprised to find China among the high-growth countries of Exhibit 3. After all, isn't China a centrally planned socialist economy that has generally followed policies inconsistent with growth and prosperity?

Even though the Communist Party is in charge of the government, the Chinese economy has experienced remarkable change in recent years. Following a meeting of the Communist Party Congress in 1978, China began to introduce reforms that have dramatically changed the structure of the economy. ***Today, there are essentially two Chinese economies: (1) agriculture, small businesses, and "special economic zones," and (2) state enterprises. The activities in the first category take place within a now relatively free economy, while those in the second continue to be centrally planned.***

Initially, China took several important steps toward the economic liberalization of its agricultural sector. Collective farms were dismantled and replaced with what the Chinese refer to as a contract responsibility system. Under this system, individual families are permitted to lease land for fifteen years or more in exchange for supplying the state with a fixed amount of production at a designated price (which is generally below the market price). Amounts produced above the required quota belong to the individual farmers and may be either directly consumed or sold at a free-market price.

Even though the legal ownership of land remains with the state, the system of long-term leases provides farmers with something akin to a private-property right. This is particularly true since renewing the lengthy leases is now virtually automatic. Because the state quota is relatively low—approximately 15 percent—and the farmers are permitted to keep all of what they produce above the fixed quota, the effective marginal tax rate is zero. Clearly, this provides a strong incentive for them to expand their output. Markets play a key role in the allocation of agricultural products. Currently, more than 85 percent of the grain output (rice, wheat, and barley) is produced privately and sold at market-determined prices. Restrictions on individual stock breeding, household sideline occupations, the transport of agricultural goods, and trade fairs (marketplaces) have been removed. Farmers are also now permitted to own tractors and trucks, and even hire laborers to work in their leased fields.

Success in China's agriculture led to reforms in other sectors. Restrictions on the operation of small-scale service and retail businesses were relaxed in the 1980s. As a result, private restaurants, stores, and repair shops sprang up and began to compete with state-operated enterprises. By the mid-1980s, Chinese cities were teeming with sidewalk vendors, restaurants, small retail businesses, and hundreds of thousands of individuals providing personal services.

China also established so-called special economic zones. Approximately 20 percent of the people in the Chinese labor force now work in these zones. They are permitted to establish businesses, engage in trade with foreigners, maintain bank accounts in foreign currencies, and undertake investment without having to obtain government approval. Taxes in the special zones are generally quite low. Consequently, during the past decade, the zones attracted a large amount of investment from abroad, which has contributed to the growth of the Chinese investment rate. Economic activity in these regions has also made a sizable contribution to the growth of the trade sector, which has tripled as a share of the economy since 1980. With China's entry into the World Trade Organization, it will almost surely become more fully integrated into the world economy in the future.

Liberalizing China's economic system has surely contributed substantially to its growth. However, it is possible that some of the growth has been exaggerated. This was the case for the former Soviet Union and the countries of Eastern Europe during the 1970s and 1980s. Because centrally planned economies do not rely on product prices to allocate goods and services, output is measured by the physical quantities of goods produced and inputs used. These factors might not reliably reflect the value of what is actually being produced. Also, as China has moved away from a command/barter economy in recent years toward greater reliance on markets, some productive activities that were not counted (or were counted only at a depressed level) are now being counted as part of GDP. This will also tend to exaggerate the growth of GDP. Therefore China's growth figures should be interpreted with caution.

Although economics cannot provide us with a precise recipe for economic growth, it does reveal important sources of such growth: (1) investment in physical and human capital, (2) technological advances, and (3) institutions and policies consistent with efficient economic organization.

Investment in Physical and Human Capital

Equipment can have a substantial impact on a person's ability to produce. Even Robinson Crusoe on an uninhabited island can catch more fish with a net than he can with his hands. Farmers working with modern tractors and plows can cultivate many more acres than could their great-grandparents, who probably worked with hoes. Similarly, education and training that upgrade the knowledge and skills of workers can vastly improve their productivity. For example, a cabinetmaker, skilled after years of training and experience, can build cabinets far more rapidly and efficiently than a neophyte.

Investment in both physical capital (machines) and human capital (knowledge and skills) can expand the productive capacity of a worker. In turn, people who produce more goods and services valued by others will tend to have higher incomes. Other things being constant, countries using a larger share of their resources to produce tools, machines, and factories will tend to grow more rapidly. Correspondingly, allocation of more resources to education and training will also enhance economic growth. But investment is not a free lunch. When more resources are used to produce machines and factories and develop skills, fewer resources are available to produce current-consumption goods. Economics is about trade-offs.

Technological Progress

Technological advancement
The introduction of new techniques or methods that increase output per unit of input.

Technological advancement—the adoption of new, improved techniques or methods of production—enables workers to produce more output with the same amount of resources. Clearly, improved technology—the result of using brainpower to discover economical new products and/or less costly methods of production—has substantially enhanced our production possibilities.

During the last 250 years, the substitution of power-driven machines for human labor; the development of miracle grains, fertilizer, and new sources of energy; and improvements in transportation and communication have vastly improved living standards. Technology continues to affect the availability of goods and services. Just think of the new products introduced during the last 50 years: CD players, microcomputers, word processors, microwave ovens, video cameras, cell phones, DVDs, heart bypass surgery, hip replacements, automobile air conditioners, and so on. These products have vastly changed the quality of our lives. Today, technological progress and entrepreneurial ingenuity are perhaps more important than ever before.

But new and improved products do not just happen. As we discussed in Chapter 2, innovators play a vitally important role in the discovery, development, and dissemination of technological improvements. Innovators are people who are good at figuring out how to apply scientific knowledge in a practical manner. For example, Henry Ford played only a minor role in the invention and development of the automobile. Nonetheless, he literally "put America on wheels" with his innovative assembly line production techniques that made low-cost production of automobiles possible. More recently, Fred Smith, the president and founder of FedEx, realized that the computer age would generate a strong demand for a rapid delivery system. He figured out how to combine both ground and air transportation into a network delivery system capable of transporting a package virtually overnight anywhere in the world. Without innovators like Ford, Smith, and millions of others operating on a smaller scale, scientific breakthroughs are merely ideas waiting to be exploited.

Interestingly, modern technology is available to all nations—rich and poor alike. Poor nations do not have to invest in research and development—they can emulate (or import at a low cost) the proven technologies of the developed countries. This actually places low-

Henry Ford started not only Ford Motor Co., but also the company that eventually became General Motors. His major contribution was an innovation (the assembly line shown here). As a source of economic progress, innovations are often even more important than inventions.

income countries at an advantage. They do not have to discover technologically superior products and production methods. Instead, they can merely emulate those that have been successful in the more advanced countries. This is one reason that countries like South Korea, Taiwan, Hong Kong, Singapore, and even Ireland, which were relatively poor just a few years ago, dominate the list of the world's fastest-growing economies (see Exhibit 3 for evidence on this point).

Although technology is an important source of growth, it is also important to keep its contribution in perspective. If technology were the primary factor determining wealth creation, most low-income countries would be growing more rapidly than developed nations. This hasn't been the case, however. Many low-income countries continue to perform poorly even though the proven technologies of high-income industrial countries are readily available to them (see Exhibit 3). Clearly, access to modern technology does not guarantee growth. In fact, it is of little value when the institutional and policy environments undermine the potential attractiveness of entrepreneurial and innovative business activity.

Institutional Environment

Following the approach outlined in a classic article by Nobel laureate Robert Solow, traditional models of economic growth have stressed the importance of inputs.[4] In fact, the growth of output has often been attributed to the growth of the human capital and physical capital inputs, plus an unexplained residual that was credited to improvements in technology. Clearly, investment in capital goods, education, and technology are important. By themselves, however, they do not necessarily produce economic growth. Centrally planned economies like the former Soviet Union illustrate this point. These economies had both very high rates of capital formation and rapid improvements in schooling levels. Despite this growth of inputs, however, their economic performance was unimpressive. Slow growth and poor living standards eventually led to their collapse.

During the last two decades, there has been renewed interest in how institutions and policies affect economic growth. Building on the work of Peter Bauer and Douglass C. North, two renowned economists who focused on this area, "new growth theory" stresses how vital the economic environment is to the development and efficient use of resources. Proponents of the new growth theory, such as Robert Barro of Harvard University and Gerald Scully of the University of Texas, argue that inappropriate institutions and policies

[4]Robert Solow, "A Contribution to the Theory of Economic Growth," *Quarterly Journal of Economics* 70, no. 1 (February 1956): 65–94.

OUTSTANDING ECONOMIST	Douglass C. North (1920–)

The 1993 recipient of the Nobel Prize in economics, Douglass C. North is best known for his application of both economic theory and statistical analysis to topics in the field of economic history. A professor at Washington University in St. Louis, North showed in his work that the development of both patent laws and the corporation as a legal entity were important sources of economic growth during the seventeenth and eighteenth centuries. His analysis of the link between institutional change and economic progress has played an important role in the development of new growth theory.

can cause growth to fall well below its potential.[5] Furthermore, the more recent approach stresses that when nations foster a sound economic environment, people will develop their skills (human capital), and investors—both foreign and domestic—will supply the necessary physical capital. In many ways, this recent view is a return to the approach of Adam Smith, who also stressed the importance of policies and institutions.

WHAT INSTITUTIONS AND POLICIES WILL PROMOTE GROWTH?

A number of factors are important for economic growth, but a few are vital. The left side of the Thumbnail Sketch shows the primary sources of growth we just discussed, including appropriate institutions and policies. The right side lists the six primary ingredients related to growth-promoting policies and institutions. Let's consider each of the six next.

Secure Property Rights and Political Stability

As we discussed, private ownership rights legally protect people against those who would use violence, theft, and fraud to take things that do not belong to them. Private ownership rights change an economy's incentive structure. *When the property rights of all citizens— including the vitally important property right to their labor—are clearly defined and securely enforced, production and trade replace plunder as the means of acquiring wealth. When property ownership rights are well defined and enforced, people get ahead by helping and cooperating with others.* Employers, for example, have to provide prospective employees and other resource suppliers with at least as good a deal as they can get elsewhere. To succeed, business owners will have to develop and provide potential customers with goods and services that they value highly (relative to their cost). Moreover, private owners have an incentive to maintain and conserve their assets. An owner who fails to maintain the owned assets properly will see the value of those assets, and his or her wealth, decline.

Throughout history, people have searched for and established other forms of ownership that they thought would be more humanitarian or more productive. These experiences

---

[5]For additional information on the importance of institutions as a source of growth, see Peter T. Bauer, *Dissent on Development: Studies and Debates in Development Economics* (Cambridge, MA: Harvard University Press, 1972); Douglass C. North, *Institutions, Institutional Change, and Economic Performance* (Cambridge, MA: Cambridge University Press, 1990); Robert Barro and Xavier Sala-i-Martin, *Economic Growth* (New York: McGraw-Hill, 1995); and Gerald Scully, *Constitutional Environments and Economic Growth* (Princeton: Princeton University Press, 1992).

Sources of Economic Growth
1. Investment in physical and human capital
2. Advancements in technology
3. Institutions and policies that improve economic efficiency

Key Institutions and Policies That Enhance Efficiency and Growth
1. Secure property rights and political stability
2. Competitive markets
3. Free trade
4. Open capital markets
5. Stable money and prices
6. Relatively low marginal tax rates

have ranged from unsuccessful to disastrous. To date, we do not know of any institutional arrangement that provides individuals with as much freedom and incentive to use resources productively and efficiently as does private ownership.[6]

A volatile political climate undermines the security of property rights. Historically, some governments have confiscated the physical and financial assets of their citizens, imposed punitive taxes on them, and used regulations to punish those out of favor with the current political regime. Countries with a history like this will find it difficult to restore confidence and reestablish the security of property rights.

Unfortunately, the political climate of many poor, less-developed countries is highly unstable. In some cases, prejudice, injustice, and highly unequal wealth status create a fertile environment for political upheaval. In other instances, political corruption and a history of favoritism to a ruling class provide the seeds for unrest. Regardless of its source, one thing is clear: potential political upheaval that reduces the security of property rights will repel capital investment and retard economic growth. In recent years, this factor has contributed to the dismal economic performance of several nations, including the Democratic Republic of Congo, Haiti, Nicaragua, Russia, and Iraq.

Competitive Markets

As Adam Smith stressed long ago, when competition is present, even self-interested individuals will tend to promote the general welfare. Conversely, when competition is weakened, business firms have more leeway to raise prices and pursue their own objectives and less incentive to innovate and develop better ways of doing things. Competition is a disciplining force for both buyers and sellers. In a competitive environment, producers must provide goods at a low cost and serve the interests of consumers because, if they don't, other suppliers will. Firms that develop improved products and figure out how to produce them at a low cost will succeed. Sellers that are unwilling or unable to provide consumers with quality goods at competitive prices will be driven from the market. This process leads to improved products and production methods and directs resources toward projects that create more value. It is a powerful stimulus for economic progress. Policies that allow free entry into businesses and occupations and the freedom to exchange goods and services promote competition and economic progress. In contrast, business subsidies, price controls, and entry restraints stifle competition and hinder economic progress.

---

[6]For evidence that a legal system that protects property rights, enforces contracts, and relies on rule-of-law principles for the settlement of disputes among parties promotes economic growth, see Stephen Knack and Philip Keefer, "Institutions and Economic Performance: Cross-Country Tests Using Alternative Institutional Measures," *Economics and Politics* 7 (1995): 207–27.

Free International Trade

As we have learned, international trade allows the residents of countries to use more of their resources to supply to the world market goods that they can produce at a low cost and use the proceeds from their sale to purchase goods that are expensive to produce domestically. Together, trading partners are able to produce more goods and services and purchase a wider variety of them at more economical prices. International competition also keeps domestic producers on their toes—they will be less likely to "gouge" consumers with high prices, for example.

On the other hand, policies that restrict international trade stifle this process and retard economic progress. Obviously, tariffs (taxes on imported goods) and quotas fall into this category because they limit the ability of domestic citizens to trade with people in other countries. So, too, do exchange rate controls. When a nation fixes the exchange rate value of its currency at an artificially high level—a level above the market exchange rate—the volume of international trade that other countries are willing to conduct with it will fall, and economic progress will slow. (We will explain how this works in upcoming chapters.)

An Open Capital Market

If investment is going to increase the wealth of a nation, capital must be channeled into productive projects. When the value of the additional output derived from an investment exceeds the cost of the investment, the project will increase the value of the resources and thereby create wealth. In contrast, if the value of the additional output is less than the cost of the investment, undertaking the project will reduce the wealth of the nation. If a nation is going to realize its potential, it must have a mechanism capable of attracting savings and channeling them into wealth-creating projects. A competitive capital market performs this function.

When a nation's capital market is integrated with the world capital market, it will be able to attract savings (financial capital) from throughout the world at the cheapest possible price (or interest rate). Similarly, its citizens will have access to the most attractive investment opportunities, regardless of where those opportunities are located. *As a result, in a competitive capital market, private investors have a strong incentive to evaluate projects carefully and allocate their funds to projects they expect will yield the highest rates of return. In turn, profitable projects will tend to increase the wealth not only of the investor but also of the nation.*

In contrast, when governments fix interest rates and tax some activities heavily while subsidizing others, they undermine the ability of the capital market to bring savers and investors together and channel funds into wealth-creating projects. If investment funds are allocated by governments rather than capital markets, political clout rather than the expected rate of return will determine which projects are undertaken. More money will be channeled into unproductive and unprofitable activities rather than activities leading to the economy's growth.

Eastern European countries and the former Soviet Union are prime examples. For four decades (1950–1990), the investment rates (as a share of GDP) of these countries were among the highest in the world. These countries channeled approximately one-third of GDP into investment. But even these high rates of investment did little to improve living standards. Without a free capital market, the investment funds were often channeled toward unproductive political and military projects favored by central planners rather than more productive projects that would have increased the availability of consumer goods and enhanced economic growth.

Stable Money and Prices

A stable monetary environment provides the foundation for the efficient operation of a market economy. In contrast, monetary and price instability make both the price level and relative prices unpredictable, generate uncertainty, and undermine the security of contractual exchanges. When prices increase 20 percent one year, 50 percent the next year, 15 percent the year after that, and so on, the ability of individuals and businesses to develop sensible long-term plans and investment decisions is undermined. Many investors and business decision makers will move their activities to countries with a more stable environment. Foreigners will invest elsewhere, and citizens will often go to great lengths to get their savings (potential funds for investment) out of the country. As a result, the potential gains from capital formation and business activities that might have been realized won't materialize.

Relatively Low Marginal Tax Rates

High marginal tax rates take a large share of the rewards generated by productive activities, making it less attractive for people to work and undertake profitable business projects. People who are not permitted to keep much of what they earn tend not to earn very much. Some of them, perhaps those with working spouses, will drop out of the labor force to work at home where their labor is not taxed. Others will simply work fewer hours, retire earlier, or take jobs with longer vacations or a more preferred location.

High taxes also reduce economic efficiency. Because they create a large gap between an employer's cost of hiring a worker and the employee's take-home pay, they tend to drive these transactions into the underground economy, or "black" markets, where the legal structure is less certain and property rights less secure. High tax rates also encourage people to purchase items that are tax deductible, even though they are not valued as much as nondeductible goods of similar price. Worse yet, high tax rates can drive a nation's most productive citizens abroad where taxes are lower. All of these things will retard a country's economic growth.

 Governments can promote economic progress by establishing an environment that encourages entrepreneurship, investment, skill development, and technological improvements. Key elements of this are protecting individuals and their property; enforcing contracts; fostering competitive markets, free international trade, and open capital markets; and keeping money (prices) stable and taxes low.

Government and the Environment for Prosperity

ROLE OF GOVERNMENT AND ECONOMIC PROGRESS

Throughout this text, we have analyzed how governments influence the efficiency of resource use and the growth of income. Both the preceding section and the accompanying key to economic prosperity statement highlight functions of government that are vitally important for the smooth operation of markets and the efficient allocation of resources. These activities might be called the core functions of government. Although there is room for debate about the precise activities that constitute these core functions, two general categories emerge: (1) activities that protect people and their property from plunder and (2) provision of a limited set of public goods that, for various reasons, are difficult to provide through markets.

As we have learned, when governments create a legal, monetary, and regulatory environment for the efficient operation of markets, they enhance economic growth. However, a government that provides public goods such as roads, national defense, and public education also promotes growth.

But, as governments move beyond these core functions and grow, the beneficial effects wane and eventually become negative. There are four major reasons that expanding the size of the government will eventually retard growth.

1. As the size of the government expands, the marginal cost of taxation gets higher and higher. The disincentive effects and excess burden of taxation (deadweight losses) will increase as tax rates rise. (For more detail on this topic, review the material on the excess burden of taxation and the Laffer curve analysis of Chapter 4.) Therefore, even if the productivity of a government's expenditures did not decline, the net gains derived from them would diminish as the government grows and the deadweight losses caused by taxation increase.

2. As the government expands relative to the private sector, diminishing returns will reduce the benefits derived from government activity. A government that concentrates on those functions for which it is best-suited (the core functions discussed above) and performs them well will clearly enhance the smooth operation of markets and stimulate economic growth. However, as the government grows, it will become more and more involved in activities for which it is ill-suited. This will adversely affect economic growth. Providing private goods to individual citizens—goods like food, housing, medical service, and child care—fall into this category. There are good reasons to expect that governments will allocate these goods less efficiently than markets will.

3. Government is less innovative and slower to respond to change than the private sector is. To a large degree, growth is a discovery process. Profits earned in markets give entrepreneurs a strong incentive to develop better products, adopt improved technologies quickly, and figure out better ways of doing things.[7] In markets, entrepreneurs gain by constantly channeling resources toward uses that are more highly valued. There is no similar mechanism within the government that will persistently direct resources toward productive activities and away from wasteful ones. In the public sector, the incentive to innovate is weaker and the adjustment to change slower.

Markets, on the other hand, impose swift and sure punishment on those with high costs and those who use their resources unproductively. The private sector takes less time to weed out errors (bad investments, for example) and adjust to changing circumstances, new information, and improved technologies. As it relates to economic growth, this is a major shortcoming of the political process associated with government activities.

4. As the government grows, it invariably becomes more heavily involved in the redistribution of income and regulatory activism. In turn, these activities discourage productive activities and encourage wasteful rent seeking. As we discussed in Chapter 6, government income transfers and discriminatory regulations will induce individuals to shift resources away from wealth-creating activities toward the pursuit of government favors. This shift will retard economic growth and lead to income levels well below the economy's potential.

In summary, while government activities that focus on the areas where it has a comparative advantage will enhance growth, continued expansion will eventually exert a negative impact on the economy. **Exhibit 4** illustrates the implications with regard to the expected relationship between the size of government and economic growth, *assuming that governments undertake activities based on their rate of return.* As the size of government, measured on the horizontal axis, expands from zero (complete anarchy), initially the growth rate of the economy—measured on the vertical axis—increases. The *A* to *B* range of the curve illustrates this situation. As government continues to grow as a share of the economy, expenditures are channeled into less-productive (and later counterproductive) activities, causing the rate of economic growth to diminish and eventually decline. The range of the curve beyond *B* illustrates this point.[8] Thus, our analysis indicates that there is a set of activities and size of government that will maximize economic growth. Expansion of government beyond (and outside of) these functions will retard growth.

---

[7]Israel Kirzner and Joseph Schumpeter have contributed the classic literature on this topic. See Israel Kirzner, *Competition and Entrepreneurship* (Chicago: University of Chicago Press, 1973); and Joseph Schumpeter, *The Theory of Economic Development* (1912; translated by R. Opie, 1934; repr., Transaction Publishers, 1961).

[8]In the real world, governments may not undertake activities based on their rate of return and comparative advantage. Many governments that are small relative to the size of the economy fail to focus on the core activities that are likely to enhance economic growth. Thus, one would expect that the relationship between size of government and economic growth will be a loose one. The empirical evidence is consistent with this view.

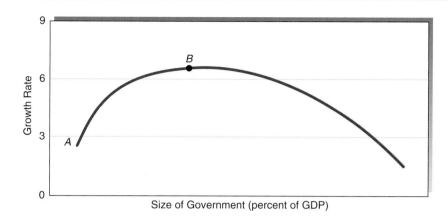

EXHIBIT 4
Economic Growth Curve and Government Size

If a government undertakes activities in the order of their productivity, its expenditures will promote economic growth (the growth rate will move from *A* to *B*). Additional expenditures, however, will eventually retard growth (the growth rate will move along the curve to the right of *B*).

Optimum Size of Government and Economic Growth—Empirical Evidence

How large is the growth-maximizing size of government? Do large governments actually retard economic growth? These are complex questions, but they have been addressed by several researchers.

Exhibit 5 sheds light on these issues. This exhibit presents data on the relationship between size of government (*x*-axis) and economic growth (*y*-axis) for the twenty-three long-standing members of the Organization for Economic Cooperation and Development

EXHIBIT 5
Government Spending and Economic Growth among the Twenty-Three OECD Countries: 1960–1999

Here we show the relationship between size of government and the growth of real GDP for the twenty-three longtime OECD members during each decade since 1960. The data indicate that a 10 percent increase in government expenditures as a share of GDP reduces the annual rate of growth by approximately 1 percent. The data also imply that the size of government in these countries is beyond the range that maximizes economic growth.

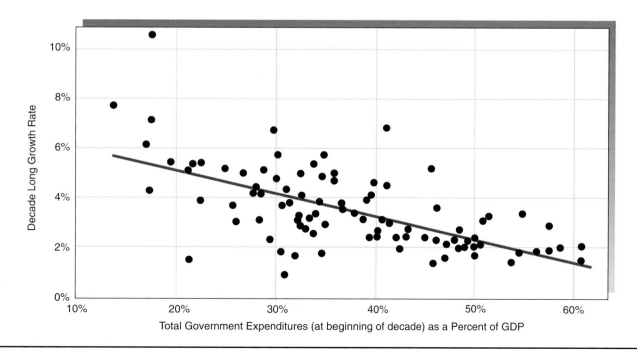

Sources: OECD, *OECD Economic Outlook* (various issues); and World Bank, *World Development Indicators,* CD-ROM, 2001.

(OECD). The exhibit contains four dots (observations) for each of the twenty-three countries—one for each of the four decades during the period 1960–1999. Thus, there are ninety-two total dots. Each dot represents a country's total government spending as a share of GDP *at the beginning of the decade* and its accompanying growth of real GDP *during that decade*. Government expenditures ranged from a low of about 15 percent of GDP in some countries to a high of more than 60 percent in others. As the plotted line in the exhibit shows, there is a clearly observable negative relationship between size of governments and long-term real GDP growth. Countries with higher levels of government spending grew less rapidly. The line drawn through the points of Exhibit 5 indicates that a 10-percentage-point increase in government expenditures as a share of GDP leads to approximately a 1-percentage-point reduction in economic growth.

Exhibit 6 presents data on growth during the 1990–2003 period for the OECD countries with the largest and smallest governments. As the upper part of the exhibit shows, seven "big government" countries—Sweden, Denmark, France, Finland, Austria, Italy, and Belgium—had total government expenditures of 48 percent or more of GDP during the period 1999–2003. Within this group, Italy had the lowest growth rate—1.5 percent—and Austria had the highest—2.2 percent. The average growth rate for the seven nations was 1.8 percent. The bottom frame of Exhibit 6 shows the government spending of three "small government" countries—Australia, Ireland, and the United States. Spending was less than 37 percent of GDP in these countries. Growth rates ranged from the 2.9 percent for the United States to 6.8 percent for Ireland. The average growth rate in the small-government group was 4.3 percent. Note that this was more than *twice* the average of the group with high levels of government spending. The highest growth rate among the big-government group, Austria's 2.2 percent, was still lower than any of the small-government countries.

Exhibits 5 and 6 utilize cross-country data, but time series data for specific countries have also been used to investigate the link between size of government and growth. Edgar Peden estimates that for the United States, the "maximum productivity growth occurs when government expenditures represent about 20 percent of GDP." Gerald Scully estimates that the growth-maximizing size of government (combined federal, state, and local) is "between

EXHIBIT 6
Growth During 1990–2003: Big-Versus Small-Government Countries

The average annual growth rate during 1990–2003 of OECD countries with the largest governments (spending greater than 48 percent of GDP) was 1.8 percent—substantially less than the 4.3 percent average for those with small governments (spending less than 37 percent of GDP).

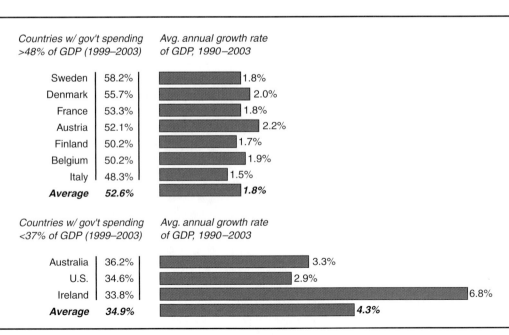

Countries w/ gov't spending >48% of GDP (1999–2003)		Avg. annual growth rate of GDP, 1990–2003
Sweden	58.2%	1.8%
Denmark	55.7%	2.0%
France	53.3%	1.8%
Austria	52.1%	2.2%
Finland	50.2%	1.7%
Belgium	50.2%	1.9%
Italy	48.3%	1.5%
Average	*52.6%*	*1.8%*

Countries w/ gov't spending <37% of GDP (1999–2003)		Avg. annual growth rate of GDP, 1990–2003
Australia	36.2%	3.3%
U.S.	34.6%	2.9%
Ireland	33.8%	6.8%
Average	*34.9%*	*4.3%*

Source: OECD, OECD Economic Outlook (June 2004).

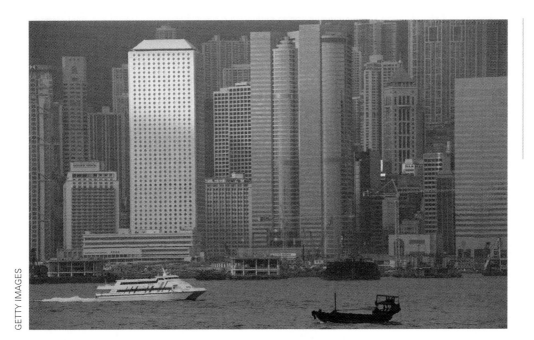

Hong Kong is a modern economic miracle. Its real income per person in 2002 was more than eight times its 1960 figure (see Exhibit 2). The economy of Hong Kong is one of the most free, if not the freest, in the world. Will it remain that way now that it is part of China?

21.5 percent and 22.9 percent of gross national product (GNP)." Although the methodology of these studies differs, they do have one thing in common: they indicate that in the ranges observed, countries with larger governments tend to grow less rapidly.[9]

ECONOMIC FREEDOM AND GROWTH

Since the time of Adam Smith, economists have generally argued that freer economies are likely to be more productive. Is this really true? Economic freedom is complex and multidimensional. Therefore, it is difficult to measure. In the mid-1980s, the Fraser Institute began work on a special project designed to develop a cross-country measure of economic freedom. Several leading scholars, including Nobel laureates Milton Friedman, Gary Becker, and Douglass North, participated in the endeavor. This eventually led to the development of the Economic Freedom of the World (EFW) index that is now published annually by a worldwide network of more than fifty institutes.[10]

The EFW index uses thirty-eight separate components to measure the consistency of a nation's institutions and policies with personal choice, freedom of exchange, and protection of private property. To achieve a high EFW rating, a country must provide secure protection of privately owned property, evenhanded enforcement of contracts, and a stable monetary environment. It also must keep taxes low, refrain from creating barriers to both domestic and international trade, and rely more fully on markets rather than governments to allocate goods and resources. In many respects, the EFW index reflects the institutional factors listed in the Thumbnail Sketch.

[9]For additional information on the relationship between size of government and growth, see James Gwartney, Robert Lawson, and Randall Holcombe, "The Scope of Government and the Wealth of Nations," *The Cato Journal* (Fall 1998), 163–90; Edgar Peden, "Productivity in the United States and Its Relationship to Government Activity: An Analysis of 57 Years, 1929–1986," *Public Choice* 69 (1991): 153–73; and Gerald Scully, *What Is the Optimal Size of Government in the United States?* (Dallas, Tex.: National Center for Policy Analysis, 1994).

[10]For additional details, see James Gwartney and Robert Lawson, *Economic Freedom of the World: 2004 Annual Report* (Vancouver: Fraser Institute, 2004) and the Web site http://www.freetheworld.com/.

EXHIBIT 7
Income and Growth of the Most- and Least-Free Economies of the World

Source: Derived from World Bank, *World Development Indicators,* CD-ROM, 2004, and James Gwartney and Robert Lawson, *Economic Freedom of the World: 2004 Annual Report* (Vancouver: Fraser Institute, 2004). The Economic Freedom of the World (EFW) ratings incorporate thirty-eight components that are rated on a 10-point scale. There were ninety-nine countries with ratings throughout the 1980–2000 period.

TEN FREEST ECONOMIES, 1980–2000	AVERAGE EFW RATING, 1980–2000	2002 GDP PER CAPITA (1995 US$)	GROWTH RATE GDP PER CAPITA, 1980–2002 (%)
Hong Kong	8.7	23,833	3.7
Singapore	8.3	21,296	4.2
United States	8.0	31,660	1.9
Switzerland	7.9	26,579	0.7
Canada	7.5	26,114	1.6
United Kingdom	7.5	23,166	2.2
Netherlands	7.4	25,778	1.8
Luxembourg	7.3	54,201	4.0
Germany	7.3	24,004	1.7
Australia	7.3	25,032	1.9
Average:	**7.7**	**$28,166**	**2.4**

TEN LEAST-FREE ECONOMIES, 1980–2000			
Iran	4.2	5,923	1.2
Brazil	4.2	6,878	0.4
Syria	4.0	3,205	0.7
Ghana	4.0	1,882	0.5
Nigeria	4.0	758	–1.1
Nicaragua	3.9	2,187	–1.4
Uganda	3.9	1,229	2.2
Algeria	3.8	5,101	0.0
Myanmar	3.7	1,121	2.7
Congo, Democratic Republic of	3.6	578	–4.9
Average:	**3.9**	**$2,886**	**0.0**

The EFW ratings (zero to ten scale) are available for ninety-nine countries throughout the 1980–2002 period. **Exhibit 7** presents data on the 2002 per capita GDP and the rate of economic growth for the ten countries with the highest and lowest EFW ratings during 1980–2000. Among the ninety-nine countries, Hong Kong, Singapore, the United States, and Switzerland headed the list of the most persistently free economies. At the other end of the spectrum, the Democratic Republic of Congo, Myanmar, Algeria, Uganda, and Nicaragua had the least-free economies. If institutional and policy factors are important, then the free economies should outperform those that are less free. As Exhibit 7 shows, this was indeed the case. The average per capita income of the ten freest economies was $28,166—nearly ten times the figure for the ten least-free economies. Correspondingly, the per capita GDP of the ten freest economies increased at an average rate of 2.4 percent during the 1980–2002 period. Income per person increased in all of the free economies. In contrast, the average growth rate of the ten least-free economies was zero, and three of the ten actually experienced reductions in income over the twenty-two-year period.

Exhibit 8 presents data for the average per capita GDP and growth according to the economic freedom rating for all of the ninety-nine countries. The same pattern emerges: the freer economies both achieved higher per capita income levels and grew more rapidly. The countries with an economic freedom rating of 7.0 or more during the 1980–2000 period had an average per capita GDP of $27,195, approximately eleven times the average

EXHIBIT 8
Economic Freedom, Income, and Growth

The average income levels and growth rates for countries with different levels of economic freedom are shown here. Countries with more economic freedom during the period 1980–2000 had both higher income levels and more rapid growth rates than those with less economic freedom.

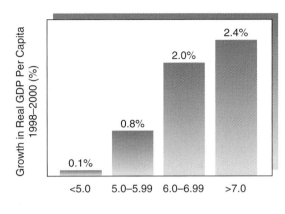

Source: Derived from James Gwartney and Robert Lawson, *Economic Freedom of the World: 2004 Annual Report*. The *Economic Freedom of the World: 2004 Annual Report* is also available on the Web at http://www.freetheworld.com/.

for the countries with an EFW rating of less than 5.0. Similarly, the average annual growth rate of the top group was 2.4 percent, compared to 0.1 percent for the bottom group. Although these data are not adjusted for other factors, such as initial income level, demographic factors, investment, and years of schooling, more comprehensive analysis indicates that even after these factors are taken into consideration, countries with more economic freedom tend to achieve higher income levels and grow more rapidly.[11]

LOOKING AHEAD

International trade and global financial markets have an increasingly important effect on our lives and our ability to achieve high levels of income. The next two chapters will focus on these topics.

[11]For additional details on how economic freedom affects performance, see Niclas Berggren, "The Benefits of Economic Freedom: A Survey," *Independent Review* 8, no. 2, (Fall 2003): 193–221; and James Gwartney and Robert Lawson, *Economic Freedom of the World: 2004 Annual Report* (Vancouver: Fraser Institute, 2004), Chapter 2.

KEY POINTS

▼ Economic growth increases the production possibilities of an economy. The growth of per capita real GDP means more goods and services per person, which typically leads to higher living standards and improvements in life expectancy, literacy, and health.

▼ Even seemingly small differences in growth rates sustained over two or three decades will substantially alter relative incomes. For example, if Country A and Country B have the same initial income but the growth rate of A is 2 percentage points greater than that of B, after thirty-five years the income level of Country A will be twice that of B.

▼ The growth picture of LDCs is clearly one of diversity. Over the last several decades, the fastest-growing countries in the world have been LDCs. These rapidly growing countries have closed the income gap relative to their wealthier counterparts. At the same time, other LDCs are doing very poorly and falling further and further behind.

▼ Economic growth is a complex process. Economists stress the importance of three major sources of economic progress: (1) investment in physical and human capital, (2) technological advances, and (3) institutional and policy changes that improve the efficiency of economies.

▼ The following are important for the efficiency of economic organization: (1) secure property rights and political stability, (2) competitive markets, (3) monetary stability, (4) freedom to trade with foreigners, (5) a capital market that directs investment toward productive projects, and (6) relatively low tax rates.

▼ When governments focus on the core activities of providing (1) a legal and enforcement structure that protects people and their property from aggression by others and (2) a limited set of public goods, they promote economic growth. However, when they expand into activities for which they are ill-suited, they deter growth.

▼ Countries with more economic freedom tend to grow more rapidly.

CRITICAL ANALYSIS QUESTIONS

1. How does economic growth influence the living standards of people? Does it really make much difference whether an economy grows at 2 percent or 4 percent annually? Discuss.

2. How does the role of government influence economic growth? As the size of government increases as a share of the economy, how is the growth rate of real GDP likely to be affected? Explain.

*3. "Without aid from the industrial nations, poor countries are caught in the poverty trap. Because they are poor, they are unable to save and invest; and, lacking investment, they remain poor." Evaluate this view.

4. More than 200 years ago, Adam Smith argued that the wealth of nations depends upon gains from (a) specialization and trade, (b) expanding the size of the market, and (c) discovering better (more productive) ways of doing things. Explain why you either agree or disagree with Smith's view.

5. Are the rich countries getting richer while the poor are getting poorer? Discuss.

6. What must an entrepreneur do to introduce an innovative product? What determines whether the new product will be a success or failure? How important is innovation as a source of economic growth? Discuss.

7. When investment is allocated by political decision makers, are innovative ideas likely to be supported? Are unproductive investments likely to be terminated? Discuss.

*8. "Since government-operated firms do not have to make a profit, they can usually produce at a lower cost and charge a lower price than privately owned enterprises." Evaluate this view.

9. "Governments can promote economic growth by using taxes and subsidies to direct investment funds

toward high-tech, heavy manufacturing, and other growth industries that will enhance the future income of the nation." Evaluate this view.

*10. What impact do natural resources have on economic growth? Will it be possible for a country with few natural resources to grow rapidly? Why or why not?

11. "The institutional environment is the key to economic growth. If a nation creates an environment conducive to economic growth, people will supply and develop the resources and technology." Evaluate this view. Is the proper economic environment more important than the supply of resources? Why or why not?

*12. The diversity of goods available to consumers today is much greater than in the past. How does this influence consumer welfare? Do the GDP growth figures capture the impact of the increased diversity? Why or why not?

13. How would you define economic freedom? Would you expect countries with more economic freedom to grow more rapidly than those with less economic freedom? Why or why not?

14. Suppose that you have just been appointed to a high-level position in the economic analysis unit of the State Department. The secretary of state has asked you to prepare a memo describing the key policies and economic arrangements that less-developed countries should follow in order to achieve rapid growth and high income levels. Briefly describe your response. Be sure to indicate why each factor you mention is important if a nation is going to attain a high level of economic progress.

*Asterisk denotes questions for which answers are given in Appendix B.

PART 4

"The world is becoming a global village"

International Economics

The volume of international trade has grown dramatically in recent decades. Although the same general principles apply to both domestic and international trade, the latter also involves the exchange of one currency for another. Thus, this part will analyze the impact of both international trade and the operation of the foreign exchange market.

Gaining from International Trade

Chapter Focus

■ How has the volume of international trade changed in recent decades?

■ Under what conditions can a nation gain from international trade?

■ What effects do trade restrictions have on an economy?

■ How have open economies performed relative to those that are more closed?

■ What accounts for the political popularity of trade restraints?

■ Do trade restrictions create jobs? Does trade with low-wage countries depress wage rates in high-wage countries like the United States?

The evidence is overwhelmingly persuasive that the massive increase in world competition—a consequence of broadening trade flows—has fostered markedly higher standards of living for almost all countries who have participated in cross-border trade. I include most especially the United States.

—*Alan Greenspan*[1]

[1]Alan Greenspan, speech before the Alliance for the Commonwealth Conference on International Business (Boston, Massachusetts, June 2, 1999).

We live in a shrinking world. The breakfast of many Americans includes bananas from Honduras, coffee from Brazil, or hot chocolate made from Nigerian cocoa beans. Americans often drive a car produced by a Japanese or European manufacturer that consumes gasoline refined from petroleum extracted in Saudi Arabia or Venezuela. Similarly, many Americans work for companies that sell a substantial number of their products to foreigners.

Spurred by cost reductions in transportation and communications, the volume of international trade has grown rapidly in recent decades. It may surprise some people that most international trade is not between the governments of different nations but rather between people and firms located in different countries. Why do people engage in international trade? The expectation of gain provides the answer. Domestic producers are often able to sell their products to foreigners at attractive prices, and domestic consumers sometimes find that the best deals are available from foreign suppliers. Like other voluntary exchanges, international trade occurs because both the buyer and the seller expect to gain and generally do. If both parties did not expect to gain, they would not agree to the exchange. ■

THE TRADE SECTOR OF THE UNITED STATES

As **Exhibit 1** illustrates, the size of the trade sector of the United States has grown rapidly during the last several decades. In 1960, total exports of goods and services accounted for 3.6 percent of the U.S. economy, while imports summed to 4.1 percent. By 1980, both exports and imports were approximately 6 percent of the economy. In 2003, exports accounted for 10 percent of total output, while imports summed to 15 percent. Thus, U.S. international trade (exports + imports) in goods and services has approximately doubled as a share of the economy since 1980 and tripled since 1960.

Who are the major trading partners of Americans? **Exhibit 2** shows the share of U.S. trade (exports + imports) with each of its ten leading trading partners. These ten countries

---

EXHIBIT 1
The Growth of the Trade Sector in the United States: 1960–2003

During the past several decades, international trade has persistently risen as a share of GDP. Imports of goods and services as a share of GDP rose from 4 percent in 1960 to 6 percent in 1980 and almost 15 percent in 2003. Similarly, exports increased from 4 percent of GDP in 1960 to 6 percent in 1980 and 10 percent in 2003.

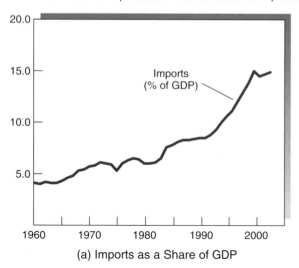

(a) Imports as a Share of GDP

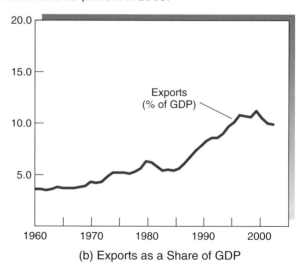

(b) Exports as a Share of GDP

Source: http://www.economagic.com. The figures are based on data for real imports, exports, and GDP.

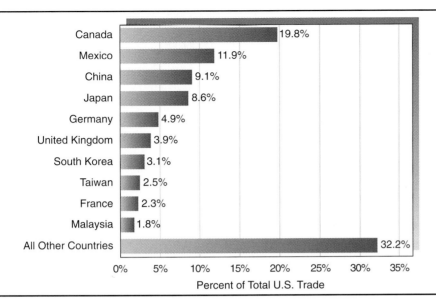

EXHIBIT 2
The 2002 Leading Trading Partners of the United States

Canada, Mexico, China, and Japan are the leading trading partners of the United States. Approximately one-half of all U.S. trade involves imports or exports to these four countries.

account for approximately two-thirds of the total volume of U.S. trade. Canada, Mexico, China, and Japan are the four largest trading partners of Americans. Nearly half of all U.S. trade is with these four countries. The U.S. also conducts a substantial volume of trade with the nations of the European Union, particularly Germany, the United Kingdom, and France.

What are the leading imports and exports of the United States? Capital goods like automobiles, computers, semiconductors, telecommunications equipment, and industrial machines are bought and sold in worldwide markets. The U.S. both imports and exports substantial quantities of these goods. Civilian aircraft, electrical equipment, chemicals, and plastics are also among the leading products exported by the United States. Crude oil, textiles, toys, sporting goods, and pharmaceuticals are major products it imports.

Clearly, the impact of international trade differs across industries. In some industries, domestic producers find it very difficult to compete with their rivals abroad. For example, approximately 90 percent of the shoes purchased by Americans and nearly two-thirds of the radio and television sets, watches, and motorcycles are produced abroad. A high percentage of the clothing and textile products, paper, cut diamonds, and VCRs consumed in the United States are also imported. On the other hand, a large proportion of the aircraft, power-generating equipment, scientific instruments, construction equipment, and fertilizers produced in the United States are exported to purchasers abroad.

GAINS FROM SPECIALIZATION AND TRADE

As we discussed in Chapter 2, the law of **comparative advantage** explains why a group of individuals, regions, or nations can gain from specialization and exchange. *International trade leads to mutual gains because it allows residents of different countries to: (1) specialize in the production of those things they do best, and (2) import goods foreign producers are willing to supply at a lower cost than domestic producers.* Resources and labor-force skills differ substantially across countries, and these differences influence costs. A good that is quite costly to produce in one country might be cheaply produced in another. For example, the warm, moist climate of Brazil, Colombia, and Guatemala makes coffee production in these countries more economical than in other places. Countries such as Saudi Arabia and Venezuela with rich oil fields can produce petroleum cheaply. Countries with an abundance of fertile land, such as Canada and

Comparative advantage
The ability to produce a good at a lower opportunity cost than others can produce it. Relative costs determine comparative advantage.

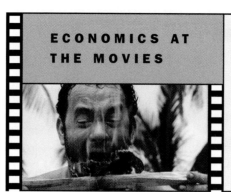

ECONOMICS AT THE MOVIES

Cast Away (2000)

In *Cast Away,* Tom Hanks is stranded alone on an island for four years. Hanks must be self-sufficient and produce everything he consumes. Because he's unable to specialize and trade with others, his standard of living while on the island is clearly meager.

Australia, are able to produce products as wheat, feed grains, and beef at a low cost. In contrast, land is scarce in Japan, a nation with a highly skilled labor force. The Japanese, therefore, specialize in manufacturing, using their comparative advantage to produce cameras, automobiles, and electronic products for export. With international trade, the residents of different countries can gain by specializing in the production of goods they can produce economically. They can then sell those goods in the world market and use the proceeds to import other goods expensive to produce domestically.

The failure to comprehend the principle of mutual gains from trade is often a source of "fuzzy" economic thinking. Because of this, we will take the time to illustrate the principle in detail. To keep things simple, let's consider a case involving only two countries, the United States and Japan, and two products, food and clothing. Furthermore, let's assume that labor is the only resource used to produce these products. In addition, since we want to illustrate that gains from trade are nearly always possible, we are going to assume that Japan has an **absolute advantage**—that the Japanese workers are more efficient than the Americans—at producing both food and clothing. **Exhibit 3** illustrates this situation. Perhaps due to their prior experience or higher skill levels, Japanese workers can produce three units of food per day, compared to only two units per day for U.S. workers. Similarly, Japanese workers are able to produce nine units of clothing per day, compared to one unit of clothing per day for U.S. workers.

Can two countries gain from trade if one of them can produce both goods with fewer resources? The answer is "Yes." As long as the *relative* production costs of the two goods

Absolute advantage
A situation in which a nation, as the result of its previous experience and/or natural endowments, can produce more of a good (with the same amount of resources) than another nation.

EXHIBIT 3
Gains from Specialization and Trade

Columns 1 and 2 indicate the daily output of either food or clothing of each worker in the United States and Japan. If the United States moves three workers from the clothing industry to the food industry, it can produce six more units of food and three fewer units of clothing. Similarly, if Japan moves one worker from food to clothing, clothing output will increase by 9 units, while food output will decline by three units. With this reallocation of labor, the United States and Japan are able to increase their aggregate output of both food (three additional units) and clothing (six additional units).

COUNTRY	OUTPUT PER WORKER DAY		POTENTIAL CHANGE IN OUTPUT[a]	
	FOOD (1)	CLOTHING (2)	FOOD (3)	CLOTHING (4)
United States	2	1	+6	−3
Japan	3	9	−3	+9
Change in Total			+3	+6

[a]Change in output if the United States shifts three workers from the clothing to the food industry and if Japan shifts one worker from the food to the clothing industry.

differ between Japan and the United States, gains from trade will be possible. Consider what would happen if the United States shifted three workers from the clothing industry to the food industry. This reallocation of labor would allow the United States to expand its food output by six units (two units per worker), while clothing output would decline by three units (one unit per worker). Suppose Japan reallocates labor in the opposite direction. When Japan moves one worker from the food industry to the clothing industry, Japanese clothing production expands by nine units, while food output declines by three units. The exhibit shows that this reallocation of labor *within* the two countries has increased their joint output by three units of food and six units of clothing.

The source of this increase in output is straightforward: aggregate output expands because the reallocation of labor permits each country to specialize more fully in the production of those goods that it can produce at a *relatively* low cost. Our old friend, the opportunity-cost concept, reveals the low-cost producer of each good. If Japanese workers produce one additional unit of food, they sacrifice the production of three units of clothing. Therefore, in Japan the opportunity cost of one unit of food is three units of clothing. On the other hand, one unit of food in the United States can be produced at an opportunity cost of only a half-unit of clothing. American workers are therefore the low-opportunity-cost producers of food, even though they cannot produce as much food per day as the Japanese workers. Simultaneously, Japan is the low-opportunity-cost producer of clothing. The opportunity cost of producing a unit of clothing in Japan is only a third of a unit of food, compared to two units of food in the United States. The reallocation of labor illustrated in Exhibit 3 expanded joint output because it moved resources in both countries toward areas where they had a comparative advantage.

To reiterate: as long as the relative costs of producing the two goods differ in the two countries, gains from specialization and trade will be possible. Both countries will find it cheaper to trade for goods they can produce only at a high opportunity cost. For example, both countries will gain if the United States trades food to Japan for clothing at a trading ratio greater than one unit of food to one half-unit of clothing (the U.S. opportunity cost of food) but less than one unit of food to three units of clothing (the Japanese opportunity cost of food). Any trading ratio between these two extremes will permit the United States to acquire clothing more cheaply than it could be produced within the country and simultaneously permit Japan to acquire food more cheaply than it could be produced domestically.

How Trade Expands Consumption Possibilities

Because trade permits nations to expand their joint output, it also allows each nation to expand its consumption possibilities. The production possibilities concept can be used to illustrate this point. Suppose that there were 200 million workers in the United States and 50 million in Japan. Given these figures and the productivity of workers indicated in Exhibit 3, **Exhibit 4** presents the production possibilities curves for the two countries. If the United States used all of its 200 million workers in the food industry, it could produce 400 million units of food per day—two units per worker—and zero units of clothing (N). Alternatively, if the United States used all its workers to produce clothing, daily output would be 200 million units of clothing and no food (M). Intermediate output combinations along the production possibilities line (MN) between these two extreme points also could be achievable. For example, the United States could produce 150 million units of clothing and 100 million units of food (US_1).

Part (b) of Exhibit 4 illustrates the production possibilities of the 50 million Japanese workers. Japan could produce 450 million units of clothing and no food (R), 150 million units of food and no clothing (S), or various intermediate combinations, like 225 million units of clothing and 75 million units of food (J_1). The slope of the production possibilities constraint reflects the opportunity cost of food relative to clothing. Because Japan is the high-opportunity-cost producer of food, its production possibilities constraint is steeper than the constraint for the United States.

In the absence of trade, the consumption of each country is constrained by its production possibilities. Trade, however, expands the consumption possibilities of both. As we

EXHIBIT 4
The Production Possibilities of the United States and Japan Before Specialization and Trade

Here we illustrate the daily production possibilities of a U.S. labor force with 200 million workers and a Japanese labor force with 50 million workers, given the cost of producing food and clothing presented in Exhibit 3. In the absence of trade, consumption possibilities will be restricted to points such as US_1 in the United States and J_1 in Japan along the production possibilities curve of each country.

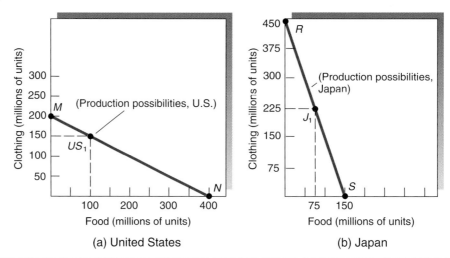

(a) United States

(b) Japan

previously said, both countries can gain from specialization if the United States trades food to Japan at a price greater than one unit of food equals one half-unit of clothing but less than one unit of food equals three units of clothing. Suppose that they agree on an intermediate price of one unit of food equals one unit of clothing. As part (a) of **Exhibit 5** shows, when the United States specializes in the production of food (where it has a comparative advantage) and trades food for clothing (at the price ratio where one unit of food equals one unit of clothing), it can consume along the line ON. If the United States insisted on self-sufficiency, it would be restricted to consumption possibilities like US_1 (100 million units of food and 150 million units of clothing) along its production possibilities constraint of MN. With trade, however, the United States can achieve a combination like US_2 (200 million units of food and 200 million units of clothing) along the line ON. Trade permits the United States to expand its consumption of both goods.

Simultaneously, Japan is able to expand its consumption of both goods when it is able to trade clothing for food at the one-to-one price ratio. As part (b) of Exhibit 5 illustrates, Japan can specialize in the production of clothing and consume along the constraint RT when it can trade one unit of clothing for one unit of food. Without trade, consumption in Japan would be limited to points like J_1 (75 million units of food and 225 million units of clothing) along the line RS. With trade, however, it is able to consume combinations like J_2 (200 million units of food and 250 million units of clothing) along the constraint RT.

Look what happens when Japan specializes in clothing and the United States specializes in food. Japan can produce 450 million units of clothing, export 200 million to the United States (for 200 million units of food), and still have 250 million units of clothing remaining for domestic consumption. Simultaneously, the United States can produce 400 million units of food, export 200 million to Japan (for 200 million units of clothing), and still have 200 million units of food left for domestic consumption. Again, after specialization and trade, the United States is able to consume at the point of US_2 and Japan at point J_2, consumption levels that would be unattainable without trade. Specialization and exchange permit the two countries to expand their joint output, and, as a result, both countries can increase their consumption of both commodities.

EXHIBIT 5
Consumption Possibilities with Trade

The consumption possibilities of a country can be expanded with specialization and trade. If the United States can trade one unit of clothing for one unit of food, it can specialize in the production of food and consume along the *ON* line (rather than its original production possibilities constraint, *MN*). Similarly, when Japan is able to trade one unit of clothing for one unit of food, it can specialize in the production of clothing and consume any combination along the line *RT*. For example, with specialization and trade, the United States can increase its consumption from *US₁* to *US₂*, gaining 50 million units of clothing and 100 million units of food. Simultaneously, Japan can increase consumption from *J₁* to *J₂*, a gain of 125 million units of food and 25 million units of clothing.

(a) United States

(b) Japan

The implications of the law of comparative advantage are clear: trade between nations will lead to an expansion in total output and mutual gain for each trading partner when each country specializes in the production of goods it can produce at a relatively low cost and uses the proceeds to buy goods that it could produce only at a high cost. It is comparative advantage that matters. As long as there is some variation in the relative opportunity cost of goods across countries, each country will always have a comparative advantage in the production of some goods.

Some Real-World Considerations

To keep things simple, we ignored the potential importance of transportation costs, which, of course, reduce the potential gains from trade. Sometimes transportation and other transaction costs, both real and artificially imposed, exceed the potential for mutual gain. In this case, exchange does not occur.

We also assumed that the cost of producing each good was constant in each country. This is seldom the case. Beyond some level of production, the opportunity cost of producing a good will often increase as a country produces more and more of it. Rising marginal costs as the output of a good expands will limit the degree to which a country will specialize in the production of a good. This situation would be depicted by a production possibilities curve that was convex, or bowed out from the origin. In a case like this, there will still be gains from trade, but generally such a situation won't lead to one country completely specializing in the production of the good.

International Trade

When people are permitted to engage freely in international trade, they are able to achieve higher income levels and living standards than would otherwise be possible.

Of course, domestic markets offer opportunities for specialization and trade also. This is particularly true for large countries like the United States. For example, most Americans specialize in relatively few productive activities and use the income from those activities to purchase most of the goods and services we consume. Many of these goods are domestically produced, but international trade makes it possible for people to buy and sell in an even larger market. Thus, it expands the opportunity for gains from trade. As we just explained, trading partners will be able to produce a larger joint output and consume a larger, more diverse bundle of goods when they each specialize in areas where they have a comparative advantage. Open markets also lead to gains from other sources. We will briefly discuss three of them.

1. More gains from large-scale production.   International trade makes it possible for both domestic producers and consumers to derive larger gains from the lower per-unit costs that often accompany large-scale production, marketing, and distribution activities. When economies of scale are important in an industry, successful domestic firms will be able to produce larger outputs and achieve lower unit costs than they would if they were unable to sell their products internationally. This is particularly important for firms located in small countries. For example, textile manufacturers in Malaysia, Taiwan, and South Korea would face much higher per-unit costs if they could not sell abroad because the domestic markets of these countries are too small to support large-scale production. There simply aren't enough buyers. However, if the firms can access the world market, where there are many more buyers, they can operate on a large scale and compete quite effectively.

Domestic consumers also benefit because international trade often makes it possible for them to acquire goods at lower prices from large-scale producers in other countries. The aircraft industry vividly illustrates this point. Given the huge design and engineering costs it takes to produce a single jet, no firm would be able to produce them economically if it weren't able to sell them abroad. Because of international trade, however, consumers around the world are able to purchase planes economically from large-scale producers like Boeing, which is based in the United States.

2. Gains from more competitive markets.   International trade promotes competition and encourages production efficiency and innovation. Competition from abroad keeps domestic producers on their toes and gives them a strong incentive to improve the quality of their products. The experience of the U.S. auto industry illustrates this point. Faced with stiff competition from Japanese firms during the 1980s, U.S. auto makers worked hard to improve the quality of their vehicles. As a result, the reliability of the automobiles and light trucks available to American consumers—including those produced by domestic manufacturers—is now much better than it used to be.

International trade also allows technologies and innovative ideas developed in one country to be disseminated to others. In many cases, local entrepreneurs will emulate production procedures and products that have been successful in other places and even further improve or adapt them for local markets. Dynamic competition of this type is an important source of growth and prosperity, particularly for less-developed countries.

3. More pressure to adopt sound institutions.   Not only do firms in open economies face more intense competition, so, too, do their governments. The gains from trade and the prosperity that results from free trade motivate political officials to establish sound institutions and adopt constructive policies. If they do not, both labor and capital will move toward more favorable environments. For example, neither domestic nor foreign investors will want to put their funds in countries characterized by hostile business conditions, monetary instability, legal uncertainty, high taxes, and inferior public services. When labor and capital are free to move elsewhere, implementing government policies that penalize success and undermine productive activities becomes more costly. This aspect of free trade is generally overlooked, but it may well be one of its most beneficial attributes.

SUPPLY, DEMAND, AND INTERNATIONAL TRADE

Like other things, international trade can be analyzed within the supply and demand framework. An analysis of supply and demand in international markets can show us how trade influences prices and output in domestic markets.

Consider the market for a good that U.S. producers are able to supply at a low cost. Using soybeans as an example, **Exhibit 6** illustrates the relationship between the domestic and world markets. The price of soybeans is determined by the forces of supply and demand in the world market. In an open economy, domestic producers are free to sell and domestic consumers are free to buy the product at the world market price (P_w). At this price, U.S. producers will supply Q_p, and U.S. consumers will purchase Q_c. Reflecting their low cost (comparative advantage), U.S. soybean producers will export $Q_p - Q_c$ units at the world market price.

Let's compare this open-economy outcome with the outcome that would occur in the absence of trade. If U.S. producers were not allowed to export soybeans, the domestic price would be determined by the domestic supply (S_d) and demand (D_d) only. A lower "no-trade" price (P_n) would emerge.

EXHIBIT 6
Producer Benefits from Exports

The price of soybeans and other internationally traded commodities is determined by the forces of supply and demand in the world market (b). If U.S. soybean producers are prohibited from selling to foreigners, the domestic price will be P_n (a). Free trade permits the U.S. soybean producers to sell Q_p units at the higher world price (P_w). The quantity $Q_p - Q_c$ is the amount U.S. producers export. Compared to the no-trade situation, the producers' gain from the higher price ($P_w bcP_n$) exceeds the cost imposed on domestic consumers ($P_w acP_n$) by the triangle *abc*.

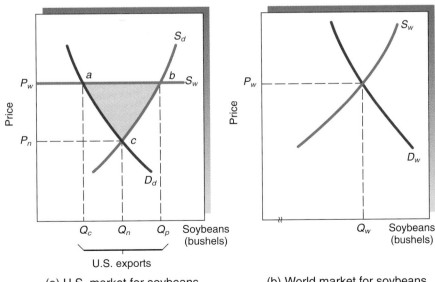

(a) U.S. market for soybeans   (b) World market for soybeans

EXHIBIT 7
Consumer Benefits from Imports

In the absence of trade, the domestic price of shoes would be P_n. Since many foreign producers have a comparative advantage in the production of shoes, international trade leads to lower prices. At the world price P_w, U.S. consumers will demand Q_c units, of which $Q_c - Q_p$ are imported. Compared to the no-trade situation, consumers gain $P_n abP_w$, while domestic producers lose $P_n acP_w$. A net gain of *abc* results.

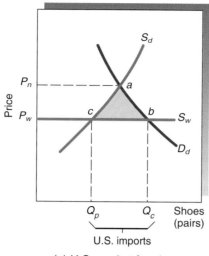

(a) U.S. market for shoes

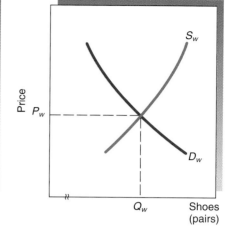

(b) World market for shoes

Who are the winners and losers as the result of free trade in soybeans? Clearly, soybean producers gain. Free trade allows domestic producers to sell a larger quantity (Q_p rather than Q_n). As a result, the net revenues of soybean producers will rise by $P_w bcP_n$. On the other hand, domestic consumers of soybeans will have to pay a higher price under free trade. Soybean consumers will lose (1) because they have to pay P_w rather than P_n for the Q_c units they purchase, and (2) because they lose the consumer surplus on the $Q_n - Q_c$ units now purchased at the higher price. Thus, free trade imposes a net cost of $P_w acP_n$ on consumers. As you can see in Exhibit 6, however, the gains of soybean producers outweigh the losses to the consumers by the triangle *abc*. In other words, free trade leads to a net welfare gain.

This exporting example makes it seem like free trade benefits producers relative to consumers, but this ignores the secondary effects: if foreigners do not sell goods to Americans, they will not have the purchasing power necessary to purchase goods from Americans. U.S. imports—the purchase of goods from low-cost foreign producers—provides foreigners with the dollar purchasing power necessary to buy U.S. exports. In turn, the lower prices in the import-competitive markets will benefit the U.S. consumers who appeared at first glance to be harmed by the higher prices (compared to the no-trade situation) in export markets.

Using shoes as an example, **Exhibit 7** illustrates the situation when the United States is a net importer. In the absence of trade, the price of shoes in the domestic market would be P_n, the intersection of the domestic supply and demand curves. However, the world price of shoes is P_w. In an open economy, many U.S. consumers would take advantage of the low shoe prices available from foreign producers. At the lower world price, U.S. consumers would purchase Q_c units of shoes, importing $Q_c - Q_p$ from foreign producers.

Compared to the no-trade situation, free trade in shoes results in lower prices and greater domestic consumption. The lower prices lead to a net consumer gain of $P_n abP_w$. Domestic producers lose $P_n acP_w$ in the form of lower sales prices and reductions in output. However, the net gain of the shoe consumers exceeds the net loss of producers by *abc*.

International competition will direct resources toward their area of comparative advantage. If domestic producers have a comparative advantage in the production of a good, they will be able to compete effectively in the world market and profit from the export of goods to foreigners. In turn, the exports will generate the purchasing power necessary to buy goods that foreigners can supply more economically.

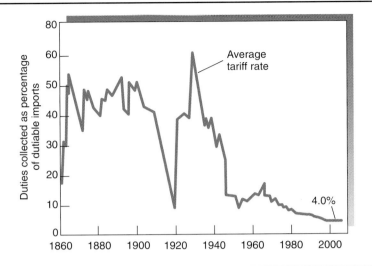

THE ECONOMICS OF TRADE RESTRICTIONS

Despite the potential benefits of free trade, almost all nations have erected trade barriers. Tariffs, quotas, and exchange rate controls are the most commonly used trade-restricting devices. Let's consider how various types of trade restrictions affect the economy.

Economics of Tariffs

A **tariff** is nothing more than a tax on imports from foreign countries. As **Exhibit 8** shows, average tariff rates of between 30 percent and 50 percent of product value were often levied on products imported to the United States prior to 1945. The notorious Smoot-Hawley Tariff Act of 1930 pushed the average tariff rate upward to 60 percent. Many economists believe that this legislation contributed significantly to the length and severity of the Great Depression. During the past sixty years, however, tariff rates in the United States have declined substantially. In 2002, the average tariff rate on imported goods was only 4 percent.

Exhibit 9 shows the impact of a tariff on automobiles. In the absence of a tariff, the world market price of P_w would prevail in the domestic market. At that price, U.S. consumers purchase Q_1 units. Domestic producers supply Q_{d_1}, while foreigners supply $Q_1 - Q_{d_1}$ units to the U.S. market. When the United States levies a tariff, t, on automobiles, Americans can no longer buy cars at the world price. U.S. consumers now have to pay $P_w + t$ to purchase an automobile from foreigners. At that price, domestic consumers demand Q_2 units (Q_{d_2} supplied by domestic producers and $Q_2 - Q_{d_2}$ supplied by foreigners). The tariff results in a higher domestic price and lower level of domestic consumption.

The tariff benefits domestic producers and the government at the expense of consumers. Because domestic producers don't have to pay the tariff, they will expand their output in response to the higher (protected) market price. In effect, the tariff acts as a subsidy to domestic producers. Domestic producers gain the area S (Exhibit 9) in the form of additional net revenues. The tariff raises revenues equal to the area T for the government. The areas U and V represent costs imposed on consumers and resource suppliers that do not benefit the government. Simply put, U and V represent *deadweight losses:* consumer and producer surpluses that could have been gained if the tariff hadn't been imposed.

As a result of the tariff, resources that could have been used to produce other U.S. goods more efficiently (compared to producing them abroad) are diverted to automobile production. Ultimately, we end up producing fewer products in areas where we have a comparative advantage and more products in areas where we are a high-cost producer. Because of this, some of the gains from specialization and trade go unrealized.

Tariff
A tax levied on goods imported into a country.

EXHIBIT 9
The Impact of a Tariff

Here we illustrate the impact of a tariff on automobiles. In the absence of the tariff, the world price of automobiles is P_w:
U.S. consumers purchase Q_1 units (Q_{d_1} from domestic producers plus $Q_1 - Q_{d_1}$ from foreign producers). The tariff makes it
more costly for Americans to purchase automobiles from foreigners. Imports decline and the domestic price increases.
Higher prices reduce consumer surplus by the areas $S + U + T + V$. Producers gain the area S, and the tariff generates T
tax revenues for the government. The areas U and V are deadweight losses. Consumers lose the surplus associated with
these two areas, but producers and the government don't gain it.

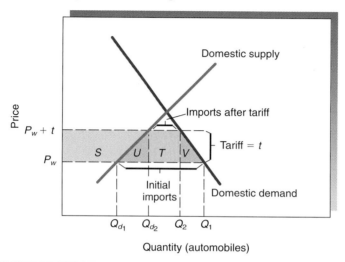

The Economics of Quotas

Import quota
A specific limit or maximum
quantity (or value) of a good
permitted to be imported into
a country during a given
period.

An **import quota**, like a tariff, is designed to restrict foreign goods and protect domestic
industries. A quota places a ceiling on the amount of a product that can be imported during a given period (typically a year). The United States imposes quotas on several products, including brooms, shoes, sugar, dairy products, and peanuts. For example, since
1953, the United States has imposed an annual peanut quota of 1.7 million pounds. That's
equivalent to just two imported peanuts per American. Like tariffs, the primary purpose of
quotas is to protect domestic industries from foreign competition.

Using peanuts as an example, **Exhibit 10** illustrates the impact of a quota. If there
were no trade restraints, the domestic price of peanuts would be equal to the world market
price (P_w). Under those circumstances, Americans would purchase Q_1 units. At the price
P_w, domestic producers would supply Q_{d_1}, and the amount $Q_1 - Q_{d_1}$ would be imported
from foreign producers.

Now consider what happens when a quota limits imports to $Q_2 - Q_{d_2}$, a quantity well
below the free-trade level of imports. Since the quota reduces the foreign supply of
peanuts to the domestic market, the price of the quota-protected product increases (to P_2).
At the higher price, U.S. consumers will reduce their purchases to Q_2, and domestic producers will happily expand their production to Q_{d_2}. With regard to the welfare of consumers, the impact of a quota is similar to that of a tariff. Consumers lose the area $S +
U + T + V$ in the form of higher prices and the loss of consumer surplus. Similarly, do-
mestic producers gain the area S, while the areas U and V represent deadweight losses in
the form of reductions in consumer surplus, gains that buyers would have derived in the
absence of the quota.

While the adverse impact of a quota on consumer welfare is similar to that of a tariff,
there is a big difference with regard to the area T. Under a tariff, the U.S. government
would collect revenues equal to T, representing the tariff rate multiplied by the number of
units imported. With a quota, however, these revenues will go to foreign producers, who

EXHIBIT 10
The Impact of a Quota

Here we illustrate the impact of a quota, such as the one the United States imposes on peanuts. The world market price of peanuts is P_w. If there were no trade restraints, the domestic price would also be P_w, and the domestic consumption would be Q_1. Domestic producers would supply Q_d units, while $Q_1 - Q_d$ would be imported. A quota limiting imports to $Q_2 - Q_{d_2}$ would push up the domestic price to P_2. At the higher price, the amount supplied by domestic producers increases to Q_{d_2}. Consumers lose the sum of the area $S + U + T + V$, while domestic producers gain the area S. In contrast with tariffs, quotas generate no revenue for the government. The area T goes to foreign producers, who are granted permission to sell in the U.S. market.

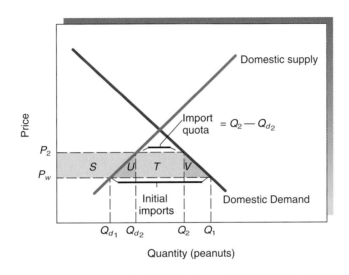

Quantity (peanuts)

are granted licenses (quotas) to sell various amounts in the U.S. market. Clearly, this right to sell at a premium price (since the domestic price exceeds the world market price) is extremely valuable. Thus, foreign producers will compete for the permits. They will hire lobbyists, make political contributions, and engage in other rent-seeking activities in an effort to secure the right to sell at a premium price in the U.S. market.

In many ways, quotas are more harmful than tariffs. With a quota, foreign producers are prohibited from selling additional units regardless of how much lower their costs are relative to those of domestic producers. In contrast to a tariff, a quota brings in no revenue for the government. While a tariff transfers revenue from U.S. consumers to the Treasury, quotas transfer these revenues to foreign producers. Rewarding domestic producers with higher prices and foreign producers with valuable import permits will create *two* strong interest groups. Both groups will lobby hard to keep the quota in place. As a result, lifting the quota will often be more difficult than lowering a tariff would be.

In addition to tariffs and quotas, governments sometimes use regulations and political pressure to restrain foreign competition. For example, the United States prohibits foreign airlines from competing in the domestic air travel market. Japanese regulations make it illegal for domestic automobile dealers to sell both foreign and domestically produced vehicles; this makes it more difficult for foreign manufacturers to establish the dealer networks they need to effectively penetrate the Japanese market. Like tariffs and quotas, regulatory barriers such as these reduce the supply to domestic markets and the gains from potential trades. Overall output is reduced, and domestic producers benefit at the expense of domestic consumers.

Exchange Rate Controls as a Trade Restriction

Some countries fix the exchange rate value of their currency above the market rate and impose restrictions on exchange rate transactions.[2] At the official (artificially high) exchange rate, the country's export goods will be extremely expensive to foreigners. As a result, foreigners will purchase goods elsewhere, and the country's exports will be small. In turn, the low level of exports will make it extremely difficult for domestic residents to obtain the foreign currency they need to purchase imports. Exchange rate controls both reduce the volume of trade and lead to black-market currency exchanges. Indeed, a large black-market premium indicates that the country's exchange rate policy is substantially limiting the ability of its citizens to trade with foreigners. While exchange rate controls have declined in popularity, they are still an important trade barrier in countries such as Myanmar and Zimbabwe.

WHY DO NATIONS ADOPT TRADE RESTRICTIONS?

As social philosopher Henry George noted over a century ago, trade restraints act like blockades. Why would political officials want to erect blockades against their own people? As we consider this question, we will take a look at three arguments often raised by the proponents of trade restrictions: the national-defense, infant-industry, and antidumping arguments. Finally, we will look at the politics of trade restrictions and analyze how the nature of the restraints influences their political popularity.

The National-Defense Argument

Protective tariffs are as much applications of force as are blockading squadrons, and their objective is the same—to prevent trade. The difference between the two is that blockading squadrons are a means whereby nations seek to prevent their enemies from trading; protective tariffs are a means whereby nations attempt to prevent their own people from trading.

—Henry George[3]

According to the national-defense argument, certain industries—aircraft, petroleum, and weapons, for example—are vital to a nation's defense. Therefore, these industries and their inputs should be protected from foreign competitors so that a domestic supply of necessary materials would be available in case of an international conflict. Would we want to be entirely dependent on Arabian or Russian petroleum? Would complete dependence on French aircraft be wise? Many Americans would answer "no," even if it meant imposing trade restrictions that would lead to higher prices on products they buy.

Although the national-defense argument has some validity, it is often abused. Relatively few industries are truly vital to our national defense. If a resource is important for national defense, often it would make more sense to stockpile the resource during peacetime rather than follow protectionist policies to preserve a domestic industry. Furthermore, fostering an economy robust enough to produce the mass quantity of goods necessary to sustain a war effort in the first place is, itself, part of a strong defense.

The Infant-Industry Argument

Infant-industry advocates believe that new domestic industries should be protected from foreign competition for a period of time so that they will have a chance to develop. As the new industry matures, it will be able to stand on its own feet and compete effectively with foreign producers, at which time the protection can be removed.

The infant-industry argument has a long and often notorious history. Alexander Hamilton used it to argue for the protection of early U.S. manufacturing. The major problem with the argument is that the protection, once granted, will be difficult to remove. For example, a century ago, this argument was used to gain tariff protection for the newly

---

[2]The most common exchange rate restriction is that individuals are required to obtain approval from the government before they engage in transactions involving foreign currency.

[3]Henry George, *Protection or Free Trade* (Washington, D.C.: U.S. Government Printing Office, 1886), 37.

APPLICATIONS IN ECONOMICS

Do More Open Economies Perform Better?

Economic theory indicates that more open economies will perform better than those with sizeable trade restrictions. Is this really true? In order to address this question, a measure of trade openness—the freedom of individuals to engage in voluntary exchange across national boundaries—is needed. Economist Charles Skipton, in a recent research project, developed a trade openness index (TOI) for eighty-one countries during the 1980–1999 period.[1] To achieve a high rating on the zero to ten TOI scale (with ten indicating more openness to free trade), a country had to maintain low tariff rates and a freely convertible currency (no exchange rate controls) as well as refrain from imposing quotas and other regulations reducing the size of its trade sector.

Exhibit 11 shows the ten countries with the highest and lowest trade openness ratings. The ratings reflect the *average* degree of openness for the entire 1980–1999 period. This is important because the gains from increased openness can only be realized over time. Expanding the openness of trade is a long-term growth strategy, not a short-term "quick fix," in other words. Hong Kong, Singapore, Belgium, Canada, and the Netherlands head the list of the most open of the eighty-one economies. By way of comparison, the United States ranked sixteenth. At the other end of the spectrum, the TOI indicates that Bangladesh, Burundi, Madagascar, Pakistan, and India were the least open economies during the period.

As Exhibit 11 shows, the 2002 average GDP per person of $26,518 of the ten most open economies was more than eight times the comparable figure for the ten least

(continued)

EXHIBIT 11
Trade Openness, Income, and Growth

	TOI	2002 GDP Per Capita (1995 DOLLARS)	GROWTH RATE, 1980–2002
10 Most Open Economies, 1980–1999			
Singapore	9.9	$21,296	4.2
Hong Kong	9.9	23,833	3.7
Belgium	9.2	24,418	1.7
Canada	8.9	26,114	1.6
Netherlands	8.9	25,778	1.8
Luxembourg	8.7	54,201	4.0
Malaysia	8.4	8,080	3.4
Norway	8.4	32,414	2.5
Australia	8.2	25,880	2.0
United Kingdom	8.1	23,166	2.2
Average	**8.9**	**$26,518**	**2.7**
Ten Least Open Economies, 1980–1999			
Algeria	3.4	$5,101	−0.0
Belize	3.4	5,386	2.1
Tanzania	3.3	513	1.0
Argentina	3.2	9,633	−0.6
Syria	3.1	3,205	0.7
India	2.8	2,365	3.6
Pakistan	2.8	1,719	2.3
Madagascar	2.8	659	−2.1
Burundi	1.4	561	−0.9
Bangladesh	0.9	1,501	2.1
Average	**2.7**	**$3,064**	**0.8**

Source: The trade openness index data are from Charles Skipton, *The Measurement of Trade Openness.* Doctoral Dissertation, Florida State University, 2003 (Table 4.6). The per capita GDP and growth Bank, World Development Indicators, CD-ROM, 2004. The per capita income figures were divided by the purchasing power parity method.

(continued)

open economies. Moreover, the more open economies also grew more rapidly. During 1980–2002, real GDP per person in the ten most open economies expanded at an annual rate of 2.7 percent, compared to 0.8 percent in the ten least open economies. The per capita GDP in every one of the most open economies grew at least 1.6 percent annually. Of course, the data of Exhibit 11 do not take into account other cross-country differences that theory indicates will influence growth. However, Skipton found that even after the differences in countries' inflation rates, legal struc-

tures, and similar factors were taken into account, trade openness continued to have a strong positive impact on both per capita GDP and growth rates.[2]

---

[1]Charles Skipton, "The Measurement of Trade Openness" (doctoral dissertation, Florida State University, 2003).

[2]For additional information on the relationship between international trade and economic growth, see Jeffrey A. Frankel and David Romer, "Does Trade Cause Growth?" *American Economic Review* (June 1999): 379–399; and Jeffrey D. Sachs and Andrew Warner, "Economic Reform and the Process of Global Integration." *Brookings Papers on Economic Activity*, no. 1 (1995): 1–95.

---

emerging steel industry in the United States. Over time, the steel industry developed and became very powerful, both politically and economically. Despite its maturity, the tariffs remained. To this day, legislation continues to provide the steel industry with various protections that limit competition from abroad.

The Antidumping Argument

Dumping

Selling a good in a foreign country at a lower price than it's sold for in the domestic market.

Dumping involves the sale of goods by a foreign firm at a price below cost or below the price charged in the firm's home-base market. Dumping is illegal and if a domestic industry is harmed, current law provides relief in the form of antidumping duties (tariffs imposed against violators). In addition, under the recently enacted Byrd Amendment, the revenues collected from the antidumping duties are transferred to the firms and unions lodging antidumping complaints, further increasing their incentive to levy such charges.[4]

Proponents of the antidumping argument argue that foreign producers will temporarily cut prices, drive domestic firms out of the market, and then use their monopoly position to gouge consumers. However, there is reason to question the effectiveness of this strategy. After all, the high prices would soon attract competitors, including other foreign suppliers.

Antidumping cases nearly always involve considerable ambiguity. The prices charged in the home market generally vary, and the production costs of the firms charged with dumping are not directly observable. This makes it difficult to tell whether a dumping violation has really occurred. Furthermore, aggressive price competition is an integral part of the competitive process. When demand is weak and inventories are large, firms will lower the prices of their products below their average total cost of production. Domestic firms are permitted to engage in this practice, and consumers benefit from it. Why shouldn't foreign firms be allowed to do the same?

One thing is for sure: antidumping legislation gives politicians another way to channel highly visible benefits to powerful business and labor interests—another open invitation for rent seeking. Moreover, the dumping charges are adjudicated by International Trade Commission and U.S. Department of Commerce officials. Consequently, it's naive to believe that political considerations won't be an important element underlying the charges that are levied and how they are resolved. Unsurprisingly, the number of claimants bringing charges of dumping has increased substantially in recent years.

---

[4]In effect, the Byrd Amendment provides subsidies to firms and unions willing to lend their support to antidumping charges and places them at a competitive advantage relative to those who fail to support the petitions. Thus, it encourages the filing of antidumping charges. In August 2004, the World Trade Organization ruled that the Byrd Amendment was a violation of international trade rules and authorized Japan, Europe, Korea, and several other countries to levy specific levels of retaliation duties against U.S. products.

Special Interests and the Politics of Trade Restrictions

Regardless of the arguments made by the proponents of trade restrictions, in truth, the restrictions are primarily special-interest related. (See the quotation to the right from Professor Weidenbaum.) *Trade restrictions typically provide highly visible, concentrated benefits for a small group of people, while imposing on the general citizenry costs that are widely dispersed and difficult to identify.* As we discussed in Chapter 6, the political process handles such issues poorly. It often leads to their adoption, even when they lower income levels and living standards.

The politics of trade restrictions are straightforward and play out over and over again. Well-organized business and labor interests gain substantially from restrictions that limit competition from abroad. Because their personal gain is large, they will feel strongly about the issue and generally vote for or against candidates on the basis of their positions on trade restriction. Most important, the special-interest groups will be an attractive source of political contributions. When it comes to consumers, on the other hand, even if the total cost of the restrictions is quite large, it will be spread thinly among them; most consumers will be unaware that they are paying slightly higher prices for various goods because of the restrictions.

As you can see, courting special-interest groups helps politicians solicit campaign contributions and generate votes. On the other hand, little political gain can be derived from poorly organized and largely uninformed consumers. Given this incentive structure, the adoption of trade restrictions is not surprising.

The U.S. tariff code itself is a reflection of the politics of trade restrictions. It is both lengthy (the schedule fills 3,825 pages) and highly complex. This makes it difficult for even a well-educated citizen to figure out how it works. High tariffs are imposed on some products (for example, apparel, tobacco, and footwear), while low tariffs are imposed on others. Highly restrictive quotas limit the import of a few commodities, most notably agricultural products. Even though this complex system of targeted trade restrictions is costly to administer, it is no accident. It reflects the rent seeking of special-interest groups and the political side payments, particularly campaign contributions, made to politicians.

> *Protectionism is a politician's delight because it delivers visible benefits to the protected parties while imposing the costs as a hidden tax on the public.*
>
> —Murray L. Weidenbaum[5]

TRADE BARRIERS AND POPULAR TRADE FALLACIES

Fallacies abound in the area of international trade. Why? Failure to consider the secondary effects of international trade is part of the answer. Key elements of international trade are closely linked; you cannot change one element without changing the other. For example, you cannot reduce imports without simultaneously reducing the demand for exports. The political incentive structure is also a contributing factor. As business, labor, and political leaders seek to gain from trade restrictions, they will often use half-truths and wrong-headed ideas to achieve their political objectives. Two of the most popular trade fallacies involve the effects of imports on employment and the impact of trade with low-wage countries. Let's take a closer look at both.

Trade Fallacy 1: Trade restrictions that limit imports save jobs and expand employment.   Like most fallacies, this one has just enough truth to give it some credibility. When tariffs, quotas, and other trade barriers limit imports, they are likely to foster employment in the industries shielded from competition. But this is only half of the story: simultaneously, jobs in other domestic sectors will be destroyed. Here's how: When trade barriers reduce the amount of goods Americans buy from foreigners, sales to foreigners will also fall. This is because our imports provide foreigners with the dollars they need to buy our exports. Because foreigners cut back on the items they would normally buy from us, other U.S. sectors will suffer job losses because they're selling less.

---

[5]Murray L. Weidenbaum, personal correspondence with the authors. Professor Weidenbaum is a former chairman of the President's Council of Economic Advisers and longtime director of the Center for the Study of American Business of Washington University.

Furthermore, when trade restrictions are imposed on a resource domestic producers use as an input, they will have to pay a higher price for it than their foreign rivals. This will increase their costs and make it more difficult for them to compete internationally. As a result, they will have to lay off some of their employees. The import quotas imposed on steel during 2002–2004 vividly illustrate this point. The quotas helped the domestic steel industry, but they virtually wiped out the domestic industry producing steel barrels, a product the U.S. had exported prior to the quota being imposed. The quota also increased costs and reduced the competitiveness of industries that were major users of steel, like the automobile- and appliance-manufacturing industries. Employment in those industries fell as well. The same phenomenon occurred after the United States imposed sugar quotas. The import quotas pushed domestic sugar prices to two or three times the world price. As a result, several large candy makers relocated abroad so that they could buy sugar at the lower world price. Again, the jobs lost in U.S. industries using sugar were offset by any increase in employment by U.S. sugar producers.

On balance, there is no reason to expect that trade restrictions will either create or destroy jobs. Instead, they will reshuffle them. The restrictions artificially direct workers and other resources toward the production of things that we do poorly, as shown by our inability to compete effectively in the world market. Simultaneously, employment will decline in areas where American firms would be able to compete successfully in the world market if it were not for the side effects of the restrictions. In other words, more Americans will be employed producing things we do poorly and fewer will be employed producing things we do well. As a result, our overall income level will be lower than it would have been otherwise.

Unfortunately, the jobs "saved" by the import quotas are more visible than those destroyed in other sectors. This increases the political popularity of trade restraints and perpetuates the fallacy that the restraints increase employment. But it does not change the reality of the situation. As Exhibit 1 shows, imports increased from 6 percent of GDP in 1980 to 15 percent in 2003. If the growth of imports destroys jobs, as the proponents of trade restrictions argue, the rapid import growth should have adversely affected U.S. employment. But this was not the case. On the contrary, civilian employment in the United States rose from 99 million in 1980 to 119 million in 1990 and 137 million in 2003. Far from retarding employment, the unprecedented growth of imports during the last two decades was associated with unprecedented employment growth.

Trade Fallacy 2: Free trade with low-wage countries like Mexico and China will reduce the wages of Americans. Many Americans believe that, without trade restrictions, their wages will fall to the wage levels of workers in poor countries. How can Americans compete with workers in countries like Mexico and China who are willing to work for $1 or less per hour? This fallacy stems from a misunderstanding of both the source of high wages and the law of comparative advantage. Workers in the United States are well educated, possess high skill levels, and work with large amounts of capital equipment. These factors contribute to their high productivity, which is the source of their high wages. Similarly, in countries like Mexico and China, wages are low precisely because productivity is low. Workers are less skilled in these countries, and there is less capital equipment to make them more productive.

The key thing to remember, though, is that gains from trade emanate from comparative advantage, not absolute advantage (see Exhibits 3, 4, and 5). The United States cannot produce *everything* more cheaply than Mexico or China merely because U.S. employees are more productive and work with more capital. Neither can the Mexicans and Chinese produce *everything* more cheaply merely because their wage rates are low compared to those of U.S. workers.

As long as there are differences between countries when it comes to their comparative advantages, gains from trade will be possible, no matter what the wages of the employees in the two countries are. Trade reflects relative advantage, not wage levels. We can illustrate this point using trade between individuals. No one argues that trade between doctors and lawn service workers, for example, will cause the wages of doctors to fall. Because of their different skills and costs of providing alternative goods, both high-wage doctors and low-wage lawn care workers can gain from trade. The same is also true for trade between rich and poor nations.

If foreigners (including low-wage foreigners) have a comparative advantage and can sell us a product for less than we ourselves can produce it, we can gain by buying it. This will give us more resources to invest in and produce other things. Perhaps an extreme example will illustrate this point. Suppose a foreign producer is willing to supply us automobiles free of charge (perhaps because its employees were willing to work for nothing). Would it make sense to impose tariffs or quotas to keep the automobiles from coming into the country? Of course not. Resources that were previously used to produce automobiles would then be freed up to produce other goods, and the real income and availability of goods would expand. It makes no more sense to erect trade barriers to keep out cheap foreign goods than it would to keep out the free autos.

THE CHANGING NATURE OF GLOBAL TRADE

Since World War II, there has been a gradual reduction in tariff rates and other trade barriers. Liberalized trade policies and lower transportation and communication costs have propelled the growth of international trade. The growth of trade—some might say the globalization of the economy—has also resulted in a changing institutional environment. This section will focus on the institutions of international trade and the prospects for future trade liberalization.

GATT and the WTO

Following World War II, the major industrial nations of the world established the **General Agreement on Tariffs and Trade (GATT)**. For almost five decades, GATT played a central role in reducing tariffs and relaxing quotas. The average tariff rates of GATT members fell from approximately 40 percent in 1947 to less than 5 percent in 1998, for example.

Following 1993, GATT was given a new name: the **World Trade Organization (WTO)**. This organization of almost 150 countries is now responsible for monitoring and enforcing the trade agreements developed through GATT. The WTO gives member nations a forum in which to discuss trade rules, and it settles trade disputes among them.

NAFTA and Other Regional Trade Agreements

Canada has been a major trading partner of the United States for many decades. On the other hand, U.S. trade with Mexico was small prior to the 1990s. Historically, Mexico has been a relatively closed economy. This began to change in the mid-1980s, when Mexico began cutting its tariff rates and unilaterally removing other trade barriers. In 1988, the United States and Canada negotiated a trade agreement designed to reduce barriers limiting both trade and the flow of capital between the two countries. A few years later, the United States, Canada, and Mexico finalized the **North American Free Trade Agreement (NAFTA)**, which took effect in 1994. As the result of NAFTA, the tariffs of most goods moving among the three countries have now been eliminated. The agreement will eventually remove restrictions on financial investments, liberalize trade in services like banking, and establish uniform legal requirements for the protection of intellectual property. In addition to its participation in NAFTA, Mexico has also adopted a free-trade agreement with the European Union. During the last fifteen years, Mexico has moved from one of the world's more protectionist countries to one of its more open economies.

As **Exhibit 12** shows, U.S. trade with both Mexico and Canada has grown rapidly in recent years. Measured as a share of GDP, trade with Mexico jumped from 1.4 percent in 1990 to 2.6 percent in 2003. During the same period, trade with Canada rose from 3.8 percent of GDP to 4.3 percent. This growth of trade, particularly with Mexico, has not been without controversy. Business and labor groups often blame employment contractions and plant closings on competition with Mexican firms. The news media generally give such stories ample exposure. However, there is no evidence that increased trade with Mexico has adversely affected the U.S. economy. During the last decade, the growth rate of the

General Agreement on Tariffs and Trade (GATT)
An organization formed after the Second World War to set the rules for the conduct of international trade and reduce trade barriers among nations.

World Trade Organization (WTO)
The new name given to GATT in 1994; the WTO is currently responsible for monitoring and enforcing multilateral trade agreements among its 133 member countries.

North American Free Trade Agreement (NAFTA)
A comprehensive trade agreement between the United States, Mexico, and Canada that went into effect in 1994. Under the agreement, tariff barriers were to continue to be phased out until 2004.

EXHIBIT 12
U.S. Trade with Canada and Mexico, 1980–2003

Measured as a share of GDP, U.S. trade with both Canada and Mexico has increased sharply during the last fifteen years.

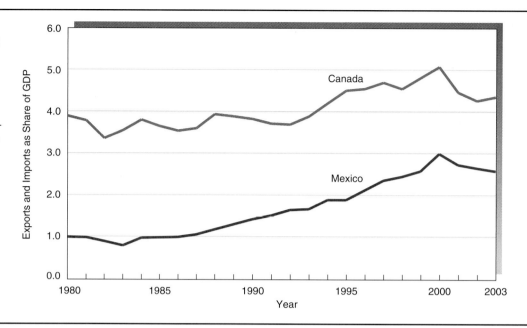

Source: *Statistical Abstract of the United States* (various years) and http://www.bea.gov.

U.S. has been strong and the unemployment rate relatively low. Clearly, the dire predictions about the "jobs going to Mexico" have not been realized.

The Future of Free Trade

For several decades following World War II, the United States and most other high-income countries were leaders among those pursuing and promoting more liberal trade policies. In contrast, India, China, and most of the less-developed economies of Africa and Latin America imposed sizeable trade restraints, and they were reluctant to relax them.

Since 1980, the situation has changed dramatically. Observing the success of open economies like Hong Kong and Singapore, many less-developed countries unilaterally reduced many of their trade restrictions during the last two decades. On average, the tariff rates of less-developed countries are now less than half their levels in the early 1980s. Exchange rate controls are becoming increasingly rare, and capital market controls are much less restrictive than they were a decade ago. Today, many leaders in less-developed countries recognize that free trade is the surest route to higher income levels and improved living standards. These countries are often the fiercest advocates of trade liberalization.

By contrast, the United States, Japan, and European Union nations have agricultural price support programs contrary to free trade. It will take considerable effort to reduce, let alone remove, the price supports and subsidies to agriculture interests. To date, these countries have been unwilling to do so, and their resistance has become a major stumbling block on the road to trade liberalization. Furthermore, protectionist proponents—particularly those in high-income countries like the Unites States—have successfully lobbied to impose labor and environmental regulations that block trade liberalization. Meanwhile, the Internet and other technological changes continue to reduce transport and communications costs, and thereby encourage the movement of goods, ideas, and people across national boundaries. All of this promises to enliven trade issues in the years ahead.

LOOKING AHEAD

There are many similarities between domestic trade and trade across national boundaries, but there is also a major difference: international trade generally involves exchanging foreign currencies. The next chapter deals with the foreign exchange market and other dimensions of international finance.

! KEY POINTS

▼ The volume of international trade has grown rapidly in recent decades. In the United States, international trade (imports plus exports) summed to 25 percent of GDP in 2003, compared to 12 percent in 1980 and 6 percent in 1960.

▼ Comparative advantage rather than absolute advantage is the source of gains from trade. As long as relative production costs of goods differ, trading partners will be able to gain from trade. Specialization and trade make it possible for trading partners to produce a larger joint output and expand their consumption possibilities.

▼ Exports and imports are linked. The exports of a nation are the primary source of purchasing power used to purchase imported goods. When a nation restricts imports, it simultaneously limits the ability of foreigners to acquire the purchasing power necessary to buy its exports.

▼ International specialization and trade result in lower prices for imported products and higher domestic prices for exported products. However, the net effect is an expansion in the aggregate output and consumption possibilities of trading nations.

▼ Import restrictions, such as tariffs and quotas, reduce the supply of foreign goods to domestic markets. This causes domestic price to rise. Essentially, the restrictions are a subsidy to producers (and workers) in protected industries at the expense of (a) consumers and (b) producers (and workers) in export industries. Jobs protected by import restrictions are offset by jobs destroyed in export-related industries.

▼ Trade restrictions generally provide concentrated benefits to the producers in industries they're designed to protect. The costs are spread thinly among consumers in the form of higher prices. Even though the impact of trade restrictions on the economy as a whole is harmful, they help politicians reward special-interest groups for campaign contributions and support. This makes them attractive to politicians.

▼ Persistently open economies have grown more rapidly and achieved higher per capita income levels than economies more closed to international trade.

CRITICAL ANALYSIS QUESTIONS

1. Why do American households and businesses buy things from foreigners? What are the characteristics of the items we buy from foreigners? What are the characteristics of the things we sell to foreigners?

*2. "Trade restrictions limiting the sale of cheap foreign goods in the United States are necessary to protect the prosperity of Americans." Evaluate this statement made by an American politician.

3. Suppose as the result of the Civil War that the United States had been divided into two countries and that, through the years, high trade barriers had grown up between the two. How might the standard of living in the "divided" United States have been affected? Explain.

*4. Can both of the following statements be true? Why or why not?
   a. "Tariffs and import quotas promote economic inefficiency and reduce the real income of a nation. Economic analysis suggests that nations can gain by eliminating trade restrictions."
   b. "Economic analysis suggests that there is good reason to expect that trade restrictions will exist in the real world."

5. "The average American is hurt by imports and helped by exports." Do you agree or disagree with this statement?

*6. "An increased scarcity of a product benefits producers and harms consumers. In effect, tariffs and other trade restrictions increase the domestic scarcity of products by reducing the supply from abroad. Such policies benefit domestic producers of the restricted product at the expense of domestic consumers." Evaluate this statement.

7. Suppose that a very high tariff were placed on steel imported into the United States. How would that affect employment in the U.S. auto industry? (*Hint:* Think about how higher steel prices will impact the cost of producing automobiles.)

*8. "Getting more Americans to realize that it pays to make things in the United States is the heart of the competitiveness issue." (This is a quote from an American business magazine.)

   a. Would Americans be better off if more of them paid higher prices in order to "buy American" rather than purchase from foreigners? Would U.S. employment be higher? Explain.
   b. Would Californians be better off if they bought goods produced only in California? Would the employment in California be higher? Explain.

9. How do tariffs and quotas differ? Can you think of any reason why foreign producers might prefer a quota rather than a tariff? Explain your answer.

*10. It is often alleged that Japanese producers receive subsidies from their government permitting them to sell their products at a low price in the U.S. market. Do you think we should erect trade barriers to keep out cheap Japanese goods if the source of their low price is governmental subsidies? Why or why not?

11. In recent years, the European Union has reduced trade barriers among its members, and most EU members now use a common currency. What impact will these changes have on European economies?

*12. Does international trade cost American jobs? Does interstate trade cost your state jobs? What is the major effect of international and interstate trade?

13. "The U.S. is suffering from an excess of imports. Cheap foreign products are driving American firms out of business and leaving the U.S. economy in shambles." Evaluate this view.

*14. The United States uses an import quota to maintain the domestic price of sugar well above the world price. Analyze the impact of the quota. Use supply and demand analysis to illustrate your answer. To whom do the gains and losses of this policy accrue? How does the quota affect the efficiency of resource allocation in the United States? Why do you think Congress is supportive of this policy?

15. As U.S. trade with low-wage countries like Mexico increases, will wages in the United States be pushed down? Why or why not? Are low-wage workers in the United States hurt when there is more trade with Mexico? Discuss.

*16. "Tariffs not only reduce the volume of imports, they also reduce the volume of exports." Is this statement true or false? Explain your answer.

17. "Physical obstacles like bad roads and stormy weather increase transaction costs and thereby reduce the volume of trade. Tariffs, quotas, exchange rate controls, and other human-made trade restrictions have similar effects." Evaluate this statement. Is it true? Why or why not?

*Asterisk denotes questions for which answers are given in Appendix B.

International Finance and the Foreign Exchange Market

Chapter Focus

■ What determines the exchange rate value of the dollar relative to other currencies? Why do exchange rates change?

■ What is a fixed exchange rate? If a country is going to maintain a fixed exchange rate, what must it do?

■ What information is included in the balance-of-payments accounts of a nation? Will the balance-of-payments accounts of a country always be in balance?

■ Will a healthy economy run a balance-of-trade surplus? Does a balance-of-trade deficit indicate that a nation is in financial trouble?

Currencies, like tomatoes and football tickets, have a price at which they are bought and sold. An exchange rate is the price of one currency in terms of another, such as the price of a French franc in U.S. dollars or German marks.

—Gary Smith[1]

[1]Gary Smith, *Macro Economics* (New York: W. H. Freeman, 1985), 514.

T rade across national boundaries is complicated by the fact that nations generally use different currencies to buy and sell goods in their respective domestic markets. The British use pounds, the Japanese yen, the Mexicans pesos, and twelve European countries use the euro, and so on. Therefore, when a good or service is purchased from a seller in another country, it is generally necessary for someone to convert one currency to another.

As we previously discussed, the forces of supply and demand will determine the exchange rate value of currencies in the absence of government intervention. This chapter will focus more directly on the foreign exchange market. We will consider how exchange rates both exert an effect on and are influenced by the flow of trade and the flow of capital across national boundaries. We will also analyze alternative exchange rate regimes and consider some of the recent changes in the structure of currency markets around the world. ■

THE FOREIGN EXCHANGE MARKET

Foreign exchange market
The market in which the currencies of different countries are bought and sold.

When trading parties live in different countries, an exchange will often involve a currency transaction. Currency transactions take place in the **foreign exchange market**, the market where currencies of different countries are bought and sold. Suppose you own a sporting goods shop in the United States and are preparing to place an order for athletic shoes. You can purchase them from either a domestic or a foreign manufacturer. If you decide to purchase the shoes from a British firm, either you will have to change dollars into pounds at a bank and send them to the British producer, or the British manufacturer will have to go to a bank and change your dollar check into pounds. In either case, purchasing the British shoes will involve an exchange of dollars for pounds.

Suppose the British producer has offered to supply the shoes for 30 pounds per pair. How can you determine whether this price is high or low? To compare the price of the British-supplied shoes with the price of those produced domestically, you must know the **exchange rate** between the dollar and the pound. *The exchange rate is one of the most important prices because it enables consumers in one country to translate the prices of foreign goods into units of their own currency. Specifically, the dollar price of a foreign good is determined by multiplying the foreign product price by the exchange rate (the dollar price per unit of the foreign currency).* For example, if it takes $1.50 to obtain 1 pound, then the British shoes priced at 30 pounds would cost $45 (30 times the $1.50 price of the pound).

Exchange rate
The domestic price of one unit of foreign currency. For example, if it takes $1.50 to purchase one English pound, the dollar-to-pound exchange rate is 1.50.

Suppose that the exchange rate is $1.50 = 1 pound and that you decide to buy 200 pairs of athletic shoes from the British manufacturer at 30 pounds ($45) per pair. You will need 6,000 pounds in order to pay the British manufacturer. If you contact an American bank that handles foreign exchange transactions and write the bank a check for $9,000 (the $1.50 exchange rate multiplied by 6,000), it will supply the 6,000 pounds. The bank will typically charge a small fee for handling the transaction.

Where does the American bank get the pounds? The bank obtains the pounds from British importers who want dollars to buy things from Americans. *Note that the U.S. demand for foreign currencies (such as the pound) is generated by the demand by Americans for things purchased from foreigners. On the other hand, the U.S. supply of foreign exchange reflects the demand by foreigners for things bought from Americans.*

Exhibit 1 presents data on the exchange rate—the cents required to purchase a European euro, Japanese yen, British pound, and Canadian dollar—during 1990–2003. Under the flexible rate system present in most industrial countries, the exchange rate between currencies changes from day to day and even from hour to hour. Thus, the annual exchange rate data given in Exhibit 1 are really averages for each year.

Appreciation
An increase in the value of the domestic currency relative to foreign currencies. An appreciation makes foreign goods cheaper for domestic residents.

An **appreciation** in the value of a nation's currency means that fewer units of the currency are now required to purchase one unit of a foreign currency. For example, as Exhibit 1 shows, it took 144.01 cents to purchase a British pound in 2001, down from 165.71 cents in 1998. As the result of this appreciation in the value of the dollar relative to the British

YEAR	EURO	JAPANESE YEN	BRITISH POUND	CANADIAN DOLLAR	INDEX OF EXCHANGE RATE VALUE OF THE DOLLAR[a]
1990		0.691	178.49	85.7	71.4
1992		0.789	176.42	82.7	76.9
1994		0.979	153.21	73.2	90.9
1996		0.919	156.16	73.3	97.5
1998		0.764	165.71	67.4	115.9
2000	92.3	0.927	151.59	67.3	119.4
2001	89.6	0.823	144.01	64.6	125.9
2002	94.5	0.798	150.24	63.7	126.8
2003	113.2	0.863	163.48	71.4	119.3

EXHIBIT 1
Foreign Exchange Rates, 1990–2003

[a]January 1997 = 100. In addition to the currencies listed above, the index also includes twenty-two other currencies.
Source: http://www.economagic.com.

pound, goods purchased from British suppliers became less expensive to Americans.[2] At the same time, the prices of American goods to British consumers moved in the opposite direction. An appreciation of the U.S. dollar relative to the British pound is the same thing as a depreciation in the British pound relative to the dollar.

When a **depreciation** occurs, it will take more units of the domestic currency to purchase a unit of foreign currency. Between 2001 and 2003, the dollar depreciated against the British pound (see Exhibit 1). In 2003, it took 163.48 cents to purchase a British pound, up from 144.01 in 2001. Similarly, it took 113.2 cents to purchase a euro in 2003, up from only 89.6 in 2001. As the number of cents required to purchase a foreign currency increases, the foreign goods become more expensive for Americans.

Exhibit 1 also provides an index of the foreign exchange value of the dollar against twenty-six major currencies. This broad index provides evidence of what is happening to the dollar's general exchange rate value.[3] An increase in the index implies an appreciation in the dollar, whereas a decline is indicative of a depreciation. Between 1996 and 2001, the dollar appreciated by approximately 30 percent against these twenty-six currencies. Between 2001 and 2003, however, the index indicates that the dollar depreciated by approximately 6 percent (down to 119.3 from 125.9) relative to this broad bundle of currencies. Frequently, people will use the terms "strong" and "weak" when referring to the exchange rate value of a currency. A currency is said to be strong when it has been appreciating in value; a weak currency is one that has been depreciating on the foreign exchange market.

A pure **flexible exchange rate** system is one in which market forces alone determine the foreign exchange value of the currency. The exchange rate system in effect since 1973 might best be described as a managed flexible-rate regime. It is flexible because all the major industrial countries allow the exchange rate value of their currencies to float. But the system is also "managed" because the major industrial nations have from time to time attempted to alter supply and demand in the foreign exchange market by buying and selling various currencies. Compared to the total size of this market, however, these transactions have generally been small. Thus, the exchange rate value of major currencies like the U.S. dollar, British pound, Japanese yen, and new European euro is determined primarily

Depreciation
A reduction in the value of the domestic currency relative to foreign currencies. A depreciation makes foreign goods more expensive for domestic residents.

Flexible exchange rates
Exchange rates that are determined by the market forces of supply and demand. They are sometimes called floating exchange rates.

[2]Because an appreciation means a lower price of foreign currencies, some may think it looks like a depreciation. Just remember that a lower price of the foreign currency means that one's domestic currency will buy more units of the foreign currency and thus more goods and services from foreigners.

[3]In the construction of this index, the exchange rate of each currency relative to the dollar is weighted according to the proportion of U.S. trade with the country. For example, the index weights the U.S. dollar–Japanese yen exchange rate more heavily than the U.S. dollar–Swiss franc exchange rate because the volume of U.S. trade with Japan exceeds the volume of trade with Switzerland.

by market forces. Several countries link their currency to major currencies like the U.S. dollar, English pound, or Japanese yen. As we proceed, we will investigate alternative methods of linking currencies and analyze the operation of different regimes.

DETERMINANTS OF THE EXCHANGE RATE

To simplify our explanation of how the exchange rate is determined, let's assume that the United States and Great Britain are the only two countries in the world. When Americans buy and sell with each other, they use dollars. Therefore, American sellers will want to be paid in dollars. Similarly, when the British buy and sell with each other, they use pounds. As a result, British sellers will want to be paid in pounds.

In our two-country world, the demand for pounds in the exchange rate market originates from the purchases by Americans of British goods, services, and assets (both real and financial). For example, when U.S. residents purchase men's suits from a British manufacturer, travel in the United Kingdom, or purchase the stocks, bonds, or physical assets of British business firms, they demand pounds from (and supply dollars to) the foreign exchange market to pay for these items.

Correspondingly, the supply of foreign exchange (pounds in our two-country case) originates from sales by Americans to foreigners. When Americans sell goods, services, or assets to the British, for example, the British buyers will supply pounds (and demand dollars) in the exchange rate market in order to acquire the dollars required to pay for the items they purchase from Americans.[4]

Exhibit 2 illustrates the demand and supply curves of Americans for foreign exchange—British pounds in our two-country case. The demand for pounds is downward

EXHIBIT 2
Equilibrium in the Foreign Exchange Market

The dollar price of the pound is measured on the vertical axis. The horizontal axis indicates the flow of pounds to the foreign exchange market. The equilibrium exchange rate is $1.50 = 1 pound. At the equilibrium price, the quantity of pounds demanded just equals the quantity supplied. A higher dollar price per pound ($1.80 = 1 pound) will lead to an excess supply of pounds, causing the dollar price of the pound to fall. On the other hand, a lower dollar price per pound ($1.20 = 1 pound) will result in an excess demand for pounds, causing the pound to appreciate.

[4]We analyze the foreign exchange market in terms of the demand for and supply of foreign currencies. Alternatively, this analysis could be done in terms of the supply of and demand for dollars. Since one currency is traded for another, the same actions that generate a demand for foreign exchange simultaneously generate a supply of dollars. Correspondingly, the same exchanges that create a supply of foreign currencies simultaneously generate a demand for dollars in the foreign exchange market.

sloping because a lower dollar price of the pound—meaning a dollar will buy more pounds—makes British goods cheaper for American importers. The goods produced by one country are generally good substitutes for the goods of another country. This means that when foreign (British) goods become cheaper, Americans will increase their expenditures on imports (and therefore the quantity of pounds demanded will increase). Thus, as the dollar price of the pound declines, Americans will both buy more of the lower-priced (in dollars) British goods and demand more pounds, which are required for the purchases.

Similarly, the supply curve for pounds is dependent on the sales by Americans to the British (that is, the purchase of American goods by the British). An increase in the dollar price of the pound means that a pound will purchase more dollars and more goods priced in dollars. Thus, the price (in pounds) of American goods, services, and assets to British purchasers declines as the dollar price of the pound increases. As this happens, the British will purchase more from Americans and therefore supply more pounds to the foreign exchange market. Thus, the supply curve for pounds will slope upward to the right.

As Exhibit 2 shows, equilibrium is present at the dollar price of the pound that brings the quantity demanded and quantity supplied of pounds into balance, $1.50 = 1 pound in this case. *The market-clearing price of $1.50 per pound not only equalizes demand and supply in the foreign exchange market, it also equalizes (1) the value of U.S. purchases of items supplied by the British with (2) the value of items sold by U.S. residents to the British.* Demand and supply in the currency market are merely the mirror images of these two factors.

What would happen if the price of the pound were above equilibrium—$1.80 = 1 pound, for example? At the higher dollar price of the pound, British goods would be more expensive for Americans. Americans would cut back on their purchases of shoes, glassware, textile products, financial assets, and other items supplied by the British, and the quantity of pounds demanded by Americans would therefore decline. Simultaneously, the higher dollar price of the pound would make U.S. exports cheaper for the British. For example, an $18,000 American automobile would cost British consumers 12,000 pounds when 1 pound trades for $1.50, but it would cost only 10,000 pounds when 1 pound exchanges for $1.80. If the dollar price of the pound were $1.80, the British would supply more pounds to the foreign exchange market than Americans would demand. As you can see in Exhibit 2, this excess supply of pounds would cause the dollar price of the pound to decline until equilibrium is restored at the $1.50 = 1 pound price.

At a price below equilibrium, such as $1.20 = 1 pound, an opposite set of forces would be present. The lower dollar price of the pound would make English goods cheaper for Americans and American goods more expensive for the British. At the $1.20 price for a pound, the purchases of Americans from the British would exceed their sales to them, leading to an excess demand for pounds. In turn, the excess demand would cause the dollar price of the pound to rise until equilibrium was restored at $1.50 = 1 pound.

The implications of the analysis are general. In our multicountry and multicurrency world, the demand for foreign currencies in exchange for dollars reflects the purchases by Americans of goods, services, and assets from foreigners. The supply of foreign currencies in exchange for dollars reflects the sales by Americans of goods, services, and assets to foreigners. The equilibrium exchange rate will bring the quantity of foreign exchange demanded by Americans into balance with the quantity supplied by foreigners. It will also bring the purchases by Americans from foreigners into balance with the sales by Americans to foreigners.

WHY DO EXCHANGE RATES CHANGE?

When exchange rates are free to fluctuate, the market value of a nation's currency will appreciate and depreciate in response to changing market conditions. Any change that alters the quantity of goods, services, or assets bought from foreigners relative to the quantity sold to them will alter the exchange rate. What types of change will alter the exchange-rate value of a currency?

EXHIBIT 3
The Growth of U.S. Income and Imports

Other things being constant, if incomes grow in the United States, U.S. imports will grow. The increase in the imports will increase the demand for pounds, causing the dollar price of the pound to rise (from $1.50 to $1.80).

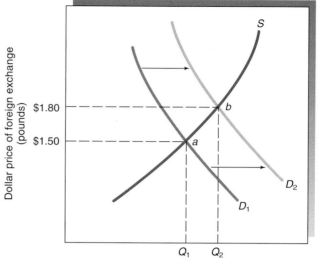

Quantity of foreign exchange (pounds)

Changes in Income

An increase in domestic income will encourage the nation's residents to spend a portion of their additional income on imports. When the income of a nation grows rapidly, the nation's imports tend to rise rapidly as well. As **Exhibit 3** illustrates, an increase in imports also increases the demand for foreign exchange (the pound in our two-country case). As the demand for pounds increases, the dollar price of the pound rises (from $1.50 to $1.80). This depreciation of the dollar reduces the incentive of Americans to import British goods and services, while increasing the incentive of the British to purchase U.S. exports. These two forces will restore equilibrium in the foreign exchange market at a new, higher dollar price of the pound.

Just the opposite takes place when the income of a trading partner (Great Britain in our example) increases. Rapid growth of income abroad will lead to an increase in U.S. exports, causing the supply of foreign exchange (and demand for dollars) to increase. This will cause the dollar to appreciate—the dollar price of the pound will fall, in other words.

What will happen if both countries are growing? Other things being constant, it is the relative growth rate that matters. A country that grows more rapidly than its trading partners will increase its imports relative to its exports, which will cause the exchange rate value of its currency to fall. Conversely, sluggish growth of a country's income relative to its trading partners will lead to a decline in imports relative to exports, which will cause the exchange rate value of its currency to rise. Granted, it seems paradoxical that sluggish growth relative to one's trading partners will cause a country's currency to appreciate, but that's in fact what happens.

Differences in Rates of Inflation

Other things being constant, domestic inflation will cause the value of a nation's currency to depreciate, whereas deflation will cause its currency to appreciate. Suppose that prices in the United States rise by 50 percent while our trading partners are experiencing stable prices. The domestic inflation will cause U.S. consumers to increase their demand for imported goods (and foreign currency). In turn, the inflated domestic prices will cause foreigners to reduce their purchases of U.S. goods, thereby reducing the supply of foreign currency to the exchange market. As **Exhibit 4** illustrates, the exchange rate will adjust to this set of circumstances. In our two-country example, the dollar will depreciate relative to the pound.

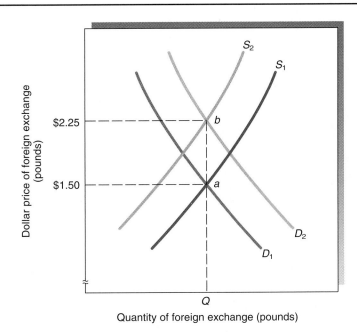

EXHIBIT 4
Inflation with Flexible Exchange Rates

If prices were stable in Britain while the price level increased 50 percent in the United States, the U.S. demand for British products (and pounds) would increase, whereas U.S. exports to Britain would decline, causing the supply of pounds to fall. These forces would cause the dollar to depreciate relative to the pound.

Exchange rate adjustments permit nations with even high rates of inflation to engage in trade with countries experiencing relatively stable prices.[5] A depreciation in a nation's currency in the foreign exchange market compensates for the nation's inflation rate. For example, if inflation increases the price level in the United States by 50 percent, and the value of the dollar in exchange for the pound depreciates (such that the value of the foreign currency increases 50 percent), then the prices of American goods measured in pounds are unchanged to British consumers. Thus, when the exchange rate value of the dollar changes from $1.50 = 1 pound to $2.25 = 1 pound, the depreciation in the dollar restores the original prices of U.S. goods to British consumers even though the price level in the United States has increased by 50 percent.

When domestic prices are increasing more rapidly than those of one's trading partners, the value of the domestic currency will tend to depreciate in the foreign exchange market. On the other hand, if a nation's inflation rate is lower than that of its trading partners, then its currency will tend to appreciate.

Changes in Interest Rates

Financial investments will be quite sensitive to changes in real interest rates—that is, interest rates adjusted for the expected rate of inflation. International loanable funds will tend to move toward areas where the expected real rate of return (after compensation for differences in risk) is highest. ***Thus, increases in real interest rates relative to a nation's trading partners will tend to cause that nation's currency to appreciate.*** For example, if real interest rates rise in the United States relative to Britain, British citizens will demand dollars (and supply their currency, pounds) in the foreign exchange market to purchase the high-yield American assets. The increase in demand for the dollar and supply of pounds will then cause the dollar to appreciate relative to the British pound.

[5]However, high rates of inflation are likely to cause greater variability in the foreign exchange value of a currency across time periods. In turn, this increased variability of the exchange rate will generate uncertainty and reduce the volume of international trade—particularly transactions involving a time dimension. Thus, exchange rate instability is generally harmful to the health of an economy.

An American consumer purchases an auto from a Japanese manufacturer.

An American vacationer buys a ticket on British Airways.

A foreign student pays tuition to Harvard.

A foreign investor purchases a bond from a U.S. corporation.

How will each of these transactions influence the demand for and supply of foreign currencies in exchange for the dollar?

In contrast, when real interest rates in other countries increase relative to rates in the United States, short-term financial investors will move to take advantage of the higher yields abroad. As investment funds move from the United States to other countries, there will be an increase in the demand for foreign currencies and an increase in the supply of dollars in the foreign exchange market. A depreciation in the dollar relative to the currencies of the countries with the higher real interest rates will be the result.

Changes in the Investment Climate

The inflow and outflow of capital will also be influenced by the quality of the investment environment. The monetary and legal climate is particularly important here. Countries that follow monetary policies consistent with price stability and establish legal systems that provide for the protection of property rights and evenhanded enforcement of contracts will tend to attract capital. In turn, the inflow of capital will strengthen the demand for the domestic currency and thereby cause it to appreciate. In contrast, when investors are concerned about the stability of the monetary climate and fairness of the legal system, they will move their financial capital elsewhere. This outflow of capital will cause the domestic currency to depreciate in the foreign exchange market.

Other things being constant, the currency of a country will tend to appreciate when its policy environment is improving. On the other hand, it will tend to depreciate if investors

THUMBNAIL SKETCH

What Factors Cause a Nation's Currency to Appreciate or Depreciate?

These factors will cause a nation's currency to appreciate:
1. Slow growth of income (relative to one's trading partners) that causes imports to lag behind exports
2. A rate of inflation that is lower than those of one's trading partners
3. Domestic real interest rates that are higher than real interest rates abroad
4. A shift toward sound policies that attract an inflow of capital

These factors will cause a nation's currency to depreciate:
1. Rapid growth of income (relative to one's trading partners) that stimulates imports relative to exports
2. A rate of inflation that is higher than those of one's trading partners
3. Domestic real interest rates that are lower than real interest rates abroad
4. Movement toward unsound policies that cause an outflow of capital

believe that the nation's policy environment is deteriorating. The accompanying Thumbnail Sketch summarizes the major forces that cause a nation's currency to appreciate or depreciate when exchange rates are determined by market forces.

INTERNATIONAL FINANCE AND ALTERNATIVE EXCHANGE RATE REGIMES

There are three major types of exchange rate regimes: (1) flexible rates, (2) fixed-rate, unified currency, and (3) pegged exchange rates. So far, we have focused on the operation of a flexible-rate regime. We now consider the other two.

Fixed-Rate, Unified Currency System

Obviously, the fifty states of the United States have a unified currency, the dollar. In addition, the U.S. dollar has been the official currency of Panama for almost a century. Ecuador adopted the U.S. dollar as its official currency in 2000, and El Salvador did so in 2001. The currency of Hong Kong is also closely linked to the U.S. dollar. Hong Kong has a **currency board** that has the power to create currency only in exchange for a specific quantity of U.S. dollars (7.7 HK dollars = 1 U. S. dollar).[6] Countries that adopt the currency board approach do not conduct monetary policy. Instead, they merely accept the monetary policy of the nation to which their currency is tied—the United States in the case of Hong Kong. Thus, the United States, Panama, Ecuador, El Salvador, and Hong Kong have a unified currency regime.

Twelve countries of the European Union—Austria, Belgium, Finland, France, Germany, Greece, Ireland, Italy, Luxembourg, Netherlands, Portugal, and Spain—have also established a unified currency regime. The official currency in each of these countries is the euro. In turn, the foreign exchange value of the euro relative to other currencies, such as the dollar and yen, is determined by market forces (flexible exchange rates).

Currency board
An entity that (1) issues a currency with a fixed designated value relative to a widely accepted currency (for example, the U.S. dollar), (2) promises to continue to redeem the issued currency at the fixed rate, and (3) maintains bonds and other liquid assets denominated in the other currency that provide 100 percent backing for all currency issued.

---

[6]A currency board like that of Hong Kong does two things. First, it issues domestic currency at a fixed rate in exchange for a designated foreign currency. Second, the foreign currency is then invested in bonds denominated in that currency. This means that the money issued by the currency board is backed 100 percent by the foreign currency. Therefore, the holders of the money issued by the currency board know that it will always have sufficient funds to exchange the domestic currency for the foreign one at the fixed rate. In essence, the country with a currency board accepts the monetary policy of the nation to which its currency is tied.

The distinguishing characteristic of a fixed-rate, unified currency regime is the presence of only one central bank with the power to expand and contract the supply of money. For the dollar, that central bank is the Federal Reserve System; for the euro, it is the European Central Bank. Those linking their currency at a fixed rate to the dollar or the euro are no longer in a position to conduct monetary policy. For example, the former central banks of the countries now using the euro no longer have the power to create money. In essence, they are now branches of the European Central Bank, much like the regional and district Federal Reserve banks are branches of the Fed.

A pure gold standard system, in which each country sets the value of its currency in terms of gold and fully backs its domestic money supply with gold, is also a fixed-rate, unified system. In this case, the world supply of gold (rather than a central bank) determines the total supply of money. If a country's purchases from foreigners exceeded its sales to them, its supply of gold would fall, which would reduce the domestic supply of money. This would put downward pressure on the domestic price level and bring the payments to and receipts from foreigners back into balance. Things would change in the opposite direction if a country was selling more to foreigners than it was purchasing from them. In this case, the excess of sales relative to purchases would lead to an inflow of gold, expansion in the domestic money supply, and higher domestic prices. International financial arrangements approximated those of a gold standard during the period between the American Civil War and the establishment of the Federal Reserve System in 1913.

Fixed exchange rate
An exchange rate that is set at a determined amount by government policy.

Between 1944 and 1971, most of the world operated under a system of **fixed exchange rates**, in which each nation fixed the price of its currency relative to others. In essence, this was a quasi-unified system. It was unified in the sense that the value of one currency was fixed relative to others over lengthy time periods. But it was not a fully unified system because each country continued to exercise control over its monetary policy. Nations maintained reserves with the **International Monetary Fund**, which could be drawn on when payments to foreigners exceeded receipts from them. This provided each with some leeway in its conduct of monetary policy. However, a country running persistent payment deficits would eventually deplete its reserves. This constrained the country's monetary independence and provided its policy makers with an incentive to keep its monetary policy approximately in line with that of its trading partners. Under this fixed exchange rate regime, nations often imposed tariffs, quotas, and other trade barriers in an effort to keep their payments and receipts in balance at the fixed rate. Various restrictions on the convertibility of currencies were also common. These problems eventually led to the demise of the system.

International Monetary Fund (IMF)
An international banking organization, currently with more than 180 member nations, designed to oversee the operation of the international monetary system. Although it does not control the world supply of money, it does hold currency reserves for member nations and makes currency loans to national central banks.

Pegged Exchange Rate Regime

A **pegged exchange rate system** is one in which a country commits itself to the maintenance of a specific exchange rate (or exchange rate range) relative to another currency (like the U.S. dollar) or a bundle of currencies. In contrast to the currency board approach, however, countries adopting the pegged exchange rate continue to conduct monetary policy. Thus, an excess of purchases from foreigners relative to sales to them does not automatically force the country to reduce its domestic money supply.

Pegged exchange rate system
A commitment to use monetary and fiscal policy to maintain the exchange rate value of the domestic currency at a fixed rate or within a narrow band relative to another currency (or bundle of currencies).

However, maintaining the pegged rate will restrict the independence of monetary policy. A country can either (1) follow an independent monetary policy and allow its exchange rate to fluctuate or (2) tie its monetary policy to maintain the fixed exchange rate. It cannot, however, maintain the convertibility of its currency at the fixed exchange rate while following a monetary policy more expansionary than the country to which its currency is tied. Attempts to do so will lead to a financial crisis—a situation in which falling foreign currency reserves eventually force the country to forgo the pegged exchange rate.

This is precisely what happened in Mexico during 1989–1994. Mexico promised to exchange the peso for the dollar at a pegged rate, but it also expanded its domestic money supply much more rapidly than the United States. In the early 1990s, this led to a higher rate of inflation in Mexico than in the United States. Responding to the different inflation rates, more and more people shifted away from the Mexican peso and toward the dollar. By December 1994, Mexico's foreign exchange reserves were virtually depleted. As a result, it could no longer maintain the fixed exchange rate with the dollar. Mexico devalued its currency, triggering a crisis that affected several other countries following similar policies.

More recently, much the same thing happened in Brazil and several Asian countries (Thailand, South Korea, Indonesia, and Malaysia). As Mexico did, these countries sought to maintain fixed exchange rates (or rates within a narrow band), while following monetary and fiscal policies that were inconsistent with the fixed rate. As their reserves declined, they were forced to abandon their exchange rate pegs. This was extremely disruptive to these economies. Imports suddenly became much more expensive and therefore less affordable. Businesses (including banks) that had borrowed money in dollars (or some other foreign currency) were unable to repay their loans as the result of the sharp decline in the exchange rate value of the domestic currency. These economies experienced sharp economic declines during 1997–1998.

Both economic theory and real-world experience indicate that either a purely flexible exchange rate regime or a fixed-rate unified regime with a single central bank will work reasonably well. On the other hand, a pegged exchange rate regime is something like a time bomb. Pushed by political considerations, monetary policy makers in most countries are unable to follow a course consistent with the maintenance of pegged rates. Failure to do so, however, eventually leads to abandonment of the peg and a financial crisis.

BALANCE OF PAYMENTS

Just as countries calculate their gross domestic product (GDP) so that they have a general idea of their domestic level of production, most countries also calculate their balance of international payments in order to keep track of transactions across national boundaries. The **balance of payments** summarizes the transactions of a country's citizens, businesses, and governments with foreigners. Balance-of-payments accounts are kept according to the principles of basic bookkeeping. Any transaction that creates a demand for foreign currency (and a supply of the domestic currency) in the foreign exchange market is recorded as a debit, or minus, item. Imports are an example of a debit item. Transactions that create a supply of foreign currency (and demand for the domestic currency) on the foreign exchange market are recorded as a credit, or plus, item. Exports are an example of a credit item. *Because the foreign exchange market will bring quantity demanded and quantity supplied into balance, it will also bring the total debits and total credits into balance.*

Exhibit 5 summarizes the balance-of-payments accounts of the United States for 2003. As the exhibit shows, the transactions can be grouped into one of three basic categories: the current account, capital account, or official reserve account. Let's take a look at each of these major categories.

Current-Account Transactions

Current-account transactions involve only current exchanges of goods and services and current income flows (and gifts). They do not involve changes in the ownership of either real or financial assets. **Current-account** transactions are dominated by the trade in goods and services. The export and import of merchandise goods are the largest components in the current account. When U.S. producers export their products, foreigners will supply their currency in exchange for dollars in order to pay for the U.S.-produced goods. Because U.S. exports generate a supply of foreign exchange and demand for dollars in the foreign exchange market, they are a credit (plus) item. In contrast, when Americans import goods, they will demand foreign currencies and supply dollars in the foreign exchange market. Thus, imports are a debit (minus) item.

In 2003, the United States exported $713.1 billion of merchandise goods, compared to imports of $1,260.7 billion. The difference between the value of a country's merchandise exports and the value of its merchandise imports is known as the **balance of merchandise trade** (or *balance of trade*). If the value of a country's merchandise exports

Balance of payments
A summary of all economic transactions between a country and all other countries for a specific time period, usually a year. The balance-of-payments account reflects all payments and liabilities to foreigners (debits) and all payments and obligations received from foreigners (credits).

Current account
The record of all transactions with foreign nations that involve the exchange of merchandise goods and services, current income derived from investments, and unilateral gifts.

Balance of merchandise trade
The difference between the value of merchandise exports and the value of merchandise imports for a nation. It is also called simply the *balance of trade* or *net exports*. The balance of merchandise trade is only one component of a nation's total balance of payments and its current account.

EXHIBIT 5
U.S. Balance of Payments, 2003 (in Billions of Dollars)

		DEBITS	CREDITS	BALANCE
CURRENT ACCOUNT				
1	U.S. merchandise exports		713.1	
2	U.S. merchandise imports	−1260.7		
3	Balance of merchandise trade (1 + 2)			−547.6
4	U.S. service exports		307.4	
5	U.S. service imports	−256.3		
6	Balance on service trade (4 + 5)			51.1
7	Balance on goods and services (3 + 6)			−496.5
8	Income receipts of Americans from abroad		294.4	
9	Income receipts of foreigners in the United States	−261.1		
10	Net income receipts			33.3
11	Net unilateral transfers			−67.4
12	Balance on current account (7 + 10 + 11)			−530.6
CAPITAL ACCOUNT				
13	Foreign investment in the United States (capital inflow)		580.6	
14	U.S. investment abroad (capital outflow)[a]	−297.1		
15	Balance on capital account (13 + 14)			283.5
OFFICIAL RESERVE TRANSACTIONS				
16	U.S. official reserve assets	−1.5		
17	Foreign official assets in the U.S.		248.6	
18	Balance, Official Reserve Account (16 + 17)			247.1
19	Total (12 + 15 + 18)			0.0

[a]Statistical discrepancy is included in this figure.
Source: http://www.economagic.com.

falls short of the value of its merchandise imports, it is said to have a balance-of-trade deficit. In contrast, the situation in which a nation exports more than it imports is referred to as a trade surplus. In 2003, the United States ran a merchandise-trade deficit of $547.6 billion (line 3 of Exhibit 5).

The export and import of services are also sizable. Service trade involves the exchange of items like insurance, transportation, banking services, and items supplied to foreign tourists. Like the export of merchandise goods, service exports generate a supply of foreign exchange and demand for dollars. For example, a Mexican business that is insured by an American company will supply pesos and demand dollars to pay its premiums for the service. Thus, service exports are recorded as credits in the balance-of-payment accounts of exporting nations. On the other hand, the import of services from foreigners generates a demand for foreign currency and a supply of dollars in the exchange market. Therefore, service imports are a debit item.

As Exhibit 5 illustrates, in 2003, U.S. service exports were $307.4 billion, compared with service imports of $256.3 billion. Thus, the United States ran a $51.1 billion surplus on its service trade transactions (line 6 of Exhibit 5). When we add the balance of service exports and imports to the balance of merchandise trade, we obtain the **balance on goods and services**. In 2003, the United States ran a $496.5 billion deficit (the sum of the $547.6 billion merchandise-trade deficit and the $51.1 billion service surplus) in the goods and services account.

Balance on goods and services
The exports of goods (merchandise) and services of a nation minus its imports of goods and services.

Two other relatively small items are also included in current-account transactions: (1) net income from investments and (2) unilateral transfers. Americans have made substantial investments in stocks, bonds, and real assets in other countries. As these investments abroad generate income, dollars will flow from foreigners to Americans. This flow of income to Americans will supply foreign currency (and create a demand for dollars) in the foreign exchange market. Thus, the net income to Americans is entered as a credit in the U.S. current account. Correspondingly, foreigners earn income from their investments in the United States. This net income to foreigners is recorded as a debit in the U.S. current account because the supply of dollars to the foreign exchange market creates a demand for foreign exchange.

As Exhibit 5 shows, in 2003, Americans earned $294.4 billion from investments abroad, while foreigners earned $261.1 billion from their investments in the United States. On balance, Americans earned $33.3 billion more on their investments abroad than foreigners earned on their investments in the United States. This $33.3 billion net inflow of investment income reduced the size of the deficit on current-account transactions.

Gifts to foreigners, such as U.S. aid to a foreign government or private gifts from U.S. residents to their relatives abroad, generate a demand for foreign currencies and supply of dollars in the foreign exchange market. Thus, they are a debit item. Correspondingly, gifts to Americans from foreigners are a credit item. Because the U.S. government and private U.S. citizens gave $67.4 billion more to foreigners than we received from them, this net unilateral transfer was entered as a debit item on the current account in 2003.

Balance on Current Account

The difference between (1) the value of a country's current exports (both goods and services) and earnings from its investments abroad and (2) the value of its current imports (again, both goods and services) and the earnings of foreigners on their domestic assets (plus net unilateral transfers to foreigners) is known as the **balance on current account**. The current-account balance provides a summary of all current-account transactions. As with the balance of trade, when the value of the current-account debit items (import-type transactions) exceeds the value of the credit items (export-type transactions), we say that the country is running a current-account deficit. Alternatively, if the credit items are greater than the debit items, the country is running a current-account surplus. In 2003, the United States ran a current-account deficit of $530.6 billion.

Because trade in goods and services dominates current-account transactions, the trade and current-account balances are closely related. Countries with large trade deficits (surpluses) almost always run substantial current-account deficits (surpluses).

Capital Account Transactions

In contrast with current-account transactions, **capital account** transactions focus on changes in the ownership of real and financial assets. These transactions are composed of (1) direct investments by Americans in real assets abroad (or by foreigners in the United States) and (2) loans to and from foreigners. When foreigners make investments in the United States—for example, by purchasing stocks, bonds, or real assets from Americans—their actions will supply foreign currency and generate a demand for dollars in the foreign exchange market. Thus, these capital inflow transactions are a credit.

On the other hand, capital outflow transactions are recorded as debits. For example, if a U.S. investor purchases a shoe factory in Mexico, the Mexican seller will want to be paid in pesos. The U.S. investor will supply dollars (and demand pesos) on the foreign exchange market. Since U.S. citizens will demand foreign currency (and supply dollars) when they invest in stocks, bonds, and real assets abroad, these transactions enter into the balance-of-payments accounts as a debit. In 2003, foreign investments in the United States (capital inflow) summed to $580.6 billion, while U.S. investments abroad (capital

Balance on current account
The import-export balance of goods and services, plus net investment income earned abroad, plus net private and government transfers. If the value of the nation's export-type items exceeds the value of the nation's import-type items plus net unilateral transfers to foreigners, a current-account surplus is present. If the value of a nation's export-type items is less than the value of the nation's import-type items plus net unilateral transfers to foreigners, a current-account deficit is present.

Capital account
The record of transactions with foreigners that involve either (1) the exchange of ownership rights to real or financial assets or (2) the extension of loans.

outflow) totaled $297.1 billion.[7] Since the capital inflow exceeded the outflow, the United States ran a $283.5 billion capital account surplus in 2003.

Official Reserve Account

Official reserve account
The record of transactions between central banks.

As we noted earlier, the current exchange rate regime is not a pure flexible-rate system. Countries with pegged exchange rates will often engage in official reserve transactions in an effort to maintain their pegged rate. These transactions are debited and credited in a country's **official reserve account**. Even countries with flexible exchange rates may engage in official reserve transactions in order to influence their exchange rate. When a nation's currency is appreciating rapidly, a country may try to slow the appreciation by purchasing foreign financial assets. Conversely, when a currency is depreciating, the country may attempt to halt the depreciation by using some of its foreign currency reserves to purchase the domestic currency in the foreign exchange market. Because of the credibility and widespread use of the U.S. dollar, these official reserve transactions often involve assets denominated in dollars, particularly bonds issued by the U.S. Treasury.

Although these official reserve transactions are modest relative to the size of the foreign exchange market, in dollar terms they are sizable. In 2003, U.S. purchases of foreign reserves were small, only $1.5 billion. But the foreign purchases of dollar assets, mostly Treasury bonds, were $248.6 billion.[8] Thus, the United States ran a surplus of $247.1 billion on official reserve transactions in 2003.

The impact on the U.S. economy of the purchases of U.S. financial assets by foreign central banks is much like that of other capital inflows. These foreign purchases, like other capital inflows, will result in a higher exchange rate value of the dollar and lower domestic interest rates than would otherwise be the case. Domestic interest rates will fall because the capital inflow will raise the supply of loanable funds. Like capital account surpluses, official reserve account surpluses reflect positively on the U.S. economy. If foreign central banks did not have confidence in both the economy and the monetary policy of the United States, they would not want to purchase and hold U.S. financial assets.

The Balance of Payments Must Balance

The sum of the debit and credit items of the balance-of-payments accounts must balance. Thus, the following identity must hold:

$$\text{Current-Account Balance} + \text{Capital Account Balance} + \text{Official Reserve Account Balance} = 0$$

However, the specific components of the accounts need not balance. For example, the debit and credit items of the current account need not be equal. Specific components may run either a surplus or a deficit. Nevertheless, since the balance of payments as a whole must balance, a deficit in one area implies a surplus in another. Similarly, even though market forces will bring about an overall balance, there is no reason to expect that the trade flows between any two countries will be in balance. See the accompanying Myths of Economics box feature on this topic.

---

[7]The statistical discrepancy is also included in the investments abroad category. This item was approximately $12 billion in 2003. International transactions—particularly those conducted in cash—can be difficult to monitor. As we noted when discussing the money supply, 60 percent or more of the U.S. currency supply circulates abroad. Because this "outflow" of currency is not included in balance-of-payments accounts, such movements would contribute to the statistical discrepancy. Illegal drug trade may also increase the size of this item.

[8]Official reserve purchases of dollar assets in 2003 were substantially larger than in other recent years. Approximately 80 percent of these purchases were undertaken by three countries—China, Japan, and Taiwan. China has a pegged exchange rate and its purchases reflect its desire to maintain the pegged rate. The dollar was depreciating against the yen in 2003, and the Japanese purchases reflect an effort to slow this process. Finally, most believe that the official reserve purchases of Taiwan reflect its desire to increase the credibility of its currency during a time of uncertainty about its future relationship with mainland China.

MYTHS IN ECONOMICS

"If other countries are treating us fairly, our exports to them should be approximately equal to our imports from them."

Many American politicians like to bash countries like Japan and China that export much more to us than they import from us. Some have even called for tariffs, quotas, and other trade restraints designed to bring imports and exports with these countries into balance. This view is based on a misconception about bilateral trade balances. Flexible exchange rates will bring total purchases from foreigners into balance with total sales to them. However, there is no reason to expect imports and exports to any specific country to be in balance with each other any more than we would expect the trade between individuals to balance.

Consider the trade "deficits" and "surpluses" of a doctor who likes to golf. The doctor can be expected to run a trade deficit with sporting goods stores, golf caddies, and course operators. Why? These suppliers sell items that the golfer-doctor purchases in sizable quantities. The doctor, on the other hand, probably sells few items that the sporting goods store purchases. Similarly, the doctor can be expected to run trade surpluses with medical insurers, elderly patients, and those with chronic illnesses. These trading partners are major purchasers of the services provided by the doctor, although the doctor might purchase very little from them.

The same principles are at work across nations. A nation will tend to run trade deficits with countries that are low-cost suppliers of items it imports and trade surpluses with countries that buy a lot of the things it exports. This is the major factor underlying the large U.S. bilateral trade deficits with Japan and China. Japan is a major importer of resources like oil and a major exporter of high-tech manufacturing goods. Americans import a lot of the latter, but they export very little of the former. Thus, we tend to run bilateral trade deficits with Japan. Similarly, China is a low-cost producer of labor-intensive items like toys and textile products, items that are costly for a high-wage country like the United States to produce domestically. On the other hand, the United States is a low-cost producer of high-tech products and grains like wheat and corn that are purchased in only small quantities by poor countries like China. These factors underlie the U.S. bilateral trade deficit with China.

In recent years, the United States has run trade surpluses with the Netherlands, Australia, Belgium, Luxembourg, Brazil, and the United Kingdom. Do these bilateral trade surpluses indicate that the United States treats these countries unfairly? Of course not. The surpluses merely reflect that these countries import substantial amounts of items supplied economically by U.S. producers and export only small amounts of items imported intensively by Americans. It might make for good politics to bash those with whom we run bilateral trade deficits, but the argument is nonetheless based on unsound economic analysis.

If a nation is experiencing a current-account deficit, it must experience an offsetting surplus on the sum of its capital account and official reserve account balances. This has been the case for the United States in recent years.

In 2003, the United States ran a $530.6 billion current-account deficit and a $283.5 billion capital account surplus. The difference between these two figures—a $247.1 billion deficit—was exactly offset by a $247.1 billion surplus in the official reserve account. Thus, the deficits and surpluses of the current-, capital, and official reserve accounts summed to zero, as shown in Exhibit 5 (line 19).

Under a pure flexible-rate system, official reserve transactions would be zero. Under these conditions, a capital account surplus (inflow of capital) would mean that the current account must have a deficit. Similarly, a capital account deficit (outflow of capital) would mean that the current account must have a surplus.

With flexible exchange rates, changes in the net inflow of capital will influence the current-account balance. If a nation is experiencing an increase in net foreign investment, perhaps as the result of attractive investment opportunities, this increase in the capital account surplus (inflow of capital) will enlarge the current-account deficit. In contrast, capital flight (outflow of capital) will move the current account toward a surplus.

ARE TRADE DEFICITS BAD AND TRADE SURPLUSES GOOD?

The word "deficit" suggests things like excessive spending relative to income, bank overdrafts, indebtedness, and a future day of reckoning. Thus, there is an understandable tendency to believe that trade deficits must be bad and surpluses good. However, factors that often lead to trade deficits provide reason for caution. A trade deficit is present when a nation's imports exceed its exports. Many times, this occurs because a nation is growing more rapidly than its trading partners. Rapid domestic growth stimulates imports, while slow growth abroad weakens demand for a nation's exports. This combination often causes a trade deficit. Trade deficits can also result because an economy offers more attractive investment opportunities than are available elsewhere. The attractive investment environment will lead to an inflow of capital, which will cause the nation's currency to appreciate. In turn, the currency appreciation will stimulate imports relative to exports and thereby shift the trade balance toward a deficit. In essence, trade (and current account) deficits are the flip side of capital inflows. Thus, rapid economic growth and an attractive investment environment—both of which are generally associated with a strong economy—are major causes of trade (and current account) deficits.

Exhibit 6 presents data on the foreign exchange value of the dollar, current-account balance, and inflow of capital for the United States over the last three decades. (*Note:* Although the data in the middle frame are for the current-account balance, the trade balance figures would be virtually identical because trade in goods and services is the dominant component of the current account.) The link between the inflow of capital and the current-account deficit is clearly visible. Prior to 1981, net foreign investment in the United States was relatively small and so too was the current-account deficit. However, as the U.S. economy grew briskly following the 1982 recession, net foreign investment (bottom panel) in the United States increased sharply. Simultaneously, the U.S. dollar appreciated and the current-account deficit widened. As the U.S. economy slowed during the late 1980s and the recession of the early 1990s, net capital inflow fell to a trickle, and the current account actually registered a small surplus in 1991. But as the U.S. economy recovered from the 1990 recession and and grew rapidly during the 1990s, once again net foreign investment increased substantially, the U.S. dollar appreciated, and the current account moved toward a large deficit.

As the middle and lower panels illustrate, net foreign investment (net inflow of capital) and the current-account deficit are almost mirror images. When net foreign investment increases, the current-account (trade) balance shifts toward a deficit. Correspondingly, when net foreign investment shrinks, so, too, does the current-account deficit. This is the expected outcome under a flexible-rate system. With flexible rates, the overall payments to and receipts from foreigners must balance. Thus, a deficit in one area is not an isolated event. If a nation runs a current-account (trade) deficit, it must also run a capital account surplus of equal magnitude.

Can a country continue to run current-account (and trade) deficits? Perhaps surprisingly, the answer is "Yes." Trade deficits are primarily a reflection of the inflow of capital. The inflow can and will continue as long as investors find the U.S. economy an attractive place in which to invest. Foreigners will be happy to supply investment capital to the U.S. economy as long as they can earn competitive returns. And there is no reason why this cannot continue indefinitely. The historical evidence is consistent with this view. The United States experienced trade deficits and capital inflows year after year from 1820 to 1870. During that period, investment opportunities in the New World were more attractive than those in Europe, so Europeans were quite willing to continue financing undertakings in the New World.

When considering the significance of the U.S. trade deficit, one should keep two points in mind: First, no legal entity is responsible for the trade deficit. It reflects an aggregation of the voluntary choices of businesses and individuals.[9] Thus, it is not like a

---

[9]As the late Herbert Stein, a former chairman of the President's Council of Economic Advisers, once put it: "The trade deficit does not belong to any individual or institution. It is a pure-statistical aggregate, like the number of eggs laid in the U.S. or the number of bald-headed men living here." See Herbert Stein, "Leave the Trade Deficit Alone," *Wall Street Journal*, March 11, 1987.

EXHIBIT 6
The Exchange Rate, Current-Account Balance, and Net Foreign Investment

Here we show the relationship between the exchange rate, the current-account deficit, and net foreign investment (capital inflow). The shaded areas represent recessions.

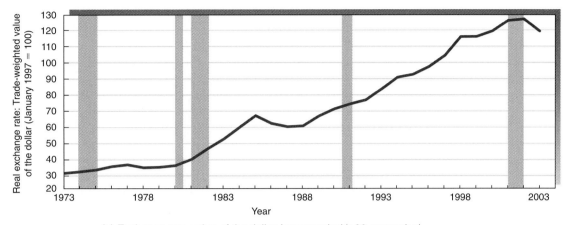

(a) Exchange-rate value of the dollar (compared with 26 currencies)

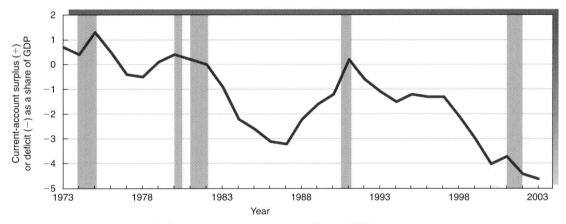

(b) Current-account balance as a share of GDP

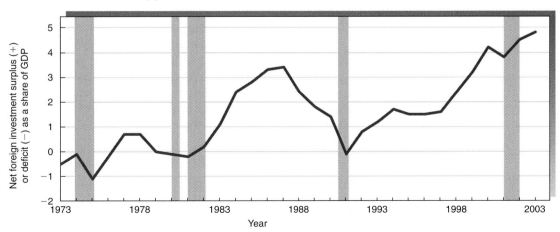

(c) Net foreign investment as a share of GDP

Note: Data are given in billions of dollars.
Source: http://www.bea.doc.gov and http://www.stls.frb.org.

business loss or even the budget deficit of a government. Second, the U.S. economy is characterized by a relatively stable monetary and legal environment and tax rates that are generally lower than other high-income industrial countries. This makes the United States an attractive place in which to invest. At the same time, the savings rate of the United States is low and the growth of the labor force more rapid than in Japan and Europe. To a large degree, the U.S. current-account deficit reflects this combination of factors—an attractive domestic investment environment, labor force growth, and a low saving rate. As long as these conditions remain in place, the trade deficit is likely to continue.

The Future

The shape of financial and exchange rate regimes is likely to change substantially in the years ahead. Much of Europe has already moved toward a unified currency. As the euro gains credibility, other European countries are likely to adopt the euro as their domestic currency as well. It would not be surprising to see a similar trend in North and South America. Brazil, Mexico, and several other countries in the Americas may well seek currency stability through some form of linkage with the dollar. A substantial share of international trade is also conducted in Japanese yen. In the future, the dollar, euro, and yen, perhaps along with two or three other currencies, may well emerge as the dominant currencies used throughout the world for domestic and international trade. These developments make this an exciting time to follow international finance.

KEY POINTS

▼ Because countries generally use different currencies, international trade usually involves the conversion of one currency to another. The currencies of different countries are bought and sold in the foreign exchange market. The exchange rate is the price of one national currency in terms of another.

▼ The dollar demand for foreign exchange arises from the purchase (import) of goods, services, and assets by Americans from foreigners. The supply of foreign currency in exchange for dollars arises from the sale (export) of goods, services, and assets by Americans to foreigners. The equilibrium exchange rate will bring these two forces into balance.

▼ With flexible exchange rates, the following will cause a nation's currency to appreciate: (1) rapid growth of income abroad (and/or slow domestic growth), (2) low inflation (relative to one's trading partners), (3) rising domestic real interest rates (and/or falling rates abroad), and (4) improvement in the investment

environment. The reverse of these conditions will cause a nation's currency to depreciate.

▼ There are three major types of exchange rate regimes: (1) flexible rates, (2) fixed-rate, unified currency, and (3) pegged exchange rates. Both flexible-rate and fixed-rate, unified currency systems work quite well. Pegged-rate systems, however, often lead to problems because they require that the nation follow a monetary policy consistent with maintaining the pegged rate. Political pressure often makes this difficult to do.

▼ The balance-of-payments accounts provide a summary of transactions with foreigners. There are three major balance-of-payments components: (1) the current account, (2) capital account, and (3) official reserve account. The balances of these three components must sum to zero, but the individual components of the accounts need not be in balance.

▼ Under a pure flexible-rate system, there will be no official reserve account transactions. Under these circumstances, the current and capital accounts must balance. Therefore, an inflow of capital will shift the current account toward a deficit, while an outflow of capital will move the current account toward a surplus.

▼ There is no reason to believe that trade deficits are bad and surpluses good. Countries that grow rapidly and follow policies that investors find attractive will tend to experience an inflow of capital and a trade deficit.

▼ There is no reason to expect that bilateral trade between countries will balance.

CRITICAL ANALYSIS QUESTIONS

*1. If the dollar depreciates relative to the Japanese yen, how will this affect the dollar price of a Japanese camera produced by Nikon, for example? How will this change influence the quantity of Nikon cameras purchased by Americans?

2. How will the purchases of items from foreigners compare with the sales of items to foreigners when the foreign exchange market is in equilibrium? Explain.

3. Will a flexible exchange rate bring the imports of goods and services into balance with the exports of goods and services? Why or why not?

*4. The accompanying chart indicates an actual newspaper quotation of the exchange rate of various currencies. On February 2, did the dollar appreciate or depreciate against the British pound? How did it fare against the Canadian dollar?

	U.S. Dollar Equivalent	
	February 1	**February 2**
British pound	1.755	1.746
Canadian dollar	0.6765	0.6775

*5. Suppose that the exchange rate between the United States and Mexico freely fluctuates in the open market. Indicate whether each of the following would cause the dollar to appreciate or depreciate relative to the peso.
   a. An increase in the quantity of drilling equipment purchased in the United States by Pemex, the Mexican oil company, as a result of a Mexican oil discovery
   b. An increase in the U.S. purchase of crude oil from Mexico as a result of the development of Mexican oil fields
   c. Higher real interest rates in Mexico, inducing U.S. citizens to move their financial investments from U.S. to Mexican banks

   d. Lower real interest rates in the United States, inducing Mexican investors to borrow dollars and then exchange them for pesos
   e. Inflation in the United States and stable prices in Mexico
   f. An increase in the inflation rate from 2 percent to 10 percent in both the United States and Mexico
   g. An economic boom in Mexico that induces Mexicans to buy more U.S.-made automobiles, trucks, electric appliances, and television sets
   h. Attractive investment opportunities in Mexico that induce U.S. investors to buy stock in Mexican firms

6. Explain why the current-account balance and capital account balance must sum to zero under a pure flexible-rate system.

7. Rapidly growing strong economies often experience trade deficits, whereas economies with sluggish growth often have trade surpluses. Can you explain this puzzle?

*8. In recent years, a substantial share of the domestic capital formation in the United States has been financed by foreign investors. Is this dependence on foreign capital dangerous? What would happen if the inflow of foreign capital came to a halt?

*9. Suppose that the United States were running a current-account deficit. How would each of the following changes influence the size of the current-account deficit?
   a. A recession in the United States
   b. A decline in the attractiveness of investment opportunities in the United States
   c. An improvement in investment opportunities abroad

10. Several politicians have suggested that the federal government should run a sizable budget surplus during the next decade in order to "save Social Security." If the federal government ran a sizable budget surplus in the years immediately ahead, what impact would this have on interest rates, the inflow of capital, the current-account deficit, and the foreign exchange value of the dollar? Explain the reasoning underlying your answer.

*11. If foreigners have confidence in the U.S. economy and therefore move to expand their investments in the United States, how will the U.S. current-account balance be affected? How will the exchange rate value of the dollar be affected?

12. Is a trade surplus indicative of a strong, healthy economy? Why or why not?

*13. "Changes in exchange rates will automatically direct a country to a current-account balance under a flexible exchange rate system." Is this statement true or false?

*14. In recent years, many American political figures have been highly critical of the fact that U.S. imports from Japan have consistently exceeded U.S. exports to Japan.
   a. Under a flexible exchange rate system, is there any reason to expect that the imports from a given country will tend to equal the exports to that country?
   b. Can you think of any reason why the United States might persistently run a trade deficit with a country such as Japan?

*15. In recent years, the central banks of both Japan and China have purchased large amounts of U.S. Treasury bonds. These purchases increase the exchange rate value of the dollar relative to the Japanese yen and Chinese yuan. Are these purchases harmful to the U.S. economy? Why or why not?

*Asterisk denotes questions for which answers are given in Appendix B.

Selected Economic Indicators:
An International Comparison

ADDENDUM

EXHIBIT A1.
Income, Growth, and Other Indicators of Economic Performance

Here we present data on 2002 per capita GDP, growth of income per person (1990–2002), inflation, investment rate, and economic freedom for fifty-nine countries. Which countries had the highest income levels in 2002? Which grew the most rapidly? What were the inflation rates, investment levels, and economic freedom values of the countries with the highest income levels and growth rates?

	POPULATION 2002 (IN MILLIONS)	PER CAPITA GDP 2002, U.S. DOLLARS (a)	REAL GROWTH OF PER CAPITA GDP 1990–2002	ANNUAL RATE OF INFLATION 1990–2002 (b)	INVESTMENT (% OF GDP) 1990–2002	ECONOMIC FREEDOM INDEX, 2002 (c)
HIGH-INCOME INDUSTRIAL						
Australia	19.7	28,260	2.3	1.9	22.5	7.9
Austria	8.0	29,220	1.8	1.9	23.4	7.5
Belgium	10.3	27,570	1.6	2.0	20.5	7.4
Canada	31.4	29,480	1.7	1.6	19.6	7.9
Denmark	5.4	30,940	1.9	2.0	19.1	7.6
Finland	5.2	26,190	1.5	2.0	20.2	7.7
France	59.5	26,920	1.4	1.6	19.7	6.8
Germany	82.5	27,100	1.3	1.9	22.0	7.3
Hong Kong	6.8	26,910	2.5	2.5	28.2	8.7
Ireland	3.9	36,360	6.1	3.8	19.6	7.8
Italy	57.7	26,430	1.4	3.7	19.3	7.0
Japan	127.2	26,940	1.0	−0.2	28.4	7.0
Netherlands	16.1	29,100	1.9	2.5	21.5	7.7
Singapore	4.2	24,040	3.6	0.9	33.6	8.6
Spain	40.9	21,460	2.2	4.2	23.5	7.1
Sweden	8.9	26,050	1.5	2.1	17.6	7.3
Switzerland	7.3	30,010	0.1	1.5	21.4	8.2
United Kingdom	59.2	26,150	2.0	3.0	16.9	8.2
United States	288.4	35,750	1.7	2.1	18.1	8.2
AFRICA						
Botswana	1.7	8,170	2.5	8.4	26.4	7.4
Cameroon	15.8	2,000	−0.6	3.8	16.5	5.6
Cote d'Ivoire	16.5	1,520	−0.9	6.8	11.7	5.8
Ghana	20.3	2,130	1.9	25.5	20.5	6.3
Kenya	31.3	1,020	−0.9	12.5	15.5	6.4
Mauritius	1.2	10,810	4.1	6.1	26.3	7.2
Nigeria	132.8	860	−0.3	25.5	19.8	5.7
South Africa	45.3	10,070	−0.2	9.6	16.0	6.8
Tanzania	35.2	580	0.8	17.9	19.9	6.3
Zambia	10.2	840	−1.1	49.4	13.7	6.6
Zimbabwe	13.0	2,370	−1.9	37.3	17.6	3.4

(continued)

EXHIBIT A1. (continued)

	POPULATION 2002 (IN MILLIONS)	PER CAPITA GDP 2002, U.S. DOLLARS (a)	REAL GROWTH OF PER CAPITA GDP 1990–2002	ANNUAL RATE OF INFLATION 1990–2002 (b)	INVESTMENT (% OF GDP) 1990–2002	ECONOMIC FREEDOM INDEX, 2002 (c)
ASIA						
Bangladesh	135.7	1,700	3.0	3.7	20.0	5.9
China	1280.4	4,580	8.6	5.3	34.3	5.7
India	1048.6	2,670	3.6	7.2	22.3	6.3
Indonesia	211.7	3,230	2.6	13.8	25.4	5.8
Malaysia	24.3	9,120	3.7	3.2	33.6	6.5
Pakistan	144.9	1,940	1.2	8.7	16.3	5.7
Philippines	79.9	4,170	0.9	8.2	21.7	6.6
Korea, Rep.	47.6	16,950	5.0	4.4	33.4	7.1
Thailand	61.6	7,010	3.5	3.4	32.9	6.7
SOUTH/CENTRAL AMERICA						
Argentina	36.5	10,880	1.4	10.8	17.5	5.8
Brazil	174.5	7,770	1.1	157.6	19.8	6.2
Chile	15.6	9,820	4.3	7.7	23.0	7.3
Colombia	43.7	6,370	0.5	18.4	17.4	5.3
Dominican Republic	8.6	6,640	3.7	11.0	22.4	6.6
Guatemala	12.0	4,080	1.1	10.7	15.6	6.4
Mexico	100.8	8,970	1.3	15.9	19.2	6.5
Peru	26.7	5,010	1.9	30.1	20.1	6.8
Venezuela	25.1	5,380	−1.0	36.5	17.1	4.6
MIDDLE EAST/ MEDITERRANEAN						
Egypt	66.4	3,810	2.1	7.8	18.7	6.2
Greece	10.6	18,720	2.2	8.5	21.2	6.9
Iran	65.5	6,690	2.8	24.6	23.9	6.0
Israel	6.6	19,530	1.4	8.9	22.0	6.6
Syria	17.0	3,620	2.2	6.5	22.3	5.4
Turkey	69.6	6,390	1.1	67.7	23.2	5.5
EASTERN EUROPE						
Bulgaria	8.0	7,130	0.0	74.1	15.6	6.0
Hungary	10.2	13,400	1.4	17.6	21.6	7.3
Poland	38.6	10,560	3.1	20.5	20.6	6.4
Romania	22.3	6,560	−0.4	87.9	19.5	5.4
Russia	144.1	8,230	−2.3	130.8	20.1	5.0

Source: World Bank, *World Development Indicators CD-ROM,* 2004; and James Gwartney and Robert Lawson, *Economic Freedom of the World, 2004 Annual Report* (Vancouver: Fraser Institute, 2004).

(a) These figures were derived by the purchasing power parity method.

(b) The GDP deflator was used to derive the compound annual rate of inflation during the period.

(c) For the 123 countries covered by the index, the ratings ranged from a low of 2.5 to a high of 8.7. Higher ratings indicate that the institutions and policies of the country are more consistent with those of market organization.

EXHIBIT A2
The Growth of International Trade as a Share of the Economy, 1980–2002: A Cross-Country Comparison

Here we show the size of the trade sector (exports plus imports) as a share of GDP in 1980, 1990, and 2002. The final column indicates the growth of trade as a share of GDP during the period. The countries are arrayed from the highest to lowest growth of trade (as a share of the economy). Review the countries with the most rapid growth of the trade sector in recent decades. Has trade been growing?

	TRADE (EXPORTS + IMPORTS) AS A PERCENT OF GDP			% CHANGE IN TRADE AS A SHARE OF GDP, 1980–2002
	1980	1990	2002	
Ghana	17.6	42.7	97.5	453.3
China	15.5	31.9	54.8	253.7
Argentina	11.5	15.0	40.5	250.7
Turkey	17.1	30.9	59.7	249.5
Mexico	23.7	38.3	56.4	138.1
Thailand	54.5	75.8	122.2	124.2
Iran	29.7	45.5	60.3	102.6
India	15.7	15.7	30.8	95.8
Malaysia	111.0	147.0	210.7	89.9
Philippines	52.0	60.8	98.4	89.0
Spain	32.0	36.0	58.5	83.1
Ireland	106.5	109.3	181.6	70.5
Bulgaria	66.4	69.8	112.9	70.0
Nigeria	48.6	72.2	81.3	67.3
Hong Kong	179.2	256.7	293.3	63.7
Hungary	80.3	59.7	131.1	63.2
Canada	54.6	52.0	82.5	51.0
Germany	45.8	50.2	67.0	46.5
Brazil	20.4	15.2	29.4	44.5
Bangladesh	23.4	19.7	33.3	42.5
Austria	74.1	78.0	103.1	39.1
Sweden	58.3	57.4	80.5	38.1
Chile	49.8	66.0	68.0	36.5
Belgium	118.5	139.7	160.5	35.4
Colombia	31.8	35.4	40.7	28.2
Denmark	65.5	66.6	83.9	28.0
Australia	33.0	33.5	41.8	26.4
Dominican Republic	48.1	77.5	60.6	25.9
France	43.2	43.5	52.1	20.5
Syria	54.8	56.3	65.1	18.8
Indonesia	54.4	49.1	63.9	17.6
Italy	46.1	39.4	52.8	14.5
United States	20.7	20.6	23.6	14.2
Netherlands	103.8	104.6	118.1	13.9
Mauritius	104.4	135.6	117.5	12.5
Switzerland	72.8	72.0	81.8	12.4
Korea, Rep.	73.3	59.4	78.6	7.2
Finland	64.9	46.7	68.3	5.3
South Africa	62.2	43.0	64.5	3.7
Cote d'Ivoire	76.2	58.8	78.7	3.4
Pakistan	36.6	38.9	37.7	3.1
United Kingdom	52.0	50.6	53.4	2.7
Tanzania	39.5	50.1	40.3	2.1
Romania	75.3	42.9	76.7	1.8
Poland	59.2	50.2	59.5	0.4
Cameroon	55.6	37.5	55.2	−0.7
Guatemala	47.1	45.9	44.3	−6.1
Greece	51.4	45.9	47.4	−7.8
Zimbabwe	49.9	45.7	45.8	−8.1
Venezuela	50.6	59.6	45.7	−9.6
Kenya	67.0	57.0	56.4	−15.9
Zambia	86.8	72.5	70.6	−18.6
Peru	41.8	29.6	33.8	−19.3
Israel	103.1	80.1	83.0	−19.5
Japan	27.8	19.8	21.0	−24.6
Singapore	439.0	361.2	325.4	−25.9
Botswana	119.5	104.9	87.5	−26.8
Egypt	73.4	52.8	38.8	−47.1
Russia	n/a	36.1	58.7	n/a

Source: World Bank, *World Development Indicators CD-ROM*, 2004.

PART
5

Microeconomics focuses on the choices of consumers, the operation of firms, the structure of markets, and the choices of resource suppliers and employers.

Core Microeconomics

Consumers are the ultimate judge of both products and business firms. Their choices will determine which will survive and which will fail. The competitive process is highly dynamic. Numerous businesses come and go. Each year, newly incorporated businesses account for approximately 10 percent of the total. Approximately 1 percent of businesses file for bankruptcy during a typical year. In addition, many others close their doors or sell their assets to other, more successful (or more optimistic) operators.

CHAPTER 19

Consumer Choice and Elasticity

The most famous law in economics, and the one economists are most sure of, is the law of demand. On this law is built almost the whole edifice of economics.

—David R. Henderson[1]

A thing is worth whatever a buyer will pay for it.

—Publilius Syrus,
first century B.C.[2]

Chapter Focus

■ What are the fundamental postulates underlying consumer choice?

■ How does the law of diminishing marginal utility help explain the law of demand?

■ How do the demand curves of individuals translate into a market demand curve?

■ What is demand elasticity? What does it measure? Why is it important?

[1]David R. Henderson, "Demand," in *The Concise Encyclopedia of Economics*, ed. David R. Henderson, http://www.econlib.org/library/CEE.html.

[2]Quoted in Michael Jackman, ed., *Macmillan Book of Business and Economic Quotations* (New York: Macmillan, 1984), 150.

The statement of David Henderson highlights the central position of the law of demand in economics. As Publilius Syrus noted more than 2,000 years ago, demand reflects the willingness of individuals to pay for what is offered in the market. In this section, we begin our examination of microeconomic markets for specific products with an analysis of the demand side of markets. In essence we will be going "behind" the market demand curve to see how it is made up of individual consumer demands and what factors determine the choices of individual consumers.[3]

FUNDAMENTALS OF CONSUMER CHOICE

Each of us must decide how to allocate our limited income among the many possible things we could purchase. The prices of goods, *relative to each other*, are very important determining factors. If your favorite cereal doubled in price, would you switch to a different brand? Would your decision be different if all cereals, not just yours, doubled in price? Your choice *between* brands of cereal will be affected only by the change in relative prices. If the prices of all cereals rose by a proportional amount, you might quit purchasing cereal, but this would not give you a strong reason to switch to a different brand. Relative prices measure opportunity cost. If cereal is $5 per box when movie tickets are $10, you must give up two boxes of cereal to purchase a movie ticket.

Several fundamental principles underlie the choices of consumers. Let's take a closer look at the key factors influencing consumer behavior.

1. Limited income necessitates choice. Because of scarcity, we all have limited incomes. The limited nature of our income requires us to make choices about which goods we will and will not buy. When more of one good or service is bought, we must buy less of some other goods if we are to stay within our budget.

2. Consumers make decisions purposefully. The goals that underpin consumer choice can usually be met in alternative ways. If two products cost the same, a consumer will choose to buy the one expected to have the higher benefit. On the other hand, if two products yield equal benefits, the consumer will choose to buy the cheaper one. Fundamentally, we assume that consumers are rational—that they are able to weigh the costs and benefits of alternative choices.

3. One good can be substituted for another. Consumers can achieve *utility*—that is, satisfaction—from many different alternatives. Either a hamburger or a taco might satisfy your hunger, while going either to a movie or to a football game might satisfy your desire for entertainment. With $600, you might either buy a new TV set or take a short vacation. No single good is so precious that some of it will not be given up in exchange for a large enough quantity of other goods. Even seemingly unrelated goods are sometimes substituted one for another. For example, high water prices in Southern California have led residents there to substitute cactus gardens and flow constrictor shower heads for the relatively more expensive water. In Montana, where household electricity in recent years cost nearly twice as much as in nearby Washington, people substitute natural gas, fuel oil, insulation, and wool sweaters for the relatively more expensive electricity.

4. Consumers must make decisions without perfect information, but knowledge and past experience will help. In Chapter 1, we noted that information is costly to acquire. Asking family and friends, searching through magazines such as *Consumer Reports,* and contacting your local Better Business Bureau are all ways of gathering information about products and potential sellers. The time and effort consumers spend acquiring information will be directly related to the value derived from it. Predictably,

---

[3]You may want to review the section on demand in Chapter 3 before proceeding with this chapter.

consumers will spend more time and money to inform themselves when they are buying "big ticket" items such as automobiles or air-conditioning systems than when they are buying pencils or paper towels.

While no one has perfect foresight, experience—your own and that of others—will help you make better-informed choices. You have a pretty good idea of what to expect when you buy a cup of coffee at your favorite restaurant or ten gallons of gasoline at a service station you patronize regularly. Your expectations might not always be fulfilled precisely the same way every time (for example, the coffee may be stronger than expected or the gasoline may make your car's engine knock), but even then, you will gain valuable information that will help you project the outcome of future choices more accurately.

5. The law of diminishing marginal utility applies: as the rate of consumption increases, the marginal utility derived from consuming additional units of a good will decline. Utility is a term economists use to describe the subjective personal benefits that result from taking an action. The **law of diminishing marginal utility** states that the **marginal** (or additional) **utility** derived from consuming successive units of a product will eventually decline as the rate of consumption increases. For example, the law says that even though you might like ice cream, your marginal satisfaction from additional ice cream will eventually decline as you eat more and more of it. Ice cream at lunchtime might be great. An additional helping for dinner might also be good. However, after you have had it for lunch and dinner, another serving as a midnight snack will be less attractive. When the law of diminishing marginal utility sets in, the additional utility derived from still more units of ice cream declines.

The law of diminishing marginal utility explains why, even if you really like a certain product, you will not spend your entire budget on it. As you increase your consumption of any good, including those that you like a lot, the utility you derive from each additional unit will become smaller and smaller and eventually it will be less than the cost of the unit. At that point, you will not want to purchase any more units of the good.

Law of diminishing marginal utility
The basic economic principle that, as the consumption of a product increases, the marginal utility derived from consuming more of it (per unit of time) will eventually decline.

Marginal utility
The additional utility, or satisfaction, derived from consuming an additional unit of a good.

MARGINAL UTILITY, CONSUMER CHOICE, AND THE DEMAND CURVE OF AN INDIVIDUAL

The law of diminishing marginal utility helps us understand the law of demand and the shape of the demand curve. The height of an individual's demand curve at any specific unit is equal to the maximum price the consumer would be willing to pay for that unit—its **marginal benefit** to the consumer—given the number of units he or she has already purchased. Although marginal benefit is measured in dollars, the dollar amount reflects the opportunity cost of the unit in terms of other goods forgone. If a consumer is willing to pay, at most, $5 for an additional unit of the product, this indicates a willingness to give up, at most, $5 worth of other goods. *Because a consumer's willingness to pay for a unit of a good is directly related to the utility derived from consuming the unit, the law of diminishing marginal utility implies that a consumer's marginal benefit, and thus the height of the demand curve, falls with the rate of consumption.*

Exhibit 1 shows this relationship for a hypothetical consumer Jones, relative to her weekly consumption of frozen pizza. Because of the law of diminishing marginal utility, each additional pizza consumed per week will generate less marginal utility for Jones than the previous pizza. For this reason, Jones's maximum willingness to pay—her marginal benefit—will fall as the quantity consumed increases. In addition, the steepness of Jones's demand curve, or its responsiveness to a change in price—its elasticity—is a reflection of how rapidly Jones's marginal utility diminishes with additional consumption. An individual's demand curve for a good whose marginal value declines more rapidly will be steeper.

Given what we now know about a consumer's maximum willingness to pay for additional units of a good, we are now in a position to discuss the choice of how many units the consumer will choose to purchase at various prices. *At any given price, consumers*

Marginal benefit
The maximum price a consumer will be willing to pay for an additional unit of a product. It is the dollar value of the consumer's marginal utility from the additional unit, and therefore it falls as consumption increases.

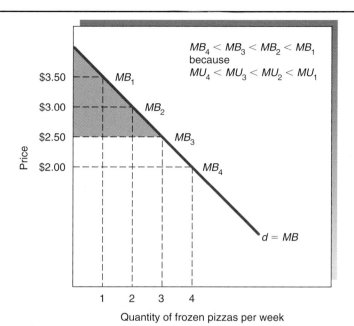

EXHIBIT 1
Diminishing Marginal Utility and the Individual's Demand Curve

An individual's demand curve, Jones's demand for frozen personal pizzas in this case, reflects the law of diminishing marginal utility. Because marginal utility (*MU*) falls with increased consumption, so does the consumer's maximum willingness to pay—marginal benefit (*MB*). A consumer will purchase until *MB* = *Price*, so at a price of $2.50 per pizza, Jones would purchase three pizzas and receive a consumer surplus shown by the shaded triangle.

will purchase all units of a good for which their maximum willingness to pay—their marginal benefit—is greater than the price. They will stop at the point where the next unit's marginal benefit would be less than the price. Although there are some problems related to dividing up certain kinds of goods (for example, it is hard to purchase half a car), we can generally say that a consumer will purchase all units of a good up to the point where the marginal benefit from it equals the price of the good (*MB* = *P*).

Returning to Exhibit 1, if the price of frozen pizza were $2.50, Jones would purchase three frozen pizzas per week.[4] Remember from Chapter 3 that consumer surplus is defined as the difference between the maximum price the consumer is willing to pay and the price actually paid. Jones's maximum willingness to pay for the first unit is $3.50, which, at a price of $2.50, generates $1.00 of consumer surplus for Jones. When a consumer has purchased all units to the point where *MB* = *P*, total consumer surplus is maximized. It is shown by the total triangular area under the demand curve that lies above the price. Total consumer surplus for Jones is shown as the shaded area in Exhibit 1.

Within this framework, how would a consumer respond to a decline in the price of a good? The consumer will increase purchases to the point where marginal benefit diminishes to the level of the new lower price. If marginal utility declines rapidly with consumption, the consumer will expand his or her purchases only slightly. If marginal utility declines less rapidly, it will take a larger expansion in purchases to reach this point. If the price were to rise, the consumer would cut back on purchases, eliminating those for which marginal benefit were now less than the price. This link between marginal benefit and maximum willingness to pay is the basis for the law of diminishing marginal utility, which underlies a person's demand curve for a product. The shape and steepness of the curve, for example, depends upon his or her marginal utility.

---

[4]Jones would certainly purchase the second unit because *MB* > *P*. For the third unit, *MB* = *P*, so Jones would be indifferent to buying the unit or not purchasing it. For a good that is easily divisible, say, pounds of roast beef, the consumer would continue purchasing up to 2.9999 pounds. Thus, economists are comfortable with simply concluding that the consumer will purchase this final unit, implying that Jones will purchase three frozen pizzas.

Consumer Equilibrium with Many Goods

The last time you were at the mall, you probably saw something, perhaps a nice billfold, that you liked. After all, there are many things we would like—many different alternatives that would give us utility. Next, you looked at the price tag: "Fifty dollars, wow! That's too much." What you were really saying was, "I like the billfold, but not as much as the $50 worth of other goods that I would have to give up for it." Consumer choice is a constant comparison of value relative to price. Consider another example: perhaps you prefer steak to less costly hamburger. Even if you do, your happiness might be better served if you were to buy the hamburger and then spend the extra money you saved on something else.

The idea that consumers choose among products by comparing their relative marginal utility (*MU*) to price (*P*) can be expressed more precisely. A consumer with a limited amount of income to spend on a group of products is not likely to do the following math, but will act as though he or she had, and will end up with

$$\frac{MU_A}{P_A} = \frac{MU_B}{P_B} = \cdots = \frac{MU_n}{P_n}$$

In this formula, *MU* represents the marginal utility derived from the last unit of a product, and *P* represents the price of the good. The subscripts $_{A, B, \ldots, n}$ indicate the different products available to the consumer. ***This formula implies that the consumer will maximize his or her satisfaction (or total utility) by ensuring that the last dollar spent on each commodity yields an equal degree of marginal utility. Alternatively stated, the last unit of each commodity purchased should provide the same marginal utility per dollar spent on it.*** Thus, if the price of a gallon of ice cream is twice as high as the price of a liter of Coke, a consumer will purchase these items to the point where the marginal utility of the last gallon of ice cream is twice as high as the marginal utility of the last liter of Coke.

Perhaps the best way to grasp this point is to think about what happens when your ratios of marginal utility to price are not equal for two goods. Suppose that you are at a local restaurant eating buffalo chicken wings and drinking Coke. For simplicity, assume that a large Coke and an order of wings each costs $2. With your $10 budget, you decide to purchase four orders of wings and one large Coke. When you finish your Coke, there are still lots of wings left. You have already eaten so many wings, though, that those remaining do not look as attractive. You could get more utility with fewer wings and another Coke, but it is too late. You have not spent your $10 in a way that gets you the most for your money. Instead of satisfying the above condition, you find that the marginal utility of wings is lower than the marginal utility of a Coke, and because they both have the same price ($2), this implies that

$$\frac{MU_{wings}}{P_{wings}} < \frac{MU_{Coke}}{P_{Coke}}$$

If you had purchased fewer wings and more Coke, your total utility would have been higher. Spending more on Coke would have lowered its marginal utility, decreasing the value of the right side of the equation. Simultaneously, spending less on wings would have raised the marginal utility of wings, increasing the value of the left side of the equation. You will maximize your utility—and get the most "bang for the buck" from your budget—when you make these values (the ratios) equal.

The equation can also be used to illustrate the law of demand. Beginning with a situation in which the two sides were equal, suppose that the price of wings increased. It would lower the value of *MU/P* for wings below the *MU/P* for Coke. In response, you would reallocate your budget, purchasing fewer of the more costly wings and more Coke. Thus, we have the law of demand—as the price of wings rises, you will purchase less of them. When people try to spend their money in a way that gives them the greatest amount of satisfaction, the consumer decision-making theory outlined here is difficult to question. In the next section, we will take the theory a little further.

Price Changes and Consumer Choice

The demand curve or schedule shows the amount of a product that consumers are willing to buy at alternative prices during a specific time period. The law of demand states that the amount of a product bought is inversely related to its price. We have seen how the law of demand can be derived from fundamental principles of consumer behavior. Now, we go further and distinguish two different phenomena underlying a consumer's response to a price change. First, as the price of a product declines, the lower opportunity cost will induce consumers to buy more of it—even if they have to give up other products. This tendency to substitute a product that has become cheaper for goods that are now relatively more expensive is called the **substitution effect** of a price change.

Second, if a consumer's money income is fixed, a reduction in the price of a product will increase his or her real income—the amount of goods and services he or she is able to purchase with that fixed amount of money income. If your rent were to decline by $100 per month, for example, that would allow you to buy more of a number of other goods. This increase in your real income has the same effect as if the rent had remained the same but your income had risen by $100 per month. As a result, this second way in which a price change affects consumption is called the **income effect**. Typically, consumers will respond to the income effect by buying more of the cheaper product and other products as well because they can better afford to do so. Substitution and income effects generally work in the same direction—in other words, in the same way; they both cause consumers to purchase more of a good as its price falls and less of a good as its price rises. (Both the income and substitution effects are derived graphically in the addendum to this chapter, titled "Consumer Choice and Indifference Curves.") [5]

Substitution effect
That part of an increase (decrease) in amount consumed that is the result of a good being cheaper (more expensive) in relation to other goods because of a reduction (increase) in price.

Income effect
That part of an increase (decrease) in amount consumed that is the result of the consumer's real income being expanded (contracted) by a reduction (rise) in the price of a good.

Time Costs and Consumer Choice

You may have heard the saying that "time is money." It is certainly true that time has value and that this value can sometimes be measured in dollars. As we have learned, the monetary price of a good is not always a complete measure of its cost to the consumer. Consuming most goods requires not only money, but time as well; and time, like money, is scarce to the consumer. So a lower time cost, like a lower money price, will make a product more attractive. For example, patients in a dentist's office would prefer a shorter wait before receiving care. One study showed that dental patients are willing to pay more than $5 per minute saved to shorten their time spent in waiting rooms.[6] Similarly, commodities such as automatic dishwashers, prepared foods, air travel, and taxi service are demanded mainly for the time savings they offer. People are often willing to pay relatively high money prices for goods that help them save time.

Time costs, unlike money prices for goods, differ among individuals. They are higher for persons with higher wage rates, for example. Other things being equal, high-wage consumers choose fewer time-intensive (and more time-saving) commodities than people with lower time costs and wages. For example, high-wage consumers are overrepresented among airplane and taxicab passengers but underrepresented among television watchers, chess players, and long-distance bus travelers. Can you explain why? You can, if you understand how both money and time costs influence the choices of consumers.

Failure to account for time costs can lead to bad decisions. For example, which is cheaper for consumers: (1) waiting in line three hours to purchase a $25 concert ticket or (2) buying the same ticket for $40 without standing in line? A consumer whose time is worth more than $5 per hour will find that $40 without the wait in line is less costly. As you can see, time costs matter. For example, when government-imposed price ceilings (discussed in Chapter 4) create shortages, rationing by waiting in line is frequently used. For many consumers, the benefit of the lower price due to the ceiling will be largely, if not entirely, offset by their increased time cost of having to wait in line.

---

[5]The substitution effect will always work in this direction. The income effect, however, may work in the reverse direction for some types of goods known as inferior goods. These will be addressed later in this chapter.

[6]Rexford E. Santerre and Stephen P. Neun, *Health Economics: Theories, Insights and Industry Studies* (Orlando, Fla.: Harcourt, 2000), 113.

EXHIBIT 2
Individual and Market Demand Curves

The market demand curve is merely the horizontal sum of the individual demand curves. It will slope downward to the right just as individual demand curves do.

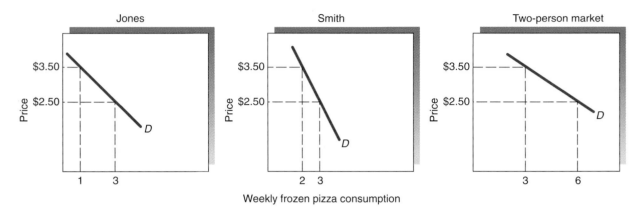

Weekly frozen pizza consumption

MARKET DEMAND REFLECTS THE DEMAND OF INDIVIDUAL CONSUMERS

The market demand schedule is the relationship between the market price of a good and the amount demanded by all the individuals in the market area. Because individual consumers purchase less at higher prices, the amount demanded in a market area as a total is also inversely related to price.

Exhibit 2 shows the relationship between individual demand and market demand for a hypothetical two-person market. The individual demand curves for both Jones and Smith are shown. Jones and Smith each consume three frozen pizzas per week at a price of $2.50. The amount demanded in the two-person market is six pizzas. If the price rises to $3.50 per pizza, the amount demanded in the market will fall to three pizzas, one demanded by Jones and two by Smith. *The market demand is simply the horizontal sum of the individual demand curves of consumers—in this case, Smith and Jones.*

In the real world, however, there can be millions of consumers in a market. But the relationship between the demand curves of individuals and the market demand curve will still be just like the one shown in Exhibit 2. At any given price, the amount purchased in the market will be the sum of the amounts purchased by each consumer in the market. Furthermore, the total amount demanded in the market will decline as price increases because individual consumers will purchase fewer units at the higher prices. The market demand curve reflects the collective choices of the individual consumers.

ELASTICITY OF DEMAND

Price elasticity of demand
The percentage change in the quantity of a product demanded divided by the percentage change in the price that caused the change in quantity. The price elasticity of demand indicates how responsive consumers are to a change in a product's price.

Although it is important to recognize that consumers will buy less of a product as its price increases, for many purposes, it is also important to know whether the increase will lead to a large or small reduction in the amount purchased. Economists have designed a tool called the price elasticity of demand to measure this sensitivity of amount purchased in response to a change in price. The equation for the **price elasticity of demand** is as follows:

$$Price\ elacticity\ of\ demand = \frac{Percentage\ change\ in\ quantity\ demanded}{Percentage\ change\ in\ price} = \frac{\%\Delta Q}{\%\Delta P}$$

This ratio is often called the *elasticity coefficient*. To express it more briefly, we use the notation %ΔQ to represent percentage change in quantity and %ΔP to represent percentage change in price. (The Greek letter delta [Δ] means "change in.") The law of demand states that an increase in a product's price lowers the quantity of it purchased, whereas a decrease in price raises it. Because a change in price causes the quantity demanded to change in the opposite direction, the price elasticity coefficient is always negative, although economists often ignore the sign and use the absolute value of the coefficient.

To see how the concept of elasticity works, suppose that the price of the Ford Explorer rises 10 percent, while other prices remain the same. Ford could expect Explorer sales to fall substantially—perhaps 30 percent—as sport-utility vehicle (SUV) buyers respond by switching to other SUVs whose prices have not changed. This strong response by buyers means that the demand for the Explorer is elastic.

Now consider a different situation. Suppose that, because of a new tax, the price of not only the Explorer *but of all new SUVs* rises 10 percent. In this case, consumers' options are much more limited. They can't simply switch to a cheaper close substitute as they could when the price of the Explorer alone rose. They might either simply pay the extra money for a new SUV or settle for a used SUV instead. Because of this, the 10 percent rise in the price of all new SUVs will lead to a smaller consumer response, perhaps a 5 percent decline in sales of new SUVs.

To calculate the elasticity coefficient for the Explorer in our example above, we begin with the 30 percent decline in quantity demanded and divide by the 10 percent rise in the price that caused the decline. Thus, the elasticity of demand for the Explorer would be:

$$\frac{\%\,\Delta Quantity}{\%\,\Delta Price} = \frac{-30\%}{+10\%} = -3$$

(or 3.0 if we ignore the minus sign). This means that the percentage change in quantity demanded is three times the percentage change in price.

To calculate the demand elasticity for *all* SUVs (our second example), we see that the percentage change in quantity, 5 percent, divided by the percentage change in price, 10 percent, gives us $-1/2$, or -0.5. When it comes to the price elasticity of demand for all SUVs, the percentage change in quantity demanded (using our hypothetical numbers) is only half the percentage change in price, not three times the percentage change in price as it was with the Explorer.

Often, we will have to derive the percentage change in quantity and price. If you know the quantities that will be purchased at two different prices, you can then derive the percentage change in both the price and the quantity. For example, suppose that a price change from P_0 to P_1 causes a change in quantity demanded from Q_0 to Q_1. The change in quantity demanded would therefore be $Q_0 - Q_1$. To calculate the percentage change in quantity, we divide the actual change by the midpoint (or average) of the two quantities.[7] Although it is often easy to find the midpoint without a formula (halfway between $4 and $6 is $5), it can also be found as $(Q_0 + Q_1)/2$. Finally, because 0.05 is simply 5 percent, we multiply by 100. Thus, we can express the percentage change in quantity demanded as:

$$\frac{Q_0 - Q_1}{(Q_0 + Q_1)/2} \times 100$$

Similarly, when the change in price is $P_0 - P_1$, the *percentage* change in price is

$$\frac{P_0 - P_1}{(P_0 + P_1)/2} \times 100$$

Dividing the resulting percentage change in quantity by the percentage change in price gives us the elasticity.

---

[7]This formula uses the average of the starting point and the ending point of the change so that it will give the same result whether we start from the lower or the higher price. This arc elasticity formula is not the only way to calculate elasticity, but it is the most frequently used.

There is a more direct way to compute elasticity using this same sort of approach. Dividing the percentage change in quantity by the percentage change in price and simplifying yields the following:

$$\frac{(Q_0 - Q_1)/(Q_0 + Q_1)}{(P_0 - P_1)/(P_0 + P_1)}$$

(Because each term is multiplied by 100 and the denominator of each term contains a 2, these factors cancel out of the final expression.)

A numerical example will help you understand this. Suppose that Trina's Cakes can sell fifty specialty cakes per week at $7 each, or it can sell seventy specialty cakes at $6 each per week. The percentage difference in quantity is the difference in the quantity demanded ($50 - 70 = -20$) divided by the midpoint (60) times 100. The result is a -33.33 percent change in quantity ($-20 \div 60 \times 100 = -33.33$).

Now that we've calculated the percentage change in quantity demanded of cakes, let's calculate the percentage change in the price. The percentage change in price is the difference in the two prices ($7 - $6 = $1) divided by the midpoint price ($6.50) times 100, or a 15.38 percent change in price ($1 \div 6.5 \times 100 = 15.38$). Dividing the percentage change in quantity by the percentage change in price ($-33.33 \div 15.38$) gives an elasticity coefficient of -2.17. Alternatively, we could have expressed this directly as:

$$\frac{[(50 - 70)/(50 + 70)]}{[(7 - 6)/(7 + 6)]} = \frac{-20/120}{1/13} = \frac{-1/6}{1/13} = \frac{-13}{6} = -2.17$$

The same result is obtained either way. The elasticity of 2.17 (ignoring the sign) indicates that the percentage change in quantity is just over twice the percentage change in price.

The elasticity coefficient lets us make a precise distinction between elasticity and inelasticity. When the elasticity coefficient is greater than 1 (ignoring the sign), as it was for the demand for Trina's Cakes, demand is elastic. When it is less than 1, demand is inelastic. Demand is said to be of *unitary elasticity* if the price elasticity is exactly 1.

Graphic Representation of Price Elasticity of Demand

Exhibit 3 presents demand curves of varying elasticity. A demand curve that is completely vertical is said to be *perfectly inelastic*. In the real world, such demand is nonexistent because the substitutes for a good become more attractive as the price of that good rises. Moreover, because of the income effect, we should expect that a higher price will always reduce the quantity demanded, other things remaining the same. (Unlike our falling rent example earlier in the chapter, this example can be thought of as a "negative" income effect. When the price of a good rises, it leaves you with less overall buying power, not more.) Still, the (mythical) perfectly inelastic demand curve is shown in part (a) of Exhibit 3.

The more inelastic the demand, the steeper the demand curve *over any specific price range*. As you can see, the demand for cigarettes (shown in part b of Exhibit 3) is highly inelastic; a big change in price doesn't change quantity demanded much. People who crave nicotine will be very willing to pay the higher price. On the other hand, the demand for apples (shown in part d) is relatively elastic. People will find it easy to switch to oranges or bananas, for example, if the price of apples skyrockets.

When demand elasticity is unitary, as part (c) shows, a demand curve that is convex to the origin will result. When a demand curve is completely horizontal, an economist would say that it is *perfectly elastic*. Demand for the wheat marketed by a single wheat farmer, for example, would approximate perfect elasticity (part e).

Because elasticity is a relative concept, the elasticity of a straight line demand curve will differ at each point along the demand curve. As **Exhibit 4** shows, the elasticity of a straight-line demand curve (one with a constant slope) will range from highly elastic to highly inelastic. In this exhibit, when the price rises from $10 to $11, sales decline from 20 to 10. According to the formula, the price elasticity of demand is -7.0. Demand is very elastic in this region. In contrast, demand is quite inelastic in the $1 to $2 price range. As

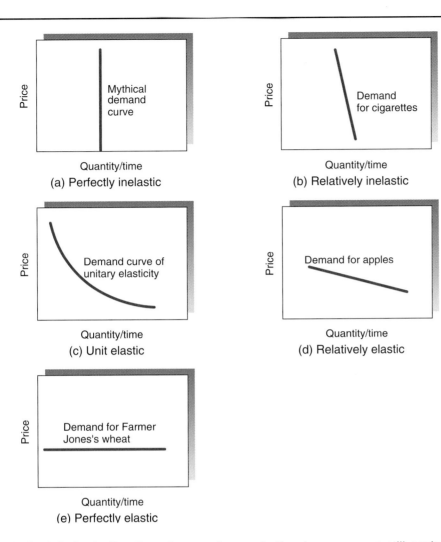

EXHIBIT 3
Price Elasticity
of Demand

(a) Perfectly inelastic: Despite an increase in a product's price, consumers still purchase the same amount of it. Substitution and income effects prevent this from happening in the real world, though.
(b) Relatively inelastic: A percentage increase in a product's price results in a smaller percentage reduction in its sales. The demand for cigarettes has been estimated to be highly inelastic.
(c) Unit elastic: The percentage change in quantity demanded of a product is equal to the percentage change in its price. A curve with a decreasing slope results. Sales revenue (price times quantity sold) is constant.
(d) Relatively elastic: A percentage increase in a product's price leads to a larger percentage reduction in purchases of it. When good substitutes are available for a product (as in the case of apples), the amount of it purchased will be highly sensitive to price changes.
(e) Perfectly elastic: Consumers will buy all of Farmer Jones's wheat at the market price, but none will be sold above the market price.

the price increases from $1 to $2, the amount demanded declines from 110 to 100. The ten-unit change in quantity is the same, but it is a smaller *percentage* change. And the $1 change in price is the same, but it is now a larger *percentage* change. The elasticity of demand in this range is only −0.14; demand in this example is highly inelastic.

How Large Are the Demand Elasticities of Various Products?

Economists have estimated the price elasticity of demand for many products. As **Exhibit 5** shows, the elasticity of demand varies substantially among products. The demand is highly inelastic for several products—salt, toothpicks, matches, light bulbs, and newspapers, for example—in their normal price range. On the other hand, the demand curves for fresh tomatoes, Chevrolet automobiles, and fresh green peas are highly elastic. The demand for movies, housing, private education, radios, and television sets is near 1.0 (unitary).

EXHIBIT 4
Slope of the Demand Curve Versus Price Elasticity

With this straight line (constant slope) demand curve, demand is more elastic in the high price range. The formula for elasticity shows that, when price rises from $1 to $2 and quantity falls from 110 to 100, demand is inelastic. A price rise of the same magnitude (but of a smaller percentage), from $10 to $11, leads to a decline in quantity of the same size (but of a larger percentage), so that elasticity is much greater. (Price elasticities are negative, but economists often ignore the sign and look only at the absolute value.)

EXHIBIT 5
Estimated Price Elasticity of Demand for Selected Products

INELASTIC		APPROXIMATELY UNITARY ELASTICITY	
Salt	– 0.1	Movies	– 0.9
Matches	– 0.1	Housing, owner occupied, long run	– 1.2
Toothpicks	– 0.1	Shellfish, consumed at home	– 0.9
Airline travel, short run	– 0.1	Oysters, consumed at home	– 1.1
Gasoline, short run	– 0.2	Private education	– 1.1
Gasoline, long run	– 0.7	Tires, short run	– 0.9
Residential natural gas, short run	– 0.1	Tires, long run	– 1.2
Residential natural gas, long run	– 0.5	Radio and television receivers	– 1.2
Coffee	– 0.25		
Fish (cod), consumed at home	– 0.5	**ELASTIC**	
Tobacco products, short run	– 0.45	Restaurant meals	– 2.3
Legal services, short run	– 0.4	Foreign travel, long run	– 4.0
Physician services	– 0.6	Airline travel, long run	– 2.4
Dental services	– 0.7	Fresh green peas	– 2.8
Taxi, short run	– 0.6	Automobiles, short run	– 1.2–1.5
Automobiles, long run	– 0.2	Chevrolet automobiles	– 4.0
		Fresh tomatoes	– 4.6

Sources: Hendrick S. Houthakker and Lester D. Taylor, *Consumer Demand in the United States, 1929–1970* (Cambridge, Mass.: Harvard University Press, 1966, 1970); Douglas R. Bohi, *Analyzing Demand Behavior* (Baltimore: Johns Hopkins University Press, 1981); Hsaing-tai Cheng and Oral Capps Jr., "Demand for Fish," *American Journal of Agricultural Economics*, August 1988; U.S. Department of Agriculture; and Rexford E. Santerre and Stephen P. Neun, *Health Economics: Theories, Insights and Industry Studies* (Orlando, Fla.: Harcourt, 2000).

Why Do the Price Elasticities of Demand Vary?

The primary determinants of a product's price elasticity of demand are the availability of good substitutes and to some extent the share of the typical consumer's total budget expended on a product. Let's consider each of these factors.

Availability of Substitutes *The most important determinant of the price elasticity of demand is the availability of substitutes. When good substitutes for a product are available, a price increase induces many consumers to switch to other products. Demand is elastic.* For example, if the price of felt tip pens increases, many consumers will switch to pencils, ballpoint pens, or (for children) crayons. If the price of apples increased, consumers might substitute oranges, bananas, peaches, or pears.

When good substitutes are unavailable, the demand for a product tends to be inelastic. Medical services are an example. When we are sick, most of us find witch doctors, faith healers, palm readers, and aspirin to be highly imperfect substitutes for the services of a physician. Not surprisingly, the demand for physician services is inelastic.

The availability of substitutes increases as the product class becomes more specific, thus increasing price elasticity. For example, as Exhibit 5 shows, the price elasticity of Chevrolets, a narrow product class, exceeds that of the broad class of automobiles in general. If the price of Chevrolets alone rises, many substitute cars are available. But if the prices of all automobiles rise together, consumers have fewer good substitutes.

Product's Share of the Consumer's Total Budget If the expenditures on a product are quite small relative to the consumer's budget, the income effect will be small even if there is a substantial increase in the price of the product. This will make demand less elastic. Compared to one's total budget, expenditures on some commodities are minuscule. Matches, toothpicks, and salt are good examples. Most consumers spend only $1 or $2 per year on each of these items. A doubling of their price would exert little influence on a family's budget. Therefore, even if the price of such a product were to rise sharply, consumers will still not find it worthwhile to spend much time and effort looking for substitutes.

Exhibit 6 provides a graphic illustration of both elastic and inelastic demand curves. In part (a), the demand curve for ballpoint pens is elastic because there are good

---

EXHIBIT 6
Inelastic and Elastic Demand

As the price of ballpoint pens (a) rose from $1.00 to $1.50, the quantity purchased plunged from 100,000 to 25,000. The percentage reduction in quantity is larger than the percentage increase in price. Thus, the demand for the pens is elastic. In contrast, an increase in the price of cigarettes from $1.00 to $1.50 results in only a small reduction in the number purchased (b). Because the demand for cigarettes is inelastic, the percentage reduction in quantity is smaller than the percentage increase in price.

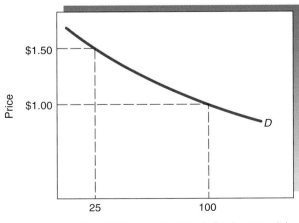

(a) Ballpoint pens per week (in thousands)

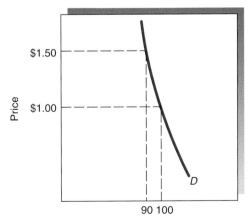

(b) Cigarette packs per week (in millions)

substitutes—for example, pencils and felt tip pens. Therefore, when the price of the pens increases from $1.00 to $1.50, the quantity purchased of them declines sharply from 100,000 to only 25,000. The calculated price elasticity equals −3.0. The fact that the absolute value of the coefficient is greater than 1 confirms that the demand for ballpoint pens is elastic over the price range shown.

Part (b) of Exhibit 6 shows the demand curve for cigarettes. Because most smokers do not find other products to be a good substitute, the demand for cigarettes is highly inelastic. If a unit of six cigarettes is worth a dollar, a substantial increase in price (from $1.00 to $1.50) leads to only a small reduction in the quantity demanded. The price elasticity coefficient is −0.26, substantially less in absolute value than 1, confirming that the demand for cigarettes is inelastic. (*Exercise:* Use the price elasticity formula to verify the values of these elasticity coefficients.)

Time and Demand Elasticity

As changing market conditions raise or lower the price of a product, both consumers and producers will respond. However, the response will not be instantaneous, and it is likely to become larger over time. *In general, when the price of a product increases, consumers will reduce their consumption by a larger amount in the long run than in the short run. Thus, the demand for most products will be more elastic in the long run than in the short run. This relationship between elasticity and the length of the adjustment period is sometimes referred to as the second law of demand.*

The first law of demand says that buyers will respond predictably to a price change, purchasing more when the price is lower than when the price is higher, if other things remain the same. The second law of demand says that the response of buyers will be greater after they have had time to adjust more fully to a price change.

HOW DEMAND ELASTICITY AND PRICE CHANGES AFFECT TOTAL EXPENDITURES (OR REVENUES) ON A PRODUCT

By looking at demand elasticity, we can determine changes in total consumer spending on a product when its price changes. We can do this in three different ways: by looking at (1) changes in an individual's total spending, using the demand elasticity from his or her demand curve for the product, (2) changes in the total combined spending of all consumers, using the elasticity from the total market demand curve, or (3) changes in total consumer spending on the product, using the demand curve facing that firm that produces it. In other words, this third method allows us to look at elasticity based not on what consumers spend, but on what the producer receives from selling the product.

Total expenditures (or revenues) simply amount to the price of the product times the number of units of it purchased (or sold).

Total Expenditures	=	Price	×	Quantity
?	=	↑	×	↓
?	=	↓	×	↑

Because total expenditures are equal to the price times the quantity, and because the price and the quantity move in opposite directions, the net effect of a price change on the total spending on a product depends upon whether the (percentage) price change or the (percentage) quantity change is greater.

When demand is inelastic, the price elasticity coefficient is less than 1. This means that the percentage change in price is greater than the percentage change in quantity. *Therefore, when demand is inelastic, the change in the price will dominate and, as a result, the price and total expenditures will change in the same direction.* In other words, when the price of an inelastic product (say, cigarettes) increases, spending on it will increase, too—and vice versa. On the other hand, when demand is elastic, the change in quantity will be greater than the change in the price. *As a result, the impact of the change in quantity will dominate, and therefore the price and expenditures will move in oppo-*

EXHIBIT 7
Demand Elasticity and How Changes in Price Affect Total Consumer Expenditures or a Firm's Total Revenue

PRICE ELASTICITY OF DEMAND	NUMERICAL ELASTICITY COEFFICIENT (IN ABSOLUTE VALUE)	IMPACT OF RAISING PRICE ON TOTAL CONSUMER EXPENDITURES OR A FIRM'S TOTAL REVENUE	IMPACT OF LOWERING PRICE ON TOTAL CONSUMER EXPENDITURES OR A FIRM'S TOTAL REVENUE
Elastic	1 to ∞	decrease	increase
Unit Elastic	1	unchanged	unchanged
Inelastic	0 to 1	increase	decrease

site directions. In other words, when the price of an elastic product (say, a ballpoint pen) increases, spending on it will decrease—and vice versa.

When demand elasticity is unitary, the change in quantity demanded will be equal in magnitude to the change in price. With regard to their impact on total expenditures, these two effects will exactly offset each other. ***Thus, when price elasticity of demand is equal to 1, total expenditures will remain unchanged as price changes.***

Exhibit 7 summarizes the relationship between changes in the price of a product and changes in total spending on it when demand is elastic, inelastic, and unit elastic. The demand curves shown in Exhibit 6 can also be used to show the link between elasticity and changes in total spending. In the case of cigarettes (part b), the price elasticity of demand for the price increase from $1.00 to $1.50 is 0.26, indicating that demand is inelastic. This increase in cigarette prices leads to an increase in spending on the product from $100 million ($1.00 × 100 million units) to $135 million ($1.50 × 90 million units). If the change had occurred in the opposite direction, with the price falling from $1.50 to $1.00, total expenditures would have declined.

The price elasticity of demand for a ballpoint pen when its price increases from $1.00 to $1.50 (part a of Exhibit 6) is 3.0, indicating that demand is elastic. This increase in the price of ballpoint pens lowers total consumer spending on the product from $100,000 ($1.00 × 100,000 pens) to $37,500 ($1.50 × 25,000 pens). If the change had occurred in the opposite direction, with the price falling from $1.50 to $1.00, total expenditures would have risen.

You can see how important it is for business decision makers to understand the concept of elasticity. When a firm increases the price of its product, its revenues may rise, fall, or remain the same. If the demand for the firm's product is inelastic, the higher price will expand the firm's total revenue. However, if the demand for the firm's product is elastic, a price increase will lead to substantially lower sales and a decline in total revenue. In the case of unitary elasticity, the price increase will leave total revenue unchanged.

Beyond the price elasticity of demand, two other elasticity relationships are important in any given market. We therefore end this chapter with a brief discussion of income elasticity of demand and price elasticity of supply.

INCOME ELASTICITY

Increases in consumer income will increase the demand (the quantity demanded at each price) for most goods. Income elasticity tells us how responsive the demand for a product is to income changes. **Income elasticity** is defined as:

$$Income\ elasticity = \frac{Percentage\ change\ in\ quantity\ demanded}{Percentage\ change\ in\ income}$$

As **Exhibit 8** shows, although the income elasticity coefficients for products vary from one good to another, they are normally positive. In fact, the term **normal good** refers to any good with a positive income elasticity of demand. Some normal goods have lower

Income elasticity
The percentage change in the quantity of a product demanded divided by the percentage change in consumer income that caused the change in quantity demanded. It measures the responsiveness of the demand for a good to a consumer's change in income.

Normal good
A good that has a positive income elasticity, so that, as consumer income rises, demand for the good rises, too.

EXHIBIT 8
Estimated Income Elasticity of Demand for Selected Products

LOW-INCOME ELASTICITY		HIGH-INCOME ELASTICITY	
Margarine	−0.20	Private education	2.46
Fuel	0.38	New cars	2.45
Electricity	0.20	Recreation and amusements	1.57
Fish (haddock)	0.46	Alcohol	1.54
Food	0.51		
Tobacco	0.64		
Hospital care	0.69		

Sources: Hendrick S. Houthakker and Lester D. Taylor, *Consumer Demand in the United States, 1929–1970* (Cambridge, Mass.: Harvard University Press, 1966); L. Taylor, "The Demand for Electricity: A Survey," *Bell Journal of Economics* (Spring 1975); F. W. Bell, "The Pope and the Price of Fish," *American Economic Review* 58 (December 1968); and Rexford E. Santerre and Stephen P. Neun, *Health Economics: Theories, Insights and Industry Studies* (Orlando, Fla.: Harcourt, 2000).

income elasticities than others, however. In general, goods that people regard as "necessities" will have low income elasticities (between 0 and 1). Significant quantities are purchased even at low incomes, and, as income increases, spending on these items will increase by less than a proportional amount. It is understandable that items such as fuel, electricity, bread, tobacco, economy clothing, and potatoes have a low income elasticity.

Goods that consumers regard as "luxuries" generally have a high (greater than 1) income elasticity. For example, private education, new automobiles, recreational activities, donations to environmental groups, swimming pools, and vacation air travel are all highly income elastic. As the consumer's income increases, the demand for these goods expands even more rapidly, and therefore spending on these items increases as a proportion of income.

A few commodities, such as margarine, low-quality meat cuts, and bus travel, actually have a negative income elasticity. Economists refer to goods with a negative income elasticity as **inferior goods**. As income expands, the demand for inferior goods will decline. Conversely, as income declines, the demand for inferior goods will increase.

Inferior good
A good that has a negative income elasticity, so that, as consumer income rises, the demand for the good falls.

PRICE ELASTICITY OF SUPPLY

Price elasticity of supply
The percentage change in quantity supplied, divided by the percentage change in the price that caused the change in quantity supplied.

The **price elasticity of supply** is the percentage change in quantity supplied, divided by the percentage change in the price causing the supply response. Because this measures the responsiveness of sellers to a change in price, it is analogous to the price elasticity of demand. However, the price elasticity of supply will be positive because the quantity producers are willing to supply is directly related to price. Like demand elasticity, time plays a role once again. Supply elasticities will be greater when suppliers have a longer time to respond to a price change. In the next two chapters, we will discuss more fully the factors that determine supply elasticity. For now, it is important simply to recognize the concept of supply elasticity and the fact that suppliers (like buyers) will be more responsive to a price change when they have had more time to adjust to it.

LOOKING AHEAD

Market demand indicates how strongly consumers desire a good or service. In the following chapter, we will turn to a firm's costs of production—costs that arise because resources are demanded for alternative uses. These two topics—consumer demand and the cost of production—are central to understanding how markets work and the conditions necessary for the efficient allocation of resources.

KEY POINTS

▼ Consumers will try to allocate their limited incomes among a multitude of goods in a way that maximizes their utility. The role of relative prices, information, and preferences, as well as the law of diminishing marginal utility help explain the choices consumers make and the downward slope of a person's demand curve for products.

▼ The market demand curve for a product is the horizontal sum of people's individual demand curves.

▼ The price elasticity of demand measures the responsiveness of the quantity of a product purchased to a change in its price.

▼ The availability of substitutes is the primary determinant of the price elasticity of demand for a product. When there are good substitutes available, and the item is a sizable component of the consumer's budget, its demand will tend to be elastic. When only poor substitutes are available, demand will tend to be inelastic.

▼ Typically, the price elasticity of a product will increase as consumers have had more time to adjust to a change in its price. This direct relationship between the size of the elasticity coefficient and the length of the adjustment period is often referred to as the *second law of demand.*

▼ The concept of elasticity helps us determine how a change in price will affect total consumer expenditures on a product or a firm's total revenues derived from it. When the demand for a product is elastic, a price change will cause total spending on it to change in the opposite direction. When demand for a product is inelastic, a change in price will cause total spending on it to change in the same direction.

▼ The concept of elasticity can also be applied to consumer income (which is called the income elasticity of demand) and supply (which is called the price elasticity of supply).

CRITICAL ANALYSIS QUESTIONS

*1. Suppose that, in an attempt to raise more revenue, Nowhere State University (NSU) increases its tuition. Will this necessarily result in more revenue? Under what conditions will revenue (a) rise, (b) fall, or (c) remain the same? Explain this, focusing on the relationship between the increased revenue from students who enroll at NSU despite the higher tuition and the lost revenue from lower enrollment. If the true price elasticity were −1.2, what would you suggest the university do to expand revenue?

*2. A bus ticket between two cities costs $50 and the trip will take twenty-eight hours, whereas an airplane ticket costs $300 and takes three hours. Mary values her time at $12 per hour, and Michele values her time at $8 per hour. Will Mary take the bus or the plane? Which will Michele take? Explain.

*3. Recent research confirms that the demand for cigarettes is inelastic, but it also indicates that smokers with incomes in the lower half of all incomes respond to a given price increase by reducing their purchases by amounts that are more than four times as large as the purchase reductions made by smokers in the upper half of all incomes. How can the income and substitution effects of a price change help explain this finding?

4. A consumer is currently purchasing three pairs of jeans and five T-shirts per year. The price of jeans is $30, and T-shirts cost $10. At the current rate of consumption, the marginal utility of jeans is 60, and the marginal utility of T-shirts is 30. Is this consumer maximizing his utility? Would you suggest that he buy more jeans and fewer T-shirts, or more T-shirts and fewer jeans?

5. A few years ago, when residential electricity in the state of Washington cost about half as much as in nearby Montana, the average household in Washington used about 1,200 kilowatt-hours per month, whereas Montanans used about half that much per household. Do these data provide us with two points on the average household's demand curve for residential electricity in this region? Why or why not?

*6. The wealthy are widely believed to have more leisure time than the poor. However, even though we are a good deal wealthier today than our great-grandparents were 100 years ago, we appear to live more hectic lives and have less free time. Can you explain why?

7. What are the major determinants of a product's price elasticity of demand? Studies indicate that the demand for Florida oranges, Bayer aspirin, watermelons, and airfares to Europe are elastic. Why?

8. Most systems of medical insurance substantially lower the out-of-pocket costs consumers have to pay for additional units of physician services and hospitalization. Some reduce these costs to zero. How does this method of payment affect the consumption levels of medical services? Might this method of organization result in "too much" consumption of medical services? Discuss.

*9. Are the following statements true or false? Explain your answers.
   a. A 10 percent reduction in price that leads to a 15 percent increase in the amount purchased indicates a price elasticity of more than 1.
   b. A 10 percent reduction in price that leads to a 2 percent increase in total expenditures indicates a price elasticity of more than 1.
   c. If the percentage change in price is less than the resultant percentage change in quantity demanded, demand is elastic.

*10. Respond to the following questions: If you really like pizza, should you try to consume as much pizza as possible? If you want to succeed, should you try to make the highest possible grade in your economics class?

*11. Sue loves ice cream but cannot stand frozen-yogurt desserts. In contrast, Carole likes both foods and can hardly tell the difference between the two. Who will have the more elastic demand for yogurt?

*12. Patsy's Specialty Bakery projects the following demand for Patsy's pies:

Price ($)	Quantity Purchased
9	130
10	110
11	95

   a. Calculate the price elasticity of demand between $9 and $10. Is demand in this range elastic or inelastic?
   b. Calculate the price elasticity of demand between $10 and $11. Is demand in this range elastic or inelastic?

13. Suppose Bobby, the owner-manager of Bobby's Red Hot BBQ restaurant, projects the following demand for his Baby Back Rib platter:

Price ($)	Quantity Purchased (per night)
9	110
11	100
13	80

   a. Calculate the price elasticity of demand between $9 and $11.
   b. Is the price elasticity of demand between $9 and $11 elastic, unit elastic, or inelastic?
   c. Will Bobby's total revenue rise if he increases the price from $9 to $11?
   d. Calculate the price elasticity of demand between $11 and $13.
   e. Is the price elasticity of demand between $11 and $13 elastic, unit elastic, or inelastic?
   f. Will Bobby's total revenue rise if he increases the price from $11 to $13?

*Asterisk denotes questions for which answers are given in Appendix B.

ADDENDUM: CONSUMER CHOICE AND INDIFFERENCE CURVES

Advanced Material

In many classes, this material will be optional.

In the text of this chapter, we used marginal utility analysis to develop the demand curve of an individual. In developing the theory of consumer choice, economists usually rely on a more formal technique—*indifference curve* analysis. Because this technique is widely used at a more advanced level, many instructors like to include it in their introductory course. In this addendum, we use indifference curve analysis to develop the theory of demand in a more formal—some would say more elegant—manner.

What Are Indifference Curves?

There are two elements in every choice: (1) preferences (the desirability of various goods) and (2) opportunities (the attainability of various goods). The **indifference curve** relates to the former: the preferences of an individual. It separates better (more preferred by this individual) bundles of goods from inferior (less preferred) bundles, providing a diagrammatic picture of how an individual ranks alternative consumption bundles.

To illustrate indifference curves, we begin with the title character from the classic *Robinson Crusoe*, by Daniel Defoe, published in 1719 and thought to be the first English novel. Crusoe was shipwrecked on a desert island. In **Exhibit A1**, we assume that he is initially consuming eight fish and eight breadfruit per week (point *A*). This initial bundle provides him with a certain level of satisfaction (utility). He would, however, be willing to trade this initial bundle for certain other consumption alternatives if the

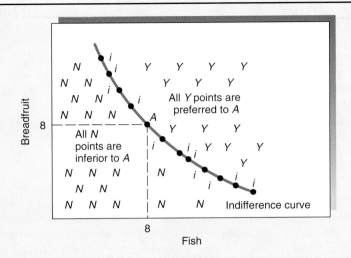

EXHIBIT A1
**Indifference Curve of
Robinson Crusoe**

The curve generated by
connecting Crusoe's "I do
not care" answers sepa-
rates the combinations of
fish and breadfruit that he
prefers to the bundle *A*
from those that he judges
to be inferior to *A*. The *i*
points map out an indifference curve.

opportunity presented itself. Since he likes both fish and
breadfruit, he would especially like to obtain bundles to
the northeast of point *A* in the diagram, since they represent more of both goods. However, he would also be willing to give up some breadfruit if in return he received a
compensatory amount of fish. Similarly, if the terms of
trade were right, he would be willing to exchange fish for
breadfruit. The trade-offs he is just willing to make—those
that would make him no better and no worse off—lie
along the indifference curve. Of course, he is happy to
move to any bundle on a higher indifference curve.

Starting from point *A* (eight fish and eight breadfruit),
we ask Crusoe if he is willing to trade that bundle for various other bundles. He answers "Yes" (*Y*), "No" (*N*), or "I
do not care" (*i*). Exhibit A1 shows the pattern of his responses. Crusoe's "I do not care" answers indicate that the
original bundle (point *A*) and each alternative indicated by
an *i* are valued equally by Crusoe. These *i* points, when
connected, form the indifference curve. This line separates
the preferred bundles of fish and breadfruit from the less-
valued combinations. Note that such a curve is likely to be
entirely different for any two people. The preferences of
individuals vary widely.

We can establish a new indifference curve for the individual by starting from any point not on the original
curve and following the same procedure. If we start with a
point (a consumption bundle) to the northeast of the original indifference curve, all points on the new curve will
have a higher level of satisfaction for Crusoe than any on
the old curve. The new curve will probably have about the
same shape as the original.

Characteristics of Indifference Curves

In developing consumer theory, economists assume that
the preferences of consumers exhibit certain properties.
These properties enable us to make statements about the
general pattern of indifference curves. What are these

properties, and what do they imply about the characteristics of indifference curves?

**1. More goods are preferable to fewer goods—
thus, bundles on indifference curves lying farthest
to the northeast of a diagram are always preferred.**
Assuming the consumption of only two commodities
that are both desired, the individual will always prefer a
bundle with more of one good (without loss of the other)
to the original bundle. This means that combinations to the
northeast of a point on the diagram will always be
preferred to points lying to the southwest.

**2. Goods are substitutable—therefore, indifference
curves slope downward to the right.**   As we discussed
in this chapter, individuals are willing to substitute one good
for another. Crusoe will be willing to give up some
breadfruit if he is compensated with enough fish. Stated
another way, there will be some amount of additional fish
such that Crusoe will stay on the same indifference curve,
even though his consumption of breadfruit has declined.
However, in order to remain on the same indifference curve,
Crusoe must always acquire more of one good to compensate for the loss of the other. The indifference curve for
goods thus will always slope downward to the right (run
northwest to southeast).

**3. The value a consumer puts on a good declines as
he or she consumes more of it—therefore, indifference curves are always convex when viewed from
below.**   The slope of the indifference curve represents
the willingness of the individual to substitute one good for
the other. Economists refer to the amount of one good that
is just sufficient to compensate the consumer for the loss
of a unit of the other good as the **marginal rate of
substitution.** It is equal to the slope of the indifference
curve. Reflecting the principle of diminishing marginal
utility, the marginal rate of substitution of a good will

decline as the good is consumed more intensively relative to other goods. Suppose Crusoe remains on the same indifference curve while continuing to expand his consumption of fish relative to breadfruit. As his consumption of fish increases (and his consumption of breadfruit declines), his valuation of fish relative to breadfruit will decline. It will take more and more units of fish to compensate for the loss of still another unit of breadfruit. The indifference curve will become flatter, reflecting the decline in the marginal rate of substitution of fish for breadfruit as Crusoe consumes more fish relative to breadfruit.

Of course, just the opposite will happen if Crusoe's consumption of breadfruit increases relative to that of fish—if he moves northwest along the same indifference curve. In this case, as breadfruit is consumed more intensively, Crusoe's valuation of it will decline relative to that of fish, and the marginal rate of substitution of fish for breadfruit will rise (the indifference curve will become steeper and steeper). Therefore, since the valuation of a good declines as it is consumed more intensively, indifference curves must be convex when viewed from the origin.

4. Indifference curves are everywhere. We can construct an indifference curve starting from any point on the diagram. This simply means that any two bundles of goods can be compared by the individual.

5. Indifference curves cannot cross—if they did, rational ordering would be violated. If indifference curves crossed, our postulate that more goods are better than fewer goods would be violated. **Exhibit A2** shows this point. The crossing of the indifference curves implies that points Y and Z are equally preferred because they both are on the same indifference curve as X. Consumption bundle Y, though, represents more of both fish and breadfruit than bundle Z, so Y must be preferred to Z. Whenever indifference curves cross, this type of internal inconsistency (irrational ranking) will arise. So, the indifference curves of an individual must not cross.

The Consumer's Preferred Bundle

Used together with the opportunity constraint of the individual, indifference curves can be used to indicate the most preferred consumption alternatives available to an individual. The **consumption opportunity constraint** separates consumption bundles that are attainable from those that are unattainable.

Assuming that Crusoe could produce only for himself, his consumption opportunity constraint would look like the production possibilities curves discussed in Chapter 2. What would happen if natives from another island visited Crusoe and offered to make exchanges with him? If a barter market existed that permitted Crusoe to exchange fish for breadfruit at a specified exchange rate, his options would resemble those of the market constraint shown by **Exhibit A3**. First, let us consider the case where Crusoe inhabits a barter economy in which the current market exchange rate is two fish to one breadfruit. Suppose that, as a result of his expertise as a fisherman, Crusoe specializes in this activity and is able to bring sixteen fish to the market per week. What consumption alternatives will be open to him? Because two fish can

EXHIBIT A2
Indifference Curves Cannot Cross

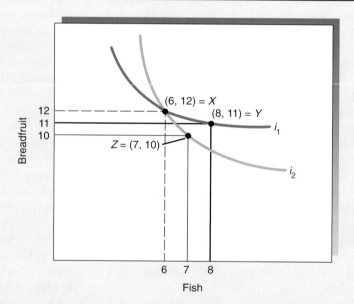

If the indifference curves of an individual crossed, they would show the inconsistency pictured here. Points X and Y must be equally valued, since they are both on the same indifference curve (i_1). Similarly, points X and Z must be equally preferred, since they are both on the indifference curve (i_2). If this is true, Y and Z must also be equally preferred, since they are both equally preferred to X. However, point Y represents more of both goods than Z, so Y has to be preferred to Z. When indifference curves cross, this type of internal inconsistency always arises.

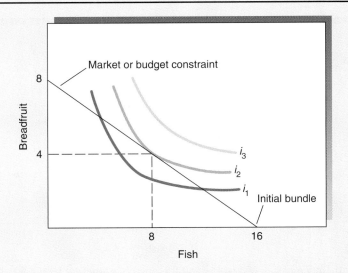

Consumer Maximization in a Barter Economy

Suppose that the set of indifference curves shown here outlines Crusoe's preferences. The slope of the market (or budget) constraint indicates that two fish trade for one breadfruit in this barter economy. If Crusoe produces sixteen fish per week, he will trade eight fish for four breadfruit in order to move to the consumption bundle (eight fish and four breadfruit) that maximizes his level of satisfaction.

be bartered in the market for one breadfruit, Crusoe will be able to consume sixteen fish, or eight breadfruit, or any combination on the market constraint indicated by the line between these two points. For example, if he trades two of his sixteen fish for one breadfruit, he will be able to consume a bundle consisting of fourteen fish and one breadfruit. Assuming that the set of indifference curves of Exhibit A3 outlines Crusoe's preferences, he will choose to consume eight fish and four breadfruit. Of course, it will be possible for Crusoe to choose many other combinations of breadfruit and fish, but none of the other attainable combinations would enable him to reach as high a level of satisfaction. Because he is able to bring only sixteen fish to the market, it would be impossible for him to attain an indifference curve higher than i_2.

Crusoe's indifference curve and the market constraint curve will coincide (they will be tangent) at the point at which his attainable level of satisfaction is maximized. At that point (eight fish and four breadfruit), the rate at which Crusoe is willing to exchange fish for breadfruit (as indicated by the slope of the indifference curve) will be just equal to the rate at which the market will *permit* him to exchange the two (the slope of the market constraint). If the two slopes differ at a point, Crusoe will always be able to find an attainable combination that will permit him to reach a *higher* indifference curve. He will always move down the market constraint when it is flatter than his indifference curve, and up if the market constraint is steeper.

Crusoe in a Money Economy

As far as the condition for maximization of consumer satisfaction is concerned, moving from a barter economy to a money income economy changes little. **Exhibit A4** shows this point. Initially, the price of fish is $1, and the price of breadfruit is $2. The market therefore permits an

exchange of two fish for one breadfruit, just as was the case in Exhibit A3. In Exhibit A4, we assume that Crusoe has a fixed money income of $16. At this level of income, he confronts the same market constraint (usually called a **budget constraint** in an economy with money) as in Exhibit A3. Given the product prices and his income, Crusoe can choose to consume sixteen fish, or eight breadfruit, or any combination indicated by a line (the budget constraint) connecting these two points. Given his preferences, Crusoe will again choose the combination of eight fish and four breadfruit if he wishes to maximize his level of satisfaction. As was true for the barter economy, when Crusoe maximizes his satisfaction (moves to the highest attainable indifference curve), the rate at which he is willing to exchange fish for breadfruit will just equal the rate at which the market will permit him to exchange the two goods. Stated in more technical terms, when his level of satisfaction is at a maximum, Crusoe's marginal rate of substitution of fish for breadfruit, as indicated by the slope of the indifference curve at E_1, will just equal the price ratio (P_F/P_b, which is also the slope of the budget constraint).

What will happen if the price of fish increases? Exhibit A4 also answers this question. Since the price of breadfruit and Crusoe's *money* income are constant, a higher fish price will have two effects. First, it will make Crusoe poorer, even though his money income will be unchanged. His budget constraint will turn clockwise around point A, illustrating that his consumption options are now more limited—that is, his real income has declined. Second, the budget line will be steeper, indicating that a larger number of breadfruit must now be sacrificed to obtain an additional unit of fish. It will no longer be possible for Crusoe to attain indifference curve i_2. The best he can do is indifference curve i_1, which he can attain by choosing the bundle of five fish and three breadfruit.

EXHIBIT A4
Consumer Maximization in a Money Economy

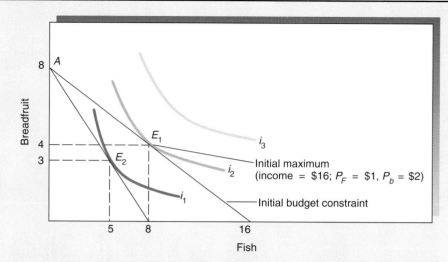

Suppose that Crusoe's income is $16 per day, the price of fish (P_F) is $1, and the price of breadfruit (P_b) is $2. Thus, Crusoe confronts exactly the same price ratio and budget constraint as in Exhibit A3. Assuming that his preferences are unchanged, he will again maximize his satisfaction by choosing to consume eight fish and four breadfruit. What will happen if the price of fish rises to $2? Crusoe's consumption opportunities will be reduced. His budget constraint will turn clockwise around point A, reflecting the higher price of fish. His fish consumption will decline to five units. (*Note:* Because Crusoe's real income has been reduced, his consumption of breadfruit will also decline.)

Using the information supplied by Exhibit A4, we can now locate two points on Crusoe's demand curve for fish. When the price of fish was $1, Crusoe chose eight fish; when the price rose to $2, Crusoe reduced his consumption to five (see **Exhibit A5**). Of course, other points on Crusoe's demand curve could also be located if we considered other prices for fish.

The demand curve of Exhibit A5 is constructed on the assumption that the price of breadfruit remains $2 and that Crusoe's money income remains constant at $16. If either of these factors were to change, the entire demand curve for fish, shown by Exhibit A5, would shift.

The indifference curve is a useful way to show how a person with a fixed budget chooses between two goods. In the real world, of course, people have hundreds, or even thousands, of goods to choose from, and the doubling of only one price usually has a small impact on a person's overall consumption and satisfaction possibilities. In our

EXHIBIT A5
Crusoe's Demand for Fish

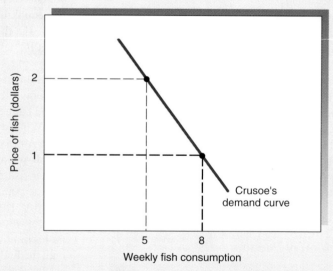

As Exhibit A4 shows, when the price of fish is $1, Crusoe chooses eight units. When the price of fish increases to $2, he reduces his consumption to five units. This gives us two points on Crusoe's demand curve for fish. Other points on the demand curve could be derived by confronting Crusoe with still other prices of fish. (*Note:* Crusoe's money income [$16] and the price of breadfruit [$2] are unchanged in this analysis.)

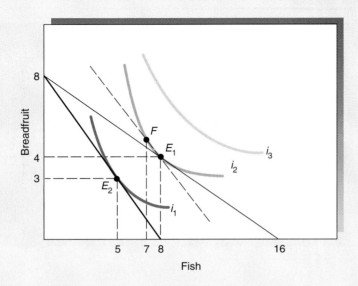

EXHIBIT A6
Income and
Substitution Effects
of a Price Change

Here we break down Crusoe's response to the rise in the price of fish from $1 to $2 (see Exhibit A4) into the substitution and income effects. The move from E_1 to F shows the substitution effect, whereas the move from F to E_2 reflects the income effect.

simple example, the twofold increase in the price of fish makes Crusoe much worse off, because he spends a large portion of his budget on the item.

Income and Substitution Effects of a Price Change

In the text, we indicated that, when the price of a product rises, the amount consumed will change as a result of both an *income effect* and a *substitution effect*. Indifference curve analysis can be used to separate these two effects. **Exhibit A6** is similar to Exhibit A4. Both exhibits show Crusoe's response to an increase in the price of fish from $1 to $2 when money income ($16) and the price of breadfruit ($2) are held constant. Exhibit A6, however, breaks down his total response into the substitution effect and the income effect. The reduction in the consumption of fish solely because of the substitution (price) effect, holding Crusoe's real income (level of utility) constant, can be found by constructing a line tangent to Crusoe's original indifference curve (i_2), and having a slope indicating the higher price of fish. This line (the broken line in Exhibit A6), which is parallel to Crusoe's actual budget constraint (the line containing point E_2), reflects the higher price of fish. It is tangent to the original indifference curve i_2, so Crusoe's real income is held constant. As this line indicates, Crusoe's consumption of fish would

fall from eight to seven, due strictly to the fact that fish are now more expensive. This move from E_1 to F is a pure substitution effect.

Real income, though, has actually been reduced. As a result, Crusoe will be unable to attain point F on indifference curve i_2. The best he can attain is point E_2, which decreases his consumption of fish by another two units to five. Since the broken line containing F and the budget constraint containing E_2 are parallel, the relative price of fish and breadfruit is held constant as Crusoe moves from F to E_2. This move from F to E_2 is thus a pure income effect. (*Note:* Because the consumption of both goods drops in this move, when income falls but the prices do not change, both goods must be normal goods.) This reduction in the consumption of fish (and breadfruit) in the move from F to E_2 is due entirely to the decline in Crusoe's real income.

Indifference curve analysis highlights the assumptions and considerations that enter into consumer decisions. The logic of the proof that there is an inverse relationship between the price and the amount demanded is both elegant and reassuring. It is elegant because of the internal consistency of the logic and the precision of the analysis. It is reassuring because it conforms with our expectations, which are based on the central postulate of economics—that incentives matter in a predictable way.

CHAPTER

20

Costs and the Supply of Goods

From the standpoint of society as a whole, the "cost" of anything is the value that it has in alternative uses.

—Thomas Sowell[1]

Chapter Focus

■ Why are business firms used by societies everywhere to organize production?

■ How are firms organized in market economies?

■ What are explicit and implicit costs, and how do they guide the behavior of the firm?

■ How does economic profit differ from accounting profit? Why is this difference important?

■ How will increases in output influence the firm's costs in the short run? How will costs vary with output in the long run?

■ What are the major factors that would cause the firm's cost curves to shift?

[1]Thomas Sowell, *Basic Economics* (New York: Basic Books, 2000), 10.

Demand and supply interact to determine the market price of a product. In the preceding chapter, we showed that the demand for a product reflects the strength of consumer desire for that product. In this chapter, we will focus on the cost of production. The resources needed to produce one good could be used to produce other goods instead. As Thomas Sowell asserts in the quotation that begins this chapter, the cost to society of anything is the value that it has in alternative uses. The market for resources makes that cost clear to producers. The maker of soccer balls, for example, must compete against producers of other goods when purchasing the machines, materials, and labor needed to produce the balls. In turn, the firm incurs costs as these resources are purchased.

Costs carry an important message: they tell producers the value of the resources in the production of other things. Further, the message comes with an important incentive attached. If the per-unit cost of producing a good exceeds its price, producers will suffer losses. Under these conditions, they are unlikely to continue supplying the good because doing so will reduce their income and wealth. Thus, supply and the cost of production are closely linked. For example, a producer who faces a cost of $1,500 to produce a high-quality TV set is unlikely to continue supplying the sets for very long if their market price is $1,000. In the long run, firms will continue to supply a good only if they can sell it for a price that covers their per-unit cost.

In this chapter, we will lay the foundation for a detailed investigation of the links between costs, business output, and market supply. What do economists count as costs, and why? How do costs guide the owners and managers of firms in a market economy? Why are costs important to managers, even when they personally do not pay those costs? We will discuss these and related questions in this chapter. ▨

THE ORGANIZATION OF THE BUSINESS FIRM

The business firm is an entity designed to organize raw materials, labor, and machines with the goal of producing goods and/or services. Firms (1) purchase productive resources from households and other firms, (2) transform them into a different commodity, and (3) sell the transformed product or service to consumers.

Every society, no matter what type of economy it has, relies on business firms to organize resources and transform them into products. In market economies, most business firms choose their own price, output level, and methods of production. They reap the benefits of sales revenues, but they also must pay the costs of the resources they use. In socialist countries, governments often set the selling prices of goods and services and constrain the actions of business firms in various other ways. Firms typically do not pay all their bills from their revenues, and they are often not allowed to keep revenues that exceed costs. In any case, the business firm is the entity used to organize production in capitalist and socialist economies alike. In this chapter, we will focus on the organization and behavior of firms in a market economy.

Incentives, Cooperation, and the Nature of the Firm

In capitalist countries, most firms are privately owned. Owners risk their wealth on the success of the business. If the firm is successful and earns profits, these financial gains go to the owners. Conversely, if the firm suffers losses, the owners must bear the consequences. Because the owners receive what remains after the revenue of the firm is used to pay the contractual costs, they are called **residual claimants**.

In a market economy, the property right of owners to the residual income of the firm plays a very important role: it provides owners with a strong incentive to organize and structure their business in a manner that will keep the cost of producing output low (relative to its value). The wealth of these residual claimants is directly influenced by the success or failure of the firm. Thus, they have both the authority and a strong incentive to see that resources under their direction are used efficiently and directed toward production of goods that are valued more highly than their costs.

Residual claimants
Individuals who personally receive the excess, if any, of revenues over costs. Residual claimants gain if the firm's costs are reduced or revenues increase.

443

Team production
A production process in which employees work together under the supervision of the owner or the owner's representative.

There are two ways of organizing productive activity: contracting and **team production,** in which workers are hired by a firm to work together under the supervision of the owner, or the owner's representative—a manager. Most business firms use both contracting and team production.

In principle, all production could be accomplished solely through contracting. For example, a builder might have a house built by contracting with one person to pour the concrete, another to construct the wooden part of the house, a third to install the roofing, a fourth to do the electrical wiring, and so on. No employees would have to be involved in such a project. More commonly though, goods and services are produced with some combination of contracting and the use of team production by employees of a firm.

Why do firms use team production? If contracting alone is used to produce something, the producer must, for each project, (1) determine what needs to be produced and how, given the circumstances, current technology, and prices, (2) search out reliable suppliers, and (3) negotiate and enforce the contracts. The entrepreneur who wants to produce by this method must have specialized knowledge in a variety of areas and must devote a great deal of time and effort to the planning and contracting processes. Not many people have the expertise or the time to perform all these tasks by themselves except on a small scale. Team production for certain tasks can be more practical and less costly.

Accordingly, a builder with multiple projects is likely to hire knowledgeable, experienced workers to plan the construction process, purchase materials, and build the structures. The builder will then contract with others to obtain materials and more specialized labor services.

The firm can reduce many of the transaction costs associated with contracting by using team production. Team production, however, comes with another set of problems. Team members—the employees working for the firm—must be monitored and given incentives to avoid shirking, or working at less than the expected rate of productivity. Taking long work breaks, paying more attention to their own convenience than to work results, and wasting time when diligence is called for are examples of **shirking**. A worker will shirk more when the costs of doing so are shifted to other team members, including the owners of the firm. Hired managers, even including those at the top, must be monitored and given incentives to avoid shirking.

Shirking
Working at less than the expected rate of productivity, which reduces output. Shirking is more likely when workers are not monitored, so that the cost of lower output falls on others.

Imperfect monitoring and imperfect incentives are always a problem with team production. It is part of a larger class of what economists call **principal-agent problems**. A person taking a car to an auto mechanic confronts this problem. The mechanic wants to get the job done quickly and make as much money on it as possible. The car owner wants to get the job done quickly also, but wants the problem fixed in a lasting way, at the lowest possible cost. Because the mechanic typically knows far more about the job than the customer, it is hard for the customer to monitor the mechanic's work. There is a possibility, therefore, that the mechanic may charge a large amount for a "quick fix" that will not last.

Principal-agent problem
The incentive problem that occurs when the purchaser of services (the principal) lacks full information about the circumstances faced by the seller (the agent) and cannot know how well the agent performs the purchased services. The agent may to some extent work toward objectives other than those sought by the principal paying for the service.

The owner of a firm is in a similar situation. It is often difficult to monitor the performance of individual employees and motivate them in a way that will encourage high productivity. Nonetheless, the ability of the firm to use resources effectively and succeed in a competitive market depends crucially upon resolving these problems. To keep costs low and the value of output high, a firm must discover and use an incentive structure that motivates managers and workers, and discourages shirking. The problem extends all the way to the top.

Even top-level executives hired to manage a firm do not have the same objectives as owners—who care mainly about profit maximization—unless, of course, the managers are the owners. So the judgments of executives, too, are influenced by what is in their personal best interests. They want perks, personal job security, and other benefits that may not be consistent with profit maximization for the firm. The problem becomes more serious as firms grow larger and acquire more managers and employees. Ultimately, it is the job of the owners, as residual claimants, to develop an incentive structure to minimize the principal-agent problem. For the owner, the saying "the buck stops here" always applies.

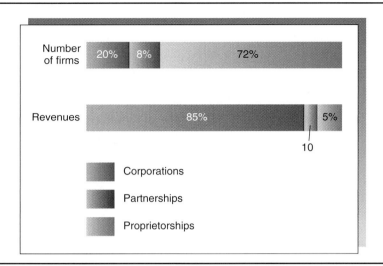

Source: Statistical Abstract of the United States, 2003, Table 732. (Data are for 2000.)

EXHIBIT 1
How Business Firms Are Organized

Nearly three out of every four firms are proprietorships, but only 5 percent of all business revenue is generated by proprietorships. Corporations account for only one out of every five firms, but generate 85 percent of all revenues.

Three Types of Business Firms

Business firms can be organized in one of three ways: as a proprietorship, a partnership, or a corporation. The structure chosen determines how the owners share the risks and liabilities of the firm and how they participate in making decisions.

A **proprietorship** is a business firm that is owned by a single individual who is fully liable for the debts of the firm. In addition to assuming the responsibilities of ownership, the proprietor often works directly for the firm, providing managerial and other labor services. Many small businesses, including neighborhood grocery stores, barbershops, and farms, are business proprietorships. As **Exhibit 1** shows, proprietorships account for 72 percent of the business firms in the United States. Because most proprietorships are small, however, they account for less than 5 percent of all business revenues.

A **partnership** consists of two or more persons who are co-owners of a business firm. The partners share risks and responsibilities in an agreed-upon manner. There is no difference between a proprietorship and a partnership in terms of owner liability. In both cases, the owners are fully liable for all business debts incurred by the firm. Many law, medical, and accounting firms are organized along partnership lines. However, this form of business structure accounts for only 8 percent of the total number of firms and 10 percent of all business revenues.

The business firms that are **corporations** account for more than 85 percent of total business revenue, even though they constitute only 20 percent of all firms. What accounts for the attractiveness of this business structure? From its start, by an Act of the British Parliament in 1862, the corporation, or "joint stock company," as it is also called, grew in importance for two main reasons. First, although the stockholders of the corporation are the legal owners, their liability is limited to the value of their shares of the corporation. If a corporation owes you money, you cannot directly sue the stockholders. Of course, you can sue the corporation. However, if a corporation goes bankrupt, you and others to whom the firm owes money may simply be out of luck. This limited liability makes it possible for corporations to attract investment funds from a large number of "owners" who do not participate in the day-to-day management of the firm.

Second, ownership can easily be transferred under the corporate structure. The shares, or ownership rights, of an owner who dies can be sold by the heirs to another owner without disrupting the business firm. Because of this, the corporation is an ongoing concern. Similarly, stockholders who become unhappy with the way a corporation is run can bail out merely by selling their stock.

The stockholders of large corporations, through their elected board of directors, usually hire managers—trained and experienced experts—to operate the firm. Will the managers operate the firm efficiently and satisfy customers? Offering consumers value at

Proprietorship
A business firm owned by an individual who possesses the ownership right to the firm's profits and is personally liable for the firm's debts.

Partnership
A business firm owned by two or more individuals who possess ownership rights to the firm's profits and are personally liable for the debts of the firm.

Corporation
A business firm owned by shareholders who possess ownership rights to the firm's profits, but whose liability is limited to the amount of their investment in the firm.

a low cost is the ticket to profitability. In an owner-managed firm, the owner's property right to the residual income provides a strong incentive both to reduce costs and to please consumers. This is not necessarily so for the managers of a corporation.

For a large corporation with many stockholders—millions in some cases—the situation is complex. Stockholders own the residual income (profits), but professional managers operate the firm. Stockholders want managers to cut costs while increasing output and revenues, but managers might want high salaries for themselves, large offices, first-class travel, and other expensive perks. They might also prefer the power and prestige associated with expanding the business (by taking over another firm, perhaps), even if it might reduce profitability. Can the stockholders control the actions of managers and direct them toward the pursuit of profitability? Direct control by many stockholders is unlikely. Few of them own enough shares to give them the incentive or information they would need to exercise direct control. Most find it too expensive even to attend the annual shareholders' meeting, much less to monitor managers closely. Instead, stockholders elect a board of directors, which in turn appoints the company's high-level managers. As the following section describes, however, not all is lost when stockholders don't directly run the company themselves. Internal corporate policies and competition for control of the firm by outsiders help mitigate principal-agent problems when managers run the company instead.

COSTS, COMPETITION, AND THE CORPORATION

Three major factors in a market economy promote cost efficiency and customer service within the corporation, limiting the power of corporate managers to shirk on their duties to shareholders:

1. Competition among firms for investment funds and customers. Even without direct control of their corporation, stockholders (and the investment advisers, pension fund managers, and others hired to help them) have an incentive to monitor the corporation's management in order to anticipate problems and search for constructive changes. Investors who are the first to spot a profitable new management strategy can buy stock early, before others realize the opportunity, and bid the price up. A rising stock price is both a signal of approval to good managers and an incentive to manage the corporation well. Conversely, when managers' decisions are contrary to the interests of stockholders, the opposite occurs: the stock price will fall. Knowing that stock prices can plummet motivates stockholders (along with professional managers of stock holdings) to be the first to spot a problem with the company. This way they can dump their stock before everyone else does, and thus prior to the share price falling. Some investment firms even specialize in selling shares "short" (writing contracts to deliver shares of the stock later, when they expect the stock price to be lower than its current level) if they believe a company is overvalued on the market. So managers get constant feedback via stock price changes, which can be just as important as current profits to stockholders and boards of directors.

Similarly, consumers have an incentive to monitor the quality and price of the firm's output. No one forces them to buy the corporation's product, so if other firms supply superior products or offer lower prices, consumers can take their business elsewhere. Because investors are free to buy and sell the company's shares and customers to buy its products or those of other firms, the ability of managers to benefit personally at the expense of either customers or stockholders is limited. While some managers are still able to enrich themselves at stockholders' expense, at least temporarily, the recent cases of corporations like Tyco and Enron show that their actions tend to catch up with them.

2. Compensation and management incentives. The compensation of managers can be structured to bring the interests of managers more into harmony with those of shareholders. Corporations usually tie the compensation of managers to the market success of the business. The salary increases and bonuses of most high-level managers are directly related to the firm's profitability and the price of its shares.

How important are these incentives? In recent years, salaries have constituted only about 10 percent of the compensation of chief executive officers (CEOs). The other 90 percent has been in the form of bonuses, often stock awards and stock options (the right to buy shares at a certain price). Both forms of payment have a "vesting period," which means they will be granted only if the CEO stays with the firm for a certain amount of time and meets specific goals. Policies like these encourage corporate managers to maximize the the firm's profits—and, not coincidentally, the value of its shares—both strongly in the interest of shareholders. Managers who develop a good track record

© BONNIE KAMIN/PHOTOEDIT

of adding value to the firm gain not only more pay and greater job security, but also better job offers should they later decide to switch firms.

Incentive pay brings with it another unwanted incentive for managers, though: the incentive to gain personally by manipulating the firm's accounting records to make its financial performance look better than it really is. (See the accompanying Applications in Economics feature: "Cooking the Books.") However, stockholders and portfolio managers, and especially investors who specialize in selling stocks short when they think the firm is overvalued, will be scrutinizing the records to detect phony accounting designed to mislead investors.

3. The threat of corporate takeover. Managers who do not serve the interests of their shareholders leave the firm vulnerable to a takeover. This is a move by an outside person or group, noticing the bad management, to gain control of the firm. As we previously noted, shareholders who lose confidence in the firm's management can exit the arrangement by selling their shares. When a significant number of shareholders follow this course of action, the market value of the firm's stock will decline. This will make it an attractive prospect for takeover specialists shopping for a poorly run business, the value of which could be substantially increased by a new and better management team.

Consider a firm currently earning $1.50 per share. At present, the market value of the firm's stock is $15 per share. If the firm's earnings are low because the current management team is pursuing its own objectives at the expense of profitability, then a corporate takeover could lead to substantial gain for someone. Suppose outsiders believe they can restructure the firm, improve the management, and double the firm's earnings. They then "tender" a takeover bid—make an offer to buy the shareholders' stock or persuade them to pressure the board of directors to sell out. Suppose they offer $20 per share. This is more than the current market value of the firm, so shareholders and the board will be tempted to accept the offer and gain wealth from the sale. If the takeover team gains control of the firm, improves its performance, and increases its earnings to $3 per share, then the stock value of the firm will rise accordingly (to $30 per share).

Of course, the current managers have an incentive to resist the takeover. After all, they are likely to lose their jobs if the potential new owners are successful. Unfortunately for them, though, the shareholders or their board of directors will ultimately decide whether or not to accept the offer. The takeover threat helps keep current managers from straying too far from a strategy to maximize profit. Some corporate managers have instituted policies to help defend their firms against takeovers. However, limiting the power of shareholders this way can significantly lower the stock price of a badly managed

Corporate managers are more likely to serve the interests of customers and stockholder because of the following: competition for investment funds and consumer sales, the threat of a takeover, and managerial compensation packages based on stock and stock options.

APPLICATIONS IN ECONOMICS

Cooking the Books: How the Market Responds to Criminal Behavior

"Cooking the books" refers to the practice of using accounting procedures in an intentionally misleading way. By cooking the books, a corporation's profits—or at least what appear to be its profits—can be increased. Stockholders are always looking for shares of high-profit firms, so a recent record of high profits will increase the demand for the corporation's stock shares and drive up their price. Cooking the books can be artificially encouraging to shareholders in the short term, but it can conceal problems and even lead to disaster in the long term.

© TIM JOHNSON/BLOOMBERG NEWS/LANDOV

Enron, the energy-trading company, is a dramatic example. High-level executives in the firm used misleading accounting procedures to make Enron look highly profitable when, in fact, it was not. Moreover, Arthur Andersen, a highly respected accounting firm, audited Enron's books and certified their accuracy, knowing there were irregularities. As a result, Enron's stock price climbed, along with the value of its managers' stock options—even though the company was really on its way to bankruptcy. These executives were then able to cash in on their stock options to enrich themselves while the company lay on the path to ruin.

When Enron made some of its accounting procedures public in November 2001, market participants took quick action, selling their shares. The stock price then plummeted. In light of its true financial position, Enron filed for bankruptcy less than a month later. At the beginning of the year, its stock had been worth $60 billion. By the end of the year, it was nearly worthless. By July 2004, Enron was employing about 9,000 workers, down from 32,000 at its peak, and its bankruptcy plan had been approved by a federal judge. The Justice Department had filed criminal charges against thirty-one members of Enron's management, including its chief executive.

Arthur Andersen, Enron's accounting firm, faced similar consequences. Many of the auditing firm's clients quickly stopped doing business with it. One of its partners was subsequently convicted of obstructing justice, and the firm announced it would no longer audit public companies in the U.S. Its reputation as a trusted accounting company was ruined, and criminal charges were brought against several Arthur Andersen executives.

company.[2] Moreover, managers thought to be doing a bad job will have to make it extraordinarily difficult for a takeover to occur in order to avoid being ousted.

How Well Does the Corporate Structure Work?

Perhaps history provides the best answer to this question. If the corporate structure were not an effective form of business organization, it would not have continued to survive, nor would it be so prevalent today. Rival forms of business organization, including proprietorships, partnerships, consumer cooperatives, employee ownership, and mutually owned companies can and do compete in the marketplace for investment funds and customers. In certain industries, some of these alternative forms of business organization are dominant. Nonetheless, in most industries, the corporate structure is the dominant form of business organization (see Exhibit 1). This is strong evidence that, despite its defects, the corporation is generally a cost-efficient, consumer-sensitive form of organization.

---

[2]Economists Paul Gompers, Joy Ishii, and Andrew Metrick, in "Corporate Governance and Equity Prices" (NBER working paper 8449, released August 2001), find that "firms with weaker shareholder rights earned significantly lower returns, were valued lower, had poorer operating performance, and engaged in greater capital expenditure and takeover activity." However, some of the same actions that favor managers—large "golden parachute" retirement plans, for example—can also be guarantees that increase the ability of a company's directors to hire or retain good managers, as shown by Dino Falaschetti, "Golden Parachutes: Credible Commitments or Evidence of Shirking?," *Journal of Corporate Finance* 8 (2002): 150–78.

THE ECONOMIC ROLE OF COSTS

Consumers would like to have more economic goods, but resources to produce them are scarce. How much of each desired good should be produced? Every economic system must balance consumers' competing desires. When decisions are made in the political arena, the budget process performs this balancing function. Legislators, a central planning committee, or a monarch decide which goods will be produced and which will be forgone. Taxes and budgets are set accordingly.

In a market economy, though, consumer demand and production costs are central to performing this balancing function. ***The demand for a product represents the voice of consumers instructing firms to produce the good. On the other hand, a firm's costs represent the desire of consumers not to sacrifice goods that could be produced if the same resources were employed elsewhere.*** A profit-seeking firm will try to produce only those units of output buyers are willing to pay full cost for. Proper measurement and interpretation of costs by the firm are critical to both the firm's profitability and the efficient use of resources.

Calculating Economic Costs and Profits

We can reasonably assume that business firms in a market setting, regardless of their size, are concerned first with profit. Profit is simply the firm's total revenue minus its total costs. But to state profit correctly, costs must be measured properly. Most people, including some who are in business, think of costs as amounts paid for raw materials, labor, machines, and similar inputs. However, this concept of cost, which stems from accounting procedures, excludes some important components of the firm's costs. When cost is miscalculated, so, too, is profit because it is merely revenue minus cost. Bad economic decisions can result from miscalculating cost and profit.

The key to understanding the economist's concept of profit is to remember the idea of *opportunity cost*—the highest valued alternative forgone by the resource owner when the resource is used. These costs may either be explicit or implicit. **Explicit costs** result when the firm makes a monetary payment to resource owners. Money wages, interest, and rental payments are a measure of what the firm gives up to employ the services of labor and capital resources. These are relatively easy to track. But firms also incur **implicit costs**—those associated with the use of resources owned by the firm. For example, the owners of small proprietorships often work for their own businesses, for little or no pay. These businesses incur an implicit cost—an opportunity cost—associated with the use of this resource (the owners' labor services). The highest valued alternative forgone in this case is the maximum amount of money the owners could have made doing something else. The **total cost** of production is the sum of these explicit and implicit costs incurred by the employment of all resources involved in the production process.

Accounting statements generally omit the implicit cost of equity capital—the cost of funds supplied by the firm's owners. If a firm borrows financial capital from a bank or other private source, it will have to pay interest. Accountants properly record this interest expense as a cost. In contrast, when the firm acquires financial capital by issuing stock, accountants don't record this as an expense. Essentially, this is because the stockholders *are* the firm's owners. Either way, acquiring capital has an opportunity cost. People who supply capital to a firm expect to earn at least a normal rate of return—a return comparable to what they could have earned if they had chosen other investment opportunities. Banks will demand interest payments, for example. Stockholders will demand a share of the company's profits, or dividends. Or they might expect the price of the stock they purchase to rise measurably, thereby enhancing their wealth.

When calculating the normal rate of return, economists use the normal return on financial capital as a basis for determining the implicit **opportunity cost of equity capital**. If the normal rate of return on financial capital is 10 percent, equity investors will refuse funds to firms that persistently fail to earn a 10 percent rate of return on capital assets.

Explicit costs
Payments by a firm to purchase the services of productive resources.

Implicit costs
The opportunity costs associated with a firm's use of resources that it owns. These costs do not involve a direct money payment. Examples include wage income and interest forgone by the owner of a firm who also provides labor services and equity capital to the firm.

Total cost
The costs, both explicit and implicit, of all the resources used by the firm. Total cost includes a normal rate of return for the firm's equity capital.

Opportunity cost of equity capital
The rate of return that must be earned by investors to induce them to supply financial capital to the firm.

How Do Economic and Accounting Profit Differ?

Economic profit
The difference between the firm's total revenues and its total costs, including both the explicit and implicit cost components.

Economists include both explicit and implicit costs when they measure total cost. **Economic profit** is total revenues minus total costs, including both the explicit and implicit cost components. Economic profit will be positive only if the earnings of the business exceed the opportunity cost of all the resources used by the firm, *including the opportunity cost of assets owned by the firm and any unpaid labor services supplied by the owner*. In contrast, economic losses result when the earnings of the firm are insufficient to cover explicit and implicit costs. That is why the **normal profit rate** is zero economic profit, yielding just the competitive rate of return on the capital (and labor) of owners. A higher rate would draw more competitors and their investors into the market; a lower rate would cause competitors and their investors to exit the market.

Normal profit rate
Zero economic profit, providing just the competitive rate of return on the capital (and labor) of owners. An above-normal profit will draw more entry into the market, whereas a below-normal profit will lead to an exit of investors and capital.

Remember, zero economic profits do not imply that the firm is about to go out of business. On the contrary, they indicate that the owners are receiving exactly the normal profit rate, or the competitive market rate of return on their investment. They are earning no more and no less than they could earn elsewhere on what they use in the firm.

Whenever accounting procedures omit implicit costs, like those associated with owner-provided labor services or capital, the firm's opportunity costs of production will be understated. This understatement of cost leads to an overstatement of profits. Therefore, the **accounting profits** of a firm are generally greater than the firm's economic profits (see the Applications in Economics feature on accounting costs). For most large corporations, though, omitting the implicit costs of services provided by an owner isn't an issue. In this case, the accounting profits approximate the returns to the firm's equity capital. High accounting profits (measured as a rate of return on a firm's assets), relative to those of other firms, suggest that a firm is earning an economic profit. Correspondingly, a low rate of accounting profit implies economic losses. Either positive or negative economic profits, of course, call for a change in output. Such a change, however, will take time.

Accounting profits
The sales revenues minus the expenses of a firm over a designated time period, usually one year. Accounting profits typically make allowances for changes in the firm's inventories and depreciation of its assets. No allowance is made, however, for the opportunity cost of the equity capital of the firm's owners, or other implicit costs.

SHORT-RUN AND LONG-RUN TIME PERIODS

A firm cannot instantly adjust its output. Time plays an important role in the production process. All of a firm's resources can be expanded (or contracted) over time, but for specialized or heavy equipment, expanding (and contracting) availability quickly is likely to be very expensive or even impossible. Economists often speak of the **short run** as a time period so short that the firm is unable to alter its present plant size. In the short run, the firm is typically stuck with its existing plant and heavy equipment. These assets are "fixed" for a given time period, in other words. The firm can alter output, however, by applying larger or smaller amounts of "variable" resources, like labor and raw materials. In this way, the existing plant capacity can be used more or less intensively in the short run.

Short run (in production)
A time period so short that a firm is unable to vary some of its factors of production. The firm's plant size typically cannot be altered in the short run.

How long is the short run? *The short run is that period of time during which at least one factor of production, usually the size of the firm's plant, cannot be changed.* The length varies from industry to industry. A trucking firm might be able to hire more drivers and buy or rent more trucks and double its hauling capacity in a few months. In other industries, particularly those that use assembly lines and mass-production techniques (for example, the automotive factory supplying trucks), increasing production capacity might take a year or even several years.

Long run (in production)
A time period long enough to allow the firm to vary all of its factors of production.

The **long run** is a time period long enough for existing firms to alter the size of their plants and for new firms to enter (or exit) the market. All of the firm's resources are variable in the long run. In the long run, firms can expand their output by increasing the sizes of their plants—perhaps by adding on to them or by constructing entirely new facilities.

An example might help you understand the distinction between the short- and long-run time periods: If a battery manufacturer hired 200 additional workers and ordered more raw materials in order to squeeze more production out of its existing plant, it would be making a short-run adjustment. In contrast, if the manufacturer built an additional plant (or expanded the size of its current facility) and installed additional heavy equipment, it would be making a long-run adjustment.

CATEGORIES OF COSTS

To describe various aspects of the firm's costs and the relationship of those costs to the level of output, even without detailed knowledge of the production process, we need some definitions. We have emphasized that in the short run some of a firm's factors of production, such as the size of its plant, will be fixed. Other productive resources will be variable. In the short run, then, we can break the firm's costs into these two categories—fixed and variable. Each category of costs behaves differently. Seeing that behavior graphically will help us understand how the profit-maximizing level of the firm's output is determined. It will be important to distinguish between a firm's total costs and its per-unit costs, called "average" costs.

Each of the firm's fixed costs, and their sum, called **total fixed cost** (*TFC*), will remain unchanged when output rises or falls in the short run. For example, a firm's insurance premiums, its property taxes, and, most significantly, the opportunity cost of using its fixed assets will be present whether the firm produces a large or small amount of output. These costs will not vary with output. They are "fixed" as long as the firm remains in business. Fixed costs will be present at all levels of output, including zero output. They can be avoided only if the firm goes out of business.

What will happen to **average fixed cost** (*AFC*), fixed costs per unit, as output expands? Remember that the firm's fixed cost will be the same whether output is 1, 100, or 1,000. The *AFC* is simply fixed cost divided by output. It's the firm's fixed cost spread across all of the units produced. As output increases, *AFC* declines because the fixed cost will be spread over more and more units (see part a of **Exhibit 2**).

Total fixed cost
The sum of the costs that do not vary with output. They will be incurred as long as a firm continues in business and the assets have alternative uses.

Average fixed cost
Total fixed cost divided by the number of units produced. It always declines as output increases.

APPLICATIONS IN ECONOMICS

Economic and Accounting Costs: A Hypothetical Example

The revenue-cost statement for a corner grocery store owned and operated by Terry Smith is presented here.

TOTAL REVENUE	
Sales (groceries)	$170,000
Costs (explicit)	
Groceries, wholesale	$76,000
Utilities	4,000
Taxes	6,000
Advertising	2,000
Labor services (employees)	12,000
Total (explicit) costs	$100,000
Net (accounting) profit	$70,000
Additional (implicit) costs	
Interest (personal investment)	$ 7,000
Rent (Terry's building)	18,000
Salary (Terry's labor)	50,000
Total (implicit) costs	$75,000
TOTAL EXPLICIT AND IMPLICIT COSTS	$175,000
ECONOMIC PROFIT (TOTAL REVENUE MINUS EXPLICIT AND IMPLICIT COSTS)	−$5,000

Terry works full-time as the manager, chief cashier, and janitor. Terry has $140,000 worth of refrigeration and other equipment invested in the store. Last year, his total sales were $170,000, and suppliers and employees were paid $100,000. His revenues therefore exceeded explicit costs by $70,000. This is what was recorded on the books as profit.

But did Terry really make a profit last year? Let's look at his opportunity costs and see: If Terry didn't have $140,000 of his own money invested in equipment, he could be earning 5 percent interest on the money, which would add up to $7,000 each year. Similarly, if the building he owns weren't being used as a grocery store, it could be rented to someone else for $1,500 per month. Rental income forgone is therefore $18,000 per year. In addition, because Terry is tied up working in the grocery store, a $50,000 managerial position with the local Safeway is forgone. Considering the interest, rental, and salary income that Terry had to forgo to operate the grocery store last year, his implicit costs were $75,000. This makes his total costs—both explicit and implicit—$175,000. (Recall that explicit costs were $100,000.) That's $5,000 *less* than his actual revenues of $170,000. As a result, Terry incurred an economic loss of $5,000, despite the accounting profit of $70,000 recorded on the store's books.

EXHIBIT 2
The General Characteristics of Short-Run Cost Curves

(a) Average fixed cost

(b) Marginal cost

(c) Average total cost

Average fixed costs (a) will be high for small rates of output, but they will always decline as output expands. Marginal cost (b) will rise sharply as the plant approaches its production capacity, *q*. As graph (c) shows, *ATC* will be a U-shaped curve because *AFC* will be high for small rates of output, and *MC* will be high as the plant's production capacity is approached.

Total variable cost
The sum of those costs that rise as output increases. Examples of variable costs are wages paid to workers and payments for raw materials.

Average variable cost
The total variable cost divided by the number of units produced.

Average total cost
Total cost divided by the number of units produced. It is sometimes called per-unit cost.

Marginal cost
The change in total cost required to produce an additional unit of output.

Some costs vary with output. For example, additional output can usually be produced by hiring more workers and buying more raw materials. The sum of those and other costs that rise as output increases are the firm's **total variable cost** (*TVC*). At any given level of output, the firm's **average variable cost** (*AVC*) is the total variable cost divided by output. It's the firm's variable cost spread across all of the units produced.

We have noted that total cost (*TC*) includes explicit and implicit costs. At the same time, the total cost of producing a good is also the sum of the fixed and variable costs at each output level. At zero output, total cost will equal total fixed cost. As output expands from zero, variable cost and fixed cost must be added to obtain total cost. **Average total cost** (*ATC*), sometimes referred to as unit cost, can be found by dividing total cost by the total number of units produced. *ATC* is also equal to the sum of the average fixed and average variable costs. It indicates the amount of revenue per unit of output needed to cover total cost.

The economic way of thinking focuses on what happens "at the margin." How much does it cost to produce an additional unit? **Marginal cost** (*MC*) is the change in total cost that results from the production of one additional unit. The profit-conscious decision maker recognizes *MC* as the addition to cost that must be covered by additional revenue if producing the marginal unit is to be profitable. In the short run, as illustrated by part (b) of Exhibit 2, *MC* will generally decline at first if output is increased, reach a minimum, and then increase. The rising *MC* simply reflects the fact that it becomes increasingly difficult to squeeze additional output from a plant as the facility's maximum capacity (the dotted line of part b of Exhibit 2) is approached. The accompanying Thumbnail Sketch summarizes how the firm's various costs are related to one another.

OUTPUT AND COSTS IN THE SHORT RUN

As a firm changes its rate of output in the short run, how will its unit cost be affected? First, look at this question intuitively. In the short run, the firm can vary its output by using its fixed plant size more (or less) intensively. Exhibit 2 shows two ways that this can result in high unit costs. First, when the output rate of a plant is small relative to its capacity, the facility is being underutilized, causing *AFC* to be high and *ATC* to be high, too. It will be costly to operate a large plant, with its high fixed costs, substantially below its production capacity. Alternatively, overutilization can also cause high unit costs. An overutilized plant will mean congestion—time spent by workers waiting for machines and similar costly delays. Requiring output beyond the least-cost, or designed, output level of a plant will lead to high *MC* and therefore to high *ATC*.

Thus, the ATC curve will be U-shaped, as pictured in part (c) of Exhibit 2. ATC will be high for both an underutilized plant and an overutilized plant. It will be high for an underutilized plant because average fixed cost will be high. It will be high for an overutilized plant because marginal cost will be high.

THUMBNAIL SKETCH

Compact Glossary on Cost

Term	Symbol	Equation	Definition
Fixed cost			Cost that is independent of the output level
Variable cost			Cost that varies with the output level
Total fixed cost	TFC		Cost of the fixed inputs (equals sum of quantity times unit price for each fixed input)
Total variable cost	TVC		Cost of the variable inputs (equals sum of quantity times unit price for each variable input)
Total cost	TC	$TC = TFC + TVC$	Cost of all inputs (equals fixed costs plus variable costs)
Marginal cost	MC	$MC = \Delta TC \div \Delta q$	Change in total cost resulting from a one-unit rise in output (q) [equals the change in total cost divided by the change in output]
Average fixed cost	AFC	$AFC = TFC \div q$	Total fixed cost per unit of output (equals total fixed cost divided by total output)
Average variable cost	AVC	$AVC = TVC \div q$	Total variable cost per unit of output (equals total variable cost divided by total output)
Average total cost	ATC	$ATC = AFC + AVC$	Total cost per unit of output (equals average fixed cost plus average variable cost)

Diminishing Returns and Production in the Short Run

Our analysis of the changes in unit cost as the output rate rises reflects a long-established economic law. This **law of diminishing returns** states that, as more and more units of a variable factor are applied to a fixed amount of other resources, output will eventually increase by smaller and smaller amounts. Therefore, the impact on output of additional units of the variable factor will diminish. The cost per unit of adding the variable factor may be the same, but the added output per dollar spent falls. The impact on cost per unit of output is clear: when the returns to the variable factor are rising, marginal costs (the additions to total variable cost needed to add a unit of output) are falling. Similarly, when the returns to the variable factor are falling, marginal cost is rising.

The law of diminishing returns is as famous in economics as the law of gravity is in physics. It is based on common sense and real-life observation. Have you ever noticed that, as you apply a single resource more intensively, the resource eventually tends to accomplish less and less? Consider a wheat farmer who applies fertilizer (a variable resource) more and more intensively to an acre of land (a fixed factor). At some point, the application of additional 100-pound units of fertilizer will expand the wheat yield by successively smaller amounts.

Essentially, the law of diminishing returns is a constraint imposed by nature. If it were not valid, it would be possible to raise all the world's food on an acre of the best land, or even in a flowerpot. Logically, then, there would be no point in cultivating any of the less-fertile land. We would be able to increase output simply by applying another unit of labor and fertilizer to the world's most fertile flowerpot! In the real world, of course, this is not the case; the law of diminishing returns is valid and it restricts our options.

Exhibit 3 illustrates the law of diminishing returns numerically. Column 1 indicates the quantity of the variable resource, labor in this example, that is combined with a specified amount of the fixed resource. Column 2 shows the **total product** that will result as the utilization rate of labor increases. Column 3 provides data on the **marginal product**, the

Law of diminishing returns
The postulate that, as more and more units of a variable resource are combined with a fixed amount of other resources, using additional units of the variable resource will eventually increase output only at a decreasing rate. Once diminishing returns are reached, it will take successively larger amounts of the variable factor to expand output by one unit.

Total product
The total output of a good that is associated with each alternative utilization rate of a variable input.

Marginal product
The increase in the total product resulting from a unit increase in the employment of a variable input. Mathematically, it is the ratio of the change in total product to the change in the quantity of the variable input.

EXHIBIT 3
The Law of Diminishing Returns (Hypothetical Data)

(1) UNITS OF THE VARIABLE RESOURCE, LABOR (PER DAY)	(2) TOTAL PRODUCT (OUTPUT)	(3) MARGINAL PRODUCT	(4) AVERAGE PRODUCT
0	0		—
1	8	8	8.0
2	20	12	10.0
3	34	14	11.3
4	46	12	11.5
5	56	10	11.2
6	64	8	10.7
7	70	6	10.0
8	74	4	9.3
9	75	1	8.3
10	73	−2	7.3

Average product
The total product (output) divided by the number of units of the variable input required to produce that output level.

change in total output associated with each additional unit of labor. Without the application of labor, output will be zero. As additional units of labor are applied, total product (output) rises. As the first three units of labor are applied, total product increases by successively larger amounts (8, then 12, then 14). Beginning with the fourth unit, however, diminishing returns are confronted. When the fourth unit is added, marginal product—the change in the total product—declines to 12 (down from 14, when the third unit was applied). As additional units of labor are applied, marginal product continues to decline. It is increasingly difficult to squeeze a larger total product from the fixed resources (for example, plant size and equipment). Eventually, marginal product becomes negative (beginning with the tenth unit). Column 4 of Exhibit 3 provides data for the **average product** of labor, which is simply the total product divided by the units of labor applied. Note that the average product increases as long as the marginal product is greater than the average product. Whenever the marginal unit's contribution is greater than the average, it must cause the average to rise. (A good analogy would be your grade point average. If the grade you get in this course is higher than your overall grade point average, your grade point average has to go up.) Here, this is true through the first four units. The marginal product of the fifth unit of labor, though, is 10, less than the average product for the first four units of labor (11.5). Therefore, beginning with the fifth unit, the average product declines as additional labor is applied. When marginal productivity is below the average, it brings down the average product.

Using the data from Exhibit 3, **Exhibit 4** illustrates the law of diminishing returns graphically. Initially, the total product curve (part a) increases quite rapidly. As diminishing marginal returns are confronted (beginning with the fourth unit of labor), total product increases more slowly. Eventually, a maximum output (75) is reached with the application of the ninth unit of labor. The marginal product curve (part b) reflects the total product curve. Geometrically, marginal product is the slope—the rate of increase—of the total product curve. That slope, the marginal product, reaches its maximum here with the application of three units of labor. Beyond three units, diminishing returns are present. Eventually, at ten units of labor, the marginal product becomes negative. When marginal product becomes negative, total product is necessarily declining. The average product curve rises as long as the marginal product curve is above it, since each added unit of labor is raising the average. The average product reaches its maximum at four units of labor. Beyond that, each additional unit of labor brings down the average product, and the curve declines.

Diminishing Returns and the Shape of the Cost Curves

What impact will diminishing returns have on a firm's costs? Once a firm confronts diminishing returns, larger and larger additions of the variable factor are required to

EXHIBIT 4
The Law of Diminishing Returns

As units of variable input (labor) are added to a fixed input, total product will increase, first at an increasing rate and then at a declining rate (a). This will cause both marginal and average product curves (b) to rise at first and then decline. Note that the marginal product curve intersects the average product curve at its maximum (when four units of labor are used). The smooth curves indicate that labor can be increased by amounts of less than a single unit.

expand output by one unit. This will cause marginal costs (MC) to rise. As MC continues to increase, eventually it will exceed average total cost. Until that point, MC is below ATC, bringing ATC down. When MC is greater than ATC, the additional units cost more than the average, and ATC must increase. As suggested above, think about what happens when you get a grade on an exam above your current class average. Your class average goes up. What happens if a unit of above-average cost is added to output? Average total cost rises. The firm's *MC* curve therefore crosses the *ATC* curve at the *ATC*'s lowest point. For output rates beyond the minimum *ATC,* the rising *MC* causes *ATC* to increase.

Exhibit 5 numerically illustrates the effect of the law of diminishing returns on a firm's short-run cost curve. Here, we assume that Royal Roller Blades, Inc. combines units of a variable input with a fixed factor to produce units of output (pairs of inline skates). Columns 2, 3, and 4 indicate how the total cost schedules vary as output is expanded. Total fixed costs (*TFC*), representing the opportunity cost of the fixed factors of production, are $50 per day at all levels of output. For the first four units of output, total variable costs (*TVC*) increase at a decreasing rate—by $15 with the production of the first unit, $10 with the production of the second unit, $9 with the third, and so on. Why? In this range, there are increasing returns to the variable input. Beginning with the fifth unit of output, however, diminishing marginal returns are present. From this point on, *TVC* and *TC* increase by successively larger amounts as output is expanded.

Columns 5 through 8 of Exhibit 5 are the average and marginal cost schedules. For small output rates, the *ATC* of producing roller blades is high, primarily because of the high *AFC*. Initially, *MC* is less than *ATC,* so *ATC* is falling. When diminishing returns set in for output rates beginning with five units, however, *MC* rises. Beginning with the sixth unit of output, *MC* exceeds *AVC,* causing *AVC* to rise. Beginning with the eighth unit of output, *MC* exceeds *ATC,* causing it also to rise. *ATC* thus reaches its minimum at seven

EXHIBIT 5
The Numerical Short-Run Cost Schedules of Royal Roller Blades, Inc.

	TOTAL COST DATA (PER DAY)			AVERAGE/MARGINAL COST DATA (PER DAY)			
(1) OUTPUT PER DAY	(2) TFC	(3) TVC	(4) TC (2) + (3)	(5) AFC (2) ÷ (1)	(6) AVC (3) ÷ (1)	(7) ATC (4) ÷ (1)	(8) MC Δ(4) ÷ Δ(1)
0	$50	$ 0	$ 50	—	—	—	—
1	50	15	65	$50.00	$15.00	$65.00	$15
2	50	25	75	25.00	12.50	37.50	10
3	50	34	84	16.67	11.33	28.00	9
4	50	42	92	12.50	10.50	23.00	8
5	50	52	102	10.00	10.40	20.40	10
6	50	64	114	8.33	10.67	19.00	12
7	50	79	129	7.14	11.29	18.43	15
8	50	98	148	6.25	12.25	18.50	19
9	50	122	172	5.56	13.56	19.11	24
10	50	152	202	5.00	15.20	20.20	30
11	50	202	252	4.55	18.36	22.91	50

units of output. Look carefully at the data of Exhibit 5 to be sure that you fully understand the relationships among the various cost curves. Do you understand how columns 4 to 8 are derived from columns 1 to 3?

Using the numeric data of Exhibit 5, **Exhibit 6** graphically illustrates the total, the average, and the marginal cost curves. Note that the *MC* curve intersects both the *AVC* and *ATC* curves at their minimum points (part b). As *MC*, driven up by diminishing returns, continues to rise above *ATC*, unit costs rise higher and higher as output increases beyond seven units.

In sum, the firm's short-run cost curves reflect the law of diminishing marginal returns. Assuming that the price of the variable resource is constant, *MC* declines so long as the marginal product of the variable input is rising. This results because, in this range, smaller and smaller additions of the variable input are required to produce each extra unit of output. The situation is reversed, however, when diminishing returns are confronted. Once diminishing returns set in, more and more units of the variable factor are required to generate each additional unit of output. *MC* will rise, because the marginal product of the

EXHIBIT 6
Costs in the Short Run

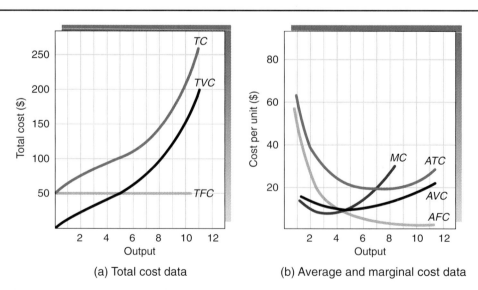

(a) Total cost data

(b) Average and marginal cost data

Using data from Exhibit 5, this exhibit shows the general shape of the firm's short-run total cost curves (a), and average and marginal cost curves (b). Note that when output is small (for example, two units), *ATC* will be high because the *AFC* is so high. Similarly, when output is large (for example, eleven units), per-unit cost (*ATC*) will be high because additional units will be extremely costly to produce at this point. Thus, the short-run *ATC* curve will be U-shaped.

variable resource is declining. Eventually, *MC* exceeds *AVC* and *ATC,* causing these costs also to rise. A U-shaped, short-run average total cost curve results.

OUTPUT AND COSTS IN THE LONG RUN

The short-run analysis relates costs to output *for a specific size of plant.* Firms, though, are not committed forever to their existing plants. In the long run, a firm can alter its plant size and all other factors of production. All resources used by the firm are variable in the long run. Thus, there are no fixed and variable cost categories in the long run.

How will the firm's choice of plant size affect per-unit production costs? **Exhibit 7** illustrates the short-run *ATC* curves for three different plant sizes, ranging from small to large. If these three plant sizes were the only possible choices, which one should the firm choose as it plans for the future? The answer depends on the rate of output the firm expects to produce from the plant. The smallest plant would have the lowest cost if an output rate of less than q_1 were produced. The medium-size plant would provide the least-cost method of producing output rates between q_1 and q_2. For any output level greater than q_2, the largest plant would be the most cost-efficient.

The long-run **ATC** *curve shows the minimum average cost of producing each output level when the firm is free to choose among all possible plant sizes. It can best be thought of as a planning curve, because it reflects the expected per-unit cost of producing alternative rates of output while plants are still in the blueprint stage.*

Exhibit 7 illustrates the long-run *ATC* curve when only three plant sizes are possible, and the planning curve *ABCD* is thus mapped out. Of course, given sufficient time, firms can usually choose among many plants of various sizes. **Exhibit 8** presents the long-run

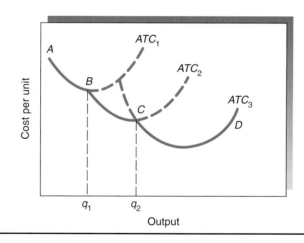

EXHIBIT 7
Long-Run Average Total Cost

The short-run average total cost curves are shown for three alternative plant sizes. If these three were the only possible plant sizes, the long-run average total cost curve would be *ABCD*.

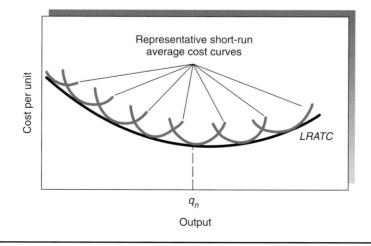

EXHIBIT 8
The Planning Curve (*LRATC*)

When many different plant sizes are possible, the long-run average total cost curve (*LRATC*) can be mapped out. When firms are able to plan large volumes of output, using mass-production methods will generally lead to lower per-unit costs. This helps explain why the *LRATC* has a downward-sloping portion.

When firms are able to plan large volumes of output, using mass-production methods will generally lead to lower per-unit costs. This helps explain why the *LRATC* has a downward-sloping portion.

planning curve under these circumstances. It is a smooth curve, with each short-run *ATC* curve tangent to it.

It is important to keep in mind that no single plant size could produce the alternative output rates at the costs indicated by the planning curve **LRATC** *in Exhibit 8.* Any of the planning curve options are, of course, available to the firm before a plant size is chosen and the plant is built. But it can *operate* in the short run only *after* a plant size has been chosen and put in place. The *LRATC* curve outlines the *possibilities* available in the planning stage. It shows the expected output and average total costs of production for the firm depending on the plant size it chooses.

Economies and Diseconomies of Scale

Do larger firms have lower minimum unit costs than smaller ones? The answer to this question depends on which industries are being considered. There is a sound basis, though, for expecting some initial reductions in per-unit cost from large-scale production methods. Why? Large firms typically produce a large total volume of output.[3] Volume of output denotes the total number of units of a product that the firm expects to produce.[4] There are three major reasons why planning a larger volume generally reduces, at least initially, unit costs: (1) economies accompanying the use of mass-production methods, (2) higher productivity as a result of specialization and "learning by doing," and (3) economies in promotion and purchasing. Let's consider each of these factors.

Mass-production techniques usually are economical only when large volumes of output are planned, since they tend to involve large development and setup costs. Once the production methods are established, though, marginal costs are low. For example, the use of molds, dies, and assembly line production methods reduce the per-unit cost of automobiles only when the planned volume is in the millions. High-volume methods, although cheaper to use for high rates of output and high volumes, will typically require high fixed costs and therefore cause unit costs to be far higher for low volumes of production.

Large-scale operation also allows the specialized use of labor and machines. In a giant auto plant, hundreds of different jobs must be done, and many of them require a training period for each worker. In a small plant, the same worker might do ten or twenty of these jobs, so each worker would have a much longer, more costly training period. Even then, the worker doing so many tasks might never fully develop the same level of proficiency of the more specialized worker. Baseball players improve by playing baseball, and pianists by playing the piano. Similarly, the employees of a firm improve their skills as they experience "learning by doing" in their jobs. Even better, concentration on a narrower range of tasks can help workers discover or develop cost-reducing techniques. The result of greater size and specialization is often more output per unit of labor.

Large firms are also able to achieve lower costs by spreading fixed costs (like the costs of advertising, developing specialized equipment, and searching out and negotiating better input prices, for example) over many more units. For example, both McDonald's and General Motors are able to spread these costs over a large number of stores and volume of sales. The cost advantages of scale come in many forms.

[3] Throughout this section, we assume that firms with larger plants necessarily plan a larger volume of output than do their smaller counterparts. Reality approximates these conditions. Firms choose large plants because they are planning to produce a large volume.

[4] Note the distinction between rate and volume of output. Rate of output is the number of units produced during a specific period (for example, the next six months). Volume is the total number of units produced during all time periods. For example, Boeing might produce two 777 airplanes per month (rate of output) while planning to produce a volume of two hundred 777s during the expected life of the model. Increasing the rate (reducing the time period during which a given output is produced) tends to raise costs, whereas increasing the volume (total amount produced) tends to lower costs.

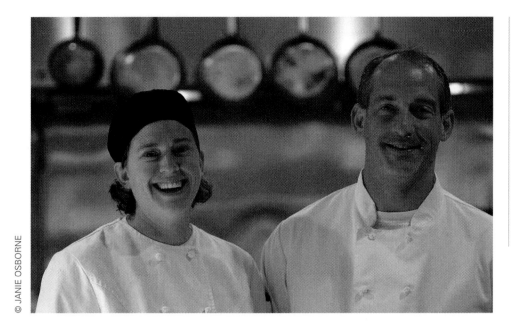

© JANIE OSBORNE

The consistently high quality of gourmet restaurants like the Savory Olive in Bozeman, Montana, can seldom be duplicated by chain restaurants, in part because a gourmet chef must make decisions daily about which locally available fresh ingredients will be used and how they will be used to produce a constantly innovative menu, delivered by an attentive and dedicated staff. Firms like the Savory Olive operate with diseconomies of scale.

Economic theory explains why, at least initially, larger firms have lower unit costs than comparable smaller firms. Declining unit costs mean that **economies of scale** are present over the initial range of outputs. The long-run *ATC* curve is falling.

What about *dis*economies of scale? As output continues to expand, is there reason to believe that larger firms will eventually have higher average total costs than smaller ones? The underlying causes of diseconomies of scale are less obvious, but they do occur. As a firm gets bigger and bigger, beyond some point bureaucratic inefficiencies *may* result. Inflexible procedures tend to replace managerial genius. Innovation requires clearance from more levels of management and becomes more difficult and costly. Motivating the workforce, carrying out managerial directives, and monitoring results of plans are also more complex when the firm is larger, and principal-agent problems grow as the number of employees increases and more levels of communication and monitoring are needed.

Circumstances vary, so diseconomies of scale set in at lower levels of firm size for some kinds of firms than for others. For example, firms in the fast-food industry can be very large and remain efficient; economies of scale apparently outweigh the diseconomies, even for giants like McDonald's. But in the fine-dining segment of the restaurant industry, the best restaurants seem to be small. Customers demand individual attention, and a constantly changing, innovative menu that takes advantage of the constantly changing array of locally available fresh ingredients, with consistently high quality as the only constant, is important. There are few truly gourmet restaurant chains because diseconomies seem to set in at a much smaller size at these firms. The bottom line for diseconomies of scale is this: for some firms, bureaucratic inefficiencies, principal-agent problems, difficulties with innovation, and similar problems that increase with firm size cause long-run average total costs to rise beyond some output level. However, there is considerable variation among industries and even among firms in the same industry concerning the precise output level at which diseconomies of scale begin to occur.

It is important to note that scale economies and diseconomies stem from sources different from those of increasing and diminishing returns. ***Economies and diseconomies of scale are long-run concepts. They relate to conditions of production when all factors are variable. In contrast, increasing and diminishing returns are short-run concepts, applicable only when the firm has at least one fixed factor of production.***

Economies of scale
Reductions in the firm's per-unit costs associated with the use of large plants to produce a large volume of output.

Alternative Shapes of the *LRATC*

Exhibit 9 outlines three different long-run average total cost (*LRATC*) curves, each describing real-world conditions in differing industries. For a firm described by the cost curve in part (a), both economies and diseconomies of scale are present. Higher per-unit

EXHIBIT 9
Three Different Types of Long-Run Average Total Cost Curves

For one type of *LRATC* curve, economies of scale are present for output levels less than *q,* but immediately beyond *q,* diseconomies of scale occur (a). In another instance, economies of scale are important until some minimum output level (q_1) is attained. Once the minimum level has been attained, there is a wide range of output levels (q_1 to q_2) consistent with the minimum *ATC* for the industry (b). In the third situation, economies of scale exist for all relevant output levels (c). As we will see later, this type of *LRATC* curve has important implications for how industries are structured.

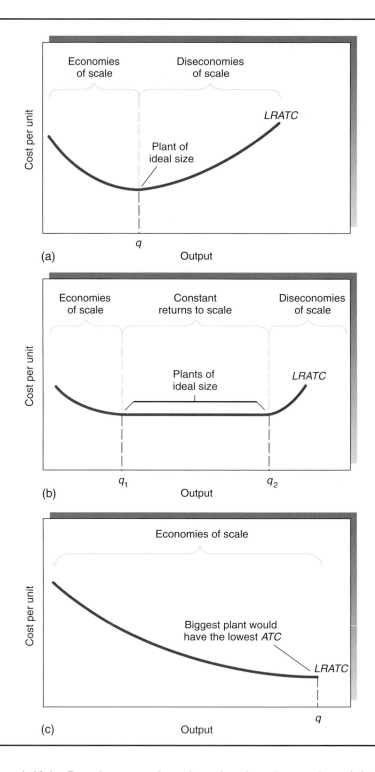

Constant returns to scale
Unit costs that are constant as the scale of the firm is altered. Neither economies nor diseconomies of scale are present.

costs will result if the firm chooses a plant size other than the one that minimizes the cost of producing output *q.* If each firm in an industry faces the same cost conditions, we can generalize and say that all plants larger or smaller than this ideal size will experience higher unit costs. A very narrow range of plant sizes would be expected in industries with the *LRATC* depicted by part (a). Some agricultural products and retail lines approximate these conditions.

Part (b) demonstrates the general shape of the *LRATC* that economists believe is present in most industries. Initially, economies of scale exist, but once a minimum efficient scale is reached, wide variation in firm size is possible. Firms smaller than the minimum efficient size would have higher per-unit costs, but firms larger than that would not gain a cost advantage. **Constant returns to scale** are present for a broad range of output rates (between q_1 and q_2), in other words. This situation is consistent with real-world conditions in many industries. For example, small firms can be as efficient as larger ones in the apparel, lumber, and publishing industries, as well as in several retail industries.

In part (c) of Exhibit 9, economies of scale exist for all relevant output levels. The larger the firm size, the lower the per-unit cost. The *LRATC* for local telephone service can approximate the curve shown here.

WHAT FACTORS CAUSE COST CURVES TO SHIFT?

When we drew the general shapes of a firm's cost curves in both the long run and short run, we assumed that certain other factors—resource prices, taxes, regulations, and technology—remained constant as the firm altered its rate of output. Let's now consider how these other factors would affect production costs if they did not remain constant but changed either in response to increasing production or for some reason unrelated to the firm's output decisions.

Prices of Resources

If the price of resources used should rise, the firm's cost curves will shift upward, as **Exhibit 10** shows. Higher resource prices will increase the cost of producing each alternative output level. For example, what happens to the cost of producing automobiles when the price of steel rises? The cost of producing automobiles also rises. Conversely, lower resource prices will reduce costs and shift the cost curves downward at every plant size.

Taxes

Taxes are a component of a firm's cost. Suppose that an excise tax of 20 cents were levied on the seller for each gallon of gasoline sold. What would happen to the seller's costs? They would increase, just as they did in Exhibit 10. The firm's average total and marginal cost curves would shift upward by the amount of the tax. If the tax were an annual business license fee instead, it would raise the average cost, but not the variable cost.

Regulations

The government often imposes health, safety, environmental, and production regulations on business firms. Regulations might require businesses to provide a certain number of water fountains and restrooms for customers and workers. Federal regulations under the Americans with Disabilities Act compel many firms to make their facilities accessible to people in wheelchairs. Other regulations force firms to build certain features into their products. Strong bumpers and air bags in automobiles are examples. Although regulations

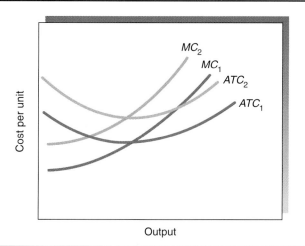

EXHIBIT 10
Higher Resource Prices and Cost

An increase in resource prices will cause the firm's cost curves to shift upward.

have their benefits, they are also costly. Just processing the paperwork that must be submitted to regulators is costly, and so are the compulsory changes themselves. Like tax increases, increases in regulatory compliance costs will shift cost curves upward. In some cases, only fixed costs will be affected; in other instances, variable costs will be altered as well. In both cases, the firm's *ATC* will be higher.

Technology

Improvements in technology often make it possible to produce a specific amount of output with fewer resources. Computers and robots have lowered costs in many industries. The Internet has made it easy to find and outsource many business-to-business services ranging from building maintenance and bookkeeping to the purchase of manufacturing components. Small firms can gain from specialization without being large themselves, and even large firms are participating. Federated Department Stores, which owns Bloomingdale's, Bon-Macy's, and Burdines-Macy's among others, now contracts with a specialty firm to manage all of its building facilities worldwide. Federated expects to save $150 million per year as the result of this change.[5] The *Wall Street Journal* reported that Micropub Systems of Rochester, New York, can install an entire brewery in ninety-six square feet, allowing the premium local brews to be made and delivered at lower cost than those currently available from the largest national brewers.[6] As **Exhibit 11** shows, a technological improvement will shift the firm's cost curves downward, reflecting the lower amount of resources needed to produce different levels of output.

THE ECONOMIC WAY OF THINKING ABOUT COSTS

When economists analyze the firm's costs, they often present a highly mechanical—some would say unrealistic—view that doesn't take into account the subjective nature of costs and the uncertainty about the future payoffs of many choices decision makers really face.

It is important to keep in mind that costs are incurred when choices are made. When business decision makers choose to purchase raw materials, hire new employees, or renew the lease on a plant, they incur costs. All these decisions, like other choices, must be made under conditions of uncertainty. Of course, past experience can help business decision makers anticipate the likely costs of various decisions. But the world is constantly changing; the future may differ substantially from the past.

EXHIBIT 11
Egg Production Costs and Technological Change

Suppose an egg producer discovers (or develops) a "super" mineral water that makes it possible to get more eggs from the same number of chickens. Because of this technological improvement, various output levels of eggs can now be produced with less feed, space, water, and labor. Costs will be reduced. The egg producer's *ATC* and *MC* curves will shift downward.

[5]"Economies of Scale: Spend to Save," *Chain Store Age* 76, no. 2 (February 2000): 2B.

[6]Thomas Petzinger Jr., "The Rise of the Small and Other Trends to Watch This Year," *Wall Street Journal*, January 9, 1998.

MYTHS OF ECONOMICS

"A good business decision maker will never sell a product for less than its production costs."

This statement contains a grain of truth. A profit-seeking entrepreneur will not undertake a project knowing the costs can't be covered. However, the statement fails to emphasize (1) the time dimension of the production process and (2) the uncertainty associated with business decisions. The production process takes time. Raw materials must be purchased, employees hired, and plants equipped. Retailers must contract with suppliers. As these decisions are made, costs result. Many of the firm's costs of production are incurred long before its product is ready for marketing.

Even a good business decision maker is not always able to predict the future because market conditions can change quickly and unexpectedly. At the time the product is ready for sale, buyers might be unwilling to pay a price that will cover the seller's past costs of production. These past costs, however, are now sunk costs and no longer relevant. Decisions must now be made on the basis of the firm's current cost and revenues.

Should a grocer refuse to sell oranges that are about to spoil because their wholesale cost cannot be covered? The grocer's current opportunity cost of selling the oranges at this point is nearly zero. The alternative would be to throw them in the garbage next week. Almost any price, even one far below past costs, will be better than letting the oranges spoil.

Consider another example. Suppose a couple who owns a house plans to relocate temporarily. Should they refuse to rent the house they're moving out of for $500 (if this is the best offer available) because their monthly house payment is $800? Of course not. The house payment will go on, regardless of whether or not they rent the house. If the homeowners can cover their opportunity costs (perhaps wear and tear plus a $60 monthly fee for a property management service), they will gain by renting rather than leaving the house vacant.

Past mistakes provide useful lessons for the future, but they cannot be reversed. Bygones are bygones, even if they resulted in business loss. There is no need to fret over spilt milk, burnt toast, or yesterday's business losses.

Opportunity costs are expected costs—they represent the highest valued option that the decision maker expects to give up as the result of a choice. Think for a moment of what the cost curves developed in this chapter really mean. The firm's short-run *MC* curve represents the opportunity cost of expanding output, *given the firm's current plant size*. The firm's long-run *ATC* curve represents the opportunity cost per unit of output associated with varying plant sizes and rates of output, *given that the alternative plants are still on the drawing board*. Opportunity costs look forward, reflecting expectations of what will be forgone as a result of current decisions. At the time decisions must be made, neither the short-run *MC* nor the long-run *ATC* can be determined from accounting records, since accounting costs look backward. Accounting figures yield valuable information about historical costs, but, as the following section illustrates, they must be interpreted carefully when they are used to forecast future costs.

What Are Sunk Costs?

Sunk costs are the historical costs of past decisions that cannot be reversed. Sunk costs give managers hindsight when it comes to making current decisions, but the specific costs themselves are no longer relevant. When past choices cannot be reversed—no refund is available, for example—money that has been spent is gone for good. Today's choices must be based on the costs and benefits expected under *current and future* market conditions, if mistakes are to be avoided (see the accompanying Myths of Economics feature).

To minimize costs, business decision makers need to realize that sunk costs are, indeed, *sunk*. A simple example will emphasize this point. Suppose that the firm in Exhibit 5 pays $100,000 to purchase and install a roller blade–producing machine. The machine is expected to last ten years. The company's books record the cost of the machine as $10,000 each year under the heading of depreciation. The machine can be used only to make roller blades, though. Because dismantling and reinstallation costs are high, it cannot be leased or sold to another firm. Also, it has no scrap value. In other words, there are no alternative uses for the machine. The machine's annual production of roller blades will generate $50,000 of revenues for the firm when it is employed with raw

Sunk costs
Costs that have already been incurred as a result of past decisions. They are sometimes referred to as historical costs.

materials and other factors of production that cost $46,000. Thus, the net revenue generated by the machine is $4,000.

Should the firm continue to use the machine? Its depreciation figures suggest that the machine is costing the firm $10,000 annually, compared to the $4,000 net revenue it generates. Put another way, the machine is reducing the firm's profit by $6,000 annually. The machine's depreciation cost, however, is a sunk cost. It was incurred when the machine was purchased and installed, which is over and done with now. The *current* opportunity cost of the machine is therefore precisely zero. In other words, the firm is not giving up anything by continuing to use it today. Since using the machine generates $4,000 of additional net revenue, the firm can gain by continuing to use it. Of course, if market conditions are not expected to improve, the firm will not purchase a similar machine or replace the machine when it wears out, but this should not influence its decision whether to continue operating the one it already has. The irrelevance of sunk costs helps explain why it often makes sense to continue using older equipment (it has a low opportunity cost), even if it would not be wise to purchase similar equipment again.

How Will Cost Influence Supply?

Economists are interested in cost because they seek to explain firms' supply decisions. A strictly profit-maximizing firm will compare the expected revenues derived from a decision or a course of action with the expected costs. If the expected revenues exceed costs, then the course of action will be chosen because it will expand profits (or reduce losses).

For short-run supply decisions, the marginal cost of producing additional units is what should be considered. To maximize profits, the decision maker should compare the expected marginal costs with the expected additional revenue from larger sales. If the latter exceeds the former, output (the quantity supplied) should be expanded.

Marginal costs are central to the choice of short-run output, whereas expected average total cost is vital to a firm's long-run supply decision. Before entering an industry (or purchasing capital assets for expansion or replacement), a profit-maximizing decision maker will compare the expected market price with the expected long-run average total cost. Profit-seeking potential entrants will supply the product if, and only if, they expect the market price to exceed their long-run average total cost. Similarly, existing firms will continue to supply a product in the long run only if they expect that the market price will enable them at least to cover their long-run average total cost.

LOOKING AHEAD

In this chapter, we outlined several basic principles that affect costs for business firms. We will use these basic principles in the chapters that follow when we analyze the price and output decisions of firms under alternative market structures.

KEY POINTS

▼ The business firm is used to organize productive resources and transform them into goods and services. There are three major types of business structure—proprietorships, partnerships, and corporations.

▼ To solve the principal-agent problem, which tends to reduce worker efficiency in team production, every firm must provide work incentives and monitoring.

▼ The demand for a product indicates the intensity of consumers' desires for the item. The (opportunity) cost of producing the item indicates the intensity of consumers' desires for other goods that could have been produced instead, with the same resources.

▼ In economics, total cost includes not only explicit payments for resources employed by the firm, but also the implicit costs associated with the use of productive resources owned by the firm (like the opportunity cost of the firm's equity capital or owner-provided services) that could be used elsewhere.

▼ Because accounting methods omit the cost of equity capital (and sometimes other implicit costs), they tend to understate the opportunity cost of producing a good and overstate the firm's economic profit.

▼ Economic profit (or loss) results when a firm's sales revenues exceed (or are less than) its total costs, both explicit and implicit. Firms that are earning the market (or "normal") rate of return on their assets will therefore make zero economic profit.

▼ The firm's short-run average total cost (*ATC*) curve will tend to be U-shaped.

▼ The law of diminishing returns explains why a firm's short-run marginal and average total costs will eventually rise. When diminishing marginal returns are present, successively larger amounts of the variable input will be required to increase output by one more unit. As this happens, marginal cost will rise.

▼ The long-run *ATC* (*LRATC*) reflects the costs of production for plants of various sizes. When economies of scale are present, *LRATC* will decline. When constant returns to scale are experienced, *LRATC* will be constant. When diseconomies of scale are present, *LRATC* will rise.

▼ Changes in: (1) resource prices, (2) taxes, (3) regulations, and (4) technology will cause the cost curves of firms to shift.

▼ Sunk costs are costs that have already been incurred and cannot be recovered. Sunk costs give managers hindsight when it comes to making current decisions, but the specific costs themselves are no longer directly relevant for current and future decisions.

CRITICAL ANALYSIS QUESTIONS

*1. What is economic profit? How might it differ from accounting profit? Explain why firms that are making zero economic profit are likely to continue in business.

*2. Which of the following statements do you think reflect sound economic thinking? Explain your answer.
   a. "I paid $400 for this economics course. Therefore, I'm going to attend the lectures even if they are useless and boring."
   b. "Because we own rather than rent, and the house is paid for, housing doesn't cost us anything."
   c. "I own 100 shares of stock that I can't afford to sell until the price goes up enough for me to get back at least my original investment."
   d. "Private education is costly to produce, whereas public schooling is free."

3. Suppose a firm produces bicycles. Will the firm's accounting statement reflect the opportunity cost of the bicycles? Why or why not? What costs would an accounting statement reveal? Should current decisions be based on accounting costs? Explain.

4. What is the principal-agent problem? When will the principal-agent problem be most severe? Why might there be a principal-agent problem between the stockholder-owners and the managers of a large corporation?

*5. "If a firm maximizes profit, it must minimize the cost of producing the profit-maximizing output." Is this statement true or false? Explain your answer.

6. What are some of the advantages of the corporate business structure of ownership for large business firms? What are some of the disadvantages? Is the corporate form of business ownership cost-efficient? In a market economy, how would you tell whether the corporate structural form was efficient?

*7. Explain the factors that cause a firm's short-run average total costs initially to decline, but eventually to increase, as the rate of output rises.

8. Which of the following are relevant to a firm's decision to increase output: (a) short-run average total cost, (b) short-run marginal cost, (c) long-run average total cost? Justify your answer.

9. Economics students often confuse (a) diminishing returns related to the variable factors of production and (b) diseconomies of scale. Explain the difference between the two, and give one example of each.

10. "Firms that make a profit have increased the value of the resources they used; their actions created wealth. In contrast, the actions of firms that make losses reduce wealth. The discovery and undertaking of profit-making opportunities are key ingredients of economic progress." Evaluate the statement.

*11. Is profit maximization consistent with the self-interest of corporate owners? Is it consistent with the self-interest of corporate managers? Is there a conflict between the self-interests of owners and those of managers?

*12. What is the opportunity cost of (a) borrowed funds and (b) equity capital? Under current tax law, firms can record as an expense the opportunity cost of borrowed funds, but not equity capital. How does this tax law affect the amount of debt the firm wants to incur, compared to the amount of money it raises by selling equity?

13. Why do economists consider normal returns to capital to be a cost? How does economic profit differ from normal profit?

*14. Draw a U-shaped, short-run *ATC* curve for a firm. Construct the accompanying *MC* and *AVC* curves.

15. What is shirking? If the managers of a firm are attempting to maximize its profits, will they have an incentive to limit shirking? How might they go about doing so?

16. What are implicit costs? Do implicit costs contribute to the opportunity cost of production? Should an implicit cost be counted as cost? Give three examples of implicit costs. Does the firm's accounting statement take implicit costs into account? Why or why not?

*17. Consider a machine purchased one year ago for $12,000. The machine is being depreciated $4,000 per year over a three-year period. Its current market value is $5,000, and the expected market value of the machine one year from now is $3,000. If the interest rate is 10 percent, what is the expected cost of holding the machine during the next year?

*18. Investors seeking to take over a firm often bid a positive price for the business even though it is currently experiencing losses. Why would anyone ever bid a positive price for a firm operating at a loss?

19. Fill in the blanks in the following table:
   a. What happens to total product when marginal product is negative?
   b. What happens to average product when marginal product is greater than average product?
   c. What happens to average product when marginal product is less than average product?
   d. At what point does marginal product begin to decrease?
   e. At what point does marginal cost begin to increase?
   f. Summarize the relationship between marginal product and marginal cost.
   g. What happens to marginal costs when total product begins to fall?
   h. What is happening to average variable costs when they equal marginal costs?
   i. Marginal costs equal average variable costs between what output levels?
   j. What is happening to average total costs when they equal marginal costs?
   k. Marginal costs equal average total costs between what output levels?

---

*Asterisk denotes questions for which answers are given in Appendix B.

Units of Variable Input	Total Product	Marginal Product	Average Product	Price of Input	Total Variable Cost	Average Variable Cost	Total Fixed Cost	Total Cost	Average Total Cost	Marginal Cost
0	0	___	___	$1	___	___	$2	___	___	___
1	6	___	___	$1	___	___	$2	___	___	___
2	15	___	___	$1	___	___	$2	___	___	___
3	27	___	___	$1	___	___	$2	___	___	___
4	37	___	___	$1	___	___	$2	___	___	___
5	45	___	___	$1	___	___	$2	___	___	___
6	50	___	___	$1	___	___	$2	___	___	___
7	52	___	___	$1	___	___	$2	___	___	___
8	50	___	___	$1	___	___	$2	___	___	___

Price Takers and the Competitive Process

CHAPTER 21

Chapter Focus

■ How do firms that are price takers differ from those that are price searchers?

■ What determines the output of a price taker?

■ How do price takers respond to changes in price in the short run? In the long run?

■ How does time influence the elasticity of supply?

■ What must firms do in order to make profits? How do profits and losses influence the supply and market price of a product?

■ How does competition provide an incentive for producers to supply goods that consumers want at a low cost?

Competition means decentralized planning by many separate persons.

—Friedrich A. von Hayek[1]

[I]t is competition that drives down costs and prices, induces firms to produce the goods consumers want, and spurs innovation and the expansion of new markets. . . .

—President's Council of Economic Advisers[2]

---

[1]F. A. von Hayek, "The Use of Knowledge in Society," *American Economic Review* 35 (September 1945): 521.

[2]President's Council of Economic Advisers, *Economic Report of the President,* 1996 (Washington, D.C.: U.S. Government Printing Office, 1996), 155.

I n the previous chapter, we focused on cost conditions of business firms. In this chapter and the next two, we will take a closer look at the price and output decisions of the firm, and analyze how they are influenced by market conditions. We will also consider how the structure of a market—for example, the number of firms, the control they have over price, and the ease of entry into the market—influences the decision making of firms. What determines the profitability of firms, and how does the level of profit influence the market supply? When goods and services are allocated by markets, will resources be allocated efficiently? Is there any reason to believe that there will be a link between market allocation and economic prosperity? These are the major questions that we will address in the next several chapters. ■

PRICE TAKERS AND PRICE SEARCHERS

Price takers
Sellers who must take the market price in order to sell their product. Because each price taker's output is small relative to the total market, price takers can sell all their output at the market price, but they are unable to sell any of their output at a price higher than the market price.

This chapter will focus on markets in which the firms are **price takers**: they simply take the price that is determined in the market. *In a price-taker market, the firms all produce identical products (for example, wheat, eggs, or regular unleaded gasoline), and each seller is small relative to the total market. Thus, the output of any single firm has little or no effect on the market price. Each firm can sell all its output at the market price, but cannot sell any of its output at a higher price.* When a firm is a price taker, there is no pricing decision to be made. Price takers try to choose the output level that will maximize profit, given their costs and the price determined by the market.

Price takers, like all other profit-seeking firms, cannot thrive (or even survive) in a competitive environment unless they are sensitive to cost. However, price-taker markets and price-searcher markets have differing degrees of competition, differing ease of entry, and perhaps differing scale economies, too. To compete, each firm has to provide a high level of delivered benefits per dollar, compared to what consumers can find elsewhere. No firm can force consumers to purchase its product, and all products have many substitutes. Successful firms are those that stay ahead of competitors and potential competitors.

APPLICATIONS IN ECONOMICS

The Aalsmeer Flower Auction: An Illustration of a Competitive Market

© DAVE BARTRUFF/CORBIS

The Aalsmeer Flower Auction, located near Amsterdam, is a highly competitive market with a large number of both buyers and sellers. Approximately 5,000 growers from the Netherlands and other countries like Israel, Kenya, and Zambia supply their products to this market. On a typical day, several thousand buyers representing wholesale florists around the world participate in the auction. More than 18 million flowers and 2 million plants are sold each day from a building equal in size to 125 football fields.

The 50,000 daily transactions are made possible by the Dutch auction system. Under this system, a clock runs backward from the highest to the lowest price per unit. The buyer pushes a button indicating his or her willingness to purchase when the clock reaches an acceptable per-unit price. The purchaser is the first buyer to push the button. Flowers and plants auctioned in the morning at Aalsmeer will be available in shops around the world within twenty-four hours.

In the real world, most firms are not price takers. In most cases, firms that lower their prices are able to attract additional customers. Correspondingly, firms are usually able to increase their prices, at least a little, without losing all their customers. For example, if Nike increased the price of its athletic shoes by 10 percent, the number of shoes sold would decline, but it would not fall to zero. Firms like Nike are not price takers. They are **price searchers**: they choose the price that they will charge for their product, but the quantity that they are able to sell is very much related to that price. To maximize their profits, price searchers must not only decide how much to produce, but also what price to charge. We will examine markets in which the firms are price searchers in the following two chapters.

If most real-world firms are price searchers, not price takers, why take the time to analyze the latter? There are several reasons. First, even though most firms are not price takers, there are a number of important markets, particularly in agriculture, in which the firms do essentially take the price determined in the market. Second, the price-taker model helps clarify the relationship between the decision making of individual firms and the market supply in both price-taker and price-searcher markets. Finally, and perhaps most important, the study of markets in which firms are price takers enhances our knowledge of **competition as a dynamic process**. Understanding how the competitive process works when firms are price takers will also contribute to our understanding of the process as it applies to many price searchers.

Historically, the term **pure competition** has been used to refer to markets in which firms are price takers. However, these markets are increasingly referred to as "price-taker markets" because this expression is more descriptive. Furthermore, this label avoids the implication that competitive forces are necessarily less pure or less intense in price-searcher markets. Often this is not the case. Many price searchers use a broad array of competitive weapons—for example, quality of product, style, convenient location, advertising, and price—all in an effort to attract consumers. When **barriers to entry** are low, the competitive process is just as important in price-searcher markets as it is when the firms are price takers.

Nonetheless, it should be noted that price-taker markets and purely competitive markets are really alternative names for the same thing. So when you hear people talk about pure competition or purely competitive markets, they mean markets with characteristics like those analyzed in this chapter.

WHAT ARE THE CHARACTERISTICS OF PRICE-TAKER MARKETS?

Consider the situation of Les Parrot, a Texas cattle rancher. In the financial pages of the local newspaper, he finds that the current market price of quality steers is 88 cents per pound. Even if his ranch is quite large, there is little that Parrot can do to change the market price of beef cattle. After all, there are tens of thousands of farmers who raise cattle. Thus, Parrot supplies only a small portion of the total cattle market. The amount that he sells will exert little or no effect on the market price of cattle. Parrot is a price taker.

Price searchers
Firms that face a downward-sloping demand curve for their product. The amount the firm is able to sell is inversely related to the price it charges.

Competition as a dynamic process
Rivalry or competitiveness between or among parties (for example, producers or input suppliers) to deliver a better deal to buyers in terms of quality, price, and product information.

Pure competition
A market structure characterized by a large number of small firms producing an identical product in an industry (market area) that permits complete freedom of entry and exit. Also called price-taker markets.

Barriers to entry
Obstacles that limit the freedom of potential rivals to enter and compete in an industry or market.

Producers in the wheat-farming and beef cattle markets are price takers. If they are going to sell their output, they must do so at the price determined by the market. Because individual producers are small relative to the total market, they can sell as many units as they like at the market price.

EXHIBIT 1
The Price Taker's
Demand Curve

The market forces of sup-
ply and demand determine
price (b). Price takers have
no control over price. Thus,
the demand for the product
of the firm is perfectly
elastic (a).

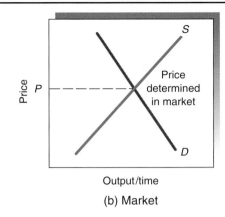

(a) Firm

(b) Market

The firms in a market will be price takers when the following four conditions are met:

1. All the firms in the market are producing an identical product (for example, beef, or cattle, of a given grade).

2. A large number of firms exist in the market.

3. Each firm supplies only a very small portion of the total amount supplied to the market.

4. No barriers limit the entry or exit of firms in the market.

When these conditions are met, firms selling in the market must accept the market price. This is why they are called price takers. **Exhibit 1** illustrates the relationship between the market forces (part b) and the demand curve facing the price-taking firm (part a). If the firm sets a price above the market level, consumers will simply buy from other sellers. Why pay the higher price when the identical good is available elsewhere at a lower price? For example, if the price of wheat were $5.00 per bushel, a farmer would be unable to find buyers for wheat at $5.50 per bushel. A firm would gain nothing by setting its price below the market level, because any small firm in the market can already sell as much as it wants at the market price. A price reduction would only reduce revenues. A firm that is a price taker thus faces a perfectly elastic demand for its product. (In Exhibit 1, note that a lowercase *d* is used to denote the demand curve faced by the *firm,* whereas an uppercase *D* indicates the *market* demand curve.)

HOW DOES THE PRICE TAKER MAXIMIZE PROFIT?

The firm's output decision is based on comparing benefits with costs. A firm that decides to enter a market will expand its output as long as the benefits (additional revenues) from the production and sales of the additional units exceed their marginal costs. How will changes in output change the firm's costs? In the preceding chapter, we discovered that the firm's short-run marginal costs will eventually increase as the firm expands its output by working its fixed plant facilities more intensively. The law of diminishing marginal returns assures us that this will be the case. Eventually, both the firm's short-run marginal and average total cost curves will turn upward.

Marginal revenue (*MR*)
The incremental change in total revenue derived from the sale of one additional unit of a product.

What about the benefits or additional revenues from output expansion? **Marginal revenue (*MR*)** is the change in the firm's total revenue per unit of output. It is the additional revenue derived from the sale of an additional unit of output. Mathematically,

$$MR = \text{Change in total revenue/Change in output}$$

Since the price taker sells all units at the same price, its marginal revenue will be equal to the market price.

In the short run, the price taker will expand its output until marginal revenue (price) just equals marginal cost. This decision-making rule will maximize the firm's profits (or minimize its losses).

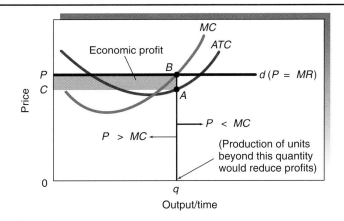

EXHIBIT 2
Profit Maximization
When the Firm Is a
Price Taker

The price taker will
maximize profits by
producing the output level
q, where *P = MC*.

Exhibit 2 helps explain why. Since the firm can sell as many units as it would like at the market price, the sale of one additional unit will increase revenue by the price of the product. Does the firm gain by producing an extra unit? The answer is "Yes," as long as the marginal revenue (price, for the price taker) is greater than or equal to the marginal cost of that unit. Profit is simply the difference between total revenue and total cost. Profit will increase as long as the production and sale of a unit add more to revenue than to cost. Thus, the firm will gain from an increase in output as long as marginal revenue exceeds marginal cost. Eventually, however, as the firm produces a larger and larger quantity with its fixed-size plant, marginal costs will rise and exceed the price and marginal revenues. When the production of an additional unit adds more to cost than it adds to revenue, the firm's profit will be reduced if the unit is produced. Thus, the profit of the price taker is maximized at the output rate at which $P = MR = MC$. In Exhibit 2, this occurs at output level q.

A profit-maximizing firm with the cost curves shown in Exhibit 2 would produce exactly q units. The total revenue of the firm would be the sales price of each unit, P, multiplied by output sold, q. Total revenue is represented by the area $P0qB$. The firm's total cost, on the other hand, can be found by multiplying the average total cost (ATC) by the output level. Total cost is represented by the area $C0qA$. Because the firm's total revenues exceed its total costs, it is making short-run economic profit (the shaded area).

In the real world, of course, decisions are not made by entrepreneurs who spend time drawing demand and marginal cost curves. Many entrepreneurs have never even heard of these concepts. A business decision maker who has never heard of the $P = MR = MC$ rule for profit maximization, however, probably has another rule that yields approximately the same outcome. For example, the rule might be to produce those units, and only those units, that add more to revenue than to cost. This ensures maximum profit (or minimum loss). It also happens to be the point at which $P = MR = MC$. Why? To stop short of that point would mean that the firm would not be producing some profitable units that would add more to revenue than to cost. Similarly, the firm should not go beyond that point because producing more units would add more to cost than to revenue. This commonsense rule thus leads to the same outcome as our model, even when the decision maker knows none of the technical jargon of economics. No wonder economics is sometimes thought of as "organized common sense."

Just how accurate is the price taker's competitive model in predicting behavior in real markets? Do other models, which assume that sellers collude to eliminate competition, yield better predictions? Direct scientific evidence would help us answer these questions. As the Applications in Economics feature about the significance of competition shows, this evidence has, indeed, been produced repeatedly in recent decades by people working in the relatively new subdiscipline of experimental economics. The evidence indicates that the general implications of the price-taker model are valid under a variety of circumstances.

APPLICATIONS IN ECONOMICS

Experimental Economics: The Significance of Competition

A normal economic event observed in the real world can have more than one potential cause. An economist seeking to isolate the effect of a single variable—a change in price, for example—must therefore try to either hold other potential causal factors constant or adjust for their expected impact. This is not an easy task. In other disciplines, scientists use carefully designed laboratory experiments, which hold other factors constant, to test and verify the basic principles on which their science is built.

In the mid-twentieth century, economists also began to conduct laboratory experiments. A good many experiments have been conducted to investigate the predictive power of the price-taker model. In one of the earliest, conducted in 1956 by leading experimental economist Vernon Smith, then at Purdue University, individuals were brought into a laboratory setting and arbitrarily assigned roles as buyers and sellers in a gamelike setting. Each buyer was given a different "limit price" (a maximum price he or she was allowed to pay) for a paper asset. Any buyer who could purchase the paper commodity for less than the limit price received a cash payment equal to the difference between the limit price and the amount actually paid. Each buyer gained financially by purchasing at lower prices—just as buyers and sellers do in real markets. The sellers were treated similarly. Each had a "limit price" (a minimum selling price) and received in cash any extra revenue above that price. In turn, buyers and sellers were free to make verbal offers and enter into exchanges at any mutually agreeable price.

The price-taker model predicts that all mutually advantageous trades among buyers and sellers will occur and that, as trades occur, the price of the good will converge toward a single price—the market price. Prior to the work in experimental economics, many economists thought this model was relevant only under highly restrictive conditions. Experimental researchers, however, have found that outcomes approximating those of the price-taker model generally emerge even when the strict assumptions of the model are absent. For example, even if the number of sellers is relatively small, say ten to fifteen, outcomes similar to those predicted by the price-taker model generally occur.

Participants in these experiments are often startled to discover that their competitive trading generated the largest possible joint income gain and, furthermore, that the competitive model presented in this chapter predicted this occurrence. Vernon Smith, who now directs the Interdisciplinary Center for Economic Studies at George Mason University, cites cases in which, after the experiment, participants describe the experimental market as "unorganized, unstable, chaotic, and confused." Generally, they are amazed when shown that their actions (trades) achieved the maximum income for the group, and that a sealed envelope, given to them prior to the experiment, predicted the approximate amount of their (maximum) joint gain.

At first, Smith himself was surprised that efficient outcomes were achieved under a wide variety of conditions, but after numerous experiments, he stated:

> In many experimental markets, poorly informed, error-prone, and uncomprehending human agents interact through the trading rules to produce social algorithms which demonstrably approximate the wealth maximizing outcomes traditionally thought to require complete information and cognitively rational actors.[1]

In addition to analyzing the exchange process, experimental research has addressed numerous other topics, including the impact of alternative auction rules, the likelihood of a stock market or real estate bubble, and the provision of public goods. In 2002, Vernon Smith was awarded the Nobel Prize for his path-breaking work in this area. Clearly, experimental economics is now one of the most exciting and fruitful areas of current economic research.

[1]Vernon L. Smith, "Economics in the Laboratory," *Journal of Economic Perspectives* 8, no. 1 (Winter 1994): 118.

Profit Maximizing—A Numeric Example

Exhibit 3 uses numeric data to illustrate profit-maximizing decision making for a firm that is a price taker. Put yourself in the place of the owner of this firm. Your short-run total and marginal cost schedules have the general characteristics we discussed in the previous chapter. Since the firm confronts a market price of $5 per unit, its marginal revenue is $5. Total revenue thus increases by $5 per additional unit of output produced and sold. You will maximize your profit when you supply an output of 15 units.

There are two ways to look at this profit-maximizing output rate. First, profit is equal to the difference between total revenue and total cost. Thus, profit will be maximized at the output rate at which this difference (*TR* minus *TC*) is greatest. Column 6 of Exhibit 3

(1) OUTPUT (PER DAY)	(2) TOTAL REVENUE (*TR*)	(3) TOTAL COST (*TC*)	(4) MARGINAL REVENUE (*MR*)	(5) MARGINAL COST (*MC*)	(6) PROFIT (*TR* − *TC*)
0	$ 0.00	$ 25.00	$0.00	$ 0.00	$−25.00
1	5.00	29.80	5.00	4.80	−24.80
2	10.00	33.75	5.00	3.95	−23.75
3	15.00	37.25	5.00	3.50	−22.25
4	20.00	40.25	5.00	3.00	−20.25
5	25.00	42.75	5.00	2.50	−17.75
6	30.00	44.75	5.00	2.00	−14.75
7	35.00	46.50	5.00	1.75	−11.50
8	40.00	48.00	5.00	1.50	− 8.00
9	45.00	49.25	5.00	1.25	− 4.25
10	50.00	50.25	5.00	1.00	− 0.25
11	55.00	51.50	5.00	1.25	3.50
12	60.00	53.25	5.00	1.75	6.75
13	65.00	55.75	5.00	2.50	9.25
14	70.00	59.25	5.00	3.50	10.75
15	75.00	64.00	5.00	4.75	11.00
16	80.00	70.00	5.00	6.00	10.00
17	85.00	77.25	5.00	7.25	7.75
18	90.00	85.50	5.00	8.25	4.50
19	95.00	95.00	5.00	9.50	0.00
20	100.00	108.00	5.00	13.00	− 8.00
21	105.00	125.00	5.00	17.00	−20.00

EXHIBIT 3
Profit Maximization for a Price Taker: A Numeric Illustration

provides this information. For small output rates (less than eleven units), you and your firm would actually experience losses. But at fifteen units of output, an $11 profit is earned ($75 total revenue minus $64 total cost). A look at the profit figures of column 6 shows that it's impossible to earn a profit larger than $11 at any other rate of output.

In **Exhibit 4,** part (a) presents the total revenue and total cost approach in graph form. (However, the curves are drawn smoothly, as though output could be increased by tiny amounts, not just in whole-unit increments like those shown in Exhibit 3.) Profits will be greatest when the total revenue line lies above the total cost curve by the largest vertical amount. That takes place, of course, at fifteen units of output.

You can also use the marginal approach to determine the profit-maximizing rate of output for the firm. Remember, as long as price (marginal revenue) exceeds marginal cost, production and sale of additional units will add to the firm's profit (or reduce its losses). A look at columns 4 and 5 of Exhibit 3 reveals that *MR* is greater than *MC* for the first fifteen units of output. Producing these units will expand the firm's profit. In contrast, producing any unit beyond fifteen adds more to cost than to revenue. Profit will therefore decline if you expand output beyond fifteen units. Given the firm's cost and revenue schedule, you will maximize profit by producing fifteen, and only fifteen, units per day.

Part (b) of Exhibit 4 graphically illustrates the marginal approach. Note here that the output rate (fifteen units) at which the marginal cost and marginal revenue curves intersect coincides with the output rate in part (a) at which the total revenue curve exceeds the total cost curve by the largest amount. Beyond that output rate, *MR* is less than *MC,* so profit will decline.

Losses and When to Go Out of Business

Suppose that market changes cause the price to drop below a firm's average total cost at all possible output levels. How will a profit maximizer (or loss minimizer) respond to this situation? The answer to this question depends both on the firm's current sales revenues relative to its variable cost and on its expectations about the future. The firm's owner has three options: (1) continue to operate in the short run, (2) shut down temporarily, or (3) go out of business.

EXHIBIT 4
The Firm's Profit-Maximizing Output Level—Total and Marginal Approaches

Using the data of Exhibit 3, we can find the profit-maximizing output of a price taker using either the total approach or the marginal approach. Using the total approach, we find that profits are maximized when the firm's total revenues exceed its total costs by the greatest amount (a). Using the marginal approach, we find that profits are maximized by comparing marginal revenue and marginal costs (b).

(a) Total revenue/total cost approach

(b) Marginal revenue/marginal cost approach

Shutdown
A temporary halt in the operation of a firm. Because the firm anticipates operating in the future, it does not sell its assets and go out of business. The firm's variable cost is eliminated by the shutdown, but its fixed costs continue.

Going out of business
The sale of a firm's assets, and its permanent exit from the market. By going out of business, a firm is able to avoid its fixed costs, which would continue during a shutdown.

If the firm anticipates that the lower market price is temporary, it may want to continue operating in the short run as long as it can cover its variable cost.[3] **Exhibit 5** illustrates why. The firm shown in this exhibit would minimize its loss at output level q, where $P = MR = MC$. But at q, total revenues $(0qBP_1)$ are less than total costs $(0qAC)$. The firm faces short-run economic losses. Even if it shuts down completely, it will still incur fixed costs, *unless the firm goes out of business*. If it anticipates that the market price will increase enough to allow the firm to cover its average total costs in the future, it may not want to terminate operations and sell its assets. It may choose to produce q units in the short run, even though it will incur losses. At price P_1, producing output q is clearly more advantageous than shutting down, because the firm is able to cover its variable costs and have revenue remaining to pay some of its fixed costs. If it were to shut down but not sell out, the firm would lose the entire amount of its fixed cost.

What if the market price drops below the firm's average variable cost (for example, to P_2)? When this happens, not only is the firm not covering its fixed costs, it's not fully covering its variable, or per-unit, costs either. In other words, the more units the firm produces, the more money it loses. Under these circumstances, a temporary **shutdown** is preferable to short-run operation. Even if the firm's owner expects the market price to increase later, enabling the firm to survive and prosper in the future, shutting down in the short run will

---

[3]Keep in mind the opportunity-cost concept. The firm's fixed costs are opportunity costs that do not vary with the level of output. They can be avoided if, and only if, the firm goes out of business. To specify fixed costs, we need to know (1) how much the firm's fixed assets would bring if they were sold or rented to others and (2) any other costs, such as operating license fees and debts, that could be avoided if the firm declared bankruptcy and/or went out of business. Since fixed costs can be avoided if the firm goes out of business, the firm will foresee greater losses from operating even in the short run if it does not expect conditions to improve.

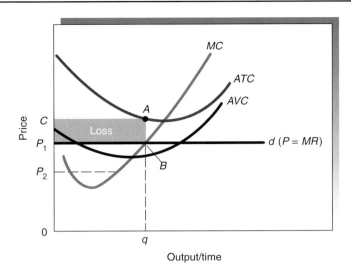

EXHIBIT 5
Operating with Short-Run Losses

A firm making losses will operate in the short run if it (1) can cover its variable costs now and (2) expects price to be high enough in the future to cover all its costs.

hold the line on its losses. The firm will still have to pay its fixed costs, but it won't be taking an additional loss on each unit it produces. Temporary shutdowns are actually regularly planned in some markets. For example, many ski resorts, golf courses, hotels, and restaurants in vacation areas plan to shut down in slow seasons, operating only when tourists or other seasonal purchasers provide enough demand. The price-taker model predicts that these firms will operate only when they expect to cover at least their variable costs.

The firm's third option is **going out of business** immediately. If the firm is sold, even the losses resulting from its fixed costs can be avoided. When market conditions are not expected to change for the better, going out of business is the preferred option.

THE FIRM'S SHORT-RUN SUPPLY CURVE

© RUSSELL SOBEL

The price taker that intends to stay in business will maximize profits (or minimize losses) when it produces the output level at which **P = MR = MC** *and variable costs are covered. Therefore, the portion of the firm's short-run marginal cost curve that lies above its average variable cost is the short-run supply curve of the firm.*

Exhibit 6 illustrates that, as the market price increases, the firm will expand output along its *MC* curve. If the market price were less than P_1, the firm would shut down immediately because it would be unable to cover even its variable costs. Shutting down will hold its loss to the payment of fixed costs only. If the market price is P_1, however, a price equal to the firm's average variable cost, the firm may supply output q_1 in the short run. Economic losses will result, but the firm would incur similar losses if it shut down completely. As the market price increases to P_2, the firm will happily expand output along its *MC* curve to q_2. At P_2, price is equal to average total costs. At this point, the firm is making a "normal rate of return," or zero economic profits. Higher prices will result in a still larger short-run output. For example, when the price rises to P_3, the firm will supply Q_3 units. At this price, economic profits will result. At still higher prices, output will be expanded even more. As long as price exceeds average variable cost, higher prices will cause the firm to expand output along its *MC* curve, which therefore becomes the firm's short-run supply curve.

A Temporary Shutdown
A firm will temporarily shut down if it cannot cover its variable cost but does not want to go out of business because it expects to be able to operate profitably in the future. This ice-cream store in Morgantown, West Virginia, closes for several months each winter and reopens during the summer. During these short-run shutdowns, the store still pays its fixed costs, such as its rent, taxes, and insurance. The store avoids only variable costs during the winter months.

EXHIBIT 6
The Short-Run Supply Curve for the Firm and the Market

As price increases, firms will expand output along their *MC* curve. Thus, the firm's *MC* curve is also its supply curve (a). When resource prices are constant, the short-run market supply (a) is merely the sum of the supply produced by all the firms in the market (b).

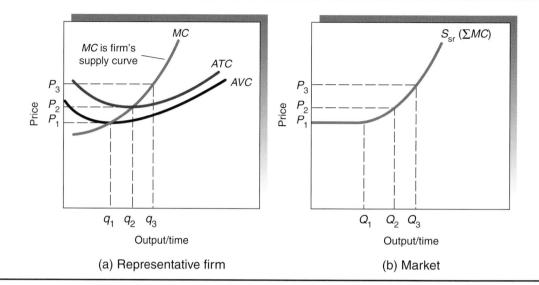

(a) Representative firm

(b) Market

THE SHORT-RUN MARKET SUPPLY CURVE

The short-run market supply curve shows the total quantity supplied at alternative market prices. ***When the firms are price takers, the short-run market supply curve is the horizontal summation of the marginal cost curves (ΣMC) above the level of average variable cost for all of the firms in the market. Since individual firms will supply a larger amount at a higher price, the short-run market supply curve will slope upward to the right.***

Exhibit 6 illustrates this relationship. As the price of the product rises from P_1 to P_2 to P_3, the individual firms expand their output along their marginal cost curves. Since the individual firms supply a larger output as the market price increases, the total amount supplied to the market also expands.

Our construction of the short-run market supply curve assumes that the prices of the resources used by the industry do not change with industry output. When the entire industry (rather than just a single firm) expands output, resource prices may rise. The reason, of course, is that when just one firm expands, it has a minuscule effect on the market for resources, but when the entire industry expands output, the rise in resource demand is larger, so resource prices are more likely to rise. When this happens, the short-run market supply curve (reflecting the higher prices of purchased inputs) will be slightly more inelastic (steeper) than the sum of the supply curves of the individual firms.

PRICE AND OUTPUT IN PRICE-TAKER MARKETS

The short-run market supply curve, together with the demand curve for the industry's product, will determine the market price. At the short-run equilibrium market price, each firm will have expanded output until marginal costs are equal to the market price. In the short run, the firms may experience either profits or losses, but they will not have enough time to alter the size of their plants.

In the long run, however, firms will have the opportunity to expand the sizes of their plants. Firms will also be able to enter and exit the industry in the long run. As long-run adjustments are made, output in the whole industry may either expand or contract.

Long-Run Equilibrium

In addition to the balance between quantity supplied and quantity demanded necessary for short-run equilibrium, firms that are price takers can earn the normal rate of return, and only the normal rate, when the market is in long-run equilibrium. Why? ***If economic profit***

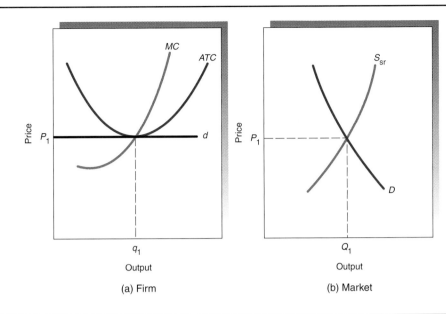

EXHIBIT 7
Long-Run Equilibrium in a Price-Taker Market

The two conditions necessary for equilibrium in a price-taker market are depicted here. First, quantity supplied and quantity demanded must be equal in the market (b). Second, the firms in the industry must earn zero economic profit (the "normal rate of return") at the established market price (a).

(a) Firm

(b) Market

is present, new firms will enter the industry to capture some of those profits. Current producers will have an incentive to expand the scale of their operations to capture some of the additional profits, too. This increase in supply will put downward pressure on prices. In contrast, if firms in the industry are suffering economic losses, they will leave the market. This decrease in supply will put upward pressure on prices.

Therefore, as **Exhibit 7** shows, when a price-taker market is in long-run equilibrium, the quantity supplied and the quantity demanded will be equal at the market price (part b), and each firm in the industry will be earning normal (zero) economic profit (that is, its minimum *ATC* will just equal the market price) (part a). Firms will have no incentive to alter either their output levels or their plant sizes. Neither will there be incentive for net investment to flow into or away from the industry.

How Will the Market Respond to an Increase in Demand?

Suppose that a price-taker market is in equilibrium. What will happen if there is an increase in demand? **Exhibit 8** shows us. Suppose that an entrepreneur introduces a fantastic new candy. Consumers go wild over it. However, since it sticks to people's teeth, the market demand for toothpicks increases from D_1 to D_2, pushing toothpick prices upward from P_1 to P_2. What impact will the higher market price have on the output level of toothpick-producing firms? It will increase (from q_1 to q_2 in part a of the exhibit) as the firms expand output along their *MC* curves. In the short run, the toothpick producers will make economic profits. The profits will attract new toothpick producers to the industry and cause the existing firms to expand the scale of their plants. Hence, the market supply will increase (shift from S_1 to S_2) and eventually eliminate the short-run profits. If the prices of resources supplied to the industry are unchanged, the market supply will continue to expand (shift to the right) until the price of toothpicks returns to its initial level (P_1), even though output has expanded to Q_3.

How Will the Market Respond to a Fall in Demand?

Economic profits attract new firms to an industry. In contrast, economic losses (when they are expected to continue) encourage capital and entrepreneurship to move out of the industry and into other areas where the profitability potential is more favorable. Economic losses mean that the owners of capital in the industry (or firms that purchase the services of the capital) are earning less than the market rate of return. The opportunity cost of continuing in the industry exceeds the gain.

EXHIBIT 8
Market Response to Increased Demand

A new candy that sticks to people's teeth causes the demand for toothpicks to increase to D_2 (b). Toothpick prices rise to P_2, inducing firms to expand output. Toothpick firms make short-run profits (a), which draw new competitors into the industry. The toothpick supply then expands (shifts from S_1 to S_2). If cost conditions are unchanged, the expansion in supply will continue until the market price of toothpicks declines to its initial level of P_1.

(a) Firm

(b) Market

Exhibit 9 shows market forces reacting to economic losses. Initially, assume that an equilibrium price exists in the industry. The firms are able to cover their average costs of production. Now suppose that consumer incomes fall, lowering the product's demand and its market price. At the new, lower price, firms in the industry will not be able to cover their costs of production. In the short run, they will reduce output along their *MC* curves. The lower output by the individual firms results in a lower quantity supplied in the market.

In the face of short-run losses, the inflow of capital will decline and the industry's capital assets will shrink as firms fail to replace equipment when it wears out. Some firms will leave the industry as their fixed costs become variable—when machinery wears out and needs to be replaced, for example—and they are no longer able to cover their variable costs at the prevailing price. Others will reduce the scale of their operations, producing only those units for which the new, lower revenues can still justify the production costs. These factors will cause the industry supply to decline, indicated by the shift from S_1 to S_2. What impact will this have on price? It will rise. Over time, given no other shifts in demand, the short-run market supply curve will decline—continue shifting to the left—until the price rises enough that the firms remaining in the industry can once again earn "normal profits." At that point, a new long-run equilibrium is established. For a real-world example of how a market adjusts to changing demand and cost conditions, see the Applications in Economics feature on coffee production in a price takers' market.

The Long-Run Market Supply Curve

The *long-run market supply curve* shows the minimum price at which firms will supply various market output levels, given enough time to adjust the sizes of their plants (or other fixed factors) and to enter or exit the industry. The shape of the curve depends on what happens to the cost of production as the *industry's* output is altered. Three possibilities emerge, although one is far more likely than the other two.

Long-Run Supply in Constant-Cost Industries   If resource prices remain unchanged, the long-run market supply curve will be perfectly elastic. In terms of economics, this describes a **constant-cost industry**. Exhibits 8 and 9 both depict constant-cost industries.

Constant-cost industry
An industry for which factor prices and costs of production remain constant as market output is expanded. The long-run market supply curve is therefore horizontal in these industries.

EXHIBIT 9
The Impact of a Fall in Demand

Lower market demand will cause the price to fall and short-run losses to occur. The losses will cause some firms to go out of business and others to reduce their output. In the long run, the market supply will fall, causing the market price to rise. The supply will continue to decline and price will continue to rise until the short-run losses have been eliminated.

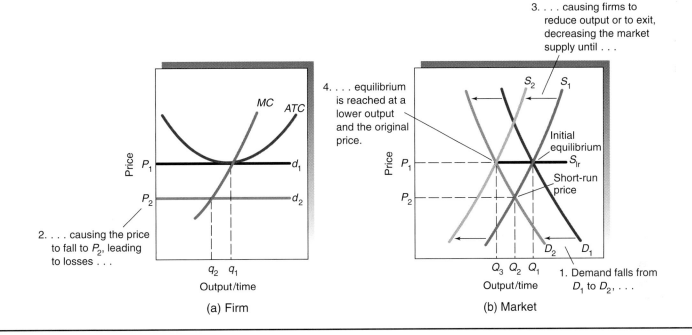

3. . . . causing firms to reduce output or to exit, decreasing the market supply until . . .

4. . . . equilibrium is reached at a lower output and the original price.

Initial equilibrium

Short-run price

2. . . . causing the price to fall to P_2, leading to losses . . .

1. Demand falls from D_1 to D_2, . . .

(a) Firm

(b) Market

Coffee Production in a Price Takers' Market

Sellers in the world's coffee market are price takers. Hundreds of thousands of farmers produce coffee beans, and no grower has a significant impact on the world price. Each grower selling in the world market takes the price as given and is free to respond to any price change. Changes can be dramatic in the coffee market. For example, the market price rose from less than $1 per pound on average early in the 1990s to nearly $2 in early 1997.

As growing coffee became more profitable, coffee production around the world expanded. For example, Vietnamese growers more than quadrupled their coffee production, from 92,000 tons in 1990 to 487,000 tons in 1999. By 2000, Vietnam had become the world's second-largest coffee-producing nation.

But the greater supply of coffee turned out to be more than consumers were willing to buy. In 1997, the market price fell, along with the price paid to growers. By August 2001, coffee bean prices were averaging less than $.60 per pound. Many growers couldn't cover their costs at such low prices and began growing other crops. Some landowners in Indonesia, for example, planted rice. Others, especially in Central and Latin America, began to plant organic and other specialty coffees, with lower yields but higher prices. Still other producers, including some in Vietnam, simply abandoned the least-profitable plantations, at least temporarily. In Mexico, more than an estimated 300,000 coffee farmers—unable to cover even their variable costs—left their farms to seek other opportunities.

The world coffee market illustrates very clearly how producers in price-taker markets can quickly expand production when rising prices are seen or expected but also contract production when prices and profits fall.

Source: The information presented is from Howard LaFranchi, "Economic Upheaval over Coffee," *Christian Science Monitor*, August 15, 2001, and from the BBC Web site at http://www.bbc.co.uk/worldservice/business/story_fdh200301.shtml (accessed September 17, 2001), and from the Web site of the International Coffee Organization at http://www.ico.org/, "Coffee Crisis" section (accessed June 16, 2004).

As Exhibit 8 shows, higher demand causes prices to increase *temporarily*. With time, however, the higher prices and profits will stimulate expansion and additional production, which will push the market price down to its initial level (and profitability to its normal rate). Because resource prices and the minimum per-unit cost remain constant as the market output expands, the larger supply will not require a permanent price increase. Similarly, Exhibit 9 illustrates the impact of a decline in demand in a constant-cost industry. Again, because resource prices and production costs are unaffected by the change in market output, the reduction in demand lowers the price in the short run, but not in the long run. Thus, in a constant-cost industry, the *long-run market supply curve* (S_{lr}) is perfectly elastic.

A constant-cost industry is most likely to arise when the industry's demand for resource inputs is quite small relative to the total demand for these resources. For example, the demand of the matches industry for wood, chemicals, and labor is very small relative to the total demand for these resources. Thus, doubling the output of matches would have very little effect on the price of the resources used by the industry. Matches therefore approximate a constant-cost industry.

Increasing-cost industry
An industry for which costs of production rise as output is expanded. In these industries, even in the long run, higher market prices will be needed to induce firms to expand total output in such industries. As a result, the long-run market supply curve in these industries will slope upward to the right.

Long-Run Supply in Increasing-Cost Industries

In most industries, an increase in market demand and *industry* output will lead to higher per-unit production costs for all the firms in the industry. Economists refer to such industries as **increasing-cost industries**. The rising output and expanded resource demand in such industries result in higher prices for at least some resources, causing the firms' cost curves to shift upward. For example, a rising demand for housing places upward pressure on the prices of lumber, window frames, building sites, and construction labor, causing the cost of housing to rise. Similarly, an increase in demand (and market output) for beef will typically cause the prices of feed grains, hay, and grazing land to rise. Thus, the production costs of beef rise as more of it is produced.

For an increasing-cost industry, an expansion in market demand will bid up resource prices, causing the per-unit cost of the firms to rise. As a result, the market price will have to increase in order to induce firms to supply the larger output. The long-run market supply curve for the product will therefore slope upward.

Exhibit 10 depicts an increasing-cost industry. Greater demand causes higher prices and a larger market output. As the industry expands, the price of resources (factors of production) rises so that costs increase. What happens to the firm's cost curves? Both the average and marginal cost curves rise (shift to ATC_2 and MC_2). Greater production costs necessitate a higher long-run price (P_2), so the long-run supply curve slopes upward to the right.

Decreasing-cost industry
An industry for which costs of production decline as the industry expands. The market supply is therefore inversely related to price. Such industries are atypical.

Long-Run Supply in Decreasing-Cost Industries

Sometimes, factor prices will decline when the market output of a product is expanded. The lower resource prices will reduce the unit costs of the firms, placing them in a position to supply a larger market output at a lower price. In such **decreasing-cost industries**, the long-run (but not the short-run) market supply curve will slope downward to the right. For example, as the electronics industry expands, suppliers of certain components may be able to adopt large-scale production techniques that will lead to lower component prices. If rising electronics demand leads to reduced component cost (and if other resource prices do not rise to offset the reductions), then the cost curves of the electronics firms will shift downward. Under these circumstances, the industry supply curve for electronics products—reflecting the lower cost—will slope downward to the right.

In most industries, however, increases in demand and expansion in market output cause higher rather than lower input prices. Thus, increasing-cost industries are the norm, and decreasing-cost industries are rare.

Supply Elasticity and the Role of Time

It takes time for firms to adjust to a change in the price of a product. In the short run, firms are stuck with the existing sizes of their plants. If the price increases in the short run, they can expand output only by utilizing their existing plants more intensely. Thus, their output response will be limited. In the long run, however, they will have time to build new plants. This will allow them to expand output by a larger amount in response to an increase in price. Thus, the market supply curve will be more elastic in the long run than in the short run.

In central areas of large cities, the supply of parking spaces can be expanded only by using higher-cost space and higher-cost techniques, such as taller parking garages that use a large portion of the building for access ramps. As a result, the unit cost of parking spaces increases as the total number is expanded. Thus, provision of parking space is an increasing-cost industry.

© HOA QUI/INDEX STOCK IMAGES

The short- and long-run distinction offers a convenient two-stage analysis, but in the real world there are many intermediate production "runs." The delivery rates for some factor inputs that could not be easily increased in a one-week time period can be increased over a two-week period. It might take two weeks, for example, to hire reliable workers who need no special skills. Expanding other factors might take a month, and still others, six months. Ordering a new custom-made machine tool at Boeing or hiring a competent new manager to expand an eastern Montana ranch operation might take a year. More precisely, the cost penalty for quicker availability is greater for some productive resources than others. In any case, a faster expansion usually means that greater cost penalties are encountered when a firm demands earlier availability of resources it needs for production.

When a firm has a longer time period to plan its output and adjust all of its productive inputs to their desired utilization levels, it will be able to produce any specific new rate of output at a lower cost. ***Because it is less costly to expand output slowly in response to a***

EXHIBIT 10
Increasing Costs and Long-Run Supply

4. . . . profits disappear for the firm and a new equilibrium results at a higher price and output, . . .

(a) Firm

2. . . . causing the price to rise temporarily to P_3 leading to profits, . . .

3. . . . causing added output from current and new producers, increasing the market supply, lowering price, and raising cost until . . .

5. . . . reflected in a new, long-run market equilibrium.

1. Demand rises from D_1 to D_2, . . .

(b) Market

demand increase, the expansion of output by firms will increase with time, as long as the price exceeds the cost. Therefore, the elasticity of the market supply curve will be greater when firms have more time to adjust their output.

Exhibit 11 shows the impact of time on producers' responses to an increase in price caused by greater demand. When the price of a product increases from P_1 to P_2, the immediate supply response of the firms is small, reflecting the high cost of hasty expansion. After one week, firms are willing to expand output only from Q_1 to Q_2. After one month, because of cost reductions made possible by the longer production-planning period, firms are willing to offer Q_3 units at the price P_2. After three months, the rate of output expands to Q_4. In the long run, when it is possible to adjust all inputs to the desired utilization levels (after a six-month time period, for example), firms are willing to supply Q_5 units of output at the market price of P_2. The supply curve for products is typically more elastic over a longer time period than over a shorter period.

THE ROLE OF PROFITS AND LOSSES

The price-taker model highlights the role of profits and losses: economic profits result when a firm or entrepreneur increases the value of resources. Business firms purchase resources and use them to produce a product or service that is sold to consumers. Costs are incurred as the business pays workers and other resource owners for the resources required to produce the product. If the sales revenue of the business firm exceeds the costs of employing all the resources required to produce the firm's output, then the firm will make a profit. *In essence, profit is a reward that business owners will earn if they produce a good that consumers value more (as measured by their willingness to pay) than the resources required for the good's production (as measured by the cost of bidding the resources away from their alternative uses).*

For example, suppose that it costs a shirt manufacturer $20,000 per month to lease a building, rent the required machines, and purchase the labor, cloth, buttons, and other materials necessary to produce and market 1,000 shirts per month. Thus, the average cost of the shirts is $20 (the $20,000 monthly cost divided by the 1,000 monthly output). If the manufacturer sells the 1,000 shirts for $22 each, its actions create wealth. Consumers value the shirts more than they value the resources required for their production. The manufacturer's $2 profit per shirt is a reward received for increasing the value of the resources.

In contrast, losses are a penalty imposed on businesses that reduce the value of resources. Losses indicate that the value of the resources used by the firm (as measured by their cost) exceeds the price consumers are willing to pay for the product supplied. Losses, along with bankruptcies, are the market's way of providing signals and incentives to bring such wasteful activities to a halt.

EXHIBIT 11
Time and the Elasticity of Supply

The elasticity of the market supply curve usually increases when suppliers have more time to adjust to a change in the price.

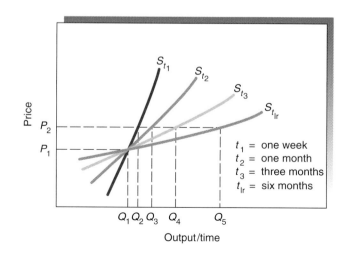

t_1 = one week
t_2 = one month
t_3 = three months
t_{lr} = six months

We live in a world of changing tastes and technology, imperfect knowledge, and uncertainty. Business decision makers cannot be sure of either future market prices or costs of production. Their decisions must be based on expectations. Nonetheless, the reward-penalty structure of a market economy is clear. *Firms that anticipate correctly the products and services for which future demand will be most urgent (relative to production costs), and produce and market them efficiently will make economic profits. Those that are inefficient and allocate resources incorrectly to areas of weak demand (relative to costs) will be penalized with losses.*

The firms most adept at giving consumers value for their money thrive and expand. Those less successful in doing so tend to shrink or even to disappear from the market. Free entry and the competitive process will protect the consumer from arbitrarily high prices. When profits are present, profit-seeking entrepreneurs will put more resources into these markets, supply will expand, and eventually the price will be driven down to the unit cost.

The Market Process in Action

When entry barriers are low, even small firms are often able to challenge and compete successfully against rivals that are much larger. Michael Dell's success in the personal computer market vividly illustrates this point. In 1984, Dell began producing and marketing personal computers while he was still a student at the University of Texas. At the age of nineteen, he began operations from his dormitory room with an investment of $1,000.[4] Then, as now, Dell Computer took orders for PCs, bought component parts from competing sellers, and custom-built the machines almost immediately to fill each order for quick delivery directly to consumers. This business strategy made it possible for the firm to keep inventories low and build the latest technical innovations into its products as soon as they were available. In contrast, IBM, Compaq, and Apple, the dominant firms during the 1980s, built specific PC models by the thousands and marketed them through retailers.

Dell's sales grew year after year and the firm eventually became the industry leader. By the first quarter of 2004, it was selling computers at a rate of $46 billion per year and Michael Dell was one of the world's richest individuals. On the other hand, IBM had exited from the PC market, a struggling Compaq had been bought out by Hewlett-Packard, and Apple's market share had declined substantially.

Although Dell Computer is not a price taker, it operates in a market with low entry barriers. Just as the price-taker model indicates, the low entry barriers will keep prices low and make sure that Dell and other producers in the industry stay on their toes. If Dell's cost efficiency were to fall or if it raised its prices significantly, rivals would expand, and new firms would be lured into the market. A higher price would be an open invitation for others to step in and steal Dell's customers, just as Dell has taken customers from others during the past two decades. And who knows, there may be another young college student among you with the engineering and an entrepreneurial genius needed to discover an even better way to make PCs.

COMPETITION PROMOTES PROSPERITY

 Competition motivates businesses to produce efficiently, cater to the views of consumers, and search for innovative improvements.

Competition

The price-taker model highlights the importance of the competitive process. Competition puts pressure on producers to operate efficiently and use resources wisely. Each competing firm will have a strong tendency to produce its products as cheaply as possible. Holding quality constant, pursuit of profit will encourage each firm to minimize the cost of production—to use the set of resources least valued in other uses that can produce the desired output. Firms that fail to keep costs low will be driven from the market.

---

[4]These and other facts about Dell are from Michael Dell and Andrew Fisher, "It's Crunch Time for Your Competitors," *Financial Times* (London), Sept. 5, 2001, and also from the Dell Web site at http://www1.us.dell.com/content/topics/global.aspx/corp/pressoffice/en/2004/2004_05_13_rr_000?c=us&l=en&s=corp.

| OUTSTANDING ECONOMIST | Friedrich A. von Hayek (1899–1992) |

Remarkably, the writings of this 1974 Nobel Prize recipient spanned seven decades. Friedrich von Hayek's work on knowledge and markets helped us understand the competitive process and the fatal defects of central planning. Von Hayek also made important contributions to our understanding of monetary theory, law and economics, business cycles, and capital theory. He is also well known for the idea that market exchanges create an "extended order" where perfect strangers who never meet nonetheless cooperate with one another to achieve their individual goals. The market process described in this chapter is an integral part of that cooperative network.

Similarly, firms in competitive markets will be motivated to discover and produce goods that are valued more highly than the resources required to produce them. Thus, resources are drawn to those uses where they are most productive, as judged by the consumers' willingness to pay. The ability of firms freely to expand or contract their businesses and enter or exit markets means that resources will not be trapped unproductively in a particular industry when they're valued more highly elsewhere.

If firms are going to be successful in competitive markets, they must also be innovative and forward looking. The production techniques and product offerings that lead to success today will not necessarily pass the competitive market test tomorrow. Producers who survive in a competitive environment cannot become complacent. On the contrary, they must be willing to experiment and quick to adopt improved methods.

In competitive markets, business firms must serve the interests of consumers. As Adam Smith noted more than 200 years ago, competition harnesses personal self-interest and channels it into activities that enhance our living standards. Smith stated:

> It is not from the benevolence of the butcher, the brewer, or the baker, that we expect our dinner, but from their regard to their own self-interest. We address ourselves, not to their humanity but to their self-love, and never talk to them of our own necessities, but of their advantages.[5]

Sellers, of course, profit when they supply products valued more highly than the resources needed to make them. But their actions also help the rest of us get more value from those resources than we would otherwise. Paradoxical as it may seem, personal self-interest—a characteristic many view as less than admirable—is a powerful source of economic progress when it is directed by the competitive market process.

LOOKING AHEAD

Consumers often seek variety in product design, style, durability, service, and location. Differentiating products slightly gives firms some control over the prices they can charge for them. In the next two chapters, we will examine markets in which the firms are price searchers. We will also consider the impact entry barriers have on markets and pricing.

---

[5]Adam Smith, *An Inquiry into the Nature and Causes of the Wealth of Nations* (1776; Cannan's ed., Chicago: University of Chicago Press, 1976), 18.

KEY POINTS

▼ A firm facing a perfectly elastic demand for its product is a price taker. A firm that can raise its price without losing all of its customers (and that must lower its price in order to sell more units) is a price searcher.

▼ To maximize profit, a price taker will expand its output as long as the sale of additional units adds more to revenues than to costs. Therefore, the profit-maximizing price taker will produce the output level at which marginal revenue (and price) equals marginal cost.

▼ The price taker's short-run marginal cost curve (above its average variable cost) is its supply curve. The short-run market supply curve is the horizontal summation of the marginal cost curves (above *AVC*) of the firms in the industry.

▼ A firm that experiences losses but that anticipates being able to cover its costs in the long run will operate in the short run if it can cover its average variable costs. Conversely, the firm will shut down if it cannot cover its average variable costs. A firm that does not anticipate being able to cover its average total cost even in the long run will minimize losses by immediately going out of business.

▼ When the market price exceeds the firm's average total cost, it will earn an economic profit. When entry barriers are absent, profits will attract new firms into the industry and stimulate the existing firms to expand. This increasing market supply continues and puts downward pressure on the price until it reaches the level of average total cost, eliminating the economic profit.

▼ When the market price is less than the firm's average total cost, the resulting losses imply that the resources could be used elsewhere to produce more value. Losses will cause firms to leave the industry or to reduce the scale of their operations. This declining market supply continues and puts upward pressure on price until the firms remaining in the market are able to earn normal returns (zero economic profit).

▼ As the output of an industry expands in response to rising demand, "fixed" resources like the size of the firm's plant will make it costly for firms to expand output quickly. The diminishing returns and rising marginal costs of firms explains why the short-run market supply curve slopes upward to the right.

▼ Normally, as industry output expands, rising factor prices push the costs of each firm upward, causing the long-run market supply curve to also slope upward to the right. However, in the long run, firms can alter the size of their plants and other resources that are fixed in the short run. As a result, the market supply curve is generally more elastic in the long run than the short run.

▼ Firms earn economic profit by producing goods that can be sold for more than the cost of the resources required to produce them. Profit is a reward people get for increasing the value of resources. Conversely, losses are a penalty imposed on those who use resources in a way that reduces their value.

▼ Competition motivates producers to operate efficiently and heed the views of consumers. Competition and the market process harness self-interest and direct producers toward wealth-creating activities.

CRITICAL ANALYSIS QUESTIONS

*1. Farmers are often heard to complain about the high costs of machinery, labor, and fertilizer, suggesting that these costs drive down their profits. Does it follow that if, for example, the price of fertilizer fell by 10 percent, farming (a highly competitive industry with low barriers to entry) would be more profitable? Explain.

*2. If the firms in a price-taker market are making short-run profits, what will happen to the market price in the long run? Explain.

3. "In a price-taker market, if a business operator produces efficiently—that is, if the cost of producing the good is minimized—the operator will be able to make at least a normal profit." True or false? Explain.

4. Suppose the government of a large city levies a 5 percent sales tax on hotel rooms. How will the tax affect (a) prices of hotel rooms, (b) the profits of hotel owners, and (c) gross (including the tax) expenditures on hotel rooms?

*5. If coffee suppliers are price takers, how will an unanticipated increase in demand for their product affect each of the following, in a market that was initially in long-run equilibrium?
   a. The short-run market price of the product
   b. Industry output in the short run
   c. Profitability in the short run
   d. The long-run market price in the industry
   e. Industry output in the long run
   f. Profitability in the long run

*6. Suppose that the development of a new drought-resistant hybrid seed corn leads to a 50 percent increase in the average yield per acre without increasing the cost to the farmers who use the new technology. If the producers in the corn production industry were price takers, what would happen to the following?
   a. The price of corn
   b. The profitability of corn farmers who quickly adopt the new technology
   c. The profitability of corn farmers who are slow to adopt the new technology
   d. The price of soybeans, a substitute product for corn

7. "When the firms in the industry are just able to cover their cost of production, economic profit is zero. Therefore, if demand falls, causing prices to go down even a little bit, all of the firms in the industry will be driven out of business." True or false? Explain.

8. Why does the short-run market supply curve for a product slope upward to the right? Why does the long-run market supply curve generally slope upward to the right? Why is the long-run market supply curve generally more elastic than the short-run supply curve?

*9. How does competition among firms affect the incentive of each firm to (a) operate efficiently (produce at a low per-unit cost) and (b) produce goods that consumers value? What happens to firms that fail to do these two things?

10. Will firms in a price-taker market be able to earn profits in the long run? Why or why not? What determines profitability? Discuss.

*11. During the summer of 1988, drought conditions throughout much of the United States substantially reduced the size of the corn, wheat, and soybean crops, three commodities for which demand is inelastic. Use the price-taker model to determine how the drought affected (a) prices of the three commodities, (b) revenue from the three crops, and (c) the profitability of those farming the three crops.

12. Why is competition in a market important? Is there a positive or negative effect on the economy when strong competitive pressures drive various firms out of business? Discuss.

13. Do business firms in competitive markets have a strong incentive to serve the interests of consumers? Are they motivated by a strong desire to help consumers? Are "good intentions" necessary if individuals are going to engage in actions that are helpful to others? Discuss.

*14. The accompanying table presents the expected cost and revenue data for the Tucker Tomato Farm. The Tuckers produce tomatoes in a greenhouse and sell them wholesale in a price-taker market.
   a. Fill in the firm's marginal cost, average variable cost, average total cost, and profit schedules.
   b. If the Tuckers are profit maximizers, how many tomatoes should they produce when the market price is $500 per ton? Indicate their profits.
   c. Indicate the firm's output level and maximum profit if the market price of tomatoes increases to $550 per ton.
   d. How many units would the Tucker Tomato Farm produce if the price of tomatoes fell to $450 per ton? What would be the firm's profits? Should the firm stay in business? Explain.

COST AND REVENUE SCHEDULES FOR TUCKER TOMATO FARM, INC.

OUTPUT (TONS PER MONTH)	TOTAL COST	PRICE PER TON	MARGINAL COST	AVERAGE VARIABLE COST	AVERAGE TOTAL COST	PROFITS (MONTHLY)
0	$1,000	$500	____	____	____	____
1	1,200	500	____	____	____	____
2	1,350	500	____	____	____	____
3	1,550	500	____	____	____	____
4	1,900	500	____	____	____	____
5	2,300	500	____	____	____	____
6	2,750	500	____	____	____	____
7	3,250	500	____	____	____	____
8	3,800	500	____	____	____	____
9	4,400	500	____	____	____	____
10	5,150	500	____	____	____	____

15. In the accompanying table, you are given information about two firms that compete in a price-taker market. Assume that fixed costs for each firm are $20.
    a. Complete the table.
    b. What is the lowest price at which firm A will produce?
    c. How many units of output will it produce at that price? (Assume that it cannot produce fractional units.)
    d. What is the lowest price at which firm B will produce?
    e. How many units of output will it produce?
    f. How many units will firm A produce if the market price is $20?
    g. How many units will firm B produce at the $20 price? (Assume that it cannot produce fractional units.)
    h. If each firm's total fixed costs are $20 and the price of output is $20, which firm would earn a higher net profit or incur a smaller loss?
    i. How much would that net profit or loss be?

FIRM A

QUANTITY	TOTAL VARIABLE COST	MARGINAL COST	AVERAGE VARIABLE COST
1	$ 24	___	___
2	30	___	___
3	38	___	___
4	48	___	___
5	62	___	___
6	82	___	___
7	110	___	___

FIRM B

QUANTITY	TOTAL VARIABLE COST	MARGINAL COST	AVERAGE VARIABLE COST
1	$ 8	___	___
2	10	___	___
3	16	___	___
4	24	___	___
5	36	___	___
6	56	___	___
7	86	___	___

*Asterisk denotes questions for which answers are given in Appendix B.

CHAPTER 22

Price-Searcher Markets with Low Entry Barriers

[T]he price to the price searcher is not determined for him as if by some impersonal market mechanism. Instead he must search out the optimal (wealth-maximizing) price. And, not knowing the demand schedule exactly, he will have to resort to retrial-and-error search processes.

—Armen A. Alchian and William R. Allen[1]

Chapter Focus

■ What are the characteristics of competitive price-searcher markets? How are price and output determined in such markets?

■ Is there a linkage between innovative actions by some firms and business failures by others? Are business failures bad for the economy?

■ Can markets be competitive when they consist of only one or two suppliers?

■ Why is the role of the entrepreneur left out of economic models? How do the actions of entrepreneurs influence economic progress?

■ Why do some economists criticize price-searcher behavior when entry barriers are low, while others like the results?

■ Is price discrimination bad?

[1]Armen A. Alchian and William R. Allen, *University Economics*, 2d ed. (Belmont, Calif.: Wadsworth Publishing, 1967), 113.

As we noted in the previous chapter, markets set the price in price-taker markets. Price-taker firms decide what output to produce, but they do not have a pricing decision to make. In this chapter, we will focus on markets in which entry barriers are low, but firms can alter the price charged for their output. If firms reduce their price, they will be able to sell more units. Correspondingly, they can raise their price and lose some, but not all, of their customers. Thus, the firm has to decide what price to charge for the goods and services that it sells. ■

COMPETITIVE PRICE-SEARCHER MARKETS

Markets that are characterized by (1) low entry barriers and (2) firms that face a downward-sloping demand curve are called **competitive price-searcher markets**.[2] The low entry barriers ensure that these markets are competitive, and the firm's downward–sloping demand curve means that the sellers in these markets have to search for the price and output combination that will maximize their profits.

In contrast with price-taker markets, in which the firms produce identical products, price searchers produce **differentiated products**. For example, ice cream from Häagen-Dazs is not identical to ice cream from Ben and Jerry's, Breyers, or Baskin-Robbins. The products supplied by the alternative sellers may differ in their design, dependability, location, packaging, and a multitude of other factors. This product differentiation explains why the firms confront a downward-sloping demand curve. Because some consumers are willing to pay more to get the specific product they like best, the firm will not lose all its customers to rivals if it raises its price.

Rival firms, however, supply products that are quite similar. Therefore, when a price searcher raises its price, some of its customers will switch to the substitutes. *Because good substitutes are readily available from other suppliers, the demand curve faced by the firms in competitive price-searcher markets will be highly elastic.*

Given the low entry barriers, new entrants will be attracted if an activity is profitable. Thus, sellers in competitive price-searcher markets face competition from both firms that are already in the market and potential new entrants. Clearly, competition in these markets will be intense. Sometimes economists use the term **monopolistic competition** to describe markets quite similar to those of the competitive price-searcher model, but because there is nothing "monopolistic" about these markets, we believe that this term is misleading. Competitive price searcher is much more descriptive of the conditions in these markets. However, students should be aware that the expression "monopolistic competition" is often used to describe markets very much like those analyzed in this chapter.

Although the price searcher can set the price for its products, the quantity sold at alternative prices will be determined by market forces. Therefore, to find the profit-maximizing price and quantity combination, price searchers must try to estimate not just one market price, but how buyers will respond to the various prices that might be charged. In essence, the firm must try to figure out what the demand curve for its product looks like. Clearly, the price searcher confronts a more complex set of decisions than the price taker. And the complexity does not end with the firm's pricing decision.

For the price searcher, demand is not simply a given. The firm, by changing product quality, style, location, and service (among many other factors), and by advertising, can alter the demand for its products. It can increase demand by drawing customers from rivals if it can convince consumers that its products provide more value. When an airline adopts a more generous frequent-flier program or a soap manufacturer provides "cents-off" coupons, each is trying to make its product a little more attractive than rival products to certain potential customers. The precise effects of these decisions cannot easily be predicted, but they nonetheless can make the difference between profit and loss for the firm. In the real world, most firms occupy the complex and risky territory of the price searcher.

Competitive price-searcher market
A market in which the firms have a downward-sloping demand curve, and entry into and exit from the market are relatively easy.

Differentiated products
Products distinguished from similar products by characteristics like quality, design, location, and method of promotion.

Monopolistic competition
A term often used by economists to describe markets characterized by a large number of sellers that supply differentiated products to a market with low barriers to entry. Essentially, it is an alternative term for a competitive price-searcher market.

---

[2]It is important to distinguish between the demand curve faced by the firm and the market demand curve. The competitive price-searcher model focuses on the *firm's* demand curve.

In the highly competitive market for custom-fitted golf clubs, firms use competitive weapons such as style, swingweight, variable length and club-shaft flexibility, advertising, and celebrity endorsements. Firms in this market are price searchers.

Price and Output in Competitive Price-Searcher Markets

How does a price searcher decide what price to charge and what level of output to produce? For the price searcher, reducing prices in order to expand output and sales has two conflicting influences on total revenue. As **Exhibit 1** illustrates, the increase in sales (from q_1 to q_2) due to the lower price will, by itself, add to the revenue of the price searcher. The price reduction, however, also applies to units *that would otherwise have been sold at a higher price* (P_1, rather than the lower price, P_2). This factor by itself will cause a reduction in total revenue. As the price is gradually lowered to sell additional units, these two conflicting forces will eventually result in marginal revenue (a change in total revenue) that is less than the selling price of the additional units. Because the price of units that could have been sold at the higher price will now be lower, the price searcher's marginal revenue will be less than the price of its product. As Exhibit 1 shows, the marginal revenue curve of the price searcher will always lie below the firm's demand curve.[3] (Remember, the lowercase *d* is used when the reference is to the *firm's* demand curve.)

Any firm can increase profits by expanding output as long as marginal revenue exceeds marginal cost. Therefore, a price searcher will lower price and expand output until marginal revenue is equal to marginal cost.

Exhibit 2 illustrates the profit-maximizing price and output. The price searcher will increase profit by expanding its output to q, where marginal revenue is equal to marginal cost and price P can be charged. Beyond q, the price reduction required to sell additional units will reduce the firm's profit. For any output level less than q (for example, R), a price reduction and sales expansion will add more to total revenues than to total costs. At output R, marginal revenues exceed marginal costs. Therefore, profits will be greater if the price

---

[3]For a straight-line demand curve, the marginal revenue curve will bisect any line from the *y*-axis to the demand curve, drawn parallel to the *x*-axis. For example, the *MR* curve will divide the line P_2F into two equal parts, P_2E and *EF*.

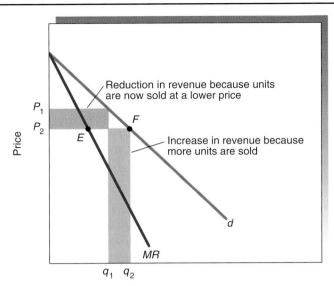

EXHIBIT 1
Marginal Revenue of a Price Searcher

When a firm faces a downward-sloping demand curve, a price reduction that increases sales will exert two conflicting influences on total revenue. First, total revenue will rise because of an increase in the number of units sold (from q_1 to q_2). However, revenue losses from the lower price (P_2) on units that could have been sold at a higher price (P_1) will at least partially offset the additional revenues from increased sales. Therefore, the marginal revenue curve will lie inside the firm's demand curve.

is reduced and output can be expanded. On the other hand, if output exceeds q (for example, S), selling additional units beyond q will add more to costs (MC) than to revenues (MR). At output S, the firm will gain by raising the price to P, even though the price rise will result in the loss of some customers. Profits will be maximized by charging price P and producing the output level q, where $MC = MR$.

The firm in Exhibit 2 is making an economic profit. Total revenues $PAq0$ exceed the firm's total costs $CBq0$ at the profit-maximizing output level. Given the low barriers to entry, profits will attract rivals. Other firms will enter this market and attempt to produce a similar product (or provide a similar service).

What will the entry of new rivals do to the demand for the products of the firms already in the market? These new rivals will draw customers away from existing firms and thereby reduce the demand for their output. As long as new entrants expect to make economic profits, additional competitors will be attracted to the market. This entry of new

EXHIBIT 2
The Price Searcher's Price and Output

A price searcher maximizes its profits by producing output q, for which $MR = MC$, and charging price P. The firm is making economic profits. What impact will these profits have if this is a typical firm?

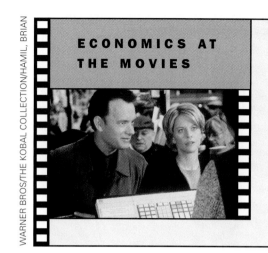

ECONOMICS AT THE MOVIES

You've Got Mail (1998)

Tom Hanks is opening a huge bookstore in Manhattan that could put Meg Ryan's small children's bookstore out of business. Can you show how the demand curve facing Ryan's bookstore would be affected by the opening of the new store in this competitive price-searcher market?

firms into the market will continue until competition among rivals shifts the demand curve in far enough to eliminate the economic profit. As **Exhibit 3** illustrates, when long-run equilibrium is present in a competitive price-searcher market, the price will equal per-unit cost. Firms will produce at the *MR = MC* output level, but they will be unable to earn economic profits because competitive pressures will force the price down to the per-unit cost level.

If losses are present in a specific market, with time, some of the firms in the market will go out of business. As firms leave, some of their previous customers will buy from other firms. The demand curve facing the remaining firms in the industry will then shift outward until the economic losses are eliminated and the long-run, zero-profit equilibrium illustrated by Exhibit 3 is restored.

Consider the role of profits and losses in competitive price-searcher markets. Profits will attract both new firms and additional investment capital into the market. In turn, the increased availability of the product (and similar products) will drive down the price until the profits are eliminated. Conversely, economic losses will cause competitors to exit the market and investment capital to move elsewhere. This will reduce the supply of the product and eventually make it possible for the firms remaining in the market to charge a price sufficient to cover their unit costs. ***Thus, firms in competitive price-searcher markets can make either economic profits or losses in the short run. But, after long-run adjustments occur, only a normal profit (that is, zero economic profit) will be possible because of the competitive conditions.***

EXHIBIT 3
Competitive Price-Searcher and Long-Run Normal Profit

Because firms are free to enter and exit the market, competition will eventually drive down prices to the level of average total cost for price searchers.

DYNAMIC COMPETITION, INNOVATION, AND BUSINESS FAILURES

Business failures and cutbacks in output and employment are generally reported under the heading of negative news about the economy. Clearly, they are often painful for the parties directly involved. Owners often lose a substantial amount of their wealth, and employees are forced to search for alternative job opportunities. From the standpoint of the entire economy, however, business failures play an important role that is often overlooked: they weed out inefficient, high-cost producers and release resources so they can be employed more productively elsewhere. The assets and workers of firms that fail become available for use by others supplying goods that are more highly valued by consumers. Without this release of resources, the expansion of both profitable firms and the entire economy would be slowed.

Business failures occur for a variety of reasons, including poor management and misjudgment of market conditions. One of the most important sources of business failure is innovative behavior by rival firms. Suppose that an innovative firm introduces a new improved product or comes up with a lower-cost method of supplying a good. The actions of the innovator will reduce the demand for goods supplied by rival firms. Facing intense competition from the innovator, rival firms that are unable to do as well for buyers will experience losses and will eventually be driven out of business. Viewed from this perspective, business failures are often merely the flip side of innovative actions that improve products and reduce costs for consumers.

The great Austrian economist Joseph Schumpeter referred to the competition that occurs when new products, technologies, and better forms of organization are developed as "creative destruction." Dynamic competition of this type is both widespread and highly important in competitive price-searcher markets. It is constantly leading to the expansion of some firms and the contraction of others. Examples abound. In early 2001, Lucent, a high-technology firm, announced that its sales had fallen 28 percent, while rival Nortel Networks experienced a 34 percent increase. Lucent's failure to adopt a new generation of optical-technology production quickly forced it to lay off 16,000 of its employees. As a result, these workers were available to other firms and pursuits.

Important changes were also taking place in the retail sector that year. J. C. Penney announced it would shut forty-seven stores eleven months after it had closed forty-five others. In 2002, Kmart filed for bankruptcy. Meanwhile, Wal-Mart, Costco, and Target were rapidly expanding across the United States, "the way the Huns blew into Europe," as one news report put it.[4]

Numerous businesses come and go. Each year, newly incorporated businesses account for about 10 percent of the total number of businesses. At the same time, approximately 1 percent of businesses file for bankruptcy, and many others close their doors or sell their assets to other, more successful (or at least more optimistic) operators. *It is important to recognize that business failures do not destroy either the assets owned by the firm or the talents of its workers. Instead, they release these resources for more productive use by other firms.*

CONTESTABLE MARKETS AND THE COMPETITIVE PROCESS

If firms can easily enter a market with little risk of suffering a substantial loss of wealth, competition is likely to be intense, even if there are only a few firms operating within it. Markets in which firms can enter and exit with minimal risk are known as **contestable markets**.[5] Even if entering a contestable market requires a substantial amount of capital, this won't be

Contestable market
A market in which the costs of entry and exit are low, so a firm risks little by entering. Efficient production and zero economic profits should prevail in a contestable market.

---

[4]Steve Syre and Charles Stein, "Capitalism's Messy Ways Still Come Up Rosy," *Boston Globe,* January 26, 2001, and David Hayes, "Sprint Will Slice 1,100 More Jobs," *Knight-Ridder/Tribune Business News,* June 17, 2004.

[5]The classic article on this topic is William J. Baumol's "Contestable Markets: An Uprising in the Theory of Industry Structure," *American Economic Review* 72 (March 1982): 1–15.

Airliners are extremely expensive, so their cost might be a barrier to entry. But airplanes can also be leased and are highly mobile among markets, as are pilots, flight attendants, and office workers. These highly mobile resources allow firms to enter and exit a given transportation market with relative ease. Such a market is contestable.

© DAVE BARTRUFF/INDEX STOCK IMAGERY

a major deterrent if the funds can largely be recovered should the firm need to exit. This will be the case when the assets necessary to compete in a market can be either leased for short time periods or resold at something near their original purchase price.

When airport landing rights and facilities are available, an airline route is a classic example of a contestable market. Consider the case of the airline route between Salt Lake City, Utah, and Albuquerque, New Mexico. Only Delta Airlines provides nonstop service on this route, since there is so little traffic. Furthermore, there would seem to be high barriers to entry, since it takes multimillion-dollar airplanes to compete, as well as facilities for reservations, ticketing, baggage handling, and so on. Given that Delta is the only supplier on the route, one might expect the price to be high and service relatively poor. However, if firms can easily rent facility space at airports, then the barriers to entry are much lower than the equipment costs suggest. The nonstop Salt Lake City–Albuquerque market, for example, can be entered by other airlines simply by shifting aircraft, personnel, and equipment from other routes and locations. Moreover, airlines often rent or lease their planes. This reduces both the amount of initial capital needed to enter a market and the risk of losing it should the venture fail.

Delta is well aware that other firms can easily enter this market. Some of its rivals already serve both Salt Lake City and Albuquerque, and, in fact, provide service between the two via connecting flights. Delta knows that if it raises prices much above cost on the route, other firms will enter the market. The very threat of competition encourages Delta to provide quality service at an attractive price.

In a contestable market, potential competition, as well as actual entry, will discipline sellers. When entry and exit are not expensive, even a firm alone in a market faces the serious prospect of competition. Two important conditions will be present in contestable markets: (1) prices above the level necessary to achieve zero economic profits will not be sustained, and (2) the costs of production will be kept to a minimum. This is because production inefficiencies and prices that are above costs present a profitable opportunity for new entrants. Predictably, profit-seeking rivals will enter and drive the price down to the level of per-unit costs.

The contestable market model has important policy implications. If policy makers are concerned that a market is not sufficiently competitive, they should take a close look at its entry barriers and what might be done to make it contestable. Much of economists' enthusiasm for deregulation can be traced to the fact that regulation often impedes market entry. Many economists believe that deregulating markets to make entry easier can lead to lower prices and better performance than other alternatives, including directly regulating prices.

COMPLEX DECISION MAKING AND THE ENTREPRENEUR

Scientific models simplify conditions in order to help us understand complex relationships. Economic models like the price-taker and price-searcher models are no exception. But these models leave out some important elements of the business decision-making process. Furthermore, they gloss over the complexity of other decisions that must be made by real-world entrepreneurs.

Will profits increase if prices are raised (or lowered)? To get an answer to this question, real-world business decision makers cannot go into a back room and look at a demand-cost diagram. Instead, they must search for clues, experiment with actual price changes, and interpret what they see, often using a great deal of "seat-of-the-pants" judgment. Our model doesn't reveal precisely how this is done, but it highlights the fact that entrepreneurs are strongly motivated to find the profit-maximizing price. Those that are most successful will at least approximate this objective, and the outcome will be as if they had deliberately chosen the $MR = MC$ price and output combination of our model.

Although the competitive price-searcher model explains how entrepreneurs will react to profits and losses in a specific market, it does not explain how and when new products will be developed or new production techniques applied. How will consumers react to a potential new product? Can it be produced profitably? Will a new production process or alternative technology reduce cost? Can per-unit costs be reduced if the firm offers a different combination of products and services? Here, again, the marginal principle applies: if the change adds more to revenue than it does to cost, it should be made. But how much of a change should be made? Up to the point where $MC = MR$, of course. Identifying this point for each potential change, however, is difficult. Such decisions generally involve an important variable that is omitted from our economic models: entrepreneurship.

The Left-Out Variable: Entrepreneurship

Entrepreneurial judgment is necessary when there is no decision rule that can be applied using only information that is freely available. For this reason, we are unable to incorporate fully the function of the entrepreneur into economic models. There simply is no way to model these complex decisions that involve uncertainty, discovery, and business judgment. All we can do is note the importance of entrepreneurial judgment and recognize that our models are limited because they are unable to capture this critical element of both business success and economic progress.

If we cannot put entrepreneurship into our models, what can we say about its function? One way to answer this question is to consider a generalized job description for an entrepreneurial position. An investor who lacks the desire, or perhaps the skill, to be an entrepreneur but nonetheless wants to be in business, might provide some of the capital to launch a business and hire someone else to act as the entrepreneur. A hypothetical newspaper ad to find such a person might read like this:

> *Wanted: Entrepreneur.* Diverse skills required. Must be (1) alert to new business opportunities and new problems before they become obvious; (2) willing to back judgments with hard work and creative effort before others recognize the correctness of judgments; (3) able to make correct decisions and convince others of their validity, so as to attract additional financial backing; and (4) able to recognize one's own inevitable mistakes and to back away from incorrect decisions without wasting additional resources. Exciting, exhausting, high-risk position. Pay will be very good for success, and very poor for failure.

Entrepreneurship is not for the fainthearted or the lazy. Entrepreneurs are at the center of the action in the real world, even if they do not have a place in most economic models.[6]

---

[6] For a more complete overview of entrepreneurship and references on the topic, see Mark Crosson, "Entrepreneurship," in *The New Palgrave: A Dictionary of Economics*, ed. John Eatwell et al. (New York: Stockton Press, 1987), 151-153.

APPLICATIONS IN ECONOMICS

Entrepreneurs at the Helm of Some Bizarre Occupations[7]

*These innovative people see a need
and find a niche in the market*
BY DAVID YOUNG (*CHICAGO TRIBUNE*)

Mike Turk lost a coin toss and wound up with a thousand teak trophy bases he couldn't get rid of. So he bolted Army surplus hand grenades to them and sold them for $15 apiece as desk ornaments. Joseph Tokarski, a postal worker contemplating a post-retirement business, developed a machine to clean up Canada goose droppings.

"There are two important dimensions to being an entrepreneur: The first is risk and the second is innovation," said Sumaria Mohan-Neill, professor of entrepreneurship at Roosevelt University's College of Business Administration. "To succeed, a person has to be innovative. Some would call it bizarre," she added.

Turk and Tokarski are among what may be scores of entrepreneurs around Chicago who have found unusual business niches and somehow make their living at bizarre occupations. They manufacture odd products, they provide unusual services and some sell the grotesque. Sometimes these entrepreneurs accidentally find their callings; sometimes out of desperation they gravitate to odd occupations after losing their regular jobs; and in some cases, they are able to turn their hobbies into going business concerns.

"People leverage their knowledge," said Steven C. Michael, business administration professor at the University of Illinois' College of Commerce in Urbana. According to Michael, entrepreneurs have a vision of their mission and are able to sell that to other people, but they also have to be flexible enough to change course.

"Entrepreneurs don't spot markets. They spot needs and assemble the skills to fill them," says Michael, and that's the genesis of Magic Mound Mover, Joseph Tokarski's business. Tokarski said he developed a vacuum system to clean up the backyard scat from his own dogs because no one else in the family would do the chore. The device worked so well that he decided to mount it on a golf cart and go after a problem common in Midwestern open spaces: Canada goose droppings. A little advertising in local newspapers and by word of mouth has resulted in jobs with apartment complexes, park districts and school systems cleaning up after the ubiquitous geese.

Similarly, coming up with a clever idea to solve a problem played a big role for Turk, who was working in the family-owned surplus business Surplus Trading Corp. in Benton Harbor, Mich. Only for Turk, the problem was what to do with 1,000 teak trophy bases he acquired on the toss of a coin that determined their price. "We have all kinds of ways of doing deals in the surplus business," concedes Turk, who over the years has bought and sold 85 dozen women's panties from Victoria's Secret, 60 cases of olive oil and 500 pounds of hard candy. But he couldn't unload the teak at any price, so he decided to turn them into novelty items. He bolted Army surplus hand grenades to the bases and attached plaques that read, "Complaint Department: Take a number." The number is attached to the detonating pin. He has sold hundreds of them.

Turk and Tokarski are lucky ones; the failure rate for entrepreneurs is high, possibly as much as 70 to 80 percent, according to business scholars.

"Complaint Department: Take a number." (Pull the pin of the hand grenade.)

© MIKE TURK/SURPLUS TRADING COMPANY

---

[7] David Young, "Risky, Odd, Bizarre: Even–Entrepreneur's Spot Needs," *Chicago Tribune*, Jan. 30, 1999, 1. Reprinted by permission.

APPLICATIONS IN ECONOMICS

Five Entrepreneurs Who Have Changed Our Lives

Compared to movie stars and athletes, business entrepreneurs seldom command quite as much respect in our society. Often, their contributions are either overlooked or misunderstood. Of course, everyone knows that highly successful entrepreneurs make a lot of money. Remember, however, that trade helps both the buyers and the sellers. Consumers benefit, too, by purchasing the products and services of successful entrepreneurs. If they didn't, they wouldn't buy them.

Entrepreneurship often comes from unusual sources—people who have an ability to think about and institute unconventional ideas. Many entrepreneurs have had an enormous impact on our lives, far more than most of us realize. Let's take a closer look at the impact of five leading entrepreneurs.

Fred Smith

In 2004, Fred Smith was named "CEO of the Year" by *Chief Executive* magazine. Smith's business career began when he was in college in the 1960s, with the observation that computers were going to become a major part of people's lives. More important, he predicted a logical consequence: if computers were going to replace people for many tasks, the computers would have to be in good working order every day. If something went wrong, they had to be fixed immediately, and parts had to be available right away. As Smith describes it now, computer companies needed a "logistics system that provided the parts and pieces wherever that computer was located whenever it was needed."

Smith developed the idea and described the system in a paper for a business strategy course while studying in the MBA program at Yale. Perhaps because it seemed farfetched at the time, he reports that the professor gave him a "gentleman's C." In the following decade, however, Smith founded Federal Express—now officially FedEx—and actually created the express delivery system outlined in his paper. Beginning in 1973, FedEx created a giant network of airplane and truck transportation capable of providing overnight delivery around the world. Smith's chief innovation was the development of a transportation system with a "central switch" or "central junction." For FedEx, that was Memphis, Tennessee. When one looks at moving an item from Detroit to Minneapolis via Memphis, it seems inefficient, says Smith. "But when you take all of the transactions on the network together, it's tremendously efficient."

FedEx has revolutionized the express mail and package delivery system, consistently earning a profit. It has absorbed several companies in related businesses, and its annual revenue now exceeds $25 billion. Furthermore, FedEx has forced competitors, from the U.S. Postal Service to United Parcel Service, to become more efficient and make major changes in their operations. In the process, Smith transformed the lives of millions of shippers, who now use the term "FedEx" as a verb and know they can get a package anywhere "absolutely positively overnight"—to quote one of the company's past advertising slogans. He can take great pride in the fact that the market gave him a much higher grade than his old MBA professor.

For more detail, see Gretchen Morgenson, ed., "Fred Smith," in *Forbes Great Minds of Business* (New York: John Wiley, 1997), 35–71; and William J. Holstein, "Leader of the Pack," *Chief Executive* (June 2004).

Pleasant Rowland

Even though she had never run a business or studied in an MBA program, Pleasant Rowland used her life savings to start a company selling a popular line of dolls and books known as The American Girl. Today, the Pleasant Company is a $250-million-a-year business.

Rowland was motivated by a mission: to give girls ages 7 to 12 the chance to experience the love of dolls and the fun of reading she remembered from her childhood. Rowland's idea began to take shape one Christmas season when she tried to find some dolls for her nieces, then ages 8 and 10. The dolls she found—Cabbage Patch babies and Barbie dolls—seemed of mediocre quality, and they failed to evoke "what it meant to be a girl growing up in America." She had already been thinking about American history. While visiting Colonial Williamsburg, Virginia, she fell in love with the historic buildings and streets. She began to wonder, "Isn't there some way that I can make the magic of this historic place come alive for little girls?"

Her idea was a subtle one, creating a distinctive line of dolls that reflect authentic American history and serve as appealing role models. She had to find designers and craftspeople who could create dolls that captured the imagination and love of young girls, dolls with often poignant stories—a girl who pioneered in the West or one who escaped slavery in the South. Rowland shaped her products as she went along, drawing on all her talents and unswayed by those who thought she was on the wrong track. She had been a teacher and a writer, so she knew how to communicate with children. She knew that her kind of doll wasn't suited for garish Saturday morning television commercials, where she would be battling against giant companies like Hasbro and Mattel. She didn't have enough money to compete with those companies anyway. So she marketed her dolls through a catalog, writing her own copy in a "softer" voice.

(continued)

(continued)

Rowland turned out to be right; there was a void in the market, and her dolls helped fill it. Books and a magazine, *The American Girl,* naturally followed. Rowland put it this way: "I don't think I'm in the doll business or the book business or the direct-mail business. I'm in the little girl business." By following her convictions, she found an audience ready to purchase what she wanted to provide.

Mattel bought into Rowland's approach as well. In 1998, she sold Pleasant Company and American Girl to Mattel for $700 million and took on a new career—philanthropy. By 2004, Pleasant Company (recently renamed American Girl) had sold more than 8 million American Girl dolls and 90 million books.

For more detail, see Gretchen Morgenson, ed., "Pleasant Rowland," in *Forbes Great Minds of Business* (New York: John Wiley, 1998), 121–55; and Julie Sloan, "How We Got Started: Pleasant Rowland," *Fortune Small Business* (October 2002).

William "Bill" Gates III

Even as a child, Bill Gates loved computers. At the early age of fifteen, he earned $20,000 by writing a computer program to help manage traffic. He entered Harvard at the age of seventeen, and, while still an undergraduate, developed BASIC for the first microcomputer, the MITS Altair. Convinced that eventually most offices and homes would have a microcomputer, Gates, along with his friend Paul Allen, created Microsoft in 1975. The focus of the business was the development of software designed to make microcomputers both more useful and more user-friendly.

Gates quickly earned a reputation as a programming genius. When IBM decided to enter the personal computer (PC) market in 1980, it contracted with Gates to provide the basic operating software for its computers, a system now known as MS-DOS. Gates reserved the rights to sell his MS-DOS software to other firms. As IBM (and IBM clones) grew to dominate the PC market during the 1980s, Gates's fortune rose as well. Microsoft developed into the dominant firm in the computer software industry, and today, its programs run more than 90 percent of the world's computers. Microsoft has moved beyond MS-DOS, of course, but its Windows software continues to be among the most popular in the world. Near the end of 2001, Gates's personal fortune was estimated at more than $50 billion. This was after giving $21 billion to his charitable foundation, and losing more than $9 billion that year in the falling stock market.

Probably still the world's richest man in 2004, Bill Gates attributes his success to his workaholic nature. He continues to work long hours and is still actively involved in the operation and strategic decision making of Microsoft, even as his charitable activities have increased. If you have ever used a computer, you have almost certainly benefited from programs Gates created. His remarkable programming genius has changed the way we use personal computers both at home and in the workplace.

For more detail, see Gene N. Landrum, *Profiles of Genius* (Buffalo, N.Y.: Prometheus Books, 1993); and Robert F. Hartley, *Management Mistakes and Successes* (New York: John Wiley, 1994).

Sergey Brin and Larry Page

For years, Internet users have struggled to find billions of bits of information scattered across the World Wide Web. More than anyone, two Stanford computer science graduate students—Sergey Brin and Larry Page—have changed that by getting information to users more quickly and easily on Google.com.

Brin and Page were in their early twenties when they dropped out of graduate school. Using their credit cards and those of their parents and friends, they formed Google, Inc. in a garage in Menlo Park, California. ("Googol" is the number 1 followed by 100 zeros.)

Google's computers are constantly searching the Web, downloading a huge number of files into the company's databases, and updating them regularly. The sophisticated programs Brin and Page developed sort and quickly bring the most important and reliable information to the top of users' screens. Information seekers love it. The keywords they type in for their searches also target the advertising that generates the firm's revenue. Unlike, say, a newspaper, which delivers the same ads to every reader, Google links advertising to the user's particular interests according to the topic being searched. Users see fewer ads, but advertisers get more targeted exposure of their messages.

By 2000, Google had become the world's top search engine, handling 18 million hits a day. The following year, the firm turned its first annual profit: $7 million on sales of $86 million. In 2002, Google was processing 70 million hits per day, and Google, Inc. had expanded its business to sell additional Web-related and wireless business and personal services.

By 2004, first-quarter profits alone were $64 million, and Google announced plans to sell stock to the public. That plan was innovative also. Instead of simply hiring a firm to sell its shares, Page and Brin decided to sell them by means of a "Dutch auction," whereby anyone, including

APPLICATIONS IN ECONOMICS

individual investors, can bid on the shares. The bidder specifies a price as high or low as he or she wants, and the number of shares to be purchased at that price. Market analysts predicted that total share values, and thus the capital raised by Google, would reach $20 billion to $30 billion; a few estimates ran well above that.

The two founders of Google have not yet earned their doctorates, but they *have* earned a fortune. They did it by designing a system that benefits millions of people every day.

For more detail, see "Google Shows Wall Street a Better Way to Sell Stock," Today's Debate, *USA Today*, sec. A, May 7, 2004.

ENTREPRENEURSHIP AND ECONOMIC PROGRESS

 The entrepreneurial discovery and development of improved products and production processes is a central element of economic progress.

Entrepreneurship

Discovery and development of improved products and production methods propel economic progress. Think of the new products that have been introduced during the last fifty years; microwave ovens, videocassette recorders, color television sets, personal computers, fax machines, cellular telephone service, DVD and MP3 players, and better coronary artery bypass techniques come to mind. Innovations like these have had an enormous impact on our lives. But no one knows what the next innovative breakthrough will be or precisely which production techniques will minimize per-unit costs. Better ways of doing things do not just happen; they must be discovered and developed by entrepreneurs.

Is the entrepreneur's new, visionary idea the greatest thing since the development of the fast-food chain? Or is it simply another dream that will soon vaporize? In a market economy, it is relatively easy to try new business ideas. A person needs only to win the support of a few investors willing to finance the innovative new product or production technology. However, competition holds entrepreneurs and the investors who support them accountable: their ideas face a "reality check" imposed by production costs and consumers' willingness to pay. Consumers are the ultimate judge and jury. If they do not value an innovative new product or service enough to cover its cost, that product or service will not survive in the marketplace.

Furthermore, today's successful product may not pass tomorrow's competitive test. Therefore, entrepreneurs must be good at anticipating, identifying, and quickly adopting improved ideas, be they their own or others'. They must constantly face the ongoing reality of dynamic change in a competitive world.

Entrepreneurial Decision Making and the Structure, Size, and Scope of Firms

Entrepreneurs must also figure out the type of business structure, scale of operation, and scope of activities that keeps per-unit costs low. Their pursuit of profit encourages them to do so. Unlike other economic systems, a market economy does not mandate or limit the types of firms that are permitted to compete. Any form of business organization is permissible. An owner-operated firm, a partnership, a corporation, an employee-owned firm, a consumer cooperative, a commune, or any other form of business is free to enter the market. To be successful, however, a business structure must be cost-effective. A form of business organization that results in high per-unit cost will be driven from a competitive market by lower-cost rivals.

The same is true for the size of a firm. For some products, a business must be quite large to take full advantage of economies of scale. When per-unit costs decline as output increases, small businesses tend to have higher production costs (and therefore higher prices) than their larger counterparts. When this is the case, consumers interested in getting the maximum value for their money will tend to buy from the lower-priced, larger firm. In contrast, when personalized service and individualized products are valued highly, small firms, often organized as individual proprietorships or partnerships, are likely to be more cost-effective. It is up to the entrepreneur to discover the scale of operation that best fits the circumstances of each market.

The scope of a business is another variable that requires entrepreneurial decision making. Should a gasoline station stand alone, or should its scope be expanded to include auto repair services? Or should it instead be combined with a convenience store to create more value relative to cost? Unlimited combinations of business activities are possible. Differences in locations and other circumstances will often influence how well each is received. A new and better combination of products and services in the right place can generate a profit, at least until others catch on and provide close substitutes. In contrast, a business that chooses the wrong scope of operation will earn less and is likely to be driven out of the market by rivals offering combinations buyers like better. Once again, buyers have the final say.

To be successful, entrepreneurs must consistently offer consumers at least as much value for their dollar as they can get elsewhere. Put another way, they must figure out how to supply consumers with goods and services that are valued highly relative to their costs. If they do, their actions will create wealth and increase productivity. Many of the activities of entrepreneurs are omitted from our basic economic models. Nonetheless, these people play a *vital* role as agents of economic progress.

EVALUATING COMPETITIVE PRICE-SEARCHER MARKETS

Because the long-run equilibrium conditions in price-taker markets are generally consistent with ideal economic efficiency, it is useful to compare and contrast them with long-run conditions in competitive price-searcher markets. There are both similarities and differences.

First, let us consider the similarities. Because of the low entry barriers, both price takers and competitive price searchers will have a strong incentive to serve the interests of consumers. Neither will be able to earn long-run economic profits. In the long run, competition will drive prices down to the level of average total cost in both price-taker and competitive price-searcher markets. Furthermore, entrepreneurs in both price-taker and price-searcher markets have a strong incentive to manage and operate their businesses efficiently. In both cases, operational inefficiency will lead to higher costs, losses, and forced exit from the market. Similarly, price takers and competitive price searchers alike will be motivated to develop and adopt new, cost-reducing procedures and techniques because lower costs will mean higher short-run profits (or at least smaller losses).

The responses to changing demand conditions in price-taker and competitive price-searcher markets are also similar. In both cases, any increase in market demand that was not already expected leads to higher prices, short-run profits, expanded output, and the entry of new firms. With the entry of new producers and the expanded output of existing firms, the market supply will increase, putting downward pressure on the price. This process will continue until the market price falls to the level of average total cost, squeezing out all economic profit. Correspondingly, lower demand will lead to lower prices and short-run losses, causing output to fall and some firms to exit. As the market supply declines, prices will rise until the short-run losses are eliminated and the firms remaining in the market can again cover their costs. Thus, profits and losses direct the output decisions and market supply in both price-taker and competitive price-searcher markets.

What are some of the differences between the two market structures? As **Exhibit 4** shows, the price taker confronts a horizontal demand curve, while the demand curve of the price-searcher firm is downward sloping. This is important: it means that the marginal revenue of the price-searcher will be less than, not equal to, the price charged for the product sold. So, when the price searcher expands output until $MR = MC$, the price will still exceed the marginal cost (part b). In contrast, the price charged by a profit-maximizing price taker will equal the marginal cost (part a). In addition, when a price searcher is in long-run equilibrium, the firm's output rate will be less than the rate that minimizes average total cost. The price searcher would have a lower per-unit cost (97 cents rather than $1) if a larger output were produced, but MR would be even less.

EXHIBIT 4
Comparing Price-Taker and Price-Searcher Markets

Here we illustrate the long-run equilibrium conditions of a price taker and a price searcher when entry barriers are low. In both cases, the price is equal to the average total cost, and economic profit is zero. However, because the price searcher confronts a downward-sloping demand curve for its product, its profit-maximizing price exceeds marginal cost, and output is not large enough to minimize average total cost when the market is in long-run equilibrium. For identical cost conditions, the price of the product in a price-searcher market will be slightly higher than in a price-taker market. Some argue that this higher price is indicative of inefficiency, whereas others believe that it merely reflects the higher cost accompanying greater variety and convenience.

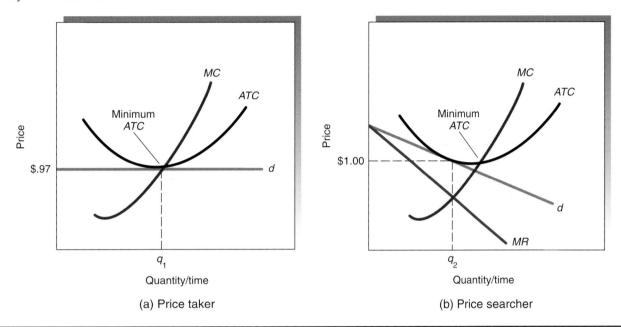

(a) Price taker

(b) Price searcher

Some argue that the slightly higher prices (and unit costs) in competitive price-searcher markets indicate that these markets allocate goods and services inefficiently. However, it is important to recognize that the higher prices reflect the fact that it is costly to provide the greater product variety and diversity found in competitive price-searcher markets. But a broader range of choices also provides benefits. The greater variety makes it possible for a wider range of consumers to obtain the quality, style, and accompanying service that best fit their preferences and specific situation.

Are the higher prices accompanying the greater diversity worth the cost? This question can't be answered with certainty, but in some cases it is clear that consumers are willing to pay for it. For example, many consumers patronize small, conveniently located stores, even though they know that the same items are available at lower prices at large supermarkets.

The two market structures also differ with regard to advertising: price searchers often advertise, but price takers do not. Like variety, advertising is costly, and in the long run, consumers cover this cost in the form of higher prices. Do advertised products provide enough information and variety to justify the higher cost from the consumer's viewpoint? We cannot know for certain. However, we do know that producers are always free to use low-priced, more uniform, and less-advertised products to lure buyers away from firms that advertise and provide variety at a higher price. Some firms do, and sometimes the strategy works; yet many consumers choose to buy advertised goods and pay the higher prices. This result suggests that many customers do find that advertised products and greater variety are worth more.

Perhaps most important, competitive price-searcher markets provide entrepreneurs with a strong incentive to innovate and discover better ways of doing things. In a dynamic setting with constantly changing opportunities for producers and buyers, this is vitally important for the efficient use of resources.

A SPECIAL CASE: PRICE DISCRIMINATION

So far, we have assumed that all sellers of a product will charge each customer the same price. Sometimes, though, price searchers can increase their revenues (and profits) by charging different prices to different groups of consumers. Businesses like hotels, restaurants, and drugstores often charge senior citizens less than other customers. Students and children are often given discounts at movie theaters and athletic events. Grocery stores commonly give discounts to customers who clip "cents-off" coupons from newspapers or magazines. Colleges often give financial aid (reduced tuition) to students from less-wealthy families. These practices are called **price discrimination**. *To gain from such a practice, price searchers must be able to do two things: (1) identify and separate at least two groups with differing elasticities of demand, and (2) prevent those who buy at the low price from reselling to the customers charged higher prices.*

Price discrimination
A practice whereby a seller charges different consumers different prices for the same product or service.

Let us take a closer look at how sellers may gain from price discrimination. Suppose that a seller has two groups of customers: one with an inelastic demand for its product and the other with an elastic demand. An increase in the price charged the first group will increase the total revenue derived from that group. At the same time, a reduction in price will increase revenues derived from the latter. Thus, a seller may be able to increase total revenue and profit by charging the first group a higher price than the second.

The pricing of airline tickets illustrates the potential of price discrimination. The airline industry has found that the demand of business fliers is substantially more inelastic than the demand of vacationers, students, and other travelers. Thus, airlines often charge higher fares to persons who are unwilling to stay over a weekend, who spend only a day or two at their destination, and who make reservations a short time before their flight. These high fares fall primarily on business travelers who are less sensitive to price. In contrast, discount fares are offered to fliers willing to make reservations well in advance, travel during off-peak hours, and stay at their destinations over a weekend before returning home. Such travelers are likely to be vacationers and students, who are highly sensitive to price.

Exhibit 5 illustrates the logic of this policy. Part (a) shows what would happen if a single price were charged to all customers. Given the demand, the profit-maximizing firm ex-

---

EXHIBIT 5
Price Discrimination

As part (a) illustrates, a $400 ticket price will maximize profits on coast-to-coast flights if an airline charges a single price. However, the airline can do still better if it raises the price to $500 for passengers with a highly inelastic demand (business travelers) and reduces the price to $300 for travelers with a more elastic demand (for example, students and vacationers). When sellers can segment their market, they can gain by (1) charging a higher price to consumers with a less elastic demand and (2) offering discounts to customers whose demand is more elastic.

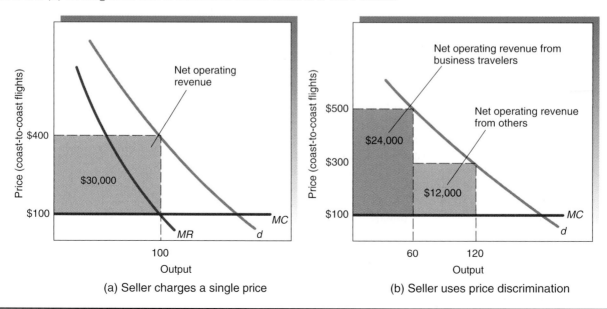

(a) Seller charges a single price

(b) Seller uses price discrimination

pands output to 100, where *MR* equals *MC*. The profit-maximizing price on coast-to-coast flights is $400, which generates $40,000 of revenue per flight. Since the marginal cost per passenger is $100, this provides the airline with net operating revenue of $30,000 with which to cover other costs.

However, as part (b) shows, although the market demand schedule is unchanged, the airline can do even better if it uses price discrimination. When it charges business travelers $500, most of these passengers continue to use the airline, since their demand is highly inelastic. On the other hand, a $100 price cut generates substantial additional ticket sales from price-sensitive vacationers, students, and others whose demands are more elastic. Therefore, with price discrimination, the airline can sell 60 tickets (primarily to business travelers) at $500 and 60 additional tickets to others at $300. Total revenue jumps to $48,000 and leaves the airline with $36,000 ($48,000 minus 120 times the $100 marginal cost per passenger) of revenue in excess of variable cost. Compared to the single-price outcome (part a), the price discrimination strategy expands profit by $6,000.

When sellers can segment their market (at a low cost) into groups with differing price elasticities of demand, price discrimination can increase profits. For *each group,* the seller will maximize profit by equating marginal cost and marginal revenue. This rule will lead to higher prices for groups with a more inelastic demand and lower prices for those with a more elastic demand. Compared to the single-price situation, price discrimination increases profitability because a higher price increases the net revenue from groups with an inelastic demand, while a lower price increases the net revenue from price-sensitive customers. With price discrimination, the number of units sold also increases (compare part a with part b) because the discounts provided to price-sensitive groups increase the quantity sold more than the higher prices charged the less-price-sensitive groups reduce sales. Of course, this will work only if the two groups can't trade with each other. Movie theaters sell children's tickets to kids, and the tickets cannot be used by adults. Notice, though, that they don't try to sell popcorn at lower prices to children because popcorn could be too easily resold to adults. Airline tickets are nontransferable, so they cannot be resold. Price discrimination can work in both of these situations because differing categories of buyers can be identified, and trade between them is prevented.

Sometimes price discrimination is subtle. Colleges engage in price discrimination by charging a high standard tuition to get additional revenue from high-income students with a more inelastic demand, while providing low-income students with scholarships based on need (tuition "discounts"). At the University of Maine, for example, when tuition at the undergraduate level ran between $12,998 and $20,738 (depending on the degree), financial aid amounted to 54 percent of tuition for students from low-income families, while for high-income students, it was only 17 percent of tuition. Partial-tuition scholarships given to students whose parents are less wealthy enable a school to attract students who have a more elastic demand. In this way, low-income students are not as frequently priced out of the market by the high standard tuition.

How do buyers fare when a seller can price discriminate? Some buyers pay more than they would if a single, intermediate price were offered. They purchase fewer units, and they are worse off. In contrast, those for whom the price discrimination process lowers the price are better off. Of course, with some products, such as airline transportation, a single buyer might be better off with some purchases and worse off with others.

On balance, however, we can expect that output will be greater with price discrimination than it would be with a single price. The market is not as understocked as it would have been in the absence of the price discrimination. So from an allocative efficiency standpoint, price discrimination gets high marks; it allows more trades, reducing the inefficiency due to price being set above marginal cost. Some of the gains that would accrue to consumers with an inelastic demand are transferred to the price searcher as increased revenue, but additional gains from trade are created by the increased output of goods that would be lost if price discrimination were prevented.

Students from low-income families are likely to be more sensitive to tuition charges than those from high-income families. Colleges often make scholarships and other forms of financial aid more readily available to low-income students. This price discrimination makes it possible for them to generate larger revenues from tuition than would otherwise be the case.

In some markets, there is an additional gain from price discrimination: production may occur that would be lost entirely if only a single price could be charged. With price discrimination, some otherwise unprofitable firms may be able to generate enough additional revenue to operate successfully in the marketplace. For example, some small towns in Montana might not provide enough revenue at a single price to enable a local physician to cover her opportunity costs. However, if she is able to discriminate on the basis of income, charging higher-income patients more than normal rates and lower-income patients less, the resulting revenues from practicing in the small town may enable her to stay in the community. In this case, all residents of the town may be better off because of the price discrimination, since it makes it possible for them to access a local physician. After all, even those being charged the highest prices are not disadvantaged if the price discrimination keeps the physician in town. They are just as able to seek physician services elsewhere as they would have been in the absence of the price-discriminating local doctor. With or without price discrimination, access to competing sellers (or buyers) protects market participants from unfair treatment.

In summary, if potential customers can be segmented into groups with different elasticities of demand and retrading can be controlled at a low cost, sellers can often gain by charging higher prices to those with the less elastic demand (and lower prices to those with a more elastic demand). Price discrimination can also increase the total gains from trade and thereby reduce allocative inefficiency. Sometimes it even allows production where none would have otherwise occurred.

LOOKING AHEAD

In this chapter, we have analyzed the choices facing price searchers and their behavior when barriers to entry are low. The following chapter will analyze the performance of price-searcher markets when the barriers to entry are relatively high.

! KEY POINTS

▼ Firms in price-searcher markets with low barriers to entry face a downward-sloping demand curve. They are free to set the prices for the products that they sell but face strong competitive pressure from existing and potential rivals.

▼ The mark of the price-searcher market with low barriers to entry is product differentiation. Price searchers use product quality, style, convenience of location, advertising, and price as competitive weapons. Because each firm competes with rivals offering similar products, each confronts a highly elastic demand curve for its products.

▼ A profit-maximizing price searcher will expand output as long as marginal revenue exceeds marginal cost, lowering its price in the process, until $MR = MC$. The price charged by the profit-maximizing price searcher will be greater than its marginal cost.

▼ Firms in competitive price-searcher markets can experience either profits or losses in the short run.

Profits will attract rival firms into the market until supply increases and the profit-maximizing price falls to the level of per-unit price. Losses will cause firms to exit the market until the price increases enough that the remaining firms can once again cover their per-unit costs. Because of the low entry barriers, the firms in competitive price-searcher markets will earn only normal returns (zero economic profit) when long-run equilibrium is present.

▼ Competition can come from potential as well as actual rivals. If entry and exit can be arranged at low cost, and if there are no legal barriers to entry, the theory of contestable markets indicates that competitive results will be approximated, even if there are only a few firms actually in the market.

▼ Although standard economic models do not include the central role of entrepreneurial decision making in a world of uncertainty, economists recognize its importance. Entrepreneurs who discover and introduce lower-cost production methods and new products that are highly valued relative to cost promote economic progress. Entrepreneurs also have a strong incentive to discover the type of business structure, firm size, and scope of operation that can best keep the per-unit cost of products or services low.

▼ Competitive price-searcher markets provide more variety but may raise costs relative to price-taker markets because (1) price exceeds marginal cost at the profit-maximizing output level; (2) long-run average cost is not minimized; and (3) advertising is costly. When barriers to entry are low, however, price searchers have an incentive to (1) produce effi-

ciently; (2) undertake production if, and only if, their actions will increase the value of resources used; and (3) be innovative in offering new product options.

▼ When a price searcher can (1) identify groups of customers that have different price elasticities of demand and (2) prevent customers from retrading the product, price discrimination may emerge. Sellers may be able to gain by charging higher prices to groups with a less elastic demand and lower prices to those with a more elastic demand. The practice generally leads to a larger output and more gains from trade than would otherwise occur.

? CRITICAL ANALYSIS QUESTIONS

1. Price searchers can set the prices of their products. Does this mean that they will charge the highest possible price for their products? What price will maximize the profits of a price searcher? How will the firm's marginal cost compare with its price at the profit-maximum output?

2. Since price searchers can set their prices, does this mean that their prices are unaffected by market conditions? In price-searcher markets with low barriers to entry, will the firms be able to make economic profit in the long run? Why or why not? What do competitive price searchers have to do to make economic profit?

*3. What determines the *variety* of styles, designs, and sizes of different products? Why do you think there are only a few different varieties of toothpicks but lots of different types of napkins on the market?

*4. How would imposing a per-unit tax of $2,000 on each new U.S. automobile affect (a) higher-quality, higher-priced cars (those selling for more than the median price) compared to (b) lower-quality,lower-priced cars? What would happen as a result to the average *quality* of automobiles if the proceeds of the tax were used to subsidize a government-operated lottery?

5. What must an entrepreneur do in order to introduce a new innovative product? What determines whether the new product will be a success or failure?

6. Is quality and style competition as important as price competition? Would you like to live in a country where government regulation restricted the use of quality and style competition? Why or why not? Do you think you would get more or less for your consumer dollar under restrictions like these? Discuss.

*7. Suppose that a price searcher is currently charging a price that maximizes the firm's total revenue. Will

this price also maximize the firm's profit? Why or why not? Explain.

*8. a. What determines whether corporations, individual proprietorships, employee-owned firms, consumer cooperatives, or some other form of business structure will dominate in a market?

b. What determines whether small firms, medium-size firms, or large firms will dominate in a market?

9. Would our standard of living be higher if the government "bailed out" troubled businesses? If a firm goes out of business, what happens to the firm's assets, workers, and customers? Are business failures bad for the economy? Why or why not?

*10. Suppose that a group of investors wants to start a business operated out of a popular Utah ski area. The group is considering either building a new hotel complex or starting a new local airline serving that market. Each new business would require about the same amount of capital and personnel hiring. The group believes each endeavor has the same profit potential. Which is the safer (less likely to result in a substantial capital loss) investment? Why? Is there an offsetting advantage to the other investments?

11. Is price discrimination harmful to the economy? How does price discrimination affect the total amount of gains from exchange? Explain. Why do colleges often charge students different prices, based on their family income?

*12. "When competition is really severe, only the big firms survive. The little guy has no chance." True or false? Explain.

13. What is the primary requirement for a market to be competitive? Is competition necessary for markets to work well? Why or why not? How does competition

influence the following: (a) the cost efficiency of producers, (b) the quality of products, and (c) the discovery and development of new products? Explain your answers.

*14. What keeps McDonald's, Wal-Mart, General Motors, or any other business firm from raising prices, selling shoddy products, and providing lousy service?

15. "The superiority of the competitive market is the positive stimuli it provides for constantly improving efficiency, innovating, and offering consumers diversity of choice." This quotation is from Alfred Kahn, the architect of transportation deregulation during the 1970s. Evaluate the statement. Is it true? Discuss.

16. The accompanying graph shows the short-run demand and cost situation for a price searcher in a market with low barriers to entry.
   a. What level of output will maximize the firm's profit level?
   b. What price will the firm charge?
   c. How much revenue will the firm receive in this situation? How much is total cost? Total profit?
   d. How will the situation change over time?

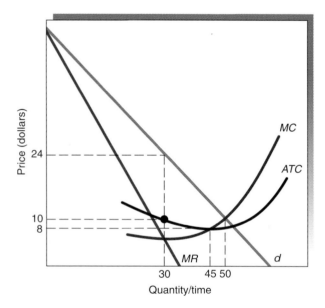

*17. Rod N. Reel owns a dealership that sells fishing boats in an open, price-searcher market. To develop his pricing strategy, Rod hired an economist to estimate his demand curve. Columns (1) and (2) of the following chart provide the data for the expected weekly quantity demanded for Rod's fishing boats at alternative prices. Rod's marginal (and average) cost of supplying each boat is constant at $5,000 per boat no matter how many boats he sells per week in this range. This cost includes all opportunity costs and represents the economic cost per boat.
   a. Find Rod's economic profits at each alternative price by calculating the difference between total revenue and total cost.
   b. Find Rod's marginal revenue and marginal cost from the sale of each additional boat.
   c. If Rod wants to maximize his profits, what price should he charge per boat?
   d. How many boats will Rod sell per week at the profit-maximizing price?
   e. What will Rod's profits be per week at this price and sales volume?
   f. At the price and sales level where profits are maximized, has Rod sold all boats that have higher marginal revenue than marginal cost?
   g. If Rod's profits are typical of all firms in the boat sales business, what might be expected to happen in the future? Will more boat dealers open in the area, or will some of the existing ones go out of business? What will happen to the profitability of the boat dealers in the future once the entry/exit has occurred?
   h. Challenge Question: Recall the relationship between elasticity of demand, price changes, and their impact on total revenues. As Rod lowers his price from $9,000 to $5,000, his total revenues keep increasing. Is demand in this price range elastic, inelastic, or unit elastic? When Rod lowers his price from $5,000 to $4,000, his total revenues stay the same. Is demand in this price range elastic, inelastic, or unit elastic? Can you guess what might happen at prices below $4,000? Explain.

---

*Asterisk denotes questions for which answers are given in Appendix B.

Price of Fishing Boats (1)	Number of Fishing Boats Sold per Week (2)	Total Revenue per Week (3)	Total Cost per Week (4)	Economic Profit per Week (5)	Marginal Revenue (6)	Marginal Cost (7)
$9,000	0	____	____	____	____	____
8,000	1	____	____	____	____	____
7,000	2	____	____	____	____	____
6,000	3	____	____	____	____	____
5,000	4	____	____	____	____	____
4,000	5	____	____	____	____	____

Price-Searcher Markets with High Entry Barriers

CHAPTER 23

Chapter Focus

■ What are the barriers to entry that protect some firms against competition from potential rivals?

■ What is a monopoly? Does it guarantee the ability to make a profit?

■ What is an oligopoly? When are oligopolists likely to collude? Why is it impossible to construct a general theory of output and price for an oligopolist?

■ Will competition keep large firms in check in markets that have high barriers to entry? What problems may arise in such markets?

■ What policy alternatives might improve the operation of markets with high barriers to entry?

"When the monopolist raises prices above the competitive level in order to reap his monopoly profits, customers buy less of the product, less is produced, and society as a whole is worse off. In short, monopoly reduces society's income."

". . .[C]ompetition is a tough weed, not a delicate flower."

—George Stigler[1]

---

[1]Both quotes are from George J. Stigler, "Monopoly," in *The Concise Encyclopedia of Economics,* ed. David R. Henderson (Indianapolis, Ind.: Liberty Fund, Inc., Library of Economics and Liberty), http://www.econlib.org/library/Enc/Monopoly.html (accessed August 31, 2004).

I n the previous two chapters, we analyzed the way firms behave in competitive markets with low barriers to entry. We now turn to the analysis of firm behavior when entry barriers are high and there are few, if any, rival firms offering the same or similar products. This chapter focuses on factors that make entry into a market more difficult, and how this can reduce the ability of markets to keep firms in check. We will also consider policy alternatives that might improve the efficiency of these markets. ■

WHY ARE ENTRY BARRIERS SOMETIMES HIGH?

What makes it difficult for potential competitors to enter a market? Under certain conditions, four factors can be important: economies of scale, government licensing, patents, and control over an essential resource. Let's consider each.

Economies of Scale

As we have learned, when the fixed costs in an industry are large, bigger firms can achieve lower average total per-unit costs than smaller firms can over the full range of output consumers are willing to buy. As our prior analysis of contestable markets indicated, however, economies of scale and high fixed costs are not a significant barrier to entry when the assets needed to enter the market can be leased, transferred to another location, or resold later without a major loss of value.

In some markets, however, this will not be the case. Airline routes may be contestable, but airplane manufacturing is not because many items of equipment are specialized for the production of a specific airplane. The cost of that equipment is a sunk cost. Except in its current use, the specialized equipment is worth little. If necessary, the incumbent firm will continue operating for a long period of time as long as it can cover its variable (operating) costs. Potential new entrants will recognize that this incentive structure will make it extremely difficult to displace the current incumbent. Thus, they will be reluctant to attempt entry, even if the current incumbent is earning economic profit. Under these circumstances, a dominant firm will tend to emerge in the industry, and if the market is not contestable, the cost advantages resulting from its size will protect it from potential rivals.

Government Licensing and Other Legal Barriers to Entry

Legal barriers are the oldest and most effective method of protecting a business firm from potential competitors. Kings once granted exclusive business rights to favored citizens or groups. Tariffs that raise the price of imported goods and quotas that limit the quantity of imports have restricted entry and reduced the competitiveness of various markets for centuries. Today, governments continue to establish barriers that restrict the right to buy and sell goods. To compete in certain parts of the communications industry in the United States (for example, to operate a radio or television station), one must obtain a government franchise. Similarly, local governments often grant exclusive franchises for the operation of cable television systems. Each of these measures reduces competition and protects the profits of favored firms.

Licensing can also limit entry and reduce competitiveness. States and cities often require the operators of liquor stores, hairstyling shops, taxicabs, funeral homes, and many other businesses to obtain a license. Sometimes these licenses cost little and are designed to ensure certain minimum standards. Often, however, they are costly to obtain and a major deterrent to the entry of potential rivals.

Licensing
A requirement that one obtain permission from the government in order to perform certain business activities or work in various occupations.

Patents

Most countries have patent laws to give inventors a property right to their inventions. A patent grants the owner the exclusive legal right to the commercial use of a newly invented product or process for a limited period of time, twenty years in the United States. Others are not allowed to copy the product or procedure without the permission of the patent holder. For example, when a pharmaceutical company is granted a patent for a newly developed drug, other potential suppliers must obtain permission from the patent holder before producing and selling the product. Others might be able to supply the drug more economically. If they want to do so, however, they will have to purchase the production and marketing rights from the originating firm as long as the patent is in effect.

Both costs and benefits for consumers come with a patent system. The entry barrier created by the grant of a patent generally leads to higher consumer prices for products that have already been developed. On the positive side, however, patents increase the potential returns to inventive activity, thus encouraging scientific research and technological improvements. According to a recent study, the average cost of developing and testing a new pharmaceutical drug is approximately $900 million.[2] Without the profit potential accompanying patents, the incentive to engage in research and develop new products would be slowed.

©MARK ANTMAN/THE IMAGEWORKS

A firm that develops a new drug can use patent protection to restrain production by others for twenty years from the time the patent is issued. Although consumers will pay higher prices than if open competition were permitted, they may benefit from additional investment in research and more rapid development of new products by firms seeking a market with patent protection.

Control over an Essential Resource

Control over a resource essential for production of a product may also insulate a firm from direct competitors. An example often cited is the Aluminum Company of America, which before World War II controlled the known supply of bauxite conveniently available to American firms. Without this critical raw material, potential competitors could not produce aluminum. Over time, however, other supplies of bauxite were discovered, and the Aluminum Company of America lost its advantage. Resource monopolies are seldom complete. Profit opportunities provide challengers with an incentive to search for mineral deposits, new technologies, and substitute resources. Over time, they are usually found.

Barriers to entry like the different ones we've just described are often temporary, but they do exist. Let's see what happens when, at least temporarily, there is a barrier to entry high enough to limit the market to only one seller.

CHARACTERISTICS OF A MONOPOLY

The word *monopoly,* derived from two Greek words, means "single seller." We will define **monopoly** as a market characterized by (1) high barriers to entry and (2) a single seller of a well-defined product for which there are no good substitutes. Even this definition is ambiguous, because "high barriers" and "good substitutes" are both relative terms. Are the barriers to entry into the automobile or steel industries high? Many observers would argue that they are. After all, it takes a great deal of capital to operate at the least-cost scale of output in both of these industries. However, there are no *physical* or *legal* restraints that prevent an entrepreneur from producing automobiles or steel. If price is well above cost and profit potential

Monopoly
A market structure characterized by (1) a single seller of a well-defined product for which there are no good substitutes and (2) high barriers to the entry of any other firms into the market for that product.

---

[2]Tufts Center for the Study of Drug Development, "Total Cost to Develop a New Prescription Drug, Including Cost of Post-Approval Research, Is $897 Million," News Release May 13, 2003, downloaded July 6, 2004, at: http://csdd.tufts.edu/NewsEvents/RecentNews.asp?newsid529.

is present, it should not be too difficult to find the necessary investment capital. Thus, some would argue that entry barriers into these industries are not particularly high.

"Good substitute" is also a subjective term. There is always some substitutability among products, even those produced by a single seller. Is a letter a good substitute for a telephone or e-mail message? For some purposes—correspondence between law firms, for example—a letter delivered by mail is a very good substitute. In other cases, when the speed of communication and immediacy of response are important, the telephone and e-mail are far superior forms of communication. Are there any good substitutes for electricity? Most of the known substitutes for electric lighting (candles, oil lamps, and battery lights, for example) are inferior to electric lights in most uses. Natural gas, fuel oil, and wood, though, are often excellent substitutes for electric heating. Also, electric utilities have found that many of their largest industrial customers can generate their own electricity, sometimes at low cost, in conjunction with other fuel-burning operations.

Monopoly, then, is always a matter of degree. Only a small fraction of all markets are served by only one seller. In a few markets, governments have allocated specific markets to a single seller. This is the case with cable television and providers of electricity in many communities. The monopoly model we discuss next will illuminate the operation of these markets. It will also help us understand markets in which there are just a few sellers and little active rivalry. When there are only two or three producers in a market, firms may seek to collude rather than compete, and thus, together, they may behave much like a monopoly.

Price and Output under Monopoly

Suppose you invent, patent, and produce a microwave device that locks the hammer of any firearm in the immediate area. This fabulous invention can be used to immobilize the weapons of terrorists or armed robbers. Since you own the exclusive patent right to the firearm lock device, you are not concerned about a competitive supplier in the foreseeable future. Although other products are competitive with your invention, they are poor substitutes. In short, you are a monopolist.

What price should you charge for your product? Because you are the only seller of this device, the demand for your product is also the market demand curve. It will be downward sloping because consumers will cut back on their purchases as the price of the firearm lock increases. As a price searcher, you will have to search out the most profitable price to charge. An expansion in output will increase profit as long as the production and sale of additional units add more to revenue than to cost. *Like other price searchers, the monopolist will expand its output until marginal revenue equals marginal cost. This profit-maximizing output rate can be sold at the price indicated on the firm's demand curve.*

Exhibit 1 graphically illustrates how a monopolist derives the profit-maximizing output rate.[3] The firm will continue to expand output as long as marginal revenue exceeds marginal cost. Therefore, output will be expanded to Q, where $MR = MC$. The monopolist will be able to sell the profit-maximizing output Q at price P, the height of the demand curve at Q. At any output less than Q, the benefits (marginal revenue) of producing the *additional* units will exceed their costs. In this range, the monopolist will gain by reducing the price and expanding output toward Q. For any output greater than Q, the monopolist's costs of producing additional units will be greater than the benefits (marginal revenue). Producing these units will reduce profits. Output rate Q and price P will maximize the firm's profit.

Exhibit 1 also depicts the profits of a monopolist. At output Q and price P, the firm's total revenue is equal to *PAQ0*, the price times the number of units sold. The firm's total cost would be *CBQ0*, the average per-unit cost multiplied by the number of units sold. The firm's profits are merely total revenue less total cost, the shaded area of Exhibit 1.

Exhibit 2 provides a numeric illustration of decision making by a profit-maximizing monopolist. At low output rates, marginal revenue exceeds marginal cost. The monopolist will continue expanding output as long as MR is greater than MC. Thus, an output rate of

---

[3]In this chapter we assume that firms are unable to use price discrimination to increase their revenues. If they could, the analysis of price discrimination from the previous chapter would help describe their decisions.

EXHIBIT 1
The Short-Run Price and Output of a Monopolist

The monopolist will reduce its price and expand its output as long as *MR* exceeds *MC*. Output *Q* will result. When the price exceeds the average total cost at any output level, a profit will be earned.

eight units per day will be chosen. (*Note:* If tiny portions of a unit could be produced and sold, then production would increase to where *MR* = *MC*.) Given the demand for the product, the monopolist can sell eight units at a price of $17.25 each. Total revenue will be $138, compared to a total cost of $108.50. The monopolist will make a profit of $29.50. The profit rate will be smaller at all other output rates. For example, if the monopolist reduces the price to $16 in order to sell nine units per day, revenue will increase by $6. However, the marginal cost of producing the ninth unit is $6.25. Since the cost of producing the ninth unit is greater than the revenue it brings in, profits will decline.

When high barriers to entry are present, they will insulate the monopolist from direct competition with rival firms producing a similar product. In markets with high entry barriers, monopoly profits will not attract—at least not quickly—rivals who will expand supply, cut prices, and spoil the seller's market.

EXHIBIT 2
Profit Maximization for a Monopolist

RATE OF OUTPUT (PER DAY) (1)	PRICE (PER UNIT) (2)	TOTAL REVENUE (1) × (2) (3)	TOTAL COST (PER DAY) (4)	PROFIT (3) − (4) (5)	MARGINAL COST (6)	MARGINAL REVENUE (7)
0	—	—	$50.00	$−50.00	—	—
1	$25.00	$25.00	60.00	−35.00	$10.00	$25.00
2	24.00	48.00	69.00	−21.00	9.00	23.00
3	23.00	69.00	77.00	−8.00	8.00	21.00
4	22.00	88.00	84.00	4.00	7.00	19.00
5	21.00	105.00	90.50	14.50	6.50	17.00
6	19.75	118.50	96.75	21.75	6.25	13.50
7	18.50	129.50	102.75	26.75	6.00	11.00
8	17.25	138.00	108.50	29.50	5.75	8.50
9	16.00	144.00	114.75	29.25	6.25	6.00
10	14.75	147.50	121.25	26.25	6.50	3.50
11	13.50	148.50	128.00	20.50	6.75	1.00
12	12.25	147.00	135.00	12.00	7.00	−1.50
13	11.00	143.00	142.25	.75	7.25	−4.00

Protected by high entry barriers, a monopolist may be able to continue earning a profit, even in the long run. Does this mean that monopolists can charge as high a price as they want? Monopolists are often accused of price gouging. In evaluating this charge, however, it is important to recognize that, like other sellers, monopolists will seek to maximize *profit,* not *price.* Consumers will buy less as the price increases. Thus, a higher price is not always best for a monopolist. Exhibit 2 illustrates this point. What would happen to the profit of the monopolist if the price were increased from $17.25 to $18.50? At the higher price, only seven units would be sold, and total revenue would equal $129.50. The cost of producing seven units would be $102.75. Thus, when the price is $18.50 and output seven units, profit is only $26.75—less than it would be at the lower price ($17.25) and larger output (eight units). The highest price is not usually the best price for the monopolist. Sometimes lower prices will mean more profit.

Will a monopolist always earn a profit? The profitability of a monopolist is limited by the demand for the product that it produces. In some cases, a monopolist—even one protected by high barriers to entry—may be unable to sell its product for a profit. For example, there are thousands of clever, patented items that are never produced because demand-cost conditions are not favorable. **Exhibit 3** illustrates this possibility. Here, the monopolist's average total cost curve is above its demand curve at every level of output. Even when operating at the *MR* = *MC* rate of output, economic losses (shaded area) will occur. While output *Q* could be sold at price *P,* this price is too low to cover the per-unit cost of the monopolist. This model explains why many small towns lack even a single bookstore, gourmet coffee shop, or any number of other specialty stores. Under these circumstances, not even a monopolist would want to operate—at least not for long.

The Monopoly Model and Decision Making in the Real World

Until now, we have proceeded as if monopolists always knew exactly what their revenue and cost curves looked like. In reality, a monopolist cannot be sure of the ever-changing demand conditions for a product. How many sales will be lost if the price is raised? How many sales will be added if the price is lowered? Monopolists often experiment with price changes, attempting to find the price at which profit will be maximized. Thus, the revenue and cost data illustrated in Exhibits 1, 2, and 3 represent *expected* revenues and costs associated with various output levels. To complicate matters further in real life, the monopolist searching for additional profits can undertake quality changes of various sorts. Buyer re-

EXHIBIT 3
How a Monopolist Can Lose Money

Even a monopolist will lose money if its average total cost curve lies everywhere above the demand curve.

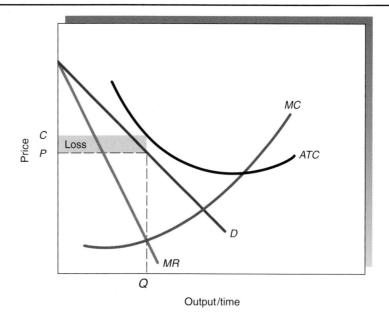

actions to potential quality changes and resulting shifts in demand and cost must also be considered by the profit-seeking monopolist.

A monopolist, like other business decision makers, seldom calculates what we have called demand, marginal revenue, and cost curves. With imperfect information, the profit-maximizing price can only be approximated. However, the monopolist has a strong incentive to find the profit-maximizing price and output rate and, when that occurs, the outcome will be as if the $MR = MC$ rule had been used to maximize profit.

As we have indicated, it is difficult for a monopolist to predict demand conditions and consumer response to quality and price changes. But life is even more complex for the next class of price searchers we consider: large firms with few rivals in a market protected by high barriers to entry.

THE CHARACTERISTICS OF AN OLIGOPOLY

In the United States, most of the output in certain industries, such as the automobile, cigarette, and aircraft industries, is produced by five or fewer dominant firms. These industries are characterized by **oligopoly**. *Oligopoly* means "few sellers." ***The distinguishing characteristics of an oligopolistic market are (1) a small number of rival firms, (2) interdependence among the sellers because each is large relative to the size of the market, (3) substantial economies of scale, and (4) high entry barriers to the market.***

Oligopoly
A market situation in which a small number of sellers constitutes the entire industry. It is competition among the few.

Interdependence among Oligopolistic Firms

Since the number of sellers in an oligopolistic industry is small, the supply decisions of one firm will significantly influence the demand, price, and profit of rivals. This adds to the complexity of the firm's decision making. A firm that is deciding what price to charge, output to produce, or quality of product to offer must consider not only the currently available substitutes, but also the potential reactions of rival producers. The business decisions of each firm depend on the policies it expects its major rivals to follow because those will influence the demand for all the rivals' products.

Substantial Economies of Scale

In an oligopolistic industry, large-scale production (relative to the total market) is generally required to achieve minimum per-unit cost. Economies of scale are present, so a small number of large-scale firms can produce enough of the product to meet the entire market demand. Using the automobile industry in the recent past as an example, **Exhibit 4** illustrates the importance of economies of scale as a source of oligopoly. It has been estimated

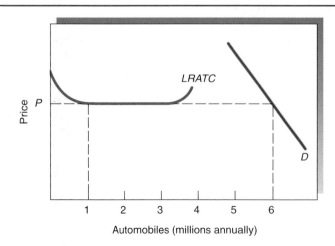

EXHIBIT 4
Economies of Scale
Oligopoly

An oligopoly exists in t[]
automobile industry b[]
cause firms do not ful[]
achieve the lower cos[]
large-scale operation[]
they are able to prod[]
approximately one-si[]
the total market.

that each firm must produce approximately 1 million automobiles annually before its per-unit cost of production is minimized. However, when the selling price of automobiles is barely sufficient to cover costs, the total quantity demanded from these producers is only 6 million. To minimize costs, then, each firm must produce at least one-sixth (1 million of the 6 million) of the output demanded. If this is true, the industry can support no more than five or six domestic firms of cost-efficient size.

Significant Barriers to Entry

As with monopoly, barriers to entry limit the ability of new firms to compete effectively in oligopolistic industries. Except where a market is contestable, economies of scale are probably the most significant entry barrier protecting firms in an oligopolistic industry. A potential competitor may be unable to start out small and gradually grow to the optimal size, since it must gain a large share of the market before it can minimize its per-unit cost. The manufacture of refrigerators, diesel engines, and automobiles seems to fall into this category. Other factors, including patent rights, control over an essential resource, and government-imposed entry restraints, can also prevent new competitors from entering profitable oligopolistic industries. The presence of high entry barriers is what distinguishes oligopoly from a competitive price-searcher market.

Identical or Differentiated Products

The products of sellers in an oligopolistic industry may be either similar or differentiated. When firms produce identical products, like milk or gasoline, there is less opportunity for nonprice competition. On the other hand, when rival firms produce differentiated products they are more likely to use style, quality, and advertising as competitive weapons. Each firm attempts to convince buyers that other products would be poor substitutes.

PRICE AND OUTPUT UNDER OLIGOPOLY

Unlike a monopolist or a price taker, an oligopolist cannot determine the product price that will deliver maximum profit simply by estimating its own costs and the *existing* market demand. The demand facing an oligopolistic firm depends also on the pricing behavior of its close rivals. Suppose, for example, that General Motors is considering how to price next year's new Chevrolet model when it comes on the market. The number of Chevrolets it can sell at each price will depend not only on buyer preferences but also on the prices (and quality) of substitutes available from Ford, Toyota, and other GM rivals. What pricing strategy will each rival use if GM puts a low price on its new model? How will each rival firm react to a higher GM price?

Economics cannot predict these complex interactions among rivals without making some strong, simplifying assumptions about how each firm reacts when another firm makes a change in price or quality. These simplifying assumptions will not be realistic for the general case, and therefore we cannot precisely predict the price and output that will emerge in an oligopoly. We can, however, zero in on a potential range of prices and the factors that will determine whether prices in the industry will be high or low relative to costs of production.

Consider a typical oligopolistic industry in which seven or eight rival firms produce the entire market output because substantial economies of scale are present. The firms produce nearly identical products and have similar costs of production. **Exhibit 5** depicts the market demand conditions and long-run costs of production of the individual firms for such an industry.

What price will prevail? We can answer this question for two extreme cases. First, suppose that each firm sets its price independently of the other firms. There is no **collusion** (no agreement among the firms to limit output and keep the price high), so each competitive firm is free to seek additional customers and profits by offering buyers a slightly better deal than its market rivals. Under these conditions, the market price would be driven down to P_c. Firms would be just able to cover their per-unit costs of production. If a single firm raised its price,

Collusion
Agreement among firms to avoid various competitive practices, particularly price reductions. It may involve either formal agreements or merely tacit recognition that competitive practices will be self-defeating in the long run. Tacit collusion is difficult to detect. In the United States, antitrust laws prohibit collusion and conspiracies to restrain trade.

EXHIBIT 5
Price and Output in an Oligopoly

If oligopolists were to act independently and compete with one another, price cutting would drive price down to P_c. In contrast, perfect cooperation among firms would lead to a higher price of P_m and a smaller output (Q_m rather than Q_c). The shaded area shows profit if firms collude. Demand here is the market demand.

its customers would switch to rival firms, which would now expand to accommodate the new customers. The firm that raised its price would lose out. It would be self-defeating for any one firm to raise its price if the other firms didn't also raise theirs.

What happens if the current price is greater than P_c, perhaps because the market has not yet adjusted fully to a recent reduction in resource prices that lowered production costs? As a result, price is above per-unit cost and the firms are making economic profit. However, any *individual firm* that reduces its price slightly, by 1 or 2 percent, for example, will gain numerous customers if the other firms maintain the higher price. The price-cutting firm will attract some new buyers to the market, but, more important, it will also lure many buyers away from rival firms charging higher prices. Thus, if the rival sellers act independently, each will have a strong incentive to reduce price in order to increase sales and gain a large share of the total market. Price will be driven down to P_c and the economic profit will be eliminated.

However, oligopolists don't always compete with one another. They have a strong incentive to collude—to raise prices and restrict output in order to maximize their joint profits. The collusion may be either formal or informal. Formal collusion might even involve the formation of a **cartel**, like the Organization of Petroleum Exporting Countries (OPEC). Under federal antitrust laws, both formal and informal collusive agreements to restrict output and raise prices are illegal in the United States. Nonetheless, let's see what would happen if oligopolists followed this course.

Exhibit 5 shows the marginal revenue curve that would accompany the market demand D for the product. Under perfect cooperation, the oligopolists would refuse to produce units for which marginal revenue to the group was less than marginal cost. Thus, they would restrict joint output to Q_m, where $MR = MC$. Market price would rise to P_m. With collusion, substantial joint profits (the shaded area of Exhibit 5) can be attained. If the collusion were perfect, the outcome would be identical to the one that would occur under monopoly.

Real-world outcomes are likely to be between the two polar case extremes of price competition and perfect collusion. Oligopolists generally recognize their interdependence and try to avoid vigorous price competition, because they know it will drive down the price to the level of per-unit costs. But there are also obstacles to collusion, which is why prices in oligopolistic industries are unlikely to rise to the monopoly level. *As a result, oligopoly prices are typically above per-unit cost but below those a monopolist would charge.*

Cartel
An organization of sellers designed to coordinate supply decisions so that the joint profits of the members will be maximized. A cartel will seek to create a monopoly in the market.

The Incentive to Collude and to Cheat

Collusion comes at the expense of buyers. Rival oligopolists can profit as a group by colluding to restrict output and raise price. To achieve the higher price, however, they must reduce total output. Output must be cut because consumers will purchase a smaller quan-

EXHIBIT 6
Gaining from Cheating

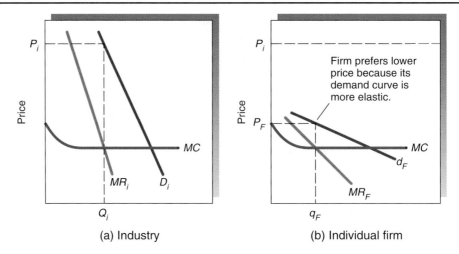

(a) Industry

(b) Individual firm

The industry demand (D_i) and marginal revenue (MR_i) curves show that the joint profits of oligopolists would be maximized at Q_i, where $MR_i = MC$. Price P_i would be best for the industry as a whole (a). However, as part (b) shows, the demand curve (d_F) facing each firm (under the assumption that no other firms cheat) will be much more elastic than D_i. Given the greater elasticity of its demand curve, an individual firm will have an incentive to cut its price to P_F and expand output to q_F, where $MR_F = MC$. In other words, an individual oligopolist can gain by secretly cutting its price and cheating on the collusive agreement—until the other firms find out and react by cutting their price.

tity at the higher price. This raises a point of conflict: none of the oligopolists want to reduce their output. Although the firms have an incentive to collude in order to achieve higher prices, each of them also has an incentive to cheat on the agreement.

Exhibit 6 explains why this is the case. An undetected price cut will enable a firm to attract (1) customers who normally wouldn't buy from any firm at the higher price and, more important, (2) customers who would normally buy from the other firms. Therefore, the demand facing each *individual firm* will be considerably more elastic than the market demand curve. As Exhibit 6 shows, the price P_i that maximizes the industry's profits will be higher than the price P_F that is best for a single oligopolist when the others stay with the higher price. If a firm can use secret rebates or other ways to undercut the price set by the collusive agreement while the other sellers maintain the higher price, it can expand its sales (beyond the level agreed upon by the cartel). This will more than make up for the reduction in per-unit profit margin from the price cut.

In oligopolistic industries, there are two conflicting tendencies. An oligopolistic firm has a strong incentive to cooperate with its rivals so that joint profit can be maximized. But it also has a strong incentive to cheat—to secretly expand output in order to increase its profit. Oligopolistic agreements, therefore, tend to be unstable. This instability exists whether the cooperative behavior is formal, as in the case of a cartel, or informal.

Obstacles to Collusion

There are certain situations in which it is more difficult for oligopolists to collude. Five major obstacles limit collusive behavior.

1. As the number of firms in an oligopolistic market increases, the likelihood of effective collusion declines.   Other things being constant, an increase in the number of major firms in an industry will make it more difficult for the oligopolists to communicate, negotiate, and enforce agreements among themselves. Furthermore, when there are more firms involved, the objectives of individual firms are more likely to conflict with those of others in the industry. Opinions about the best collusive price arrangement are likely to differ because marginal costs, unused plant capacity, and estimates of market demand elasticity will often differ among the firms. Aggressive, less mature firms might be especially interested in expanding their share of total output. As the number of firms expands, conflict arising from these and other sources will increase and make it more difficult to maintain collusive agreements.

2. When it is difficult to detect and eliminate price cuts, collusion is less attractive.

Unless a firm has a way of policing the pricing activities of rivals, it may be the "sucker" in a collusive agreement. Firms that secretly cut prices can gain a larger share of the market, while those maintaining higher prices lose customers and profits. The history of OPEC highlights this point. Cheating by members on production and sales quota agreements is not easy to monitor by the others, and it has been a persistent problem for the cartel.

Price cutting can sometimes be accomplished in ways that are difficult for the other firms to identify. For example, a firm might freely provide better credit terms, faster delivery, and other related services that improve the package offered to the buyer. In industries in which differentiated products are supplied, oligopolists can hold money prices constant and still use improvements in quality and style to provide consumers with more value. "Price cuts" like this are particularly attractive to oligopolists because they cannot be easily and quickly duplicated by rivals. As a result, collusive agreements on price are largely ineffective when quality and style are important competitive weapons. The bottom line is this: when cheating (price cutting) is profitable and difficult for rivals to detect and police, collusive agreements—both formal and informal—will be difficult to maintain.

3. Low entry barriers are an obstacle to collusion.

Unless potential new rivals can be excluded, oligopolists will be unable to sustain economic profits. Profitable collusion will attract new competitors into the market. But, if entry cannot be blocked, over time the benefits of higher prices accompanying a collusive agreement will have to be shared with more and more firms. High prices will also make it more attractive for potential rivals to develop substitutes, which will reduce the demand for the product provided by the oligopolists. Of course, these factors will not work instantaneously, but over time they will gnaw away at abnormally high prices and profits resulting from collusion.

Once again, OPEC illustrates the point. As OPEC pushed prices sharply upward in the 1970s, non-OPEC producers developed new oil fields and expanded their output from existing sources. The higher prices also encouraged energy conservation and greater use of alternative energy sources, such as coal, natural gas, and nuclear energy. By the mid-1980s, OPEC's share of world oil production had fallen to about 30 percent, down from 55 percent in 1973 when it first began to restrict output and raise oil prices. At that point,

Collusive agreements among oligopolists and cartels like OPEC are difficult to maintain because any individual cartel member would be better off if it could cheat on the agreement and charge a slightly lower price, so long as other members do not.

OPEC changed its course, expanding its output in order to recapture a larger share of the world market. As a result, oil prices declined throughout the 1985–2000 period. Despite recent increases, adjusted for inflation, the price of a barrel of crude oil in 2004 was still well below that of the mid-1980s. Furthermore, OPEC's share of world production stood at 40 percent in 2004, considerably less than during the early 1970s.

4. Unstable demand conditions are an obstacle to collusion. Honest differences of opinion among oligopolists about what is best for the industry always exist, but unstable demand increases the likelihood of conflict. One firm might want to expand because it anticipates a sharp increase in future demand, whereas a more pessimistic rival may want to hold the line on existing industrial capacity. The larger the differences in expectations about future demand, the greater the potential for conflict among oligopolistic firms. Successful collusion is more likely when demand is relatively stable.

5. Vigorous antitrust action increases the cost of collusion. Under existing antitrust laws in many nations, collusive behavior is prohibited. Secret agreements are, of course, possible. Simple informal cooperation might be conducted without discussions or collusive agreements. However, like other illegal behavior, such agreements are not legally enforceable by any firm. Vigorous antitrust action can discourage firms from making illegal agreements. As the threat of getting caught increases, participants will be less likely to attempt collusive behavior.

Uncertainty and Oligopoly

Market power
The ability of a firm that is not a pure monopolist to earn persistently large profits, indicating that it has some monopoly power. Because the firm has few (or weak) competitors, it has a degree of freedom from vigorous competition.

Game theory
A tool used to analyze the strategic choices made by competitors in a conflict situation like the decisions made by firms in an oligopoly.

Uncertainty and imprecision characterize the theory of oligopoly. We know that firms will gain if they successfully restrict output and raise prices. However, collusion is fraught with conflicts and difficulties. In some industries, these difficulties are so great that the **market power** of the oligopolists is relatively small. In other industries, oligopolistic cooperation, although not perfect, can raise prices significantly, indicating a higher degree of market power, which is, in effect, a degree of monopoly power. The use of **game theory** to analyze the costs and benefits of collusive behavior, under varying degrees of cooperation and conflict, has become an important part of economics during the last two decades. (See the accompanying Applications in Economics feature on this topic.) Although this developing field of economics does not yield precise predictions on oligopoly pricing and output, it does suggest the conditions that make it more likely that an oligopolist will be kept in check by competitive pressures.

MARKET POWER AND PROFIT—THE EARLY BIRD CATCHES THE WORM

Our analysis of both monopoly and oligopoly indicates that because entry barriers into these markets are often high, firms can sometimes earn economic profits over lengthy periods of time. Suppose a well-established firm, such as Disney or Microsoft, could use its market power to persistently earn above-normal returns. Would the current stockholders gain? Surprisingly, the answer is "No." The ownership value of a share of corporate stock in such a corporation would long ago have begun to reflect the firm's market power and expected future profitability. Many of the present stockholders paid high prices for their stock because they expected these firms to continue to be highly profitable. In other words, they have paid for any above-normal economic profits the firm is expected to earn because of its market power.

Do not expect to get rich buying the stock of monopolistic or oligopolistic firms known to be highly profitable. You are already too late. Those who owned the stock when these firms initially developed their market position have already captured the gain. The value of their stock increased at that time. After a firm's future prospects are widely recognized, subsequent stockholders fail to gain a higher-than-normal rate of return on their financial investment.

APPLICATIONS IN ECONOMICS

Oligopolistic Decision Making, Game Theory, and the Prisoner's Dilemma

In an oligopoly, a few firms compete in the same market, and the actions of each influence the demand faced by the others. One firm can gain customers at the expense of the others by cutting its price or increasing its advertising. The firms that fail to follow suit will lose customers. But if the other firms react competitively by doing the same, then all the firms lose. Thus, each firm finds itself on the horns of a dilemma—this is an example of the classic "prisoner's dilemma."

Economists have increasingly used game theory like the prisoner's dilemma to analyze strategic choices made by competitors, particularly those in an oligopoly. To understand the prisoner's dilemma, consider the hypothetical case of Al and Bob, two touring Americans who just met at a train station in a small foreign country. Al and Bob are taken prisoner and hauled into the local police station to be questioned separately. They are suspected of being the two men who robbed a local merchant, and each is told that if he makes the job of the police easier by confessing immediately, he will get only a six-month sentence. But each is also told that if he says nothing while the other confesses, then the one who did not confess immediately will get a twelve-month sentence. If neither confesses, both will be held for three months while the investigation continues. Al and Bob will not be allowed to communicate with each other. Will they confess?

To analyze such a situation, the game theorist begins by laying out the alternative outcomes and showing how they are related to choices made by the players of the game, as we do in **Exhibit 7.** For each man individually, in this version of the dilemma, the box reveals that the best choice depends on what the other does. If Al confesses, then Bob can save six months of jail time by also confessing. The same holds for Al, if he thinks Bob will confess. But if neither confesses, both serve only three months in jail.[1] The proper strategy for each prisoner depends heavily on his estimate of the likelihood that the other will confess. The

EXHIBIT 7
The Prisoner's Dilemma

		Al's Choice	
		Confess	Not Confess
Bob's Choice	Confess	6 months each	Al: 12 months Bob: 6 months
	Not Confess	Al: 6 months Bob: 12 months	3 months each

Al and Bob must each decide, without communicating with each other, whether to confess. Al knows that if Bob does not confess, then he can either confess and spend six months in jail, or not confess and spend three months. But if Bob does confess, then Al's failure to confess will cost him an additional six months in jail. Bob is in a similar situation, facing the same options under the same assumptions about whether Al confesses. Each man has an incentive to confess if he thinks the other one will, but an incentive not to confess if he thinks the other will also remain silent.

problem becomes more complex if we consider prisoners who face a series of such decisions over time and each prisoner learns what the other has done before making his or her next choice.

Firms in an oligopoly must make decisions somewhat like those of the prisoners: Should a firm cut its price in order to attract more customers—luring some of them away from its competitors—or should it keep its price high and risk losing customers to competitors who cut *their* prices? If all firms keep the price high, then as a group they will reap more profit. If all of them cut prices, then as a group they will reap less profit. But the firm that fails to cut price when the others do will lose many customers. The decision about whether or not to advertise has similar characteristics.

For example, consider the pricing policies or advertising strategies of large automakers, like Ford, General Motors, and Chrysler. Suppose the profit rate of each would be 15 percent if all the major automobile producers raised their prices (or cut their advertising expenditures) by a similar amount. In contrast, each would earn a profit rate of only 10 percent if intense competition led to lower prices and/or larger advertising expenditures. Industry profits are highest when all firms decide to charge high prices. However, if one automaker cuts its price or advertises more heavily, it will be able to steal customers away from its rivals and increase its

(continued)

---

[1]If the numbers were slightly different from those in the accompanying chart, both Al and Bob would have an incentive to confess regardless of what they thought the other would do. For example, if each were told that he would get only a one-month sentence if he confessed and the other party did not, then confession would become the dominant strategy for both Bob and Al. Under these circumstances, if Bob thought Al would remain silent, then Bob would spend only one month in jail if he confessed (compared to three months if he also remained silent). Al would be in a similar situation if he believed Bob would remain silent. On the other hand, if Bob thought Al would confess, then Bob's best option would be to confess also since confession would lead to only a six-month sentence whereas silence would result in a twelve-month jail term. The same would also be true for Al if he thought Bob would confess. Thus, in this classic prisoner's dilemma case, both men have an incentive to confess even though confession leads to more jail time for both—six months rather than three months. What is best for the individual (or firm) does not always lead to the best outcome from the viewpoint of the group (or industry).

(continued)

profit rate to 20 percent. Thus, if the firm thinks its rivals will continue to charge higher prices (or fail to match its advertising expenditures), it will be tempted to do it. If the other firms follow a similar course, however, the strategy will backfire and the profit rate of all the firms in the industry will be less than the level it would have achieved had they all charged higher prices (or spent less on advertising).

Although our simplified analysis highlights the interdependence among the firms and the importance of probability estimates concerning the strategy of rivals, the real world is much more complex. The choices of the rival firms will be repeated over and over again, although often in modified forms. A prior strategy will be modified in light of previous reactions on the part of rivals. How attractive a strategy will be will depend on its likelihood of being detected by rivals and the speed with which they will respond. In addition, the strategies of oligopolistic firms will be influenced by market conditions and the threat of foreign competition—factors that change with the passage of time. As you can see, additional assumptions will need to be made to account for these and other complex factors—factors that often change in the real world. But if the assumptions incorporated into

game theory models are not consistent with real-world conditions, the implications of the game theory analysis may well be invalid.

Economists have used game theory extensively to show how results change when the "rules of the game" change for the firms in an oligopolistic market, as well as for auction-bidding markets and other business decision-making situations. When the rules of the game are carefully defined and enforced, as they are in economic experiments held in laboratories, game theory has yielded interesting and important testable conclusions. But in open markets in the real world, empirical work using game theory has been less successful. The use of models is always difficult when the problem to be solved is complex and when human expectations about the changing strategic choices of other human beings must be taken into account. There is no question, however, that game theory can be useful for scholars and business practitioners alike, by helping them frame the issues involved in strategic decision making.[2]

[2]For a further explanation of game theory and the prisoner's dilemma, see Avinash Dixit and Barry Nalebuff, "Game Theory," in *The Concise Encyclopedia of Economics*, ed. David R. Henderson (Indianapolis, Ind.: Liberty Fund, Inc., 2002), http://www.econlib.org/library/CEE.html.

DEFECTS OF MARKETS WITH HIGH ENTRY BARRIERS

From Adam Smith's time to the present, economists have generally considered monopoly to be a problem. The attitude toward markets with few sellers and high entry barriers has been only slightly more tolerant. Generally, economists level three major criticisms at concentrated markets with high entry barriers. We will outline each of them.

1. When entry barriers are high and there are few, if any, alternative suppliers, the discipline of market forces is weakened. When entry barriers are low, consumers are well equipped to direct the behavior of suppliers. Consumer choices will

ECONOMICS AT THE MOVIES

A Beautiful Mind (2001)

A Beautiful Mind, starring Russell Crowe, tells the story of Nobel Prize–winning economist John Nash's struggle with schizophrenia. The prisoner's dilemma presented in this chapter was fundamentally shaped by Nash. His early ideas and how he came up with them are depicted in the movie, although he claims he didn't come up with the "Nash equilibrium" solution to the prisoner's dilemma in a bar, as the movie portrays.

drive firms from the market if they charge high prices, supply unattractive goods, or otherwise fail to serve the interest of consumers. If you do not like the food at a local restaurant, you eat elsewhere. If you think prices are high and the selection poor at a department store, you patronize rival firms. But consider your alternatives if you do not like the local cable television service. What can you do when the service is bad? You can voice a complaint to the company or your legislative representative, but unlike a competitive situation, you have no exit option other than sacrificing your cable service, perhaps to rely instead on satellite dish service. Cable and satellite service are imperfect substitutes, each with its own disadvantages. To the extent that consumers do not have good exit options, they must either take what the seller offers or do without. Consequently, their ability to keep sellers in check is greatly reduced.

2. Reduced competition results in allocative inefficiency. Allocative efficiency requires that additional units be produced when they are valued more highly than what it costs to produce them. When barriers to entry are low, profit-seeking producers of each good expand their output until its price is driven down to the level of per-unit costs. With high barriers to entry, however, this will not generally be the case. A monopolist or cartel that does not have to worry about rivals entering the market can often gain by restricting output and raising the price. Some units might not be produced, even though consumers value them more than their costs. Prices may exceed not only marginal costs, but also average total cost for a long period of time when entry barriers into a market are high.

3. Government grants of monopoly power will encourage rent seeking; resources will be wasted by firms attempting to secure and maintain grants of market protection. Special favors granted by the government will lead to costly activities for those who seek such favors. As we noted in Chapter 6, economists refer to such activities as rent seeking. When licenses or other entry barriers erected by the government enhance the profitability and provide protection from the rigors of market competition, people will expend scarce resources to secure and maintain these political favors. From an efficiency standpoint, these rent-seeking costs related to getting and keeping monopoly power add to the welfare losses resulting from the allocative inefficiencies we previously mentioned.

Suppose the government issues a license providing a seller with the exclusive right to sell liquor in a specific market. If this grant of monopoly power permits the licensee to earn monopoly profit, potential suppliers will expend resources trying to convince government officials that they should be granted the license. The potential monopolists will lobby government officials, make political contributions, hire representatives to do consulting studies, and undertake other actions designed to obtain the monopoly grant. Any firm that expects its rent-seeking activities to be successful will be willing to spend up to the present value of the future expected monopoly profits, if necessary, to obtain the monopoly protection. Other suppliers, of course, will also be willing to invest in rent-seeking activities. When several suppliers believe they can win, the total expenditures of all firms on rent-seeking activities can actually consume resources worth more than the economic profit expected from the monopoly enterprise.

POLICY ALTERNATIVES WHEN ENTRY BARRIERS ARE HIGH

What government policies might be used to counteract the problems that result from high barriers to entry? Economists suggest four policy options:

1. Control the structure of the industry to ensure the presence of rival firms.

2. Reduce artificial barriers that limit competition.

3. Regulate the price and output of firms in the market.

4. Supply the market with goods produced by a government firm.

Each of these policies has been used to either reduce entry barriers or counteract their negative results. We will briefly consider each of them and analyze both their potential and limitations as tools that can be used to improve the efficiency of resource use.

Antitrust Policy and Controlling the Structure of an Industry

The major problems associated with high barriers to entry and monopoly power are not present when rival sellers are present and compete. The United States, to a greater degree than most Western countries, has adopted antitrust laws designed to prevent monopoly and promote competition. Antitrust legislation began in 1890 with the passage of the Sherman Antitrust Act. Additional legislation, including the Clayton Act and the Federal Trade Commission Act of 1914, has buttressed policy in this area.

Antitrust laws give the U.S. Department of Justice the power to prosecute firms engaging in collusive behavior or other actions designed to create a monopoly or cartel. They also give the government the power to break up an existing monopoly and prevent mergers that significantly reduce competition. The Federal Trade Commission (FTC) is is allowed to bring charges under the Sherman Act. Private firms can also bring suits charging antitrust violations by a rival under the Sherman and Clayton acts and collect up to three times any actual damages caused by the rival firm. Each year, far more cases are brought by private firms against their competitors than by the two federal agencies. Rival firms can also ask the two agencies to bring antitrust cases against successful competitors who may have, or threaten to gain, monopoly power.

Economists are not in total agreement about the usefulness of antitrust action to increase the number of rival firms in an industry. Those who support policies of this type believe that only by preserving numerous competitors in a market can we be confident that monopoly has been controlled. Opponents point to the danger of protecting high-cost firms at the expense of both consumers and the more aggressive and successful firm(s) in the market. Protection of less efficient firms from successful competitors, they say, is all too common in the actual practice of antitrust policy.

Economists agree that there is one clear situation in which the application of antitrust action would be inappropriate. When substantial economies of scale are present and unit cost will be minimized only if the entire industry output is produced by a single firm, a **natural monopoly** is present. In that case, breaking up a large firm in order to increase the number of rivals in the industry would lead to higher per-unit costs. Because of their higher costs, the prices charged by the smaller firms might even exceed those of a monopolist. Therefore, using antitrust laws to expand the number of firms is not an attractive option when economies of scale in an industry produce a natural monopoly.

Natural monopoly
A market situation in which the average costs of production continually decline with increased output. In a natural monopoly, the average costs of production will be lowest when a single, large firm produces the entire output demanded by the marketplace.

Reduce Artificial Barriers to Trade

Government-imposed restraints such as licensing requirements, tariffs, and quotas often reduce the competitiveness of markets. For example, local governments often require potential entrants into the taxicab business to prove that "additional capacity is needed to serve the market." Hearings must be held to address this issue, and existing firms are allowed to explain why the new entrant is not needed. Governments also restrain entry into various occupations through the use of substantial licensing fees, complex examinations, and lengthy training requirements. When government-imposed restrictions are the source of the monopoly power, the appropriate policy action is straightforward: remove the restraints. But this is easier said than done. The restraints generally reflect the political influence of special-interest groups—the producers currently in the industry—who have a vested interest in restricting competition and keeping prices high.

If a product is traded in international markets, foreign suppliers can enhance the competitiveness of the domestic market. When the domestic market is dominated by a small number of firms, removing tariffs, quotas, and other obstacles that limit competition from abroad is particularly helpful. The competition of foreign rivals will help ensure that the domestic firms improve quality and keep their costs low.

The U.S. automobile industry illustrates the importance of this approach. Profits for U.S. producers in the highly competitive automobile segment of the industry have been low. The 2.5 percent tariff on imported autos places foreign producers at only a modest disadvantage. In contrast, there is a 25 percent tariff on imported trucks. (The tariff was implemented in 1963 to retaliate against restrictions imposed by foreign governments on U.S. frozen-chicken exports.) The higher tariff protects the same U.S. producers of cars in the truck segment of the industry. There, profits per vehicle are much higher. When General Motors began selling its newly designed line of full-size pickups in 1998 (the first full updating of those models in ten years), the profit on a well-equipped $30,000 vehicle was reported to be $8,000. The tariff keeps the price of foreign imports high, so the level of competition is lower in the U.S. market for new trucks than in the market for cars. Clearly, though, the competition from abroad has helped keep domestic auto producers on their toes. As a result, most observers believe that the overall quality of automobiles available to the American consumer, including those produced by domestic manufacturers, is higher than it would have been without the competition from abroad.

As with domestically imposed entry restraints, political considerations often make it difficult to remove obstacles that retard competition from abroad. Trade restraints that limit competition from foreign suppliers benefit primarily the owners, managers, and workers in the protected industries. These interest groups are highly concentrated and generally well organized politically. In contrast, consumers are poorly organized, and the costs imposed on them by the restraints are nearly always thinly spread among them. As we discussed in Chapter 6, the political process often works to the advantage of the concentrated interests. As a result, even when lower trade barriers are needed to increase the competitiveness of an industry, political factors often prevent them.

Regulate the Protected Producer

Can government regulation improve the allocative efficiency of a monopoly or an oligopoly? In theory, the answer to this question is clearly "Yes." **Exhibit 8** illustrates why ideal government price regulation, in the case of a monopolist, can improve resource allocation. The firm illustrated here is a natural monopoly. Its *LRATC* falls over the entire relevant range of output. Antitrust action dividing the firm into several smaller rivals will not help consumers because the unit costs of the smaller firms will be higher than if the output were produced by the monopolist. Nonetheless, from the viewpoint of allocative efficiency, the profit-maximizing monopolist will produce an output that is too small and charge a price that is too high. It will set price at P_0 and produce output Q_0, where

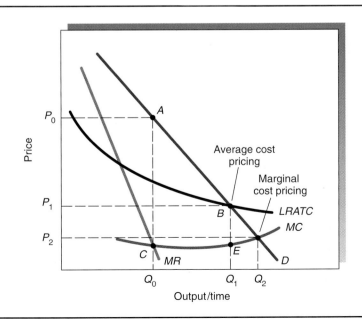

EXHIBIT 8
Regulating a Monopolist

If unregulated, a profit-maximizing monopolist with the costs indicated here will produce Q_0 units and charge P_0. If a regulatory agency forced the monopolist to reduce price to P_1, then the monopolist would expand output to Q_1. Ideally, we would like output to be expanded to Q_2, where $P = MC$, but regulatory agencies usually do not attempt to keep prices as low as P_2. Can you explain why?

$MR = MC$. Consumers, however, will value the additional units more than the opportunity cost of producing them. Let's consider the potential of two regulatory options and also analyze some of their real-world limitations.

Average Cost Pricing

If a regulatory agency forces the firm in Exhibit 8 to reduce the price to P_1, at which point the *ATC* curve intersects the market (and firm) demand curve, then the firm will expand output to Q_1. Since it cannot charge a price above P_1, the firm cannot increase its revenues by selling a smaller output at a higher price. Once the price ceiling is instituted, the firm can increase its revenues by P_1, and by only P_1, for each unit it sells. The regulated firm's *MR* is constant at P_1 for all units sold until output is increased to Q_1. Since the firm's *MC* is less than P_1 (and therefore less than *MR*), the profit-maximizing regulated firm shown here will expand output from Q_0 to Q_1. The benefits from the consumption of these units (ABQ_1Q_0) clearly exceed their costs (CEQ_1Q_0). Social welfare has improved as a result of the regulatory action (we will ignore the impact on the distribution of income). At this output level, revenues are sufficient to cover costs. The firm is making zero economic profit (or "normal" accounting profit).

Marginal Cost Pricing

Even at the Q_1 output level, marginal cost is still less than price. Additional welfare gains could be achieved if output were increased to Q_2. However, if a regulatory agency forced the monopolist to reduce the price to P_2 (so the price would equal the marginal cost at the output level Q_2), economic losses would result. Even a monopolist, unless it is subsidized, wouldn't produce the product at P_2 or any price below P_1. But how large should a subsidy be? No one has the knowledge to set this subsidy, partly because prices, technologies, and the value of output change daily. Also, who has the incentive to fight the pressures on both sides for higher (or lower) subsidies? Marginal cost pricing is seldom practical.

Problems with Regulation

Although regulating a monopoly might seem like a way to improve the efficiency of markets, both economic analysis and the history of regulation suggest that it has serious shortcomings. Why? Three factors tend to reduce the effectiveness of regulations and the probability that regulators will act on behalf of all citizens to control monopolies. Let's look at each of these factors.

1. Lack of information. When we discussed ideal regulation, we assumed that we knew what the firm's *ATC, MC,* and demand curves looked like. In reality, of course, we don't. The firms themselves have difficulty knowing their costs, and especially their demand curves, with any precision. Furthermore, both supply and demand will vary with time and place. The market for electricity is an excellent example. Because electricity cannot be stored for later use, the highly variable supply and demand conditions in that market cause the opportunity cost of power to change dramatically from one day, or even one hour, to the next. California utilities made headlines when they experienced this early in the summer of 2001. Low rainfall reduced hydropower generation, rising natural gas prices increased gas-fired generation costs, and some hot weather early in the summer added to an already growing demand. These factors combined to sharply raise the marginal cost of delivering electric power. The regulated retail power rates were far too low to cover costs in this situation, and both policy makers and regulators were slow to adjust. Later in the summer, these demand and supply factors had shifted back toward their previous levels, and the marginal cost of power had declined substantially. Meanwhile, however, the resulting power outages and utility revenue shortfalls caused serious problems.

Because estimates of demand and marginal costs are difficult to obtain, regulatory agencies usually gauge profits (or the rate of return) to determine whether the regulated price is too high or too low. The regulatory agency seeks to impose a "fair" or "normal" rate of return on the firm. If the firm is making profits (that is, an abnormally high rate of return), the regulated price must be higher than P_1 in Exhibit 8, and that price should be lowered. Alternatively, if the firm is incurring losses (less than the fair, or normal, rate of return), this indicates that the regulated price is less than P_1 and the firm should be permitted to charge a higher price.

The actual existence of profits, though, is not easily identifiable. Accounting profit, or the rate of return, is not the same as economic profit, which includes opportunity cost. Also, regulated firms have a strong incentive to adopt reporting techniques and accounting methods that conceal profits. Because of this, a regulatory agency will find it difficult or impossible to identify and impose a price consistent with allocative efficiency.

2. Cost shifting.   Regulation changes incentives, so it can affect costs. If demand is sufficient, the owners of the regulated firm can expect the long-run rate of profit to be essentially fixed, regardless of whether efficient management reduces costs or inefficient management allows costs to increase. If costs decrease, the "fair return" rule imposed by the regulatory agency will force a price reduction; if costs increase, the "fair return" rule will allow a price increase. Compared to the managers of unregulated firms, managers of regulated firms have more freedom to pursue personal objectives and less incentive to seek lower costs. Predictably, they will often fly first-class, entertain lavishly at company expense, grant unwarranted wage increases, and so on. This will lead to higher unit cost. Yet the firm's monopoly position leaves consumers unable to switch to substitute products.

3. Special-interest influence.   The difficulties of government regulation discussed so far are practical limitations a regulatory agency confronts. Unfortunately, the political element of government regulation exacerbates the problem. Regulated firms have a strong incentive to see that "friendly," "reasonable" people serve as regulators, and they will invest political and economic resources toward this end. Just as rent-seeking activities designed to gain monopoly privileges in the first place can be expected, so, too, can activities to influence regulators' decisions. Few consumers will invest the time and resources required to understand regulatory policy and make the political contributions needed to counteract the influence peddling. Over time, regulatory commissions are therefore likely to reflect the views and interests of the business and labor interests they were designed to regulate.

For the reasons we just explored, both economic reasoning and decades of experience show that although regulation has the potential to improve resource allocation, it is not a magic cure.

Supply Market with Government Production

Government-operated firms—socialized firms like the U.S. Postal Service, the Tennessee Valley Authority, and many local public utilities—present an alternative to both private monopoly and regulation. Here, too, however, both economic thinking and experience indicate that socialized firms will fail to counteract fully the problems that stem from high barriers to entry. The same perverse managerial incentives that regulated firms confront—incentives to ignore efficiency and pursue personal or professional objectives at the firm's expense—also tend to plague government-operated firms. In addition, the rational ignorance effect comes into play here. Individual voters have little incentive to acquire information about the operation of government firms because, unlike the case of a personal investment, the individual's choices will not decide which investment will be purchased with the voter's money. Predictably, the "owners" of a socialized firm (voters) will be uninformed about how well the firm is run, how it might be run better, or which other firm has a better plan. This is especially true when there are no direct competitors against which the firm's performance might easily be compared.

Government-operated firms do not provide an environment that rewards managers or investors for efficient management and reductions in cost. Unlike investors in the private sector, no small group of voters is in a position to gain a substantial amount of wealth by taking over the socialized firm and improving its management. Even more than with monopoly or oligopoly in the private sector, customers of the socialized monopoly cannot easily switch their business to other sellers. Voter-taxpayers who do not even consume the product often have to pay taxes to support its provision. When the government operates a business—particularly one with monopoly power—there is typically less investor scrutiny, less reward for efficiency, and less penalty for inefficiency or the production of inferior goods. Higher costs and lower-valued outputs are predictable results.

Government ownership, like unregulated monopoly and government regulation, is a less-than-ideal solution. Those who denounce monopoly in, for instance, the local telephone industry, seldom point to a government-operated monopoly—such as first-class mail delivery by the U.S. Postal Service—as an example of how an industry should be run.

Pulling It Together

The policy alternatives available when high barriers to entry are present are less than fully satisfying. Most of the available policy alternatives are just not very attractive. Economies of scale often make antitrust actions impractical. When larger firms have lower per-unit costs, restructuring the industry to increase the number of firms will be both costly and difficult to maintain. Rivals can also use antitrust policy against successful firms that have simply given consumers a better deal and captured a large part of the market in the process. Policy actions to stop or to punish such progress are counterproductive for customers and for economic efficiency. Lifting government restrictions such as licensing requirements, quotas, and tariffs that limit competition is perhaps the surest way to improve the performance of markets with few suppliers. But the nature of the political process, particuarly its tendency to cater to the views of well-organized interest groups, often undermines the feasibility of this option. Too often in this situation, good economics does not translate into good politics.

Regulation is also a less-than-ideal solution. Regulators do not possess the information necessary to impose an efficient outcome, and as part of the political process, they will be susceptible to manipulation by industrial and labor interests. Since public-sector managers go unchecked by private-sector consumers, they are likely to pursue political objectives at the expense of economic efficiency. This means that government operation of firms also has its problems. In short, when economies of scale are present in an industry, there is no perfect way for the government to control market power.

THE COMPETITIVE PROCESS IN THE REAL WORLD

How competitive are markets today? As George Stigler points out in the second of his chapter-opening quotations, "Competition is a tough weed, not a delicate flower." In a very real sense, every firm competes with every other firm for the consumer's additional dollar of spending. Firms in markets that appear to be unrelated often compete with one another. Sellers of compact discs, for example, compete with bookstores and local restaurants for our entertainment budgets. The suppliers of swimming pools compete with airlines, hotels, casinos, and automobile rental companies for the vacation and leisure time expenditures of consumers.

In recent decades, direct competition in almost all markets has increased. Lower transportation and communication costs have played an important role here. Lower transport costs make it more feasible for consumers to consider products offered by far-away suppliers. They also make it possible for producers to compete over a much larger geographic area, which often leads to lower per-unit costs and larger gains from economies of scale. Further, the Internet is now available to most households, and it provides even those living in small towns with quick and easy access to worldwide markets. This widening of markets reduces the market power of both buyers and sellers and, at the same time, reduces potential problems related to economies of scale.

Technological change is also a powerful force for competitive markets. Innovation and nonprice competition on product quality, design, convenience, and other factors are used constantly by firms seeking greater market share and profitability. For a firm, innovation is the key to (temporary) profits. Successful innovation can give the innovating firm some degree of relief from competition while other firms struggle to catch up. Technical improvements, like newer and better computers or ways to make and sell them, cheaper and better inventory control methods, and MP3 players, have all made fortunes for the firms developing the information technology behind them. But the advantage is always temporary. Over time, each technical and business innovation becomes available to all firms, and the consumers of all products win, even as the profits of the innovating firms wane.

The competitiveness of markets is complex and difficult to measure directly. However, like Professor Stigler, most economists believe that competition is a tough weeed. Given the importance of quality competition, broader markets, and technological discoveries, most economists also believe that the U.S. economy is more competitive today than it was, say, fifty years ago. The pervasiveness of the competitive process helps explain why profit levels, even in manufacturing industries, are considerably lower than many people think. A national sample poll of adults conducted by Opinion Research Corporation of Princeton, New Jersey, found that the average person thought profits constituted 29 percent of every dollar of sales in manufacturing. In reality, the after-tax accounting profits of manufacturing corporations are about 4 cents to 5 cents per dollar of sales. These figures also suggest that the U.S. economy, including the manufacturing sector, is relatively competitive.

LOOKING AHEAD

The last several chapters have focused on product markets. Of course, resources are required to produce products. The following chapters will focus on resource markets and the employment decisions of both business firms and resource suppliers.

KEY POINTS

▼ The four major barriers to entry into a market are economies of scale (in uncontestable markets), government licensing, patents, and control of an essential resource.

▼ A monopoly is present when there is a single seller of a well-defined product for which there are no good substitutes and the entry barriers into the market are high. Although there are only a few markets in which the entire output is supplied by a single seller, the monopoly model also helps us better understand the operation of markets dominated by a small number of firms.

▼ Like other price searchers, a profit-maximizing monopolist will lower the price and expand its output as long as marginal revenue exceeds marginal cost. At the maximum-profit output, *MR* will equal *MC*. The monopolist will charge the price on its demand curve consistent with that output.

▼ If a monopolist is earning a profit, high barriers to entry will shield it from direct competition, thereby enabling it to earn long-run economic profits. But sometimes demand and cost conditions will be such that even a monopolist will be unable to earn economic profit.

▼ An oligopolistic market is characterized by (1) a small number of rival firms, (2) interdependence among the sellers, (3) substantial economies of scale, and (4) high entry barriers to the market.

▼ There is no general theory of equilibrium price and output for oligopolistic markets. If rival oligopolists acted totally independently of their competitors, they would drive the price down to the per-unit cost of production. Alternatively, if they colluded perfectly, the price would rise to the level a monopolist would charge. The actual outcome in an oligopoly will generally fall between these two extremes.

▼ Oligopolists have a strong incentive to collude and raise their prices. However, each firm will be able to gain if it (alone) can cut its price (or improve the quality of its product) because the demand curve confronted by the firm is more elastic than the industry demand curve. This introduces a conflict that makes it difficult to maintain collusive agreements.

▼ Oligopolistic firms are less likely to collude successfully against the interests of consumers if (1) the number of rival firms is large; (2) it is costly to prohibit competitors from offering secret price cuts (or quality improvements) to customers; (3) entry barriers are low; (4) market demand conditions tend to be unstable; and/or (5) the threat of antitrust action is present.

▼ Economists criticize high barriers to market entry because (1) the ability of consumers to discipline producers is weakened, (2) the unregulated monopolist or oligopoly group can often gain by restricting output and raising price, and (3) legal barriers to entry encourage firms to engage in wasteful rent-seeking activities.

▼ When entry barriers are high and competition among rival firms weak, the major policy alternatives are: (1) antitrust action designed to maintain or increase the number of firms in the industry, (2) relaxation of regulations that limit entry and trade, (3) price regulation, and (4) provision of output by government firms. When feasible, option (2) is the most attractive alternative. Under most circumstances, all the other options have shortcomings.

▼ Competitive forces are present and growing, even in markets with high barriers to entry. Quality competition, the widening of markets, and technological change are all important elements of the competitive process.

? CRITICAL ANALYSIS QUESTIONS

*1. "Barriers to entry are crucial to the existence of long-run profits, but they cannot guarantee the existence of profits." Evaluate.

2. "Monopoly is good for producers but bad for consumers. The gains of the former offset the losses of the latter. On balance, there is no reason to think that monopoly is bad for the economy." Is this statement true? Why or why not?

*3. Do monopolists charge the highest prices for which they can sell their products? Do they maximize their average profit per sale? Are monopolistic firms always profitable? Why or why not?

4. The retail liquor industry is potentially a competitive industry. However, the liquor retailers of a southern state, with the cooperation of the state legislature, organized a trade association that sets prices for all firms. For all practical purposes, a competitive industry became a monopoly. Compare the price and output policy of a purely competitive industry with the policy that would be established by a profit-maximizing monopolist or trade association. Who benefits and who is hurt by the formation of the monopoly?

5. Does economic theory indicate that an ideal regulatory agency that forces a monopolist to charge a price equal to either marginal or average total cost will improve economic efficiency? Explain. Does economic theory suggest that a regulatory agency will in fact follow a proper regulation policy? What are some of the factors that complicate the regulatory function?

6. Is a monopolist subject to any competitive pressures? Explain. Would an unregulated monopolist have an incentive to operate and produce efficiently? Why or why not?

7. How will high entry barriers into a market influence (a) the long-run profitability of the firms, (b) the cost efficiency of the firms in the industry, (c) the likelihood that some inefficient (high-cost) firms will survive, and (d) the incentive of entrepreneurs to develop substitutes for the product supplied by the firms? Are competitive pressures present in markets with high barriers to entry? Discuss.

*8. Why is oligopolistic collusion more difficult when there is product variation than when the products of all firms are identical?

9. In large cities, taxi fares are often set above the market equilibrium rate. Sometimes the number of licenses is limited in order to maintain the above-market price. Other times licenses are automatically granted to anyone wanting to operate a taxi. When taxi fares are set above market equilibrium, compare and contrast resource allocation under the restricted license system (assume the licenses are tradable) and the free-entry system. In which case will it be easier for customers to get a taxi? In which case will

the amount of capital required to enter the taxi business be greater?

10. We have a theory to explain the equilibrium price and output for monopoly, but not for oligopoly. Why? How can game theory help us understand the decisions made by oligopolists?

***11.** Historically, the real cost of transporting both goods and people has declined substantially. What impact do lower transportation costs have on the market power of individual producers? Do you think the U.S. economy is more or less competitive today than it was 100 years ago? Explain.

***12.** "My uncle just bought 1,000 shares of Microsoft, one of the largest and most profitable companies in the United States. Given Microsoft's high profit rate, he will make a bundle from this purchase." Evaluate this statement. Is it necessarily true? Explain.

***13.** Gouge-em Cable Company is the only cable television service company licensed to operate in Backwater County. Most of its costs are access fees and maintenance expenses. These fixed costs total $640,000 monthly. The marginal cost of adding another subscriber to its system is constant at $2 per month. Gouge-em's demand curve can be determined from the data in the accompanying table.

Subscription Price	Number of Subscribers (per month)
$25	20,000
20	40,000
15	60,000
10	80,000
5	100,000
1	150,000

  a. What price will Gouge-em charge for its cable services? What are its profits at this price?
  b. Now suppose the Backwater County Public Utility Commission has the data and believes that cable subscription rates in the county are too expensive and that Gouge-em's profits are unfairly

high. What regulated price will it set so that Gouge-em makes only a normal rate of return on its investment?

14. Suppose that you produce and sell children's tables in a local market. Past experience enables you to estimate your demand and marginal cost schedules. This information is presented in the table at the bottom of this page.
  a. Fill in the missing revenue and cost schedules.
  b. Assuming you are currently charging $55 per table set, what should you do if you want to maximize profits?
  c. Given your demand and cost estimates, what price should you charge if you want to maximize your weekly profit? What output should you produce? What is your maximum weekly profit?

15. The diagram shows demand and long-run cost conditions in an industry.
  a. Explain why the industry is likely to be monopolized.
  b. Indicate the price that a profit-maximizing monopolist would charge, and label it *P*.
  c. Indicate the monopolist's output level, and label it *Q*.
  d. Indicate the maximum profits of the monopolist.
  e. Will the profits attract competitors to the industry? Why or why not? Explain.

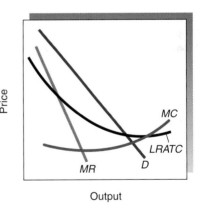

Price	Quantity Demanded (per week)	Marginal Cost	Total Revenue	Marginal Revenue	Fixed Cost	Total Cost
$60	1	$50	_____	_____	$40	_____
55	2	20	_____	_____	_____	_____
50	3	24	_____	_____	_____	_____
45	4	29	_____	_____	_____	_____
40	5	35	_____	_____	_____	_____
35	6	45	_____	_____	_____	_____

CHAPTER 24

The Supply of and Demand for Productive Resources

It is . . . necessary to attach price tags to the various factors of production . . . in order to guide those who have the day-to-day decisions to make as to what is plentiful and what is scarce.

—Professor James Meade[1]

Chapter Focus

- Why do business firms demand labor, machines, and other resources? Why is the demand for a productive resource inversely related to its price?

- How do business firms decide which resources to employ and the quantity of each that will be used?

- How is the quantity supplied of a resource related to its price in the short run? In the long run?

- What determines the market price of a resource? How do resource prices help efficiently allocate a society's resources across competing uses?

---

[1]James E. Meade was a longtime professor of economics at Cambridge University.

R ecent chapters have focused on product markets, markets in which consumers purchase goods and services supplied by business firms. Our analysis now shifts to **resource markets**, markets in which firms hire productive resources like machines and workers and use them to produce goods and services. (*Note*: Because resources are also referred to as *factors* or *inputs,* these markets are also known as *factor markets* or *input markets.*)

Just as in product markets, the forces of supply and demand combine to determine prices in resource markets. The buyers and sellers in resource markets are just the reverse of what they are in product markets. In resource markets, business firms are the purchasers; they demand resources that are used to produce goods and services. Households are the sellers; they (and firms they own) supply resources in exchange for income. The income from supplying productive resources, such as the wages received from the sale of labor services, is the major source of income for most of us. Prices in resource markets coordinate the choices of buyers and sellers and bring the amount of each resource demanded into harmony with the amount supplied. Resource prices also help allocate factors of production efficiently and channel them into the areas where they are most productive. This enables us to have higher incomes and a larger supply of consumer goods than would otherwise be the case.

As the circular flow diagram of **Exhibit 1** illustrates, there is a close relationship between product and resource markets. Households earn income by selling factors of production—for example, the services of their labor and capital—to business firms. Their offers to sell form the supply curve in resource markets (bottom loop). The income that households get from the sale of resources gives them the buying power they need to purchase goods and services in product markets. These expenditures by households generate revenue and motivate firms to produce goods and services (top loop). In turn, firms demand resources because they contribute to the production of goods and services that can be sold in product markets. ■

HUMAN AND NONHUMAN RESOURCES

Broadly speaking, there are two different types of productive inputs, nonhuman and human. **Nonhuman resources** can be broken down into physical capital, land, and natural resources. *Physical capital* consists of human-made resources, such as tools, machines, and buildings, that are used to produce other things.

Net investment can increase the supply of nonhuman resources. However, investment involves a cost. Resources used to produce machines, upgrade the quality of land, or discover natural resources could be used to produce goods and services for current consumption instead of invested for the future. Why take the roundabout path? The answer is that sometimes indirect methods of producing goods are less costly in the long run. For example, Robinson Crusoe found he could catch more fish by taking some time off from hand-fishing to build a net. Even though his initial investment of time to make the net reduced his current catch, once the net was completed he was able to more than make up for this loss. Trade-offs like these influence what people will invest in, be it fishing nets or complex machines. An investment will be undertaken only when the decision maker expects the benefits of a larger future output to more than offset the current reduction in the production of consumption goods. Just as the supply of machines can be increased with investment, so, too, can investments in better land development and soil-conservation practices improve the quantity and quality of usable land. Similarly, the supply of natural resources like oil and gas, for example, can be increased (to some extent) by making an investment in, or dedicating more resources to, exploration and development.

Human resources consist of the skills and knowledge of workers. Investments in education, training, health, and experience can enhance the skills, abilities, and ingenuity of individuals, and thereby increase their productivity. Economists call activities like these

Resource markets
Markets in which business firms demand factors of production (for example, labor, capital, and natural resources) from household suppliers. The resources are then used to produce goods and services. These markets are sometimes called factor markets or input markets.

Nonhuman resources
The durable, nonhuman inputs used to produce both current and future output. Machines, buildings, land, and raw materials are examples. Investment can increase the supply of nonhuman resources. Economists often use the term physical capital when referring to nonhuman resources.

Human resources
The abilities, skills, and health of human beings that contribute to the production of both current and future output. Investment in training and education can increase the supply of human resources.

EXHIBIT 1
The Market for Resources

Until now, we have focused on product markets, in which households demand goods and services that are supplied by firms (upper loop). We now turn to resource markets, in which firms demand factors of production—human capital (like the skills and knowledge of workers) and physical capital (like machines, buildings, and land). Factors of production are supplied by households in exchange for income (bottom loop). In resource markets, firms are buyers and households are sellers—just the reverse of their roles in product markets.

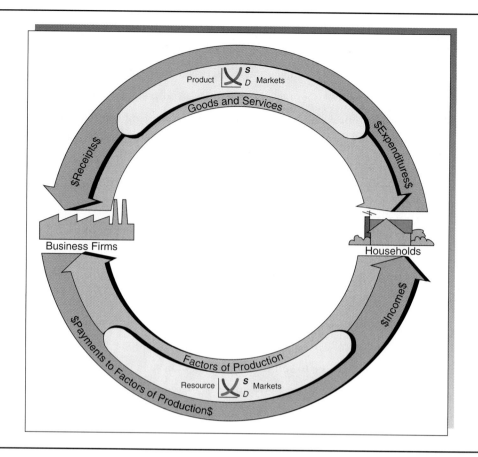

Investment in human capital
Expenditures on training, education, skill development, and health designed to increase human capital and people's productivity.

an **investment in human capital**.[2] Like physical capital, human capital also depreciates—people's skills, for example, can decline with age or lack of use. Education and training will add to the stock of human capital while depreciation detracts from it.

Decisions to invest in human capital are no different from other investment decisions we make. Consider your decision about going to college. As you know, an investment in a college education requires you to sacrifice some current earnings as well as pay for direct expenses, like tuition and books. However, you are making the investment anyway because you expect it to lead to a better job and other benefits later. A rational person will attend college only if the expected future benefits outweigh the current costs.

Human resources differ from nonhuman resources in two important respects. First, human capital is embodied in the individual. Individuals cannot be separated from their knowledge, skills, and health conditions in the same way that they can be separated from physical capital, like buildings or machines that they might own. As a result, in addition to money, a person's job choices are also affected by a job's working conditions, location, prestige, and other nonmonetary factors. Money, of course, influences people's human capital decisions. However, people will often choose to trade off some money income for better working conditions. Second, human resources cannot be bought and sold in nonslave societies. Workers sell only the *services* of their labor. They have the option of quitting, selling their labor services to another employer, or using them in some other way. Thus, we usually speak of the worker as selling (and the firm as buying) labor services.

In competitive markets, the price of resources, like the price of products, is determined by supply and demand. We will begin our analysis of resource markets by focusing on the demand for resources, both human and nonhuman.

[2]The contributions of T. W. Schultz and Gary Becker to the literature on human capital have been particularly significant. See Ronald G. Ehrenberg and Robert S. Smith, *Modern Labor Economics: Theory and Public Policy,* 8th ed. (Reading, MA: Addison-Wesley, 2003), chap. 9, for additional detail on human capital theory.

THE DEMAND FOR RESOURCES

Profit-seeking producers employ laborers, machines, raw materials, and other resources because they help produce goods and services. *The demand for a resource exists because there is a demand for goods that the resource helps to produce. The demand for each resource is thus a derived demand; it is derived from the demand of consumers for products.*

For example, an auto repair shop hires mechanics because customers demand repair service, not because the auto repair shop owner benefits simply from having mechanics around. If customers did not demand repair service, mechanics would not be employed for long. Similarly, the demand for inputs like carpenters, plumbers, lumber, and glass windows is derived from the demand of consumers for houses and other consumer products that these resources help to make. Most resources contribute to the production of numerous goods. For example, glass is used to produce windows, ornaments, dishes, light bulbs, and mirrors, among other things. The total demand for a resource is the sum at each resource price of the derived demands for each of its uses.

The demand curve for a resource shows the amount of the resource that will be used at different prices. As **Exhibit 2** shows, there is an inverse relationship between the price of a resource and the amount demanded of it. There are two major reasons that less of a resource will be demanded as its price increases: (1) producers will turn to substitute resources and (2) consumers will buy fewer goods that become more expensive as the result of higher resource costs. Let us take a closer look at each of these factors.

Derived demand
The demand for a resource; it stems from the demand for the final good the resource helps produce.

Substitution in Production

Firms will use the input combination that minimizes their costs. When the price of a resource goes up, firms will use lower-cost substitute inputs and cut back on their use of the more expensive resource.

Typically, there are many ways producers can reduce their use of a more expensive resource. For example, if the price of oak lumber increases, furniture manufacturers will use other wood varieties, metals, and plastics more intensely. Similarly, if the price of copper tubing increases, construction firms and plumbers will substitute plastic pipe for it. Sometimes producers will alter the style and dimensions of a product in order to use less of a more expensive resource. Relocation is also a substitution strategy. For example, if the price of office space and land increases in the downtown area of a large city, firms may move to the suburbs. The degree to which firms will be able to cut back on a more

EXHIBIT 2
The Demand Curve for a Resource

As the price of a resource increases, producers that use the resource intensely will (1) turn to substitute resources and (2) face higher costs, which will lead to higher product prices and lower output. At the lower rate of output, producers will use less of the resource that increased in price. Both of these factors contribute to the inverse relationship between the price and amount demanded of a resource.

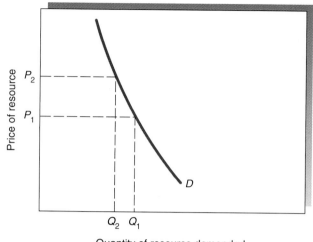

expensive resource will vary. The easier it is to turn to substitutes, the more elastic the demand for a resource is. *Other things being constant, the demand for a resource will be more elastic when more and better substitutes are available for it.*

Substitution in Consumption

An increase in the price of a resource will lead to higher costs of production and thus higher prices for the products that the input helps to produce. Faced with these higher prices, *consumers* will turn to substitute products and cut back on their purchases of the more expensive products. In turn, a smaller quantity of resources (including less of the one that rose in price) will be required to produce the smaller amount of the product demanded by consumers at the now higher price.

To illustrate the substitution-in-consumption effect, suppose the United Auto Workers negotiates a substantial wage increase for employees in the U.S. automobile industry. The large wage increase will push the costs of American automakers upward. As the price of domestically produced autos rises, many consumers will switch to substitutes, particularly automobiles produced abroad. The sales of American producers will fall, lowering the quantity of labor demanded (and employment) in the U.S. automobile industry.

Other things being constant, the more elastic the demand for a product, the more elastic the demand for the resources used to make it. This relationship stems from the derived nature of resource demand. An increase in the price of a product for which consumer demand is highly elastic will cause a sharp fall in the sales of the good. As a result, there will be a relatively sharp fall in the demand for the resources used to produce it.

In summary, the demand elasticity of a resource will vary with the ease of substitution when it comes to both production and consumption. The demand for a resource will tend to be elastic when it is easy to substitute other resources for it in production and when the demand for goods produced with it is relatively elastic. Conversely, the demand for a resource will tend to be inelastic when it is difficult to find good substitutes for it in production and the demand for the goods produced with it is more inelastic.

How Time Changes the Demand for Resources

The elasticity of resource demand is also influenced by time. It takes time for producers to fully adjust to a change in the price of a resource. Typically, a producer will be unable to

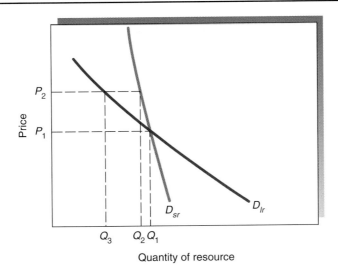

EXHIBIT 3
Time and the Demand
Elasticity of Resources

The demand for a resource
will be more elastic (1) the
easier it is for firms to
switch to substitute inputs
and (2) the more elastic
the consumer demand for
the products the resource
helps produce. As the
graph here shows, demand
for a resource in the long
run (D_{lr}) is nearly always
more elastic than demand
in the short run (D_{sr}).

immediately alter a production process or redesign a product to use less of a more
expensive input or more of an input that has declined in price. Consumers may also find it
difficult to alter their consumption patterns quickly in response to price changes. For example, if the price of cigarettes rises due to a tax increase, cigarette smokers may find it
initially hard to reduce their consumption of cigarettes very much. Over time, however,
the higher price will cause more and more smokers to smoke less. Thus, the demand for a
resource generally becomes more elastic with the passage of time.

Exhibit 3 shows how time affects the elasticity of resource demand. Since it is generally difficult to substitute quickly away from a more expensive resource, demand is relatively
inelastic in the short run. Notice how steep, or inelastic, the slope of the short-run demand
curve (D_{sr}) is. An increase in price from P_1 to P_2 will lead to only a small fall in the quantity
of the resource used (from Q_1 to Q_2). Given more time, however, producers will be able to
make a larger substitution away from the more expensive resource. The increase in price to
P_2 causes a much larger fall in the quantity demanded (to Q_3) over time. The slope of the
long-run demand curve (D_{lr}) is not so steep, as you can see, but is more elastic. In the long
run, the demand for a resource is nearly always more elastic than in the short run.

Things That Change the Demand for Resources

Like the demand schedule for a product, the entire demand curve for a resource may shift.
There are three major reasons why:

1. *A change in the demand for a product will cause a similar change in the demand for
   the resources used to make the product.* An increase in the demand for a consumer
   good simultaneously increases the demand for resources needed to make it. Conversely, a fall in the demand for a product will lower the demand for the resources
   used to make it. Recent changes in the tax-preparation industry illustrate this point.
   Starting in the mid-1990s, the demand for tax-preparation software increased
   sharply, driven by the introduction of easy-to-use software and the growing use of
   personal computers. This led to an increase in the demand for programmers to produce the tax-preparation software, and their employment increased rapidly as a result. In contrast, the higher consumer demand for tax-preparation software meant
   falling demand for tax accountants and other tax preparers. This reallocation of resources is a natural and integral part of how markets respond to changes in product
   demands.

The demand for resources is a derived demand. A more complex tax code would increase the demand for (and thus the wages of) accountants, whereas a simpler tax code would have the opposite effect.

2. *Changes in the productivity of a resource will alter demand—the higher the productivity of a resource, the greater will be the demand for it.* As the productivity of a resource increases, so does its value to potential users. Improvements in the quality of a resource—in the case of workers, their skill levels—will increase the productivity of the resource and therefore the demand for it. For example, as workers gain valuable new knowledge and/or upgrade their skills, they enhance their productivity and essentially move into a different skill category—one where demand is greater.

The productivity of a resource will also depend on the amount of other resources used in the production process. In general, additional capital will tend to increase the productivity of labor. For example, someone with a dump truck can haul more material than the same person with a wheelbarrow. The quantity and quality of the tools with which you work will significantly affect your productivity.

Improvements in technology also tend to increase the productivity of resources, including labor. For example, technological advances in word processing equipment have enhanced the productivity of secretaries, journalists, lawyers, and writers. Similarly, computers have substantially increased the productivity of typesetters, telephone operators, scientific researchers, and workers in many other occupations. The link between technological advances and worker productivity helps explain why improvements in technology generally do not exert a large negative impact on employment, even in the occupations most directly affected. Of course, when firms substitute new technology for labor services, the demand for labor will fall. However, the new technology also makes the labor more productive, which, in turn, increases the demand for labor services. This second effect will partially, and sometimes more than completely, offset the first effect.

The productivity-demand linkage sheds light on why wage rates in the United States, Canada, Western Europe, and Japan are higher than in most other areas of the world. Given the skill level of workers, the technology, and the capital equipment with which they work, individuals in these countries produce more goods and services per hour of labor than workers in most other countries. In turn, the demand for their labor (relative to supply) is greater because of their high productivity. Essentially, the workers' greater productivity leads to their higher wage rates.

3. *A change in the price of a related resource will affect the demand for the original resource.* A rise in the price of a resource will cause the demand for substitute resources to expand. For example, when the price of lumber increases, the demand for bricks will increase as home builders switch to building more brick homes and fewer wood homes. Conversely, an increase in the price of a resource that is a *complement* to a given resource will decrease the demand for the given resource. For example, higher lumber prices will tend to lower the demand for nails.

MARGINAL PRODUCTIVITY AND THE FIRM'S HIRING DECISION

How does a producer decide whether to employ additional units of a resource? As for other decisions, the marginal benefit relative to the marginal cost provides the answer. Because firms are mostly price takers in resource markets (meaning they can hire as many units of the resource as they wish without affecting the market price of the resource), the marginal cost of hiring one more worker is simply the worker's wage, whereas the marginal cost of purchasing a machine is its price. These represent the increase in the firm's costs from employing one more unit of the resource. But what about the marginal benefit of the resource to the firm? It is measured by the increase in the firm's revenue from employing one more unit of the resource. This is called the resource's **marginal revenue product** (*MRP*). A profit-maximizing firm will hire an additional unit of the resource only if the marginal revenue product exceeds the cost of employing the resource.

> **Marginal revenue product (*MRP*)**
> The change in the total revenue of a firm that results from the employment of one additional unit of a resource. The marginal revenue product of an input is equal to its marginal product multiplied by the marginal revenue of the good or service produced.

Suppose that a retail store is considering hiring a security guard for $25 per hour to help reduce shoplifting. If the security guard could prevent $20 worth of shoplifting per hour, should the profit-maximizing firm hire the guard? Because the marginal cost of employing the security guard (the wage of $25) is higher than the guard's marginal revenue product (the $20 reduction in shoplifting per hour), the wise decision is for the firm not to hire the security guard. Hiring the guard will lower the firm's profit by $5 per hour. The guard should be employed only if the reduction in shoplifting exceeds the guard's wage cost. In most situations, the direct impact of hiring an additional resource on a firm's revenue is not as clear, so let's take a closer look at the firm's decision and how marginal revenue product is determined.

Using a Variable Resource with a Fixed Resource

When an additional unit of the resource is used relative to a fixed amount of other resources, the firm's output will increase by an amount equal to the resource's **marginal product** (*MP*). Because marginal product is measured in units of physical output, it is sometimes referred to as marginal physical product. How much additional revenue can the firm derive from the employment of the resource? Recall that **marginal revenue** (*MR*) is the increase in the firm's revenue that results from the sale of each additional unit of output. Thus, a resource's marginal revenue product is equal to the marginal product of the resource multiplied by the marginal revenue of the good or service produced. *When the law of diminishing returns sets in, the marginal product of a resource will fall as employment of the resource expands. As a result, the marginal revenue product of a resource will also fall as employment expands.*

> **Marginal product (*MP*)**
> The change in total output that results from the employment of one additional unit of a resource.

> **Marginal revenue (*MR*)**
> The change in a firm's total revenue that results from the production and sale of one additional unit of output.

The relationship between the marginal revenue a firm gets from selling an additional unit of output and the price for which it is sold is different for *price-taker* firms than for *price searchers,* however. Because a price-taker firm sells all units produced at the same price, the price taker's marginal revenue will be equal to the market price of the product. The price searcher, however, must reduce the price of all units in order to expand the number of units sold. Consequently, the price searcher's marginal revenue will be less than the sales price of the units. The marginal product of a resource multiplied by the selling price of the product is called the resource's **value marginal product** (*VMP*). *For a price-taker firm, the* **MRP** *of a resource is equal to its* **VMP** *because price and marginal revenue*

> **Value of marginal product (*VMP*)**
> The marginal product of a resource multiplied by the selling price of the product it helps produce. For a price-taker firm, marginal revenue product (*MRP*) will be equal to the value marginal product (*VMP*).

EXHIBIT 4
The Short-Run Demand Schedule of a Firm

Compute-Accounting Inc. uses computer technology and data entry operators to provide accounting services in a competitive market. For each accounting statement processed, the firm receives a $200 fee (column 4). Given the firm's current fixed capital, column 2 shows how total output changes as additional data entry operators are hired. The marginal revenue product (*MRP*) schedule (column 6) indicates how hiring an additional operator affects the total revenue of the firm. Since a profit-maximizing firm will hire an additional employee if, and only if, the employee adds more to revenues than to costs, the marginal revenue product curve is the firm's short-run demand curve for the resource (see Exhibit 5).

UNITS OF VARIABLE FACTOR (DATA ENTRY OPERATORS) (1)	TOTAL OUTPUT (ACCOUNTING STATEMENTS PROCESSED PER WEEK) (2)	MARGINAL PRODUCT (CHANGE IN COLUMN 2 DIVIDED BY CHANGE IN COLUMN 1) (3)	SALES PRICE PER STATEMENT (4)	TOTAL REVENUE (2) × (4) (5)	MRP (3) × (4) (6)
0	0.0	—	$200	$ 0	—
1	5.0	5.0	200	1,000	1,000
2	9.0	4.0	200	1,800	800
3	12.0	3.0	200	2,400	600
4	14.0	2.0	200	2,800	400
5	15.5	1.5	200	3,100	300
6	16.5	1.0	200	3,300	200
7	17.0	0.5	200	3,400	100

are equal. For a price-searcher firm, however, the **MRP** *of a resource will be lower than its* **VMP** *because marginal revenue is less than price.*

Using these measures, **Exhibit 4** illustrates how a firm decides how much of a resource to employ. Compute-Accounting Inc. uses computer equipment and data entry operators to supply clients with monthly accounting statements. The firm is a price taker: it sells its service in a competitive market for $200 per statement. Given the fixed quantity of computer equipment owned by Compute-Accounting, column 2 shows how much total output (quantity of accounting statements) the firm can produce with different numbers of data entry operators. One data entry operator can process five statements per week. When two operators are employed, nine statements can be completed. Column 2 indicates how total output is expected to change as additional data entry operators are employed. Column 3 presents the marginal product schedule for data entry operators. Column 6, the *MRP* schedule, shows how the employment of each additional operator affects total revenue. Due to the law of diminishing returns, both the marginal product and the marginal revenue product of workers decline as additional operators are employed.

Because Compute-Accounting is a price taker, the marginal revenue product and the value marginal product of labor are equal. Thus, the marginal revenue product of labor (column 6) can be calculated by multiplying the marginal product (column 3) times the sales price of an accounting statement (column 4).

How does Compute-Accounting decide how many operators to employ? *Answer:* It analyzes the benefits relative to the costs. As additional operators are employed, the output of processed statements (column 2) will increase, which will expand total revenue (column 5). Employing additional operators, though, will also add to production costs because the operators must be paid. Applying the profit-maximization rule, Compute-Accounting will hire additional operators as long as their employment adds more to revenues than to costs. This will be the case as long as the *MRP* (column 6) of the data entry operators exceeds their wage rate. At a weekly wage of $1,000, Compute-Accounting would hire only one operator. If the weekly wage dropped to $800, two operators would be hired. At still lower wage rates, additional operators would be hired.

Profit-maximizing firms will expand their employment of each variable resource until the **MRP** *of the resource (the firm's additional revenue generated by the resource) is*

just equal to the price of the resource (the firm's marginal cost of employing the resource).
This profit-maximization rule applies to all firms, price takers and price searchers alike.

MRP and the Firm's Demand Curve for a Resource

Using the data in Exhibit 4, we can construct Compute-Accounting's demand curve for data entry operators. Recall that the height of a demand curve shows the maximum price (in this case, the wage) that the buyer (the firm) would be willing to pay for the unit. Because the marginal revenue product of the first data entry operator is $1,000, the firm would be willing to hire this worker only up to a maximum price of $1,000. Because of this relationship, as **Exhibit 5** shows, a firm's short-run demand curve for a resource is precisely the *MRP* curve for the resource.[3] Using this demand curve yields the identical solutions as the table. At a weekly wage of $1,000, Compute-Accounting would hire only one operator. If the weekly wage dropped to $800, two operators would be hired. At still lower wage rates, additional operators would be hired. Underlying the downward-sloping demand curve is the law of diminishing returns, which causes *MP,* and thus *MRP,* to fall as more workers are hired, when at least one factor of production is fixed.

The location of the firm's *MRP* curve depends on (1) the price of the product, (2) the productivity of the resource, and (3) the amount of other resources with which the resource is working. Changes in any one of these three factors will cause the *MRP* curve to shift. For example, if Compute-Accounting purchased additional computer equipment, making it possible for the operators to complete more statements each week, the *MRP* curve for labor would increase (shift outward). This increase in the quantity of the other resources working with labor would increase labor's productivity.

Multiple Resources and How Much to Use of Each

So far, we have analyzed the firm's hiring decision assuming that it used one variable resource (labor) and one fixed resource. Production, though, usually involves the use of many resources. How should these resources be combined to produce the product? We can answer this question by considering the conditions for either profit maximization or cost minimization.

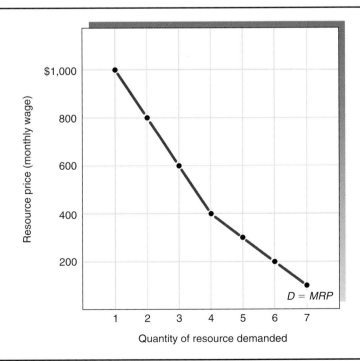

EXHIBIT 5
The Firm's Demand Curve for a Resource

The firm's demand curve for a resource will reflect the marginal revenue product (*MRP*) of the resource. In the short run, it will slope downward because the marginal product of the resource will fall as more of it is used with a fixed amount of other resources. The location of the MRP curve will depend on (1) the price of the product, (2) the productivity of the resource, and (3) the quantity of other factors working with the resource.

[3] Strictly speaking, this is true only for a variable resource that is employed with a fixed amount of another factor.

Maximizing Profits When Multiple Resources Are Used

The same decision-making considerations apply when the firm employs several factors of production. The profit-maximizing firm will expand its use of a resource as long as the *MRP* of the resource exceeds its employment cost. If we assume that resources are perfectly divisible, the profit-maximizing decision rule implies that, in equilibrium, the *MRP* of each resource will be equal to the price of the resource. Therefore, the following conditions will exist for the profit-maximizing firm:

> *MRP* of skilled labor = Price (wage rate) of skilled labor
>
> *MRP* of unskilled labor = Price (wage rate) of unskilled labor
>
> *MRP* of machine A = Price (explicit or implicit rental price) of machine A and so on, for all other factors

Cost Minimization When Multiple Resources Are Used

To maximize its profits, clearly the firm must produce the profit-maximizing output at the least possible cost. If the firm is minimizing costs, then the marginal dollar expenditure for each resource will have the same impact on output as an additional dollar expenditure on other resources used to produce the product. ***Factors of production will be employed such that the marginal product per last dollar spent on each factor is the same for all factors.***

To see why, consider a situation in which a $100 expenditure on labor caused output to rise by ten units, whereas an additional $100 expenditure on machines generated only a five-unit expansion in output. In this case, the firm can produce five more units of output by spending the $100 on labor instead of machines. By substituting labor for machines, it will reduce its *per-unit* cost.

If the marginal dollar spent on one resource increases output by a larger amount than a dollar expenditure on other resources, costs can always be reduced by substituting resources with a high marginal product per dollar expenditure for those with a low one. Substitution will continue to reduce unit costs (and add to profit) until the marginal product per dollar expenditure on each resource is equalized. This will occur because as additional units of a resource are hired, their marginal product will fall. Thus, the proportional relationship between the price of each resource and its marginal product will eventually be achieved.

Therefore, the following condition exists when per-unit costs are minimized:

$$\frac{\textbf{MP } \textit{of skilled labor}}{\textbf{Price } \textit{of skilled labor}} = \frac{\textbf{MP } \textit{of unskilled labor}}{\textbf{Price } \textit{of unskilled labor}} = \frac{\textbf{MP } \textit{of machine A}}{\textbf{Price (rental value) } \textit{of machine A}}$$

This relationship explains why workers with different skill levels earn different wages. If skilled workers are twice as productive as unskilled workers, then their wage rates will tend to be twice those of unskilled workers. For example, suppose that a construction firm hiring workers to hang doors is choosing among skilled and unskilled workers. If skilled door hangers can complete four doors per hour, while unskilled workers can hang only two doors per hour, a cost-minimizing firm would hire only skilled workers—as long as their wages are less than twice the wages of unskilled workers. On the other hand, only unskilled workers would be hired if the wages of skilled workers are more than twice that of unskilled workers. Because of competition, wages across skill categories will tend to mirror productivity differences.

Low wages do not necessarily mean low cost. In other words, it is not always cheaper to hire the lowest wage workers. It is not just wages, but rather wages *relative to productivity* that matter. If the wages of skilled workers are twice those of unskilled workers, it will still be cheaper to hire additional skilled workers if their marginal productivity (output per hour) is more than twice that of the unskilled workers.

The importance of wages relative to productivity explains why relatively few firms moved to Mexico following the passage of the North American Free Trade Agreement (NAFTA). Some forecasted there would be a "giant sucking sound" caused by the movement of both firms and jobs to Mexico. Why didn't the low wages of Mexican workers cause firms to relocate? *Answer:* Although wages are low in Mexico, so, too, is worker productivity. Because of this, many firms are able to achieve lower production costs in the high-wage United States than in low-wage Mexico. Suppose that the average wage rate of a U.S. worker is $12 per hour and average hourly productivity is thirty-six units, while the average wage is $4 per hour in Mexico and average productivity is eight units. To maximize profits (or minimize costs), a firm should choose to operate where the *MP/P* is greatest. In the United States, the firm would get three units of output (36/12) per dollar spent on labor. In Mexico, the firm would get only two units of output (8/4) per dollar spent on labor. Thus, a cost-minimizing firm would want to locate in the United States despite the higher wages, because the productivity difference more than makes up for the wage difference. Although U.S. wages are three times higher, the productivity of workers in the United States is four and a half times higher. This more than compensates for the higher wage cost.

The Main Conclusion of the Marginal Productivity Theory of Employment

Firms minimize their per-unit costs of production when they hire additional units of each resource as long as the units' marginal productivity generates revenues in excess of their costs. Firms that minimize per-unit costs and maximize profit will never pay more for a unit of input, whether it is skilled labor, a machine, or an acre of land, than the input is worth to them. The worth of a unit of input to the firm is determined by how much additional revenue (marginal revenue product) is expected from its employment.

In the real world, it's sometimes difficult to measure the marginal product of a resource. And, as we have said, the marginal product of a resource is influenced by the other factors with which it is employed. But do decision makers really think like this—in terms of equating the marginal product/price ratio (*MP/P*) for each factor of production? Probably not. Their thought process is probably going to be something more like this: "Can we reduce costs by using more of one resource and less of another?" However, regardless of how managers think about the problem, when a firm maximizes its profits and minimizes its costs, its marginal product/price ratio will be equal for all factors of production. The results will be *as if* the firm followed the cost-minimization, decision-making rule just presented. Furthermore, competitive forces will more or less force firms to follow this rule—whether or not they're aware they're following it. Firms that fail to do so will be unable to compete successfully with rivals achieving lower per-unit costs.

The marginal productivity theory explains why the demand for some resources is higher or lower than the demand for other resources. Of course, resource prices will also be influenced by the supply of resources. We now turn to that topic.

THE SUPPLY OF RESOURCES

Just as benefits and costs direct the choices of employers, so, too, will they guide the actions of resource suppliers. Resource owners will supply their services to an employer only if they perceive that the benefits of doing so exceed their costs (the value of the other things they could do with their time or resources). Because of this, employers must offer resource owners at least as good a deal as they can get elsewhere. For example, if an employer does not offer a potential employee pay, benefits, and working conditions as good as or better than others he or she can get, the employer will be unable to hire that worker.

Resource owners will supply their services to those who offer them the best employment alternative. Other things being constant, as the price of a specific resource (for example, engineering services, craft labor, or wheat farmland) increases, the incentive of potential suppliers to provide the resource increases.

An increase in the price of a resource will lure resource suppliers into the market. A decrease will cause them to shift into other activities. Therefore, as **Exhibit 6** illustrates, the supply curve for a specific resource will slope upward to the right.[4]

---

[4]Although the supply for nonhuman resources will always slope upward, the supply of labor at very high wage rates can become backward bending. As wages rise, individuals will substitute toward more work, but simultaneously the higher income will cause them to desire more leisure. At very high wage rates the income effect might dominate, causing a negative relationship between wage rates and quantity of labor supplied in this range. For example, at a wage of $10,000 per hour, many individuals would probably supply fewer hours of work than at $500 per hour!

EXHIBIT 6
The Supply of a Resource

As the price of a resource increases, individuals have a greater incentive to supply it. Therefore, a direct relationship will exist between the price of a resource and the quantity supplied.

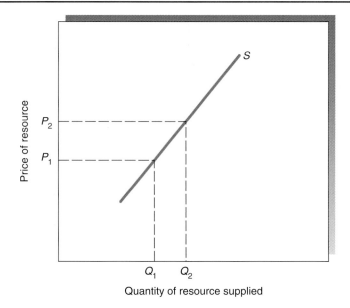

Short-Run Versus Long-Run Resource Supply

Like demand, supply in resource markets can be different in the short run than in the long run. If the wage rate for certified public accountants (CPAs) rose, for example, we would expect more workers supplying their services as CPAs. But where do these additional CPAs come from? In the short run, the additional supply must come from people who are already CPAs but are currently doing other things. The higher wages might induce some college accounting professors and some stay-at-home spouses with accounting credentials to move into employment as CPAs. In the short run, however, there isn't enough time to alter the availability of a resource through investment in human and physical capital. In contrast, in the long run, resource suppliers have time to adjust their investment choices in response to a change in resource prices. With time, the higher wages for CPAs will cause more students to major in accounting and other people to pursue the coursework needed to become CPAs. Higher resource prices will increase the quantity supplied in both the short run and the long run, but the response will be greater in the long run. Therefore, as **Exhibit 7** shows, the long-run supply of a resource will be more elastic than the short-run supply.

Short-Run Supply

Resource mobility
The ease with which factors of production are able to move among alternative uses. Resources that can easily be transferred to a different use or location are said to be highly mobile. Resources with few alternative uses are immobile.

The short-run supply response to a change in price is determined by how easily the resource can be transferred from one use to another—that is, **resource mobility**. The supply of resources with high mobility will be relatively elastic, even in the short run. On the other hand, resources that have few alternative uses (or are not easily transferable) are said to be immobile. The short-run supply of immobile resources will be highly inelastic.

Consider the mobility of labor. Within a skill category (for example, plumber, store manager, accountant, or secretary), labor will be highly mobile within the same geographic area. Movements between geographic areas and from one skill category to another are more costly to accomplish, though. Labor will thus be less mobile for movements of this variety. In addition, because it is easier for a high-skilled person to perform effectively in a lower-skill position than vice versa, short-run mobility will tend to decline as the skill level of the occupation rises. Thus, the short-run supply curve in high-skill occupations like that of an architect, mechanical engineer, and medical surgeon is usually quite inelastic.

What about the mobility of land? Land is highly mobile among uses when location doesn't matter. For example, the same land can often be used to raise corn, wheat, soybeans, or oats. As a result, the supply of land allocated to the production of each of these commodities will be highly responsive to changes in their relative prices. Undeveloped

EXHIBIT 7
Time and the Elasticity of Supply for Resources

If the wage rate for certified public accountants (CPAs) rises, for example, to P_2, we would expect more workers to supply CPA services. Because it takes time to be trained as a CPA, though, the quantity of CPA services supplied in the short run (S_{sr}) won't increase by much—just to Q_2. The supply of CPA services is therefore relatively inelastic in the short run. In the long run, though, it is more elastic and the quantity supplied increases to Q_3.

(Figure labels: S_{sr}; S_{lr}; "In the short run, quantity supplied increases to Q_2"; "Given more time, quantity supplied increases to Q_3"; vertical axis "Price (wage)" with P_2, P_1; horizontal axis "Quantity of CPA services per unit of time" with Q_1 Q_2 Q_3.)

land on the outskirts of cities is particularly mobile among uses. It can be used for agriculture, but it can also quickly be subdivided and used for a housing development or a shopping center. Because land is physically immobile, you might think its supply is unresponsive to changes in price when it comes to how desirable it is (or isn't) due to its location. You can't move it to make it more desirable and get a better price, obviously. You can, however, expand its usable space by constructing multiple-story buildings, for example. As the demand for a given location increases, higher and higher multilevel construction will be justified. This is why tall buildings are generally located in city centers, for example—because the demand for space is highest in these locations.

Machines are typically not very mobile among uses. A machine developed to produce airplane wings is seldom of much use when it comes to producing automobiles, appliances, or other products. Steel mills cannot easily be converted to produce aluminum. There are, of course, some exceptions. Trucks can typically be used to haul a variety of products. Building space can often be converted from one use to another. In the short run, however, immobility and inelasticity of supply characterize much of our physical capital.

Long-Run Supply

In the long run, the supply of resources can change substantially. Machines wear out, human skills depreciate, and even the fertility of land declines with use and erosion. These factors reduce the supply of resources. On the other hand, investment can expand the supply of productive resources, including machines, buildings, and durable assets. Correspondingly, investments in training and education can, over time, develop and improve the skills of future labor force participants. Thus, the supply of both physical and human resources in the long run is determined primarily by investment and depreciation.

As the price of a resource increases, more and more people will make the investments necessary to supply the resource. This will be true for human as well as physical resources. Examples abound. As the spread of the computer revolution pushed up the salaries of programmers, systems analysts, and computer technicians during the early 1990s, there was a sharp increase in the number of students training for jobs in these areas. In the late 1990s and early 2000s, attractive salaries for registered nurses led to both new programs and expanded enrollments. Higher salaries for lawyers stimulate law school enrollments. According to Harvard University economist Richard Freeman, a 1 percent increase in starting law salaries causes enrollment in the first year of law school to rise by 2 percent.

The long run, of course, is not a specified length of time. Investment can increase the availability of some resources fairly quickly. For example, it does not take very long to train

The supply curve for truck drivers will be considerably more elastic than the supply curve for doctors. Can you explain why?

additional over-the-road truck drivers. However, it takes a long time to train physicians, dentists, lawyers, and pharmacists. Higher earnings in these occupations may have only a small impact on their current availability. Additional investment will flow into these areas, but typically it will be several years before there is a substantial increase in the quantity supplied.

SUPPLY, DEMAND, AND RESOURCE PRICES

In a market economy, resource prices will, of course, be determined by the forces of supply and demand and bring the choices of buyers and sellers into line with each other. **Exhibit 8** illustrates how the forces of supply and demand push the market wage rates of engineers toward equilibrium, where quantity demanded and quantity supplied are equal. Equilibrium is achieved when the price (wage rate) for engineering services is P_1. Given the market conditions illustrated by Exhibit 8, an excess supply is present if the price of engineering services exceeds P_1. Some engineers will be unable to find jobs at the above-equilibrium wage. This excess supply of engineers will cause the wage rate for engineers to fall. This will cause some of the engineers to look for jobs in other fields, and quantity supplied will fall, pushing the market toward equilibrium. In contrast, if the resource price is less than P_1, excess demand is present. Employers are unable to hire the amount of engineering services they want at a below-equilibrium resource price. Rather than doing without the resource, employers will attempt to hire engineers away from other firms by bidding the price up to P_1 and thereby eliminating the excess demand.

How will a resource market adjust to an unexpected change in market conditions? Suppose that there is a sharp increase in the demand for houses, apartments, and office buildings. The increase in demand for these products will also increase the demand for resources required for their construction. Thus, the demand for resources such as steel, lumber, brick, and the labor services of carpenters, architects, and construction engineers will increase. **Exhibit 9** shows the increase in demand for new houses and buildings (part a) and the accompanying increase in demand for construction engineers. The market demand for the services of construction engineers increases from D_1 to D_2 (part b), and initially there is a sharp rise in their wages (price increases from P_1 to P_2). The higher wages will motivate additional people to get the education and training necessary to become a construction engineer. Over time, the entry of the newly trained construction engineers will

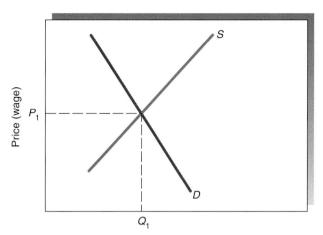

EXHIBIT 8
Equilibrium in a
Resource Market

The market demand for a resource, such as engineering services, is a downward-sloping curve, reflecting the declining *MRP* of the resource. The market supply curve slopes upward because higher resource prices (wage rates) will motivate people to supply more of the resource. Market price will move toward equilibrium (P_1), where the quantity demanded and quantity supplied are in balance.

EXHIBIT 9
Adjusting to Dynamic Change

An increase in the demand for housing and commercial buildings (part a) will lead to an increase in demand for the services of construction engineers (part b) and other resources used in the construction industry. Initially, the increase in the resource price will be substantial, jumping from P_1 to P_2 (point *a* versus point *b* in the graph). The increase will be particularly sharp if the supply of the resource is highly inelastic in the short run. The higher resource price will attract additional human capital investment and, with time, the resource supply curve will become more elastic, which will moderate the price (or wage) increase to P_3 (point *c*).

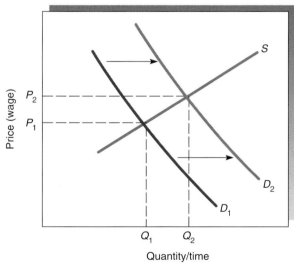

(a) Product market—new houses
and commercial buildings

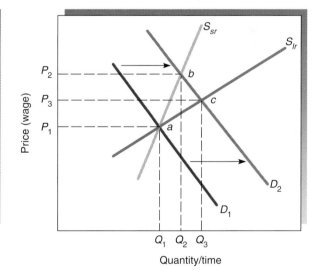

(b) Resource market—services
of construction engineers

increase the elasticity of the resource supply curve. As these new construction engineers eventually enter the occupation, the supply curve will become more elastic (S_{lr} rather than S_{sr}), which will place downward pressure on wages in the occupation (the move from *b* to *c*). Therefore, as part (b) of Exhibit 9 illustrates, the long-run price increase (to P_3) will be less than the short-run increase (to P_2).

Workers in occupations such as nursing that require substantial skill and education will generally earn higher wages than those in occupations requiring little training or experience.

The supply response and market adjustment for other resources—physical as well as human—will be similar. For example, an unexpected construction boom will generally cause sharp initial increases in the prices of lumber, bricks, and other building materials. With time, however, additional investment will increase the availability of these resources and moderate the increase in their price, just as additional investment in human capital eventually moderated the wage increases of the construction engineers. The market adjustment to an unexpected reduction in demand for a resource is the same. The price falls further in the short run than in the long run. At the lower price, some resource suppliers will use their talents in other areas, so the incentive for potential new suppliers to offer the resource will be less. With time, the quantity of the resource supplied will decline, moderating the reduction in its price. Those with the poorest alternatives (that is, lowest opportunity cost) will continue to provide the resource at the lower prices. Those with better alternatives will look for other opportunities.

THE COORDINATING FUNCTION OF RESOURCE PRICES

Throughout this text, we have stressed that profit is a reward earned by producers who increase the value of resources, whereas loss is a punishment imposed on producers who reduce the value of resources they are using. The key links in this process are the prices of the products being sold and the prices of the resources used in production. As we have learned, a firm's profits are its revenues (which are determined by the product's sales price) minus its costs (which are determined by the prices of the resources it uses). The price of the product measures the value that consumers place on that product. The price of the resources, however, measures the value that consumers place on *other products* that could be produced with those same resources. Let us explore the importance of this link in a little more detail.

As we have shown, the price of a resource will equal the resource's marginal revenue product when the resource market is in equilibrium. The resource's marginal revenue product depends upon the price consumers are willing to pay for the output (how they value it) produced by the resource. We also learned that when a firm wishes to hire a resource, it must offer the owner of the resource a price at least as attractive as the resource could have earned elsewhere—that is, the resource's *MRP* in its next best alternative employment. Thus, the price a firm pays for a resource is equal to the resource's value (as measured by the consumer) in the alternative use. If the output the firm produces with that resource can be sold at a higher price than the price of the alternative outputs, then and only then will the firm earn a profit. Thus, profit is a reward to those entrepreneurs who are able to see and act on opportunities to put resources to higher-valued uses. Because consumer tastes and preferences continuously change, though, so do product and resource prices. As a result, opportunities for their use are created and destroyed on a daily basis in a market economy.

Pulling things together, our analysis indicates that prices in resource markets play a vitally important role. These prices coordinate the actions of the firms demanding factors of production and the households supplying them. Resource prices provide users with both information about the scarcity of the resources they're using and the incentive to conserve them in production. They also provide suppliers with an incentive to learn skills and provide resources—particularly those that are intensely demanded by users. Without the use of resource markets and the price incentives they provide, efficient use and wise conservation of resources would be extremely difficult to achieve.[5]

LOOKING AHEAD

The analysis of this chapter can be applied to a broad range of economic issues. The next chapter will focus on the labor market and earnings differences among workers. Later, we will focus on the capital market and the allocation of resources over time. The operation of these two markets plays an important role in determining the distribution of income, a topic that we will also analyze in detail in a subsequent chapter.

! KEY POINTS

▼ Productive assets and services are bought and sold in resource markets. There are two broad classes of productive resources: (1) nonhuman capital and (2) human capital.

▼ The demand for resources is derived from the demand for products that the resources help produce. The quantity of a resource demanded is inversely related to its price because of substitutions made by both producers and consumers.

▼ The demand curve for a resource, like the demand for a product, can shift. The major factors that increase the demand for a resource are an increase in (1) demand for products that use the resource, (2) the productivity of the resource, and (3) the price of substitute resources.

▼ Profit-maximizing firms will hire additional units of a resource up to the point where the marginal revenue product (*MRP*) of the resource equals its price. With multiple inputs, firms will expand their use of each until the marginal product divided by the price (*MP/P*) is equal across all inputs. When real-world

decision makers minimize per-unit costs, the outcome will be as if they had followed these mathematical procedures, even though they may not consciously have done so.

▼ The amount of a resource supplied will be directly related to its price. The supply of a resource will be more elastic in the long run than in the short run. In the long run, investment can increase the supply of both physical and human resources.

▼ The prices of resources are determined by supply and demand. Changes in the market prices of resources will influence the decisions of both users and suppliers. Higher resource prices give users a greater incentive to turn to substitutes and suppliers a greater incentive to provide more of the resource.

▼ Changes in resource prices in response to changing market conditions are essential for the efficient allocation of resources in a dynamic world. Profit is a reward to the entrepreneur who is able to see and act on opportunities to put resources to higher-valued uses.

---

[5]Analysis of energy consumption under central planning illustrates this point. The centrally planned economies used more energy per unit of output and their energy consumption was less responsive to changes in price than it was in economies that used markets to allocate energy. For evidence on these points, see Mikhail S. Bernstam, *The Wealth of Nations and the Environment* (London: Institute of Economic Affairs, 1991).

? CRITICAL ANALYSIS QUESTIONS

1. "The demand for resources is a derived demand." What is meant by that statement? Why is the employment of a resource inversely related to its price?

2. How does a firm decide whether or not to employ an additional unit of a resource? What determines the combination of skilled and unskilled workers employed by a firm?

*3. Use the information in Exhibit 4 of this chapter to answer the following:
   a. How many employees (operators) would Compute-Accounting hire at a weekly wage of $250 if it were attempting to maximize profits?
   b. What would the firm's maximum profit be if its fixed costs were $1,500 per week?
   c. Suppose that there were a decline in demand for accounting services that reduced the market price per monthly statement to $150. At this demand level, how many employees would Compute-Accounting hire at $250 per week in the short run? Would Compute-Accounting be able to stay in business at the lower market price? Explain.

*4. Are productivity gains the major source of higher wages? If so, how does one account for the rising real wages of barbers, who, by and large, have used the same techniques for a half-century? (*Hint:* Do not forget opportunity cost and supply.)

5. Are the following statements both correct? Are they inconsistent with each other? Explain.
   a. "Firms will hire a resource only if they can make money by doing so."
   b. "In a market economy, each resource will tend to be paid according to its marginal product. Highly productive resources will command high prices, whereas less productive resources will command lower prices."

*6. Many school districts pay teachers on the basis of their highest degree earned and number of years of service (seniority). They often find it quite easy to fill the slots for English and history teachers, but very difficult to find the required number of math and science teachers. Can you explain why?

7. Suppose that you were the manager of a large retail store that was currently experiencing a shoplifting problem. Every hour, approximately $15 worth of merchandise was being stolen from your store. Suppose that a security guard would completely eliminate the shoplifting in your store. If you were interested in maximizing your profits, should you hire a security guard if the wage rate of security guards

were $20 per hour? Why or why not? What does this imply about the relationship between average shoplifting per hour in the economy and the wage rates of security guards?

*8. A dressmaker uses labor and capital (sewing machines) to produce dresses in a competitive market. Suppose the last unit of labor hired cost $1,000 per month and increased output by 100 dresses. The last unit of capital hired (rented) cost $500 per month and increased output by 80 dresses. Is the dressmaker minimizing costs? If not, what changes need to be made?

9. A firm is considering moving from the United States to Mexico. The firm pays its U.S. workers $12 per hour. Current U.S. workers have a marginal product of forty, whereas the Mexican workers have a marginal product of ten. How low would the Mexican wage have to be for the firm to reduce its wage cost per unit of output by moving to Mexico?

*10. "The earnings of engineers, doctors, and lawyers are high because lots of education is necessary to practice in these fields." Evaluate this statement.

11. Other things being constant, what impact will a highly elastic demand for a product have on the elasticity of demand for the resources used to produce the product? Explain.

*12. The following chart provides information on a firm that hires labor competitively and sells its product in a competitive market.

Units of Labor	Total Output	Marginal Product	Product Price	Total Revenue	*MRP*
1	14	___	$5	___	___
2	26	___	$5	___	___
3	37	___	$5	___	___
4	46	___	$5	___	___
5	53	___	$5	___	___
6	58	___	$5	___	___
7	62	___	$5	___	___

   a. Fill in the missing figures.
   b. How many units of labor would be employed if the market wage rate were $40? Why?
   c. What would happen to employment if the wage rate rose to $50? Explain.

13. Leisure Times Inc. employs skilled workers and capital to install hot tubs. The capital includes the tools and equipment workers use to construct and install the tubs. The installation services are sold in

a competitive market for $1,200 per hot tub. Leisure Times is able to hire workers for $2,200 per month, including the cost of wages, fringe benefits, and employment taxes. As additional workers are hired, the increase in the number of hot tubs installed is shown in the table.

Number of Workers Employed	Number of Hot Tubs Installed (per month)
1	5
2	12
3	18
4	23
5	27
6	30
7	32
8	33
9	34

a. Indicate the marginal product and *MRP* schedules of the workers.

b. What quantity of workers should Leisure Times employ to maximize its profit?

c. If a construction boom pushes the wages of skilled workers up to $2,500 per month, how many workers would Leisure Times employ to maximize its profit?

d. Suppose that strong demand for hot tubs pushes the price of installation services up to $1,500 per month. How would this affect employment of the skilled workers if the wage rate of the workers remained at $2,500 per month?

14. A recent flyer on a university campus stated that consumers should boycott sugar due to the low wages earned by laborers on sugar cane farms in Florida. If you use the notion of derived demand, what impact would a boycott on sugar have on the wages of the farm laborers in the short run? In the long run?

*Asterisk denotes questions for which answers are given in Appendix B.

CHAPTER

25

Earnings, Productivity, and the Job Market

How can I be overpaid? The boss wouldn't pay me that amount if I wasn't worth it.

—Jackie Gleason[1]

Chapter Focus

- Why do some people earn more than others?

- Are earnings differences according to race and gender the result of employment discrimination?

- Why are wages higher in the United States than in India or China?

- What is the source of higher wages? Why has the growth rate of both wages and income per capita increased during the past decade?

- Does automation destroy jobs?

---

[1]The above statement was made in response to a question about the amount he was being paid for the popular television show *The Honeymooners*, which ran during the 1950s and 1960s.

T
he earnings of U.S. workers are among the highest in the world. However, they vary widely. An unskilled laborer may earn $8 per hour, or even less. Lawyers and physicians often earn $150 per hour, or more. Dentists and even economists might receive $100 per hour. How can these variations in earnings be explained? Why are the earnings of Americans so high? How have earnings changed in recent years, and what are the factors underlying these changes? This chapter will address these topics and related issues. ■

WHY DO EARNINGS DIFFER?

The earnings of individuals in the same occupation or with the same amount of education often differ substantially. So do the earnings of people in the same family. For example, one researcher found that the average annual earnings differential between brothers was $29,564, compared with $32,742 for men paired randomly.[2] The earnings of people with the same intelligence, level of training, or amount of experience also typically differ.

Several factors combine to determine a person's earning power. Some seem to be the result of good or bad luck. Others are clearly the result of conscious decisions people make. In the previous chapter, we analyzed how the market forces of supply and demand operate to determine resource prices. Wages are a resource price, and therefore the supply and demand model can be used to examine earnings differentials among workers.

For simplicity, we have proceeded as if employees earned only money payments. In reality, most workers receive a compensation package that includes **fringe benefits** as well as money wages. The fringe benefit component typically includes things like medical insurance, life insurance, pension benefits, and paid vacation days. When we use the terms wages and earnings in the following discussions, we are referring to the total compensation package that includes both wages and fringe benefits.

The **real earnings** of all employees in a competitive market economy would be equal if: (1) all individuals were identical in preferences, skills, and background, (2) all jobs were equally attractive, and (3) workers were perfectly mobile among jobs. Given these conditions, if higher real wages existed in an area of the economy, the supply of workers in that area would expand until the wage differential were eliminated. Similarly, low wages in an area would cause workers to exit until wages there returned to normal. Of course, that's not the way things work in the real world. We all know that earnings differences are a fact of life. There are three reasons for this, and we'll discuss each next.

Fringe benefits
Benefits other than normal money wages that are supplied to employees in exchange for their labor services. Higher fringe benefits come at the expense of lower money wages.

Real earnings
Earnings adjusted for differences in the general level of prices across time periods or geographic areas. When real earnings are equal, the same bundle of goods and services can be purchased with the earnings.

Earnings Differentials Due to Nonidentical Workers

Workers differ in several important respects that affect both the supply of and demand for their services. In turn, these factors affect their wage rates. Let's consider these differences.

1. Worker productivity and specialized skills. The demand for employees who are highly productive is greater than the demand for those who are less productive. People who can operate a machine more skillfully, hit a baseball more consistently, or sell life insurance policies with greater regularity are more valuable to employers. Compared to their less skillful counterparts, these employees contribute more to the firm's revenue. Put another way, the marginal revenue product (*MRP*) of the more productive employees is higher than the *MRP* of less productive ones. In competitive labor markets, workers earn a wage equal to their marginal revenue product. As a result, the labor services of more productive workers will command higher wages in the marketplace.

Worker productivity is the result of a combination of factors, including native ability, parental training, hard work, and investment in human capital. The link between higher productivity and higher earnings motivates people to invest in themselves in order to

---

[2]Christopher Jencks, *Inequality* (New York: Basic Books, 1972), 220. Salary figures are in 2003 dollars.

EXHIBIT 1
Demand, Supply, and Wage Rates for Skilled and Unskilled Workers

The productivity—and therefore marginal product (*MP*)—of skilled workers is greater than that of unskilled workers. As a result, as part (a) illustrates, the demand for skilled workers (D_s) will exceed the demand for unskilled workers (D_u). Education and training generally enhance skills. Because upgrading one's skills through investments in human capital is costly, the supply of skilled workers (S_s) is smaller than the supply of unskilled workers at any given wage (part b). As part (c) illustrates, the wages of skilled workers are high relative to those of unskilled workers due to the strong demand and small supply of skilled workers relative to unskilled workers. (*Note:* The quantity of skilled labor employed may be far smaller, far larger, or, by accident, equal to the quantity of unskilled labor hired.)

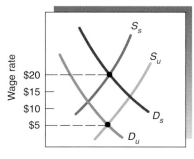

(a) Demand for skilled and unskilled labor

(b) Supply of skilled and unskilled labor

(c) Wages of skilled and unskilled labor

upgrade their knowledge and skills. If additional worker productivity didn't lead to higher earnings, people would have little incentive to incur the costs of doing so, including paying to go to college or get additional training.

Exhibit 1 shows the demand, supply, and wage rates for skilled versus unskilled workers. The productivity of skilled workers exceeds that of unskilled workers, and so does the demand for them. The vertical distance between the demand curve for skilled workers (D_s) and the demand curve for unskilled workers (D_u), shown in part (a), reflects the higher marginal product (*MP*) of skilled workers. Because human capital investments (education, training, and so on) are costly, the supply of skilled workers (S_s) will be smaller than the supply of unskilled workers (S_u). This is shown in part (b). The vertical distance between the two supply curves is the wage differential employers will need to pay skilled workers for the costs they incurred to acquire their skills.

Wages are determined by demand relative to supply (part c). Since the demand for skilled workers is large while their supply is small, the equilibrium wage of skilled workers will be high ($20 per hour). In contrast, since the supply of unskilled workers is large relative to the demand, their wage rates will be substantially lower ($5 per hour).

The skills one person gains from a year of education, vocational school, or on-the-job training might be better or worse than those of someone else. Therefore, we should not expect a rigid relationship to exist between years of education (or training) and skill level. On average, however, there is a strong positive relationship between investment in education and earnings.

Exhibit 2 presents annual earnings data according to educational level for year-round, full-time workers in 2001. Notice that the earnings of both men and women increased consistently with additional schooling. High school graduates earned almost 50 percent more than their counterparts with less than a high school education. Male college graduates working full-time, year-round earned $70,253, compared to $37,362 for men with only a high school education. In the case of women, college graduates earned $45,290, compared to $26,660 for those who only graduated from high school. The earnings of both men and women continued to increase as they earned master's and doctoral degrees.

In addition to education, a person's intelligence, native ability, and motivation also affect his or her productivity and earnings. Research shows, however, that much of the extra income earned by high-wage earners is, in fact, the result of the knowledge and skills they acquired by making an investment in additional education. (See the accompanying Applications in Economics feature, "A College Degree as a Job Market Signal.") Other studies show that on-the-job training enhances the earnings of workers.

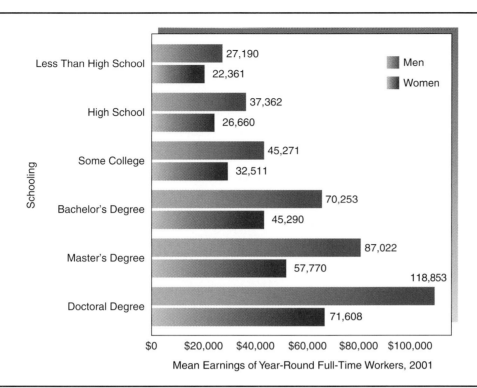

EXHIBIT 2
Education and Earnings

The accompanying graph presents data for the mean annual earnings of year-round, full-time workers based on their gender and education. Note that the earnings of both men and women increased with additional education. Even though the data are for full-time workers, the earnings of women were only about two-thirds those of men with similar education.

Source: U.S. Department of Commerce, *Current Population Reports,* P-60 Series. "Money Income in the United States: 2002," Table 9.

APPLICATIONS IN ECONOMICS

A College Degree as a Job Market Signal: Why You Should Take More Math

"Why should I take this difficult course?" "When will I ever use this?" Students often complain about taking courses not directly related to their future career. This complaint often reflects an incomplete understanding of exactly why college graduates do better in the job market than those without a college degree. A college degree increases a person's earnings because of both (1) human capital—knowledge that will directly increase job productivity and (2) signaling—"signs" to employers about a person's attitude and motivational characteristics, as well as his or her general analytical skills.

Suppose that an employer is looking for an employee who is a very good analytical problem solver. Without a way to directly observe this ability, the employer will likely look for indicators that signal this attribute. For example, even if a job doesn't directly require calculus, persons with a good calculus grade are likely to possess better problem-solving skills than those with a poor grade (or those who dodged the subject). Thus, employers may favor job applicants with good calculus grades, even if calculus isn't directly used on the job.

In other words, even if a college degree added nothing to the knowledge or skills required to do a particular job, it could still help employers identify people with abilities that are difficult to observe. Similarly, students who are admitted to and graduate from elite universities like Harvard and Yale are likely to have superior abilities relative to those attending lower-level schools. Because of this signaling device, even mediocre graduates from top universities often have better entry-level job market prospects than exceptional students from lesser-known schools. The signaling function also explains why students who choose majors others think are "hard" (like engineering, economics, or finance) generally do better in the job market than those choosing "easy" majors (like physical education, marketing, or social work).

"When will I ever use this stuff?" "When will a good grade in challenging courses like math and economics matter?" The answer to these questions is, "Soon!" They will matter most when you're searching for a job at the beginning stages of your career—when it's still difficult for employers to judge your true abilities.

An investment in human capital and development of specialized skills can protect high-wage workers from the competition of others willing to offer their services at a lower price. Few persons could develop the specialized skills of a Steven Spielberg, Tiger Woods, or Oprah Winfrey. Similarly, the supply of heart surgeons, trial lawyers, engineers, business entrepreneurs, and many other specialized workers is limited in occupations in which specific skills, knowledge, and human capital investments contribute to job performance.

What about the large salaries received by CEOs of major corporations? Decisions made by CEOs can have a huge financial impact on their companies' profitability. Because of this, a good CEO can be particularly valuable when a company is in trouble, facing new competitors, or confronting a changing technological or regulatory environment. A CEO who turns losses into profits is worth millions to the stockholders of a major corporation.

The annual earnings of star athletes, entertainers, and television personalities often run into the millions of dollars. What is the marginal revenue product of a superstar entertainer like Cameron Diaz? How many more people will go see a movie starring Diaz rather than another actress less known or less talented? If an additional 2 million or 3 million people spend $8 to attend a movie, this will generate $16 million or $24 million of additional revenue. It is easy to see how hiring a "box office" star will generate a lot more money for a movie company. In turn, competitive labor markets will ensure that big stars get paid their marginal revenue product.

Economic studies have found that the marginal revenue product of many sports and entertainment superstars is pretty much in line with their salaries.[3] However, there may be another factor at work here. The earnings in some markets resemble tournaments. In tournaments, only the top-ranked person receives the big payoff, while those who finish second receive much less. This type of compensation is called **tournament pay**.[4] This name refers to reward systems structured like golf tournaments, in which a slight difference in productivity (perhaps one or two shots) is associated with a difference in pay of several hundred thousand dollars.

Tournament pay
A form of compensation in which the top performer (or performers) receives much higher rewards than other competitors, even if the others perform at only a slightly lower level.

What is the marginal revenue product of entertainment stars like Cameron Diaz? Do the earnings of star entertainers, athletes, and even business executives reflect the tournament pay nature of markets in these areas?

HUBERT BOESL/DPA/LANDOV

[3]Paul M. Sommers and Noel Quinton, "Pay and Performance in Major League Baseball: The Case of the First Family of Free Agents," *Journal of Human Resources* (Summer 1982): 426–35.

[4]Edward Lazear and Sherwin Rosen, "Rank Order Tournaments as an Optimum Labor Contract," *Journal of Political Economy* 89 (October 1981): 841–64; and Robert Frank and Phillip Cook, *The Winner-Take-All Society* (New York: The Free Press, 1995).

In this type of environment, workers basically subject themselves to a lottery where the winner (the person with the highest productivity) receives compensation higher than his or her marginal revenue product, while the losers receive less than their marginal revenue product. There are some constraints as to how low the compensation of the losers can be, however, because if their wages are depressed too low, they will shift to alternative job opportunities.

The tournament pay environment creates a strong incentive for potential superstars to expend considerable effort to become a top performer. As a result, many people spend long hours developing skills that will increase their chances of becoming a "star" in athletics, entertainment, professions, and business. The tournament system also encourages those who are unwilling to make such sacrifices to follow another path. Is this good or bad? Economics does not answer that question; it merely explains how these markets work.

2. Worker preferences.   An important source of earnings differentials that is sometimes overlooked is worker preferences. People have different objectives in life. Some want to make a great deal of money. Many are willing to work two jobs or very long hours, undergo agonizing training and many years of education, or sacrifice social and family life to make money. Others might be "workaholics" because they enjoy their jobs. Still others might be satisfied with just enough money to get by, preferring to spend more time with their family, the Boy Scouts, watching television, on vacation, with a hobby, or at the local tavern.

Economics doesn't dictate that one set of worker preferences is more desirable than another, any more than it suggests that people should eat more spinach and less pastrami. It does, however, show that worker preferences in the areas of money, work, and skill development will contribute to differences in earnings. Other things being constant, persons who are more highly motivated by monetary objectives will be more likely to do the things necessary to command higher wage rates. But economics makes no judgments about whether this is good or bad.

3. Race and gender.   Discrimination on the basis of race or gender also contributes to earnings differences among people. **Employment discrimination** can directly limit the earnings opportunities of minorities and women. Employment discrimination occurs when minority or women employees are treated differently than similarly productive whites or men. Of course, the earnings of minorities or women can differ from those of whites or men, respectively, for reasons other than employment discrimination. Nonemployment discrimination—including access to high-quality education or specialized training, for example—can limit the opportunities of minority groups and women to acquire human capital, enhancing their productivity and earnings. Other factors, like the limited opportunities that can result from growing up in a low-income or single-parent family, can also influence skill development and educational achievement. In a later section in this chapter, we will analyze the impact of employment discrimination in more detail.

Employment discrimination
Unequal treatment of persons on the basis of their race, gender, or religion, restricting their employment and earnings opportunities compared to others of similar productivity. Employment discrimination may stem from the prejudices of employers, customers, fellow employees, or all three.

Earnings Differentials Due to Nonidentical Jobs

When people evaluate employment alternatives, they consider working conditions as well as wage rates. Is a job dangerous? Does it offer the opportunity to acquire the experience and training that will enhance future earnings? Is the work strenuous and nerve-racking? Are the working hours, job location, and means of transportation convenient? These factors are what economists call **nonpecuniary job characteristics**. People will accept jobs with undesirable working conditions if the wages are high enough, compared to potential job alternatives with better working conditions. Because the higher wages, in essence, compensate workers for the unpleasant nonpecuniary attributes of a job, economists refer to wage differences stemming from this source as **compensating wage differentials**.

Examples abound of higher wages that compensate various workers for less-attractive working conditions. Because of the dangers involved, aerial window washers (those who hang from windows twenty stories up) earn higher wages than other window washers. Sales jobs involving a great deal of out-of-town travel typically pay more than similar jobs that aren't so inconvenient. Because the jobs are both physically demanding and sometimes dangerous, the wages of coal miners and sewer workers are generally higher than

Nonpecuniary job characteristics
Working conditions, prestige, variety, location, employee freedom and responsibilities, and other nonwage characteristics of a job that influence how employees evaluate the job.

Compensating wage differentials
Wage differences that compensate workers for risk, unpleasant working conditions, and other undesirable nonpecuniary aspects of a job.

those in other occupations available to low-skilled workers. Jobs in attractive locations pay less than similar jobs in less-attractive areas. For example, American truck drivers in postwar Iraq earned $80,000 per year tax free, which is much more than they could have earned in the United States. This high rate of compensation was the result of the dangerous conditions they faced in Iraq. Compensating factors even influence the earnings of economists. When economists work for colleges or universities, they generally enjoy a more independent and intellectually stimulating work environment than when they are employed in the business sector. Unsurprisingly, the earnings of academic economists are typically lower than those of business economists. However, it is important to remember that the academic economist with the lower earnings has chosen this job over business-sector employment. Thus, the lower earnings do not imply that the worker is worse off.

Earnings Differentials Due to the Immobility of Labor

It is costly to move to a new location or train for a new occupation in order to get a job. As a result, labor, like other resources, isn't perfectly mobile. Some wage differentials therefore result because wages have not yet adjusted fully to changes in market conditions.

For example, as we've learned, when strong demand leads to wage increases, more and more people will train for the occupation in high demand. Eventually, supply will increase and moderate the wage increases. But this process will take time. Just the opposite will happen when demand falls. When the demand for workers in a given occupation or skill category falls, wages are likely to fall sharply in the short run. With time, some workers will move into other occupations, which eventually moderates the reduction in wages. But this will also take time. Some of the wage differences reflect the fact that this adjustment process doesn't happen instantly.

Institutional barriers can also limit the mobility of labor. Licensing requirements, for example, limit the mobility of labor into many occupations—medicine, taxicab driving, architecture, and mortuary science among them. Since minimum wages raise the cost to employers of hiring workers, they may retard the ability of low-skilled workers to obtain employment in certain sectors of the economy. These restrictions on labor mobility will also influence the size of wage differentials. Labor unions often promote policies designed to increase the demand for union labor and reduce the labor supply in unionized job categories. Their actions, though, often limit the ability of nonunionized workers (and firms) to enter and compete in the unionized sectors of the economy. To the extent that unions are successful, they hamper the mobility of nonunionized workers and create higher wages for those who are unionized. For more on this topic, see the special topic "Do Labor Unions Increase the Wages of Workers?" later in this book.

THUMBNAIL SKETCH

What Are the Sources of Earnings Differentials?

Differences in Workers

1. Productivity and specialized skills that reflect native ability, parental training, and investment in human capital (education)
2. Worker preferences (the trade-off that workers are willing to make between money earnings and other factors)
3. Race and gender discrimination

Differences in Jobs

1. Location of job
2. Working conditions (such as job safety and comfort in the workplace)

3. Opportunity for training and skill-enhancing work experience

Immobility of Resources

1. Temporary disequilibrium resulting from market changes
2. Institutional restrictions (for example, occupational licensing and union-imposed restraints)

America's Millionaires[1]

The number of millionaires has been expanding rapidly. In 1975, there were only 350,000 households with a net worth of $1 million or more. By 1996, the figure had grown to 3.5 million. Only about one-third of the increase was due to inflation. The growth in the number of millionaires is expected to continue. Forecasts indicate that, by 2005, there will be 5.6 million millionaire households—5.2 percent of the total (1 out of every 20). Who are these millionaires?

- In terms of age, millionaires are typically in their late 50s. They tend to be older than the general population because it takes time to accumulate wealth of this magnitude. In addition, older workers have higher earnings, enabling them to increase wealth more rapidly.
- Not surprisingly, millionaires tend to be well educated. About 80 percent have a college degree. In fact, nearly two-fifths have a graduate degree. Those with more education have higher earnings, which is an important source for acquiring wealth.
- Millionaires are disproportionately self-employed entrepreneurs. While less than one-fifth of the workforce is self-employed, two-thirds of the millionaires fall into this category. To a degree, the income and wealth of millionaires are rewards that compensate them for assuming the greater financial risks that accompany self-employment and business ownership than those that accompany working for a salary.
- The vast majority of millionaires achieved their status through saving and investment. They save on average 20 percent of their income. Most of them are first-generation rich. Less than 20 percent received more than 10 percent of their wealth through an inheritance.

[1]Based on Thomas J. Stanley and William D. Danko, *The Millionaire Next Door: The Surprising Secrets of America's Wealthy* (New York: Longstreet Press, 1996).

Sources of Wage Differentials: A Summary

As the accompanying Thumbnail Sketch shows, wage differentials stem from many sources, which can be categorized in three main ways: differences in workers, differences in jobs, and immobility of resources. Many of the wage differentials in these categories play an important allocative role, compensating people for (1) human capital investments that increase their productivity or (2) unfavorable working conditions. Other wage differentials reflect, at least partially, locational preferences or the desires of individuals for higher money income rather than nonmonetary benefits. Still other differentials, like those related to discrimination and occupational restrictions, are unrelated to worker productivity or preferences and do not promote efficient production.

The analysis above focuses on factors that contribute to differences in real earnings. Nominal earnings will also be influenced by differences in the cost of living. In a large, geographically diverse country like the United States, the cost of living varies substantially across cities, regions, and communities. In cities like New York and San Francisco, the level of prices can be 50 percent or even 100 percent higher than in other parts of the country. Put another way, the quantity of goods and services that can be purchased with $50,000 of earnings is substantially less in New York City than in rural Georgia or Kansas. Geographical cost-of-living differences therefore also contribute to wage differences.

THE ECONOMICS OF EMPLOYMENT DISCRIMINATION

How does employment discrimination affect the job opportunities available to women and minorities? Do employers gain from discrimination? Economics sheds light on both these questions. There are two outlets for labor market discrimination: wage rates and employment restrictions. **Exhibit 3** illustrates the impact of wage discrimination. When nonminority workers are preferred to minority workers (or male to female workers), the demand for the latter groups falls and the wages of these people decline.

EXHIBIT 3
The Impact of Direct Wage Discrimination

If there is employment discrimination against minorities or women, then the demand for their services will decline, and their wage rate will fall from W_w to W_m.

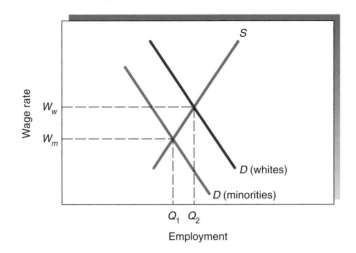

Essentially, there are two labor markets—one market for the favored group and another for the group against which the discrimination is directed. The favored group, such as whites, is preferred, but the less expensive labor of minority workers is a substitute productive resource. Both white and minority employees are employed, but the whites are paid a higher wage rate.

Exclusionary practices are another form of employment discrimination. Either in response to outside pressure or because of their own views, employers might primarily hire whites and men for certain types of jobs. When minority and female workers are excluded from a large number of occupations, they are crowded into a smaller number of remaining jobs and occupations. If entry restraints prevent people from becoming supervisors, plumbers, electricians, and airline pilots, they will be forced to accept alternatives. Thus, the supply of labor in the unrestricted occupations increases, causing wage rates in these occupations to fall. In turn, the exclusionary practices reduce supply and push wages up in occupations and industries dominated by white men.

Discrimination is costly to employers when they are merely reflecting their own prejudices. ***If employers can hire equally productive minority employees (or women) at a lower wage than whites (or men), then the profit motive gives them a strong incentive to do so. Hiring the higher-wage whites when similar minority employees are available will increase the costs of firms that discriminate.*** Employers who hire employees regardless of their race or gender will have lower costs and higher profits than rival firms that try to fill positions with (mostly) white men. Thus, competitive forces tend to reduce the profitability of firms that discriminate.

Discriminatory hiring practices can stem from factors other than the employer prejudice, however. If either the firm's employees or its customers have a preference for or against various groups, this may lead to discriminatory hiring, even if the employer is totally unbiased. When discrimination is customer based, a worker from a favored group will be able to bring in more revenue for the firm. For example, adult nightclubs that hire attractive young women as dancers will generate more revenue than those that hire dancers from all age and gender groups. Similarly, Chinese restaurants that hire all (or almost all) Chinese servers are likely to do better than if the ethnic and racial composition of their employees mirrors that of the labor force. Historically, customer-based discrimination has often gone unchallenged. This appears to be changing. In a highly publicized case, the Hooters restaurant chain was charged with discriminating against male servers. Although the Equal Employment Opportunity Commission dropped its four-year investigation, Hooters agreed to pay $3.75 million in damages and begin hiring male servers as the result of privately filed lawsuits in Illinois and Maryland.

How Much Impact Does Employment Discrimination Have on Earnings?

If we want to isolate the impact of employment discrimination, we must (1) adjust for differences between groups in education, experience, and other productivity-related factors and (2) then make comparisons between similarly qualified groups of employees who differ only with regard to race (or gender).

How do the earnings of minorities compare with those of similarly productive whites? **Exhibit 4** presents the actual wages of minorities relative to whites and the "productivity-adjusted" minority/white wage ratio. The adjusted ratio is an estimate of how the wages of minorities would compare with those of whites if the two groups had the same productivity characteristics (schooling, work experience, marital status, regional location, and union and industry status). In 2000–2003, the actual wages of black men were 79 percent of the wages of white men. When the workforce characteristics of black men were taken into account, however, the adjusted hourly earnings of black men rose to 86 percent of the earnings of white men. This implies that productivity-related factors accounted for a little more than one-quarter of the wage differential between the two groups. A 14 percent differential, which may well be the result of employment discrimination, remained after adjustment for the productivity characteristics.[5]

Mexican-Americans constitute the second-largest minority group in the United States. Even though the actual wages of Mexican-American men were only 67 percent of the wages of white men, their "adjusted" earnings were 93 percent of those for whites. These data were not adjusted for the ability to speak English. Adjustment for this factor would almost certainly further narrow the differential. This suggests that when Mexican-American men possess the same worker characteristics as white men, their earnings are nearly on par with those of their white counterparts. Interestingly, adjustment for productivity factors reduces the wages of Asian-Americans relative to whites. Asian-Americans have greater productivity characteristics, particularly educational levels, than whites. As a result, the "adjusted" earnings of Asian-Americans are lower than their actual earnings figures.

Turning to the data for women, the productivity-adjusted wage rates of minority women relative to white women are between 94 percent and 98 percent for each of the

EXHIBIT 4
The Actual and Productivity-Adjusted Wages of Minorities Compared to Whites: 2000–2003.

	MEN		WOMEN	
	ACTUAL	ADJUSTED	ACTUAL	ADJUSTED
White	100	100	100	100
African-American	79	86	90	94
American Indian	82	92	87	95
Asian-American[a]	100	94	103	97
Mexican-American	67	93	75	98
Other Hispanic	79	92	85	95

[a]Primarily Chinese-Americans and Japanese-Americans.
Source: These data were supplied by David Macpherson. They were derived from the 2000–2003 *Current Population Surveys*. The data were adjusted for years of schooling, work experience, region, industry, sector of employment, union status, and marital status.

[5]The figures presented in Exhibit 4 do not control for the lower average quality of schooling received by blacks. Other researchers using more refined data have found that productivity factors account for a larger share of the earnings differential between whites and blacks. For evidence on this point, see Francine D. Blau and Lawrence M. Kahn, "Race and Gender Pay Differentials," in *Research Frontiers in Industrial Relations and Human Resources*, ed. David Lewin, Olivia S. Mitchell, and Peter D. Scherer, 381–416 (Madison, Wis.: Industrial Relations Research Association, 1992); and Derek A. Neal and William R. Johnson, "The Role of Premarket Factors in Black-White Wage Differences," *Journal of Political Economy* (October 1996): 869–95. For a detailed explanation of how the adjusted ratios of Exhibit 4 were derived and information on the significance of productivity factors and employment discrimination on the basis of gender, see David A. Macpherson and Barry T. Hirsch, "Wages and Gender Composition: Why Do Women's Jobs Pay Less?" *Journal of Labor Economics* (July 1995).

groups included in Exhibit 4. This implies that employment discrimination on the basis of race adds little to earnings differentials that may reflect discrimination on the basis of gender. For an analysis of earnings differences according to gender, see the special topic "Is Discrimination Responsible for the Earnings Differences between Men and Women?" later in this book.

LINK BETWEEN PRODUCTIVITY AND EARNINGS

Link between Productivity and Earnings

 In a market economy, productivity and earnings are closely linked. To earn a large income, one must provide large benefits to others.

In a competitive market setting, productivity—that is, output per worker—and earnings are closely linked. When workers are more productive, the demand for their services will be higher, and therefore they will be able to command higher wages. ***High productivity is the source of high wages. When the output per hour of workers is high, the real wages of the workers will also be high.***

In turn, the linkage between productivity and earnings provides individuals with a strong incentive to develop their talents and utilize their resources in ways that are helpful to others. As the value of the goods and services supplied to others increases, there will also be a tendency for one's earnings to increase. If you want to make a large income, you had better figure out how to provide services that are highly valued. Self-interest is a powerful motivator and, as Adam Smith noted long ago, competitive markets can bring it into harmony with economic progress.

Productivity differences are an important source of differences in earnings among individuals. They are also an important source of earnings differences across countries. For example, the earnings per worker are vastly greater in the United States than they are in India or China because the output of U.S. workers is much greater than the output of their counterparts in those countries. The average worker in the United States is better educated, works with more productive machines, and benefits from more efficient economic organization than the average person in India or China. Thus, the value of the output produced by the average U.S. worker is approximately fifteen times that produced by the average worker in India or China. American workers earn more because they produce more. If they did not produce more, they would not be able to earn more.

Labor-saving equipment can improve productivity. But profit-maximizing firms will adopt automated production methods and high-tech equipment only when they reduce costs. Cost-effective automation releases labor and other resources so that they can be used to expand production in other areas. In turn, the higher worker productivity and expansion in production makes higher income levels and living standards possible.

GETTY IMAGES

Productivity differences also affect earnings across time. Today, American workers are substantially more productive than they were fifty years ago.[6] The output of goods and services per hour of U.S. workers in 2003 was approximately twice the level of the mid-1950s. Similarly, average real earnings (total compensation) per hour in 2003 were approximately double those of fifty years ago. Earnings rose because productivity increased. If productivity had not increased, the increase in earnings would not have been possible.

Increased physical capital, improvements in the skill level of the labor force, and advances in technology drive productivity and earnings growth. For several decades, both the educational level of American workers and the capital equipment per worker have steadily increased. Technological advances have also enhanced productivity and contributed to the growth of output and income. Some people argue that technology and **automation** adversely affect workers (see the accompanying Myth of Economics feature). In fact, just the opposite is true. ***Once you recognize that higher output is the source of higher earnings, the value of new production technology is apparent: better technology makes it possible for workers to produce more and earn more.*** For example, accountants can handle more business accounts using microcomputers than they can with pencils and calculators. A secretary can prepare more letters with a word processor than a typewriter.

Automation
A production technique that reduces the amount of labor required to produce a good or service. It is beneficial to adopt the new labor-saving technology only if it reduces the cost of production.

Productivity, Wages, and the Computer Revolution

What has been happening to the growth of productivity, and how has this influenced the wages of workers? **Exhibit 5** presents data on the change in both productivity (output per hour) and real hourly compensation of the United States for the period 1948–1973, 1974–1995, and 1996–2003. Predictably, productivity growth and increases in real compensation per hour have moved together. During the period 1948–1973, both productivity and real hourly compensation grew at a rapid rate—approximately 3 percent annually.

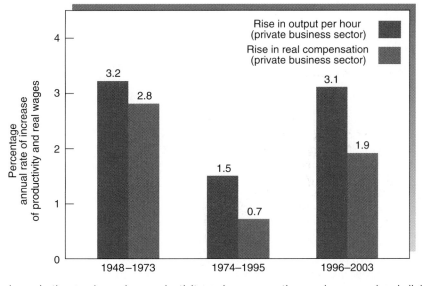

EXHIBIT 5
Productivity and Employee Compensation in the United States, 1948–2003

As shown in the graph, worker productivity and compensation per hour are closely linked. Between 1974 and 1995, the growth of both productivity and real compensation per hour slowed substantially compared to the growth figures achieved during the 1948–1973 period. However, worker productivity and real hourly compensation rebounded during the 1996–2003 period.

Source: Bureau of Labor Statistics, http://www.bls.gov/.

---

[6]For more on productivity growth, see Kevin J. Stiroh, "What Drives Productivity Growth?" *Economic Policy Review* (Federal Reserve Bank of New York) (March 2001): 37–59.

MYTHS IN ECONOMICS

"Automation Is the Major Cause of Unemployment. If We Keep Allowing Machines to Replace People, We Are Going to Run Out of Jobs."

Machines are substituted for people if, and only if, the machines reduce costs of production. Why did the automatic elevator replace human elevator operators or the power shovel virtually eliminate human ditchdiggers? Because each is a cheaper method of accomplishing a task.

When automation and technological improvements reduce the cost of producing a good, they allow us to obtain each unit of the product with fewer resources. If the demand for the product is inelastic, consumers will spend less on the good and therefore have more of their income available for spending on other things.

Consider the following example. Suppose that someone develops a new toothpaste that really prevents cavities and sells it for half the price of other brands. If the demand for toothpaste is inelastic, at the lower price consumers will spend less on this product than they did before. Furthermore, the decline in cavities will lower the demand for and spending on dental services. Will the lower toothpaste and dental care expenditures reduce employment? The lower level of spending on dental care will mean that households now have more income to spend on other goods and services. As a result, they will spend more on clothes, recreation, vacations, personal computers, education, and other items. This additional spending, which would not have taken place without lower dental costs, will generate additional demand and employment in these sectors, and employment will decline in the dental care sector. Although jobs will be reshuffled, there's no reason to expect that total employment will decline.

What would happen to employment if a technological improvement reduced production costs and the demand for the product were elastic? Under these circumstances, a cost-saving invention can lead to higher employment, even in the industry affected by the invention. This was essentially what happened in the automobile industry when Henry Ford's mass-production techniques reduced the cost (and price) of cars. When the price of automobiles fell 50 percent, consumers bought three times as many cars. Even though the worker-hours per car fell by 25 percent between 1920 and 1930, employment in the industry increased by approximately 50 percent during the decade.

More recently, the same thing happened in the computer-manufacturing industry. As technological improvements reduced the cost of producing various types of computer equipment, the lower costs and lower prices for computer products generated such a large increase in sales that employment in the computer-manufacturing sector actually increased.

Of course, technological advances can diminish the earnings of individual people or groups. Home appliances, like automatic washers and dryers, dishwashers, and microwave ovens, have reduced the job opportunities of maids. Voice recognition technology has lowered the demand for telephone operators. In the future, videotaped lectures may reduce the earnings and opportunities of college professors. It is understandable why groups directly affected in this manner often fear and oppose automation.

Focusing on the loss of specific jobs, however, can be misleading. Clearly, running out of jobs is not a problem. Jobs represent obstacles—tasks that must be accomplished to loosen the bonds of scarcity. As long as our ability to produce goods and services falls short of our consumption desires, there will be jobs. A society running out of jobs would be in an enviable position: It would be nearing the impossible goal—victory over scarcity!

In contrast, both sagged badly during the period 1974–1995. Productivity growth averaged only 1.5 percent annually and hourly real compensation rose at an annual rate of only 0.7 percent over the two decades (1974–1995). Although the reasons for slow productivity growth during this period are not entirely clear, most economists believe that slower improvement in the educational quality of the workforce, environmental regulations, and the inflation of the 1970s were contributing factors. Beginning in the mid-1990s, both productivity and real compensation rebounded. During the period 1996–2003, productivity and hourly compensation grew at annual rates of 3.1 percent and 1.9 percent, respectively.[7]

---

[7]One explanation for the slower growth in compensation than productivity is that the compensation measure does not account for the improvements in working conditions, such as job comfort and safety, that have occurred over the past few decades.

What accounts for the recent rebound in the growth of productivity? Will productivity continue to grow rapidly over the next decade or so? Most economists believe that the recent acceleration in productivity growth is largely the result of the computer revolution and related technological innovations.[8] Information technology and investment in computer equipment soared during the 1990s, and productivity began to grow more rapidly. Approximately three-fifths of the productivity growth during the decade was due to this increase in investment, one study found.[9]

Furthermore, some believe that the pace of technological change has quickened and new technologies now spread throughout the economy more rapidly. As measured by price reductions, the speed of innovations in computer technology has certainly increased in recent years. For example, the price of computers in the second half of the 1990s fell at nearly twice the rate as that of the first half of the decade. A recent study estimated that about one-third of the recent productivity growth was due to a single factor: increased efficiency in the production of computers and semiconductors.[10]

Is the computer revolution going to continue, or have we already witnessed its major impact? Will the speedup of technological change continue at a rapid rate, or perhaps even accelerate, in the decades immediately ahead? It is too early to determine the answers to these questions. If the development and dissemination of technological improvements do continue at a rapid rate, higher rates of productivity growth can be expected. This will help us achieve higher income levels and living standards more quickly. However, the rapid growth of technology may also mean changing work requirements, more job switching, and less career stability. (See the accompanying feature "Are Lifetime Jobs Disappearing?")

APPLICATIONS IN ECONOMICS

Are Lifetime Jobs Disappearing?[1]

Workers in earlier generations could typically expect to have a long-term career with one firm. This is no longer the case. Today's workers believe they will have to switch employers more often than their parents did. In 1983, the average full-time male worker expected to remain with his current employer for an additional 18.6 years. By 1998, this figure had fallen to 14.7 years. A similar pattern exists for women. Their expected time of employment with their current employer dropped from 15.9 years in 1983 to 12.8 years in 1998.

Why might there be more job switching and shorter periods of employment with the same firm in the future? Two trends seem to be pushing things in that direction. First, employment is expanding in the service sector but declining in manufacturing. On average, workers in manufacturing have been with their current employer more than two years longer than workers in the service sector. Thus, movement of employment toward the service sector tends to reduce the average length of job tenure.

Second, technological advances and rapid growth of productivity can also reduce job tenure. Workers in industries with larger productivity increases had shorter periods of job tenure during the last two decades. Technological advances tend to both replace some workers with machines and change the nature of jobs, which often means that current employees do not have the skills required to handle them. Thus, to the extent that productivity grows more rapidly in the future, it may also mean more job switching and shorter periods of job tenure with the same employer.

---

[1]Leora Friedberg and Michael Owyang. "Explaining the Evolution of Pension Structure and Job Tenure." Working Paper 2002-022b, Federal Reserve Bank of St. Louis (October 2002).

---

[8]For a discussion of the new–economy perspective, see Kevin J. Stiroh, "Is There a New Economy?" *Challenge* (July/August 1999): 82–101.

[9]Stephen D. Oliner and Daniel E. Sichel, "Information Technology and Productivity: Where Are We Now and Where Are We Going?" *Economic Review* (Federal Reserve Bank of Atlanta) (Third Quarter 2002): 15–44.

[10]Ibid.

LOOKING AHEAD

As we have learned, productivity and earnings are influenced by both human capital and physical capital investments. This chapter focused on the labor market. The following chapter will analyze investment choices and the operation of the capital market.

KEY POINTS

▼ The real earnings of individuals would be equal if (1) all individuals were identical in preferences, skills, and background, (2) all jobs were equally attractive, and (3) workers were perfectly mobile among jobs. Earnings differences among individuals result from the absence of these conditions.

▼ Wage differences play an important allocative role. They generally compensate people for (1) investments in education and training that enhance productivity and the development of highly specialized skills and (2) unfavorable working conditions and/or job locations. Wage differences can also result from differences in workers' preferences, employment discrimination, and institutional factors that restrict worker mobility.

▼ Employment discrimination reduces the wages of people being discriminated against by either lowering the demand for their services or restricting their entry into various job categories. Productivity differences also contribute to earnings differentials between groups. Research indicates that the earnings of African-American and Mexican-American men are, respectively, approximately 86 percent

and 93 percent those of white men of similar productivity.

▼ Productivity is the ultimate source of high wages and earnings. Workers in the United States (and other high-income industrial countries) earn high wages because their output per hour is high as the result of (1) greater worker knowledge and skills (human capital) and (2) the use of modern machinery (physical capital).

▼ Automated methods of production will be adopted only if they reduce costs. Although automation might reduce employment in a specific industry, it also releases resources that can be employed in other areas. Improved technology permits us to achieve larger output and income levels than would otherwise be possible.

▼ During the last seven years, the growth of productivity in the United States has increased well above the growth rate achieved during the prior twenty years. If the acceleration in productivity continues, increases in wages in the years ahead will be more rapid than during the 1974–1995 period.

CRITICAL ANALYSIS QUESTIONS

1. Why do some people earn higher wages than others? Why are wages in some occupations higher than in others? How do wage differentials influence the allocation of resources? Explain.

*2. Why are real wages in the United States higher than in other countries? Is the labor force itself responsible for the higher wages of American workers? Explain.

3. What explains the earnings differences between (a) a lawyer and a minister, (b) an accountant and

an elementary school teacher, (c) a business executive and a social worker, (d) a country lawyer and a Wall Street lawyer, (e) an experienced, skilled craftsperson and a twenty-year-old high school dropout, and (f) an upper-story and a ground-floor window washer?

4. a. If minority employees are discriminated against, how will this affect their earnings? Use supply and demand analysis to explain your answer.

b. If the average earnings differ between two groups of employees (for example, whites and blacks), does this mean that the group with the lower earnings is experiencing employment discrimination? Why or why not?

5. Is there a relationship between the growth of productivity and changes in wage rates? Can higher earnings be achieved without higher productivity? Why or why not? Discuss.

*6. "Jobs are the key to economic progress. Unless we create more jobs, our standard of living will fall." Is this statement true or false? Explain.

7. "If Jones has a skill that is highly valued, she will be able to achieve high market earnings. In contrast, Smith may work just as hard or even harder, and still earn only a low income."
a. Does hard work necessarily lead to a high income?
b. Why are the incomes of some workers high and others low?
c. Do you think the market system of wage determination is fair? Why or why not?
d. Can you think of a more equitable system? If so, explain why it is more equitable.

*8. People who have invested heavily in human capital (for example, lawyers, doctors, and even college professors) generally have higher wages, but they also generally work more hours than other workers. Can you explain why?

*9. "If individuals had identical abilities and opportunities, earnings would be equal." Is this statement true or false?

*10. Other things being constant, how will the following influence the hourly earnings of employees? Explain your answer.

a. The employee must work the midnight to 8:00 A.M. shift.
b. The job involves split shifts (work three hours, off two hours, work three additional hours, and so on).
c. The employer provides low-cost child care services on the premises.
d. The job is widely viewed as prestigious.
e. The job requires employees to move often from city to city.
f. The job requires substantial amounts of out-of-town travel.

*11. Consider two occupations (A and B) that employ people with the same skills and abilities. When employed, workers in the two occupations work the same number of hours per day. In occupation A, employment is stable throughout the year, while employment in B is characterized by seasonal layoffs. In which occupation will the hourly wage rate be highest? Why? In which occupation will the annual wage be highest? Why?

12. "Technological change eliminates thousands of jobs every year. Unless something is done to slow the growth of technology, ordinary workers will face a bleak future of low wages and high unemployment." Explain why you either agree or disagree with this statement.

13. If an individual is motivated primarily by the desire to make money, will he or she have an incentive to be helpful to others? Will he or she have an incentive to develop skills that others value highly? Why or why not?

*Asterisk denotes questions for which answers are given in Appendix B.

CHAPTER

26

Investment, the Capital Market, and the Wealth of Nations

To produce capital, people must forgo the opportunity to produce goods for current consumption. People can choose whether to spend their time picking apples or planting apple trees. In the first case there are more apples today; in the second, more apples tomorrow.

—*Steven Landsburg*[1]

Chapter Focus

- Why do people invest? Why are capital resources often used to produce consumer goods?

- What is the interest rate? Why are investors willing to pay interest to get loanable funds? Why are lenders willing to loan funds?

- Why is the interest rate so important when costs and revenues are evaluated across time periods?

- When is an investment profitable? How do profitable and unprofitable investments influence the wealth of nations?

- How does the capital market influence growth and prosperity?

[1]Steven E. Landsburg, *Price Theory and Applications* (Fort Worth, Tex.: Dryden Press, 1992), 581.

I n the previous chapter, we noted that there is a close relationship between productivity and earnings. In turn, productivity is influenced by investment choices: consider choices about whether to construct an office building, purchase a harvesting machine, or go to law school. The returns derived from investments like these are usually spread over several years (or even decades). Some investment costs, such as maintenance expenses, can also be incurred over a lengthy time period. Why should we expect profit-seeking individuals and corporate decision makers to pay now to create benefits later—sometimes much later? How can people compare the benefits and costs of an activity when both are spread across lengthy periods of time? Why is the method of allocating investment a vitally important determinant of economic progress? As we explain the investment process and capital markets, this chapter will help you answer these questions. ■

WHY PEOPLE INVEST

Capital is a term used by economists to describe long-lasting resources that are valued because they can help us produce goods and services in the future. As we previously discussed, there are two broad categories of capital: (1) *physical capital:* nonhuman resources, like buildings, machines, tools, and natural resources, and (2) *human capital:* human resources, that is, the knowledge and skills of people. **Investment** is the purchase, construction, or development of a capital resource. Thus, investment expands the availability of capital resources.

Saving is income not spent on current consumption. *Investment and saving are closely linked. In fact, the two words describe different aspects of the capital formation process. Saving refers to the nonconsumption of income, whereas investment refers to the use of the unconsumed income to produce a capital resource.* Sometimes saving and investment are conducted by the same person, as when a farmer saves current income (refrains from spending it on consumption goods) in order to purchase a new tractor (an investment good).

It is important to recognize that saving is required for investment. Someone must save—refrain from consumption—in order to provide the resources for investment. When investors finance a project with their own funds, they are also saving (refraining from current consumption). Investors, however, do not always use their own funds to finance investments. Sometimes they will borrow funds from others. When this is the case, it is the lender rather than the investor who is doing the saving.

Considering the alternative use of resources also highlights the link between investment and saving. Resources used to produce capital will be unavailable for the direct production of consumption goods. The opportunity cost of investing more and using more of our resources to produce capital resources today is that fewer current resources will be available to produce consumption goods.

Why would anyone want to delay consumption in order to undertake an investment? After all, consumption is the ultimate objective of all production. However, we can sometimes produce more consumption goods by first using resources to produce capital resources and then using these resources to produce the desired consumer goods. Using capital to produce consumption goods makes sense only when it allows us to produce more consumption goods than we otherwise could.

Perhaps a simple illustration can highlight the potential gains from using capital to produce consumption goods. Suppose that Robinson Crusoe can catch fish by either (1) combining his labor with natural resources (direct production) or (2) constructing a net and eventually combining his labor with this capital resource (indirect production). Let's assume that Crusoe can catch 2 fish per day by hand-fishing, but 3 fish per day if he constructs and uses a net that will last for 310 days. Now suppose it will take Crusoe 55 days to build the net. The opportunity cost of constructing the net will be 110 fish (2 fish per day not caught for each of the 55 days he spends building the net). As the accompanying chart shows, if Crusoe invests in the capital resource (the net), his output during the next year (including the 55 days required to build the net) would be 930 fish (3 per day for 310 days). Alternatively, hand-fishing during the year would lead to an output of only 730 fish (2 fish per day for 365 days).

Capital
Resources that enhance our ability to produce output in the future.

Investment
The purchase, construction, or development of capital resources, including both nonhuman capital and human capital. Investments increase the supply of capital.

Saving
Current income that is not spent on consumption goods. Savings deposited by some individuals allow resources to be devoted to investments (such as the making of tractors or other equipment used in production).

NUMBER OF FISH CAUGHT		
	WITHOUT NET	WITH NET
Per day	2	3
Annually	730	930

In other words, Crusoe's investment in the net will enhance his productivity by 200 fish annually. In the short term, however, investing in the net will require a sacrifice. During the fifty-five days it takes to construct the net, Crusoe's production of consumption goods will decline.

How can Crusoe or any other investor know if the value of the larger future output is worth the short-term cost? Most of us have a preference for goods now rather than later. For example, if you are a typical person, you would prefer a sleek new sports car now rather than the same car ten years from now. On average, individuals possess a **positive rate of time preference**. That is, other things being the same, people subjectively value more highly goods obtained sooner than goods obtained later.

Positive rate of time preference
The desire of consumers for goods now rather than in the future.

When only Crusoe is involved, the attractiveness of the investment in the fishing net depends upon his time preference. If he places a high value on a couple of fish per day during the next fifty-five days, as indeed he may if he is on the verge of starvation, the cost of the investment may well exceed the value of the larger future output. If Crusoe could find someone who would loan him fish while he built the net, however, he could consume the borrowed fish now while building the net, and pay later with the extra fish made possible by the net. If such a loan is available, the attractiveness of the investment (building the net instead of hand-fishing now) will be influenced by the price of borrowing fish. Is the cost of borrowing fish in order to maintain his consumption while he constructs the net worth the extra cost? To answer this question, Crusoe must consider the cost of paying for earlier availability—he must consider, in effect, the interest rate.

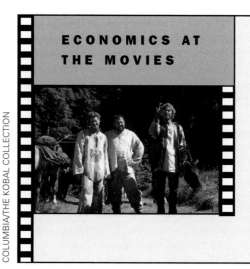

ECONOMICS AT THE MOVIES

COLUMBIA/THE KOBAL COLLECTION

A Knight's Tale (2001)

After winning a jousting competition, Heath Ledger tries to persuade two other peasants to invest their winnings in preparing for an even larger, upcoming competition to win an even bigger prize, rather than spending the winnings right away (as the two peasants want to do). The three clearly differ when it comes to their rate of time preference. This scene illustrates the trade-off between consuming now versus investing for the future.

INTEREST RATES

The interest rate links the future to the present. It allows individuals to evaluate the value today—the present value—of future income and costs. In essence, it is the market price of earlier availability. From the viewpoint of a potential borrower, the interest rate is the premium that must be paid in order to acquire goods sooner and pay for them later. From the lender's viewpoint, it is a reward for waiting—a payment for supplying others with current purchasing power. The interest rate allows the lender to calculate the future benefit (future payments earned) of extending a loan or saving funds today.

In a modern economy, people often borrow funds to finance current investments and consumption. Because of this, the interest rate is often defined as the price of loanable funds. This definition is correct. But we should remember that it is the earlier availability of goods and services purchased, not the money itself, that is desired by the borrower.

How Interest Rates Are Determined

Interest rates are determined by the demand for and supply of loanable funds. Investors demand funds in order to finance capital assets they believe will increase output and generate profit. Simultaneously, consumers demand loanable funds because they have a positive rate of time preference: they prefer earlier availability.

The demand of investors for loanable funds stems from the productivity of capital. Investors are willing to borrow in order to finance the use of capital in production because they expect that expanding future output will provide them with more than enough resources to repay the amount borrowed—the principal—and interest on the loan. Our prior example of Robinson Crusoe illustrates this point. Remember, Crusoe could increase his output by 200 fish this year if he could take off fifty-five days from hand-fishing to build a net. But doing so would reduce Crusoe's fish production by 2 fish per day while he was constructing the net. Suppose a fishing crew from a neighboring island visited Crusoe and offered to lend him 110 fish so he could undertake the capital investment project (building the net). If Crusoe could borrow the 110 fish (the principal) in exchange for, say, 165 fish one year later (110 fish to repay the principal and 55 as interest on the loan), the investment project would be highly profitable. Crusoe could repay the funds borrowed, plus the 50 percent interest rate, and still have 145 additional fish (the 200 additional fish caught minus the 55 fish paid in interest).

Crusoe's demand for loanable fish—and, more generally, the demand of investors for loanable funds—stems directly from the productivity of the capital investment. Crusoe can gain by borrowing to finance the construction of a fishing net only because the net enables him to expand his total output during the year. Similarly, investors can gain by borrowing funds to undertake investment projects only when the capital assets they purchase permit them to expand output (or reduce costs) by enough to make the interest payments and still have more output than they would have without the investment.

As **Exhibit 1** illustrates, the interest rate brings the choices of investors and consumers wanting to borrow funds into harmony with the choices of lenders willing to supply funds. Higher interest rates make it more costly for investors to undertake capital spending projects and for consumers to buy now rather than later. Both investors and consumers will therefore curtail their borrowing as the interest rate rises. Investors will borrow less because some investment projects that would be profitable at a low interest rate

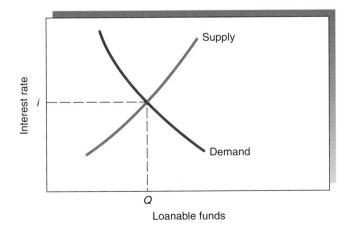

**EXHIBIT 1
Determining the Interest Rate**

The demand for loanable funds stems from the consumer's desire for earlier availability and the productivity of capital. As the interest rate rises, current goods become more expensive in comparison with future goods. Therefore, borrowers will demand fewer loanable funds. On the other hand, higher interest rates will stimulate lenders to supply additional funds to the market.

will be unprofitable at higher rates. Some consumers will reduce their current consumption rather than pay the high interest premium when the interest rate increases. Therefore, the amount of funds demanded by borrowers is inversely related to the interest rate.

The interest rate also rewards people (lenders) willing to reduce their current consumption in order to provide loanable funds to others. If some people are going to borrow in order to undertake an investment project (or consume more than their current income), others must curtail their current consumption by an equal amount. In essence, the interest rate provides lenders with the incentive to reduce their current consumption so that borrowers can either invest or consume beyond their current income. Higher interest rates give people who are willing to save (willing to supply loanable funds) the ability to purchase more goods in the future in exchange for sacrificing current consumption. Even though people have a positive rate of time preference, they will give up current consumption to supply funds to the loanable funds market if the price is right. Higher interest rates will induce people to save more. Therefore, as the interest rate rises, the quantity of funds supplied to the loanable funds market will increase.

As Exhibit 1 illustrates, the interest rate will bring the quantity of funds demanded into balance with the quantity supplied. *At the equilibrium interest rate, the quantity of funds borrowers demand for investment and consumption now (rather than later) will just equal the quantity of funds lenders save. So the interest rate brings the choices of borrowers and lenders into harmony.*

The Money Rate Versus the Real Rate of Interest

We have emphasized that the interest rate is a premium paid by borrowers for earlier availability and a reward received by lenders for delaying consumption. However, during a period of inflation—a general increase in prices—the nominal interest rate, or **money rate of interest**, is a misleading indicator of how much borrowers are paying and lenders are receiving. Inflation reduces the purchasing power of a loan's principal. Rising prices mean that when the borrower repays the principal in the future, the repayment amount will not purchase as much as it would have when the funds were initially loaned.

When inflation is common, lenders will recognize that they are being repaid with dollars of less purchasing power. Unless they are compensated for the anticipated inflation by an upward adjustment in the interest rate, they will supply fewer funds to the loanable funds market. At the same time, when borrowers anticipate inflation, they will want to purchase goods and services now before they become even more expensive in the future. Thus, they are willing to pay an **inflationary premium**, an additional amount of interest that reflects the expected rate of future price increases. For example, if borrowers and lenders fully anticipate a 5 percent rate of inflation, they will be just as willing to agree on a 9 percent interest rate as they were earlier to agree on a 4 percent interest rate when both anticipated price stability.

Unlike when the general price level is stable, the supply of loanable funds will decline (the supply curve will shift to the left) and the demand will increase (the demand curve will shift to the right) once decision makers anticipate future inflation. The money interest rate thus rises, overstating the "true" cost of borrowing and the yield from lending. This true cost is the **real rate of interest**, which is equal to the money rate of interest minus the inflationary premium. It reflects the real burden to borrowers and payoff to lenders in terms of their being able to buy goods and services.

Our analysis indicates that high rates of inflation will raise the money rate of interest. The real world is consistent with this view. Money interest rates rose to historical highs in the United States as inflation soared to double-digit rates during the 1970s. These same nominal rates fell to the 5 percent range as inflation fell below 2 percent in the 1990s. Cross-country comparisons also illustrate the link between inflation and high interest rates. The lowest money interest rates in the 1990s and early 2000s were found in nations such as Germany, Switzerland, and Japan, all with low rates of inflation. In contrast, the highest money interest rates were observed in Russia, Brazil, Turkey, and other countries with high rates of inflation during the period.

Money rate of interest
The rate of interest in monetary terms that borrowers pay for borrowed funds. During periods when borrowers and lenders expect inflation, the money rate of interest exceeds the real rate of interest.

Inflationary premium
A component of the money interest rate that reflects compensation to the lender for the expected decrease, due to inflation, in the purchasing power of the principal and interest during the course of the loan. It is determined by the expected rate of future inflation.

Real rate of interest
The money rate of interest minus the expected rate of inflation. The real rate of interest indicates the interest premium, in terms of real goods and services, that one must pay for earlier availability.

Interest Rates and Risk

So far, we've assumed that there is only a single interest rate present in the loanable funds market. In the real world, of course, there are many interest rates. There is the mortgage rate, the prime interest rate (the rate charged to business firms with strong credit ratings), the consumer loan rate, and the credit card rate, to name only a few.

Interest rates in the loanable funds market will differ mainly because of differences in the risks associated with the loans. It is riskier, for example, to loan money to an unemployed worker than to a well-established business with substantial assets. Similarly, credit card loans are riskier than loans secured by an asset. An example of a secured loan is a mortgage loan on a house. If the borrower defaults, the lender can repossess the house. The risk also increases with the duration of the loan. The longer the time period, the more likely that the ability of the borrower to repay the loan or market conditions will change—perhaps unfavorably.

As **Exhibit 2** shows, the money rate of interest on a loan has three components. The pure-interest component is the real price one must pay for earlier availability. The inflationary-premium component reflects the expectation that the loan will be repaid with dollars of less purchasing power as the result of inflation. The risk-premium component reflects the probability of default—the risk imposed on the lender by the possibility that the borrower may be unable to repay the loan.

THE PRESENT VALUE OF FUTURE INCOME AND COSTS

If you deposited $100 today in a savings account earning 6 percent interest, you would have $106 one year from now. To put it another way, the present value of $106 one year from now is equal to the amount ($100) you would have to invest today in order to get $106 a year later. ***The interest rate allows us to make this calculation. The interest rate connects the value of dollars (and capital assets) today with the value of dollars (expected income and receipts) in the future. It is used to "discount" the value of a dollar received in the future so that its present worth can be determined today.***

The **present value (PV)** of a payment received one year from now can be expressed as follows:

Present value (PV)
The current worth of future income after it is discounted to reflect the fact that revenues in the future are valued less highly than revenues now.

$$PV = \frac{\textit{Receipts One Year from Now}}{1 + \text{Interest Rate}}$$

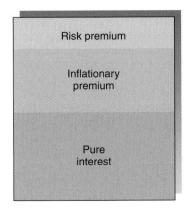

Risk premium

Inflationary premium

Pure interest

EXHIBIT 2
The Three Components of Money Interest

The money interest rate reflects three components: pure interest, inflationary premium, and risk premium. When decision makers expect a high rate of inflation while the loan is outstanding, the inflationary premium will be substantial. Similarly, the risk premium will be large when the probability of default by the borrower is substantial.

If the interest rate is 6 percent, the current value of $100 to be received one year from now is

$$PV = \frac{100}{1.06} = 94.34$$

If you put $94.34 in a savings account yielding 6 percent interest, during the year the account would earn $5.66 interest (6 percent of $94.34) and grow to $100 one year from now. Thus, the present value of $100 to be received a year from now is $94.34.

Discounting
The procedure used to calculate the present value of future income, which is inversely related to both the interest rate and the amount of time that passes before the funds are received.

Economists use the term **discounting** to describe this procedure of reducing the value of a dollar to be received in the future to its present worth. Clearly, the value of a dollar in the future is inversely related to the interest rate. For example, if the interest rate is 10 percent, the present value of $100 received one year from now would be only $90.91 ($100 divided by 1.10). At still higher interest rates, the present value of $100 a year from now would be even lower.

The present value of $100 received two years from now is

$$PV = \frac{100}{(1 + Interest\ Rate)^2}$$

If the interest rate is 6 percent, $100 received two years from now would be equal to $89 today ($100 divided by 1.06^2). In other words, $89 invested today would yield $100 two years from now.

The present-value procedure can be used to determine the current value of any future income (or cost) stream. If R represents receipts received at the end of various years in the future (indicated by the subscripts) and i represents the interest rate, the present value of the future income stream is

$$PV = \frac{R}{(1 + i)} + \frac{R_2}{(1 + i)^2} + \cdots + \frac{R_n}{(1 + i)^n}$$

Exhibit 3 shows the present value of $100 received at various times in the future at several different discount rates. The chart clearly illustrates two points. First, the present value of income received in the future declines with the interest rate. The present value of the $100 received a year from now, when discounted at a 4 percent interest rate, is $96.15, compared to $98.04 when a 2 percent discount rate is used. Second, the present value of the $100 also declines as the date of its receipt is set further into the future. If the discount rate is 6 per-

EXHIBIT 3
The Present Value of $100 to be Received in the Future

The columns indicate the present value of $100 to be received a designated number of years in the future at different discount (interest) rates. For example, at a discount rate of 2 percent, the present value of $100 to be received five years from now is $90.57. Note that the present value of the $100 declines as either the interest rate or the number of years in the future increases.

PRESENT VALUE OF $100 TO BE RECEIVED
A DESIGNATED NUMBER OF YEARS
IN THE FUTURE AT ALTERNATIVE DISCOUNT RATES

YEARS IN THE FUTURE	2 PERCENT	4 PERCENT	6 PERCENT	8 PERCENT	12 PERCENT	20 PERCENT
1	98.04	96.15	94.34	92.59	89.29	83.33
2	96.12	92.46	89.00	85.73	79.72	69.44
3	94.23	88.90	83.96	79.38	71.18	57.87
4	92.39	85.48	79.21	73.50	63.55	48.23
5	90.57	82.19	74.73	68.06	56.74	40.19
6	88.80	79.03	70.50	63.02	50.66	33.49
7	87.06	75.99	66.51	58.35	45.23	27.08
8	85.35	73.07	62.74	54.03	40.39	23.26
9	83.68	70.26	59.19	50.02	36.06	19.38
10	82.03	67.56	55.84	46.32	32.20	16.15
15	74.30	55.53	41.73	31.52	18.27	6.49
20	67.30	45.64	31.18	21.45	10.37	2.61
30	55.21	30.83	17.41	9.94	3.34	0.42
50	37.15	14.07	5.43	2.13	0.35	0.01

cent, the present value of $100 received a year from now is $94.34, compared to $89 if the $100 is received two years from now. If the $100 is received five years from now, its current worth is only $74.73. *So the present value of a future dollar payment is inversely related to both the interest rate and how far in the future the payment will be received.*

To see in a more personal way the importance of interest and the value of saving, consider what you could gain by saving just $1,000 per year ($83.33 per month) for ten years in a tax-free individual retirement account. If you begin at age twenty-five and continue only until age thirty-five (putting nothing into the account after that), and the account returns 8 percent annually, it will be worth $168,627 when you reach age sixty-five. In contrast, if you wait until age thirty-five and then save $1,000 per year for thirty years (not ten years of savings as before) with the same 8 percent annual return, by age sixty-five your account will be worth only $125,228. Ten years of saving, starting at age twenty-five, yields far more than thirty years of saving at the same amount each year but waiting to start until age thirty-five. Which savings plan is more attractive to you?

PRESENT VALUE, PROFITABILITY, AND INVESTMENT

Investment decisions, like saving decisions, require us to compare costs and benefits over time. Investment involves an up-front cost of acquiring a machine, skill, or other asset expected to generate additional output and revenue in the future. How can an investor know if the expected future revenues will be sufficient to cover the costs? The discounting procedure helps provide the answer. It permits the investor to place both the costs and the expected future revenues of an investment project in present-value terms. If the present value of the revenue derived from the investment exceeds the present value of the cost, it makes sense to undertake the investment. If the revenues and costs of such an investment turn out as expected, the investor will earn a profit, and the project will create wealth.

On the other hand, if the cost of the project exceeds the discounted value of the future receipts, the project is a loser. The losses reflect that the project diminished the value of the resources. Investments like these are counterproductive.

Let's pencil in the figures for a hypothetical investment option and determine whether it is a good investment. Suppose that a truck rental firm is contemplating the purchase of a new $40,000 truck. Past experience indicates that after figuring in the truck's operational and maintenance expenses, the firm can rent it out for a net revenue of $12,000 annually (received at the end of each year). The firm will be able to do this every year for four years—the expected life of the vehicle.[2] Since the firm can borrow and lend funds at an interest rate of 8 percent, we will discount the future expected income at an 8 percent rate. **Exhibit 4** illustrates the calculation. Column 4 shows how much $12,000, available at year-end for each of the next four years, is worth today. In total, the present value of the expected rental receipts is $39,744—less than the purchase price of the truck. Therefore, the project should not be undertaken.

YEAR (1)	EXPECTED FUTURE INCOME RECEIVED AT YEAR-END (2)	DISCOUNTED VALUE PER DOLLAR (8 PERCENT RATE) (3)	PRESENT VALUE OF INCOME (4)
1	$12,000	$0.926	$11,112
2	12,000	0.857	10,284
3	12,000	0.794	9,528
4	12,000	0.735	8,820
Total			$39,744

EXHIBIT 4
The Discounted Present Value of $12,000 of Truck Rental Receipts for Four Years (Interest Rate = 8 Percent)

[2]For the sake of simplicity, we assume that the truck has no scrap value at the end of four years.

APPLICATIONS IN ECONOMICS

Would You Like to Become a Millionaire?

In the previous chapter, we indicated that approximately one out of every twenty American households has assets worth a million dollars or more. The proportion of millionaires among those fifty-five to sixty-four years of age is even higher. Many millionaires earned large incomes in business, professional, and other activities, but some achieved this status even though their incomes were not very much different from those of other Americans. They did so by saving and investing regularly throughout their lives.

How could a person become a millionaire without making a huge income? Saving and compound interest provide the answer. The real rate of return on a broad portfolio of stock has averaged more than 7 percent during the last 200 years. Moreover, stock investments over 35- to 40-year periods have consistently earned a real return in this range. A real return of 7 percent is highly realistic for even a novice investor. Those with more entrepreneurial talent might well do better. If a 25-year-old began putting money into a tax-free retirement account, pension fund, or similar investment earning a 7 percent real return, how much would the person have to save annually in order for the funds to be worth a million dollars (measured in the purchasing power of today's dollar) when he or she reaches age 65? The answer is $5,009. Put another way, a person (or household) with an income of $50,000 (which is only slightly above the U.S. average) could achieve millionaire status by saving just 10 percent of it annually. A 5 percent savings rate would do the job with $100,000 of income annually. The power of compound interest illustrates that millionaire status is well within the reach of many Americans willing to save and invest for many years.

If the interest rate in our example had been 6 percent, the results would have been different. The present value of the future rental income would have been $41,580.[3] It pays to purchase a capital good whenever the present value of the income generated by it exceeds its purchase price. At the lower interest rate, the investment project would have been productive (and profitable).

Expected Future Earnings and Asset Values

The present value of the expected revenue from a project minus the cost of an investment will tell us whether the project should be undertaken. However, *once an investment project has been completed,* the present value of the expected future net earnings will determine the market value of the asset. If the present value of the expected net earnings rises (or falls), so too will the value of the asset.

The value of an asset is equal to the present value of the expected net revenues that can be earned by the asset. If the asset is expected to generate a constant annual net income each year in the future, its value would be equal to:

$$Asset\ Value\ =\ \frac{Annual\ Net\ Income\ from\ the\ Asset}{Interest\ Rate}$$

What is the market value of a tract of land that is expected to generate $1,000 of rental income net of costs each year indefinitely into the future? If the market interest rate is 10 percent, investors would be willing to pay $10,000 for the land ($1,000 divided by .10).

---

[3]The derivation of this figure is shown in the following tabulation:

YEAR	EXPECTED FUTURE INCOME (DOLLARS)	DISCOUNTED VALUE PER DOLLAR (6% RATE)	PRESENT VALUE OF INCOME (DOLLARS)
1	12,000	0.943	11,316
2	12,000	0.890	10,680
3	12,000	0.840	10,080
4	12,000	0.792	9,504
Total			41,580

When purchased at this price, the land would provide an investor with the 10 percent market rate of return. Similarly, if an asset generates $2,500 of net earnings annually and the market interest rate is 10 percent, the asset would be worth $25,000 ($2,500 divided by .10). There is a direct relationship between the expected future earnings generated by an asset and the asset's market value. ***As the present value of the future earnings of an asset increases, so, too, does the market value of the asset.***

This link between expected future earnings and the price of an asset motivates asset owners to make sure that the assets are being used wisely. Some entrepreneurial investors are particularly good at (1) identifying a business that is poorly operated, (2) purchasing the business at a depressed price, (3) improving the operational efficiency of the firm, and then (4) reselling the business at a handsome profit. Suppose that a poorly run business currently has net earnings of $1 million per year. What is the market value of the business? If the firm is expected to continue earning $1 million per year, the market value of the firm would be $10 million if the interest rate is 10 percent. Suppose that an alert entrepreneur buys the business for $10 million and improves the operational efficiency of the firm. As the result of these changes, the annual net earnings of the firm increase to $2 million per year. Now how much is the firm worth? If the $2 million annual earnings are expected to continue into the future, the net present value of the firm would rise to $20 million. Thus, the entrepreneur would be able to sell the firm for a very substantial profit. You can see from this example that business managers and asset owners have a strong incentive to use the resources under their control efficiently. If they don't, the value of the assets will decline, and the business will be vulnerable to a takeover by those who do.

Investors and Corporate Investments

In modern market economies, investors typically are not entrepreneurs who personally decide which factories to expand, which machine tools to build, and which research investments to undertake. Instead corporate officers, under the scrutiny of corporate boards of directors, make the entrepreneurial capital investment choices. Nevertheless, individual investors (buyers and sellers of stock) influence that process through the stock market. Stock market investors who believe that a corporation is currently making decisions likely to increase its future profits will buy more of the corporation's stock, driving up its price. Similarly, stockholders who believe that the corporation's current investment decisions will reduce future profits have an incentive to "bail out" by selling their stock holdings, reducing the market value of the stock. Either way, the price of a corporation's shares gives corporate officers fast feedback on what investors think of their decisions.

Do corporate officers respond to stock price changes? Normally they do. Often they own stock themselves, and the value of their pay package generally depends on the stock price. Also, the members of the corporate board (which hires and fires the officers) are typically large shareholders. Thus, the corporate officers have a strong incentive to act on the feedback from the stock market. The choices of individual buyers (and nonbuyers) of the firm's products are the ultimate judge of its performance. However, the choices of investors and their fund managers provide early information about the expected success of business ventures.

INVESTING IN HUMAN CAPITAL

Investments in human capital (like the decision to go to college, for example) are the same as other investment decisions. As with physical capital, discounting can also help us gauge whether or not to make a human capital investment.

Exhibit 5 shows the human capital decision confronting Juanita, an eighteen-year-old high school graduate thinking about pursuing a bachelor's degree in business administration. Just as an investment in a truck involves a cost in order to generate a future income, so does a degree in business administration. If Juanita does not go to college, she will be

EXHIBIT 5
Investing in Human
Capital

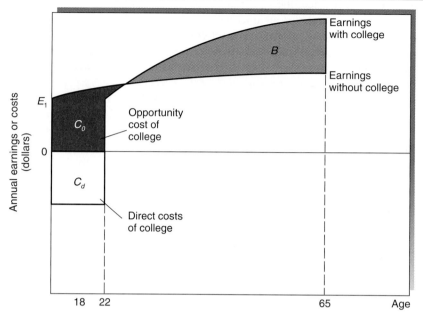

Juanita, an eighteen-year-old who has just finished high school, is trying to decide whether or not to go to college and get a business degree. If Juanita goes to college and majors in business administration, she will incur the direct cost (C_d) of the college education—tuition, books, transportation, and so on—plus the opportunity cost (C_o) of earnings she forgoes while in college. However, with a business degree, she can expect to earn an additional amount of income (B) during her career. If the discounted present value of the additional future earnings exceeds the discounted value of the direct and indirect costs of a college education, the business degree will be a profitable investment for Juanita.

able to begin work immediately, starting at annual earnings of E_1. But if she goes to college, she will incur direct costs (C_d) in the form of tuition, books, transportation, and related expenses. She will also bear the opportunity cost (C_o) of lower earnings while she's in college. However, studying business will expand Juanita's knowledge and skills, and enable her to earn more money later (see the areas in the exhibit labeled "Earnings with college" versus "Earnings without college"). Will the higher future income be worth the cost? To answer this question, Juanita must project the additional income she would earn by getting a business degree, discount each year's additional income, and compare the total with the discounted value of the cost of getting the degree—including the opportunity cost of the earnings she forgoes while attending college. If the discounted present value of Juanita's additional future income exceeds the discounted present value of the cost, acquiring the degree is a worthwhile investment.

Of course, nonmonetary considerations might also be important to Juanita. For example, Juanita might prefer having a degree and working in the business world (rather than in the jobs available to high school graduates) even if she did not make more money. Thus, the nonmonetary attractiveness of business may induce her to pursue the business degree, even if the monetary rate of return is low (or even negative).

Like choosing to purchase a new machine, choosing a human capital investment project such as Juanita's degree involves cost, the possibility of profit, and uncertainty. The same principles apply to both types of decisions. Giving due consideration to nonmonetary factors as a potential "benefit," human capital investors, like physical capital investors, will undertake only those projects that they think will yield benefits greater than their costs.

UNCERTAINTY, ENTREPRENEURSHIP, AND PROFIT

As we previously discussed, firms and individual investors can sometimes earn persistent economic profits—returns in excess of the opportunity cost of funds—if they can restrict entry into various industries and occupations. Economic profits, however, can also be earned in competitive markets with no entry restrictions. ***In competitive markets, there are two sources of economic profit: uncertainty and entrepreneurship.***

First, let's talk about how uncertainty enables people to earn an economic profit. Investment opportunities put people in a position to earn a handsome return, but they also expose them to additional uncertainty. We live in a world of uncertainty, imperfect information, and dynamic change. Unanticipated changes, changes that no one could have foreseen, create winners and losers. If people didn't care about the uncertainty related to different investment projects, they wouldn't demand higher returns for higher-risk projects. Most people, though, dislike uncertainty. They would prefer to know that they'll collect $1,000 rather than take a 50-50 chance of collecting either nothing or $2,000. To accept the uncertainty associated with riskier investments, they will demand a premium—an economic profit. For example, compared to government bonds, the returns on stocks are considerably more uncertain. This uncertainty of return is one reason that stocks have historically yielded a higher average return than bonds.

Entrepreneurship is a second source of economic profit. Some people are better than others at identifying entrepreneurial opportunities. At any given time, there are infinite numbers of potential investment projects to choose from in the economy. Investing in some of them will increase the value of resources and lead to handsome returns. Investing in others will actually reduce the value of resources, generating losses. Entrepreneurship involves the ability to recognize and undertake economically beneficial projects that have gone unnoticed by others. Creativity, foresight, and leadership are important aspects of entrepreneurship. Naturally, risk is involved. Unfortunately, all too frequently, the entrepreneur's vision turns out to have been a mirage. What appeared to be a profitable opportunity turns out to be an expensive mistake.

The great Harvard economist Joseph Schumpeter believed that entrepreneurship and innovation were the moving forces behind capitalism. According to Schumpeter, the entrepreneurial discovery of new, improved ways of doing things drove economic progress and improved living standards. As Schumpeter put it,

> The fundamental impulse that sets the capitalist engine in motion comes from the new consumer's goods, the new methods of production or transportation, and new markets, and the new forms of industrial organization that capitalist enterprise creates.[4]

OUTSTANDING ECONOMIST	Joseph Schumpeter (1883–1950)	

Born in Austria, Joseph Schumpeter was a longtime professor of economics at Harvard University. Generally recognized as one of the top five economists of this century, Schumpeter is perhaps best known for his views on entrepreneurship and the future of capitalism. He believed that the discovery and introduction of new and better products and organizational methods were constantly making the old ways of doing things obsolete. He referred to this process as "creative destruction" and argued that it was the primary fuel of economic progress.

[4]Joseph A. Schumpeter, *Capitalism, Socialism, and Democracy* (New York: Harper Torchbooks, 1950), 83.

The introduction of new products often makes older ones obsolete. Examples abound: the personal computer replaced the typewriter, digital music players replaced the phonograph, and digital cameras are replacing film models. Joseph Schumpeter referred to outcomes of this type as "creative destruction." How does creative destruction influence the living standards of people like you?

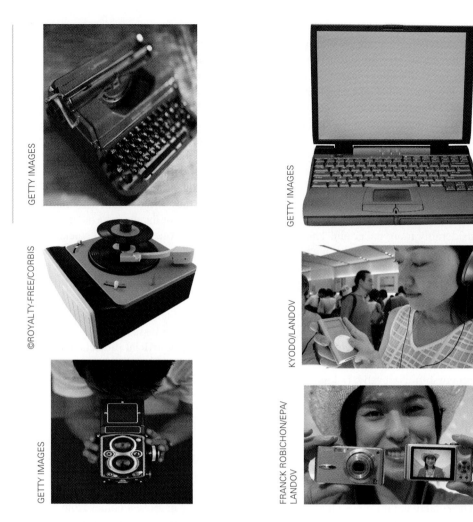

To finance their investments, would-be entrepreneurs usually have to use their own money and the money of co-venturers, in addition to whatever they can borrow. Entrepreneurs with successful track records find it easier to get capital for their investment projects. As a result, in a market economy, successful entrepreneurs will have a greater say about which projects will be undertaken and which will not.

Returns to Physical and Human Capital

Both interest and profit perform important allocative functions. Interest induces people to give up current consumption, a sacrifice that is necessary for capital formation. Economic profit provides both human and physical capital decision makers with the incentive to (1) undertake investments yielding an uncertain return and (2) discover and undertake beneficial (wealth-creating) investment opportunities.

Income reflects the returns from both human capital and physical capital. As **Exhibit 6** shows, approximately four-fifths of the national income in the United States is earned by employees and self-employed workers. The earnings in these two categories primarily reflect a return on human capital. The other one-fifth—income in the form of interest, corporate profits, and rents—reflects mostly returns to physical capital.[5] These shares of human and physical capital have been relatively constant for several decades.

---

[5]As used here, rent is income derived by owners who lease (rent) assets like buildings and equipment to another party for a period of time.

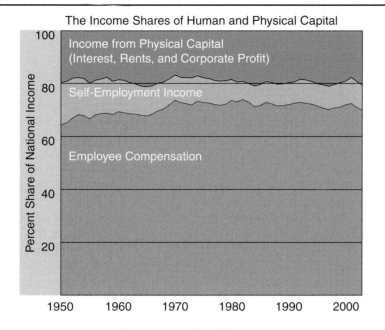

The Income Shares of Human and Physical Capital

Source: http://www.bea.doc.gov/.

EXHIBIT 6
The Income Shares of Human and Physical Capital

The share of national income earned by employees, self-employed proprietors, and owners of physical capital (interest, corporate profits, and rents) is shown here. Employee compensation and self-employment income represent primarily returns to human capital. These two components have constituted approximately 80 percent of total national income in the United States for several decades.

THE CAPITAL MARKET AND THE WEALTH OF NATIONS

 If the potential gains from innovative ideas and human ingenuity are going to be fully realized, it must be relatively easy for individuals to try their innovative and potentially ingenious ideas, but difficult to continue if the idea is a bad one.

Innovation and the Capital Market

Improved knowledge about how to transform resources into desired goods and services is the main reason that our output today is far greater than our ancestors' a century or two ago. Predictably, further improvements in our knowledge and and the innovative applications of those improvements will propel growth and prosperity in the future, as well. The human ingenuity and entrepreneurial talent capable of pushing the frontier of economic progress outward are found everywhere and often come from unexpected sources. For example, college dropout Ted Turner, the founder of CNN, transformed the way people around the world received news during the last two decades of the twentieth century. A relatively unsuccessful marketer of milk shake machines (Ray Kroc) perfected the franchising business and developed McDonald's into the world's largest restaurant chain. A plainspoken owner of a small retail store in one of the poorest states (Sam Walton, founder in Arkansas of Wal-Mart) became America's largest retailer.

It is impossible to determine who will come up with the next innovative idea that will promote human progress. This makes it vitally important that individuals from all backgrounds and walks of life be able to try out their ideas at a relatively low cost. Of course, counterproductive projects can waste substantial amounts of resources. Thus, if a nation is going to get the most out of its resources, it must also have a mechanism that will bring unsound projects to a halt.

Competitive capital markets perform these two functions. In a market economy, it is relatively easy to try out a new idea. Entrepreneurs do not have to convince a majority of the populace or key political leaders that their idea is sound. They can undertake the project if they can get the required financing. This can be achieved by either putting up one's own money or convincing financiers of the project's profit potential merits. Once the project is undertaken, in order to continue, it will have to pass the market test. If the revenues derived from sale of the output produced are insufficient to cover the cost, it will be difficult to keep the project afloat. Losses will soon drive unprofitable business ventures from the market. Conversely, if a project is profitable, this will encourage operation on a larger scale.

The modern capital market also accommodates lenders with widely varying preferences and goals. For example, a person wanting to save for retirement that will begin only ten years from now may nonetheless be willing to buy a new twenty-year bond from General Motors or some other private firm because the bond market makes it relatively easy to sell the bond to another person if the bondholder desires to do so. Varying preferences for risk are also accommodated. Some people want to supply savings in exchange for a fixed rate of return. People who purchase bonds and maintain savings deposits are examples. Others are willing to supply funds in exchange for an uncertain return linked to the success or failure of a business or investment project. Stockholders and partnership investors fall into this category. Still others supply funds to the capital market when they use their own funds to purchase a business or acquire additional schooling.

Private investors, ranging from small-business owners to corporate stockholders to venture capitalists, place their own funds at risk in the capital market. This provides them with a strong incentive to search for, discover, and undertake profitable projects—those that generate revenues that exceed costs. In turn, profit indicates that people value the output more than the resources utilized. Thus, profitable investments tend to increase not only the wealth of the investor, but also the wealth of the nation.

In an uncertain world, of course, mistakes will occur. Sometimes projects will be undertaken that prove unprofitable. If investors were unwilling to take chances, many innovative ideas and worthwhile but risky projects would never be tested. In a world of uncertainty, mistaken investments are a necessary price that must be paid for fruitful innovations to occur. The capital market will at least ensure that the mistakes are self-correcting. Unexpected losses will signal investors to terminate unprofitable and unproductive projects, and investors whose own wealth is at stake will be very sensitive and responsive to these signals.

In summary, the capital market will tend to direct savings toward entrepreneurial activities that are profitable. When property rights are clearly defined and enforced, profitable projects will also be productive—they will create wealth. Properly guided investment in both physical and human capital is an important source of productivity and income growth. Other things being constant, countries that invest more and channel more of their investments into productive projects today will tend to have a higher income tomorrow.

Without a private capital market, it is hard to see how investment funds could be consistently channeled into wealth-creating projects. In today's dynamic world, economic

The capital market will channel the savings of individuals into the finance of investment goods like trucks and earth-moving equipment. Does it make any difference whether these investment projects are profitable? Why or why not?

©BILL ARON/PHOTO EDIT

©JOHN B. BOYKIN/CORBIS

growth is driven by discovery and innovation. Given the pace of dynamic change and the diversity of entrepreneurial talent that exists in the world, the knowledge required for making sound decisions about how capital should be allocated is far beyond the scope of any single gifted leader, industrial planning committee, or government agency. Perhaps more important, when investment funds are allocated by the government rather than by the market, an entirely different set of criteria comes into play. The individual voter, unlike a partner or an owner of stock, has little incentive to be alert for new opportunities or wary of investment mistakes made by government officials. Furthermore, the citizen-voter can neither (1) invest more upon discovery of an attractive project nor (2) opt out (sell) when problems are detected. Consequently, voters in economies like these are in a weak position to monitor and direct government investment effectively. Most simply remain on the sidelines. As they do so, the political clout of special interests replaces market returns as the basis for allocating funds. Predictably, investment projects that reduce wealth rather than enhance it become more likely.

The experience of Eastern Europe and the former Soviet Union provides a vivid illustration of what happens when political factors replace economic considerations in the allocation of investment. At one time, the investment rates of these countries were among the highest in the world. Their central planners, in fact, channeled approximately one-third of the national output into capital formation. Living standards were kept low to finance these investments. But even these high rates of investment did little to improve living standards over time. Government planners and state enterprises were slow to incorporate scientific breakthroughs. Available consumer goods generally reflected outdated technologies. Funds were often wasted on political boondoggles and high-visibility projects favored by important political leaders. Misdirection of investment and failure to keep up with dynamic change eventually led to the collapse of the system.

LOOKING AHEAD

As the preceding two chapters have stressed, investment in physical and human capital will influence the wealth and income of both individuals and nations. Differences among individuals with regard to these factors will also contribute to income inequality. In the next chapter, we will consider the issue of income inequality in some detail.

KEY POINTS

▼ We can often produce more consumption goods by first using our resources to produce physical and human capital resources and then using these capital resources to produce the desired consumption goods. Because resources used to produce capital goods will be unavailable for the direct production of consumption goods, saving is necessary for investment.

▼ The interest rate is the price of earlier availability. It is the premium that borrowers must pay to lenders to acquire goods now rather than later.

▼ The demand for loanable funds reflects the productivity of capital resources and the positive rate of time preference. The market interest rate will bring the quantity of funds demanded by borrowers into balance with the quantity supplied by lenders.

▼ During inflationary times, the money rate of interest incorporates an inflationary premium reflecting the expected future increase in the price level. When inflation is expected, the money rate of interest exceeds the real rate of interest.

▼ The money rate of interest on a specific loan reflects three basic factors—the pure interest rate, an inflationary premium, and a risk premium that is directly related to the probability of default by the borrower.

▼ The interest rate allows individuals to put a current value on future revenues and costs. The discounting procedure can be used to calculate the present value of an expected net income stream from a potential investment project. If the present value of the expected revenues exceeds the present value of the expected costs—and if things turn out as expected—the project will be profitable.

▼ The present value of expected future net earnings will determine the market value of existing assets. An increase in the expected future earnings of an asset will increase the market value of the asset. Conversely, a decrease in the expected future earnings of an asset will reduce the market value of the asset.

▼ Economic profit plays a central role in allocating capital and determining which investment projects will be undertaken. In a competitive environment, economic profit reflects uncertainty and entrepreneurship—the ability to recognize and undertake profitable projects that have gone unnoticed by others.

▼ To grow and prosper, a nation must have a mechanism that will attract savings and channel them into investments that create wealth. The capital market performs this function in a market economy. When property rights are clearly defined and enforced, profits and losses will channel investment into projects that promote economic progress.

CRITICAL ANALYSIS QUESTIONS

*1. How would the following changes influence the rate of interest in the United States?
  a. An increase in the positive time preference of lenders
  b. An increase in the positive time preference of borrowers
  c. An increase in domestic inflation
  d. Increased uncertainty about a nuclear war
  e. Improved investment opportunities in Europe

2. "Any return to capital above the pure interest yield is unnecessary. The pure interest yield is sufficient to provide capitalists with the earnings necessary to replace their assets and to compensate for their sacrifice of current consumption. Any return above that is pure gravy; it is excess profit." Do you agree with this view? Why or why not?

3. How are human and physical capital investment decisions similar? How do they differ? What determines the profitability of a physical capital investment? Do human capital investors make profits? If so, what is the source of the profit? Explain.

*4. A lender made the following statement to a borrower: "You are borrowing $1,000, which is to be repaid in twelve monthly installments of $100 each. Your total interest charge is $200, which means your interest rate is 20 percent." Is the effective interest rate on the loan really 20 percent? Explain.

5. In a market economy, investors have a strong incentive to undertake profitable investments. What makes an investment profitable? Do profitable investments create wealth? Why or why not? Do all investments create wealth? Discuss.

*6. Over long periods of time, the rate of return of an average investment in the stock market has exceeded the return on high-quality bonds. Is the higher return on stocks surprising? Why or why not?

7. The interest rates charged on outstanding credit card balances are generally higher than the interest rate that banks charge customers with a good credit rating. Why do you think the credit card rate is so high? Should the government impose an interest rate ceiling of, say, 10 percent? If it did, who would be hurt and who would be helped? Discuss.

*8. If the money rate of interest on a low-risk government bond is 10 percent and the inflation rate for the last several years has been steady at 4 percent, what is the estimated real rate of interest?

9. Suppose that you are contemplating the purchase of a commercial lawn mower at a cost of $10,000. The expected lifetime of the machine is three years. You can lease the asset to a local business for $4,000 annually (payable at the end of each year) for three years. The lessee is responsible for the upkeep and maintenance of the machine during the three-year period. If you can borrow (and lend) money at an interest rate of 8 percent, will the investment be a profitable undertaking? Is the project profitable at an interest rate of 12 percent? Provide calculations in support of your answer.

*10. Alicia's philosophy of life is summed up by the proverb, "A penny saved is a penny earned." She plans and saves for the future. In contrast, Mike's view is, "Life is uncertain; eat dessert first." Mike wants as much as possible now.
  a. Who has the higher rate of time preference?

b. Do people like Alicia benefit from the presence of people like Mike? Explain.

c. Do people like Mike benefit from the presence of people like Alicia? Explain.

*11. Some countries with very low incomes per capita are unable to save very much. Are people in these countries helped or hurt by people in high-income countries with much higher rates of saving?

*12. According to a news item, the owner of a lottery ticket paying $3 million over twenty years is offering to sell the ticket for $1.2 million cash now. "Who knows?" the ticket owner explained. "We might not even be here in twenty years, and I do not want to leave it to the dinosaurs."

a. If the ticket pays $150,000 per year at the end of each year for the next twenty years, what is the present value of the ticket when the appropriate rate for discounting the future income is thought to be 10 percent?

b. If the discount rate is in the 10 percent range, is the sale price of $1.2 million reasonable?

c. Can you think of any disadvantages of buying the lottery earnings rather than a bond?

13. Suppose that you are moving into a new apartment you expect to rent for five years. The owner of the apartment offers to provide you with a used refrigerator for free and promises to maintain and repair the refrigerator during the next five years. You also have the option of buying a new, energy-efficient refrigerator (with a free, five-year maintenance agreement) for $700. The new refrigerator will reduce your electric bill by $150 per year and will have a market value of $200 after five years. If necessary, you can borrow money from the bank at an 8 percent rate of interest. Which option should you choose?

*14. Suppose that you are considering whether to enroll in a summer computer training program that costs $2,500. If you take the program, you will have to give up $1,500 of earnings from your summer job. You figure that the program will increase your earnings by $500 per year for each of the next ten years. Beyond that, it is not expected to affect your earnings. If you take the program, you will have to borrow the funds at an 8 percent rate of interest. From a strictly monetary viewpoint, should you enroll in the program?

15. "In a world of uncertainty, it is important that entrepreneurs be able to introduce new products and try out innovative ideas. But it is also important that unproductive projects be brought to a halt." Evaluate this statement.

*16. Will political officials be more likely than private investors and entrepreneurs to channel funds into wealth-creating projects? Why or why not? Discuss.

*Asterisk denotes questions for which answers appear in Appendix B

CHAPTER

27

Income Inequality and Poverty

All animals are equal, but some animals are more equal than others.

—*George Orwell*[1]

Chapter Focus

■ How do resource prices and income differences influence the incentive of people to develop resources and use them productively?

■ How much income inequality is there in the United States? Has the degree of inequality changed in recent years?

■ How much income mobility exists? Do the rich stay rich while the poor stay poor?

■ How widespread is poverty? How has the poverty rate changed in recent decades? Did the War on Poverty help reduce the poverty rate?

■ Is there too much income inequality? Should the government try to reduce inequality? Why or why not?

[1]George Orwell, *Animal Farm* (New York: Harcourt and Brace Company, 1946), p. 112.

Differences in resource prices and the productivity of individuals will cause incomes to vary. Of course, economic inequality is present in all societies. Neither politics nor central planning will eliminate it. Nonetheless, most of us are troubled by the extremes of inequality—the extravagant luxury of some and the grinding poverty of others. How much inequality is there in the United States? Do wealthy families continually enjoy high incomes? Are those in poverty unable to escape it? What effect have income transfer programs had on the welfare of the poor? Do these income transfer programs lessen the incentive for both the poor and nonpoor to earn income? This chapter focuses on these questions and related issues. ▪

HOW MUCH INCOME INEQUALITY EXISTS IN THE UNITED STATES?

Money income is only one component of economic well-being. Factors such as leisure, non-cash transfer benefits, the nonmonetary advantages and disadvantages of a job, and the expected stability of future income also affect people's economic welfare. Money income is quite important, however, because it makes it possible to buy market goods and services. It is also easy to measure and is therefore widely used as a yardstick of economic well-being and inequality prevailing in society.

Exhibit 1 presents data on money income in the United States. First, look at the share of *before-tax* annual money income by quintile—that is, by each fifth of the total population of families—ranked from the lowest to the highest. If there were total income equality, each quintile (20 percent) of families would generate 20 percent of the aggregate income. Given the differences in education, skills, ability, work effort, ages, family sizes, and other factors among families, clearly we would not expect this to be the case. Some

EXHIBIT 1
Share of Money Income by Quintile During Selected Years, 1950–2001

	LOWEST 20 PERCENT OF RECIPIENTS	SECOND QUINTILE	THIRD QUINTILE	FOURTH QUINTILE	TOP 20 PERCENT OF RECIPIENTS
FAMILY INCOME BEFORE TAXES					
1950	4.5	12.0	17.4	23.4	42.7
1960	4.8	12.2	17.8	24.0	41.3
1970	5.4	12.2	17.6	23.8	40.9
1980	5.1	11.6	17.5	24.3	41.6
1990	4.6	10.8	16.6	23.8	44.3
2001	4.2	9.7	15.4	22.9	47.7
IMPACT OF TAXES AND TRANSFERS ON 2001 HOUSEHOLD INCOME					
BEFORE	3.5	8.7	14.6	23.0	50.1
AFTER	4.4	10.4	16.3	24.0	44.9

Source: Bureau of the Census, *Current Population Survey,* Series P-60; *Statistical Abstract of the United States, 1995,* table 733; Congressional Budget Office; 1994, Green Book; and Bureau of the Census, *Money Income in the United States: 2002.*

families will be able to generate more income than others. It is, however, informative to look at the shares of income by quintile.

The figures show that before-tax income inequality fell throughout the 1950s and 1960s. In other words, the income gap between the top and bottom earning quintiles closed. For example, in 1970, the top quintile earned 40.9 percent of the aggregate money income, down from 42.7 percent in 1950. During the same period, the share of income earned by the lowest quintile rose from 4.5 percent in 1950 to 5.4 percent in 1970.

Beginning in the 1970s, however, this trend reversed. During the last three decades, the share of income earned by the top quintile has steadily risen, while that earned by the bottom group has fallen.[2] By 2001, the share of before-tax money income of the top group had risen to 47.7 percent, while that earned by the bottom 20 percent of families had fallen to 4.2 percent. Thus, in 2001, the top quintile of families earned approximately 11 times as much before-tax money income as the bottom quintile of families.

Low-income families are the primary beneficiaries of noncash transfer programs that provide people with food (food stamps), health care, and housing. Correspondingly, under a system of progressive taxation, which the United States has, taxes take a larger share of income as one's earnings increase. As a result, we would expect *after-tax and transfer* incomes to be more equal than before-tax incomes. Using household data, Exhibit 1 shows that this is indeed the case. After taxes and transfers, the bottom quintile of households received 4.4 percent of the total income in 2001 (compared to 3.5 percent of the before-tax income), and the top quintile of families received 44.9 percent (compared to 50.1 percent before taxes). Notice that taxes and transfers increased the income share of every quintile except the top group. As you can see, taxes and transfers do, in fact, reduce income inequality. [*Note:* Household income is used here because after-tax and family transfer-income data are unavailable. In addition to families, households include individuals living by themselves and unrelated persons living together.]

A market economy does not have a central distributing agency that carves up the economic pie and allocates slices to various individuals. Rather, each individual produces his or her own slice of the pie. If one person's income grows, it does not mean that another's must shrink. The distribution of income is actually a result of many individual efforts and decisions. We now turn to consider what factors underlie the distribution of income in the United States.

The Factors Affecting Income Distribution

How meaningful are the data of Exhibit 1? If all families (and households) were similar except with regard to the amount of income they earned, the use of annual income data as an index of inequality would be quite reasonable. However, the fact is that the aggregate data lump together (1) small and large families, (2) prime-age earners and elderly retirees, (3) multi-earner families and families without any current earners, and (4) husband-wife families and single-parent families.

Consider just one factor: the impact of age and the pattern of lifetime income. Typically, the annual income of young people is low, particularly if they are going to school or are getting training. Many people under 25 years of age studying to be lawyers, doctors, engineers, and economists will have low annual incomes during this phase of their lives. But this does not mean they are poor—at least not in the usual sense. After completing their formal education and acquiring work experience, these people move into their prime working years. At this point, their annual incomes are generally quite high, particularly in families in which both spouses are employed outside the home. Remember, however, that this is also a time when families are purchasing homes and providing for their children, which is costly. Consequently, the economic well-being of these people as measured by their earnings may well be overstated. In other words, although these people are earning

---

[2]A reduction in the share of income earned by the bottom quintile income group does not imply that their income level fell. It merely indicates that their income did not grow as rapidly as that of other groups, particularly the top quintile. The inflation-adjusted income of the bottom quintile of earners has increased in recent decades.

more at this stage in their lives, they also have more responsibilities. Finally, people reach the retirement phase, characterized by less work, more leisure, and smaller family sizes. Even families that are quite well-off tend to experience incomes well below average during the retirement phase. *Given the life cycle of income, lumping together families of different ages (phases of their life-cycle earnings) results in substantial inequality in the annual income figures. This would be so even if the incomes of families over a lifetime were approximately equal.*

Exhibit 2 highlights major differences between high- and low-income families that underlie the distributional data of Exhibit 1. The typical high-income family (top 20 percent) is headed by a well-educated person in the prime working-age phase of life. His or her income is supplemented by the earnings of other family members, particularly working spouses. In contrast, people with little education, nonworking retirees, younger workers (under age 35), and single-parent families are substantially overrepresented among low-income families (the bottom 20 percent of income recipients). In 2001, 34 percent of the householders in the lowest income quintile failed to complete high school, compared to only 3 percent for the highest income quintile. Although only 9 percent of the household heads in the bottom quintile completed college, 58 percent of the householders in the top group did so. Seventy-nine percent of the high-income families had household heads in the prime working-age category (age 35 to 64), compared with only 44 percent of the low-income families. Only one parent was present in 49 percent of the low-income families, whereas 93 percent of the high-income group were dual-parent families. High-income families are also larger than low-income families, which might surprise you. In 2001, there were 3.4 persons per family in the top income quintile, compared to only 2.9 persons per family in the bottom quintile.

There was a striking difference between low- and high-income families in the percentage of hours each group worked. No doubt, much of this difference reflected factors like family size, the age of the wage earners, whether or not both spouses worked, and whether two spouses are present in the home. In high-income families, the average number of workers per family was 2.2, compared with 0.80 for low-income families. Among married-couple families, a wife working full time was present only 13 percent of the time in low-income families, compared to 63 percent of the time in high-income families. As

	BOTTOM 20 PERCENT OF INCOME RECIPIENTS	TOP 20 PERCENT OF INCOME RECIPIENTS	
EDUCATION OF HOUSEHOLDER			**EXHIBIT 2**
Percent with less than high school	34	3	**Differing**
Percent with college degree or more	9	58	**Characteristics of**
AGE OF HOUSEHOLDER			**High- and Low-income**
(PERCENT DISTRIBUTION)			**Families, 2001**
Under 35	32	13	
35–64	44	79	
65 and over	24	8	
FAMILY STATUS			
Married-couple family (percent of total)	51	93	
Single-parent family (percent of total)	49	7	
PERSONS PER FAMILY	2.9	3.4	
EARNERS PER FAMILY	0.80	2.2	
Percent of married-couple families in which wife works full time	13	63	
PERCENT OF TOTAL HOURS WORKED			
SUPPLIED BY GROUP	10	25	

Source: U.S. Department of Commerce, *Money Income in the United States:* 2001 (Washington, DC: Government Printing Office, 2002).

we would expect, couples who decide not to have the wife work full-time pay for this choice by falling down the income distribution ladder.

In terms of their work effort, the top 20 percent of income recipients contributed 25 percent of the total number of hours worked in the economy, whereas the bottom 20 contributed only 10 percent of the total work time. In other words, high-income families worked 2.5 times as many hours as low-income families. As we noted on page 590, they also earned approximately 11 times as much before-tax income. This implies that the earnings per hour worked by the top income recipients were only about 4.4 times the earnings per hour worked by the low-income recipients. Clearly, differences in the amount of time worked were a major factor contributing to the income inequality of Exhibit 1.

In summary, Exhibit 2 sheds a great deal of light on the distributional data presented in Exhibit 1. ***Those with high incomes are far more likely to be well-educated, dual-parent families with both parents working outside the home in their prime earning years. In contrast, those with low incomes are often single-parent families headed by a poorly educated adult who is either youthful or elderly. The household heads of those families with little income are often either out of the labor force or working only part-time.*** Given these factors, it is not surprising that the top 20 percent of recipients have substantially higher incomes, both before and after taxes, than the bottom quintile.

Why Has Income Inequality Increased?

Exhibit 1 indicates that there has been an increase in income inequality in the United States during the last couple of decades. Why has the gap between the rich and the poor been growing? Research in this area shows that at least four factors have contributed to the rise in inequality.

1. The Increasing Proportion of Single-parent and Dual-earner Families The nature of the family and the allocation of work responsibilities within the family have changed dramatically in recent decades. In 2002, more than one-fourth (28 percent) of all families with children were headed by a single parent, double the figure of the mid-1960s. At the same time, the labor force participation rate of married women increased from 40 percent in 1970 to 62 percent in 2002.

As a result, today we now have more single-parent families and more dual-earner families. Both of these changes tend to promote income inequality. Consider two hypothetical families, the Smiths and the Browns. In 1970, both were middle-income families with two children and one parent working earning $40,000 (in 2005 dollars). Now consider their 2005 counterparts. The Smiths of 2005 are divorced, and one of them, probably Mrs. Smith, is trying to work part-time and take care of the two children. The probability is very high that the single-parent Smith family of 2005 will be in the low- rather than the middle-income category. The Smiths may well be in the bottom quintile of the income distribution. In contrast, the Browns of 2005 both work outside the home, and each earns $40,000 annually. Given their dual incomes, the Browns are now a high- rather than a middle-income family. Along with many other dual-income families (see Exhibit 2), the Browns' 2005 family income will probably place them in the top quintile of income recipients.

Even if there were no changes in earnings between skilled and less-skilled workers, the recent changes within the family would increase the income inequality among families and households. Today, more single-parent families like the Smiths fall into the low-income quintile, while more dual-earner families like the Browns fall into the high-income quintile. The gap between the earnings of these two groups has therefore increased the overall income inequality in the United States.

2. Earnings Differentials between Skilled and Less-skilled Workers In 1970, workers with little education who were willing to work hard, often in a hot and sweaty environment, received high wages. This is less true today. In 1974, the annual earnings of men who graduated from college were only 27 percent higher than the earnings of male high school graduates—hardly a huge payoff for the time and cost of a college degree.

Since 1974, however, things have changed dramatically. By the mid-1980s, the earnings premium of male college graduates relative to male high school grads rose to the 50–60 percent range, approximately twice the premium of 1974. By 2002, the income premium of male college graduates relative to high school graduates rose to 85 percent. Similarly, during the last two decades, the earnings of women college graduates have increased sharply relative to women with only a high school education.

Why have the earnings of persons with more education (and skill) risen relative to those with less education (and skill)? Deregulation of the transportation industry and the declining power of unions may have reduced the number of high-wage, blue-collar jobs available to workers with little education. International competition has also played a role because, increasingly, American workers must compete in a global economy. Furthermore, innovations and cost reductions in both communications and transportation have made it easier for firms to hire workers in different locations. Firms producing goods that require substantial amounts of low-skilled labor can easily move to places like Korea, Taiwan, and Mexico, where low-skilled labor is cheaper. In contrast, the United States is more attractive than most other countries to firms requiring substantial amounts of high-skilled, well-educated workers. Globalization has, therefore, reduced the demand for American workers with few skills and little education but increased the demand for high-skilled workers with college degrees. This has made for a wider earnings gap among workers in high-income countries like the United States. However, it is worth noting that this process enhances income levels in low-income countries and thereby reduces *worldwide* income inequality.[3]

3. The Increasing Number of Markets Characterized by a Few People at the Top with Very High Earnings As we discussed in the chapter on wage differentials, the market compensation of star entertainers and athletes, the most talented professionals, and top business executives is often like that of winner-take-all tournaments. At any point in time, a few people at the top have huge earnings, while most others in these areas have modest or even low incomes. As transportation and communication costs have declined, markets have increasingly become national and even global, rather than local. This increases the incomes of a few people at the top, but it also increases the degree of income inequality.

4. Sharply Lower Marginal Tax Rates than in the 1970s Prior to 1981, high-income Americans confronted top marginal tax rates of up to 70 percent (50 percent of their earnings). This encouraged high-income earners to structure their business affairs and invest in ways that sheltered much of their income from the Internal Revenue Service. As we indicated in Chapter 4, the taxable incomes of the top 10 percent of earners expanded sharply when the top marginal tax rates were reduced to the 30 percent range during the 1980s. Some of this increase in income reflected greater work effort due to the increased incentive to earn. Much of it, however, merely reflected the fact that people were engaging in fewer activities to shelter their earnings from taxes. The flip side of fewer tax shelter activities accompanying lower marginal tax rates led to an increase in the visible income of the rich. As more of the income of the rich is observable, money income statistics such as those of Exhibit 1 will register an increase in income inequality.

INCOME MOBILITY AND INEQUALITY IN ECONOMIC STATUS

Statistics on the distribution of annual income fail to reveal **income mobility**—movement up and down the income ladder. Therefore, they may be misleading. Consider two countries with identical distributions of annual income. In both cases, the annual income of the top quintile of income recipients is ten times greater than the bottom quintile. Now, suppose that in the first country—we will refer to it as Static—the same people are at the top

Income mobility
Movement of individuals and families either up or down income-distribution rankings when comparisons are made at two different points in time. When substantial income mobility is present, a person's current position in the rankings will not be a very good indicator of what his or her position will be a few years in the future.

---

[3]For additional information on the relationship between international trade and income inequality, see Gary Burtless, "International Trade and the Rise in Earnings Inequality," *Journal of Economic Literature* (June 1995): 800–816; and Symposium on "Income Inequality and Trade," *Journal of Economic Perspectives* (Summer 1995).

of the income distribution year after year. Similarly, the poor people of Static remain poor year after year. Static is characterized by an absence of income mobility. In contrast, earners in the second country, which we will call Dynamic, are constantly changing places. Indeed, during every five-year period, each family spends one year in the upper-income quintile, one year in each of the three middle-income quintiles, and one year in the bottom-income quintile. In Dynamic, no one is rich for more than one year (out of each five), and no one is poor for more than a year. Obviously, the nature of economic inequality in Static is vastly different from that in Dynamic. You would not know it, though, by looking at their identical annual income distributions.

The contrast between Static and Dynamic highlights an important point: income mobility is an important facet of economic inequality. Until recently, detailed data on income mobility were sparse. This is now beginning to change.[4] **Exhibit 3** presents data on the mobility of family income between 1988 and 1998 in the United States. The data compare the relative income positions of the *same families* at two different points in time. Based on their 1988 income, each family was placed into income quintiles ranked from highest to lowest. Later, the 1998 real-income level of the *same families* was used once again to group the income of each by quintiles.

The first row of Exhibit 3 shows the relative income position in 1998 of people in the top quintile of income recipients in 1988. Approximately one-half (53 percent) of those with incomes in the top quintile in 1988 were able to maintain this lofty position 10 years later. Slightly less than one-half (47 percent) of the top income group in 1988 had fallen to a lower income quintile by 1998. However, less than 1 in 10 of the high-income individuals fell to one of the bottom two quintiles of the 1998 income distribution. This suggests that once families are able to achieve high-income status, they rarely fall back to a very low level of income.

The bottom row of Exhibit 3 tracks the experience of those in the lowest-income quintile in 1988. Slightly more than half (53 percent) of the families in the lowest-income quintile remained there in 1998. Nearly one-quarter (23 percent) moved up to one of the top three income quintiles in 1998. Among those in the next-to-lowest income quintile in 1988, nearly two-fifths (38 percent) had moved up to one of these higher-income groupings by 1998.

The income mobility data reveal something concealed by the annual figures: there is considerable movement up and down the economic ladder. Relative income positions often change over time. A sizable portion of those with a high relative income during one year subsequently find themselves in a lower income position. At the same time, many of

---

EXHIBIT 3
Income Mobility—Income Ranking, 1988 and 1998

INCOME STATUS OF FAMILY, 1988	PERCENTAGE DISTRIBUTION BY INCOME STATUS OF FAMILY IN 1998				
	HIGHEST QUINTILE	NEXT-HIGHEST QUINTILE	MIDDLE QUINTILE	NEXT-LOWEST QUINTILE	LOWEST QUINTILE
Highest Quintile	53.2	23.2	14.9	5.7	3.0
Next-Highest Quintile	25.8	31.1	23.7	12.9	6.5
Middle Quintile	12.6	27.5	28.3	20.7	10.9
Next-Lowest Quintile	4.3	11.0	22.6	36.3	25.7
Lowest Quintile	4.3	6.4	12.4	23.6	53.3

Source: Katherine Bradbury and Jane Katz, "Women's Labor Market Involvement and Family Income Mobility When Marriages End," *New England Economic Review,* Fourth Quarter 2002, pages 41–74.

---

[4]For a review of the literature on income mobility, see Isabel V. Sawhill and Daniel P. McMurrer, *Income Mobility in the United States* (Washington, DC: Urban Institute, 1996). For an early classic work on this topic, see Greg J. Duncan et al., *Years of Poverty, Years of Plenty: The Changing Fortunes of American Workers and Families* (Ann Arbor: Institute for Social Research, University of Michigan, 1984).

GETTY IMAGES

Generational Mobility: There is a weak positive correlation between the earnings of fathers and sons. If a father has lifetime earnings 20 percent above the average of his generation, a son can expect to earn about 8 percent more. There is virtually no correlation between the earnings of grandparents and their grandchildren. Apparently, there is some truth in the old saying, "From shirtsleeves to shirtsleeves in three generations."

those with low relative incomes during a given year move up to higher-income quintiles in subsequent years.

Many economists argue that differences in household expenditures are a more accurate indicator of economic status than annual income precisely because of this. If your income or earnings prospects in the future are good, you're likely to spend more than your current income. On the other hand, if your future income is expected to be lower, you're likely to save more, causing spending to be less than your current income. To a large degree, current expenditures reflect long-term economic status.

What do expenditures reveal about the degree of inequality in the United States? The expenditure statistics indicate that the degree of inequality is significantly smaller than the corresponding figure for annual income. For example, in recent years, the household expenditures of the bottom 20 percent of households have summed to approximately 7 percent of the total. This is substantially greater than their income share both before and after taxes. Correspondingly, the expenditures of the top 20 percent of households have constituted approximately 38 percent of the total, well below their income share. Moreover, the share of household expenditures by quintile has been relatively constant during the last four decades. This suggests that the increase in inequality as measured by the annual income data is a reflection of dynamic change, temporary fluctuations in annual income, and measurement issues rather than a true increase in economic inequality.

POVERTY IN THE UNITED STATES

In an affluent country like the United States, income inequality and poverty are related issues. Poverty could be defined in strictly relative terms—the bottom one-fifth of all income recipients, for example. However, this definition would not be very helpful because it would mean that poverty would never fall below what these 20 percent earn.

The official definition of poverty in the United States is based on the perceived minimum income necessary to provide food, clothing, shelter, and basic necessities economically for a family to survive. This **poverty threshold income level** varies with family size and composition, and it is adjusted annually for changes in prices. The official poverty threshold is based only on money income. (See the Measures of Economic Activity feature for additional details on how the poverty rate is measured.)

Who are the poor? **Exhibit 4** presents data on both the number of poor families and the poverty rate for 1959, 1976, and 2003. In 2003, 7.6 million families, 10.0 percent of

Poverty threshold income level
The level of money income below which a family is considered to be poor. It differs according to family characteristics (for example, number of family members) and is adjusted when consumer prices change.

MEASURES OF ECONOMIC ACTIVITY

How Is the Poverty Rate Calculated?

Families and individuals are classified as poor or nonpoor based on the poverty threshold income level originally developed by the Social Security Administration (SSA) in 1964. Consumption survey data showed that low- and median-income families of three or more persons spent approximately one-third of their income on food. Because of this, the SSA established the poverty threshold income level at three times the cost of an economical, nutritionally adequate food plan. A slightly larger multiple was used for smaller families and individuals living alone. The poverty threshold figure varies according to family size, because the food costs vary by family size and composition. It is adjusted annually to account for rising prices. The following chart illustrates how the poverty threshold for a family of four has increased as prices have risen from 1959 to 2004:

1959	$2,973
1970	3,968
1980	8,414
1990	13,359
2004	18,850

Even though the poverty threshold income level is adjusted for prices, it is actually an absolute measure of economic status. As real income increases, the poverty threshold declines relative to the income of the general populace.

The official poverty rate is the number of persons or families living in households with a money income below the poverty threshold as a percentage of the total. Only money income is considered. Income received in the form of noncash benefits, like food stamps, medical care, and housing subsidies, is completely ignored in the calculation of the official poverty rate. Because of this omission, the official rate tends to overstate the degree of poverty. To remedy this deficiency, the Bureau of the Census has developed several alternative measures of poverty that count the estimated value of noncash benefits as income. In addition to the official poverty rate, the bureau now publishes annual data for the "adjusted" poverty rates that include a valuation for various noncash benefits. Of course, including these benefits reduces the poverty rate. For example, the official poverty rate for families was 10.0 percent in 2003, but the adjusted poverty rate that included the value of the noncash food, housing, and medical benefits was only 7.4 percent.

The poverty rate is calculated each year based on a survey of about 60,000 households designed to reflect the population of the United States. The two major sources for comprehensive data on this topic are the Bureau of the Census annual publications, *Money Income in the United States* and *Poverty in the United States*.

EXHIBIT 4

The Changing Composition of the Poor and Poverty Rates, Selected Groups: 1959, 1976, and 2003

	1959	1976	2003
Number of Poor Families (in millions)	8.3	5.3	7.6
Percent of Poor Families Headed by a:			
Female	23	48	51
Black	26	30	27
Elderly person (age 65 and over)	22	14	10
Person who worked at least some during the year	70	55	48
Poverty Rate			
All families	18.5	10.1	10.0
Married couple families	15.8	7.2	5.4
Female-headed families	42.6	32.5	28.0
All individuals	22.4	11.7	12.5
Whites	18.1	9.1	10.5
Blacks	55.1	31.1	24.4
Children (under age 18)	27.3	16.0	17.6

Sources: U.S. Department of Commerce, *Characteristics of the Population Below the Poverty Level: 1982, Table 5;* and *Poverty in the United States: 2003, (P60-226).*

the total, were classified as poor. Half of these families were headed by a woman. As Exhibit 4 shows, there has been a substantial change in the composition of the poverty population during the last four decades. In 1959, elderly persons and the working poor formed the core of the poverty population. Twenty-two percent of the poor families were headed by an elderly person in 1959 versus only 10 percent by 2003. In 1959, 70 percent of the heads of poor families worked at least part of the year, but in 2003, only 48 percent of them worked at least part of the year.

During the last several decades, the proportion of families headed by women in the United States has increased while the proportion of husband-wife families has decreased. Since the poverty rate of families headed by women is several times higher than the rate for husband-wife families (28.0 percent compared with 5.4 percent in 2003), an increase in family instability tends to push the poverty rate upward. It also tends to increase the number of households headed by women among poor families. In 2003, 51 percent of the poor families were headed by a woman, compared to only 23 percent in 1959.

Rather than calculating the poverty rate of families, one could measure the poverty rate of individuals. The poverty rate of individuals is, in fact, somewhat higher than the poverty rate of families. In 2003, 12.5 percent of people in the United States were classified as poor, compared to 10.0 percent for families. The poverty rate of blacks in 2003 was 24.4 percent, compared to 10.5 percent for whites. Nonetheless, 70 percent of the people in poverty were white. Perhaps the most tragic consequence of poverty is its impact on children. Little progress has been made in this area during the last two decades. In 2003, 17.6 percent of the children in the United States lived in poverty, up from 16.0 percent in 1976.

Just as people move up and down the income distribution ladder, there is movement into and out of poverty. A large proportion of poor families remain poor for only a brief period of time. For example, 34.2 percent of the U.S. population was poor for two consecutive months between 1996 and 1999. However, only 2.0 percent of the population were poor during the entire period. In fact, the median duration of poverty spells during 1996–1999 was only 4 months. Many of these short-term spells of poverty were the result of factors like medical problems or job changes. In fact, poverty is a long-term problem for only a small number of families in the United States.

Transfer Payments and the Poverty Rate

In the mid-1960s, it was widely believed that an increase in income transfers directed toward the poor would substantially reduce, if not eliminate, the incidence of poverty. The 1964 *Economic Report of the President* argued that poverty could be virtually eliminated if the federal government increased its expenditures on transfer programs by approximately 2 percent of aggregate income. Following the declaration of the "War on Poverty" by President Lyndon Johnson's administration, transfer expenditures increased rapidly. Measured in 1982–1984 dollars, **means-tested income transfers**—those limited to people with incomes below a certain cutoff point—tripled, expanding from $24 billion in 1965 to $70 billion in 1975. After 1975, transfer expenditures continued to expand, but the rate of increase was slower. Measured as a share of aggregate income, means-tested transfers jumped from 1.5 percent in 1965 to 5.2 percent in 2000.

Did the expansion in government income transfers reduce the poverty rate as the 1964 *Economic Report of the President* anticipated? **Exhibit 5** shows the poverty rate from 1947 through 2003. Interestingly, the poverty rate declined substantially during the period prior to the War on Poverty. It fell from 32 percent in 1947 to 13.9 percent in 1965. The downward trend continued for a few more years, reaching 10 percent in 1968. However, shortly after the War on Poverty was initiated, the downward trend in the poverty rate came to a halt. Since 1968, the poverty rate has fluctuated within a narrow band around the 10 percent level. In 2003, it was 10.0 percent—the same as it was in 1968. When noncash benefits like Medicaid and food stamps were counted as income, the poverty rate was lower, but the overall pattern is still much the same. This is particularly remarkable when you consider that over this same time span, real income per person in the United States approximately doubled.

Means-tested income transfers
Transfers that are limited to persons or families with an income below a certain cutoff point. Eligibility is thus dependent on low-income status.

**EXHIBIT 5
The Poverty Rate,
1947–2003**

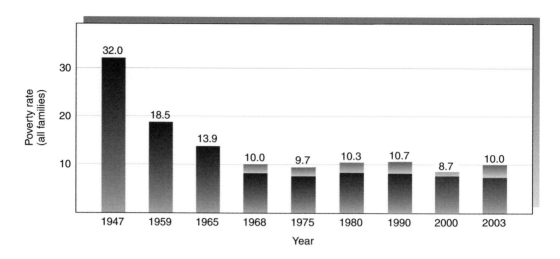

The official poverty rate of families fell sharply during the 1950s and 1960s, but it has remained near 10 percent since 1968. The shaded area of the bars show the additional decline in the poverty rate when noncash benefits are counted as income. When the value of these noncash transfer benefits is added, the poverty rate ranges from 7 percent to 8 percent. This statistic remained unchanged throughout most of the 1968–2003 period.

Sources: U.S. Department of Commerce, *Characteristics of the Population Below the Poverty Level: 1982, Table 5*; and *Poverty in the United States: 2002,* (P60-226).

Samaritan's dilemma
The dilemma that occurs when assisting low-income citizens with transfers reduces the opportunity cost of choices that lead to poverty. Providing income transfers to the poor and discouraging behavior that leads to poverty are conflicting goals.

Implicit marginal tax rate
The amount of additional (marginal) earnings that must be paid explicitly in taxes or implicitly in the form of lower income supplements. The marginal tax rate establishes the fraction of an additional dollar earned that an individual is permitted to keep, so it is an important determinant of the incentive to work.

Why wasn't the War on Poverty more effective? One reason is because means-tested income transfers generate two major side effects that reduce their effectiveness. ***First, transfer programs that significantly reduce the hardship of poverty also reduce the opportunity cost of choices that often lead to poverty.*** This factor is sometimes called the Samaritan's dilemma. To the extent that antipoverty programs reduce the negative effects of, for example, births by unmarried mothers, abandonment of children by fathers, dependence on drugs or alcohol, or dropping out of school, they inadvertently encourage people to make choices that result in these conditions. Of course, this is not the intent of the transfers, but nonetheless it is one of their side effects. In the short run, these secondary effects are probably not very important. Over the longer term, however, their negative consequences can be substantial.

Second, income-linked transfers reduce the incentive of low-income individuals to help themselves. When the size of transfers is linked to income, larger transfers tend to increase the implicit marginal tax rate imposed on the poor. The implicit marginal rate is the amount of additional (marginal) earnings that must be paid explicitly in taxes or—in the case of the poor—implicitly in the form of lower income supplements. The marginal tax rate determines the fraction of an additional dollar earned that an individual is permitted to keep, so it is an important determinant of the incentive to work. Participants in the food stamp program, for example, have their food stamp benefits reduced by $30 for every $100 of income they earn. Consequently, every $100 of additional income leads to only a $70 increase in well-being (spendable net income) after the reduction in food stamp benefits is taken into account. When a person qualifies for several programs like food stamps, Medicaid, and housing benefits, the problem is compounded, and the combined implicit marginal tax rate can frequently exceed 50 or 60 percent. In some cases, the rate may exceed 100 percent. In other words, if recipients work, the money they make can actually reduce the family's economic status. Because the high implicit marginal tax rates reduce the incentive of poor families to work and earn, transfers often merely replace income that otherwise would have been earned. When this is the case, they add little or nothing to the *net* income of the poor.

Estimating the Costs of Redistribution

The U.S. government has numerous income transfer programs, including many that are unrelated to helping the poor. In 2003, income transfers and subsidy programs intended to help various groups purchase food, housing, and health care summed to 22 percent of aggregate income. As we discussed in Chapter 6, politicians will often be able to gain by proposing programs that provide concentrated benefits to readily identifiable groups (for example, farmers, senior citizens, or unemployed workers) while imposing a small personal cost on disparate groups like taxpayers and consumers in general. Because of this, the presence and size of transfer programs is not surprising.

Income transfers are also costly in terms of the economy's overall output level. The higher marginal tax rates needed to finance transfers and subsidies mean that taxpayers get to keep less of what they earn. Furthermore, recipients often qualify for larger transfers

---

APPLICATIONS IN ECONOMICS

Competition for Transfers and the Net Gain of Recipients

As the data of this chapter show, the achievements of antipoverty transfer programs fell short of initial expectations. Indeed, the economic way of thinking would lead a person to believe that it's difficult to transfer income to a group of recipients in a way that will significantly improve their long-term well-being. The unintended consequences that alter people's incentives explain why this is true.

Governments must establish criteria to determine who should get the transfers, subsidies, and other political favors and who should not. Without these criteria, benefit programs would exhaust their budgets. Typically, governments require potential recipients to do something, own something, buy something, or be something in order to qualify for the transfer. But, as people take the steps necessary to qualify, they erode much of the benefit.

Consider the case in which the recipients have to do something (for example, fill out forms, take an exam, submit a detailed proposal, lobby government officials, endure delays, or contribute to selected political campaigns) in order to obtain the transfer. These actions are costly and will reduce the recipient's net gain. In some cases, almost all of the gain may be eroded. Perhaps a simple example will help illustrate this important point. Suppose the U.S. government decided to give away a $50 bill between 9 a.m. and 5 p.m. each week day to anyone willing to show up at one of six teller windows at the U.S. Department of Treasury. Certainly, a line would emerge. How much time would people be willing to wait in the line? A person whose time was worth $5 per hour would be willing to spend up to 10 hours waiting in line for the $50. But it might take longer than 10 hours if there were enough other people, whose

time was worth less, say $3 or $4 per hour. And everyone would find that the waiting consumed much of the value of the $50 transfer. If the government's objective is to make the recipients $50 richer, it will fail. In fact, some of those waiting in line for the $50 bill will gain very little. For example, if the wait were 10 hours, the net benefit of a person with an opportunity cost of $4.90 would be only $1. So it is with real-world transfers. When you consider the cost of what has to be done for someone to qualify for the transfer, the net gain of the recipient is often small.

In other cases, the government will require recipients to own something (for example, land with an acreage allotment to grow wheat, a license to operate a taxicab, or a permit to sell in a restricted market) in order to qualify for a transfer or subsidy. Recipients will gain when programs like this are initiated or unexpectedly expanded. But once programs of this type are established, people will bid up the price of the asset needed to acquire the subsidy. The higher price of the asset, such as the taxicab license or the land with a wheat allotment, will capture the value of the expected future subsidy. Once this happens, the rate of return in the business or occupation (for example, farming or operating a taxicab) will be driven down to the normal level. The current recipients don't benefit from the subsidy program continuing at the expected benefit level. Essentially, they paid for the expected benefit of the subsidy when they purchased the asset needed to get it.

Interestingly, even though they don't benefit, current recipients will fight to keep the program going if it is threatened. Repealing (or reducing) the subsidies will be harmful because it will reduce the value of the asset they currently hold. This explains why eliminating farm subsidies, for example, is difficult even though the subsidies do not make farming more profitable for the current operators.

(continued)

APPLICATIONS IN ECONOMICS

(continued)

Economist Gordon Tullock refers to this as the *transitional gains trap*, because, once programs like these get started, they will be difficult to eliminate even though current recipients aren't benefiting from them.[1]

Sometimes recipients are required to purchase a good or service in order to qualify for a subsidy. For example, the Medicare and Medicaid programs subsidize health care purchases made by senior citizens and the poor. Several states provide educational subsidies for college tuition or the purchase of textbooks. As we discussed in Chapter 4, subsidizing the purchase of a good will increase its demand and lead to higher prices. As a result, some of the benefits of such subsidies will accrue to the suppliers rather than the purchasers. Again, the subsidized recipients will not gain as much as it might appear.

Finally, sometimes the government requires that recipients be something in order to qualify for the subsidy. Programs of this type are often intended to help protect people against the adverse effects of certain events such as unemployment or catastrophic storms. Unfortunately, the programs also encourage choices that increase the ad-

verse effects of such events. For example, consider the impact of subsidized insurance premiums for those living in hurricane-prone areas. These subsidies reduce the owners' personal cost of rebuilding their properties after a hurricane. But the lower personal costs also encourage people to build in hurricane-prone areas. As more of them do so, the overall cost of damage from hurricanes increases. The impact of unemployment insurance is much the same. The benefits paid to the unemployed will reduce the opportunity cost of continuing a job search while unemployed. As a result, periods of unemployment will be longer and the rate of unemployment higher than would have otherwise been the case.

The ability of transfers to improve the well-being of a designated group is more limited than is generally recognized. Transfer programs alter incentives and generate unintended consequences that erode some, if not most, of the benefits derived by the recipients. Thus, the net gains of the intended beneficiaries are often much less than they appear to be.

---

[1]See Gordon Tullock, "The Transitional Gains Trap," *Bell Journal of Economics* 6 (Autumn 1975), 671–678.

---

if their income is lower, which motivates them to earn even less. Thus, transfer programs typically weaken the incentive of both taxpayer-donors and the subsidy recipients to work and earn. As a result, the cost of the transfers will be greater than the amount of income transferred. A study by economists Sam Allgood and Arthur Snow sought to measure the loss of output due to the lower supply of labor associated with higher marginal tax rates accompanying income transfers.[5] Allgood and Snow estimated that it costs between $1.26 and $3.22 in terms of lost output for every additional dollar redistributed from the top 60 percent of income recipients to the bottom 40 percent.

Helping transfer recipients achieve long-term well-being is also more difficult than it first appears. Competition for the transfers and subsidies will often erode much of the recipient's gain. See the Application in Economics "Competition for Transfers and the Net Gain of Recipients" for more about how this works.

INCOME INEQUALITY: SOME CONCLUDING THOUGHTS

Is there too much inequality in the United States? Should transfer programs be expanded or contracted? These are normative questions that positive economics cannot definitively answer. Economics can help identify and quantify the cost (in terms of lost output) and the expected effectiveness of alternative programs, but it can't make a judgment about whether that cost or amount is good or bad. Many people, including a good number of

---

[5]See Sam Allgood and Arthur Snow, "The Marginal Cost of Raising Tax Revenue and Redistributing Income," *Journal of Political Economy* (December 1998). This study builds on earlier work by Edgar K. Browning and William Johnson, "The Trade-off between Equality and Efficiency," *Journal of Political Economy* (April 1984); and Charles L. Ballard, "The Marginal Efficiency Cost of Redistribution," *American Economic Review* (December 1988).

economists, would like to see income inequality reduced. Some dimensions of U.S. public policy are directed toward this. The progressive income tax system, the **Earned Income Tax Credit** (a tax credit that provides supplementary payments to workers with low incomes), and means-tested programs like food stamps, Medicaid, and housing subsidies are examples.

The problem is that the political process is multidimensional. It represents a diverse set of forces, including powerful special-interest groups. Therefore, it shouldn't surprise you that the political record in this area, like others, is mixed. Social Security, the largest income transfer program, redirects income toward the elderly, today a group with above-average levels of both income and wealth. Agriculture subsidies constitute another large transfer program; the bulk of these benefits go to large farmers with incomes well above the average. Another sizable share of government transfers is allocated to business interests, including many that are large and highly profitable. Thus, many of the income transfers are from those with modest incomes to those with incomes well above the average.

Finally, it is important to recognize that income in a market economy is not like manna from heaven. It is something people produce and earn by providing others with goods and services they are willing to pay for. The allocation of income reflects the choices of individuals with differing preferences, talents, educational levels, entrepreneurial skills, rate of saving, and so on. Wage differentials, profits, losses, and interest rates coordinate the choices of these vastly different individuals and bring them into harmony with one another. Income inequality is a natural outgrowth of this process. Indeed, policies that modify the process can generate perverse, counterproductive incentives.

When it comes to issues of fairness, some people argue that the process—the system, in other words—that generates the outcomes is more important than the actual result. Do all people in the economy have an opportunity to acquire education and training? Are people from all segments of society free to compete in business and labor markets? Do incomes reflect their choices, voluntary exchanges, and productive efforts? These questions are about opportunity, economic freedom, and how income is acquired. Many people believe that these things, rather than the income distribution patterns that result from them, are the key elements of economic fairness.

Perhaps the following example will illustrate the difference between the process and pattern view. Suppose a million people purchase a $10 lottery ticket, and the proceeds are used to finance a $10 million jackpot for one person. This activity will clearly increase income inequality. But is it unfair? Those who adhere to the process view would stress that the outcome merely reflects the voluntary choices of participants who were well aware of the rules of the game prior to their purchasing a ticket. According to this view, it is the process rather than the outcome that is the primary determinant of fairness.

Economics provides insight into both the allocative role and sources of differences in income. It also indicates that it will be costly, in terms of lost output, to redistribute income through taxes and transfers. Of course, this does not reveal whether there is too much inequality or whether the government should play a larger or smaller role in the allocation of income. It does, however, enable us to address these normative issues in a more thoughtful way.

Earned Income Tax Credit
A feature of the personal income tax system that provides supplementary payments to workers with low incomes.

LOOKING AHEAD

Income transfers are the focal point of many current policy issues, including Social Security and health care. The special topics in the following section analyze this issue and other topics.

KEY POINTS

▼ In 2001, the bottom 20 percent of families earned 4.2 percent of aggregate income; the top 20 percent of families earned approximately 11 times that amount (47.7 percent). After taxes and transfers are taken into account, the top quintile of households earn nearly 10 times the income of the bottom quintile.

▼ A substantial percentage of the inequality in annual income reflects differences in age, education, family size, marital status, number of earners in the family, and time worked. Young inexperienced workers, students, single-parent families, and retirees are over-represented among those with low current incomes.

▼ Income inequality has risen during the last 25 years. The following four factors contributed to this increase: (1) an increase in the proportion of both single-parent *and* dual-earner families, (2) an increase in earnings differentials on the basis of skill and education, (3) more "winner-take-all" markets, and (4) increases in the reported income of those in the top tax brackets due to lower marginal tax rates.

▼ The tracking of household income over time indicates that there is considerable movement of individuals both up and down the income spectrum. The data on the distribution of income at a particular point in time can be misleading because they do not reflect this movement up and down the income ladder.

▼ One-tenth of American families were officially classified as poor in 2003. Those living in poverty were generally younger, less educated, less likely to be working, and more likely to be living in families headed by a woman than those who were not poor. There is considerable movement both into and out of poverty. A relatively small proportion of families constitute the long-term poor.

▼ During the last several decades, income transfers—including means-tested transfers—have expanded rapidly both in real dollars and as a share of personal income. As a weapon against poverty, transfers have been largely ineffective. Even though per capita income increased by more than 100 percent between 1965 and 2002, there was little reduction in the overall poverty rate during this period.

▼ Income transfers large enough to improve the economic status of the poor will (1) encourage behavior that increases the risk of poverty and/or (2) create high implicit marginal tax rates that reduce the recipient's incentive to earn.

▼ Positive economics cannot determine how much inequality should be present. The nature of the income-generating process as well as the pattern of income distribution is relevant to the issue of fairness.

CRITICAL ANALYSIS QUESTIONS

1. Do you think the current distribution of income in the United States is too unequal? Why or why not? What criteria do you think should be used to judge the fairness of the distribution of income? Is the final outcome more important than the process that generates the income?

*2. Is annual money income a good measure of economic status? Is a family with an $80,000 annual income able to purchase twice the quantity of goods and services as a family with $40,000 of annual income? Is the standard of living of the $80,000 family twice as high as that of the $40,000 family? Discuss.

3. What is income mobility? If there is substantial income mobility in a society, how does this influence the importance of income distribution data?

*4. Consider a table such as Exhibit 3 in which the family income of parents is grouped by quintiles down the first column, and that of their offspring is grouped by quintiles across the other columns. If there were no intergenerational mobility in this country, what pattern of numbers would appear in the table? If the nation had attained complete equality of opportunity, what pattern of numbers would emerge? Explain.

5. Do individuals have a property right to income they acquire from market transactions? Is it a proper function of government to tax some people in order to provide benefits to others? Why or why not? Discuss.

*6. Because income transfers to the poor typically increase the implicit marginal tax rate they confront, does a $1,000 transfer payment necessarily increase the income of poor recipients by $1,000? Why or why not?

*7. Sue is a single parent with two children. She is considering a job that pays $800 per month. She is currently drawing monthly cash benefits of $300, food stamp benefits of $100, and Medicaid benefits valued at $80. If she accepts the job, she will be liable for employment taxes of $56 per month and lose all transfer benefits. What is Sue's implicit marginal tax rate for this job?

8. What groups are overrepresented among those with relatively low incomes? Do the poor in the United States generally stay poor? Why or why not?

9. Some people argue that taxes exert little effect on people's incentive to earn income. Suppose you were required to pay a tax rate of 50 percent on all money income you earn while in school. Would this affect your employment? How might you minimize the personal effects of this tax?

10. Large income transfers are targeted toward the elderly, farmers, and the unemployed, regardless of their economic condition. Why do you think this is so? Do you think there would be less income inequality if the government levied higher taxes in order to make larger income transfers? Why or why not?

11. The outcome of a state lottery game is certainly a very unequal distribution of the prize income. Some players are made very rich, while others lose their money. Using this example, discuss whether the fairness of the process or the fairness of the outcome is more important, and how they differ.

12. "Means-tested transfer payments reduce the current poverty rate. However, they also create an incentive structure that discourages self-sufficiency and self-improvement. Thus, they tend to increase the future poverty rate. Welfare programs essentially purchase a lower poverty rate today in exchange for a higher poverty rate in the future." Evaluate this statement.

13. Was the poverty rate increasing or decreasing prior to the War on Poverty initiated by the Johnson administration? As income transfer programs accompanying the War on Poverty increased beginning in the latter half of the 1960s, what happened to the poverty rate?

14. Suppose one family has $100,000 while another has only $20,000. Is this outcome fair? What is your initial reaction? Compare and contrast your views depending upon the following:
   a. The family with the higher income has both a husband and wife working, while the other family has chosen for the wife to remain home with the children rather than work in the labor force.
   b. The family with the higher income is headed by a person who completed a college degree, while the other family is headed by someone who dropped out of high school.
   c. The family with the higher income derived most of its income from the farm subsidy program.
   d. The family with the higher income received it as an inheritance from parents who just died.

---

*Asterisk denotes questions for which answers are given in Appendix B.

6
PART

Economics is about how the real world works

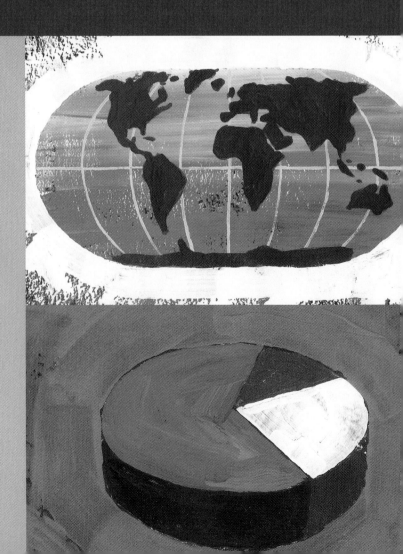

Applying the Basics: Special Topics in Economics

P A R T **6**

Economics has a lot to say about current issues and real world events. What impact will the internet have on your life? Why does the current social security system face problems and what might be done to minimize them? Is ownership of stock risky? Why is the unemployment rate higher in Europe than the United States? What might be done to improve the quality of health care and education? How can we best protect the environment? This section will focus on these topics and several other current issues.

Government Spending and Taxation

[A] wise and frugal government, which shall restrain men from injuring one another, shall leave them otherwise free to regulate their own pursuits of industry and improvement, and shall not take from the mouth of labor the bread it has earned. This is the sum of good government. . . .

—Thomas Jefferson[1]

A taxpayer is someone who works for the federal government but doesn't have to take a civil service examination.

—Ronald Reagan

Focus

- How has government spending per person changed historically in the United States?

- How has the composition of government spending changed in recent decades?

- Do taxes measure the cost of government?

- Do the rich pay their fair share of taxes? Do they pay a smaller share of taxes today than they did a couple of decades ago?

- How does the size of government in the United States compare with the size of governments of other countries?

[1]First Inaugural Address, March 4, 1801.

In Chapters 5 and 6, we analyzed the economic role of government and the operation of the political process. We learned that while the political process and markets are alternative ways of organizing the economy, a sound legal system, secure property rights, and stable monetary regime are vitally important for the efficient operation of markets. We also noted that there may be advantages of using government to provide certain classes of goods that are difficult to supply efficiently through markets. However, as public-choice analysis indicates, the political process is not a corrective device. Even democratic representative government will often result in the misuse of resources—spending on programs that are counterproductive. This feature will take a closer look at government in the United States and will provide some additional details with regard to the characteristics of both its spending and taxation. ■

GOVERNMENT EXPENDITURES

As we noted in Chapter 6, total government spending (federal, state, and local) sums to approximately one-third of the U.S. economy. Government spending on the purchase of goods and services, including the payments made to employees, accounts for about 20 percent of the total economy, while spending on transfer payments sums to nearly 15 percent of total income. Moreover, government spending has risen rapidly during the last seventy-five years. Measured as a share of the economy, government spending rose from less than 10 percent in 1929 to nearly 35 percent in 2002. The bulk of this increase in spending has taken place at the federal level.

Approximately three-fifths of the spending by government now takes place at the federal level. Federal expenditures on just four things, (1) income transfers (including Social Security and other income security programs), (2) health care, (3) national defense, and (4) net interest on the national debt, accounted for 85 percent of federal spending in 2003. (See Chapter 6, Exhibit 2.) This means that expenditures on everything else—the federal courts, national parks, highways, education, job training, agriculture, energy, natural resources, federal law enforcement, and numerous other programs—were less than 15 percent of the federal budget. Major spending categories at the state and local level include education, public welfare and health, transportation and highways, utilities, and law enforcement.

Government Spending per Person, 1792–2003

Article 1, section 8 of the U.S. Constitution outlined a limited set of functions that the federal government was authorized to perform. These included the authority to raise up an army and navy, establish a system of weights and measures, issue patents and copyrights, operate the Post Office, and regulate the value of money that it issued. Beyond this, the federal government was not authorized to do much else. The founders of the United States were skeptical of governmental powers, and they sought to limit those powers, particularly those at the federal level. (See the quotation by Thomas Jefferson at the beginning of this feature.)

During the United States' first 125 years, the constitutional limitations worked pretty much as planned; the economic role of the federal government was quite limited, and its expenditures were modest. In the nineteenth century, except during times of war, most government expenditures were undertaken at the state and local level. The federal government spent funds on national defense and transportation (roads and canals), but not much else.

Exhibit 1 presents data on real federal spending per person (measured in terms of the purchasing power of the dollar in 2000). Just prior to the Civil War, real federal expenditures were $50 per person, not much different than the $40 figure of 1800. Federal spending per person rose sharply during the Civil War, but it soon receded and remained in a range between $90 and $150 throughout the 1870–1916 period. Thus, prior to World War I, federal expenditures per person were low and the growth of government was modest.

EXHIBIT 1
Real Federal Expenditures per Capita: 1792–2003

Real federal spending per person (measured in 2000 dollars) was generally less than $50 prior to the Civil War, and it ranged from $90 to $150 throughout the 1870–1916 period. However, beginning with the spending buildup for World War I in 1917, real federal spending per person soared, reaching $6,938 in 2003—roughly sixty times the level of 1916.

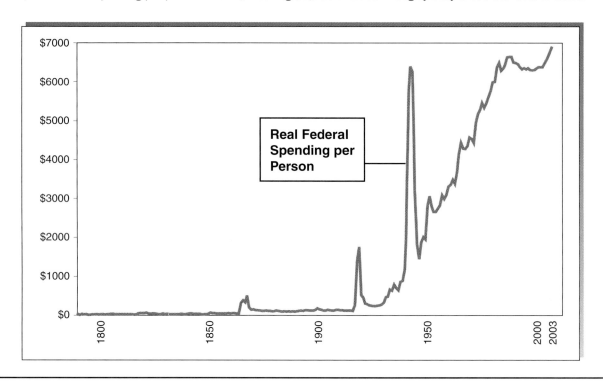

Source: U.S. Census Bureau, *Historical Statistics of the United States* (Washington, D.C.: U.S. Dept. of Commerce, U.S. Bureau of the Census, 1975) and *Economic Report of the President* (Washington, D.C.: U.S. Government Printing Office, 2004).

Beginning with the World War I spending of 1917, however, the situation changed dramatically. Federal spending remained well above the prewar levels during the 1920s and rose rapidly during the 1930s. It soared during World War II, and after receding at the end of the war, federal spending continued to grow rapidly throughout the 1950–1990 period. After a brief reduction during the 1990s, per capita real federal spending is once again on the upswing. In 2003, it amounted to $6,940, roughly sixty times the $112 figure of 1916. The additional government expenditures came with a cost. On average, Americans paid more federal taxes in one week during 2003 than they paid during the entire year in 1916.

How Has the Composition of Federal Spending Changed?

Not only has federal spending grown rapidly, there has also been a dramatic shift in the composition of that spending. Since 1960, spending on defense has fallen as both a share of the budget and as a share of the economy, while expenditures on health care, transfer payments, and subsidies have soared.

As **Exhibit 2** illustrates, defense expenditures constituted more than half (52.2 percent) of federal spending in 1960. By 2000, defense spending was only 16.5 percent of the federal budget. Because of the war in Iraq, defense spending has risen slightly since 2000 to 18.8 percent of the federal budget. In contrast, government expenditures on income transfers (including Social Security, agriculture subsidies, and other income transfer programs) and health care (primarily Medicare and Medicaid) rose from 21.5 percent of the federal budget in 1960 to 59.2 percent in 2003.

EXHIBIT 2
The Changing Composition of Federal Spending

In 2003, national defense expenditures accounted for only 18.8 percent of the federal budget, down from 52.2 percent in 1960. In contrast, spending on income transfers and health care rose from 21.5 percent of the federal budget in 1960 to 59.2 percent in 2003.

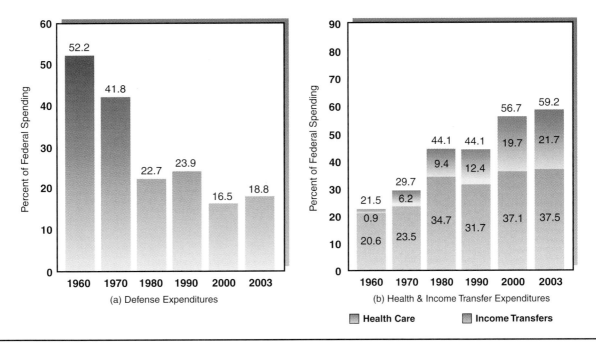

(a) Defense Expenditures

(b) Health & Income Transfer Expenditures

☐ **Health Care**   ☐ **Income Transfers**

Source: Economic Report of the President (Washington, D.C.: U.S. Government Printing Office, 2004).

Thus, there has been a dramatic change in the composition of federal spending during the last four decades. In contrast with earlier times, national defense is no longer the primary focus of the federal government. In essence, the federal government has become an entity that taxes working-age Americans in order to provide income transfers and health care benefits primarily for senior citizens. Furthermore, spending on the elderly is almost certain to increase once the baby boomers begin to retire, starting around 2010.

TAXES AND THE FINANCE OF GOVERNMENT

I'm proud to be paying taxes in the United States. The only thing is—I could be just as proud for half the money.

—Comedian Arthur Godfrey

Government expenditures must be financed through taxes, user charges, or borrowing.[2] Borrowing is simply another name for future taxes that will have to be levied to pay the interest on the borrowed funds. Thus, it affects the timing but not the level of taxes. In the United States, taxes are by far the largest source of government revenue. The power to tax sets governments apart from private businesses. Of course, a private business can put whatever price tag it wishes on its products; but no private business can force you to buy them. With its power to tax, a government can force citizens to pay, whether or not they receive something of value in return. As government expenditures have increased, so, too, have taxes. Taxes now take more than one-third of the income generated by Americans.

---

[2]In addition to user charges, taxes, and borrowing, the operations of government might be financed by printing money. But this is also a type of tax (it is sometimes called an "inflation tax") on those who hold money balances.

EXHIBIT 3
Sources of Government Revenue

Almost half of federal revenues are derived from the personal income tax. The payroll tax and corporate income tax are also major sources of federal revenue. The major revenue sources of state and local governments are sales and excise taxes, personal income taxes, user charges, grants from the federal government, property taxes.

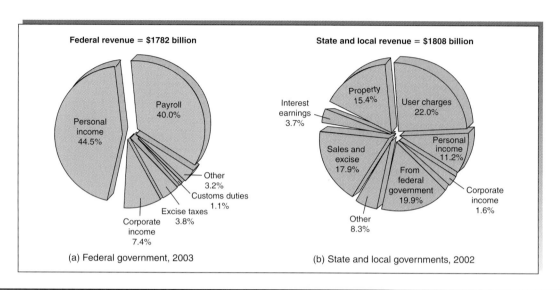

(a) Federal government, 2003

(b) State and local governments, 2002

Source: Economic Report of the President, 2004, and *Statistical Abstract of the United States*, 2003. http://www.census.gov.

Types of Taxes

Exhibit 3 indicates the major revenue sources for the federal and state and local levels of government. At the federal level, the personal income tax accounts for almost half of all revenue. Although income from all sources is covered by the income tax, only earnings derived from labor are subject to the payroll tax. Payroll taxes on the earnings of employees and self-employed workers finance Social Security, Medicare, and unemployment compensation benefits. The payroll tax accounts for 40 percent of federal revenue. The remaining sources of revenue, including the corporate income tax, excise taxes, and customs duties, account for less than 20 percent of federal revenue.

Both sales and income taxes are important sources of revenue for state governments. A sales tax is levied by forty-five of the fifty states (Alaska, Delaware, Montana, New Hampshire, and Oregon are the exceptions). State and local governments derive about 18 percent of their revenue from this source. Personal income taxes are imposed by forty-two states (Alaska, Florida, Nevada, New Hampshire, South Dakota, Texas, Washington, and Wyoming are the exceptions), and they provide approximately 11 percent of state and local government revenue.[3] Property taxes (levied mostly at the local level), grants from the federal government, and user charges (prices for services provided by the government) also provide substantial revenues for state and local governments.

Taxes and the Cost of Government

There are no free lunches. Regardless of how they are financed, activities undertaken by the government will incur costs. When governments purchase resources and other goods and services to provide rockets, education, highways, health care, and other goods, the resources used by the government will be unavailable to produce goods and services in the

---

[3]New Hampshire does levy a tax on income derived from dividends and interest.

private sector. As a result, private-sector output will be lower. This reduction in private-sector output is an opportunity cost of government. Furthermore, this cost will be present whether government activities are financed by taxes or borrowing.

Moreover, a tax dollar extracted from an individual or a business ends up costing the private economy much more than just one dollar. There are two main reasons why this is the case.

First, the collection of taxes is costly. The administration, enforcement, and compliance of tax legislation requires a sizable volume of resources, including the labor services of many highly skilled experts. The IRS itself employs 100,000 people. In addition, an army of bookkeepers, tax accountants, and lawyers is involved in the collection process. According to the Office of Management and Budget, each year individuals and businesses spend more than 6.7 billion hours (the equivalent of 3.3 million full-time year-round workers) keeping records, filling out forms, and learning the tax rules and other elements of the tax-compliance process.[4] More than half of U.S. families now retain tax-preparation firms like H&R Block and Jackson Hewitt to help them file the required forms and comply with the complex rules. Businesses spend roughly $5 billion each year in tax-consulting fees to the four largest accounting firms, to say nothing of the fees paid to other accounting, law, and consulting firms. In total, the resources involved amount to between 3 percent and 4 percent of national income (or 12 to 15 percent of the revenues collected). If these resources were not tied up with the tax-collection process, they could be employed producing goods and services for consumption.

Second, taxes impose an additional burden on the economy because they eliminate some productive exchanges (and cause people to undertake some counterproductive activities). As we noted in Chapter 4, economists refer to this as an excess burden (or deadweight loss) because it imposes a burden over and above the tax revenue transferred to the government. It results because taxes distort incentives. When buyers pay more and sellers receive less due to the payment of a tax, trade and the production of output become less attractive and decline. Individuals will spend less time on productive (but taxed) market activities and more time on tax-avoidance and untaxed activities, such as leisure. Research indicates that these deadweight losses add between 9 percent and 16 percent to the cost of taxation.[5] This means that $1 in taxes paid to the government imposes a cost of somewhere between $1.20 and $1.30 on the economy. Thus, the cost of a $100 million government program financed with taxes is really somewhere between $120 million and $130 million. As a result, the government's supply of goods and services generally costs the economy a good bit more than either the size of the tax bill or the level of government spending implies.

When the burden of taxation is considered, it is also important to recognize that all taxes are paid by people. Politicians often speak of imposing taxes on "business" as if part of the tax burden could be transferred from individuals to a nonperson (business). This is not the case. Business taxes, like all other taxes, are paid by individuals. A corporation or business firm might write the check to the government, but it merely collects the money from someone else—from its customers in the form of higher prices, its employees in the form of lower wages, or its stockholders in the form of lower dividends—and transfers the money to the government.

How Has the Structure of the Personal Income Tax Changed?

The personal income tax is the largest single source of revenue for the federal government. The rate structure of the income tax is progressive; taxpayers with larger incomes face higher tax rates. However, the structure of the rates has changed substantially since 1960. In the early 1960s, there were twenty-four marginal tax brackets ranging from a low of 20 percent to a high of 91 percent. The Kennedy-Johnson tax cut reduced the lowest marginal

---

[4]Office of Management and Budget, *Information Collection Budget of the United States Government*, fiscal year 2004. Also see Tax Foundation *Special Brief* by Arthur Hall, March 1996.

[5]The classic article on this topic is Edgar K. Browning, "The Marginal Cost of Public Funds," *Journal of Political Economy* 84, no. 2 (April 1976): 283–98.

rate to 14 percent and the top rate to 70 percent. The rate reductions during the Reagan years cut the top marginal rate initially to 50 percent in 1981 and later to approximately 30 percent during the period 1986–1988. During the 1990s, the top rate was increased to 39.6 percent, but the tax reductions during the administration of George W. Bush rolled back the top rate to 35 percent.

Thus, since the late 1980s, Americans with the highest incomes have paid sharply lower top marginal tax rates—rates in the 30 to 40 percent range, compared to top rates of 91 percent in the early 1960s and 70 percent prior to 1981. These reductions in the top rate make it tempting to jump to the conclusion that high-income Americans are now getting a free ride—that they now shoulder a smaller share of the personal income tax burden than in the past. But such a conclusion would be fallacious.

Exhibit 4 presents the Internal Revenue Service data on the share of the personal income tax paid by various classes of high-income taxpayers, as well as those in the bottom half of the income distribution, for the years 1963, 1980, 1990, and 2002. These data show that the share of the personal income tax paid by high-income Americans has increased substantially since 1963, and the increase has been particularly sharp since 1980. For example, the top 1 percent of earners paid 33.7 percent of the personal income tax in 2002, up from 19.1 percent in 1980 and 18.3 percent in 1963. The top 10 percent of income recipients paid 65.7 percent of the personal income tax in 2002, compared to 49.3 percent in 1980 and 47 percent in 1963. At the same time, the share of the personal income tax paid by the bottom half of the income recipients has steadily fallen from 10.4 percent of the total in 1963 to 7.1 percent in 1980 and 3.5 percent in 2002.

What is going on here? How can one explain the fact that high-income Americans are now paying more of the personal income tax even though their rates are now sharply lower than those in effect prior to 1981? Two major factors provide the answer. First, when marginal rates are cut by a similar percentage, the "incentive effects" are much greater in the top tax brackets. For example, when the top rate was cut from 91 percent to 70 percent during the Kennedy-Johnson years, high-income taxpayers in this bracket got to keep $30 out of every $100 of additional earnings after the tax cut, compared to only $9 before the rates were reduced. Thus, their incentive to earn additional income increased by a whopping 233 percent (30 minus 9 divided by 9)! On the other hand, the rate reduction in the lowest tax bracket from 20 percent to 14 percent meant that the low-

---

EXHIBIT 4

Share of Federal Income Taxes Paid by Various Groups, 1963–2002

Even though marginal tax rates have been reduced substantially during the last four decades, upper-income Americans pay a much larger share of the federal income tax today than was previously the case. In 2002, the richest 1 percent of Americans paid 33.7 percent of the federal income tax, up from 18.3 percent in 1963 and 19.1 percent in 1980. The richest 5 percent of Americans paid over half of the personal income tax, while the entire bottom half of the income distribution (the bottom 50 percent) paid only 3.5 percent of the total.

INCOME GROUP	SHARE OF TOTAL FEDERAL PERSONAL INCOME TAX PAID			
	1963	1980	1990	2002
Top 1%	18.3%	19.1%	25.1%	33.7%
Top 5%	35.6%	36.8%	43.6%	53.8%
Top 10%	47.0%	49.3%	55.4%	65.7%
Top 25%	68.8%	73.0%	77.0%	83.9%
Top 50%	89.6%	93.0%	94.2%	96.5%
Bottom 50%	10.4%	7.1%	5.8%	3.5%

Source: Internal Revenue Service (also available online at the Tax Foundation's Web site: http://www.taxfoundation.org/prtopincometable.html).

income taxpayers in this bracket now got to keep $86 of each additional hundred dollars that they earned compared to $80 prior to the tax cut. Their incentive to earn increased by a modest 7.5 percent (86 minus 80 divided by 80). Because the rate reductions increased the incentive to earn by much larger amounts in the top tax (and therefore highest income) brackets, the income base on which high-income Americans were taxed expanded substantially as their rates were reduced. As a result, the tax revenues collected from them declined only modestly. In the very highest brackets, the rate reductions actually increased the revenues collected from high-income Americans. (See Laffer Curve analysis of Chapter 4.) In contrast, the incentive effects were much weaker in the lower tax brackets and, as a result, rate reductions led to approximately proportional reductions in revenues collected from low- and middle-income taxpayers. This combination of incentive effects shifts the share of taxes paid toward those with higher incomes, the pattern observed in Exhibit 4.

Second, both the standard deduction and personal exemption have been increased substantially during the last couple of decades. This means that Americans are now able to earn more income before they face any tax liability. In 2002, for example, 30 percent (approximately 40 million returns) of those filing an income tax return either had zero tax liability or actually received funds from the IRS as the result of the **Earned Income Tax Credit**. This change in the structure of the personal income tax explains why people in the bottom half of income now pay such a small percentage of the personal income tax: 3.5 percent in 2002 compared to 10.4 percent in 1963.[6]

> **Earned Income Tax Credit**
> A provision of the tax code that provides a credit or rebate to persons with low earnings (income from work activities). The credit is eventually phased out if the recipient's earnings increase.

Income Levels and Overall Tax Payments

In addition to the personal income tax, the federal government also derives sizable revenues from payroll, corporate income, and excise taxes. How is the overall burden of federal taxes allocated among the various income groups? **Exhibit 5** presents Congressional Budget Office estimates for the average amount of federal taxes paid in 2001 according to income. On average, the top quintile (20 percent) of earners are estimated to pay 26.8 percent of their income in federal taxes. The average federal tax rate for the quintile with the next-highest level of income falls to 19.3 percent, and the average tax rate continues to fall as income declines. The average tax rate of the bottom quintile is 5.4 percent, about one-fifth of the average rate for the top quintile of earners. Clearly, the federal tax system is highly progressive, meaning that it takes a larger share of the income of those with higher incomes than from those with lower income levels.

Does the Growth of Income Benefit the Federal Government?

The federal personal income tax brackets are indexed for inflation. Therefore, the tax brackets are widened as inflation increases the nominal incomes of individuals and families. However, no adjustment is made for increases in real incomes. Under a progressive tax system, a larger and larger share of income will be taxed at higher rates as real incomes rise. As a result, the growth of real income will automatically increase federal revenues more than proportionally. Thus, under the current progressive tax structure, the growth of real income will increase federal revenues as a share of total income if no offsetting action is taken. Some economists, particularly those with a public-choice perspective, argue that these automatic tax increases accompanying economic growth adversely affect the efficiency of political decision making. They believe that elected political officials would make better (more efficient) choices if they had to vote for higher taxes in order to adopt new spending programs and expand the relative size of government.

---

[6]The data of Exhibit 4 consider only the tax liability of taxpayers. They do not reflect the payments from the IRS to taxpayers as the result of the Earned Income Tax Credit, which was established in the mid-1980s. If these payments to taxpayers were taken into consideration, the net taxes paid by the bottom half of income recipients would have been less than 1 percent in 2002. Thus, the data of Exhibit 4 actually understate the reduction in the net share of taxes paid by the bottom half of income recipients during the last two decades.

EXHIBIT 5
Total Federal Taxes as a Share of Income, 2001

The federal income tax structure is highly progressive. Federal taxes take 26.8 percent of the income generated by the top quintile (20 percent) of earners, compared to 15.2 percent from the middle-income quintile and 5.4 percent from the lowest quintile of earners.

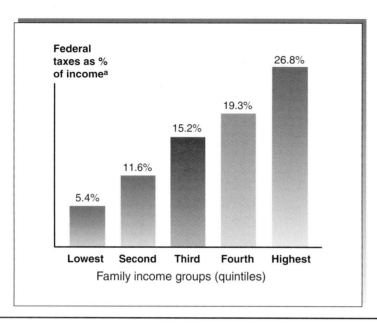

[a]Total federal taxes include income, payroll, and excise taxes.
Source: Congressional Budget Office, *Effective Federal Tax Rates: 1979–2001,* April 2004, http://www.cbo.gov/showdoc.cfm?index=5324&sequence=0.

SIZE OF GOVERNMENT: THE U.S. VERSUS OTHER COUNTRIES

There is substantial variation in the size of government across countries. As **Exhibit 6** illustrates, the relative size of government in most other high-income industrial countries is greater than that of the United States. In 2003, government spending summed to 58 percent of the economy in Sweden and 56 percent in Denmark. Government spending in France, Belgium, and Austria exceeded 50 percent of the economy. Compared to the United States, government was also quite large in Germany, Netherlands, and Italy. The size of government in Australia and Ireland was similar to that of the U.S., about 36 percent of the economy. Interestingly, the size of government was substantially smaller in South Korea, Singapore, Thailand, and Hong Kong—four Asian nations that have achieved rapid growth and substantial increases in living standards during the last four decades. As we proceed, we will return to this topic and investigate the effect of the size and functions of government on the growth and prosperity of nations.

The Future

A major share of government spending in the United States is now directed toward the elderly. The Social Security and Medicare programs constitute a huge share of federal spending. Once the baby boomers move into the retirement phase of life, beginning around 2010, federal expenditures on both of these programs are likely to balloon. This will make it very difficult to control the growth of government in the decades immediately ahead.

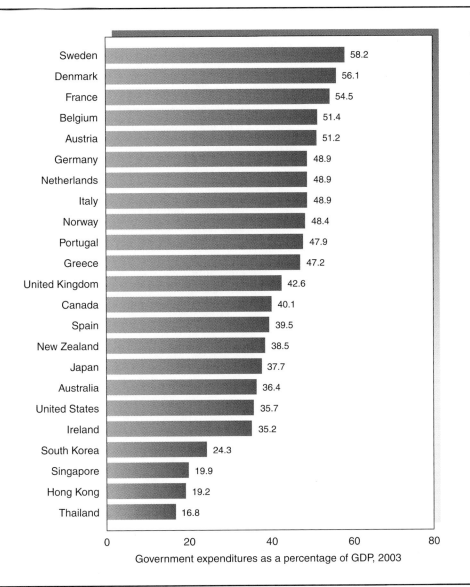

EXHIBIT 6
The Size of Governments—An International Comparison

The size of governments varies substantially across countries. In Sweden, government spending sums to almost three-fifths of the economy, compared to 35.7 percent in the United States and less than 20 percent in Singapore, Hong Kong, and Thailand.

Country	Value
Sweden	58.2
Denmark	56.1
France	54.5
Belgium	51.4
Austria	51.2
Germany	48.9
Netherlands	48.9
Italy	48.9
Norway	48.4
Portugal	47.9
Greece	47.2
United Kingdom	42.6
Canada	40.1
Spain	39.5
New Zealand	38.5
Japan	37.7
Australia	36.4
United States	35.7
Ireland	35.2
South Korea	24.3
Singapore	19.9
Hong Kong	19.2
Thailand	16.8

Government expenditures as a percentage of GDP, 2003

Source: OECD, *OECD Economic Outlook*, No. 75, June 2004, Annex Table 25, and International Monetary Fund, *International Financial Statistics* and *Government Finance Statistics Yearbook*. The data for Singapore and Hong Kong are for 2002 and 2001, respectively.

KEY POINTS

▼ During the first 125 years of U.S. history, federal expenditures per person were small and they grew at a relatively slow rate. But the size and nature of government has changed dramatically during the past 100 years. Today, the real (adjusted for inflation) spending per person of the federal government is roughly sixty times the level of 1916.

▼ During the last four decades, the composition of federal spending has shifted away from national defense and toward spending on income transfers and health care.

▼ As the size of government has grown, taxes have increased. Taxes impose a burden on the economy over

and above the revenue transferred to the government because of (1) the administration and compliance costs and (2) the deadweight losses that accompany taxation.

▼ Overall, the federal tax system of the United States is highly progressive. Taxes as a percentage of income are approximately five times greater for the top quintile (20 percent) of families than for the bottom quintile.

▼ The size of government of the United States is smaller than that of the major Western European countries, but larger than for a number of high-growth Asian economies.

CRITICAL ANALYSIS QUESTIONS

*1. How do taxes influence the efficiency of resource use? How much does it cost for the government to raise an additional dollar (or $1 billion) of tax revenue?

2. During the last four decades, a smaller share of the federal budget has been allocated to national defense and a larger share to income transfers and health care. Does economics indicate that this change will help Americans achieve higher living standards?

3. Because the structure of the personal income tax is progressive, a larger share of income is taxed at higher rates as income grows. Therefore, economic growth automatically results in higher taxes unless offsetting legislative action is taken. Do you think this is an attractive feature of the current tax system? Why or why not?

4. Compared to the situation prior to 1981, the marginal tax rates imposed on individuals and families with high incomes are now lower. What was the top marginal personal income tax rate in 1980? What is the top rate now? Are you in favor of or opposed to the lower marginal rates? Why?

*5. As the result of changes during the last two decades, the bottom half of income recipients now pay little or no personal income tax. Rather than paying taxes, many of them now receive payments back from the IRS as the result of the Earned Income Tax Credit and Child Tax Credit programs. Do you think the increase in the number of people who pay no taxes will affect the efficiency of the political process? Why or why not?

*Asterisk denotes questions for which answers are given in Appendix B.

The Internet: How Is It Changing the Economy?

Focus

- Why is the development of the Internet an important economic phenomenon?

- How is the Internet changing product markets?

- What is the effect of the Internet on the labor market?

The Internet is kind of like a gold rush where there really is gold.

—Bill Gates[1]

[1]Bill Gates, *Microsoft Magazine,* January/February 1996.

The Internet is a gigantic library, super shopping mall, and extensive transportation system all wrapped into one. Far more documents can be obtained over the Internet than from even the largest brick-and-mortar library facility. Although a large mall can provide you with access to hundreds of shops in a given locality, the Internet provides access to millions of businesses located around the world. And for only a small fee, you can open your own shop in the world's super mall.

Music, movies, software, and financial services can be transported almost instantaneously over the Internet, something unheard of just a couple of decades ago. For example, online sales of goods and services such as airline tickets, computers, and books totaled $114 billion in 2003. This figure is expected to rise to $316 billion, or 12 percent of all projected retail sales, by 2010.[2] The Web is also influencing labor markets by changing how people find new jobs as well as how labor services are provided. ▪

USE OF THE INTERNET

As **Exhibit 1** shows, the number of Web sites on the Internet has exploded in the past decade. In 1992, there were only 16,000 Web sites, but by 2004 there were more than 39 million sites. This tremendous growth in the number of Web sites has been matched by a dramatic rise in the number of Internet users. By October 2004, more than two-thirds of the population, or 200 million people, were using the Internet in the United States. The typical user employs the Internet intensively. The average user spends more than seven hours a week surfing the Web and visits twenty-two different Web sites per week.[3]

As **Exhibit 2** demonstrates, the use of the Internet has become a worldwide phenomenon. About one-third of the Internet users reside in Asia, compared to a little more than one-quarter in both North America and Europe. Residents of Latin America, the Middle East, and Africa account for a relatively small portion of the total users.

ECONOMIC GAINS FROM THE INTERNET

Why is the development of the Internet an important economic phenomenon? There are good reasons to believe that the Internet has improved productivity and efficiency—that it has helped us generate more value from available resources. There are three major sources of economic gains from the Internet.

1. Gains from broader and more competitive markets. As we have previously discussed, gains from trade and competition are important sources of growth and prosperity. The Internet promotes the realization of gains from both. The cost of establishing an Internet firm is low, often only a few hundred dollars. The costs of identifying potential suppliers via the Internet are also low, and with the development of more efficient search devices, they are declining. Via the Internet, firms are able to compete over a much larger geographic area than they could a decade ago, and buyers are better able to purchase from sellers who are located far away. A case in point: a farm family in West Texas was able to start a successful business selling tumbleweeds to New York restaurants wanting southwestern décor. Markets are becoming more competitive and the location of both buyers and sellers less relevant. This is particularly true for goods that can be transported economically, either through the Internet or via other means of transportation.

---

[2]Carrie A. Johnson, "US eCommerce Overview: 2004 to 2010," August 2004, *Forrester Research Report,* Forrester Research Inc., Cambridge, Mass.

[3]The current number of Internet users as well as usage patterns can be obtained from http://www.nielsen-netratings.com/.

EXHIBIT 1
Number of Web Sites, 1992–2004

The number of Web sites rose dramatically between 1992 and 2004. By 2004, there were 39 million Web sites.

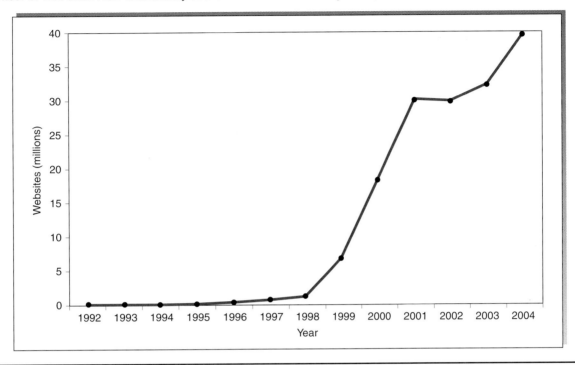

Source: http://www.zooknic.com/.

EXHIBIT 2
The Geographic Distribution of Internet Use, 2004

About one-third of Internet users live in Asia. About one-quarter reside in Europe, and another quarter are in North America.

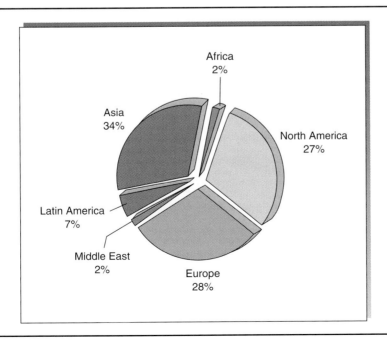

Source: http://www.internetworldstats.com/.

2. Gains from lower transaction costs. Transaction costs are an obstacle to the realization of gains from trade. The Internet, however, often reduces the cost of transactions, including the cost of information. Think about, for example, the software you are able to download and the time and money it saves you from having to go to a store to buy it. The U.S. economy has already reaped substantial gains from these lower transcation costs. But as use of the Internet increases, there is reason to believe that the future gains will be even greater.

3. Gains from networking. Like the telephone of an earlier era, the Internet is a networking system. Telephones were not very valuable when only a few people had one, but their value increased dramatically as more and more people acquired them. The Internet has this same characteristic. The value of the system to current users increases as more and more people join the network. Growth of the network will make it more likely that Internet sellers will be offering products you want to buy and that potential Internet buyers will be searching for goods you are willing to sell.

KEY SECTORS OF INTERNET GROWTH

Exhibit 3 shows that the Internet is now extensively used in several consumer product markets. The percentage of sales conducted online is about one-fifth or more in retail markets such as travel, books, and computer hardware and software. The rapid rise in the importance of the Internet in these markets is the result of the relatively low transportation costs for these items as well as the availability of information about these standardized products online. A much smaller percentage of the sales of automobiles, food, apparel, and toys and music items are conducted online. The low market penetration for online firms in the food market is partly because customers can't observe the condition of these items. Similarly, the sale of clothing over the Internet is hampered by the fact that one can't examine the fit of clothing online.

The Internet is also quickly transforming how banking is conducted. The number of households engaged in online banking has been rapidly increasing. In 2003, 19 million households paid their bills online, but this figure is projected to rise to 61 million by 2008.[4]

EXHIBIT 3
Online Market Penetration, 2004

The percentage of sales conducted online is about one-fifth or more in the travel, books, and computer hardware and software markets. The market share for online firms in the automobile, food, apparel, and toys and music/video markets is much smaller.

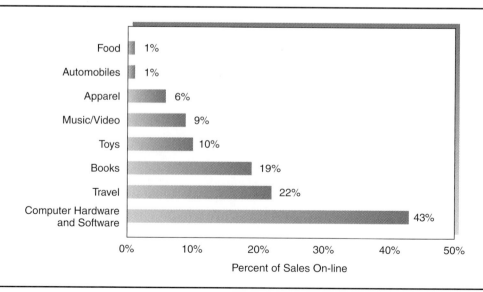

Source: Shop.org and Boston Consulting Group, State of Online Retailing 7.0, May 2004.

[4]http://www.clickz.com/.

The Web has revolutionized the market for used consumer durables. The Web site eBay has made it much easier for people to buy or sell used goods. Sales are conducted by an online auction process, and eBay earns money by charging a commission for each sale completed. Prior to purchasing an item on eBay, prospective buyers can examine earlier customers' ratings of a given seller. The ease with which trades can be conducted on the eBay Web site enabled the company to grow to 114.0 million users in 2004. Unlike most Internet firms, eBay has been profitable since its inception.[5]

MORE EFFICIENT CONSUMER MARKETS

The Internet helps create value in final product markets by either reducing sellers' costs or improving the matches between sellers and consumers.[6] First, several factors help online retail firms achieve lower costs. Their handling costs will often be lower because it will not be necessary for the firms to unpack products or put them on display. Losses due to shoplifting, which often are about 3 percent of sales, are eliminated. Web-based firms are generally able to use low-cost warehouses rather than expensive stores in urban or suburban areas. Online retailers often have lower sales comissions on their products than traditional brick-and-mortar firms do.

Second, the Internet can improve matches between sellers and consumers by making information about goods easier to get. The Internet is an excellent source of information for consumers about available goods and services because an individual can get very specific information about a product or service at a low cost any time of day or night. Web shoppers can obtain information from online versions of product catalogs, product reviews, and price comparisons. Sites like Amazon.com and eopinions.com also allow users to rate how well they like different products and provide product recommendations to customers based on their past purchases. Web shoppers can get product samples of books, music, and software, which can help them better decide whether to purchase products or not.

The Web can also make it easier for consumers to obtain access to hard-to-find goods, particularly specialty products and goods with unique characteristics. For example, it is very expensive for a chain such as The Gap to maintain a large inventory of its products at many different locations. As a consequence, each Gap store branch has only a limited inventory of different styles and sizes of jeans. This results in some consumers having to make compromises on the jeans they purchase. Online firms, however, can take advantage of economies of scale of centralized inventories and stock a much wider variety of products. This enables Web-based firms to provide a better match to customers' preferences.

Dell Computers provides the best example of the effect of product customization. Prior to Dell, the typical personal computer manufacturer forecasted demand for various computer models and then produced these computers in batches. The computers were then distributed to wholesalers and retail stores. Changes in inventories and prices were used to create a balance between supply and demand. Dell uses a different business model. Online, Dell customers can customize their computer purchases on several dimensions such as the processor, memory, hard disk size, monitor, and so on. After the order is placed, the computer is made and then shipped directly to the customer. As a result, Dell does not need to manufacture all possible configurations of its computers and therefore is able to achieve lower costs.

A major problem, of course, with purchasing goods online is that consumers can't touch, taste, smell, or try on the goods before purchasing them. A potential solution is hybrid stores that act as a showroom for a broad range of products. These stores have for display only a few of each product available for sale. Shoppers can examine the products and then place their order either in the store or later at home online.

---

[5]http://www.ebay.com/.

[6]For an overview of the effect of the Internet on product markets, see Severin Borenstein and Garth Saloner, "Economics and Electronic Commerce," *Journal of Economic Perspectives*, winter 2001: 3–12. This section is partly derived from this article.

Will Internet firms eventually dominate product markets? It depends on whether they are an efficient method of supplying goods and services. When Internet firms have lower costs or provide consumers with other benefits (for example, broader selection, faster delivery, or greater customization), they will be able to compete effectively. With time, they may even dominate some sectors of the economy. On the other hand, when traditional retailers have lower costs and provide consumers with other benefits (immediate access to goods, inspection of the items, and/or local service contacts, for example), they will survive and prosper. In a market economy, consumers are the ultimate judge. Their choices will determine which firms, be they traditional or online, will expand and prosper and which will be driven from the market.

MORE EFFICIENT INPUT MARKETS AND PRODUCTION PROCESSES

The ability of the Internet to improve matches between buyers and sellers also applies to business-to-business transactions. In fact, a higher volume of business-to-business transactions is being conducted on the Web today than business-to-consumer transactions. Some online firms serve as intermediaries between companies. For example, some Web sites auction off goods such as steel and advertising space. Other online companies have set up exchanges for a wide variety of goods. One such exchange is Covisint, which was started by DaimlerChrysler, Ford, and General Motors to handle their transactions with parts suppliers. Because these three companies purchase about $250 billion worth of parts each year, this Web site has the potential to become one of the largest firms on the Internet.[7]

These intermediaries can take the form of exchanges, online auctions, and brokers. The intermediaries can often reduce the buyer's search costs and facilitate one-stop shopping and thereby reduce the need for costly contacts with multiple suppliers.

Many companies are also increasingly conducting "reverse auctions" online. Vendors that supply inputs bid on the prices they will charge the companies conducting the auctions. In other words, instead of bidding to buy products online, vendors are bidding to sell their products online (which is why they are called "reverse" auctions). Sun Microsystems' Web site, for example, allows programmers and other vendors to bid on contracts to solve Sun's clients' software problems.

The Internet can also lower sales costs between companies. For example, switching to an electronic version of the purchasing process from a paper one can substantially reduce the cost of buying goods and services. The cost of completing a paper transaction has been estimated to be roughly $50 per transaction. In addition, improved information from a firm's suppliers about the availability of their products can enable the firm to lower its inventory of inputs and thus its costs. In addition, the Web can be used to take advantage of differences in time zones. For example, software projects can often be transferred over the Internet from programmers in the United States to their counterparts in India at the end of the workday. Via the Web, radiologists in India examine emergency medical scans overnight, so U.S. radiologists can get some sleep. Being able to outsource work anywhere around the world is also cost-effective for firms.

LABOR MARKETS AND THE INTERNET: FASTER AND BETTER EMPLOYEE-EMPLOYER MATCHES[8]

The explosive growth of the Internet has changed how people search for jobs and firms hire workers. There are now more than 3,000 job search sites. Monster.com, the leading

---

[7]David Lucking-Reiley and Daniel F. Spulber, "Business to Business Electronic Commerce," *Journal of Economic Perspectives,* winter 2001: 55–68.

[8]This section draws on David H. Autor, "Wiring the Labor Market," *Journal of Economic Perspectives,* winter 2001: 25–40.

job-posting site, indicated in October 2004 that it had more than 800,000 job openings posted on its site and the résumés of more than 25 million job seekers. Currently, the Internet is used in 15 percent of all job searches by unemployed workers. Half of job seekers with Internet access use it in their job search. Today, more people use the Internet to look for jobs than search methods such as contacting friends or relatives and using private employment agencies.

Job-posting Web sites have several advantages over traditional newspaper help-wanted ads. They contain more job openings and are easier to search. The job openings can be more current because employers can post ads immediately as well as edit them after their initial posting. Online jobs sites also permit individuals to advertise their skills to potential employers. Lastly, the cost to advertise a job opening is lower. The cost of a 30-day advertisement on Monster.com is less than 5 percent of the cost of a job advertisement in one issue of the Sunday *New York Times*.

Job-posting software on sites can also help match job seekers with employers. Software can compare the résumés of job seekers with descriptions of open positions. If an appropriate match occurs, then both the employer and the job seeker can be notified. Some Web programs advise applicants of new employment opportunities based on the job openings he or she has applied for in the past. Employers can also screen candidates by administering personality and skills tests over the Internet.

Because matches between employers and prospective employees can be made more quickly, it's possible that the Internet has the potential to reduce frictional unemployment in the economy. Moreover, online screening of candidates can lead to better matches, and better matches lead to higher productivity for firms.

The Internet's effect on employee turnover is less clear, however. On the one hand, better and faster matches can be made, as we have pointed out. On the other hand, because the Internet enables employed workers to easily search for a new position, turnover may increase. In fact, 7 percent of the employed indicate that they routinely use the Internet to search for potential new job opportunities.

The Delivery of Labor Services and the Training of Employees

The Internet has changed how workers provide labor services to employers. Remote access to documents and e-mail will permit some workers to provide part or all of their work at home or other locations. In 2001, about 15 percent of workers reported working at home at least once per week.[9] Less time is spent commuting, leaving more time for work activities that add economic value.

The Internet has also changed how workers obtain their skills. Students, of course, can now go to school and get their degrees online. Many employers provide formal and informal training to their workers online. This training plays an important role in workers' earnings. The online delivery of skills training has the potential to reduce the cost and increase the convenience of getting such training.

CONCLUDING THOUGHT

The Internet is an important technological change—perhaps as important as the development of electricity, the railroad, or the automobile. There are reasons to believe that it will improve economic efficiency and help us achieve higher living standards. It has increased the interaction of people around the world. It may also change lifestyles and alter cultural values around the globe. It will be exciting to follow these developments in the decades immediately ahead.

---

[9]http://www.bls.gov/.

KEY POINTS

▼ The use of the Internet has grown dramatically in the past decade and is now a worldwide phenomenon.

▼ The Internet tends to improve productivity and the efficiency of resource use because it (1) increases the breadth and competitiveness of markets, (2) lowers transaction costs, and (3) becomes more valuable as additional users and Web sites are added.

▼ The Internet can improve the operation of product markets by reducing costs and improving the matches between buyers and sellers. Costs are reduced due to lower distribution and production costs. Matches are improved through better information about available goods, greater access to goods, and increased customization.

▼ The volume of business-to-business sales being conducted on the Internet is even greater than the volume of retail-to-consumer sales. The Internet is making inputs cheaper and input markets more competitive, and is helping streamline production processes.

▼ The Internet has become an integral part of the job search process. Quicker and improved matches between employers and employees have the potential to reduce unemployment. The Internet also makes it possible for many employees to work at home and other locations and get training online.

CRITICAL ANALYSIS QUESTIONS

1. What effect does the Internet have on the efficiency of markets? Explain. How is the Internet likely to influence productivity and the growth of output in the years immediately ahead?

*2. The share of airline tickets bought over the Internet has grown rapidly, whereas the percentage of groceries purchased online remains minuscule. What factors likely explain this difference?

3. Indicate how the production, marketing, and distribution of each of the following are likely to be influenced by the development of the Internet: (a) popular music, (b) movies, (c) automobiles, (d) commercial employment agencies, (e) beautician services, and (f) health care. Briefly explain your response.

*Asterisk denotes questions for which answers are given in Appendix B.

The Economics of Social Security

Focus

- Why is Social Security headed for problems?

- Will the Social Security Trust Fund lighten the tax burden of future generations?

- Does Social Security transfer income from the rich to the poor? How does it impact the economic status of blacks, Hispanics, and those with fewer years of life expectancy?

- Should the Social Security system be reformed?

The federal government's handling of [Social Security] pension monies is very different from that of private pension plans.

—Mark Weinberger[1]

[1]Mark Weinberger, *Social Security: Facing the Facts* (Washington, DC: Cato Institute, 1996), 2.

The ongoing debate about the future structure of Social Security is particularly important to younger people. It is their lives that will be most affected by how this issue is handled. In the United States, the program is officially known as Old Age and Survivors Insurance (OASI). It offers protection against the loss of income that usually accompanies old age or the death of a breadwinner. In spite of its official title, Social Security is not based on principles of insurance. Private insurance and pension programs invest the current payments of customers in buildings, farms, or other real assets. Alternatively, they buy stocks and bonds that finance the development of real assets. These real assets generate income that allows the pension fund (or insurance company) to fulfill its future obligations to its customers.

Social Security does not follow this saving-and-investment model. Instead, most of the funds flowing into the system are paid out to current retirees and survivors in the program. In essence, the Social Security system is an intergenerational income-transfer program. Most of the taxes collected from the present generation of workers are paid out to current beneficiaries. Thus, the system is based on "pay-as-you-go," rather than on the savings and investment principle.

The Social Security retirement program is financed by a flat-rate payroll tax of 10.6 percent applicable to employee earnings up to a cutoff level. In 2005, the earnings cutoff was $90,000. Thus, employees earning $90,000 or more paid $9,540 in Social Security taxes to finance the OASI retirement program.[2] The income cutoff is adjusted upward each year by the growth rate of nominal wages. Although the payroll tax is divided equally between employee and employer, it is clearly part of the employee's compensation package, and most economists believe that the burden of this tax falls primarily on the employee. The formula used to determine retirement benefits favors those with lower earnings during their working years. However, as we will discuss later, the redistributive effects toward those with lower incomes are more apparent than real.

When the program began in 1935, not many people lived past age 65, and the nation had lots of workers and few eligible retirees. As **Exhibit 1** illustrates, there were 16 workers for every Social Security beneficiary as recently as 1950. That ratio has declined sharply through the years. As a result, higher and higher taxes per worker have been required just to maintain a constant level of benefits. There are currently 3.3 workers per Social Security retiree. By 2030, however, that figure will decline to only 2.2.

Because there were many workers per beneficiary during the early years of Social Security, it was possible to provide retirees with generous benefits while maintaining a relatively low rate of taxation. Many of those who retired in the 1960s and 1970s received real benefits of three or four times the amount they paid into the system, far better than they could have done had they invested the funds privately. The era of high returns, however, is now over. The program has matured, and the number of workers per beneficiary has declined. Payroll taxes have risen greatly over the decades, and still higher taxes will be necessary merely to fund currently promised benefits.

Studies indicate that those now age 40 and younger can expect to earn a real rate of return of about 2 percent on their Social Security tax dollars, substantially less than what they could earn from personal investments. Thus, Social Security has been a good deal for current and past retirees. It is not, however, a very good deal for today's middle-aged and younger workers. ▪

---

[2]Additional payroll taxes are levied for the finance of disability programs (1.8 percent) and Medicare (2.9 percent). Thus, although the total payroll tax sums to 15.3 percent, only revenues from the 10.6 percent rate are used to finance the benefits to retirees and surviving dependents. Note that the earnings cutoff does not apply to the Medicare portion of the payroll tax.

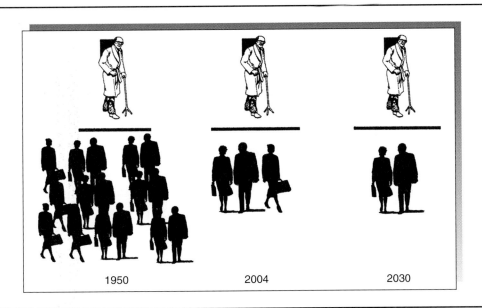

1950   2004   2030

EXHIBIT 1
Workers per Social Security Beneficiary

In 1950, there were 16 workers per Social Security beneficiary. By 2004, the figure had fallen to only 3.3. By 2030, there will be only 2.2 workers per retiree. As the worker/beneficiary ratio falls under a pay-as-you-go system, either taxes must be increased or benefits reduced (or both).

Source: 2004 Annual Report of the Board of Trustees of the Federal Old Age and Survivors Insurance and Disability Insurance Trust Funds (Washington, DC: Government Printing Office, 2004), p. 47.

WHY IS SOCIAL SECURITY HEADED FOR PROBLEMS?

The flow of funds into and out of a pay-as-you-go retirement system is sensitive to demographic conditions. The Social Security system is currently enjoying a period of highly favorable demographics. The U.S. birthrate was low during the Great Depression and World War II. The Great Depression and World War II group is now retiring, and because it is a relatively small generation, payments to it are also relatively small. The birthrate rose sharply during the two decades following World War II. These baby boomers are now in their prime working years, and their large numbers are expanding the flow of revenues into the Social Security retirement system.

However, as **Exhibit 2** shows, the situation will change dramatically when the baby boomers start retiring around 2011. Their retirement, combined with rising life expectancies, will substantially increase the number of retirees relative to the number of workers. As we previously noted, the number of workers per Social Security retiree will fall from the current 3.3 level to only 2.2 in 2030.

Exhibit 3 illustrates the effect of demographics on the pay-as-you-go Social Security system. Currently, the funds flowing into the system (pushed up by the large baby boom generation) exceed the expenditures on benefits for retirees (pulled down by the small Great Depression and World War II generation). But the retirement of the baby boomers around 2011 will begin pushing the expenditures of the system upward at a rapid rate. The current surplus of revenues from the payroll tax relative to retirement benefits will dissipate around 2018. After 2018, the deficits will grow larger and larger as the number of beneficiaries relative to workers continues to grow in the decades ahead.

The revenues derived from the payroll tax have exceeded the benefits paid to current retirees since the mid-1980s (see Exhibit 3). Currently, only about 80 percent of the revenues are required for the payments to current beneficiaries. Thus, the system is currently running a surplus—about $138 billion per year. The surpluses are projected to continue for approximately another decade. If other elements of the federal budget were in balance, the Social Security surpluses could be used to pay off some of the federal government's outstanding debt. In turn, the debt reduction would reduce the government's future interest payments, which would make it easier to deal with rising Social Security expenditures when the baby boomers retire. However, this has not been the case. Most of the Social

EXHIBIT 2
U.S. Population Aged 65 and Over, 1980–2000 and Projections to 2030

As shown here, the growth rate of the elderly population will accelerate after 2010 as the baby boomers move into the retirement phase of life. This will place strong pressure on both the Social Security and Medicare programs.

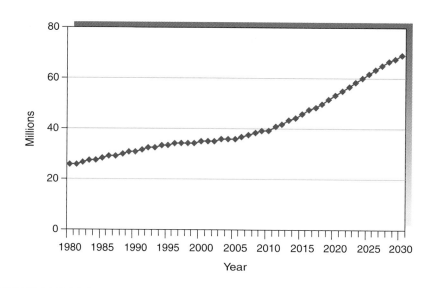

Source: http://www.census.gov/.

Security surpluses since 1980 have been used to finance current government operations rather than retiring the government debt.

WILL THE TRUST FUND LIGHTEN THE FUTURE TAX BURDEN?

Under current law, the surpluses are channeled into the Social Security Trust Fund (SSTF). The Trust Fund uses the revenue to buy special nonmarketable bonds from the U.S. Treasury. By 2018, the Social Security Trust Fund is expected to grow to more than $5 trillion. Social Security actuaries calculate that this will provide sufficient funds for payment of promised benefits until 2042.

EXHIBIT 3
The Forthcoming Deficit between Payroll Tax Revenues and Social Security Benefit Expenditures

Given current payroll taxes and retirement benefit levels, the system will run larger and larger deficits in the 2018–2030 period and beyond.

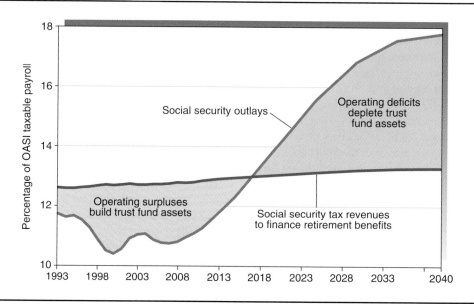

Source: Social Security Administration 2004 OASDI Annual Trustees Report, http://www.ssa.gov/.

Will a large trust fund make it easier to deal with the retirement of the baby boomers? Some people are surprised to learn that there is little reason to believe that it will. Unlike the bonds, stocks, and physical assets held by a private pension fund or insurance company, the SSTF bonds will not generate a stream of future income for the federal government. Neither are they a "pot of money" set aside for the payment of future benefits. Instead, the trust fund bonds are an IOU from one government agency—the Treasury—to another—the Social Security Administration. The federal government is both the payee and recipient of the interest and principal represented by the SSTF bonds. ***No matter how many bonds are in the trust fund, their net asset value to the federal government is zero!***

Thus, the number of IOUs in the trust fund is largely irrelevant.[3] The size of the trust fund could be doubled or tripled, but that would not give the government any additional funds for the payment of benefits. Correspondingly, the trust fund could be abolished, and the government would not be relieved of any of its existing obligations or commitments. To redeem the bonds and thereby provide the Social Security system with funds to cover future deficits, the federal government will have to raise taxes, cut other expenditures, or borrow from the public. These options will not change with the depletion of the trust fund.

THE REAL PROBLEM OF THE CURRENT SYSTEM

The real problem faced by the pay-as-you-go Social Security system will arise in about 2018 when the revenues from the payroll tax will begin to fall short of the benefits promised to retirees. The deficits of the system will become larger and larger throughout the 2020s and 2030s. Under current law, revenues will be sufficient to pay only about three-quarters of promised benefits by 2030, and less in later years.

There are only four ways to cover future shortfalls: (1) cut benefits, (2) increase taxes, (3) cut spending in other areas, or (4) borrow. None of these options are attractive and, regardless of how the gap is filled, a slowdown in the rate of economic growth is likely to occur. If benefits are reduced, current beneficiaries and persons near retirement will—quite correctly—feel that a commitment made to them has been broken. It will also be difficult to cover the shortfall with higher taxes. Once the baby boom generation retires, approximately a 50 percent increase in the payroll tax or a 30 percent increase in the personal income tax will be needed to cover Social Security deficits. Tax increases of this magnitude will have a negative effect on the economy. Neither will it be easy to cut expenditures in other areas of the federal budget. Defense spending was already cut substantially as a share of the economy during the 1990s, and it is likely to be pushed upward in the future by external threats, including those arising from terrorism. Furthermore, the growth of the elderly population is sure to put upward pressure on Medicare spending, another major federal program. Finally, borrowing to cover the shortfall will put upward pressure on interest rates, and taxes will have to be higher in the future merely to cover the interest obligations. Thus, it merely delays the problem.

Not even robust economic growth would eliminate the future shortfall. Retirement benefits are indexed to the average growth in nominal wages. If higher productivity enables *real* (inflation-adjusted) wages to rise quickly, then Social Security benefits will rise, too. For example, if inflation is zero, and real wages start growing at 2 percent a year instead of their previous level of 1 percent, then the formula used to calculate Social Security benefits will also begin to push up those benefits more rapidly. Higher economic growth may temporarily improve Social Security's finances, but under current law the improvement will not last.[4]

---

[3]Of course, the SSTF bonds represent funds borrowed by the Treasury from the Social Security system. This increases the legitimacy of claims on these funds by future Social Security recipients. It also indicates that the trust fund is similar to what is called budget authority, which provides the legal permission for the government to spend funds on an item.

[4]See Garth Davis, "Faster Economic Growth Will Not Solve the Social Security Crisis," Heritage Center for Data Analysis, Feb. 3, 2000.

WHO IS HELPED AND WHO IS HURT BY SOCIAL SECURITY?

When Social Security was established in 1935, the population was growing rapidly, only a few Americans lived to age 65, and the labor force participation rate of women was low. Social Security was designed for that world. But today's world is dramatically different. Several aspects of the system now seem outdated, arbitrary, and, in some cases, unfair.

Does Social Security Help the Poor?

Social Security has gained many supporters because of the belief that it redistributes wealth from rich to poor. The system is financed with a flat tax rate up to the cutoff limit, but the formula used to calculate benefits disproportionately favors workers with low lifetime earnings.[5] However, other aspects of the system tend to favor those with higher incomes. First, workers with more education and high earnings tend to live longer than those with less education and lower earnings. As **Exhibit 4** shows, the age-adjusted mortality rate of persons with less than a high school education is 8 to 10 percent higher than the average for all Americans. As years of schooling increase, mortality rates fall. The age-adjusted mortality rate of college graduates is 21 percent below the average for all Americans, whereas the rate for persons with advanced degrees is 32 percent below the average. Given the strong correlation between education and earnings, the age-adjusted mortality figures indicate that, on average, Americans with higher earnings live longer than their counterparts with less education and lower earnings. As a result, high-wage workers will, on average, draw Social Security benefits for a longer period of time than low-wage workers. Correspondingly, low-wage

EXHIBIT 4
Mortality Rates by Level of Education

As shown here, the age-adjusted mortality rates are lower for people with more education. Because of the close link between education and income, people with higher incomes tend to live longer and, therefore, draw Social Security benefits for a longer period of time than people with less education and income.

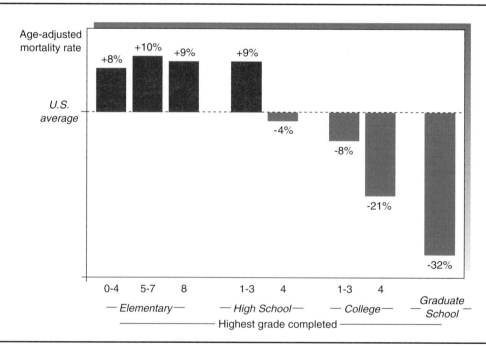

Source: Center for Data Analysis, Heritage Foundation.

[5]Retirement benefits are based on the best 35 years of earnings from a worker's career. Benefits are calculated by taking 90 percent of the first $7,524 a year of earnings, 32 percent of earnings between $7,524 and $45,348, and just 15 percent of earnings above $45,348 up to the earnings cutoff of $90,000. Therefore, as base earnings rise, benefits fall as a percentage of average earnings (and payroll taxes paid) during one's lifetime. For example, the retirement benefits of persons with base annual earnings of $10,000 sum to 76 percent of their average working year earnings. In contrast, the retirement benefits of those with base earnings of $60,000 are only 35 percent of their average preretirement earnings. These figures are based on the formula for 2005. The figures are adjusted each year for the growth of nominal wages.

workers are far more likely to pay thousands of dollars in Social Security taxes and then die before, or soon after, becoming eligible for retirement benefits.

Second, low-wage workers generally begin full-time work at a younger age. Many work full-time and pay Social Security taxes for years while future high-wage workers are still in college and graduate school. Low-wage workers generally pay more into the system earlier, and therefore forego more interest, than high-wage workers.

Third, labor participation tends to fall as spousal earnings increase. As a result, couples with a high-wage worker are more likely to gain from Social Security's spousal benefit provision, which provides the nonworking spouse with benefits equal to 50 percent of those the working spouse receives.

Two recent studies taking these and other related factors into consideration suggest that Social Security may actually transfer wealth from low-wage to high-wage workers. A study using data from the Social Security Administration and the Health and Retirement Study found that when Social Security benefits are assessed for family units, rather than for individuals, the progressiveness of the system disappears. Another study adjusted for differences in mortality rates, patterns of lifetime income, and other factors. It found that if a 2 percent real interest rate (discount rate) is used to evaluate the pattern of taxes paid and benefits received, the redistributive effects of Social Security are essentially neutral. However, at a more realistic 4 percent real interest rate, Social Security actually favors higher-income households.[6]

Social Security Adversely Affects Blacks and Other Groups with Below-average Life Expectancy

Currently, the average retiree reaching age 65 can expect to spend 18 years receiving Social Security benefits, after more than 40 years of paying into the system. But what about those people who do not make it into their 80s, or even to the normal retirement age of 65? Unlike private financial assets, Social Security benefits cannot be passed on to heirs. Thus, those who die before age 65 or soon thereafter, receive little or nothing from their payroll tax payments.

Social Security was not set up to transfer income from some ethnic groups to others, but under its current structure, it does so, nonetheless. Because of the shorter life expectancies of black Americans the Social Security system adversely affects their economic welfare. Compared to whites and Hispanics, blacks are far more likely to pay a lifetime of payroll taxes and then die without receiving much in the way of benefits. Thus, the system works to their disadvantage. On the other hand, Social Security is particularly favorable to Hispanics because of their above-average life expectancy and the progressive nature of the benefit formula. As a result, Hispanics derive a higher return than whites and substantially higher than blacks.[7]

Exhibit 5 presents the expected real returns for people born in 1975, according to gender, marital status, and ethnicity.[8] Single black men who were born in 1975 can expect to derive a real annual return of *negative* 1.3 percent on their Social Security tax payments, compared to returns of 0.2 percent for single white men and 1.6 percent for single

---

[6]See Alan Gustman and Thomas Steinmeier, "How Effective Is Redistribution Under The Social Security Benefit Formula?" *Journal of Public Economics* 82 (October 2001): 1–28; and Julia Lynn Coronado, Don Fullerton, and Thomas Glass, "Long Run Effects of Social Security Reform Proposals on Lifetime Progressivity," in *The Distributional Aspects of Social Security and Social Security Reform,* eds. Martin Feldstein and Jeffrey B. Liebman (Chicago: University of Chicago Press, 2002).

[7]For additional details on the redistributive effects of Social Security across ethnic groups, see William W. Beach and Gareth Davis, "More for Your Money: Improving Social Security's Rate of Return," in *Improving Retirement Security: A Handbook for Reformers,* ed. David C. John, (Washington DC: Heritage Foundation, 2000) 25–64 and Martin Feldstein and Jeffrey Liebman, "The Distributional Effects of an Investment-based Social Security System," in *The Distributional Aspects of Social Security and Social Security Reform,* eds. Martin Feldstein and Jeffrey B. Liebman (Chicago: University of Chicago Press, 2002).

[8] It is common to calculate a rate of return on financial investments by comparing initial investments with the stream of projected future income (or benefits). Social Security is not like a regular financial investment since there is no accumulation of assets and no legal right to benefits. Nonetheless, a rate of return can be calculated by comparing the payroll taxes a worker pays with the future benefits he or she is promised. The rate-of-return figures of Exhibit 5 were derived in this manner. They assume that the current tax level and promised future benefits will be maintained. However, as we previously noted, projections indicate that current tax rates will cover only about three-fourths of promised benefits by 2030. Thus, higher taxes will be required to maintain the promised benefit levels. In turn, the higher taxes will lower rates of return. Therefore, the figures of Exhibit 5 probably overstate the rates of return for the various groups.

EXHIBIT 5
Rates of Return by Gender, Marital Status, and Ethnicity

The earnings of blacks are lower than whites, but their life expectancies are shorter. The latter effect dominates when it comes to Social Security payouts. As a result, blacks get a lower rate of return from Social Security than whites. On the other hand, the earnings of Hispanics are lower than whites', but their life expectancies are a little longer. Consequently, their returns from Social Security are higher than whites' and substantially higher than blacks'.

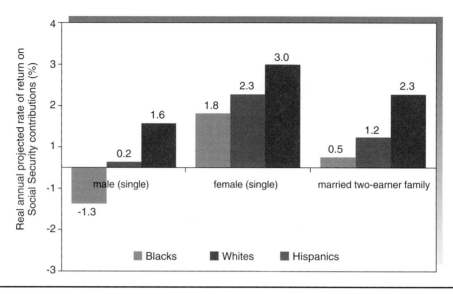

Source: Center for Data Analysis, Heritage Foundation.

Hispanic men. Similarly, a two-earner black couple born in 1975 can expect a real return of 0.5 percent, compared to returns of 1.2 percent and 2.3 percent for white and Hispanic couples born during the same year. A similar pattern exists when comparisons are made for people born in other years.

The Social Security retirement system also works to the disadvantage of those with life-shortening diseases. People with diabetes, heart disease, AIDS, and other diseases often spend decades paying 10.6 percent of their earnings into the system, only to die with loved ones unable to receive benefits from the Social Security taxes they have paid. (People with life-shortening diseases may receive disability insurance, but if they die before retirement, they collect nothing from their payments into the retirement system.)

Discrimination against Working Women

When Social Security was established, relatively few married women worked outside the home. Therefore, people were permitted to receive benefits based on either their own earnings or 50 percent of the benefits earned by their spouse, whichever was greater. This provision, which is still in place today, imposes a heavy penalty on women in the workforce. In the case of many working married women, the benefits based on the earnings of their spouses are approximately equal to, or in some cases greater than, benefits based on their own earnings. Thus, the payroll tax takes a big chunk of the earnings of many working women without providing them with any significant additional benefits.

PERSONAL RETIREMENT ACCOUNTS AND SOCIAL SECURITY REFORM

When the number of workers is growing rapidly and each successive generation is larger than the one that preceded it, a pay-as-you-go system can work well and yield a reasonable return. But we are now in an era when the number of retirees is growing more

THE WIZARD OF ID

The projected real rate of return on Social Security taxes for persons born after 1950 is approximately 2 percent, far below the real rate of return on private-sector investments.

rapidly than the number of workers. In this environment, Social Security is not a good investment. As we previously mentioned, today's typical worker can expect a return of only 2.0 percent from the taxes paid into the system. Social Security uses a worker's highest 35 earning years to calculate benefits. Going back to 1873 (this is as far back as calculations can be made), the average real rate of return derived from a fixed annual payment over a 35-year period into the stock market has been 6.4 percent. The highest return over a 35-year period was 9.5, while the lowest was 2.7 percent.[9] Even this latter figure is higher than can be expected from Social Security. Social Security's low rate of return, along with its structure that sometimes seems outdated, has fostered an environment for change.

When the number of workers is small relative to the number of retirees, a system in which people finance their own retirement by saving and investing during their working years becomes more attractive. In varying degrees, several countries have already moved toward systems based on personal retirement accounts (PRAs). Beginning in the early 1980s, Chile shifted to a retirement system based on saving and investing through PRAs rather than pay-as-you-go. The Chilean plan was so successful that other Latin American countries, including Mexico, Bolivia, Colombia, and Peru, adopted similar plans in the 1990s. High-income countries have also moved in this direction. In 1986, the United Kingdom began allowing workers to channel 4.6 percentage points of their payroll tax into PRAs in exchange for accepting a lower level of benefits from the pay-as-you-go system. The PRA option is highly popular. Three-fourths of British workers now choose it. Other countries that now permit at least some substitution of PRAs for payroll taxes and pay-as-you-go benefits include the Netherlands, Australia, Sweden, and Germany.

A shift to a retirement security system based, at least partially, on personal saving accounts raises a number of issues. We will mention four of the most important.

1. Degree of Investor Choice   Historical evidence indicates that, when held over a lengthy time period, a diverse holding of stocks is a low-risk investment that will generally outperform government bonds. (See the following Special Topic feature.) Furthermore, mutual funds now make it possible for even a small, novice investor to hold a diverse stock portfolio while still keeping administrative costs low. However, there is no assurance that investors, if left to their own discretion will choose to hold a diverse portfolio. Some proponents of PRAs say that providing individuals with a good deal of discretion concerning how their funds are invested is a good idea. Others say it is necessary to restrict people's choices in order to ensure that their retirement funds are not squandered on risky investments. The issue here is primarily about striking a balance between an attractive rate of return and minimal risk that the funds will be wiped out if invested unwisely or if the stock market were to crash.

---

[9]See Liqun Liu, Andrew J. Rettenmaier, and Zijun Wang, "Social Security and Stock Market Risk," NCPA Policy Report No. 244, National Center for Policy Analysis, July 23, 2001.

2. Share of Payroll Tax Allocated to PRAs and Current System

How much of the payroll tax should workers be permitted to allocate into PRAs? Several plans would permit individuals to channel between 2 and 6 percentage points (out of the current 10.6 percent rate) into a PRA-based system in exchange for accepting lower benefits from the current system. Over time, other plans call for fully substituting a PRA-based system for the current pay-as-you-go system. Obviously, this issue is about the relative importance of the two systems in the future.

3. Protecting the Benefits of Current Retirees and People Near Retirement

The benefits promised to current retirees and people near retirement age must be protected. Because most of the payroll tax is needed to finance current benefits, permitting workers to channel more than 1 or 2 percentage points into PRAs would create an immediate shortfall for the current system. Therefore, the transition to a system based more on personal investment may well require an increase in taxes and/or additional borrowing.

4. Property Rights and PRAs

Most plans currently under consideration would give people the property rights to the funds in their accounts and allow them to be passed along to their heirs in case of death prior to their retirement. However, funds drawn from a PRA during one's retirement years would generally have to be converted to a lifetime annuity, an insurance instrument paying the retiree a regular income for the remainder of his or her life.

Policy makers are now searching for ways to provide income security for future retirees without having to increase payroll taxes to levels that will retard work incentives and endanger future economic growth. Personal retirement accounts may help achieve this objective. The disincentive effects of having to make payments into a PRA—which can enhance the retiree's income and be passed along to his or her heirs—are much less severe than those associated with higher taxes. Furthermore, PRAs will tend to encourage saving and investment, which will help grow the economy.

KEY POINTS

▼ Social Security does not follow the saving-and-investment model. Rather, most of the funds flowing into the system are paid out to current retirees and survivors.

▼ Although the current tax revenues exceed the payments to retirees, this will change dramatically as the baby boomers begin to move into the retirement phases of their lives. Beginning in about 2018, the system's current surplus will become a deficit, which will persist for several decades.

▼ The current surplus of the Social Security system is used to purchase U.S. Treasury bonds. However, because the federal government is both the payee and recipient of these bonds, their net asset value to the federal government is zero. The bonds will not reduce the level of future taxes needed to cover the Social Security deficit when the baby boomers begin to retire.

▼ The big problem with the current pay-as-you-go system is that large tax increases, spending cuts, and/or additional borrowing will be needed to cover the Social Security deficits following the retirement of the baby boom generation. Dealing with these deficits is likely to adversely affect the economy.

▼ Although the Social Security benefit formula favors those with lower lifetime earnings, low-wage workers have lower life expectancies, begin work at a younger age, and gain less from the spousal benefit provisions of the current system. These latter factors largely, if not entirely, offset the egalitarian effects of the benefit formula.

▼ Because of their shorter life expectancies, blacks get a lower rate of return from Social Security than whites and a substantially lower return than Hispanics.

? CRITICAL ANALYSIS QUESTIONS

1. Is the Social Security system based on the same principles as private insurance? Why or why not?

*2. Why does the Social Security system face a crisis? Are there real assets in the Social Security Trust Fund that can be used to pay future benefits? Will the trust fund help avert higher future taxes and/or benefit reductions when the baby boomers retire? Why or why not?

3. Do you think workers should be permitted to invest all or part of their Social Security contribution in private investment funds? What are the advantages and disadvantages of a private option system? If given the opportunity, would you choose the private option or stay with the current system? Why?

4. How does Social Security affect the economic well-being of blacks relative to whites and Hispanics? Explain.

5. Does the current Social Security system promote income equality? Why or why not?

6. The Social Security payroll tax is split equally between the employee and the employer. Would it make any difference if the entire tax was imposed on employees? Would employees be helped if all the tax was imposed on employers? (*Hint:* You may want to consult the section on tax incidence in Chapter 4.)

*Asterisk denotes questions for which answers are given in Appendix B.

SPECIAL TOPIC 4

The Stock Market: Its Function, Performance, and Potential as an Investment Opportunity

Though the stock market functions as a voting machine in the short run, it acts as a weighing machine in the long run.

—Ben Graham,[1]
Securities Analyst

Focus

- What is the economic function of the stock market?

- What determines the price of a stock? Can experts forecast the future direction of stock prices?

- Can an ordinary investor profit from stock market investments? If so, how and under what circumstances?

---

[1]As quoted by Warren Buffett in Carol Loomis, "Warren Buffett on the Stock Market," *Fortune,* December 10, 2001, 80–87.

The market for corporate shares is called the stock market. The stock market makes it possible for investors, including small investors, to share in the profits (and the risks) of large businesses. About one-half of all households now own stock, either directly or indirectly through shares in an equity mutual fund. In recent years, changes in stock prices have often been front-page news. This feature will focus on the economic functions of the stock market and analyze its potential as an investment tool through which people can build their wealth. ■

THE ECONOMIC FUNCTIONS OF THE STOCK MARKET

The stock market performs several important functions in a modern economy. Let's consider three of the most important.

1. The stock market provides investors, including those who are not interested in participating directly in the operation of the firm, with an opportunity to own a fractional share of the firm's future profits.   As a firm earns profits, its shareholders may gain as the result of both dividend payments and increases in the market value of the stock. Ownership of stock is risky. There is no guarantee that any firm will be profitable in the future. But the shareholders' potential losses are limited to the amount of their initial investment. Beyond this point, shareholders are not responsible for the debts of the corporations that they own.

2. New stock issues are often an excellent way for firms to obtain funds for growth and product development.   Essentially, there are three ways for a firm to obtain additional financing. It can use retained earnings (profits earned but not paid out to stockholders), it can borrow money, or it can sell stock. When borrowing, the firm promises to repay the lender a specific amount, including principal and interest. On the other hand, new stock issues provide the firm with additional financing, while the owner of the stock acquires an ownership right to a fraction of the future revenues generated by the firm.

Newly issued stocks are sold to the public through specialized firms. A firm that issues new stock sells it in the **primary market**. When news reports tell us about how stock prices are changing, they are referring to **secondary markets**, where previously issued stocks are traded. Secondary markets make it easy to buy and sell listed stock. This is important to the primary market. The initial buyers want to know that their stock will be easy to sell later. Entry is more attractive when exit will be easy. This will help the corporation issuing new stock to sell it for a higher price.

A stock exchange is a secondary market. It is a place where stockbrokers come to arrange trades for buyers and sellers. The largest and best-known stock market is the New York Stock Exchange, where more than 2,500 stocks are traded. There are other such markets in the United States, as well as in London, Tokyo, and other trading centers around the world.

3. Stock prices provide information about the quality of business decisions. Changing stock prices reward good decisions and penalize bad ones. It pays for a stockholder, especially a large one, to be alert to whether the firm's decisions are good or bad. Those who spot a corporation's problems early can sell part or all of their stock in that firm before others notice and lower the price by selling their own stock. Similarly, those who first notice decisions that will be profitable can gain by increasing their holdings of the stock. Stockholder alertness benefits the corporation, too. The firm's board of directors can utilize the price changes resulting from investor vigilance to reward good management decisions. They often do so by tying the compensation of the top corporate officers to stock performance. How? Rather than paying these officers entirely in the form of salaries, a board of directors can integrate **stock options** into the compensation package

Primary market
The market in which financial institutions aid in the sale of new securities.

Secondary market
The market in which financial institutions aid in the buying and selling of existing securities.

Stock options
The option to buy a specified number of shares of the firm's stock at a designated price. The designated price is generally set so that the options will be quite valuable if the firm's shares increase in price but of little value if their price falls. Thus, when used to compensate top managers, stock options provide a strong incentive to follow policies that will increase the value of the firm.

of top executives. When good decisions drive the stock price up, the executives' options will be very valuable. On the other hand, if bad decisions cause the stock price to fall, then the options will have little or no value.

STOCK MARKET PERFORMANCE: THE HISTORICAL RECORD

On the whole, investors in American stocks have done exceedingly well. Furthermore, this has been true over a lengthy period of time. During the last two centuries, after adjustment for inflation, corporate stocks have yielded a real return of approximately 7 percent per year, compared to a real return of about 3 percent for bonds. The historic returns derived from savings accounts and money market mutual funds are even lower. A 7 percent real return may not sound particularly good, but when it is compounded, it means that the real value of your investment will double every ten years. In contrast, it will take twenty-three years to double your money at a 3 percent interest return.[2]

The Standard and Poor's 500 Index is one measure of the performance of the broad stock market. This index factors in the value of dividends as if they were reinvested in the market. Thus, it provides a measure of the rate of return received by investors in the form of both dividends and changes in share prices. **Exhibit 1** presents data on the real rate of return earned by stockholders each year since 1950 as measured by the changes in the S&P 500 Index during the year. The compound annual nominal rate of return of the S&P 500 was 11.4 percent during the fifty-three-year period. Even after adjustment for inflation, the real compound annual return was 7.6 percent for the entire period. The returns during the 1980s and 1990s were even higher.

Exhibit 1 highlights one of the risks that accompanies the ownership of stock: the returns and therefore the value of the stock can be quite volatile. The broad stock market, as measured by the S&P 500, provided double-digit returns during thirty-three of the fifty-three years between 1950 and 2003, but the returns were negative during thirteen of those

EXHIBIT 1
Annual Return for Stocks, 1950–2003

During the past fifty-three years, the broad S&P 500 Index indicates that stock investors earned an 11.4 percent compound annual rate of return. Double-digit returns were earned in thirty-three of the fifty-three years, whereas returns were negative during only thirteen of the years.

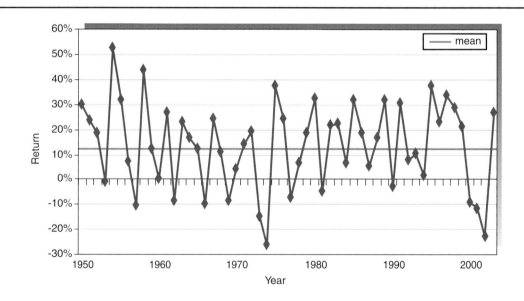

Source: Global Financial Data, http://www.globalfindata.com.

[2]You can approximate the number of years it will take to double your funds at alternative interest rates by simply dividing the yield into 70. This is sometimes referred to as the rule of 70.

years. Stock market investors can never be sure what return they will earn or what the value of their stock holdings will be at a specified time in the future.

But this volatility is a big reason that stocks yield a significantly higher return than saving accounts, money market certificates, or short-term government bonds, all of which guarantee you a given amount in the future. Since most people value the additional certainty in the yields that bonds and savings accounts provide over stocks, the average return on stocks has to be higher to attract investors away from the more predictable investments.

THE INTEREST RATE, THE VALUE OF FUTURE INCOME, AND STOCK PRICES

Underlying today's price of a firm's stock is the present value of the firm's expected future net earnings, or profit. What those future profits are worth to an investor today depends on three things: (1) the expected size of future net earnings, (2) when these earnings will be achieved, and (3) how much the investor discounts the future income. The last depends on the interest rate. As we noted in an earlier chapter, the present-value procedure can be used to determine the current value of any future income (or cost) stream. If D represents dividends (and gains from a higher stock price) earned in various years in the future (indicated by the subscripts) and i represents the discount or interest rate, the present value of the future income stream is

$$PV = \frac{D_1}{(1 + i)} + \frac{D_2}{(1 + i)^2} + \ldots + \frac{D_n}{(1 + i)^n}$$

As this formula shows, a higher interest rate will reduce the present value of future revenues (returns), including those derived from stocks. This is true even if the size of the future returns is not affected by changes in the interest rate.

Stock analysts often stress that lower interest rates are good for the stock market. This should not be surprising because the lower rates of interest will increase the value of future income (and capital gains). For a specific annual income stream in perpetuity, the present value is equal simply to R/i, where R is the annual revenue stream and i is the interest rate. Thus, for example, when the interest rate is 12.5 percent, the discounted value of $10 of future income to be received each year in perpetuity is $80 ($10 divided by 0.125), eight times the stream of earnings. But when the interest rate is 5 percent, the discounted value of this same income stream is $200 ($10 divided by 0.05), or twenty times the stream of earnings. Therefore, if the $10 represented the expected future income stream from a share of stock, the present value of the income stream would be higher when the interest rate was lower. Other things being constant, lower interest rates will increase the value of future income and thereby increase the market value of stocks.

How can one tell whether stock prices are high or low? The answer to that question depends on both the interest rate and expectations about the future income generated by the stock (or bundle of stocks). The price–earnings (P/E) ratio provides information on the price of a stock relative to its current earnings. It is interesting to look at the historic path of the P/E ratio and observe how it has responded to changes in interest rates and business-cycle conditions. Of course, the latter is likely to influence the future earnings prospects of business firms.

Exhibit 2 presents data on the P/E ratio over the 1950–2004 period for the stocks included in the S&P 500 Index. The P/E ratio average during this lengthy period was 16. From the early 1950s through the mid-1990s, the P/E ratio ranged from a low of 8 to a high of 24. During the 1960s, the economy grew rapidly and both the inflation and interest rates were relatively low. Throughout most of that period, the P/E ratio was near 20. The 1970s was a period of both high inflation and high interest rates. As we just indicated, high interest rates will reduce the value of future income. Reflecting this factor, the P/E ratio during the 1970s was near 10 throughout the decade, considerably lower than during the 1960s.

EXHIBIT 2
Price–Earnings Ratio, 1950–2004

Since 1950, the average price–earnings ratio of the S&P 500 Index has been 16. This ratio was between 8 and 24 throughout the 1951–1997 period. It was persistently near the lower end of this range (between 8 and 10) during the 1970s. It rose during the period 1985–1997 and eventually soared above 30 during the period 1998–2002. A combination of stock price declines and higher earnings as the economy recovered from the 2001 recession caused the price–earnings ratio to recede to 21 in 2004.

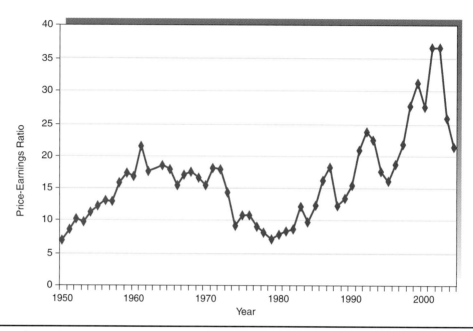

Source: http://www.globalfindata.com/.

As the economy grew rapidly, and both the inflation rate and interest rates declined and remained at a low level during the 1984–1997 period, the P/E ratio rose sharply. By the mid-1990s, it had risen to the 20 to 25 range, quite high by historical standards. But the stock market continued to boom, and, by 1999, the P/E ratio had risen to an extremely high level, 31.2. By the late 1990s, there was considerable talk of a "stock market bubble," high stock prices that could not be maintained because they were out of line with the future earning prospects of business firms. The bubble burst and stock prices fell sharply. As a result, the S&P 500 lost nearly 50 percent of its value during 2000–2002 (see Exhibit 1). As the economy recovered from the recession of 2001, corporate earnings picked up in 2004, and the P/E ratio receded to near 20. Measured by the yardstick of history, the P/E ratio was still quite high at year-end 2004, but at least it had declined into a range that had been observed several times in the past.

THE RANDOM WALK THEORY OF THE STOCK MARKET

Random walk theory
The theory that current stock prices already reflect known information about the future. Therefore, the future movement of stock prices will be determined by surprise occurrences. This will cause them to change in a random fashion.

Most economists adhere to the **random walk theory** of stock prices. According to this theory, current stock prices already reflect information that is known or can be forecast with any degree of accuracy about the future state of corporate earnings, interest rates, the health of the economy, and other factors that influence stock prices. In other words, current stock prices will already reflect the best information currently available. In the future, the direction of stock prices will be driven by surprise occurrences—things that differ from what people are currently anticipating. By their very nature, these factors are unpredictable. If they were predictable, they would already be reflected in current stock prices.

The random walk theory applies to the price of a specific stock as well as to the market as a whole. The prices of specific stocks will reflect their future earnings prospects.

The stock prices of firms with attractive future profit potential will be high relative to their current earnings. Consequently, their current prices will already reflect their attractive future earnings prospects. The opposite will be true for firms with poor future prospects. Although numerous factors affect the future price of any specific stock, changes in the current price will be driven by changes that differ from current expectations. Thus, because the future prices of both specific stocks and the market as a whole are driven by unexpected and unpredictable factors, no one can consistently forecast their future path with any degree of accuracy.

HOW THE ORDINARY INVESTOR CAN BEAT THE EXPERTS

Historically, ordinary Americans have often refrained from investing in the stock market because of the risks involved. But there are ways this risk can be reduced, particularly for long-term investments. The value of any specific stock can rise or fall by a huge amount within a relatively short time period. But the risk accompanying these movements can be reduced by holding a diverse **portfolio**, a collection of stocks characterized by relatively small holdings of a large number of companies in different markets and industries. **Equity mutual funds** make this possible. They provide the ordinary investor with a low-cost method of owning a diverse bundle of stocks. An equity mutual fund is a corporation that buys and holds shares of stock in many firms. This diversification puts the law of large numbers to work for you. While some of the investments in a diversified portfolio will do poorly, others will do extremely well. The performance of the latter will offset that of the former, and the rate of return will converge toward the average. Remember, the average real return of equities has been substantially higher than for bonds, savings accounts, and other readily accessible methods of saving.

    As **Exhibit 3** shows, there was a huge increase in the quantity of funds flowing into mutual funds during the 1990s. The value of mutual fund investments increased from $246 billion in 1990 to approximately $4 trillion in 1999–2000. Although equity mutual fund investments declined as stock prices fell during 2000–2002, they rebounded to $3.7 trillion by year-end 2003. They now account for about 30 percent of all publicly traded U.S. stocks.

Portfolio
All the stocks, bonds, or other securities held by an individual or corporation for investment purposes.

Equity mutual fund
A corporation that pools the funds of investors, including small investors, and uses them to purchase a bundle of stocks.

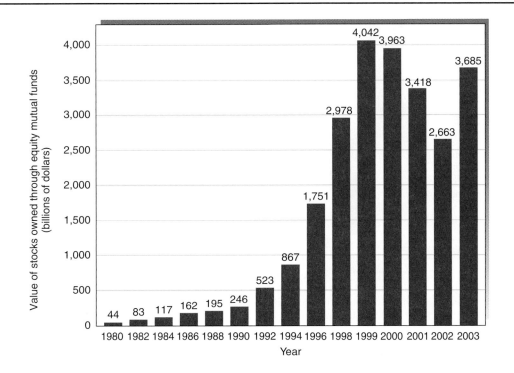

EXHIBIT 3
Value of Equity Mutual Funds

The amount of money that people put into U.S. equity mutual funds, in order to hold shares in the ownership of stocks, rose dramatically in the 1990s. Purchasing shares in a mutual fund is a simple way for an individual to buy and hold an interest in a large variety of stocks with one purchase.

Source: Investor Company Institute, http://www.ici.org/.

A second source of risk facing the stock market investor is the possibility that nearly all stocks in the market can rise or fall together when expectations about the entire economy change. This has happened on several occasions. For example, on October 19, 1987, the stocks listed in the Dow Jones Industrial Average lost more than 22 percent of their value in just one trading day. More recently, the high-tech stocks listed on the NASDAQ exchange lost about 70 percent of their value during 2000 and 2001. However, the risks accompanying such short-term movements can be substantially reduced if an investor either continually adds to or holds a diverse portfolio of stocks over a lengthy period of time, say, thirty or thirty-five years.

Exhibit 4 illustrates this point. This exhibit shows the highest and lowest real returns (the returns adjusted for inflation) earned from stock market investments for periods of varying lengths between the years 1871 and 2000. The exhibit assumes that the investor paid a fixed amount annually into a mutual fund that mirrored the Standard & Poor's 500 Index, a basket of stocks thought to represent the market as a whole. Clearly, huge swings are possible when stocks are held for only a short time period. During the 1871–2000 period, the single-year returns of the S&P 500 ranged from 47.2 percent to –35.5 percent. Even over a five-year period, the compound annual returns ranged from 29.8 percent to –16.7 percent. Note that the "best returns" and "worst returns" converged as the length of the investment period increased. When a thirty-five-year period was considered, the compound annual return for the best thirty-five years between 1871 and 2000 was 9.5 percent, compared to 2.7 percent for the worst thirty-five years.[3] Thus, the annual real return of stocks during the worst-case scenario was about the same as the real return for bonds. Furthermore, the annual real rate of return from the stock investments during the period was 7 percent—more than twice the comparable rate for bonds.

EXHIBIT 4
Stocks Are Less Risky When Held for a Lengthy Time Period

This exhibit shows the best and the worst annualized real performance for each investment period from 1871 to 2000. It shows that there is less risk of a low or negative return when an investment in a portfolio of stocks (S&P 500) is held for a longer period of time.

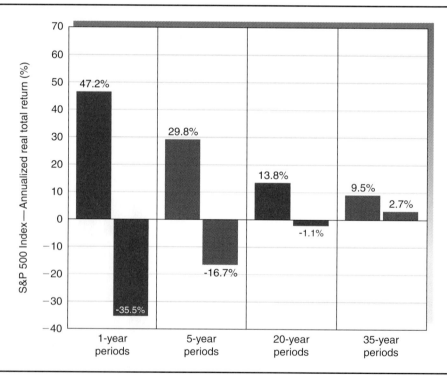

Source: Liqun Liu, Andrew J. Rettenmaier, and Zijun Wang, "Social Security and Market Risk," National Center for Policy Analysis Working Paper Number 244, July 2001. The returns are based on the assumption that an individual invests a fixed amount for each year in the investment period.

[3]See Liqun Liu, Andrew J. Rettenmaier, and Zijun Wang, "Social Security and Market Risk," National Center for Policy Analysis Working Paper Number 244, July 2001.

Are stocks riskier than bonds? If held for only a short time—five years, for example—stocks are more risky. However, when held over lengthy periods, such as twenty or thirty years, historically the rate of return on stocks has been both higher and less variable than that of bonds. What does this imply for people in their twenties and thirties who are saving for their retirement? Where should they put their funds?

The bottom line is this: when held over a lengthy period, a diverse portfolio of stocks has yielded a high rate of return, and the variation in that return has been low. Thus, for the long-term investor, such as a person saving for his or her retirement years, a diverse portfolio of stocks is not particularly risky.

The Advantages of Indexed Mutual Funds

When purchasing a mutual fund, the investor can choose either a managed or an indexed fund. A **managed equity mutual fund** is one in which an "expert," generally supported by a research staff, tries to pick and choose the stock holdings of the fund in a manner that will maximize its rate of return. In contrast, an **indexed equity mutual fund** merely holds stocks in the same proportion as they exist in a broad stock market index like the Standard & Poor's 500 or the Dow Jones Industrials.

In the case of indexed funds, neither comprehensive research nor extensive stock trading are needed because the fund merely seeks to mirror the index and earn the rate of return of the broad market that it represents. Thus, because they do not spend much on either research or stock trading, the operating costs of indexed funds are substantially lower than they are for managed funds. Therefore, they are able to charge lower fees, which means that a larger share of the investor's money flows directly into the purchase of stock.

As a result, the average rate of return yielded by a broad indexed fund beats the return of almost all managed mutual funds when comparisons are made over periods of time such as a decade. This is not surprising because, as the random walk theory indicates, not even the experts will be able to forecast consistently the future direction of stock prices with any degree of accuracy. Over the typical ten-year period, the S&P 500 Index has yielded a higher return than 85 percent of actively managed funds. And over twenty-year periods, mutual funds indexed to the S&P 500 have generally outperformed about 98 percent of actively managed funds.[4] Thus, the odds are very low, about 1 in 50, that you or anyone else will be able to select an actively managed fund that will do better than the market average *over the long run.*

Managed equity mutual fund
An equity mutual fund that has a portfolio manager who decides what stocks will be held in the fund and when they will be bought or sold. A research staff generally provides support for the fund manager.

Indexed equity mutual fund
An equity mutual fund that holds a portfolio of stocks that matches their share (or weight) in a broad stock market index such as the S&P 500. The overhead of these funds is usually quite low because their expenses on stock trading and research are low.

---

[4]See Jeremy J. Siegel, *Stocks for the Long Run,* 3rd ed. (New York: McGraw-Hill, 2002): 342–43.

Should You Invest in a Fund Because of Its Past Performance?

People marketing mutual funds often encourage customers to invest in mutual funds that have yielded high rates of return in the past. This sounds like a good strategy, but history indicates that it is not. Mutual funds with outstanding records over a five- or ten-year period often perform poorly in the future. Examples of this abound. On average, the top funds during the 1970s underperformed during the 1980s. For example, the top fund (Twentieth Century Growth) during the '70s fell to 176th place in the '80s. The second-place fund in the '70s (Templeton Growth) fell to 126th place in the '80s. The fund "44 Wall Street" was in fourth place in the '70s, but fell to 309th place in the '80s.

The same pattern has presented itself in recent years. The top twenty managed equity funds of the 1980s outperformed the S&P 500 Index by 3.9 percent per year over the course of the decade. But if investors entering the market in 1990 thought they would beat the market by choosing the "hot" funds of the '80s, they would have been disappointed. The top twenty funds of the 1980s underperformed the S&P 500 by 1.2 percent per year during the 1990s. The "hot" funds in the late 1990s ended up in similar shape. For example, during the period 1998–1999, the top-performing managed fund in the marketplace was Van Wagoner's Emerging Growth fund. During this time, the Emerging Growth fund yielded an astonishing 105.52 percent average annual return. But over the two-year period 2000–2001, the fund ranked 1,106th, earning an average annual return of *minus* 43.54 percent.[5]

Why is past performance such an unreliable indicator? Two factors provide insight on the answer to this question. First, some of the mutual funds with above-average returns during a period were merely lucky. After all, if you flip a coin 100 times, you will not always get 50 heads and 50 tails. Sometimes, the coin will come up heads maybe 60 times out of 100. But this does not mean you can expect 60 heads during the next sequence of 100. So it is with stock market mutual funds. Given that there are a large number of funds, some of them will have above-average performance for a time period. But this does not mean that the above-average performance can be expected in the future.

Second, a strategy that works well in one environment, inflationary conditions, for example, is often disastrous when conditions change. For example, mutual funds with substantial holdings of gold mining companies did exceedingly well during the inflationary 1970s. But their performance was disastrous during the 1980s and 1990s as the inflation was brought under control. Similarly, some mutual funds that performed well during the bull market of the 1990s were among the worst performers during the bear market that began in 2000.

Virtually none of the experts are able to consistently "beat the market average" over lengthy time periods and changing market conditions. Thus, broad market indexes outperform the stock pickers in the long run. This is something you will not often hear from brokerage firms and other experts trying to sell their services to you. But knowing this will make you a smarter investor.

KEY POINTS

▼ The stock market makes it possible for investors without either specialized business skills or the time to become involved in the operation of a business firm to share in the risks and opportunities that accompany the ownership of corporate businesses.

▼ During the last two centuries, after adjustment for inflation, corporate stocks have yielded a real return of approximately 7 percent per year, compared to a real return of about 3 percent for bonds and even lower yields for savings accounts and money market mutual funds.

[5]Burton G. Malkiel, *A Random Walk Down Wall Street: The Time Tested Strategy for Sucessful Investing* (New York: W.W. Norton & Company, 2003), 189-190.

▼ Most economists adhere to the random walk theory of stock prices. According to this theory, current stock prices already reflect all information about factors influencing stock prices that is known or can be forecast with any degree of accuracy. Thus, the future direction of stock prices will be driven by surprise occurrences and, as a result, no one will be able to forecast future stock prices with any degree of accuracy.

▼ Buying and selling individual stocks without specialized knowledge for a quick profit is very risky. But holding a diverse portfolio of unrelated stocks and holding them for long periods of time greatly reduces the risk of investing in the stock market.

▼ An equity mutual fund that is tied to a broad stock market index like the S&P 500 provides an attractive method for long-term investors to obtain relatively high yields with minimal risk. Indexed mutual funds have substantially lower operating costs than managed funds because they engage in less trading and have no need for either a market expert or research staff.

? CRITICAL ANALYSIS QUESTIONS

*1. A friend just inherited $50,000. She informs you of her investment plans and asks for your advice. "I want to put it into the stock market and use it for my retirement in thirty years. What do you think is the best plan that will provide high returns at a relatively low risk?" What answer would you give? Explain.

2. Suppose that more expansionary monetary policy leads to inflation and higher nominal interest rates. How is this likely to affect the value of stocks? Explain.

*3. Microsoft stock rose from less than $10 in 1995 to more than $100 per share in 2000. Microsoft has made sizable profits but never paid a dividend. Why were people willing to pay such a high price knowing that they might not get dividends for many years?

4. If an investment adviser gives you some hot new stock tip, is it likely to be a "sure thing"? Why or why not? If you have a stockbroker and purchase the stocks promoted by the broker, are you likely to earn a high return on your stock investments? Why or why not?

*5. The stocks of some corporations that have never made a profit, especially those in high-technology industries, have risen in price. What causes investors to be willing to buy these stocks?

6. The stock market is generally a leading business-cycle indicator. Can you explain why stock prices are likely to fall before the economy goes into a recession and rise before it begins to recover? (*Hint:* Will stock prices reflect current or future earnings?)

7. In 2003, the taxes on dividends from stocks were reduced and brought into line with the tax treatment of capital gains. Other things being constant, what is the expected effect of a dividend tax reduction on stock prices? Explain. What other changes might be expected as the result of the more favorable tax treatment of dividends?

---

*Asterisk denotes questions for which answers are given in Appendix B.

SPECIAL TOPIC

5

The Federal Budget and the National Debt

The attractiveness of financing spending by debt issue to the elected politicians should be obvious. Borrowing allows spending to be made that will yield immediate political payoffs without the incurring of any immediate political cost.

—*James Buchanan*[1]

Focus

- How large is the national debt? Will the debt have to be paid off?

- Who owns the national debt?

- How are future generations affected by debt financing?

- How does the government debt of the United States compare with the government debt of other countries?

- Are budget deficits the result of the political incentive structure?

---

[1]James Buchanan, *The Deficit and American Democracy* (Memphis, Tenn.: P. K. Steidman Foundation, 1984).

Historically, attitudes toward government debt have undergone dramatic swings. Prior to the Keynesian revolution, there was a virtual consensus that budget deficits were irresponsible and therefore should be avoided, except perhaps during wartime emergencies. In contrast, during the 1960–1980 Keynesian era, deficits were perceived as an important policy tool that could be used to stimulate growth and help promote stability. But concern about the potential harmful effects of debt financing rose again with the large budget deficits and growth of the national debt during the 1980s. This feature will analyze both the economics and politics of debt financing. ■

DEFICITS, SURPLUSES, AND THE NATIONAL DEBT

When the federal government uses debt rather than taxes and user charges to pay for its expenditures, the United States Treasury fills this gap by borrowing in the loanable funds market. When borrowing funds, the Treasury generally issues interest-bearing bonds. These bonds comprise the **national debt**. In effect, the national debt consists of outstanding loans from financial investors to the general fund of the U.S. Treasury.

The federal budget exerts a direct effect on the national debt. The budget deficit or surplus is a "flow" concept (like water running into or out of a bathtub), whereas the national debt is a "stock" figure (like the amount of water in the tub at a point in time). A budget deficit increases the size of the national debt by the amount of the deficit. Conversely, a budget surplus allows the federal government to pay off bondholders and thereby reduce the size of the national debt. In essence, the national debt represents the cumulative effect of all the prior budget deficits and surpluses.

The creditworthiness of an organization is dependent upon the size of its debt relative to its income base. Therefore, when analyzing the significance of budget deficits, surpluses, and the national debt, it makes sense to consider their size relative to the entire economy. **Exhibit 1** presents data for the 1950–2003 period for both the federal budget deficit and the national debt as a percentage of GDP. Because the defense effort of World War II was largely financed with debt rather than taxes, the national debt was quite large during the period immediately following the war. As part (a) of Exhibit 1 shows, budget deficits averaged less than 1 percent of GDP during the 1950–1974 period. Historically, real output in the United States has grown at an annual rate of approximately 3 percent. When the budget deficit as a percentage of GDP is less than the growth of real output, the federal debt will decline relative to the size of the economy. This is precisely what happened during the 1950–1974 period. Budget deficits were present, and they pushed up the nominal national debt (from $257 billion at year-end 1950 to $493 billion at the end of 1974). But GDP grew even more rapidly. By 1974, the national debt had fallen to 32 percent of GDP, down from 87 percent in 1950 (and 127 percent in 1946).

From the mid-1970s to the mid-1990s, federal deficits were both large and continuous. The budget deficits averaged nearly 4 percent of GDP during 1974–1995 (part a of Exhibit 1). Pushed along by the large deficits, the national debt rose from 32 percent of GDP in 1974 to 67 percent in 1995. However, as the economy grew rapidly in the 1990s, the budget deficits were eventually transformed into surpluses. By 2001, the outstanding federal debt had fallen to 57 percent of GDP. Propelled by the large deficits of 2002–2003, federal debt as a share of GDP is once again rising, and this upward trend is expected to continue in the years immediately ahead.

WHO OWNS THE NATIONAL DEBT?

As **Exhibit 2** illustrates, more than two-fifths (42.4 percent) of the national debt is held by agencies of the federal government. For example, Social Security Trust Funds are often used to purchase U.S. bonds. When the debt is owned by a government agency, it is little more

National debt
The sum of the indebtedness of the federal government in the form of outstanding interest-earning bonds. It reflects the cumulative effect of budget deficits and surpluses.

EXHIBIT 1

Budget Deficits, Surpluses, and the National Debt as a Percentage of GDP

Throughout most of the 1950s and 1960s, federal budget deficits were small as a percentage of GDP, and occasionally the government ran a budget surplus (a). During this period, the national debt declined as a proportion of GDP (b). During the period 1974–1995, budget deficits were quite large, causing the national debt to increase as a percentage of GDP. During the period 1996–2001, the national debt fell as a share of the economy, but, propelled by the large deficits of recent years, the federal debt/GDP ratio is once again increasing.

(a) Federal budget deficit or surplus as a percentage of GDP

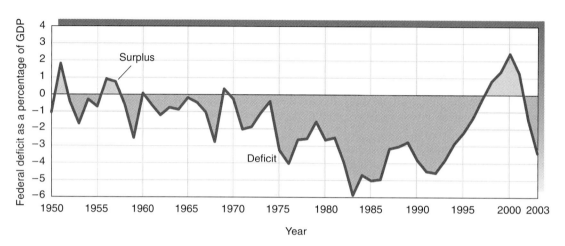

(b) Gross and net federal debt as a percentage of GDP

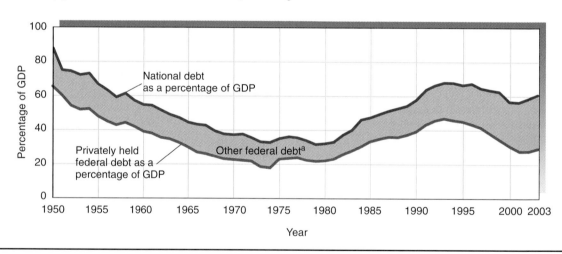

ᵃFederal debt held by U.S. government agencies and Federal Reserve banks.
Source: http://www.economagic.com/.

than an accounting transaction indicating that one government agency (for example, the Social Security Administration) is making a loan to another (the U.S. Treasury). Even the interest payments in this case represent little more than an internal government transfer.

Another 9.7 percent of the public debt is held by the Federal Reserve System. When the Fed purchases U.S. securities, it creates money. The bonds held by the Fed, therefore, are indicative of prior government expenditures that have been paid for with "printing-press" money—money created by the central bank. As in the case of the securities held by government agencies, the interest on the bonds held by the Fed is returned to the Treasury after the Fed has covered its costs of operation. The U.S. Treasury both pays and receives almost all of the interest, approximately $30 billion in 2003, on the bonds held by the

EXHIBIT 2
Who Owns the National Debt?

Of the $6.73 trillion national debt, a little more than half is held by government agencies (primarily the Social Security Trust Fund) and Federal Reserve banks. Of the $3.22 trillion federal debt held privately, 55.9 percent is owned by domestic investors and 44.1 percent by foreigners.

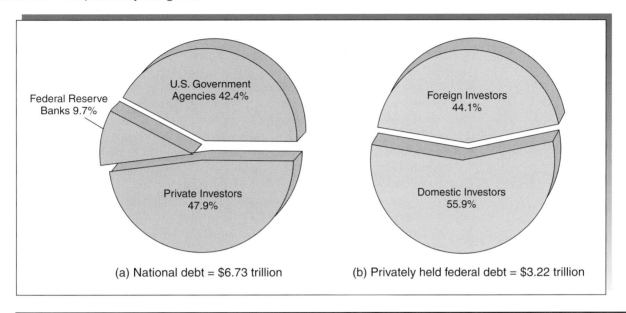

(a) National debt = $6.73 trillion   (b) Privately held federal debt = $3.22 trillion

Source: http://www.economagic.com/. These data can also be found in the *Federal Reserve Bulletin*.

Federal Reserve. Thus, the bonds held by the Fed, like those held by U.S. government agencies, do not create a net interest liability for the U.S. Treasury.

In contrast, **privately held government debt** imposes a net interest burden on the federal government. In the case of the privately held debt—that is, the bonds held by individuals, insurance companies, mutual funds, and other investors—the federal government will have to impose taxes to meet the future interest payments on these bonds. Therefore, it is important to distinguish between (1) the total national debt and (2) the privately held government debt. Only the latter imposes a net interest obligation on the federal government. Currently, the privately held portion of the national debt constitutes less than half of the total. Thus, the total national debt ($6.73 trillion at year-end 2003) vastly overstates the net debt obligations of the federal government. Of the $3.22 trillion privately held debt, 55.9 percent is owned by domestic investors and 44.1 percent by foreigners. The portion owned by foreigners is sometimes referred to as **external debt**.

Part (b) of Exhibit 1 presents data on the size of the privately held federal debt as a percentage of GDP for the 1950–2003 period. Measured as a share of GDP, the general trend of the privately held debt has been similar to that for the national debt as a whole. However, in recent years the privately held debt has gradually declined as a share of the total. In 2003, the privately held federal debt stood at 29 percent of GDP, up from 18 percent in 1974.

HOW DOES DEBT FINANCING INFLUENCE FUTURE GENERATIONS?

The impact of the national debt on future generations has been a point of controversy for decades.[2] Opponents of debt financing often charge that we are mortgaging the future of our children and grandchildren—that debt financing permits us to consume today and then

Privately held government debt
The portion of the national debt owed to domestic and foreign investors. It does not include bonds held by agencies of the federal government or the Federal Reserve.

External debt
The portion of the national debt owed to foreign investors.

[2]See Richard H. Fink and Jack High, eds., *A Nation in Debt: Economists Debate the Federal Budget Deficit* (Frederick, Md.: University Publications of America, 1987), for an excellent set of readings summarizing this debate.

send the bill to future generations. In the 1960s and 1970s, the overwhelming bulk of the national debt was held by domestic investors. During this era, Keynesians argued that there was little reason for concern because, "We owe it to ourselves." Today, new classical economists take the position that debt affects the timing, but not the magnitude, of taxes. Like Keynesians, the new classical economists do not believe that debt financing exerts much effect on the welfare of future generations. Who is right?

When analyzing the issue of debt financing, it is important to keep two points in mind. First, in the case of domestically held debt, our children and grandchildren will indeed pay the taxes to service the debt, but they will also receive the interest payments. Admittedly, those paying the taxes and receiving the interest payments will not always be the same people. Some will gain and others will lose. But both those who gain and those who lose will be members of the future generation.

Second, debt financing of a government activity cannot push the opportunity cost of the resources used by government onto future generations. If current GDP is $10 trillion and the federal government spends $2 trillion on goods and services, then only $8 trillion will be available for consumption and investment by individuals, businesses, and state and local governments. This will be true regardless of whether the federal government finances its expenditures with taxes or debt. When the government builds a highway, constructs an antimissile defense system, or provides police protection, it draws resources with alternative uses away from the private sector. This cost is incurred in the present; it cannot be avoided through debt financing.

If the opportunity cost of resources occurs during the current period, does this mean that the welfare of future generations is unaffected by debt financing? Not necessarily. Debt financing influences future generations primarily through its potential impact on saving and capital formation. If lots of factories, machines, houses, technical knowledge, and other productive assets are available to future generations, then their productive potential will be high. Alternatively, if fewer productive assets are passed along to the next generation, then their productive capability will be less. Thus, the true measure of how government debt influences future generations involves knowledge of its impact on capital formation.

The effect of budget deficits on capital formation is a complex issue. Consider an economy operating at its normal productive capacity. If government expenditures were held constant, how would the substitution of debt financing for current taxation influence capital formation? As our discussion of fiscal policy models implies, economists differ in their responses to this question. We will consider two major theories: the traditional view that budget deficits reduce future capital stock and the opposing new classical view that such deficits exert no significant future effect.

The Traditional View: Budget Deficits Reduce the Future Capital Stock

Most economists embrace the traditional view that budget deficits will retard private investment and thereby reduce the welfare of future generations. Suppose that the government substitutes borrowing for current taxation. For example, consider what would happen if the government cut the current taxes of each household by $1,000 and borrowed the funds to replace the lost revenues. As a result, the after-tax income of each household increases by $1,000. Of course, the households may save some of the $1,000 addition to their disposable income, but they are also likely to spend some of it on consumption goods, according to the traditional view. If they do not save all the $1,000, the additional government borrowing will increase the demand for loanable funds relative to the supply and thereby push real interest rates upward.[3] In turn, the higher real interest rates will retard private investment, which will reduce the physical capital available to future

---

[3]Alternatively, one could approach this topic from the viewpoint of how households value the government bonds relative to the future tax liability implied by the bonds. If bondholders recognize the asset value of the government bonds while taxpayers fail to recognize fully the accompanying tax liability, then the general populace will have an exaggerated view of its true wealth position. Wealth is an important determinant of consumption. When people think they are wealthier, they will consume more and save less than they would if they had fully recognized their future tax liability. Of course, the increase in consumption and reduction in savings would place upward pressure on the real rate of interest. This is simply an alternative way of viewing the substitution of government debt for current taxation.

generations. To the extent that future generations work with less capital (fewer productivity-enhancing tools and machines), their productivity and wages will be lower than would have been the case had the budget deficits not crowded out private investment.

In addition, the higher interest rates will attract foreign investors. But investments in the United States will require dollars. As foreigners increase their investments in the United States, they will demand dollars in the foreign exchange market. This strong demand will cause the dollar to appreciate relative to other currencies. In turn, the appreciation in the exchange rate value of the dollar will make U.S. exports more expensive to foreigners and foreign goods cheaper for Americans. These relative price changes will retard exports and stimulate imports. Predictably, net exports will decline.

The inflow of capital from abroad will dampen both the increase in interest rates and the reduction in domestic investment. However, it will also increase the asset holdings of foreigners in the United States. That means the returns on these assets will generate income for foreigners rather than Americans. As a result of financing the debt with foreign funds, future generations of Americans will inherit both a smaller stock of physical capital and less income from that capital (because the share owned by foreigners has increased). Succeeding generations will be less well-off as a result.

In summary, we can say that the traditional view argues that the substitution of debt financing for current taxation will increase current consumption, push up real interest rates, and retard private investment. In addition, the higher real interest rates will lead to an increase in net foreign investment, appreciation in the exchange rate value of the dollar, and a decline in net exports (imports will increase relative to exports). According to the traditional view, budget deficits will retard the growth rate of capital formation, particularly capital owned by Americans, and reduce national income and future living standards of Americans.

The New Classical View: Budget Deficits Exert Little Effect on Future Capital Stock

Not all economists accept the traditional view of budget deficits. An alternative theory, most closely associated with Robert Barro of Harvard University, encompasses the new classical perspective of fiscal policy.[4] This new classical view stresses that additional debt implies an equivalent amount of future taxes. If, as the new classical model assumes, individuals fully anticipate the added future tax liability accompanying the debt, current consumption will be unaffected when governments substitute debt for taxes. According to this view, when future taxes (debt) are substituted for current taxes, people will save the reduction in current taxes so that they will have the required income to pay the higher future taxes implied by the additional debt. Continuing with our previous example, the new classical theory implies that households receiving a $1,000 reduction in current taxes financed by issuing bonds (which imply higher future taxes) will save all the $1,000 increase in their current disposable income. This increase in saving, triggered by the anticipation of the higher future taxes, allows the additional government debt to be financed without an increase in the real rate of interest. Since there is no increase in interest rates, private investment is unaffected. Neither is there an influx of foreign capital. Under these circumstances, the substitution of debt for taxes exerts little or no effect on either capital formation or the welfare of future generations.

Empirical Evidence on the Impact of the Deficit

What does the empirical evidence indicate about the validity of the two theories? Empirical studies have found little, if any, relationship between year-to-year changes in the budget deficit and real interest rates. New classical economists argue that these findings support their theory.

---

[4]See Robert Barro, "Are Government Bonds Net Wealth?" *Journal of Political Economy* 82 (November–December 1974): 1095–1117; and "The Ricardian Approach to Budget Deficits," *Journal of Economic Perspectives* 2 (spring 1989).

However, the experience with the large budget deficits subsequent to 1980 would appear to support the traditional theory. As the size of the budget deficit increased substantially during the 1980s, Americans increased their current consumption expenditures and substantially reduced their domestically financed capital formation. Simultaneously, there was an inflow of net foreign investment and a reduction in net exports (imports increased relative to exports). This pattern is precisely what the traditional theory predicts will happen when debt financing is substituted for current taxation. Empirical work on the linkage between (1) the budget deficit on the one hand and (2) interest rates, consumption, and inflow of capital on the other is continuing. At this point, most economists believe that the bulk of the evidence is more consistent with the traditional view.

GOVERNMENT DEBT: A CROSS-COUNTRY COMPARISON

How does the national debt of the United States compare with that of other countries? **Exhibit 3** provides data on net government debt as a share of GDP for several high-income industrial nations. Among the industrial nations, the net public debt/GDP ratio in 2000 was lowest, 3 percent, for Australia. The parallel figures for the United Kingdom and Canada were 34 percent and 35 percent, respectively. The debt/GDP ratio of the United States was 46 percent, slightly higher than for France and slightly lower than for Germany.

Among industrial countries, the debt/GDP ratio is highest in Belgium and Italy. In both countries, the outstanding government debt stood at 94 percent of GDP at year-end 2003. Of course, a large outstanding debt means higher taxes to finance the interest payments. As a share of the economy, the interest payments on government debt in Italy and Belgium are more than twice the level of the United States. Moreover, as the size of a

EXHIBIT 3
The Government Debt of Industrial Countries

The net public debt of the United States lies in the middle group among the high-income industrial countries.

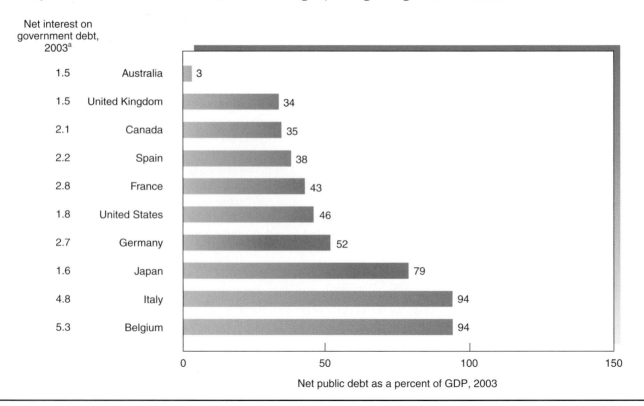

Net interest on government debt, 2003[a]	Country	Net public debt as a percent of GDP, 2003
1.5	Australia	3
1.5	United Kingdom	34
2.1	Canada	35
2.2	Spain	38
2.8	France	43
1.8	United States	46
2.7	Germany	52
1.6	Japan	79
4.8	Italy	94
5.3	Belgium	94

Source: OECD, *OECD Economic Outlook,* June 2004, Annex Tables 31 and 33.
[a]As a percentage of GDP.

nation's debt gets larger and larger, eventually global credit markets will apply some discipline. Countries with large debt/GDP ratios will have to pay higher real interest rates in order to induce investors to purchase their bonds. At some point, credit markets will more or less force governments to bring their spending more closely in line with revenues. This happened in Ireland in 1986 and Belgium in 1994.

SOCIAL SECURITY, BUDGET DEFICITS, AND THE NATIONAL DEBT

As conventionally measured, the budget deficit includes the revenues and expenditures of government trust funds, including the Social Security Trust Fund. Under legislation adopted in 1983, Social Security payroll tax rates were set at levels designed to generate surpluses for the years prior to the retirement of the baby boom generation. Currently, the revenues flowing into the Social Security system are about $150 billion more than the benefits paid out. Thus, the inclusion of Social Security in the budget calculation makes the deficit appear smaller or the surplus appear larger than it would otherwise. For example, if the Social Security surplus had not been included in the budgetary figures, the 2003 federal deficit would have been approximately 5 percent rather than 3.3 percent of GDP.

This is important because the current Social Security surplus will swing to a deficit once the baby boomers start retiring, beginning around 2010. As this happens, rather than reducing the federal government's overall budget deficit, the Social Security system will add to it. This will make it even more difficult for the federal government to balance its budget.

Interestingly, the "implicit debt" accompanying the Social Security and Medicare programs is substantially greater than the outstanding bonds of the federal government. At current tax rates, the revenues flowing into the Social Security system are sufficient to cover only about 70 percent of the promised benefits. Thus, 30 percent of the promised Social Security benefits are unfunded. These unfunded benefits amount to between $5 trillion and $11 trillion. The same is true of Medicare. At current rates, Medicare taxes will fall short of the promised future benefits by between $13 trillion and $38 trillion.[5] Thus, the implicit debt (promised benefits that exceed the tax revenue that will be generated at current rates) of the Social Security and Medicare programs is several times larger than the outstanding federal debt.

Like outstanding federal debt, these unfunded liabilities will mean higher taxes (or broken promises) in the future. This is a point that is often overlooked in discussions about the size of the national debt.

THE POLITICAL ECONOMY, DEMOGRAPHICS, AND DEBT FINANCING

Debt financing reflects an interesting combination of economics, politics, and demographics. Prior to 1960, almost everyone—including the leading figures of both political parties—thought that the government should balance its budget, except perhaps during times of war. In essence, there was widespread implicit agreement, something like a constitutional rule, that the federal budget should be balanced. Against this political background, both deficits and surpluses were small relative to the size of the economy during times of peace.

The Keynesian revolution changed all of this. Rather than balancing the budget, Keynesians argued that the budget should be shifted toward deficit when stimulus was needed and toward surplus when there was concern about inflation. In essence, the Keynesian Revolution released political decision makers from the discipline imposed by a balanced budget. Freed from this constraint, politicians persistently spent more than they were willing to tax.[6] Since 1960, there have been only two brief periods of budget surplus, one in 1969 and the other in 1998–2001.

[5]See National Center for Policy Analysis, "How Large Is the Federal Government's Debt?" Report No. 263, October 30, 2003.

[6]See James M. Buchanan and Richard Wagner, *Democracy in Deficit: The Political Legacy of Lord Keynes* (New York: Academic Press, 1977), for a detailed account of the changes wrought by the Keynesian revolution.

From a public-choice viewpoint, the political attractiveness of spending compared to taxation is not surprising. Politicians have a strong incentive to spend money on programs that benefit the voters of their district and special-interest groups that will help them win reelection. On the other hand, politicians do not like to levy taxes because they impose a visible cost on voters. Borrowing provides politicians with an attractive alternative. Because deficits push the taxes into the future, they impose a less visible cost than current taxation. Thus, borrowing allows politicians to supply voters with immediate benefits without having to impose a parallel visible cost in the form of higher taxes or user charges.

The same is true for unfunded promises to provide future benefits like those of Social Security and Medicare. Like borrowing, this technique makes it possible for politicians to take credit for the promised benefits now without having to levy the equivalent amount of taxes. Thus, the political popularity of both debt financing and unfunded promised benefits is a reflection of the political incentive structure—the desire of elected officials to spend and their reluctance to tax. Unless the incentive structure is changed—for example, by requiring a two-thirds or three-fourths majority to approve spending measures or additional borrowing—debt financing can be expected to continue.

DEMOGRAPHIC CHANGES AND BUDGET DEFICITS

During the 1990s, rapid economic growth substantially increased the revenues of the federal government. At the same time, defense expenditures were reduced substantially in the aftermath of the Cold War. Both of these factors helped shift the federal budget from a deficit to a surplus. In addition, demographic changes of the 1990s were highly favorable to both rapid income growth and lower levels of government spending. As the baby boomers moved into the prime earning years of life during the decade, this promoted the rapid growth of both income and government revenue. At the same time, the growth of retirees drawing Social Security and Medicare expanded slowly during the 1990s because the birthrate was low during the Great Depression and World War II (1930–1945). This combination of factors—a larger share of the population in the peak earning years of life and a smaller share in the retirement phase—exerted a highly favorable effect on the federal budget during the 1990s.

The surpluses of the late 1990s were quickly transformed into deficits by a combination of recession, tax reductions, and rapid increases in government spending triggered in part by the response to the attacks of September 11, 2001, and the war in Iraq. Moreover, the underlying conditions are almost sure to worsen in the near future. Beginning in 2010, the baby boomers will start moving into the retirement phase of their lives. When this happens, there will be upward pressure on government expenditures for health care and Social Security, while income growth is likely to slow because a shrinking number of people will be in the prime working years of their lives. Given these unfavorable demographic conditions and the political incentive for elected officials to spend more than they are willing to tax, sizable budget deficits can be expected in the years ahead.

KEY POINTS

▼ The national debt is the sum of the outstanding bonds of the U.S. Treasury. Budget deficits increase the national debt, whereas surpluses reduce it. The national debt reflects the cumulative effect of all prior budget deficits and surpluses.

▼ A little more than half of the national debt is owned by U.S. government agencies and Federal Reserve banks. For this portion of the debt, the government both pays and receives the interest (except for the expenses of the Fed). Only the privately held federal debt—the portion of the national debt owned by domestic and foreign investors—generates a net interest obligation for the government.

▼ Budget deficits affect future generations through their impact on capital formation. According to the traditional view, the substitution of debt financing for taxes will increase real interest rates and reduce the rate of capital formation—particularly capital owned by Americans. Thus, the traditional view indicates that future generations are adversely affected.

▼ In contrast with the traditional view, the new classical theory argues that people will increase their saving in anticipation of the higher future taxes implied by additional debt. In the new classical model, the substitution of debt for taxes leaves interest rates, consumption, and investment unaffected.

▼ Measured as a share of GDP, the net outstanding debt of the United States falls in the middle group among high-income industrial countries.

▼ Currently, inclusion of Social Security in the budget calculations makes the deficit appear smaller than it would be if these funds were omitted.

▼ Politicians find debt financing attractive because it allows them to spend without levying the equivalent amount of taxes. Thus, political considerations make it difficult to achieve balanced budgets. This factor, along with increased spending on Social Security and Medicare as the baby boomers begin retiring in the years following 2010 are likely to result in large and persistent deficits in the years ahead.

CRITICAL ANALYSIS QUESTIONS

*1. Does the national debt have to be paid off at some time in the future? What will happen if it is not?

2. "The national debt is a mortgage against the future of our children and grandchildren. We are forcing them to pay for our current consumption of goods and services." Evaluate this statement.

*3. When government bonds are held by foreigners, the interest income from the bonds goes to foreigners rather than to Americans. Would Americans be better off if we prohibited the sale of bonds to foreigners?

4. How is the Social Security system currently influencing the size of the budget deficit? If it is not reformed, how will Social Security influence the budget deficit a decade from now? Is this a cause for concern? Why or why not?

*5. Would you predict that government expenditures would be higher or lower if taxes (or user charges) were required for the finance of all expenditures? Why? Do you think the government would spend

funds more or less efficiently if it could not issue debt? Explain.

6. Suppose that the federal government ran a sizable budget surplus during the next decade. Compared to balancing the budget, how would this surplus affect interest rates, saving, and investment? Compare and contrast the traditional view and the new classical view.

*7. Does an increase in the national debt increase the supply of money (M1)? Can the money supply increase when the U.S. Treasury is running a budget surplus?

8. "Given the incentive of elected political officials to spend and their reluctance to tax, two-thirds approval of the House and Senate should be required for both spending measures and increases in government debt." Do you think this is a good idea? Why or why not?

*Asterisk denotes questions for which answers are given in Appendix B.

SPECIAL TOPIC

6

Labor Market Policies and Unemployment: A Cross-Country Analysis

If work does not pay, people will be reluctant to work.

—OECD Jobs Strategy Report[1]

Focus

- Why are unemployment rates substantially higher in Europe than in the United States?

- How do the structure of labor markets and level of unemployment benefits influence the rate of unemployment?

- How have the United Kingdom and New Zealand altered the structure of their labor markets?

[1]OECD, *OECD Jobs Strategy: Making Work Pay* (Paris: OECD, 1997), 7.

A s we noted in Chapter 8, the natural rate of unemployment is the minimum unemployment rate that a country will be able to achieve and sustain over an extended period. This rate is influenced by policies and institutional arrangements. The natural rate of unemployment will be higher when the policies of a country (1) push wages above equilibrium, (2) make it more costly for employers to hire and dismiss employees, and (3) make it less costly for job seekers to continue searching for a better job offer. ■

CROSS-COUNTRY VARIATIONS IN UNEMPLOYMENT RATES

Exhibit 1 presents the standardized unemployment rates during the periods 1990–1996 and 1997–2003 for the five most populous European countries, plus Australia, Canada, Japan, and the United States. These countries are all members of the Organization for Economic Cooperation and Development (OECD). They are perhaps the nine most important market economies in the world. Note how the unemployment rates in France, Germany, Italy, and Spain were substantially higher than those of the United States and Japan during both the 1990–1996 and 1997–2003 periods. The unemployment rate for the countries of the Euro area averaged 9.8 percent during 1990–1996 and 9.2 percent during 1997–2003. By way of comparison, the unemployment rate of the United States was 6.3 percent during 1990–1996 and 4.9 percent during 1997–2003. Similarly, even though the Japanese economy stagnated throughout most of the 1990s, Japan's unemployment rate was still only about half that of the Euro area during 1997–2003.

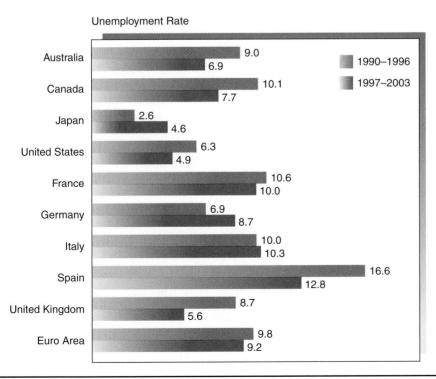

EXHIBIT 1
The Standardized Unemployment Rates of Nine Major Industrial Economies, 1990–2003

In recent years, the rate of unemployment in Europe (particularly in France, Italy, and Spain) has been substantially higher than in the United States and Japan.

Source: OECD, *OECD Economic Outlook,* June 2004, annex table 14. The Euro Area figures are for 1991–2003.

The European unemployment rates have generally been near or above 10 percent throughout most of the last two decades. These persistently high unemployment rates indicate that they are the result of long-run factors rather than short-run business conditions. The price stability data are also consistent with this view. The nine economies of Exhibit 1 expanded in the 1990s, and the inflation rate of each was low and relatively stable—neither rising nor falling. Under these circumstances, unemployment will move toward the natural rate, the lowest sustainable unemployment rate consistent with the economy's institutional structure. Put another way, the persistently high unemployment rates throughout most of Europe suggest that policies are being followed that result in a high natural rate of unemployment.

The picture is much the same with regard to the growth of employment. While employment in the United States between 1980 and 1990 increased by 19.6 percent, the employment growth in the five most populous European countries was only 6 percent. Similarly, U.S. employment increased by 17 percent between 1991 and 2003 compared to only 7.5 percent in the Euro area. Why has the unemployment rate been so high and the growth of employment so slow in Europe? Most economists believe that labor market policies provide a major part of the answer.

THE STRUCTURE OF LABOR MARKETS

Labor market structural characteristics and policies differ substantially among countries. Compared to the United States and Japan, the labor markets of most European countries are characterized by (1) higher rates of unionization, (2) greater regulation, and (3) more generous unemployment assistance.[2] Let us look at the cross-country data and consider how each of these factors will influence the rate of unemployment.

Centralized Wage-Setting

Exhibit 2 indicates both the percentage of the nonfarm labor force that is unionized and the share of employees whose wages are set by collective bargaining. Among the nine countries, the unionization rate is highest for Italy, Canada, and the United Kingdom; it is lowest for France, the United States, and Spain. However, the structure of unions differs substantially across countries. Therefore, membership is often a misleading indicator of the role of unions in the wage-setting process.

Collective bargaining in the United States, Canada, and Japan is decentralized—it takes place at the company or plant level. Unions in Japan are almost exclusively of the "company union" variety. They seldom set wages for an entire industry. Although unions in the United States and Canada may operate across an entire industry, the bargaining process is nearly always between a union and a single employer, or, in some cases, a single plant of the employer. These contracts do not apply to other firms. Under these circumstances, the union density (membership) and the share of workers whose wages are set by collective bargaining are similar (see Exhibit 2).

In contrast, the wage-setting process is highly centralized throughout most of Europe as well as in Australia. Negotiations between a union (or federation of unions) and an association of employers set the wages for all or most workers in various industries, occupations, and/or regions. Statutory legislation extends these agreements to both nonunion employees and nonassociation employers who neither participate in the bargaining process nor agree to the wage contracts. Sometimes political officials are also actively involved in the wage-setting process.

[2]For additional information on the impact of labor market policies on unemployment, see Charles Bean, "European Unemployment: A Survey," *Journal of Economic Literature,* 1995, no. 2:573–619; Edward Bierhanzl and James Gwartney, "Regulation, Unions, and Labor Markets," *Regulation* (summer 1998): 40–53; OECD, *Making Work Pay: Taxation, Benefits, Employment and Unemployment* (Paris: OECD, 1997); and Horst Siebert, "Labor Market Rigidities: At the Root of Unemployment in Europe," *Journal of Economic Perspectives,* 1997, no. 3:37–54.

EXHIBIT 2
The Share of Employees Whose Wages Are Set by Collective Bargaining: 1980 and 2000/2001

Centralized collective bargaining agreements that set wages for all workers in an industry and/or occupation are far more common in Europe than in the United States, Canada, and Japan. Note how the wages of the overwhelming bulk of workers are set by centralized collective bargaining in France, Germany, Italy, and Spain.

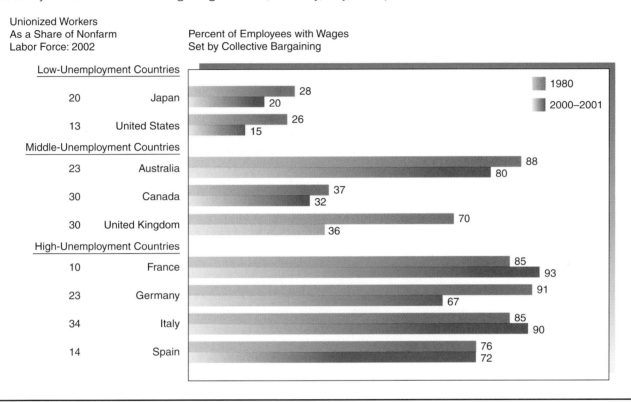

Sources: http://www.oecd.org/; http://www.eurofound.eu.it/; http://www.abs.gov.au/; http://www.unionstats.com/; and http://www.statcan.ca/. Unionization data for France and Spain are for 2001. Collective bargaining data for Australia is for 2002 and Canada is for 2001.

Therefore, as Exhibit 2 shows, the share of employees whose wages are set by collective bargaining in Australia and the populous countries of Europe (except for the United Kingdom in recent years) is far greater than union membership. For example, although union members were only 10 percent of the French labor force in 2002, collective bargaining set the wages for 93 percent of the employees. In Australia, Italy, Germany, and Spain, the pattern was the same. In all of these countries, highly centralized "agreements" set the wages of most workers—both union and nonunion—within various industry and occupational categories. This explains why the proportion of employees whose wages are set by collective bargaining is so much higher in these countries than union workers as a share of the workforce.

Does it make any difference whether wages are set at the firm level or for an entire industry, occupation, or region? Economic theory indicates that it does. When union members (and unionized firms) compete with nonunion workers and firms, market forces continue to play an important role. If the unionized workers push wages significantly above the competitive level, it will be more difficult for their employers to compete effectively with nonunion rivals. Thus, higher wages for union members would lead to employment reductions in the unionized sector. This will temper the bargaining process.

In contrast, the discipline of market forces is eroded when the wages for all workers and firms in an industry, an occupation, and a region are set centrally. A union that can set the wages of all firms in an industry will have considerable monopoly power. As wages are pushed up, the costs of both union and nonunion employers will rise. As a result, there will be less opportunity for nonunion firms to expand and hire workers willing to work at a lower wage. Of course, market forces will not be totally absent. Higher wages will encourage the substitution of capital for labor and make it more difficult for domestic firms to compete in international markets. Some firms will move production operations to other countries, where the services of workers of similar skill are available at a lower cost. Thus, when unions with a substantial degree of monopoly power are able to push wages to high levels, their actions will cause high rates of unemployment and a slow rate of employment growth like that experienced by European countries during the last two decades.

Centralized wage setting will have fewer adverse effects in small countries with labor forces that are relatively homogeneous in skills and education. In large countries with regional differences in cost of living and greater diversity among labor force participants, centrally determined wage rates will predictably lead to a substantial excess supply of workers in some areas and excess demand in others. In fact, unions and employers in high-wage regions can use the centralized wage-setting process to foist higher costs on rival firms and workers in regions where wages, reflecting educational and skill levels, would normally be lower. By pushing wages up in those regions, lower-wage and lower-skilled workers are priced out of the market and rendered less competitive. The incentive for capital to move toward the low-wage regions is thus reduced.

Northern and southern Italy illustrate the significance of this strategy. Workers in southern Italy generally have fewer skills and less education than their counterparts in the North. Because of centralized labor contracts, however, wages in the various job categories are the same in both regions. As a result, workers in the South are less competitive, and the incentive for capital to move toward that region is substantially reduced. Obviously, the northern workers and their union representatives find this arrangement highly attractive. In the South, however, the results are disastrous. In recent years, unemployment rates in southern Italy have ranged between 15 percent and 25 percent—two or three times the rates of the North. Centralized wage setting has also reduced the competitiveness of low-skilled workers in several regions of Spain. As in Italy, the policy has led to both a high overall rate of unemployment and substantial regional disparity.

Dismissal and Mandated Severance Pay Regulations

Severance pay
Pay by an employer to an employee upon the termination of employment with the firm.

European labor markets are also characterized by regulations that make it more costly for employers to both hire and dismiss workers. Minimum-wage laws, high payroll taxes, and restrictions on the hours of work all make it more expensive for a potential employer to hire workers, particularly those with few skills. Regulations can also make it more costly to dismiss employees. Laws that require employers to provide lengthy notification and several months of **severance pay** when dismissing an employee illustrate this point.

Exhibit 3 presents data on the restrictiveness of hiring and dismissal regulations in the world's nine major market economies. They are based on the responses of employers in the different countries with regard to how regulations influence the cost of both hiring and dismissing workers. Higher ratings on the zero-to-ten scale are reflective of less restrictive labor market regulations. Among the nine countries, the United States received the highest rating. The labor market regulations of the four high-unemployment European countries, along with Japan, were rated as the most restrictive. The regulations of Australia, Canada, and the United Kingdom fell between these two extremes.

Lengthy periods of prior notification and mandated severance pay are far more common in countries with highly regulated labor markets. So are regulations that require employers to obtain approval from government agencies in order to dismiss a large number of employees. In addition, several European countries require political approval for mass layoffs. For example, employers in Italy, Spain, and France must convince various political officials that a business necessity is present before they are permitted to reduce their workforce by a sizable amount.[3]

---

[3]Although there is no general notification requirement in the United States, employers with 100 or more full-time employees are required to give sixty-day notice to employees dismissed as the result of a plant closing or mass layoff.

EXHIBIT 3
The Restrictiveness of Hiring and Dismissal Regulations

Regulations that make it more costly to hire workers and limit the ability of employers to lay off or dismiss employees are substantially more restrictive in the four high-unemployment European economies than in the United States. For example, in France, Italy, and Spain, most employers have to obtain permission from political authorities before they can dismiss workers and cut back employment. How will regulations that make it difficult to dismiss workers affect the incentive of employers to hire additional employees?

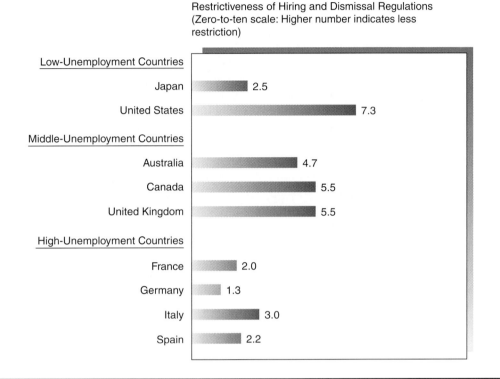

Restrictiveness of Hiring and Dismissal Regulations
(Zero-to-ten scale: Higher number indicates less restriction)

Low-Unemployment Countries

Japan — 2.5
United States — 7.3

Middle-Unemployment Countries

Australia — 4.7
Canada — 5.5
United Kingdom — 5.5

High-Unemployment Countries

France — 2.0
Germany — 1.3
Italy — 3.0
Spain — 2.2

Source: James Gwartney and Robert Lawson, *Economic Freedom of the World: 2004 Annual Report* (Vancouver, BC: Fraser Institute, 2004). The original data were from the World Economic Forum, *Global Competitiveness Report*, 2004.

Proponents argue that regulations that limit the ability of employers to dismiss workers will help protect workers against arbitrary dismissal and provide them with greater job security. However, regulations that make it more costly to dismiss workers also make it more costly to hire them. When dismissal costs are high, employers will be reluctant to add workers during periods of strong demand because it will be costly to dismiss them if future conditions are less favorable. Thus, firms will often find that it is cheaper to expand output—particularly if the expansion is expected to be temporary—by using more capital, contracting out, or hiring part-time workers not covered by the dismissal regulations.

Furthermore, restrictive dismissal policies reduce the competition between workers with jobs and those seeking employment. They make it more expensive for employers to substitute current job seekers for established workers. In essence, the restrictions make it extremely difficult for new entrants to find jobs and acquire labor force experience. High unemployment among younger workers is an important secondary effect. The data are consistent with this view. The unemployment rate of persons age fifteen to twenty-four years has often exceeded 25 percent during the last decade in the four European countries that impose the most severe restrictions on the dismissal of workers.

The Impact of Unemployment Benefits

Unemployment benefits reduce the opportunity cost of job searches and thereby encourage more lengthy "spells" of unemployment. When set at a high level, they can become an attractive source of income in comparison to work. The generosity of the benefit levels

Business is brisk in this German unemployment office. Compared to those in the United States, unemployment benefits are more generous in Germany and several other European countries. See Exhibit 4. Higher unemployment benefits reduce the opportunity cost of job searches, which leads to more lengthy periods of unemployment and higher unemployment rates than would otherwise be the case.

PHOTO BY SEAN GALLUP/GETTY IMAGES

Replacement rate
The share of previous earnings replaced by unemployment benefits.

may also influence unemployment in more subtle ways. Employers in seasonal and other industries offering erratic employment will often be able to pay lower wages because the benefits provide employees with income supplements when they are not working. In essence, the benefits subsidize businesses that offer unstable employment and encourage the expansion of such employment.[4] More generous benefits also tend to reduce the political repercussions of high unemployment rates. This is particularly important when the government is an active participant in the wage-setting process, as is the case throughout much of Europe. When the benefit levels are high, political officials will have less reason to resist the wage demands of unions, even if the higher wages mean fewer jobs and higher rates of unemployment. Therefore, there are good reasons to expect that countries with more generous unemployment benefits will experience higher rates of unemployment.

Unemployment benefit systems are highly complex. Interestingly, the initial **replacement rate** among the major industrial countries is quite similar. However, there is considerable variation with regard to the length of time persons are permitted to draw benefits. The shortest duration periods for the benefits are found in Italy, the United States, the United Kingdom, Canada, and Japan, where the benefits for most unemployed workers expire in a year or less.[5] (*Note*: In the United States, unemployment benefits expire after twenty-six weeks.) In contrast, unemployed workers are permitted to draw benefits for two years or more in Spain, France, Germany, and Australia.

The replacement rate often varies with previous level of earnings, family size and situation, previous length of employment, and duration of unemployment. The OECD has calculated the replacement rate of member countries for recipients at two different income levels, three family situations, and three time periods of unemployment. The average replacement rates for these eighteen different categories provide a reasonably good "index of generosity" for the unemployment system of each country.[6]

---

[4]In several countries, including the United States, employers with more erratic employment patterns are required to pay a higher payroll tax for unemployment insurance. However, the higher tax is generally insufficient to cover the additional benefits paid to the workers laid off or dismissed by these firms.

[5]Historically, Italy has used a system of mandated severance pay as a substitute for unemployment benefits. This accounts for its extremely low replacement rate during the 1980s and early 1990s.

[6]The OECD figures cover the replacement rate for the first year of unemployment, years two and three, and years four and five. Because the benefits will expire after six months or one year in many countries, this average replacement rate for most countries is substantially lower than the initial replacement rate. For example, unemployment benefits initially replace 60 percent of earnings in the United States. However, since the benefits can be drawn for only six months, the average replacement rate over the five-year time period is much lower than the initial figure.

As **Exhibit 4** shows, the unemployment benefits are generally more attractive (and less restrictive with regard to eligibility) in Europe, Australia, and Canada than in the United States and Japan. The average replacement rates of the United States and Japan generally range from one-half to one-third the replacement rates of France, Germany, and Spain. It is also interesting to note that the replacement rate of the United Kingdom has been trending downward and is now only slightly above the rates for the U.S. and Japan. On the other hand, Canada's replacement rate has increased sharply in recent years and it now looks much like the rates of the high-unemployment European economies.

EXHIBIT 4
The Average Replacement Rate of Unemployment Benefits in Nine Major Industrial Economies

Unemployment benefits are more generous in most European countries than in the United States and Japan. Note that, during the last two decades, the benefit levels have increased substantially in Canada and declined significantly in the United Kingdom.

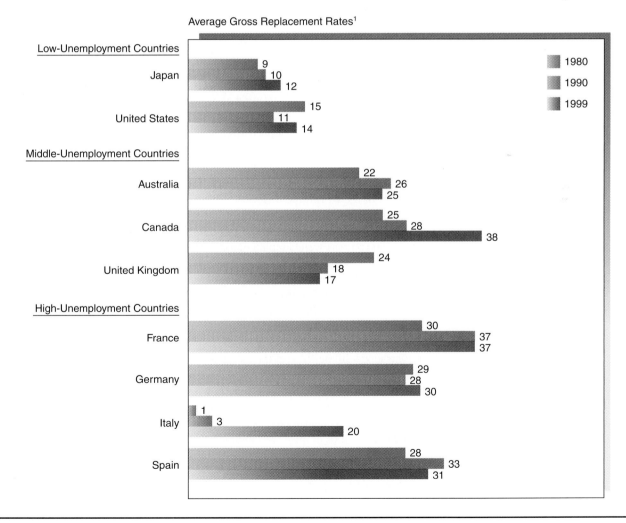

Average Gross Replacement Rates[1]

[1] Average for two earnings levels (2/3 average and average earnings), three family situations (single, married with dependent spouse, and married with working spouse), and three duration periods (1 year, 1–3 years, and 3–5 years).
Sources: OECD, *OECD Jobs Strategy: Making Work Pay,* 1997, figure 2; OECD, *Implementing the OECD Jobs Strategy: Member Countries' Experience,* table 5; and OECD, *Benefits and Wages,* 2002, table 3.11.

Pulling It Together

Compared to France, Germany, Italy, and Spain, the United States and Japan have more decentralized labor markets, less restrictive dismissal regulations, and less generous unemployment benefits. Economic theory indicates that each of these factors will enhance the flexibility of labor markets and help keep unemployment rates low. In contrast, policies that make it more costly to employ workers and less costly for persons to remain unemployed will lead to higher rates of unemployment. Of course, the regulations were not designed to push the unemployment rate upward. Nonetheless, when perverse incentives were created, higher unemployment was a secondary effect.

The evidence supports this view. While the unemployment rates of the United States and Japan averaged 4.9 and 4.6 respectively during 1997–2003, Germany's unemployment rate was 8.7 percent, France's 10.0 percent, Italy's 10.3 percent, and Spain's 12.8 percent. (See Exhibit 1.) Thus, the unemployment rates of the four more heavily regulated labor markets were approximately twice those of the less regulated labor markets of the United States and Japan.

Labor Market Reforms in the United Kingdom and New Zealand

If a country moved toward a more liberal labor market, would it make any difference? The experience of the United Kingdom and New Zealand sheds light on this issue. During the 1980s and 1990s, these two countries adopted major reforms designed to protect the rights of workers and make their labor markets more competitive.

In the United Kingdom, the reforms focused on promotion of democratic decision making and the protection of workers' rights. The Employment Act of 1980 required secret-ballot approval prior to the establishment of a closed shop. Later, legislation was adopted (1) requiring worker approval every five years for the continuation of a closed shop and (2) making strike action to establish a closed shop unlawful. Nonunion members were also granted legal protection against dismissal and discriminatory actions as the result of their nonunion status. Union members were given the right to join the union of their choice and granted protection against unions seeking to discipline them for failure to support a strike. These changes both weakened the monopoly power of unions and led to a more decentralized wage-setting process. Union membership in the United Kingdom fell from 50 percent of the workforce in 1980 to 30 percent in 2002. More important, centralized bargaining became less commonplace. The share of employees having their wages set by collective bargaining contracts fell from 70 percent in 1980 to 36 percent in 2002. The labor market reforms were supplemented with less generous unemployment benefits. As Exhibit 4 indicates, the average replacement rate in the United Kingdom fell from 24 percent in 1980 to 18 percent in 1990 and 17 percent in 1999.

In New Zealand, the Employment Contracts Act of 1991 restructured the labor market even more rapidly than the reforms in the United Kingdom. This act allowed all employees to "choose whether or not to associate with other employees for advancing the employees' collective employment interests." Employees were granted the right to negotiate labor contracts, with or without the assistance of an agent. Most significant, although rights to strike and lockout were explicitly recognized, these weapons were permitted only at the expiration of labor contracts and then only after employee approval was obtained at the enterprise level. This effectively changed the wage-setting process in New Zealand from a centralized to a decentralized system. As in the United Kingdom, union membership fell, and the share of employees having their wages set by union contracts declined from 67 percent in 1990 to 31 percent in 1995 and 22 percent in 2002.[7]

How have the labor markets of these two countries reacted to economic liberalization? In the United Kingdom, the economy expanded rapidly throughout most of the 1980s and the unemployment rate declined. Following the recession in the early 1990s, the economy rebounded nicely and by 1998, the rate of unemployment in the United

---

[7]See Raymond Harbridge, Robyn May, and Glen Thickett, "The Current State of Pay: Collective Bargaining and Union Membership under the ERA 2000," *New Zealand Journal of Industrial Relations* 28 (June 2003): 140–49.

Kingdom had receded to less than 6 percent, a rate that it had not achieved since the 1970s. And it has remained at a low level, averaging 5.1 percent during the first four years of the new century. The UK unemployment rate now stands in stark contrast to the double-digit rates of the other populous European countries. Furthermore, the average annual growth rate of real GDP during the last decade has been about 1 percentage point higher in the United Kingdom than in France and Germany.

Similar results were achieved in New Zealand. The unemployment rate of New Zealand fell from 10 percent during 1991–1993 to an average of 5.1 percent during 2001–2003. New Zealand now has one of the highest growth rates among the high-income industrial countries. During 1993–2003, New Zealand's real GDP expanded at a 3.6 percent annual rate, up from 2.4 percent during the 1980s. The experiences of both the United Kingdom and New Zealand indicate that if a country is willing to liberalize its labor market, it will be able to achieve and maintain both substantially lower rates of unemployment and strong economic growth.

Labor Markets in the United States and Canada

Comparisons between the United States and Canadian labor markets are also revealing. Although the Canadian labor market is less regulated and more decentralized than those of the major European economies, it is clearly less liberal than that of the United States. Compared to the United States, the share of employees with wages set by collective bargaining is greater, dismissal regulations are more restrictive, and unemployment benefits are more generous in Canada. Furthermore, the Canadian labor market has been drifting toward the European model. During the last decade, Canada has enacted legislation that makes it more difficult for employers to dismiss workers and reduce the size of their workforce. As Exhibit 4 shows, it has also substantially increased the benefits available to unemployed workers.

These factors show up in the unemployment statistics. During the 1960s and 1970s, the Canadian average unemployment rate was virtually the same as that of the United States. This is no longer true. During the 1980s, the Canadian average rate of unemployment was about 2 percent greater than the rate of the United States, and during the last decade, the gap has widened to approximately 3 percent (see Exhibit 1). Like the unemployment gap between the United Kingdom and the other large European economies, the differential unemployment rate between the United States and Canada also illustrates the link between labor market policies and the natural rate of unemployment.

! KEY POINTS

▼ During the last decade, the major European economies (with the exception of the United Kingdom) have experienced substantially higher unemployment rates than the United States and Japan.

▼ When used in large and diverse labor markets, a centralized wage-setting process will push wage rates above market levels in various regions and skill categories. This will tend to cause higher rates of unemployment. Similarly, regulations that make it more costly to dismiss workers will also make employers more reluctant to hire employees. This will lead to sluggish employment growth and high rates of unemployment, particularly for youthful workers seeking to enter the workforce.

▼ High unemployment benefits will reduce the opportunity cost of job searches and thereby cause more lengthy spells of unemployment.

▼ Compared to those of the United States and Japan, the labor markets of Italy, Spain, France, and Germany are characterized by centralized wage-setting processes, more restrictive dismissal regulations, and high unemployment benefit replacement rates. Economic theory indicates that such policies will lead to high rates of unemployment like those experienced by these four countries.

▼ Recent reforms in the United Kingdom and New Zealand have increased the competitiveness of labor markets in these countries. The rates of unemployment in both countries have declined and are now significantly lower than the rates of countries that have followed more restrictive labor market practices.

▼ Compared to the labor market of the United States, the Canadian labor market is characterized by a larger degree of unionization, more restrictive dismissal practices, and more generous unemployment benefits. The data also indicate that the natural rate of unemployment is higher in Canada than in the United States.

? CRITICAL ANALYSIS QUESTIONS

*1. Compared to the situation in which a union is able to organize only a portion of the firms in an industry, how does the ability to set wages for an entire industry influence the power of a labor union? What does this suggest about the relative strength of unions in Europe versus those in the United States and Japan?

2. Should the U.S. provide more generous unemployment benefits to unemployed workers? Why or why not? Can you think of a policy alternative that would help workers deal with spells of unemployment that would have less perverse incentives than the current system? Discuss.

3. Suppose legislation were passed requiring all employers in the United States to pay dismissed workers one week of severance pay for every year they were employed by the firm. What effect would this have on (a) the dismissal rate of employees, (b) the productivity of employees, and (c) the unemployment rate of youthful workers? Discuss.

4. Do you think that the United States should move toward the European labor market model characterized by more extensive collective bargaining, greater government regulation, and more generous unemployment benefits? Why or why not?

*Asterisk denotes questions for which answers are given in Appendix B.

Institutions, Policies, and the Irish Miracle

Focus

■ What were Ireland's tax, trade, and monetary policies like during the period 1965–1985? How did these policies change in the late 1980s?

■ How did Ireland's change in policy direction in the late 1980s affect its economic performance?

■ What can other countries learn from the experience of Ireland?

Fifteen years ago Ireland was deemed an economic failure, a country that after years of mismanagement was suffering from an awful cocktail of high unemployment, slow growth, high inflation, heavy taxation and towering public debts. Yet within a few years it had become the "Celtic Tiger", a rare example of a developed country with a growth record to match East Asia's, as well as enviably low unemployment and inflation, a low tax burden and a tiny public debt.

—The Economist [1]
October 16, 2004

[1]*Economist* Special Report, "The Luck of the Irish," *The Economist*, October 16, 2004.

Economic analysis indicates that institutions and policies exert a major effect on the growth and prosperity of nations. Countries that provide an institutional and policy environment that allows people to engage freely in trade and keep what they earn will encourage productive activity and attract investment. Key ingredients of such an environment are protection of individuals and their property, openness to trade, low taxes, monetary and price stability, and a legal system that enforces contracts in an evenhanded manner. The experience of Ireland over the last four decades vividly illustrates the importance of these factors.

Prior to the late 1980s, Ireland followed policies that were inconsistent with strong growth and prosperity. Between 1965 and 1985, government expenditures increased substantially as a share of the economy. Taxes were high and monetary policy was erratic. By 1987, Ireland was on the verge of collapse. Real growth had fallen sharply. Unemployment soared to more than 17 percent during the period 1985–1987. People were leaving the country in search of opportunity. At that point, however, Ireland made a dramatic change in policy direction. ▪

IRELAND'S U-TURN

As Ireland faced a financial crisis in the mid-1980s, it began to shift toward policies consistent with growth and prosperity. Government spending was slashed, tax rates were lowered, monetary policy became more stable, and trade became more open. Let us take a closer look at each one of these factors.

1. Smaller government. As **Exhibit 1** shows, Ireland's government spending persis-tently rose as a share of the economy during the period 1965–1986. By the mid-1980s, government spending had risen to more than 50 percent of GDP. Propelled by the growth of spending and budget deficits, the outstanding debt of the Irish government soared to 120 percent of GDP in 1986. An attempt in 1983 to balance the budget by raising taxes had failed, throwing the economy into recession and leading to even higher levels of government debt. The government's credit rating was plunging in international markets.

Mostly out of desperation, the Irish government cut its expenditures sharply in 1987. Government employment was reduced by about 10 percent between 1986 and 1989. As Exhibit 1 shows, total government outlays fell from 54 percent of GDP in 1986 to 42 percent in 1989. They continued to recede in the 1990s, reaching 32 percent of GDP in 2000.

It is interesting to compare and contrast the size of government in Ireland with that of France, Germany, and Italy. In the late 1980s, government spending summed to approximately half of GDP in all of these countries. But fifteen years later, the picture was dramatically different. While government spending continued at or near the 50 percent level in the three large European economies, it was reduced to only about one-third of the Irish economy.

2. Lower tax rates. As the size of government shrank, the taxburden on both individuals and businesses was systematically reduced. As **Exhibit 2** shows, the top marginal rate imposed on personal income was cut from 65 percent in 1984 to 58 percent in 1986 and 48 percent in 1992. The Irish government continued to reduce taxes, and by 2000 the top marginal personal income tax rate had fallen to 42 percent.

Corporate taxes were also reduced. The top corporate rate was reduced from 50 percent in 1986 to 40 percent in the early 1990s and 32 percent in the latter part of the decade. In 2003, the corporate tax rate was sliced to 12.5 percent, by far the lowest rate among the members of the European Union.

Even though Ireland has reduced taxes, it has kept spending roughly in line with revenues during the last decade. Although budget deficits have been present during some years, they have been largely offset by surpluses in other years. As a result, Ireland's outstanding government debt has declined sharply relative to the size of the economy. In 2003, Ireland's government debt/GDP ratio was 32 percent, down from 112 percent in 1987.

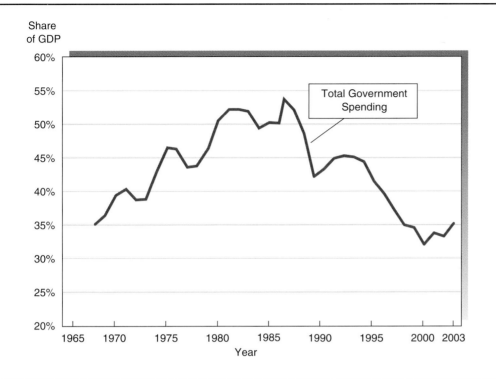

Source: OECD, *OECD Economic Outlook* (various issues), and OECD, *OECD Historical Statistics, 1960–1982.*

EXHIBIT 1
The Rise and Fall of Ireland's Government Expenditures

Measured as a share of GDP, Ireland's government spending rose rapidly during the period 1968–1986. Confronting a financial crisis in 1987, the size of government was sharply curtailed, and it continued to decline throughout the 1990s. By 2000, government spending had fallen to 32 percent of GDP, down from more than 50 percent in the mid-1980s.

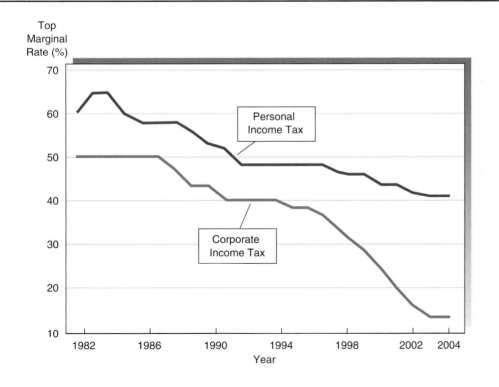

EXHIBIT 2
Ireland's Top Marginal Tax Rates, 1980–2004

In the midst of the 1987 financial crisis, Ireland not only reduced government spending, it also cut taxes. Personal and corporate tax rates were also reduced several times during the 1990s. Ireland's highest personal income tax bracket is now 42 percent, and its corporate income tax rate is now only 12.5 percent. The Irish tax rates are now the lowest in Europe.

Source: Price Waterhouse, *Individual Taxes: A Worldwide Summary* (various issues).

EXHIBIT 3
Ireland's Inflation Rate

After fluctuating substantially during the 1970s and the first half of the 1980s, Ireland's inflation rate has been much lower in recent years. It has averaged 3 percent and has been much more steady during the last fifteen years.

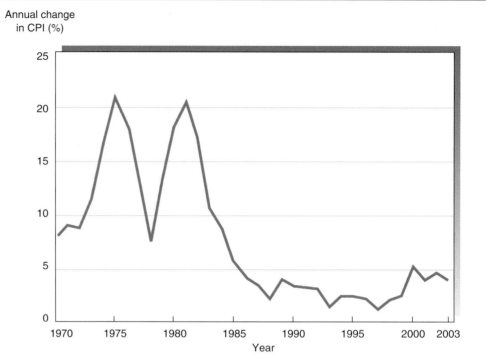

Annual change in CPI (%)

Source: OECD, *OECD Historical Statistics, 1960–1980,* table 8. 11, and OECD, *OECD Economic Outlook,* June 2004.

3. Sound monetary policy and price stability.   During the 1970s and into the mid-1980s, Ireland's monetary policy was highly erratic. As **Exhibit 3** shows, Ireland's inflation rate jumped from less than 10 percent in 1972 to more than 20 percent in 1975. Then, after receding to 10 percent in 1978, it once again soared to more than 20 percent in the early 1980s. Since that time, monetary policy has improved substantially. Ireland's monetary authorities brought the inflation rate down to less than 5 percent in the late 1980s, and they have kept it there. Since 1987, inflation has averaged 3 percent a year, down from 12.7 percent during the period 1970–1986. Obviously, the lower and more stable rate of inflation makes it easier for both investors and business decision makers to plan for the future.

4. Openness to international trade.   When Ireland joined the European Union (EU) in 1973, it was required to harmonize its trade policy with that of the EU over the next decade. By the mid-1980s, Irish tariffs were phased out and replaced by those of the EU. Ireland benefited both from free trade within the EU and from EU tariff rates, which were lower than those previously imposed by the Irish government. **Exhibit 4** illustrates the response to the increased openness of the Irish economy. Ireland's international trade (imports + exports) rose from 101 percent of GDP in 1986 to 121 percent in 1993. During the last decade, the size of the Irish trade sector has continued to grow rapidly. During the first four years of this century (2000–2003), Ireland's trade sector has averaged 170 percent of its GDP, more than 50 percent greater than during the 1980s. Once heavily dependent upon neighboring Britain as a trading partner, Ireland's trade is now more diversified. Britain now accounts for only 25 percent of Irish exports, down from 47 percent in 1979.

THE IMPACT OF THE POLICY U-TURN

What impact has the change in policy direction had on the Irish economy? The turnaround since the late 1980s has been remarkable. As **Exhibit 5** shows, the annual growth rate of real GDP rose from 2.3 percent in the period 1982–1987 to 4.8 percent in the period 1988–1993. From 1994 to 2003 the Irish economy grew at a remarkable rate of 7.9 percent.

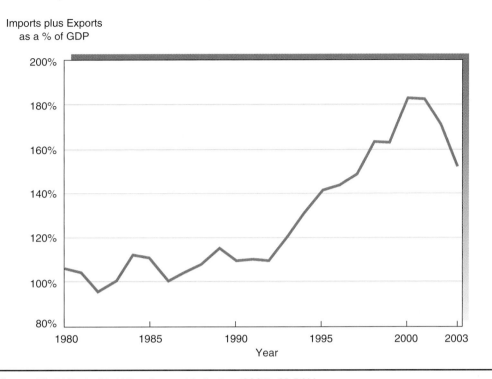

Imports plus Exports
as a % of GDP

Year

Source: World Bank, *World Development Indicators* (2001), CD-ROM.

EXHIBIT 4
Ireland's Trade Sector,
1980–2003

The size of the international trade sector (exports + imports) increased substantially as a share of the Irish economy during the 1990s.

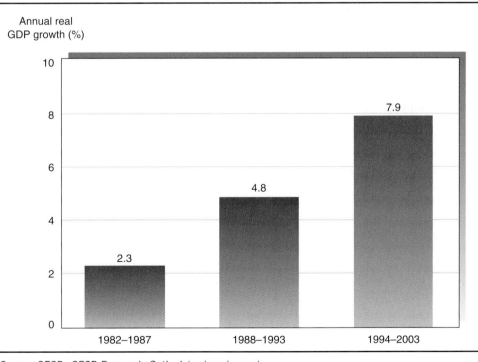

Annual real
GDP growth (%)

EXHIBIT 5
Ireland's Rate of
Economic Growth

Ireland's economy has responded to the sounder policies of the last fifteen years. Its average annual rate of growth increased from 2.3 percent in the period 1982–1987 to 4.8 percent in the period 1988–1993 and 7.9 percent during the period 1994–2003. The Irish economy is now one of the fastest growing in the world.

Source: OECD, *OECD Economic Outlook* (various issues).

Since 1990, Ireland has been one of the fastest-growing economies in the world. Its growth rate stands in stark contrast with that of other Western European economies, which have generally been growing at an annual rate of around 1.5 percent. Ireland's growth has dramatically changed its relative income position. Along with Greece, Spain, and Portugal, Ireland was one of the poorest countries in the European Union in the late 1980s. This is no longer the case. In 2002, Ireland's per capita income was $28,040, higher than the figure for France ($26,180), Germany ($26,200), and the United Kingdom ($25,870).[2] Ireland's per capita GDP is now the second-highest in the European Union, trailing only that of Luxembourg.

There has also been a dramatic change in the performance of the Irish labor market. During the first four years of this century, the unemployment rate of Ireland averaged 4.3 percent, compared to an average of 14.5 percent during the first four years of the 1990s. Ireland's low rate of unemployment stands in stark contrast with most other EU countries, which continue to experience unemployment rates at or near double-digit levels.

Lessons from the Irish Experience

Although Ireland's economic performance in the last fifteen years is often referred to as the "Irish miracle," it is not really a miracle. Instead, it is the result of sound policies that release the creative energies of people. It illustrates what can be achieved when countries get the institutional and policy environment right.

It is true that the Irish economy had a couple of things going for it that are often absent in other countries. It inherited rule-of-law principles and a common-law legal system from the English. Its judiciary system has been relatively free of favoritism for several decades. Its location between the large and relatively open economies of North America and Europe makes it a particularly attractive place for business activity. But these factors were present when the economy was stagnating in the 1970s and 1980s, too.

The Irish economy began to grow rapidly only after its policy U-turn. As Ireland opened its economy to international trade, restrained government spending, cut taxes, and shifted to a monetary policy more consistent with price stability, growth picked up, and foreign investment began to increase. This inflow of foreign investment contributed substantially to Ireland's success. As the policy environment improved and became more credible, many corporations, both large and small, opened operations in Ireland. Even though Ireland has only 1 percent of the European population, it now attracts approximately one-quarter of the U.S. investment in Europe. More than 1,100 multinational companies do business in Ireland, and they are now exporting about $60 billion of goods each year. Ireland is now a major producer of both computers and pharmaceutical products. Currently, one-third of all personal computers sold in Europe are manufactured in Ireland. The Irish case highlights the potential importance of foreign investment as a source of growth when a country, particularly one with low income, adopts a sound combination of policies.

The Irish growth experience is not unique, however. Several countries, including Hong Kong, Singapore, Taiwan, and New Zealand (since the late 1980s), have followed similar paths. In recent decades, all of these countries have instituted relatively sound policies, and they have been rewarded with rapid growth rates and high income levels. The Irish economic experience is neither a miracle nor a mystery. Most important, it is one available to other countries willing to adopt and maintain sound policies and institutions.

---

[2]These per capita income figures are from the World Bank, *World Development Report: 2004,* appendix table 1. They were derived by the purchasing power parity method.

KEY POINTS

▼ During the 1970s and most of the 1980s, the Irish economy was characterized by a high and growing level of government expenditures, high taxes, high and variable rates of inflation, and restrictions that limited international trade. By 1987, sluggish growth and a high level of government debt placed the economy on the verge of collapse.

▼ Beginning in the late 1980s, Ireland sharply reduced government spending, lowered tax rates, adopted a more stable monetary policy, and increased trade openness. Propelled by the policy U-turn, Ireland became one of the world's fastest-growing economies during the period 1990–2003.

▼ The experience of Ireland illustrates the substantial gains that can be achieved by adopting sound spending, tax, trade, and monetary policies.

CRITICAL ANALYSIS QUESTIONS

1. Why has Ireland grown more rapidly than other European economies during the last decade? If Mexico were to follow policies like those of Ireland during the 1990s, could it achieve a similar rate of economic growth? Why or why not? Discuss.

*2. How will the policy environment of a country influence its ability to attract foreign investment? How will foreign investment influence the growth rate of a country? Discuss.

3. If Ireland had not had a relatively sound legal system, would its policy U-turn have been as effective? Why or why not?

* Asterisk denotes questions for which answers are given in Appendix B.

SPECIAL
TOPIC

8

The Economics of Health Care

Focus

- How much do Americans spend on health care?

- Who pays the bill for health-care services? Why is this important?

- Why have the prices of health-care services risen so rapidly in recent decades?

- What is likely to happen to health-care prices and expenditures in the future?

- What can be done to improve the delivery of health-care services?

Americans increasingly have been driven to pay for their health care through third-party insurers and to purchase that insurance, when possible, from their employers. This, in turn, has led to rising health care costs while making it harder for Americans without employer-provided insurance to obtain coverage.

—Michael Tanner[1]

[1]Michael Tanner, "What's Wrong with the Current System," in *Empowering Health Care Consumers Through Tax Reform,* ed. Grace-Marie Arnett (Ann Arbor: University of Michigan Press, 1999).

There is considerable dissatisfaction with the operation of the health-care industry in the United States. This is not without justification. Both the expenditures on and prices of health care have soared in recent decades. **Exhibit 1** presents the expenditure figures *as a share of GDP*. Health-care spending, including both private and government, jumped from 5.1 percent of GDP in 1960 to 8.8 percent in 1980 and 14.9 percent in 2002. What are the factors underlying this growth of health-care spending? Is this growth likely to continue in the future? Is the health-care industry in need of fundamental reform? This special topic feature will investigate these questions and related issues.

Some categories of health-care spending have substantial public-good components. This is true for expenditures on pure research and activities that retard, and in some cases, eliminate the incidence of communicable diseases. In these cases, health-care spending can generate spillover benefits for the general population, and it would be difficult, if not impossible, to exclude nonpaying consumers from the receipt of these benefits. As we discussed in Chapter 5, under these conditions, the market may produce less than the ideal quantity, and therefore there is a strong case for government action promoting the supply of such goods. The National Institutes of Health and the Centers for Disease Control and Prevention are examples of government organizations that justify their funding primarily on the basis of the public-good nature of their services. However, the vast majority of health-care spending, including that of the government, involves private goods—goods for which the benefits accrue primarily to the consumer. Thus, this feature will focus on the government's involvement in financing this category of health-care service. ▪

THE STRUCTURE OF THE HEALTH-CARE INDUSTRY

As we discussed in Chapter 6, goods and services may be produced by either private or government-operated firms. Correspondingly, they may be paid for by the consumer directly or by the taxpayer or some other third party. (See Exhibit 4 of Chapter 6.) Because it alters incentives, the structure of production and payment affects the operation of an industry.

Health care in many countries, including Canada and most of the high-income countries of Europe, is a socialized industry.[2] In these countries, hospitals are operated by the government, and their services are financed by taxes. Physicians, nurses, and other health-care workers are government employees. Of course, socialization does not eliminate the prob-

**EXHIBIT 1
Health-care
Expenditures as a
Share of GDP**

Total expenditures (including both private and government-financed) on health care as a share of GDP have persistently increased during the last four decades. In 2002, the United States spent 14.9 percent of its GDP on health care, up from 8.8 percent in 1980 and 5.1 percent in 1960.

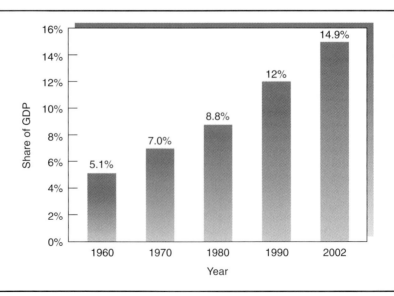

Source: http://www.cms.hhs.gov/.

[2]For a cross-national comparison of spending on health care, see Uwe E. Reinhardt, "Health Care for Aging Baby Boom: Lessons from Abroad," *Journal of Economic Perspectives*, spring 2000, 71–83.

lems of scarcity and rationing. Resources must be attracted to the health-care industry, and this will involve a cost. No country is able to provide as much health care, free of charge, as its citizens would like. Therefore, when price plays a secondary role, alternative methods must be utilized to allocate health-care services. As a result, countries with socialized medicine are characterized by waiting lists for basic medical procedures, an absence (or highly restricted availability) of services such as MRIs that involve expensive equipment, and widespread use of political rules and regulations to determine who will receive and who will be denied various types of health care. When patients in countries with socialized medicine are unable to obtain treatment or lack confidence in that treatment, those who can afford to do so often travel to other locations to purchase the health services they want.

In the United States, there is widespread use of both private and government-operated enterprises in the health-care industry. The services of doctors are generally supplied privately, but hospitals are often operated by the government, particularly local governments. Many communities, however, also have hospitals that are operated privately. Some of the private hospitals are for-profit businesses, whereas others are operated by charitable institutions. In contrast with most other industries, in the United States, nearly 85 percent of health-care spending is paid for by a third party—either the taxpayer or a private insurance company.

The Medicare and Medicaid programs have covered the bulk of the health-care costs of the elderly and the poor since the programs were established in the mid-1960s. Medicare's hospitalization program (Part A) uses a 2.9 percent tax on the wages and salaries of current workers to finance virtually all of the cost of hospitalization incurred by the elderly (persons age sixty-five and over). Medicare's Supplementary Medical Insurance (Part B) covers outpatient medical services. It is financed 75 percent by general revenues and 25 percent by beneficiary premiums. The Medicaid program is financed by general revenues, and it provides low-income families with access to health care either free or at a nominal cost.

Exhibit 2 presents data for real expenditures (measured in 2003 dollars) on the Medicare and Medicaid programs. From the very beginning, spending on the programs rose rapidly. By 1970, combined spending on the two summed to $44 billion. Real expenditures on the Medicare program doubled between 1970 and 1980 and then doubled again between 1980 and 1990. During the 1990s, real expenditures increased by another 80 percent. In 2002, the total expenditures on Medicare summed to $263 billion. Real spending on Medicaid has increased even more rapidly than Medicare. In 2002, government spending on Medicaid ($151 billion) was more than twelve times the level it was in 1970.

Health-care spending, mostly for Medicare and Medicaid, consumed 21.7 percent of the federal budget in 2003, up from 9.4 percent in 1980 and 0.9 percent in 1960. This makes it the second-largest item in the federal budget, greater than the spending on national defense and only slightly less than expenditures on Social Security. If the present

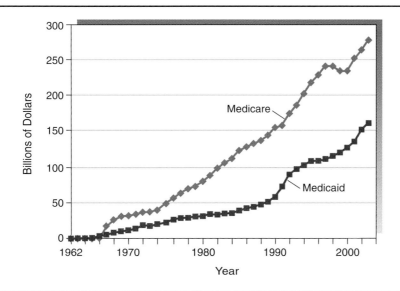

EXHIBIT 2
Real Expenditures on Medicare and Medicaid (Measured in 2003 Dollars)

Expenditures on both Medicare and Medicaid have soared during the last three decades. Adjusted for inflation, the 2002 expenditures on Medicare were more than three times the level of 1980 and eight times the figure for 1970. The real Medicaid expenditures in 2002 were twelve times the level of 1970.

Source: http://www.gpoaccess.gov/usbudget/fy05/hist.html.

trend continues, health-care spending will be the largest item in the federal budget in the near future. (See Exhibit 2 of Special Topic 1, "Government Spending and Taxation.")

Discrimination against the Direct Purchase of Health Insurance

Health insurance is also an integral part of the health-care industry in the United States. About two-thirds of nonelderly adults have health insurance through group plans offered by their employers. Employee compensation in the form of health insurance is not subject to taxation. This makes group health insurance programs provided through employers particularly attractive.[3] Interestingly, this favorable tax treatment of employer-provided health insurance is a historical relic dating back to the wage and price controls of World War II. Because health insurance benefits were not counted as wages, employers were able to use them as a means to increase workers' compensation and attract additional employees, while still complying with the wage controls imposed during the war.

In contrast with employer-provided policies, both personal medical bills and the direct purchase of health insurance by an individual or family must be paid for with after-tax dollars. When employees are provided with additional income rather than health insurance benefits, the income is subject to both payroll and personal income taxes. This makes the direct purchase of health insurance far more costly than purchasing health care through an employer. For example, a lower-middle-income family confronting a 15 percent federal income tax and the 15.3 percent payroll tax would have to earn approximately $12,000 of additional income in order to purchase an $8,400 health insurance policy. A family in the 28 percent federal tax bracket would have to earn approximately $14,000 more to purchase the policy. If state and local income and payroll taxes apply, these figures will be even higher.

This discriminatory tax treatment encourages employees to demand and employers to provide low-deductible, small co-payment health insurance policies. In essence, health-care expenses covered in this manner are tax deductible, whereas those paid for out of pocket or through the direct purchase of health insurance are not.[4] As a result of this distortion, more health-care bills are paid for by third-party insurers, and fewer are covered directly by the health-care consumer or through high-deductible insurance plans. As we will see in a moment, this affects the efficiency of health-care delivery.

The linking of health insurance to employment also reduces employee mobility and increases the number of people without any health insurance coverage. When employees lose their job or change jobs, they often lose their health insurance. Because purchasing a policy with after-tax dollars is so expensive, many unemployed workers remain uncovered until they are able to find a new job. Furthermore, the discriminatory tax treatment of direct purchase policies reduces the competitiveness of the health insurance industry. Unsurprisingly, the industry is dominated by a relatively small number of companies offering primarily "one size fits all" group plans.

THIRD-PARTY PAYMENTS AND HEALTH-CARE INFLATION

After the Medicare and Medicaid programs were established in the mid-1960s, third- party payment of health-care expenditures grew rapidly, whereas the share of medical bills paid directly by the consumer declined. As **Exhibit 3** shows, 55.2 percent of the 1960 medical expenditures were paid directly by consumers. Third parties financed only 44.8 percent of the 1960 total. Through the years, the share paid out of pocket has declined while that financed by third parties has risen. By 2002, third-party payments accounted for 84.1 percent of the medical care purchases, 44.1 percent by the government, and 40.0 percent by private insurers. Only 15.9 percent of the medical bills in 2002 were paid for directly by consumers.

Economic theory indicates that the growth of subsidies to health-care consumers and the accompanying expansion of third-party payments will push prices upward. There are two reasons why this will be the case. First, subsidies like those provided by Medicare and Med-

---

[3]In addition to the favorable tax treatment, economies that result from the group purchase of health insurance may also make employer-provided plans more attractive.

[4]Out-of-pocket health-care expenses can be deducted only if the taxpayer files an itemized return. Even in this case, only health-care expenses in excess of 7.5 percent of the taxpayer's adjusted gross income are deductible.

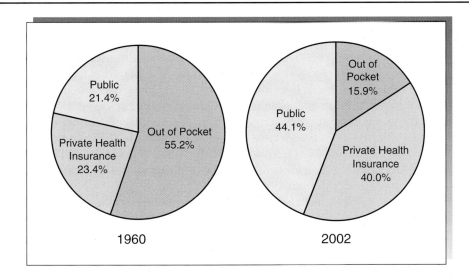

EXHIBIT 3
Out-of-pocket Versus Third-party Payments for Medical Care, 1960 and 2002

In 1960, out-of-pocket medical care expenditures of consumers accounted for 55 percent of the total, while private insurance and government programs paid 45 percent of the medical bills. By 2002, the out-of-pocket payments had fallen to only 15.9 percent of expenditures, whereas those covered by a third party had risen to 84.1 percent of the total. Third-party payments for a service reduce the incentive to economize on the service and lead to both higher prices and spending levels for it.

Source: http://www.cms.hhs.gov/.

icaid, will increase the demand for medical care. (When someone else is footing part of the bill for a service, consumers are more likely purchase it.) In turn, the stronger demand will lead to higher prices. Unfortunately, the supply of many health-care services is highly inelastic, particularly in the short run. In the health-care industry, the short run may be quite lengthy. This is perhaps most evident in the case of the services of doctors. Training for doctors is long and rigorous; an increase in doctors' fees will not quickly increase the supply of practicing physicians and reverse the upward movement of prices. This is particularly true when medical schools, perhaps unduly influenced by the American Medical Association, are reluctant to expand the size of their classes. Thus, the increase in demand generated by Medicare and Medicaid will tend to push the prices of health-care services upward.

Second, the growth of third-party payments has an enormous effect on the incentive of consumers to economize and shop for low-cost services and producers to provide the goods at a low price. In a normal market, consumers will shop around and patronize those suppliers that provide the most value per dollar spent. In turn, this shopping by consumers motivates suppliers to control their costs and offer their services at attractive prices. But when someone else is paying all or most of the bill, the incentive to economize is eroded. Rather than search for value relative to cost, consumers will attempt to purchase from the "best available" supplier, pretty much regardless of price.

Perhaps the following example will help explain why substituting third-party payments for out-of-pocket spending leads to higher prices. Suppose that the government, insurance companies, or some other third party were willing to pay 90 percent of costs associated with purchasing hairstyling services. Think how the behavior of both potential consumers and suppliers in the hairstyling business would be altered. Because someone else was paying most of the bill, many consumers would get their hair styled more often, search for the very best stylists—even if they were quite expensive—and patronize those providing extra services (those that, say, offer shoulder massages, pleasant surroundings, and valet parking). The strong demand would make it possible for hairstylists to raise their prices, and many of them would begin providing the "extras" designed to convince consumers that their services were the best. All of these adjustments would drive the price of hairstyling services upward and cause the third-party expenditures to soar.

Of course, health care is a far more serious matter than hairstyling, but our simple example, nonetheless illustrates what happens when someone else is paying the bill. *Economic theory indicates that when a third party is paying more and more of the bill, the demand for the service will increase, the incentive to economize will decline, and both the prices and expenditures on the service will rise rapidly.*

The evidence is consistent with this view. **Exhibit 4** shows the ratio of the medical care price index to the overall Consumer Price Index. If the prices of medical services increase more than the prices of other consumer purchases, this ratio will rise. Note that this has been the case year after year. Since the passage of the Medicare and Medicaid programs in 1965, the prices of medical services have doubled relative to the general Consumer Price Index. Thus, during this lengthy time span, on average, the prices of health-care services rose at twice the rate of other consumer items. Furthermore, there is no evidence that the health-care inflation is about to subside. In fact, the increase in medical prices relative to the general index of consumer prices has accelerated since 1980. Moreover, the prices of prescription drugs, which rose less than the Consumer Price Index during the 1960s and 1970s, have also been increasing more rapidly than the CPI since 1980. (See the accompanying Applications in Economics, "Could imports from Canada reduce the drug prices of Americans?" for an analysis of a widely debated proposal some people think would reduce the cost of prescription drugs for Americans.)

Over time, third-party payees, including both insurance companies and the government, will take steps to restrain expenditures. They may limit the amount paid for various services, require consumers to patronize only certain providers, make it more difficult to obtain permission for costly procedures, impose delays, and the like. This is essentially the route taken by the "managed-care movement" of the 1990s. Regulatory controls of this type, however, will be difficult to implement successfully because they will generally conflict with the interest of both consumers and health-care providers. As the managed-care experience already indicates, this path will tend to result in unhappy consumers and decisions that, with the benefit of hindsight, are clearly inappropriate and in some cases life-threatening. Controlling costs through rules and regulations imposed by a third party is an imperfect substitute for competition and the freedom of the consumer to choose how to spend his or her money.

IS THE U.S. HEADED FOR A HEALTH-CARE CRISIS?

How are health-care prices and expenditures likely to change in the future? **Exhibit 5** provides insight on this question. Between 1995 and 2015, the number of Americans aged seventy and over is projected to increase by 7.4 million (31 percent). But the baby boom generation, those people born during the years following World War II, will begin reaching age seventy in 2015. During the two decades following 2015, the U.S. population age seventy and over will expand by 26.8 million, from 31.2 million to 58 million, a whopping increase of 86 percent.

This huge increase in elderly Americans has enormous implications for the health-care industry. Because health-care expenses are much higher for people in their seventys than for people in their sixties and younger, this growth of Americans aged seventies and

EXHIBIT 4
Ratio of Health-care Price Indexes Relative to the Consumer Price Index

The ratio of medical care prices to the general level of consumer prices more than doubled between 1965 and 2003. After increasing less rapidly than the Consumer Price Index during the period 1960–1980, prescription drug prices rose more rapidly than the CPI during the last two decades.

Source: http://www.bls.gov.

APPLICATIONS IN ECONOMICS

Could imports from Canada reduce the drug prices of Americans?

American pharmaceutical companies often make their products available at lower prices in countries other than the United States. This price discrimination can often be used to increase the net revenues of the companies. In many poor countries, very few units would be sold if the drugs were priced at the same level as in the United States. Under these circumstances, the lower prices make it possible for the companies to generate more revenue. In other instances, the lower prices may reflect volume sales and the bargaining power of a government-operated health service. This may well be the case in Canada.

Legislation currently prohibits Americans from importing pharmaceutical drugs from other countries. This prohibition makes it easier for the drug companies to practice price discrimination. In the age of the Internet, however, buyers have greater access to sellers in distant markets. Thus, it is fairly common for Americans to purchase pharmaceutical products from suppliers in other countries, particularly Canada.

If various drugs are, for example, 50 percent cheaper in Canada, it is tempting to think that huge savings could be achieved if a large share of Americans simply purchased their drugs in Canada. Unfortunately, this is unlikely to be the case. The pharmaceutical companies will not continue to sell their products at lower prices in other countries if large quantities are then sold back into the American market. Remember, price discrimination works only when you can prevent resale to customers who will otherwise be charged higher prices. If the pharmaceutical companies cannot limit the resale of their products to Americans, predictably they will eliminate their "discount prices" in other smaller and less lucrative markets. The Canadian market, for example, is only about one-tenth the size of the U.S. market. Drug manufacturers are not going to endanger their profits in the U.S. market by selling at lower prices in the much smaller Canadian market. Thus, the primary effect of increased movement of pharmaceutical products across national boundaries will be higher prices and more limited supplies in the foreign markets rather than significantly lower prices in the U.S. market.[1]

[1]For additional details on this topic, see Robert J. Barro, "Drugs Via Canada: The Side Effects Could Hurt," *Business Week*, August 23–30, 2004.

over will increase both the demand for medical services and the share of those services financed by third parties. This will push both health-care prices and expenditures upward. It will also cause Medicare expenditures to soar and necessitate the need for higher taxes to finance the program. Unless reform is undertaken, the health-care inflation and spending growth of recent decades will not only continue, but, many believe, it will reach crisis proportions.

AVERTING THE CRISIS: HOW TO MOVE TOWARD A CONSUMER-DRIVEN SYSTEM

Perverse public policy is the primary factor underlying the soaring expenditures and rising prices in the health-care industry. By promoting third-party payment of health-care expenses and the purchase of medical insurance through employers, health-care policy has (1) eroded the incentive of health-care consumers and providers to economize, (2) undermined the operation of health-care markets, and (3) made it more costly for persons without a job to obtain health insurance. Without fundamental reforms, political officials can be expected to impose more and more regulations on the industry, including price controls, in an effort to control the soaring expenditure levels. The experience of other countries indicates where this will lead. The health-care industry is too large, complex, and diverse to be planned and regulated centrally. Efforts at central planning will waste resources and produce disappointing results.

If health care is to become more efficient and cost-effective, greater reliance must be put on consumer choice and the direct payment of medical expenses. How can this be achieved? Several policy changes would be helpful, but the following five alternatives are particularly important.

EXHIBIT 5

Growth in the U.S. Population Age seventy and over, 1995–2035

Between 1995 and 2015, the number of persons over age seventy is projected to increase by 7.4 million. But during the two decades following 2015, the U.S. population over age seventy will increase by 26.8 million as the baby boomers move into this age group. Because the medical expenses of persons over age seventy are exceedingly high, the rapid growth of this group during the years following 2015 will put enormous pressure on the Medicare program.

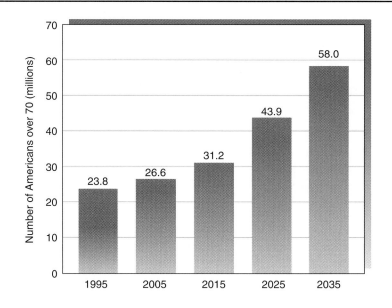

Source: http://www.census.gov/.

1. Equalize the tax treatment of out-of-pocket medical expenses and the direct purchase of health insurance with employer-purchased health insurance. As we discussed above, health insurance purchased through an employer is tax-free, whereas medical bills and personal health insurance policies purchased out-of-pocket must be paid for with after-tax income. The most reasonable and politically feasible method of correcting this distortion is to make out-of-pocket medical expenses and the purchase of personal health insurance tax deductible. This deductibility would not be of much value to taxpayers with low incomes or those filing the short tax forms. However, these taxpayers could be given a 30 percent tax credit—a tax saving similar to that of employer-provided plans—for medical insurance purchases and out-of-pocket medical-bill payments. This would also make it cheaper for people without access to employer-provided insurance to purchase coverage and pay their medical bills directly.

Medical savings accounts
Special savings accounts that individuals could use for the payment of medical bills or the purchase of a catastrophic (high-deductible) health insurance plan. Unfavorable tax treatment compared to employer-provided health insurance and other regulatory restrictions currently reduce their use.

2. Encourage medical savings accounts (MSAs) and the direct payment of medical bills from MSAs. Important action was recently taken in this area. Beginning in 2004, MSAs were given the same status as insurance purchased through employers. Approximately 250 million nonelderly Americans are now eligible for these accounts. An MSA allows people with high-deductible insurance plans ($1,000 or more) to contribute up to $2,600 per year for a single person ($5,150 for a married couple) to a savings account to cover future medical bills. Employers making contributions into the accounts of their employees can record the contributions as a business expense. A person with an MSA has a property right to the account, and its ownership is not dependent on his or her employment. Funds can be withdrawn from these accounts for the direct payment of medical bills not covered by the high-deductible policies. Balances in the accounts can earn interest tax-free and be rolled over from year to year. Accumulated balances can either be used in retirement or passed on to heirs.

Like insurance premiums, MSAs involve setting aside funds on a regular basis for coverage of future medical bills. But they also make it possible for individuals and their families to take more control over their health-care expenditures. People will economize on their use of these funds, just as they economize on other expenditures. As the use of MSAs expands, the incidence of third-party payments will decline. With time, as more and more health-care consumers shop for value, medical suppliers will become more cost sensitive. Administrative costs are also likely to decline as the share of out-of-pocket health-care spending increases. Clearly, MSAs are a step in the right direction.

3. Encourage the purchase of catastrophic health insurance, and discourage the purchase of health insurance plans with small co-payments. MSAs are designed to be used with a high-deductible, modest co-payment insurance plan that can be purchased at an economical price. Insurance works well when it compensates people for losses resulting from unpredictable events outside of their control that seldom occur. When such events do occur, large losses are imposed on the unfortunate parties. Under these circumstances, the premiums of those experiencing little or no damage can be used to compensate those experiencing large losses. Large medical expenses such as those resulting from a severe injury or a catastrophic illness like diabetes or cancer generally fall into this category. It makes sense to promote the purchase of health insurance providing protection against large medical bills resulting from catastrophic illnesses and injuries. High-deductible policies, for example, those that cover most medical expenses in excess of $3,000 per year, are relatively cheap. In 2001, such a policy could be purchased for an annual premium of approximately $1,500. A system of tax credits could be utilized to encourage all (or at least most) citizens to purchase policies of this type.

In contrast, insurance works poorly when the "losses" are widespread among the insurees, and when the actions of those insured influence the size of the benefits they derive. Most everyone can expect to experience medical problems ranging from routine illnesses like colds, flus, and common childhood diseases to minor injures. There are several alternative ways of dealing with them, some of which are far more costly than others. Predictably, insurance will work poorly for medical costs of this type. Furthermore, policies requiring only a small co-payment for routine medical services promote the third-party payment system that retards economizing behavior.

4. Shift Medicare at least partly from a reimbursement plan to a defined-benefit plan. Under this approach, Medicare recipients would receive a specific amount each year to pay their medical bills directly and purchase private insurance. All Medicare recipients would be required to purchase at least a catastrophic insurance plan. The funds not used in one year could be rolled over for use in subsequent years. This approach would increase the freedom of Medicare recipients to choose the combination of medical services and payment methods that best fits their needs.

5. Put more emphasis on the supply side of the health-care market. Each year the government spends several hundred billion dollars subsidizing the demand for medical care—that is, helping people purchase it. But very little is spent encouraging additional supply. However, without additional supply, demand subsidies merely reallocate scarce health-care services among consumers. The subsidy recipients, primarily the elderly and those with low incomes, get more medical care, whereas others receive less. Furthermore, the primary beneficiaries of the demand-side subsidies are health-care suppliers, who receive higher prices for their services. Supply-side programs would focus more on the training of health-care providers. For example, they might provide more aid for the growth and development of medical schools. In fact, only one new medical school has been established in the United States during the last two decades. Aid to low-income students qualified to attend medical and nursing schools might also be expanded. In contrast with demand subsidies, programs that expand the supply of medical personnel would make it easier to control future costs.

If we want to avert a future health-care crisis, the current system must be reformed. The five proposals outlined above would lead to (1) more direct payment (and less third-party payment) of health-care expenses, (2) lower costs for catastrophic insurance protection (but higher costs for low-deductible, high co-payment coverage), and (3) a greater effort to expand the supply of medical services rather than stimulate demand for them. No doubt, these reforms will not solve all of our health-care problems, but economic analysis suggests that they are a move in the right direction.

KEY POINTS

▼ Spending on health care has soared in recent decades. Measured as a share of the economy, total health-care spending rose from 5.1 percent in 1960 to 8.8 percent in 1980 and 14.9 percent in 2002.

▼ After Medicare and Medicaid were established in the mid-1960s, the direct expenditures of health-care consumers gradually declined, and those made by third-party payees expanded. The out-of-pocket spending of consumers accounted for only 15.9 percent of health-care spending in 2002, down from 55 percent in 1960.

▼ The growth of subsidies to health-care consumers and greater reliance on third-party payments in recent decades (1) increased the demand for medical services and (2) reduced the incentive of both health-care consumers and providers to economize. Both factors have contributed to the health-care inflation and soaring expenditures in recent decades.

▼ As the baby boom generation grows older, the number of persons over age seventy will increase sharply between 2015 and 2035. Under the current Medicare program, this will increase the demand for health-care services and the share of medical payments financed by third parties. Unless reform is undertaken, this will mean both more health-care inflation and substantially higher taxes to finance Medicare.

▼ Health-care reform emphasizing (1) direct, rather than third-party, payment of medical bills, (2) catastrophic insurance protection (but not low-deductible, high co-payment plans), and (3) the expansion of the supply (rather than the demand) of health care would help minimize, if not avert, a crisis that is likely to occur when the baby boomers retire.

CRITICAL ANALYSIS QUESTIONS

1. How does the substitution of third-party payments by insurance companies and the government for the out-of-pocket purchase of health care by consumers influence the demand and price of medical services? Explain.

*2. When an employer provides health insurance benefits as part of the compensation package, does this represent a gift by employers to their employees? Do employees earn these benefits? Why or why not? Justify your response.

3. Do individuals have a right to free health care? Do they have a right to force others to provide them with free health care? Discuss.

*4. How did the Medicare and Medicaid programs influence the cost of medical services purchased by Americans who were neither poor nor elderly? Explain.

5. Consider the five reform proposals suggested by the authors at the end of this feature. Indicate why you believe each is either a good or a bad idea. Explain your answers.

6. Are there things that individuals can do to improve their personal health and, as a result, reduce their expenditures on health care? Give some examples.

*Asterisk denotes questions for which answers are given in Appendix B.

School Choice:
Can It Improve the Quality
of Education in America?

Focus

■ How has spending on education changed in recent decades? How does
the educational spending of the United States compare with that of
other countries?

■ How do student achievement scores today compare with those of the
past? How does student performance in the United States compare
with that of other countries?

■ What does economics have to say about the structure of education?

■ How can the quality of education be improved?

*Real reform will only come from
pressure from outside the system, generated by empowered
parents with expanded school
choice.*

—Howard Fuller[1]

---

[1]Former School Superintendent, Milwaukee School District, *USA Today,* August 25, 1995.

*I*ncreasingly, brains rather than brawn or resources are the basis of economic development and individual wealth. A good education is more important than ever to economic success. There is, however, widespread concern about the quality of education in the United States. Is a lack of spending the cause of low student achievement in the United States? What are the sources of the deficiencies in the current educational system? How can we reform the educational process? This special topic will investigate these questions and related issues. ▪

EDUCATIONAL SPENDING AND STUDENT PERFORMANCE

One source of the dissatisfaction with the education system in the United States is low student performance. As **Exhibit 1** demonstrates, achievement scores fell in the 1970s, changed little during the 1980s, and rose slightly during the 1990s. Clearly, the average achievement scores of high school graduates today are well below those of students thirty-five years ago.

Cross-country comparisons of achievement scores also illustrate the weak performance of U.S. schools. **Exhibit 2** shows the mathematics achievement scores from the 2000 Program of International Student Assessment, which compared achievement in thirty-one countries. Fifteen-year-olds in the United States scored 7 points below the country average and 64 points below Japan. The achievement scores for science also show that U.S. students lag well behind those of most developed countries.

Do the performance patterns reflect expenditures? **Exhibit 3** presents data on real spending per pupil on public elementary and secondary education for the 1970–2002 period. As the graph illustrates, educational spending has been steadily increasing. *Measured in 2002 dollars,* expenditures per pupil in public elementary and secondary schools in the United States increased from $4,181 in 1970 to $8,865 in 2002. Thus, real spending per pupil has more than doubled during the last three decades.

How does U.S. spending on education compare with that of other countries? **Exhibit 4** presents international data for government spending on primary education for 2001, the latest year for which the figures are available. As these figures show, spending per pupil in the United States is among the highest in the world. The United States spent $7,560 per primary student, which was 57 percent more than the average across twenty-seven countries.[2] Thus, lack of spending does not explain the lower performance level of U.S. students compared to other countries.

EXHIBIT 1
Average Combined SAT Score, 1967–2002

The achievement scores of American students dropped in the 1970s, changed little in the 1980s, and rose modestly during the 1990s.

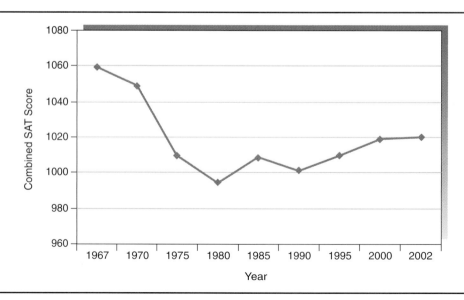

Source: Statistical Abstract of the United States, 2003.

[2]The United States spent $8,779 per secondary pupil, which is 31 percent above the OECD average.

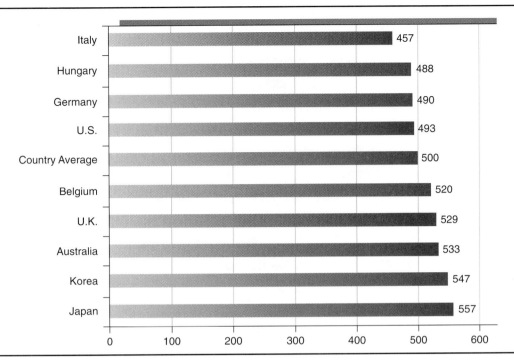

Source: OECD, *Education at a Glance,* 2004.

EXHIBIT 2

Average Mathematics Achievement Scores of fifteen-year-olds: A Cross-country Comparison

The mathematics achievement scores of fifteen-year-old American students lag behind those of other countries.

ECONOMICS AND THE STRUCTURE OF THE EDUCATIONAL SYSTEM

Why are U.S. schools doing so poorly? Many economists believe that part of the answer lies with the structure of the school system. As we discussed in Chapter 6 (see Exhibit 4 in Chapter 6), the operation of a market is influenced by who pays for the good (the consumer or a third party) and who produces it (private or government-operated firms). When consumers pay directly for goods and services, they will shop among suppliers and patronize those that provide them with the most value per unit of expenditure. In turn, their choices will provide profit-seeking firms operating in open markets with a strong incentive to operate efficiently, keep their prices down, and cater to the preferences of consumers. As we have stressed throughout, this combination of forces—economizing behavior by consumers and competition among suppliers—is vitally important for the efficient allocation of resources.

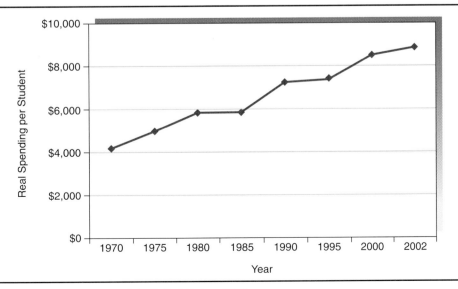

EXHIBIT 3

Real Spending per Elementary and Secondary Pupil, 1970–2002

Real spending per pupil on public elementary and secondary schools more than doubled during the 1970–2002 period.

Source: Statistical Abstract of the United States, 2003.

EXHIBIT 4
Spending per Primary Student, 2001:
A Cross-country Comparison

Spending per primary student in the United States is among the highest in the world.

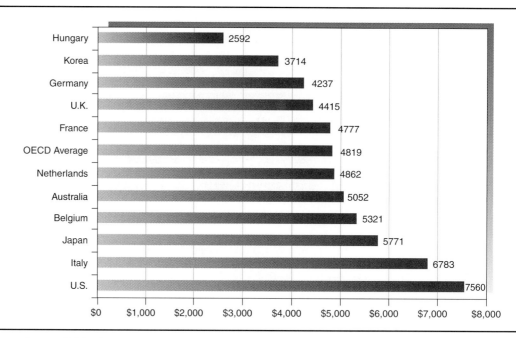

Source: OECD, *Education at a Glance*, 2004.

The structure of the U.S. schooling market undermines both of these forces. In essence, public schools are government-operated firms with substantial monopoly power. They are protected from the competition of rivals because "free" education is available only to those who attend the local district public school. The effect of economizing behavior on the part of consumers is largely eroded. If students (and their parents) choose a non-public school, they have to pay for their own education. They lose the government subsidy that would be theirs if they attended public schools. This makes it very costly to switch to rival suppliers. Thus, a public school has to be very bad before it loses many customers.

Furthermore, like the managers of other government-operated firms, school administrators have a strong incentive to build the case for larger government funding. Predictably, they will confront politicians controlling their budgets with the image that marvelous things can be accomplished with additional funds and that any reduction in funding will have drastic consequences. In contrast, the incentive to innovate and figure out how to provide students with a better education at a lower cost is weakened. After all, school revenues come from the politicians, not consumers.

Perhaps a thought experiment will help illuminate some of the problems with the current educational structure. Suppose that the restaurant industry in the United States were set up in the way that public schools are in the United States. A system of local "restaurant districts" would be established. Taxes would be levied to finance the cost of the government-operated restaurants in each district. Citizens would not be allowed to patronize public restaurants outside their local district. If customers chose to patronize private restaurants, they would have to pay for the food *twice*—once as a taxpayer and again as a consumer. Thus, if a private restaurant were to survive, it would have to figure out how to attract customers from the tax-financed restaurants that were giving food away to district residents.

Clearly, there would be major problems with this organizational structure. Since the managers of the government-operated restaurants would derive their funds from the government, predictably they would spend more time satisfying those with political clout (including worker unions) and less time catering to the needs and preferences of customers. The incentive to keep costs low would be weak. Similarly, there would be little reason for restaurant operators to innovate, figure out how to do things better, or search for ways to provide their "customers" with better service. After all, a lower quality of service would merely highlight the need for additional funding of the public-sector restaurants. Since consumers could not take their funding and go elsewhere, they would be in a weak position to discipline the district restaurants that were not doing a good job. The outcome of this organizational structure is predictable. Compared to the current system based on customer choice and competition, restaurant food costs would rise and quality would deteriorate. There would be a disconnect between the preferences of consumers and the product supplied and, as a result, consumers would get less for their food expenditure dollar.

The performance of U.S. education at the college and university level is also instructive. Here, the structure is quite different than at the elementary and secondary level. At higher education levels, students have a much greater opportunity to choose among a variety of colleges and universities. Financial aid that can be used at either private or government-operated schools is more readily available. Thus, competition between private and government-operated schools (and among public schools) is much stronger at the college level. In contrast with the international standing of elementary and secondary schools, U.S. higher education leads the world in the variety of programs offered, the eminence of researchers, quality of facilities, and percentage of high school graduates attending college.

ALTERNATIVE WAYS OF INCREASING COMPETITION AND EXPANDING THE OPTIONS OF CONSUMERS

After years of disappointing results from the growth of educational expenditures, interest has grown in alternative approaches. In recent years, several states have adopted programs providing students and parents with options to the traditional public school system. The following section will briefly consider three of the most common alternatives: school vouchers, charter schools, and choice for children attending failing schools.

School Vouchers

Under a pure voucher plan, rather than financing schools directly, the government would give parents a certificate equal to the current educational expenditures per pupil. The parents could then use the voucher to finance their child's education at the public or private school they think is best for their child.

In essence, a voucher plan would put competition to work to improve the schools. Because their revenues would be dependent upon their ability to attract students, schools would compete for students, and parents would be free to choose among schools. The competition among schools would encourage innovative ideas and the discovery of more effective teaching techniques. It would also mean competition for first-rate educators. The demand for outstanding teachers would increase, which would increase salaries and help attract quality people to the teaching profession. Perhaps just as important, the demand for poor teachers would decline, and many would shift to other careers.

A voucher system would also encourage diversity, which would allow a larger number of Americans to choose and receive a type of schooling that is more consistent with their preferences. Some parents would choose a highly structured school; others would prefer a less-structured school. Some would select a school that stresses religious values; others would opt for secular education. Some would choose a school with a traditional college prep program, while others would support schools that provide technical and vocational training. Under a system of parental choice, each of these diverse preferences could be satisfied.

Three major objections are typically raised against a voucher system. First, some opponents charge that the primary beneficiaries would be high-income Americans who already send their children to private schools. (*Note:* About 10 percent of the students at the elementary and secondary level currently attend private schools, while approximately 90 percent attend public schools.) Second, other opponents fear that a voucher plan would increase the racial imbalance among schools. Third, still others argue that vouchers would drain funds away from the public schools, and thereby cause their quality to deteriorate.

A modified voucher targeted toward low- and middle-income families would overcome each of these objections. For example, low-income families with children in a private school might be given a voucher equal to the full cost per pupil of public spending on education, while the voucher grants to middle-income families might be equal to, say, two-thirds of the public school cost; the grants to high-income families might be even smaller. Above a certain income level, perhaps no aid would be given to high-income families with children in private schools. This type of voucher plan would enhance the educational opportunities available to the children of low- and middle-income families without providing a windfall gain to high-income families sending their children to private schools.

The modified voucher plan would also promote racial and economic balance among schools. Since blacks and other minorities are overrepresented among the low-income families receiving the highest valued vouchers, those groups would also be overrepresented among families shifting to private schools (and high-quality public schools outside the district).

Furthermore, the modified plan should ameliorate fears that public schools would be put at a financial disadvantage. Except in the case of low-income students the per-pupil aid to public schools would always exceed that given students attending private schools. Moreover, if middle- or high-income students were to move from a public to a private school, the per-pupil funding remaining with public schools would actually increase. Given the superior aid that this plan would provide for public relative to private schools, the inability of a public school to compete would speak volumes about the efficiency of its operation and the quality of education it was providing.

Charter Schools

Charter schools are another mechanism that might be used to expand parental choice and introduce competitive forces in the public school system. Charter schools are publicly funded but run independently of the traditional public school system. They operate under a contract ("charter") with a government agency. The supervising agency usually requires the charter schools to meet a variety of standards, including financial, safety, and educational outcomes.

Charter schools differ from voucher programs in some important ways. Religious schools are not permitted to be charter schools. Charter schools are not permitted to charge tuition, as all of their students are subsidized by public funds. Because existing private schools charge tuition, they are not allowed to be charter schools (though conversions to a charter school are permitted in some states). In contrast, vouchers are allowed to be used at private schools.

Like the voucher programs, charter schools would increase the choices available to parents regarding the types of schools their children could attend. Charter schools that offer a wide variety of programs have been established. Some schools focus on mathematics and science, others on the arts; some are directed at African-American students; and still others focus on the development of leadership skills among girls.

Choices for Students in Failing Schools

As we noted earlier, in most states, primary and secondary education is a monopoly. Students are assigned to a particular public school, and it is virtually impossible to escape the grasp of a failing school, particularly for children of parents with low incomes. One solution to this problem is to provide students in a failing school with a voucher that would cover their cost of attending an alternative private or public school of their choice.

This would increase the incentive of schools to cater to the needs of students and empower those currently trapped in failing schools with a strong weapon: the ability to take their business elsewhere. It would also provide a strong incentive for weaker public schools to improve. If they did not, like other businesses in a competitive environment, they would lose customers.

The Growth of Choice Programs

In 2001, Congress passed an educational bill providing parents with children in failing schools grants of up to $1,000 for the purchase of after-school tutoring, summer school programs, or other educational materials. But when it comes to school choice, state and local governments are leading the way. Innovative programs include the following:

- Florida's A-Plus Education Plan (which allows students in failing schools to switch to private or other public schools)

- State and locally funded school voucher programs in Milwaukee, Cleveland, and elsewhere

- Privately funded efforts to offer scholarships to low-income families in some of the country's worst-performing school districts

During the 2003–2004 school year, nearly 700,000 students attended charter schools. Charter schools are now available in forty-one states. In 2004, thirty states permitted public school choice in some or all school districts. In addition, Arizona, Illinois, Iowa, Minnesota, and Pennsylvania now allow taxpayers a tax deduction (or tax credit) for donations to organizations that provide scholarships to students or for parents who spend personal funds on private school expenses. Choice is also expanding in other countries. Voucher programs that pay some or all of the tuition at private primary and secondary schools already exist in Chile, Colombia, the Netherlands, Sweden, and even post-communist Russia.

THE EFFECT OF STRUCTURAL CHANGE

It is too early for a full evaluation of voucher programs and charter schools. Structural changes of this type will be felt in the long run—over a time period long enough for suppliers to innovate and for the competitive process to yield better ways of doing things. In spite of these limitations, some interesting results are beginning to emerge from early research in this area.[3] First, African-American students tend to earn modestly higher achievement test scores after one to two years in voucher programs. On the other hand, evidence of systematic improvements in the achievement scores of children from other racial groups is limited.

Second, the impact of charter schools on student achievement is inconclusive. In Arizona, charter school students score higher on reading and math exams than those in traditional public schools after the first year of operation. In North Carolina, Texas, and Florida, student achievement gains in both reading and math are lower in first-year charter schools than traditional public schools. However, these negative effects diminish as charter schools mature. After two to four years, achievement scores are equal between charter schools and traditional public schools in Florida and Texas. Preliminary evidence from Texas shows that, after six years, charter school achievement scores surpass those of traditional public schools. In North Carolina, achievement scores in charter schools also improve after the first year, but traditional public schools still have higher achievement after five years.

Third, most parents of students in charter schools and voucher programs indicate they are highly satisfied with their children's schools. The satisfaction level of parents with children in voucher programs and charter schools exceeds that of parents with children in traditional public schools in the same community.

Lastly, targeted voucher programs do appear to modestly increase racial integration in highly segregated communities. These programs are placing minority children in voucher schools that have a lower percentage of minority students. In contrast, charter schools have racial distributions that are similar to those in local public schools.[4]

[3] The following discussion is based on Brian P. Gill, P. Michael Timpane, Karen E. Ross, and Dominic J. Brewer, *Rhetoric Versus Reality: What We Know and What We Need to Know About Vouchers and Charter Schools* (Santa Monica, CA: RAND, 2001); and Tim R. Sass, "Charter Schools and Student Achievement in Florida" (working paper, Florida State University, October 2004).

[4] There is some evidence that greater choice resulting from smaller school districts enhances quality. Most of the students graduating from high school during the 1960s (when SAT scores were much higher) were educated in districts that were much smaller than districts are now. Today, choice is expanded by multiple school districts within cities because this makes it easier for parents to improve the educational opportunities of their children by moving to districts with better schools. In contrast, when school districts cover an entire city, it is costly for parents to express their preferences for schools. Harvard University economist Caroline Hoxby compared results in metropolitan areas that have lots of school districts with those that have only a small number (often only one). Her findings indicate that average achievement levels were higher and expenditure levels lower in cities with more choice. Furthermore, the effect of choice on school productivity was largest in those states where districts have greater financial independence. See Caroline Hoxby, "Does Competition Among Public Schools Benefit Students and Taxpayers?" *American Economic Review*, December 2000, 1209–38, and "Would School Choice Change the Teaching Profession?" *Journal of Human Resources*, Fall 2002, 846–91.

CONCLUSION

During the last three decades, educational expenditures have increased substantially, but the performance of schools, as measured by the achievement level of students, has been poor. Given the structure of the schooling system, this is not surprising. There is little incentive for government firms operating in a protected market to provide high-quality service at a low cost. On the other hand, competition among rival suppliers works quite well in most markets. Many people believe that it would also work well in education and help improve public schools.

KEY POINTS

▼ Real spending per student has risen over the past several decades, but student performance on basic skill exams is now well below the levels of the late 1960s. The United States spends more on primary and secondary education than most countries, but its students have performed below international averages on measures of student achievement.

▼ Economic analysis indicates that the structure of the educational system may be a contributing factor to the poor performance in recent decades. Education is provided by government-operated firms with substantial monopoly power. Because competition is largely absent and educational consumers have limited choices, the incentive to produce efficiently and cater to the needs of parents and students is weak.

▼ Vouchers, charter schools, and choice for students at failing schools are three possible reforms of the educational system. These changes generally expand the choices of consumers and increase competition among schools.

▼ In the short time that they have been operating, charter schools and voucher programs appear to have had modest effects on student achievement. However, parents with children in charter schools and voucher programs indicate a higher level of satisfaction with their children's schools than parents with children in traditional public schools.

CRITICAL ANALYSIS QUESTIONS

1. "The best solution to reverse the decline in student performance in recent decades is to increase spending on education." Evaluate this statement.

*2. How does the lack of competition in the provision of education affect the quality and cost of education? Explain.

3. Should parents have the right to choose which schools their children attend? Why or why not? Discuss.

4. Consider the three reform proposals discussed by the authors at the end of this special topic. Indicate why you believe each is either a good or a bad idea. Explain your answers.

5. Currently, students attending state colleges and universities are heavily subsidized, but those attending private higher educational institutions are not. Do you think this is fair? Would you like to see a voucher system applied to higher education? Why or why not?

---

*Asterisk denotes questions for which answers are given in Appendix B.

Is Discrimination Responsible for the Earnings Differences between Men and Women?

Focus

- Why are the earnings of women substantially lower than those of men? Is it because of employment discrimination?

- How has the economic status of women changed in recent decades?

- How have the educational choices and career goals of women changed? Will this affect their future earnings?

Over the past 25 years, the gender pay gap has narrowed dramatically and women have increasingly entered traditionally male occupations.

—Francine D. Blau and Lawrence M. Kahn[1]

---

[1]Francine D. Blau and Lawrence M. Kahn, "Gender Differences in Pay," *Journal of Economic Perspectives*, fall 2000.

A half-century ago, the typical American woman spent most of her time at home caring for her children, preparing food, and doing laundry, cleaning, and other chores for her family. Fewer than one in four married women worked outside the household in 1950. Today, the situation is dramatically different. Most women, including those who are married, work outside the home. This special topic analyzes earnings differences of men and women and the changing economic role of women. ▨

EMPLOYMENT DISCRIMINATION AND THE EARNINGS OF WOMEN

During the last several decades, there has been a dramatic shift in the household versus market work choices of women. As **Exhibit 1** shows, the labor force participation rate of women rose from 37.6 percent in 1960 to 60.6 percent in 2002. Married women accounted for most of the increase.

Exhibit 1 also shows that the female/male (F/M) earnings ratio for full-time workers was approximately 60 percent from 1960 to 1980. In other words, women earned only 60 percent of what men did. Since the early 1980s, though, the earnings of women have steadily increased relative to men. Nevertheless, by 2002, women working full-time still earned only 76.6 percent as much as their male counterparts. However, women employed full-time also worked approximately 10 percent fewer hours than men. Once you make adjustments for the fewer number of hours they worked, the hourly earnings of women were approximately 80 percent of those of their male counterparts in 2002.

Why are the earnings of women so low compared to those of men? Most people blame employment discrimination. Evidence appears to support this view. The characteristics of minorities relative to whites—age, education, marital status, location, and lan-

EXHIBIT 1
Labor Force Experience of Women, 1960–2002

Between 1960 and 2002, the labor force participation of women rose from 37.6 to 60.6 percent. However, the F/M earnings ratio fluctuated around 60 percent during the period 1960–1980, before climbing throughout the 1980s and 1990s. By 2002, the F/M earnings ratio had risen to 76.6 percent. The hourly earnings ratio of women relative to men was approximately 80 percent in 2002.

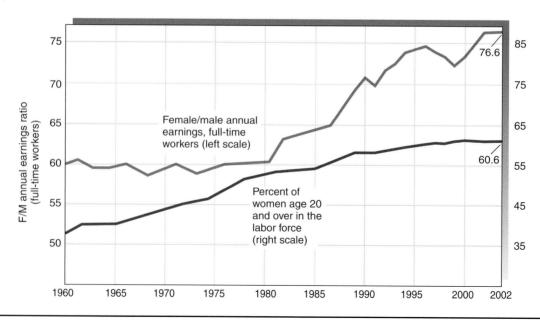

Source: http://www.census.gov/ and http://www.bls.gov/.

guage—differ more markedly from one another than these same characteristics do between men and women. So they don't explain the earnings differences between them. Women are also crowded into a few low-paying jobs, occupational data show. Until recently, more than half of all women were employed in just four occupations—as clerical workers, teachers, nurses, and food service workers.

MARITAL STATUS AND THE EARNINGS OF WOMEN

Still, attributing all or most of the pay differences between men and women to employment discrimination is an argument that's less than airtight. The very size of the difference makes the argument suspect. If an employer could really hire women who were willing and able to do the same work as men for 15 or 20 percent less, the profit motive would give them a strong incentive to do so. Even employers (both men and women) who don't consider themselves to be "sexist" would jump at the chance to cut their wage cost so dramatically. Of course, as more and more employers substituted women for men workers, the F/M earnings gap would close.

It might be helpful to think about the problem in a historical light. Prior to the last decade or so, married men typically pursued paid employment aggressively because they were expected to be the family's primary breadwinner. Because they shouldered most of the responsibility for "bringing home the bacon," they were more likely to (1) participate continuously in the labor force, (2) relocate if necessary to get a higher-paying job, and (3) accept jobs with long working hours, uncertain schedules, and out-of-town travel.

In contrast, married women, who were traditionally more responsible for running the households and rearing children, sought part-time work and jobs with more flexible hours.[2] Because women expected to drop out of the labor force from time to time (say, to care for young children or when their families' financial needs became less burdensome), jobs skills they could take to different employers at different times were worth getting. It's therefore not surprising that women were concentrated in nursing, teaching, and secretarial positions.

How important are gender differences when it comes to specialization within the family and pay differences today? **Exhibit 2** shows the median annual earnings of women relative to men in 2002, according to their marital status. Clearly, married women earn substantially less than married men. Even when working full-time, year-round, married women earn only 71 percent as much as men. However, the earnings gap between men and women is substantially less among those who have never married. In fact, in 2002 the female/male annual earnings ratio for full-time, year-round workers was 96 percent for people who've never married. In other words, the earnings of never-married women were only 4 percent less than the earnings of never-married men. So, although employment discrimination may well contribute to the wage differences between men and women, factors related to marital status, perhaps differences in preferences and past educational choices based on career objectives, are also highly important.

THE CHANGING CAREER OBJECTIVES OF WOMEN

Although the career objectives of men and women have differed substantially in the past, those differences have narrowed in recent years. In 1968, a national survey of women fourteen to twenty-four years of age found that only 27 percent expected to be working at age thirty-five. In contrast, a similar survey of young women in 1979 found that 72 percent expected to be working at that age.[3] These figures show there was a dramatic increase during the 1970s in the number of young women preparing for a career and lifetime of labor force participation. While this upward trend may have slowed, it has almost certainly continued during the last couple of decades.

---

[2]For an analysis of how family specialization influences the employment and earnings of women, see James P. Smith and Michael P. Ward, "Women in the Labor Market and in the Family," *Journal of Economic Perspectives,* winter 1989: 9–23.

[3]See Chapter 7 of the *Economic Report of the President,* 1987. The numbers presented here are from table 7-3 of the report.

EXHIBIT 2
Female/Male Earnings According to Marital Status, 2002

Although the female/male earnings ratio varies considerably with marital status and time worked, the earnings of never-married women were 96 percent of those of never-married men in 2002—a ratio that is much higher than for other marital status groupings. This suggests that differences in specialization within the traditional husband-wife family contribute substantially to earnings differentials according to gender.

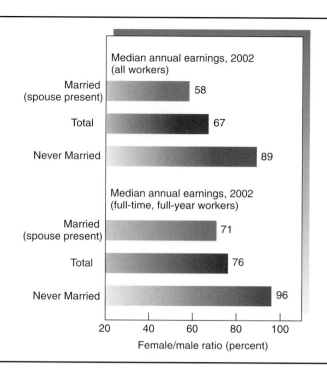

Source: Author calculations from March 2003 Current Population Survey.

As the percentage of women planning for a career rose, their educational choices also changed dramatically. In the early 1970s, women were much less likely than men to study and prepare for engineering, medicine, law, and similar high-paying fields traditionally dominated by men. But, as **Exhibit 3** shows, the percentage of women earning degrees in these fields and others, such as accounting, veterinary medicine, dentistry, medicine, law, architecture, pharmacy, and economics, increased dramatically in the 1970s and 1980s. By the 1990s, parity was achieved in several of these areas. Increasingly, women, like men, are planning for careers in diverse areas, including high-paying professions such as these.

The gender composition of new college graduates also suggests that women are increasingly planning for a career in the marketplace. During the last four decades, the percentage of women as a share of new college graduates has increased dramatically. As Exhibit 4 shows, only 39 percent of those completing an undergraduate degree in 1961 were women. By 1980 that figure had risen to 49 percent, and by 2002 it had jumped to 58 percent. Today, nearly three out of every five graduating seniors are women, compared to less than two out of five four decades ago.

EXHIBIT 3
Women as a Percentage of Persons Earning Selected Professional Degrees, 1970–1971, 1987–1988, and 2000–2001

FIELD OF STUDY	1970–71	1987–88	2000–01
Engineering	0.8	15.3	19.9
Dentistry	1.2	26.1	38.6
Optometry	2.4	34.3	54.5
Law	7.3	40.4	47.3
Veterinary Medicine	7.8	50.0	69.8
Medicine	9.2	33.0	45.3
Accounting	10.1	52.6	60.5
Economics	11.2	32.8	34.1
Architecture	12.0	38.7	35.8
Pharmacy	25.2	59.7	66.1

Source: Commission of Professionals in Science and Technology, *Professional Women and Minorities* (Washington, D.C.: CPST, 1987); and U.S. Department of Education, *Digest of Education Statistics,* 1990 and 2002, (Washington, D.C.: U.S. Government Printing Office).

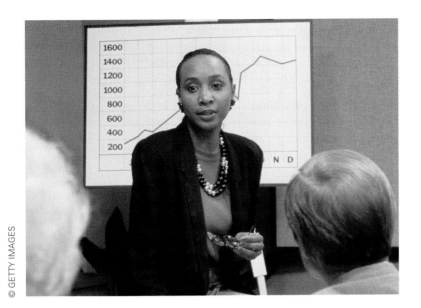

© GETTY IMAGES

During the 1970s, an increasing proportion of women began to plan for full-time, long-term labor force participation. Reflecting this commitment, the career and educational choices of women shifted toward higher-paying professions (see Exhibit 3). As this happened, the earnings of women began to increase steadily relative to men (see Exhibit 1).

The fact that men are now a minority among current college graduates is not particularly surprising. Jobs in fields like construction and heavy manufacturing offer attractive earnings opportunities, but they are also generally physically demanding and require employees to work either outdoors or in a less than ideal environment. Given their greater physical strength and perhaps a stronger preference for outdoor working conditions, men are more likely than women to find these physically demanding jobs attractive and face a higher opportunity cost of forgoing them because they pay well given the skill required. As a result, men will be more likely than women to choose these jobs rather than pursue a college degree.

It is interesting to think about women's career choices in light of societal changes in the United States over the last four decades. In 1962, equal pay legislation was passed requiring employers to pay equal wage rates to men and women doing the same jobs. In 1964, civil rights legislation was passed prohibiting employers from discriminating on the basis of both gender and race. Nonetheless, in the 1960s and 1970s, there was little change in the earnings of women relative to men. However, as the career objectives of women—perhaps pushed along by earlier legislative actions—began to change during the 1970s, the educational choices of men and women started to become more similar (see Exhibit 3).[4] Soon thereafter, the earnings of women began to rise relative to men (see Exhibit 1).

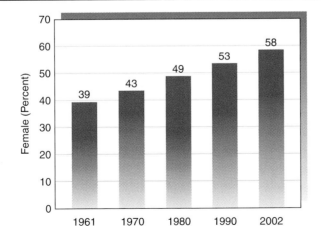

EXHIBIT 4
Women as a Percentage of Persons Graduating from College, 1961–2002

During the last four decades, women have constituted an increasing share of college graduates. Now, almost three out of every five graduating seniors are women. Does this indicate that colleges discriminate against men? What does it mean?

Source: U.S. Department of Education, *Digest of Education Statistics, 2002* (Washington, D.C.: U.S. Government Printing Office, 2003), table 246. The data are for persons graduating with a four-year degree.

IMPLICATIONS FOR THE FUTURE

Clearly, the increased representation of women during the past several decades among both college graduates and those preparing themselves for careers indicates that women are increasingly committed to working in the marketplace. As the current generation of highly trained, well-educated young women acquire experience and move into the prime earning years of life, the upward trend in the F/M earnings ratio can be expected to continue in the years ahead.

---

[4]For additional details on recent changes in the male/female earnings gap, see Francine D. Blau and Lawrence M. Kahn, "Gender Differences in Pay," *Journal of Economic Perspectives,* fall 2000: 75–99; and June O'Neill, "The Gender Gap in Wages, circa 2000," *American Economic Review,* May 2003: 309–14.

! KEY POINTS

▼ The annual earnings of women working full-time are approximately 77 percent of what men's are. Among those who've never married, the female/male earnings ratio is 96 percent.

▼ In addition to employment discrimination, differences in specialization within the family, educational choices, and career goals contribute to the earnings differences between men and women.

▼ As the educational and career choices of women have become more like those of men during the last two decades, the earnings of women have risen relative to those of men. This trend is likely to continue in the future as more and more women prepare for and acquire experience in high-paying fields that have traditionally been dominated by men.

? CRITICAL ANALYSIS QUESTIONS

1. Is employment discrimination the major cause of earnings differences between men and women? Carefully justify your answer.

*2. Between 1960 and 1990, the labor force participation rate of married women approximately doubled. What impact did this influx of married workers into the labor force have on (a) the average years of work experience of women relative to men, (b) the mean hours of work time of women relative to men, and (c) the female/male earnings ratio?

3. Physical strength is important on some jobs. Do you think differences in physical strength between men

and women contribute to earnings differences according to gender? Why or why not? Do they also influence the share of men relative to women who will pursue a college education? Explain.

*4. In 2002, the median earnings of single men working full-time, year-round were only 70 percent of their married counterparts. Does this indicate that employment discrimination existed against single men and in favor of married men?

---

* Asterisk denotes questions for which answers are given in Appendix B.

Do Labor Unions Increase the Wages of Workers?

Focus

- How much of the U.S. workforce is unionized?

- Can unions increase the wages of their members? What makes a union strong? What factors limit the power of a union?

- Can unions increase the wages of all workers?

The rise and decline of private sector unionization were among the more important features of the U.S. labor market during the twentieth century.

—*Barry T. Hirsch and Edward J. Schumacher*[1]

[1]Barry T. Hirsch and Edward J. Schumacher, "Private Sector Union Density and the Wage Premium: Past, Present, and Future," *Journal of Labor Research,* Summer 2001: 487.

A labor union is an organization of employees, usually working in either the same occupation or same industry, who have consented to joint bargaining with employers about their wages, working conditions, grievance procedures, and other elements of employment. The primary objective of a labor union is to improve the welfare of its members. Unions have historically been controversial. Some see them as a necessary shield protecting workers from employer greed. Others charge that unions are monopolies seeking to provide their members with benefits at the expense of other workers, consumers, and economic efficiency. Still others argue that the economic influence of unions—both for good and for bad—is vastly overrated. This feature will consider the impact of unions on the wages of their members and those of other workers. ■

Labor union
A collective organization of employees who bargain as a unit with employers.

UNION MEMBERSHIP AS A SHARE OF THE WORKFORCE

Historically, the proportion of the U.S. labor force belonging to a labor union has fluctuated substantially. In 1910, approximately 10 percent of nonfarm employees belonged to a union. As **Exhibit 1** shows, this figure rose to 18 percent in 1920. In the aftermath of the First World War, union membership declined, falling to 12 percent of nonfarm workers by 1929. Pushed along by favorable legislation adopted during the Great Depression, union membership rose from 13.5 percent of nonfarm employees in 1935 to 30.4 percent in 1945. By 1954, nearly a third of nonfarm workers in the United States were unionized.

Since the mid-1950s, however, union membership has waned. As Exhibit 1 illustrates, it declined slowly as a share of the workforce during the period 1955–1970, and then more rapidly during the last two decades. By 2003, union members constituted only 13.1 percent of nonfarm employees, down from 24 percent in 1979 (and 32 percent in 1954).

EXHIBIT 1
Union Membership as a Share of Nonagricultural Employment

Between 1910 and 1935, union membership fluctuated between 12 percent and 18 percent of nonagricultural employment. During the 1935–1945 period, union membership increased sharply to approximately one-third of the nonfarm workforce. Since the mid-1950s, union membership has declined as a percentage of nonfarm employment, and the decline has been particularly sharp since 1979.

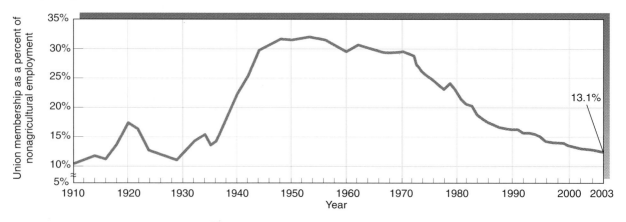

Source: Leo Troy and Neil Sheflin, *Union Source Book: Membership, Structure, Finance, Directory* (West Orange, NJ: Industrial Relations and Information Services, 1985); and Barry T. Hirsch, David A. Macpherson, and Wayne G. Vroman, "Estimates of Union Density by State," *Monthly Labor Review,* July 2001.

Several factors have contributed to this decline. First, much of the recent employment growth has been in sectors where unions have been traditionally weak. Such sectors include relatively small firms (fewer than 100 employees) in service and high-tech industries. Small firms are costly for unions to organize and thus tend to be nonunion. Also, in recent decades, employment has grown rapidly in the less-organized Sunbelt, while stagnating in the more heavily unionized Northeast and upper Midwest. This regional growth pattern has retarded the growth of union membership. Second, competition has eroded union strength in several important industries. Foreign producers have increased their market share in steel, mining, automobiles, and other heavy-manufacturing industries. Employment has therefore been shrinking in these areas of traditional union strength. Deregulation in the transportation and communication industries has further reduced the membership of unions. As these industries have become more competitive, unionized firms have faced increased competition from nonunion producers. Finally, union membership has declined, in part, because workers have reduced their demand for unions over time. Consistent with a falling desire for union representation, opinion surveys reveal that workers believe that unions are less effective in improving their lot now than they were in the past.[2]

To some extent, several of these trends reflect the impact of unions on the wages of their members. Business investment and employment will tend to move toward geographic areas, industries, and classes of firms in which wages are lower *relative to productivity*. Therefore, when unions increase the wages of their members *relative to nonunion workers of similar productivity*, they also retard the growth of employment in unionized sectors.

As **Exhibit 2** shows, there is substantial variation in the incidence of union membership across gender, racial, and occupational groups. Men are more likely than women to belong to a union. In 2003, 14.3 percent of employed men were union members, compared to only 11.4 percent of employed women. The incidence of unionization among blacks (16.5 percent) was higher than for whites (12.5 percent) or Hispanics (10.7 percent). There is substantial variation in unionization according to occupation. Less than 10 percent of the workers in sales, clerical, and service occupations were unionized in 2003. In contrast, about 20 percent of the workers in construction, extraction, production, transportation, and material moving occupations belonged to a union.

The biggest difference in unionization is found when the private and public sectors are compared. Although only 8.2 percent of the private wage and salary workers are unionized, 37.2 percent of the government employees belong to a union. And while the share of the private workforce belonging to a union has been shrinking, unionization has been increasing in the public sector. In fact, the proportion of government employees belonging to a union has more than tripled since 1960.

There is also substantial variation in the rate of unionization among states. **Exhibit 3** indicates the share of wage and salary employees who are unionized for the ten states with the lowest and highest unionization rates. Southern states constitute most of the group of ten with the lowest incidence of union membership. Fewer than 5 percent of employees are unionized in North Carolina, South Carolina, and Arkansas. Heading the list of states with the highest rate of unionization are New York, Hawaii, Alaska, Michigan, and Washington. The rate of unionization tends to be high in the industrial states of the Northeast and upper Midwest. All ten states with the lowest incidence of unionization have **right-to-work laws**, legislation that prohibits collective bargaining agreements requiring a worker to join a union as a condition of employment. In contrast, none of the ten states with the highest rate of union membership has right-to-work legislation.[3]

Right-to-work laws
Laws that prohibit union shops, the requirement that employees must join a union as a condition of employment. Each state has the option to adopt (or reject) right-to-work legislation.

[2]For several recent studies examining the decline in unionism, see "Symposium on the Future of Private Sector Unions in the United States: Part I," *Journal of Labor Research,* spring 2001; and "Symposium on the Future of Private Sector Unions in the United States: Part II," *Journal of Labor Research,* summer 2001.

[3]In 1947, Congress passed the Taft-Hartley Act; Section 14-B allows states to adopt right-to-work laws. Currently, twenty-two states, mostly in the Sunbelt, have such legislation.

EXHIBIT 2
The Incidence of Union Membership by Sex, Race, Occupation, and Sector

The incidence of unionism is higher among (a) men than women and (b) blacks than whites or Hispanics. Technical, sales, clerical, and service workers are far less likely to be unionized than are craft, operator, and repair workers. As a share of the workforce, unionization among government employees is four times that of private-sector workers.

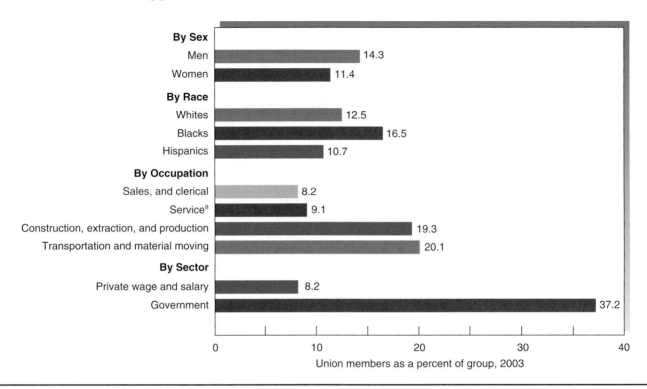

ᵃExcluding protective service workers.
Source: Barry T. Hirsch and David A. Macpherson, *Union Membership and Earnings Data Book: Compilations from the Current Population Survey,* 2004 edition (Washington, D.C.: The Bureau of National Affairs, 2004).

HOW DO UNIONS INFLUENCE WAGES?

The union-management bargaining process often leaves people with the impression that wages are established primarily by the talents of those sitting at the bargaining table. It might appear that market forces play a relatively minor role. However, as both union and management are well aware, market forces provide the setting in which the bargaining is conducted. They often tip the balance of power one way or the other.

High wages increase the firm's costs. When union employers face stiff competition from nonunion producers or foreign competitors, they will be less able to pass along higher wage costs to their customers. Competition in the product market thus limits the bargaining power of a union. Changing market conditions also affect the balance of power between unions and management. When the demand for a product is strong, the demand for labor will be high, and the firm will be much more willing to consent to a significant wage increase. When demand is weak, however, the product inventory level of the firm (or industry) is more likely to be high. Under these circumstances, wage increases will be more difficult to obtain because the firm will be much less vulnerable to a **strike** on the part of the union. (*Note:* When we speak of wage rates, we are referring to the total compensation package, including both fringe benefits and money wages.)

A union can use three basic strategies to increase the wages of its members: supply restrictions, bargaining power, and increased demand for union labor. We will examine each of these in turn.

Strike
An action of unionized employees in which they (1) discontinue working for the employer and (2) take steps to prevent other potential workers from offering their services to the employer.

EXHIBIT 3

States with the Lowest and Highest Incidence of Union Members as a Percentage of All Wage and Salary Employees

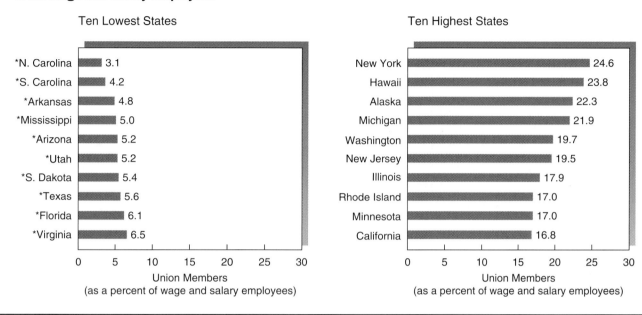

Ten Lowest States

State	
*N. Carolina	3.1
*S. Carolina	4.2
*Arkansas	4.8
*Mississippi	5.0
*Arizona	5.2
*Utah	5.2
*S. Dakota	5.4
*Texas	5.6
*Florida	6.1
*Virginia	6.5

Union Members
(as a percent of wage and salary employees)

Ten Highest States

State	
New York	24.6
Hawaii	23.8
Alaska	22.3
Michigan	21.9
Washington	19.7
New Jersey	19.5
Illinois	17.9
Rhode Island	17.0
Minnesota	17.0
California	16.8

Union Members
(as a percent of wage and salary employees)

*Indicates state has a right-to-work law.
Source: Barry T. Hirsch and David A. Macpherson, *Union Membership and Earnings Data Book: Compilations from the Current Population Survey,* 2004 Edition (Washington, DC: The Bureau of National Affairs, 2004), table 4a.

Supply Restrictions

If a union can successfully reduce the supply of competitive labor, higher wage rates will automatically result. Licensing requirements, long apprenticeship programs, immigration barriers, high initiation fees, refusal to admit new members to the union, and prohibition of nonunion workers from holding jobs are all practices that unions have used to limit the supply of labor to various occupations and jobs. Craft unions, in particular, have been able to restrict the supply of workers in various occupations and boost the wages of their members.

Part (a) of **Exhibit 4** illustrates the effect of supply restrictions on wage rates. Successful exclusionary tactics will reduce the supply, shifting the supply curve from S_0 to S_1. Facing the supply curve S_1, employers will consent to the wage rate W_1. Compared to a free-entry market equilibrium, the wage rate has increased from W_0 to W_1, but employment has declined from E_0 to E_1. At the higher wage rate, W_1, an excess supply of labor, AB, will result. The restrictive practices will prevent this excess supply from undercutting the above-equilibrium wage rate. Because of the exclusionary practices, the union will be able to obtain higher wages for E_1 employees. Other employees willing to accept work even at wage rate W_0 will be forced into other areas of employment.

Bargaining Power

Must unions restrict entry? Why can't they simply use their bargaining power, enhanced by the the threat of a strike, to raise wages? If they have enough economic power, this will be possible. A strike by even a small percentage of vital employees can sometimes halt the flow of production. For example, a work stoppage by airline pilots can force major airlines to cancel their flights. Because the pilots perform an essential function, an airline cannot operate without their services, even though they constitute only 10 percent of all airline employees.

If the union is able to obtain an above-free-entry wage rate, the effect on employment will be similar to a reduction in supply. As part (b) of Exhibit 4 illustrates, employers will hire fewer workers at the higher wage rate obtained through bargaining power. Employment

EXHIBIT 4
Supply Restrictions, Bargaining Power, and Wage Rates

The impact of higher wages obtained by restricting supply is very similar to that obtained through bargaining power. As illustrated in part (a), when union policies reduce the supply of one type of labor, higher wages result. Similarly, when bargaining power is used in order to obtain higher wages (part b), employment declines and an excess supply of labor results.

(a) Supply restriction

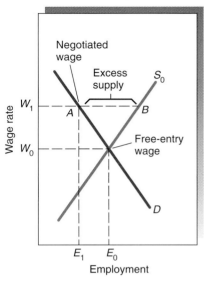

(b) Bargaining power

will decline below the free-entry level (from E_0 to E_1) as a result of the rise in wages. An excess supply of labor, *AB,* will exist, at least temporarily. More employees will seek the high-wage union jobs than employers will choose to hire. Nonwage methods of rationing jobs will become more important.

Increased Demand

Unions can attempt to increase the demand for union labor by appealing to consumers to buy only union-produced goods. Union-sponsored promotional campaigns instructing consumers to "look for the union label" or "buy American" are generally designed to increase the demand for union-made products.

Most people, however, are primarily interested in getting the most for their consumer dollar. Thus, the demand for union labor is usually determined primarily by factors outside the union's direct control, such as the availability of substitute inputs and the demand for the product. Unions, though, can sometimes use their political power to increase the demand for their services. They may be able to induce legislators to pass laws that reduce competition from nonunion and/or foreign workers. In some areas, required inspections on construction projects will be undertaken only if the electrical or plumbing services have been performed by "licensed" (mostly union) craft workers. Unions are often supportive of import restrictions designed to increase the demand for products that they produce. In 2002, the steel workers successfully lobbied for higher tariffs restricting the entry of foreign-produced steel. Garment workers have used their political muscle to raise tariffs and reduce import quotas for clothing produced abroad. Practices that increase the demand for goods and services produced by union labor will increase product prices as well as the wages of unionized workers. Thus, it is not surprising that both management and labor of unionized firms often join together to support various restrictions designed to reduce the competitiveness of goods produced by nonunion employees and foreigners.

WHAT GIVES A UNION STRENGTH?

Not all unions are able to raise the wages of their workers. What are the factors that make a union strong? *Simply stated, if a union is to be strong, the demand for its labor must be inelastic. This will enable the union to command large wage increases while suffering only modest reductions in employment.* In contrast, when the demand for union labor is elastic, a substantial rise in wages will mean a large loss in jobs.

There are four major determinants of the demand elasticity for a factor of production: (1) the availability of substitutes, (2) the elasticity of product demand, (3) the share of the input as a proportion of total cost, and (4) the supply elasticity of substitute inputs.[4] We now turn to the importance of each of these conditions as a determinant of union strength.

Availability of Good Substitute Inputs

When it is difficult to substitute other inputs for unionized labor in the production of a good, the union is strengthened. The demand for union labor is then more inelastic, and employment cuts tend to be small if the union is able to use its bargaining power and the threat of a strike to push wages up. In contrast, when there are good substitutes for union labor, employers will turn to the substitutes and cut back on their use of union labor as it becomes more expensive. Under these circumstances, higher union wages will price the union workers out of the market and lead to a sharp reduction in their employment.

Some employers may be able to automate various production operations—in effect, substituting machines for union workers if their wages increase. When machines are a good substitute for union labor, the demand for union labor will be elastic, which will reduce the union's ability to push wages above the market level.

The best substitute for union labor is generally nonunion labor. Thus, the power of unions to gain more for their members will be directly related to their ability to insulate themselves from competition with nonunion labor. When employers are in a position to substitute nonunion labor for unionized workers, the market power of the union will be substantially reduced.

Within a given plant, a union will negotiate the wages and employment conditions for all workers, both union and nonunion. However, as union wages rise, it may be economical for unionized firms to contract with nonunion firms to handle specific operations or to supply various components used in production. Thus, contracting out often permits employers to indirectly substitute nonunion for union workers. In addition, many large firms in automobile, textile, and other manufacturing industries operate both union and nonunion plants. They may be able to substitute nonunion for union labor by shifting more and more of their production to their nonunion plants, including those located overseas or in right-to-work states where unions are generally weaker.

© BRIAN HAIMER / PHOTO EDIT

The Elasticity of Demand for Products Produced by Unionized Firms

Wages are a component of costs. An increase in the wages of union members will almost surely lead to higher prices for goods produced with union labor. Unless the demand for the good produced by union labor is inelastic, the output and employment of unionized firms will decline if the union pushes up wages (and costs). If a union is going to have a significant effect on wages (without undermining employment opportunities), its workers must produce a good for which the demand is inelastic.

Our analysis implies that a union will be unable to significantly increase wages above the free-market rate when producing a good that competes with similar (or identical) goods produced by nonunion labor or foreign producers. The demand for the good produced by union labor will almost surely be highly elastic when the same product is available from nonunion and foreign producers. Thus, if higher union wages push up costs, the market share of unionized firms will shrink and their employment will fall substantially.

Deregulation of the trucking industry opened the market to nonunion trucking firms. This led to a sharp reduction in the employment of unionized truck drivers (Teamsters) in the early 1980s. Can you explain why?

---

[4]Alfred Marshall, *Principles of Economics,* 8th ed. (New York: Macmillan, 1920).

For example, the strength of the Teamsters union was substantially eroded when deregulation subjected the unionized segment of the trucking industry to much more intense competition from nonunion firms in the early 1980s. With deregulation, nonunion firms with lower labor costs entered the industry. Given their labor-cost advantage, many of the new entrants cut their prices and were able to gain a larger market share. In contrast, the output and employment of unionized trucking firms declined. More than 100,000 Teamsters lost their jobs. Given the sharp fall in the employment of their members, the Teamsters eventually agreed to wage concessions and a lower fringe benefit package.[5]

Unionized Labor as a Share of the Cost of Production

If the unionized labor input constitutes only a small share of the total production cost of a product, demand for that labor typically will be relatively inelastic. For example, because the wages of plumbers and airline pilots constitute only a small share of the total cost of production in the housing and air travel industries, respectively, a doubling or even tripling of their wages would result in only a 1 percent or 2 percent increase in the cost of housing or air travel. A large increase in the price of these inputs would have little impact on the product price, output, and employment. This factor has sometimes been called "the importance of being unimportant" because when the expenditures on a unionized resource are small relative to total cost, the position of the union is strengthened.

The Supply Elasticity of Substitute Inputs

We have just explained that if wage rates in the unionized sector are pushed upward, firms will look for substitute inputs, and the demand for these substitutes will increase. If the supply of these substitutes (like nonunion labor) is inelastic, however, their price will rise sharply in response to an increase in demand. In turn, the higher price will reduce the attractiveness of the substitutes. An inelastic supply of substitutes will thus strengthen the union by making the demand for union labor more inelastic.

THE WAGES OF UNION AND NONUNION EMPLOYEES

The precise effect of unions on the wages of their members is not easy to determine. To isolate the union effect, one must eliminate differences in other factors. Comparisons must be made between union and nonunion workers who have similar productivity (skills) and who are working in similar jobs.

Exhibit 5 provides estimates of the union-nonunion wage differential adjusted for productivity characteristics.[6] The union-nonunion wage differential widened during the 1970s. Union workers received a 22 percent premium compared with similar nonunion workers during the 1977–1978 period, up from an 18 percent premium during 1973–1974. Since the late 1970s, the union-nonunion premium has been shrinking. On average, union workers earned a little less than 20 percent more than similar nonunion employees during the periods 1983–1984 and 1994–1995. By 2002–2003, the union premium had fallen to 14.9 percent.

Our theory indicates that some unions will be much stronger than others—that is, better able to achieve higher wages for their members. In some occupations, the size of the union-nonunion differential will be well above the average, while in other occupations, unions will have little effect on wages. Strong unions, such as those of electricians, plumbers, tool and die makers, metal craft workers, truckers (prior to deregulation), and commercial airline pilots, are able to raise the wages of their members substantially more than the average for all unions. Economists have found that the earnings of unionized mer-

---

[5]A study of the deregulation of the trucking industry found that the wage premium of unionized truckers fell by approximately 30 percent in the regulated sector of the industry. More drivers were employed, but the percentage of drivers who were union members fell from 60 percent prior to deregulation to 25 percent currently. See Barry T. Hirsch and David A. Macpherson, "Earnings and Employment in Trucking: Deregulating a Naturally Competitive Industry," in *Regulatory Reform and Labor Markets,* ed. James Peoples (Dordrecht, Netherlands: Kluwer Publishers, 1998).

[6]Barry T. Hirsch and David A. Macpherson, *Union Membership and Earnings Data Book: Compilations from the Current Population Survey,* 2004 edition (Washington, D.C.: The Bureau of National Affairs, 2004).

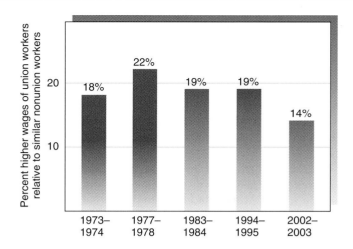

EXHIBIT 5
The Wage Premium of Union Workers, 1973–2003

The wages of union workers have been between 14 and 19 percent higher than those of similar nonunion workers during the last two decades. This union-nonunion wage differential is lower than it was during the late 1970s.

Source: Barry T. Hirsch and David A. Macpherson, *Union Membership and Earnings Data Book: Compilations from the Current Population Survey,* 2004 edition (Washington, D.C.: The Bureau of National Affairs, 2004).

chant seamen, postal workers, and rail, auto, and steel workers, for example, exceed the wages of similarly skilled nonunion workers by 25 percent or more.

Unionization appears to have had the least effect on the earnings of cotton-textile, footwear, furniture, hosiery, clothing, and retail sales workers. In these areas, the power of the union has been considerably limited by the existence of a substantial number of nonunion firms. The demands of union workers in these industries are moderated by the fear that unionized employers will be at a competitive disadvantage relative to nonunion employers in the industry.

Unions, Profitability, and Employment in the Unionized Sector

If unions increase the wages of unionized firms above the competitive market level, the costs of those firms will rise unless (as seems unlikely) there is a corresponding increase in productivity. In the short run, the higher costs will reduce the profitability of the unionized firm. Research indicates that this was true during the 1970s. Barry Hirsch found that as the union-nonunion wage premium increased during the 1970s, the profitability of unionized firms lagged behind the profitability of other firms.[7]

If unions are able to transfer profits from unionized firms to union workers, clearly this is a two-edged sword. For a time, workers enjoy higher wages. In the long run, however, investment will move away from areas of low profitability. Like other mobile resources, capital can be exploited in the short run, but this will not be the case in the long run. Therefore, to the extent that the profits of unionized firms are lower, investment expenditures on fixed structures, research, and development will flow into the nonunion sector and away from unionized firms. As a result, the growth of both productivity and employment will tend to lag in the unionized sector. Investment, production, and employment will all shift away from unionized operations and toward nonunion firms. The larger the wage premium of unionized firms, the greater the incentive will be to shift production toward nonunion operations. The findings of Peter Linneman, Michael Wachter, and William Carter are highly supportive of this view.[8] They found that industries with the largest union wage premiums were precisely the industries with the largest declines in the employment of unionized workers.

---

[7]Barry T. Hirsch, *Labor Unions and the Economic Performance of Firms* (Kalamazoo, Mich: Upjohn Institute for Employment Research, 1991). Also see Barry T. Hirsch, "What Do Unions Do for Economic Performance?" *Journal of Labor Research,* summer 2004: 415–55.

[8]Peter D. Linneman, Michael L. Wachter, and William Carter, "Evaluating the Evidence on Union Employment and Wages," *Industrial and Labor Relations Review,* October 1990. Linneman, Wachter, and Carter estimate that increases in the union wage premium were responsible for up to 64 percent of the decline in the union share of employment during the last two decades.

THE IMPACT OF UNIONS ON THE WAGES OF ALL WORKERS

Although unions have increased the average wages of their members, there is no reason to believe that they have increased the overall average wages for both union and nonunion workers. At first glance, this may seem paradoxical. However, the economic way of thinking enhances our understanding of this issue. As unions push wages up in the unionized sector, employers in this sector will hire fewer workers. Unable to find jobs in the high-wage union sector, some workers will shift to the nonunion sector. This increase in labor supply will depress the wages of nonunion workers. As a result, higher wages for union members do not necessarily mean higher overall average wages for workers.

If labor unions increased the wages of all workers, we would expect labor's share of income to be directly related to union membership. This has not been the case. Even though union membership rose sharply during the 1940s, reached a peak in the 1950s, and has been declining ever since, there was virtually no change in the share of income received by labor (human capital) during this entire period. Similarly, if unions were the primary source of high wages, the real wages of workers would be higher in highly unionized countries, such as Australia, France, and Italy, than they are in the United States. But this is not what we observe.

The real source of high wages is high productivity, not labor unions. Increases in the general level of wages are dependent upon increases in productivity per hour. Income is simply the flip side of output (productivity). Of course, improvements in (1) technology, (2) the machines and tools available to workers (physical capital), (3) worker skills (human capital), and (4) the efficiency of economic organization provide the essential ingredients for higher levels of productivity. ***Higher real wages can be achieved only if the production of goods and services is expanded. Although unions can increase the wages of union workers, they cannot increase the wages of all workers unless their activities increase the total productivity of labor.***

! KEY POINTS

▼ Union membership as a share of nonfarm employees fluctuated substantially during the last century. During the 1910–1935 period, union workers constituted between 12 and 18 percent of nonfarm employees. Unionization increased rapidly during the two decades following 1935, however, soaring to one-third of the workforce in the mid-1950s. Since then, union membership has waned, falling to only 13.1 percent of employees in 2003.

▼ A union can use three basic methods to increase the wages of its members: (1) restrict the supply of competitive inputs, including nonunion workers; (2) apply bargaining power enforced by a strike or threat of one; and (3) increase the demand for the labor service of union members.

▼ If a union is going to increase the wages of its members without experiencing a significant reduction in employment, the demand for union labor must be inelastic. The strength of a union is enhanced if (1) there is an absence of good substitutes for the services of union employees, (2) the demand for the product produced by the union labor is highly inelastic, (3) the union labor input is a small share of the total cost of production, and (4) the supply of available substitutes is highly inelastic. An absence of these conditions weakens the power of the union.

▼ Studies suggest that the wage premium of union members relative to similar nonunion workers rose during the 1970s, but has fallen during the last two decades. In the period 2002–2003, union workers earned about 15 percent more, on average, than similar nonunion workers.

▼ Even though unions have increased the average wage of their members, there is no indication that they have either increased the average wage of all workers or increased the share of national income going to labor (human capital rather than physical capital).

▼ The real wages of workers are a reflection of their productivity rather than the share of the workforce that is unionized.

CRITICAL ANALYSIS QUESTIONS

*1. Suppose that Florida migrant workers are effectively unionized. What will be the effect of the unionization on (a) the price of Florida oranges, (b) the profits of Florida fruit growers in the short run and in the long run, (c) the mechanization of the fruit-picking industry, and (d) the employment of migrant farmworkers?

2. Assume that the primary objective of a union is to raise the wages of its members.
   a. Discuss the conditions that will help the union achieve this objective.
   b. Why might a union be unable to meet its goal?

*3. "If a union is unable to organize all the major firms in an industry, it is unlikely to exert a major effect on the wages of union members." Indicate why you either agree or disagree.

4. Evaluate the following statements.
   a. "An increase in the price of steel will be passed along to consumers in the form of higher prices for automobiles, homes, appliances, and other products made with steel." Do you agree or disagree?
   b. "An increase in the price of craft union labor will be passed along to consumers in the form of higher prices of homes, repair and installation services, appliances, and other products that require craft union labor." Do you agree or disagree?
   c. Are the interests of labor unions in conflict primarily with the interests of union employers? Explain.

*5. "Unions provide the only protection available to working men and women. Without unions, employers would be able to pay workers whatever they wanted." True or false?

*6. A survey of firms in your local labor market reveals that the average hourly wage rate of unionized production workers is $1.50 higher than the average wage rate of nonunion production workers. Does this indicate that unionization increases the wage rates of workers in your area by $1.50? Why or why not?

*7. Even though the wage scale of union members is substantially greater than the minimum wage, unions have generally been at the forefront of those lobbying for higher minimum rates. Why do you think unions fight so hard for a higher minimum wage?

*Asterisk denotes questions for which answers are given in Appendix B.

How Does Government Regulation Affect Your Life?

Sometimes things are not what they seem. And sometimes the illusion is more satisfying than the reality.

—*William R. Allen*[1]

Focus

■ How does regulation influence our lives?

■ How does the regulation of health and safety differ from traditional economic regulation?

■ What does public choice analysis suggest about the motivation for regulatory activities and differences between their stated objectives and actual effects?

■ Who bears the cost of regulation? How do regulatory costs compare to their benefits?

[1]William R. Allen, *The Midnight Economist: Little Essays on Big Truths* (Sun Lakes, Ariz.: Thomas Horton and Daughters, 1997), 133.

A
s we saw in Chapter 5, markets often are not perfectly efficient. When property rights fail to hold resource users, polluters, or consumers fully accountable, ideal efficiency will not result. Government regulation might improve efficiency in such cases. Regulation might also improve economic efficiency in a market that is not fully competitive. However, the actual outcomes of regulation often differ substantially from stated objectives. The regulatory process is complex and people often adjust to it in unforeseen ways. Further, efficiency is not the only reason why people seek to influence the regulatory process. Some people may promote regulations in order to seek advantages at the expense of others. For example, producers might find regulations to be a useful way to increase the costs of rival firms, or even to keep them out of the market altogether. In those cases, regulatory restrictions may reduce economic efficiency. This special topic feature takes a closer look at how regulation affects our lives. ■

REGULATION OF BUSINESS

Regulatory activity in the United States has a large effect on the economy. In 2000, federal regulatory agencies spent $18.9 billion on regulatory activities, and Americans spent far more than that to comply with the regulations, according to a 2001 study by economists Mark Crain and Thomas Hopkins for the U.S. Small Business Administration[2]. They estimated the additional cost of complying with federal regulations at $843 billion in 2000. Crain and Hopkins's estimate excluded taxes paid but included private-sector paperwork required by federal regulations, including record keeping required by tax regulations. Economic regulation accounts for 49 percent of the total, and environmental regulations generated another 23 percent. Crain and Hopkins also cite estimates that the cost of resources devoted to lobbying for and against regulatory change in 2000 was $290 billion, approximately 3 percent of GDP. Regulation can have benefits, but clearly it has substantial costs.

The trend for staffing and spending by federal regulatory agencies has been mostly upward since 1970, except in the early 1980s. From 1970 to 2000, the number of government employees involved in the regulatory process rose 86 percent to nearly 130,000, while regulatory agency budgets grew 203 percent.

Traditional Economic Regulation

Regulation of business activity is not a new development. In 1887, Congress established the Interstate Commerce Commission (ICC), and provided it with the authority to regulate both prices and levels of service in the railroad industry. In 1935, the trucking industry was also brought under the ICC's regulatory jurisdiction. State regulatory commissions began to oversee local delivery of electricity, natural gas, and telephone services as early as 1907. Federal commissions were formed during the 1930s to regulate interstate telephone service, broadcasting, airlines, natural gas pipelines, and other industries. The activities of these commissions focus on **economic regulation**. They usually control the product price or the structure of a particular industry rather than specifying the production processes used by business firms.

Sometimes economic regulation is promoted to protect consumers in markets characterized by large-scale production and natural monopoly. In other instances, it is designed to preserve "orderly competition" in industries with high fixed costs and low variable costs. Railroad transport is an example of the latter. Regardless of their original purpose, regulations that fix prices and restrict entry stifle the competitive process. With time, such regulation often ends up protecting inefficient producers and limiting the options of consumers.

Economic regulation
Regulation of product price or industrial structure, usually imposed on a specific industry. By and large, the production processes used by the regulated firms are unaffected by this type of regulation.

---

[2]W. Mark Crain and Thomas D. Hopkins, *The Impact of Regulatory Costs on Small Firms,* a report for The Office of Advocacy, U.S. Small Business Administration, http://www.sba.gov/advo/research/rs207tot.pdf.

Later, we will see some examples of this. During the late 1970s, high costs generated widespread dissatisfaction with economic regulations in several industries. Major steps toward deregulation in the ground and air transportation industries resulted. Consumers benefited substantially. Airline deregulation, for example, brought more competition and reduced average airline ticket prices by about 40 percent from their levels in 1978, spurring large increases in airline traffic. Regulatory reform continues in other markets.

Recent Health and Safety Regulation of Business

Health and safety regulation
Legislation designed to improve the health, safety, and environmental conditions available to workers and/or consumers. The legislation usually mandates production procedures, minimum standards, and/or product characteristics to be met by producers and employers.

Although there has been some movement toward less economic regulation, **health and safety regulations** have been expanding. In the late 1960s and early 1970s, people had great faith in the ability of government to improve the quality of life. The economy was prospering, and people turned their attention toward policies to reduce health hazards and preserve environmental quality. As the nation became wealthier, reducing air and water pollution and other externalities became more feasible and more desirable. In addition, activist groups with a distrust of market results sought regulation to protect individuals against risks from occupational hazards, as well as risks from newly developed drugs and other consumer products.

Reflecting these forces, the new health and safety regulations have expanded rapidly. The expenditures, employment, and powers of such agencies as the Occupational Safety and Health Administration (OSHA), Consumer Product Safety Commission (CPSC), Food and Drug Administration (FDA), and Environmental Protection Agency (EPA) have grown. Their regulatory authority cuts across industries and involves them more in the actual operation of individual firms. In contrast with economic regulation, the health and safety mandates frequently specify in detail the production methods that the regulated firms and industries must use.

THE POLITICAL ECONOMY OF REGULATION

Regulation involves complex forces, both political and economic. Public-choice analysis provides insights regarding political support of regulation, how the regulatory process works, and why its results are not always what we might hope. Five factors stand out.

1. The demand for regulation often stems from special-interest effects and redistribution goals, not the pursuit of economic efficiency. An individual (or business firm) can seek wealth by producing more value, net of cost. But regulation introduces another possibility. Sellers can gain from regulatory policies that either reduce competition in their market or increase the costs of rival firms. For their part, buyers can gain, at least in the short run, if a law forces producers to supply goods below cost. Regulations allow those most able to influence the political process to increase their personal wealth.

Public choice analysis (see Chapter 6) indicates that special-interest groups, like well-organized, concentrated groups of buyers or sellers, will exert a disproportionate influence on the political process. Furthermore, the regulators themselves often constitute a politically powerful interest group. Regulatory bureaucrats are key figures in the process. Their cooperation is important to those who are regulated. These factors suggest that there will be demand for economic regulation, even if it reduces economic efficiency.

2. Over time, agencies that regulate a specific industry will often adopt the views of the business interests they are supposed to regulate. Once again, the special-interest effect indicates why we should expect this, even if the regulation initially was designed to police the actions of a group of firms. The personal payoff derived by individual consumers (and taxpayers) from a change in regulatory actions is likely to be small. Often they are lulled into thinking that because a regulatory agency exists, the "public interest" is served. In contrast, firms (and employees) in regulated industries are vitally interested in the structure and composition of regulatory commissions and agencies. Favorable actions by these regulators of their industry could result in larger profits, higher-paying jobs, and insulation from the uncertainties of competition. Thus, firms and employee groups, recognizing their potential gain, will invest both economic and political resources to influence the actions of regulatory agencies. In return for their organized support, political officials will have a strong incentive to favor their position when setting policy and making appointments to regulatory agencies.

3. The glare of publicity can elicit strong, but uninformed, voter sentiment, especially when it comes to public health, safety, and the environment. But this sentiment can lead to regulations that ignore trade-offs. The rational ignorance effect indicates that voters have little incentive to learn policy details or how likely results may differ from the announced intent of a proposed policy, when each voice or vote is not likely to affect the policy outcome. The result is often a tendency to be swayed by emotional arguments without checking closely to see whether the policy they favor will actually work as they intend. For example, public enthusiasm for recycling is so great that city governments often adopt high-cost regulations like mandatory curbside recycling of household wastes to reduce environmental harms from taking the materials to a landfill. Yet mandatory recycling has a number of strikes against it. First, curbside recycling requires an additional set of trucks that must circulate through city streets picking up the recyclables. They increase pollution and congestion, use additional energy, and place financial burdens on the taxpayer. Second, recycling is a manufacturing process like any other, and it emits some pollutants, as all manufacturing does. And, third, although recycling may reduce the amount of waste that goes into landfills (or in some places, the amount that is incinerated), the nation's landfill capacity is large and growing, not declining. These facts[3] are well-known to specialists, but not to the public. Indeed, the public's convictions about this topic are so strong, but its knowledge so superficial, that even bringing up these arguments can lead to rancor and resentment. Politicians are unlikely to challenge the conventional "wisdom" of voters in such a situation.

4. Regulation is inflexible and slow to react to dynamic change. Changing market conditions often make regulatory procedures obsolete. For example, the advent of trucking vastly changed the competitiveness of the ground transportation industry, which previously was dominated by railroad interests. Yet price, entry, and route regulations for both trucking firms and railroads continued for years after competitive forces eliminated the monopoly power of railroad firms. Similarly, city building codes that may have been appropriate when they were adopted have become obsolete and now retard the introduction of new, more efficient materials and procedures. In many cities, regulatory procedures have prevented builders from introducing such cost-saving materials as plastic pipes, preconstructed septic tanks, and prefabricated housing units. Other local restraints are also common. Existing firms prefer to avoid costly change or new competitors, and some regulations are used primarily to stifle competition. (See the accompanying feature on regulation of limousine services.) In any case, change is costly, so it is understandable that politicians often wait until there is a strong constituency pushing for change before taking political action to change an outmoded regulation.

5. When approval has to be obtained from regulators, it will be difficult to introduce new products, including those that might potentially save lives. The activities and management of a regulatory agency, the Food and Drug Administration, for example, will come under severe scrutiny if it inadvertently permits a dangerous product on the market. The victims of such a product are specific persons and the product's harm can often be seen. In contrast, regulators face few problems if they keep a highly beneficial product—including one that would save lives—off the market. Who will know that a specific drug or other product—one that most people have never heard about because the

---

[3]See Daniel K. Benjamin, "Eight Great Myths of Recycling," *PERC Policy Series,* PS-28, September 2003, http://www.perc.org/publications/policyseries/recycling.php.

APPLICATIONS IN ECONOMICS

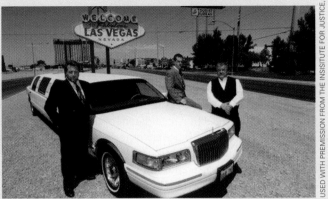

Limousines and Restraints on Entry*

Occupational and business licensing by state and local governments often restricts entry and reduces competition. John West, an auto mechanic in Las Vegas, felt the brunt of such regulation when he tried to start a limousine business. His experience shows how existing companies, with help from a state agency, often use regulation to keep out competition.

Las Vegas, one of the fastest growing cities in the country and well-known for its entertainment complexes, would be an excellent location for a limousine business, West decided a few years ago. He had worked on limousines and thought he could improve life for himself and his family by starting his own limousine service. But he almost went bankrupt in an effort to obtain permission from the state of Nevada.

To operate a limousine service in Nevada, a person must obtain a "certificate of public convenience and necessity" from the Transportation Services Authority (TSA). It permits existing limousine companies to intervene in the approval process. The TSA commissioners can turn down applicants if the commissioners think that a new entrant will have an "unreasonable and adverse effect" on the present limousine business. In effect, the existing companies can operate as a cartel and pressure the TSA to keep out competition. In John West's case, the TSA delayed action on his application for a year, while the existing limousine companies ("intervenors") demanded extensive information from him, including lists of prospective clients. Then the TSA abruptly and arbitrarily rejected West's application. Of course, the primary effect of such regulations is less competition and higher fares.

In 1998, the Institute for Justice, a private nonprofit organization that defends economic freedom, supported West and two other would-be limousine drivers in challenging the practices of the TSA in court. On May 16, 2001, Judge Jon Parraguirre of Nevada's Clark County ruled that the TSA had violated the rights of the applicants. The judge said, "The right to earn a living in one's chosen profession is a liberty interest protected by the due process clauses of both the U.S. and Nevada constitutions."

The cartel didn't give up, however. Very quickly, owners of existing limousine companies went to the Nevada legis-

Rey Vinole, John West, and Ed Wheeler challenged regulations limiting entry into the Las Vegas limousine market. Their legal victory changed the rules to open up entry.

lature and campaigned for a law limiting entry to the limousine business. The law would have restricted the number of licenses for limousine service and would have divided these licenses among existing operators. However, the proposed law was not passed.

The Institute for Justice assists people in many occupations who face licensing restraints. In 1999, it litigated the case of JoAnne Cornwell, a provider of African hairbraiding services. Regulations of the state of California had prohibited her from opening a salon because she is not a licensed cosmetologist. Obtaining a California cosmetology license would require 1,600 hours of training, none of which actually teaches skills relevant to her specialty. A federal court struck down the California law.

While certain licensing regulations have been successfully challenged in some states, occupational and business licensing appears to be on the increase. Economist Morris M. Kleiner says that more than 800 occupations are licensed in at least one state, ranging from fortune-tellers in Maryland to rainmakers in Arizona, and the percentage of workers covered by licensing is increasing. Regulation of entry is clearly an avenue for cartels to reduce potential competition by excluding competitors.

---

*This feature is based on http://www.ij.org/cases/economic/ and Morris M. Kleiner, "Occupational Licensing," *Journal of Economic Perspectives* 14, no. 4: 189–202.

tests are still being conducted—*might* have saved an individual's life? Yet if a drug can save 1,000 lives per year, then an extra year of delay in bringing it to the market will have the effect of causing the deaths of 1,000 people. However, the cost to the regulatory agency of the former error is much greater than that of the latter. As a result, regulatory agencies will predictably apply tests that take too long and are too restrictive from the viewpoint of economic efficiency and consumer welfare.

THE COSTS OF REGULATION

Regulators create benefits by ordering producers to do things such as emit less pollution, make workplaces accessible to handicapped workers, and reduce noise levels in the workplace. Of course, as they do so, costs are incurred. The major cost of health and safety regulation is felt in the form of higher production costs and thus higher prices. And, of course, the process of regulation itself is costly: employment and operating costs of regulatory agencies must be met, which means higher taxes. When costs are borne by others, and mostly "off budget," there is little incentive to regulate in the most economical manner. The costs can be surprisingly high. The U.S. EPA has estimated that when contractors are hired to clean up Superfund hazardous waste sites, the indirect costs—costs to EPA of such things as formulating and enforcing the rules—amount to more than $500 (measured in 2004 dollars) for every hour spent by a worker involved in the cleanup. These figures—essentially overhead—are in addition to all payments to the firms and their employees actually planning and undertaking the work at each site.[4] For this and other reasons, the Superfund program is an example of inefficient regulation, open to severe criticism of its effectiveness. (See the accompanying feature, "Superfund: A Highly Inefficient Cleanup Program.")

The primary cost of health and safety regulation, however, comes in the form of higher operating costs for firms striving to meet the new standards. In effect, these higher costs are like a tax. As **Exhibit 1** illustrates, the higher cost shifts the supply curve to the left for a good affected by the regulation. Higher prices and a decline in the output of the product result. Who pays the cost? As with any tax, the burden is shared by buyers and sellers according to the elasticity of supply and demand. When consumers have more options available to substitute for the taxed good, their demand is more elastic and they will pay a smaller portion of the tax. In Exhibit 1, the new price ($P_2 + t$) will be closer to P_1 when demand is more elastic. On the other hand, sellers will pay a smaller portion when the supply curve is more elastic, indicating that resource suppliers in the industry have reasonably attractive options to move their resources to other industries. The burden imposed on sellers includes reduced profits for investors and lower wages (and employment) for workers in the industry. In the short run, when resources employed in the industry have few alternative uses, the short-run supply is likely to be inelastic. In the long run, of course, capital and labor are quite mobile among users, resulting in a supply curve that is more elastic.

Sometimes the opportunity cost of health and safety regulation is exceedingly difficult to calculate. For example, former FDA official Henry I. Miller reports that FDA testing requirements and approval delays helped increase the time from synthesis of a new drug to

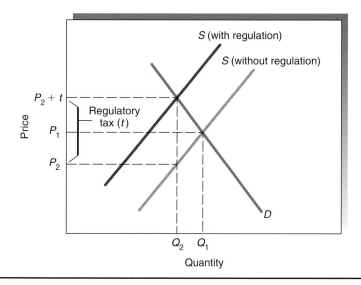

EXHIBIT 1
The Regulation "Tax"

Regulation that requires businesses to adopt more costly production techniques is similar to a tax. If the regulation increases per-unit costs by t, the supply curve shifts upward by that amount. Higher prices and a smaller output result.

[4]These figures are from an EPA statement in the *Federal Register* 57, no. 152 (August 6, 1992).

APPLICATIONS IN ECONOMICS

Superfund: A Highly Inefficient Cleanup Program*

A classic case of wasteful regulation is the EPA's Superfund program, which was enacted in 1980 to clean up hazardous waste sites. Reducing human health risks was the major selling point for the legislation. Yet little in the way of human health benefits could be demonstrated by 1996, when researchers James T. Hamilton and W. Kip Viscusi wrote *Calculating Risks?* (Cambridge, Mass.: MIT Press, 1999). They analyzed the Superfund program in general and 150 Superfund hazardous waste sites in particular. Hamilton and Viscusi's conclusions included a number of discouraging findings:

- Most supposed Superfund "risks" do not pose a threat to human health now, and they will do so in the future only if people violate commonsense precautions and actually inhabit contaminated sites and disregard known risks there.

- Even if the risks of exposure did occur, there is less than a 1 percent chance that the risks are as great as EPA estimates, due to extreme assumptions made by the EPA about the dangers.

- Cancer risk is the main concern at Superfund sites, but cleanups are expected to avert only 0.1 case of cancer at the majority of sites. Without any cleanup, only 10 of the 150 sites studied were estimated to have one or more expected cases.

- Average cleanup cost per site in the study was $26 million (in 1993 dollars).

- Replacing extreme EPA assumptions about each risk component with more reasonable averages for each component brought the estimated median cost per cancer case averted to more than $7 billion; at eighty-seven of the ninety-six sites having the necessary data available, the cost per cancer case averted (only some of which would mean a life saved) was more than $100 million.

- Other federal programs commonly consider a life saved to be worth about $5 million. Diverting expenditures from most Superfund sites to other sites or other risk-reduction missions could save many more lives or save the same number of lives at far less cost.

Why do we observe such apparent inefficiencies in environmental programs? EPA site managers have little reason to consider that forcing people to spend more money at Superfund sites means spending less on other important goals for society. As Supreme Court Justice Stephen Breyer has put it, each agency decision maker has "tunnel vision."

In Breyer's words, tunnel vision is a "classic administrative disease" that arises "when an agency so organizes or subdivides its tasks that each employee's individual conscientious performance effectively carries single-minded pursuit of a single goal too far, to the point where it brings about more harm than good." Breyer calls this trying to achieve "the last 10 percent." Thus agency and program officials will try to push beyond the efficient point of cleanup. Indeed, Hamilton and Viscusi estimate that 95 percent of Superfund expenditures are directed at the last 0.5 percent of the risk. In other words, 99.5 percent of the benefits could be gained with the proper allocation of only 5 percent of the resources actually used. The inefficiency of Superfund cleanups clearly demonstrates the importance of encouraging decision makers to consider opportunity cost and to think at the margin as they set the standards at Superfund sites. It also demonstrates the cost we pay when our political process fails to use economic thinking.

---

*This feature is based on Richard L. Stroup, "Politics or Sound Policy?" *Regulation* 24, no. 2: 50–51; and Stephen Breyer, *Breaking the Vicious Circle: Toward Effective Risk Regulation* (Cambridge, Mass.: Harvard University Press, 1993), 10–11.

FDA-approved marketing from 8.1 years in 1970 to 15.2 years in 2000. Further, he says "the United States's $800 million tab for each drug approved is by far the most expensive in the world."[5] In addition to these costs, there are two other major opportunity costs of this regulation: (1) some drugs that have a limited profit potential are never developed because of the expensive tests and delays, and (2) people who could have been helped by a drug—had it been approved—have to forgo it for several years. Deaths often result from these delays.

Health and safety regulations often stem from a problem of lack of information. Many people are unaware of the precise effects of drugs, air pollution, or workplace hazards. Even when the information is available to experts, consumers may never receive it because

---

[5]Henry I. Miller, "Why It Takes a Village (To Afford a Prescription)," Policy Matters 02-51, November 2002, http://www.aei.brookings.org/policy/page.php?id=120.

When the FDA announces the approval of a new life-saving drug after several years of testing, the public can be better assured of its safety and effectiveness. However, this assurance involves costs. This expensive and time-consuming approval process means both higher drug prices and additional pain, suffering, and even loss of life for those who might have been helped by a more rapid approval of the drug.

of the cost of communicating information, particularly highly technical information. A case can be made, therefore, that we should let the experts decide which drugs, how much air pollution, and what forms of workplace safety should be sought.

Ironically, however, choosing regulation to protect citizens who do not understand the danger introduces a related problem: when regulators make the decisions, most of the incentive for individuals to learn about comparative risks is removed. Yet these same individuals, now with less incentive to learn about the risks being regulated, ultimately, as voters, control the political process and influence the regulatory agency's decisions.

The same lack of information that generates much of the demand for health and safety regulation also makes it difficult to evaluate the effectiveness of each regulatory activity. Current health and safety regulations in the United States produce high costs as well as large benefits, but these costs and benefits can be only crudely estimated. When Robert Hahn and John Hird estimated the sum of the costs and benefits from health and safety regulations, they could not state with confidence whether the benefits exceeded the costs. Hahn and Hird concluded that the annual costs of these regulations in the late 1980s may have exceeded the benefits by as much as $65 billion, or that, alternatively, benefits may have exceeded costs by as much as $104 billion. They suggest that the benefits of health and safety regulation are probably larger than the costs, but only by a small amount. More recently, Hahn and other respected economists from three Washington, D.C., research organizations jointly published a critique of federal regulations. It stated that a "substantial share" of the regulations are "ineffective."[6]

Case Study: The Costs and Benefits of Fuel Conservation Regulation[7]

Fear of global warming—which some scientists think could be caused by rising levels of carbon dioxide in the air—combined with a concern about the possibility of declining oil availability in the future and possible disruptions in that supply, have led to louder calls for regulations requiring more fuel-efficient cars. Legislation that would require automakers to boost substantially their average mileage per gallon (mpg) of gasoline is repeatedly put before Congress. Would tighter regulations mandating greater fuel economy reduce fuel usage significantly? And, if so, at what cost? A look at the history of fuel efficiency regulation is informative. Responding to sharp worldwide increases in petroleum prices,

[6]Robert W. Hahn and John A. Hird, "The Costs and Benefits of Regulation: Review and Synthesis," *Yale Journal on Regulation* 8 (winter 1991): 233–78; and Robert W. Crandall et al., *An Agenda for Federal Regulatory Reform* (Washington, D.C.: AEI and Brookings, 1997).

[7]This case study was written with the assistance of Jane S. Shaw, Senior Fellow at the Property and Environment Research Center, Bozeman, Montana.

Congress began mandating fuel economy standards in 1975, although the actual effects of the legislation did not occur until the mid-1980s. The experience with this legislation provides insights with regard to both the expected impact of tighter standards and possible unintended consequences that often accompany regulation.

The initial Corporate Average Fuel Economy (CAFE) standards were intended to conserve energy and make the United States less dependent on foreign oil. However, price ceilings on gasoline prices were in place then, and if Congress had simply allowed gasoline prices to rise, people would have adjusted in ways best suited to their personal circumstances. Some would simply have driven less; others would have saved on gasoline by buying smaller cars or having more tune-ups. Some living far from their workplaces might have bought larger cars and carpooled; others might have moved to places where they would have a shorter commute.

Indeed, well before the CAFE standards had an impact, people began to respond to higher gasoline prices by purchasing fuel-efficient cars. According to the 1986 *Economic Report of the President,* average fuel economy in the United States increased by 43 percent between 1973 and 1979, as consumers responded to higher fuel prices. By the time the fuel efficiency standards influenced the design of cars, which probably occurred with the 1986 model year, much fuel economy had already been achieved, and gasoline prices were going down.

By that time, fuel prices had fallen and some consumers wanted larger cars, but the CAFE standards forced automakers to offer smaller cars. Although car companies could make some reductions in fuel usage by such steps as redesigning transmissions or fuel injection systems, they had to reduce vehicle weight to meet the standards. Robert W. Crandall of the Brookings Institution and John Graham of the Harvard School of Public Health estimated that model year 1989 cars were on average 500 pounds lighter than they would have been without the CAFE standards.[8]

A serious problem with lighter cars is that they are less safe than larger cars. A study published in 2000 by the National Academy of Sciences found that downsizing cars "probably resulted in an additional 1,300 to 2,600 traffic fatalities in 1993."[9]

There have been other unintended consequences of CAFE standards. To sell enough small cars to raise the fuel economy average, domestic automakers reduced small car prices and raised prices for large cars. Buying decisions were distorted, and consumers paid more on balance for their cars. Because Congress required the car companies to calculate average fuel economy separately for their domestic-manufactured cars and their imports, companies could not use their smaller, more fuel-efficient imports to bring down their domestic fleets' average. This encouraged small-car production in the United States, even though it might have been cheaper to produce these cars overseas. At the same time, Ford moved some of its large-car production out of the country in order to more easily meet the overall standards. Predictably, the CAFE regulations also led to major lobbying efforts by the auto industry firms, moving additional creative skills and energy away from productive activity.

Did the CAFE standards effectively reduce fuel use? Technology has improved, but fuel prices fell after they were deregulated in 1981. Consumers chose to use the new technology to enhance the performance, size, and safety of the cars more than fuel economy. From 1981 to 2003, the EPA says that while fuel economy rose slightly (20.5 to 20.8 miles per gallon on average), horsepower rose from 102 to 197 on average, and vehicle weight from 3,201 to 3,974 pounds. With new, larger cars more expensive as a result of the standards, some people kept their old cars longer, increasing gas consumption (and pollution). At the same time, the lower prices of small cars probably increased the total number of cars purchased. More cars on the road meant greater fuel consumption, and so did the fact that the marginal cost of driving in a small, higher-mileage car was lower than it would have been; and smaller car sizes led people to share fewer rides. Robert A. Leone of Boston University estimates that a 2 or 3 cent tax on gasoline beginning in 1984

---

[8]Robert W. Crandall and John D. Graham, "The Effect of Fuel Economy Standards on Automobile Safety," *Journal of Law and Economics* 32, no. 1 (April 1989): 97–118.

[9]Two of the thirteen members of the committee dissented with this finding on page 111 of the report, *Effectiveness and Impact of Corporate Average Fuel Economy (CAFE) Standards* (Washington, D.C.: National Academy Press, 2002), http://www.nap.edu/books/0309076013/html/.

would have saved as much fuel as the CAFE standards, and at a substantially lower cost to society.

The experience with CAFE highlights both the inflexibility of regulation and the unforeseen and unwanted side effects that often accompany it. It is not easy to mandate a specific outcome without triggering adverse consequences. As a result, regulation is generally less effective than it might first appear.

FUTURE DIRECTIONS FOR REGULATORY POLICY

Most people concede that regulation, both economic and social, is like a two-edged sword. Regulations can be beneficial, but typically they are costly and can even be counterproductive. Some regulations are far more costly than others, even when their main goals are similar. **Exhibit 2** demonstrates this point. A group of well-known risk researchers analyzed several hundred federal regulations that save lives, issued by several agencies. The researchers estimated the cost per year of life saved by each regulation and averaged the cost for each agency. Some of these cost estimates for various agencies are presented here. The researchers estimated that the median cost of Federal Aviation Administration (FAA) regulations *per life year* saved was $23,000. In contrast, that of the Environmental Protection Agency was $7,600,000, or 330 times the cost of a life year saved by regulations of the FAA. Clearly, if some resources had been shifted from EPA regulatory activities to those of the FAA, more lives could have been saved for the same cost.

The cost also varied widely among the rules within each agency. The researchers suggest that if the least costly methods to save lives were chosen, the same expenditures could save tens of thousands of additional lives per year, or alternatively, the same number of lives could be saved while expenditures could be reduced by tens of billions of dollars per year.

Regulation would significantly improve if the regulations that generate large gains relative to their costs could be adopted while those that generate few, if any, benefits could be modified or eliminated. However, it is not easy to do this, especially because regulations are the business of many agencies. The leaders of each agency believe strongly in the narrow agency mission, and can usually generate vocal public support from citizens who like the idea of uncompromising regulations to achieve the narrow goals they care most about. Predictably, each agency's leadership will lobby for larger budgets and greater authority. Still, while there is strong support for the continuation and expansion of social regulatory activities, the voices favoring regulatory reform, and even deregulation, are growing louder and bringing more evidence to the table to support their position. Over time, we can expect that improved empirical evidence of the effectiveness of specific regulatory policies will continue to emerge and, in some cases, will reduce the cost and improve the effectiveness of regulatory activities.

Agency	Median Cost per Life Year Saved
Federal Aviation Administration	$23,000
Consumer Product Safety Commission	$68,000
National Highway Transportation Safety Administration	$78,000
Occupational Safety and Health Administration	$88,000
Environmental Protection Agency	$7,600,000

EXHIBIT 2
Regulations and Differences in the Cost of Saving Lives

Source: T. O. Tengs et al., "Five Hundred Life-Saving Interventions and Their Cost-Effectiveness," *Risk Analysis* 15 (1995): 369–90.

▼ Traditional economic regulation has generally sought to fix prices and/or influence entry into specific industries. During the 1970s, widespread dissatisfaction with regulation of this type led to significant deregulation in the trucking and airline industries. This deregulation resulted in new entry, intense competition, and discount prices.

▼ Regulation involves a complex set of economic and political forces. Public choice analysis provides some insight regarding how the regulatory process can be expected to work. Five key points emerge:

1. The demand for regulation often stems from special-interest and redistribution considerations.

2. With the passage of time, agencies that regulate a specific industry are likely to adopt the views of the interest groups they are supposed to regulate.

3. The glare of publicity can bring out strong but uninformed voter sentiment, especially in the case of public health, safety, and environment regulations, leading to regulations that ignore trade-offs.

4. Regulation is inflexible; it will be slow to adjust to changing conditions.

5. Approval of a dangerous product will cause more problems for a regulatory agency than a failure to approve a highly beneficial product. As a result, agencies approving new products (for example, medical drugs) will generally apply tests that are too restrictive from the viewpoint of consumer welfare.

▼ While economic regulation has been relaxed in recent years, health and safety regulation has expanded rapidly. Health and safety regulation seeks to provide a cleaner, safer, healthier environment for workers and consumers. Pursuit of this objective is costly, bringing about higher product prices and higher taxes, as well as unintended safety problems. Since the costs, and particularly the benefits, are often difficult to measure and evaluate, the efficiency of social regulatory programs is both controversial and the subject of much current research.

? CRITICAL ANALYSIS QUESTIONS

*1. Legislation mandating stronger side and door panels to protect drivers and passengers against side collisions presumably makes cars both safer and more expensive. The same could be said for air bags. Are laws like these necessary for auto safety? Do they save lives and make auto travel safer? Why or why not?

2. "Without legal safety requirements, products such as lawn mowers would be unsafe." Evaluate this statement.

*3. Will health and safety legislation mandating workplace and product safety standards reduce the profitability of the regulated firms? Who bears the cost and who gains the benefits of such legislation?

4. "Regulations on the introduction of new drugs should be strengthened. Fewer people would die if more research were required prior to the introduction of new drugs. Only an economist could possibly disagree. Sure, it would cost more, but saving even one life would be worth more than whatever it costs." Evaluate this statement.

*5. "People cannot be expected to make good decisions on their own regarding auto safety. Only experts know enough to make such decisions." Evaluate this statement.

6. "Safety regulation is not an economic question. Where lives and health are at stake, economics has no place." Evaluate this statement.

*7. "If we force increased safety measures in the workplace by regulation, business may bear the cost in the short run, but capital will receive the market rate of return in the long run." Evaluate this statement, and explain your reasoning.

*Asterisk denotes questions for which answers are given in Appendix B.

Resource Management: How Property Rights and Markets Replace Conflict with Cooperation

Focus

- Should there be exploration for oil in the Arctic National Wildlife Refuge?

- How much timber should be harvested from our forests?

- In the absence of strict regulations, will private choices focus only on profit at the expense of environmental quality?

- Will markets cause us to run out of natural resources like oil and minerals?

- How can we protect the environment against threats posed by new technologies and economic growth?

If Fido digs up your flower bed, your recourse is to find Fido's owner and hold him accountable for the damages. . . . Where property rights [for animals] are lacking, problems are inevitable because costs are imposed on unwilling recipients.

—Terry L. Anderson and
Donald R. Leal[1]

In nearly every case, environmental problems stem from insecure, unenforceable, or nonexistent property rights.

—Jane S. Shaw[2]

[1]Terry L. Anderson and Donald R. Leal, *Free Market Environmentalism* (New York: Palgrave, 2001), 27.
[2]Jane S. Shaw, "Private Property Rights: Hope for the Environment," *Liberty* 2, no. 2 (November 1988), 55.

ewspaper headlines are full of conflicts over natural resource and environmental issues like those suggested above. People compete for limited environmental resources just like they do in the rest of an economy. In Chapter 1, we noted that competition was an outgrowth of scarcity. In Chapter 3, we learned that when resources are privately owned and individuals seek what they want in markets, competition leads to cooperation rather than conflict. Nonetheless, even though markets promote prosperity and the efficient use of resources, many people have a hard time seeing these positive effects. Indeed, some people believe markets are the very source of most environmental problems. After reading the first three chapters of this book, however, you should have no trouble recognizing that markets work well for environmental matters—as long as property rights are enforced and owners are held accountable when the rights of others are violated as a result of how they use their property.

The fact that industrialized nations like the United States have grown less polluted as they have become richer and more productive bolsters the argument that markets benefit the environment. The U.S. Environmental Protection Agency, for example, recently reported that the levels of all six major air pollutants fell dramatically in the United States since 1970. As **Exhibit 1** shows, they declined an average of 51 percent, even though GDP went up by 176 percent.[3] This success shows that industrialization and environmental quality are not mutually exclusive goals. It shows how entrepreneurs—guided by Adam Smith's invisible hand—find ways to improve the quality of the environment and profit, too. ▪

PROPERTY RIGHTS: THE KEY TO ENVIRONMENTAL QUALITY

Sometimes property rights are lacking or hard to enforce. This can, indeed, have a negative effect on the environment. The next special topic will focus on how governments respond to environmental threats and opportunities. But first let us review the functions of property rights, this time in the context of environmental concerns.

Why Private Ownership Is Important

The private ownership of natural resources, together with the organization of production provided by markets, encourages resource conservation, improves the quality of the environment, and reduces conflict by turning competition into cooperation:

1. When resources are privately owned, owners have an incentive to share their access with others who are willing to pay. The price these people will pay for the resources gives buyers and sellers an incentive to conserve them. Because the owners face the opportunity cost of alternative ways in which their resources might be used, they will be more sensitive to the desires of others. In turn, this sensitivity will tend to promote cooperation among potential resource users and reduce the likelihood of conflict between them.

The case of the Rainey Preserve in Louisiana is a vivid illustration of this point.[4] The Rainey Preserve provides nesting grounds for snowy egrets and other rare birds. It is owned by the National Audubon Society. When the potential of its energy reserves (mainly natural gas) became known in the 1940s, the society chose, after much negotiation, to allow drilling for natural gas and oil there from the 1940s until economically recoverable deposits ran out in 1999.

Although the society and the drilling companies had different goals, they were able to cooperate because strong property rights guaranteed that neither could force the other to

---

[3]Environmental Protection Agency, *Clean Air Status Report: Three Decades of Progress* (Washington, D.C.: September 22, 2004), http://www.epa.gov/adminweb/leavitt/acidrain922.pdf.

[4]For the full story of the Rainey Preserve, see Pamela Snyder and Jane S. Shaw, "PC Drilling in a Wildlife Refuge," *Wall Street Journal,* September 7, 1995; and John Flicker, "Don't Desecrate the Arctic Refuge," *Wall Street Journal,* September 18, 1995.

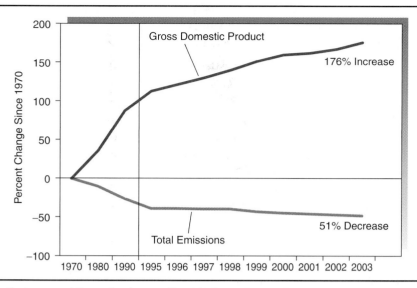

Source: Environmental Protection Agency, *Clean Air Status Report: Three Decades of Progress* (Washington, D.C.: September 22, 2004), http://www.epa.gov/adminweb/leavitt/acidrain922.pdf.

EXHIBIT 1
Economic Prosperity in the Face of Declining Emissions

Economic progress and a clean environment are not mutually exclusive goals. As the figure shows, pollution in the United States in the last quarter-century fell, even though the GDP grew dramatically.

act in ways outside its interests. Audubon experts and the biologists for the oil companies worked out methods of drilling and production that could be conducted without harming the snowy egrets and other birds and animals. The companies had to meet the society's strict stipulations; they were not allowed to drill during nesting season, for example. The stipulations were costly to the oil companies, so the society agreed to charge the companies much less to drill than it might have. However, by doing so, the society protected the natural habitat.

The cooperation between the National Audubon Society and the oil companies benefited both organizations. Revenues for the society totaled more than $25 million over the years, helping it pursue its mission, both at Rainey and elsewhere. The producers of natural gas earned revenues that would have been lost if they had not met the Audubon Society's terms.

It is interesting to compare the cooperation that resulted in the Rainey Preserve, which is privately owned by the National Audubon Society, with the constant conflict resulting from the discovery of oil and other energy resources in the government-owned Arctic National Wildlife Refuge in Alaska. The society has vigorously opposed oil drilling in the refuge, arguing that drilling in even a small portion of the preserve would be an environmental disaster.

Why is the National Audubon Society so hostile toward drilling on government land when it permitted drilling on its own land? The difference is that the government, not the society, is the owner of the refuge. In contrast with the situation in the Rainey Preserve, failing to develop the energy resources of the Arctic National Wildlife Refuge will not impose a cost on the Audubon Society or other nonowners. Thus, the group opposes development there, and the issue becomes one of conflict rather than cooperation. For the record, officials of the National Audubon Society argue that the Arctic Refuge, with its cold climate and fragile tundra, may be less suited to drilling than the lush semitropical environment of the Rainey Preserve. This is debatable, but, in any case, we can be reasonably sure that if Audubon or another private party owned the refuge, constructive negotiations would be going on, with a serious search for mutually beneficial solutions.

© GEORGE D. LEPP/CORBIS

The National Audubon Society preserves wildlife habitat at the Paul J. Rainey Preserve in Louisiana. Working with oil company biologists and insisting on preservation above all, Audubon approved putting technologies into place that preserved the habitat while natural gas drilling ensued. The drilling added more than $25 million to the society's treasury, enhancing its ability to maintain the preserve as well as other wildlife habitats.

2. A resource owner has a strong incentive to exercise good stewardship. Private ownership of property provides owners with the incentive to take good care of things. If the resource is well cared for, it will be more valuable and add more to the personal wealth of its owner. If the owner does not take good care of the resource, he or she will personally bear the cost of that negligence as the property deteriorates or is polluted. Without private ownership, the direct personal incentive to exercise good care is generally absent.

The case of Ravenna Park, a private park initially developed by Mr. and Mrs. R. W. Beck, provides an interesting example of how ownership affects stewardship.[5] In 1887, the Becks bought land covered with large fir trees, some as big as 400 feet tall and 20 feet in diameter, just north of the city of Seattle. They built a pavilion for concerts, made trails and benches, and installed totem poles. They charged visitors 25 cents a day (about $4.00 in today's dollars) to use the park. On a good day, 8,000 to 10,000 people would pay to enter.

The Becks' Ravenna Park thrived, but as Seattle's population grew, local sentiment favored an expansion of public parks. In 1911, after condemnation proceedings, the city bought Ravenna Park. Soon thereafter, the giant trees began to disappear. The Seattle Federation of Women's Clubs confronted the city's park superintendent, who admitted that one of the best-known large trees had been cut down because it was a "threat to public safety." While he conceded that the tree had been sold for firewood, he said that the sale had occurred only to cover the cost of cutting it. A subsequent investigation showed that many other trees had also been cut down, but the park's board promised that the cutting would stop.

By 1925, however, the big trees were all gone. Whether the park superintendent profited from their cutting or whether the trees were cut down and stolen while he looked the other way has not been settled to this day. But the contrast is clear. While the Becks were the owners and in control, the incentive to prevent such damage was stronger. Public servants did not have the same incentive, however. Their personal wealth was not harmed (and may have been enhanced) when the trees were harvested.

3. A resource owner has legal rights against anyone who would harm the resource. A private owner of a farm, a forest, or other resource has more than just the incentive to preserve the value of that resource. Private property rights also give the owner access to the courts to defend it from invasion or harm that would violate the owner's rights. Much environmental damage is prevented by the existence of this legal right. The private owner of a forest, farm, or water supply company will not sit idly by if someone is cutting down the trees or infringing the owner's property right with hazardous pollutants.

In the United States, Canada, and Great Britain, courts have, for centuries, provided a way to stop people who, by polluting, are injuring others and violating their rights. Courts can issue an injunction to stop the polluting and/or require that the owner be compensated for the harm done. Such court suits are sometimes called private law but, more generally, common law. Common law refers to the body of legal rules and traditions that have been developed over time through court decisions. Each decision helps settle the details of the law, putting everyone on notice of what is expected. This helps reduce uncertainty and the need for future legal action.

Property Rights and Environmental Protection in the Nineteenth Century[6]

It is easy to find examples of common law protections against pollution, even going back more than 100 years. In the late nineteenth century, the Carmichael family owned a 45-acre farm in Texas, with a stream running through it, bordering the state of Arkansas. The city of Texarkana, Arkansas, built a sewage system that deposited sewage in the river that ran past the front of the Carmichaels' home. They sued the city in federal court on the grounds that their property rights had been violated because the family and their livestock no longer were able to use the river and may have been exposed to disease.

The court awarded damages to the Carmichaels and granted an injunction against the city, forcing it to stop the harmful dumping. Even though the city of Texarkana was

---

[5]Terry L. Anderson and Jane S. Shaw, "Grass Isn't Always Greener in a Public Park," *Wall Street Journal,* May 28, 1985.

[6]See Roger E. Meiners and Bruce Yandle, *The Common Law: How It Protects the Environment*, PERC Policy Series PS-13 (Bozeman, Mont: PERC, May 1998), 4–10.

operating properly under state law in building a sewer system, it could not foul the water used by the Carmichaels. Indeed, the judge noted, "I have failed to find a single well-considered case where the American courts have not granted relief under circumstances such as are alleged in this bill against the city."[7] Even in the 1800s, property owners were able to protect their property from those who would damage it.

Another example of natural resource preservation achieved via the protection of property rights can be seen in England and Scotland. In contrast to the United States, fishing rights in England and Scotland are privately owned by the landowners whose property lies along the streams. The rights to fish can be sold or leased, even though the water itself is not privately owned.

Moreover, the owners of the fishing rights can take polluters to court if the pollution harms their fishing rights. After an association of anglers won a celebrated case in the early 1950s against a government-owned utility and a private firm, it has only rarely been necessary to go to court to stop pollution that damages fishing. Once established by precedent, such rights seldom need to be defended in court unless in a particular case the circumstances are new and different from previous cases. When the courts are doing their job to protect property rights, owners can often protect natural resources more effectively than do extensive bureaucratic controls and regulations. And owners have every incentive to do just that.

U.S. Property Rights and Environmental Protection in the Twentieth Century[8]

The common law tradition that protected the Carmichaels in the nineteenth century still protects us today. However, in many cases, common law rules have been superseded by government regulations. The Carmichaels sued a city polluting farther upstream in a different state, and won. In 1972, the city of Milwaukee tried to sue the state of Illinois for polluting its water. But the passage of the Clean Water Act in 1972 led a judge to dismiss the case because water pollution disputes fell under the jurisdiction of federal agencies as a result.[9]

When resources are not privately owned, no single person will benefit by filing a lawsuit against polluters, even when the source of the pollution is clear. In the United States, fish in a river might be damaged by pollution, but neither they nor the fishing rights are owned by anyone whose personal wealth depends on their protection. By and large, Americans must rely on political and bureaucratic authorities to protect their streams. In England, by contrast, where fishing rights on a stream are privately owned, the owners jealously guard the quality of the water.

4. Actions today that affect the value of a privately owned resource are immediately brought to bear on the resource owner.

Property rights provide long-term incentives for maximizing the value of a resource, even for owners with a short-term outlook. If erosion of a tract of land reduces its future productivity, the land's value falls today, reducing the owner's wealth immediately. When a potential buyer can see that there will be fewer future services from the resource, the buyer will not be willing to pay as much for that resource. Thus, the value of the asset declines immediately. In the same way, investments made now to enhance the value of the resource will increase the market value of the property and thus the owner's wealth as soon as potential buyers can see that there will be an increase in the future value of the resource. (See the accompanying feature, "Looking Ahead at the Flying D Ranch.")

Even if the owner of the resource is a corporation, actions affecting future productivity, taken today by the corporation's top managers, will affect the firm's current value. For example, if a decision today is expected to reduce the firm's future profits, the price of the firm's stock will fall quickly as the market responds to the decision. So although they might want to put short-term profits first (say, to maximize their bonuses)—rather than the long-term interests of stockholders—managers must be equally concerned about changes in the value of the corporation's stock. Moreover, because they are hired and fired by the firm's board of directors, which is normally dominated by large shareholders, they cannot afford

---

[7]*Carmichael v. City of Texarkana*, 94 F. 561, 574 (W.D. Ark. 1899).

[8]This and certain other sections of this special topic are adapted from Richard L. Stroup, *Eco-nomics*, (Washington, D.C.: Cato Institute, 2003), 22–23.

[9]Bruce Yandle, *Common Sense and Common Law for the Environment*, (Lanham, Md.: Rowman & Littlefield, 1997), 109.

to implement shortsighted policies that adversely affect the wealth of these influential shareholders. The scrutiny by investors is a direct result of the investors' property rights. As a result, corporate managers have an incentive to use the firm's resources wisely.

HOW PROPERTY RIGHTS AFFECT ENVIRONMENTAL QUALITY AND LIFE EXPECTANCY

Recent studies show that in countries where property rights receive better protection, people are healthier and live longer due to better environmental conditions. For example, economist Seth Norton found that, in countries where property rights are well protected, 93 percent of citizens, on average, have access to safe drinking water. In nations with weak property rights, only 60 percent of the population have safe drinking water. Similarly, in nations with stronger property rights, 93 percent of the people have access to sewage treatment, compared to only 48 percent in countries with weakly protected rights.[10] Life expectancy averages seventy years in nations where property rights are strong, but only fifty years in nations where they are weak.

One reason for these differences is the fact that property rights promote prosperity and growth. Certainly, wealthier nations have a greater ability to protect the health, safety, and environmental conditions of their citizens. But this is not the entire story. Norton also conducted a study looking solely at poor nations (countries with per capita income less than $5,000 in 1985).[11] He found that, even among poor nations, countries with relatively stronger property rights protection see 95 percent of their population live to age forty, whereas, in nations with weaker protection of rights, only 74 percent of the people live to age forty. In rich nations or poor, property rights make an important difference. Property rights force people to be accountable. They also foster trade, improve the environmental qualities that people value, and promote resource conservation.

MARKETS, ECONOMIZING, AND RESOURCE CONSERVATION

Technological advances have allowed us to extract more value from resources, which, in turn, has increased the demand for them. Some people worry that this higher demand for natural resources will lead to their depletion. However, other new technologies routinely

---

APPLICATIONS IN ECONOMICS

Looking Ahead at the Flying D Ranch

As television broadcasting magnate Ted Turner neared the end of a successful and innovative career, he began buying ranches in the western and southwestern United States. On the Flying D Ranch, south of Bozeman, Montana, for example, he decided not to raise traditional livestock but instead to manage the ranch largely to foster bison and elk. To do this, he decided to increase the number of trophy animals that could be hunted on the ranch over time. In 1999, he was able to charge elk hunters as much as $9,500 per

hunt. For additional fees, hunters can also kill a deer and bison during their hunts.

In all, the ranch is earning roughly $300,000 in additional revenue per year. This added revenue stream has increased the value of the ranch. Turner has been able to manage the ranch in a way that is pleasing to hunters and that encourages the proliferation of other species of wildlife in addition to elk, deer, and bison.[1]

---

[1]Terry L. Anderson and Donald R. Leal, *Enviro-Capitalists: Doing Good While Doing Well* (Lanham, Md.: Rowman & Littlefield, 1997), 75–77.

---

[10]Seth W. Norton, "Property Rights, the Environment, and Economic Well-Being," in *Who Owns the Environment?* Peter J. Hill and Roger E. Meiners, eds. (Lanham, Md.: Rowman & Littlefield, 1998), 37–54.

[11]Seth W. Norton, "Poverty, Property Rights and Human Well-Being: A Cross-National Study," *Cato Journal* 18, no. 2 (fall 1998) 233–45.

provide new ways to economize on the use of many resources, reducing the demand for them. On balance, in modern economies, resource economizing has persistently won out over increasing demand. Economist Robert McTeer found, for example, that shifts to more efficient plants, equipment, homes, and vehicles in the United States have cut the energy-to-GDP ratio by more than 50 percent since the early 1980s. A case in point: in the airline industry, the average fuel per passenger mile has fallen by about 25 percent.[12] In other words, more value is being produced with less energy.

Conservation of land, too, occurs when farmers and private landowners operate in conjunction with markets. Today people have more leisure time than they have had in decades past. Many of them want to spend some of that time in forests, mountains, and other wild lands where they can enjoy camping, hunting, fishing, hiking, and bird watching. Landowners have responded to this changing demand and profited from it. (See the accompanying feature, "Managing Forests for Nature, Too.")

Similarly, landowners have the freedom and the incentives to adopt new technologies that will make their land more productive—with positive environmental benefits. New technologies, for example, have helped farmers increase their per-acre yields immensely. As a result, much less land is needed today for agricultural purposes, and land that at one time would have been needed for agriculture can be put to other uses. **Exhibit 2** illustrates this point. If farmers had, on average, continued with the technology present in 1910, the United States would require more than four times as much agricultural land now to feed today's population. Far less land would be left for other uses, including the natural habitat that improves environmental quality. In fact, when we look at nations today where farmland is not privately owned and people have no incentive to maximize its productivity, we

© KEVIN FLEMING/CORBIS

Ted Turner converted the Flying D Ranch in Montana from a cattle to a bison ranch and managed the land for natural wildlife, greatly increasing the elk herd there. Guided hunts add an estimated $300,000 to ranch revenues each year, substantially increasing the value of the ranch.

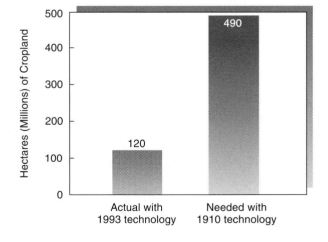

EXHIBIT 2
How Technology Has Lowered the Need for Cropland in the United States

Private property rights motivated U.S. farmers to adopt many technological advancements during the twentieth century. Without the incentives and the subsequent technology adoption, producing the food the world needed in 1993 would have required more than four times the amount of cropland, and much less land would have been available for other uses, including natural habitats for wildlife and recreation for humans.

Source: Indur Goklany, "Factors Affecting Environmental Impacts: The Effect of Technology on Long-term Trends in Cropland, Air Pollution and Water-related Diseases," *Ambio* 25, no. 8 (December 1996), 498.

---

[12]Robert D. McTeer, "The Gas in Our Tanks," *Wall Street Journal,* May 11, 2004.

APPLICATIONS IN ECONOMICS

Managing Forests for Nature, Too

Tom Bourland faced a challenge. As a wildlife biologist at International Paper Company, one of the world's largest private forest owners, Bourland wanted the forests to teem with birds and wild animals such as deer, bears, beaver, and woodpeckers. He didn't want his company simply to produce wood and pulp. Experimental efforts by the company proved that it was possible to enrich the forests in Louisiana and east Texas with wildlife, but doing so was costly. How could he make improving the wildlife habitat an integral part of International Paper's goals?

Bourland found a way. He knew that hunters, fishers, and campers love the woods as well as he does and would pay for the opportunity to use them, especially if the woods were natural—full of wild animals, diverse vegetation, and clean-running streams. So he began a program to improve and market the recreational opportunities of the land. Revenues from recreational access to International Paper's land rose from a quarter of a million dollars in 1983 to $5.5 million in 1998. The rising revenues from his program gave Bourland the clout he needed in the company's boardroom to further enhance the habitat. His success illustrates the adage one hears in conservation circles: "If it pays, it stays."[1]

---

[1]For more about Bourland's project, see Terry L. Anderson and Donald R. Leal, *Enviro-Capitalists: Doing Good While Doing Well* (Lanham, Md.: Rowman & Littlefield, 1997), 4–8.

---

see that food output per acre is much less than it is where farmland is privately owned. Lower productivity per acre means that more land must be devoted to farming and less to other uses, including natural habitats and wildlife.

Resource Markets Allow Changes to Be Made More Quickly and Smoothly

We saw earlier that to satisfy consumers, firms must be able to innovate. However, what makes good sense for consumers at one time and place might not make sense at all in another time or place. In market economies, decision-makers who quickly recognize the benefits of changing what they produce, or how they produce it, can reap profits—at least until others see the opportunity and change their own output to better match the new circumstances. Market prices provide the information and incentive to guide these changes. In contrast, when buyers do not have access to alternatives, as in countries with heavy government control, change is less likely. This failure to innovate can have negative environmental effects.

Competition and the innovation that it fosters are so integral to a market system that it may be hard to imagine a system without innovation. However, the planned economies of Eastern Europe were, by and large, such a system. The Trabant automobile, produced in East Germany between 1959 and 1989, illustrates what happens without innovation. In those years, central planners ran East Germany, and private property rights were largely missing from the economic scene. Managers had little incentive to innovate and little freedom to act. Production plans were dictated by central planners, and managers were mainly rewarded for meeting quantitative output goals.

It wasn't until after the Berlin wall came down in 1989 that many Americans saw the Trabant. An American auto magazine, *Car and Driver,* brought the Trabant over to have a look at it. On the positive side, the editors reported that the car provided basic transportation and was easy to fix (similar things were said about the Model T Fords in the early twentieth century). But its top speed was sixty-six miles per hour, it was noisy, and the editors said it had "no discernible handling." It spewed "a plume of oil and gray exhaust smoke" and didn't have a gas gauge. In fact, the Trabant's exhaust was so noxious that the Environmental Protection Agency refused to let the *Car and Driver* staff drive it on public streets.[13]

---

[13]Rich Ceppos, "The Car Who Came in from the Cold," *Car and Driver,* December 1990, 89–97.

The Trabant was backward, dirty, and inefficient because its design was the same as when it was first manufactured in 1959. The last model was introduced in 1964, and, because market pressures were absent, there had been no technological change or innovation related to it. In contrast, the Volkswagen—the "people's car" of West Germany—was marketed worldwide and continually updated. It had been rather primitive in 1959 also, but, by 1989, the VW was far more efficient and caused little pollution. Pollution control laws were a factor in reducing emissions, but fuel economy and performance alone would have brought some of the reduction. The safety, comfort, performance, and pollution control of the VW changed constantly for the better while the Trabant stagnated.

© STEFAN SAUER/DPA LANDOV

The Trabant was produced in East Germany from 1959 to 1989, almost without innovation or improvement. In contrast, in competitive market economies like that of West Germany, even cars like the Volkswagen saw substantial improvements, including large reductions in polluting emissions, during the same time period.

Differing Product Choices Reflect Local Differences in Resource Prices

Proper resource conservation differs not only over time but sometimes also over space. An excellent solution to a problem in one situation might not work well in a different setting. Consider, for example, cloth versus disposable diapers: Cloth diapers can be used again and again, but they must be washed and dried each time. This requires hot water and detergent, disposal of waste water, and perhaps heat to dry the diapers. And if a diaper service is used, transportation to and from the customer also can generate pollution. Disposable diapers are used only once. Each new diaper is produced by a manufacturing process that requires new cellulose fiber and plastic liners, and disposal requires transportation and space in a landfill.

Are cloth diapers or disposable diapers better for the environment? In a place where water and the energy to heat it are scarce but landfill space is plentiful—the rural West, for example—disposable diapers may be better for the environment. But where landfill space is scarcer and more expensive, but water is abundant—urban areas in the East, for example—cloth diapers may be environmentally better.

If those who make and those who buy diapers pay the full cost of their resource use, market prices will automatically signal the relative resource costs for the specific situation. For example, higher water prices signal scarce supply, making water conservation more valuable in the West. This encourages the use of disposable diapers. Price signals encourage users to pick the product that, in their specific circumstance, imposes less total cost—including environmental cost—on the society.[14]

Strong Property Rights Are Highly Productive, but They Can Be Costly, Too

Private property rights benefit both the individual and society, but not everything is privately owned. One reason is that sometimes defining and defending property rights is extremely expensive. Thus, at times, a resource isn't valuable enough for anyone to make the effort to establish private property rights to it. At other times, even when rights are established, protecting them against certain threats—pollution from many sources simultaneously, for example—can be difficult without the help of government regulation. In the next and final special topic, we will look at some of those problems. We will see that political solutions to environmental problems have promise but are also imperfect.

[14]Mark Duda and Jane S. Shaw, *A New Environmental Tool? Assessing Life Cycle Assessment,* Contemporary Issues Series 81 (St. Louis, Mo.: Center for the Study of American Business, August 1996).

KEY POINTS

▼ Property rights, when properly defined, defended, and tradable, encourage people to cooperate to develop and conserve environmental resources as well as earn profits.

▼ Private ownership encourages entrepreneurial changes and new technologies that, on balance, have led to natural resource conservation.

▼ Countries with stronger property rights have fewer environmental problems, and their citizens have longer life expectancies. Countries with weaker property rights have more environmental problems, and their citizens have shorter life spans.

CRITICAL ANALYSIS QUESTIONS

*1. "Private ownership of a natural resource, such as a lake in the woods, results in personal, selfish enjoyment for just one owner. Society would be better off if such a resource were available for everyone to enjoy." Evaluate this statement.

*2. "Corporations should not be allowed to own forests. Corporate managers are just too shortsighted. Their philosophy is to make a profit now, regardless of the future consequences. For example, they will be inclined to cut down trees that have been growing thirty years to get revenue now, even though another twenty years' growth would yield a very high rate of return. The long-run health of our forests is too important to entrust them to this sort of management." Evaluate this statement.

3. "If more nations become as rich as the United States, the pressures placed on natural systems will quickly become intolerable. Our world cannot sustain such increases in consumption." What evidence can you cite for or against this view?

*4. "People want clean air and clean water in their rivers, but they cannot buy them in a market. Government regulation is the only way to provide them." Evaluate this statement.

5. "Without tighter regulation, economic growth will inevitably cause us to be buried in our own waste and choked by our own pollution." What does the history of the last century tell us about this concern? How can the economic way of thinking help us avoid this pessimistic possibility?

---

* Asterisk denotes questions for which answers are given in Appendix B.

Difficult Environmental Cases and the Role of Government

Focus

- Why do people seek governmental regulation to improve the environment in a market economy?

- What can economics tell us about an effective policy on global warming and climate change? Will economic growth help with this problem or make matters worse?

- How can the government utilize market-like policies to reduce the cost of environmental policy?

- How does the Endangered Species Act cause problems for efforts to save listed species?

- Why does federal ownership of our national parks pose problems for park managers serving the public? Are there ways to lessen those problems?

"A little richer is a lot safer."

—Aaron Wildavsky[1]

[1]Aaron Wildavsky, "Riskless Society," *The Concise Encyclopedia of Economics,* Library of Economics and Liberty, retrieved December 3, 2004, from the World Wide Web, http://www.econlib.org/library/Enc/RisklessSociety.html.

P rivate property rights can promote prosperity and cooperation and at the same time protect the environment, but do they protect the environment sufficiently? In recent years, especially since the late 1960s in the United States, people have increasingly turned to the government to achieve additional environmental improvements. Sometimes people turned to government because property rights failed to hold polluters accountable for the costs they were imposing on others. In these "external cost" cases, government may be able to improve accountability and protect rights more efficiently by regulation.

In other instances, people want the government to force others to help pay for desired environmental amenities (for example, green spaces, hiking trails, or wilderness lands). In this special topic we will look more closely at the possibilities for achieving environmental goals through governmental control of pollution and of natural resources, as well as the problems that arise from government action in these areas. ▨

GOVERNMENT REGULATION AND THE ENVIRONMENT

As we noted in the previous special topic, courts guided by common law can protect individuals and their property against invasions by others, including polluters. However, it is sometimes difficult—if not impossible—to define, establish, and protect property rights. This is particularly true when there is either a large number of polluters or a large number of persons harmed by the emissions, or both. In these large-number cases, high transaction costs undermine the effectiveness of the property rights–market exchange approach. For example, consider the air quality in a large city such as Los Angeles or Denver. Millions of people are harmed when pollutants are put into the air. But millions of people also contribute to the pollution as they drive their cars. Markets will be unable to handle large-number cases like this efficiently. More direct regulations may generate a superior outcome.

Although government regulation is an alternative method of protecting the environment, as we discussed in the special topic on regulation, there are also problems with the regulatory approach. It has a number of deficiencies. First, government regulation is often sought precisely because the harms are uncertain and the source of the problem cannot be demonstrated, so relief from the courts is difficult to obtain. But when the harms are uncertain, so are the benefits of reducing them. Second, by its very nature, regulation overrides or ignores the information and incentives provided by market signals. Accountability of regulators for the costs they impose then is lacking, as accountability for polluters is missing in the market sector when secure and tradable property rights are not in place. The tunnel vision of regulators is not properly constrained by readily observable costs. Third, regulation allows special interests to use political power to achieve objectives that may be quite different from the environmental goals originally announced. A look at the global warming issue illustrates all of these problems and the uncertainties that they generate.

CLIMATE CHANGE AND THE UNCERTAINTY PROBLEM

The headline-grabbing problem of global warming generates a legitimate reason for considering governmental intervention. Yet the global nature of the problem and the scientific uncertainties associated with it put into question the potential net benefits from government regulation. It is a complex and increasingly costly problem that is worth examining in some detail.

Fuels such as coal, oil, and natural gas emit carbon dioxide when they burn. In contrast with harmful pollutants, these emissions cause no direct harm. Carbon dioxide is not a pollutant in the normal sense, but rather a gas that is an essential food for plants, and thus is necessary to life on this planet. It also allows plants to use less water and be more resistant to drought. Yet, as the world has become more industrialized, more carbon dioxide has been building up in the atmosphere. Although carbon dioxide represents a tiny part of the atmosphere, it is a "greenhouse" gas. In fact, there are two reasons to call it that. Not only is it purchased in compressed gas form by owners of greenhouses as a fertilizer for their plants (because it spurs their growth), it also, along with other gases such as methane and nitrous oxide, acts as an invisible blanket that traps some heat on earth that would otherwise be radiated into space.

Higher levels of carbon dioxide may be contributing to the 1 degree Fahrenheit of warming the earth has experienced over the past century. Further increases might cause the earth to warm more dramatically, changing weather patterns and perhaps leading to rising sea levels around the globe. If the "worst-case scenarios" suggested by some scientists were to materialize, certain communities would face flooding of their lands and serious ecological disruption. Therefore, some scientists and many environmentalists support an international treaty known as the Kyoto Protocol. The treaty requires industrial nations to control the total amount of emissions of carbon dioxide within their borders to no more than they produced in 1990.

Our knowledge of regulation should make us wary of this protocol. To begin with, a lot of critical information is still missing. Scientists don't know what causes major changes in the earth's temperature. Global temperatures changed significantly long before the Industrial Revolution began to pump up fossil-fuel consumption. Two periods in the past 2,000 years stand out: the Medieval Optimum (a warm period from about 700 AD to 1200) and the Little Ice Age (a period of temperatures significantly colder, on average, than today, from about 1560 to 1850). Thus, the earth has experienced both warming and cooling trends in the past, and the current warming trend may well be unrelated to the emissions of carbon dioxide and other greenhouse gases into the atmosphere.

Most predictions of significant temperature increases are based on giant computer models of the earth's atmosphere, but these models are full of information gaps. The effects of clouds and water vapor in warming or cooling the earth and the role of oceans in absorbing carbon dioxide are especially important. The models assume that the effects of water vapor (which is, in fact, a far more important greenhouse gas than carbon dioxide) and clouds are positive and will increase the warming effect. But it is quite possible that the water vapor won't increase to the extent the models assume, and that clouds, on balance, will do little to add to warming or might even be a force for cooling.

We cannot even be sure whether a warmer world would, on the whole, be better or worse. Some people—particularly those distant from the equator—would gain. The warming would be greater in colder climates, closer to the north and south poles than to the equator, and would be greater at night than in the daytime. The warmer climate may well

Coal-fired power generators put large amounts of carbon dioxide into the air. Carbon dioxide is a greenhouse gas that may be warming the earth significantly.

lengthen the growing season, and the higher levels of carbon dioxide may enhance productivity in the agricultural sector. On the other hand, certain diseases might become more prevalent, but economist Thomas Gale Moore has shown that warmer climates are generally more healthy on balance.[2]

The opportunity cost of attempting to slow the warming under the Kyoto Protocol would be extremely high—much economic growth would be reduced—and the expected effect on world temperatures extremely small. Economist William Nordhaus has estimated[3] that accepting the Kyoto Protocol would cost the United States alone about $125 billion each year for the next century. Yet these expenditures will have almost no effect, partly because developing countries will be allowed to increase their carbon emissions without limit. Richard Lindzen, a prominent climatologist at Massachusetts Institute of Technology, says: "Kyoto, itself, will have no discernible impact on global warming regardless of what one believes about climate change."[4]

Government regulation tends to encourage special interests, and Kyoto is no exception. The billions of dollars going into global warming research give scientists an incentive to maintain climate change as a public issue. As Lindzen puts it, "Alarm is felt to be essential to the maintenance of funding." Scientists, however, are certainly not the only special-interest group in support of the Kyoto treaty. A voluntary program for American business has some firms holding claims to greenhouse gas reductions that could be worth millions if Kyoto is ratified by the U.S. and if an enforced "cap-and-trade" scheme of the sort discussed below were to be implemented. This prospect has made those firms strong advocates of Kyoto and other such measures.

Global Warming Risks: The Adaptation Strategy

The estimated costs, the special-interest involvement, and the scientific uncertainties leave many economists unwilling to recommend strong regulations to reduce emissions of carbon dioxide. Some have proposed, instead, an approach called adaptation. See the accompanying feature, "Fighting the Risks of Global Warming: Mitigation or Adaptation?"

Instead of accepting the Kyoto Protocol, which would greatly reduce national income, nations might be better off if they deal with the uncertainties of global warming through growth and development. As the late Aaron Wildavsky implied in the quotation at the opening of this special topic, wealthier people can better handle all sorts of risks. They purchase better health care, enjoy better nutrition, drive safer cars, and pay for routine safety measures of all sorts. A more prosperous country is more resilient when faced with major threats, whether from a new disease, an earthquake, an asteroid striking the earth, or global warming. For example, a rich citizenry might respond to a potential flooding problem due to global warming with dikes like those that protect lowlands in the Netherlands. A poor society has fewer options and less resilience. And richer people are far more willing and able to make sacrifices to gain greater environmental quality of all sorts. Economic development accomplishes all these goals on behalf of health and environmental safety.

MARKET-LIKE SCHEMES: REDUCING THE COST OF SPECIFIC REGULATIONS

Policy makers who want to take action now on global warming recognize that any actions will impose severe costs. Some emitters of carbon dioxide, however, can cut back on their emissions at much lower costs than others. To take advantage of this fact, some have proposed market-like incentive schemes, such as a tax on the carbon content of fuels. They

---

[2]Thomas Gale Moore, *Climate of Fear* (Washington, D.C.: Cato Institute, 1998).

[3]William D. Nordhaus, "Global Warming Economics," *Science* 294 (November 9, 2001): 1283–84.

[4]Richard S. Lindzen, "Climate Alarm—Where Does It Come From?" Speech to the Houston Forum, September 9, 2004 (verified by Richard Lindzen in personal correspondence with Richard Stroup on November 26, 2004).

APPLICATIONS IN ECONOMICS

Fighting the Risks of Global Warming: Mitigation or Adaptation?

Given the possibility of serious harm from global warming, what should be done? The Kyoto Protocol attempts *mitigation*—reducing carbon emissions in order to keep global temperatures from rising as much as they otherwise would. In contrast, *adaptation* means making changes as actual problems—such as coastal flooding or an increase in malaria—begin to occur.

Climate change researcher Indur Goklany suggests that perhaps the latter is wiser. In a study published in *Energy & Environment*, Goklany examines four risk factors—hunger,

malaria, water shortages, and coastal flooding—that could be worsened if global temperatures increase significantly. He concludes that taking action now to address these already serious problems, independently from global warming, would cost far less than trying to reduce temperature increases, and the payoff in improved human lives would long precede the impact of the Kyoto Protocol. Economic logic suggests that a larger payoff obtained sooner for a smaller cost is the better bet.

Source: Indur Goklany, "Relative Contributions of Global Warming to Various Climate Sensitive Risks, and Their Implications for Adaptation and Mitigation," *Energy & Environment,* 2003.

have been influenced by the apparent success of some "market-based mechanisms" in reducing traditional pollutants at relatively low cost. Such mechanisms have some of the incentive effects of markets, but they also have severe limits.

There are two major "market-like" approaches to controlling pollution.

1. Pollution charges or taxes.   Under this approach, the government levies fees on polluters. Ideally for efficiency, these charges would just equal the costs of pollution borne by others downwind or downstream. Facing a pollution tax, a polluter has an incentive to reduce the contaminants it is putting into the air or water or soil. As emissions decrease, the payment of the pollution tax by the company will also decrease. The incentive to reduce emissions continues only to the point where the cost of cutting back further would exceed the cost savings from the reduced emission charges. At that point, the company will pay tax on the remaining emissions.

This process will result in efficient emission controls only if the emission charges properly represent the marginal cost of the pollutant to those harmed. But it is difficult or impossible for the regulator to know this cost without market trades to provide information. In a true property-rights situation, would-be polluters could negotiate with those who would be harmed by the pollution and decide whether to stop the pollution or compensate those harmed. In the nineteenth century, for example, Wisconsin paper mills bought land for miles downstream from their mills so that the effluent from their manufacturing would not harm the property and violates the rights of others.

Only a few pollution charges have been adopted in the United States. Companies oppose these fees because they are an added cost of doing business. Governments are not happy with them, either. Such taxes are proposed to replace other taxes, and if the emission charge does reduce pollution, the government will get less revenue over time. Reluctance on the part of governments to impose them has held back their implementation.

2. Emission standards and tradable permits.   Under this approach, a pollution-control authority (such as the Environmental Protection Agency) sets the total amount of emissions (a "cap") allowed in an area. But then it assigns (or perhaps sells) permits allowing emission of that amount of pollution. These permits are then tradable.

Such a program, sometimes called "cap-and-trade," gives each emitter an incentive to reduce or even eliminate emissions. If a company can cheaply reduce emissions below its allowed level, it can sell emissions permits ("credits") to other companies that face higher costs and thus can save money by buying permits from low-cost reducers. The total reduction in pollution will not change, but the overall costs of meeting the standard may be much lower. The result is efficiency in attaining specified emission levels.

The best-known example in the United States is the "cap-and-trade" program established in the Clean Air Act Amendments of 1990. This act authorized the Environmental Protection Agency to establish a nationwide system for trading sulfur dioxide emission reductions among power plants. This program is lowering the long-run costs to electric utilities of meeting the legislated targets. The utilities that face the highest cost of emission control are purchasing permits from those who can more easily control emissions.

Such schemes can play a useful role, but they have drawbacks. For one thing, deciding on the appropriate amount of pollution reduction is difficult. To set the allowable emissions at an efficient level, the EPA or other authority needs accurate information about both the cost of controlling emissions and the benefit (harms avoided) of doing so. But the cost to those affected is subjective, depending in part on their ability to avoid damage by moving or changing what they are doing. If they have a property right to be pollution-free (beyond some level of acceptable emissions), then they can decide what price to put on trading away that property right by their acceptance of added pollution. But that can't happen under this approach.

Offers and trades to accept more pollution are not allowed in "cap-and-trade" programs. Instead, the regulator chooses a level of pollution that must not be exceeded. But without trades it is difficult to know the appropriate level, especially in the case of nationwide standards. The willingness and ability of citizens to pay for environmental quality is strongly dependent on their income and the cost of environmental quality. Citizens who are poor, or who can experience better environmental quality only at a very high price, will not be willing to sacrifice as much for the same result. So it is difficult to know how pollution-free an area should be, taking into account both environmental goals and the benefits to all concerned from the polluting activity.

As we noted in Chapter 5, even things that are worth doing, such as reducing levels of pollution, are seldom worth doing perfectly. At some point, the benefits of achieving still lower levels of pollution will not be worth the cost. Indeed, policy analysts familiar with the formation of the 1990 Clean Air Act negotiations say that the standard chosen, a reduction of 10 million tons of sulfur dioxide per year around the country, was arbitrary. So even though the trades reduced the costs of meeting the standard, the standard may have been unreasonable—or too lax for that matter. In fact, since the major problem the program addressed—acid rain—turned out to be smaller than many people expected, the overall program was probably unnecessarily costly in spite of the trades.[5]

Regulation has an additional limitation that common law court solutions do not. After a court orders a reduction in pollution, the polluter and the receptor (the person affected) can then trade property rights if they wish. For example, a court may order a factory owner to halve the factory's pollution to protect a downwind farmer. However, the farmer might be willing to accept all the pollution in exchange for a payment. Under common law, the freedom exists to make such a trade.

With regulation, however, this kind of mutually beneficial trade is forbidden. A "cap-and-trade" program allows polluters to reduce compliance costs by trading with *one another,* but it does not allow people affected by pollution to negotiate with emitters on increases in the level of pollution, even though such negotiation might better achieve what both want. *In sum, emissions trading can reduce the cost of reaching chosen goals; but an efficient way to reach a badly chosen goal can be worse than no action at all.*

PROPERTY RIGHTS AS A TOOL FOR GOVERNMENT POLICY

Not all "market-like" schemes have such flaws. When the government recognizes the power of private property rights, there is potential for successful government policy. Ocean fisheries are one example where progress is being made.

---

[5]Robert W. Crandall, "Is There Progress in Environmental Policy?" *Contemporary Economic Policy* 12, no. 1 (1994): 80–83.

Ocean Fisheries: A Lack of Property Rights Causes Overfishing[6]

Overfishing in the oceans is a classic example of overexploitation of a resource that is not privately owned. This is typically called the "tragedy of the commons."[7] Without ownership of the fish or of fishing rights, each fisher has little to gain from holding back, since others will get most of the fish left in the water. To cope with this tragedy of the commons, governments try to institute regulations that protect the fish. Since the 1970s, the U.S. government has regulated fishing in coastal waters. Even so, at least a third of U.S. fisheries are known to be overfished.

One reason is that the regulations encouraged a wasteful and dangerous "race to fish." To preserve the stock of fish, governments reduced the length of the fishing seasons (often to just a few days) and set limits on the kinds of gear that could be used. This meant that boats went out to sea in dangerous weather, took all the fish they could, even immature fish, and faced accidents and capsizing as their gear became entangled with other fishers' gear.

Fortunately, a strategy increasingly used around the world has been developed to replace limits on season length with property rights strategies. A prominent example is the adoption of ITQs, or individual transferable quotas, which give fishers ownership of a portion of the annual allowable catch. For example, as economist Don Leal puts it in one case, "an individual who holds a 0.1 percent share in the South Atlantic wreckfish fishery is entitled to 7,400 pounds of wreckfish for the season if the total allowable catch is 7,400,000 pounds."[8] Regulators could be mistaken in setting the quota, of course. However, unlike the case of air pollution, the fishery itself will give them rapid feedback. If the stock of fish falls, regulators can drop the total allowable catch to let the fishery recover. When they own ITQs, fishers support such limits, to maintain the value of their fishing rights over time.

ITQs (known as individual fishing quotas, or IFQs, in the United States) come very close to being private property rights, and in New Zealand they are genuine private property. These property rights provide healthy incentives both in the short run and over time. So far, however, IFQs in the United States are not secure property rights; that is, they may be revised or retracted by the federal government. This limits the incentive for holders of IFQs to invest now to enhance the future value of the fishery and their IFQs.

WEAKENING PROPERTY RIGHTS: THE ENDANGERED SPECIES ACT[9]

Although ITQs are—at least potentially—a recognition of private property rights, governmental regulation often ignores or overrides private property rights. This is the case with the Endangered Species Act in the United States.

The intent of the Endangered Species Act (ESA), which Congress passed in 1973, was to help save species from extinction. The act was popular because there was evidence that animals such as bald eagles, grizzly bears, and condors were declining in number, and the public wanted to save them. To do so, the law gave a government agency, the U.S. Fish and Wildlife Service (FWS), enormous power over landowners and public land managers when listed species are nearby. Under the law, the agency can prohibit owners from doing anything that might disturb the habitat of an animal species listed as endangered. Farming, building, cutting trees, clearing brush, and even walking on the land have been prohibited.

Certainly, the law has benefited specific colonies and populations of many listed species. But the implementation of the law has had a negative effect on land management

[6]This section is based in large part on information found in Donald R. Leal, *Homesteading the Oceans: The Case for Property Rights in U.S. Fisheries,* found at http://www.perc.org/ps19pr.htm, and personal communications with Leal.

[7]Garrett Hardin, "The Tragedy of the Commons," *The Concise Encyclopedia of Economics,* Library of Economics and Liberty, http://www.econlib.org/library/Enc/TragedyoftheCommons.html.

[8]Dnald R. Leal, "Fencing the Fishery—A Primer on Ending the Race for Fish," found online at http://perc.org/publications/guidespractical/fence_fishery.php.

[9]Sources for this section are: Thomas R. Bourland and Richard L. Stroup, "Rent Payments as Incentives: Making Endangered Species Welcome on Private Land," *Journal of Forestry* 94, no. 4 (April 1996): 18–21; and Richard L. Stroup and Jane S. Shaw, "Technology and the Protection of Endangered Species," in *The Half-Life of Policy Rationales: How New Technology Affects Old Policy Issues,* eds. Fred E. Foldvary and Daniel B. Klein (New York: New York University Press, 2003).

in two ways. First, by severely weakening the property rights of landowners when a listed species is on or near the property, the ESA changes their incentives, reducing their willingness to protect endangered species. Second, by giving regulators a way to save species that is low-cost to them but high-cost to the landowner—forcing landowners to set aside land—the law discourages agency officials from seeking ways to save species that would cost less for the society as a whole. These negative forces probably outweigh the benefits of the law.

Consider the red-cockaded woodpecker, a bird that is in danger of extinction because its favorite habitat, very old pine trees throughout the South, has been diminishing over time. Under Fish and Wildlife Service regulations, the trees that red-cockaded woodpeckers nest in must be left standing for some decades beyond the time they would normally be harvested for wood. Once a bird has built a nest, most uses of the land are forbidden within several hundred yards. Many acres of forage must be available around the nest.

Many landowners dread the possibility that any listed species will be found on their land because it will lead the Fish and Wildlife Service to impose tight restrictions. Landowners can take subtle management steps to make their land unattractive to the listed species. In the case of the woodpecker, there is evidence that they do so. Economists Dean Lueck and Jeffrey Michael found that landowners located close to colonies of red-cockaded woodpeckers in North Carolina cut down their trees sooner than did those who were far away from the woodpeckers. By logging before they normally would, they kept trees from growing old enough to attract the woodpeckers and thus trigger severe restrictions on the use of their land. The unwanted secondary effect of the ESA has been a systematic reduction in habitat for listed and candidate species—precisely the opposite of the goal of the law.[10]

Prior to the ESA's passage in 1973, which weakened property rights with serious unwanted results for listed species, landowners often were quite willing to help preserve declining wildlife. In the 1920s, when fears arose that eastern bluebirds were in danger of extinction, for example, landowners allowed volunteers to place and maintain hundreds of thousands of specially designed bluebird nest boxes on their land. Because owners did not fear the loss of their rights, they usually cooperated voluntarily. The bluebird has recovered and has never had to be listed under the ESA.

Preservation of endangered species such as the red-cockaded woodpecker can be achieved at a much lower cost if the incentive structure encourages local landowners to assist in their protection. Unfortunately, the incentives generated by the Endangered Species Act encourage just the opposite.

© AP PHOTO/TEXAS PARKS & WILDLIFE DEPT., GLEN MILLS

---

[10]Dean Lueck and Jeffrey A. Michael, "Preemptive Habitat Destruction under the Endangered Species Act," *Journal of Law & Economics* 46 (2003): 27–60.

Many similar efforts, large and small, have gained landowner cooperation with little or no payment. But finding a landowner willing to help a species now listed under the current ESA is difficult. Few want to attract species that could bring government control of their land. In fact, some will no longer even welcome hikers who might discover and report an endangered species on the land.

GOVERNMENT OWNERSHIP OF RESOURCES AND PROVISION OF SERVICES

Much government intervention in environmental matters has to do with establishing regulations to control pollution. But the government also owns many natural resources and is involved in protecting environmental quality through parks, refuges, and other lands it owns. When resources are not privately owned and traded in open markets, however, the vital flow of information and incentives that prices bring is missing. That is the case with our national parks.[11] Mismanagement, even by highly qualified, well-intended professionals, is the natural result.

Most of the funds for the national parks are tax dollars appropriated by Congress. Park visitors pay only a small fraction of the cost of the services they receive. In 1995, for example, proceeds from national park recreation fees covered only 7.5 percent of the cost of park operations. Thus, park managers have little information about how much the various services are worth to visitors. Without good information about what visitors want, park managers allocate their budgets with information missing that would be crucial to a private business serving the public. Should the roads, buildings, and sewers be improved? Or should more rangers be hired for interpretive programs? Should campgrounds be kept open and operating hours lengthened—should new ones be added? The Park Service cannot know the answers, because a market is lacking. And because the Park Service's funding is dependent on decisions in Congress, it spends more time figuring out what the relevant congressmen want than what park visitors want.

Even when park managers have good information, the proper incentive to use it may not be present. This was the case in 1996 when the superintendent of Yellowstone Park closed a campground. The park was short on cash, and the superintendent was trying to reduce his spending. In fact, the campground in question was profitable—that is, it earned more than it cost to operate. The problem was that while his budget paid the cost of keeping the campground open, the revenues went to the U.S. Treasury, not to Yellowstone. So the superintendent closed the campground to save money, even though doing so deprived visitors of a campground that was providing net earnings for the Treasury. The superintendent needed resources to protect the park and repair sewers and roads, but the campground was draining park resources to feed the national treasury.

In contrast, for owners of private campgrounds, amusement parks, museums, and other attractions that also draw visitors, information is always flowing, and managers always have an incentive to respond to that information. These owners must pay for the resources they use, and they collect the needed revenue from customers. If people don't come to a private museum, its revenues fall. In response, its owners must do something to attract customers who are willing to pay the full cost (or, alternatively, philanthropists who will cover the costs for them), or they will have to close their doors.

The National Park Service may be starting to realize that it needs better information and better incentives. In the 1990s, a number of states found that when their park systems relied on the visitors, not the state legislature, for revenues, they began to provide services that visitors wanted and were willing to pay for. By 1997, sixteen state park systems relied on user fees for more than half their operating budgets.[12] Two systems, those in Vermont and New Hampshire, got their entire operating budgets from user fees.

---

[11]Donald R. Leal and Holly L. Fretwell, "Back to the Future to Save Our Parks," PERC Policy Series, Issue Number PS-10, June 1997, found at: http://www.perc.org/publications/policyseries/back_future_full .php.

[12]Leal and Fretwell, op. cit.

Following the lead of the state parks, a federal demonstration program raised fees for access to national parks and allows the parks to use 80 percent of those fees rather than send them to the Treasury in Washington. This way, the park managers directly benefit by serving their visitors. The new fees have led to major repair and rehabilitation of roads and trails.

CONCLUSION

People turn to government to get what they can't get in markets. In many cases, they are seeking to get what they want with a subsidy from others. Government can provide protection from harms, as in regulation that reduces pollution, or production of goods and services, as in the provision of national parks. Government can indeed shift the cost of services from some citizens to others, and can do the same with benefits from its programs. There is little reason, however, to expect a net increase in efficiency when government steps in. That is true in environmental matters, as in all other areas of citizen concern.

! KEY POINTS

▼ When it is difficult to assign and enforce private property rights, markets often result in outcomes that are inefficient. This is often the case when large numbers of persons engage in actions that impose harm on others. Government regulation has some promise but also poses some problems of its own.

▼ There is much uncertainty regarding global warming. Scientists agree on some facts but disagree on many others. In their search for research funding, they, like all scientists studying risks with policy implications, have a strong incentive to keep the public highly concerned about the importance of the risks they study.

▼ Market like schemes can reduce the costs of reaching a chosen environmental goal, but the programs do not help in choosing the right goal.

▼ The Endangered Species Act, by weakening private property rights, discourages landowners from attracting and providing habitat for listed species.

▼ Federal ownership of national parks, as with other lands, has brought troublesome results along with benefits, but there seems to be progress in moving closer to market solutions that provide better information and incentives for federal managers.

? CRITICAL ANALYSIS QUESTIONS

*1. The movie *The Perfect Storm* is set in a situation where a very short fishing season forces the fishers to go to sea despite the dangerous conditions. Explain how a move to ITQs could solve that problem.

2. "The national parks belong to us all. No one should be charged money to enter." Evaluate, using the economic way of thinking.

*3. "The buildup of carbon dioxide and other gases in the air threatens to warm the planet and cause enormous damage worldwide. We must immediately stop this buildup for the sake of future generations." Why do many economists disagree with this statement? Are they not concerned with the future? Explain.

*4. "Unlike a marketplace, where pollution is profitable, government control of resources and pollution can take into account the desires of all the people." Evaluate, using economic thinking.

General Business and Economic Indicators for the United States

SECTION 1
Gross Domestic Product and Its Components

Year	Personal Consumption Expenditures (Billions)	Gross Private Domestic Investment (Billions)	Government Consumption and Gross Investment (Billions)	Net Exports (Billions)	Gross Domestic Product (Billions)	Real GDP 2000 Prices	Real GDP Annual Growth Rate (Percent)	Real GDP Per Capita
1960	$ 331.7	$ 78.9	$ 111.6	$ 4.2	$ 526.4	$2,501.8	2.5	$13,840
1961	342.1	78.2	119.5	4.9	544.7	2,560.0	2.3	13,932
1962	363.3	88.1	130.1	4.1	585.6	2,715.2	6.1	14,552
1963	382.7	93.8	136.4	4.9	617.8	2,834.0	4.4	14,971
1964	411.4	102.1	143.2	6.9	663.6	2,998.6	5.8	15,624
1965	443.8	118.2	151.5	5.6	719.1	3,191.1	6.4	16,420
1966	480.9	131.3	171.8	3.9	787.8	3,399.1	6.5	17,290
1967	507.8	128.6	192.7	3.6	832.6	3,484.6	2.5	17,533
1968	558.0	141.2	209.4	1.4	910.0	3,652.7	4.8	18,196
1969	605.2	156.4	221.5	1.4	984.6	3,765.4	3.1	18,573
1970	648.5	152.4	233.8	4.0	1,038.5	3,771.9	0.2	18,391
1971	701.9	178.2	246.5	0.6	1,127.1	3,898.6	3.4	18,771
1972	770.6	207.6	263.5	−3.4	1,238.3	4,105.0	5.3	19,555
1973	852.4	244.5	281.7	4.1	1,382.7	4,341.5	5.8	20,484
1974	933.4	249.4	317.9	−0.8	1,500.0	4,319.6	−0.5	20,195
1975	1,034.4	230.2	357.7	16.0	1,638.3	4,311.2	−0.2	19,961
1976	1,151.9	292.0	383.0	−1.6	1,825.3	4,540.9	5.3	20,822
1977	1,278.6	361.3	414.1	−23.1	2,030.9	4,750.5	4.6	21,565
1978	1,428.5	438.0	453.6	−25.4	2,294.7	5,015.0	5.6	22,526
1979	1,592.2	492.9	500.8	−22.5	2,563.3	5,173.4	3.2	22,982
1980	1,757.1	479.3	566.2	−13.1	2,789.5	5,161.7	−0.2	22,666
1981	1,941.1	572.4	627.5	−12.5	3,128.4	5,291.7	2.5	23,007
1982	2,077.3	517.2	680.5	−20.0	3,255.0	5,189.3	−1.9	22,346
1983	2,290.6	564.3	733.5	−51.7	3,536.7	5,423.8	4.5	23,146
1984	2,503.3	735.6	797.0	−102.7	3,933.2	5,813.6	7.2	24,593
1985	2,720.3	736.2	879.0	−115.2	4,220.3	6,053.7	4.1	25,382
1986	2,899.7	746.5	949.3	−132.7	4,462.8	6,263.6	3.5	26,024
1987	3,100.2	785.0	999.5	−145.2	4,739.5	6,475.1	3.4	26,664
1988	3,353.6	821.6	1,039.0	−110.4	5,103.8	6,742.7	4.1	27,514
1989	3,598.5	874.9	1,099.1	−88.2	5,484.4	6,981.4	3.5	28,221
1990	3,839.9	861.0	1,180.2	−78.0	5,803.1	7,112.5	1.9	28,429
1991	3,986.1	802.9	1,234.4	−27.5	5,995.9	7,100.5	−0.2	28,007
1992	4,235.3	864.8	1,271.0	−33.2	6,337.8	7,336.6	3.3	28,556
1993	4,477.9	953.4	1,291.2	−65.0	6,657.4	7,532.7	2.7	28,940
1994	4,743.3	1,097.1	1,325.5	−93.6	7,072.2	7,835.5	4.0	29,741
1995	4,975.8	1,144.0	1,369.2	−91.4	7,397.7	8,031.7	2.5	30,128
1996	5,256.8	1,240.3	1,416.0	−96.2	7,816.8	8,328.9	3.7	30,881
1997	5,547.4	1,389.8	1,468.7	−101.6	8,304.3	8,703.5	4.5	31,886
1998	5,879.5	1,509.1	1,518.3	−159.9	8,747.0	9,066.9	4.2	32,833
1999	6,282.5	1,625.7	1,620.8	−260.5	9,268.4	9,470.3	4.4	33,904
2000	6,739.4	1,735.5	1,721.6	−379.5	9,817.0	9,817.0	3.7	34,760
2001	7,055.0	1,614.3	1,825.6	−367.0	10,128.0	9,890.7	0.8	34,661
2002	7,376.1	1,579.2	1,956.6	−424.9	10,487.0	10,074.8	1.9	34,953
2003	7,760.9	1,665.8	2,075.5	−498.1	11,004.1	10,381.3	3.0	35,664

Source: http://www.economagic.com.

	GDP Deflator		Consumer Price Index	
Year	Index (2000 = 100)	Annual Percentage Change	Index (1982–84 = 100)	Percentage Change
1960	21.0	1.4	29.6	1.0
1961	21.3	1.1	29.9	1.1
1962	21.6	1.4	30.3	1.2
1963	21.8	1.1	30.6	1.2
1964	22.1	1.5	31.0	1.3
1965	22.5	1.8	31.5	1.6
1966	23.2	2.8	32.5	3.0
1967	23.9	3.1	33.4	2.8
1968	24.9	4.3	34.8	4.3
1969	26.1	5.0	36.7	5.5
1970	27.5	5.3	38.8	5.8
1971	28.9	5.0	40.5	4.3
1972	30.2	4.3	41.8	3.3
1973	31.8	5.6	44.4	6.2
1974	34.7	9.0	49.3	11.1
1975	38.0	9.4	53.8	9.1
1976	40.2	5.8	56.9	5.7
1977	42.8	6.4	60.6	6.5
1978	45.8	7.0	65.2	7.6
1979	49.5	8.3	72.6	11.3
1980	54.0	9.1	82.4	13.5
1981	59.1	9.4	90.9	10.3
1982	62.7	6.1	96.5	6.1
1983	65.2	4.0	99.6	3.2
1984	67.7	3.8	103.9	4.3
1985	69.7	3.0	107.6	3.5
1986	71.3	2.2	109.6	1.9
1987	73.2	2.7	113.6	3.7
1988	75.7	3.4	118.3	4.1
1989	78.6	3.8	124.0	4.8
1990	81.6	3.9	130.7	5.4
1991	84.4	3.5	136.2	4.2
1992	86.4	2.3	140.3	3.0
1993	88.4	2.3	144.5	3.0
1994	90.3	2.1	148.2	2.6
1995	92.1	2.0	152.4	2.8
1996	93.9	1.9	156.9	2.9
1997	95.4	1.7	160.5	2.3
1998	96.5	1.1	163.0	1.6
1999	97.9	1.4	166.6	2.2
2000	100.0	2.2	172.2	3.4
2001	102.4	2.4	177.1	2.8
2002	104.1	1.7	179.9	1.6
2003	106.0	1.8	184.0	2.3

SECTION 2
Prices and Inflation

Source: http://www.economagic.com.

SECTION 3
Population and
Employment

	POPULATION AND LABOR FORCE			
YEAR	CIVILIAN NONINSTITUTIONAL POPULATION AGE 16+ (MILLIONS)	CIVILIAN LABOR FORCE (MILLIONS)	CIVILIAN LABOR FORCE PARTICIPATION RATE (PERCENT)	CIVILIAN EMPLOYMENT/ POPULATION RATIO (PERCENT)
1959	115.3	68.4	59.3	56.0
1960	117.2	69.6	59.4	56.1
1961	118.8	70.5	59.3	55.4
1962	120.2	70.6	58.8	55.5
1963	122.4	71.8	58.7	55.4
1964	124.5	73.1	58.7	55.7
1965	126.5	74.5	58.9	56.2
1966	128.1	75.8	59.2	56.9
1967	129.9	77.3	59.6	57.3
1968	132.0	78.7	59.6	57.5
1969	134.3	80.7	60.1	58.0
1970	137.1	82.8	60.4	57.4
1971	140.2	84.4	60.2	56.6
1972	144.1	87.0	60.4	57.0
1973	147.1	89.4	60.8	57.8
1974	150.1	91.9	61.3	57.8
1975	153.2	93.8	61.2	56.1
1976	156.2	96.2	61.6	56.8
1977	159.0	99.0	62.3	57.9
1978	161.9	102.3	63.2	59.3
1979	164.9	105.0	63.7	59.9
1980	167.7	106.9	63.8	59.2
1981	170.1	108.7	63.9	59.0
1982	172.3	110.2	64.0	57.8
1983	174.2	111.6	64.0	57.9
1984	176.4	113.5	64.4	59.5
1985	178.2	115.5	64.8	60.1
1986	180.6	117.8	65.3	60.7
1987	182.8	119.9	65.6	61.5
1988	184.6	121.7	65.9	62.3
1989	186.4	123.9	66.5	63.0
1990	189.2	125.8	66.5	62.8
1991	190.9	126.3	66.2	61.7
1992	192.8	128.1	66.4	61.5
1993	194.8	129.2	66.3	61.7
1994	196.8	131.1	66.6	62.5
1995	198.6	132.3	66.6	62.9
1996	200.6	133.9	66.8	63.2
1997	203.1	136.3	67.1	63.8
1998	205.2	137.7	67.1	64.1
1999	207.8	139.4	67.1	64.3
2000	212.6	142.6	67.1	64.4
2001	215.1	143.7	66.8	63.7
2002	217.6	144.9	66.6	62.7
2003	221.2	146.5	66.2	62.3

Source: http://www.bls.gov.

Year	UNEMPLOYMENT RATES			
	ALL WORKERS	BOTH SEXES, AGE 16 TO 19	MEN AGE 20+	WOMEN AGE 20+
1959	5.5	14.6	4.7	5.2
1960	5.5	14.7	4.7	5.1
1961	6.7	16.8	5.7	6.3
1962	5.5	14.7	4.6	5.4
1963	5.7	17.2	4.5	5.4
1964	5.2	16.2	3.9	5.2
1965	4.5	14.8	3.2	4.5
1966	3.8	12.8	2.5	3.8
1967	3.8	12.9	2.3	4.2
1968	3.6	12.7	2.2	3.8
1969	3.5	12.2	2.1	3.7
1970	4.9	15.3	3.5	4.8
1971	5.9	16.9	4.4	5.7
1972	5.6	16.2	4.0	5.4
1973	4.9	14.5	3.3	4.9
1974	5.6	16.0	3.8	5.5
1975	8.5	19.9	6.8	8.0
1976	7.7	19.0	5.9	7.4
1977	7.1	17.8	5.2	7.0
1978	6.1	16.4	4.3	6.0
1979	5.8	16.1	4.2	5.7
1980	7.1	17.8	5.9	6.4
1981	7.6	19.6	6.3	6.8
1982	9.7	23.2	8.8	8.3
1983	9.6	22.4	8.9	8.1
1984	7.5	18.9	6.6	6.8
1985	7.2	18.6	6.2	6.6
1986	7.0	18.3	6.1	6.2
1987	6.2	16.9	5.4	5.4
1988	5.5	15.3	4.8	4.9
1989	5.3	15.0	4.5	4.7
1990	5.6	15.5	5.0	4.9
1991	6.8	18.7	6.4	5.7
1992	7.5	20.1	7.1	6.3
1993	6.9	19.0	6.4	5.9
1994	6.1	17.6	5.4	5.4
1995	5.6	17.3	4.8	4.9
1996	5.4	16.7	4.6	4.8
1997	4.9	16.0	4.2	4.4
1998	4.5	14.6	3.7	4.1
1999	4.2	13.9	3.5	3.8
2000	4.0	13.1	3.3	3.6
2001	4.7	14.7	4.2	4.1
2002	5.8	16.5	5.3	5.1
2003	6.0	17.5	5.6	5.1

Source: http://www.bls.gov.

SECTION 4
Money Supply, Interest Rates, and Federal Finances

	MONEY SUPPLY					FEDERAL BUDGET			NATIONAL DEBT[1]	
YEAR	M1 (BILLIONS)	ANNUAL CHANGE (PERCENT)	M2 (BILLIONS)	ANNUAL CHANGE (PERCENT)	Aaa BONDS (PERCENT)	FISCAL YEAR OUTLAYS (BILLIONS)	FISCAL YEAR RECEIPTS (BILLIONS)	SURPLUS/ DEFICIT (BILLIONS)	BILLIONS OF DOLLARS	PERCENT OF GDP
1960	$140.7	0.5	$ 312.4	4.9	4.4	$ 92.2	$ 92.5	$ 0.3	$ 210.3	40.0%
1961	145.2	3.2	335.5	7.4	4.4	97.7	94.4	(3.3)	211.1	38.8%
1962	147.8	1.8	362.7	8.1	4.3	106.8	99.7	(7.1)	218.3	37.3%
1963	153.3	3.7	393.2	8.4	4.3	111.3	106.6	(4.7)	222.0	35.9%
1964	160.3	4.6	424.7	8.0	4.4	118.5	112.6	(5.9)	222.1	33.5%
1965	167.8	4.7	459.2	8.1	4.5	118.2	116.8	(1.4)	221.7	30.8%
1966	172.0	2.5	480.2	4.6	5.1	134.5	130.8	(3.7)	221.5	28.1%
1967	183.3	6.5	524.8	9.3	5.5	157.5	148.8	(8.7)	219.9	26.4%
1968	197.4	7.7	566.8	8.0	6.2	178.1	153.0	(25.1)	237.3	26.1%
1969	203.9	3.3	587.9	3.7	7.0	183.6	186.9	3.3	224.0	22.8%
1970	214.4	5.2	626.5	6.6	8.0	195.6	192.8	(2.8)	225.5	21.7%
1971	228.3	6.5	710.3	13.4	7.4	210.2	187.1	(23.1)	237.5	21.1%
1972	249.2	9.2	802.3	13.0	7.2	230.7	207.3	(23.4)	251.0	20.3%
1973	262.9	5.5	855.5	6.6	7.4	245.7	230.8	(14.9)	265.7	19.2%
1974	274.2	4.3	902.1	5.4	8.6	269.4	263.2	(6.2)	263.1	17.5%
1975	287.1	4.7	1,016.2	12.6	8.8	332.3	279.1	(53.2)	309.7	18.9%
1976	306.2	6.7	1,152.0	13.4	8.4	371.8	298.1	(73.7)	382.7	21.0%
1977	330.9	8.0	1,270.3	10.3	8.0	409.2	355.6	(53.6)	444.1	21.9%
1978	357.3	8.0	1,366.0	7.5	8.7	458.7	399.6	(59.1)	491.6	21.4%
1979	381.8	6.9	1,473.7	7.9	9.6	504.0	463.3	(40.7)	524.7	20.5%
1980	408.5	7.0	1,599.8	8.6	11.9	590.9	517.1	(73.8)	591.1	21.2%
1981	436.7	6.9	1,755.4	9.7	14.2	678.2	599.3	(78.9)	664.9	21.3%
1982	474.8	8.7	1,910.3	8.8	13.8	745.8	617.8	(128.0)	790.1	24.3%
1983	521.4	9.8	2,126.5	11.3	12.0	808.4	600.6	(207.8)	981.7	27.8%
1984	551.6	5.8	2,309.9	8.6	12.7	851.9	666.5	(185.4)	1,151.9	29.3%
1985	619.8	12.4	2,495.7	8.0	11.4	946.4	734.1	(212.3)	1,337.5	31.7%
1986	724.6	16.9	2,732.3	9.5	9.0	990.5	769.2	(221.3)	1,549.8	34.7%
1987	750.2	3.5	2,831.4	3.6	9.4	1,004.1	854.4	(149.7)	1,677.7	35.4%
1988	786.6	4.9	2,994.4	5.8	9.7	1,064.5	909.3	(155.2)	1,822.4	35.7%
1989	792.8	0.8	3,158.4	5.5	9.3	1,143.7	991.2	(152.5)	1,970.6	35.9%
1990	824.8	4.0	3,279.2	3.8	9.3	1,253.2	1,032.0	(221.2)	2,177.1	37.5%
1991	896.9	8.7	3,379.1	3.0	8.8	1,324.4	1,055.0	(269.4)	2,430.4	40.5%
1992	1,025.0	14.3	3,432.8	1.6	8.1	1,381.7	1,091.3	(290.4)	2,703.3	42.7%
1993	1,129.9	10.2	3,484.7	1.5	7.2	1,409.5	1,154.4	(255.1)	2,922.7	43.9%
1994	1,150.5	1.8	3,497.7	0.4	8.0	1,461.9	1,258.6	(203.3)	3,077.9	43.5%
1995	1,127.0	−2.0	3,641.4	4.1	7.6	1,515.8	1,351.8	(164.0)	3,230.3	43.7%
1996	1,079.3	−4.2	3,817.0	4.8	7.4	1,560.6	1,453.1	(107.5)	3,343.1	42.8%
1997	1,072.5	−0.6	4,031.9	5.6	7.3	1,601.3	1,579.3	(22.0)	3,347.8	40.3%
1998	1,096.1	2.2	4,384.1	8.7	6.5	1,652.6	1,721.8	69.2	3,262.9	37.3%
1999	1,124.0	2.5	4,649.0	6.0	7.0	1,702.9	1,827.5	124.6	3,135.7	33.8%
2000	1,087.9	−3.2	4,932.7	6.1	7.6	1,788.8	2,025.2	236.4	2,898.4	29.5%
2001	1,179.3	8.4	5,448.6	10.5	7.1	1,863.8	1,991.2	127.4	2,785.5	27.5%
2002	1,217.2	3.2	5,794.5	6.3	6.5	2,011.0	1,853.2	(157.8)	2,936.2	28.0%
2003	1,293.4	6.3	6,062.5	4.6	5.7	2,157.6	1,782.3	(375.3)	3,257.5	29.6%

[1]National debt is debt held by private investors at year end.

Source: http://www.economagic.com and http://www.whitehouse.gov/omb/.

FEDERAL, STATE, AND LOCAL GOVERNMENT[1]

SECTION 5
Size of Government as a Share of GDP

YEAR	EXPENDITURES (% OF GDP)	REVENUES (% OF GDP)	PURCHASES OF GOODS AND SERVICES (% OF GDP)	NON-DEFENSE PURCHASES OF GOODS AND SERVICES (% OF GDP)	TRANSFER PAYMENTS TO PERSONS (% OF GDP)
1960	23.3%	25.5%	21.2%	11.1%	5.3%
1961	24.3%	25.5%	21.9%	11.6%	5.8%
1962	24.4%	25.7%	22.2%	11.8%	5.6%
1963	24.5%	26.3%	22.1%	12.2%	5.5%
1964	24.0%	25.1%	21.6%	12.5%	5.3%
1965	23.7%	25.1%	21.1%	12.6%	5.3%
1966	24.5%	25.7%	21.8%	12.7%	5.3%
1967	26.4%	26.1%	23.1%	13.1%	6.0%
1968	27.1%	27.7%	23.0%	13.2%	6.4%
1969	27.1%	28.8%	22.5%	13.4%	6.5%
1970	28.4%	27.6%	22.5%	14.1%	7.4%
1971	28.9%	26.9%	21.9%	14.4%	8.1%
1972	28.7%	28.0%	21.3%	14.3%	8.3%
1973	27.9%	28.2%	20.4%	14.0%	8.3%
1974	29.1%	28.8%	21.2%	14.8%	9.0%
1975	31.0%	27.0%	21.8%	15.5%	10.3%
1976	30.1%	27.7%	21.0%	14.9%	10.0%
1977	29.4%	27.9%	20.4%	14.4%	9.5%
1978	28.5%	28.1%	19.8%	14.1%	9.1%
1979	28.3%	28.4%	19.5%	13.9%	9.1%
1980	30.2%	28.6%	20.3%	14.3%	10.0%
1981	30.8%	29.3%	20.1%	13.8%	10.0%
1982	33.0%	28.8%	20.9%	14.0%	10.8%
1983	33.0%	28.3%	20.7%	13.7%	10.7%
1984	31.9%	28.3%	20.3%	13.1%	9.9%
1985	32.4%	28.8%	20.8%	13.5%	9.9%
1986	32.7%	28.9%	21.3%	13.9%	9.9%
1987	32.4%	29.6%	21.1%	13.7%	9.7%
1988	31.7%	29.4%	20.4%	13.4%	9.6%
1989	31.6%	29.7%	20.0%	13.4%	9.7%
1990	32.3%	29.4%	20.3%	13.9%	10.1%
1991	33.0%	29.3%	20.6%	14.2%	10.4%
1992	33.8%	29.1%	20.1%	14.1%	11.8%
1993	33.3%	29.2%	19.4%	13.9%	12.0%
1994	32.4%	29.5%	18.7%	13.7%	11.8%
1995	32.4%	29.9%	18.5%	13.8%	11.8%
1996	31.9%	30.4%	18.1%	13.6%	11.8%
1997	30.9%	30.7%	17.7%	13.5%	11.4%
1998	30.1%	31.1%	17.4%	13.4%	11.1%
1999	29.6%	31.2%	17.5%	13.6%	10.8%
2000	29.4%	31.8%	17.5%	13.8%	10.8%
2001	30.2%	30.7%	18.0%	14.1%	11.5%
2002	30.8%	28.2%	18.7%	14.5%	12.1%
2003	30.9%	27.6%	18.9%	14.4%	12.1%

[1]There are some differences across reporting agencies with regard to accounting procedures and the treatment of government enterprises. This results in some differences in statistical measures of the size of government.
Source: http://www.bea.doc.gov.

SECTION 6
Share of Federal Income Taxes Paid by Income Groupings

	FEDERAL INCOME TAX SHARE BY PERCENTILES				
YEAR	TOP 1%	TOP 5%	TOP 10%	NEXT 40%	BOTTOM 50%
1980	19.1%	36.8%	49.3%	43.7%	7.0%
1981	17.6%	35.1%	48.0%	44.6%	7.5%
1982	19.0%	36.1%	48.6%	44.1%	7.3%
1983	20.3%	37.3%	49.7%	43.1%	7.2%
1984	21.1%	38.0%	50.6%	42.1%	7.4%
1985	21.8%	38.8%	51.5%	41.4%	7.2%
1986	25.7%	42.6%	54.7%	38.9%	6.5%
1987	24.8%	43.3%	55.6%	38.3%	6.1%
1988	27.6%	45.6%	57.3%	37.0%	5.7%
1989	25.2%	43.9%	55.8%	38.4%	5.8%
1990	25.1%	43.6%	55.4%	38.8%	5.8%
1991	24.8%	43.4%	55.8%	38.7%	5.5%
1992	27.5%	45.9%	58.0%	36.9%	5.1%
1993	29.0%	47.4%	59.2%	36.0%	4.8%
1994	28.9%	47.5%	59.4%	35.8%	4.8%
1995	30.3%	48.9%	60.7%	34.6%	4.6%
1996	32.3%	51.0%	62.5%	33.2%	4.3%
1997	33.2%	51.9%	63.2%	32.5%	4.3%
1998	34.8%	53.8%	65.0%	30.8%	4.2%
1999	36.2%	55.5%	66.5%	29.5%	4.0%
2000	37.4%	56.5%	67.3%	28.8%	3.9%
2001	33.9%	53.3%	64.9%	31.1%	4.0%
2002	33.7%	53.8%	65.7%	30.8%	3.5%

Source: Internal Revenue Service.

Answers to Selected Critical Analysis Questions

APPENDIX
B

CHAPTER 1: THE ECONOMIC APPROACH

2. Production of scarce goods always involves a cost; there are no free lunches. When the government provides goods without charge to consumers, other citizens (taxpayers) will bear the cost of their provision. Thus, provision by the government affects how the costs will be covered, not whether they are incurred.

4. For most taxpayers, the change will reduce the after-tax cost of raising children. Other things being constant, one would predict an increase in the birthrate.

5. False. Intentions do not change the effect of the policy. If the policy runs counter to sound economics, it will lead to a counterproductive outcome even if that was not the intention of the policy. Bad policies are often advocated by people with good intentions.

7. Raising the price of new cars by requiring safety devices, which customers would not have purchased if given the choice, slows the rate of sales for new cars. Thus the older, less safe cars are driven longer, partially offsetting the safety advantage provided by the newer, safer cars. Also, drivers act a bit differently—they may take more risks—when they believe the safety devices will provide protection should they have an accident. In fact, economist Gordon Tullock says that the greatest safety device of all might be a dagger built into the center of the steering wheel, pointed directly at the driver's chest!

8. Money has nothing to do with whether an individual is economizing. Any time a person chooses, in an attempt to achieve a goal, he or she is economizing.

9. Positive economics can help one better understand the likely effects of alternative policies. This will help one choose alternatives that are less likely to lead to disappointing results.

10. Association is not causation. It is likely that a large lead, near the end of the game, caused the third team to play more, rather than the third team causing the lead.

14. This is a question that highlights the importance of marginal analysis. In responding to the question, think about the following. After pollution has already been reduced substantially, how much will it cost to reduce it still more? If the quality of air and water were already high, how much gain would result from still less pollution?

CHAPTER 2: SOME TOOLS OF THE ECONOMIST

2. This is an opportunity cost question. Even though the productivity of brush painters has changed only slightly, rising productivity in other areas has led to higher wages in other occupations, thereby increasing the opportunity cost of being a house painter. Since people would not supply house painting services unless they were able to meet their opportunity costs, higher wages are necessary to attract house painters from competitive (alternative) lines of work.

4. The statement reflects the view that "exchange is a zero sum game." This view is false. No private business can force customers to buy. Consumers purchase various goods and services from businesses because they gain by doing so. If they did not gain, they would not continue to purchase items from a business. Similarly, the business firms also gain from their production and sale activities. Mutual gain provides the foundation for voluntary exchange, including that between business firms and their customers.

8. Yes. This question highlights the incentive of individuals to conserve for the future when they have private ownership rights. The market value of the land will increase in anticipation of the future harvest as the trees grow and the expected day of harvest grows closer. Thus, with transferable private property, the tree farmer will be able to capture the value added by his planting and holding the trees for a few years, even if the actual harvest does not take place until well after his death.

9. In general, it sanctions all forms of competition except for the use of violence (or the threat of violence), theft, or fraud.

11. If consumer demand for beef fell, the profitability of cattle herding would fall as well. Many cattle farmers would let their cattle herds dwindle and quit keeping cattle altogether. The result would be a smaller population of cattle, not a larger one. Because cattle are privately owned, an increase in their value in human consumption results in more cattle being kept, whereas a decrease would result in fewer cattle. To "save the cows," you should eat more beef!

12. Those who get tickets at the lower price gain, whereas those who are prevented from offering a higher price to ticket holders may not get a ticket even though both the prospective buyer and some ticket holders would have gained from the exchange at the higher price. Ticket holders may simply break the law or may sell at the regulated price only to buyers willing to provide them with other favors. Price controls, if they are effective, always reduce the gains from trade.

17. The opportunity cost of those individuals will rise, and they will likely consume less leisure.

CHAPTER 3: SUPPLY, DEMAND, AND THE MARKET PROCESS

1. Choices (a) and (b) would increase the demand for beef; (c) and (d) would affect primarily the supply of beef, rather than the demand; (e) leads to a change in quantity demanded, not a change in demand.

4. Prices reflect marginal value, not total value. The marginal value of a good is the maximum amount a consumer would be willing to pay for a specific unit. The height of the demand curve reflects the value consumers place on each unit. The total value is the total benefit consumers derive from all units consumed. The area under the demand curve for the number of units consumed reflects the total value. Water provides an example of a good with high total value but low marginal value. With regard to the last question, are there more nurses or professional wrestlers?

8. Neither markets nor the political process leaves the determination of winners and losers to chance. Under market organization, business winners and losers are determined by the decentralized choices of millions of consumers who use their dollar votes to reward firms that provide preferred goods at a low cost and penalize others who fail to do so. Under political decision-making, the winners and losers are determined by political officials who use taxes, subsidies, regulations, and mandates to favor some businesses and penalize others.

10. **a.** Profitable production increases the value of resources owned by people and leads to mutual gain for resource suppliers, consumers, and entrepreneurs. **b.** Losses reduce the value of resources, which reduces the well-being of at least some people. There is no conflict.

12. The supply curve is constructed under the assumption that other things are held constant. A reduction in the supply of oranges such as would occur under adverse weather conditions would lead to both a higher price and smaller total quantity supplied. This is perfectly consistent with economic theory.

14. Questions for thought. What happened to the cost of producing calculators during the period? How would this affect the supply curve and price of the calculators?

17. Business firms do have a strong incentive to serve the interest of consumers, but this is not what motivates them. Instead, they are motivated by self-interest and the pursuit of income, but they must provide consumers with a quality product if they are going to be successful. Good intentions are not required for people to engage in actions that are helpful to others.

CHAPTER 4: SUPPLY AND DEMAND: APPLICATIONS AND EXTENSIONS

1. An increase in demand for housing will also increase the demand for the resources required for its production, including the services of carpenters, plumbers, and electricians. This will lead to higher wages and an increase in employment for people in these groups.

4. Agreement of both buyer and seller is required for an exchange. Price ceilings push prices below equilibrium and thereby reduce the quantity sellers are willing to offer. Price floors push prices above equilibrium and thereby reduce the quantity consumers wish to buy. Both decrease the actual quantity traded in the market.

6. **a.** Decreases; **b.** Increases; **c.** Decreases; **d.** Increases

11. The deadweight loss is the loss of the potential gains of buyers and sellers emanating from trades that are squeezed out by the tax. It is an excess burden because even though the exchanges that are squeezed out by the tax impose a cost on buyers and sellers, they do not generate tax revenue (because the trades do not take place).

14. The employment level of low-skilled workers with large families would decline. Some would attempt to conceal the presence of their large family in order to get a job.

16. No. As the tax rate approaches the revenue maximum point, the higher rates substantially reduce the number of trades that take place. This is why the higher rates do not raise much additional revenue. As rates increase toward the revenue maximum point, the lost gains from trade are large and the additions to revenue are small. Thus, rates in this range are highly inefficient.

17. **a.** The quantity of cigarettes sold legally will decline sharply. The evidence is consistent with this view. After the tax hike was instituted, the number of cigarette-tax stamps issued by the city of New York fell by approximately 50 percent.

    b. Because the quantity of cigarettes sold legally in New York City will decline sharply, the revenues raised from the tax may actually decline.

    c. Internet purchases will increase. Approximately 80 percent of the cigarettes sold through the Internet are from Indian reservations, which are exempt from state sales tax.

    d. The incidence of smoking by New Yorkers may not decline very much because there are good substitutes available for cigarettes purchased in New York City, namely cigarettes purchased through the Internet or in states with a lower cigarette tax. Thus, the cost of smoking for New Yorkers may not rise very much. Predictably, the tax will lead to a sharp increase in both the legal purchase and illegal smuggling of cigarettes into New York City from localities (such as Virginia and North Carolina) that impose a much lower tax on cigarettes.

CHAPTER 5: DIFFICULT CASES FOR THE MARKET AND THE ROLE OF GOVERNMENT

1. When payment is not demanded for services, potential customers have a strong incentive to attempt a "free ride." However, when the number of nonpaying customers becomes such that the sales revenues of sellers are diminished (and in some cases eliminated), the sellers' incentive to supply the good is thereby reduced (or eliminated).

4. The antimissile system is a public good for the residents of Washington, D.C. Strictly speaking, none of the other items is a public good because each could be provided to some consumers (paying customers, for example) without being provided to others.

9. By reducing output below the efficient level, sellers of toasters would no longer produce or exchange some units of the good, despite the fact that the consumers value the marginal units more than it costs to produce them.

11. A public good reflects the characteristics of the good, not the sector in which it is provided. Elementary education is not a public good because it is relatively easy to exclude nonpaying customers and establish a one-to-one link between payment for and receipt of the good.

14. A government intervention would be efficient if the benefits from the intervention exceeded the cost of the intervention. All opportunity costs (such as tax money required, resources utilized, and deadweight losses.) would need to be considered in the comparison. A government intervention would be considered inefficient if the costs exceeded the benefits.

CHAPTER 6: THE ECONOMICS OF COLLECTIVE DECISION-MAKING

2. Corporate officers, while they surely care about the next few months and the profits during that time, care also about the value of the firm and its stock price. If the stock price rises sufficiently in the next few months—as it will if investors believe that current investments in future-oriented projects (planting new trees, for example) are sound—then the officers will find their jobs secure even if current profits do not look good. Rights to the profits from those (future) trees are saleable now in the form of the corporation's stock. There is no such mechanism to make the distant fruits of today's investments available to the political entrepreneurs who might otherwise fight for the future-oriented project. Only if the project appeals to today's voters, and only if they are willing to pay today for tomorrow's benefits, will the program be a political success. In any case, the wealth of the political official is not directly enhanced by his or her successful fight for the project.

4. The problem is not so much that the "wrong guys" won the last election as it is the incentive structure confronted by political decision-makers. Even if the "right people" were elected, they would be unlikely to improve the efficiency of government, at least not very much, given the strong incentive to support special interest and short-sighted policies and the weak incentives for operational efficiency when decisions are made by the political process.

6. True. Because each individual computer customer both decides the issue (what computer, if any, will be purchased) and bears the consequences of a mistaken choice, each has a strong incentive to acquire information needed to make a wise choice. In contrast, each voter recognizes that one vote, even if mistaken, will not decide the congressional election. Thus, a voter has little incentive to search for information to make a better-informed choice.

8. It is difficult for the voter to know what a candidate will do once elected, and the rationally ignorant voter is usually unwilling to spend the time and effort required to understand issues because the probability that any single vote will decide the issue is exceedingly small. Special-interest voters, on the other hand, will know which candidate has promised them the most on their issue. Also, the candidate who is both competent and prepared to ignore special interests will have a hard time getting these facts to voters without financial support from special-interest groups. Each voter has an incentive to be a "free rider" on the "good government" issue. Interestingly, controlling government on behalf of society as a whole is a public good. As in the case of other public goods, there is a tendency for too little of it to be supplied.

10. No. The government is merely an alternative form of organization. Government organization does not permit us to escape either scarcity or competition. It merely affects the nature of the competition. Political competition (for example, voting, lobbying,

political contributions, and politically determined budgets) replaces market competition. Neither is there any reason to believe that government organization modifies the importance of personal self-interest.

12. When the welfare of a special-interest group conflicts with that of a widely dispersed, unorganized majority, the legislative political process can reasonably be expected to work to the benefit of the special interest.

16. The presence of the sugar price supports and highly restrictive import quotas reflect the special-interest nature of the issue. Even though there are far more sugar consumers than growers, politicians apparently gain more by supporting the sugar growers and soliciting their political contributions rather than representing the interests of consumers. Government action in this area has almost certainly reduced the income levels and living standards of Americans.

CHAPTER 7: TAKING THE NATION'S ECONOMIC PULSE

1. Choices (a), (c), (f), (g), and (h) will exert no effect on GDP; (b) and (d) will increase GDP by the amount of the expenditure; and (e) will increase GDP by $250 (the commission on the transaction).

3. Since the furniture was produced last year, the sale does not affect GDP this year. It reduces inventory investment by $100,000 and increases consumption by $100,000, leaving GDP unchanged.

5. The reliability of GDP comparisons over long periods of time is reduced because the leisure and human costs may change substantially between the two years, and because the types of goods available for consumption during the two years may be vastly different.

7. $8.05

9. **a.** $1,000; **b.** $600; **c.** $200; **d.** 0; **e.** $20,000

11. **a.** False. Inventory investment indicates whether the holdings of unsold goods are rising or falling. A negative inventory investment merely indicates that there was a reduction in the size of inventories during the period. **b.** False. If gross investment is less than the depreciation of capital goods during the period, net investment would be negative. Net investment in the United States was negative for several years during the Great Depression of the 1930s. **c.** Not necessarily. Rather, it may be the result of an increase in prices, population, or hours worked.

12. Neither the receipts nor the expenditures on payouts would count toward GDP because they are merely transfers—they do not involve production. However, expenditures on operations, administration, and government-provided goods and services from lottery proceeds would add to GDP.

14. **a.** 0; **b.** 0; **c.** $300; **d.** $500; **e.** $300; **f.** 0; **g.** 0; **h.** 0

16. **a.** $2,506.7 billion; **b.** $3,776.4 billion; **c.** 54.0; **d.** $5,803.8 billion; **e.** 108.6; **f.** $9,817 billion; and **g.** $10,381.2 billion

CHAPTER 8: ECONOMIC FLUCTUATIONS, UNEMPLOYMENT, AND INFLATION

2. Job seekers do not know which employers will offer them the more attractive jobs. They find out by searching. Job search is "profitable" and consistent with economic efficiency as long as the marginal gain from search exceeds the marginal cost of searching. The job search process will lead to a better match between the skills of employees and the requirements of the available jobs.

3. Individuals (e) and (f) would be classified as employed; (a), (b), and (c) would be classified as unemployed; (d) is not in the labor force.

6. When the actual unemployment rate is equal to the natural rate of unemployment, cyclical unemployment is absent and potential GDP is at its sustainable rate.

7. a. 60 percent; **b.** 8.3 percent; **c.** 55 percent

8. No. It means that there were no jobs available at wage rates acceptable to the potential workers who were unemployed. Thus, they continued to search for more attractive opportunities.

10. a. $646,552; $925,926; $581,395; $417,537; $400,000 **b.** 1940; **c.** The real salary rose because the price level fell between 1920 and 1940.

13. The wages people earn are also prices (prices for labor services) and, like other prices, they usually rise as the general level of prices increases. The statement ignores this factor. It implicitly assumes that money wages are unaffected by inflation—that they would have increased by the same amount (6 percent) even if prices would have been stable. Generally, this will not be the case.

CHAPTER 9: AN INTRODUCTION TO BASIC MACROECONOMIC MARKETS

4. If the inflation rate unexpectedly falls from 3 percent to zero, the real wages of union members will rise. If other unions have similar contracts, the unemployment rate will increase because employment costs have risen relative to product prices. Profit margins will be cut, and producers will respond by reducing output and laying off workers. In contrast, if the inflation rate rises to 8 percent, profit margins will improve, producers will expand their output, and the unemployment rate will decline.

6. An increase in the real interest rate will make it more attractive for foreigners to purchase bonds and make other investments in the United States. As a result, there will be an increase in the inflow of capital from abroad.

8. When the price level is higher than decision-makers had anticipated, real wages will be lower and the level of employment higher than would have been the case if the price level had been anticipated accurately. Profit margins will increase; the actual rate of unemployment will fall below the natural rate. The high current rate of output will not be sustainable because real wages will rise as there is opportunity to renegotiate existing contracts.

10. They are all equal.

12. $10,000; $20,000

13. Inversely; an increase in interest rates is the same thing as a reduction in bond prices.

16. a. 5,700; **b.** No, because the actual price level will be 110, higher than what was anticipated. **c.** Actual unemployment will be less than the natural rate because the unexpected high level of prices will improve profit margins, reduce real wage rates, and cause the firms to expand output in the short run.

CHAPTER 10: WORKING WITH OUR BASIC AGGREGATE DEMAND AND AGGREGATE SUPPLY MODEL

1. Choice (a) would decrease *AD*; (b), (c), and (d) would increase it; and (e) would leave it unchanged. For the "why" part of the question, see the *Factors That Shift Aggregate Demand* section at the beginning of the chapter.

2. Choices (a), (b), (c), and (d) will reduce *SRAS*; (e) will increase it.

4. When an economy is operating at less than full employment, weak demand for investment and resources will tend to reduce (a) the real rate of interest and (b) resource prices relative to product prices and thereby restore normal profit and the incentive of firms to produce the long-run potential output level. If resource prices and the real interest rate were inflexible downward, the self-correcting mechanism would not work.

6. At the lower-than-expected inflation rate, *real wages* (and costs) will increase relative to product prices. This will squeeze profit margins and lead to reductions in output and employment, causing the unemployment rate to rise.

8. Tightness in resource markets will result in rising resource prices relative to product prices, causing the *SRAS* to shift to the left. Profit margins will decline, output rate will fall, and long-run equilibrium will be restored at a higher price level. The above-normal output cannot be maintained because it reflects input prices that people would not have agreed to and output decisions they would not have chosen if they had anticipated the current price level (and rate of inflation). Once they have a chance to correct these mistakes, they do so; and output returns to the economy's long-run potential.

9. Real wages will tend to increase more rapidly when the unemployment rate is low because a tight labor market (strong demand) will place upward pressure on wages.

12. The increase in demand for exports will increase aggregate demand. In the short run, this unanticipated expansion in demand will tend to increase output and employment while exerting modest upward pressure on the price level. In the long run, the primary impact will be a higher price level, with no change in output and employment.

15. A substantial reduction in defense expenditures will tend to reduce aggregate demand (shift *AS* to the left) in the short run. As a result, there may be some temporary increase in unemployment. However, if fewer resources are required to provide for national defense in the future, more resources will be available to produce other things that will enhance living standards.

18. The assets destroyed (such as World Trade Center and a portion of the Pentagon) by the attack reduced the productive assets of the U.S. and thereby adversely affected potential real output. However, these assets were a relatively small share, less than 0.01 percent, of U.S. capital assets. Thus, the direct effect on potential output was small. But there were also indirect effects, such as increased expenditures on national defense and domestic security. The opportunity cost of these indirect effects reduced the future potential output of *consumer* goods and thereby adversely affected the future living standard of Americans. These indirect effects, may well be larger than the effect of the assets destroyed.

CHAPTER 11: KEYNES AND THE EVOLUTION OF MACROECONOMICS

2. **a.** Increase current consumption, as the expectation of rising future prices will induce consumers to buy now

   b. Decrease current consumption, as people will attempt to save more for hard times

   c. Increase current consumption, as the result of an increase in disposable income

   d. May have little effect; however, the tendency will be toward a reduction in consumption, since households have an incentive to save more at the higher interest rate

   e. Decrease consumption, as falling stock prices will reduce the wealth of consumers

   f. and **g.** Increase consumption, as the young and the poor typically have a higher marginal propensity to consume than the elderly and wealthy

4. The multiplier principle is the concept that a change in one of the components of aggregate demand—investment, for example—will lead to a far greater change in the equilibrium level of income. Because the multiplier equals 1/(1- MPC), its size is determined by the marginal propensity to consume. The multiplier makes stabilizing the economy more difficult, because relatively small changes in aggregate demand have a much greater effect on equilibrium income.

7. They do not. The Keynesian model assumes that wages and prices are inflexible downward. It will take an increase in aggregate expenditures to restore full employment.

8. In the Keynesian *AE* model, the consumption function will shift downward by the increase in saving. The multiplier will magnify the decline in consumption, and the expected result is a sharp reduction in output. In the *AD-AS* model, the increase in saving will lead to lower real interest rates, which will tend to stimulate both investment and consumption and thereby at least partially offset the effect of the higher saving (and lower consumption) of households.

10. Both consumers and investors are likely to spend cautiously until they are convinced that a real recovery is under way. See Exhibit 2 of Chapter 10 for evidence that consumer sentiment remained weak during the initial phase of the expansions from these recessions. Further, investment spending will also be weak because many firms will initially have substantial excess productive capacity. Thus, consumption and investment can be expected to grow slowly during the initial phase of a recovery.

12. You would expect the multiplier to be smaller in Canada because Canadians would be expected to spend a larger share of their additions to income on imports, rather than domestic goods. This will reduce the size of the multiplier.

15. **a.** Business inventories will decline, which will induce firms to expand output and employment.

    b. Inventories will rise, which will cause firms to reduce both output and employment.

    c. $5,500

    d. The rate of unemployment would be high.

    e. Equilibrium output would increase to $6,000. Note that the MPC is 0.5 and the multiplier is equal to 2. Thus, the $250 increase in investment expands total expenditures by $500.

CHAPTER 12: FISCAL POLICY

2. The crowding-out effect is the theory that budget deficits will lead to higher real interest rates, which retard private spending. The crowding-out effect indicates that fiscal policy will not be nearly as potent as the simple Keynesian model implies. The new classical theory indicates that anticipation of higher future taxes (rather than higher interest rates) will crowd out private spending when government expenditures are financed by debt.

4. Automatic stabilizers are built-in features (unemployment compensation, corporate profit tax, progressive income tax) that tend automatically to promote a budget deficit during a recession and a budget surplus (or smaller deficit) during an inflationary boom. Automatic stabilizers have the major advantage of providing needed restraint, or stimuli, without congressional approval—which, in turn, minimizes the problem of proper timing.

6. Either an increase in government expenditures or a reduction in taxes should be employed to shift the budget toward a larger deficit (or smaller surplus).

8. This statement depicts the views of many economists three decades ago. Today, most economists recognize that it is naive. Given our limited ability to accurately forecast

future economic conditions, timing fiscal policy is more difficult than was previously thought. Political considerations—remember, the government is merely an alternative form of social organization, not a corrective device—reduce the likelihood that fiscal policy will be used as a stabilization tool. Changes in interest rates and private spending may offset fiscal actions and thereby reduce the potency of fiscal policy. All factors considered, it is clear that the use of fiscal policy to stabilize the economy is both difficult and complex.

10. There is a major defect in this view. If the budget deficits stimulated demand and thereby output and employment, we would have expected the inflation rate to accelerate. This was not the case; in fact, the inflation rate declined. The failure of the inflation rate to accelerate during the expansion of the 1980s strongly suggests that factors other than demand stimulus were at work.

13. Yes. Only the lower rates would increase the incentive to earn marginal income and thereby stimulate aggregate supply.

15. In the Keynesian model, investment is determined by factors other than the interest rate. Thus, budget deficits would not exert much effect on capital formation. In the crowding-out model, capital formation would be reduced because the budget deficits would lead to higher interest rates, which would crowd out private investment. In the new classical model, households will save more, and, as a result, budget deficits could be financed without either an increase in the interest rate or a reduction in capital formation.

CHAPTER 13: MONEY AND THE BANKING SYSTEM

1. A liquid asset is one that can easily and quickly be transformed into money without experiencing a loss of its market value. Assets such as high-grade bonds and stocks are highly liquid. In contrast, illiquid assets cannot be easily and quickly converted to cash without some loss of their value. Real estate, a family-owned business, business equipment, and artistic works are examples of illiquid assets.

3. Money is valuable because of its scarcity relative to the availability of goods and services. The use of money facilitates (reduces the cost of) exchange transactions. Money also serves as a store of value and a unit of account. Doubling the supply of money while holding output constant, would simply cause its purchasing power to fall without enhancing the services that it performs. In fact, fluctuations in the money supply generally create uncertainty about the future value of money and thereby reduce its ability to serve as a reliable store of value, accurate unit of account, and medium of exchange for time-dimension contracting.

6. **a.** There is no change; currency held by the public increases, but checking deposits decrease by an equal amount. **b.** Bank reserves decrease by $100. **c.** Excess reserves decrease by $100, minus $100 multiplied by the required reserve ratio.

8. Answers (b), (e), and (f) will reduce the money supply; (a) and (c) will increase it. If the Treasury's deposits (or the deposits of persons who receive portions of the Treasury's spending) are considered part of the money supply, then (d) will leave the money supply unchanged.

10. While the transformation of deposits into currency does not directly affect the money supply, it does reduce the excess reserves of banks. The reduction in excess reserves will cause banks to reduce their outstanding loans and thereby shrink the money supply. Therefore, an increase in the holding of currency relative to deposits will tend to reduce the supply of money.

12. There are two major reasons. First, the money supply can be altered quietly via open market operations, whereas a reserve requirement change focuses attention on Fed

policy. Second, open market operations are a fine-tuning method, whereas a reserve requirement change is a blunt instrument. Generally, the Fed prefers quiet, marginal changes to headline-grabbing, blunt changes that are more likely to disrupt markets.

13. **a.** False; statements of this type often use "money" when they are really speaking about wealth (or income).

    b. False; the checking deposit also counts as money. In addition, the deposit increases the reserves of the receiving bank and thereby places it in a position to extend additional loans that would increase the money supply.

    c. False; only an increase in the availability of goods and services valued by people will improve Americans' standard of living. Without an additional supply of goods and services, more money will simply lead to a higher price level.

16. **a.** Money supply increases by $100,000; **b.** $80,000; **c.** $500,000; **d.** no; there will be some leakage in the form of additional currency holdings by the public and additional excess reserve holdings by banks.

18. **a.** Money supply will increase by $2 billion; **b.** $1.8 billion; **c.** $20 billion; **d.** The leakages in the form of currency held by the public and additions to bank reserves cause the actual money multiplier to be less than the potential multiplier.

CHAPTER 14: MODERN MACROECONOMICS AND MONETARY POLICY

2. Choices (a) and (c) would increase your incentive to hold money deposits; (b) and (d) would reduce your incentive to hold money.

3. **a.** The cost of obtaining the house is $100,000.

    b. The cost of holding it is the interest forgone on the $100,000 sales value of the house.

    c. The cost of obtaining $1,000 is the amount of goods one must give up in order to acquire the $1,000. For example, if a pound of sugar sells for 50 cents, the cost of obtaining $1,000 in terms of sugar is 2,000 pounds.

    d. As in the case of the house, the cost of holding $1,000 is the interest forgone.

7. **a.** Bank reserves will decline; **b.** Real interest rates will rise; **c.** Spending on consumer durables will fall; **d.** The dollar will appreciate because the higher interest rates will attract bond purchases by foreigners; **e.** Exports will decline because the appreciation of the dollar will make U.S. goods more expensive for foreigners; **f.** The higher real interest rates will tend to reduce real asset prices; and **g.** Real GDP will fall.

10. If the time lag is long and variable (rather than short and highly predictable), it is less likely that policy makers will be able to time changes in monetary policy so that they will exert a *countercyclical* effect on the economy. The policy makers will be more likely to make mistakes and thereby exert a destabilizing influence.

11. Association does not reveal causation. Decision-makers, including borrowers and lenders, will eventually anticipate a high rate of inflation and adjust their choices accordingly. As the expected rate of inflation increases, the demand for loanable funds will increase and the supply will decrease. This will lead to higher nominal interest rates. Thus, economic theory indicates that the causation tends to run the opposite direction from that indicated by the statement.

12. Aggregate demand will decline as individuals and businesses reduce spending in an effort to build up their money balances (demand more money).

14. a.

	Real GDP	MS	PL
United States			
	9,817.00	x	x
	9,864.06	8.36	2.40
	10,087.39	3.22	1.46
	10,395.36	6.24	1.73
Chile			
	40,575.00	x	x
	42,012.57	11.44	3.40
	43,908.23	9.08	2.22
	45,663.61	11.28	3.22
Turkey			
	124,583.00	x	x
	115,477.02	46.35	54.50
	124,437.78	36.66	43.56
	131,877.93	43.07	22.99

b. Turkey

c. Turkey

d. Chile

CHAPTER 15: STABILIZATION POLICY, OUTPUT, AND EMPLOYMENT

2. During the last four decades, the United States has experienced less economic instability than it did in earlier periods. There is reason to believe that a more stable monetary policy is the primary factor underlying this increase in stability.

5. For (a) and (b), the actual and natural rates of unemployment will be equal. For (c), the actual rate will be less than the natural rate. For (d), the actual rate will exceed the natural rate.

7. Here are three practical problems that limit the effectiveness of discretionary macro policy as a stabilization tool: (1) inability to forecast the future direction of the economy with a high degree of accuracy, (2) lengthy and uncertain time lags between when a policy change is instituted and when the primary effects are felt, and (3) political factors that make it difficult to alter fiscal policy quickly.

9. The Great Depression certainly demonstrated that the economy's self-correcting mechanism does not work instantaneously and that it is unable to offset the impact of perverse macroeconomic policy. Most significantly, it highlights the importance of monetary stability and the damage that occurs when counterproductive policies are undertaken.

11. **a.** Keep the inflation rate at a low and highly predictable level; **b.** No; **c.** Both nominal interest rates and the general level of prices will rise.

CHAPTER 16: ECONOMIC GROWTH AND THE WEALTH OF NATIONS

3. A few years ago, many people believed that this view was essentially true. However, this is no longer the case. Foreign aid has played an insignificant role in the progress of most of the high-growth LDCs. In some cases, it has adversely affected economies. In the past, aid has disrupted markets and retarded the incentive of producers in less-developed countries. Furthermore, attractive investment alternatives will draw investment from abroad even if domestic saving is inadequate. Thus, the efficacy of aid as a tool to promote economic growth is highly questionable.

8. When considering the answer to this question, think about the following. Is there an opportunity cost of the capital used by government firms? Do government firms have a strong incentive to keep costs low? Are government firms innovative?

10. Natural resources are neither a necessary nor a sufficient condition for economic growth. Other than their harbors, neither Hong Kong nor Singapore has significant natural resources. Likewise, Japan has few natural resources, and it imports almost all of its industrial energy supply. Nonetheless, the growth rates of all three have been among the most rapid in the world since 1960. In contrast, many resource-rich countries, such as Nigeria, Venezuela, Ghana, and Bolivia, have poor records of economic growth. Without sound institutions and policies, even resource-rich countries tend to stagnate. On the other hand, countries that follow sound policies are able to import the resources required for growth and prosperity.

12. The increase in diversity provides consumers with more options and thereby improves their welfare. For the most part, the GDP figures fail to capture the impact of this factor.

CHAPTER 17: GAINING FROM INTERNATIONAL TRADE

2. Availability of goods and services, not jobs, is the source of economic prosperity. When a good can be purchased cheaper abroad than it can be produced at home, a nation can expand the quantity of goods and services available for consumption by specializing in the production of those goods for which it is a low-cost producer and trading them for the cheap (relative to domestic costs) foreign goods. Trade restrictions limiting the ability of Americans to purchase low-cost goods from foreigners stifle this process and thereby reduce the living standard of Americans.

4. Statements (a) and (b) are not in conflict. Since trade restrictions are typically a special-interest issue, political entrepreneurs can often gain by supporting them even when they promote economic inefficiency.

6. True. The primary effect of trade restrictions is an increase in domestic scarcity. This has distributional consequences, but it is clear that, as a whole, a nation will be harmed by the increased domestic scarcity that accompanies the trade restraints.

8. **a.** No. Americans would be poorer if we used more of our resources to produce things for which we are a high-opportunity-cost producer and less of our resources to produce things for which we are a low-opportunity-cost producer. Employment might either increase or decrease, but the key point is that it is the value of goods produced, not employment, that generates income and provides for the wealth of a nation. The answer to (b) is the same as (a).

10. In thinking about this issue, consider the following points. Suppose that the Japanese were willing to give products such as automobiles, electronic goods, and clothing to us free of charge. Would we be worse off if we accepted the gifts? Should we try to keep the free goods out? What is the source of real income—jobs or goods and services? If the gifts make us better off, doesn't it follow that partial gifts would also make us better off?

12. Although trade reduces employment in import-competing industries, it expands employment in export industries. On balance, there is no reason to believe that trade either promotes or destroys jobs. The major effect of trade is to permit individuals, states, regions, and nations to generate a larger output by specializing in the things they do well and trading for those things that they would produce only at a high cost. A higher real income is the result.

14. The quota reduces the supply of sugar to the domestic market and drives up the domestic price of sugar. Domestic producers benefit from the higher prices at the expense of domestic consumers (see Exhibit 17-9). Studies indicate that the quota

expanded the gross income of the 11,000 domestic sugar farmers by approximately $130,000 per farm in the mid-1980s, at the expense (in the form of higher prices of sugar and sugar products) of approximately $6 per year to the average domestic consumer. Since the program channels resources away from products for which the United States has a comparative advantage, it reduces the productive capacity of the United States. Both the special interest nature of the issue and rent-seeking theory explain the political attractiveness of the program.

16. True. If country A imposes a tariff, other countries will sell less to A and therefore acquire less purchasing power in terms of A's currency. Thus, they will have to reduce their purchases of A's export goods.

CHAPTER 18: INTERNATIONAL FINANCE AND THE FOREIGN EXCHANGE MARKET

1. The Japanese cameras will become more expensive, and the quantity purchased by Americans will decline.

4. On February 2, the dollar appreciated against the British pound and depreciated against the Canadian dollar.

5. Scenarios (a) and (g) would cause the dollar to appreciate; (b), (c), (d), (e), and (h) would cause the dollar to depreciate; (f) would leave the exchange rate unchanged.

8. Some people fear that foreign investment makes the U.S. vulnerable because foreigners might decide to suddenly sell their assets and leave. When you consider this argument, it is important to recognize that foreign and domestic investors are influenced by pretty much the same considerations. Anything that would cause foreigners to withdraw funds would also cause domestic investors to do likewise. In fact, the vulnerability runs the other way. If foreign investors were to leave, the assets financed by their funds would remain. Thus, they would be in a weak position to impose harm on the U.S. economy.

9. Each of the changes would reduce the size of the current-account deficit.

11. The current-account balance will move toward a larger deficit (or smaller surplus), and the dollar will appreciate.

13. False. Flexible exchange rates bring the sum of the current and capital accounts into balance, but they do not necessarily lead to balance for either component.

14. a. No. The exchange rate will bring the sum of the current and capital accounts into balance, but it will not bring about either an overall merchandise trade balance or a trade balance with a specific country.

    b. Compared to the United States, Japan has a high savings rate. High-income countries with high savings rates tend to invest substantially abroad. To pay for these investments, Japan must run a current-account surplus. Its trading partners—particularly those with a low saving rate, such as the United States—will do the opposite. In addition, Japan is a major importer of natural resources and raw materials, two product areas where the United States does not generally have a comparative advantage. Because the United States is generally not a low-cost producer of the primary products imported by the Japanese, the United States tends to export fewer goods and services to Japan than it imports.

15. These purchases increase the foreign-exchange value of the dollar, which makes imports cheaper relative to exports and thereby enlarges the trade deficit. Politicians often charge that this reduces output and employment. However, the bond purchases are an inflow of capital that will also result in lower U.S. interest rates, which will tend to stimulate output and employment. Thus, there is little reason to believe that the net affect will be either substantial or harmful.

CHAPTER 19: CONSUMER CHOICE AND ELASTICITY

1. Revenue will rise (fall) if students who enroll pay more (less) extra revenue than is lost due to lower enrollment. Revenue will remain the same if those who enroll pay just enough more to offset the loss from reduced enrollment. A price elasticity of 1.2 implies that raising tuition rates would reduce tuition revenue.

2. If your opportunity cost of time is more than $10, it will make sense to take the plane. Thus, Mary will take the plane and Michele the bus.

3. It is likely that the income effect of cigarette price changes is much larger for low-income smokers than for high-income smokers, perhaps because expenditures on cigarettes are a larger proportion of the household budget for those with lower incomes. Thus, the income effect will be larger for this group.

6. Both income and time constrain our ability to consume. Since, in a wealthier society, time becomes more binding and income less binding, time-saving actions will be more common in a wealthier society. As we engage in time-saving actions (fast food, automatic appliances, air travel, and so on) in order to shift the time restraint outward, our lives become more hectic.

9. All three statements are true.

10. The answer to the first question is "No." Even for things we like, we will experience diminishing returns. Eventually, the cost of additional units of pizza will exceed their benefits. And, in answer to the second question, perfection in any activity is generally not worth the cost. For example, reading every page of this text three, four, or five times may improve your grade, but it may not be worth it. One function of a text is to structure the material (highlighted points, layout of graphs, and so on) so that the reader will be able to learn quickly (at a lower cost).

11. Carole

12. **a.** minus 1.59; elastic

    b. minus 1.54; elastic

CHAPTER 20: COSTS AND THE SUPPLY OF GOODS

1. The economic profit of a firm is its total revenue minus the opportunity cost of all resources used in the production process. Accounting profit often excludes the opportunity cost of certain resources—particularly the equity capital of the firm and any labor services provided by an owner-manager. Zero economic profit means that the resources owned by the firm are earning their opportunity cost—that is, the rate of return is as high as the highest valued alternative forgone. Thus, the firm would not gain by pursuing other lines of business.

2. **a.** The amount paid for the course is a sunk cost. It is not directly relevant to whether one should attend the lectures. **b.** There is an opportunity cost of one's house even if it is paid for. **c.** The decline in the price of the stock is a sunk cost and therefore it is not directly relevant to whether or not to sell at this time. **d.** There is an opportunity cost of public education even if it is provided free to the consumer.

5. True. If it could produce the output at a lower cost, its profit would be greater.

7. At low output, the firm's plant (a fixed cost) is underutilized, implying a high average cost. As output rises toward the designed output level, average cost falls, but then rises as the designed or optimal output for that size plant is surpassed and diminishing returns set in.

11. Because owners receive profits, clearly profit maximization is in their interest. Managers, if they are not owners, have no property right to profit and therefore no direct interest in profit maximization. Since a solid record of profitability tends to increase the market value (salary) of corporate managers, they do have an indirect incentive to pursue profits. However, corporate managers may also be interested in gaining power, having nice offices, hiring friends, expanding sales, and other activities, which may conflict with profitability. Thus, owners need to provide incentives for managers to seek profits, and to monitor the results.

12. **a.** The interest payments; **b.** The interest income forgone. The tax structure encourages debt rather than equity financing since the firm's tax liability is inversely related to its debt/equity ratio.

14. Check list. Did your marginal cost curve cross the *ATC* and *AVC* curves at their low points? Does the vertical distance between the *ATC* and *AVC* curves get smaller and smaller as output increases? If not, redraw the three curves correctly. See Exhibit 6b.

17. $2,500: the $2,000 decline in market value during the year plus $500 of potential interest on funds that could be obtained if the machine were sold new. Costs associated with the decline in the value of the machine last year are sunk costs.

18. Because they believe they will be able to restructure the firm and provide better management so that the firm will have positive net earnings in the future. If the firm is purchased at a low enough price, this will allow the new owners to cover the opportunity cost of their investment and still earn an economic profit. Alternatively, they may expect to sell off the firm's assets, receiving more net revenue than the cost of purchasing the firm.

CHAPTER 21: PRICE TAKERS AND THE COMPETITIVE PROCESS

1. In a highly competitive industry such as agriculture, lower resource prices might improve the rate of profit in the short run, but in the long run, competition will drive prices down until economic profit is eliminated. Thus, lower resource prices will do little to improve the long-run profitability in such industries.

2. The market price will decline because the profits will attract new firms (and capital investment) into the market and supply will increase, driving down the price until the profits are eliminated.

5. **a.** Increase; **b.** Increase; **c.** Increase: firms will earn economic profit; **d.** Rise (compared with its initial level) if coffee is an increasing-cost industry, but return to initial price if it is a constant-cost industry; **e.** Increase even more than it did in the short run; **f.** Economic profit will return to zero.

6. **a.** Decline; **b.** Increase; **c.** Decline; **d.** Decline

9. Competition virtually forces firms to operate efficiently and produce goods and services that consumers value highly relative to cost. Firms that fail to do so will find it difficult to compete, and eventually losses will drive them from the market.

11. **a.** The reduction in supply led to higher prices. **b.** Since demand is inelastic, the total revenue from sales increased. **c.** Overall, the profitability of farming increased, although some of the producers that were hardest hit by the drought experienced losses because of their sharp reduction in output.

14. **b.** Six or seven tons—$250 profit; **c.** seven or eight tons—$600 profit; **d.** five or six tons—$50 loss. Since the firm can cover its variable cost, it should stay in business if it believes that the low ($450) price is temporary.

CHAPTER 22: PRICE-SEARCHER MARKETS WITH LOW ENTRY BARRIERS

3. The amount of variety is determined by the willingness of consumers to pay for variety relative to the cost of providing it. If consumers value variety highly and the added costs of producing different styles, designs, and sizes is low, there will be a lot of variety. Alternatively, if consumers desire similar products, or if variation can be produced only at a high cost, little variety will be present. Apparently, consumers place a substantial value (relative to cost) on variety in napkins, but not in toothpicks.

4. The tax would increase the price of lower-quality (and lower-priced) automobiles by a larger percentage than higher-quality automobiles. Consumers would substitute away from the lower-quality autos after their relative price had increased. This substitution would increase the average quality of automobiles sold. Since the funds from the tax would be rebated to citizens through the lottery, one would expect this substitution effect to dominate any possible income effect.

7. No. A firm that maximizes *total* revenue would expand output as long as marginal revenue is positive. When marginal costs are positive, the revenue-maximizing price would be lower (and the output greater) than the price that would maximize the firm's profits.

8. In any of these cases, the answer is competition. To survive, a given type and size of firm must be able to produce at a low cost. Those firms with high per-unit cost will be driven from the market.

10. Building the new resort is more risky (and less attractive) because if the market analysis is incorrect, and demand is insufficient, it probably will be difficult to find other uses for the newly built resort. If the airline proves unprofitable, however, the capital (airplanes) should be extremely mobile. However, the resort would have one offsetting advantage: if demand were stronger than expected, and profits larger, it would take competitors longer to enter the market (build a new resort), and they would be more reluctant to make the more permanent investment.

12. In a competitive setting, only the big firms will survive if economies of scale are important. When economies of scale are unimportant, small firms will be able to compete effectively.

14. Competition provides the answer. If McDonald's fails to provide an attractively priced, tasty sandwich with a smile, people will turn to Burger King, Wendy's, Dairy Queen, and other rivals. If Wal-Mart does not provide convenience and value, people will turn to Kmart, Target, and other retailers. Similarly, as recent experience has shown, even a firm as large as General Motors will lose customers to Ford, Honda, Toyota, Chrysler, Volkswagen, and other automobile manufacturers if it fails to please the customer as much as rival suppliers do.

17. **a.** Total revenue: $0; $8,000; $14,000; $18,000; $20,000; $20,000; Total cost: $0; $5,000; $10,000; $15,000; $20,000; $25,000; Economic profit: $0; $3,000; $4,000; $3,000; $0; $5,000 (loss)

   b. Marginal revenue: $8,000; $6,000; $4,000; $2,000; $0; Marginal cost: $5,000; $5,000; $5,000; $5,000; $5,000

   c. Profit-maximizing price: $7,000

   d. Rod will sell 2 boats at the profit-maximizing price of $7,000.

   e. Rod's economic profits will be $4,000 per week.

   f. Yes, boats 1 and 2 are the only boats for which marginal revenue is higher than marginal cost.

g. Because of the existence of economic profit, more boat dealers will open up in the area. This will result in more competition and lower prices. The entry will continue until boat dealers' economic profits fall to zero.

h. When demand is elastic, lowering price increases total revenue; thus, Rod's demand is elastic between the prices of $9,000 and $5,000. When demand is, lowering price leaves revenue unchanged; thus, Rod's demand is unitary elastic between the prices of $5,000 and $4,000. One could also assume that Rod's demand would eventually become inelastic below a price of $4,000 because the elasticity of demand keeps falling as one moves down along a demand curve. When this happens, Rod's total revenue will begin to fall as he continues to lower price. For example, at a price of $3,000, Rod may sell 6 boats per week, resulting in only $18,000 in revenue, which is less than the revenue Rod receives at a price of $4,000.

CHAPTER 23: PRICE-SEARCHER MARKETS WITH HIGH ENTRY BARRIERS

1. The statement is true. Profits cannot exist in the long run without barriers to entry because without barriers new entrants seeking the profits would increase supply, drive down price, and eliminate the profits. But barriers to entry are no guarantee of profits. Sufficient demand is also a necessary condition.

3. No; No; No.

8. Because use of product variation and quality improvements to obtain a larger share of the market will be more difficult to monitor and control than a simple price reduction

11. Reductions in the cost of transportation generally increase competition because they force firms to compete with distant rivals and permit consumers to choose among a wider range of suppliers. As a result, the U.S. economy today is generally more competitive, in the rivalry sense, than it was 100 years ago.

12. The stock price, when the uncle bought the stock, no doubt reflected the well-known profits of Microsoft. The previous owners of the stock surely would not have sold it at a price that failed to reflect its high expected rate of future profit. Thus, there is no reason to believe that the stock purchase will earn a high rate of return for the uncle.

13. **a.** $15, profit = $110,000; **b.** $10

CHAPTER 24: THE SUPPLY OF AND DEMAND FOR PRODUCTIVE RESOURCES

3. **a.** Five; **b.** $350; **c.** Four. The firm will operate in the short run, but it will go out of business in the long run unless the market prices rise.

4. Yes. General increases in the productivity of the labor force will cause a general increase in wages. The higher general wage rates will increase the opportunity cost of barbering and cause the supply of barbers to decline. The reduction in the supply of barbers will place upward pressure on the wages of barbers, even if technological change and worker productivity have changed little in barbering.

6. The job opportunities outside of teaching are more attractive for persons with math and science training than for those with English and history degrees. Therefore, the same salary that attracts a substantial number of English and history teachers will be insufficient to attract the required number of math and science teachers.

8. No. The dressmaker needs to employ more capital and less labor because the marginal dollar expenditures on the former are currently increasing output by a larger amount than the latter.

10. Other things being constant, a lengthy training requirement to perform in an occupation reduces supply and places upward pressure on the earnings level. However, resource prices, including those for labor services, are determined by both demand and supply. When demand is weak, earnings will be low, even though a considerable amount of education may be necessary to perform in the occupation. For example, the earnings of people with degrees in English literature and world history are generally low, even though most people in these fields have a great deal of education.

12. **b.** 4; **c.** Employment would decline to 3.

CHAPTER 25: EARNINGS, PRODUCTIVITY, AND THE JOB MARKET

2. U.S. workers are more productive. By investing in human capital, the laborers are somewhat responsible, but the superior tools and physical capital that are available to U.S. workers also contribute to their higher wages.

6. Although this statement, often made by politicians, sounds true, in fact, it is false. Output of goods and services valued by consumers, not jobs, is the key to economic progress and a high standard of living. Real income cannot be high unless real output is high. If job creation were the key to economic progress, it would be easy to create millions of jobs. For example, we could prohibit the use of farm machinery. Such a prohibition would create millions of jobs in agriculture. However, it would also reduce output and our standard of living.

8. The opportunity cost of leisure (nonwork) for higher-wage workers is greater than it is for lower-wage workers.

9. False. Several additional factors, including differences in preferences (which would influence time worked, the trade-off between money wage and working conditions, and evaluation of alternative jobs), differences in jobs, and imperfect labor mobility, would result in variations in earnings.

10. Scenarios (a), (b), (e), and (f) will generally increase hourly earnings; (c) and (d) will generally reduce hourly earnings.

11. Hourly wages will be highest in B because the higher wages will be necessary to compensate workers in B for the uncertainty and loss of income during layoffs. Annual earnings will be higher in A in order to compensate workers in A for the additional hours they will work during the year.

CHAPTER 26: INVESTMENT, THE CAPITAL MARKET, AND THE WEALTH OF NATIONS

1. All the changes would increase interest rates in the United States.

4. No. The average outstanding balance during the year is only about half of $1,000. Therefore, the $200 interest charge translates to almost a 40 percent annual rate of interest.

6. Hints: Which has been considered to be more risky—purchasing a bond or a stock? How does risk influence the expected rate of return?

8. 6 percent

10. **a.** Mike; **b.** Yes, people who save a lot are able to get a higher interest rate on their savings as the result of people with a high rate of time preference; **c.** Yes, people who want to borrow money will be able to do so at a lower rate when there are more people (like Alicia) who want to save a lot.

11. They are helped. This question is a lot like prior questions involving Alicia and Mike. Potential gains from trade are present. If obstacles do not restrain trade, the low-income countries will be able to attract savings (from countries with a high saving rate) at a lower interest rate than would exist in the absence of trade. Similarly, people in the high-income countries will be able to earn a higher return than would otherwise be possible. Each can gain because of the existence of the other.

12. **a.** Approximately $1.277 million; **b.** Yes; **c.** The lottery earnings are less liquid. Because there is not a well-organized market transforming lottery earnings into present income, the transaction costs of finding a "buyer" (at a price equal to the present value of the earnings) for the lottery earnings "rights" may be higher than for the bond, if one wants to sell in the future.

14. No. The present value of the $500 annual additions to earnings during the next 10 years is less than the cost of the schooling.

16. Consider the following when answering this question: whose money is being invested by each of the two entities? If a private investment project goes bad, who is hurt? If a private project is successful, who reaps the gain? Answer the same two questions for political officials.

CHAPTER 27: INCOME INEQUALITY AND POVERTY

2. Differences in family size, age of potential workers, nonmoney "income," taxes, and cost-of-living among areas reduce the effectiveness of annual money income as a measure of economic status. In general, high-income families are larger, are more likely to be headed by a prime-age worker, have less nonmoney income (including leisure), pay more taxes, and reside in higher-cost-of-living areas (particularly large cities). Thus, money income comparison between high- and low-income groups often overstates the economic status of the former relative to the latter.

4. If there were no intergenerational mobility, the diagonal numbers would all be 100 percent. If there were complete equality of opportunity and outcomes, the numbers in each column and row would be 20 percent.

6. No. The increase in marginal tax rates will reduce the incentive of the poor to earn income. Therefore, their income will rise by $1,000 minus the reduction in their personal earnings due to the disincentive effects of the higher marginal tax rates.

7. 67 percent

SPECIAL TOPIC 1: GOVERNMENT SPENDING AND TAXATION

1. Taxes reduce economic efficiency because they eliminate some exchanges and thereby reduce the gains from these transactions. Because of (a) the deadweight losses accompanying the elimination of exchanges and (b) the cost of collecting taxes, the costs of additional tax revenue will be greater than the revenue transferred to the government. Studies indicate that it costs between $1.20 and $1.30 for each dollar of tax revenue raised by the government.

5. As we discussed in Chapter 6, the political process works better when there is a close relationship between who pays for and who benefits from government programs. An increase in the number of people who pay no income taxes is likely to weaken this relationship. While those with low incomes pay payroll taxes, the revenues from this tax are earmarked for the finance of the Social Security and Medicare programs. Thus, expansions in government are financed primarily by the personal income tax. In the future, exemption of large numbers of people from this tax is likely to make it

more difficult to control the growth of government. If you do not have to help pay for more government spending, why would you oppose it?

SPECIAL TOPIC 2: THE INTERNET: HOW IS IT CHANGING THE ECONOMY?

2. Airline tickets can be "transported" electronically; groceries cannot. Customers can observe the ticket information on-line, but they cannot observe the condition of fruits, vegetables, and other grocery products via the Internet.

SPECIAL TOPIC 3: THE ECONOMICS OF SOCIAL SECURITY

2. The pay-as-you-go Social Security system will face a crisis sometime around 2018 when the inflow of tax revenue will be insufficient to cover the promised benefits. Although the Social Security Trust Fund has bonds, they are merely an IOU from the Treasury to the Social Security Administration. To redeem these bonds and provide additional funds to finance Social Security benefits, the federal government will have to raise taxes (or pay the interest on additional Treasury bonds it sells), or cut other expenditures, or both. Thus, the presence of the SSTF bonds does not do much to alleviate the crisis.

SPECIAL TOPIC 4: THE STOCK MARKET: ITS FUNCTION, PERFORMANCE, AND POTENTIAL AS AN INVESTMENT OPPORTUNITY

1. History shows that in the U.S. stock market, fairly high returns can be gained at a relatively low risk by people who hold a diverse portfolio of stocks in unrelated industries for a period of 20 years or more. An indexed equity mutual fund is an option that would allow a person to purchase a diverse portfolio while keeping commission costs low.

3. The expectation of high profits in the future drove up the price of the stock, despite the lack of dividend payment in the first years of the firm. Investors are equally happy with high dividends or the equivalent in rising stock value due to the firm's retaining its profits for further investment.

5. Investors are buying such a stock for its rising value (price), which reflects expected future earnings and dividends.

SPECIAL TOPIC 5: THE FEDERAL BUDGET AND THE NATIONAL DEBT

1. No. Both private corporations and governments can, and often do, have continual debt outstanding. Borrowers can continue to finance and refinance debt as long as lenders have confidence in their ability to pay. This will generally be the case as long as the interest liability is small relative to income (or the potential tax base).

3. No. Remember, trade is a positive-sum game. Bonds are sold to foreigners because they are offering a better deal (acceptance of a lower interest rate) than is available elsewhere. Prohibiting the sale of bonds to foreigners would result in higher real interest rates and less investment, both of which would adversely affect Americans.

5. Lower; voters do not enjoy paying taxes and, therefore, voter dissatisfaction places a restraint on higher taxes, which would also restrain expenditures if the budget had to

be balanced. More efficiently; the restraint of tax increases would tighten the budget constraint and make the reality of opportunity cost more visible to both voters and politicians.

7. No. Yes.

SPECIAL TOPIC 6: LABOR MARKET POLICIES AND UNEMPLOYMENT: A CROSS-COUNTRY ANALYSIS

1. The ability to organize only a portion of the firms in an industry leaves the organized firms in competition with the unorganized firms. When organized firms pay higher wages, they find it harder to compete with nonunion firms due to higher costs. This restricts the ability of the union to raise wages in the organized firms. Because competition from nonunion firms is less prevalent in Europe than in the United States, European unions are better able than their counterparts in the United States to increase the wages of union members.

SPECIAL TOPIC 7: INSTITUTIONS, POLICIES, AND THE IRISH MIRACLE

2. Foreign investors have options. To attract foreign investment, a country will not only have to follow sound policies (for example, low taxes, trade openness, maintenance of monetary and price stability, minimal regulation), but it will also have to earn credibility that the sound policies will be maintained in the future. The foreign investment will supplement investment financed by domestic saving and thereby help a country achieve higher rates of capital formation and worker productivity than it would otherwise. In turn, rapid growth of productivity is the primary source of rapid growth in income.

SPECIAL TOPIC 8: THE ECONOMICS OF HEALTH CARE

2. Health insurance benefits are a component of the employee's compensation package. Unless the employer values the services of the employee by an amount greater than or equal to the total cost of the employee's compensation, the worker will not be hired. Thus, like other components of the compensation package, health insurance benefits are earned by employees.

4. Medicare and Medicaid increased both total health-care spending and the share of that spending paid by a third party. Both of these factors increased the demand for and prices of medical services, thereby making them more expensive for people who do not qualify for these programs.

SPECIAL TOPIC 9: SCHOOL CHOICE: CAN IT IMPROVE THE QUALITY OF EDUCATION IN AMERICA?

2. The incentive is weak to keep costs low because the suppliers (public schools) don't face competition from rivals. Because consumers cannot take their funding and go elsewhere, they are in a weak position to discipline the district schools that are not doing a good job. Furthermore, a lower quality of service can often be used as an argument for more government funding. Economics indicates that an absence of competitive forces will lead to higher costs and lower quality of the product or service supplied. There is no reason to expect that education will be an exception.

SPECIAL TOPIC 10: IS DISCRIMINATION RESPONSIBLE FOR THE EARNINGS DIFFERENCES BETWEEN MEN AND WOMEN?

2. (a) The average years of work experience of women relative to men would decline because many of the women entering the labor force would have little prior work experience.

(b) The average hours of work of women would also decline because many of the married women would be looking for part-time employment and hours that were complementary with their historic household responsibilities.

(c) The increased labor force participation of married women would cause the female/male earnings ratio to fall.

4. Not necessarily. Compared with married men, single men tend to be younger, have fewer dependents, be more likely to drop out of the labor force, and be less likely to receive earnings-enhancing assistance from another person. All these factors will reduce their earnings relative to married men.

SPECIAL TOPIC 11: DO LABOR UNIONS INCREASE THE WAGES OF WORKERS?

1. If the union is able to raise the wages of the farm workers: (a) the cost of Florida oranges will rise, causing supply to decline and price to rise in the long run; (b) profits of the Florida orange growers will decline in the short run, but in the long run they will return to the normal rate; (c) mechanization will be encouraged; and (d) the employment of fruit pickers will decline—particularly in the long run.

3. If only part of an industry is unionized, if the union pushes up the wages of the unionized firms, this will increase their cost and make it difficult for them to compete effectively with their nonunion rivals. Thus, the union will be unable to increase wages much without experiencing a substantial reduction in the employment of its members.

5. False. Competition constrains both employers and employees. Employers must compete with other employers for labor services. To gain the labor services of an employee, an employer must offer a compensation package superior to one that the employee can get elsewhere. If the employer does not offer a superior package, the employee will work for a rival employer or choose self-employment. Similarly, employees must compete with other employees. Therefore, their ability to demand whatever wage they would like is also restrained. Thus, competition prevents both the payment of low (below-market) wages by employers and the imposition of high (above-market) wages by employees.

6. Not necessarily. Adjustment must be made for differences in (a) the productivity characteristics of the union and nonunion workers, and (b) the types of jobs they occupy (for example, work environment, job security, likelihood of layoff, and so on). Adjustment for these factors may either increase or reduce the $1.50 differential.

7. Remember, union members compete with other workers, including less-skilled workers. An increase in the minimum wage makes unskilled, low-wage workers more expensive. A higher minimum wage increases the demand for high-skilled employees who are good substitutes for the low-skilled workers. Union members are overrepresented among the high-skilled group helped by an increase in the minimum wage. Therefore, while union leaders will generally pitch their support for a higher minimum wage in terms of a desire that all workers be paid a "decent wage," the effect of the legislation on union members suggests that self-interest rather than altruism underlies their support for the legislation.

SPECIAL TOPIC 12: HOW DOES GOVERNMENT REGULATION AFFECT YOUR LIFE?

1. Making cars safer is good, but if the cost has previously kept consumers from demanding the safety measures, it is possible that they are not worth the cost to many consumers. Some very expensive cars, such as Mercedes-Benz, had airbags when there was no requirement, but Volkswagen did not. Should only the more costly cars be sold? If so, then some people, probably the less affluent, will drive older, even less safe cars. This is not a clear-cut issue.

3. Profitability may be adversely affected in the short run, but in the long run, prices will rise enough for the firms to cover their opportunity cost of production. Consumers bear the cost of such legislation and get the associated benefits, large or small.

5. Experts often do know far more about the technical options than do consumers, although consumers can and do read the advice of experts. Suppliers of safer products also make it a point to advertise data and expert opinion indicating their products are indeed safer. Nevertheless, experts usually do understand the technologies better. On the other hand, experts cannot know about how products will be used. A consumer may prefer to pay for a high degree of safety for the family car, which will carry the whole family at high speeds over long distances, while preferring a much cheaper, less-reliable car for running errands near home. Such choices are hard to allow if all vehicles are strictly regulated for safety. Decision-maker knowledge (and incentives) is, in some cases, better with consumer choice than with thorough and strict regulation.

7. The statement is essentially true. In the short run, capital may be invested in an industry such that it cannot easily be moved elsewhere. If customer demand is elastic, the industry may bear a large part of the cost burden in the short run. In the long run, however, capital is mobile. Factories don't have to be replaced, for example. If costs in the industry are high relative to the revenues, then capital will migrate over time to other industries, and supply in the regulated industry will fall until the price that buyers will pay is again high enough to provide the market rate of return to capital.

SPECIAL TOPIC 13: RESOURCE MANAGEMENT: HOW PROPERTY RIGHTS AND MARKETS REPLACE CONFLICT WITH COOPERATION

1. Issues for thought: Are resources scarce when supplied by nature? If so, what process should be used to ration them among competing demanders? If a resource is owned by the government rather than privately, how will this affect the incentive to care for and conserve the resource for the future? Do you think that government-owned property like the national forests and parks are better cared for than, for example, Disney World?

2. If an investment, such as letting the trees grow another 20 years, yields a higher return than other investments, then the stock price will fall if the trees are cut too soon, or will go higher if a new, more profitable investment path (letting the trees grow) is announced. Either way, the stock price immediately rewards good long-term decisions relative to bad, shortsighted ones.

4. *Hint:* What is the role of common law protection of property rights, when a polluter violates the rights of a property owner downwind or downstream?

SPECIAL TOPIC 14: DIFFICULT ENVIRONMENTAL CASES AND THE ROLE OF GOVERNMENT

1. The ITQ would allow fishers to fish at their own speed without fear of losing their quota to others.

3. The cost of stopping the buildup would be very large. Avoiding the buildup would be very costly. That large opportunity cost could accomplish instead much else that would help future generations. The forecasted risks are only speculatively the result of the buildup and would occur mostly far in the future. And a warmer world has advantages as well as disadvantages.

4. In a market with strong property rights in place, a polluter would have to be concerned about harming others and being sued by them for damages. Without strong property rights in place, regulation might help. Or it might not. In any case, regulators need information available only in a market to judge how tightly to regulate if the regulator is seeking efficiency.

Absolute advantage   A situation in which a nation, as the result of its previous experience and/or natural endowments, can produce more of a good (with the same amount of resources) than another nation.

Accounting profits   The sales revenues minus the expenses of a firm over a designated time period, usually one year. Accounting profits typically make allowances for changes in the firm's inventories and depreciation of its assets. No allowance is made, however, for the opportunity cost of the equity capital of the firm's owners, or other implicit costs.

Activists   Economists who believe that discretionary changes in monetary and fiscal policy can reduce the degree of insability in output and employment.

Adaptive-expectations hypothesis   The hypothesis that economic decision makers base their future expectations on actual outcomes observed during recent periods. For example, according to this view, the rate of inflation actually experienced during the past two or three years would be the major determinant of the rate of inflation expected for the next year.

Administrative lag   The time period after the need for a policy change is recognized but before the policy is actually implemented.

Aggregate demand curve   A downward-sloping curve showing the relationship between the price level and the quantity of domestically produced goods and services all households, business firms, governments, and foreigners (net exports) are willing to purchase.

Aggregate supply curve   The curve showing the relationship between the nation's price level and quantity of goods supplied by its producers. In the short run, it is probably an upward-sloping curve, but in the long run the aggregate supply curve is vertical.

Anticipated change   A change that is foreseen by decision makers in time for them to make an adjustment.

Anticipated inflation   An increase in the general level of prices that was expected by most decision makers.

Appreciation   An increase in the value of domestic currency relative to foreign currencies. An appreciation makes foreign goods cheaper for domestic residents.

Automatic stabilizers   Built-in features that tend automatically to promote a budget deficit during a recession and a budget surplus during an inflationary boom, even without a change in policy.

Automation   A production technique that reduces the amount of labor required to produce a good or service. It is beneficial to adopt the new labor-saving technology only if it reduces the cost of production.

Autonomous expenditures   Expenditures that do not vary with the level of income. They are determined by factors (such as business expectations and economic policy) that are outside the basic aggregate expenditure model.

Average fixed cost   Total fixed cost divided by the number of units produced. It always declines as output increases.

Average product   The total product (output) divided by the number of units of the variable input required to produce that output level.

Average tax rate (ATR)   Tax liability divided by taxable income. It is the percentage of income paid in taxes.

Average total cost   Total cost divided by the number of units produced. It is sometimes called per-unit cost.

Average variable cost   The total variable cost divided by the number of units produced.

Balance of merchandise trade   The difference between the value of merchandise exports and the value of merchandise imports for a nation. It is also called simply the *balance of trade* or *net exports.* The balance of merchandise trade is only one component of a nation's total balance of payments and its current accounts.

Balance of payments   A summary of all economic transactions between a country and all other countries for a specific time period, usually a year. The balance-of-payments account reflects all payments and liabilities to foreigners (debits) and all payments and obligations received from foreigners (credits).

Balance on current account   The import-export balance of goods and services, plus net investment income earned abroad, plus net private and government transfers. If the value of the nation's export-type items exceeds (is less than) the value of the nation's import-type items plus net unilateral transfers to foreigners, a current-account surplus (deficit) is present. If the value of a nation's export-type items is less than the value of the nation's import-type items plus net unilateral transfers to foreigners, a current-account deficit is present.

Balance on goods and services   The exports of goods (merchandise) and services of a nation minus its imports of goods and services.

Balanced budget   A situation in which current government revenue from taxes, fees, and other sources is just equal to current government expenditures.

Bank reserves   Vault cash plus deposits of banks with Federal Reserve banks.

Barriers to entry   Obstacles that limit the freedom of potential rivals to enter and compete in an industry or market.

Black market   A market that operates outside the legal system, either where illegal goods are sold or legal goods are sold at illegal prices or terms.

Budget deficit   A situation in which total government spending exceeds total government revenue during a specific time period, usually one year.

Budget surplus   A situation in which total government spending is less than total government revenue during a time period, usually a year.

Business cycle   Fluctuations in the general level of economic level of activity as measured by variables such as the rate of unemployment and changes in real GDP.

Capital   Man-made resources (such as tools, equipment, and structures) that are used to produce other goods and services. They enhance our ability to produce in the future.

Capital account   The record of transactions with foreigners that involve either (1) the exchange of ownership rights to real or financial assets or (2) the extension of loans.

Capitalism An economic system in which productive resources are owned privately and goods and resources are allocated through market prices.

Cartel An organization of sellers designed to coordinate supply decisions so that the joint profits of the members will be maximized. A cartel will seek to create a monopoly in the market.

Central bank An institution that regulates the banking system and controls the supply of a country's money.

Ceteris paribus A Latin term meaning "other things constant," used when the effect of one change is being described, recognizing that if other things changed, they also could affect the result. Economists often describe the effects of one change, knowing that in the real world, other things might change and also exert an effect.

Choice The act of selecting among alternatives.

Civilian labor force The number of people 16 years of age and over who are either employed or unemployed. In order to be classified as unemployed, one must be looking for a job.

Classical economists Economists from Adam Smith to the time of Keynes who focused their analyses on economic efficiency and production. With regard to business instability, they thought market prices and wages would decline during a recession quickly enough to bring the economy back to full employment within a short period of time.

Collective decision making The method of organization that relies on public-sector decision making (voting, political bargaining, lobbying, and so on) to resolve basic economic questions.

Collusion Agreement among firms to avoid various competitive practices, particularly price reductions. It may involve either formal agreements or merely tacit recognition that competitive practices will be self-defeating in the long run. Tacit collusion is difficult to detect. In the United States, antitrust laws prohibit collusion and conspiracies to restrain trade.

Commercial banks Financial institutions that offer a wide range of services (for example, checking accounts, savings accounts, and loans) to their customers. Commercial banks are owned by stockholders and seek to operate at a profit.

Comparative advantage The ability to produce a good at a lower opportunity cost than others can produce it. Relative costs determine comparative advantage.

Compensating wage differentials Wage differences that compensate workers for risk, unpleasant working conditions, and other undesirable nonpecuniary aspects of a job.

Competition as a dynamic process Rivalry or competitiveness between or among parties (for example, producers or input suppliers), each of which seeks to deliver a better deal to buyers in terms of quality, price, and product information.

Competitive price-searcher market A market where the firms have a downward-sloping demand curve, and entry into and exit from the market are relatively easy.

Complements Products that are usually consumed jointly (for example, bread and butter, hot dogs and hot dog buns). A decrease in the price of one will cause an increase in demand for the other.

Constant returns to scale Unit costs that are constant as the scale of the firm is altered. Neither economies nor diseconomies of scale are present.

Constant-cost industry An industry for which factor prices and costs of production remain constant as market output is expanded. The long-run market supply curves is therefore horizontal in these industries.

Consumer price index (CPI) An indicator of the general level of prices. It attempts to compare the cost of purchasing the market basket bought by a typical consumer during a specific period to the cost of purchasing the same market basket during an earlier period.

Consumer sentiment index A measure of the optimism of consumers based on their responses to a set of five questions about their current and expected future personal economic situation. Conducted by the University of Michigan, it is based on a representative sample of U.S. households.

Consumer surplus The difference between the maximum price consumers are willing to pay and the price they actually pay. It is the net gain derived by the buyers of the good.

Consumption function A fundamental relationship between disposable income and consumption. When disposable income increases, current consumption expenditures rise, but by a smaller amount than the increase in income.

Contestable market A market in which the costs of entry and exit are low, so a firm risks little by entering. Efficient production and zero economic profits should prevail in a contestable market.

Corporation A business firm owned by shareholders who possess ownership rights to the firm's profits, but whose liability is limited to the amount of their investment in the firm.

Countercyclical policy A policy that tends to move the economy in an opposite direction from the forces of the business cycle. Such a policy would stimulate demand during the contraction phase of the business cycle and restrain demand during the expansion phase.

Credit Funds acquired by borrowing.

Credit unions Financial cooperative organizations of individuals with a common affiliation (such as an employer or a labor union). They accept deposits, including checkable deposits, pay interest (or dividends) on them out of earnings, and lend funds primarily to members.

Crowding-out effect A reduction in private spending as a result of higher interest rates generated by budget deficits that are financed by borrowing in the private loanable funds market.

Currency Medium of exchange made of metal or paper.

Currency board An entity that (1) issues a currency with a fixed designated value relative to a widely accepted currency (for example, the U.S. dollar), (2) promises to continue to redeem the issued currency at the fixed rate, and (3) maintains bonds and other liquid assets denominated in the other currency that provide 100 percent backing for all currency issued.

Current account The record of all transactions with foreign nations that involve the exchange of merchandise goods and services, current income derived from investments, and unilateral gifts.

Cyclical unemployment Unemployment due to recessionary business conditions and inadequate labor demand.

Deadweight loss The loss of gains from trade to buyers and sellers that occurs when a tax is imposed. The deadweight loss imoses a burden on both buyers and sellers over and above the actual payment of the tax.

Decreasing-cost industry An industry for which costs of production decline as the industry expands. The market supply is therefore inversely related to price. Such industries are atypical.

Demand deposits Non-interest-earning checking deposits that can be either withdrawn or made payable on demand to a third party. Like currency, these deposits are widely used as a means of payment.

Demand for money A curve that indicates the relationship between the interest rate and the quantity of money people want to hold. Because higher interest rates increase the opportunity cost of holding money, the quantity demanded of money will be inversely related to the interest rate.

Deposit Expansion multiplier The multiple by which an increase in reserves will increase the money supply. It is inversely related to the required reserve ratio.

Depository institutions Businesses that accept checking and savings deposits and use a portion of them to extend loans and make investments. Banks, savings and loan associations, and credit unions are examples.

Depreciation A reduction in the value of the domestic currency relative to foreign currencies. A depreciation makes foreign goods more expensive for domestic residents. The estimated amount of physical capital (for example, machines and buildings) that is worn out or used up producing goods during the period.

Depression A prolonged and very severe recession.

Derived demand The demand for a resource; it stems from the demand for the final good the resource helps to produce.

Differentiated products Products distinguished from similar products by characteristics like quality, design, location, and method of promotion.

Discount rate The interest rate the Federal Reserve charges banking institutions for borrowing funds.

Discounting The procedure used to calculate the present value of future income, which is inversely related to both the interest rate and the amount of time that passes before the funds are received.

Discretionary fiscal policy A change in laws or appropriation levels that alters government revenues and/or expenditures.

Disposable income The income available to individuals after personal taxes. It can be either spent on consumption or saved.

Division of labor A method that breaks down the production of a product into a series of specific tasks, each performed by a different worker.

Dumping Selling a good in a foreign country at a lower price than it's sold for in the domestic market.

Earned Income Tax Credit A provision of the tax code that provides a credit or rebate to persons with low earnings (income from work activities). The credit is eventually phased out if the recipient's earnings increase.

Economic efficiency A situation that occurs when (1) all activities generating more benefit than cost are undertaken, and (2) no activities are undertaken for which the cost exceeds the benefit.

Economic profit The difference between the firm's total revenues and its total costs, including both the explicit and implicit cost components.

Economic regulation Regulation of product price or industrial structure, usually imposed on a specific industry. By and large, the production processes used by the regulated firms are unaffected by this type of regulation.

Economic theory A set of definitions, postulates, and principles assembled in a manner that makes clear the "cause-and-effect" relationships.

Economies of scale Reductions in the firm's per-unit costs associated with the use of large plants to produce a large volume of output.

Economizing behavior Choosing the option that offers the greatest benefit at the least possible cost.

Employment discrimination Unequal treatment of persons on the basis of their race, sex, or religion, restricting their employment and earnings opportunities compared to others of similar productivity. Employment discrimination may stem from the prejudices of employers, customers, fellow employees, or all three.

Employment/population ratio The number of people 16 years of age and over employed as civilians divided by the total civilian population 16 years of age and over. The ratio is expressed as a percentage.

Entrepreneur A person who introduces new products or improved technologies and decides which projects to undertake. A successful entrepreneur's actions will increase the value of resources and expand the size of the economic pie.

Equation of exchange $MV - PY$, where M is the money supply, V is the velocity of money, P is the price level, and Y is the output of goods and services produced in an economy.

Equilibrium A state in which the conflicting forces of supply and demand are in balance. When a market is in equilibrium, the decisions of consumers and producers are brought in to harmony with one another, and the quantity supplied will equal the quantity demanded.

Equilibrium A balance of forces permitting the simultaneous fulfillment of plans by buyers and sellers.

Equity mutual fund A corporation that pools the funds of investors, including small investors, and uses them to purchase a bundle of stocks.

Escalator clause A contractual agreement that periodically and automatically adjusts money wage rates upward as the price level rises. They are sometimes referred to as a cost-of-living adjustment or COLA.

Excess burden of taxation Another term for deadweight loss. It reflects losses that occur when beneficial activities are forgone because they are taxed.

Excess reserves Actual reserves that exceed the legal requirement.

Exchange rate The domestic price of one unit of foreign currency. For example, if it takes $1.50 to purchase one English pound, the dollar-to-pound exchange rate is 1.50.

Expansionary fiscal policy An increase in government expenditures and/or a reduction in tax rates such that the expected size of the budget deficit expands.

Expansionary monetary policy A shift in monetary policy designed to stimulate aggregate demand. Bond purchases by the Fed, the creation of additional bank reserves, and an increase in the growth rate of the money supply generally indicate a shift to a more expansionary monetary policy.

Expenditure multiplier The ratio of the change in equilibrium output to the independent change in investment, consumption, or government spending that brings about the change. Numerically, the multiplier is equal to 1 *divided by* (1-MPC) when the price level is constant.

Explicit costs Payments by a firm to purchase the services of productive resources.

Exports Goods and services produced domestically but sold to foreigners.

External Benefits Spillover effects that generate benefits for nonconsenting third parties.

External costs Spillover effects that reduce the well-being of nonconsenting third parties.

External debt The portion of the national debt owed to foreign investors.

Externalities Spillover effects of an activity that influence the well-being of nonconsenting third parties.

Fallacy of composition Erroneous view that what is true for the individual (or the part) will also be true for the group (or the whole).

Federal Deposit Insurance Corporation (FDIC) A federally chartered corporation that insures the deposits held by commercial banks, savings and loans, and credit unions.

Federal funds market A loanable funds market in which banks seeking additional reserves borrow short-term (generally for seven days or less) funds from banks with excess reserves. The interest rate in this market is called the federal funds rate.

Federal Open Market Committee (FOMC) A committee of the Federal Reserve system that establishes Fed policy with regard to governement securities—the primary mechanism used to control the money supply. It is comprised of the 7 members of the Board of Governors and the 12 district bank presidents of the Fed.

Federal Reserve System The central bank of the United States; it carries out banking regulatory policies and is responsible for the conduct of monetary policy.

Fiat money Money that has neither intrinsic value nor the backing of a commodity with intrinsic value; paper currency is an example.

Final market goods and services Goods and services purchased by their ultimate user.

Fiscal policy The use of government taxation and expenditure policies for the purpose of achieving macroeconomic goals.

Fixed exchange rate An exchange rate that is set at a determined amount by government policy.

Flexible exchange rates Exchange rates that are determined by the market forces of supply and demand. They are sometimes called floating exchange rates.

Foreign exchange market The market in which the currencies of different countries are bought and sold.

Fractional reserve banking A system that permits banks to hold reserves of less than 100 percent against their deposits.

Franchise A right or license granted to an individual to market a company's goods or services or use its brand name. The individual firms are independently firms owned but must meet certain conditions to continue to use the name.

Free rider A person who receives the benefit of a good without paying for it. Because of their nonexcludable nature, public goods are subject to free-rider problems.

Frictional unemployment Unemployment due to constant changes in the economy that prevent qualified unemployed workers from being immediately matched up with existing job openings. It results from the imperfect information and search activities related to suitably matching employees with employers.

Fringe benefits Benefits other than normal money wages that are supplied to employees in exchange for their labor services. Higher fringe benefits come at the expense of lower money wages.

Full employment The level of employment that results from the efficient use of the labor force after allowance is made for the normal (natural) rate of unemployment due to information

cost, dynamic changes, and the structural conditions of the economy. For the United States, full employmentis thought to exist when approximately 95 percent of the labor force is employed.

Game theory A tool used to analyze the strategic choices made by competitors in a conflict situation like the decisions made by firms in an oligopoly.

GDP deflator A price index that reveals the cost during the current period of purchasing the items included in GDP relative to the cost during a base year (currently, 2000). Unlike the consumer price index (CPI) the GDP deflator also measures the prices of capital goods and other goods and services purchased by businesses and governments. Because of this, it is thought to be a more accurate measure of changes in the general level of prices than the CPI.

General Agreement on Tariffs and Trade (GATT) An organization formed following the Second World War to set the rules for the conduct of international trade and reduce barriers to trade among nations.

Going out of business The sale of a firm's assets and its permanent exit from the market. By going out of business, a firm is able to avoid fixed costs, which would continue during a shutdown.

Goods and services market A highly aggregated market encompassing the flow of all final-user goods and services. The market counts all items that enter into GDP. Thus, real output in this market is equal to real GDP.

Gross domestic product (GDP) The market value of all final goods and services produced within a country during a specific period.

Gross national product (GNP) The total market value of all final goods and services produced by the citizens of a country. It is equal to GDP minus the net income of foreigners.

Health and safety regulation Legislation designed to improve the health, safety, and environmental conditions available to workers and/or consumers. The legislation usually mandates production procedures, minimum standards, and/or product characteristics to be met by producers and employers.

Human resources The abilities, skills, and health of human beings that can contribute to the production of both current and future output. Investment in training and education can increase the supply of human resources.

Impact lag The time period after a policy change is implemented but before the change begins to exert its primary effects.

Implicit costs The opportunity costs associated with a firm's use of resources that it owns. These costs do not involve a direct money payment. Examples include wage income and interest forgone by the owner of a firm who also provides labor services and equity capital to the firm.

Implicit marginal tax rate The amount of additional (marginal) earnings that must be paid explicitly in taxes or implicitly in the form of lower income supplements. The marginal tax rate establishes the fraction of an additional dollar earned that an individual is permitted to keep, it is an important determinant of the incentive to work.

Import quota A specific limit or maximum quantity (or value) of a good permitted to be imported into a country during a given period.

Imports Goods and services produced by foreigners but purchased by domestic consumers, businesses, and governments.

Income effect   That part of an increase (decrease) in amount consumed that is the result of the consumer's real income being expanded (contracted) by a reduction (rise) in the price of a good.

Income elasticity   The percentage change in the quantity of a product demanded divided by the percentage change in consumer income that caused the change in quantity demanded. It measures the responsiveness of the demand for a good to a consumer's change in income.

Income mobility   Movement of individuals and families either up or down income-distribution rankings when comparisons are made at two different points in time. When substantial income mobility is present, a person's current position in the ranking will not be a very good indicator of what his or her position will be a few years in the future.

Increasing-cost industry   An industry for which costs of production rise as output is expanded. In these industries, even in the long run, higher market prices will be needed to induce the firms to expand the total output in such industries. As a result, the long-run market supply curve in such industries will slope upward to the right.

Index of leading indicators   An index of economic variables that historically has tended to turn down prior to the beginning of a recession and turn up prior to the beginning of a business expansion.

Indexed equity mutual fund   An equity mutual fund that holds a portfolio of stocks that matches their share (or weight) in a broad stock market index such as the S&P 500. The overhead of these funds is usually quite low because their expenses on stock trading and research are low.

Indirect business taxes   Taxes that increase the business firm's costs of production and, therefore, the prices charged to consumers. Examples would be sales, excise, and property taxes.

Inferior good   A good that has a negative income elasticity, so that, as consumer income rises, the demand for that good falls.

Inflation   A continuing rise in the general level of prices of goods and services. The purchasing power of the monetary unit, such as the dollar, declines when inflation is present.

Inflationary premium   A component of the money interest rate that reflects compensation to the lender for the expected decrease, due to inflation, in the purchasing power of the principal and interest during the course of the loan. It is determined by the expected rate of future inflation.

Innovation   The successful introduction and adoption of a new product or process; the economic application of inventions and marketing techniques.

Intermediate goods   Goods purchased for resale or for use in producing another good or service.

International Monetary Fund (IMF)   An international banking organization, with more than 180 member nations, designed to oversee the operation of the international monetary system. Although it does not control the world supply of money, it does hold currency reserves for member nations and makes currency loans to national central banks.

Invention   The creation of a new product or process, often facilitated by the knowledge of engineering and science.

Inventory investment   Changes in the stock of unsold goods and raw materials held during a period.

Investment   The purchase, construction, or development of resources, including physical assets, such as plants and machinery, and human assets, such as better education. Investment expands an economy's resources. The process of investment is sometimes referred to as capital formation.

Investment in human capital   Expenditures on training, education, skill development, and health designed to increase human capital and people's productivity.

Invisible hand principle   The tendency of market prices to direct individuals pursuing their own interests to engage in activities promoting the economic well-being of the society.

Labor force participation rate   The number of people in the civilian labor force 16 years of age or over who are either employed or actively seeking employment as a percentage of the total civilian population 16 years of age and over.

Labor union   A collective organization of employees who bargain as a unit with employers.

Laffer curve   A curve illustrating the relationship between the tax rate and tax revenues. Tax revenues will be low at both very high and very low tax rates. Thus, when tax rates are quite high, lowering them can increase tax revenue.

Law of comparative advantage   A principle that states that individuals, firms, regions, or nations can gain by specializing in the production of goods that they produce cheaply (at a low opportunity cost) and exchanging them for goods they cannot produce cheaply (at a high opportunity cost).

Law of demand   A principle that states there is an inverse relationship between the price of a good and the quantity of it buyers are willing to purchase. As the price of a good increases, consumers will wish to purchase less of it. As the price decreases, consumers will wish to purchase more of it.

Law of diminishing marginal utility   The basic economic principle that, as the consumption of a product increases, the marginal utility derived from consuming more of it (per unit of time) will eventually decline.

Law of diminishing returns   The postulate that, as more and more units of a variable resource are combined with a fixed amount of other resources, using additional units of the variable resource will eventually increase output only at a decreasing rate. Once diminishing returns are reached, it will take successively larger amounts of the variable factor to expand output by one unit.

Law of supply   A principle that states there is a direct relationship between the price of a good and the quantity of it producers are willing to supply. As the price of a good increases, producers will wish to supply less.

Less-developed countries (LDCs)   Low-income countries generally characterized by rapid population growth and an agriculture-household sector that dominates the economy. Sometimes these countries are referred to as developing countries.

Licensing   A requirement that one obtain permission from the government in order to perform certain business activities or work in various occupations.

Liquid asset   An asset that can be easily and quickly converted to purchasing power.

Loanable funds market   A general term used to describe the market that coordinates the borrowing and lending decisions of business firms and households. Commercial banks, savings and loan associations, the stock and bond markets, and insurance companies are important financial institutions in this market.

Logrolling   The exchange between politicians of political support on one issue for political support on another issue.

Long run   A time period of sufficient length to enable decision makers to adjust fully to a market change.

Long run (in production)   A time period long enough to allow the firm to vary all factors of production.

Loss A deficit of sales revenue relative to the opportunity cost of production. Losses are a penalty imposed on those who produce goods even though they are valued less than the resources required for their production.

M1 (money supply)   The sum of (1) currency in circulation (including coins), (2) checkable deposits maintained in depository institutions, and (3) traveler's checks.

M2 (money supply)   Equal to M1 plus (1) savings deposits, (2) time deposits (accounts of less than $100,000) held in depository institutions, and (3) money market mutual fund shares.

Macroeconomics   The branch of economics that focuses on how human behavior affects outcomes in highly aggregated markets, such as the markets for labor or consumer products.

Managed Equity Mutual Fund   An equity mutual fund that has a portfolio manager who decides what stocks will be held in the fund and when they will be bought or sold. A research staff generally provides support for the fund manager.

Marginal   Term used to describe the effects of a change in the current situation. For example, the marginal cost is the cost of producing an additional unit of a product, given the producer's current facility and production rate.

Marginal benefit   The maximum price a consumer would be willing to pay for an additional unit of a product. It is the dollar value of the consumer's marginal utility from the additional unit, and therefore it falls as consumption increases.

Marginal cost   The change in total cost required to produce an additional unit of output.

Marginal product (MP)   The change in total output that results from the employment of one additional unit of a resource. The increase in the total product resulting from a unit increase in the employment of a variable input. Mathematically, it is the ratio of the change in total product to the change in the quantity of the variable input.

Marginal propensity to consume (MPC)   Additional current consumption divided by additional current disposable income.

Marginal revenue (MR)   The change in a firm's total revenue that results from the production and sale of one additional unit of output. The incremental change in total revenue derived from the sale of one additional unit of a product.

Marginal revenue product (MRP)   The change in the total revenue of a firm that results from the employment of one additional unit of a resource. The marginal revenue product of an input is equal to its marginal product multiplied by the marginal revenue of the good or service produced.

Marginal tax rate (MTR)   The additional tax liability a person faces divided by his or her additional taxable income. It is the percentage of an extra dollar of income earned that must be paid in taxes. It is the marginal tax rate that is relevant in personal decision making.

Marginal utility   The additional utility, or satisfaction, derived from consuming of an additional unit of a good.

Market   An abstract concept encompassing the forces of supply and demand, and the interaction of buyers and sellers with the potential for exchange to occur.

Market Organization A method of organization in which private parites make thir own plans and decisions with the guidance of unregulated market prices. The basic economic questions of consumption, production, and distribution are answered through these decentralized decisions.

Market power   The ability of a firm that is not a pure monopolist to earn unusually large profits, indicating that it has some monopoly power. Because the firm has few (or weak) competitors, it has a degree of freedom from the discipline of vigorous competition.

Means-tested income transfers   Transfers that are limited to persons or families with an income below a certain cutoff point. Eligibility is thus dependent on low-income status.

Medical savings accounts   Special savings accounts that individuals could use for the payment of medical bills or the purchase of a catastrophic (high deductibility) health insurance plan. Unfavorable tax treatment compared to employer-provided health insurance and other regulatory restrictions currently reduce their use.

Medium of exchange   An asset that is used to buy and sell goods or services.

Microeconomics   The branch of economics that focuses on how human behavior affects the conduct of affairs within narrowly defined units, such as individual households or business firms.

Middleman   A person who buys and sells goods or services or arranges trades. A middleman reduces transaction costs.

Minimum wage   Legislation requiring that workers be paid at least the stated minimum hourly rate of pay.

Monetarists   Economists who believe that (1) monetary instability is the major cause of fluctuations in real GDP and (2) rapid growth of the money supply is the major cause of inflation.

Monetary base   The sum of currency in circulation plus bank reserves (vault cash and reserves with the Fed). It reflects the stock of U.S. securities held by the Fed.

Monetary policy   The deliberate control of the money supply, and, in some cases, credit conditions, for the purpose of achieving macroeconomic goals.

Money interest rate   The percentage of the amount borrowed that must be paid to the lender in addition to the repayment of the principal. The money interest overstates the real cost of borrowing during an inflationary period. When inflation is anticipated, an inflationary premium will be incorporated into this rate. The money interest rate is often referred to as the nominal interest rate.

Money market mutual funds   Interest-earning accounts offered by brokerage firms that pool depositors' funds and invest them in highly liquid short-term securities. Since these securities can be quickly converted to cash, depositors are permitted to write checks (which reduce their share holdings) against their accounts.

Money rate of interest   The rate of interest in monetary terms that borrowers pay for borrowed funds. During periods when borrowers and lenders expect inflation, the money rate of interest exceeds the real rate of interest.

Money supply   The supply of currency, checking account funds, and traveler's checks. These items are counted as money because they are used as the means of payment for purchases.

Monopolistic competition   A term often used by economists to describe markets characterized by a large number of sellers that supply differentiated products to a market with low barriers to entry. Essentially, it is an alternative term for a competitive price-searcher market.

Monopoly   A market structure characterized by (1) a single seller of a well-defined product for which there are no good substitutes and (2) high barriers to the entry of any other firms into the market for that product.

National debt   The sum of the indebtedness of the federal government in the form of outstanding interest-earning bonds. It reflects the cumulative effect of budget deficits and surpluses.

National income   The total income earned by the nationals (citizens) during a period. It is the sum of employee compensation, self-employment income, rents, interest, and corporate profits.

Natural monopoly   A market situation in which the average costs of production continually decline with increased output. In a natural monopoly, the average costs of production will be lowest when a single, large firm produces the entire output demanded by the marketplace.

Natural rate of unemployment   The "normal" unemployment rate due to frictional and structural conditions in labor markets. It is the unemployment rate that occurs when the ecnonmy is operating at a sustainable rate of output. The current natural rate of unemployment in the United States is thought to be approximately 5 percent.

Net exports   Exports minus imports.

Net income of foreigners   The income that foreigners earn by contributing labor and capital resources to the production of goods within the borders of a country minus the income the nationals of the country earn abroad.

New classical economists   Economists who believe that there are strong forces pushing a market economy toward full-employment equilibrium and that macroeconomic policy is an ineffective tool with which to reduce economic instability.

Nominal GDP   GDP expressed at current prices. It is often called money GDP.

Nominal values   Values expressed in current dollars.

Nonactivists   Economists who believe that discretionary macroeconomic policy adjustments in response to cyclical conditions are likely to increase, rather than reduce instability. Nonactivists favor steady and predictable policies regardless of business conditions.

Nonpecuniary job characteristics   Working conditions, prestige, variety, location, employee freedom and responsibilities, and other nonwage characteristics of a job that influence how employees evaluate the job.

Normal good   A good that has a positive income elasticity, so that, as consumer income rises, demand for that good rises, too.

Normal profit rate   Zero economic profit, providing just the competitive rate of return on the capital (and labor) of owners. An above-normal profit rate will draw more entry into the market, while a below-normal rate will cause an exit of investors and capital.

Normative economics   Judgments about "what ought to be" in economic matters. Normative economic views cannot be proven false, because they are based on value judgments.

North American Free Trade Agreement (NAFTA)   A comprehensive trade agreement between the United States, Mexico, and Canada that went into effect in 1994. Under the agreement, tariff barriers were to continue to be phased out until 2004.

Objective   A fact based on observable phennomenon that is not influenced by differeces in personal opinion.

Official reserve account   The record of transactions between central banks.

Oligopoly   A market situation in which a small number of sellers constitutes the entire industry. It is competition among the few.

Open market operations   The buying and selling of U.S. government securities in the open market by the Federal Reserve.

Opportunity cost   The highest valued alternative that must be sacrificed as a result of choosing an option.

Opportunity cost of equity capital   The rate of return that must be earned by investors to induce them to continue to supply financial capital to the firm.

Opportunity cost of production   The total economic cost of producing a good or service. The cost component includes the opportunity cost of all resources, including those owned by the firm. The opportunity cost is equal to the value of the production of other goods sacrificed as the result of producing the good.

Other checkable deposits   Interest-earning deposits that are also available for checking.

Partnership   A business firm owned by two or more individuals who possess ownership rights to the firm's profits and are personally liable for the debts of the firm.

Pegged exchange-rate system   A commitment to use monetary and fiscal policy to maintain the exchange-rate value of the domestic currency at a fixed rate or within a narrow band relative to another currency (or bundle of currencies).

per capita GDP   Income per person. Increases in income per person are vital for the achievement of higher living standards.

Permanent income hypothesis   The hypothesis that people's consumption depends on their long-run expected (permanent) income rather than on current income.

Personal consumption   Household spending on consumer goods and services during the current period. Consumption is a flow concept.

Personal income   The total income received by domestic households and noncorporate businesses. It is available for consumption, saving, and payment of personal taxes.

Phillips Curve   A curve that illustrates the relationship between the rate of inflation and the rate of unemployment.

Pork-barrel legislation   A package of spending projects benefiting local areas financed through the federal government. The costs of the projects typically exceed the benefits in total, but the projects are intensely desired by the residents of a particular district who get the benefits without having to pay much of the costs.

Portfolio   All the stocks, bonds, or other securities held by an individual or corporation for investment purposes.

Positive economics   The scientific study of "what is" among economic relationships.

Positive rate of time preference   The desire of consumers for goods now rather than in the future.

Potential deposit expansion mulitpllier   The maximum potential increase in the money supply as a ratio of the new reserves injected into the banking system. It is equal to the inverse of the required ratio.

Potential output   The level of output that can be achieved and sustained into the future, given the size of the labor force, its expected productivity, and natural rate of unemployment consistent with the efficient operation of the labor market. Actual output may differ from the economy's potential output.

Poverty threshold income level The level of money income below which a family is considered to be poor. It differs according to family characteristics (for example, number of family members) and is adjusted when consumer prices change.

Present value (PV) The current worth of future income after it is discounted to reflect the fact that revenues in the future are valued less highly than revenues now.

Price ceiling A legally established maximum price sellers can charge for a good or resource.

Price controls Government-mandated prices that are generally imposed in the form of maximum or minimum legal prices.

Price discrimination A practice wherby a seller charges different consumers different prices for the same product or service.

Price elasticity of demand The percent change in the quantity of a product demanded divided by the percent change in the price causing the change in quantity. The price elasticity of demand indicates the degree of consumer response to variation in price.

Price elasticity of supply The percentage change in quantity supplied, divided by the percentage change in the price that caused the change in quantity supplied.

Price floor A legally established minimum price that buyers must pay for a good or resource.

Price searchers Firms that face a downward sloping demand curve for their product. The amount that the firm is able to sell is inversely related to the price that it charges.

Price takers Sellers who must take the market price in order to sell their product. Because each price taker's output is small relative to the total market, price takers can sell all their output at the market price, but they are unable to sell any of their output at a price higher than the market price.

Primary market The market in which financial institutions aid in the sale of new securities.

Principal-agent problem The incentive problem that occurs when the purchaser of services (the principal) lacks full information about the circumstances faced by the seller (the agent) and thus cannot know how well the agent performs the purchased services. The agent may to some extent work toward objectives other than those sought by the principal paying for the service.

Private investment The flow of private sector expenditures on durable assets (fixed investment) plus the addition to inventories (inventory investment) during a period. These expenditures enhance our ability to provide consumer benefits in the future.

Private property rights Property rights that are exclusively held by an owner and protected against invasion by others. Private property can be transferred, sold, or mortgaged at the owners' discretion.

Privately held government debt The portion of the national debt owed to domestic and foreign investors. It does not include bonds held by agencies of the federal government or the Federal Reserve.

Producer surplus The difference between the minimum price suppliers are willing to accept and the price they actually receive. It measures the net gains to producers and resource suppliers from market trade. It is not the same as profit.

Production possibilities curve A curve that outlines all possible combinations of total output that could be produced, as-suming (1) a fixed amount of productive resources, (2) a given amount of technical knowledge, and (3) full and efficient use of those resources. The slope of the curve indicates the amount of one product that must be given up to produce more of the other.

Productivity The average output produced per worker during a specific time period. It is usually measured in terms of output per hour worked.

Profit An excess of sales revenue relative to the opportunity cost of production. The cost component includes the opportunity cost of all resources, including those owned by the firm. Therefore, profit accrues only when the value of the good produced is greater than the value of the resources used for its production.

Progressive tax A tax in which the average tax rate rises with income. People with higher incomes will pay a higher percentage of their income in taxes.

Property rights The right to use, control, and obtain the benefits from a good or service.

Proportional tax A tax in which the average tax rate is the same at all income levels. Everyone pays the same percentage of income in taxes.

Proprietorship A business firm owned by an individual who possesses the ownership right to the firm's profits and is personally liable for the firm's debts.

Public goods Goods for which rivalry among consumers is absent and exclusion of non-paying customers is difficult.

Public-choice analysis The study of decision making as it affects the formation and operation of collective organizations, such as governments. In general, the principles and methodology of economics are applied to political science topics.

Pure competition A market structure characterized by a large number of small firms producing an identical product in an industry (market area) that permits complete freedom of entry and exit. Also called price-taker markets.

Quantity theory of money A theory that hypothesizes that a change in the money supply will cause a proportional change in the price level because velocity and real output are unaffected by the quantity of money.

Random walk theory The theory that current stock prices already reflect known information about the future. Therefore, the future movement of stock prices will be determined by surprise occurrences. This will cause them to change in a random fashion.

Rational ignorance effect Because it is highly unlikely that an individual vote will decide the outcome of an election, a rational individual has little or no incentive to search for and acquire the information needed to cast an informed vote.

Rational-expectations hypothesis The hypothesis that economic decision makers weigh all available evidence, including information concerning the probable effects of current and future economic policy, when they form their expectations about future economic events (such as the probable future inflation rate).

Rationing Allocating a limited supply of a good or resource among people who would like to have more of it. When price performs the rationing function, the good or resource is allocated to those willing to give up the most "other things" in order to get it.

Real balance effect   The increase in wealth that occurs when the price level falls and the purchasing power of money increases (assuming the supply of money in the economy is stable). The wealth effect leads to an inverse relationship between price (level) and quantity demanded in the goods and services market: when the price level falls, people will demand more goods and services.

Real earnings   Earnings adjusted for differences in the general level of prices across time periods or geographic areas. When real earnings are equal, the same bundle of goods and services can be purchased with the earnings.

Real GDP   GDP adjusted for changes in the price level.

Real interest rate   The interest rate adjusted for expected inflation; it indicates the real cost of borrowing and lending money afer inflation has been factored in.

Real rate of interest   The money rate of interest minus the expected rate of inflation. The real rate of interest indicates the interest premium. In terms of real goods and services, that one must pay for earlier availability.

Real values   Values that have been adjusted for the effects of inflation.

Recession   A downturn in economic activity characterized by declining real GDP and rising unemployment. In an effort to be more precise, many economists define a recession as two consecutive quarters in which there is a decline in real GDP.

Recognition lag   The time period after a policy change is needed from a stabilization standpoint but before the need is recognized by policy-makers.

Regressive tax   A tax in which the average tax rate falls with income. People with higher incomes will pay a lower percentage of their income in taxes.

Rent-seeking   Actions by individuals and interest groups designed to restructure public policy in a manner that will either directly or indirectly redistribute more income to themselves or the projects they promote.

Repeat-purchase item   An item purchased often by the same buyer.

Replacement rate   The share of previous earnings replaced by unemployment benefits.

Required reserves   The minimum amount of reserves that a bank is required by law to keep on hand to back up its deposits. If reserve requirements were 15 percent, the banks would be required to keep $150,000 in reserves against each $1 million of deposits.

Required reserve ratio   A percentage of a specified liability category (for example, checkable deposits) that banking institutions are required to hold as reserves against that type of liability.

Residual claimants   Individuals who personally receive the excess, if any, of revenues over costs. Residual claimants gain if the firm's costs are reduced or revenues increased.

Resource   An input used to produce economic goods. Land, labor, skills, natural resources, and capital are examples. Throughout history, people have struggled to transform available, but limited, resources into things they would like to have—economic goods.

Resoure market   The market for inputs used to produce goods and services. A highly aggregated market encompassing all resources (labor, physical capital, land, and entrepreneurship) contributing to the production of current output. The labor market is the largest component of this market.

Resource markets   Markets in which business firms demand factors of production (for example, labor, capital, and natural resources) from household suppliers. The resources are then used to produce goods and services. These markets are sometimes called factor markets or input markets.

Resource mobility   The ease with which factors of production are able to move among alternative uses. Resources that can easily be transferred to a different use or location are said to be highly mobile. Resources with few alternative uses are immobile.

Restrictive fiscal policy   A reduction in government expenditures and/or an increase in tax rates such that the expected size of the budget deficit declines (or the budget surplus increases).

Restrictive monetary policy   A shift in monetary policy designed to reduce aggregate demand and place downward pressure on the general level of prices (or the rate of inflation). Bond sales by the Fed, a decline in bank reserves, and a reduction in the growth rate of the money supply are generally indicative of a restrictive monetary policy.

Ricardian equivalence   The view that a tax reduction financed with government debt will exert no impact on current consumption and aggregate demand because people will fully recognize the higher future taxes implied by the additional debt.

Right-to-work laws   Laws that prohibit the union shop, the requirement that employees must join a union as a condition of employment. Each state has the option to adopt (or reject) right-to-work legislation.

Rule of 70   If a variable grows at a rate of x percent per year, $70/x$ will approximate the number of years required for the variable to double.

Samaritan's dilemma   The dilemma that occurs when assisting low-income citizens with tranfers reduces the opportunity cost of choices that lead to poverty. Providing income transfers to the poor and discouraging behavior that leads to poverty are conflicting goals.

Saving   Current income that is not spent on consumption goods. Savings deposited by some individuals allow resources to be devoted to investments (such as the making of tractors or other equipment used in production). The portion of after-tax income that is not spent on consumption. Saving is a "flow" concept.

Savings and loan associations   Financial institutions that accept deposits in exchange for shares that pay dividends. Historically, these funds have been channeled into residential mortgage loans. Under banking legislation adopted in 1980, S&Ls are permitted to offer a broad range of services similar to those of commercial banks.

Say's Law   The view that production creates its own demand. Demand will always be sufficient to purchase the goods produced because the income payments to the resource suppliers will equal the value of the goods produced.

Scarcity   Fundamental concept of economics that indicates that there is less of a good freely available from nature than people would like.

Scientific thinking   Development of a theory from basic postulates and testing it against events in the real world. Good theories are consistent with and help explain real-world events. Theories that are inconsistent with the real world are invalid and must be rejected.

Secondary effects   The indirect impact of an event or policy that may not be easily and immediately observable. In the area of policy, these effects are often both unintended and overlooked.

Secondary market The market in which financial institutions aid in the buying and selling of existing securities.

Severance pay Pay by an employer to an employee upon the termination of employment with the firm.

Shirking Working at less than the expected rate of productivity, which reduces output. Shirking is more likely when workers are not monitored, so that the cost of lower output falls on others.

Short run (in production) A time period so short that a firm is unable to vary some of its factors of production. The firm's plant size typically cannot be altered in the short run.

Shortage A condition in which the amount of a good offered for sale by producers is less than the amount demanded by buyers at the existing price. An increase in price would eliminate the shortage.

Shortsightedness effect The misallocation of resources that results because public-sector action is biased (1) in favor of proposals yielding clearly defined current benefits in exchange for difficult-to-identify future costs and (2) against proposals with clearly identifiable current costs but yielding less concrete and less obvious future benefits.

Shutdown A temporary halt in the operation of a business firm. Because the firm anticipates operating in the future, it does not sell its assets and go out of business. The firm's variable cost is eliminated by the shutdown, but its fixed costs continue.

Socialism A system of economic organization in which (1) the ownership and control of the basic means of production rest with the state, and (2) resource allocation is determined by centralized planning rather than by market forces.

Special-interest issue An issue that generates substantial individual benefits to a small minority while imposing a small individual cost on many other voters. In total, the net cost to the majority might either exceed or fall short of the net benefits to the special-interest group.

Stock options The option to buy a specified number of shares of the firm's stock at a designated price. The designated price is generally set so that the options will be quite valuable if the firm's shares increase in price, but of little value if their price falls. Thus, when used to compensate top managers, stock options provide a strong incentive to follow policies that will increase the value of the firm.

Store of value An asset that will allow people to transfer purchasing power from one period to the next.

Strike An action of unionized employees in which they (1) discontinue working for the employer and (2) take steps to prevent other potential workers from offering their services to the employer.

Structural unemployment Unemployment due to the structural characteristics of the economy that mke it difficult for jobseekers to find employment and for employers to hire workers. Although job openings are available, they generally require skills that many unemployed workers do not have.

Subjective An opinion based on personal preferences and value judgements.

Subsidy A payment the government makes to either the buyer or seller, usually on a per-unit basis, when a good or service is purchased or sold.

Substitutes Products that serve similar purposes. An increase in the price of one will cause an increase in demand for the other (hamburgers and tacos, butter and margarine, Microsoft Xbox and Sony Playstation, Chevrolets and Fords, are examples).

Substitution effect That part of an increase (decrease) in amount consumed that is the result of a good being cheaper (more expensive) in relation to other goods because of a reduction (increase) in price.

Sunk costs Costs that have already been incurred as a result of past decisions. They are sometimes referred to as historical costs.

Supply shock An unexpected event that temporarily increases or decreases aggregate supply.

Supply-side economists Modern economists who believe that changes in marginal tax rates exert important effects on aggregate supply.

Surplus A condition in which the amount of a good offered for sale by producers is greater than the amount that buyers will purchase at the existing price. A decline in price would eliminate the surplus.

Tariff A tax levied on goods imported into a country.

Tax base The level or quantity of the economic activity that is taxed. Higher tax rates reduce the level of the tax base because they make the activity less attractive.

Tax incidence The way the burden of a tax is distributed among economic units (consumers, producers, employees, employers, and so on). The actual tax burden does not always fall on those who are statutorily assigned to pay the tax.

Tax rate The per-unit amount of the tax or the percentage rate at which the economic activity is taxed.

Team production A production process in which employees work together under the supervision of the owner or the owner's representative.

Technological advancement The introduction of new techniques or methods that increase output per unit of input.

Technology The techological knowledge available in an economy at any given time. The level of technology determines the amount of output we can generate with out limited resources.

Total cost The costs, both explicit and implicit, of all the resources used by the firm. Total cost includes an imputed normal rate of return for the firm's equity capital.

Total fixed cost The sum of the costs that do not vary with output. They will be incurred as long as a firm continues in business and the assets have alternative uses.

Total product The total output of a good that is associated with alternative utilization rates of a variable input.

Total variable cost The sum of those costs that rise as output increases. Examples of variable costs are wages paid to workers and payments for raw materials.

Tournament pay A form of compensation where the top performer (or performers) receives much higher rewards than other competitors, even if the others perform at only a slightly lower level.

Trade deficit The situation when a country's imports of goods and services are greater than its exports.

Trade surplus The situation when a country's exports of goods and services are greater than its imports.

Transfer payments Payments to individuals or institutions that are not linked to the current supply of a good or service by the recipient.

Transaction costs The time, effort, and other resources needed to search out, negotiate, and consummate an exchange.

Unanticipated change   A change that decision-makers could not reasonably foresee. Thus, choices made prior to the change did not take it into account.

Unanticipated inflation   An increase in the general level of prices that was not expected by most decision makers.

Underground economy   Unreported barter and cash transactions that take place outside recorded market channels. Some are otherwise legal activities undertaken to evade taxes. Others involve illegal activities, such as trafficking in drugs and prostitution.

Unemployed   The term used to describe a person not currently employed who is either (1) actively seeking employment or (2) waiting to begin or return to a job.

Unemployment rate   The percentage of people in the labor force who are unemployed. Mathematically, it is equal to the number of people unemployed/number of persons in the labor force x 100.

Unit of account   A unit of measurement used by people to post prices and keep track of revenues and costs.

User charges   Payments that users (consumers) are required to make if they want to receive certain services provided by the government.

Utility   The subjective benefit or satisfaction a person expects from a choice or course of action.

Value of marginal product (VMP)   The marginal product of a resource multiplied by the selling price of the product it helps to produce. For a price-taker firm, marginal revenue product (*MRP*) will be equal to the value marginal product (*VMP*).

Velocity of money   The average number of times a dollar is used to purchase final goods and services during a year. It is equal to GDP divided by the stock of money.

World Trade Organization (WTO)   The new name given to GATT in 1994; the WTO is currently responsible for monitoring and enforcing the multilateral trade agreements among its 133 member countries.

sales, 608
statutuory vs. actual incidence, 96–97
subsidies and, 104
types of, 612
team production, 444–445
Teamsters' union, 702
technological advances
affect of, on aggregate supply, 219
competition and, 527
economic growth and, 352–353
productivity rates and, 561–563
resource productivity and, 536
unemployment and, 562
technological progress
entrepreneurs and, 499–500
technology, 43
changes in, and supply, 70
production possibilities and, 43–44
telecommuting, 621
thinking at the margin, 13–14
time
elasticity of supply for resources and, 543
influence of, on demand for resources, 534–535
preference, positive rate of, 568
time costs
affect of, on consumer choice, 425
time factor
in production process, 451–452
supply elasticity and, 480–481
time lags, 329–330, 342
total cost (TC), 451
total fixed cost (TFC), 450–451
total product, 455
total value, 60
total variable cost (TVC), 449–450
Tournament pay, 554–555
Trabant automobile, 726–727
trade
as natural human endeavor, 84
balance of, 403
current-account balance and, 405
domestic, 376
flow of capital and, 209
free, and economic growth, 356
gains from, 45, 52–53
increased output and, 45
innovation and, 47–48
law of comparative advantage and, 45–47
legal restrictions on, 44
mass production and, 47
middlemen and, 34
of services, 404
see also international trade, 370
transaction costs as barrier to, 34
value creation and, 32–34
trade barriers
reduction of artificial, 522–523
trade deficit
flow of capital and, 209
impact of, 408, 410
meanings of, 209

myths about, 407
net capital inflow and, 210
reasons for, 408
trade fallacies, 385–387
trade openness
economic performance and, 383–384
Trade Openness Index (TOI), 384
trade restrictions, 379–382
anti-dumping argument for, 384
economic performance and, 383–384
employment issues and, 385–386
exchange-rate controls, 382
fallacies about, 385–387
impact of, 380
import quotas, 380–381
infant-industry argument for, 382, 384
national-defense argument for, 382
reasons for, 382, 384
regulatory barriers, 381
relaxation of, 388
secondary effects from, 15
special interests and, 385
tariffs, 379
wages and, 386–387
trade sector
growth of U.S., 370
of United States, 370–371
trade surpluses, 209, 408, 410
trade-offs, 7, 10, 30
economic efficiency and, 109–110
trading partners
affect of, on aggregate demand, 217
tragedy of the commons, 742
transaction costs, 34
as barrier to trade, 34
middlemen and, 34
on Internet, 618
transfer incomes, 586
transfer payments, 126
affect of, on income inequalities, 586
affect of, on output levels, 595–596
competition for, 595–596
criteria for receiving, 595–596
GDP and, 151
growth of, 126
increases in, 597
poverty rate and, 593–594, 596
side effects of, 594
special interest groups and, 597
transfer programs
costs of, 595–596
noncash, 586
transitional gains trap, 596
traveler's checks, 280
Tullock, Gordon, 596
Turner, Ted, 583, 724

U

U.S. Constitution, 142–143
U.S. dollar
foreign exchange value of, 395
use of, outside of U.S., 295, 298

U.S. economy
growth rate of, 190
impact of foreign purchases on, 406
U.S. education system
at level of higher education, 687
charter schools and, 688
choice programs and, 688–689
expenditures on, 685
impact of structural changes on, 689
reform of, 687–688
school vouchers and, 687–688
structure of, 685–686
student achievement in, 684–685
U.S. Fish and Wildlife Service (FWS), 735
U.S. Government
size and growth of, 125, 127
size of, 612
U.S. labor force
union membership of, 698–699
U.S. securities, 293
U.S. tariffs, 379
U.S. trade
with Canada, 388
with Mexico, 388
U.S. trade deficit, 408, 410
U.S. Treasury
Fed and, 293–295
vs. Federal Reserve System, 294
Ukraine
black markets in, 94
unanticipated changes, 215
business cycles and, 228
market adjustments and, 222–227
unanticipated inflation, 184–185
uncertainty
economic profits and, 581
underground economy, 160–161
Underwriters Laboratories (UL), 120
unemployment
actual vs. natural, 200
automation and, 566
cyclical, 178
during Great Depression, 237
frictional, 176–178
increases in, during recessions, 171
job search process and, 177
Keynesian model and, 242, 244
Keynesian view of, 238
minimum wage and, 91–92
myths about, 177
natural rate of, 179–181, 201, 655
rate of, 173, 229
reasons for, 175–176
structural, 178
types of, 176–178
Unemployment benefits
impact of, 659, 661
Unemployment compensation, 266
unemployment programs, 180
unemployment rate
actual vs. natural, 181
cross-country variations in, 655–656
defined, 173
derivation of, 174

THE EIGHT GUIDEPOSTS TO ECONOMIC THINKING

These eight guideposts provide the foundation for the economic way of thinking (they are discussed in Chapter 1). To do well in this course you will need to understand and be able to apply these ideas to a wide range of issues.

1. The Use of Scarce Resources Is Costly; Trade-offs Must Always Be Made.

2. Individuals Choose Purposefully—They Try to Get the Most From Their Limited Resources.

3. Incentives Matter—Choice Is Influenced in a Predictable Way by Changes in Incentives.

4. Individuals Make Decisions at the Margin.

5. Although Information Can Help Us Make Better Choices, Its Acquisition Is Costly.

6. Economic Actions Often Generate Secondary Effects in Addition to Their Immediate Effects.

7. The Value of a Good or Service Is Subjective.

8. The Test of a Theory Is Its Ability to Predict.

SPECIAL TOPICS

These Special Topics covered in the "Applying the Basics" section use the basic concepts to analyze important current-day topics.

1. Government Spending and Taxation

2. The Internet: How Is It Changing the Economy?

3. The Economics of Social Security

4. The Stock Market: Its Function, Performance, and Potential as an Investment Opportunity

5. The Federal Budget and the National Debt

6. Labor Market Policies and Unemployment: A Cross-Country Analysis

7. Institutions, Policies, and the Irish Miracle

8. The Economics of Health Care

9. School Choice: Can It Improve the Quality of Education in America?

10. Is Discrimination Responsible for the Earnings Difference between Men and Women?

11. Do Labor Unions Increase the Wages of Workers?

12. How Does Government Regulation Affect Your Life?

13. Resource Management: How Property Rights and Markets Replace Conflict with Cooperation

14. Difficult Environmental Cases and the Role of Government